THE HERITAGE SHAKESPEARE

EDITED, WITH AN INTRODUCTION TO EACH PLAY
AND A GLOSSARY, BY

PETER ALEXANDER

*Regius Professor of English Language and Literature
in the University of Glasgow*

HISTORIES

William Shakespeare

THE
HISTORIES

with an introduction by JAMES G. MCMANAWAY

and wood-engravings by JOHN FARLEIGH

NEW YORK · THE HERITAGE PRESS

The text of the Heritage Shakespeare is that of
Collins Tudor Shakespeare, edited by PROFESSOR PETER ALEXANDER,
and first published in 1951; it is here used with the permission of
Wm. Collins Sons & Co., Ltd., Glasgow, Scotland.
This volume of *Histories* is the second of three presenting
the complete plays of Shakespeare. The volume of *Comedies* contains
Professor Alexander's General Introduction,
and reproduces the preliminary matter of the First Folio.
The third volume comprises the *Tragedies.*

Contents

ACKNOWLEDGMENTS

The text of the Tudor Shakespeare has been corrected in some places, particularly in *Richard III*. Professor Dover Wilson in the course of his recension of that play pointed out that here and there I had failed to give effect to the general principles that guided me in my treatment of the Quarto and Folio versions. These corrections I gratefully acknowledge.

In the introductions to the individual Histories I have also drawn in places on Professor Wilson's introductions to his 'New Shakespeare' and his studies elsewhere, as I have on Dr. Tillyard's *Shakespeare's History Plays* and *Elizabethan World Picture*, as well as on studies by Professor Harbage, Professor Hardin Craig, Professor Reyher, Dr. Rossiter, and others.

In my desire to refer interested readers to the body of scholarly work that has recently been published in elucidation of the political and social ideas of the Elizabethan age, I have not omitted, I hope, to emphasize the dramatic context which Shakespeare provided for these ideas—a context which the reader should also always have in mind.

P. A.

Preface

BY JAMES G. McMANAWAY

S HAKESPEARE's Chronicle History Plays have no exact coun-
terpart in any other national literature. These plays, when
new, caused terrific excitement, and the first audiences learned
much of their English history from them. "How would it have
joyed brave *Talbot* (the terror of the French) to thinke that
after he had lyne two hundred yeares in his Tombe, hee
should triumphe againe on the Stage [*1 Henry VI*], and have
his bones newe embalmed with the teares of ten thousand spectators at least (at severall times), who, in the Tragedian that
represents his person, imagine they behold him fresh bleeding?" Thus wrote Thomas Nashe in 1592, when English patri-
otism was ablaze after the defeat of the Spanish Armada.

Shakespeare's representation of historical event, such as the
choosing of the Red Rose and the White in *1 Henry VI*, and
his interpretation of the characters of Prince Hal, Hotspur,
and Richard III, imposed themselves indelibly on Elizabethan
minds and those of succeeding generations. As early as 1618-
1621, Richard Corbet testified to the fusion in the popular
mind of Shakespeare's poetry with historical fact, when in
Iter Boreale he described a conducted tour over Bosworth
Field:

> Mine host was full of ale and history;
> Why, he could tell
> The inch where Richmond stood, where Richard fell:
> Besides what of his knowledge he could say,
> He had authenticke notice from the Play; . . .
> But chiefly by that one perspicuous thing,
> Where he mistook a player for a King.
> For when he would have sayd, King Richard dyed,
> And call'd—A horse! a horse!—he, Burbidge cry'de.

And not even the latest and most laudatory biography of
Richard III can efface the memory of Shakespeare's bloody
tyrant,

Cheated of feature by dissembling nature,
Deform'd, unfinish'd, sent before my time
Into this breathing world scarce half made up,
And that so lamely and unfashionable
That dogs bark at me as I halt by them.

Long before Shakespeare's death, however, Chronicle Histories were beginning to seem a little old-fashioned, so that Ben Jonson could poke fun at plays which

With three rustie swords,
And helpe of some few foot-and-halfe-foote words,
Fight over Yorke, and Lancasters long jarres.

The tremendous figure of Sir John Falstaff continued to keep *1 Henry IV* on the stage, perhaps because his Rabelaisian vigor made the play seem a comedy rather than a history. *Henry VIII* retained its popularity because of the opportunities it afforded for stage spectacle. And Englishmen have turned repeatedly to *Henry V*, especially in time of trial. No one who saw Sir Laurence Olivier's color picture of that play during the dark days of World War II can ever forget the prophetic twang of English bowstrings at Agincourt.

In recent years the History Plays, from *Richard II* through *3 Henry VI*, and occasionally *King John* and *Henry VIII*, have been presented at several of the Shakespeare Festivals with notable success, and it has become clear that even in his earliest years Shakespeare could handle the confused narrative of the Wars of the Roses with great theatrical effectiveness.

In view of the fact that, at the beginning of his dramatic career, Shakespeare seems to have been known best for his History Plays—if, indeed, he was not the first who wrote in this vein—there has been a serious effort to understand Shakespeare's purpose in writing the plays and to relate the ideas of the young dramatist to the great tragedies of his full maturity.

First, one may inquire what the History Plays meant to the Elizabethan audience and, after that, what significance they have today. The earliest plays, those dealing with the reign of the saintly but ineffectual Henry VI, told the story of an England that was plunged from greatness to impotence because it was at war with itself. Its chief nobility, the descendants of Edward III, whose duty was to obey the king and under him to rule the people, had thrown off their allegiance because of

ambition and envy and personal hatred. And Parts 1, 2, and 3
of *Henry VI* depict the miseries of civil war. These are epit-
omized in *3 Henry VI*, II. v. King Henry has been sent apart
from a battle by his termagant Queen, and as he longs to exchange his lot for that of a simple shepherd, "*Enter* [from
the battle] *a Son that hath kill'd his Father.*"

> SON.   Ill blows the wind that profits nobody.
> This man whom hand to hand I slew in fight
> May be possessed with some store of crowns;
>
> .   .   .   .
>
> Who's this? O God! It is my father's face,
> Whom in this conflict I unwares have kill'd.
> O heavy times, begetting such events!
> From London by the King was I press'd forth;
> My father, being the Earl of Warwick's man,
> Came on the part of York, press'd by his master;
> And I, who at his hands receiv'd my life,
> Have by my hands of life bereaved him.
> Pardon me, God, I knew not what I did.

Then, "*Enter* Father, *bearing of his* Son.*"

> FATHER.   Thou that so stoutly hath resisted me,
> Give me thy gold, if thou hast any gold;
> For I have bought it with an hundred blows.
> But let me see. Is this our foeman's face?
> Ah, no, no, no, it is mine only son!
>
> .   .   .   .
>
> O, pity, God, this miserable age!

Civil war is an unnatural, monstrous thing. Elizabeth's subjects saw in many lands the nobility arrayed against their king
and against each other, and friends and families in deadly
strife. The cause might be religious, as in France and Germany,
or dynastic. So that while Englishmen thanked God and their
Queen for the years of domestic peace they enjoyed, the
thoughtful could hardly forget for a day that there were pre-
tenders to the crown with quite as valid a claim as Elizabeth's;
furthermore, their ruler was unmarried and childless—there
was no sure, peaceful succession to the throne. And while po-
tential claimants schemed with adherents at home and sought
military support abroad, the general populace was itself divided, Anglican against Papist, and Puritan against both. England was thickly strewn with the seeds of imminent civil war.

And ever in the shadows lurked the power of Spain. What could History teach from the Wars of the Roses?

Elizabeth's Council fostered the apologists of the Tudor dynasty and the chroniclers as Henry VII had done, and the English people were indoctrinated by Edward Hall and Raphael Holinshed with the idea that the Houses of York and Lancaster had been providentially united by the marriage of Henry VII and Elizabeth of York.

Shakespeare tells the story in *Richard II* and *Richard III*. Richard II was a weak king, unfit to rule, but he was the anointed king and God's vicegerent on earth, so that when Henry Bolingbroke dethroned him he was committing not only the crime of treachery to his king, but, worse yet, the sin of impiety towards God. And England, by acquiescing in the deposition of Richard, became equally guilty with Bolingbroke and was doomed to expiate the sin in decades of bloodshed. The Tudor doctrine of the sanctity of kingship and of the subjects' duty of passive obedience is stated in *Richard II*, IV. i. As the Duke of York proclaims Bolingbroke king, "Henry, fourth of that name," and the new monarch ascends the regal throne, the Bishop of Carlisle bursts forth:

Marry, God forbid!
. . . .
What subject can give sentence on his king?
And who sits here that is not Richard's subject?
. . . .
And shall the figure of God's majesty,
His captain, steward, deputy elect,
Anointed, crowned, planted many years,
Be judg'd by subject and inferior breath . . . ?
        O, forfend it, God. . . .
I speak to subjects, and a subject speaks,
Stirr'd up by God, thus boldly for his king.
My Lord of Hereford here [Bolingbroke], whom you call king,
Is a foul traitor to proud Hereford's king;
And if you crown him, let me prophesy—
The blood of English shall manure the ground,
And future ages groan for this foul act;
. . . .
And in this seat of peace tumultuous wars
Shall kin with kin and kind with kind confound;
Disorder, horror, fear, and mutiny,

Shall here inhabit, and this land be call'd
The field of Golgotha and dead men's skulls.
O, if you raise this house against this house,
It will the woefullest division prove
That ever fell upon this cursed earth.

The Biblical language of Carlisle here and of the "Son that hath kill'd his Father," quoted above, is not accidental. In the year that the nine-year-old Edward VI became king, the Council of Regency caused to be published and sent to every parish in England a book called *Certayne Sermons, or Homilies appoynted by the Kynges Maiestie, to be declared and redde, by all persones, Vicars, or Curates, every Sondaye in their churches, where thei have cure.* The tenth homily, in three parts, to be read on each of three consecutive Sundays, is "an exhortation concerning good order and obedience to Rulers and Magistrates." It expounds the doctrines of the divine right of kings, nonresistance, passive obedience, and the wickedness of rebellion. The Homilies were reprinted at least ten times before Edward's death. Naturally their use was dispensed with during the reign of Mary, but when Elizabeth succeeded her in November 1558, the Homilies were printed again (in 1559), and their use proclaimed.

The series of Homilies was extended in 1563 by the publication of *The Seconde Tome* and again, about 1570, upon the suppression of the rebellion of the Northern Earls, by the issuance of a six-part tract, *An Homilie against disobedience and wylful rebellion.* This refers directly to the recent uprising and concludes with a formal prayer, "A Thankesgeving for the suppression of the last rebellion." Nine times every year Shakespeare and every regular church attendant in England—and the regular church attendance of every subject was required by law—would hear a portion of the homily on Obedience or of the special homily on Disobedience and Wilful Rebellion. There was no escape from indoctrination in these themes that are so prominent in Shakespeare's Histories.

The idea of royal authority under God and of the relationship between king and subject was in harmony with Elizabethan concepts of the universe, which find their best statement in Richard Hooker's *Of the Lawes of Ecclesiastical Politie* (1594-97), and are everywhere reflected in Shakespeare's thought. The universe is the handiwork of an omniscient and omnipotent creator. Below him is the angelic hierarchy. A little lower than the angels is man, who by the exercise of reason has dominion over the earth. Then come the beasts of the field and the fowls of the air, of which the lion and the eagle are, respectively, kings. Vegetative life is lower still, and at the bottom is inanimate creation, the best of which are gold, the king of metals, and the diamond, hardest and most brilliant of precious stones. In every category, there is gradation: kings, princes, dukes, earls, lords, knights, esquires, and commoners. Whatever the symbol of the universe, whether a ladder from earth to the deity or the great chain of being, each thing in creation had its appointed place and properties, and any effort to change was as impious as Lucifer's revolt in Heaven. In *Henry V*, Exeter and the Archbishop of Canterbury describe human society in terms of a musical composition and of a hive of bees.

> EXETER. For government, though high, and low, and lower,
> Put into parts, doth keep in one consent,
> Congreeing in a full and natural close,
> Like music.
> CANTERBURY. Therefore doth heaven divide
> The state of man in divers functions,
> Setting endeavour in continual motion;
> To which is fixed as an aim or butt
> Obedience; for so work the honey bees,
> Creatures that by a rule in nature teach
> The act of order to a peopled kingdom.
> They have a king, and officers of sorts,
> Where some like magistrates correct at home;
> Others like merchants venture trade abroad;
> Others like soldiers, armed in their stings,
> Make boot upon the summer's velvet buds,
> Which pillage they with merry march bring home
> To the tent-royal of their emperor;
> Who, busied in his majesty, surveys
> The singing masons building roofs of gold,
> The civil citizens kneading up the honey,
> The poor mechanic porters crowding in
> Their heavy burdens at his narrow gate,
> The sad-ey'd justice, with his surly hum,
> Delivering o'er to executors pale
> The lazy yawning drone.

PREFACE

Ulysses echoes the figure of the beehive in his great speech to the Grecian leaders in *Troilus and Cressida* [see *The Tragedies*] and then drives home the reason for their long failure to capture Troy. In their pride and passion, the Greek leaders have ignored authority.

> The heavens themselves, the planets, and this centre,
> Observe degree, priority, and place,
> Insisture, course, proportion, season, form,
> Office, and custom, in all line of order;
>
> . . . .
>   But when the planets
> In evil mixture to disorder wander,
> What plagues and what portents, what mutiny,
> What raging of the sea, shaking of earth,
> Commotion in the winds! Frights, changes, horrors,
> Divert and crack, rend and deracinate,
> The unity and married calm of states
> Quite from their fixture!

"Take but degree away," he continues, "untune that string, And hark what discord follows!" A state of universal warfare, in which the seas would threaten the land, "the rude son should strike his father dead," or, rather, "right and wrong . . . Should lose their names, and so should justice too." Raw power would dominate, will would degenerate into appetite; "And appetite, an universal wolf, So doubly seconded with will and power, Must make perforce an universal prey, And last eat up himself." Chaos would come again.

Against this background of religion and philosophy, Shakespeare tells the story of England's kings, and in the process he foreshadows the titanic struggles in which Othello and Macbeth and Lear are to go to their deaths. For these kings and their unruly henchmen are first of all human beings, men, proud men, "dressed in a little brief authority," but compounded of good and evil as other men are, stirred by like passions, seduced by the same temptations, and capable, on occasion, of the same unpredictable generosity and compassion and heroism.

In holding the mirror up to nature, the Histories reflect the panorama of English life. There are melodramatic despots like the Machiavellian Richard III, who lusts for power and revels in his skill in manipulating friend and foe alike; sensitive lovers of the beautiful like Richard II, who in a later age might have won fame as a Renaissance Maecenas but who lacked the common sense and the iron devotion to duty needful in a king; crafty politicians like Henry IV, plagued by the crime that brought him to the throne and wanting the magnanimity to win and hold the loyalty of his subjects. Other kings there are, ambitious nobles and proud prelates; vengeful queens, like Margaret, and queens right royal, like Katharine of Aragon.

Not all the people are kings and nobles, however, nor are all the scenes laid in court and cloister. Simpcox, the beggar who is "miraculously" cured of blindness and lameness at St. Albans, Jack Cade and his followers, and Horner the armourer and his man Peter, though they come from much lower levels of society, speak an English as racy and authentic as that used by Henry V, homely, but with a tang of its own. These are the predecessors of Falstaff's companions in *1* and *2 Henry IV* and *Henry V*, and, especially, of Mouldy, Shadow, Bullcalf, and Feeble in the press scene in *2 Henry IV*. "By my troth, I care not," says Feeble after he has been pricked to go to the wars; "a man can die but once; we owe God a death. I'll ne'er bear a base mind. An't be my destiny, so; an't be not, so. No man's too good to serve's Prince; and let it go which way it will, he that dies this year is quit for the next." Prince Hamlet acquits himself only a little better:

. . . we defy augury: there is a special providence in the fall of a sparrow. If it be now, 'tis not to come; if it be not to come, it will be now; if it be not now, yet it will come—the readiness is all.

Scenes and lines like those in which the Hostess describes the death of Falstaff:

Nay, sure, he's not in hell: he's in Arthur's bosom, if ever man went to Arthur's bosom. 'A made a finer end, and went away an it had been any christom child; 'a parted ev'n just between twelve and one, ev'n at the turning o' th' tide; for after I saw him fumble with the sheets, and play with flowers, and smile upon his fingers' end, I knew there was but one way; for his nose was as sharp as a pen, and 'a babbl'd of green fields. 'How now, Sir John!' quoth I. 'What, man, be o' good cheer.' So 'a cried out 'God, God, God!' three or four times. Now I, to comfort him, bid him 'a should not think of God; I hop'd there was no need to trouble himself with any such thoughts yet. So 'a bade me lay more clothes on his feet; I put my hand into the bed and felt them, and they were as cold as any stone; then I felt to his knees, and so upward and upward, and all was as cold as any stone.

reveal that the playwright whose blank verse and rhymes are so varied and exuberant in *Romeo* and the early comedies had developed a supple prose that is adequate to any purpose of mirth or pathos.

From the outset of his career as playwright, Shakespeare had a matchless way with words and an architect's skill in construction. It was also a part of his genius to share the thoughts and passions of his characters and to hear and reproduce their individual accents. His Bolingbroke could no more speak the lines of Richard II than Prince Hal could make Falstaff's analysis of Honour, or Hamlet suffer the torments of Othello and utter them in the cadences of the Moor of Venice. These gifts were Shakespeare's birthright. The years of acting and writing taught him other things. *Richard III*, which is in some respects an anticipation of *Macbeth* (as *Richard II* is of *Hamlet* and *Julius Caesar*) is a closely knit play centering about one titanic figure. The high tension of the play can be traced in part to something that had not been prominent in earlier plays: the repeated identification of Richard with loathsome or dangerous animals. He is a *hell-hound, poisonous toad, foul hunch-back'd toad, bottled spider, hedge-hog, abortive, rooting hog* (in allusion to his crest, a Boar). And the recurring epithets serve the double purpose of characterizing the King and sustaining a unity of tone.

In *Richard II*, simple characterization by iterative or cluster imagery gives way to far subtler use of images. Sometimes the author indicates the symbolic meaning of a situation or incident, as when the gardeners while discussing their tasks reveal Richard to be a heedless gardener who has suffered "noisome weeds" to grow rank and "suck the soil's fertility from wholesome flowers." At other times, Shakespeare puts images in the mouths of his characters that make them disclose facets of their own natures. Thus when Richard, shortly before his death, hears music, he ponders the irony of his situation. Now, a prisoner, he has "the daintiness of ear to check time broke in a disorder'd string," whereas formerly, "for the concord of [his] state and time," he had not "an ear to hear [his] true time broke." Still another of the new uses of imagery is to have characters give their estimate of a situation. An unforgettable instance occurs at the castle in Wales, when Richard hears the summons to come down from the walls to parley with Bolingbroke. Dramatizing the situation—and himself—he cries out:

> Down, down, I come, like glist'ring Phaethon,
> Wanting the manage of unruly jades.
> In the base court? Base court, where kings grow base,
> To come at traitors' calls, and do them grace.

The self-identification of Richard with Phaethon, a pretender to the lordship of the sun's chariot, is especially significant, for throughout the play the sanctity of kingship is spoken of in terms of sun imagery.

With a greater technical and poetic skill came a wider experience of life and a more profound insight into personality. The panorama of life exhibited in his plays astounded even the earliest critics. Writing in 1664, the Marchioness of Newcastle marveled at the great variety of his characters and at Shakespeare's exact knowledge of them all, high and low alike:

> Yet *Shakespear* did not want Wit, to Express to the Life all Sorts of Persons, of what Quality, Profession, Degree, Breeding, or Birth soever; nor did he want Wit to Express the Divers, and Different Humours, or Natures, or Several Passions in mankind; and so Well he hath Express'd in his Playes all Sorts of Persons, as one would think he had been Transformed into every one of those Persons he hath Described; and as sometimes one would think he was Really himself the Clown or Jester he Feigns, so one would think, he was also the King, and Privy Counsellor; also as one would think he was Really the Coward he Feigns, so one would think he was the most Valiant and Experienced Souldier; Who would not think he had been such a man as his Sir *John Falstaff?* and who would not think he had been *Harry* the Fifth? and certainly *Julius Caesar, Augustus Caesar,* and *Antonius,* did never Really Act their parts Better, if so Well, as he hath Described them, and I believe that *Antonius* and *Brutus* did not Speak Better to the People, than he hath feign'd them.

PREFACE

The Marchioness concludes with the statement that Cleopatra, Nan Page, Beatrice, Mrs. Quickly, and others are presented so truly that "one would think [Shakespeare] had been Metamorphosed from a Man to a Woman."

The variety of characters in *1* and *2 Henry IV* and *Henry V* is almost incredible, and so is their vitality. Hotspur, Glendower, Lady Percy, Hostess Quickly and Doll Tearsheet, even Bardolph, Pistol, Justice Shallow, and Fluellen seem colorless in comparison with Sir John Falstaff. A fat, cowardly, boastful drunkard, he should be despised or abhorred. But by his zest for life and his ready wit he dominates two plays, and the account of his death casts a shadow upon a third play. It has been said of Mercutio that Shakespeare had to kill him off early in *Romeo and Juliet* to keep him from running away with the play. Shylock, who should have been a comic villain, made such an appeal to Shakespeare's humanity ("Hath not a Jew eyes?") that he got out of hand and almost turned a romantic comedy into a tragedy of racial antipathy. Falstaff is the last of Shakespeare's characters to break the mold in which he should have been cast. He captured Shakespeare's imagination so completely that his partisans cannot to this day forgive Prince Hal, by whom Sir John's heart was "fracted and corroborate." Not many actors in these pallid times have the temerity to attempt the portrayal of this greatest of comic creations.

Living in the midst of social and economic revolution in a world torn by the bitterest of religious and political conflicts, the Elizabethans were stirred by the hope of wealth and empire in the New World of the Americas. They watched Shakespeare's English Histories in the theatre, and they read them, as they read Greek and Roman history, for an understanding of how good and evil men had managed affairs of state and had been transformed, for better or worse, by the quest or the use of power. The dangers faced by Shakespeare's England seemed no less terrible then than atomic warfare appears today. It was under continual threat by Spain and the Papacy; we grapple with the problems of the Cold War and Coexistence. The Battle of the Coral Sea helps us to understand the significance of the Spanish Armada to the Elizabethans. Gettysburg and Yorktown give meaning to Bosworth Field and Agincourt. It is not by accident that in this age of insecurity, when men are competing for the mastery of interplanetary space, there has been a quickening of American interest in History. Not the issues only of the Civil War, but the statesmen, the military leaders, the great campaigns, and the crucial battles, are being reappraised in an unparalleled flood of books. And not in a hundred years has there been so close a scrutiny of the struggle for American independence. We have needed inspiration from the suffering and heroism of Valley Forge, King's Mountain, Shiloh, and the Wilderness, and from the fortitude and nobility of Washington and Lincoln, just as we have needed the rediscovery and the reaffirmation of the principles and ideals upon which America was founded. A rootless generation is seeking to re-establish its roots. Today, as in the age of Shakespeare, when Right and Wrong seem almost to have lost their names and naked power threatens to become a universal wolf and eat up mankind, thoughtful people turn naturally to biography and history, seeking in the historians and the poets a truer insight into human nature and a clearer hope of the triumph of the human spirit.

A Note on the Illustrations

BY JOHN FARLEIGH

IN THE ILLUSTRATION of these ten Historical Plays I have preferred to see them as one theme—the history of England from King John to King Henry VIII—with the personality and drama of each king in each play, one inevitably leading on to the other. I have done this, partly accepting the unquestioned Tudor propaganda and partly with the knowledge of the greatness and beauty of the Plantagenets, and of how much they contributed to English culture.

I have tried in each frontispiece to summarise the essence of the play, and in each end-piece to lead on to the next—hoping that this might create the varied pattern that is English history. The combination of Shakespeare and English history is so great a matter that the illustrator can scarcely count on doing justice to them both; but it is my contribution.

As far as is possible I have incorporated the actual portraits of the kings, although I would not claim to have perfected the contemporary detail. I had no wish to make the series a source of reference for students of costume, but have used authentic detail in so far as it colours the action. Colour is used more as a symbol to build up atmosphere and has no period significance.

And now to the individual engravings:

King John. The death of Arthur: perhaps a gloomy note to start on, but there is a darkness belonging to that period that one does not feel later. Hubert, the intended executioner, is shocked at finding the body and looks round in fear. The image of the king is traced against the background of the castle—aloof and detached from his own crime. The end-piece shows the loss of the crown jewels in The Wash—typical of the carelessness of King John as the murder is of his cruelty.

King Richard II. A sensitive man brought down by treachery, one out of his time. The scene is "down court, down king," presaging his abdication and death. The end-piece is a play on the King's words to Bolingbroke (Act IV, Scene 1)—

> Now is this golden crown like a deep well
> That owes two buckets, filling one another;
> The emptier ever dancing in the air,
> The other down, unseen, and full of water.

xix

That bucket down and full of tears am I,
Drinking my griefs, whilst you mount up on high.

And, of course, the murder of Richard is indicated.

King Henry IV, Part 1. The revolt of the Percys resulting finally in the Battle of Shrewsbury, with the character of King Henry V already emerging in the young Prince of Wales. Percy Hotspur must have captured Shakespeare's sympathy and imagination, for his death in battle has much of tragedy in it. The full picture shows Prince Hal saving King Henry IV from Hotspur at Shrewsbury; Percy is shown with his crescent on his helm. The end-piece is intended to convey the fall of Percy Hotspur—his arms reversed and his fallen helmet—with something of the nostalgic pathos of such scenes.

King Henry IV, Part 2. The disillusion and dissolution of the King are symptomatic. Prince Henry moves slowly from his irresponsible youth to the dawn of his kingship. Turning his back on the past, he tries on the crown while the king lies dying. His character has grown throughout these two plays, and at the end of this play he already emerges as an important figure. End-piece: the arms of Prince Hal rising above the relics of the gaming table. One remembers his rebuke to Falstaff, "I know thee not, old man."

King Henry V. The character of King Henry V has now emerged, at the provocation of the French court, and, to their surprise, he leads his army across to France. The first of the royal heroes in these plays, he must have been favoured by Shakespeare. Here are the great heroic speeches. Henry is shown delivering his famous address at Southampton before setting off in all the bravura of his youth and attainment. The end-piece of the lion and the lily symbolizes his marriage to Katherine of France.

King Henry VI, Part 1. Crowned young upon the early death of Henry V, the King is from the first set apart and alone. Disinclined from war, a scholar, out of his time, he was from the first moment of his crowning surrounded by factious and scheming nobles—this is the motif of the frontispiece. The end-piece—the red and white roses of York and Lancaster—indicates the beginning of the War of the Roses.

King Henry VI, Part 2. The quarrels of the nobles, treason, plots—the ambition and activity of the Queen, so misguided, and separated from her husband. She won all battles except when the King was present, and she almost lost England. The King is seen, as ever, apart, with the Queen—close to Suffolk, her favourite—in the background. The plotting goes on while the King remains apart, preferring a treaty to a battle. The end-piece of traitors' heads on the gateway to London Bridge is the expected footnote to this play.

A NOTE ON THE ILLUSTRATIONS

King Henry VI, Part 3. The King has bartered his crown to the House of York for his life. It is the Battle of Tewkesbury, led by the Queen and forced upon King Henry. The King is seen still alone, pensive and resting on a staff. It is the end of a monarch who favoured treaties while men yet understood only force. The end-piece is a portrait of Edward IV; he holds the white rose—the House of York has now taken over from the House of Lancaster.

King Richard III. I have accepted Shakespeare's villain, though to-day Richard III has been considerably recast. He is in his tent before the last battle and haunted by his many victims; he sees the crown taken from him. A veritable villain, but a soldier and fearless—except for this moment—up to the end. The end-piece of the crown found on the thorn-bush is an indication of the depth to which he had brought the idea of kingship.

King Henry VIII. The Tudors have taken over from the Plantagenets. Shown with all the swagger of the coming Elizabethan age, Henry is seen conversing intimately with Wolsey, the arch-plotter, the churchman. The first obvious emergence of the Church in affairs temporal—the dark curtains in the background will fall for Wolsey before the play is out. The end-piece gives, as it were, a glimpse of the sun shortly to rise in the glory of Elizabeth's reign—foretold in Cranmer's baptismal speech at the end of the play.

And so the illustrations do not end the drama here so much as look into the future, or rather the present when Shakespeare was writing his plays. The end of each play is the beginning of the next stage in history. The end of the book that contains so significant a part of English history is but the beginning of a new phase, the glory of the Elizabethan era.

The Life and Death of
King John

KING JOHN

KING JOHN stands first among the Histories, because Heminge and Condell arranged this group according to the dates of the kings who give their titles to the plays. The place of this play in the chronology of Shakespeare's work is, however, still a subject of scholarly dispute.

Scholars have long favoured a date soon after 1594 for the play and regarded it as Shakespeare's rehandling of a play published in two parts in 1591 named *The Troublesome Raigne of King John*. A preliminary address to the reader of *The Troublesome Raigne* commends King John to his attention as an English patriot too little regarded by his countrymen, who have, so the writer implies, been applauding a heathen conqueror like Tamburlaine, when they might have been better employed admiring the courage of this Christian and champion of English liberties.

The accounts found in modern histories of King John and his doings present a man so little like a Christian or a champion of English liberties that one must pause for a little to ask why the Elizabethans regarded John so differently. To-day one hears of John as a man not without the abilities that often go with cunning and greed or the policy that need take no reckoning of honesty or shame; a man, however, that neither ability nor policy could deliver from the visitations his wickedness brought on him. The most humiliating, had he been capable of shame, was his submission to Pope Innocent the Third. The dispute over the election to the See of Canterbury led to a Papal interdict and later excommunication; John was willing to end a quarrel in which he was worsted by surrendering his crown to Pandulf the Papal Legate and receiving it again as a vassal of the Pope. The Pope, however, could not deliver him from his other great submission. John appealed to the Pope to release him from the obligations imposed on him by Magna Carta; but while the country had not been willing to resist the Pope, when the cause of his displeasure seemed ecclesiastical, the baronage would not accept the Papal ruling on Magna Carta. Had

3

Innocent not later admitted the validity of the Charter, the nobles would have recognized Louis, the son of Philip the Second of France, as King of England. Innocent the Third had made his great power felt in England as in so many of the countries of Europe; the Pope's integrity had triumphed over John's duplicity; but the nobility of England did not recognize the Pope's claim to rule not only the Church, but the whole political world, and they were not prepared to allow John as the Pope's nominee to rule more tyranically than he had done before his submission to Pandulf. When, therefore, we find the author of *The Troublesome Raigne* introduce John to his readers as a champion of English liberties and tell us how

> For Christs true faith indur'd he many a storme
> And set himself against the Man of Rome,
> Untill base treason (by a damned wight)
> Did all his former triumphs put to flight—

we have to look for some strong current of political thought that could so transport this king from the censure of his contemporaries to the admiration of the Elizabethans.

The events that prompted the transformation were the Reformation and the rise of the new national state. In John's reign the ideas now summarized in the words "Englishman" and "Frenchman" had not yet taken shape; the concepts that shaped European society were feudal not national. By the reign of Henry the Eighth France and England were no longer merely parts of a feudal Europe but nations, and the ecclesiastical jurisdiction of Rome in England was now in dispute. It was in these new conditions that John Bale, a churchman who had become the determined enemy of Rome, presented the story of King John as a warning to his countrymen of the pretensions and dangers of the Roman claims. He cast his exhortation into the form of a play in which figure not only persons like John and Pandulf and Stephen Langton, but abstract personages like Civil Order and Sedition, and representative characters like Nobility, Clergy, and England herself. It cannot be said that John acts the part of a hero, for there is little or no action in the production, but he serves as the mouthpiece for a sustained complaint against the tyranny of Rome and the wickedness of her clergy. He surrenders in lamenting strains to the Cardinal, and is soon afterwards poisoned by the monk Dissimulation. There follows a long epilogue-like scene in which the dead king's virtues are celebrated; Nobility now acknowledges its fault in failing to serve the king with the loyalty his office rightly demanded; and the figure of Imperial Majesty, now dominating the scene, orders to the satisfaction of Civil Order the immediate execution of Sedition.

Bale first shaped his historical morality in the days of Henry the Eighth. He had, however, to take himself to the continent on the fall of Cromwell, and again on the accession of Mary; but he lived to give his final revisions to the piece after the accession of Elizabeth. Edward the Sixth had made him Bishop of Ossory, and his last years under Elizabeth he enjoyed as a prebendary of Canterbury. His writings were many but his *King Johan* is for students of drama his most interesting work; it exhibits the temper common to the extreme partisans of both sides in this religious controversy, and explains how King John almost ceased to be a historical figure and assumed the attributes of the herald of the new age in England that was anti-papal and national.

Compared with Bale's *King Johan* the anonymous *Troublesome Raigne of King John* is a play full of the action and stir characteristic of the pieces that were making the London playhouses of the 1590's both popular and paying ventures; but it carries on the tradition about John established in the reign of Henry the Eighth. That the tradition should assume new life immediately after the defeat of the Armada was not unnatural: England had had to meet the armed aggression of their religious and national enemies, and the anonymous author of *The Troublesome Raigne* was as whole-hearted as Bale in his championship of King John,

A warlike Christian and your countryman,

although he had not been quite as happy in his warfare as his compatriots of these later days.

If *The Troublesome Raigne* is indeed, as many scholars hold, an original play, it is, however imperfect as a drama, an important document in the history of the Elizabethan stage. It would have claims to be the first History, in the sense in which we may call Shakespeare's *Henry VI* or *Richard III* Histories, and the forerunner of a line of plays that have robbed it of its dramatic interest but not of its priority. And this priority gives it for students of the drama a peculiar interest; for its author, in spite of much ineptitude, reveals, were he indeed its creator, powers of construction and invention that Shakespeare himself was to acknowledge in what is regarded as his rehandling of the work.

Even that most obdurate of Shakespeare's critics, Tolstoi, while denouncing the immoral view of life he discovers in the plays, cannot refrain from commending one feature of Shakespeare's art and singles out for special praise "the masterly development of the scenes, which constitutes Shakespeare's speciality." This was an art that Tolstoi himself had perfected in his great novels, and he recognized instinctively the technical accomplishment of the older master; although at the same time he regarded Shakespeare's outlook with the same dissatisfaction that his own masterpieces now inflicted on him. In this speciality, however, the author of *The Troublesome Raigne* may be fairly held to have anticipated Shakespeare and even to have instructed him; for Shakespeare's *King John* follows *The Troublesome Raigne* almost scene for scene. There are of course innumerable refinements in the treatment, but on the whole the scenic structure of the plays is the same. Whatever his deficiencies the anonymous author of *The Troublesome Raigne* must be given high commendation for his constructive powers.

Nor should what may be called his powers of invention be overlooked. He felt impelled, even if only by his need of dramatic incident, to treat many more events in the reign of John than Bale included; and the author of *The Troublesome Raigne* was faced with this difficulty that the more he dwelt on the details of John's doings the less of a hero the king became. In addition to the surrender to the Papacy, there was the revolt of the nobility, only touched on indirectly by Bale, and above all the disposal of Arthur. Whatever John's contemporaries in England may have felt about Richard's lawful successor to the throne, the Elizabethans could not disregard Arthur's claim; and it was clear to them that John was ridding himself of the rightful heir. Such a deliberate and cold-blooded bit of business, especially when taken in conjunction with surrender elsewhere, however politic, could do little to attract the sympathy even of John's countrymen, and nothing to make him a rallying point for patriots. The author of *The Troublesome Raigne* however was equal to the situation: by a bold and dexterous stroke he transferred the burden of England's honour to a character created expressly for its support. The creation of the Bastard Falconbridge, as King Richard's illegitimate son, fills the gap in the centre of the picture left by John's very marginal transactions, and allows the dramatist the necessary support for his national sympathies. The author of *The Troublesome Raigne* must therefore be credited not merely with the power with which he develops his scenes but with the inventiveness that the creation of Falconbridge reveals.

Unfortunately this power of construction, admittedly one of the most important gifts in those who write for the theatre, and the further ability to establish a harmony between plot and characterization, are not matched with an equal skill in handling his verse or vocabulary. The author has filled his lines with what look like his pickings among the odds and ends of other plays; unless we suppose that this play so attracted contemporary dramatists that its expressions echo through their subsequent productions.

It is impossible to lay down rules for the mixture of gifts and defects that any man may draw from Nature's lottery; but it must be admitted that the author of *The Troublesome Raigne* exhibits a most unusual combination of skill and clumsiness. So remarkable indeed are the contrasts in attainment revealed by the various aspects of the play that it would be simpler to account for them by supposing that the author was not an original creator at all but merely an imitator of a more gifted writer's work. Two considerations however have always discouraged the suggestion that *The Troublesome Raigne* is no more than a copy of Shakespeare's *King John*: the idea that Shakespeare was a great genius but no innovator, and the conviction that Shakespeare had written little or nothing for the stage before 1591.

That the most gifted writers may be the greatest of borrowers is a familiar paradox. Men of genius have the gift of turning the oddest suggestions to account. The reply attributed to Molière when charged with plagiarism, *Je prends mon bien où je le trouve*, is the answer of a man whose originality needed no defence, although sources and analogues can be found for almost every work he wrote. What a man cannot borrow, however keen his eye for *son bien*, are his powers of construction and integration; these are the signs of the born poet or artist, for such powers cannot be acquired, though they may be developed. Yet it is precisely here that the author of *The Troublesome Raigne* is supposed to have shown the way to Shakespeare. In all that can be put under the heading of vocabulary or versification or atmosphere the plays are worlds apart; in their construction and unity of impression they are as close together as two very differing pieces can be.

As to the date of publication of *The Troublesome Raigne* ruling out Shakespeare's priority, that is an argument that is less convincing than it once was. The possibility that Shakespeare had made a beginning as a dramatist some time before 1591 is now admitted. *King John* as we now have it may seem more mature than what we may surmise of his powers in 1590 warrants. Such assumptions are unfortunately in our present state of knowledge difficult to assess. The whole question therefore must be considered still an open one. It is however difficult to attribute to an unknown dramatist the powers characteristic of a born playwright, especially as he was never, so far as we know, to exercise them again in so remarkable a fashion. It is simpler to suppose he took his framework from the man who we know excelled in such constructions. Yet the simpler explanation need not necessarily be the true one, and *The Troublesome Raigne* may be just another of those things that criticism, even in its dreams, finds it difficult to imagine.

KING JOHN
PRINCE HENRY, *his son*
ARTHUR, DUKE OF BRITAINE, *son of Geffrey, late Duke of
Britaine, the elder brother of King John*
EARL OF PEMBROKE
EARL OF ESSEX
EARL OF SALISBURY
LORD BIGOT
HUBERT DE BURGH
ROBERT FAULCONBRIDGE, *son to Sir Robert Faulconbridge*
PHILIP THE BASTARD, *his half-brother*
JAMES GURNEY, *servant to Lady Faulconbridge*
PETER OF POMFRET, *a prophet*

KING PHILIP OF FRANCE
LEWIS, *the Dauphin*
LYMOGES, *Duke of Austria*
CARDINAL PANDULPH, *the Pope's legate*
MELUN, *a French lord*
CHATILLON, *ambassador from France to King John*

QUEEN ELINOR, *widow of King Henry II and mother to
King John*
CONSTANCE, *mother to Arthur*
BLANCH OF SPAIN, *daughter to the King of Castile and niece
to King John*
LADY FAULCONBRIDGE, *widow of Sir Robert Faulconbridge*

Lords, Citizens of Angiers, Sheriff, Heralds, Officers, Soldiers, Executioners, Messengers, Attendants

SCENE:

England and France

King John

ACT I. SCENE 1

KING JOHN'S *palace*

Enter KING JOHN, QUEEN ELINOR, PEMBROKE, ESSEX,
SALISBURY, *and others, with* CHATILLON

KING JOHN. Now, say, Chatillon, what would France with
us?
CHATILLON. Thus, after greeting, speaks the King of France
In my behaviour to the majesty,
The borrowed majesty, of England here.
ELINOR. A strange beginning—'borrowed majesty'!
KING JOHN. Silence, good mother; hear the embassy.
CHATILLON. Philip of France, in right and true behalf
Of thy deceased brother Geffrey's son,
Arthur Plantagenet, lays most lawful claim
To this fair island and the territories,
To Ireland, Poictiers, Anjou, Touraine, Maine,
Desiring thee to lay aside the sword
Which sways usurpingly these several titles,
And put the same into young Arthur's hand,
Thy nephew and right royal sovereign.
KING JOHN. What follows if we disallow of this?
CHATILLON. The proud control of fierce and bloody war,
To enforce these rights so forcibly withheld.
KING JOHN. Here have we war for war, and blood for blood,
Controlment for controlment—so answer France.
CHATILLON. Then take my king's defiance from my mouth—
The farthest limit of my embassy.
KING JOHN. Bear mine to him, and so depart in peace;
Be thou as lightning in the eyes of France;
For ere thou canst report I will be there,
The thunder of my cannon shall be heard.
So hence! Be thou the trumpet of our wrath

And sullen presage of your own decay.
An honourable conduct let him have—
Pembroke, look to 't. Farewell, Chatillon.

Exeunt CHATILLON *and* PEMBROKE

ELINOR. What now, my son! Have I not ever said
    How that ambitious Constance would not cease
    Till she had kindled France and all the world
    Upon the right and party of her son?
    This might have been prevented and made whole
    With very easy arguments of love,
    Which now the manage of two kingdoms must
    With fearful bloody issue arbitrate.
KING JOHN. Our strong possession and our right for us!
ELINOR. Your strong possession much more than your right,
    Or else it must go wrong with you and me;
    So much my conscience whispers in your ear,
    Which none but heaven and you and I shall hear.

Enter a SHERIFF

ESSEX. My liege, here is the strangest controversy
    Come from the country to be judg'd by you
    That e'er I heard. Shall I produce the men?
KING JOHN. Let them approach.   *Exit* SHERIFF
    Our abbeys and our priories shall pay
    This expedition's charge.

Enter ROBERT FAULCONBRIDGE *and* PHILIP, *his bastard brother*

    What men are you?
BASTARD. Your faithful subject I, a gentleman
    Born in Northamptonshire, and eldest son,
    As I suppose, to Robert Faulconbridge—
    A soldier by the honour-giving hand
    Of Cœur-de-lion knighted in the field.
KING JOHN. What art thou?
ROBERT. The son and heir to that same Faulconbridge.
KING JOHN. Is that the elder, and art thou the heir?
    You came not of one mother then, it seems.
BASTARD. Most certain of one mother, mighty king—
    That is well known—and, as I think, one father;
    But for the certain knowledge of that truth

I put you o'er to heaven and to my mother.
Of that I doubt, as all men's children may.
ELINOR. Out on thee, rude man! Thou dost shame thy mother,
  And wound her honour with this diffidence.
BASTARD. I, madam? No, I have no reason for it—
  That is my brother's plea, and none of mine;
  The which if he can prove, 'a pops me out
  At least from fair five hundred pound a year.
  Heaven guard my mother's honour and my land!
KING JOHN. A good blunt fellow. Why, being younger born,
  Doth he lay claim to thine inheritance?
BASTARD. I know not why, except to get the land.
  But once he slander'd me with bastardy;
  But whe'er I be as true begot or no,
  That still I lay upon my mother's head;
  But that I am as well begot, my liege—
  Fair fall the bones that took the pains for me!—
  Compare our faces and be judge yourself.
  If old Sir Robert did beget us both
  And were our father, and this son like him—
  O old Sir Robert, father, on my knee
  I give heaven thanks I was not like to thee!
KING JOHN. Why, what a madcap hath heaven lent us here!
ELINOR. He hath a trick of Cœur-de-lion's face;
  The accent of his tongue affecteth him.
  Do you not read some tokens of my son
  In the large composition of this man?
KING JOHN. Mine eye hath well examined his parts
  And finds them perfect Richard. Sirrah, speak,
  What doth move you to claim your brother's land?
BASTARD. Because he hath a half-face, like my father.
  With half that face would he have all my land:
  A half-fac'd groat five hundred pound a year!
ROBERT. My gracious liege, when that my father liv'd,
  Your brother did employ my father much—
BASTARD. Well, sir, by this you cannot get my land:
  Your tale must be how he employ'd my mother.
ROBERT. And once dispatch'd him in an embassy
  To Germany, there with the Emperor
  To treat of high affairs touching that time.

Th' advantage of his absence took the King,
And in the meantime sojourn'd at my father's;
Where how he did prevail I shame to speak—
But truth is truth: large lengths of seas and shores
Between my father and my mother lay,
As I have heard my father speak himself,
When this same lusty gentleman was got.
Upon his death-bed he by will bequeath'd
His lands to me, and took it on his death
That this my mother's son was none of his;
And if he were, he came into the world
Full fourteen weeks before the course of time.
Then, good my liege, let me have what is mine,
My father's land, as was my father's will.

KING JOHN. Sirrah, your brother is legitimate:
Your father's wife did after wedlock bear him,
And if she did play false, the fault was hers;
Which fault lies on the hazards of all husbands
That marry wives. Tell me, how if my brother,
Who, as you say, took pains to get this son,
Had of your father claim'd this son for his?
In sooth, good friend, your father might have kept
This calf, bred from his cow, from all the world;
In sooth, he might; then, if he were my brother's,
My brother might not claim him; nor your father,
Being none of his, refuse him. This concludes:
My mother's son did get your father's heir;
Your father's heir must have your father's land.

ROBERT. Shall then my father's will be of no force
To dispossess that child which is not his?

BASTARD. Of no more force to dispossess me, sir,
Than was his will to get me, as I think.

ELINOR. Whether hadst thou rather be a Faulconbridge,
And like thy brother, to enjoy thy land,
Or the reputed son of Cœur-de-lion,
Lord of thy presence and no land beside?

BASTARD. Madam, an if my brother had my shape
And I had his, Sir Robert's his, like him;
And if my legs were two such riding-rods,
My arms such eel-skins stuff'd, my face so thin

That in mine ear I durst not stick a rose
Lest men should say 'Look where three-farthings goes!'
And, to his shape, were heir to all this land—
Would I might never stir from off this place,
I would give it every foot to have this face!
I would not be Sir Nob in any case.

ELINOR. I like thee well. Wilt thou forsake thy fortune,
Bequeath thy land to him and follow me?
I am a soldier and now bound to France.

BASTARD. Brother, take you my land, I'll take my chance.
Your face hath got five hundred pound a year,
Yet sell your face for fivepence and 'tis dear.
Madam, I'll follow you unto the death.

ELINOR. Nay, I would have you go before me thither.

BASTARD. Our country manners give our betters way.

KING JOHN. What is thy name?

BASTARD. Philip, my liege, so is my name begun:
Philip, good old Sir Robert's wife's eldest son.

KING JOHN. From henceforth bear his name whose form
thou bearest:
Kneel thou down Philip, but rise more great—
Arise Sir Richard and Plantagenet.

BASTARD. Brother by th' mother's side, give me your hand;
My father gave me honour, yours gave land.
Now blessed be the hour, by night or day,
When I was got, Sir Robert was away!

ELINOR. The very spirit of Plantagenet!
I am thy grandam, Richard: call me so.

BASTARD. Madam, by chance, but not by truth; what though?
Something about, a little from the right,
In at the window, or else o'er the hatch;
Who dares not stir by day must walk by night;
And have is have, however men do catch.
Near or far off, well won is still well shot;
And I am I, howe'er I was begot.

KING JOHN. Go, Faulconbridge; now hast thou thy desire:
A landless knight makes thee a landed squire.
Come, madam, and come, Richard, we must speed
For France, for France, for it is more than need.

BASTARD. Brother, adieu. Good fortune come to thee!

For thou wast got i' th' way of honesty.

Exeunt all but the BASTARD

A foot of honour better than I was;
But many a many foot of land the worse.
Well, now can I make any Joan a lady.
'Good den, Sir Richard!'—'God-a-mercy, fellow!'
And if his name be George, I'll call him Peter;
For new-made honour doth forget men's names:
'Tis too respective and too sociable
For your conversion. Now your traveller,
He and his toothpick at my worship's mess—
And when my knightly stomach is suffic'd,
Why then I suck my teeth and catechize
My picked man of countries: 'My dear sir,'
Thus leaning on mine elbow I begin
'I shall beseech you'—That is question now;
And then comes answer like an Absey book:
'O sir,' says answer 'at your best command,
At your employment, at your service, sir!'
'No, sir,' says question 'I, sweet sir, at yours.'
And so, ere answer knows what question would,
Saving in dialogue of compliment,
And talking of the Alps and Apennines,
The Pyrenean and the river Po—
It draws toward supper in conclusion so.
But this is worshipful society,
And fits the mounting spirit like myself;
For he is but a bastard to the time
That doth not smack of observation—
And so am I, whether I smack or no;
And not alone in habit and device,
Exterior form, outward accoutrement,
But from the inward motion to deliver
Sweet, sweet, sweet poison for the age's tooth;
Which, though I will not practise to deceive,
Yet, to avoid deceit, I mean to learn;
For it shall strew the footsteps of my rising.
But who comes in such haste in riding-robes?
What woman-post is this? Hath she no husband
That will take pains to blow a horn before her?

Enter LADY FAULCONBRIDGE, *and* JAMES GURNEY

O me, 'tis my mother! How now, good lady!
What brings you here to court so hastily?
LADY FAULCONBRIDGE. Where is that slave, thy brother?
    Where is he
That holds in chase mine honour up and down?
BASTARD. My brother Robert, old Sir Robert's son?
    Colbrand the giant, that same mighty man?
    Is it Sir Robert's son that you seek so?
LADY FAULCONBRIDGE. Sir Robert's son! Ay, thou unrever-
    end boy,
    Sir Robert's son! Why scorn'st thou at Sir Robert?
    He is Sir Robert's son, and so art thou.
BASTARD. James Gurney, wilt thou give us leave awhile?
GURNEY. Good leave, good Philip.
BASTARD. Philip—Sparrow! James,
    There's toys abroad—anon I'll tell thee more.
                                        Exit GURNEY

    Madam, I was not old Sir Robert's son;
    Sir Robert might have eat his part in me
    Upon Good Friday, and ne'er broke his fast.
    Sir Robert could do: well—marry, to confess—
    Could he get me? Sir Robert could not do it:
    We know his handiwork. Therefore, good mother,
    To whom am I beholding for these limbs?
    Sir Robert never holp to make this leg.
LADY FAULCONBRIDGE. Hast thou conspired with thy brother
    too,
    That for thine own gain shouldst defend mine honour?
    What means this scorn, thou most untoward knave?
BASTARD. Knight, knight, good mother, Basilisco-like.
    What! I am dubb'd; I have it on my shoulder.
    But, mother, I am not Sir Robert's son:
    I have disclaim'd Sir Robert and my land;
    Legitimation, name, and all is gone.
    Then, good my mother, let me know my father—
    Some proper man, I hope. Who was it, mother?
LADY FAULCONBRIDGE. Hast thou denied thyself a Faulcon-
    bridge?

BASTARD. As faithfully as I deny the devil.

LADY FAULCONBRIDGE. King Richard Cœur-de-lion was thy
  father.
  By long and vehement suit I was seduc'd
  To make room for him in my husband's bed.
  Heaven lay not my transgression to my charge!
  Thou art the issue of my dear offence,
  Which was so strongly urg'd past my defence.

BASTARD. Now, by this light, were I to get again,
  Madam, I would not wish a better father.
  Some sins do bear their privilege on earth,
  And so doth yours: your fault was not your folly;
  Needs must you lay your heart at his dispose,
  Subjected tribute to commanding love,
  Against whose fury and unmatched force
  The aweless lion could not wage the fight
  Nor keep his princely heart from Richard's hand.
  He that perforce robs lions of their hearts
  May easily win a woman's. Ay, my mother,
  With all my heart I thank thee for my father!
  Who lives and dares but say thou didst not well
  When I was got, I'll send his soul to hell.
  Come, lady, I will show thee to my kin;
  And they shall say when Richard me begot,
  If thou hadst said him nay, it had been sin.
  Who says it was, he lies; I say 'twas not.   *Exeunt*

ACT II. SCENE 1

France. Before Angiers

Enter, on one side, AUSTRIA *and forces; on the other,*
KING PHILIP OF FRANCE, LEWIS *the Dauphin,*
CONSTANCE, ARTHUR, *and forces*

KING PHILIP. Before Angiers well met, brave Austria.
  Arthur, that great forerunner of thy blood,
  Richard, that robb'd the lion of his heart

And fought the holy wars in Palestine,
By this brave duke came early to his grave;
And for amends to his posterity,
At our importance hither is he come
To spread his colours, boy, in thy behalf;
And to rebuke the usurpation
Of thy unnatural uncle, English John.
Embrace him, love him, give him welcome hither.

ARTHUR. God shall forgive you Cœur-de-lion's death
The rather that you give his offspring life,
Shadowing their right under your wings of war.
I give you welcome with a powerless hand,
But with a heart full of unstained love;
Welcome before the gates of Angiers, Duke.

KING PHILIP. A noble boy! Who would not do thee right?

AUSTRIA. Upon thy cheek lay I this zealous kiss
As seal to this indenture of my love:
That to my home I will no more return
Till Angiers and the right thou hast in France,
Together with that pale, that white-fac'd shore,
Whose foot spurns back the ocean's roaring tides
And coops from other lands her islanders—
Even till that England, hedg'd in with the main,
That water-walled bulwark, still secure
And confident from foreign purposes—
Even till that utmost corner of the west
Salute thee for her king. Till then, fair boy,
Will I not think of home, but follow arms.

CONSTANCE. O, take his mother's thanks, a widow's thanks,
Till your strong hand shall help to give him strength
To make a more requital to your love!

AUSTRIA. The peace of heaven is theirs that lift their swords
In such a just and charitable war.

KING PHILIP. Well then, to work! Our cannon shall be bent
Against the brows of this resisting town;
Call for our chiefest men of discipline,
To cull the plots of best advantages.
We'll lay before this town our royal bones,
Wade to the market-place in Frenchmen's blood,
But we will make it subject to this boy.

CONSTANCE. Stay for an answer to your embassy,
 Lest unadvis'd you stain your swords with blood;
 My Lord Chatillon may from England bring
 That right in peace which here we urge in war,
 And then we shall repent each drop of blood
 That hot rash haste so indirectly shed.

Enter CHATILLON

KING PHILIP. A wonder, lady! Lo, upon thy wish,
 Our messenger Chatillon is arriv'd.
 What England says, say briefly, gentle lord;
 We coldly pause for thee. Chatillon, speak.
CHATILLON. Then turn your forces from this paltry siege
 And stir them up against a mightier task.
 England, impatient of your just demands,
 Hath put himself in arms. The adverse winds,
 Whose leisure I have stay'd, have given him time
 To land his legions all as soon as I;
 His marches are expedient to this town,
 His forces strong, his soldiers confident.
 With him along is come the mother-queen,
 An Ate, stirring him to blood and strife;
 With her her niece, the Lady Blanch of Spain;
 With them a bastard of the king's deceas'd;
 And all th' unsettled humours of the land—
 Rash, inconsiderate, fiery voluntaries,
 With ladies' faces and fierce dragons' spleens—
 Have sold their fortunes at their native homes,
 Bearing their birthrights proudly on their backs,
 To make a hazard of new fortunes here.
 In brief, a braver choice of dauntless spirits
 Than now the English bottoms have waft o'er
 Did never float upon the swelling tide
 To do offence and scathe in Christendom. [*Drum beats*]
 The interruption of their churlish drums
 Cuts off more circumstance: they are at hand;
 To parley or to fight, therefore prepare.
KING PHILIP. How much unlook'd for is this expedition!
AUSTRIA. By how much unexpected, by so much
 We must awake endeavour for defence,

For courage mounteth with occasion.
Let them be welcome then; we are prepar'd.

Enter KING JOHN, ELINOR, BLANCH, *the* BASTARD,
PEMBROKE, *and others*

KING JOHN. Peace be to France, if France in peace permit
  Our just and lineal entrance to our own!
  If not, bleed France, and peace ascend to heaven,
  Whiles we, God's wrathful agent, do correct
  Their proud contempt that beats His peace to heaven!
KING PHILIP. Peace be to England, if that war return
  From France to England, there to live in peace!
  England we love, and for that England's sake
  With burden of our armour here we sweat.
  This toil of ours should be a work of thine;
  But thou from loving England art so far
  That thou hast under-wrought his lawful king,
  Cut off the sequence of posterity,
  Outfaced infant state, and done a rape
  Upon the maiden virtue of the crown.
  Look here upon thy brother Geffrey's face:
  These eyes, these brows, were moulded out of his;
  This little abstract doth contain that large
  Which died in Geffrey, and the hand of time
  Shall draw this brief into as huge a volume.
  That Geffrey was thy elder brother born,
  And this his son; England was Geffrey's right,
  And this is Geffrey's. In the name of God,
  How comes it then that thou art call'd a king,
  When living blood doth in these temples beat
  Which owe the crown that thou o'er-masterest?
KING JOHN. From whom hast thou this great commission,
    France,
  To draw my answer from thy articles?
KING PHILIP. From that supernal judge that stirs good
    thoughts
  In any breast of strong authority
  To look into the blots and stains of right.
  That judge hath made me guardian to this boy,
  Under whose warrant I impeach thy wrong,

And by whose help I mean to chastise it.

KING JOHN. Alack, thou dost usurp authority.

KING PHILIP. Excuse it is to beat usurping down.

ELINOR. Who is it thou dost call usurper, France?

CONSTANCE. Let me make answer: thy usurping son.

ELINOR. Out, insolent! Thy bastard shall be king,
That thou mayst be a queen and check the world!

CONSTANCE. My bed was ever to thy son as true
As thine was to thy husband; and this boy
Liker in feature to his father Geffrey
Than thou and John in manners—being as like
As rain to water, or devil to his dam.
My boy a bastard! By my soul, I think
His father never was so true begot;
It cannot be, an if thou wert his mother.

ELINOR. There's a good mother, boy, that blots thy father.

CONSTANCE. There's a good grandam, boy, that would blot
thee.

AUSTRIA. Peace!

BASTARD. Hear the crier.

AUSTRIA. What the devil art thou?

BASTARD. One that will play the devil, sir, with you,
An 'a may catch your hide and you alone.
You are the hare of whom the proverb goes,
Whose valour plucks dead lions by the beard;
I'll smoke your skin-coat an I catch you right;
Sirrah, look to 't; i' faith I will, i' faith.

BLANCH. O, well did he become that lion's robe
That did disrobe the lion of that robe!

BASTARD. It lies as sightly on the back of him
As great Alcides' shows upon an ass;
But, ass, I'll take that burden from your back,
Or lay on that shall make your shoulders crack.

AUSTRIA. What cracker is this same that deafs our ears
With this abundance of superfluous breath?
King Philip, determine what we shall do straight.

KING PHILIP. Women and fools, break off your conference.
King John, this is the very sum of all:
England and Ireland, Anjou, Touraine, Maine,
In right of Arthur, do I claim of thee;

Wilt thou resign them and lay down thy arms?

KING JOHN. My life as soon. I do defy thee, France.
Arthur of Britaine, yield thee to my hand,
And out of my dear love I'll give thee more
Than e'er the coward hand of France can win.
Submit thee, boy.

ELINOR. Come to thy grandam, child.

CONSTANCE. Do, child, go to it grandam, child;
Give grandam kingdom, and it grandam will
Give it a plum, a cherry, and a fig.
There's a good grandam!

ARTHUR. Good my mother, peace!
I would that I were low laid in my grave:
I am not worth this coil that's made for me.

ELINOR. His mother shames him so, poor boy, he weeps.

CONSTANCE. Now shame upon you, whe'er she does or no!
His grandam's wrongs, and not his mother's shames,
Draws those heaven-moving pearls from his poor eyes,
Which heaven shall take in nature of a fee;
Ay, with these crystal beads heaven shall be brib'd
To do him justice and revenge on you.

ELINOR. Thou monstrous slanderer of heaven and earth!

CONSTANCE. Thou monstrous injurer of heaven and earth,
Call not me slanderer! Thou and thine usurp
The dominations, royalties, and rights,
Of this oppressed boy; this is thy eldest son's son,
Infortunate in nothing but in thee.
Thy sins are visited in this poor child;
The canon of the law is laid on him,
Being but the second generation
Removed from thy sin-conceiving womb.

KING JOHN. Bedlam, have done.

CONSTANCE. I have but this to say—
That he is not only plagued for her sin,
But God hath made her sin and her the plague
On this removed issue, plagued for her
And with her plague; her sin his injury,
Her injury the beadle to her sin;
All punish'd in the person of this child,
And all for her—a plague upon her!

ELINOR. Thou unadvised scold, I can produce
  A will that bars the title of thy son.
CONSTANCE. Ay, who doubts that? A will, a wicked will;
  A woman's will; a cank'red grandam's will!
KING PHILIP. Peace, lady! pause, or be more temperate.
  It ill beseems this presence to cry aim
  To these ill-tuned repetitions.
  Some trumpet summon hither to the walls
  These men of Angiers; let us hear them speak
  Whose title they admit, Arthur's or John's.

Trumpet sounds. Enter citizens upon the walls

CITIZEN. Who is it that hath warn'd us to the walls?
KING PHILIP. 'Tis France, for England.
KING JOHN. England for itself.
  You men of Angiers, and my loving subjects—
KING PHILIP. You loving men of Angiers, Arthur's subjects,
  Our trumpet call'd you to this gentle parle—
KING JOHN. For our advantage; therefore hear us first.
  These flags of France, that are advanced here
  Before the eye and prospect of your town,
  Have hither march'd to your endamagement;
  The cannons have their bowels full of wrath,
  And ready mounted are they to spit forth
  Their iron indignation 'gainst your walls;
  All preparation for a bloody siege
  And merciless proceeding by these French
  Confront your city's eyes, your winking gates;
  And but for our approach those sleeping stones
  That as a waist doth girdle you about
  By the compulsion of their ordinance
  By this time from their fixed beds of lime
  Had been dishabited, and wide havoc made
  For bloody power to rush upon your peace.
  But on the sight of us your lawful king,
  Who painfully with much expedient march
  Have brought a countercheck before your gates,
  To save unscratch'd your city's threat'ned cheeks—
  Behold, the French amaz'd vouchsafe a parle;
  And now, instead of bullets wrapp'd in fire,

To make a shaking fever in your walls,
They shoot but calm words folded up in smoke,
To make a faithless error in your ears;
Which trust accordingly, kind citizens,
And let us in—your King, whose labour'd spirits,
Forwearied in this action of swift speed,
Craves harbourage within your city walls.
KING PHILIP. When I have said, make answer to us both.
Lo, in this right hand, whose protection
Is most divinely vow'd upon the right
Of him it holds, stands young Plantagenet,
Son to the elder brother of this man,
And king o'er him and all that he enjoys;
For this down-trodden equity we tread
In warlike march these greens before your town,
Being no further enemy to you
Than the constraint of hospitable zeal
In the relief of this oppressed child
Religiously provokes. Be pleased then
To pay that duty which you truly owe
To him that owes it, namely, this young prince;
And then our arms, like to a muzzled bear,
Save in aspect, hath all offence seal'd up;
Our cannons' malice vainly shall be spent
Against th' invulnerable clouds of heaven;
And with a blessed and unvex'd retire,
With unhack'd swords and helmets all unbruis'd,
We will bear home that lusty blood again
Which here we came to spout against your town,
And leave your children, wives, and you, in peace.
But if you fondly pass our proffer'd offer,
'Tis not the roundure of your old-fac'd walls
Can hide you from our messengers of war,
Though all these English and their discipline
Were harbour'd in their rude circumference.
Then tell us, shall your city call us lord
In that behalf which we have challeng'd it;
Or shall we give the signal to our rage,
And stalk in blood to our possession?
CITIZEN. In brief: we are the King of England's subjects;

For him, and in his right, we hold this town.

KING JOHN. Acknowledge then the King, and let me in.

CITIZEN. That can we not; but he that proves the King,
To him will we prove loyal. Till that time
Have we ramm'd up our gates against the world.

KING JOHN. Doth not the crown of England prove the King?
And if not that, I bring you witnesses:
Twice fifteen thousand hearts of England's breed—

BASTARD. Bastards and else.

KING JOHN. To verify our title with their lives.

KING PHILIP. As many and as well-born bloods as those—

BASTARD. Some bastards too.

KING PHILIP. Stand in his face to contradict his claim.

CITIZEN. Till you compound whose right is worthiest,
We for the worthiest hold the right from both.

KING JOHN. Then God forgive the sin of all those souls
That to their everlasting residence,
Before the dew of evening fall, shall fleet
In dreadful trial of our kingdom's king!

KING PHILIP. Amen, Amen! Mount, chevaliers; to arms!

BASTARD. Saint George, that swing'd the dragon, and e'er since
Sits on's horse back at mine hostess' door,
Teach us some fence! [To AUSTRIA] Sirrah, were I at home,
At your den, sirrah, with your lioness.
I would set an ox-head to your lion's hide,
And make a monster of you.

AUSTRIA. Peace! no more.

BASTARD. O, tremble, for you hear the lion roar!

KING JOHN. Up higher to the plain, where we'll set forth
In best appointment all our regiments.

BASTARD. Speed then to take advantage of the field.

KING PHILIP. It shall be so; and at the other hill
Command the rest to stand. God and our right!   *Exeunt*

Here, after excursions, enter the HERALD OF FRANCE,
with trumpets, to the gates

FRENCH HERALD. You men of Angiers, open wide your gates

And let young Arthur, Duke of Britaine, in,
Who by the hand of France this day hath made
Much work for tears in many an English mother,
Whose sons lie scattered on the bleeding ground;
Many a widow's husband grovelling lies,
Coldly embracing the discoloured earth;
And victory with little loss doth play
Upon the dancing banners of the French,
Who are at hand, triumphantly displayed,
To enter conquerors, and to proclaim
Arthur of Britaine England's King and yours.

Enter ENGLISH HERALD, *with trumpet*

ENGLISH HERALD. Rejoice, you men of Angiers, ring your
    bells:
King John, your king and England's, doth approach,
Commander of this hot malicious day.
Their armours that march'd hence so silver-bright
Hither return all gilt with Frenchmen's blood.
There stuck no plume in any English crest
That is removed by a staff of France;
Our colours do return in those same hands
That did display them when we first march'd forth;
And like a jolly troop of huntsmen come
Our lusty English, all with purpled hands,
Dy'd in the dying slaughter of their foes.
Open your gates and give the victors way.
CITIZEN. Heralds, from off our tow'rs we might behold
From first to last the onset and retire
Of both your armies, whose equality
By our best eyes cannot be censured.
Blood hath bought blood, and blows have answer'd blows;
Strength match'd with strength, and power confronted
    power;
Both are alike, and both alike we like.
One must prove greatest. While they weigh so even,
We hold our town for neither, yet for both.

Enter the two KINGS, *with their powers, at several doors*

KING JOHN. France, hast thou yet more blood to cast away?
Say, shall the current of our right run on?
Whose passage, vex'd with thy impediment,
Shall leave his native channel and o'erswell
With course disturb'd even thy confining shores,
Unless thou let his silver water keep
A peaceful progress to the ocean.

KING PHILIP. England, thou hast not sav'd one drop of blood
In this hot trial more than we of France;
Rather, lost more. And by this hand I swear,
That sways the earth this climate overlooks,
Before we will lay down our just-borne arms,
We'll put thee down, 'gainst whom these arms we bear,
Or add a royal number to the dead,
Gracing the scroll that tells of this war's loss
With slaughter coupled to the name of kings.

BASTARD. Ha, majesty! how high thy glory tow'rs
When the rich blood of kings is set on fire!
O, now doth Death line his dead chaps with steel;
The swords of soldiers are his teeth, his fangs;
And now he feasts, mousing the flesh of men,
In undetermin'd differences of kings.
Why stand these royal fronts amazed thus?
Cry 'havoc!' kings; back to the stained field,
You equal potents, fiery kindled spirits!
Then let confusion of one part confirm
The other's peace. Till then, blows, blood, and death!

KING JOHN. Whose party do the townsmen yet admit?

KING PHILIP. Speak, citizens, for England; who's your king?

CITIZEN. The King of England, when we know the King.

KING PHILIP. Know him in us that here hold up his right.

KING JOHN. In us that are our own great deputy
And bear possession of our person here,
Lord of our presence, Angiers, and of you.

CITIZEN. A greater pow'r than we denies all this;
And till it be undoubted, we do lock
Our former scruple in our strong-barr'd gates;
King'd of our fears, until our fears, resolv'd,
Be by some certain king purg'd and depos'd.

BASTARD. By heaven, these scroyles of Angiers flout you,
  kings,
  And stand securely on their battlements
  As in a theatre, whence they gape and point
  At your industrious scenes and acts of death.
  Your royal presences be rul'd by me:
  Do like the mutines of Jerusalem,
  Be friends awhile, and both conjointly bend
  Your sharpest deeds of malice on this town.
  By east and west let France and England mount
  Their battering cannon, charged to the mouths,
  Till their soul-fearing clamours have brawl'd down
  The flinty ribs of this contemptuous city.
  I'd play incessantly upon these jades,
  Even till unfenced desolation
  Leave them as naked as the vulgar air.
  That done, dissever your united strengths
  And part your mingled colours once again,
  Turn face to face and bloody point to point;
  Then in a moment Fortune shall cull forth
  Out of one side her happy minion,
  To whom in favour she shall give the day,
  And kiss him with a glorious victory.
  How like you this wild counsel, mighty states?
  Smacks it not something of the policy?
KING JOHN. Now, by the sky that hangs above our heads,
  I like it well. France, shall we knit our pow'rs
  And lay this Angiers even with the ground;
  Then after fight who shall be king of it?
BASTARD. An if thou hast the mettle of a king,
  Being wrong'd as we are by this peevish town,
  Turn thou the mouth of thy artillery,
  As we will ours, against these saucy walls;
  And when that we have dash'd them to the ground,
  Why then defy each other, and pell-mell
  Make work upon ourselves, for heaven or hell.
KING PHILIP. Let it be so. Say, where will you assault?
KING JOHN. We from the west will send destruction
  Into this city's bosom.
AUSTRIA. I from the north.

KING PHILIP. Our thunder from the south
Shall rain their drift of bullets on this town.
BASTARD. [*Aside*] O prudent discipline! From north to south,
Austria and France shoot in each other's mouth.
I'll stir them to it.—Come, away, away!
CITIZEN. Hear us, great kings: vouchsafe awhile to stay,
And I shall show you peace and fair-fac'd league;
Win you this city without stroke or wound;
Rescue those breathing lives to die in beds
That here come sacrifices for the field.
Persever not, but hear me, mighty kings.
KING JOHN. Speak on with favour; we are bent to hear.
CITIZEN. That daughter there of Spain, the Lady Blanch,
Is niece to England; look upon the years
Of Lewis the Dauphin and that lovely maid.
If lusty love should go in quest of beauty,
Where should he find it fairer than in Blanch?
If zealous love should go in search of virtue,
Where should he find it purer than in Blanch?
If love ambitious sought a match of birth,
Whose veins bound richer blood than Lady Blanch?
Such as she is, in beauty, virtue, birth,
Is the young Dauphin every way complete—
If not complete of, say he is not she;
And she again wants nothing, to name want,
If want it be not that she is not he.
He is the half part of a blessed man,
Left to be finished by such as she;
And she a fair divided excellence,
Whose fulness of perfection lies in him.
O, two such silver currents, when they join,
Do glorify the banks that bound them in;
And two such shores to two such streams made one,
Two such controlling bounds, shall you be, Kings,
To these two princes, if you marry them.
This union shall do more than battery can
To our fast-closed gates; for at this match
With swifter spleen than powder can enforce,
The mouth of passage shall we fling wide ope
And give you entrance; but without this match,

The sea enraged is not half so deaf,
Lions more confident, mountains and rocks
More free from motion—no, not Death himself
In mortal fury half so peremptory
As we to keep this city.

BASTARD. Here's a stay
That shakes the rotten carcass of old Death
Out of his rags! Here's a large mouth, indeed,
That spits forth death and mountains, rocks and seas;
Talks as familiarly of roaring lions
As maids of thirteen do of puppy-dogs!
What cannoneer begot this lusty blood?
He speaks plain cannon-fire, and smoke and bounce;
He gives the bastinado with his tongue;
Our ears are cudgell'd; not a word of his
But buffets better than a fist of France.
Zounds! I was never so bethump'd with words
Since I first call'd my brother's father dad.

ELINOR. Son, list to this conjunction, make this match;
Give with our niece a dowry large enough;
For by this knot thou shalt so surely tie
Thy now unsur'd assurance to the crown
That yon green boy shall have no sun to ripe
The bloom that promiseth a mighty fruit.
I see a yielding in the looks of France;
Mark how they whisper. Urge them while their souls
Are capable of this ambition,
Lest zeal, now melted by the windy breath
Of soft petitions, pity, and remorse,
Cool and congeal again to what it was.

CITIZEN. Why answer not the double majesties
This friendly treaty of our threat'ned town?

KING PHILIP. Speak England first, that hath been forward
first
To speak unto this city: what say you?

KING JOHN. If that the Dauphin there, thy princely son,
Can in this book of beauty read 'I love,'
Her dowry shall weigh equal with a queen;
For Anjou, and fair Touraine, Maine, Poictiers,
And all that we upon this side the sea—

Except this city now by us besieg'd—
Find liable to our crown and dignity,
Shall gild her bridal bed, and make her rich
In titles, honours, and promotions,
As she in beauty, education, blood,
Holds hand with any princess of the world.

KING PHILIP. What say'st thou, boy? Look in the lady's face.

LEWIS. I do, my lord, and in her eye I find
A wonder, or a wondrous miracle,
The shadow of myself form'd in her eye;
Which, being but the shadow of your son,
Becomes a sun, and makes your son a shadow.
I do protest I never lov'd myself
Till now infixed I beheld myself
Drawn in the flattering table of her eye.

                                        [*Whispers with* BLANCH]

BASTARD. [*Aside*] Drawn in the flattering table of her eye,
Hang'd in the frowning wrinkle of her brow,
And quarter'd in her heart—he doth espy
Himself love's traitor. This is pity now,
That hang'd and drawn and quarter'd there should be
In such a love so vile a lout as he.

BLANCH. My uncle's will in this respect is mine.
If he see aught in you that makes him like,
That anything he sees which moves his liking
I can with ease translate it to my will;
Or if you will, to speak more properly,
I will enforce it eas'ly to my love.
Further I will not flatter you, my lord,
That all I see in you is worthy love,
Than this: that nothing do I see in you—
Though churlish thoughts themselves should be your
    judge—
That I can find should merit any hate.

KING JOHN. What say these young ones? What say you, my
    niece?

BLANCH. That she is bound in honour still to do
What you in wisdom still vouchsafe to say.

KING JOHN. Speak then, Prince Dauphin; can you love this
    lady?

LEWIS. Nay, ask me if I can refrain from love;
  For I do love her most unfeignedly.
KING JOHN. Then do I give Volquessen, Touraine, Maine,
  Poictiers, and Anjou, these five provinces,
  With her to thee; and this addition more,
  Full thirty thousand marks of English coin.
  Philip of France, if thou be pleas'd withal,
  Command thy son and daughter to join hands.
KING PHILIP. It likes us well; young princes, close your
  hands.
AUSTRIA. And your lips too; for I am well assur'd
  That I did so when I was first assur'd.
KING PHILIP. Now, citizens of Angiers, ope your gates,
  Let in that amity which you have made;
  For at Saint Mary's chapel presently
  The rites of marriage shall be solemniz'd.
  Is not the Lady Constance in this troop?
  I know she is not; for this match made up
  Her presence would have interrupted much.
  Where is she and her son? Tell me, who knows.
LEWIS. She is sad and passionate at your Highness' tent.
KING PHILIP. And, by my faith, this league that we have
  made
  Will give her sadness very little cure.
  Brother of England, how may we content
  This widow lady? In her right we came;
  Which we, God knows, have turn'd another way,
  To our own vantage.
KING JOHN. We will heal up all,
  For we'll create young Arthur Duke of Britaine,
  And Earl of Richmond; and this rich fair town
  We make him lord of. Call the Lady Constance;
  Some speedy messenger bid her repair
  To our solemnity. I trust we shall,
  If not fill up the measure of her will,
  Yet in some measure satisfy her so
  That we shall stop her exclamation.
  Go we as well as haste will suffer us
  To this unlook'd-for, unprepared pomp.
              Exeunt all but the BASTARD

BASTARD. Mad world! mad kings! mad composition!
John, to stop Arthur's title in the whole,
Hath willingly departed with a part;
And France, whose armour conscience buckled on,
Whom zeal and charity brought to the field
As God's own soldier, rounded in the ear
With that same purpose-changer, that sly devil,
That broker that still breaks the pate of faith,
That daily break-vow, he that wins of all,
Of kings, of beggars, old men, young men, maids,
Who having no external thing to lose
But the word 'maid,' cheats the poor maid of that;
That smooth-fac'd gentleman, tickling commodity,
Commodity, the bias of the world—
The world, who of itself is peised well,
Made to run even upon even ground,
Till this advantage, this vile-drawing bias,
This sway of motion, this commodity,
Makes it take head from all indifferency,
From all direction, purpose, course, intent—
And this same bias, this commodity,
This bawd, this broker, this all-changing word,
Clapp'd on the outward eye of fickle France,
Hath drawn him from his own determin'd aid,
From a resolv'd and honourable war,
To a most base and vile-concluded peace.
And why rail I on this commodity?
But for because he hath not woo'd me yet;
Not that I have the power to clutch my hand
When his fair angels would salute my palm,
But for my hand, as unattempted yet,
Like a poor beggar raileth on the rich.
Well, whiles I am a beggar, I will rail
And say there is no sin but to be rich;
And being rich, my virtue then shall be
To say there is no vice but beggary.
Since kings break faith upon commodity,
Gain, be my lord, for I will worship thee.   *Exit*

ACT III. SCENE 1

France. The FRENCH KING'S *camp*

Enter CONSTANCE, ARTHUR, *and* SALISBURY

CONSTANCE. Gone to be married! Gone to swear a peace!
  False blood to false blood join'd! Gone to be friends!
  Shall Lewis have Blanch, and Blanch those provinces?
  It is not so; thou hast misspoke, misheard;
  Be well advis'd, tell o'er thy tale again.
  It cannot be; thou dost but say 'tis so;
  I trust I may not trust thee, for thy word
  Is but the vain breath of a common man:
  Believe me I do not believe thee, man;
  I have a king's oath to the contrary.
  Thou shalt be punish'd for thus frighting me,
  For I am sick and capable of fears,
  Oppress'd with wrongs, and therefore full of fears;
  A widow, husbandless, subject to fears;
  A woman, naturally born to fears;
  And though thou now confess thou didst but jest,
  With my vex'd spirits I cannot take a truce,
  But they will quake and tremble all this day.
  What dost thou mean by shaking of thy head?
  Why dost thou look so sadly on my son?
  What means that hand upon that breast of thine?
  Why holds thine eye that lamentable rheum,
  Like a proud river peering o'er his bounds?
  Be these sad signs confirmers of thy words?
  Then speak again—not all thy former tale,
  But this one word, whether thy tale be true.
SALISBURY. As true as I believe you think them false
  That give you cause to prove my saying true.
CONSTANCE. O, if thou teach me to believe this sorrow,
  Teach thou this sorrow how to make me die;
  And let belief and life encounter so
  As doth the fury of two desperate men
  Which in the very meeting fall and die!
  Lewis marry Blanch! O boy, then where art thou?
  France friend with England; what becomes of me?

Fellow, be gone: I cannot brook thy sight;
This news hath made thee a most ugly man.
SALISBURY. What other harm have I, good lady, done
But spoke the harm that is by others done?
CONSTANCE. Which harm within itself so heinous is
As it makes harmful all that speak of it.
ARTHUR. I do beseech you, madam, be content.
CONSTANCE. If thou that bid'st me be content wert grim,
Ugly, and sland'rous to thy mother's womb,
Full of unpleasing blots and sightless stains,
Lame, foolish, crooked, swart, prodigious,
Patch'd with foul moles and eye-offending marks,
I would not care, I then would be content;
For then I should not love thee; no, nor thou
Become thy great birth, nor deserve a crown.
But thou art fair, and at thy birth, dear boy,
Nature and Fortune join'd to make thee great:
Of Nature's gifts thou mayst with lilies boast,
And with the half-blown rose; but Fortune, O!
She is corrupted, chang'd, and won from thee;
Sh' adulterates hourly with thine uncle John,
And with her golden hand hath pluck'd on France
To tread down fair respect of sovereignty,
And made his majesty the bawd to theirs.
France is a bawd to Fortune and King John—
That strumpet Fortune, that usurping John!
Tell me, thou fellow, is not France forsworn?
Envenom him with words, or get thee gone
And leave those woes alone which I alone
Am bound to under-bear.
SALISBURY. Pardon me, madam,
I may not go without you to the kings.
CONSTANCE. Thou mayst, thou shalt; I will not go with thee;
I will instruct my sorrows to be proud,
For grief is proud, and makes his owner stoop.
To me, and to the state of my great grief,
Let kings assemble; for my grief's so great
That no supporter but the huge firm earth
Can hold it up.   [*Seats herself on the ground*]
Here I and sorrows sit;

Here is my throne, bid kings come bow to it.

Enter KING JOHN, KING PHILIP, LEWIS, BLANCH,
ELINOR, *the* BASTARD, AUSTRIA, *and attendants*

KING PHILIP. 'Tis true, fair daughter, and this blessed day
Ever in France shall be kept festival.
To solemnize this day the glorious sun
Stays in his course and plays the alchemist,
Turning with splendour of his precious eye
The meagre cloddy earth to glittering gold.
The yearly course that brings this day about
Shall never see it but a holiday.
CONSTANCE. [*Rising*] A wicked day, and not a holy day!
What hath this day deserv'd? what hath it done
That it in golden letters should be set
Among the high tides in the calendar?
Nay, rather turn this day out of the week,
This day of shame, oppression, perjury;
Or, if it must stand still, let wives with child
Pray that their burdens may not fall this day,
Lest that their hopes prodigiously be cross'd;
But on this day let seamen fear no wreck;
No bargains break that are not this day made;
This day, all things begun come to ill end,
Yea, faith itself to hollow falsehood change!
KING PHILIP. By heaven, lady, you shall have no cause
To curse the fair proceedings of this day.
Have I not pawn'd to you my majesty?
CONSTANCE. You have beguil'd me with a counterfeit
Resembling majesty, which, being touch'd and tried,
Proves valueless; you are forsworn, forsworn;
You came in arms to spill mine enemies' blood,
But now in arms you strengthen it with yours.
The grappling vigour and rough frown of war
Is cold in amity and painted peace,
And our oppression hath made up this league.
Arm, arm, you heavens, against these perjur'd kings!
A widow cries: Be husband to me, heavens!
Let not the hours of this ungodly day
Wear out the day in peace; but, ere sunset,

Set armed discord 'twixt these perjur'd kings!
Hear me, O, hear me!
AUSTRIA. Lady Constance, peace!
CONSTANCE. War! war! no peace! Peace is to me a war.
O Lymoges! O Austria! thou dost shame
That bloody spoil. Thou slave, thou wretch, thou coward!
Thou little valiant, great in villainy!
Thou ever strong upon the stronger side!
Thou Fortune's champion that dost never fight
But when her humorous ladyship is by
To teach thee safety! Thou art perjur'd too,
And sooth'st up greatness. What a fool art thou,
A ramping fool, to brag and stamp and swear
Upon my party! Thou cold-blooded slave,
Hast thou not spoke like thunder on my side,
Been sworn my soldier, bidding me depend
Upon thy stars, thy fortune, and thy strength,
And dost thou now fall over to my foes?
Thou wear a lion's hide! Doff it for shame,
And hang a calf's-skin on those recreant limbs.
AUSTRIA. O that a man should speak those words to me!
BASTARD. And hang a calf's-skin on those recreant limbs.
AUSTRIA. Thou dar'st not say so, villain, for thy life.
BASTARD. And hang a calf's-skin on those recreant limbs.
KING JOHN. We like not this: thou dost forget thyself.

Enter PANDULPH

KING PHILIP. Here comes the holy legate of the Pope.
PANDULPH. Hail, you anointed deputies of heaven!
To thee, King John, my holy errand is.
I Pandulph, of fair Milan cardinal,
And from Pope Innocent the legate here,
Do in his name religiously demand
Why thou against the Church, our holy mother,
So wilfully dost spurn; and force perforce
Keep Stephen Langton, chosen Archbishop
Of Canterbury, from that holy see?
This, in our foresaid holy father's name,
Pope Innocent, I do demand of thee.
KING JOHN. What earthly name to interrogatories

Can task the free breath of a sacred king?
Thou canst not, Cardinal, devise a name
So slight, unworthy, and ridiculous,
To charge me to an answer, as the Pope.
Tell him this tale, and from the mouth of England
Add thus much more, that no Italian priest
Shall tithe or toll in our dominions;
But as we under heaven are supreme head,
So, under Him that great supremacy,
Where we do reign we will alone uphold,
Without th' assistance of a mortal hand.
So tell the Pope, all reverence set apart
To him and his usurp'd authority.

KING PHILIP. Brother of England, you blaspheme in this.

KING JOHN. Though you and all the kings of Christendom
  Are led so grossly by this meddling priest,
  Dreading the curse that money may buy out,
  And by the merit of vile gold, dross, dust,
  Purchase corrupted pardon of a man,
  Who in that sale sells pardon from himself—
  Though you and all the rest, so grossly led,
  This juggling witchcraft with revenue cherish;
  Yet I alone, alone do me oppose
  Against the Pope, and count his friends my foes.

PANDULPH. Then by the lawful power that I have
  Thou shalt stand curs'd and excommunicate;
  And blessed shall he be that doth revolt
  From his allegiance to an heretic;
  And meritorious shall that hand be call'd,
  Canonized, and worshipp'd as a saint,
  That takes away by any secret course
  Thy hateful life.

CONSTANCE. O, lawful let it be
  That I have room with Rome to curse awhile!
  Good father Cardinal, cry thou 'amen'
  To my keen curses; for without my wrong
  There is no tongue hath power to curse him right.

PANDULPH. There's law and warrant, lady, for my curse.

CONSTANCE. And for mine too; when law can do no right,
  Let it be lawful that law bar no wrong;

Law cannot give my child his kingdom here,
For he that holds his kingdom holds the law;
Therefore, since law itself is perfect wrong,
How can the law forbid my tongue to curse?

PANDULPH. Philip of France, on peril of a curse,
Let go the hand of that arch-heretic,
And raise the power of France upon his head,
Unless he do submit himself to Rome.

ELINOR. Look'st thou pale, France? Do not let go thy hand.

CONSTANCE. Look to that, devil, lest that France repent
And by disjoining hands hell lose a soul.

AUSTRIA. King Philip, listen to the Cardinal.

BASTARD. And hang a calf's-skin on his recreant limbs.

AUSTRIA. Well, ruffian, I must pocket up these wrongs,
Because—

BASTARD. Your breeches best may carry them.

KING JOHN. Philip, what say'st thou to the Cardinal?

CONSTANCE. What should he say, but as the Cardinal?

LEWIS. Bethink you, father; for the difference
Is purchase of a heavy curse from Rome
Or the light loss of England for a friend.
Forgo the easier.

BLANCH. That's the curse of Rome.

CONSTANCE. O Lewis, stand fast! The devil tempts thee here
In likeness of a new untrimmed bride.

BLANCH. The Lady Constance speaks not from her faith,
But from her need.

CONSTANCE. O, if thou grant my need,
Which only lives but by the death of faith,
That need must needs infer this principle—
That faith would live again by death of need.
O then, tread down my need, and faith mounts up:
Keep my need up, and faith is trodden down!

KING JOHN. The King is mov'd, and answers not to this.

CONSTANCE. O be remov'd from him, and answer well!

AUSTRIA. Do so, King Philip; hang no more in doubt.

BASTARD. Hang nothing but a calf's-skin, most sweet lout.

KING PHILIP. I am perplex'd and know not what to say.

PANDULPH. What canst thou say but will perplex thee more,
If thou stand excommunicate and curs'd?

KING PHILIP. Good reverend father, make my person yours,
  And tell me how you would bestow yourself.
  This royal hand and mine are newly knit,
  And the conjunction of our inward souls
  Married in league, coupled and link'd together
  With all religious strength of sacred vows;
  The latest breath that gave the sound of words
  Was deep-sworn faith, peace, amity, true love,
  Between our kingdoms and our royal selves;
  And even before this truce, but new before,
  No longer than we well could wash our hands,
  To clap this royal bargain up of peace,
  Heaven knows, they were besmear'd and overstain'd
  With slaughter's pencil, where revenge did paint
  The fearful difference of incensed kings.
  And shall these hands, so lately purg'd of blood,
  So newly join'd in love, so strong in both,
  Unyoke this seizure and this kind regreet?
  Play fast and loose with faith? so jest with heaven,
  Make such unconstant children of ourselves,
  As now again to snatch our palm from palm,
  Unswear faith sworn, and on the marriage-bed
  Of smiling peace to march a bloody host,
  And make a riot on the gentle brow
  Of true sincerity? O, holy sir,
  My reverend father, let it not be so!
  Out of your grace, devise, ordain, impose,
  Some gentle order; and then we shall be blest
  To do your pleasure, and continue friends.
PANDULPH. All form is formless, order orderless,
  Save what is opposite to England's love.
  Therefore, to arms! be champion of our church,
  Or let the church, our mother, breathe her curse—
  A mother's curse—on her revolting son.
  France, thou mayst hold a serpent by the tongue,
  A chafed lion by the mortal paw,
  A fasting tiger safer by the tooth,
  Than keep in peace that hand which thou dost hold.
KING PHILIP. I may disjoin my hand, but not my faith.
PANDULPH. So mak'st thou faith an enemy to faith;

And like a civil war set'st oath to oath,
Thy tongue against thy tongue. O, let thy vow
First made to heaven, first be to heaven perform'd,
That is, to be the champion of our Church.
What since thou swor'st is sworn against thyself
And may not be performed by thyself,
For that which thou hast sworn to do amiss
Is not amiss when it is truly done;
And being not done, where doing tends to ill,
The truth is then most done not doing it;
The better act of purposes mistook
Is to mistake again; though indirect,
Yet indirection thereby grows direct,
And falsehood cures, as fire cools fire
Within the scorched veins of one new-burn'd.
It is religion that doth make vows kept;
But thou hast sworn against religion
By what thou swear'st against the thing thou swear'st,
And mak'st an oath the surety for thy truth
Against an oath; the truth thou art unsure
To swear swears only not to be forsworn;
Else what a mockery should it be to swear!
But thou dost swear only to be forsworn;
And most forsworn to keep what thou dost swear.
Therefore thy later vows against thy first
Is in thyself rebellion to thyself;
And better conquest never canst thou make
Than arm thy constant and thy nobler parts
Against these giddy loose suggestions;
Upon which better part our pray'rs come in,
If thou vouchsafe them. But if not, then know
The peril of our curses light on thee
So heavy as thou shalt not shake them off,
But in despair die under the black weight.
AUSTRIA. Rebellion, flat rebellion!
BASTARD. Will't not be?
Will not a calf's-skin stop that mouth of thine?
LEWIS. Father, to arms!
BLANCH. Upon thy wedding-day?
Against the blood that thou hast married?

What, shall our feast be kept with slaughtered men?
Shall braying trumpets and loud churlish drums,
Clamours of hell, be measures to our pomp?
O husband, hear me! ay, alack, how new
Is 'husband' in my mouth!—even for that name,
Which till this time my tongue did ne'er pronounce,
Upon my knee I beg, go not to arms
Against mine uncle.

CONSTANCE. O, upon my knee,
Made hard with kneeling, I do pray to thee,
Thou virtuous Dauphin, alter not the doom
Forethought by heaven!

BLANCH. Now shall I see thy love. What motive may
Be stronger with thee than the name of wife?

CONSTANCE. That which upholdeth him that thee upholds,
His honour. O, thine honour, Lewis, thine honour!

LEWIS. I muse your Majesty doth seem so cold,
When such profound respects do pull you on.

PANDULPH. I will denounce a curse upon his head.

KING PHILIP. Thou shalt not need. England, I will fall from
thee.

CONSTANCE. O fair return of banish'd majesty!

ELINOR. O foul revolt of French inconstancy!

KING JOHN. France, thou shalt rue this hour within this hour.

BASTARD. Old Time the clock-setter, that bald sexton Time,
Is it as he will? Well then, France shall rue.

BLANCH. The sun's o'ercast with blood. Fair day, adieu!
Which is the side that I must go withal?
I am with both: each army hath a hand;
And in their rage, I having hold of both,
They whirl asunder and dismember me.
Husband, I cannot pray that thou mayst win;
Uncle, I needs must pray that thou mayst lose;
Father, I may not wish the fortune thine;
Grandam, I will not wish thy wishes thrive.
Whoever wins, on that side shall I lose:
Assured loss before the match be play'd.

LEWIS. Lady, with me, with me thy fortune lies.

BLANCH. There where my fortune lives, there my life dies.

KING JOHN. Cousin, go draw our puissance together.

Exit BASTARD

France, I am burn'd up with inflaming wrath,
A rage whose heat hath this condition
That nothing can allay, nothing but blood,
The blood, and dearest-valu'd blood, of France.
KING PHILIP. Thy rage shall burn thee up, and thou shalt turn
To ashes, ere our blood shall quench that fire.
Look to thyself, thou art in jeopardy.
KING JOHN. No more than he that threats. To arms let's hie!

Exeunt severally

SCENE 2

France. Plains near Angiers

Alarums, excursions. Enter the BASTARD *with* AUSTRIA's *head*

BASTARD. Now, by my life, this day grows wondrous hot;
Some airy devil hovers in the sky
And pours down mischief. Austria's head lie there,
While Philip breathes.

Enter KING JOHN, ARTHUR, *and* HUBERT

KING JOHN. Hubert, keep this boy. Philip, make up:
My mother is assailed in our tent,
And ta'en, I fear.
BASTARD. My lord, I rescued her;
Her Highness is in safety, fear you not;
But on, my liege, for very little pains
Will bring this labour to an happy end.   *Exeunt*

SCENE 3

France. Plains near Angiers

Alarums, excursions, retreat. Enter KING JOHN, ELINOR,
ARTHUR, *the* BASTARD, HUBERT, *and* LORDS

KING JOHN. [*To* ELINOR] So shall it be; your Grace shall stay behind,

So strongly guarded. [*To* ARTHUR] Cousin, look not sad;
Thy grandam loves thee, and thy uncle will
As dear be to thee as thy father was.
ARTHUR. O, this will make my mother die with grief!
KING JOHN. [*To the* BASTARD] Cousin, away for England!
haste before,
And, ere our coming, see thou shake the bags
Of hoarding abbots; imprisoned angels
Set at liberty; the fat ribs of peace
Must by the hungry now be fed upon.
Use our commission in his utmost force.
BASTARD. Bell, book, and candle, shall not drive me back,
When gold and silver becks me to come on.
I leave your Highness. Grandam, I will pray,
If ever I remember to be holy,
For your fair safety. So, I kiss your hand.
ELINOR. Farewell, gentle cousin.
KING JOHN. Coz, farewell.

Exit BASTARD

ELINOR. Come hither, little kinsman; hark, a word.
KING JOHN. Come hither, Hubert. O my gentle Hubert,
We owe thee much! Within this wall of flesh
There is a soul counts thee her creditor,
And with advantage means to pay thy love;
And, my good friend, thy voluntary oath
Lives in this bosom, dearly cherished.
Give me thy hand. I had a thing to say—
But I will fit it with some better time.
By heaven, Hubert, I am almost asham'd
To say what good respect I have of thee.
HUBERT. I am much bounden to your Majesty.
KING JOHN. Good friend, thou hast no cause to say so yet,
But thou shalt have; and creep time ne'er so slow,
Yet it shall come for me to do thee good.
I had a thing to say—but let it go:
The sun is in the heaven, and the proud day,
Attended with the pleasures of the world,
Is all too wanton and too full of gawds
To give me audience. If the midnight bell
Did with his iron tongue and brazen mouth

Sound on into the drowsy race of night;
If this same were a churchyard where we stand,
And thou possessed with a thousand wrongs;
Or if that surly spirit, melancholy,
Had bak'd thy blood and made it heavy-thick,
Which else runs tickling up and down the veins,
Making that idiot, laughter, keep men's eyes
And strain their cheeks to idle merriment,
A passion hateful to my purposes;
Or if that thou couldst see me without eyes,
Hear me without thine ears, and make reply
Without a tongue, using conceit alone,
Without eyes, ears, and harmful sound of words—
Then, in despite of brooded watchful day,
I would into thy bosom pour my thoughts.
But, ah, I will not! Yet I love thee well;
And, by my troth, I think thou lov'st me well.
HUBERT. So well that what you bid me undertake,
Though that my death were adjunct to my act,
By heaven, I would do it.
KING JOHN. Do not I know thou wouldst?
Good Hubert, Hubert, Hubert, throw thine eye
On yon young boy. I'll tell thee what, my friend,
He is a very serpent in my way;
And wheresoe'er this foot of mine doth tread,
He lies before me. Dost thou understand me?
Thou art his keeper.
HUBERT. And I'll keep him so
That he shall not offend your Majesty.
KING JOHN. Death.
HUBERT. My lord?
KING JOHN. A grave.
HUBERT. He shall not live.
KING JOHN. Enough!
I could be merry now. Hubert, I love thee.
Well, I'll not say what I intend for thee.
Remember. Madam, fare you well;
I'll send those powers o'er to your Majesty.
ELINOR. My blessing go with thee!
KING JOHN. [To ARTHUR] For England, cousin, go;

Hubert shall be your man, attend on you
With all true duty. On toward Calais, ho!   *Exeunt*

SCENE 4

France. The FRENCH KING'S *camp*

Enter KING PHILIP, LEWIS, PANDULPH, *and attendants*

KING PHILIP. So by a roaring tempest on the flood
  A whole armado of convicted sail
  Is scattered and disjoin'd from fellowship.
PANDULPH. Courage and comfort! All shall yet go well.
KING PHILIP. What can go well, when we have run so ill.
  Are we not beaten? Is not Angiers lost?
  Arthur ta'en prisoner? Divers dear friends slain?
  And bloody England into England gone,
  O'erbearing interruption, spite of France?
LEWIS. What he hath won, that hath he fortified;
  So hot a speed with such advice dispos'd,
  Such temperate order in so fierce a cause,
  Doth want example; who hath read or heard
  Of any kindred action like to this?
KING PHILIP. Well could I bear that England had this praise,
  So we could find some pattern of our shame.

Enter CONSTANCE

  Look who comes here! a grave unto a soul;
  Holding th' eternal spirit, against her will,
  In the vile prison of afflicted breath.
  I prithee, lady, go away with me.
CONSTANCE. Lo now! now see the issue of your peace!
KING PHILIP. Patience, good lady! Comfort, gentle Con-
  stance!
CONSTANCE. No, I defy all counsel, all redress,
  But that which ends all counsel, true redress—
  Death, death; O amiable lovely death!
  Thou odoriferous stench! sound rottenness!
  Arise forth from the couch of lasting night,
  Thou hate and terror to prosperity,

And I will kiss thy detestable bones,
And put my eyeballs in thy vaulty brows,
And ring these fingers with thy household worms,
And stop this gap of breath with fulsome dust,
And be a carrion monster like thyself.
Come, grin on me, and I will think thou smil'st,
And buss thee as thy wife. Misery's love,
O, come to me!
KING PHILIP. O fair affliction, peace!
CONSTANCE. No, no, I will not, having breath to cry.
O that my tongue were in the thunder's mouth!
Then with a passion would I shake the world,
And rouse from sleep that fell anatomy
Which cannot hear a lady's feeble voice,
Which scorns a modern invocation.
PANDULPH. Lady, you utter madness and not sorrow.
CONSTANCE. Thou art not holy to belie me so.
I am not mad: this hair I tear is mine;
My name is Constance; I was Geffrey's wife;
Young Arthur is my son, and he is lost.
I am not mad—I would to heaven I were!
For then 'tis like I should forget myself.
O, if I could, what grief should I forget!
Preach some philosophy to make me mad,
And thou shalt be canoniz'd, Cardinal;
For, being not mad, but sensible of grief,
My reasonable part produces reason
How I may be deliver'd of these woes,
And teaches me to kill or hang myself.
If I were mad I should forget my son,
Or madly think a babe of clouts were he.
I am not mad; too well, too well I feel
The different plague of each calamity.
KING PHILIP. Bind up those tresses. O, what love I note
In the fair multitude of those her hairs!
Where but by a chance a silver drop hath fall'n,
Even to that drop ten thousand wiry friends
Do glue themselves in sociable grief,
Like true, inseparable, faithful loves,
Sticking together in calamity.

CONSTANCE. To England, if you will.
KING PHILIP. Bind up your hairs.
CONSTANCE. Yes, that I will; and wherefore will I do it?
  I tore them from their bonds, and cried aloud
  'O that these hands could so redeem my son,
  As they have given these hairs their liberty!'
  But now I envy at their liberty,
  And will again commit them to their bonds,
  Because my poor child is a prisoner.
  And, father Cardinal, I have heard you say
  That we shall see and know our friends in heaven;
  If that be true, I shall see my boy again;
  For since the birth of Cain, the first male child,
  To him that did but yesterday suspire,
  There was not such a gracious creature born.
  But now will canker sorrow eat my bud
  And chase the native beauty from his cheek,
  And he will look as hollow as a ghost,
  As dim and meagre as an ague's fit;
  And so he'll die; and, rising so again,
  When I shall meet him in the court of heaven
  I shall not know him. Therefore never, never
  Must I behold my pretty Arthur more.
PANDULPH. You hold too heinous a respect of grief.
CONSTANCE. He talks to me that never had a son.
KING PHILIP. You are as fond of grief as of your child.
CONSTANCE. Grief fills the room up of my absent child,
  Lies in his bed, walks up and down with me,
  Puts on his pretty looks, repeats his words,
  Remembers me of all his gracious parts,
  Stuffs out his vacant garments with his form;
  Then have I reason to be fond of grief.
  Fare you well; had you such a loss as I,
  I could give better comfort than you do.
  I will not keep this form upon my head,
                              [*Tearing her hair*]
  When there is such disorder in my wit.
  O Lord! my boy, my Arthur, my fair son!
  My life, my joy, my food, my all the world!
  My widow-comfort, and my sorrows' cure!   *Exit*

KING PHILIP. I fear some outrage, and I'll follow her.   *Exit*
LEWIS. There's nothing in this world can make me joy.
   Life is as tedious as a twice-told tale
   Vexing the dull ear of a drowsy man;
   And bitter shame hath spoil'd the sweet world's taste,
   That it yields nought but shame and bitterness.
PANDULPH. Before the curing of a strong disease,
   Even in the instant of repair and health,
   The fit is strongest; evils that take leave
   On their departure most of all show evil;
   What have you lost by losing of this day?
LEWIS. All days of glory, joy, and happiness.
PANDULPH. If you had won it, certainly you had.
   No, no; when Fortune means to men most good,
   She looks upon them with a threat'ning eye.
   'Tis strange to think how much King John hath lost
   In this which he accounts so clearly won.
   Are not you griev'd that Arthur is his prisoner?
LEWIS. As heartily as he is glad he hath him.
PANDULPH. Your mind is all as youthful as your blood.
   Now hear me speak with a prophetic spirit;
   For even the breath of what I mean to speak
   Shall blow each dust, each straw, each little rub,
   Out of the path which shall directly lead
   Thy foot to England's throne. And therefore mark:
   John hath seiz'd Arthur; and it cannot be
   That, whiles warm life plays in that infant's veins,
   The misplac'd John should entertain an hour,
   One minute, nay, one quiet breath of rest.
   A sceptre snatch'd with an unruly hand
   Must be boisterously maintain'd as gain'd,
   And he that stands upon a slipp'ry place
   Makes nice of no vile hold to stay him up;
   That John may stand then, Arthur needs must fall;
   So be it, for it cannot be but so.
LEWIS. But what shall I gain by young Arthur's fall?
PANDULPH. You, in the right of Lady Blanch your wife,
   May then make all the claim that Arthur did.
LEWIS. And lose it, life and all, as Arthur did.
PANDULPH. How green you are and fresh in this old world!

John lays you plots; the times conspire with you;
For he that steeps his safety in true blood
Shall find but bloody safety and untrue.
This act, so evilly borne, shall cool the hearts
Of all his people and freeze up their zeal,
That none so small advantage shall step forth
To check his reign but they will cherish it;
No natural exhalation in the sky,
No scope of nature, no distemper'd day,
No common wind, no customed event,
But they will pluck away his natural cause
And call them meteors, prodigies, and signs,
Abortives, presages, and tongues of heaven,
Plainly denouncing vengeance upon John.
LEWIS. May be he will not touch young Arthur's life,
But hold himself safe in his prisonment.
PANDULPH. O, sir, when he shall hear of your approach,
If that young Arthur be not gone already,
Even at that news he dies; and then the hearts
Of all his people shall revolt from him,
And kiss the lips of unacquainted change,
And pick strong matter of revolt and wrath
Out of the bloody fingers' ends of John.
Methinks I see this hurly all on foot;
And, O, what better matter breeds for you
Than I have nam'd! The bastard Faulconbridge
Is now in England ransacking the Church,
Offending charity; if but a dozen French
Were there in arms, they would be as a call
To train ten thousand English to their side;
Or as a little snow, tumbled about,
Anon becomes a mountain. O noble Dauphin,
Go with me to the King. 'Tis wonderful
What may be wrought out of their discontent,
Now that their souls are topful of offence.
For England go; I will whet on the King.
LEWIS. Strong reasons makes strong actions. Let us go;
If you say ay, the King will not say no. *Exeunt*

KING JOHN

ACT IV. SCENE 1

England. A castle

Enter HUBERT *and* EXECUTIONERS

HUBERT. Heat me these irons hot; and look thou stand
  Within the arras. When I strike my foot
  Upon the bosom of the ground, rush forth
  And bind the boy which you shall find with me
  Fast to the chair. Be heedful; hence, and watch.
EXECUTIONER. I hope your warrant will bear out the deed.
HUBERT. Uncleanly scruples! Fear not you. Look to't.
                    Exeunt EXECUTIONERS
  Young lad, come forth; I have to say with you.

Enter ARTHUR

ARTHUR. Good morrow, Hubert.
HUBERT. Good morrow, little Prince.
ARTHUR. As little prince, having so great a title
  To be more prince, as may be. You are sad.
HUBERT. Indeed I have been merrier.
ARTHUR. Mercy on me!
  Methinks no body should be sad but I;
  Yet, I remember, when I was in France,
  Young gentlemen would be as sad as night,
  Only for wantonness. By my christendom,
  So I were out of prison and kept sheep,
  I should be as merry as the day is long;
  And so I would be here but that I doubt
  My uncle practises more harm to me;
  He is afraid of me, and I of him.
  Is it my fault that I was Geffrey's son?
  No, indeed, is't not; and I would to heaven
  I were your son, so you would love me, Hubert.
HUBERT. [*Aside*] If I talk to him, with his innocent prate
  He will awake my mercy, which lies dead;
  Therefore I will be sudden and dispatch.
ARTHUR. Are you sick, Hubert? You look pale to-day;
  In sooth, I would you were a little sick,

That I might sit all night and watch with you.
I warrant I love you more than you do me.
HUBERT. [*Aside*] His words do take possession of my
    bosom.—
    Read here, young Arthur.   [*Showing a paper*]
    [*Aside*] How now, foolish rheum!
    Turning dispiteous torture out of door!
    I must be brief, lest resolution drop
    Out at mine eyes in tender womanish tears.—
    Can you not read it? Is it not fair writ?
ARTHUR. Too fairly, Hubert, for so foul effect.
    Must you with hot irons burn out both mine eyes?
HUBERT. Young boy, I must.
ARTHUR. And will you?
HUBERT. And I will.
ARTHUR. Have you the heart? When your head did but
    ache,
    I knit my handkerchief about your brows—
    The best I had, a princess wrought it me—
    And I did never ask it you again;
    And with my hand at midnight held your head;
    And, like the watchful minutes to the hour,
    Still and anon cheer'd up the heavy time,
    Saying 'What lack you?' and 'Where lies your grief?'
    Or 'What good love may I perform for you?'
    Many a poor man's son would have lyen still,
    And ne'er have spoke a loving word to you;
    But you at your sick service had a prince.
    Nay, you may think my love was crafty love,
    And call it cunning. Do, an if you will.
    If heaven be pleas'd that you must use me ill,
    Why, then you must. Will you put out mine eyes,
    These eyes that never did nor never shall
    So much as frown on you?
HUBERT. I have sworn to do it;
    And with hot irons must I burn them out.
ARTHUR. Ah, none but in this iron age would do it!
    The iron of itself, though heat red-hot,
    Approaching near these eyes would drink my tears,
    And quench his fiery indignation

Even in the matter of mine innocence;
Nay, after that, consume away in rust
But for containing fire to harm mine eye.
Are you more stubborn-hard than hammer'd iron?
An if an angel should have come to me
And told me Hubert should put out mine eyes,
I would not have believ'd him—no tongue but Hubert's.
HUBERT. [*Stamps*] Come forth.

Re-enter EXECUTIONERS, *with cord, irons, etc.*

Do as I bid you do.
ARTHUR. O, save me, Hubert, save me! My eyes are out
Even with the fierce looks of these bloody men.
HUBERT. Give me the iron, I say, and bind him here.
ARTHUR. Alas, what need you be so boist'rous rough?
I will not struggle, I will stand stone-still.
For heaven sake, Hubert, let me not be bound!
Nay, hear me, Hubert! Drive these men away,
And I will sit as quiet as a lamb;
I will not stir, nor wince, nor speak a word,
Nor look upon the iron angrily;
Thrust but these men away, and I'll forgive you,
Whatever torment you do put me to.
HUBERT. Go, stand within; let me alone with him.
EXECUTIONER. I am best pleas'd to be from such a deed.
Exeunt EXECUTIONERS
ARTHUR. Alas, I then have chid away my friend!
He hath a stern look but a gentle heart.
Let him come back, that his compassion may
Give life to yours.
HUBERT. Come, boy, prepare yourself.
ARTHUR. Is there no remedy?
HUBERT. None, but to lose your eyes.
ARTHUR. O heaven, that there were but a mote in yours,
A grain, a dust, a gnat, a wandering hair,
Any annoyance in that precious sense!
Then, feeling what small things are boisterous there,
Your vile intent must needs seem horrible.
HUBERT. Is this your promise? Go to, hold your tongue.
ARTHUR. Hubert, the utterance of a brace of tongues

Must needs want pleading for a pair of eyes.
Let me not hold my tongue, let me not, Hubert;
Or, Hubert, if you will, cut out my tongue,
So I may keep mine eyes. O, spare mine eyes,
Though to no use but still to look on you!
Lo, by my troth, the instrument is cold
And would not harm me.
HUBERT. I can heat it, boy.
ARTHUR. No, in good sooth; the fire is dead with grief,
Being create for comfort, to be us'd
In undeserved extremes. See else yourself:
There is no malice in this burning coal;
The breath of heaven hath blown his spirit out,
And strew'd repentant ashes on his head.
HUBERT. But with my breath I can revive it, boy.
ARTHUR. An if you do, you will but make it blush
And glow with shame of your proceedings, Hubert.
Nay, it perchance will sparkle in your eyes,
And, like a dog that is compell'd to fight,
Snatch at his master that doth tarre him on.
All things that you should use to do me wrong
Deny their office; only you do lack
That mercy which fierce fire and iron extends,
Creatures of note for mercy-lacking uses.
HUBERT. Well, see to live; I will not touch thine eye
For all the treasure that thine uncle owes.
Yet I am sworn, and I did purpose, boy,
With this same very iron to burn them out.
ARTHUR. O, now you look like Hubert! All this while
You were disguis'd.
HUBERT. Peace; no more. Adieu.
Your uncle must not know but you are dead:
I'll fill these dogged spies with false reports;
And, pretty child, sleep doubtless and secure
That Hubert, for the wealth of all the world,
Will not offend thee.
ARTHUR. O heaven! I thank you, Hubert.
HUBERT. Silence; no more. Go closely in with me.
Much danger do I undergo for thee.   *Exeunt*

KING JOHN

SCENE 2

England. KING JOHN'S *palace*

Enter KING JOHN, PEMBROKE, SALISBURY, *and other* LORDS

KING JOHN. Here once again we sit, once again crown'd,
  And look'd upon, I hope, with cheerful eyes.
PEMBROKE. This once again, but that your Highness pleas'd,
  Was once superfluous: you were crown'd before,
  And that high royalty was ne'er pluck'd off,
  The faiths of men ne'er stained with revolt;
  Fresh expectation troubled not the land
  With any long'd-for change or better state.
SALISBURY. Therefore, to be possess'd with double pomp,
  To guard a title that was rich before,
  To gild refined gold, to paint the lily,
  To throw a perfume on the violet,
  To smooth the ice, or add another hue
  Unto the rainbow, or with taper-light
  To seek the beauteous eye of heaven to garnish,
  Is wasteful and ridiculous excess.
PEMBROKE. But that your royal pleasure must be done,
  This act is as an ancient tale new told
  And, in the last repeating, troublesome,
  Being urged at a time unseasonable.
SALISBURY. In this the antique and well-noted face
  Of plain old form is much disfigured;
  And like a shifted wind unto a sail
  It makes the course of thoughts to fetch about,
  Startles and frights consideration,
  Makes sound opinion sick, and truth suspected,
  For putting on so new a fashion'd robe.
PEMBROKE. When workmen strive to do better than well,
  They do confound their skill in covetousness;
  And oftentimes excusing of a fault
  Doth make the fault the worse by th' excuse,
  As patches set upon a little breach
  Discredit more in hiding of the fault
  Than did the fault before it was so patch'd.

SALISBURY. To this effect, before you were new-crown'd,
  We breath'd our counsel; but it pleas'd your Highness
  To overbear it; and we are all well pleas'd,
  Since all and every part of what we would
  Doth make a stand at what your Highness will.
KING JOHN. Some reasons of this double coronation
  I have possess'd you with, and think them strong;
  And more, more strong, when lesser is my fear,
  I shall indue you with. Meantime but ask
  What you would have reform'd that is not well,
  And well shall you perceive how willingly
  I will both hear and grant you your requests.
PEMBROKE. Then I, as one that am the tongue of these,
  To sound the purposes of all their hearts,
  Both for myself and them—but, chief of all,
  Your safety, for the which myself and them
  Bend their best studies—heartily request
  Th' enfranchisement of Arthur, whose restraint
  Doth move the murmuring lips of discontent
  To break into this dangerous argument:
  If what in rest you have in right you hold,
  Why then your fears—which, as they say, attend
  The steps of wrong—should move you to mew up
  Your tender kinsman, and to choke his days
  With barbarous ignorance, and deny his youth
  The rich advantage of good exercise?
  That the time's enemies may not have this
  To grace occasions, let it be our suit
  That you have bid us ask his liberty;
  Which for our goods we do no further ask
  Than whereupon our weal, on you depending,
  Counts it your weal he have his liberty.
KING JOHN. Let it be so. I do commit his youth
  To your direction.

Enter HUBERT

[*Aside*] Hubert, what news with you?
PEMBROKE. This is the man should do the bloody deed:
  He show'd his warrant to a friend of mine;
  The image of a wicked heinous fault

Lives in his eye; that close aspect of his
Doth show the mood of a much troubled breast,
And I do fearfully believe 'tis done
What we so fear'd he had a charge to do.
SALISBURY. The colour of the King doth come and go
Between his purpose and his conscience,
Like heralds 'twixt two dreadful battles set.
His passion is so ripe it needs must break.
PEMBROKE. And when it breaks, I fear will issue thence
The foul corruption of a sweet child's death.
KING JOHN. We cannot hold mortality's strong hand.
Good lords, although my will to give is living,
The suit which you demand is gone and dead:
He tells us Arthur is deceas'd to-night.
SALISBURY. Indeed, we fear'd his sickness was past cure.
PEMBROKE. Indeed, we heard how near his death he was,
Before the child himself felt he was sick.
This must be answer'd either here or hence.
KING JOHN. Why do you bend such solemn brows on me?
Think you I bear the shears of destiny?
Have I commandment on the pulse of life?
SALISBURY. It is apparent foul-play; and 'tis shame
That greatness should so grossly offer it.
So thrive it in your game! and so, farewell.
PEMBROKE. Stay yet, Lord Salisbury, I'll go with thee
And find th' inheritance of this poor child,
His little kingdom of a forced grave.
That blood which ow'd the breadth of all this isle
Three foot of it doth hold—bad world the while!
This must not be thus borne: this will break out
To all our sorrows, and ere long I doubt.   *Exeunt* LORDS
KING JOHN. They burn in indignation. I repent.
There is no sure foundation set on blood,
No certain life achiev'd by others' death.

Enter a MESSENGER

A fearful eye thou hast; where is that blood
That I have seen inhabit in those cheeks?
So foul a sky clears not without a storm.
Pour down thy weather—how goes all in France?

MESSENGER. From France to England. Never such a pow'r
  For any foreign preparation
  Was levied in the body of a land.
  The copy of your speed is learn'd by them,
  For when you should be told they do prepare,
  The tidings comes that they are all arriv'd.
KING JOHN. O, where hath our intelligence been drunk?
  Where hath it slept? Where is my mother's care,
  That such an army could be drawn in France,
  And she not hear of it?
MESSENGER. My liege, her ear
  Is stopp'd with dust: the first of April died
  Your noble mother; and as I hear, my lord,
  The Lady Constance in a frenzy died
  Three days before; but this from rumour's tongue
  I idly heard—if true or false I know not.
KING JOHN. Withhold thy speed, dreadful occasion!
  O, make a league with me, till I have pleas'd
  My discontented peers! What! mother dead!
  How wildly then walks my estate in France!
  Under whose conduct came those pow'rs of France
  That thou for truth giv'st out are landed here?
MESSENGER. Under the Dauphin.
KING JOHN. Thou hast made me giddy
  With these ill tidings.

      Enter the BASTARD *and* PETER OF POMFRET

  Now! What says the world
  To your proceedings? Do not seek to stuff
  My head with more ill news, for it is full.
BASTARD. But if you be afear'd to hear the worst,
  Then let the worst, unheard, fall on your head.
KING JOHN. Bear with me, cousin, for I was amaz'd
  Under the tide; but now I breathe again
  Aloft the flood, and can give audience
  To any tongue, speak it of what it will.
BASTARD. How I have sped among the clergymen
  The sums I have collected shall express.
  But as I travell'd hither through the land,
  I find the people strangely fantasied;

Possess'd with rumours, full of idle dreams,
Not knowing what they fear, but full of fear;
And here's a prophet that I brought with me
From forth the streets of Pomfret, whom I found
With many hundreds treading on his heels;
To whom he sung, in rude harsh-sounding rhymes,
That, ere the next Ascension-day at noon,
Your Highness should deliver up your crown.
KING JOHN. Thou idle dreamer, wherefore didst thou so?
PETER. Foreknowing that the truth will fall out so.
KING JOHN. Hubert, away with him; imprison him;
And on that day at noon whereon he says
I shall yield up my crown let him be hang'd.
Deliver him to safety; and return,
For I must use thee.

       Exit HUBERT *with* PETER

O my gentle cousin,
Hear'st thou the news abroad, who are arriv'd?
BASTARD. The French, my lord; men's mouths are full of it;
Besides, I met Lord Bigot and Lord Salisbury,
With eyes as red as new-enkindled fire,
And others more, going to seek the grave
Of Arthur, whom they say is kill'd to-night
On your suggestion.
KING JOHN. Gentle kinsman, go
And thrust thyself into their companies.
I have a way to win their loves again;
Bring them before me.
BASTARD. I will seek them out.
KING JOHN. Nay, but make haste; the better foot before.
O, let me have no subject enemies
When adverse foreigners affright my towns
With dreadful pomp of stout invasion!
Be Mercury, set feathers to thy heels,
And fly like thought from them to me again.
BASTARD. The spirit of the time shall teach me speed.
KING JOHN. Spoke like a sprightful noble gentleman.

         Exit BASTARD

Go after him; for he perhaps shall need
Some messenger betwixt me and the peers;

And be thou he.
MESSENGER. With all my heart, my liege.   *Exit*
KING JOHN. My mother dead!

Re-enter HUBERT

HUBERT. My lord, they say five moons were seen to-night;
  Four fixed, and the fifth did whirl about
  The other four in wondrous motion.
KING JOHN. Five moons!
HUBERT. Old men and beldams in the streets
  Do prophesy upon it dangerously;
  Young Arthur's death is common in their mouths;
  And when they talk of him, they shake their heads,
  And whisper one another in the ear;
  And he that speaks doth gripe the hearer's wrist,
  Whilst he that hears makes fearful action
  With wrinkled brows, with nods, with rolling eyes.
  I saw a smith stand with his hammer, thus,
  The whilst his iron did on the anvil cool,
  With open mouth swallowing a tailor's news;
  Who, with his shears and measure in his hand,
  Standing on slippers, which his nimble haste
  Had falsely thrust upon contrary feet,
  Told of a many thousand warlike French
  That were embattailed and rank'd in Kent.
  Another lean unwash'd artificer
  Cuts off his tale, and talks of Arthur's death.
KING JOHN. Why seek'st thou to possess me with these fears?
  Why urgest thou so oft young Arthur's death?
  Thy hand hath murd'red him. I had a mighty cause
  To wish him dead, but thou hadst none to kill him.
HUBERT. No had, my lord! Why, did you not provoke me?
KING JOHN. It is the curse of kings to be attended
  By slaves that take their humours for a warrant
  To break within the bloody house of life,
  And on the winking of authority
  To understand a law; to know the meaning
  Of dangerous majesty, when perchance it frowns
  More upon humour than advis'd respect.
HUBERT. Here is your hand and seal for what I did.

KING JOHN. O, when the last account 'twixt heaven and
  earth
Is to be made, then shall this hand and seal
Witness against us to damnation!
How oft the sight of means to do ill deeds
Make deeds ill done! Hadst not thou been by,
A fellow by the hand of nature mark'd,
Quoted and sign'd to do a deed of shame,
This murder had not come into my mind;
But, taking note of thy abhorr'd aspect,
Finding thee fit for bloody villainy,
Apt, liable to be employ'd in danger,
I faintly broke with thee of Arthur's death;
And thou, to be endeared to a king,
Made it no conscience to destroy a prince.
HUBERT. My lord—
KING JOHN. Hadst thou but shook thy head or made a
  pause,
When I spake darkly what I purposed,
Or turn'd an eye of doubt upon my face,
As bid me tell my tale in express words,
Deep shame had struck me dumb, made me break off,
And those thy fears might have wrought fears in me.
But thou didst understand me by my signs,
And didst in signs again parley with sin;
Yea, without stop, didst let thy heart consent,
And consequently thy rude hand to act
The deed which both our tongues held vile to name.
Out of my sight, and never see me more!
My nobles leave me; and my state is braved,
Even at my gates, with ranks of foreign pow'rs;
Nay, in the body of the fleshly land,
This kingdom, this confine of blood and breath,
Hostility and civil tumult reigns
Between my conscience and my cousin's death.
HUBERT. Arm you against your other enemies,
I'll make a peace between your soul and you.
Young Arthur is alive. This hand of mine
Is yet a maiden and an innocent hand,
Not painted with the crimson spots of blood.

Within this bosom never ent'red yet
The dreadful motion of a murderous thought
And you have slander'd nature in my form,
Which, howsoever rude exteriorly,
Is yet the cover of a fairer mind
Than to be butcher of an innocent child.
KING JOHN. Doth Arthur live? O, haste thee to the peers,
Throw this report on their incensed rage
And make them tame to their obedience!
Forgive the comment that my passion made
Upon thy feature; for my rage was blind,
And foul imaginary eyes of blood
Presented thee more hideous than thou art.
O, answer not; but to my closet bring
The angry lords with all expedient haste.
I conjure thee but slowly; run more fast.   *Exeunt*

SCENE 3

England. Before the castle

Enter ARTHUR, *on the walls*

ARTHUR. The wall is high, and yet will I leap down.
Good ground, be pitiful and hurt me not!
There's few or none do know me; if they did,
This ship-boy's semblance hath disguis'd me quite.
I am afraid; and yet I'll venture it.
If I get down and do not break my limbs,
I'll find a thousand shifts to get away.
As good to die and go, as die and stay.   [*Leaps down*]
O me! my uncle's spirit is in these stones.
Heaven take my soul, and England keep my bones!
                                                      [*Dies*]

Enter PEMBROKE, SALISBURY, *and* BIGOT

SALISBURY. Lords, I will meet him at Saint Edmundsbury;
It is our safety, and we must embrace
This gentle offer of the perilous time.
PEMBROKE. Who brought that letter from the Cardinal?

SALISBURY. The Count Melun, a noble lord of France,
Whose private with me of the Dauphin's love
Is much more general than these lines import.
BIGOT. To-morrow morning let us meet him then.
SALISBURY. Or rather then set forward; for 'twill be
Two long days' journey, lords, or ere we meet.

Enter the BASTARD

BASTARD. Once more to-day well met, distemper'd lords!
The King by me requests your presence straight.
SALISBURY. The King hath dispossess'd himself of us.
We will not line his thin bestained cloak
With our pure honours, nor attend the foot
That leaves the print of blood where'er it walks.
Return and tell him so. We know the worst.
BASTARD. Whate'er you think, good words, I think, were
best.
SALISBURY. Our griefs, and not our manners, reason now.
BASTARD. But there is little reason in your grief;
Therefore 'twere reason you had manners now.
PEMBROKE. Sir, sir, impatience hath his privilege.
BASTARD. 'Tis true—to hurt his master, no man else.
SALISBURY. This is the prison. What is he lies here?
PEMBROKE. O death, made proud with pure and princely
beauty!
The earth had not a hole to hide this deed.
SALISBURY. Murder, as hating what himself hath done,
Doth lay it open to urge on revenge.
BIGOT. Or, when he doom'd this beauty to a grave,
Found it too precious-princely for a grave.
SALISBURY. Sir Richard, what think you? Have you beheld,
Or have you read or heard, or could you think?
Or do you almost think, although you see,
That you do see? Could thought, without this object,
Form such another? This is the very top,
The height, the crest, or crest unto the crest,
Of murder's arms; this is the bloodiest shame,
The wildest savagery, the vilest stroke,
That ever wall-ey'd wrath or staring rage
Presented to the tears of soft remorse.

PEMBROKE. All murders past do stand excus'd in this;
   And this, so sole and so unmatchable,
   Shall give a holiness, a purity,
   To the yet unbegotten sin of times,
   And prove a deadly bloodshed but a jest,
   Exampled by this heinous spectacle.
BASTARD. It is a damned and a bloody work;
   The graceless action of a heavy hand,
   If that it be the work of any hand.
SALISBURY. If that it be the work of any hand!
   We had a kind of light what would ensue.
   It is the shameful work of Hubert's hand;
   The practice and the purpose of the King;
   From whose obedience I forbid my soul,
   Kneeling before this ruin of sweet life,
   And breathing to his breathless excellence
   The incense of a vow, a holy vow,
   Never to taste the pleasures of the world,
   Never to be infected with delight,
   Nor conversant with ease and idleness,
   Till I have set a glory to this hand
   By giving it the worship of revenge.
PEMBROKE. ⎫
BIGOT.   ⎬ Our souls religiously confirm thy words.

Enter HUBERT

HUBERT. Lords, I am hot with haste in seeking you.
   Arthur doth live; the King hath sent for you.
SALISBURY. O, he is bold, and blushes not at death!
   Avaunt, thou hateful villain, get thee gone!
HUBERT. I am no villain.
SALISBURY. Must I rob the law?   *[Drawing his sword]*
BASTARD. Your sword is bright, sir; put it up again.
SALISBURY. Not till I sheathe it in a murderer's skin.
HUBERT. Stand back, Lord Salisbury, stand back, I say;
   By heaven, I think my sword's as sharp as yours.
   I would not have you, lord, forget yourself,
   Nor tempt the danger of my true defence;
   Lest I, by marking of your rage, forget
   Your worth, your greatness and nobility.

BIGOT. Out, dunghill! Dar'st thou brave a nobleman?
HUBERT. Not for my life; but yet I dare defend
  My innocent life against an emperor.
SALISBURY. Thou art a murderer.
HUBERT. Do not prove me so.
  Yet I am none. Whose tongue soe'er speaks false,
  Not truly speaks; who speaks not truly, lies.
PEMBROKE. Cut him to pieces.
BASTARD. Keep the peace, I say.
SALISBURY. Stand by, or I shall gall you, Faulconbridge.
BASTARD. Thou wert better gall the devil, Salisbury.
  If thou but frown on me, or stir thy foot,
  Or teach thy hasty spleen to do me shame,
  I'll strike thee dead. Put up thy sword betime;
  Or I'll so maul you and your toasting-iron
  That you shall think the devil is come from hell.
BIGOT. What wilt thou do, renowned Faulconbridge?
  Second a villain and a murderer?
HUBERT. Lord Bigot, I am none.
BIGOT. Who kill'd this prince?
HUBERT. 'Tis not an hour since I left him well.
  I honour'd him, I lov'd him, and will weep
  My date of life out for his sweet life's loss.
SALISBURY. Trust not those cunning waters of his eyes,
  For villainy is not without such rheum;
  And he, long traded in it, makes it seem
  Like rivers of remorse and innocency.
  Away with me, all you whose souls abhor
  Th' uncleanly savours of a slaughter-house;
  For I am stifled with this smell of sin.
BIGOT. Away toward Bury, to the Dauphin there!
PEMBROKE. There tell the King he may inquire us out.
                                    Exeunt LORDS

BASTARD. Here's a good world! Knew you of this fair work?
  Beyond the infinite and boundless reach
  Of mercy, if thou didst this deed of death,
  Art thou damn'd, Hubert.
HUBERT. Do but hear me, sir.
BASTARD. Ha! I'll tell thee what:
  Thou'rt damn'd as black—nay, nothing is so black—

Thou art more deep damn'd than Prince Lucifer;
There is not yet so ugly a fiend of hell
As thou shalt be, if thou didst kill this child.

HUBERT. Upon my soul—

BASTARD. If thou didst but consent
   To this most cruel act, do but despair;
   And if thou want'st a cord, the smallest thread
   That ever spider twisted from her womb
   Will serve to strangle thee; a rush will be a beam
   To hang thee on; or wouldst thou drown thyself,
   Put but a little water in a spoon
   And it shall be as all the ocean,
   Enough to stifle such a villain up
   I do suspect thee very grievously.

HUBERT. If I in act, consent, or sin of thought,
   Be guilty of the stealing that sweet breath
   Which was embounded in this beauteous clay,
   Let hell want pains enough to torture me!
   I left him well.

BASTARD. Go, bear him in thine arms.
   I am amaz'd, methinks, and lose my way
   Among the thorns and dangers of this world.
   How easy dost thou take all England up!
   From forth this morsel of dead royalty
   The life, the right, and truth of all this realm
   Is fled to heaven; and England now is left
   To tug and scamble, and to part by th' teeth
   The unowed interest of proud-swelling state.
   Now for the bare-pick'd bone of majesty
   Doth dogged war bristle his angry crest
   And snarleth in the gentle eyes of peace;
   Now powers from home and discontents at home
   Meet in one line; and vast confusion waits,
   As doth a raven on a sick-fall'n beast,
   The imminent decay of wrested pomp.
   Now happy he whose cloak and cincture can
   Hold out this tempest. Bear away that child,
   And follow me with speed. I'll to the King;
   A thousand businesses are brief in hand,
   And heaven itself doth frown upon the land.   *Exeunt*

KING JOHN

ACT V. SCENE 1

England. KING JOHN's *palace*

Enter KING JOHN, PANDULPH, *and attendants*

KING JOHN. Thus have I yielded up into your hand
  The circle of my glory.
PANDULPH. [*Gives back the crown*] Take again
  From this my hand, as holding of the Pope,
  Your sovereign greatness and authority.
KING JOHN. Now keep your holy word; go meet the French;
  And from his Holiness use all your power
  To stop their marches fore we are inflam'd.
  Our discontented counties do revolt;
  Our people quarrel with obedience,
  Swearing allegiance and the love of soul
  To stranger blood, to foreign royalty.
  This inundation of mistemp'red humour
  Rests by you only to be qualified.
  Then pause not; for the present time's so sick
  That present med'cine must be minist'red
  Or overthrow incurable ensues.
PANDULPH. It was my breath that blew this tempest up,
  Upon your stubborn usage of the Pope;
  But since you are a gentle convertite,
  My tongue shall hush again this storm of war
  And make fair weather in your blust'ring land.
  On this Ascension-day, remember well,
  Upon your oath of service to the Pope,
  Go I to make the French lay down their arms.   *Exit*
KING JOHN. Is this Ascension-day? Did not the prophet
  Say that before Ascension-day at noon
  My crown I should give off? Even so I have.
  I did suppose it should be on constraint;
  But, heaven be thank'd, it is but voluntary.

Enter the BASTARD

BASTARD. All Kent hath yielded; nothing there holds out
  But Dover Castle. London hath receiv'd,

Like a kind host, the Dauphin and his powers.
Your nobles will not hear you, but are gone
To offer service to your enemy;
And wild amazement hurries up and down
The little number of your doubtful friends.

KING JOHN. Would not my lords return to me again
After they heard young Arthur was alive?

BASTARD. They found him dead, and cast into the streets,
An empty casket, where the jewel of life
By some damn'd hand was robbed and ta'en away.

KING JOHN. That villain Hubert told me he did live.

BASTARD. So, on my soul, he did, for aught he knew.
But wherefore do you droop? Why look you sad?
Be great in act, as you have been in thought;
Let not the world see fear and sad distrust
Govern the motion of a kingly eye.
Be stirring as the time; be fire with fire;
Threaten the threat'ner, and outface the brow
Of bragging horror; so shall inferior eyes,
That borrow their behaviours from the great,
Grow great by your example and put on
The dauntless spirit of resolution.
Away, and glister like the god of war
When he intendeth to become the field;
Show boldness and aspiring confidence.
What, shall they seek the lion in his den,
And fright him there, and make him tremble there?
O, let it not be said! Forage, and run
To meet displeasure farther from the doors
And grapple with him ere he come so nigh.

KING JOHN. The legate of the Pope hath been with me,
And I have made a happy peace with him;
And he hath promis'd to dismiss the powers
Led by the Dauphin.

BASTARD. O inglorious league!
Shall we, upon the footing of our land,
Send fair-play orders, and make compromise,
Insinuation, parley, and base truce,
To arms invasive? Shall a beardless boy,
A cock'red silken wanton, brave our fields

And flesh his spirit in a warlike soil,
Mocking the air with colours idly spread,
And find no check? Let us, my liege, to arms.
Perchance the Cardinal cannot make your peace;
Or, if he do, let it at least be said
They saw we had a purpose of defence.
KING JOHN. Have thou the ordering of this present time.
BASTARD. Away, then, with good courage!
Yet, I know
Our party may well meet a prouder foe.   *Exeunt*

SCENE 2

England. The DAUPHIN'S *camp at Saint Edmundsbury*

Enter, in arms, LEWIS, SALISBURY, MELUN,
PEMBROKE, BIGOT, *and soldiers*

LEWIS. My Lord Melun, let this be copied out
And keep it safe for our remembrance;
Return the precedent to these lords again,
That, having our fair order written down,
Both they and we, perusing o'er these notes,
May know wherefore we took the sacrament,
And keep our faiths firm and inviolable.
SALISBURY. Upon our sides it never shall be broken.
And, noble Dauphin, albeit we swear
A voluntary zeal and an unurg'd faith
To your proceedings; yet, believe me, Prince,
I am not glad that such a sore of time
Should seek a plaster by contemn'd revolt,
And heal the inveterate canker of one wound
By making many. O, it grieves my soul
That I must draw this metal from my side
To be a widow-maker! O, and there
Where honourable rescue and defence
Cries out upon the name of Salisbury!
But such is the infection of the time
That, for the health and physic of our right,
We cannot deal but with the very hand

Of stern injustice and confused wrong.
And is't not pity, O my grieved friends!
That we, the sons and children of this isle,
Were born to see so sad an hour as this;
Wherein we step after a stranger-march
Upon her gentle bosom, and fill up
Her enemies' ranks—I must withdraw and weep
Upon the spot of this enforced cause—
To grace the gentry of a land remote
And follow unacquainted colours here?
What, here? O nation, that thou couldst remove!
That Neptune's arms, who clippeth thee about,
Would bear thee from the knowledge of thyself
And grapple thee unto a pagan shore,
Where these two Christian armies might combine
The blood of malice in a vein of league,
And not to spend it so unneighbourly!

LEWIS. A noble temper dost thou show in this;
And great affections wrestling in thy bosom
Doth make an earthquake of nobility.
O, what a noble combat hast thou fought
Between compulsion and a brave respect!
Let me wipe off this honourable dew
That silverly doth progress on thy cheeks.
My heart hath melted at a lady's tears,
Being an ordinary inundation;
But this effusion of such manly drops,
This show'r, blown up by tempest of the soul,
Startles mine eyes and makes me more amaz'd
Than had I seen the vaulty top of heaven
Figur'd quite o'er with burning meteors.
Lift up thy brow, renowned Salisbury,
And with a great heart heave away this storm;
Commend these waters to those baby eyes
That never saw the giant world enrag'd,
Nor met with fortune other than at feasts,
Full of warm blood, of mirth, of gossiping.
Come, come; for thou shalt thrust thy hand as deep
Into the purse of rich prosperity
As Lewis himself. So, nobles, shall you all,

That knit your sinews to the strength of mine.

Enter PANDULPH

And even there, methinks, an angel spake:
Look where the holy legate comes apace,
To give us warrant from the hand of heaven
And on our actions set the name of right
With holy breath.
PANDULPH. Hail, noble prince of France!
The next is this: King John hath reconcil'd
Himself to Rome; his spirit is come in,
That so stood out against the holy Church,
The great metropolis and see of Rome.
Therefore thy threat'ning colours now wind up
And tame the savage spirit of wild war,
That, like a lion fostered up at hand,
It may lie gently at the foot of peace
And be no further harmful than in show.
LEWIS. Your Grace shall pardon me, I will not back:
I am too high-born to be propertied,
To be a secondary at control,
Or useful serving-man and instrument
To any sovereign state throughout the world.
Your breath first kindled the dead coal of wars
Between this chastis'd kingdom and myself
And brought in matter that should feed this fire;
And now 'tis far too huge to be blown out
With that same weak wind which enkindled it.
You taught me how to know the face of right,
Acquainted me with interest to this land,
Yea, thrust this enterprise into my heart;
And come ye now to tell me John hath made
His peace with Rome? What is that peace to me?
I, by the honour of my marriage-bed,
After young Arthur, claim this land for mine;
And, now it is half-conquer'd, must I back
Because that John hath made his peace with Rome?
Am I Rome's slave? What penny hath Rome borne,
What men provided, what munition sent,
To underprop this action? Is't not I

That undergo this charge? Who else but I,
And such as to my claim are liable,
Sweat in this business and maintain this war?
Have I not heard these islanders shout out
'Vive le roi!' as I have bank'd their towns?
Have I not here the best cards for the game
To win this easy match, play'd for a crown?
And shall I now give o'er the yielded set?
No, no, on my soul, it never shall be said.

PANDULPH. You look but on the outside of this work.

LEWIS. Outside or inside, I will not return
Till my attempt so much be glorified
As to my ample hope was promised
Before I drew this gallant head of war,
And cull'd these fiery spirits from the world
To outlook conquest, and to win renown
Even in the jaws of danger and of death.

[*Trumpet sounds*]

What lusty trumpet thus doth summon us?

Enter the BASTARD, *attended*

BASTARD. According to the fair play of the world,
Let me have audience: I am sent to speak.
My holy lord of Milan, from the King
I come, to learn how you have dealt for him;
And, as you answer, I do know the scope
And warrant limited unto my tongue.

PANDULPH. The Dauphin is too wilful-opposite,
And will not temporize with my entreaties;
He flatly says he'll not lay down his arms.

BASTARD. By all the blood that ever fury breath'd,
The youth says well. Now hear our English King;
For thus his royalty doth speak in me.
He is prepar'd, and reason too he should.
This apish and unmannerly approach,
This harness'd masque and unadvised revel,
This unhair'd sauciness and boyish troops,
The King doth smile at; and is well prepar'd
To whip this dwarfish war, these pigmy arms,
From out the circle of his territories.

That hand which had the strength, even at your door,
To cudgel you and make you take the hatch,
To dive like buckets in concealed wells,
To crouch in litter of your stable planks,
To lie like pawns lock'd up in chests and trunks,
To hug with swine, to seek sweet safety out
In vaults and prisons, and to thrill and shake
Even at the crying of your nation's crow,
Thinking this voice an armed Englishman—
Shall that victorious hand be feebled here
That in your chambers gave you chastisement?
No. Know the gallant monarch is in arms
And like an eagle o'er his aery tow'rs
To souse annoyance that comes near his nest.
And you degenerate, you ingrate revolts,
You bloody Neroes, ripping up the womb
Of your dear mother England, blush for shame;
For your own ladies and pale-visag'd maids,
Like Amazons, come tripping after drums,
Their thimbles into armed gauntlets change,
Their needles to lances, and their gentle hearts
To fierce and bloody inclination.
LEWIS. There end thy brave, and turn thy face in peace;
We grant thou canst outscold us. Fare thee well;
We hold our time too precious to be spent
With such a brabbler.
PANDULPH. Give me leave to speak.
BASTARD. No, I will speak.
LEWIS. We will attend to neither.
Strike up the drums; and let the tongue of war,
Plead for our interest and our being here.
BASTARD. Indeed, your drums, being beaten, will cry out;
And so shall you, being beaten. Do but start
And echo with the clamour of thy drum,
And even at hand a drum is ready brac'd
That shall reverberate all as loud as thine:
Sound but another, and another shall,
As loud as thine, rattle the welkin's ear
And mock the deep-mouth'd thunder; for at hand—
Not trusting to this halting legate here,

Whom he hath us'd rather for sport than need—
Is warlike John; and in his forehead sits
A bare-ribb'd death, whose office is this day
To feast upon whole thousands of the French.
LEWIS. Strike up our drums to find this danger out.
BASTARD. And thou shalt find it, Dauphin, do not doubt.

Exeunt

SCENE 3

England. The field of battle

Alarums. Enter KING JOHN *and* HUBERT

KING JOHN. How goes the day with us? O, tell me, Hubert.
HUBERT. Badly, I fear. How fares your Majesty?
KING JOHN. This fever that hath troubled me so long
Lies heavy on me. O, my heart is sick!

Enter a MESSENGER

MESSENGER. My lord, your valiant kinsman, Faulconbridge,
Desires your Majesty to leave the field
And send him word by me which way you go.
KING JOHN. Tell him, toward Swinstead, to the abbey there.
MESSENGER. Be of good comfort; for the great supply
That was expected by the Dauphin here
Are wreck'd three nights ago on Goodwin Sands;
This news was brought to Richard but even now.
The French fight coldly, and retire themselves.
KING JOHN. Ay me, this tyrant fever burns me up
And will not let me welcome this good news.
Set on toward Swinstead; to my litter straight;
Weakness possesseth me, and I am faint. *Exeunt*

SCENE 4

England. Another part of the battlefield

Enter SALISBURY, PEMBROKE, *and* BIGOT

SALISBURY. I did not think the King so stor'd with friends.

PEMBROKE. Up once again; put spirit in the French;
  If they miscarry, we miscarry too.
SALISBURY. That misbegotten devil, Faulconbridge,
  In spite of spite, alone upholds the day.
PEMBROKE. They say King John, sore sick, hath left the
  field.

Enter MELUN, *wounded*

MELUN. Lead me to the revolts of England here.
SALISBURY. When we were happy we had other names.
PEMBROKE. It is the Count Melun.
SALISBURY. Wounded to death.
MELUN. Fly, noble English, you are bought and sold;
  Unthread the rude eye of rebellion,
  And welcome home again discarded faith.
  Seek out King John, and fall before his feet;
  For if the French be lords of this loud day,
  He means to recompense the pains you take
  By cutting off your heads. Thus hath he sworn,
  And I with him, and many moe with me,
  Upon the altar at Saint Edmundsbury;
  Even on that altar where we swore to you
  Dear amity and everlasting love.
SALISBURY. May this be possible? May this be true?
MELUN. Have I not hideous death within my view,
  Retaining but a quantity of life,
  Which bleeds away even as a form of wax
  Resolveth from his figure 'gainst the fire?
  What in the world should make me now deceive,
  Since I must lose the use of all deceit?
  Why should I then be false, since it is true
  That I must die here, and live hence by truth?
  I say again, if Lewis do win the day,
  He is forsworn if e'er those eyes of yours
  Behold another day break in the east;
  But even this night, whose black contagious breath
  Already smokes about the burning crest
  Of the old, feeble, and day-wearied sun,
  Even this ill night, your breathing shall expire,
  Paying the fine of rated treachery

Even with a treacherous fine of all your lives,
If Lewis by your assistance win the day.
Commend me to one Hubert, with your King;
The love of him—and this respect besides,
For that my grandsire was an Englishman—
Awakes my conscience to confess all this.
In lieu whereof, I pray you, bear me hence
From forth the noise and rumour of the field,
Where I may think the remnant of my thoughts
In peace, and part this body and my soul
With contemplation and devout desires.

SALISBURY. We do believe thee; and beshrew my soul
But I do love the favour and the form
Of this most fair occasion, by the which
We will untread the steps of damned flight,
And like a bated and retired flood,
Leaving our rankness and irregular course,
Stoop low within those bounds we have o'erlook'd,
And calmly run on in obedience
Even to our ocean, to our great King John.
My arm shall give thee help to bear thee hence;
For I do see the cruel pangs of death
Right in thine eye. Away, my friends! New flight,
And happy newness, that intends old right.

Exeunt, leading off MELUN

SCENE 5

England. The French camp

Enter LEWIS *and his train*

LEWIS. The sun of heaven, methought, was loath to set,
But stay'd and made the western welkin blush,
When English measure backward their own ground
In faint retire. O, bravely came we off,
When with a volley of our needless shot,
After such bloody toil, we bid good night;
And wound our tott'ring colours clearly up,
Last in the field and almost lords of it!

Enter a MESSENGER

MESSENGER. Where is my prince, the Dauphin?
LEWIS. Here; what news?
MESSENGER. The Count Melun is slain; the English lords
  By his persuasion are again fall'n off,
  And your supply, which you have wish'd so long,
  Are cast away and sunk on Goodwin Sands.
LEWIS. Ah, foul shrewd news! Beshrew thy very heart!
  I did not think to be so sad to-night
  As this hath made me. Who was he that said
  King John did fly an hour or two before
  The stumbling night did part our weary pow'rs?
MESSENGER. Whoever spoke it, it is true, my lord.
LEWIS. Well; keep good quarter and good care to-night;
  The day shall not be up so soon as I
  To try the fair adventure of to-morrow.   *Exeunt*

SCENE 6

An open place near Swinstead Abbey

Enter the BASTARD *and* HUBERT, *severally*

HUBERT. Who's there? Speak, ho! speak quickly, or I shoot.
BASTARD. A friend. What art thou?
HUBERT. Of the part of England.
BASTARD. Whither dost thou go?
HUBERT. What's that to thee? Why may I not demand
  Of thine affairs as well as thou of mine?
BASTARD. Hubert, I think.
HUBERT. Thou hast a perfect thought.
  I will upon all hazards well believe
  Thou art my friend that know'st my tongue so well.
  Who art thou?
BASTARD. Who thou wilt. And if thou please,
  Thou mayst befriend me so much as to think
  I come one way of the Plantagenets.
HUBERT. Unkind remembrance! thou and eyeless night
  Have done me shame. Brave soldier, pardon me

That any accent breaking from thy tongue
Should scape the true acquaintance of mine ear.
BASTARD. Come, come; sans compliment, what news abroad?
HUBERT. Why, here walk I in the black brow of night
To find you out.
BASTARD. Brief, then; and what's the news?
HUBERT. O, my sweet sir, news fitting to the night,
Black, fearful, comfortless, and horrible.
BASTARD. Show me the very wound of this ill news;
I am no woman, I'll not swoon at it.
HUBERT. The King, I fear, is poison'd by a monk;
I left him almost speechless and broke out
To acquaint you with this evil, that you might
The better arm you to the sudden time
Than if you had at leisure known of this.
BASTARD. How did he take it; who did taste to him?
HUBERT. A monk, I tell you; a resolved villain,
Whose bowels suddenly burst out. The King
Yet speaks, and peradventure may recover.
BASTARD. Who didst thou leave to tend his Majesty?
HUBERT. Why, know you not? The lords are all come back,
And brought Prince Henry in their company;
At whose request the King hath pardon'd them,
And they are all about his Majesty.
BASTARD. Withhold thine indignation, mighty heaven,
And tempt us not to bear above our power!
I'll tell thee, Hubert, half my power this night,
Passing these flats, are taken by the tide—
These Lincoln Washes have devoured them;
Myself, well-mounted, hardly have escap'd.
Away, before! conduct me to the King;
I doubt he will be dead or ere I come.   *Exeunt*

SCENE 7

The orchard at Swinstead Abbey

Enter PRINCE HENRY, SALISBURY, *and* BIGOT

PRINCE HENRY. It is too late; the life of all his blood

Is touch'd corruptibly, and his pure brain,
Which some suppose the soul's frail dwelling-house,
Doth by the idle comments that it makes
Foretell the ending of mortality.

Enter PEMBROKE

PEMBROKE. His Highness yet doth speak, and holds belief
  That, being brought into the open air,
  It would allay the burning quality
  Of that fell poison which assaileth him.
PRINCE HENRY. Let him be brought into the orchard here.
  Doth he still rage?   *Exit* BIGOT
PEMBROKE. He is more patient
  Than when you left him; even now he sung.
PRINCE HENRY. O vanity of sickness! Fierce extremes
  In their continuance will not feel themselves.
  Death, having prey'd upon the outward parts,
  Leaves them invisible, and his siege is now
  Against the mind, the which he pricks and wounds
  With many legions of strange fantasies,
  Which, in their throng and press to that last hold,
  Confound themselves. 'Tis strange that death should sing.
  I am the cygnet to this pale faint swan
  Who chants a doleful hymn to his own death,
  And from the organ-pipe of frailty sings
  His soul and body to their lasting rest.
SALISBURY. Be of good comfort, Prince; for you are born
  To set a form upon that indigest
  Which he hath left so shapeless and so rude.

Re-enter BIGOT *and attendants, who bring in*
KING JOHN *in a chair*

KING JOHN. Ay, marry, now my soul hath elbow-room;
  It would not out at windows nor at doors.
  There is so hot a summer in my bosom
  That all my bowels crumble up to dust.
  I am a scribbled form drawn with a pen
  Upon a parchment, and against this fire
  Do I shrink up.
PRINCE HENRY. How fares your Majesty?

KING JOHN. Poison'd—ill-fare! Dead, forsook, cast off;
And none of you will bid the winter come
To thrust his icy fingers in my maw,
Nor let my kingdom's rivers take their course
Through my burn'd bosom, nor entreat the north
To make his bleak winds kiss my parched lips
And comfort me with cold. I do not ask you much;
I beg cold comfort; and you are so strait
And so ingrateful you deny me that.
PRINCE HENRY. O that there were some virtue in my tears,
That might relieve you!
KING JOHN. The salt in them is hot.
Within me is a hell; and there the poison
Is as a fiend confin'd to tyrannize
On unreprievable condemned blood.

Enter the BASTARD

BASTARD. O, I am scalded with my violent motion
And spleen of speed to see your Majesty!
KING JOHN. O cousin, thou art come to set mine eye!
The tackle of my heart is crack'd and burnt,
And all the shrouds wherewith my life should sail
Are turned to one thread, one little hair;
My heart hath one poor string to stay it by,
Which holds but till thy news be uttered;
And then all this thou seest is but a clod
And module of confounded royalty.
BASTARD. The Dauphin is preparing hitherward,
Where God He knows how we shall answer him;
For in a night the best part of my pow'r,
As I upon advantage did remove,
Were in the Washes all unwarily
Devoured by the unexpected flood. [*The* KING *dies*]
SALISBURY. You breathe these dead news in as dead an ear.
My liege! my lord! But now a king—now thus.
PRINCE HENRY. Even so must I run on, and even so stop.
What surety of the world, what hope, what stay,
When this was now a king, and now is clay?
BASTARD. Art thou gone so? I do but stay behind
To do the office for thee of revenge,

And then my soul shall wait on thee to heaven,
As it on earth hath been thy servant still.
Now, now, you stars that move in your right spheres,
Where be your pow'rs? Show now your mended faiths,
And instantly return with me again
To push destruction and perpetual shame
Out of the weak door of our fainting land.
Straight let us seek, or straight we shall be sought;
The Dauphin rages at our very heels.

SALISBURY. It seems you know not, then, so much as we:
The Cardinal Pandulph is within at rest,
Who half an hour since came from the Dauphin,
And brings from him such offers of our peace
As we with honour and respect may take,
With purpose presently to leave this war.

BASTARD. He will the rather do it when he sees
Ourselves well sinewed to our defence.

SALISBURY. Nay, 'tis in a manner done already;
For many carriages he hath dispatch'd
To the sea-side, and put his cause and quarrel
To the disposing of the Cardinal;
With whom yourself, myself, and other lords,
If you think meet, this afternoon will post
To consummate this business happily.

BASTARD. Let it be so. And you, my noble Prince,
With other princes that may best be spar'd,
Shall wait upon your father's funeral.

PRINCE HENRY. At Worcester must his body be interr'd;
For so he will'd it.

BASTARD. Thither shall it, then;
And happily may your sweet self put on
The lineal state and glory of the land!
To whom, with all submission, on my knee
I do bequeath my faithful services
And true subjection everlastingly.

SALISBURY. And the like tender of our love we make,
To rest without a spot for evermore.

PRINCE HENRY. I have a kind soul that would give you thanks,
And knows not how to do it but with tears.

BASTARD. O, let us pay the time but needful woe,
  Since it hath been beforehand with our griefs.
  This England never did, nor never shall,
  Lie at the proud foot of a conqueror,
  But when it first did help to wound itself.
  Now these her princes are come home again,
  Come the three corners of the world in arms,
  And we shall shock them. Nought shall make us rue,
  If England to itself do rest but true.   *Exeunt*

The Tragedy of
King Richard the Second

KING RICHARD THE SECOND

SOON after the beginning of 1595, when the London companies had settled down once again to regular playing after the long break caused by the plague-ridden condition of the capital, Shakespeare made a start with his second tetralogy of plays on English history.

Shakespeare, in writing *Richard II*, was shaping a play on history in the manner he had already achieved in *Richard III;* he was not putting on the stage a piece of political propaganda; and although the play was very soon to be regarded, if not as a political manifesto, at least as good publicity for the attitude of a party at court, it is clear its first hearers regarded it as untainted by subversive doctrine. Sir Edmund Chambers discovered a reference to its performance at the house of Sir Edward Hoby on 9 December 1595. Sir Robert Cecil, the son of Burghley the Secretary of State, was among the guests at the supper and entertainment, and there can be no question either of his or his host's loyalty to the reigning monarch; yet, very soon after, both the Queen herself and the Essex party, which was now dissatisfied with existing conditions and was later to offer a show of armed resistance to constituted authority, regarded the play as the vehicle of political instruction.

In 1601 William Lambarde, a scholarly man of antiquarian and historical bent, who was in charge of the records in the Tower of London, was submitting to Her Majesty at Greenwich an account of his stewardship, and turning over for her satisfaction the documents entrusted to his care. When they came to the reign of Richard the Second, the Queen said to Lambarde: "I am Richard the Second, know ye not that?" Lambarde understood the implication of the remark perfectly, for he replied by deploring the conduct of Essex, who, in spite of the favours shown him by his sovereign, had attempted to defy her authority and actually tried to raise the City of London to armed rebellion. To this the Queen replied:

86

He that will forget God, will also forget his benefactors; this tragedy was played forty times in open streets and houses.

The Queen and Lambarde were looking back on recent events that were associated in their minds with the fate of Richard the Second, and the Queen's comment on the play was in part at least prompted by the strange manner in which the performance of Shakespeare's play formed a feature in the preparations for the Essex rising.

On 18 February 1601 Augustine Phillips, a member of Shakespeare's company, appeared before a court to explain why the Lord Chamberlain's servants had on 7th February, the afternoon before Essex made his attempt to raise London against the government, put on a performance of *Richard II*. This play showed the deposition of a ruler and might be regarded, in the circumstances, so the authorities thought, as an incitement to the public to support the coming attempt by the Essex faction to take over the government from its lawful sovereign. That the authorities were correct in their surmise that the play was intended to stir the spectators to acquiesce, if not to participate, in the coming venture, the evidence of Phillips fully confirmed; but at the same time he was able to satisfy the court that the actors themselves were innocent of any such intention. He explained to the court that on 6th February several gentlemen, who were now at the time of his examination known to have been implicated with Essex, requested the players to substitute for the play they had in mind for Saturday the old play of *Richard II*. The players had, Phillips continued, pointed out that this piece was so old and so long out of use that the house would be thin and the takings poor. The conspirators, for so they turned out, to meet this objection, offered a special fee of forty shillings above the takings at the doors; and accepting this offer the company put on *Richard II* as requested. As it was unlikely that the servants of the Lord Chamberlain, who was one of the Queen's most loyal and able ministers, would be deliberately engaged in so subversive a plot, the explanation offered by Phillips seems to have cleared the company of any complicity in the affair.

At the trials of Essex and others, this performance of *Richard II* was urged against them as evidence of their intentions and as a pointer to the highly treasonable nature of their conduct. Sir Edward Coke the attorney general protested to the court that had the Queen fallen into the hands of the accused she would not have long remained alive; for he added

> Note but the precedents of former ages, how long lived Richard the Second after he was surprised in the same manner? The pretence was alike for the removing of certain counsellors, but yet shortly after it cost him his life.

Essex had pleaded that he had no designs against Her Majesty's safety; he aimed only at removing some of those who in his judgment were misdirecting her and self-seeking in their advice. Coke suggested that the choice of play indicated a more sinister intention.

That the play was regarded by the Queen as providing an unedifying example to the people of treasonable practices can hardly have been unknown to the players themselves. When the play came to be printed in Quarto in 1597 the deposition scene, which may be regarded as the very heart of the action, was omitted, doubtless because the official licenser disapproved of it. It was however still presented on the stage, for we can hardly suppose that the conspirators would have felt they were getting value for their forty shillings with this vital scene omitted. Further, another publication dealing with the reign of Henry the Fourth had brought those held responsible for its issue before the courts. In January 1599 John Hayward published an historical account *The First Part of the Life and Raigne of King Henrie IV*, and added a dedication to Essex himself, in which the Earl is described as not merely important in the judgment of the present but likely to prove more so in that of the future. Even Essex felt that the dedication would displease the Queen and he asked for its cancellation. The book was eventually suppressed and its author imprisoned. This publication with the Earl's name so prominently attached to it, and the belief that he had frequently attended in earlier years Shakespeare's play on Richard's fall and expressed his approval of the piece, all told against him at his trial. Hayward's fate as well as the excision of the deposition scene in the Quarto of 1597 can hardly have escaped the notice of the actors. That the players however performed the play without ulterior political motives and that Shakespeare had written the play without any intention of inciting his contemporaries to rebellion may be taken as established.

So far is modern criticism from finding anything subversive in *Richard II* that many commentators now tend to regard it as the glorification of a royal martyr deposed and done to death by a conspiracy of ruthless worldlings. Some feel that Shakespeare is insisting that this violation of the sanctity of Richard's office was the crime that was eventually to be visited on the country in the Wars of the Roses. The other view that the fault was in Richard himself and in his abuse of his office is neglected or minimized in face of Shakespeare's remarkable portrait of this character in whom the elements were so strangely mixed. Shakespeare had before him in his sources both views, and it may be hazarded that one of his chief interests as a dramatist was his creation of a character that explains the very diverse accounts of the tragedy; while Shakespeare could not fail to take account of the consequences of the events of the reign he gives his main attention to the character of the king himself.

Shakespeare found in the Chronicles of Hall and Holinshed that Richard unlike his predecessors adopted an attitude to his office that was to become more familiar to later generations; Richard began to assume that he was king by divine right and that his conduct could not be questioned by any of his subjects whatever their degree or office. Coming to the throne as a boy and having endured for many years the far from paternal attentions of his uncles, Richard once he had disposed of his masters found his freedom too much for him and acted extravagantly and arbitrarily often just to gratify his mere caprice. There were naturally not wanting those who fed his vanity and turned his folly to their own advantage. In the Parliament of 1397, Holinshed tells us, Sir John Bushy, addressing the king,

did not attribute to him titles of honour, due and accustomed, but invented unused terms and such strange names as were rather agreeable to the divine majesty of God than to any earthly potentate. The prince being desirous enough of all honour, and more ambitious than was requisite, seemed to like well of his speech and gave good ear to his talk.

Bushy is one of the favourites who are represented in Shakespeare and elsewhere as a principal cause of the king's undoing. Carried away by their adulation Richard becomes despotic: "Whatsoever he then did, none durst speak a word contrary thereunto."

In a play still extant in manuscript and written just before Shakespeare's *Richard II* the plot turns on the struggle between the favourites, who are ruining the king and his kingdom, on one side, and Thomas of Woodstock, who is the king's uncle and Duke of Gloucester, on the other. Woodstock is Lord Protector of the Realm and represented in the play as the plain blunt man who tries by his advice and example to save the king from his own folly and to counter the devices of those who batten on his favours. In the final act Woodstock, who has been seized by the king, is murdered by his orders; the friends of the Protector rally to his aid, too late to save him alive, but in force sufficient to overthrow the favourites. The finale is missing from the manuscript, so that we can only guess how Richard conducts himself in the conclusion in which his misleaders pay the penalty for his crimes.

As Mr. Rossiter, the latest editor of this play that he calls *Woodstock*, observes,

> there is not a word of condemnation in this play for those who do, and very practically, "call to account the doings of the prince."

This he thinks curious so insistent were the *Homilies* of the author's time on the duty of the subjects' suffering patiently the wrongs and injuries inflicted on them by the ruler. A loyal subject was exhorted to refer the judgment of his cause only to God. The author of *Woodstock* seems to Mr. Rossiter unorthodox in so ignoring the current teaching of the day, and contrasts his attitude with Shakespeare's; for in

Richard II both Gaunt and York give expression to the doctrine of non-resistance.

But this seems to miss Shakespeare's dramatic use of the doctrine of his times. Gaunt and York do, it is true, use the current formulas of the age; but Shakespeare's play goes far beyond anything that the author of *Woodstock* ventured on. Shakespeare does not hesitate to show us not only the king's deposition but even his violent end. Shakespeare is not like the author of *Woodstock* in the difficulty the latter makes for himself in the final act, where all the punishment must fall on the favourites, and the king presumably makes his peace with his uncles. Shakespeare presents us with the full consequences of the king's misguided and reckless policy; nor does he in any way minimize the king's responsibility for the fatal conclusion. Indeed Shakespeare's play might be taken as a lesson for those who trust to divine right to protect them from their follies. Certainly Elizabeth did not regard the piece as a lesson against calling to account the doings of the prince; she was convinced it might be regarded as an example to those who presumed to take the judgment of their ruler into their own hands. Elizabeth therefore while she may have thought the divinity of rulers a suitable doctrine to disseminate also observed the advice of that earlier adherent to the faith, the Bishop of Carlisle:

> The means that heaven yields must be embrac'd,
> And not neglected.

Shakespeare does not make his king the crude creation of *Woodstock*, nor does he represent the opposition as a set of high-minded dispensers of justice. The distracted mind of York, torn between loyalty and necessity; the appeal of the dying Gaunt; the assertion of his rights by the plundered Bolingbroke; all are presented as the very natural reactions to Richard's conduct. The circumstances are such that Bolingbroke might with some justice make in his last days the defence Shakespeare gives him:

> necessity so bow'd the state
> That I and greatness were compell'd to kiss.

Shakespeare, if he does justice to the opposition and does not spare the king the consequences of his misrule, treats

Richard very differently from the author of *Woodstock;* for Richard had his disinterested admirers, and Shakespeare has not omitted their contribution to our understanding of the king.

In compiling his account of the reign of Richard the Second, the historian Holinshed acknowledged his debt to two French sources on which amongst others he drew. In his margin he refers to "an old French pamphlet belonging to John Stow" and in another marginal reference he mentions "a French pamphlet which belongeth to Master John Dee." These pamphlets once belonging to Stow and Dee are still in existence and identifiable, the first being in the British Museum, the other in the library at Lambeth. Stow's pamphlet is called *La Chronicque de la Traison et Mort de Richart Deux roy Dengleterre,* while Dee's has as title *Histoire du Roy d'Angleterre Richard.* The author of this latter work was a French gentleman Jean Créton who had crossed with a companion to England to go with Richard on his Irish expedition "for recreation and to see the country." He went through the rather futile Irish campaign, came back with Salisbury to find England in the hands of Bolingbroke, and was one of the few at Richard's side in the last agonizing moments at Flint Castle before the arrival of Bolingbroke. Créton's account of the hostility and desire for vengeance against the king and his supporters shown by the followers of Bolingbroke transmits something of the chill that even the bravest of Richard's party felt in so helpless a position. Bolingbroke sent Créton back safely to France; there Créton completed his story from an account given him by another of his compatriots who had witnessed the very last stages of Richard's reign. It had been conjectured that his informant may have been the author of *La Traison;* for the moment the identification is not material. We know that Créton is an honest witness and followed with his own eyes the king's progress till Bolingbroke handed him over to the keeping of the authorities of the city of London; and the author of *La Traison,* whoever he was, seems also to have witnessed some of the events he describes and to have regarded them with the same feelings of indignation and pity that they stirred in Créton.

These French witnesses to Richard's character and fortunes coloured the account Shakespeare found in Holinshed. Shakespeare may even have turned them over for himself. Following Professor Reyher's study of the sources of *Richard II*, Professor Dover Wilson finds details in the play that seem to come directly from Créton or *La Traison*, and perhaps from a third French source *La Chronicque de Richard II*, which is derived in part from *La Traison*. These accounts were not easily come by in England, for their anti-Lancastrian sentiment was not acceptable to Henry the Fourth and his descendants. Professor Dover Wilson finds himself driven to conjecture that some unknown historian drew on them as he put together a stage version of the reign; but why we should suppose some unknown writer should have access to such sources while Shakespeare was denied them can be explained only by a view of Shakespeare's life and habits that is conjectural. The poet Daniel knew *La Traison*; why should Shakespeare find it beyond his reach? We can hardly suppose *Richard II* was produced without much meditation not merely on the technical problems its presentation raised but also on the mystery with which the strange character and his unhappy fate confront us. For it is the presentation of Richard that dictates the lines of the whole design.

Shakespeare could not have said of the king as Créton did: "Never did I see anything in him save catholic faith and justice"; but the dramatist could understand very well how a man like Créton felt in this way about Richard, and Shakespeare in his portrait has not omitted the qualities that inspired these personal loyalties. He equally understood the detestation with which the king's enemies regarded him; but the poet could not say with Créton that Bolingbroke was like Pilate washing his hands of the blood he was shedding nor regard Bolingbroke's followers as so many Judases betraying their master. He could however show Richard himself directing the same reproaches to his former vassals that the French chroniclers heaped on all who went over to the house of Lancaster. Had Richard been as Créton saw him all "catholic faith and justice" such reproaches would not have been as they are in Shakespeare's context as much a criticism of Richard's nature as his enemies' conduct. Richard sees himself in a part he is not able to sustain, but he cannot but draw applause for the animation with which he plays it out.

Here as so often elsewhere Shakespeare preserves a wonderful balance between the elements that mix in his protagonist—but his subject did not permit the dramatist to leave on his listeners the final impression that transforms all that has gone before. There is no scene in the Tragedies like that between the gardener and his helpers leading to his discussion with the Queen. In many of the plays there are characters who play a chorus-like part but they are usually themselves involved in the action. The gardener may be said to be entirely neutral; he sees the political situation in terms of his own craft where more than divine right is needed to

keep law and form and due proportion

in the garden that has been entrusted to him; and he feels that good husbandry is as necessary in "our sea-walled garden, the whole land," and that the absence of law and form and proportion have brought the state to confusion. The Queen's passionate outburst is very natural and entirely to the credit of her heart; but it does nothing to obliterate the truth that the compassionate gardener has spoken. What is true of the Queen's protest is equally true of Richard's; it cannot cancel the obvious, though it may discover what we cannot fail to sympathize with. There is a contradiction at the very heart of Richard's ideal of divine right, and Shakespeare makes no attempt to hide the flaw; his treatment of the political situation is as free from any mystical interpretation as the facts of history can be in the hands of the most dispassionate historian. The mystery is in Richard himself, and this Shakespeare has presented with a power and sympathy that no one is likely to surpass.

KING RICHARD THE SECOND
JOHN OF GAUNT, *Duke of Lancaster* ⎫
EDMUND OF LANGLEY, *Duke of York* ⎰ *uncles to the King*
HENRY, *surnamed* BOLINGBROKE, *Duke of Hereford, son of John of Gaunt, afterwards King Henry IV*
DUKE OF AUMERLE, *son of the Duke of York*
THOMAS MOWBRAY, *Duke of Norfolk*
DUKE OF SURREY
EARL OF SALISBURY
EARL BERKELEY
BUSHY ⎫
BAGOT ⎬ *favourites of King Richard*
GREEN ⎭
EARL OF NORTHUMBERLAND
HENRY PERCY, *surnamed* HOTSPUR, *his son*

LORD ROSS	LORD WILLOUGHBY
LORD FITZWATER	BISHOP OF CARLISLE
ABBOT OF WESTMINSTER	LORD MARSHAL
SIR STEPHEN SCROOP	SIR PIERCE OF EXTON
CAPTAIN *of a band of Welshmen*	TWO GARDENERS

QUEEN *to King Richard*
DUCHESS OF YORK
DUCHESS OF GLOUCESTER, *widow of Thomas of Woodstock, Duke of Gloucester*
LADY *attending on the Queen*

Lords, Heralds, Officers, Soldiers, Keeper, Messenger, Groom, *and other* Attendants

SCENE:

England and Wales

King Richard the Second

ACT I. SCENE 1

London. The palace

Enter King Richard, John of Gaunt, *with other* Nobles *and attendants*

King Richard. Old John of Gaunt, time-honoured Lan-
caster,
Hast thou, according to thy oath and band,
Brought hither Henry Hereford, thy bold son,
Here to make good the boist'rous late appeal,
Which then our leisure would not let us hear,
Against the Duke of Norfolk, Thomas Mowbray?
Gaunt. I have, my liege.
King Richard. Tell me, moreover, hast thou sounded him
If he appeal the Duke on ancient malice,
Or worthily, as a good subject should,
On some known ground of treachery in him?
Gaunt. As near as I could sift him on that argument,
On some apparent danger seen in him
Aim'd at your Highness—no inveterate malice.
King Richard. Then call them to our presence: face to face
And frowning brow to brow, ourselves will hear
The accuser and the accused freely speak.
High-stomach'd are they both and full of ire,
In rage, deaf as the sea, hasty as fire.

Enter Bolingbroke *and* Mowbray

Bolingbroke. Many years of happy days befall
My gracious sovereign, my most loving liege!
Mowbray. Each day still better other's happiness
Until the heavens, envying earth's good hap,
Add an immortal title to your crown!
King Richard. We thank you both; yet one but flatters us,

97

As well appeareth by the cause you come;
Namely, to appeal each other of high treason.
Cousin of Hereford, what dost thou object
Against the Duke of Norfolk, Thomas Mowbray?
BOLINGBROKE. First—heaven be the record to my speech!
In the devotion of a subject's love,
Tend'ring the precious safety of my prince,
And free from other misbegotten hate,
Come I appellant to this princely presence.
Now, Thomas Mowbray, do I turn to thee,
And mark my greeting well; for what I speak
My body shall make good upon this earth,
Or my divine soul answer it in heaven—
Thou art a traitor and a miscreant,
Too good to be so, and too bad to live,
Since the more fair and crystal is the sky,
The uglier seem the clouds that in it fly.
Once more, the more to aggravate the note,
With a foul traitor's name stuff I thy throat;
And wish—so please my sovereign—ere I move,
What my tongue speaks, my right drawn sword may
  prove.
MOWBRAY. Let not my cold words here accuse my zeal.
'Tis not the trial of a woman's war,
The bitter clamour of two eager tongues,
Can arbitrate this cause betwixt us twain;
The blood is hot that must be cool'd for this.
Yet can I not of such tame patience boast
As to be hush'd and nought at all to say.
First, the fair reverence of your Highness curbs me
From giving reins and spurs to my free speech;
Which else would post until it had return'd
These terms of treason doubled down his throat.
Setting aside his high blood's royalty,
And let him be no kinsman to my liege,
I do defy him, and I spit at him,
Call him a slanderous coward and a villain;
Which to maintain, I would allow him odds
And meet him, were I tied to run afoot
Even to the frozen ridges of the Alps,

Or any other ground inhabitable
Where ever Englishman durst set his foot.
Meantime let this defend my loyalty—
By all my hopes, most falsely doth he lie.

BOLINGBROKE. Pale trembling coward, there I throw my
    gage,
Disclaiming here the kindred of the King;
And lay aside my high blood's royalty,
Which fear, not reverence, makes thee to except.
If guilty dread have left thee so much strength
As to take up mine honour's pawn, then stoop.
By that and all the rites of knighthood else
Will I make good against thee, arm to arm,
What I have spoke or thou canst worst devise.

MOWBRAY. I take it up; and by that sword I swear
Which gently laid my knighthood on my shoulder
I'll answer thee in any fair degree
Or chivalrous design of knightly trial;
And when I mount, alive may I not light
If I be traitor or unjustly fight!

KING RICHARD. What doth our cousin lay to Mowbray's
    charge?
It must be great that can inherit us
So much as of a thought of ill in him.

BOLINGBROKE. Look what I speak, my life shall prove it
    true—
That Mowbray hath receiv'd eight thousand nobles
In name of lendings for your Highness' soldiers,
The which he hath detain'd for lewd employments
Like a false traitor and injurious villain.
Besides, I say and will in battle prove—
Or here, or elsewhere to the furthest verge
That ever was survey'd by English eye—
That all the treasons for these eighteen years
Complotted and contrived in this land
Fetch from false Mowbray their first head and spring.
Further I say, and further will maintain
Upon his bad life to make all this good,
That he did plot the Duke of Gloucester's death,
Suggest his soon-believing adversaries,

And consequently, like a traitor coward,
Sluic'd out his innocent soul through streams of blood;
Which blood, like sacrificing Abel's, cries,
Even from the tongueless caverns of the earth,
To me for justice and rough chastisement;
And, by the glorious worth of my descent,
This arm shall do it, or this life be spent.

KING RICHARD. How high a pitch his resolution soars!
Thomas of Norfolk, what say'st thou to this?

MOWBRAY. O, let my sovereign turn away his face
And bid his ears a little while be deaf,
Till I have told this slander of his blood
How God and good men hate so foul a liar.

KING RICHARD. Mowbray, impartial are our eyes and ears.
Were he my brother, nay, my kingdom's heir,
As he is but my father's brother's son,
Now by my sceptre's awe I make a vow,
Such neighbour nearness to our sacred blood
Should nothing privilege him nor partialize
The unstooping firmness of my upright soul.
He is our subject, Mowbray; so art thou:
Free speech and fearless I to thee allow.

MOWBRAY. Then, Bolingbroke, as low as to thy heart,
Through the false passage of thy throat, thou liest.
Three parts of that receipt I had for Calais
Disburs'd I duly to his Highness' soldiers;
The other part reserv'd I by consent,
For that my sovereign liege was in my debt
Upon remainder of a dear account
Since last I went to France to fetch his queen:
Now swallow down that lie. For Gloucester's death—
I slew him not, but to my own disgrace
Neglected my sworn duty in that case.
For you, my noble Lord of Lancaster,
The honourable father to my foe,
Once did I lay an ambush for your life,
A trespass that doth vex my grieved soul;
But ere I last receiv'd the sacrament
I did confess it, and exactly begg'd
Your Grace's pardon; and I hope I had it.

This is my fault. As for the rest appeal'd,
It issues from the rancour of a villain,
A recreant and most degenerate traitor;
Which in myself I boldly will defend,
And interchangeably hurl down my gage
Upon this overweening traitor's foot
To prove myself a loyal gentleman
Even in the best blood chamber'd in his bosom.
In haste whereof, most heartily I pray
Your Highness to assign our trial day.

KING RICHARD. Wrath-kindled gentlemen, be rul'd by me;
Let's purge this choler without letting blood—
This we prescribe, though no physician;
Deep malice makes too deep incision.
Forget, forgive; conclude and be agreed:
Our doctors say this is no month to bleed.
Good uncle, let this end where it begun;
We'll calm the Duke of Norfolk, you your son.

GAUNT. To be a make-peace shall become my age.
Throw down, my son, the Duke of Norfolk's gage.

KING RICHARD. And, Norfolk, throw down his.

GAUNT. When, Harry, when?
Obedience bids I should not bid again.

KING RICHARD. Norfolk, throw down; we bid.
There is no boot.

MOWBRAY. Myself I throw, dread sovereign, at thy foot;
My life thou shalt command, but not my shame:
The one my duty owes; but my fair name,
Despite of death, that lives upon my grave
To dark dishonour's use thou shalt not have.
I am disgrac'd, impeach'd, and baffl'd here;
Pierc'd to the soul with slander's venom'd spear,
The which no balm can cure but his heart-blood
Which breath'd this poison.

KING RICHARD. Rage must be withstood:
Give me his gage—lions make leopards tame.

MOWBRAY. Yea, but not change his spots. Take but my
shame,
And I resign my gage. My dear dear lord,
The purest treasure mortal times afford

Is spotless reputation; that away,
Men are but gilded loam or painted clay.
A jewel in a ten-times barr'd-up chest
Is a bold spirit in a loyal breast.
Mine honour is my life; both grow in one;
Take honour from me, and my life is done:
Then, dear my liege, mine honour let me try;
In that I live, and for that will I die.

KING RICHARD. Cousin, throw up your gage; do you begin.

BOLINGBROKE. O, God defend my soul from such deep sin!
Shall I seem crest-fallen in my father's sight?
Or with pale beggar-fear impeach my height
Before this outdar'd dastard? Ere my tongue
Shall wound my honour with such feeble wrong
Or sound so base a parle, my teeth shall tear
The slavish motive of recanting fear,
And spit it bleeding in his high disgrace,
Where shame doth harbour, even in Mowbray's face.

Exit GAUNT

KING RICHARD. We were not born to sue, but to command;
Which since we cannot do to make you friends,
Be ready, as your lives shall answer it,
At Coventry, upon Saint Lambert's day.
There shall your swords and lances arbitrate
The swelling difference of your settled hate;
Since we can not atone you, we shall see
Justice design the victor's chivalry.
Lord Marshal, command our officers-at-arms
Be ready to direct these home alarms.   *Exeunt*

SCENE 2

London. The DUKE OF LANCASTER'S *palace*

Enter JOHN OF GAUNT *with the* DUCHESS OF GLOUCESTER

GAUNT. Alas, the part I had in Woodstock's blood
Doth more solicit me than your exclaims
To stir against the butchers of his life!
But since correction lieth in those hands

Which made the fault that we cannot correct,
Put we our quarrel to the will of heaven;
Who, when they see the hours ripe on earth,
Will rain hot vengeance on offenders' heads.

DUCHESS. Finds brotherhood in thee no sharper spur?
Hath love in thy old blood no living fire?
Edward's seven sons, whereof thyself art one,
Were as seven vials of his sacred blood,
Or seven fair branches springing from one root.
Some of those seven are dried by nature's course,
Some of those branches by the Destinies cut;
But Thomas, my dear lord, my life, my Gloucester,
One vial full of Edward's sacred blood,
One flourishing branch of his most royal root,
Is crack'd, and all the precious liquor spilt;
Is hack'd down, and his summer leaves all faded,
By envy's hand and murder's bloody axe.
Ah, Gaunt, his blood was thine! That bed, that womb,
That mettle, that self mould, that fashion'd thee,
Made him a man; and though thou livest and breathest,
Yet art thou slain in him. Thou dost consent
In some large measure to thy father's death
In that thou seest thy wretched brother die,
Who was the model of thy father's life.
Call it not patience, Gaunt—it is despair;
In suff'ring thus thy brother to be slaught'red,
Thou showest the naked pathway to thy life,
Teaching stern murder how to butcher thee.
That which in mean men we entitle patience
Is pale cold cowardice in noble breasts.
What shall I say? To safeguard thine own life
The best way is to venge my Gloucester's death.

GAUNT. God's is the quarrel; for God's substitute,
His deputy anointed in His sight,
Hath caus'd his death; the which if wrongfully,
Let heaven revenge; for I may never lift
An angry arm against His minister.

DUCHESS. Where then, alas, may I complain myself?

GAUNT. To God, the widow's champion and defence.

DUCHESS. Why then, I will. Farewell, old Gaunt.

Thou goest to Coventry, there to behold
Our cousin Hereford and fell Mowbray fight.
O, sit my husband's wrongs on Hereford's spear,
That it may enter butcher Mowbray's breast!
Or, if misfortune miss the first career,
Be Mowbray's sins so heavy in his bosom
That they may break his foaming courser's back
And throw the rider headlong in the lists,
A caitiff recreant to my cousin Hereford!
Farewell, old Gaunt; thy sometimes brother's wife,
With her companion, Grief, must end her life.

GAUNT. Sister, farewell; I must to Coventry.
As much good stay with thee as go with me!

DUCHESS. Yet one word more—grief boundeth where it falls,
Not with the empty hollowness, but weight.
I take my leave before I have begun,
For sorrow ends not when it seemeth done.
Commend me to thy brother, Edmund York.
Lo, this is all—nay, yet depart not so;
Though this be all, do not so quickly go;
I shall remember more. Bid him—ah, what?—
With all good speed at Plashy visit me.
Alack, and what shall good old York there see
But empty lodgings and unfurnish'd walls,
Unpeopled offices, untrodden stones?
And what hear there for welcome but my groans?
Therefore commend me; let him not come there
To seek out sorrow that dwells every where.
Desolate, desolate, will I hence and die;
The last leave of thee takes my weeping eye.   *Exeunt*

SCENE 3

The lists at Coventry

Enter the LORD MARSHAL *and the* DUKE OF AUMERLE

MARSHAL. My Lord Aumerle, is Harry Hereford arm'd?
AUMERLE. Yea, at all points; and longs to enter in.
MARSHAL. The Duke of Norfolk, sprightfully and bold,

Stays but the summons of the appellant's trumpet.

AUMERLE. Why then, the champions are prepar'd, and stay
For nothing but his Majesty's approach.

The trumpets sound, and the KING *enters with his
nobles,* GAUNT, BUSHY, BAGOT, GREEN, *and others.
When they are set, enter* MOWBRAY, *Duke of Norfolk, in arms, defendant, and a* HERALD

KING RICHARD. Marshal, demand of yonder champion
The cause of his arrival here in arms;
Ask him his name; and orderly proceed
To swear him in the justice of his cause.

MARSHAL. In God's name and the King's, say who thou art,
And why thou comest thus knightly clad in arms;
Against what man thou com'st, and what thy quarrel.
Speak truly on thy knighthood and thy oath;
As so defend thee heaven and thy valour!

MOWBRAY. My name is Thomas Mowbray, Duke of Norfolk;
Who hither come engaged by my oath—
Which God defend a knight should violate!—
Both to defend my loyalty and truth
To God, my King, and my succeeding issue,
Against the Duke of Hereford that appeals me;
And, by the grace of God and this mine arm,
To prove him, in defending of myself,
A traitor to my God, my King, and me.
And as I truly fight, defend me heaven!

The trumpets sound. Enter BOLINGBROKE, *Duke of Hereford,
appellant, in armour, and a* HERALD

KING RICHARD. Marshal, ask yonder knight in arms,
Both who he is and why he cometh hither
Thus plated in habiliments of war;
And formally, according to our law,
Depose him in the justice of his cause.

MARSHAL. What is thy name? and wherefore com'st thou
hither
Before King Richard in his royal lists?
Against whom comest thou? and what's thy quarrel?

Speak like a true knight, so defend thee heaven!

BOLINGBROKE. Harry of Hereford, Lancaster, and Derby,
Am I; who ready here do stand in arms
To prove, by God's grace and my body's valour,
In lists on Thomas Mowbray, Duke of Norfolk,
That he is a traitor, foul and dangerous,
To God of heaven, King Richard, and to me.
And as I truly fight, defend me heaven!

MARSHAL. On pain of death, no person be so bold
Or daring-hardy as to touch the lists,
Except the Marshal and such officers
Appointed to direct these fair designs.

BOLINGBROKE. Lord Marshal, let me kiss my sovereign's hand,
And bow my knee before his Majesty;
For Mowbray and myself are like two men
That vow a long and weary pilgrimage.
Then let us take a ceremonious leave
And loving farewell of our several friends.

MARSHAL. The appellant in all duty greets your Highness,
And craves to kiss your hand and take his leave.

KING RICHARD. We will descend and fold him in our arms.
Cousin of Hereford, as thy cause is right,
So be thy fortune in this royal fight!
Farewell, my blood; which if to-day thou shed,
Lament we may, but not revenge thee dead.

BOLINGBROKE. O, let no noble eye profane a tear
For me, if I be gor'd with Mowbray's spear.
As confident as is the falcon's flight
Against a bird, do I with Mowbray fight.
My loving lord, I take my leave of you;
Of you, my noble cousin, Lord Aumerle;
Not sick, although I have to do with death,
But lusty, young, and cheerly drawing breath.
Lo, as at English feasts, so I regreet
The daintiest last, to make the end most sweet.
O thou, the earthly author of my blood,
Whose youthful spirit, in me regenerate,
Doth with a twofold vigour lift me up
To reach at victory above my head,
Add proof unto mine armour with thy prayers,

And with thy blessings steel my lance's point,
That it may enter Mowbray's waxen coat
And furbish new the name of John o' Gaunt,
Even in the lusty haviour of his son.
GAUNT. God in thy good cause make thee prosperous!
　　Be swift like lightning in the execution,
　　And let thy blows, doubly redoubled,
　　Fall like amazing thunder on the casque
　　Of thy adverse pernicious enemy.
　　Rouse up thy youthful blood, be valiant, and live.
BOLINGBROKE. Mine innocence and Saint George to thrive!
MOWBRAY. However God or fortune cast my lot,
　　There lives or dies, true to King Richard's throne,
　　A loyal, just, and upright gentleman.
　　Never did captive with a freer heart
　　Cast off his chains of bondage, and embrace
　　His golden uncontroll'd enfranchisement,
　　More than my dancing soul doth celebrate
　　This feast of battle with mine adversary.
　　Most mighty liege, and my companion peers,
　　Take from my mouth the wish of happy years.
　　As gentle and as jocund as to jest
　　Go I to fight: truth hath a quiet breast.
KING RICHARD. Farewell, my lord, securely I espy
　　Virtue with valour couched in thine eye.
　　Order the trial, Marshal, and begin.
MARSHAL. Harry of Hereford, Lancaster, and Derby,
　　Receive thy lance; and God defend the right!
BOLINGBROKE. Strong as a tower in hope, I cry amen.
MARSHAL. [*To an officer*] Go bear this lance to Thomas,
　　Duke of Norfolk.
FIRST HERALD. Harry of Hereford, Lancaster, and Derby,
　　Stands here for God, his sovereign, and himself,
　　On pain to be found false and recreant,
　　To prove the Duke of Norfolk, Thomas Mowbray,
　　A traitor to his God, his King, and him;
　　And dares him to set forward to the fight.
SECOND HERALD. Here standeth Thomas Mowbray, Duke of
　　Norfolk,
　　On pain to be found false and recreant,

Both to defend himself, and to approve
Henry of Hereford, Lancaster, and Derby,
To God, his sovereign, and to him disloyal,
Courageously and with a free desire
Attending but the signal to begin.

MARSHAL. Sound trumpets; and set forward, combatants.

[*A charge sounded*]

Stay, the King hath thrown his warder down.

KING RICHARD. Let them lay by their helmets and their
    spears,
And both return back to their chairs again.
Withdraw with us; and let the trumpets sound
While we return these dukes what we decree.

    A long flourish, while the KING *consults his Council*

Draw near,
And list what with our council we have done.
For that our kingdom's earth should not be soil'd
With that dear blood which it hath fostered;
And for our eyes do hate the dire aspect
Of civil wounds plough'd up with neighbours' sword;
And for we think the eagle-winged pride
Of sky-aspiring and ambitious thoughts,
With rival-hating envy, set on you
To wake our peace, which in our country's cradle
Draws the sweet infant breath of gentle sleep;
Which so rous'd up with boist'rous untun'd drums,
With harsh-resounding trumpets' dreadful bray,
And grating shock of wrathful iron arms,
Might from our quiet confines fright fair peace
And make us wade even in our kindred's blood—
Therefore we banish you our territories.
You, cousin Hereford, upon pain of life,
Till twice five summers have enrich'd our fields
Shall not regreet our fair dominions,
But tread the stranger paths of banishment.

BOLINGBROKE. Your will be done. This must my comfort
    be—
That sun that warms you here shall shine on me,
And those his golden beams to you here lent

Shall point on me and gild my banishment.
KING RICHARD. Norfolk, for thee remains a heavier doom,
  Which I with some unwillingness pronounce:
  The sly slow hours shall not determinate
  The dateless limit of thy dear exile;
  The hopeless word of 'never to return'
  Breathe I against thee, upon pain of life.
MOWBRAY. A heavy sentence, my most sovereign liege,
  And all unlook'd for from your Highness' mouth.
  A dearer merit, not so deep a maim
  As to be cast forth in the common air,
  Have I deserved at your Highness' hands.
  The language I have learnt these forty years,
  My native English, now I must forgo;
  And now my tongue's use is to me no more
  Than an unstringed viol or a harp;
  Or like a cunning instrument cas'd up
  Or, being open, put into his hands
  That knows no touch to tune the harmony.
  Within my mouth you have engaol'd my tongue,
  Doubly portcullis'd with my teeth and lips;
  And dull, unfeeling, barren ignorance
  Is made my gaoler to attend on me.
  I am too old to fawn upon a nurse,
  Too far in years to be a pupil now.
  What is thy sentence, then, but speechless death,
  Which robs my tongue from breathing native breath?
KING RICHARD. It boots thee not to be compassionate;
  After our sentence plaining comes too late.
MOWBRAY. Then thus I turn me from my country's light,
  To dwell in solemn shades of endless night.
KING RICHARD. Return again, and take an oath with thee.
  Lay on our royal sword your banish'd hands;
  Swear by the duty that you owe to God,
  Our part therein we banish with yourselves,
  To keep the oath that we administer:
  You never shall, so help you truth and God,
  Embrace each other's love in banishment;
  Nor never look upon each other's face;
  Nor never write, regreet, nor reconcile

This louring tempest of your home-bred hate;
Nor never by advised purpose meet
To plot, contrive, or complot any ill,
'Gainst us, our state, our subjects, or our land.
BOLINGBROKE. I swear.
MOWBRAY. And I, to keep all this.
BOLINGBROKE. Norfolk, so far as to mine enemy:
By this time, had the King permitted us,
One of our souls had wand'red in the air,
Banish'd this frail sepulchre of our flesh,
As now our flesh is banish'd from this land—
Confess thy treasons ere thou fly the realm;
Since thou hast far to go, bear not along
The clogging burden of a guilty soul.
MOWBRAY. No, Bolingbroke; if ever I were traitor,
My name be blotted from the book of life,
And I from heaven banish'd as from hence!
But what thou art, God, thou, and I, do know;
And all too soon, I fear, the King shall rue.
Farewell, my liege. Now no way can I stray:
Save back to England, all the world's my way.   *Exit*
KING RICHARD. Uncle, even in the glasses of thine eyes
I see thy grieved heart. Thy sad aspect
Hath from the number of his banish'd years
Pluck'd four away. [*To* BOLINGBROKE] Six frozen winters
    spent,
Return with welcome home from banishment.
BOLINGBROKE. How long a time lies in one little word!
Four lagging winters and four wanton springs
End in a word: such is the breath of Kings.
GAUNT. I thank my liege that in regard of me
He shortens four years of my son's exile;
But little vantage shall I reap thereby,
For ere the six years that he hath to spend
Can change their moons and bring their times about,
My oil-dried lamp and time-bewasted light
Shall be extinct with age and endless night;
My inch of taper will be burnt and done,
And blindfold death not let me see my son.
KING RICHARD. Why, uncle, thou hast many years to live.

GAUNT. But not a minute, King, that thou canst give:
    Shorten my days thou canst with sullen sorrow
    And pluck nights from me, but not lend a morrow;
    Thou can'st help time to furrow me with age,
    But stop no wrinkle in his pilgrimage;
    Thy word is current with him for my death,
    But dead, thy kingdom cannot buy my breath.
KING RICHARD. Thy son is banish'd upon good advice,
    Whereto thy tongue a party-verdict gave.
    Why at our justice seem'st thou then to lour?
GAUNT. Things sweet to taste prove in digestion sour.
    You urg'd me as a judge; but I had rather
    You would have bid me argue like a father.
    O, had it been a stranger, not my child,
    To smooth his fault I should have been more mild.
    A partial slander sought I to avoid,
    And in the sentence my own life destroy'd.
    Alas, I look'd when some of you should say
    I was too strict to make mine own away;
    But you gave leave to my unwilling tongue
    Against my will to do myself this wrong.
KING RICHARD. Cousin, farewell; and, uncle, bid him so.
    Six years we banish him, and he shall go.

Flourish. Exit KING *with train*

AUMERLE. Cousin, farewell; what presence must not know,
    From where you do remain let paper show.
MARSHAL. My lord, no leave take I, for I will ride
    As far as land will let me by your side.
GAUNT. O, to what purpose dost thou hoard thy words,
    That thou returnest no greeting to thy friends?
BOLINGBROKE. I have too few to take my leave of you,
    When the tongue's office should be prodigal
    To breathe the abundant dolour of the heart.
GAUNT. Thy grief is but thy absence for a time.
BOLINGBROKE. Joy absent, grief is present for that time.
GAUNT. What is six winters? They are quickly gone.
BOLINGBROKE. To men in joy; but grief makes one hour ten.
GAUNT. Call it a travel that thou tak'st for pleasure.
BOLINGBROKE. My heart will sigh when I miscall it so,
    Which finds it an enforced pilgrimage.

GAUNT. The sullen passage of thy weary steps
  Esteem as foil wherein thou art to set
  The precious jewel of thy home return.
BOLINGBROKE. Nay, rather, every tedious stride I make
  Will but remember me what a deal of world
  I wander from the jewels that I love.
  Must I not serve a long apprenticehood
  To foreign passages; and in the end,
  Having my freedom, boast of nothing else
  But that I was a journeyman to grief?
GAUNT. All places that the eye of heaven visits
  Are to a wise man ports and happy havens.
  Teach thy necessity to reason thus:
  There is no virtue like necessity.
  Think not the King did banish thee,
  But thou the King. Woe doth the heavier sit
  Where it perceives it is but faintly borne.
  Go, say I sent thee forth to purchase honour,
  And not the King exil'd thee; or suppose
  Devouring pestilence hangs in our air
  And thou art flying to a fresher clime.
  Look what thy soul holds dear, imagine it
  To lie that way thou goest, not whence thou com'st.
  Suppose the singing birds musicians,
  The grass whereon thou tread'st the presence strew'd,
  The flowers fair ladies, and thy steps no more
  Than a delightful measure or a dance;
  For gnarling sorrow hath less power to bite
  The man that mocks at it and sets it light.
BOLINGBROKE. O, who can hold a fire in his hand
  By thinking on the frosty Caucasus?
  Or cloy the hungry edge of appetite
  By bare imagination of a feast?
  Or wallow naked in December snow
  By thinking on fantastic summer's heat?
  O, no! the apprehension of the good
  Gives but the greater feeling to the worse.
  Fell sorrow's tooth doth never rankle more
  Than when he bites, but lanceth not the sore.
GAUNT. Come, come, my son, I'll bring thee on thy way.

Had I thy youth and cause, I would not stay.

BOLINGBROKE. Then, England's ground, farewell; sweet soil,
  adieu;
My mother, and my nurse, that bears me yet!
Where'er I wander, boast of this I can:
Though banish'd, yet a trueborn English man.   *Exeunt*

SCENE 4

London. The court

Enter the KING, *with* BAGOT *and* GREEN, *at one door; and
the* DUKE OF AUMERLE *at another*

KING RICHARD. We did observe. Cousin Aumerle,
  How far brought you high Hereford on his way?
AUMERLE. I brought high Hereford, if you call him so,
  But to the next high way, and there I left him.
KING RICHARD. And say, what store of parting tears were
  shed?
AUMERLE. Faith, none for me; except the north-east wind,
  Which then blew bitterly against our faces,
  Awak'd the sleeping rheum, and so by chance
  Did grace our hollow parting with a tear.
KING RICHARD. What said our cousin when you parted with
  him?
AUMERLE. 'Farewell.'
  And, for my heart disdained that my tongue
  Should so profane the word, that taught me craft
  To counterfeit oppression of such grief
  That words seem'd buried in my sorrow's grave.
  Marry, would the word 'farewell' have length'ned hours
  And added years to his short banishment,
  He should have had a volume of farewells;
  But since it would not, he had none of me.
KING RICHARD. He is our cousin, cousin; but 'tis doubt,
  When time shall call him home from banishment,
  Whether our kinsman come to see his friends.
  Ourself, and Bushy, Bagot here, and Green,
  Observ'd his courtship to the common people;

How he did seem to dive into their hearts
With humble and familiar courtesy;
What reverence he did throw away on slaves,
Wooing poor craftsmen with the craft of smiles
And patient underbearing of his fortune,
As 'twere to banish their affects with him.
Off goes his bonnet to an oyster-wench;
A brace of draymen bid God speed him well
And had the tribute of his supple knee,
With 'Thanks, my countrymen, my loving friends';
As were our England in reversion his,
And he our subjects' next degree in hope.

GREEN. Well, he is gone; and with him go these thoughts!
Now for the rebels which stand out in Ireland,
Expedient manage must be made, my liege,
Ere further leisure yield them further means
For their advantage and your Highness' loss.

KING RICHARD. We will ourself in person to this war;
And, for our coffers, with too great a court
And liberal largess, are grown somewhat light,
We are enforc'd to farm our royal realm;
The revenue whereof shall furnish us
For our affairs in hand. If that come short,
Our substitutes at home shall have blank charters;
Whereto, when they shall know what men are rich,
They shall subscribe them for large sums of gold,
And send them after to supply our wants;
For we will make for Ireland presently.

Enter BUSHY

Bushy, what news?

BUSHY. Old John of Gaunt is grievous sick, my lord,
Suddenly taken; and hath sent poste-haste
To entreat your Majesty to visit him.

KING RICHARD. Where lies he?

BUSHY. At Ely House.

KING RICHARD. Now put it, God, in the physician's mind
To help him to his grave immediately!
The lining of his coffers shall make coats
To deck our soldiers for these Irish wars.

ACT I. SCENE 4

Come, gentlemen, let's all go visit him.
Pray God we may make haste, and come too late!
ALL. Amen.   *Exeunt*

ACT II. SCENE 1

London. Ely House

Enter JOHN OF GAUNT, *sick, with the* DUKE OF YORK, *etc.*

GAUNT. Will the King come, that I may breathe my last
  In wholesome counsel to his unstaid youth?
YORK. Vex not yourself, nor strive not with your breath;
  For all in vain comes counsel to his ear.
GAUNT. O, but they say the tongues of dying men
  Enforce attention like deep harmony.
  Where words are scarce, they are seldom spent in vain;
  For they breathe truth that breathe their words in pain.
  He that no more must say is listen'd more
  Than they whom youth and ease have taught to glose;
  More are men's ends mark'd than their lives before.
  The setting sun, and music at the close,
  As the last taste of sweets, is sweetest last,
  Writ in remembrance more than things long past.
  Though Richard my life's counsel would not hear,
  My death's sad tale may yet undeaf his ear.
YORK. No; it is stopp'd with other flattering sounds,
  As praises, of whose taste the wise are fond,
  Lascivious metres, to whose venom sound
  The open ear of youth doth always listen;
  Report of fashions in proud Italy,
  Whose manners still our tardy apish nation
  Limps after in base imitation.
  Where doth the world thrust forth a vanity—
  So it be new, there's no respect how vile—
  That is not quickly buzz'd into his ears?
  Then all too late comes counsel to be heard
  Where will doth mutiny with wit's regard.

Direct not him whose way himself will choose.
'Tis breath thou lack'st, and that breath wilt thou lose.
GAUNT. Methinks I am a prophet new inspir'd,
And thus expiring do foretell of him:
His rash fierce blaze of riot cannot last,
For violent fires soon burn out themselves;
Small showers last long, but sudden storms are short;
He tires betimes that spurs too fast betimes;
With eager feeding food doth choke the feeder;
Light vanity, insatiate cormorant,
Consuming means, soon preys upon itself.
This royal throne of kings, this scept'red isle,
This earth of majesty, this seat of Mars,
This other Eden, demi-paradise,
This fortress built by Nature for herself
Against infection and the hand of war,
This happy breed of men, this little world,
This precious stone set in the silver sea,
Which serves it in the office of a wall,
Or as a moat defensive to a house,
Against the envy of less happier lands;
This blessed plot, this earth, this realm, this England,
This nurse, this teeming womb of royal kings,
Fear'd by their breed, and famous by their birth,
Renowned for their deeds as far from home,
For Christian service and true chivalry,
As is the sepulchre in stubborn Jewry
Of the world's ransom, blessed Mary's Son;
This land of such dear souls, this dear dear land,
Dear for her reputation through the world,
Is now leas'd out—I die pronouncing it—
Like to a tenement or pelting farm.
England, bound in with the triumphant sea,
Whose rocky shore beats back the envious siege
Of wat'ry Neptune, is now bound in with shame,
With inky blots and rotten parchment bonds;
That England, that was wont to conquer others,
Hath made a shameful conquest of itself.
Ah, would the scandal vanish with my life,
How happy then were my ensuing death!

ACT II. SCENE 1

Enter KING *and* QUEEN, AUMERLE, BUSHY, GREEN, BAGOT,
ROSS, *and* WILLOUGHBY

YORK. The King is come; deal mildly with his youth,
For young hot colts being rag'd do rage the more.
QUEEN. How fares our noble uncle Lancaster?
KING RICHARD. What comfort, man? How is't with aged
Gaunt?
GAUNT. O, how that name befits my composition!
Old Gaunt, indeed; and gaunt in being old.
Within me grief hath kept a tedious fast;
And who abstains from meat that is not gaunt?
For sleeping England long time have I watch'd;
Watching breeds leanness, leanness is all gaunt.
The pleasure that some fathers feed upon
Is my strict fast—I mean my children's looks;
And therein fasting, hast thou made me gaunt.
Gaunt am I for the grave, gaunt as a grave,
Whose hollow womb inherits nought but bones.
KING RICHARD. Can sick men play so nicely with their
names?
GAUNT. No, misery makes sport to mock itself:
Since thou dost seek to kill my name in me,
I mock my name, great king, to flatter thee.
KING RICHARD. Should dying men flatter with those that live?
GAUNT. No, no; men living flatter those that die.
KING RICHARD. Thou, now a-dying, sayest thou flatterest me.
GAUNT. O, no! thou diest, though I the sicker be.
KING RICHARD. I am in health, I breathe, and see thee ill.
GAUNT. Now He that made me knows I see thee ill;
Ill in myself to see, and in thee seeing ill.
Thy death-bed is no lesser than thy land
Wherein thou liest in reputation sick;
And thou, too careless patient as thou art,
Commit'st thy anointed body to the cure
Of those physicians that first wounded thee:
A thousand flatterers sit within thy crown,
Whose compass is no bigger than thy head;
And yet, incaged in so small a verge,
The waste is no whit lesser than thy land.

O, had thy grandsire with a prophet's eye
Seen how his son's son should destroy his sons,
From forth thy reach he would have laid thy shame,
Deposing thee before thou wert possess'd,
Which art possess'd now to depose thyself.
Why, cousin, wert thou regent of the world,
It were a shame to let this land by lease;
But for thy world enjoying but this land,
Is it not more than shame to shame it so?
Landlord of England art thou now, not King.
Thy state of law is bondslave to the law;
And thou—

KING RICHARD. A lunatic lean-witted fool,
Presuming on an ague's privilege,
Darest with thy frozen admonition
Make pale our cheek, chasing the royal blood
With fury from his native residence.
Now by my seat's right royal majesty,
Wert thou not brother to great Edward's son,
This tongue that runs so roundly in thy head
Should run thy head from thy unreverent shoulders.

GAUNT. O, spare me not, my brother Edward's son,
For that I was his father Edward's son;
That blood already, like the pelican,
Hast thou tapp'd out, and drunkenly carous'd.
My brother Gloucester, plain well-meaning soul—
Whom fair befall in heaven 'mongst happy souls!—
May be a precedent and witness good
That thou respect'st not spilling Edward's blood.
Join with the present sickness that I have;
And thy unkindness be like crooked age,
To crop at once a too long withered flower.
Live in thy shame, but die not shame with thee!
These words hereafter thy tormentors be!
Convey me to my bed, then to my grave.
Love they to live that love and honour have.

Exit, borne out by his attendants

KING RICHARD. And let them die that age and sullens have;
For both hast thou, and both become the grave.

YORK. I do beseech your Majesty impute his words

To wayward sickliness and age in him.
He loves you, on my life, and holds you dear
As Harry Duke of Hereford, were he here.
KING RICHARD. Right, you say true: as Hereford's love, so
  his;
As theirs, so mine; and all be as it is.

Enter NORTHUMBERLAND

NORTHUMBERLAND. My liege, old Gaunt commends him to
  your Majesty.
KING RICHARD. What says he?
NORTHUMBERLAND. Nay, nothing; all is said.
  His tongue is now a stringless instrument;
  Words, life, and all, old Lancaster hath spent.
YORK. Be York the next that must be bankrupt so!
  Though death be poor, it ends a mortal woe.
KING RICHARD. The ripest fruit first falls, and so doth he;
  His time is spent, our pilgrimage must be.
  So much for that. Now for our Irish wars.
  We must supplant those rough rug-headed kerns,
  Which live like venom where no venom else
  But only they have privilege to live.
  And for these great affairs do ask some charge,
  Towards our assistance we do seize to us
  The plate, coin, revenues, and moveables,
  Whereof our uncle Gaunt did stand possess'd.
YORK. How long shall I be patient? Ah, how long
  Shall tender duty make me suffer wrong?
  Not Gloucester's death, nor Hereford's banishment,
  Nor Gaunt's rebukes, nor England's private wrongs,
  Nor the prevention of poor Bolingbroke
  About his marriage, nor my own disgrace,
  Have ever made me sour my patient cheek
  Or bend one wrinkle on my sovereign's face.
  I am the last of noble Edward's sons,
  Of whom thy father, Prince of Wales, was first.
  In war was never lion rag'd more fierce,
  In peace was never gentle lamb more mild,
  Than was that young and princely gentleman.
  His face thou hast, for even so look'd he,

Accomplish'd with the number of thy hours;
But when he frown'd, it was against the French
And not against his friends. His noble hand
Did win what he did spend, and spent not that
Which his triumphant father's hand had won.
His hands were guilty of no kindred blood,
But bloody with the enemies of his kin.
O Richard! York is too far gone with grief,
Or else he never would compare between—

KING RICHARD. Why, uncle, what's the matter?

YORK. O my liege,
Pardon me, if you please; if not, I, pleas'd
Not to be pardoned, am content withal.
Seek you to seize and gripe into your hands
The royalties and rights of banish'd Hereford?
Is not Gaunt dead? and doth not Hereford live?
Was not Gaunt just? and is not Harry true?
Did not the one deserve to have an heir?
Is not his heir a well-deserving son?
Take Hereford's rights away, and take from Time
His charters and his customary rights;
Let not to-morrow then ensue to-day;
Be not thyself—for how art thou a king
But by fair sequence and succession?
Now, afore God—God forbid I say true!—
If you do wrongfully seize Hereford's rights,
Call in the letters patents that he hath
By his attorneys-general to sue
His livery, and deny his off'red homage,
You pluck a thousand dangers on your head,
You lose a thousand well-disposed hearts,
And prick my tender patience to those thoughts
Which honour and allegiance cannot think.

KING RICHARD. Think what you will, we seize into our
hands
His plate, his goods, his money, and his lands.

YORK. I'll not be by the while. My liege, farewell.
What will ensue hereof there's none can tell;
But by bad courses may be understood
That their events can never fall out good.   *Exit*

ACT II. SCENE 1

KING RICHARD. Go, Bushy, to the Earl of Wiltshire straight;
  Bid him repair to us to Ely House
  To see this business. To-morrow next
  We will for Ireland; and 'tis time, I trow.
  And we create, in absence of ourself,
  Our Uncle York Lord Governor of England;
  For he is just, and always lov'd us well.
  Come on, our queen; to-morrow must we part;
  Be merry, for our time of stay is short.

         Flourish. Exeunt KING, QUEEN, BUSHY, AUMERLE,
                     GREEN, *and* BAGOT

NORTHUMBERLAND. Well, lords, the Duke of Lancaster is
  dead.
ROSS. And living too; for now his son is Duke.
WILLOUGHBY. Barely in title, not in revenues.
NORTHUMBERLAND. Richly in both, if justice had her right.
ROSS. My heart is great; but it must break with silence,
  Ere't be disburdened with a liberal tongue.
NORTHUMBERLAND. Nay, speak thy mind; and let him ne'er
  speak more
  That speaks thy words again to do thee harm!
WILLOUGHBY. Tends that thou wouldst speak to the Duke
  of Hereford?
  If it be so, out with it boldly, man;
  Quick is mine ear to hear of good towards him.
ROSS. No good at all that I can do for him;
  Unless you call it good to pity him,
  Bereft and gelded of his patrimony.
NORTHUMBERLAND. Now, afore God, 'tis shame such wrongs
  are borne
  In him, a royal prince, and many moe
  Of noble blood in this declining land.
  The King is not himself, but basely led
  By flatterers; and what they will inform,
  Merely in hate, 'gainst any of us all,
  That will the King severely prosecute
  'Gainst us, our lives, our children, and our heirs.
ROSS. The commons hath he pill'd with grievous taxes;
  And quite lost their hearts; the nobles hath he fin'd
  For ancient quarrels and quite lost their hearts.

WILLOUGHBY. And daily new exactions are devis'd,
  As blanks, benevolences, and I wot not what;
  But what, a God's name, doth become of this?
NORTHUMBERLAND. Wars hath not wasted it, for warr'd he
    hath not,
  But basely yielded upon compromise
  That which his noble ancestors achiev'd with blows.
  More hath he spent in peace than they in wars.
Ross. The Earl of Wiltshire hath the realm in farm.
WILLOUGHBY. The King's grown bankrupt like a broken
  man.
NORTHUMBERLAND. Reproach and dissolution hangeth over
  him.
Ross. He hath not money for these Irish wars,
  His burdenous taxations notwithstanding,
  But by the robbing of the banish'd Duke.
NORTHUMBERLAND. His noble kinsman—most degenerate
  king!
  But, lords, we hear this fearful tempest sing,
  Yet seek no shelter to avoid the storm;
  We see the wind sit sore upon our sails,
  And yet we strike not, but securely perish.
Ross. We see the very wreck that we must suffer;
  And unavoided is the danger now
  For suffering so the causes of our wreck.
NORTHUMBERLAND. Not so; even through the hollow eyes of
  death
  I spy life peering; but I dare not say
  How near the tidings of our comfort is.
WILLOUGHBY. Nay, let us share thy thoughts as thou dost
  ours.
Ross. Be confident to speak, Northumberland.
  We three are but thyself, and, speaking so,
  Thy words are but as thoughts; therefore be bold.
NORTHUMBERLAND. Then thus: I have from Le Port Blanc,
  a bay
  In Brittany, receiv'd intelligence
  That Harry Duke of Hereford, Rainold Lord Cobham,
  That late broke from the Duke of Exeter,
  His brother, Archbishop late of Canterbury,

ACT II. SCENE 1

Sir Thomas Erpingham, Sir John Ramston,
Sir John Norbery, Sir Robert Waterton, and Francis
   Quoint—
All these, well furnish'd by the Duke of Britaine,
With eight tall ships, three thousand men of war,
Are making hither with all due expedience,
And shortly mean to touch our northern shore.
Perhaps they had ere this, but that they stay
The first departing of the King for Ireland.
If then we shall shake off our slavish yoke,
Imp out our drooping country's broken wing,
Redeem from broking pawn the blemish'd crown,
Wipe off the dust that hides our sceptre's gilt,
And make high majesty look like itself,
Away with me in post to Ravenspurgh;
But if you faint, as fearing to do so,
Stay and be secret, and myself will go.
Ross. To horse, to horse! Urge doubts to them that fear.
Willoughby. Hold out my horse, and I will first be there.

Exeunt

SCENE 2

Windsor Castle

Enter Queen, Bushy, *and* Bagot

Bushy. Madam, your Majesty is too much sad.
  You promis'd, when you parted with the King,
  To lay aside life-harming heaviness
  And entertain a cheerful disposition.
Queen. To please the King, I did; to please myself
  I cannot do it; yet I know no cause
  Why I should welcome such a guest as grief,
  Save bidding farewell to so sweet a guest
  As my sweet Richard. Yet again methinks
  Some unborn sorrow, ripe in fortune's womb,
  Is coming towards me, and my inward soul
  With nothing trembles. At some thing it grieves

123

More than with parting from my lord the King.

BUSHY. Each substance of a grief hath twenty shadows,
Which shows like grief itself, but is not so;
For sorrow's eye, glazed with blinding tears,
Divides one thing entire to many objects,
Like perspectives which, rightly gaz'd upon,
Show nothing but confusion—ey'd awry,
Distinguish form. So your sweet Majesty,
Looking awry upon your lord's departure,
Find shapes of grief more than himself to wail;
Which, look'd on as it is, is nought but shadows
Of what it is not. Then, thrice-gracious Queen,
More than your lord's departure weep not—more is not
seen;
Or if it be, 'tis with false sorrow's eye,
Which for things true weeps things imaginary.

QUEEN. It may be so; but yet my inward soul
Persuades me it is otherwise. Howe'er it be,
I cannot but be sad; so heavy sad
As—though, on thinking, on no thought I think—
Makes me with heavy nothing faint and shrink.

BUSHY. 'Tis nothing but conceit, my gracious lady.

QUEEN. 'Tis nothing less: conceit is still deriv'd
From some forefather grief; mine is not so,
For nothing hath begot my something grief,
Or something hath the nothing that I grieve;
'Tis in reversion that I do possess—
But what it is that is not yet known what,
I cannot name; 'tis nameless woe, I wot.

Enter GREEN

GREEN. God save your Majesty! and well met, gentlemen.
I hope the King is not yet shipp'd for Ireland.

QUEEN. Why hopest thou so? 'Tis better hope he is;
For his designs crave haste, his haste good hope.
Then wherefore dost thou hope he is not shipp'd?

GREEN. That he, our hope, might have retir'd his power
And driven into despair an enemy's hope
Who strongly hath set footing in this land.
The banish'd Bolingbroke repeals himself,

And with uplifted arms is safe arriv'd
At Ravenspurgh.
QUEEN. Now God in heaven forbid!
GREEN. Ah, madam, 'tis too true; and that is worse,
  The Lord Northumberland, his son young Henry Percy,
  The Lords of Ross, Beaumond, and Willoughby,
  With all their powerful friends, are fled to him.
BUSHY. Why have you not proclaim'd Northumberland
  And all the rest revolted faction traitors?
GREEN. We have; whereupon the Earl of Worcester
  Hath broken his staff, resign'd his stewardship,
  And all the household servants fled with him
  To Bolingbroke.
QUEEN. So, Green, thou art the midwife to my woe,
  And Bolingbroke my sorrow's dismal heir.
  Now hath my soul brought forth her prodigy;
  And I, a gasping new-deliver'd mother,
  Have woe to woe, sorrow to sorrow join'd.
BUSHY. Despair not, madam.
QUEEN. Who shall hinder me?
  I will despair, and be at enmity
  With cozening hope—he is a flatterer,
  A parasite, a keeper-back of death,
  Who gently would dissolve the bands of life,
  Which false hope lingers in extremity.

Enter YORK

GREEN. Here comes the Duke of York.
QUEEN. With signs of war about his aged neck.
  O, full of careful business are his looks!
  Uncle, for God's sake, speak comfortable words.
YORK. Should I do so, I should belie my thoughts.
  Comfort's in heaven; and we are on the earth,
  Where nothing lives but crosses, cares, and grief.
  Your husband, he is gone to save far off,
  Whilst others come to make him lose at home.
  Here am I left to underprop his land,
  Who, weak with age, cannot support myself.
  Now comes the sick hour that his surfeit made;
  Now shall he try his friends that flatter'd him.

Enter a SERVINGMAN

SERVINGMAN. My lord, your son was gone before I came.
YORK. He was—why so go all which way it will!
    The nobles they are fled, the commons they are cold
    And will, I fear, revolt on Hereford's side.
    Sirrah, get thee to Plashy, to my sister Gloucester;
    Bid her send me presently a thousand pound.
    Hold, take my ring.
SERVINGMAN. My lord, I had forgot to tell your lordship,
    To-day, as I came by, I called there—
    But I shall grieve you to report the rest.
YORK. What is't, knave?
SERVINGMAN. An hour before I came, the Duchess died.
YORK. God for his mercy! what a tide of woes
    Comes rushing on this woeful land at once!
    I know not what to do. I would to God,
    So my untruth had not provok'd him to it,
    The King had cut off my head with my brother's.
    What, are there no posts dispatch'd for Ireland?
    How shall we do for money for these wars?
    Come, sister—cousin, I would say—pray, pardon me.
    Go, fellow, get thee home, provide some carts,
    And bring away the armour that is there.
                          Exit SERVINGMAN

    Gentlemen, will you go muster men?
    If I know how or which way to order these affairs
    Thus disorderly thrust into my hands,
    Never believe me. Both are my kinsmen.
    T'one is my sovereign, whom both my oath
    And duty bids defend; t'other again
    Is my kinsman, whom the King hath wrong'd,
    Whom conscience and my kindred bids to right.
    Well, somewhat we must do.—Come, cousin,
    I'll dispose of you. Gentlemen, go muster up your men
    And meet me presently at Berkeley.
    I should to Plashy too,
    But time will not permit. All is uneven,
    And everything is left at six and seven.
                    Exeunt YORK *and* QUEEN

BUSHY. The wind sits fair for news to go to Ireland.
  But none returns. For us to levy power
  Proportionable to the enemy
  Is all unpossible.
GREEN. Besides, our nearness to the King in love
  Is near the hate of those love not the King.
BAGOT. And that is the wavering commons; for their love
  Lies in their purses; and whoso empties them,
  By so much fills their hearts with deadly hate.
BUSHY. Wherein the King stands generally condemn'd.
BAGOT. If judgment lie in them, then so do we,
  Because we ever have been near the King.
GREEN. Well, I will for refuge straight to Bristow Castle.
  The Earl of Wiltshire is already there.
BUSHY. Thither will I with you; for little office
  Will the hateful commons perform for us,
  Except like curs to tear us all to pieces.
  Will you go along with us?
BAGOT. No; I will to Ireland to his Majesty.
  Farewell. If heart's presages be not vain,
  We three here part that ne'er shall meet again.
BUSHY. That's as York thrives to beat back Bolingbroke.
GREEN. Alas, poor Duke! the task he undertakes
  Is numb'ring sands and drinking oceans dry.
  Where one on his side fights, thousands will fly.
  Farewell at once—for once, for all, and ever.
BUSHY. Well, we may meet again.
BAGOT. I fear me, never.   *Exeunt*

SCENE 3

Gloucestershire

Enter BOLINGBROKE *and* NORTHUMBERLAND, *with forces*

BOLINGBROKE. How far is it, my lord, to Berkeley now?
NORTHUMBERLAND. Believe me, noble lord,
  I am a stranger here in Gloucestershire.
  These high wild hills and rough uneven ways

Draws out our miles, and makes them wearisome;
And yet your fair discourse hath been as sugar,
Making the hard way sweet and delectable.
But I bethink me what a weary way
From Ravenspurgh to Cotswold will be found
In Ross and Willoughby, wanting your company,
Which, I protest, hath very much beguil'd
The tediousness and process of my travel.
But theirs is sweet'ned with the hope to have
The present benefit which I possess;
And hope to joy is little less in joy
Than hope enjoy'd. By this the weary lords
Shall make their way seem short, as mine hath done
By sight of what I have, your noble company.
BOLINGBROKE. Of much less value is my company
  Than your good words. But who comes here?

Enter HARRY PERCY

NORTHUMBERLAND. It is my son, young Harry Percy,
  Sent from my brother Worcester, whencesoever.
  Harry, how fares your uncle?
PERCY. I had thought, my lord, to have learn'd his health of
  you.
NORTHUMBERLAND. Why, is he not with the Queen?
PERCY. No, my good lord; he hath forsook the court,
  Broken his staff of office, and dispers'd
  The household of the King.
NORTHUMBERLAND. What was his reason?
  He was not so resolv'd when last we spake together.
PERCY. Because your lordship was proclaimed traitor.
  But he, my lord, is gone to Ravenspurgh,
  To offer service to the Duke of Hereford;
  And sent me over by Berkeley, to discover
  What power the Duke of York had levied there;
  Then with directions to repair to Ravenspurgh.
NORTHUMBERLAND. Have you forgot the Duke of Hereford,
  boy?
PERCY. No, my good lord; for that is not forgot
  Which ne'er I did remember; to my knowledge,
  I never in my life did look on him.

NORTHUMBERLAND. Then learn to know him now; this is the
    Duke.

PERCY. My gracious lord, I tender you my service,
    Such as it is, being tender, raw, and young;
    Which elder days shall ripen, and confirm
    To more approved service and desert.

BOLINGBROKE. I thank thee, gentle Percy; and be sure
    I count myself in nothing else so happy
    As in a soul rememb'ring my good friends;
    And as my fortune ripens with thy love,
    It shall be still thy true love's recompense.
    My heart this covenant makes, my hand thus seals it.

NORTHUMBERLAND. How far is it to Berkeley? And what
    stir
    Keeps good old York there with his men of war?

PERCY. There stands the castle, by yon tuft of trees,
    Mann'd with three hundred men, as I have heard;
    And in it are the Lords of York, Berkeley, and Seymour—
    None else of name and noble estimate.

Enter ROSS *and* WILLOUGHBY

NORTHUMBERLAND. Here come the Lords of Ross and Wil-
    loughby,
    Bloody with spurring, fiery-red with haste.

BOLINGBROKE. Welcome, my lords. I wot your love pursues
    A banish'd traitor. All my treasury
    Is yet but unfelt thanks, which, more enrich'd,
    Shall be your love and labour's recompense.

ROSS. Your presence makes us rich, most noble lord.

WILLOUGHBY. And far surmounts our labour to attain it.

BOLINGBROKE. Evermore thanks, the exchequer of the poor;
    Which, till my infant fortune comes to years,
    Stands for my bounty. But who comes here?

Enter BERKELEY

NORTHUMBERLAND. It is my Lord of Berkeley, as I guess.

BERKELEY. My Lord of Hereford, my message is to you.

BOLINGBROKE. My lord, my answer is—'to Lancaster';
    And I am come to seek that name in England;
    And I must find that title in your tongue

Before I make reply to aught you say.

BERKELEY. Mistake me not, my lord; 'tis not my meaning
To raze one title of your honour out.
To you, my lord, I come—what lord you will—
From the most gracious regent of this land,
The Duke of York, to know what pricks you on
To take advantage of the absent time,
And fright our native peace with self-borne arms.

Enter YORK, *attended*

BOLINGBROKE. I shall not need transport my words by you;
Here comes his Grace in person. My noble uncle!

[Kneels]

YORK. Show me thy humble heart, and not thy knee,
Whose duty is deceivable and false.

BOLINGBROKE. My gracious uncle!—

YORK. Tut, tut!
Grace me no grace, nor uncle me no uncle.
I am no traitor's uncle; and that word 'grace'
In an ungracious mouth is but profane.
Why have those banish'd and forbidden legs
Dar'd once to touch a dust of England's ground?
But then more 'why?'—why have they dar'd to march
So many miles upon her peaceful bosom,
Frighting her pale-fac'd villages with war
And ostentation of despised arms?
Com'st thou because the anointed King is hence?
Why, foolish boy, the King is left behind,
And in my loyal bosom lies his power.
Were I but now lord of such hot youth
As when brave Gaunt, thy father, and myself
Rescued the Black Prince, that young Mars of men,
From forth the ranks of many thousand French,
O, then how quickly should this arm of mine,
Now prisoner to the palsy, chastise thee
And minister correction to thy fault!

BOLINGBROKE. My gracious uncle, let me know my fault;
On what condition stands it and wherein?

YORK. Even in condition of the worst degree—
In gross rebellion and detested treason.

Thou art a banish'd man, and here art come
Before the expiration of thy time,
In braving arms against thy sovereign.
BOLINGBROKE. As I was banish'd, I was banish'd Hereford;
But as I come, I come for Lancaster.
And, noble uncle, I beseech your Grace
Look on my wrongs with an indifferent eye.
You are my father, for methinks in you
I see old Gaunt alive. O, then, my father,
Will you permit that I shall stand condemn'd
A wandering vagabond; my rights and royalties
Pluck'd from my arms perforce, and given away
To upstart unthrifts? Wherefore was I born?
If that my cousin king be King in England,
It must be granted I am Duke of Lancaster.
You have a son, Aumerle, my noble cousin;
Had you first died, and he been thus trod down,
He should have found his uncle Gaunt a father
To rouse his wrongs and chase them to the bay.
I am denied to sue my livery here,
And yet my letters patents give me leave.
My father's goods are all distrain'd and sold;
And these and all are all amiss employ'd.
What would you have me do? I am a subject,
And I challenge law—attorneys are denied me;
And therefore personally I lay my claim
To my inheritance of free descent.
NORTHUMBERLAND. The noble Duke hath been too much
abused.
Ross. It stands your Grace upon to do him right.
WILLOUGHBY. Base men by his endowments are made great.
YORK. My lords of England, let me tell you this:
I have had feeling of my cousin's wrongs,
And labour'd all I could to do him right;
But in this kind to come, in braving arms,
Be his own carver and cut out his way,
To find out right with wrong—it may not be;
And you that do abet him in this kind
Cherish rebellion, and are rebels all.
NORTHUMBERLAND. The noble Duke hath sworn his coming is

But for his own; and for the right of that
We all have strongly sworn to give him aid;
And let him never see joy that breaks that oath!
YORK. Well, well, I see the issue of these arms.
    I cannot mend it, I must needs confess,
    Because my power is weak and all ill left;
    But if I could, by Him that gave me life,
    I would attach you all and make you stoop
    Unto the sovereign mercy of the King;
    But since I cannot, be it known unto you
    I do remain as neuter. So, fare you well;
    Unless you please to enter in the castle,
    And there repose you for this night.
BOLINGBROKE. An offer, uncle, that we will accept.
    But we must win your Grace to go with us
    To Bristow Castle, which they say is held
    By Bushy, Bagot, and their complices,
    The caterpillars of the commonwealth,
    Which I have sworn to weed and pluck away.
YORK. It may be I will go with you; but yet I'll pause,
    For I am loath to break our country's laws.
    Nor friends nor foes, to me welcome you are.
    Things past redress are now with me past care.   *Exeunt*

SCENE 4

A camp in Wales

Enter EARL OF SALISBURY *and a* WELSH CAPTAIN

CAPTAIN. My Lord of Salisbury, we have stay'd ten days
    And hardly kept our countrymen together,
    And yet we hear no tidings from the King;
    Therefore we will disperse ourselves. Farewell.
SALISBURY. Stay yet another day, thou trusty Welshman;
    The King reposeth all his confidence in thee.
CAPTAIN. 'Tis thought the King is dead; we will not stay.
    The bay trees in our country are all wither'd,
    And meteors fright the fixed stars of heaven;
    The pale-fac'd moon looks bloody on the earth,

And lean-look'd prophets whisper fearful change;
Rich men look sad, and ruffians dance and leap—
The one in fear to lose what they enjoy,
The other to enjoy by rage and war.
These signs forerun the death or fall of kings.
Farewell. Our countrymen are gone and fled,
As well assur'd Richard their King is dead.   *Exit*
SALISBURY. Ah, Richard, with the eyes of heavy mind,
  I see thy glory like a shooting star
  Fall to the base earth from the firmament!
  The sun sets weeping in the lowly west,
  Witnessing storms to come, woe, and unrest;
  Thy friends are fled, to wait upon thy foes;
  And crossly to thy good all fortune goes.   *Exit*

ACT III. SCENE 1

BOLINGBROKE's *camp at Bristol*

Enter BOLINGBROKE, YORK, NORTHUMBERLAND, PERCY, ROSS,
  WILLOUGHBY, *with* BUSHY *and* GREEN, *prisoners*

BOLINGBROKE. Bring forth these men.
  Bushy and Green, I will not vex your souls—
  Since presently your souls must part your bodies—
  With too much urging your pernicious lives,
  For 'twere no charity; yet, to wash your blood
  From off my hands, here in the view of men
  I will unfold some causes of your deaths:
  You have misled a prince, a royal king,
  A happy gentleman in blood and lineaments,
  By you unhappied and disfigured clean;
  You have in manner with your sinful hours
  Made a divorce betwixt his queen and him;
  Broke the possession of a royal bed,
  And stain'd the beauty of a fair queen's cheeks
  With tears drawn from her eyes by your foul wrongs;
  Myself—a prince by fortune of my birth,

Near to the King in blood, and near in love
Till you did make him misinterpret me—
Have stoop'd my neck under your injuries
And sigh'd my English breath in foreign clouds,
Eating the bitter bread of banishment,
Whilst you have fed upon my signories,
Dispark'd my parks and fell'd my forest woods,
From my own windows torn my household coat,
Raz'd out my imprese, leaving me no sign
Save men's opinions and my living blood
To show the world I am a gentleman.
This and much more, much more than twice all this,
Condemns you to the death. See them delivered over
To execution and the hand of death.

BUSHY. More welcome is the stroke of death to me
Than Bolingbroke to England. Lords, farewell.

GREEN. My comfort is that heaven will take our souls,
And plague injustice with the pains of hell.

BOLINGBROKE. My Lord Northumberland, see them dispatch'd.   *Exeunt* NORTHUMBERLAND, *and others,*
with the prisoners

Uncle, you say the Queen is at your house;
For God's sake, fairly let her be entreated.
Tell her I send to her my kind commends;
Take special care my greetings be delivered.

YORK. A gentleman of mine I have dispatch'd
With letters of your love to her at large.

BOLINGBROKE. Thanks, gentle uncle. Come, lords, away,
To fight with Glendower and his complices.
Awhile to work, and after holiday.   *Exeunt*

SCENE 2

The coast of Wales. A castle in view

Drums. Flourish and colours. Enter the KING, *the* BISHOP
OF CARLISLE, AUMERLE, *and soldiers*

KING RICHARD. Barkloughly Castle call they this at hand?
AUMERLE. Yea, my lord. How brooks your Grace the air

After your late tossing on the breaking seas?
KING RICHARD. Needs must I like it well. I weep for joy
  To stand upon my kingdom once again.
  Dear earth, I do salute thee with my hand,
  Though rebels wound thee with their horses' hoofs.
  As a long-parted mother with her child
  Plays fondly with her tears and smiles in meeting,
  So weeping-smiling greet I thee, my earth,
  And do thee favours with my royal hands.
  Feed not thy sovereign's foe, my gentle earth,
  Nor with thy sweets comfort his ravenous sense;
  But let thy spiders, that suck up thy venom,
  And heavy-gaited toads, lie in their way,
  Doing annoyance to the treacherous feet
  Which with usurping steps do trample thee;
  Yield stinging nettles to mine enemies;
  And when they from thy bosom pluck a flower,
  Guard it, I pray thee, with a lurking adder,
  Whose double tongue may with a mortal touch
  Throw death upon thy sovereign's enemies.
  Mock not my senseless conjuration, lords.
  This earth shall have a feeling, and these stones
  Prove armed soldiers, ere her native king
  Shall falter under foul rebellion's arms.
CARLISLE. Fear not, my lord; that Power that made you king
  Hath power to keep you king in spite of all.
  The means that heaven yields must be embrac'd
  And not neglected; else, if heaven would,
  And we will not, heaven's offer we refuse,
  The proffered means of succour and redress.
AUMERLE. He means, my lord, that we are too remiss;
  Whilst Bolingbroke, through our security,
  Grows strong and great in substance and in power.
KING RICHARD. Discomfortable cousin! know'st thou not
  That when the searching eye of heaven is hid,
  Behind the globe, that lights the lower world,
  Then thieves and robbers range abroad unseen
  In murders and in outrage boldly here;
  But when from under this terrestrial ball
  He fires the proud tops of the eastern pines

And darts his light through every guilty hole,
Then murders, treasons, and detested sins,
The cloak of night being pluck'd from off their backs,
Stand bare and naked, trembling at themselves?
So when this thief, this traitor, Bolingbroke,
Who all this while hath revell'd in the night,
Whilst we were wand'ring with the Antipodes,
Shall see us rising in our throne, the east,
His treasons will sit blushing in his face,
Not able to endure the sight of day,
But self-affrighted tremble at his sin.
Not all the water in the rough rude sea
Can wash the balm off from an anointed king;
The breath of worldly men cannot depose
The deputy elected by the Lord.
For every man that Bolingbroke hath press'd
To lift shrewd steel against our golden crown,
God for his Richard hath in heavenly pay
A glorious angel. Then, if angels fight,
Weak men must fall; for heaven still guards the right.

Enter SALISBURY

Welcome, my lord. How far off lies your power?
SALISBURY. Nor near nor farther off, my gracious lord,
Than this weak arm. Discomfort guides my tongue,
And bids me speak of nothing but despair.
One day too late, I fear me, noble lord,
Hath clouded all thy happy days on earth.
O, call back yesterday, bid time return,
And thou shalt have twelve thousand fighting men!
To-day, to-day, unhappy day, too late,
O'erthrows thy joys, friends, fortune, and thy state;
For all the Welshmen, hearing thou wert dead,
Are gone to Bolingbroke, dispers'd, and fled.
AUMERLE. Comfort, my liege, why looks your Grace so
    pale?
KING RICHARD. But now the blood of twenty thousand men
Did triumph in my face, and they are fled;
And, till so much blood thither come again,
Have I not reason to look pale and dead?

All souls that will be safe, fly from my side;
For time hath set a blot upon my pride.
AUMERLE. Comfort, my liege; remember who you are.
KING RICHARD. I had forgot myself; am I not King?
Awake, thou coward majesty! thou sleepest.
Is not the King's name twenty thousand names?
Arm, arm, my name! a puny subject strikes
At thy great glory. Look not to the ground,
Ye favourites of a king; are we not high?
High be our thoughts. I know my uncle York
Hath power enough to serve our turn. But who comes
here?

Enter SCROOP

SCROOP. More health and happiness betide my liege
Than can my care-tun'd tongue deliver him.
KING RICHARD. Mine ear is open and my heart prepar'd.
The worst is worldly loss thou canst unfold.
Say, is my kingdom lost? Why, 'twas my care,
And what loss is it to be rid of care?
Strives Bolingbroke to be as great as we?
Greater he shall not be; if he serve God,
We'll serve him too, and be his fellow so.
Revolt our subjects? That we cannot mend;
They break their faith to God as well as us.
Cry woe, destruction, ruin, and decay—
The worst is death, and death will have his day.
SCROOP. Glad am I that your Highness is so arm'd
To bear the tidings of calamity.
Like an unseasonable stormy day
Which makes the silver rivers drown their shores,
As if the world were all dissolv'd to tears,
So high above his limits swells the rage
Of Bolingbroke, covering your fearful land
With hard bright steel and hearts harder than steel.
White-beards have arm'd their thin and hairless scalps
Against thy majesty; boys, with women's voices,
Strive to speak big, and clap their female joints
In stiff unwieldy arms against thy crown;
Thy very beadsmen learn to bend their bows

Of double-fatal yew against thy state;
Yea, distaff-women manage rusty bills
Against thy seat: both young and old rebel,
And all goes worse than I have power to tell.
KING RICHARD. Too well, too well thou tell'st a tale so ill.
Where is the Earl of Wiltshire? Where is Bagot?
What is become of Bushy? Where is Green?
That they have let the dangerous enemy
Measure our confines with such peaceful steps?
If we prevail, their heads shall pay for it.
I warrant they have made peace with Bolingbroke.
SCROOP. Peace have they made with him indeed, my lord.
KING RICHARD. O villains, vipers, damn'd without redemption!
Dogs, easily won to fawn on any man!
Snakes, in my heart-blood warm'd, that sting my heart!
Three Judases, each one thrice worse than Judas!
Would they make peace? Terrible hell make war
Upon their spotted souls for this offence!
SCROOP. Sweet love, I see, changing his property,
Turns to the sourest and most deadly hate.
Again uncurse their souls; their peace is made
With heads, and not with hands; those whom you curse
Have felt the worst of death's destroying wound
And lie full low, grav'd in the hollow ground.
AUMERLE. Is Bushy, Green, and the Earl of Wiltshire dead?
SCROOP. Ay, all of them at Bristow lost their heads.
AUMERLE. Where is the Duke my father with his power?
KING RICHARD. No matter where—of comfort no man speak.
Let's talk of graves, of worms, and epitaphs;
Make dust our paper, and with rainy eyes
Write sorrow on the bosom of the earth.
Let's choose executors and talk of wills;
And yet not so—for what can we bequeath
Save our deposed bodies to the ground?
Our lands, our lives, and all, are Bolingbroke's.
And nothing can we call our own but death
And that small model of the barren earth
Which serves as paste and cover to our bones.
For God's sake let us sit upon the ground
And tell sad stories of the death of kings:

How some have been depos'd, some slain in war,
Some haunted by the ghosts they have depos'd,
Some poison'd by their wives, some sleeping kill'd,
All murder'd—for within the hollow crown
That rounds the mortal temples of a king
Keeps Death his court; and there the antic sits,
Scoffing his state and grinning at his pomp;
Allowing him a breath, a little scene,
To monarchize, be fear'd, and kill with looks;
Infusing him with self and vain conceit,
As if this flesh which walls about our life
Were brass impregnable; and, humour'd thus,
Comes at the last, and with a little pin
Bores through his castle wall, and farewell, king!
Cover your heads, and mock not flesh and blood
With solemn reverence; throw away respect,
Tradition, form, and ceremonious duty;
For you have but mistook me all this while.
I live with bread like you, feel want,
Taste grief, need friends: subjected thus,
How can you say to me I am a king?
CARLISLE. My lord, wise men ne'er sit and wail their woes,
But presently prevent the ways to wail.
To fear the foe, since fear oppresseth strength,
Gives, in your weakness, strength unto your foe,
And so your follies fight against yourself.
Fear and be slain—no worse can come to fight;
And fight and die is death destroying death,
Where fearing dying pays death servile breath.
AUMERLE. My father hath a power; inquire of him,
And learn to make a body of a limb.
KING RICHARD. Thou chid'st me well. Proud Bolingbroke,
I come
To change blows with thee for our day of doom.
This ague fit of fear is over-blown;
An easy task it is to win our own.
Say, Scroop, where lies our uncle with his power?
Speak sweetly, man, although thy looks be sour.
SCROOP. Men judge by the complexion of the sky
The state in inclination of the day;

So may you by my dull and heavy eye,
My tongue hath but a heavier tale to say.
I play the torturer, by small and small
To lengthen out the worst that must be spoken:
Your uncle York is join'd with Bolingbroke;
And all your northern castles yielded up,
And all your southern gentlemen in arms
Upon his party.

KING RICHARD. Thou hast said enough.
[*To* AUMERLE] Beshrew thee, cousin, which didst lead
    me forth
Of that sweet way I was in to despair!
What say you now? What comfort have we now?
By heaven, I'll hate him everlastingly
That bids me be of comfort any more.
Go to Flint Castle; there I'll pine away;
A king, woe's slave, shall kingly woe obey.
That power I have, discharge; and let them go
To ear the land that hath some hope to grow,
For I have none. Let no man speak again
To alter this, for counsel is but vain.

AUMERLE. My liege, one word.

KING RICHARD. He does me double wrong
That wounds me with the flatteries of his tongue.
Discharge my followers; let them hence away,
From Richard's night to Bolingbroke's fair day.   *Exeunt*

SCENE 3

Wales. Before Flint Castle

Enter, with drum and colours, BOLINGBROKE, YORK,
NORTHUMBERLAND, *and forces*

BOLINGBROKE. So that by this intelligence we learn
The Welshmen are dispers'd; and Salisbury
Is gone to meet the King, who lately landed
With some few private friends upon this coast.

NORTHUMBERLAND. The news is very fair and good, my lord.
Richard not far from hence hath hid his head.

YORK. It would beseem the Lord Northumberland
  To say 'King Richard.' Alack the heavy day
  When such a sacred king should hide his head!
NORTHUMBERLAND. Your Grace mistakes; only to be brief,
  Left I his title out.
YORK. The time hath been,
  Would you have been so brief with him, he would
  Have been so brief with you to shorten you,
  For taking so the head, your whole head's length.
BOLINGBROKE. Mistake not, uncle, further than you should.
YORK. Take not, good cousin, further than you should,
  Lest you mistake. The heavens are over our heads.
BOLINGBROKE. I know it, uncle; and oppose not myself
  Against their will. But who comes here?

Enter PERCY

Welcome, Harry. What, will not this castle yield?
PERCY. The castle royally is mann'd, my lord,
  Against thy entrance.
BOLINGBROKE. Royally!
  Why, it contains no king?
PERCY. Yes, my good lord,
  It doth contain a king; King Richard lies
  Within the limits of yon lime and stone;
  And with him are the Lord Aumerle, Lord Salisbury,
  Sir Stephen Scroop, besides a clergyman
  Of holy reverence; who, I cannot learn.
NORTHUMBERLAND. O, belike it is the Bishop of Carlisle.
BOLINGBROKE. [*To* NORTHUMBERLAND] Noble lord,
  Go to the rude ribs of that ancient castle;
  Through brazen trumpet send the breath of parley
  Into his ruin'd ears, and thus deliver:
  Henry Bolingbroke
  On both his knees doth kiss King Richard's hand,
  And sends allegiance and true faith of heart
  To his most royal person; hither come
  Even at his feet to lay my arms and power,
  Provided that my banishment repeal'd
  And lands restor'd again be freely granted;
  If not, I'll use the advantage of my power

And lay the summer's dust with showers of blood
Rain'd from the wounds of slaughtered Englishmen;
The which how far off from the mind of Bolingbroke
It is such crimson tempest should bedrench
The fresh green lap of fair King Richard's land,
My stooping duty tenderly shall show.
Go, signify as much, while here we march
Upon the grassy carpet of this plain.

[NORTHUMBERLAND *advances to the Castle, with*
a trumpet]

Let's march without the noise of threat'ning drum,
That from this castle's tottered battlements
Our fair appointments may be well perus'd.
Methinks King Richard and myself should meet
With no less terror than the elements
Of fire and water, when their thund'ring shock
At meeting tears the cloudy cheeks of heaven.
Be he the fire, I'll be the yielding water;
The rage be his, whilst on the earth I rain
My waters—on the earth, and not on him.
March on, and mark King Richard how he looks.

Parle without, and answer within; then a flourish.
Enter on the walls, the KING, *the* BISHOP OF
CARLISLE, AUMERLE, SCROOP, *and* SALISBURY

See, see, King Richard doth himself appear,
As doth the blushing discontented sun
From out the fiery portal of the east,
When he perceives the envious clouds are bent
To dim his glory and to stain the track
Of his bright passage to the occident.

YORK. Yet he looks like a king. Behold, his eye,
As bright as is the eagle's, lightens forth
Controlling majesty. Alack, alack, for woe,
That any harm should stain so fair a show!

KING RICHARD. [*To* NORTHUMBERLAND] We are amaz'd;
and thus long have we stood
To watch the fearful bending of thy knee,
Because we thought ourself thy lawful King;
And if we be, how dare thy joints forget

To pay their awful duty to our presence?
If we be not, show us the hand of God
That hath dismiss'd us from our stewardship;
For well we know no hand of blood and bone
Can gripe the sacred handle of our sceptre,
Unless he do profane, steal, or usurp.
And though you think that all, as you have done,
Have torn their souls by turning them from us,
And we are barren and bereft of friends,
Yet know—my master, God omnipotent,
Is mustering in his clouds on our behalf
Armies of pestilence; and they shall strike
Your children yet unborn and unbegot,
That lift your vassal hands against my head
And threat the glory of my precious crown.
Tell Bolingbroke, for yon methinks he stands,
That every stride he makes upon my land
Is dangerous treason; he is come to open
The purple testament of bleeding war;
But ere the crown he looks for live in peace,
Ten thousand bloody crowns of mothers' sons
Shall ill become the flower of England's face,
Change the complexion of her maid-pale peace
To scarlet indignation, and bedew
Her pastures' grass with faithful English blood.

NORTHUMBERLAND. The King of Heaven forbid our lord
    the King
  Should so with civil and uncivil arms
  Be rush'd upon! Thy thrice noble cousin,
  Harry Bolingbroke, doth humbly kiss thy hand;
  And by the honourable tomb he swears
  That stands upon your royal grandsire's bones,
  And by the royalties of both your bloods,
  Currents that spring from one most gracious head,
  And by the buried hand of warlike Gaunt,
  And by the worth and honour of himself,
  Comprising all that may be sworn or said,
  His coming hither hath no further scope
  Than for his lineal royalties, and to beg
  Enfranchisement immediate on his knees;

Which on thy royal party granted once,
His glittering arms he will commend to rust,
His barbed steeds to stables, and his heart
To faithful service of your Majesty.
This swears he, as he is a prince, is just;
And as I am a gentleman I credit him.
KING RICHARD. Northumberland, say thus the King returns:
His noble cousin is right welcome hither;
And all the number of his fair demands
Shall be accomplish'd without contradiction.
With all the gracious utterance thou hast
Speak to his gentle hearing kind commends.
[*To* AUMERLE] We do debase ourselves, cousin, do we not,
To look so poorly and to speak so fair?
Shall we call back Northumberland, and send
Defiance to the traitor, and so die?
AUMERLE. No, good my lord; let's fight with gentle words
Till time lend friends, and friends their helpful swords.
KING RICHARD. O God, O God! that e'er this tongue of mine
That laid the sentence of dread banishment
On yon proud man should take it off again
With words of sooth! O that I were as great
As is my grief, or lesser than my name!
Or that I could forget what I have been!
Or not remember what I must be now!
Swell'st thou, proud heart? I'll give thee scope to beat,
Since foes have scope to beat both thee and me.
AUMERLE. Northumberland comes back from Bolingbroke.
KING RICHARD. What must the King do now? Must he
submit?
The King shall do it. Must he be depos'd?
The King shall be contented. Must he lose
The name of king? A God's name, let it go.
I'll give my jewels for a set of beads,
My gorgeous palace for a hermitage,
My gay apparel for an almsman's gown,
My figur'd goblets for a dish of wood,
My sceptre for a palmer's walking staff,
My subjects for a pair of carved saints,
And my large kingdom for a little grave,

A little little grave, an obscure grave—
Or I'll be buried in the king's high way,
Some way of common trade, where subjects' feet
May hourly trample on their sovereign's head;
For on my heart they tread now whilst I live,
And buried once, why not upon my head?
Aumerle, thou weep'st, my tender-hearted cousin!
We'll make foul weather with despised tears;
Our sighs and they shall lodge the summer corn
And make a dearth in this revolting land.
Or shall we play the wantons with our woes
And make some pretty match with shedding tears?
As thus: to drop them still upon one place
Till they have fretted us a pair of graves
Within the earth; and, therein laid—there lies
Two kinsmen digg'd their graves with weeping eyes.
Would not this ill do well? Well, well, I see
I talk but idly, and you laugh at me.
Most mighty prince, my Lord Northumberland,
What says King Bolingbroke? Will his Majesty
Give Richard leave to live till Richard die?
You make a leg, and Bolingbroke says ay.
NORTHUMBERLAND. My lord, in the base court he doth
     attend
     To speak with you; may it please you to come down?
KING RICHARD. Down, down I come, like glist'ring Phaethon,
     Wanting the manage of unruly jades.
     In the base court? Base court, where kings grow base,
     To come at traitors' calls, and do them grace.
     In the base court? Come down? Down, court! down,
          king!
     For night-owls shriek where mounting larks should sing.
                                        Exeunt from above
BOLINGBROKE. What says his Majesty?
NORTHUMBERLAND. Sorrow and grief of heart
     Makes him speak fondly, like a frantic man;
     Yet he is come.

          Enter the KING, *and his attendants, below*

BOLINGBROKE. Stand all apart,

And show fair duty to his Majesty.   [*He kneels down*]
My gracious lord—
KING RICHARD. Fair cousin, you debase your princely knee
  To make the base earth proud with kissing it.
  Me rather had my heart might feel your love
  Than my unpleas'd eye see your courtesy.
  Up, cousin, up; your heart is up, I know,
  [*Touching his own head*] Thus high at least, although
    your knee be low.
BOLINGBROKE. My gracious lord, I come but for mine own.
KING RICHARD. Your own is yours, and I am yours, and all.
BOLINGBROKE. So far be mine, my most redoubted lord,
  As my true service shall deserve your love.
KING RICHARD. Well you deserve. They well deserve to have
  That know the strong'st and surest way to get.
  Uncle, give me your hands; nay, dry your eyes:
  Tears show their love, but want their remedies.
  Cousin, I am too young to be your father,
  Though you are old enough to be my heir.
  What you will have, I'll give, and willing too;
  For do we must what force will have us do.
  Set on towards London. Cousin, is it so?
BOLINGBROKE. Yea, my good lord.
KING RICHARD. Then I must not say no.   *Flourish. Exeunt*

SCENE 4

The DUKE OF YORK'S *garden*

Enter the QUEEN *and two* LADIES

QUEEN. What sport shall we devise here in this garden
  To drive away the heavy thought of care?
LADY. Madam, we'll play at bowls.
QUEEN. 'Twill make me think the world is full of rubs
  And that my fortune runs against the bias.
LADY. Madam, we'll dance.
QUEEN. My legs can keep no measure in delight,
  When my poor heart no measure keeps in grief;
  Therefore no dancing, girl; some other sport.

LADY. Madam, we'll tell tales.
QUEEN. Of sorrow or of joy?
LADY. Of either, madam.
QUEEN. Of neither, girl;
   For if of joy, being altogether wanting,
   It doth remember me the more of sorrow;
   Or if of grief, being altogether had,
   It adds more sorrow to my want of joy;
   For what I have I need not to repeat,
   And what I want it boots not to complain.
LADY. Madam, I'll sing.
QUEEN. 'Tis well that thou hast cause;
   But thou shouldst please me better wouldst thou weep.
LADY. I could weep, madam, would it do you good.
QUEEN. And I could sing, would weeping do me good,
   And never borrow any tear of thee.

Enter a GARDENER *and two* SERVANTS

   But stay, here come the gardeners.
   Let's step into the shadow of these trees.
   My wretchedness unto a row of pins,
   They will talk of state, for every one doth so
   Against a change: woe is forerun with woe.
                [QUEEN *and* LADIES *retire*]
GARDENER. Go, bind thou up yon dangling apricocks,
   Which, like unruly children, make their sire
   Stoop with oppression of their prodigal weight;
   Give some supportance to the bending twigs.
   Go thou, and like an executioner
   Cut off the heads of too fast growing sprays
   That look too lofty in our commonwealth:
   All must be even in our government.
   You thus employ'd, I will go root away
   The noisome weeds which without profit suck
   The soil's fertility from wholesome flowers.
SERVANT. Why should we, in the compass of a pale,
   Keep law and form and due proportion,
   Showing, as in a model, our firm estate,
   When our sea-walled garden, the whole land,
   Is full of weeds; her fairest flowers chok'd up,

Her fruit trees all unprun'd, her hedges ruin'd,
Her knots disordered, and her wholesome herbs
Swarming with caterpillars?
GARDENER. Hold thy peace.
He that hath suffer'd this disorder'd spring
Hath now himself met with the fall of leaf;
The weeds which his broad-spreading leaves did shelter,
That seem'd in eating him to hold him up,
Are pluck'd up root and all by Bolingbroke—
I mean the Earl of Wiltshire, Bushy, Green.
SERVANT. What, are they dead?
GARDENER. They are; and Bolingbroke
Hath seiz'd the wasteful King. O, what pity is it
That he had not so trimm'd and dress'd his land
As we this garden! We at time of year
Do wound the bark, the skin of our fruit trees,
Lest, being over-proud in sap and blood,
With too much riches it confound itself;
Had he done so to great and growing men,
They might have liv'd to bear, and he to taste
Their fruits of duty. Superfluous branches
We lop away, that bearing boughs may live;
Had he done so, himself had borne the crown,
Which waste of idle hours hath quite thrown down.
SERVANT. What, think you the King shall be deposed?
GARDENER. Depress'd he is already, and depos'd
'Tis doubt he will be. Letters came last night
To a dear friend of the good Duke of York's
That tell black tidings.
QUEEN. O, I am press'd to death through want of speaking!
[*Coming forward*]
Thou, old Adam's likeness, set to dress this garden,
How dares thy harsh rude tongue sound this unpleasing
news?
What Eve, what serpent, hath suggested thee
To make a second fall of cursed man?
Why dost thou say King Richard is depos'd?
Dar'st thou, thou little better thing than earth,
Divine his downfall? Say, where, when, and how,
Cam'st thou by this ill tidings? Speak, thou wretch.

GARDENER. Pardon me, madam; little joy have I
  To breathe this news; yet what I say is true.
  King Richard, he is in the mighty hold
  Of Bolingbroke. Their fortunes both are weigh'd.
  In your lord's scale is nothing but himself,
  And some few vanities that make him light;
  But in the balance of great Bolingbroke,
  Besides himself, are all the English peers,
  And with that odds he weighs King Richard down.
  Post you to London, and you will find it so;
  I speak no more than every one doth know.
QUEEN. Nimble mischance, that art so light of foot,
  Doth not thy embassage belong to me,
  And am I last that knows it? O, thou thinkest
  To serve me last, that I may longest keep
  Thy sorrow in my breast. Come, ladies, go
  To meet at London London's King in woe.
  What, was I born to this, that my sad look
  Should grace the triumph of great Bolingbroke?
  Gard'ner, for telling me these news of woe,
  Pray God the plants thou graft'st may never grow!

                     Exeunt QUEEN *and* LADIES

GARDENER. Poor Queen, so that thy state might be no worse,
  I would my skill were subject to thy curse.
  Here did she fall a tear; here in this place
  I'll set a bank of rue, sour herb of grace.
  Rue, even for ruth, here shortly shall be seen,
  In the remembrance of a weeping queen.   *Exeunt*

ACT IV. SCENE 1

Westminster Hall

Enter, as to the Parliament, BOLINGBROKE, AUMERLE, NORTHUMBERLAND, PERCY, FITZWATER, SURREY, *the* BISHOP OF CARLISLE, *the* ABBOT OF WESTMINSTER, *and others;* HERALD, OFFICERS, *and* BAGOT

BOLINGBROKE. Call forth Bagot.

Now, Bagot, freely speak thy mind—
What thou dost know of noble Gloucester's death;
Who wrought it with the King, and who perform'd
The bloody office of his timeless end.

BAGOT. Then set before my face the Lord Aumerle.

BOLINGBROKE. Cousin, stand forth, and look upon that man.

BAGOT. My Lord Aumerle, I know your daring tongue
Scorns to unsay what once it hath deliver'd.
In that dead time when Gloucester's death was plotted
I heard you say 'Is not my arm of length,
That reacheth from the restful English Court
As far as Calais, to mine uncle's head?'
Amongst much other talk that very time
I heard you say that you had rather refuse
The offer of an hundred thousand crowns
Than Bolingbroke's return to England;
Adding withal, how blest this land would be
In this your cousin's death.

AUMERLE. Princes, and noble lords,
What answer shall I make to this base man?
Shall I so much dishonour my fair stars
On equal terms to give him chastisement?
Either I must, or have mine honour soil'd
With the attainder of his slanderous lips.
There is my gage, the manual seal of death
That marks thee out for hell. I say thou liest,
And will maintain what thou hast said is false
In thy heart-blood, through being all too base
To stain the temper of my knightly sword.

BOLINGBROKE. Bagot, forbear; thou shalt not take it up.

AUMERLE. Excepting one, I would he were the best
In all this presence that hath mov'd me so.

FITZWATER. If that thy valour stand on sympathy,
There is my gage, Aumerle, in gage to thine.
By that fair sun which shows me where thou stand'st,
I heard thee say, and vauntingly thou spak'st it,
That thou wert cause of noble Gloucester's death.
If thou deniest it twenty times, thou liest;
And I will turn thy falsehood to thy heart,
Where it was forged, with my rapier's point.

AUMERLE. Thou dar'st not, coward, live to see that day.

FITZWATER. Now, by my soul, I would it were this hour.

AUMERLE. Fitzwater, thou art damn'd to hell for this.

PERCY. Aumerle, thou liest; his honour is as true
  In this appeal as thou art all unjust;
  And that thou art so, there I throw my gage,
  To prove it on thee to the extremest point
  Of mortal breathing. Seize it, if thou dar'st.

AUMERLE. An if I do not, may my hands rot off
  And never brandish more revengeful steel
  Over the glittering helmet of my foe!

ANOTHER LORD. I task the earth to the like, forsworn
  Aumerle;
  And spur thee on with full as many lies
  As may be halloa'd in thy treacherous ear
  From sun to sun. There is my honour's pawn;
  Engage it to the trial, if thou darest.

AUMERLE. Who sets me else? By heaven, I'll throw at all!
  I have a thousand spirits in one breast
  To answer twenty thousand such as you.

SURREY. My Lord Fitzwater, I do remember well
  The very time Aumerle and you did talk.

FITZWATER. 'Tis very true; you were in presence then,
  And you can witness with me this is true.

SURREY. As false, by heaven, as heaven itself is true.

FITZWATER. Surrey, thou liest.

SURREY. Dishonourable boy!
  That lie shall lie so heavy on my sword
  That it shall render vengeance and revenge
  Till thou the lie-giver and that lie do lie
  In earth as quiet as thy father's skull.
  In proof whereof, there is my honour's pawn;
  Engage it to the trial, if thou dar'st.

FITZWATER. How fondly dost thou spur a forward horse!
  If I dare eat, or drink, or breathe, or live,
  I dare meet Surrey in a wilderness,
  And spit upon him whilst I say he lies,
  And lies, and lies. There is my bond of faith,
  To tie thee to my strong correction.
  As I intend to thrive in this new world,

Aumerle is guilty of my true appeal.
Besides, I heard the banish'd Norfolk say
That thou, Aumerle, didst send two of thy men
To execute the noble Duke at Calais.

AUMERLE. Some honest Christian trust me with a gage
That Norfolk lies. Here do I throw down this,
If he may be repeal'd to try his honour.

BOLINGBROKE. These differences shall all rest under gage
Till Norfolk be repeal'd—repeal'd he shall be
And, though mine enemy, restor'd again
To all his lands and signories. When he is return'd,
Against Aumerle we will enforce his trial.

CARLISLE. That honourable day shall never be seen.
Many a time hath banish'd Norfolk fought
For Jesu Christ in glorious Christian field,
Streaming the ensign of the Christian cross
Against black pagans, Turks, and Saracens;
And, toil'd with works of war, retir'd himself
To Italy; and there, at Venice, gave
His body to that pleasant country's earth,
And his pure soul unto his captain, Christ,
Under whose colours he had fought so long.

BOLINGBROKE. Why, Bishop, is Norfolk dead?

CARLISLE. As surely as I live, my lord.

BOLINGBROKE. Sweet peace conduct his sweet soul to the
bosom
Of good old Abraham! Lords appellants,
Your differences shall all rest under gage
Till we assign you to your days of trial.

Enter YORK, *attended*

YORK. Great Duke of Lancaster, I come to thee
From plume-pluck'd Richard, who with willing soul
Adopts thee heir, and his high sceptre yields
To the possession of thy royal hand.
Ascend his throne, descending now from him—
And long live Henry, fourth of that name!

BOLINGBROKE. In God's name, I'll ascend the regal throne.

CARLISLE. Marry, God forbid!
Worst in this royal presence may I speak,

Yet best beseeming me to speak the truth.
Would God that any in this noble presence
Were enough noble to be upright judge
Of noble Richard! Then true noblesse would
Learn him forbearance from so foul a wrong.
What subject can give sentence on his king?
And who sits here that is not Richard's subject?
Thieves are not judg'd but they are by to hear,
Although apparent guilt be seen in them;
And shall the figure of God's majesty,
His captain, steward, deputy elect,
Anointed, crowned, planted many years,
Be judg'd by subject and inferior breath,
And he himself not present? O, forfend it, God,
That in a Christian climate souls refin'd
Should show so heinous, black, obscene a deed!
I speak to subjects, and a subject speaks,
Stirr'd up by God, thus boldly for his king.
My Lord of Hereford here, whom you call king,
Is a foul traitor to proud Hereford's king;
And if you crown him, let me prophesy—
The blood of English shall manure the ground,
And future ages groan for this foul act;
Peace shall go sleep with Turks and infidels,
And in this seat of peace tumultuous wars
Shall kin with kin and kind with kind confound;
Disorder, horror, fear, and mutiny,
Shall here inhabit, and this land be call'd
The field of Golgotha and dead men's skulls.
O, if you raise this house against this house,
It will the woefullest division prove
That ever fell upon this cursed earth.
Prevent it, resist it, let it not be so,
Lest child, child's children, cry against you woe.
NORTHUMBERLAND. Well have you argued, sir; and, for your
    pains,
Of capital treason we arrest you here.
My Lord of Westminster, be it your charge
To keep him safely till his day of trial.
May it please you, lords, to grant the commons' suit?

BOLINGBROKE. Fetch hither Richard, that in common view
    He may surrender; so we shall proceed
    Without suspicion.
YORK. I will be his conduct.   *Exit*
BOLINGBROKE. Lords, you that here are under our arrest,
    Procure your sureties for your days of answer.
    Little are we beholding to your love,
    And little look'd for at your helping hands.

    Re-enter YORK, *with* KING RICHARD, *and* OFFICERS
                bearing the regalia

KING RICHARD. Alack, why am I sent for to a king,
    Before I have shook off the regal thoughts
    Wherewith I reign'd? I hardly yet have learn'd
    To insinuate, flatter, bow, and bend my knee.
    Give sorrow leave awhile to tutor me
    To this submission. Yet I well remember
    The favours of these men. Were they not mine?
    Did they not sometime cry 'All hail!' to me?
    So Judas did to Christ; but he, in twelve,
    Found truth in all but one; I, in twelve thousand, none.
    God save the King! Will no man say amen?
    Am I both priest and clerk? Well then, amen.
    God save the King! although I be not he;
    And yet, amen, if heaven do think him me.
    To do what service am I sent for hither?
YORK. To do that office of thine own good will
    Which tired majesty did make thee offer—
    The resignation of thy state and crown
    To Henry Bolingbroke.
KING RICHARD. Give me the crown. Here, cousin, seize the
    crown.
    Here, cousin,
    On this side my hand, and on that side thine.
    Now is this golden crown like a deep well
    That owes two buckets, filling one another;
    The emptier ever dancing in the air,
    The other down, unseen, and full of water.
    That bucket down and full of tears am I,
    Drinking my griefs, whilst you mount up on high.

BOLINGBROKE. I thought you had been willing to resign.

KING RICHARD. My crown I am; but still my griefs are mine.
You may my glories and my state depose,
But not my griefs; still am I king of those.

BOLINGBROKE. Part of your cares you give me with your
crown.

KING RICHARD. Your cares set up do not pluck my cares
down.
My care is loss of care, by old care done;
Your care is gain of care, by new care won.
The cares I give I have, though given away;
They tend the crown, yet still with me they stay.

BOLINGBROKE. Are you contented to resign the crown?

KING RICHARD. Ay, no; no, ay; for I must nothing be;
Therefore no no, for I resign to thee.
Now mark me how I will undo myself:
I give this heavy weight from off my head,
And this unwieldy sceptre from my hand,
The pride of kingly sway from out my heart;
With mine own tears I wash away my balm,
With mine own hands I give away my crown,
With mine own tongue deny my sacred state,
With mine own breath release all duteous oaths;
All pomp and majesty I do forswear;
My manors, rents, revenues, I forgo;
My acts, decrees, and statutes, I deny.
God pardon all oaths that are broke to me!
God keep all vows unbroke are made to thee!
Make me, that nothing have, with nothing griev'd,
And thou with all pleas'd, that hast all achiev'd.
Long mayst thou live in Richard's seat to sit,
And soon lie Richard in an earthly pit.
God save King Henry, unking'd Richard says,
And send him many years of sunshine days!
What more remains?

NORTHUMBERLAND. No more; but that you read
These accusations, and these grievous crimes
Committed by your person and your followers
Against the state and profit of this land;
That, by confessing them, the souls of men

 May deem that you are worthily depos'd.
KING RICHARD. Must I do so? And must I ravel out
 My weav'd-up follies? Gentle Northumberland,
 If thy offences were upon record,
 Would it not shame thee in so fair a troop
 To read a lecture of them? If thou wouldst,
 There shouldst thou find one heinous article,
 Containing the deposing of a king
 And cracking the strong warrant of an oath,
 Mark'd with a blot, damn'd in the book of heaven.
 Nay, all of you that stand and look upon me
 Whilst that my wretchedness doth bait myself,
 Though some of you, with Pilate, wash your hands,
 Showing an outward pity—yet you Pilates
 Have here deliver'd me to my sour cross,
 And water cannot wash away your sin.
NORTHUMBERLAND. My lord, dispatch; read o'er these articles.
KING RICHARD. Mine eyes are full of tears; I cannot see.
 And yet salt water blinds them not so much
 But they can see a sort of traitors here.
 Nay, if I turn mine eyes upon myself,
 I find myself a traitor with the rest;
 For I have given here my soul's consent
 T'undeck the pompous body of a king;
 Made glory base, and sovereignty a slave,
 Proud majesty a subject, state a peasant.
NORTHUMBERLAND. My lord—
KING RICHARD. No lord of thine, thou haught insulting man,
 Nor no man's lord; I have no name, no title—
 No, not that name was given me at the font—
 But 'tis usurp'd. Alack the heavy day,
 That I have worn so many winters out,
 And know not now what name to call myself!
 O that I were a mockery king of snow,
 Standing before the sun of Bolingbroke
 To melt myself away in water drops!
 Good king, great king, and yet not greatly good,
 An if my word be sterling yet in England,
 Let it command a mirror hither straight,
 That it may show me what a face I have

Since it is bankrupt of his majesty.

BOLINGBROKE. Go some of you and fetch a looking-glass.

Exit an attendant

NORTHUMBERLAND. Read o'er this paper while the glass doth
    come.

KING RICHARD. Fiend, thou torments me ere I come to hell.

BOLINGBROKE. Urge it no more, my Lord Northumberland.

NORTHUMBERLAND. The Commons will not, then, be satisfied.

KING RICHARD. They shall be satisfied. I'll read enough,
    When I do see the very book indeed
    Where all my sins are writ, and that's myself.

Re-enter attendant with glass

    Give me that glass, and therein will I read.
    No deeper wrinkles yet? Hath sorrow struck
    So many blows upon this face of mine
    And made no deeper wounds? O flatt'ring glass,
    Like to my followers in prosperity,
    Thou dost beguile me! Was this face the face
    That every day under his household roof
    Did keep ten thousand men? Was this the face
    That like the sun did make beholders wink?
    Is this the face which fac'd so many follies
    That was at last out-fac'd by Bolingbroke?
    A brittle glory shineth in this face;
    As brittle as the glory is the face;
                [*Dashes the glass against the ground*]
    For there it is, crack'd in a hundred shivers.
    Mark, silent king, the moral of this sport—
    How soon my sorrow hath destroy'd my face.

BOLINGBROKE. The shadow of your sorrow hath destroy'd
    The shadow of your face.

KING RICHARD. Say that again.
    The shadow of my sorrow? Ha! let's see.
    'Tis very true: my grief lies all within;
    And these external manner of laments
    Are merely shadows to the unseen grief
    That swells with silence in the tortur'd soul.
    There lies the substance; and I thank thee, king,
    For thy great bounty, that not only giv'st

Me cause to wail, but teachest me the way
How to lament the cause. I'll beg one boon,
And then be gone and trouble you no more.
Shall I obtain it?

BOLINGBROKE. Name it, fair cousin.

KING RICHARD. Fair cousin! I am greater than a king;
For when I was a king, my flatterers
Were then but subjects; being now a subject,
I have a king here to my flatterer.
Being so great, I have no need to beg.

BOLINGBROKE. Yet ask.

KING RICHARD. And shall I have?

BOLINGBROKE. You shall.

KING RICHARD. Then give me leave to go.

BOLINGBROKE. Whither?

KING RICHARD. Whither you will, so I were from your sights.

BOLINGBROKE. Go, some of you convey him to the Tower.

KING RICHARD. O, good! Convey! Conveyers are you all,
That rise thus nimbly by a true king's fall.

Exeunt KING RICHARD, *some Lords and a Guard*

BOLINGBROKE. On Wednesday next we solemnly set down
Our coronation. Lords, prepare yourselves.

Exeunt all but the ABBOT OF WESTMINSTER, *the*
BISHOP OF CARLISLE, *and* AUMERLE

ABBOT. A woeful pageant have we here beheld.

CARLISLE. The woe's to come; the children yet unborn
Shall feel this day as sharp to them as thorn.

AUMERLE. You holy clergymen, is there no plot
To rid the realm of this pernicious blot?

ABBOT. My lord,
Before I freely speak my mind herein,
You shall not only take the sacrament
To bury mine intents, but also to effect
Whatever I shall happen to devise.
I see your brows are full of discontent,
Your hearts of sorrow, and your eyes of tears.
Come home with me to supper; I will lay
A plot shall show us all a merry day.   *Exeunt*

ACT V. SCENE 1

London. A street leading to the Tower

Enter the QUEEN, *with her attendants*

QUEEN. This way the King will come; this is the way
To Julius Cæsar's ill-erected tower,
To whose flint bosom my condemned lord
Is doom'd a prisoner by proud Bolingbroke.
Here let us rest, if this rebellious earth
Have any resting for her true King's queen.

Enter KING RICHARD *and Guard*

But soft, but see, or rather do not see,
My fair rose wither. Yet look up, behold,
That you in pity may dissolve to dew,
And wash him fresh again with true-love tears.
Ah, thou, the model where old Troy did stand;
Thou map of honour, thou King Richard's tomb,
And not King Richard; thou most beauteous inn,
Why should hard-favour'd grief be lodg'd in thee,
When triumph is become an alehouse guest?
KING RICHARD. Join not with grief, fair woman, do not so,
To make my end too sudden. Learn, good soul,
To think our former state a happy dream;
From which awak'd, the truth of what we are
Shows us but this: I am sworn brother, sweet,
To grim Necessity; and he and I
Will keep a league till death. Hie thee to France,
And cloister thee in some religious house.
Our holy lives must win a new world's crown,
Which our profane hours here have thrown down.
QUEEN. What, is my Richard both in shape and mind
Transform'd and weak'ned? Hath Bolingbroke depos'd
Thine intellect? Hath he been in thy heart?
The lion dying thrusteth forth his paw
And wounds the earth, if nothing else, with rage
To be o'erpow'r'd; and wilt thou, pupil-like,
Take the correction mildly, kiss the rod,
And fawn on rage with base humility,

Which art a lion and the king of beasts?

KING RICHARD. A king of beasts, indeed! If aught but beasts,
I had been still a happy king of men.
Good sometimes queen, prepare thee hence for France.
Think I am dead, and that even here thou takest,
As from my death-bed, thy last living leave.
In winter's tedious nights sit by the fire
With good old folks, and let them tell thee tales
Of woeful ages long ago betid;
And ere thou bid good night, to quit their griefs
Tell thou the lamentable tale of me,
And send the hearers weeping to their beds;
For why, the senseless brands will sympathize
The heavy accent of thy moving tongue,
And in compassion weep the fire out;
And some will mourn in ashes, some coal-black,
For the deposing of a rightful king.

Enter NORTHUMBERLAND *attended*

NORTHUMBERLAND. My lord, the mind of Bolingbroke is
chang'd;
You must to Pomfret, not unto the Tower.
And, madam, there is order ta'en for you:
With all swift speed you must away to France.

KING RICHARD. Northumberland, thou ladder wherewithal
The mounting Bolingbroke ascends my throne,
The time shall not be many hours of age
More than it is, ere foul sin gathering head
Shall break into corruption. Thou shalt think
Though he divide the realm and give thee half
It is too little, helping him to all;
And he shall think that thou, which knowest the way
To plant unrightful kings, wilt know again,
Being ne'er so little urg'd, another way
To pluck him headlong from the usurped throne.
The love of wicked men converts to fear;
That fear to hate; and hate turns one or both
To worthy danger and deserved death.

NORTHUMBERLAND. My guilt be on my head, and there an
end.

Take leave, and part; for you must part forthwith.

KING RICHARD. Doubly divorc'd! Bad men, you violate
A twofold marriage—'twixt my crown and me,
And then betwixt me and my married wife.
Let me unkiss the oath 'twixt thee and me;
And yet not so, for with a kiss 'twas made.
Part us, Northumberland; I towards the north,
Where shivering cold and sickness pines the clime;
My wife to France, from whence set forth in pomp,
She came adorned hither like sweet May,
Sent back like Hallowmas or short'st of day.

QUEEN. And must we be divided? Must we part?

KING RICHARD. Ay, hand from hand, my love, and heart
from heart.

QUEEN. Banish us both, and send the King with me.

NORTHUMBERLAND. That were some love, but little policy.

QUEEN. Then whither he goes thither let me go.

KING RICHARD. So two, together weeping, make one woe.
Weep thou for me in France, I for thee here;
Better far off than near, be ne'er the near.
Go, count thy way with sighs; I mine with groans.

QUEEN. So longest way shall have the longest moans.

KING RICHARD. Twice for one step I'll groan, the way being
short,
And piece the way out with a heavy heart.
Come, come, in wooing sorrow let's be brief,
Since, wedding it, there is such length in grief.
One kiss shall stop our mouths, and dumbly part;
Thus give I mine, and thus take I thy heart.

QUEEN. Give me mine own again; 'twere no good part
To take on me to keep and kill thy heart.
So, now I have mine own again, be gone.
That I may strive to kill it with a groan.

KING RICHARD. We make woe wanton with this fond delay.
Once more, adieu; the rest let sorrow say.   *Exeunt*

SCENE 2

The DUKE OF YORK'S *palace*

Enter the DUKE OF YORK *and the* DUCHESS

DUCHESS. My Lord, you told me you would tell the rest,
  When weeping made you break the story off,
  Of our two cousins' coming into London.
YORK. Where did I leave?
DUCHESS. At that sad stop, my lord,
  Where rude misgoverned hands from windows' tops
  Threw dust and rubbish on King Richard's head.
YORK. Then, as I said, the Duke, great Bolingbroke,
  Mounted upon a hot and fiery steed
  Which his aspiring rider seem'd to know,
  With slow but stately pace kept on his course,
  Whilst all tongues cried 'God save thee, Bolingbroke!'
  You would have thought the very windows spake,
  So many greedy looks of young and old
  Through casements darted their desiring eyes
  Upon his visage; and that all the walls
  With painted imagery had said at once
  'Jesu preserve thee! Welcome, Bolingbroke!'
  Whilst he, from the one side to the other turning,
  Bareheaded, lower than his proud steed's neck,
  Bespake them thus, 'I thank you, countrymen.'
  And thus still doing, thus he pass'd along.
DUCHESS. Alack, poor Richard! where rode he the whilst?
YORK. As in a theatre the eyes of men
  After a well-grac'd actor leaves the stage
  Are idly bent on him that enters next,
  Thinking his prattle to be tedious;
  Even so, or with much more contempt, men's eyes
  Did scowl on gentle Richard; no man cried 'God save
    him!'
  No joyful tongue gave him his welcome home;
  But dust was thrown upon his sacred head;
  Which with such gentle sorrow he shook off,
  His face still combating with tears and smiles,

The badges of his grief and patience,
That had not God, for some strong purpose, steel'd
The hearts of men, they must perforce have melted,
And barbarism itself have pitied him.
But heaven hath a hand in these events,
To whose high will we bound our calm contents.
To Bolingbroke are we sworn subjects now,
Whose state and honour I for aye allow.

DUCHESS. Here comes my son Aumerle.

YORK. Aumerle that was
But that is lost for being Richard's friend,
And madam, you must call him Rutland now.
I am in Parliament pledge for his truth
And lasting fealty to the new-made king.

Enter AUMERLE

DUCHESS. Welcome, my son. Who are the violets now
That strew the green lap of the new come spring?

AUMERLE. Madam, I know not, nor I greatly care not.
God knows I had as lief be none as one.

YORK. Well, bear you well in this new spring of time,
Lest you be cropp'd before you come to prime.
What news from Oxford? Do these justs and triumphs
hold?

AUMERLE. For aught I know, my lord, they do.

YORK. You will be there, I know.

AUMERLE. If God prevent not, I purpose so.

YORK. What seal is that that hangs without thy bosom?
Yea, look'st thou pale? Let me see the writing.

AUMERLE. My lord, 'tis nothing.

YORK. No matter, then, who see it.
I will be satisfied; let me see the writing.

AUMERLE. I do beseech your Grace to pardon me;
It is a matter of small consequence
Which for some reasons I would not have seen.

YORK. Which for some reasons, sir, I mean to see.
I fear, I fear—

DUCHESS. What should you fear?
'Tis nothing but some bond that he is ent'red into
For gay apparel 'gainst the triumph-day.

YORK. Bound to himself! What doth he with a bond
   That he is bound to? Wife, thou art a fool.
   Boy, let me see the writing.
AUMERLE. I do beseech you, pardon me; I may not show it.
YORK. I will be satisfied; let me see it, I say.
                    [*He plucks it out of his bosom, and reads it*]
   Treason, foul treason! Villain! traitor! slave!
DUCHESS. What is the matter, my lord?
YORK. Ho! who is within there?

Enter a servant

   Saddle my horse.
   God for his mercy, what treachery is here!
DUCHESS. Why, what is it, my lord?
YORK. Give me my boots, I say; saddle my horse.
                                        Exit servant
   Now, by mine honour, by my life, my troth,
   I will appeach the villain.
DUCHESS. What is the matter?
YORK. Peace, foolish woman.
DUCHESS. I will not peace. What is the matter, Aumerle?
AUMERLE. Good mother, be content; it is no more
   Than my poor life must answer.
DUCHESS. Thy life answer!
YORK. Bring me my boots. I will unto the King.

His man enters with his boots

DUCHESS. Strike him, Aumerle. Poor boy, thou art amaz'd.
   Hence, villain! never more come in my sight.
YORK. Give me my boots, I say.
DUCHESS. Why, York, what wilt thou do?
   Wilt thou not hide the trespass of thine own?
   Have we more sons? or are we like to have?
   Is not my teeming date drunk up with time?
   And wilt thou pluck my fair son from mine age
   And rob me of a happy mother's name?
   Is he not like thee? Is he not thine own?
YORK. Thou fond mad woman,
   Wilt thou conceal this dark conspiracy?
   A dozen of them here have ta'en the sacrament,

And interchangeably set down their hands
  To kill the King at Oxford.
DUCHESS. He shall be none;
  We'll keep him here. Then what is that to him?
YORK. Away, fond woman! were he twenty times my son
  I would appeach him.
DUCHESS. Hadst thou groan'd for him
  As I have done, thou wouldst be more pitiful.
  But now I know thy mind: thou dost suspect
  That I have been disloyal to thy bed
  And that he is a bastard, not thy son.
  Sweet York, sweet husband, be not of that mind.
  He is as like thee as a man may be
  Not like to me, or any of my kin,
  And yet I love him.
YORK. Make way, unruly woman!   *Exit*
DUCHESS. After, Aumerle! Mount thee upon his horse;
  Spur post, and get before him to the King,
  And beg thy pardon ere he do accuse thee.
  I'll not be long behind; though I be old,
  I doubt not but to ride as fast as York;
  And never will I rise up from the ground
  Till Bolingbroke have pardon'd thee. Away, be gone.
                                        Exeunt

SCENE 3

Windsor Castle

Enter BOLINGBROKE *as King,* PERCY, *and other* LORDS

BOLINGBROKE. Can no man tell me of my unthrifty son?
  'Tis full three months since I did see him last.
  If any plague hang over us, 'tis he.
  I would to God, my lords, he might be found.
  Inquire at London, 'mongst the taverns there,
  For there, they say, he daily doth frequent
  With unrestrained loose companions,
  Even such, they say, as stand in narrow lanes

And beat our watch and rob our passengers,
Which he, young wanton and effeminate boy,
Takes on the point of honour to support
So dissolute a crew.

PERCY. My lord, some two days since I saw the Prince,
And told him of those triumphs held at Oxford.

BOLINGBROKE. And what said the gallant?

PERCY. His answer was, he would unto the stews,
And from the common'st creature pluck a glove
And wear it as a favour; and with that
He would unhorse the lustiest challenger.

BOLINGBROKE. As dissolute as desperate; yet through both
I see some sparks of better hope, which elder years
May happily bring forth. But who comes here?

Enter AUMERLE *amazed*

AUMERLE. Where is the King?

BOLINGBROKE. What means our cousin that he stares and looks
So wildly?

AUMERLE. God save your Grace! I do beseech your Majesty,
To have some conference with your Grace alone.

BOLINGBROKE. Withdraw yourselves, and leave us here alone.
Exeunt PERCY *and* LORDS
What is the matter with our cousin now?

AUMERLE. For ever may my knees grow to the earth,
[*Kneels*]
My tongue cleave to my roof within my mouth,
Unless a pardon ere I rise or speak.

BOLINGBROKE. Intended or committed was this fault?
If on the first, how heinous e'er it be,
To win thy after-love I pardon thee.

AUMERLE. Then give me leave that I may turn the key,
That no man enter till my tale be done.

BOLINGBROKE. Have thy desire.
[*The* DUKE OF YORK *knocks at the door and crieth*]

YORK. [*Within*] My liege, beware; look to thyself;
Thou hast a traitor in thy presence there.

BOLINGBROKE. [*Drawing*] Villain, I'll make thee safe.

AUMERLE. Stay thy revengeful hand; thou hast no cause to
    fear.
YORK. [*Within*] Open the door, secure, foolhardy King.
    Shall I, for love, speak treason to thy face?
    Open the door, or I will break it open.

Enter YORK

BOLINGBROKE. What is the matter, uncle? Speak;
    Recover breath; tell us how near is danger,
    That we may arm us to encounter it.
YORK. Peruse this writing here, and thou shalt know
    The treason that my haste forbids me show.
AUMERLE. Remember, as thou read'st, thy promise pass'd.
    I do repent me; read not my name there;
    My heart is not confederate with my hand.
YORK. It was, villain, ere thy hand did set it down.
    I tore it from the traitor's bosom, King;
    Fear, and not love, begets his penitence.
    Forget to pity him, lest thy pity prove
    A serpent that will sting thee to the heart.
BOLINGBROKE. O heinous, strong, and bold conspiracy!
    O loyal father of a treacherous son!
    Thou sheer, immaculate, and silver fountain,
    From whence this stream through muddy passages
    Hath held his current and defil'd himself!
    Thy overflow of good converts to bad;
    And thy abundant goodness shall excuse
    This deadly blot in thy digressing son.
YORK. So shall my virtue be his vice's bawd;
    And he shall spend mine honour with his shame,
    As thriftless sons their scraping fathers' gold.
    Mine honour lives when his dishonour dies,
    Or my sham'd life in his dishonour lies.
    Thou kill'st me in his life; giving him breath,
    The traitor lives, the true man's put to death.
DUCHESS. [*Within*] What ho, my liege, for God's sake, let
    me in.
BOLINGBROKE. What shrill-voic'd suppliant makes this eager
    cry?

DUCHESS. [*Within*] A woman, and thine aunt, great King;
'tis I.

    Speak with me, pity me, open the door.

    A beggar begs that never begg'd before.

BOLINGBROKE. Our scene is alt'red from a serious thing,

    And now chang'd to 'The Beggar and the King.'

    My dangerous cousin, let your mother in.

    I know she is come to pray for your foul sin.

YORK. If thou do pardon whosoever pray,

    More sins for this forgiveness prosper may.

    This fest'red joint cut off, the rest rest sound;

    This let alone will all the rest confound.

Enter DUCHESS

DUCHESS. O King, believe not this hard-hearted man!

    Love loving not itself, none other can.

YORK. Thou frantic woman, what dost thou make here?

    Shall thy old dugs once more a traitor rear?

DUCHESS. Sweet York, be patient. Hear me, gentle liege.

                               [*Kneels*]

BOLINGBROKE. Rise up, good aunt.

DUCHESS. Not yet, I thee beseech.

    For ever will I walk upon my knees,

    And never see day that the happy sees

    Till thou give joy; until thou bid me joy

    By pardoning Rutland, my transgressing boy.

AUMERLE. Unto my mother's prayers I bend my knee.

                               [*Kneels*]

YORK. Against them both, my true joints bended be.

                               [*Kneels*]

    Ill mayst thou thrive, if thou grant any grace!

DUCHESS. Pleads he in earnest? Look upon his face;

    His eyes do drop no tears, his prayers are in jest;

    His words come from his mouth, ours from our breast.

    He prays but faintly and would be denied;

    We pray with heart and soul, and all beside.

    His weary joints would gladly rise, I know;

    Our knees still kneel till to the ground they grow.

    His prayers are full of false hypocrisy;

    Ours of true zeal and deep integrity.

Our prayers do out-pray his; then let them have
That mercy which true prayer ought to have.
BOLINGBROKE. Good aunt, stand up.
DUCHESS. Nay, do not say 'stand up';
    Say 'pardon' first, and afterwards 'stand up.'
    An if I were thy nurse, thy tongue to teach,
    'Pardon' should be the first word of thy speech.
    I never long'd to hear a word till now;
    Say 'pardon,' King; let pity teach thee how.
    The word is short, but not so short as sweet;
    No word like 'pardon' for kings' mouths so meet.
YORK. Speak it in French, King, say 'pardonne moy.'
DUCHESS. Dost thou teach pardon pardon to destroy?
    Ah, my sour husband, my hard-hearted lord,
    That sets the word itself against the word!
    Speak 'pardon' as 'tis current in our land;
    The chopping French we do not understand.
    Thine eye begins to speak, set thy tongue there;
    Or in thy piteous heart plant thou thine ear,
    That hearing how our plaints and prayers do pierce,
    Pity may move thee 'pardon' to rehearse.
BOLINGBROKE. Good aunt, stand up.
DUCHESS. I do not sue to stand;
    Pardon is all the suit I have in hand.
BOLINGBROKE. I pardon him, as God shall pardon me.
DUCHESS. O happy vantage of a kneeling knee!
    Yet am I sick for fear. Speak it again.
    Twice saying 'pardon' doth not pardon twain,
    But makes one pardon strong.
BOLINGBROKE. With all my heart
    I pardon him.
DUCHESS. A god on earth thou art.
BOLINGBROKE. But for our trusty brother-in-law and the
    Abbot,
    With all the rest of that consorted crew,
    Destruction straight shall dog them at the heels.
    Good uncle, help to order several powers
    To Oxford, or where'er these traitors are.
    They shall not live within this world, I swear,
    But I will have them, if I once know where.

Uncle, farewell; and, cousin, adieu;
Your mother well hath pray'd, and prove you true.
DUCHESS. Come, my old son; I pray God make thee new.
Exeunt

SCENE 4

Windsor Castle

Enter SIR PIERCE OF EXTON *and a servant*

EXTON. Didst thou not mark the King, what words he
spake?
'Have I no friend will rid me of this living fear?'
Was it not so?
SERVANT. These were his very words.
EXTON. 'Have I no friend?' quoth he. He spake it twice
And urg'd it twice together, did he not?
SERVANT. He did.
EXTON. And, speaking it, he wishtly look'd on me,
As who should say 'I would thou wert the man
That would divorce this terror from my heart';
Meaning the King at Pomfret. Come, let's go.
I am the King's friend, and will rid his foe.   *Exeunt*

SCENE 5

Pomfret Castle. The dungeon of the Castle

Enter KING RICHARD

KING RICHARD. I have been studying how I may compare
This prison where I live unto the world
And, for because the world is populous
And here is not a creature but myself,
I cannot do it. Yet I'll hammer it out.
My brain I'll prove the female to my soul,
My soul the father; and these two beget
A generation of still-breeding thoughts,
And these same thoughts people this little world,

In humours like the people of this world,
For no thought is contented. The better sort,
As thoughts of things divine, are intermix'd
With scruples, and do set the word itself
Against the word,
As thus: 'Come, little ones'; and then again,
'It is as hard to come as for a camel
To thread the postern of a small needle's eye.'
Thoughts tending to ambition, they do plot
Unlikely wonders: how these vain weak nails
May tear a passage through the flinty ribs
Of this hard world, my ragged prison walls;
And, for they cannot, die in their own pride.
Thoughts tending to content flatter themselves
That they are not the first of fortune's slaves,
Nor shall not be the last; like silly beggars
Who, sitting in the stocks, refuge their shame,
That many have and others must sit there;
And in this thought they find a kind of ease,
Bearing their own misfortunes on the back
Of such as have before endur'd the like.
Thus play I in one person many people,
And none contented. Sometimes am I king;
Then treasons make me wish myself a beggar,
And so I am. Then crushing penury
Persuades me I was better when a king;
Then am I king'd again; and by and by
Think that I am unking'd by Bolingbroke,
And straight am nothing. But whate'er I be,
Nor I, nor any man that but man is,
With nothing shall be pleas'd till he be eas'd
With being nothing.   [*The music plays*]
Music do I hear?
Ha, ha! keep time. How sour sweet music is
When time is broke and no proportion kept!
So is it in the music of men's lives.
And here have I the daintiness of ear
To check time broke in a disorder'd string;
But, for the concord of my state and time,
Had not an ear to hear my true time broke.

I wasted time, and now doth time waste me;
For now hath time made me his numb'ring clock:
My thoughts are minutes; and with sighs they jar
Their watches on unto mine eyes, the outward watch,
Whereto my finger, like a dial's point,
Is pointing still, in cleansing them from tears.
Now sir, the sound that tells what hour it is
Are clamorous groans which strike upon my heart,
Which is the bell. So sighs, and tears, and groans,
Show minutes, times, and hours; but my time
Runs posting on in Bolingbroke's proud joy,
While I stand fooling here, his Jack of the clock.
This music mads me. Let it sound no more;
For though it have holp madmen to their wits,
In me it seems it will make wise men mad.
Yet blessing on his heart that gives it me!
For 'tis a sign of love; and love to Richard
Is a strange brooch in this all-hating world.

Enter a GROOM *of the stable*

GROOM. Hail, royal Prince!
KING RICHARD. Thanks, noble peer!
  The cheapest of us is ten groats too dear.
  What art thou? and how comest thou hither,
  Where no man never comes but that sad dog
  That brings me food to make misfortune live?
GROOM. I was a poor groom of thy stable, King,
  When thou wert king; who, travelling towards York,
  With much ado at length have gotten leave
  To look upon my sometimes royal master's face.
  O, how it ern'd my heart, when I beheld,
  In London streets, that coronation-day,
  When Bolingbroke rode on roan Barbary—
  That horse that thou so often hast bestrid,
  That horse that I so carefully have dress'd!
KING RICHARD. Rode he on Barbary? Tell me, gentle friend,
  How went he under him?
GROOM. So proudly as if he disdain'd the ground.
KING RICHARD. So proud that Bolingbroke was on his back!
  That jade hath eat bread from my royal hand;

This hand hath made him proud with clapping him.
Would he not stumble? would he not fall down,
Since pride must have a fall, and break the neck
Of that proud man that did usurp his back?
Forgiveness, horse! Why do I rail on thee,
Since thou, created to be aw'd by man,
Wast born to bear? I was not made a horse;
And yet I bear a burden like an ass,
Spurr'd, gall'd, and tir'd, by jauncing Bolingbroke.

Enter KEEPER *with meat*

KEEPER. Fellow, give place; here is no longer stay.
KING RICHARD. If thou love me, 'tis time thou wert away.
GROOM. What my tongue dares not, that my heart shall say.
Exit

KEEPER. My lord, will't please you to fall to?
KING RICHARD. Taste of it first as thou art wont to do.
KEEPER. My lord, I dare not. Sir Pierce of Exton,
    Who lately came from the King, commands the contrary.
KING RICHARD. The devil take Henry of Lancaster and thee!
    Patience is stale, and I am weary of it.
[Beats the KEEPER]

KEEPER. Help, help, help!

The murderers, EXTON *and servants, rush in, armed*

KING RICHARD. How now! What means death in this rude
        assault?
    Villain, thy own hand yields thy death's instrument.
        [Snatching a weapon and killing one]
    Go thou and fill another room in hell.
        [He kills another, then EXTON *strikes him down]*
    That hand shall burn in never-quenching fire
    That staggers thus my person. Exton, thy fierce hand
    Hath with the King's blood stain'd the King's own land.
    Mount, mount, my soul! thy seat is up on high;
    Whilst my gross flesh sinks downward, here to die.
        [Dies]

EXTON. As full of valour as of royal blood.
    Both have I spill'd. O, would the deed were good!
    For now the devil, that told me I did well,

Says that this deed is chronicled in hell.
This dead King to the living King I'll bear.
Take hence the rest, and give them burial here.   *Exeunt*

SCENE 6

Windsor Castle

Flourish. Enter BOLINGBROKE, *the* DUKE OF YORK, *with other* LORDS *and attendants*

BOLINGBROKE. Kind uncle York, the latest news we hear
Is that the rebels have consum'd with fire
Our town of Ciceter in Gloucestershire;
But whether they be ta'en or slain we hear not.

Enter NORTHUMBERLAND

Welcome, my lord. What is the news?
NORTHUMBERLAND. First, to thy sacred state wish I all
happiness.
The next news is, I have to London sent
The heads of Salisbury, Spencer, Blunt, and Kent.
The manner of their taking may appear
At large discoursed in this paper here.
BOLINGBROKE. We thank thee, gentle Percy, for thy pains;
And to thy worth will add right worthy gains.

Enter FITZWATER

FITZWATER. My lord, I have from Oxford sent to London
The heads of Brocas and Sir Bennet Seely;
Two of the dangerous consorted traitors
That sought at Oxford thy dire overthrow.
BOLINGBROKE. Thy pains, Fitzwater, shall not be forgot;
Right noble is thy merit, well I wot.

Enter PERCY, *with the* BISHOP OF CARLISLE

PERCY. The grand conspirator, Abbot of Westminster,
With clog of conscience and sour melancholy,
Hath yielded up his body to the grave;
But here is Carlisle living, to abide

Thy kingly doom, and sentence of his pride.
BOLINGBROKE. Carlisle, this is your doom:
   Choose out some secret place, some reverend room,
   More than thou hast, and with it joy thy life;
   So as thou liv'st in peace, die free from strife;
   For though mine enemy thou hast ever been,
   High sparks of honour in thee have I seen.

Enter EXTON, *with attendants, bearing a coffin*

EXTON. Great King, within this coffin I present
   Thy buried fear. Herein all breathless lies
   The mightiest of thy greatest enemies,
   Richard of Bordeaux, by me hither brought.
BOLINGBROKE. Exton, I thank thee not; for thou hast
      wrought
   A deed of slander with thy fatal hand
   Upon my head and all this famous land.
EXTON. From your own mouth, my lord, did I this deed.
BOLINGBROKE. They love not poison that do poison need,
   Nor do I thee. Though I did wish him dead,
   I hate the murderer, love him murdered.
   The guilt of conscience take thou for thy labour,
   But neither my good word nor princely favour;
   With Cain go wander thorough shades of night,
   And never show thy head by day nor light.
   Lords, I protest my soul is full of woe
   That blood should sprinkle me to make me grow.
   Come, mourn with me for what I do lament,
   And put on sullen black incontinent.
   I'll make a voyage to the Holy Land,
   To wash this blood off from my guilty hand.
   March sadly after; grace my mournings here
   In weeping after this untimely bier.   *Exeunt*

The First Part of
King Henry the Fourth

THE FIRST PART OF
KING HENRY THE FOURTH

SHAKESPEARE, when he planned *Richard II*, had doubtless
in mind the possibility that other plays might grow out
of his study of this period of English history. The contrasts
in character that it provided, the personal antipathies and
rival ambitions that continually create new causes of conflict,
all supplied opportunities for effective theatrical situations.
Yet Shakespeare, although he reminds his listeners from time
to time that the plays carrying on the conflict initiated in
Richard II mark stages in a story that extends beyond the
bounds of any individual play, found it necessary to give
each individual piece its own complication and resolution. To
have devised such a series of movements all in strict keeping
and all developing the political themes of the prelude between Richard and Bolingbroke would have required more
concentration perhaps than the material would allow. Even
Richard II, it has been argued, does not derive its dramatic
force from its politics, although the deposition was to leave
a legacy that was likely to lead to claims and counter-claims.
Men were naturally inclined in the confusions in which they
later found themselves to look back to events in Richard's
reign as the cause of it all. To find good excuses for present
conduct in the doings of the past is habitual in all generations; it is equally natural for those who have participated in
events where necessity seems to have driven them to acts
that are, even viewed in their historical context and most
venial aspect, unwelcome to the memory to feel that a curse
may lie on them. These common and familiar attitudes
Shakespeare develops with great advantage in the plays that
follow *Richard II;* but it is going beyond the evidence of the
plays themselves to insist that Shakespeare's main intention is
to work out the implications of Carlisle's words as if they
were the inspired message of heaven itself. The situation Carlisle feared provided of itself the opportunities for the strife

he foresaw; but it is clear that if Henry the Fifth's son had been the man his father or his grandfather was the Yorkists would have rebelled in vain. Shakespeare nowhere represents Henry the Sixth as the man specially designed by God to bring down destruction on the Lancastrians or to make amends for their treatment of Richard. One might as well suppose Shakespeare saw in the "royal saint" the outcome of Henry the Fifth's unwarranted claims on France and his pride in marrying the daughter of the none too sane King Charles the Sixth. In *Henry IV* and *Henry V* men do remember that Richard was done to death; but these recollections are generally the promptings of ambition. The Lancastrians fell as Richard the Second fell because Henry the Sixth could not cultivate his garden.

There run through *Henry IV* and *Henry V* recollections of the events of *Richard II*; but the themes round which these subsequent pieces are organized have no very direct connection with that of Richard's fall. Five years separate the composition of *Richard II* and *Henry V*; between his thirtieth and his thirty-fifth year Shakespeare's powers were maturing rapidly and winning for him his unrivalled position as the master not only of the tragic but the comic stage. *Richard II* had no room for comedy; in *Henry IV* comedy threatens to sweep the boards clear of all else, and is only stayed by what many feel to be an arbitrary and unfeeling act of authority. Falstaff was the character in *Henry IV* to whom the Elizabethan audience came to pay their tribute, and the Queen herself, if tradition can be trusted, did him the unique honour of having him brought before her not in the train of his superiors but in his private capacity as a visitor to Windsor.

The contemporary reaction to a play is not necessarily the truest or profoundest or final interpretation of its dramatic significance. We can understand perfectly why Elizabeth spoke with some anger of *Richard II* and why the followers of Essex regarded it as a lesson in rebellion. Neither party could enjoy it disinterestedly; and it may be fair to argue that the Elizabethans were so carried away by the insolence of Falstaff's wit that they ignored the place he really occupied in the hierarchy of Shakespeare's characters. Modern readings of the play have attempted to reduce him in status, and on the stage itself he has recently been played down in the interest of his social superiors who are supposed to be the dramatist's chief concern.

Much has been made in recent years of the influence of the Moralities on Elizabethan drama. The Morality treats of the struggle between man's good and bad angels for the salvation of his soul. The author of a Morality may array the opposing forces in whatever formation his fancy suggests and may multiply the figures that represent the sins and temptations that beset mankind as he may the representatives of virtue and salvation. The type is illustrated by a play which one of Shakespeare's contemporaries saw in his earliest years, *The Cradle of Security*. The leading character is a ruler Wicked-of-the-World who disports himself with three ladies, Pride, Covetousness, and Luxury; these keep him from all godly exercises and lull him to sleep in a cradle. Their attentions so transform him that he now appears masked with a swine's snout. But he does not lie in peace, for two aged figures End-of-the-World and Last Judgment carrying a mace and sword scatter the courtiers with a blow and the Prince starting up is for all his plaints carried off by wicked spirits. Bale's *King Johan* is a type intermediate between the simple Morality and the History play. Historical figures now mingle with the moral abstractions and the lesson taught is political as much as moral. Wherever there are men in society there will always be moral issues, and it may be said that in a sense the Elizabethan Histories carry on the tradition of the Moralities. Their kings and princes may like Richard the Second stand between their evil and their wiser counsellors and incline to wisdom or to folly; it is possible to say that Richard the Third as depicted by Shakespeare is just Wicked-of-the-World incarnate; he now steps out of history but the moral is unchanged. Following this line of thought modern criticism has inclined to regard *Henry IV* as a kind of Morality in which the Prince is drawn to wickedness and all disorder by Falstaff and the other irregular humorists and only saved by such counsellors as the Lord Chief Justice.

The relations of Prince Hal and the Lord Chief Justice had already provided material for the stage, and Shakespeare was recalling familiar matter when in 2 *Henry IV*, I, 5 he makes Falstaff say to the Lord Chief Justice:

> For the box of the ear that the prince gave you, he gave it like a rude prince, and you took it like a sensible lord.

The episode in which the Lord Chief Justice commits the Prince to prison for this offence the theatre had already borrowed from tradition, and Shakespeare at the close of the second part shows as a token of the new King's resolution to have law and order his retaining the Lord Chief Justice in his office. That Shakespeare had in his mind from the beginning of 1 *Henry IV* some such conclusion as that in which he shows the prince transformed into the king who casts off his irresponsible companions and turns to more sober counsellors is obvious. This transformation was to provide the ostensible theme of his play.

Shakespeare's general plan undoubtedly required the Prince to associate with characters that were hardly respectable enough for a prince to countenance, let alone for the favours of a King. Falstaff and his associates are as the Prince's opening soliloquy shows condemned from the beginning; but having provided this initial assurance Shakespeare felt free to develop the association of the Prince and his companions without misgivings. The Prince is not without touches that indicate the man of authority but to represent him as entering half-heartedly or without zest into the fooling is to stress Shakespeare's formal scheme rather than the inspiration that it provoked.

In creating his Falstaff the dramatist once again took advantage of popular tradition. The Prince of history whatever his wildness was a man long trained and exercised in arms; as a youth he had been with Richard the Second on his Irish expedition and later campaigned in Wales; such a training however is not incompatible with a taste for fun and horseplay. Tradition may have had something to work on in the Prince's doings, but when it gave him as a companion in his riots the Lollard martyr Sir John Oldcastle this was a pure extravagance of fancy. That Shakespeare some time before the printing of 1 *Henry IV* in 1598 substituted "Falstaff" for

"Oldcastle" is clear from the play on the name at 1 *Henry IV*, I, 2, "my old lad of the castle," from the retention in 2 *Henry IV* of the speech-heading *Old.* I, 2, and from Shakespeare's own disclaimer in the *Epilogue* that he had no intention of depicting the historical Oldcastle in the Prince's companion, "for Oldcastle died a martyr and this is not the man." The fame of Shakespeare's Oldcastle had roused the Cobham family to protest against this defamation of their ancestor, for Oldcastle had in 1408 married into the Cobham family and taken the title Lord Cobham. Yet the name Old-castle seems to have been still in use on the stage, though the younger Lord Cobham of Shakespeare's own day is referred to in private letters as Falstaff. The unpleasantness over Shakespeare's use of the name Oldcastle gave the rival company of the Admiral's men their cue for producing a counterblast, *The First Part of the True and Honourable History of the Life of Sir John Oldcastle, the good Lord Cobham*, and their *Prologue* assures the audience that

> It is no pampered glutton we present
> Nor aged Councellor to youthful sinne,
> But one whose vertue shone above the rest,
> A valiant Martyr and a vertuous peere.

Shakespeare's Falstaff is the Oldcastle of popular story, but in every other way his own creation.

Shakespeare first made Falstaff in the interests of the Prince. As Maurice Morgann observes: "The Prince is supposed to possess a high relish of humour and to have a temper and a force about him, which, whatever was his pursuit, delighted in excess." One cannot imagine the Prince's father taking any pleasure in Falstaff's company; but it is part of the dramatist's intention to show us the son's greater reach; he is as prepared to match himself with Falstaff as he is with Hotspur.

The Prince touches the extremes at which Hotspur and Falstaff stand. Hotspur and Falstaff are poles apart, but the Prince occupies the whole extent between; there is a capacity of sympathy and power in him as a consequence that is felt necessary for the complete man. Yet Shakespeare presents the extreme types so vividly; he paints them failings and all with such life that the ideal between is by comparison more a description of a character than the thing itself.

The difficulty Shakespeare had with his central figure lies in this that while he had to talk about the Prince's becoming a different man he has also to make it clear from the beginning that there is no change whatever. The Prodigal Son motif is not really heard in the Prince's part; he is from the start sure of himself and confident of the end he is making for. It is his father only who is troubled with anxiety about how his son will squander his patrimony. While the King is thinking gloomily of how much more honourable is Hotspur's career than the course being run by his son, the Prince himself can jest at his ease about the man who "kills me some six or seven dozen of Scots at a breakfast, washes his hands, and says to his wife 'Fie upon this quiet life! I want work.' " For the Prince feels he is if necessary as capable a workman; there is not the awe in his voice that infects even Falstaff's when Glendower and Percy and Douglas are named. The part the Prince has to play however is perhaps too obvious; it lacks the surprising turns and unexpected sallies that make Falstaff's life one long adventure. The Elizabethan public found Falstaff's infinite resource very much to their minds, and Shakespeare whatever kind of sequel he may have planned gave his public a further taste of their favourite's quality. Whether the Second part as we have it was produced rather in response to the public's enthusiasm for Falstaff than in fulfilment of a predetermined design in Shakespeare's mind can never be answered with certainty. Shakespeare however took the opportunity it provided of developing more fully some aspects of the idea that shaped the first part.

King Henry the Fourth
Henry, Prince of Wales ⎫
Prince John of Lancaster ⎬ *sons of Henry IV*
Earl of Westmoreland ⎫
Sir Walter Blunt ⎬ *friends of the King*
Thomas Percy, Earl of Worcester
Henry Percy, Earl of Northumberland
Henry Percy, *surnamed* Hotspur, *his son*
Edmund Mortimer, Earl of March
Archibald, Earl of Douglas
Scroop, Archbishop of York
Sir Michael, *friend of the Archbishop*
Owen Glendower
Sir Richard Vernon
Sir John Falstaff ⎫
Poins ⎮
Bardolph ⎬ *irregular humourists*
Peto ⎮
Gadshill ⎭

Lady Percy, *wife of Hotspur and sister of Mortimer*

Lady Mortimer, *wife of Mortimer and daughter of Glendower*

Hostess Quickly, *of the Boar's Head, Eastcheap*

Lords, Officers, Attendants, Sheriff, Vintner, Chamberlain, Drawers, Carriers, Travellers

SCENE:
England and Wales

The First Part of
King Henry the Fourth

ACT I. SCENE 1

London. The palace

Enter the KING, LORD JOHN OF LANCASTER, EARL OF
WESTMORELAND, SIR WALTER BLUNT, *and others*

KING. So shaken as we are, so wan with care,
    Find we a time for frighted peace to pant
    And breathe short-winded accents of new broils
    To be commenc'd in strands afar remote.
    No more the thirsty entrance of this soil
    Shall daub her lips with her own children's blood;
    No more shall trenching war channel her fields,
    Nor bruise her flow'rets with the armed hoofs
    Of hostile paces. Those opposed eyes
    Which, like the meteors of a troubled heaven,
    All of one nature, of one substance bred,
    Did lately meet in the intestine shock
    And furious close of civil butchery,
    Shall now in mutual well-beseeming ranks
    March all one way, and be no more oppos'd
    Against acquaintance, kindred, and allies.
    The edge of war, like an ill-sheathed knife,
    No more shall cut his master. Therefore, friends,
    As far as to the sepulchre of Christ—
    Whose soldier now, under whose blessed cross
    We are impressed and engag'd to fight—
    Forthwith a power of English shall we levy,
    Whose arms were moulded in their mothers' womb
    To chase these pagans in those holy fields
    Over whose acres walk'd those blessed feet
    Which fourteen hundred years ago were nail'd

For our advantage on the bitter cross.
But this our purpose now is twelvemonth old,
And bootless 'tis to tell you we will go;
Therefore we meet not now. Then let me hear
Of you, my gentle cousin Westmoreland,
What yesternight our Council did decree
In forwarding this dear expedience.

WESTMORELAND. My liege, this haste was hot in question
And many limits of the charge set down
But yesternight, when all athwart there came
A post from Wales loaden with heavy news;
Whose worst was that the noble Mortimer,
Leading the men of Herefordshire to fight
Against the irregular and wild Glendower,
Was by the rude hands of that Welshman taken,
A thousand of his people butchered;
Upon whose dead corpse there was such misuse,
Such beastly shameless transformation,
By those Welshwomen done, as may not be
Without much shame re-told or spoken of.

KING. It seems then that the tidings of this broil
Brake off our business for the Holy Land.

WESTMORELAND. This match'd with other did, my gracious
    Lord;
For more uneven and unwelcome news
Came from the north, and thus it did import:
On Holy-rood day, the gallant Hotspur there,
Young Harry Percy, and brave Archibald,
That ever-valiant and approved Scot,
At Holmedon met,
Where they did spend a sad and bloody hour;
As by discharge of their artillery
And shape of likelihood the news was told;
For he that brought them, in the very heat
And pride of their contention did take horse,
Uncertain of the issue any way.

KING. Here is a dear, a true industrious friend,
Sir Walter Blunt, new lighted from his horse,
Stain'd with the variation of each soil
Betwixt that Holmedon and this seat of ours;

And he hath brought us smooth and welcome news.
The Earl of Douglas is discomfited:
Ten thousand bold Scots, two and twenty knights,
Balk'd in their own blood, did Sir Walter see
On Holmedon's plains; of prisoners, Hotspur took
Mordake, Earl of Fife and eldest son
To beaten Douglas; and the Earl of Athol,
Of Murray, Angus, and Menteith.
And is not this an honourable spoil?
A gallant prize? Ha, cousin, is it not?
WESTMORELAND. In faith,
   It is a conquest for a prince to boast of.
KING. Yea, there thou mak'st me sad and mak'st me sin
   In envy that my Lord Northumberland
   Should be the father to so blest a son—
   A son who is the theme of honour's tongue;
   Amongst a grove, the very straightest plant;
   Who is sweet Fortune's minion and her pride;
   Whilst I, by looking on the praise of him,
   See riot and dishonour stain the brow
   Of my young Harry. O that it could be prov'd
   That some night-tripping fairy had exchang'd
   In cradle-clothes our children where they lay,
   And call'd mine Percy, his Plantagenet!
   Then would I have his Harry, and he mine.
   But let him from my thoughts. What think you, coz,
   Of this young Percy's pride? The prisoners
   Which he in this adventure hath surpris'd
   To his own use he keeps; and sends me word,
   I shall have none but Mordake Earl of Fife.
WESTMORELAND. This is his uncle's teaching, this is
     Worcester,
   Malevolent to you in all aspects;
   Which makes him prune himself, and bristle up
   The crest of youth against your dignity.
KING. But I have sent for him to answer this;
   And for this cause awhile we must neglect
   Our holy purpose to Jerusalem.
   Cousin, on Wednesday next our council we
   Will hold at Windsor—so inform the lords;

KING HENRY IV. PART 1

But come yourself with speed to us again,
For more is to be said and to be done
Than out of anger can be uttered.

WESTMORELAND. I will, my liege.   *Exeunt*

SCENE 2

London. The PRINCE'S *lodging*

Enter the PRINCE OF WALES *and* SIR JOHN FALSTAFF

FALSTAFF. Now, Hal, what time of day is it, lad?

PRINCE. Thou art so fat-witted with drinking of old sack,
and unbuttoning thee after supper, and sleeping upon
benches after noon, that thou hast forgotten to demand that
truly which thou wouldest truly know. What a devil hast
thou to do with the time of the day? Unless hours were cups
of sack, and minutes capons, and clocks the tongues of
bawds, and dials the signs of leaping-houses, and the
blessed sun himself a fair hot wench in flame-coloured
taffeta, I see no reason why thou shouldst be so superfluous
to demand the time of the day.

FALSTAFF. Indeed, you come near me now, Hal; for we that
take purses go by the moon and the seven stars, and not by
Phœbus, he 'that wand'ring knight so fair.' And, I prithee,
sweet wag, when thou art a king, as, God save thy Grace—
Majesty, I should say; for grace thou wilt have none—

PRINCE. What, none?

FALSTAFF. No, by my troth; not so much as will serve to be
prologue to an egg and butter.

PRINCE. Well, how then? Come, roundly, roundly.

FALSTAFF. Marry, then, sweet wag, when thou art king, let
not us that are squires of the night's body be called thieves
of the day's beauty; let us be Diana's foresters, gentlemen
of the shade, minions of the moon; and let men say we be
men of good government, being governed, as the sea is, by
our noble and chaste mistress the moon, under whose
countenance we steal.

PRINCE. Thou sayest well, and it holds well too; for the fortune of us that are the moon's men doth ebb and flow like

the sea, being governed, as the sea is, by the moon. As, for proof, now: a purse of gold most resolutely snatch'd on Monday night, and most dissolutely spent on Tuesday morning; got with swearing 'Lay by' and spent with crying 'Bring in'; now in as low an ebb as the foot of the ladder, and by and by in as high a flow as the ridge of the gallows.

FALSTAFF. By the Lord, thou say'st true, lad. And is not my hostess of the tavern a most sweet wench?

PRINCE. As the honey of Hybla, my old lad of the castle. And is not a buff jerkin a most sweet robe of durance?

FALSTAFF. How now, how now, mad wag! What, in thy quips and thy quiddities? What a plague have I to do with a buff jerkin?

PRINCE. Why, what a pox have I to do with my hostess of the tavern?

FALSTAFF. Well, thou hast call'd her to a reckoning many a time and oft.

PRINCE. Did I ever call for thee to pay thy part?

FALSTAFF. No; I'll give thee thy due, thou hast paid all there.

PRINCE. Yea, and elsewhere, so far as my coin would stretch; and where it would not, I have used my credit.

FALSTAFF. Yea, and so us'd it that, were it not here apparent that thou art heir apparent—but, I prithee, sweet wag, shall there be gallows standing in England when thou art king, and resolution thus fubb'd as it is with the rusty curb of old father antic the law? Do not thou, when thou art king, hang a thief.

PRINCE. No; thou shalt.

FALSTAFF. Shall I? O rare! By the Lord, I'll be a brave judge!

PRINCE. Thou judgest false already: I mean thou shalt have the hanging of the thieves, and so become a rare hangman.

FALSTAFF. Well, Hal, well; and in some sort it jumps with my humour as well as waiting in the court, I can tell you.

PRINCE. For obtaining of suits?

FALSTAFF. Yea, for obtaining of suits, whereof the hangman hath no lean wardrobe. 'Sblood, I am as melancholy as a gib cat or a lugg'd bear.

PRINCE. Or an old lion, or a lover's lute.

FALSTAFF. Yea, or the drone of a Lincolnshire bagpipe.

PRINCE. What sayest thou to a hare, or the melancholy of Moor Ditch?

FALSTAFF. Thou hast the most unsavoury similes, and art indeed the most comparative, rascalliest, sweet young prince. But, Hal, I prithee, trouble me no more with vanity. I would to God thou and I knew where a commodity of good names were to be bought. An old lord of the Council rated me the other day in the street about you, sir, but I mark'd him not; and yet he talk'd very wisely, but I regarded him not; and yet he talk'd wisely, and in the street too.

PRINCE. Thou didst well; for wisdom cries out in the streets, and no man regards it.

FALSTAFF. O, thou hast damnable iteration, and art indeed able to corrupt a saint. Thou hast done much harm upon me, Hal—God forgive thee for it! Before I knew thee, Hal, I knew nothing; and now am I, if a man should speak truly, little better than one of the wicked. I must give over this life, and I will give it over. By the Lord, an I do not I am a villain! I'll be damn'd for never a king's son in Christendom.

PRINCE. Where shall we take a purse to-morrow, Jack?

FALSTAFF. Zounds, where thou wilt, lad: I'll make one. An I do not, call me villain and baffle me.

PRINCE. I see a good amendment of life in thee—from praying to purse-taking.

FALSTAFF. Why, Hal, 'tis my vocation, Hal; 'tis no sin for a man to labour in his vocation.

Enter POINS

Poins!—Now shall we know if Gadshill have set a match. O, if men were to be saved by merit, what hole in hell were hot enough for him? This is the most omnipotent villain that ever cried 'Stand' to a true man.

PRINCE. Good morrow, Ned.

POINS. Good morrow, sweet Hal. What says Monsieur Remorse? What says Sir John Sack and Sugar? Jack, how agrees the devil and thee about thy soul, that thou soldest

him on Good Friday last for a cup of Madeira and a cold
capon's leg?

PRINCE. Sir John stands to his word—the devil shall have his
bargain; for he was never yet a breaker of proverbs; he
will give the devil his due.

POINS. Then art thou damn'd for keeping thy word with
the devil.

PRINCE. Else he had been damn'd for cozening the devil.

POINS. But, my lads, my lads, to-morrow morning, by four
o'clock early, at Gadshill! There are pilgrims going to
Canterbury with rich offerings, and traders riding to London with fat purses. I have vizards for you all; you have
horses for yourselves. Gadshill lies to-night in Rochester; I
have bespoke supper to-morrow night in Eastcheap. We
may do it as secure as sleep. If you will go, I will stuff
your purses full of crowns; if you will not, tarry at home
and be hang'd.

FALSTAFF. Hear ye, Yedward: if I tarry at home and go not,
I'll hang you for going.

POINS. You will, chops?

FALSTAFF. Hal, wilt thou make one?

PRINCE. Who?—I rob, I a thief? Not I, by my faith.

FALSTAFF. There's neither honesty, manhood, nor good fellowship in thee, nor thou cam'st not of the blood royal, if
thou darest not stand for ten shillings.

PRINCE. Well then, once in my days I'll be a madcap.

FALSTAFF. Why, that's well said.

PRINCE. Well, come what will, I'll tarry at home.

FALSTAFF. By the lord, I'll be a traitor then, when thou art
king.

PRINCE. I care not.

POINS. Sir John, I prithee, leave the Prince and me alone: I
will lay him down such reasons for this adventure that he
shall go.

FALSTAFF. Well, God give thee the spirit of persuasion, and
him the ears of profiting, that what thou speakest may
move, and what he hears may be believed; that the true
prince may, for recreation sake, prove a false thief; for the
poor abuses of the time want countenance. Farewell; you
shall find me in Eastcheap.

PRINCE. Farewell, thou latter spring! Farewell, All-hallown summer! *Exit* FALSTAFF

POINS. Now, my good sweet honey lord, ride with us to-morrow. I have a jest to execute that I cannot manage alone. Falstaff, Bardolph, Peto, and Gadshill, shall rob those men that we have already waylaid; yourself and I will not be there; and when they have the booty, if you and I do not rob them, cut this head off from my shoulders.

PRINCE. How shall we part with them in setting forth?

POINS. Why, we will set forth before or after them, and appoint them a place of meeting, wherein it is at our pleasure to fail; and then will they adventure upon the exploit themselves; which they shall have no sooner achieved but we'll set upon them.

PRINCE. Yea, but 'tis like that they will know us by our horses, by our habits, and by every other appointment, to be ourselves.

POINS. Tut! our horses they shall not see—I'll tie them in the wood; our vizards we will change after we leave them; and, sirrah, I have cases of buckram for the nonce, to immask our noted outward garments.

PRINCE. Yea, but I doubt they will be too hard for us.

POINS. Well, for two of them, I know them to be as true-bred cowards as ever turn'd back; and for the third, if he fight longer than he sees reason, I'll forswear arms. The virtue of this jest will be the incomprehensible lies that this same fat rogue will tell us when we meet at supper: how thirty, at least, he fought with; what wards, what blows, what extremities he endured; and in the reproof of this lives the jest.

PRINCE. Well, I'll go with thee. Provide us all things necessary, and meet me to-morrow night in Eastcheap; there I'll sup. Farewell.

POINS. Farewell, my lord. *Exit*

PRINCE. I know you all, and will awhile uphold
The unyok'd humour of your idleness;
Yet herein will I imitate the sun,
Who doth permit the base contagious clouds
To smother up his beauty from the world,

That, when he please again to be himself,
Being wanted, he may be more wond'red at
By breaking through the foul and ugly mists
Of vapours that did seem to strangle him.
If all the year were playing holidays,
To sport would be as tedious as to work;
But when they seldom come, they wish'd-for come,
And nothing pleaseth but rare accidents.
So, when this loose behaviour I throw off
And pay the debt I never promised,
By how much better than my word I am,
By so much shall I falsify men's hopes;
And, like bright metal on a sullen ground,
My reformation, glitt'ring o'er my fault,
Shall show more goodly and attract more eyes
Than that which hath no foil to set it off.
I'll so offend to make offence a skill,
Redeeming time when men think least I will.   *Exit*

SCENE 3

London. The palace

Enter the KING, NORTHUMBERLAND, WORCESTER, HOTSPUR,
SIR WALTER BLUNT, *with others*

KING. My blood hath been too cold and temperate,
    Unapt to stir at these indignities,
    And you have found me; for accordingly
    You tread upon my patience. But be sure
    I will from henceforth rather be myself,
    Mighty and to be fear'd, than my condition,
    Which hath been smooth as oil, soft as young down,
    And therefore lost that title of respect
    Which the proud soul ne'er pays but to the proud.
WORCESTER. Our house, my sovereign liege, little deserves
    The scourge of greatness to be us'd on it—
    And that same greatness too which our own hands
    Have holp to make so portly.
NORTHUMBERLAND. My lord—

KING. Worcester, get thee gone; for I do see
  Danger and disobedience in thine eye.
  O, sir, your presence is too bold and peremptory,
  And majesty might never yet endure
  The moody frontier of a servant brow.
  You have good leave to leave us; when we need
  Your use and counsel, we shall send for you.

Exit WORCESTER

  You were about to speak.
NORTHUMBERLAND. Yea, my good lord.
  Those prisoners in your Highness' name demanded,
  Which Harry Percy here at Holmedon took,
  Were, as he says, not with such strength denied
  As is delivered to your Majesty.
  Either envy, therefore, or misprision
  Is guilty of this fault, and not my son.
HOTSPUR. My liege, I did deny no prisoners.
  But I remember when the fight was done,
  When I was dry with rage and extreme toil,
  Breathless and faint, leaning upon my sword,
  Came there a certain lord, neat, and trimly dress'd,
  Fresh as a bridegroom, and his chin new reap'd
  Show'd like a stubble-land at harvest-home.
  He was perfumed like a milliner,
  And 'twixt his finger and his thumb he held
  A pouncet-box, which ever and anon
  He gave his nose and took't away again;
  Who therewith angry, when it next came there,
  Took it in snuff—and still he smil'd and talk'd—
  And as the soldiers bore dead bodies by,
  He call'd them untaught knaves, unmannerly,
  To bring a slovenly unhandsome corse
  Betwixt the wind and his nobility.
  With many holiday and lady terms
  He questioned me: amongst the rest, demanded
  My prisoners in your Majesty's behalf.
  I then, all smarting with my wounds being cold,
  To be so pest'red with a popinjay,
  Out of my grief and my impatience
  Answer'd neglectingly I know not what—

He should, or he should not—for he made me mad
To see him shine so brisk, and smell so sweet,
And talk so like a waiting-gentlewoman
Of guns, and drums, and wounds—God save the mark!—
And telling me the sovereignest thing on earth
Was parmaceti for an inward bruise;
And that it was great pity, so it was,
This villainous saltpetre should be digg'd
Out of the bowels of the harmless earth,
Which many a good tall fellow had destroy'd
So cowardly; and but for these vile guns
He would himself have been a soldier.
This bald unjointed chat of his, my lord,
I answered indirectly, as I said;
And I beseech you, let not his report
Come current for an accusation
Betwixt my love and your high Majesty.

BLUNT. The circumstance considered, good my lord,
Whate'er Lord Harry Percy then had said
To such a person, and in such a place,
At such a time, with all the rest re-told,
May reasonably die, and never rise
To do him wrong, or any way impeach
What then he said, so he unsay it now.

KING. Why, yet he doth deny his prisoners,
But with proviso and exception—
That we at our own charge shall ransom straight
His brother-in-law, the foolish Mortimer;
Who, on my soul, hath wilfully betray'd
The lives of those that he did lead to fight
Against that great magician, damn'd Glendower,
Whose daughter, as we hear, that Earl of March
Hath lately married. Shall our coffers, then,
Be emptied to redeem a traitor home?
Shall we buy treason, and indent with fears,
When they have lost and forfeited themselves?
No, on the barren mountains let him starve;
For I shall never hold that man my friend
Whose tongue shall ask me for one penny cost
To ransom home revolted Mortimer.

HOTSPUR. Revolted Mortimer!
　　He never did fall off, my sovereign liege,
　　But by the chance of war; to prove that true,
　　Needs no more but one tongue for all those wounds,
　　Those mouthed wounds, which valiantly he took
　　When on the gentle Severn's sedgy bank,
　　In single opposition hand to hand,
　　He did confound the best part of an hour
　　In changing hardiment with great Glendower.
　　Three times they breath'd, and three times did they drink,
　　Upon agreement, of swift Severn's flood;
　　Who then, affrighted with their bloody looks,
　　Ran fearfully among the trembling reeds
　　And hid his crisp head in the hollow bank
　　Bloodstained with these valiant combatants.
　　Never did base and rotten policy
　　Colour her working with such deadly wounds;
　　Nor never could the noble Mortimer
　　Receive so many, and all willingly.
　　Then let him not be slandered with revolt.
KING. Thou dost belie him, Percy, thou dost belie him;
　　He never did encounter with Glendower.
　　I tell thee
　　He durst as well have met the devil alone
　　As Owen Glendower for an enemy.
　　Art thou not asham'd? But, sirrah, henceforth
　　Let me not hear you speak of Mortimer;
　　Send me your prisoners with the speediest means,
　　Or you shall hear in such a kind from me
　　As will displease you. My Lord Northumberland,
　　We license your departure with your son.
　　Send us your prisoners, or you will hear of it.
　　　　　　　　　　Exeunt KING HENRY, BLUNT, *and train*
HOTSPUR. And if the devil come and roar for them,
　　I will not send them. I will after straight
　　And tell him so; for I will ease my heart,
　　Albeit I make a hazard of my head.
NORTHUMBERLAND. What, drunk with choler? Stay and
　　　　pause awhile.
　　Here comes your uncle.

Re-enter WORCESTER

HOTSPUR. Speak of Mortimer!
  Zounds, I will speak of him; and let my soul
  Want mercy if I do not join with him.
  Yea, on his part I'll empty all these veins
  And shed my dear blood drop by drop in the dust,
  But I will lift the down-trod Mortimer
  As high in the air as this unthankful king,
  As this ingrate and cank'red Bolingbroke.
NORTHUMBERLAND. Brother, the King hath made your
    nephew mad.
WORCESTER. Who struck this heat up after I was gone?
HOTSPUR. He will, forsooth, have all my prisoners;
  And when I urg'd the ransom once again
  Of my wife's brother, then his cheek look'd pale,
  And on my face he turn'd an eye of death,
  Trembling even at the name of Mortimer.
WORCESTER. I cannot blame him: was not he proclaim'd
  By Richard that dead is the next of blood?
NORTHUMBERLAND. He was: I heard the proclamation;
  And then it was when the unhappy King—
  Whose wrongs in us God pardon!—did set forth
  Upon his Irish expedition;
  From whence he intercepted did return
  To be depos'd, and shortly murdered.
WORCESTER. And for whose death we in the world's wide
    mouth
  Live scandaliz'd and foully spoken of.
HOTSPUR. But soft, I pray you: did King Richard then
  Proclaim my brother, Edmund Mortimer,
  Heir to the crown?
NORTHUMBERLAND. He did: myself did hear it.
HOTSPUR. Nay, then I cannot blame his cousin king,
  That wish'd him on the barren mountains starve.
  But shall it be that you that set the crown
  Upon the head of this forgetful man,
  And for his sake wear the detested blot
  Of murderous subornation—shall it be
  That you a world of curses undergo,

Being the agents or base second means,
The cords, the ladder, or the hangman rather?
O, pardon me that I descend so low
To show the line and the predicament
Wherein you range under this subtle king!
Shall it, for shame, be spoken in these days
Or fill up chronicles in time to come,
That men of your nobility and power
Did gage them both in an unjust behalf—
As both of you, God pardon it! have done—
To put down Richard, that sweet lovely rose,
And plant this thorn, this canker, Bolingbroke?
And shall it, in more shame, be further spoken
That you are fool'd, discarded, and shook off,
By him for whom these shames ye underwent?
No; yet time serves wherein you may redeem
Your banish'd honours, and restore yourselves
Into the good thoughts of the world again;
Revenge the jeering and disdain'd contempt
Of this proud king, who studies day and night
To answer all the debt he owes to you
Even with the bloody payment of your deaths.
Therefore I say—
WORCESTER. Peace, cousin, say no more.
And now I will unclasp a secret book,
And to your quick-conceiving discontents
I'll read you matter deep and dangerous,
As full of peril and adventurous spirit
As to o'er-walk a current roaring loud
On the unsteadfast footing of a spear.
HOTSPUR. If he fall in, good night, or sink or swim.
Send danger from the east unto the west,
So honour cross it from the north to south,
And let them grapple. O, the blood more stirs
To rouse a lion than to start a hare!
NORTHUMBERLAND. Imagination of some great exploit
Drives him beyond the bounds of patience.
HOTSPUR. By heaven, methinks it were an easy leap
To pluck bright honour from the pale-fac'd moon;
Or dive into the bottom of the deep,

Where fathom-line could never touch the ground,
And pluck up drowned honour by the locks;
So he that doth redeem her thence might wear
Without corrival all her dignities.
But out upon this half-fac'd fellowship!
WORCESTER. He apprehends a world of figures here,
But not the form of what he should attend.
Good cousin, give me audience for a while.
HOTSPUR. I cry you mercy.
WORCESTER. Those same noble Scots
That are your prisoners—
HOTSPUR. I'll keep them all;
By God, he shall not have a Scot of them;
No, if a Scot would save his soul, he shall not.
I'll keep them, by this hand.
WORCESTER. You start away,
And lend no ear unto my purposes.
Those prisoners you shall keep.
HOTSPUR. Nay, I will; that's flat.
He said he would not ransom Mortimer;
Forbad my tongue to speak of Mortimer;
But I will find him when he lies asleep,
And in his ear I'll holla 'Mortimer!'
Nay,
I'll have a starling shall be taught to speak
Nothing but 'Mortimer,' and give it him
To keep his anger still in motion.
WORCESTER. Hear you, cousin; a word.
HOTSPUR. All studies here I solemnly defy,
Save how to gall and pinch this Bolingbroke.
And that same sword-and-buckler Prince of Wales—
But that I think his father loves him not
And would be glad he met with some mischance—
I would have him poison'd with a pot of ale.
WORCESTER. Farewell, kinsman: I'll talk to you
When you are better temper'd to attend.
NORTHUMBERLAND. Why, what a wasp-stung and impatient
fool
Art thou to break into this woman's mood,
Tying thine ear to no tongue but thine own!

HOTSPUR. Why, look you, I am whipt and scourg'd with
    rods,
  Nettled, and stung with pismires, when I hear
  Of this vile politician, Bolingbroke.
  In Richard's time—what do you call the place?—
  A plague upon it, it is in Gloucestershire—
  'Twas where the madcap duke his uncle kept—
  His uncle York—where I first bow'd my knee
  Unto this king of smiles, this Bolingbroke—
  'Sblood!
  When you and he came back from Ravenspurgh—
NORTHUMBERLAND. At Berkeley Castle.
HOTSPUR. You say true.
  Why, what a candy deal of courtesy
  This fawning greyhound then did proffer me!
  'Look when his infant fortune came to age'
  And 'gentle Harry Percy' and 'kind cousin'—
  O, the devil take such cozeners! God forgive me!
  Good uncle, tell your tale—I have done.
WORCESTER. Nay, if you have not, to it again;
  We will stay your leisure.
HOTSPUR. I have done, i' faith.
WORCESTER. Then once more to your Scottish prisoners:
  Deliver them up without their ransom straight,
  And make the Douglas' son your only mean
  For powers in Scotland; which, for divers reasons
  Which I shall send you written, be assur'd
  Will easily be granted. [To NORTHUMBERLAND] You, my
    lord,
  Your son in Scotland being thus employ'd,
  Shall secretly into the bosom creep
  Of that same noble prelate, well belov'd,
  The Archbishop.
HOTSPUR. Of York, is it not?
WORCESTER. True; who bears hard
  His brother's death at Bristow, the Lord Scroop.
  I speak not this in estimation,
  As what I think might be, but what I know
  Is ruminated, plotted, and set down,
  And only stays but to behold the face

Of that occasion that shall bring it on.

HOTSPUR. I smell it. Upon my life, it will do well.

NORTHUMBERLAND. Before the game is afoot thou still let'st
    slip.

HOTSPUR. Why, it cannot choose but be a noble plot.
    And then the power of Scotland and of York
    To join with Mortimer, ha?

WORCESTER. And so they shall.

HOTSPUR. In faith, it is exceedingly well aim'd.

WORCESTER. And 'tis no little reason bids us speed,
    To save our heads by raising of a head;
    For, bear ourselves as even as we can,
    The King will always think him in our debt,
    And think we think ourselves unsatisfied,
    Till he hath found a time to pay us home.
    And see already how he doth begin
    To make us strangers to his looks of love.

HOTSPUR. He does, he does. We'll be reveng'd on him.

WORCESTER. Cousin, farewell. No further go in this
    Than I by letters shall direct your course.
    When time is ripe, which will be suddenly,
    I'll steal to Glendower and Lord Mortimer;
    Where you and Douglas and our pow'rs at once,
    As I will fashion it, shall happily meet,
    To bear our fortunes in our own strong arms,
    Which now we hold at much uncertainty.

NORTHUMBERLAND. Farewell, good brother. We shall thrive,
    I trust.

HOTSPUR. Uncle, adieu. O, let the hours be short
    Till fields and blows and groans applaud our sport!

                             Exeunt

ACT II. SCENE 1

Rochester. An inn yard

Enter a CARRIER *with a lantern in his hand*

FIRST CARRIER. Heigh-ho! an it be not four by the day, I'll

be hang'd; Charles' wain is over the new chimney, and yet our horse not pack'd. What, ostler!

OSTLER. [*Within*] Anon, anon.

FIRST CARRIER. I prithee, Tom, beat Cut's saddle; put a few flocks in the point; poor jade is wrung in the withers out of all cess.

Enter another CARRIER

SECOND CARRIER. Peas and beans are as dank here as a dog, and that is the next way to give poor jades the bots; this house is turned upside down since Robin Ostler died.

FIRST CARRIER. Poor fellow never joyed since the price of oats rose; it was the death of him.

SECOND CARRIER. I think this be the most villainous house in all London road for fleas; I am stung like a tench.

FIRST CARRIER. Like a tench! By the mass, there is ne'er a king christen could be better bit than I have been since the first cock.

SECOND CARRIER. Why, they will allow us ne'er a jordan; and then we leak in your chimney; and your chamber-lye breeds fleas like a loach.

FIRST CARRIER. What, ostler! come away, and be hang'd; come away.

SECOND CARRIER. I have a gammon of bacon and two razes of ginger, to be delivered as far as Charing Cross.

FIRST CARRIER. God's body! the turkeys in my pannier are quite starved. What, ostler! A plague on thee! hast thou never an eye in thy head? Canst not hear? An 'twere not as good deed as drink to break the pate on thee, I am a very villain. Come, and be hang'd! Hast no faith in thee?

Enter GADSHILL

GADSHILL. Good morrow, carriers. What's o'clock?

FIRST CARRIER. I think it be two o'clock.

GADSHILL. I prithee lend me thy lantern to see my gelding in the stable.

FIRST CARRIER. Nay, by God! Soft! I know a trick worth two of that, i' faith.

GADSHILL. I pray thee lend me thine.

SECOND CARRIER. Ay, when, canst tell? Lend me thy lantern, quoth 'a? Marry, I'll see thee hang'd first.

GADSHILL. Sirrah carrier, what time do you mean to come to London?

SECOND CARRIER. Time enough to go to bed with a candle, I warrant thee. Come, neighbour Mugs, we'll call up the gentlemen; they will along with company, for they have great charge.   *Exeunt* CARRIERS

GADSHILL. What, ho! chamberlain!

CHAMBERLAIN. [*Within*] At hand, quoth pick-purse.

GADSHILL. That's even as fair as—at hand, quoth the chamberlain; for thou variest no more from picking of purses than giving direction doth from labouring; thou layest the plot how.

Enter CHAMBERLAIN

CHAMBERLAIN. Good morrow, Master Gadshill. It holds current that I told you yesternight: there's a franklin in the Wild of Kent hath brought three hundred marks with him in gold; I heard him tell it to one of his company last night at supper, a kind of auditor; one that hath abundance of charge too—God knows what. They are up already and call for eggs and butter; they will away presently.

GADSHILL. Sirrah, if they meet not with Saint Nicholas' clerks, I'll give thee this neck.

CHAMBERLAIN. No, I'll none of it; I pray thee keep that for the hangman; for I know thou worshippest Saint Nicholas as truly as a man of falsehood may.

GADSHILL. What talkest thou to me of the hangman? If I hang, I'll make a fat pair of gallows; for if I hang, old Sir John hangs with me; and thou knowest he is no starveling. Tut! there are other Troyans that thou dream'st not of, the which for sport sake are content to do the profession some grace; that would, if matters should be look'd into, for their own credit sake, make all whole. I am joined with no foot landrakers, no long-staff six-penny strikers, none of these mad mustachio purple-hu'd malt-worms; but with nobility and tranquillity, burgomasters and great oneyers, such as can hold in, such as will strike sooner than speak, and speak sooner than drink, and drink sooner than pray. And yet, zounds, I lie; for they pray continually to their saint, the commonwealth; or, rather, not pray to her, but prey on her; for they ride up and down on her, and make her their boots.

CHAMBERLAIN. What, the commonwealth their boots? Will she hold out water in foul way?

GADSHILL. She will, she will; justice hath liquor'd her. We steal as in a castle, cocksure; we have the receipt of fern-seed, we walk invisible.

CHAMBERLAIN. Nay, by my faith, I think you are more beholding to the night than to fern-seed for your walking invisible.

GADSHILL. Give me thy hand: thou shalt have a share in our purchase, as I am a true man.

CHAMBERLAIN. Nay, rather let me have it, as you are a false thief.

GADSHILL. Go to; 'homo' is a common name to all men. Bid the ostler bring my gelding out of the stable. Farewell, you muddy knave.   *Exeunt*

SCENE 2

The highway, near Gadshill

Enter the PRINCE OF WALES *and* POINS

POINS. Come, shelter, shelter; I have remov'd Falstaff's horse, and he frets like a gumm'd velvet.

PRINCE. Stand close.

Enter FALSTAFF

FALSTAFF. Poins! Poins! And be hang'd! Poins!

PRINCE. Peace, ye fat-kidney'd rascal; what a brawling dost thou keep!

FALSTAFF. Where's Poins, Hal?

PRINCE. He is walk'd up to the top of the hill; I'll go seek him.

FALSTAFF. I am accurs'd to rob in that thief's company; the rascal hath removed my horse, and tied him I know not where. If I travel but four foot by the squier further afoot, I shall break my wind. Well, I doubt not but to die a fair death for all this, if I scape hanging for killing that rogue.

I have forsworn his company hourly any time this two
and twenty years, and yet I am bewitch'd with the rogue's
company. If the rascal have not given me medicines to
make me love him, I'll be hang'd. It could not be else: I
have drunk medicines. Poins! Hal! A plague upon you
both! Bardolph! Peto! I'll starve ere I'll rob a foot further.
An 'twere not as good a deed as drink to turn true man,
and to leave these rogues, I am the veriest varlet that ever
chewed with a tooth. Eight yards of uneven ground is
threescore and ten miles afoot with me; and the stony-
hearted villains know it well enough. A plague upon it,
when thieves cannot be true one to another! [*They
whistle*] Whew! A plague upon you all! Give me my
horse, you rogues; give me my horse, and be hang'd.

PRINCE. Peace, ye fat-guts! lie down; lay thine ear close to
the ground, and list if thou canst hear the tread of travellers.

FALSTAFF. Have you any levers to lift me up again, being
down? 'Sblood, I'll not bear mine own flesh so far afoot
again for all the coin in thy father's exchequer. What a
plague mean ye to colt me thus?

PRINCE. Thou liest: thou art not colted, thou art uncolted.

FALSTAFF. I prithee, good Prince Hal, help me to my horse,
good king's son.

PRINCE. Out, ye rogue! shall I be your ostler?

FALSTAFF. Hang thyself in thine own heir-apparent garters.
If I be ta'en, I'll peach for this. An I have not ballads
made on you all, and sung to filthy tunes, let a cup of sack
be my poison. When a jest is so forward, and afoot too!—
I hate it.

Enter GADSHILL, BARDOLPH *and* PETO *with him*

GADSHILL. Stand!

FALSTAFF. So I do, against my will.

POINS. O, 'tis our setter: I know his voice. Bardolph, what
news?

BARDOLPH. Case ye, case ye; on with your vizards: there's
money of the King's coming down the hill; 'tis going to
the King's exchequer.

FALSTAFF. You lie, ye rogue; 'tis going to the King's tavern.

GADSHILL. There's enough to make us all.

FALSTAFF. To be hang'd.

PRINCE. Sirs, you four shall front them in the narrow lane; Ned Poins and I will walk lower; if they scape from your encounter, then they light on us.

PETO. How many be there of them?

GADSHILL. Some eight or ten.

FALSTAFF. Zounds, will they not rob us?

PRINCE. What, a coward, Sir John Paunch?

FALSTAFF. Indeed, I am not John of Gaunt, your grandfather; but yet no coward, Hal.

PRINCE. Well, we leave that to the proof.

POINS. Sirrah Jack, thy horse stands behind the hedge: when thou need'st him, there thou shalt find him. Farewell, and stand fast.

FALSTAFF. Now cannot I strike him, if I should be hang'd.

PRINCE. [*Aside to* POINS] Ned, where are our disguises?

POINS. [*Aside*] Here, hard by; stand close.

Exeunt the PRINCE *and* POINS

FALSTAFF. Now, my masters, happy man be his dole, say I; every man to his business.

Enter the TRAVELLERS

FIRST TRAVELLER. Come, neighbour; the boy shall lead our horses down the hill; we'll walk afoot awhile, and ease our legs.

THIEVES. Stand!

TRAVELLERS. Jesus bless us!

FALSTAFF. Strike; down with them; cut the villains' throats. Ah, whoreson caterpillars! bacon-fed knaves! They hate us youth. Down with them; fleece them.

TRAVELLERS. O, we are undone, both we and ours for ever!

FALSTAFF. Hang ye, gorbellied knaves, are ye undone? No, ye fat chuffs; I would your store were here. On, bacons, on! What, ye knaves! young men must live. You are grand-jurors, are ye? we'll jure ye, faith.

[*Here they rob them and bind them. Exeunt*]

Re-enter the PRINCE *and* POINS *in buckram*

PRINCE. The thieves have bound the true men. Now, could

thou and I rob the thieves and go merrily to London, it would be argument for a week, laughter for a month, and a good jest for ever.

POINS. Stand close; I hear them coming.

Enter the THIEVES *again*

FALSTAFF. Come, my masters, let us share, and then to horse before day. An the Prince and Poins be not two arrant cowards, there's no equity stirring. There's no more valour in that Poins than in a wild duck.

[As they are sharing, the PRINCE and POINS set
upon them]

PRINCE. Your money!

POINS. Villains!

[They all run away, and FALSTAFF, after a blow or two,
runs away too, leaving the booty behind them]

PRINCE. Got with much ease. Now merrily to horse.
The thieves are all scatter'd, and possess'd with fear
So strongly that they dare not meet each other;
Each takes his fellow for an officer.
Away, good Ned. Falstaff sweats to death
And lards the lean earth as he walks along.
Were't not for laughing, I should pity him.

POINS. How the fat rogue roar'd!   *Exeunt*

SCENE 3

Warkworth Castle

Enter HOTSPUR *solus, reading a letter*

HOTSPUR. 'But, for mine own part, my lord, I could be well contented to be there, in respect of the love I bear your house.' He could be contented—why is he not, then? In respect of the love he bears our house—he shows in this he loves his own barn better than he loves our house. Let me see some more. 'The purpose you undertake is dangerous' —why, that's certain: 'tis dangerous to take a cold, to sleep, to drink; but I tell you, my lord fool, out of this nettle, danger, we pluck this flower, safety. 'The purpose you undertake is dangerous; the friends you have named uncertain; the time itself unsorted; and your whole plot too light for the counterpoise of so great an opposition.' Say you so, say you so? I say unto you again, you are a shallow, cowardly hind, and you lie. What a lack-brain is this! By the Lord, our plot is a good plot as ever was laid; our friends true and constant—a good plot, good friends, and full of expectation; an excellent plot, very good friends. What a frosty-spirited rogue is this! Why, my Lord of York commends the plot and the general course of the action. Zounds, an I were now by this rascal, I could brain him with his lady's fan. Is there not my father, my uncle, and myself; Lord Edmund Mortimer, my Lord of York, and Owen Glendower? Is there not, besides, the Douglas? Have I not all their letters to meet me in arms by the ninth of the next month, and are they not some of them set forward already? What a pagan rascal is this! an infidel! Ha! you shall see now, in very sincerity of fear and cold heart, will he to the King and lay open all our proceedings. O, I could divide myself and go to buffets for moving such a dish of skim milk with so honourable an action! Hang him; let him tell the King: we are prepared. I will set forward to-night.

Enter LADY PERCY

How now, Kate! I must leave within these two hours.
LADY PERCY. O my good lord, why are you thus alone?
For what offence have I this fortnight been
A banish'd woman from my Harry's bed?
Tell me, sweet lord, what is't that takes from thee
Thy stomach, pleasure, and thy golden sleep?
Why dost thou bend thine eyes upon the earth,
And start so often when thou sit'st alone?
Why hast thou lost the fresh blood in thy cheeks,
And given my treasures and my rights of thee
To thick-ey'd musing and curs'd melancholy?
In thy faint slumbers I by thee have watch'd,
And heard thee murmur tales of iron wars;
Speak terms of manage to thy bounding steed;
Cry 'Courage! To the field!' And thou hast talk'd

Of sallies and retires, of trenches, tents,
Of palisadoes, frontiers, parapets,
Of basilisks, of cannon, culverin,
Of prisoners' ransom, and of soldiers slain,
And all the currents of a heady fight.
Thy spirit within thee hath been so at war,
And thus hath so bestirr'd thee in thy sleep,
That beads of sweat have stood upon thy brow
Like bubbles in a late disturbed stream;
And in thy face strange motions have appear'd,
Such as we see when men restrain their breath
On some great sudden hest. O, what portents are these?
Some heavy business hath my lord in hand,
And I must know it, else he loves me not.
HOTSPUR. What, ho!

Enter a SERVANT

Is Gilliams with the packet gone?
SERVANT. He is, my lord, an hour ago.
HOTSPUR. Hath Butler brought those horses from the sheriff?
SERVANT. One horse, my lord, he brought even now.
HOTSPUR. What horse? A roan, a crop-ear, is it not?
SERVANT. It is, my lord.
HOTSPUR. That roan shall be my throne.
  Well, I will back him straight. O esperance!
  Bid Butler lead him forth into the park.   *Exit* SERVANT
LADY PERCY. But hear you, my lord.
HOTSPUR. What say'st thou, my lady?
LADY PERCY. What is it carries you away?
HOTSPUR. Why, my horse, my love, my horse.
LADY PERCY. Out, you mad-headed ape!
  A weasel hath not such a deal of spleen
  As you are toss'd with. In faith,
  I'll know your business, Harry, that I will.
  I fear my brother Mortimer doth stir
  About his title and hath sent for you
  To line his enterprise; but if you go—
HOTSPUR. So far afoot, I shall be weary, love.
LADY PERCY. Come, come, you paraquito, answer me
  Directly unto this question that I ask.

In faith, I'll break thy little finger, Harry,
An if thou wilt not tell me all things true.
HOTSPUR. Away.
  Away, you trifler! Love, I love thee not,
I care not for thee, Kate; this is no world
To play with mammets and to tilt with lips:
We must have bloody noses and crack'd crowns,
And pass them current too. God's me, my horse!
What say'st thou, Kate? what wouldst thou have with me?
LADY PERCY. Do you not love me? Do you not, indeed?
  Well, do not, then; for since you love me not,
I will not love myself. Do you not love me?
Nay, tell me if you speak in jest or no.
HOTSPUR. Come, wilt thou see me ride?
  And when I am o' horseback, I will swear
I love thee infinitely. But hark you, Kate:
I must not have you henceforth question me
Whither I go, nor reason whereabout.
Whither I must, I must; and, to conclude,
This evening must I leave you, gentle Kate.
I know you wise, but yet no farther wise
Than Harry Percy's wife; constant you are,
But yet a woman; and for secrecy,
No lady closer; for I well believe
Thou wilt not utter what thou dost not know,
And so far will I trust thee, gentle Kate.
LADY PERCY. How, so far?
HOTSPUR. Not an inch further. But hark you, Kate:
  Whither I go, thither shall you go too;
To-day will I set forth, to-morrow you.
Will this content you, Kate?
LADY PERCY. It must, of force.   *Exeunt*

SCENE 4

Eastcheap. The Boar's Head Tavern

Enter the PRINCE, *and* POINS

PRINCE. Ned, prithee, come out of that fat room and lend
me thy hand to laugh a little.

POINS. Where hast been, Hal?

PRINCE. With three or four loggerheads amongst three or fourscore hogsheads. I have sounded the very base-string of humility. Sirrah, I am sworn brother to a leash of drawers and can call them all by their christen names, as Tom, Dick, and Francis. They take it already upon their salvation that though I be but Prince of Wales yet I am the king of courtesy; and tell me flatly I am no proud Jack, like Falstaff, but a Corinthian, a lad of mettle, a good boy—by the Lord, so they call me—and when I am King of England I shall command all the good lads in Eastcheap. They call drinking deep, dyeing scarlet; and when you breathe in your watering, they cry 'hem!' and bid you play it off. To conclude, I am so good a proficient in one quarter of an hour that I can drink with any tinker in his own language during my life. I tell thee, Ned, thou hast lost much honour that thou wert not with me in this action. But, sweet Ned—to sweeten which name of Ned, I give thee this pennyworth of sugar, clapp'd even now into my hand by an under-skinker, one that never spake other English in his life than 'Eight shillings and sixpence' and 'You are welcome' with this shrill addition, 'Anon, anon, sir! Score a pint of bastard in the Half-moon' or so. But, Ned, to drive away the time till Falstaff come, I prithee, do thou stand in some by-room, while I question my puny drawer to what end he gave me the sugar; and do thou never leave calling 'Francis!' that his tale to me may be nothing but 'Anon.' Step aside, and I'll show thee a precedent.   *Exit* POINS

POINS. [*Within*] Francis!

PRINCE. Thou are perfect.

POINS. [*Within*] Francis!

Enter FRANCIS

FRANCIS. Anon, anon, sir. Look down into the Pomgarnet, Ralph.

PRINCE. Come thither, Francis.

FRANCIS. My lord?

PRINCE. How long hast thou to serve, Francis?

FRANCIS. Forsooth, five years, and as much as to—

POINS. [*Within*] Francis!

FRANCIS. Anon, anon, sir.

PRINCE. Five year! by'r lady, a long lease for the clinking of pewter. But, Francis, darest thou be so valiant as to play the coward with thy indenture and show it a fair pair of heels and run from it?

FRANCIS. O Lord, sir, I'll be sworn upon all the books in England, I could find in my heart—

POINS. [*Within*] Francis!

FRANCIS. Anon, sir.

PRINCE. How old art thou, Francis?

FRANCIS. Let me see, about Michaelmas next I shall be—.

POINS. [*Within*] Francis!

FRANCIS. Anon, sir. Pray stay a little, my lord.

PRINCE. Nay, but hark you, Francis: for the sugar thou gavest me—'twas a pennyworth, was't not?

FRANCIS. O Lord, I would it had been two!

PRINCE. I will give thee for it a thousand pound; ask me when thou wilt, and thou shalt have it.

POINS. [*Within*] Francis!

FRANCIS. Anon, anon.

PRINCE. Anon, Francis? No, Francis; but to-morrow, Francis; or, Francis, o' Thursday; or indeed, Francis, when thou wilt. But, Francis—

FRANCIS. My lord?

PRINCE. Wilt thou rob this leathern jerkin, crystal-button, knot-pated, agate-ring, puke-stocking, caddis-garter, smooth-tongue, Spanish-pouch—

FRANCIS. O Lord, sir, who do you mean?

PRINCE. Why, then, your brown bastard is your only drink; for, look you, Francis, your white canvas doublet will sully. In Barbary, sir, it cannot come to so much.

FRANCIS. What, sir?

POINS. [*Within*] Francis!

PRINCE. Away, you rogue! Dost thou not hear them call?
[*Here they both call him;* FRANCIS *stands amazed, not knowing which way to go*]

Enter VINTNER

VINTNER. What, stand'st thou still, and hear'st such a calling? Look to the guests within. [*Exit* FRANCIS] My lord, old Sir John, with half-a-dozen more, are at the door. Shall I let them in?

PRINCE. Let them alone awhile, and then open the door. [*Exit* VINTNER] Poins!

Re-enter POINS

POINS. Anon, anon, sir.

PRINCE. Sirrah, Falstaff and the rest of the thieves are at the door. Shall we be merry?

POINS. As merry as crickets, my lad. But hark ye: what cunning match have you made with this jest of the drawer? Come, what's the issue?

PRINCE. I am now of all humours that have showed themselves humours since the old days of goodman Adam to the pupil-age of this present twelve o'clock at midnight.

Re-enter FRANCIS

What's o'clock, Francis?

FRANCIS. Anon, anon, sir.   *Exit*

PRINCE. That ever this fellow should have fewer words than a parrot, and yet the son of a woman! His industry is up-stairs and downstairs; his eloquence the parcel of a reckon-ing. I am not yet of Percy's mind, the Hotspur of the north; he that kills me some six or seven dozen of Scots at a breakfast, washes his hands, and says to his wife 'Fie upon this quiet life! I want work.' 'O my sweet Harry,' says she 'how many hast thou kill'd to-day?' 'Give my roan horse a drench' says he; and answers 'Some fourteen,' an hour after, 'a trifle, a trifle.' I prithee call in Falstaff; I'll play Percy, and that damn'd brawn shall play Dame Mortimer his wife. 'Rivo!' says the drunkard. Call in ribs, call in tallow.

Enter FALSTAFF, GADSHILL, BARDOLPH, *and* PETO;
followed by FRANCIS *with wine*

POINS. Welcome Jack. Where hast thou been?

FALSTAFF. A plague of all cowards, I say, and a vengeance too! Marry and amen! Give me a cup of sack, boy. Ere I lead this life long, I'll sew nether-stocks, and mend them

and foot them too. A plague of all cowards! Give me a
cup of sack, rogue. Is there no virtue extant? [*He drinks*]

PRINCE. Didst thou never see Titan kiss a dish of butter,
pitiful-hearted Titan, that melted at the sweet tale of the
sun's? If thou did'st, then behold that compound.

FALSTAFF. You rogue, here's lime in this sack too! There is
nothing but roguery to be found in villainous man; yet a
coward is worse than a cup of sack with lime in it. A
villainous coward! Go thy ways, old Jack; die when thou
wilt; if manhood, good manhood, be not forgot upon the
face of the earth, then am I a shotten herring. There lives
not three good men unhang'd in England, and one of them
is fat and grows old. God help the while! A bad world, I
say. I would I were a weaver; I could sing psalms or anything. A plague of all cowards, I say still.

PRINCE. How now, woolsack! What mutter you?

FALSTAFF. A king's son! If I do not beat thee out of thy
kingdom with a dagger of lath, and drive all thy subjects
afore thee like a flock of wild geese, I'll never wear hair on
my face more. You Prince of Wales!

PRINCE. Why, you whoreson round man, what's the matter?

FALSTAFF. Are not you a coward? Answer me to that—and
Poins there?

POINS. Zounds, ye fat paunch, an ye call me coward, by the
Lord, I'll stab thee.

FALSTAFF. I call thee coward! I'll see thee damn'd ere I call
thee coward; but I would give a thousand pound I could
run as fast as thou canst. You are straight enough in the
shoulders—you care not who sees your back. Call you that
backing of your friends? A plague upon such backing!
Give me them that will face me. Give me a cup of sack;
I am a rogue if I drunk to-day.

PRINCE. O villain! thy lips are scarce wip'd since thou
drunk'st last.

FALSTAFF. All is one for that. [*He drinks*] A plague of all
cowards, still say I.

PRINCE. What's the matter?

FALSTAFF. What's the matter! There be four of us here have
ta'en a thousand pound this day morning.

PRINCE. Where is it, Jack? Where is it?

FALSTAFF. Where is it! taken from us it is: a hundred upon poor four of us.

PRINCE. What, a hundred, man?

FALSTAFF. I am a rogue if I were not at half-sword with a dozen of them two hours together. I have scap'd by miracle. I am eight times thrust through the doublet, four through the hose; my buckler cut through and through; my sword hack'd like a hand-saw—ecce signum! I never dealt better since I was a man—all would not do. A plague of all cowards! Let them speak; if they speak more or less than truth, they are villains and the sons of darkness.

PRINCE. Speak, sirs; how was it?

GADSHILL. We four set upon some dozen—

FALSTAFF. Sixteen at least, my lord.

GADSHILL. And bound them.

PETO. No, no, they were not bound.

FALSTAFF. You rogue, they were bound, every man of them; or I am a Jew else, an Ebrew Jew.

GADSHILL. As we were sharing, some six or seven fresh men set upon us—

FALSTAFF. And unbound the rest, and then come in the other.

PRINCE. What, fought you with them all?

FALSTAFF. All! I know not what you call all, but if I fought not with fifty of them, I am a bunch of radish. If there were not two or three and fifty upon poor old Jack, then am I no two-legg'd creature.

PRINCE. Pray God you have not murd'red some of them.

FALSTAFF. Nay, that's past praying for: I have pepper'd two of them; two I am sure I have paid—two rogues in buckram suits. I tell thee what, Hal, if I tell thee a lie, spit in my face, call me horse. Thou knowest my old ward: here I lay, and thus I bore my point. Four rogues in buckram let drive at me—

PRINCE. What, four? Thou saidst but two even now.

FALSTAFF. Four, Hal; I told thee four.

POINS. Ay, ay, he said four.

FALSTAFF. These four came all afront, and mainly thrust at me. I made me no more ado but took all their seven points in my target, thus.

PRINCE. Seven? Why, there were but four even now.

FALSTAFF. In buckram.

POINS. Ay, four in buckram suits.

FALSTAFF. Seven, by these hilts, or I am a villain else.

PRINCE. [*Aside to* POINS] Prithee, let him alone; we shall have more anon.

FALSTAFF. Dost thou hear me, Hal?

PRINCE. Ay, and mark thee too, Jack.

FALSTAFF. Do so, for it is worth the list'ning to. These nine in buckram that I told thee of—

PRINCE. So, two more already.

FALSTAFF. Their points being broken—

POINS. Down fell their hose.

FALSTAFF. Began to give me ground; but I followed me close, came in foot and hand, and with a thought seven of the eleven I paid.

PRINCE. O monstrous! eleven buckram men grown out of two!

FALSTAFF. But, as the devil would have it, three misbegotten knaves in Kendal green came at my back and let drive at me—for it was so dark, Hal, that thou couldest not see thy hand.

PRINCE. These lies are like their father that begets them— gross as a mountain, open, palpable. Why, thou clay-brain'd guts, thou knotty-pated fool, thou whoreson, ob-scene, greasy tallow-catch—

FALSTAFF. What, art thou mad! art thou mad? Is not the truth the truth!

PRINCE. Why, how couldst thou know these men in Kendal green, when it was so dark thou couldst not see thy hand? Come, tell us your reason; what sayest thou to this?

POINS. Come, your reason, Jack, your reason.

FALSTAFF. What, upon compulsion? Zounds, an I were at the strappado, or all the racks in the world, I would not tell you on compulsion. Give you a reason on compulsion! If reasons were as plentiful as blackberries, I would give no man a reason upon compulsion, I.

PRINCE. I'll be no longer guilty of this sin; this sanguine coward, this bed-presser, this horse-back-breaker, this huge hill of flesh—

ACT II. SCENE 4

FALSTAFF. 'Sblood, you starveling, you eel-skin, you dried neat's-tongue, you bull's pizzle, you stock-fish—O for breath to utter what is like thee!—you tailor's yard, you sheath, you bow-case, you vile standing tuck.

PRINCE. Well, breathe awhile, and then to it again; and when thou hast tired thyself in base comparisons, hear me speak but this.

POINS. Mark, Jack.

PRINCE. We two saw you four set on four, and bound them and were masters of their wealth. Mark now, how a plain tale shall put you down. Then did we two set on you four; and, with a word, out-fac'd you from your prize, and have it; yea, and can show it you here in the house. And, Falstaff, you carried your guts away as nimbly, with as quick dexterity, and roar'd for mercy, and still run and roar'd, as ever I heard bull-calf. What a slave art thou to hack thy sword as thou hast done, and then say it was in fight! What trick, what device, what starting-hole, canst thou now find out to hide thee from this open and apparent shame?

POINS. Come, let's hear, Jack; what trick hast thou now?

FALSTAFF. By the Lord, I knew ye as well as he that made ye. Why, hear you, my masters: was it for me to kill the heir-apparent? Should I turn upon the true prince? Why, thou knowest I am as valiant as Hercules; but beware instinct—the lion will not touch the true prince. Instinct is a great matter: I was now a coward on instinct. I shall think the better of myself and thee during my life—I for a valiant lion, and thou for a true prince. But, by the Lord, lads, I am glad you have the money. Hostess, clap to the doors. Watch to-night, pray to-morrow. Gallants, lads, boys, hearts of gold, all the titles of good fellowship come to you! What, shall we be merry? Shall we have a play extempore?

PRINCE. Content—and the argument shall be thy running away.

FALSTAFF. Ah, no more of that, Hal, an thou lovest me!

Enter HOSTESS

HOSTESS. O Jesu, my lord the Prince!

PRINCE. How now, my lady the hostess!
What say'st thou to me?

HOSTESS. Marry, my lord, there is a nobleman of the court at door would speak with you; he says he comes from your father.

PRINCE. Give him as much as will make him a royal man, and send him back again to my mother.

FALSTAFF. What manner of man is he?

HOSTESS. An old man.

FALSTAFF. What doth gravity out of his bed at midnight? Shall I give him his answer?

PRINCE. Prithee do, Jack.

FALSTAFF. Faith, and I'll send him packing.   *Exit*

PRINCE. Now, sirs: by'r lady, you fought fair; so did you, Peto; so did you, Bardolph. You are lions too: you ran away upon instinct; you will not touch the true prince; no, fie!

BARDOLPH. Faith, I ran when I saw others run.

PRINCE. Faith, tell me now in earnest, how came Falstaff's sword so hack'd?

PETO. Why, he hack'd it with his dagger, and said he would swear truth out of England but he would make you believe it was done in fight; and persuaded us to do the like.

BARDOLPH. Yea, and to tickle our noses with spear-grass to make them bleed, and then to beslubber our garments with it, and swear it was the blood of true men. I did that I did not this seven year before—I blush'd to hear his monstrous devices.

PRINCE. O villain! Thou stolest a cup of sack eighteen years ago, and wert taken with the manner, and ever since thou hast blush'd extempore. Thou hadst fire and sword on thy side, and yet thou ran'st away; what instinct hadst thou for it?

BARDOLPH. My lord, do you see these meteors? do you behold these exhalations?

PRINCE. I do.

BARDOLPH. What think you they portend?

PRINCE. Hot livers and cold purses.

BARDOLPH. Choler, my lord, if rightly taken.

PRINCE. No, if rightly taken, halter.

ACT II. SCENE 4

Re-enter FALSTAFF

Here comes lean Jack, here comes bare-bone. How now, my sweet creature of bombast! How long is't ago, Jack, since thou sawest thine own knee?

FALSTAFF. My own knee! When I was about thy years, Hal, I was not an eagle's talon in the waist: I could have crept into any alderman's thumb-ring. A plague of sighing and grief! it blows a man up like a bladder. There's villainous news abroad. Here was Sir John Bracy from your father: you must to the court in the morning. That same mad fellow of the north, Percy, and he of Wales that gave Amaimon the bastinado, and made Lucifer cuckold, and swore the devil his true liegeman upon the cross of a Welsh hook—what a plague call you him?

POINS. O, Glendower.

FALSTAFF. Owen, Owen—the same; and his son-in-law Mortimer, and old Northumberland, and that sprightly Scot of Scots, Douglas, that runs o' horseback up a hill perpendicular—

PRINCE. He that rides at high speed and with his pistol kills a sparrow flying?

FALSTAFF. You have hit it.

PRINCE. So did he never the sparrow.

FALSTAFF. Well, that rascal hath good mettle in him; he will not run.

PRINCE. Why, what a rascal art thou, then, to praise him so for running!

FALSTAFF. O' horseback, ye cuckoo; but afoot he will not budge a foot.

PRINCE. Yes, Jack, upon instinct.

FALSTAFF. I grant ye, upon instinct. Well, he is there too, and one Mordake, and a thousand blue-caps more. Worcester is stol'n away to-night; thy father's beard is turn'd white with the news; you may buy land now as cheap as stinking mack'rel.

PRINCE. Why, then, it is like, if there come a hot June, and this civil buffeting hold, we shall buy maidenheads as they buy hob-nails, by the hundreds.

FALSTAFF. By the mass, lad, thou sayest true: it is like we

shall have good trading that way. But tell me, Hal, art not thou horrible afeard? Thou being heir-apparent, could the world pick thee out three such enemies again as that fiend Douglas, that spirit Percy, and that devil Glendower? Art thou not horribly afraid? Doth not thy blood thrill at it?

PRINCE. Not a whit, i' faith; I lack some of thy instinct.

FALSTAFF. Well, thou wilt be horribly chid to-morrow when thou comest to thy father. If thou love me, practise an answer.

PRINCE. Do thou stand for my father, and examine me upon the particulars of my life.

FALSTAFF. Shall I? Content! This chair shall be my state, this dagger my sceptre, and this cushion my crown.

PRINCE. Thy state is taken for a join'd-stool, thy golden sceptre for a leaden dagger, and thy precious rich crown for a pitiful bald crown!

FALSTAFF. Well, an the fire of grace be not quite out of thee, now shalt thou be moved. Give me a cup of sack to make my eyes look red, that it may be thought I have wept; for I must speak in passion, and I will do it in King Cambyses' vein.

PRINCE. Well, here is my leg.

FALSTAFF. And here is my speech. Stand aside, nobility.

HOSTESS. O Jesu, this is excellent sport, i' faith!

FALSTAFF. Weep not, sweet queen, for trickling tears are vain.

HOSTESS. O, the father, how he holds his countenance!

FALSTAFF. For God's sake, lords, convey my tristful queen; For tears do stop the floodgates of her eyes.

HOSTESS. O Jesu, he doth it as like one of these harlotry players as ever I see!

FALSTAFF. Peace, good pint-pot; peace, good tickle-brain.— Harry, I do not only marvel where thou spendest thy time, but also how thou art accompanied; for though the camomile, the more it is trodden on the faster it grows, yet youth, the more it is wasted the sooner it wears. That thou art my son I have partly thy mother's word, partly my own opinion, but chiefly a villainous trick of thine eye, and a foolish hanging of thy nether lip, that doth warrant me. If then thou be son to me, here lies the point:

why, being son to me, art thou so pointed at? Shall the
blessed sun of heaven prove a micher and eat blackberries?
A question not to be ask'd. Shall the son of England prove
a thief and take purses? A question to be ask'd. There is a
thing, Harry, which thou hast often heard of, and it is
known to many in our land by the name of pitch. This
pitch, as ancient writers do report, doth defile; so doth the
company thou keepest; for, Harry, now I do not speak to
thee in drink, but in tears; not in pleasure, but in passion;
not in words only, but in woes also. And yet there is a
virtuous man whom I have often noted in thy company,
but I know not his name.

PRINCE. What manner of man, an it like your Majesty?

FALSTAFF. A goodly portly man, i' faith, and a corpulent; of
a cheerful look, a pleasing eye, and a most noble carriage;
and, as I think, his age some fifty, or, by 'r lady, inclining
to three-score. And now I remember me, his name is Falstaff. If that man should be lewdly given, he deceiveth me;
for, Harry, I see virtue in his looks. If then the tree may
be known by the fruit, as the fruit by the tree, then,
peremptorily I speak it, there is virtue in that Falstaff:
him keep with, the rest banish. And tell me now, thou
naughty varlet, tell me, where hast thou been this month?

PRINCE. Dost thou speak like a king? Do thou stand for me,
and I'll play my father.

FALSTAFF. Depose me? If thou dost it half so gravely, so
majestically, both in word and matter, hang me up by the
heels for a rabbit-sucker or a poulter's hare.

PRINCE. Well, here I am set.

FALSTAFF. And here I stand. Judge, my masters.

PRINCE. Now, Harry, whence come you?

FALSTAFF. My noble lord, from Eastcheap.

PRINCE. The complaints I hear of thee are grievous.

FALSTAFF. 'Sblood, my lord, they are false. Nay, I'll tickle
ye for a young prince, i' faith.

PRINCE. Swearest thou, ungracious boy? Henceforth ne'er
look on me. Thou art violently carried away from grace;
there is a devil haunts thee in the likeness of an old fat
man; a tun of man is thy companion. Why dost thou converse with that trunk of humours, that bolting-hutch of

beastliness, that swoll'n parcel of dropsies, that huge bombard of sack, that stuff'd cloak-bag of guts, that roasted Manningtree ox with the pudding in his belly, that reverend vice, that grey iniquity, that father ruffian, that vanity in years? Wherein is he good, but to taste sack and drink it? wherein neat and cleanly, but to carve a capon and eat it? wherein cunning, but in craft? wherein crafty, but in villainy? wherein villainous, but in all things? wherein worthy, but in nothing?

FALSTAFF. I would your Grace would take me with you; whom means your Grace?

PRINCE. That villainous abominable misleader of youth, Falstaff, that old white-bearded Satan.

FALSTAFF. My lord, the man I know.

PRINCE. I know thou dost.

FALSTAFF. But to say I know more harm in him than in myself were to say more than I know. That he is old—the more the pity—his white hairs do witness it; but that he is —saving your reverence—a whoremaster, that I utterly deny. If sack and sugar be a fault, God help the wicked! If to be old and merry be a sin, then many an old host that I know is damn'd; if to be fat be to be hated, then Pharaoh's lean kine are to be loved. No, my good lord: banish Peto, banish Bardolph, banish Poins; but, for sweet Jack Falstaff, kind Jack Falstaff, true Jack Falstaff, valiant Jack Falstaff —and therefore more valiant, being, as he is, old Jack Falstaff—banish not him thy Harry's company, banish not him thy Harry's company. Banish plump Jack, and banish all the world.

PRINCE. I do, I will.   *[A knocking heard]*

Exeunt HOSTESS, FRANCIS, *and* BARDOLPH

Re-enter BARDOLPH, *running*

BARDOLPH. O, my lord, my lord! the sheriff with a most monstrous watch is at the door.

FALSTAFF. Out, ye rogue! Play out the play: I have much to say in the behalf of that Falstaff.

Re-enter the HOSTESS

HOSTESS. O Jesu, my lord, my lord!

PRINCE. Heigh, heigh! the devil rides upon a fiddle-stick;
what's the matter?

HOSTESS. The sheriff and all the watch are at the door; they
are come to search the house. Shall I let them in?

FALSTAFF. Dost thou hear, Hal? Never call a true piece of
gold a counterfeit. Thou art essentially made, without
seeming so.

PRINCE. And thou a natural coward, without instinct.

FALSTAFF. I deny your major. If you will deny the sheriff,
so; if not, let him enter. If I become not a cart as well as
another man, a plague on my bringing up! I hope I shall
as soon be strangled with a halter as another.

PRINCE. Go, hide thee behind the arras; the rest walk up
above. Now, my masters, for a true face and good conscience.

FALSTAFF. Both which I have had; but their date is out, and
therefore I'll hide me.   *Exeunt all but the* PRINCE *and* PETO

PRINCE. Call in the sheriff.

Enter SHERIFF *and the* CARRIER

Now, master sheriff, what is your will with me?

SHERIFF. First, pardon me, my lord. A hue and cry
Hath followed certain men unto this house.

PRINCE. What men?

SHERIFF. One of them is well known, my gracious lord—
A gross fat man.

CARRIER. As fat as butter.

PRINCE. The man, I do assure you, is not here,
For I myself at this time have employ'd him.
And, sheriff, I will engage my word to thee
That I will, by to-morrow dinner-time,
Send him to answer thee, or any man,
For any thing he shall be charg'd withal;
And so let me entreat you leave the house.

SHERIFF. I will, my lord. There are two gentlemen
Have in this robbery lost three hundred marks.

PRINCE. It may be so; if he have robb'd these men
He shall be answerable; and so, farewell.

SHERIFF. Good night, my noble lord.

PRINCE. I think it is good morrow, is it not?

SHERIFF. Indeed, my lord, I think it be two o'clock.

Exeunt SHERIFF *and* CARRIER

PRINCE. This oily rascal is known as well as Paul's. Go, call him forth.

PETO. Falstaff! Fast asleep behind the arras, and snorting like a horse.

PRINCE. Hark how hard he fetches breath. Search his pockets. [*He searcheth his pocket, and findeth certain papers*] What hast thou found?

PETO. Nothing but papers, my lord.

PRINCE. Let's see what they be: read them.

PETO. [*Reads*]

Item, A capon	2s.	2d.
Item, Sauce		4d.
Item, Sack, two gallons	5s.	8d.
Item, Anchovies and sack after supper .	2s.	6d.
Item, Bread		ob.

PRINCE. O monstrous! but one halfpennyworth of bread to this intolerable deal of sack! What there is else, keep close; we'll read it at more advantage. There let him sleep till day. I'll to the court in the morning. We must all to the wars, and thy place shall be honourable. I'll procure this fat rogue a charge of foot; and I know his death will be a march of twelve-score. The money shall be paid back again with advantage. Be with me betimes in the morning; and so, good morrow, Peto.

PETO. Good morrow, good my lord.   *Exeunt*

ACT III. SCENE 1

Wales. GLENDOWER'S *castle*

Enter HOTSPUR, WORCESTER, MORTIMER, *and* GLENDOWER

MORTIMER. These promises are fair, the parties sure,
    And our induction full of prosperous hope.

HOTSPUR. Lord Mortimer, and cousin Glendower,
    Will you sit down?

And uncle Worcester—a plague upon it!
I have forgot the map.
GLENDOWER. No, here it is.
  Sit, cousin Percy; sit, good cousin Hotspur,
  For by that name as oft as Lancaster
  Doth speak of you, his cheek looks pale, and with
  A rising sigh he wisheth you in heaven.
HOTSPUR. And you in hell, as oft as he hears
  Owen Glendower spoke of.
GLENDOWER. I cannot blame him: at my nativity
  The front of heaven was full of fiery shapes,
  Of burning cressets; and at my birth
  The frame and huge foundation of the earth
  Shaked like a coward.
HOTSPUR. Why, so it would have done at the same season if
  your mother's cat had but kitten'd, though yourself had
  never been born.
GLENDOWER. I say the earth did shake when I was born.
HOTSPUR. And I say the earth was not of my mind,
  If you suppose as fearing you it shook.
GLENDOWER. The heavens were all on fire, the earth did
    tremble.
HOTSPUR. O, then the earth shook to see the heavens on fire,
  And not in fear of your nativity.
  Diseased nature oftentimes breaks forth
  In strange eruptions; oft the teeming earth
  Is with a kind of colic pinch'd and vex'd
  By the imprisoning of unruly wind
  Within her womb; which, for enlargement striving,
  Shakes the old beldam earth, and topples down
  Steeples and moss-grown towers. At your birth,
  Our grandam earth, having this distemp'rature,
  In passion shook.
GLENDOWER. Cousin, of many men
  I do not bear these crossings. Give me leave
  To tell you once again that at my birth
  The front of heaven was full of fiery shapes,
  The goats ran from the mountains, and the herds
  Were strangely clamorous to the frighted fields.
  These signs have mark'd me extraordinary;

And all the courses of my life do show
I am not in the roll of common men.
Where is he living, clipp'd in with the sea
That chides the banks of England, Scotland, Wales,
Which calls me pupil or hath read to me?
And bring him out that is but woman's son
Can trace me in the tedious ways of art
And hold me pace in deep experiments.

HOTSPUR. I think there's no man speaks better Welsh. I'll to
dinner.

MORTIMER. Peace, cousin Percy; you will make him mad.

GLENDOWER. I can call spirits from the vasty deep.

HOTSPUR. Why, so can I, or so can any man;
But will they come when you do call for them?

GLENDOWER. Why, I can teach you, cousin, to command
The devil.

HOTSPUR. And I can teach thee, coz, to shame the devil
By telling truth: tell truth, and shame the devil.
If thou have power to raise him, bring him hither,
And I'll be sworn I have power to shame him hence.
O, while you live, tell truth, and shame the devil!

MORTIMER. Come, come, no more of this unprofitable chat.

GLENDOWER. Three times hath Henry Bolingbroke made
head
Against my power; thrice from the banks of Wye
And sandy-bottom'd Severn have I sent him
Bootless home and weather-beaten back.

HOTSPUR. Home without boots, and in foul weather too!
How scapes he agues, in the devil's name?

GLENDOWER. Come, here is the map; shall we divide our
right
According to our threefold order ta'en?

MORTIMER. The Archdeacon hath divided it
Into three limits very equally:
England, from Trent and Severn hitherto,
By south and east is to my part assign'd;
All westward, Wales beyond the Severn shore,
And all the fertile land within that bound,
To Owen Glendower; and, dear coz, to you
The remnant northward lying off from Trent.

And our indentures tripartite are drawn;
Which being sealed interchangeably,
A business that this night may execute,
To-morrow, cousin Percy, you and I
And my good Lord of Worcester will set forth
To meet your father and the Scottish power,
As is appointed us, at Shrewsbury.
My father Glendower is not ready yet,
Nor shall we need his help these fourteen days.
[*To* GLENDOWER] Within that space you may have drawn
   together
Your tenants, friends, and neighbouring gentlemen.
GLENDOWER. A shorter time shall send me to you, lords;
And in my conduct shall your ladies come,
From whom you now must steal and take no leave;
For there will be a world of water shed
Upon the parting of your wives and you.
HOTSPUR. Methinks my moiety, north from Burton here,
In quantity equals not one of yours.
See how this river comes me cranking in,
And cuts me from the best of all my land
A huge half-moon, a monstrous cantle out.
I'll have the current in this place damm'd up,
And here the smug and silver Trent shall run
In a new channel, fair and evenly;
It shall not wind with such a deep indent
To rob me of so rich a bottom here.
GLENDOWER. Not wind! It shall, it must; you see it doth.
MORTIMER. Yea, but
Mark how he bears his course and runs me up
With like advantage on the other side,
Gelding the opposed continent as much
As on the other side it takes from you.
WORCESTER. Yea, but a little charge will trench him here,
And on this north side win this cape of land,
And then he runs straight and even.
HOTSPUR. I'll have it so; a little charge will do it.
GLENDOWER. I'll not have it alt'red.
HOTSPUR. Will not you?
GLENDOWER. No, nor you shall not.

HOTSPUR. Who shall say me nay?

GLENDOWER. Why, that will I.

HOTSPUR. Let me not understand you, then; speak it in
Welsh.

GLENDOWER. I can speak English, lord, as well as you,
For I was train'd up in the English court;
Where, being but young, I framed to the harp
Many an English ditty lovely well,
And gave the tongue a helpful ornament—
A virtue that was never seen in you.

HOTSPUR. Marry,
And I am glad of it with all my heart!
I had rather be a kitten and cry mew
Than one of these same metre ballad-mongers;
I had rather hear a brazen canstick turn'd,
Or a dry wheel grate on the axle-tree;
And that would set my teeth nothing on edge,
Nothing so much as mincing poetry.
'Tis like the forc'd gait of a shuffling nag.

GLENDOWER. Come, you shall have Trent turn'd.

HOTSPUR. I do not care; I'll give thrice so much land
To any well-deserving friend;
But in the way of bargain, mark ye me,
I'll cavil on the ninth part of a hair.
Are the indentures drawn? Shall we be gone?

GLENDOWER. The moon shines fair; you may away by night;
I'll haste the writer, and withal
Break with your wives of your departure hence.
I am afraid my daughter will run mad,
So much she doteth on her Mortimer.   *Exit*

MORTIMER. Fie, cousin Percy! how you cross my father!

HOTSPUR. I cannot choose. Sometime he angers me
With telling me of the moldwarp and the ant,
Of the dreamer Merlin and his prophecies,
And of a dragon and a finless fish,
A clip-wing'd griffin and a moulten raven,
A couching lion and a ramping cat,
And such a deal of skimble-skamble stuff
As puts me from my faith. I tell you what:
He held me last night at least nine hours

In reckoning up the several devils' names .
That were his lackeys. I cried 'hum' and 'well, go to'
But mark'd him not a word. O, he is as tedious
As a tired horse, a railing wife;
Worse than a smoky house; I had rather live
With cheese and garlic in a windmill, far,
Than feed on cates and have him talk to me
In any summer house in Christendom.

MORTIMER. In faith, he is a worthy gentleman,
Exceedingly well read, and profited
In strange concealments; valiant as a lion,
And wondrous affable; and as bountiful
As mines of India. Shall I tell you, cousin?
He holds your temper in a high respect,
And curbs himself even of his natural scope
When you come 'cross his humour; faith, he does.
I warrant you that man is not alive
Might so have tempted him as you have done
Without the taste of danger and reproof;
But do not use it oft, let me entreat you.

WORCESTER. In faith, my lord, you are too wilful-blame;
And since your coming hither have done enough
To put him quite besides his patience.
You must needs learn, lord, to amend this fault;
Though sometimes it show greatness, courage, blood—
And that's the dearest grace it renders you—
Yet oftentimes it doth present harsh rage,
Defect of manners, want of government,
Pride, haughtiness, opinion, and disdain;
The least of which, haunting a nobleman,
Loseth men's hearts, and leaves behind a stain
Upon the beauty of all parts besides,
Beguiling them of commendation.

HOTSPUR. Well, I am school'd: good manners be your speed!
Here come our wives, and let us take our leave.

Re-enter GLENDOWER, *with* LADY MORTIMER *and*
LADY PERCY

MORTIMER. This is the deadly spite that angers me:
My wife can speak no English, I no Welsh.

GLENDOWER. My daughter weeps: she'll not part with you;
    She'll be a soldier too, she'll to the wars.

MORTIMER. Good father, tell her that she and my aunt Percy
    Shall follow in your conduct speedily.

        [GLENDOWER *speaks to her in Welsh, and she*
                        answers him in the same]

GLENDOWER. She is desperate here; a peevish, self-will'd har-
    lotry, one that no persuasion can do good upon.

                      [*The* LADY *speaks in Welsh*]

MORTIMER. I understand thy looks: that pretty Welsh
    Which thou pourest down from these swelling heavens
    I am too perfect in; and, but for shame,
    In such a parley should I answer thee.

             [*The* LADY *speaks again in Welsh*]

    I understand thy kisses, and thou mine,
    And that's a feeling disputation;
    But I will never be a truant, love,
    Till I have learnt thy language; for thy tongue
    Makes Welsh as sweet as ditties highly penn'd,
    Sung by a fair queen in a summer's bow'r,
    With ravishing division, to her lute.

GLENDOWER. Nay, if you melt, then will she run mad.

             [*The* LADY *speaks again in Welsh*]

MORTIMER. O, I am ignorance itself in this!

GLENDOWER. She bids you on the wanton rushes lay you
    down,
    And rest your gentle head upon her lap,
    And she will sing the song that pleaseth you,
    And on your eyelids crown the god of sleep,
    Charming your blood with pleasing heaviness,
    Making such difference 'twixt wake and sleep
    As is the difference betwixt day and night
    The hour before the heavenly-harness'd team
    Begins his golden progress in the east.

MORTIMER. With all my heart I'll sit and hear her sing;
    By that time will our book, I think, be drawn.

GLENDOWER. Do so;
    And those musicians that shall play to you
    Hang in the air a thousand leagues from hence,
    And straight they shall be here; sit, and attend.

HOTSPUR. Come, Kate, thou art perfect in lying down. Come,
quick, quick, that I may lay my head in thy lap.

LADY PERCY. Go, ye giddy goose.

[*The music plays*]

HOTSPUR. Now I perceive the devil understands Welsh;
And 'tis no marvel he is so humorous.
By'r lady, he is a good musician.

LADY PERCY. Then should you be nothing but musical, for
you are altogether govern'd by humours. Lie still, ye thief,
and hear the lady sing in Welsh.

HOTSPUR. I had rather hear Lady, my brach, howl in Irish.

LADY PERCY. Wouldst thou have thy head broken?

HOTSPUR. No.

LADY PERCY. Then be still.

HOTSPUR. Neither; 'tis a woman's fault.

LADY PERCY. Now God help thee!

HOTSPUR. To the Welsh lady's bed.

LADY PERCY. What's that?

HOTSPUR. Peace! she sings.

[*Here the* LADY *sings a Welsh song*]

HOTSPUR. Come, Kate, I'll have your song too.

LADY PERCY. Not mine, in good sooth.

HOTSPUR. Not yours, in good sooth! Heart! you swear like
a comfit-maker's wife. 'Not you, in good sooth' and 'As
true as I live' and 'As God shall mend me' and 'As sure
as day.'
And givest such sarcenet surety for thy oaths
As if thou never walk'st further than Finsbury.
Swear me, Kate, like a lady as thou art,
A good mouth-filling oath; and leave 'in sooth'
And such protest of pepper-gingerbread
To velvet-guards and Sunday-citizens.
Come, sing.

LADY PERCY. I will not sing.

HOTSPUR. 'Tis the next way to turn tailor, or be redbreast
teacher. An the indentures be drawn, I'll away within
these two hours; and so come in when ye will.   *Exit*

GLENDOWER. Come, come, Lord Mortimer; you are as slow
As hot Lord Percy is on fire to go.
By this our book is drawn; we'll but seal,

And then to horse immediately.
MORTIMER. With all my heart.   *Exeunt*

SCENE 2

London. The palace

Enter the KING, *the* PRINCE OF WALES, *and* LORDS

KING. Lords, give us leave; the Prince of Wales and I
  Must have some private conference; but be near at hand,
  For we shall presently have need of you.   *Exeunt* LORDS
  I know not whether God will have it so,
  For some displeasing service I have done,
  That, in his secret doom, out of my blood
  He'll breed revengement and a scourge for me;
  But thou dost in thy passages of life
  Make me believe that thou art only mark'd
  For the hot vengeance and the rod of heaven
  To punish my mistreadings. Tell me else,
  Could such inordinate and low desires,
  Such poor, such bare, such lewd, such mean attempts,
  Such barren pleasures, rude society,
  As thou art match'd withal and grafted to,
  Accompany the greatness of thy blood
  And hold their level with thy princely heart?
PRINCE. So please your Majesty, I would I could
  Quit all offences with as clear excuse,
  As well as I am doubtless I can purge
  Myself of many I am charg'd withal;
  Yet such extenuation let me beg,
  As, in reproof of many tales devis'd,
  Which oft the ear of greatness needs must hear,
  By smiling pick-thanks and base newsmongers,
  I may, for some things true, wherein my youth
  Hath faulty wand'red and irregular,
  Find pardon on my true submission.
KING. God pardon thee! Yet let me wonder, Harry,
  At thy affections, which do hold a wing
  Quite from the flight of all thy ancestors.

Thy place in council thou hast rudely lost,
Which by thy younger brother is supplied,
And art almost an alien to the hearts
Of all the court and princes of my blood.
The hope and expectation of thy time
Is ruin'd, and the soul of every man
Prophetically do forethink thy fall.
Had I so lavish of my presence been,
So common-hackney'd in the eyes of men,
So stale and cheap to vulgar company,
Opinion, that did help me to the crown,
Had still kept loyal to possession
And left me in reputeless banishment
A fellow of no mark nor likelihood.
By being seldom seen, I could not stir
But, like a comet, I was wond'red at;
That men would tell their children 'This is he';
Others would say 'Where, which is Bolingbroke?'
And then I stole all courtesy from heaven,
And dress'd myself in such humility
That I did pluck allegiance from men's hearts,
Loud shouts and salutations from their mouths,
Even in the presence of the crowned King.
Thus did I keep my person fresh and new,
My presence, like a robe pontifical,
Ne'er seen but wond'red at, and so my state,
Seldom but sumptuous, show'd like a feast
And won by rareness such solemnity.
The skipping King, he ambled up and down
With shallow jesters and rash bavin wits,
Soon kindled and soon burnt; carded his state,
Mingled his royalty with cap'ring fools;
Had his great name profaned with their scorns,
And gave his countenance, against his name,
To laugh at gibing boys and stand the push
Of every beardless vain comparative;
Grew a companion to the common streets,
Enfeoff'd himself to popularity;
That, being daily swallowed by men's eyes,
They surfeited with honey and began

To loathe the taste of sweetness, whereof a little
More than a little is by much too much.
So, when he had occasion to be seen,
He was but as the cuckoo is in June,
Heard, not regarded, seen, but with such eyes
As, sick and blunted with community,
Afford no extraordinary gaze,
Such as is bent on sun-like majesty
When it shines seldom in admiring eyes;
But rather drowz'd and hung their eyelids down,
Slept in his face, and rend'red such aspect
As cloudy men use to their adversaries,
Being with his presence glutted, gorg'd, and full.
And in that very line, Harry, standest thou;
For thou hast lost thy princely privilege
With vile participation. Not an eye
But is aweary of thy common sight,
Save mine, which hath desir'd to see thee more;
Which now doth that I would not have it do—
Make blind itself with foolish tenderness.

PRINCE. I shall hereafter, my thrice-gracious lord,
Be more myself.

KING. For all the world
As thou art to this hour was Richard then
When I from France set foot at Ravenspurgh;
And even as I was then is Percy now.
Now, by my sceptre and my soul to boot,
He hath more worthy interest to the state
Than thou the shadow of succession;
For of no right, nor colour like to right,
He doth fill fields with harness in the realm;
Turns head against the lion's armed jaws;
And, being no more in debt to years than thou,
Leads ancient lords and reverend bishops on
To bloody battles and to bruising arms.
What never-dying honour hath he got
Against renowned Douglas! whose high deeds,
Whose hot incursions, and great name in arms,
Holds from all soldiers chief majority
And military title capital

Through all the kingdoms that acknowledge Christ.
Thrice hath this Hotspur, Mars in swathling clothes,
This infant warrior, in his enterprises
Discomfited great Douglas; ta'en him once,
Enlarged him and made a friend of him,
To fill the mouth of deep defiance up
And shake the peace and safety of our throne.
And what say you to this? Percy, Northumberland,
The Archbishop's Grace of York, Douglas, Mortimer,
Capitulate against us and are up.
But wherefore do I tell these news to thee?
Why, Harry, do I tell thee of my foes,
Which art my nearest and dearest enemy?
Thou that art like enough, through vassal fear,
Base inclination, and the start of spleen,
To fight against me under Percy's pay,
To dog his heels, and curtsy at his frowns,
To show how much thou art degenerate.

PRINCE. Do not think so; you shall not find it so;
And God forgive them that so much have sway'd
Your Majesty's good thoughts away from me!
I will redeem all this on Percy's head,
And in the closing of some glorious day
Be bold to tell you that I am your son,
When I will wear a garment all of blood,
And stain my favours in a bloody mask,
Which, wash'd away, shall scour my shame with it;
And that shall be the day, whene'er it lights,
That this same child of honour and renown,
This gallant Hotspur, this all-praised knight,
And your unthought-of Harry chance to meet.
For every honour sitting on his helm,
Would they were multitudes, and on my head
My shames redoubled! For the time will come
That I shall make this northern youth exchange
His glorious deeds for my indignities.
Percy is but my factor, good my lord,
To engross up glorious deeds on my behalf;
And I will call him to so strict account
That he shall render every glory up,

Yea, even the slightest worship of his time,
Or I will tear the reckoning from his heart.
This, in the name of God, I promise here;
The which if He be pleas'd I shall perform,
I do beseech your Majesty may salve
The long-grown wounds of my intemperature.
If not, the end of life cancels all bands;
And I will die a hundred thousand deaths
Ere break the smallest parcel of this vow.
KING. A hundred thousand rebels die in this:
Thou shalt have charge and sovereign trust herein.

Enter SIR WALTER BLUNT

How now, good Blunt! Thy looks are full of speed.
BLUNT. So hath the business that I come to speak of.
Lord Mortimer of Scotland hath sent word
That Douglas and the English rebels met
The eleventh of this month at Shrewsbury.
A mighty and a fearful head they are,
If promises be kept on every hand,
As ever off'red foul play in a state.
KING. The Earl of Westmoreland set forth to-day,
With him my son, Lord John of Lancaster;
For this advertisement is five days old.
On Wednesday next, Harry, you shall set forward;
On Thursday we ourselves will march. Our meeting
Is Bridgenorth. And, Harry, you shall march
Through Gloucestershire; by which account,
Our business valued, some twelve days hence
Our general forces at Bridgenorth shall meet.
Our hands are full of business. Let's away.
Advantage feeds him fat while men delay.   *Exeunt*

SCENE 3

Eastcheap. The Boar's Head Tavern

Enter FALSTAFF *and* BARDOLPH

FALSTAFF. Bardolph, am I not fall'n away vilely since this last

action? Do I not bate? Do I not dwindle? Why, my skin
hangs about me like an old lady's loose gown; I am withered like an old apple-john. Well, I'll repent, and that suddenly, while I am in some liking; I shall be out of heart
shortly, and then I shall have no strength to repent. An I
have not forgotten what the inside of a church is made of,
I am a peppercorn, a brewer's horse. The inside of a
church! Company, villainous company, hath been the
spoil of me.

BARDOLPH. Sir John, you are so fretful you cannot live long.

FALSTAFF. Why, there is it; come, sing me a bawdy song,
make me merry. I was as virtuously given as a gentleman
need to be; virtuous enough: swore little, dic'd not above
seven times a week, went to a bawdy-house not above
once in a quarter—of an hour, paid money that I borrowed
—three or four times, lived well, and in good compass; and
now I live out of all order, out of all compass.

BARDOLPH. Why, you are so fat, Sir John, that you must
needs be out of all compass—out of all reasonable compass,
Sir John.

FALSTAFF. Do thou amend thy face, and I'll amend my life.
Thou art our admiral, thou bearest the lantern in the poop,
but 'tis in the nose of thee; thou art the Knight of the
Burning Lamp.

BARDOLPH. Why, Sir John, my face does you no harm.

FALSTAFF. No, I'll be sworn; I make as good use of it as
many a man doth of a death's head or a memento mori: I
never see thy face but I think upon hell-fire, and Dives
that lived in purple; for there he is in his robes, burning,
burning. If thou wert any way given to virtue, I would
swear by thy face: my oath should be 'By this fire, that's
God's angel.' But thou art altogether given over, and wert
indeed, but for the light in thy face, the son of utter darkness. When thou ran'st up Gadshill in the night to catch
my horse, if I did not think thou hadst been an ignis
fatuus or a ball of wildfire, there's no purchase in money.
O, thou art a perpetual triumph, an everlasting bonfire
light! Thou hast saved me a thousand marks in links and
torches, walking with thee in the night betwixt tavern and
tavern; but the sack that thou hast drunk me would have

bought me lights as good cheap at the dearest chandler's in Europe. I have maintained that salamander of yours with fire any time this two and thirty years; God reward me for it!

BARDOLPH. 'Sblood, I would my face were in your belly!

FALSTAFF. God-a-mercy! so should I be sure to be heart-burnt.

Enter HOSTESS

How now, Dame Partlet the hen! Have you inquir'd yet who pick'd my pocket?

HOSTESS. Why, Sir John, what do you think, Sir John? Do you think I keep thieves in my house? I have search'd, I have inquired, so has my husband, man by man, boy by boy, servant by servant. The tithe of a hair was never lost in my house before.

FALSTAFF. Ye lie, hostess: Bardolph was shav'd and lost many a hair, and I'll be sworn my pocket was pick'd. Go to, you are a woman, go.

HOSTESS. Who, I? No, I defy thee. God's light, I was never call'd so in mine own house before.

FALSTAFF. Go to, I know you well enough.

HOSTESS. No, Sir John, you do not know me, Sir John. I know you, Sir John: you owe me money, Sir John; and now you pick a quarrel to beguile me of it. I bought you a dozen of shirts to your back.

FALSTAFF. Dowlas, filthy dowlas! I have given them away to bakers' wives; they have made bolters of them.

HOSTESS. Now, as I am a true woman, holland of eight shill-ings an ell. You owe money here besides, Sir John, for your diet and by-drinkings, and money lent you, four and twenty pound.

FALSTAFF. He had his part of it; let him pay.

HOSTESS. He? Alas, he is poor; he hath nothing.

FALSTAFF. How! poor? Look upon his face: what call you rich? Let them coin his nose, let them coin his cheeks. I'll not pay a denier. What, will you make a younker of me? Shall I not take mine ease in mine inn but I shall have my pocket pick'd? I have lost a seal-ring of my grandfather's worth forty mark.

HOSTESS. O Jesu, I have heard the Prince tell him, I know
not how oft, that that ring was copper!

FALSTAFF. How! the Prince is a Jack, a sneak-cup. 'Sblood,
an he were here, I would cudgel him like a dog if he
would say so.

Enter the PRINCE *marching, with* PETO; *and* FALSTAFF *meets
him, playing upon his truncheon like a fife*

FALSTAFF. How now, lad! Is the wind in that door, i' faith?
Must we all march?

BARDOLPH. Yea, two and two, Newgate fashion.

HOSTESS. My lord, I pray you hear me.

PRINCE. What say'st thou, Mistress Quickly? How doth thy
husband? I love him well; he is an honest man.

HOSTESS. Good my lord, hear me.

FALSTAFF. Prithee, let her alone, and list to me.

PRINCE. What say'st thou, Jack?

FALSTAFF. The other night I fell asleep here behind the arras
and had my pocket pick'd; this house is turn'd bawdy-
house; they pick pockets.

PRINCE. What didst thou lose, Jack?

FALSTAFF. Wilt thou believe me, Hal? Three or four bonds
of forty pound a-piece and a seal-ring of my grandfather's.

PRINCE. A trifle, some eight-penny matter.

HOSTESS. So I told him, my lord; and I said I heard your
Grace say so; and, my lord, he speaks most vilely of you,
like a foul-mouth'd man as he is, and said he would cudgel
you.

PRINCE. What! he did not?

HOSTESS. There's neither faith, truth, nor womanhood, in
me else.

FALSTAFF. There's no more faith in thee than in a stewed
prune; nor no more truth in thee than in a drawn fox; and
for womanhood, Maid Marian may be the deputy's wife of
the ward to thee. Go, you thing, go.

HOSTESS. Say, what thing? what thing?

FALSTAFF. What thing! Why, a thing to thank God on.

HOSTESS. I am no thing to thank God on, I would thou
shouldst know it; I am an honest man's wife; and setting

thy knighthood aside, thou art a knave to call me so.

FALSTAFF. Setting thy womanhood aside, thou art a beast to say otherwise.

HOSTESS. Say, what beast, thou knave, thou?

FALSTAFF. What beast! Why, an otter.

PRINCE. An otter, Sir John! Why an otter?

FALSTAFF. Why, she's neither fish nor flesh: a man knows not where to have her.

HOSTESS. Thou art an unjust man in saying so: thou or any man knows where to have me, thou knave, thou!

PRINCE. Thou say'st true, hostess; and he slanders thee most grossly.

HOSTESS. So he doth you, my lord; and said this other day you ought him a thousand pound.

PRINCE. Sirrah, do I owe you a thousand pound?

FALSTAFF. A thousand pound, Hal! A million. Thy love is worth a million: thou owest me thy love.

HOSTESS. Nay, my lord, he call'd you Jack, and said he would cudgel you.

FALSTAFF. Did I, Bardolph?

BARDOLPH. Indeed, Sir John, you said so.

FALSTAFF. Yea, if he said my ring was copper.

PRINCE. I say 'tis copper. Darest thou be as good as thy word now?

FALSTAFF. Why, Hal, thou knowest, as thou art but man, I dare; but as thou art prince, I fear thee as I fear the roaring of the lion's whelp.

PRINCE. And why not as the lion?

FALSTAFF. The King himself is to be feared as the lion. Dost thou think I'll fear thee as I fear thy father? Nay, an I do, I pray God my girdle break.

PRINCE. O, if it should, how would thy guts fall about thy knees! But, sirrah, there's no room for faith, truth, nor honesty, in this bosom of thine—it is all fill'd up with guts and midriff. Charge an honest woman with picking thy pocket! Why, thou whoreson, impudent, emboss'd rascal, if there were anything in thy pocket but tavern-reckonings, memorandums of bawdy-houses, and one poor penny-worth of sugar-candy to make thee long-winded—if thy pocket were enrich'd with any other injuries but these, I am a villain. And yet you will stand to it, you will not pocket-up wrong. Art thou not ashamed?

FALSTAFF. Dost thou hear, Hal? Thou knowest in the state of innocency Adam fell; and what should poor Jack Falstaff do in the days of villainy? Thou seest I have more flesh than another man, and therefore more frailty. You confess, then, you pick'd my pocket?

PRINCE. It appears so by the story.

FALSTAFF. Hostess, I forgive thee. Go make ready breakfast, love thy husband, look to thy servants, cherish thy guests. Thou shalt find me tractable to any honest reason. Thou seest I am pacified still. Nay, prithee, be gone. [*Exit* HOSTESS] Now, Hal, to the news at court: for the robbery, lad, how is that answered?

PRINCE. O, my sweet beef, I must still be good angel to thee: the money is paid back again.

FALSTAFF. O, I do not like that paying back; 'tis a double labour.

PRINCE. I am good friends with my father, and may do anything.

FALSTAFF. Rob me the exchequer the first thing thou doest, and do it with unwash'd hands too.

BARDOLPH. Do, my lord.

PRINCE. I have procured thee, Jack, a charge of foot.

FALSTAFF. I would it had been of horse. Where shall I find one that can steal well? O for a fine thief, of the age of two and twenty or thereabouts! I am heinously unprovided. Well, God be thanked for these rebels—they offend none but the virtuous; I laud them, I praise them.

PRINCE. Bardolph!

BARDOLPH. My lord?

PRINCE. Go bear this letter to Lord John of Lancaster,
To my brother John; this to my Lord of Westmoreland.
                                        Exit BARDOLPH
Go, Peto, to horse, to horse; for thou and I
Have thirty miles to ride yet ere dinner-time.   *Exit* PETO
Jack, meet me to-morrow in the Temple Hall
At two o'clock in the afternoon;
There shalt thou know thy charge, and there receive
Money and order for their furniture.

The land is burning; Percy stands on high;
And either we or they must lower lie.   *Exit*
FALSTAFF. Rare words! brave world! Hostess, my breakfast,
    come!
O, I could wish this tavern were my drum!   *Exit*

ACT IV. SCENE 1

The rebel camp near Shrewsbury

Enter HOTSPUR, WORCESTER, *and* DOUGLAS

HOTSPUR. Well said, my noble Scot. If speaking truth
    In this fine age were not thought flattery,
    Such attribution should the Douglas have
    As not a soldier of this season's stamp
    Should go so general current through the world.
    By God, I cannot flatter; I do defy
    The tongues of soothers; but a braver place
    In my heart's love hath no man than yourself.
    Nay, task me to my word; approve me, lord.
DOUGLAS. Thou art the king of honour:
    No man so potent breathes upon the ground
    But I will beard him.
HOTSPUR. Do so, and 'tis well.

Enter a MESSENGER *with letters*

What letters hast thou there?—I can but thank you.
MESSENGER. These letters come from your father.
HOTSPUR. Letters from him! Why comes he not himself?
MESSENGER. He cannot come, my lord, he is grievous sick.
HOTSPUR. Zounds! how has he the leisure to be sick
    In such a justling time? Who leads his power?
    Under whose government come they along?
MESSENGER. His letters bears his mind, not I, my lord.
WORCESTER. I prithee tell me, doth he keep his bed?
MESSENGER. He did, my lord, four days ere I set forth;
    And at the time of my departure thence

244

He was much fear'd by his physicians.

WORCESTER. I would the state of time had first been whole
  Ere he by sickness had been visited:
  His health was never better worth than now.

HOTSPUR. Sick now! droop now! This sickness doth infect
  The very life-blood of our enterprise;
  'Tis catching hither, even to our camp.
  He writes me here that inward sickness—
  And that his friends by deputation could not
  So soon be drawn; nor did he think it meet
  To lay so dangerous and dear a trust
  On any soul remov'd, but on his own.
  Yet doth he give us bold advertisement
  That with our small conjunction we should on,
  To see how fortune is dispos'd to us;
  For, as he writes, there is no quailing now,
  Because the King is certainly possess'd
  Of all our purposes. What say you to it?

WORCESTER. Your father's sickness is a maim to us.

HOTSPUR. A perilous gash, a very limb lopp'd off.
  And yet, in faith, it is not. His present want
  Seems more than we shall find it. Were it good
  To set the exact wealth of all our states
  All at one cast? To set so rich a main
  On the nice hazard of one doubtful hour?
  It were not good; for therein should we read
  The very bottom and the soul of hope,
  The very list, the very utmost bound
  Of all our fortunes.

DOUGLAS. Faith, and so we should;
  Where now remains a sweet reversion.
  We may boldly spend upon the hope of what
  Is to come in.
  A comfort of retirement lives in this.

HOTSPUR. A rendezvous, a home to fly unto,
  If that the devil and mischance look big
  Upon the maidenhead of our affairs.

WORCESTER. But yet I would your father had been here.
  The quality and hair of our attempt
  Brooks no division. It will be thought

By some, that know not why he is away,
That wisdom, loyalty, and mere dislike
Of our proceedings, kept the earl from hence;
And think how such an apprehension
May turn the tide of fearful faction
And breed a kind of question in our cause;
For well you know we of the off'ring side
Must keep aloof from strict arbitrement,
And stop all sight-holes, every loop from whence
The eye of reason may pry in upon us.
This absence of your father's draws a curtain
That shows the ignorant a kind of fear
Before not dreamt of.

HOTSPUR. You strain too far.
I rather of his absence make this use:
It lends a lustre and more great opinion,
A larger dare to our great enterprise,
Than if the earl were here; for men must think,
If we, without his help, can make a head
To push against a kingdom, with his help
We shall o'erturn it topsy-turvy down.
Yet all goes well, yet all our joints are whole.

DOUGLAS. As heart can think; there is not such a word
Spoke of in Scotland as this term of fear.

Enter SIR RICHARD VERNON

HOTSPUR. My cousin Vernon! welcome, by my soul.
VERNON. Pray God my news be worth a welcome, lord.
The Earl of Westmoreland, seven thousand strong,
Is marching hitherwards; with him Prince John.
HOTSPUR. No harm; what more?
VERNON. And further, I have learn'd
The King himself in person is set forth,
Or hitherwards intended speedily,
With strong and mighty preparation.
HOTSPUR. He shall be welcome too. Where is his son,
The nimble-footed madcap Prince of Wales,
And his comrades that daff'd the world aside
And bid it pass?

VERNON. All furnish'd, all in arms;
  All plum'd like estridges, that with the wind
  Bated like eagles having lately bath'd;
  Glittering in golden coats, like images;
  As full of spirit as the month of May
  And gorgeous as the sun at midsummer;
  Wanton as youthful goats, wild as young bulls.
  I saw young Harry with his beaver on,
  His cushes on his thighs, gallantly arm'd,
  Rise from the ground like feathered Mercury,
  And vaulted with such ease into his seat
  As if an angel dropp'd down from the clouds
  To turn and wind a fiery Pegasus,
  And witch the world with noble horsemanship.

HOTSPUR. No more, no more; worse than the sun in March,
  This praise doth nourish agues. Let them come.
  They come like sacrifices in their trim,
  And to the fire-ey'd maid of smoky war
  All hot and bleeding will we offer them.
  The mailed Mars shall on his altar sit
  Up to the ears in blood. I am on fire
  To hear this rich reprisal is so nigh
  And yet not ours. Come, let me taste my horse,
  Who is to bear me like a thunderbolt
  Against the bosom of the Prince of Wales.
  Harry to Harry shall, hot horse to horse,
  Meet, and ne'er part till one drop down a corse.
  O that Glendower were come!

VERNON. There is more news.
  I learn'd in Worcester, as I rode along,
  He cannot draw his power this fourteen days.

DOUGLAS. That's the worst tidings that I hear of yet.

WORCESTER. Ay, by my faith, that bears a frosty sound.

HOTSPUR. What may the King's whole battle reach unto?

VERNON. To thirty thousand.

HOTSPUR. Forty let it be:
  My father and Glendower being both away,
  The powers of us may serve so great a day.
  Come, let us take a muster speedily.
  Doomsday is near; die all, die merrily.

Douglas. Talk not of dying; I am out of fear
Of death or death's hand for this one half year.   *Exeunt*

SCENE 2

A public road near Coventry

Enter Falstaff *and* Bardolph

Falstaff. Bardolph, get thee before to Coventry; fill me a
bottle of sack. Our soldiers shall march through; we'll to
Sutton Co'fil' to-night.
Bardolph. Will you give me money, Captain?
Falstaff. Lay out, lay out.
Bardolph. This bottle makes an angel.
Falstaff. An if it do, take it for thy labour; and if it make
twenty, take them all; I'll answer the coinage. Bid my lieutenant Peto meet me at town's end.
Bardolph. I will, Captain; farewell.   *Exit*
Falstaff. If I be not ashamed of my soldiers, I am a sous'd
gurnet. I have misused the King's press damnably. I have
got, in exchange of a hundred and fifty soldiers, three hundred and odd pounds. I press me none but good house-
holders, yeomen's sons; inquire me out contracted bache-
lors, such as had been ask'd twice on the banns; such a
commodity of warm slaves as had as lief hear the devil as
a drum; such as fear the report of a caliver worse than a
struck fowl or a hurt wild-duck. I press'd me none but such
toasts-and-butter, with hearts in their bellies no bigger
than pins' heads, and they have bought out their services;
and now my whole charge consists of ancients, corporals,
lieutenants, gentlemen of companies—slaves as ragged as
Lazarus in the painted cloth, where the Glutton's dogs
licked his sores; and such as indeed were never soldiers,
but discarded unjust serving-men, younger sons to younger
brothers, revolted tapsters, and ostlers trade-fall'n; the
cankers of a calm world and a long peace; ten times more
dishonourable ragged than an old fac'd ancient. And such
have I, to fill up the rooms of them as have bought out
their services, that you would think that I had a hundred

and fifty tattered Prodigals lately come from swine-keeping, from eating draff and husks. A mad fellow met me on the way, and told me I had unloaded all the gibbets and press'd the dead bodies. No eye hath seen such scarecrows. I'll not march through Coventry with them, that's flat. Nay, and the villains march wide betwixt the legs, as if they had gyves on; for indeed I had the most of them out of prison. There's not a shirt and a half in all my company; and the half shirt is two napkins tack'd together and thrown over the shoulders like a herald's coat without sleeves; and the shirt, to say the truth, stol'n from my host at Saint Albans, or the red-nose innkeeper of Daventry. But that's all one; they'll find linen enough on every hedge.

Enter the PRINCE OF WALES *and* WESTMORELAND

PRINCE. How now, blown Jack! how now, quilt!

FALSTAFF. What, Hal! how now, mad wag! What a devil dost thou in Warwickshire? My good Lord of Westmoreland, I cry you mercy; I thought your honour had already been at Shrewsbury.

WESTMORELAND. Faith, Sir John, 'tis more than time that I were there, and you too; but my powers are there already. The King, I can tell you, looks for us all; we must away all night.

FALSTAFF. Tut, never fear me; I am as vigilant as a cat to steal cream.

PRINCE. I think, to steal cream indeed; for thy theft hath already made thee butter. But tell me, Jack, whose fellows are these that come after?

FALSTAFF. Mine, Hal, mine.

PRINCE. I did never see such pitiful rascals.

FALSTAFF. Tut, tut; good enough to toss; food for powder, food for powder; they'll fill a pit as well as better: tush, man, mortal men, mortal men.

WESTMORELAND. Ay, but, Sir John, methinks they are exceeding poor and bare—too beggarly.

FALSTAFF. Faith, for their poverty, I know not where they had that; and for their bareness, I am sure they never learn'd that of me.

PRINCE. No, I'll be sworn; unless you call three fingers in the
　ribs bare. But, sirrah, make haste; Percy is already in the
　field. *Exit*

FALSTAFF. What, is the King encamp'd?

WESTMORELAND. He is, Sir John: I fear we shall stay too
　long. *Exit*

FALSTAFF. Well,
　To the latter end of a fray and the beginning of a feast
　Fits a dull fighter and a keen guest. *Exit*

SCENE 3

The rebel camp near Shrewsbury

Enter HOTSPUR, WORCESTER, DOUGLAS, *and* VERNON

HOTSPUR. We'll fight with him to-night.

WORCESTER. It may not be.

DOUGLAS. You give him, then, advantage.

VERNON. Not a whit.

HOTSPUR. Why say you so? looks he not for supply?

VERNON. So do we.

HOTSPUR. His is certain, ours is doubtful.

WORCESTER. Good cousin, be advis'd, stir not to-night.

VERNON. Do not, my lord.

DOUGLAS. You do not counsel well;
　You speak it out of fear and cold heart.

VERNON. Do me no slander, Douglas; by my life,
　And I dare well maintain it with my life,
　If well-respected honour bid me on,
　I hold as little counsel with weak fear
　As you, my lord, or any Scot that this day lives;
　Let it be seen to-morrow in the battle
　Which of us fears.

DOUGLAS. Yea, or to-night.

VERNON. Content.

HOTSPUR. To-night, say I.

VERNON. Come, come, it may not be. I wonder much,
　Being men of such great leading as you are,
　That you foresee not what impediments

Drag back our expedition: certain horse
Of my cousin Vernon's are not yet come up;
Your uncle Worcester's horse came but to-day;
And now their pride and mettle is asleep,
Their courage with hard labour tame and dull,
That not a horse is half the half of himself.

HOTSPUR. So are the horses of the enemy
In general, journey-bated and brought low;
The better part of ours are full of rest.

WORCESTER. The number of the King exceedeth ours.
For God's sake, cousin, stay till all come in.

                            [The trumpet sounds a parley]

Enter SIR WALTER BLUNT

BLUNT. I come with gracious offers from the King,
If you vouchsafe me hearing and respect.

HOTSPUR. Welcome, Sir Walter Blunt; and would to God
You were of our determination!
Some of us love you well; and even those some
Envy your great deservings and good name,
Because you are not of our quality,
But stand against us like an enemy.

BLUNT. And God defend but still I should stand so,
So long as out of limit and true rule
You stand against anointed majesty!
But, to my charge. The King hath sent to know
The nature of your griefs; and whereupon
You conjure from the breast of civil peace
Such bold hostility, teaching his duteous land
Audacious cruelty. If that the King
Have any way your good deserts forgot,
Which he confesseth to be manifold,
He bids you name your griefs, and with all speed
You shall have your desires with interest,
And pardon absolute for yourself and these
Herein misled by your suggestion.

HOTSPUR. The King is kind; and well we know the King
Knows at what time to promise, when to pay.
My father and my uncle and myself
Did give him that same royalty he wears;

And when he was not six and twenty strong,
Sick in the world's regard, wretched and low,
A poor unminded outlaw sneaking home,
My father gave him welcome to the shore;
And when he heard him swear and vow to God
He came but to be Duke of Lancaster,
To sue his livery and beg his peace,
With tears of innocency and terms of zeal,
My father, in kind heart and pity mov'd,
Swore him assistance, and perform'd it too.
Now when the lords and barons of the realm
Perceiv'd Northumberland did lean to him,
The more and less came in with cap and knee;
Met him in boroughs, cities, villages;
Attended him on bridges, stood in lanes,
Laid gifts before him, proffer'd him their oaths,
Gave him their heirs as pages, followed him
Even at the heels in golden multitudes.
He presently—as greatness knows itself—
Steps me a little higher than his vow
Made to my father, while his blood was poor,
Upon the naked shore at Ravenspurgh;
And now, forsooth, takes on him to reform
Some certain edicts, and some strait decrees
That lie too heavy on the commonwealth;
Cries out upon abuses, seems to weep
Over his country's wrongs; and by this face,
This seeming brow of justice, did he win
The hearts of all that he did angle for;
Proceeded further: cut me off the heads
Of all the favourites that the absent King
In deputation left behind him here,
When he was personal in the Irish war.
BLUNT. Tut, I came not to hear this.
HOTSPUR. Then to the point.
In short time after, he depos'd the King;
Soon after that depriv'd him of his life;
And in the neck of that, task'd the whole state;
To make that worse, suff'red his kinsman March—
Who is, if every owner were well plac'd,

Indeed his king—to be engag'd in Wales,
There without ransom to lie forfeited;
Disgrac'd me in my happy victories;
Sought to entrap me by intelligence;
Rated mine uncle from the council-board;
In rage dismiss'd my father from the court;
Broke oath on oath, committed wrong on wrong;
And in conclusion drove us to seek out
This head of safety, and withal to pry
Into his title, the which we find
Too indirect for long continuance.
BLUNT. Shall I return this answer to the King?
HOTSPUR. Not so, Sir Walter; we'll withdraw awhile.
Go to the King; and let there be impawn'd
Some surety for a safe return again,
And in the morning early shall mine uncle
Bring him our purposes. And so, farewell.
BLUNT. I would you would accept of grace and love.
HOTSPUR. And may be so we shall.
BLUNT. Pray God you do.   *Exeunt*

SCENE 4

York. The ARCHBISHOP'S *palace*

Enter the ARCHBISHOP OF YORK, *and* SIR MICHAEL

ARCHBISHOP. Hie, good Sir Michael; bear this sealed brief
With winged haste to the Lord Marshal;
This to my cousin Scroop; and all the rest
To whom they are directed. If you knew
How much they do import, you would make haste.
SIR MICHAEL. My good lord,
I guess their tenour.
ARCHBISHOP. Like enough you do.
To-morrow, good Sir Michael, is a day
Wherein the fortune of ten thousand men
Must bide the touch; for, sir, at Shrewsbury,
As I am truly given to understand,
The King with mighty and quick-raised power

Meets with Lord Harry; and I fear, Sir Michael,
What with the sickness of Northumberland,
Whose power was in the first proportion,
And what with Owen Glendower's absence thence,
Who with them was a rated sinew too
And comes not in, o'er-rul'd by prophecies,
I fear the power of Percy is too weak
To wage an instant trial with the King.

Sir Michael. Why, my good lord, you need not fear;
There is Douglas and Lord Mortimer.

Archbishop. No, Mortimer is not there.

Sir Michael. But there is Mordake, Vernon, Lord Harry
Percy,
And there is my Lord of Worcester, and a head
Of gallant warriors, noble gentlemen.

Archbishop. And so there is; but yet the King hath drawn
The special head of all the land together:
The Prince of Wales, Lord John of Lancaster,
The noble Westmoreland, and warlike Blunt;
And many moe corrivals and dear men
Of estimation and command in arms.

Sir Michael. Doubt not, my lord, they shall be well oppos'd.

Archbishop. I hope no less, yet needful 'tis to fear;
And, to prevent the worst, Sir Michael, speed;
For if Lord Percy thrive not, ere the King
Dismiss his power, he means to visit us—
For he hath heard of our confederacy—
And 'tis but wisdom to make strong against him;
Therefore make haste. I must go write again
To other friends; and so farewell, Sir Michael.

Exeunt severally

ACT V. SCENE 1

The KING'S *camp near Shrewsbury*

Enter the KING, *the* PRINCE OF WALES, PRINCE
JOHN OF LANCASTER, SIR WALTER BLUNT, *and* SIR
JOHN FALSTAFF

KING. How bloodily the sun begins to peer
  Above yon bushy hill! The day looks pale
  At his distemp'rature.
PRINCE. The southern wind
  Doth play the trumpet to his purposes,
  And by his hollow whistling in the leaves
  Foretells a tempest and a blust'ring day.
KING. Then with the losers let it sympathize,
  For nothing can seem foul to those that win.

[*The trumpet sounds*]

Enter WORCESTER *and* VERNON

How now, my Lord of Worcester! 'Tis not well
That you and I should meet upon such terms
As now we meet. You have deceiv'd our trust,
And made us doff our easy robes of peace
To crush our old limbs in ungentle steel;
This is not well, my lord, this is not well.
What say you to it? Will you again unknit
This churlish knot of all-abhorred war,
And move in that obedient orb again
Where you did give a fair and natural light,
And be no more an exhal'd meteor,
A prodigy of fear, and a portent
Of broached mischief to the unborn times?
WORCESTER. Hear me, my liege:
  For mine own part, I could be well content
  To entertain the lag-end of my life
  With quiet hours; for I protest
  I have not sought the day of this dislike.
KING. You have not sought it! How comes it then?
FALSTAFF. Rebellion lay in his way, and he found it.
PRINCE. Peace, chewet, peace!

255

WORCESTER. It pleas'd your Majesty to turn your looks
  Of favour from myself and all our house;
  And yet I must remember you, my lord,
  We were the first and dearest of your friends.
  For you my staff of office did I break
  In Richard's time, and posted day and night
  To meet you on the way and kiss your hand,
  When yet you were in place and in account
  Nothing so strong and fortunate as I.
  It was myself, my brother, and his son,
  That brought you home, and boldly did outdare
  The dangers of the time. You swore to us—
  And you did swear that oath at Doncaster—
  That you did nothing purpose 'gainst the state,
  Nor claim no further than your new-fall'n right,
  The seat of Gaunt, dukedom of Lancaster;
  To this we swore our aid. But in short space
  It rain'd down fortune show'ring on your head;
  And such a flood of greatness fell on you,
  What with our help, what with the absent King,
  What with the injuries of a wanton time,
  The seeming sufferances that you had borne,
  And the contrarious winds that held the King
  So long in his unlucky Irish wars
  That all in England did repute him dead;
  And from this swarm of fair advantages
  You took occasion to be quickly woo'd
  To gripe the general sway into your hand;
  Forgot your oath to us at Doncaster;
  And being fed by us you us'd us so
  As that ungentle gull, the cuckoo's bird,
  Useth the sparrow—did oppress our nest,
  Grew by our feeding to so great a bulk
  That even our love durst not come near your sight
  For fear of swallowing; but with nimble wing
  We were enforc'd, for safety sake, to fly
  Out of your sight, and raise this present head;
  Whereby we stand opposed by such means
  As you yourself have forg'd against yourself,
  By unkind usage, dangerous countenance,

And violation of all faith and troth
Sworn to us in your younger enterprise.
KING. These things, indeed, you have articulate,
    Proclaim'd at market-crosses, read in churches,
    To face the garment of rebellion
    With some fine colour that may please the eye
    Of fickle changelings and poor discontents,
    Which gape and rub the elbow at the news
    Of hurlyburly innovation;
    And never yet did insurrection want
    Such water-colours to impaint his cause,
    Nor moody beggars, starving for a time
    Of pellmell havoc and confusion.
PRINCE. In both your armies there is many a soul
    Shall pay full dearly for this encounter,
    If once they join in trial. Tell your nephew
    The Prince of Wales doth join with all the world
    In praise of Henry Percy. By my hopes,
    This present enterprise set off his head,
    I do not think a braver gentleman,
    More active-valiant or more valiant-young,
    More daring or more bold, is now alive
    To grace this latter age with noble deeds.
    For my part, I may speak it to my shame,
    I have a truant been to chivalry;
    And so I hear he doth account me too.
    Yet this before my father's majesty—
    I am content that he shall take the odds
    Of his great name and estimation,
    And will, to save the blood on either side,
    Try fortune with him in a single fight.
KING. And, Prince of Wales, so dare we venture thee,
    Albeit considerations infinite
    Do make against it. No, good Worcester, no,
    We love our people well; even those we love
    That are misled upon your cousin's part;
    And will they take the offer of our grace,
    Both he and they and you, yea, every man
    Shall be my friend again, and I'll be his.
    So tell your cousin, and bring me word

What he will do. But if he will not yield,
Rebuke and dread correction wait on us,
And they shall do their office. So, be gone;
We will not now be troubled with reply.
We offer fair; take it advisedly.

Exeunt WORCESTER *and* VERNON

PRINCE. It will not be accepted, on my life:
  The Douglas and the Hotspur both together
  Are confident against the world in arms.
KING. Hence, therefore, every leader to his charge;
  For, on their answer, will we set on them;
  And God befriend us, as our cause is just!

Exeunt all but the PRINCE *and* FALSTAFF

FALSTAFF. Hal, if thou see me down in the battle, and be-
  stride me, so; 'tis a point of friendship.
PRINCE. Nothing but a colossus can do thee that friendship.
  Say thy prayers, and farewell.
FALSTAFF. I would 'twere bed-time, Hal, and all well.
PRINCE. Why, thou owest God a death.   *Exit*
FALSTAFF. 'Tis not due yet; I would be loath to pay him be-
  fore his day. What need I be so forward with him that
  calls not on me? Well, 'tis no matter; honour pricks me on.
  Yea, but how if honour prick me off when I come on?
  How then? Can honour set to a leg? No. Or an arm? No.
  Or take away the grief of a wound? No. Honour hath no
  skill in surgery, then? No. What is honour? A word.
  What is in that word? Honour. What is that honour? Air.
  A trim reckoning! Who hath it? He that died o' Wednesday. Doth he feel it? No. Doth he hear it? No. 'Tis insensible, then? Yea, to the dead. But will it not live with
  the living? No. Why? Detraction will not suffer it. Therefore I'll none of it. Honour is a mere scutcheon. And so
  ends my catechism.   *Exit*

SCENE 2

The rebel camp

Enter WORCESTER *and* VERNON

WORCESTER. O, no, my nephew must not know, Sir Richard,
  The liberal and kind offer of the King.
VERNON. 'Twere best he did.
WORCESTER. Then are we all undone.
  It is not possible, it cannot be,
  The King should keep his word in loving us;
  He will suspect us still, and find a time
  To punish this offence in other faults;
  Supposition all our lives shall be stuck full of eyes,
  For treason is but trusted like the fox,
  Who, never so tame, so cherish'd, and lock'd up,
  Will have a wild trick of his ancestors.
  Look how we can, or sad or merrily,
  Interpretation will misquote our looks,
  And we shall feed like oxen at a stall,
  The better cherish'd still the nearer death.
  My nephew's trespass may be well forgot;
  It hath the excuse of youth and heat of blood,
  And an adopted name of privilege—
  A hare-brain'd Hotspur, govern'd by a spleen.
  All his offences live upon my head
  And on his father's: we did train him on;
  And, his corruption being ta'en from us,
  We, as the spring of all, shall pay for all.
  Therefore, good cousin, let not Harry know,
  In any case, the offer of the King.
VERNON. Deliver what you will, I'll say 'tis so.
  Here comes your cousin.

Enter HOTSPUR *and* DOUGLAS

HOTSPUR. My uncle is return'd:
  Deliver up my Lord of Westmoreland.
  Uncle, what news?
WORCESTER. The King will bid you battle presently.

DOUGLAS. Defy him by the Lord of Westmoreland.
HOTSPUR. Lord Douglas, go you and tell him so.
DOUGLAS. Marry, and shall, and very willingly.　　　　*Exit*
WORCESTER. There is no seeming mercy in the King.
HOTSPUR. Did you beg any? God forbid!
WORCESTER. I told him gently of our grievances,
　Of his oath-breaking; which he mended thus,
　By now forswearing that he is forsworn.
　He calls us rebels, traitors, and will scourge
　With haughty arms this hateful name in us.

Re-enter DOUGLAS

DOUGLAS. Arm, gentlemen, to arms! for I have thrown
　A brave defiance in King Henry's teeth—
　And Westmoreland, that was engag'd, did bear it—
　Which cannot choose but bring him quickly on.
WORCESTER. The Prince of Wales stepp'd forth before the
　　King,
　And, nephew, challeng'd you to single fight.
HOTSPUR. O, would the quarrel lay upon our heads;
　And that no man might draw short breath to-day
　But I and Harry Monmouth! Tell me, tell me,
　How show'd his tasking? Seem'd it in contempt?
VERNON. No, by my soul, I never in my life
　Did hear a challenge urg'd more modestly,
　Unless a brother should a brother dare
　To gentle exercise and proof of arms.
　He gave you all the duties of a man;
　Trimm'd up your praises with a princely tongue;
　Spoke your deservings like a chronicle;
　Making you ever better than his praise,
　By still dispraising praise valued with you;
　And, which became him like a prince indeed,
　He made a blushing cital of himself,
　And chid his truant youth with such a grace
　As if he mast'red there a double spirit,
　Of teaching and of learning instantly.
　There did he pause; but let me tell the world—
　If he outlive the envy of this day,
　England did never owe so sweet a hope,

So much misconstrued in his wantonness.
HOTSPUR. Cousin, I think thou art enamoured
　On his follies. Never did I hear
　Of any prince so wild a liberty.
　But be he as he will, yet once ere night
　I will embrace him with a soldier's arm,
　That he shall shrink under my courtesy.
　Arm, arm with speed! and, fellows, soldiers, friends,
　Better consider what you have to do
　Than I, that have not well the gift of tongue,
　Can lift your blood up with persuasion.

Enter a MESSENGER

MESSENGER. My lord, here are letters for you.
HOTSPUR. I cannot read them now.
　O gentlemen, the time of life is short!
　To spend that shortness basely were too long,
　If life did ride upon a dial's point,
　Still ending at the arrival of an hour.
　An if we live, we live to tread on kings;
　If die, brave death, when princes die with us!
　Now, for our consciences, the arms are fair,
　When the intent of bearing them is just.

Enter another MESSENGER

MESSENGER. My lord, prepare; the King comes on apace.
HOTSPUR. I thank him that he cuts me from my tale,
　For I profess not talking; only this—
　Let each man do his best. And here draw I
　A sword, whose temper I intend to stain
　With the best blood that I can meet withal
　In the adventure of this perilous day.
　Now, Esperance! Percy! and set on.
　Sound all the lofty instruments of war,
　And by that music let us all embrace;
　For, heaven to earth, some of us never shall
　A second time do such a courtesy.
　　　　　　[*They embrace. The trumpets sound. Exeunt*]

SCENE 3

A plain between the camps

The KING *passes across with his power. Alarum to the battle. Then enter* DOUGLAS *and* SIR WALTER BLUNT

BLUNT. What is thy name, that in battle thus
    Thou crossest me? What honour dost thou seek
    Upon my head?
DOUGLAS. Know, then, my name is Douglas;
    And I do haunt thee in the battle thus
    Because some tell me that thou art a king.
BLUNT. They tell thee true.
DOUGLAS. The Lord of Stafford dear to-day hath bought
    Thy likeness; for instead of thee, King Harry,
    This sword hath ended him. So shall it thee.
    Unless thou yield thee as my prisoner.
BLUNT. I was not born a yielder, thou proud Scot;
    And thou shalt find a king that will revenge
    Lord Stafford's death.   [*They fight.* DOUGLAS *kills* BLUNT]

Enter HOTSPUR

HOTSPUR. O Douglas, hadst thou fought at Holmedon thus,
    I never had triumph'd upon a Scot.
DOUGLAS. All's done, all's won; here breathless lies the King.
HOTSPUR. Where?
DOUGLAS. Here.
HOTSPUR. This, Douglas? No: I know this face full well;
    A gallant knight he was, his name was Blunt;
    Semblably furnish'd like the King himself.
DOUGLAS. A fool go with thy soul whither it goes!
    A borrowed title hast thou bought too dear;
    Why didst thou tell me that thou wert a king?
HOTSPUR. The King hath many marching in his coats.
DOUGLAS. Now, by my sword, I will kill all his coats;
    I'll murder all his wardrobe, piece by piece,
    Until I meet the King.
HOTSPUR. Up, and away!
    Our soldiers stand full fairly for the day.   *Exeunt*

ACT V. SCENE 3

Alarum. Enter FALSTAFF, *solus*

FALSTAFF. Though I could scape shot-free at London, I fear the shot here: here's no scoring but upon the pate. Soft! who are you? Sir Walter Blunt. There's honour for you! Here's no vanity! I am as hot as molten lead, and as heavy too. God keep lead out of me! I need no more weight than mine own bowels. I have led my ragamuffins where they are pepper'd; there's not three of my hundred and fifty left alive, and they are for the town's end, to beg during life. But who comes here?

Enter the PRINCE OF WALES

PRINCE. What, stand'st thou idle here? Lend me thy sword.
Many a nobleman lies stark and stiff
Under the hoofs of vaunting enemies,
Whose deaths are yet unreveng'd. I prithee lend me thy
sword.
FALSTAFF. O Hal, I prithee give me leave to breathe awhile. Turk Gregory never did such deeds in arms as I have done this day. I have paid Percy, I have made him sure.
PRINCE. He is, indeed, and living to kill thee. I prithee lend me thy sword.
FALSTAFF. Nay, before God, Hal, if Percy be alive, thou get'st not my sword; but take my pistol, if thou wilt.
PRINCE. Give it me. What, is it in the case?
FALSTAFF. Ay, Hal; 'tis hot, 'tis hot; there's that will sack a
city.   [*The* PRINCE *draws it out, and finds it to
be a bottle of sack*]
PRINCE. What, is it a time to jest and dally now?
                    [*He throws the bottle at him. Exit*]
FALSTAFF. Well, if Percy be alive, I'll pierce him. If he do come in my way, so; if he do not, if I come in his willingly, let him make a carbonado of me. I like not such grinning honour as Sir Walter hath. Give me life, which if I can save, so; if not, honour comes unlook'd for, and there's an end.   *Exit*

SCENE 4

Another part of the field

Alarums. Excursions. Enter the KING, *the* PRINCE OF WALES, PRINCE JOHN OF LANCASTER, *and* WESTMORELAND

KING. I prithee,
 Harry, withdraw thyself; thou bleedest too much;
 Lord John of Lancaster, go you with him.
PRINCE JOHN. Not I, my lord, unless I did bleed too.
PRINCE. I beseech your Majesty, make up,
 Lest your retirement do amaze your friends.
KING. I will do so.
 My Lord of Westmoreland, lead him to his tent.
WESTMORELAND. Come, my lord, I'll lead you to your tent.
PRINCE. Lead me, my lord? I do not need your help;
 And God forbid a shallow scratch should drive
 The Prince of Wales from such a field as this,
 Where stain'd nobility lies trodden on,
 And rebels' arms triumph in massacres!
PRINCE JOHN. We breathe too long. Come, cousin West-
 moreland,
 Our duty this way lies; for God's sake, come.
       Exeunt PRINCE JOHN *and* WESTMORELAND
PRINCE. By God, thou hast deceiv'd me, Lancaster!
 I did not think thee lord of such a spirit;
 Before, I lov'd thee as a brother, John,
 But now I do respect thee as my soul.
KING. I saw him hold Lord Percy at the point
 With lustier maintenance than I did look for
 Of such an ungrown warrior.
PRINCE. O, this boy
 Lends mettle to us all!   *Exit*

Enter DOUGLAS

DOUGLAS. Another king! They grow like Hydra's heads.
 I am the Douglas, fatal to all those
 That wear those colours on them. What art thou,
 That counterfeit'st the person of a king?

ACT V. SCENE 4

KING. The King himself, who, Douglas, grieves at heart
  So many of his shadows thou hast met,
  And not the very King. I have two boys
  Seek Percy and thyself about the field;
  But, seeing thou fall'st on me so luckily,
  I will assay thee; so, defend thyself.
DOUGLAS. I fear thou art another counterfeit;
  And yet, in faith, thou bearest thee like a king;
  But mine I am sure thou art, who'er thou be,
  And thus I win thee.

>   *[They fight, the* KING *being in danger]*

Re-enter the PRINCE

PRINCE. Hold up thy head, vile Scot, or thou art like
  Never to hold it up again. The spirits
  Of valiant Shirley, Stafford, Blunt, are in my arms;
  It is the Prince of Wales that threatens thee,
  Who never promiseth but he means to pay.

>   *[They fight;* DOUGLAS *flies]*

  Cheerly, my lord: how fares your Grace?
  Sir Nicholas Gawsey hath for succour sent,
  And so hath Clifton. I'll to Clifton straight.
KING. Stay, and breathe awhile.
  Thou hast redeem'd thy lost opinion;
  And show'd thou mak'st some tender of my life,
  In this fair rescue thou hast brought to me.
PRINCE. O God, they did me too much injury
  That ever said I heark'ned for your death!
  If it were so, I might have let alone
  The insulting hand of Douglas over you,
  Which would have been as speedy in your end
  As all the poisonous potions in the world,
  And sav'd the treacherous labour of your son.
KING. Make up to Clifton, I'll to Sir Nicholas Gawsey. *Exit*

Enter HOTSPUR

HOTSPUR. If I mistake not, thou art Harry Monmouth.
PRINCE. Thou speak'st as if I would deny my name.
HOTSPUR. My name is Harry Percy.
PRINCE. Why, then I see

A very valiant rebel of the name.
I am the Prince of Wales; and think not, Percy,
To share with me in glory any more.
Two stars keep not their motion in one sphere,
Nor can one England brook a double reign
Of Harry Percy and the Prince of Wales.

HOTSPUR. Nor shall it, Harry, for the hour is come
To end the one of us; and would to God
Thy name in arms were now as great as mine!

PRINCE. I'll make it greater ere I part from thee,
And all the budding honours on thy crest
I'll crop to make a garland for my head.

HOTSPUR. I can no longer brook thy vanities.   [*They fight*]

Enter FALSTAFF

FALSTAFF. Well said, Hal! to it, Hal! Nay, you shall find no
boy's play here, I can tell you.

> *Re-enter* DOUGLAS; *he fights with* FALSTAFF, *who
> falls down as if he were dead;* DOUGLAS *withdraws.*
> HOTSPUR *is wounded and falls*

HOTSPUR. O, Harry thou hast robb'd me of my youth!
I better brook the loss of brittle life
Than those proud titles thou hast won of me:
They wound my thoughts worse than thy sword my flesh;
But thoughts, the slaves of life, and life, time's fool,
And time, that takes survey of all the world,
Must have a stop. O, I could prophesy,
But that the earthy and cold hand of death
Lies on my tongue. No, Percy, thou art dust
And food for—   [*Dies*]

PRINCE. For worms, brave Percy. Fare thee well, great heart!
Ill-weav'd ambition, how much art thou shrunk!
When that this body did contain a spirit,
A kingdom for it was too small a bound;
But now two paces of the vilest earth
Is room enough. This earth that bears thee dead
Bears not alive so stout a gentleman.
If thou wert sensible of courtesy,
I should not make so dear a show of zeal;

But let my favours hide thy mangled face,
And even in thy behalf, I'll thank myself
For doing these fair rites of tenderness.
Adieu, and take thy praise with thee to heaven!
Thy ignominy sleep with thee in the grave,
But not rememb'red in thy epitaph!
                    [*He spieth* FALSTAFF *on the ground*]
What, old acquaintance! Could not all this flesh
Keep in a little life? Poor Jack, farewell!
I could have better spar'd a better man.
O, I should have a heavy miss of thee,
If I were much in love with vanity!
Death hath not struck so fat a deer to-day,
Though many dearer, in this bloody fray.
Embowell'd will I see thee by and by;
Till then in blood by noble Percy lie.   *Exit*

FALSTAFF. [*Rising up*] Embowell'd! if thou embowel me
to-day, I'll give you leave to powder me and eat me too
to-morrow. 'Sblood, 'twas time to counterfeit, or that hot
termagant Scot had paid me scot and lot too. Counterfeit?
I lie, I am no counterfeit: to die is to be a counterfeit;
for he is but the counterfeit of a man who hath not the
life of a man; but to counterfeit dying, when a man
thereby liveth, is to be no counterfeit, but the true and
perfect image of life indeed. The better part of valour is
discretion; in the which better part I have saved my life.
Zounds, I am afraid of this gunpowder Percy, though he
be dead; how if he should counterfeit too, and rise? By my
faith, I am afraid he would prove the better counterfeit.
Therefore I'll make him sure; yea, and I'll swear I kill'd
him. Why may not he rise as well as I? Nothing confutes
me but eyes, and nobody sees me. Therefore, sirrah [*stabbing him*], with a new wound in your thigh, come you
along with me.   [*He takes up* HOTSPUR *on his back*]

Re-enter the PRINCE OF WALES *and*
PRINCE JOHN OF LANCASTER

PRINCE. Come, brother John, full bravely hast thou flesh'd
Thy maiden sword.
PRINCE JOHN. But, soft! whom have we here?

Did you not tell me this fat man was dead?

PRINCE. I did; I saw him dead,
Breathless and bleeding on the ground. Art thou alive?
Or is it fantasy that plays upon our eyesight?
I prithee speak; we will not trust our eyes
Without our ears: thou art not what thou seem'st.

FALSTAFF. No, that's certain: I am not a double man; but if
I be not Jack Falstaff, then am I a Jack. There is Percy
[*throwing the body down*]; if your father will do me any
honour, so; if not, let him kill the next Percy himself: I
look to be either earl or duke, I can assure you.

PRINCE. Why, Percy I kill'd myself, and saw thee dead.

FALSTAFF. Didst thou? Lord, Lord, how this world is given
to lying! I grant you I was down and out of breath, and so
was he; but we rose both at an instant, and fought a long
hour by Shrewsbury clock. If I may be believ'd, so; if not,
let them that should reward valour bear the sin upon their
own heads. I'll take it upon my death, I gave him this
wound in the thigh; if the man were alive, and would
deny it, zounds, I would make him eat a piece of my
sword.

PRINCE JOHN. This is the strangest tale that ever I heard.

PRINCE. This is the strangest fellow, brother John.
Come, bring your luggage nobly on your back.
For my part, if a lie may do thee grace,
I'll gild it with the happiest terms I have.

        [*A retreat is sounded*]

The trumpet sounds retreat; the day is ours.
Come, brother, let us to the highest of the field,
To see what friends are living, who are dead.

   Exeunt the PRINCE *and* PRINCE JOHN OF LANCASTER

FALSTAFF. I'll follow, as they say, for reward. He that rewards me, God reward him! If I do grow great, I'll grow
less; for I'll purge, and leave sack, and live cleanly, as a
nobleman should do.   *Exit*

SCENE 5

Another part of the field

The trumpets sound. Enter the KING, *the* PRINCE
OF WALES, PRINCE JOHN OF LANCASTER, WEST-
MORELAND, *with* WORCESTER *and* VERNON *prisoners*

KING. Thus ever did rebellion find rebuke.
  Ill-spirited Worcester! did not we send grace,
  Pardon and terms of love to all of you?
  And wouldst thou turn our offers contrary?
  Misuse the tenour of thy kinsman's trust?
  Three knights upon our party slain to-day,
  A noble earl, and many a creature else,
  Had been alive this hour,
  If like a Christian thou hadst truly borne
  Betwixt our armies true intelligence.
WORCESTER. What I have done my safety urg'd me to;
  And I embrace this fortune patiently,
  Since not to be avoided it falls on me.
KING. Bear Worcester to the death, and Vernon too;
  Other offenders we will pause upon.
                    Exeunt WORCESTER *and* VERNON *guarded*
  How goes the field?
PRINCE. The noble Scot, Lord Douglas, when he saw
  The fortune of the day quite turn'd from him,
  The noble Percy slain, and all his men
  Upon the foot of fear, fled with the rest;
  And falling from a hill, he was so bruis'd
  That the pursuers took him. At my tent
  The Douglas is; and I beseech your Grace
  I may dispose of him.
KING. With all my heart.
PRINCE. Then, brother John of Lancaster, to you
  This honourable bounty shall belong:
  Go to the Douglas, and deliver him
  Up to his pleasure, ransomless and free;
  His valours shown upon our crests to-day
  Have taught us how to cherish such high deeds

Even in the bosom of our adversaries.

PRINCE JOHN. I thank your Grace for this high courtesy,
  Which I shall give away immediately.

KING. Then this remains—that we divide our power.
  You, son John, and my cousin Westmoreland,
  Towards York shall bend you with your dearest speed
  To meet Northumberland and the prelate Scroop,
  Who, as we hear, are busily in arms.
  Myself, and you, son Harry, will towards Wales
  To fight with Glendower and the Earl of March.
  Rebellion in this land shall lose his sway,
  Meeting the check of such another day;
  And since this business so fair is done,
  Let us not leave till all our own be won.   *Exeunt*

The Second Part of
King Henry the Fourth

THE SECOND PART OF
KING HENRY THE FOURTH

SHAKESPEARE, if he had planned his *Henry IV* as a play in
two parts, would, it has been fairly argued, have dis-
tributed his material between them more tactfully; for the
second part especially in its treatment of the relations of the
Prince and his father repeats a situation that had not only
been already developed at length in the first part but satisfactorily concluded in the reconciliation between father
and son after the battle of Shrewsbury. Shakespeare's treatment of the battle of Shrewsbury as the episode that makes
clear to the King the worth and devotion of his son is not
based on history; it was Shakespeare's own way for effecting
the reconciliation and the establishment of the Prince's reputation. At the conclusion of the first part the Prince has
made good his promise to his father that Percy will be
merely the factor

> To engross up glorious deeds on my behalf,

and the King has acknowledged his son's prowess and loyalty. If Shakespeare had had in mind from the beginning the
scene between the Prince and his dying father in the Jerusalem chamber that comes towards the end of Part two, it is
difficult to understand why he should have concluded the
first Part with so clear a vindication of the Prince from the
reproaches of the King.

That Shakespeare had a sequel in mind however seems
obvious from the conclusion of Part one. There is no full
close, for the last speeches are concerned with directions for
immediate action and the dispositions to be adopted to meet
the rebels that were confederate with Percy but not present
at Shrewsbury. Perhaps the scene in the first Part between
the Archbishop of York and Sir Michael is an anticipation of
what Shakespeare felt might form a feature of his next play;
it prepares us for Prince John's campaign against the Archbishop, Mowbray, and Hastings. Further the Prince's promise

in his opening soliloquy in I, 2 of the first Part to throw off
his loose behaviour is considered by some as still unfulfilled
till the end of Part two. We are forewarned here, they argue, of the rejection of Falstaff and his associates that marks
the Prince's final renunciation of his irresponsible hours.

However we regard the relationship of the two parts,
whether we think of them as the single expression of a carefully premeditated theme or regard the second Part as more
casually developed and a rehandling of a topic that the
public wished to hear more about, it is clear that the second
Part follows very closely the general design of the first. The
campaign against the Archbishop and his allies takes the place
of the political complications that lead to the encounter at
Shrewsbury; and the historical and comic episodes alternate
much as in Part one. Falstaff however has a larger part and
the doings of the Archbishop and his party have little of
the interest or character that was given to rebellion by Hotspur. Indeed the rebellion in the second Part has almost as its
excuse for being introduced at all the opportunity it provides
for showing us Falstaff at the kind of roguery that is touched
on only in passing in Part one.

In Part one Falstaff and his company on their way to
Shrewsbury encounter the Prince and Westmoreland. After
a characteristic greeting the Prince says to Falstaff 'But tell
me, Jack, whose fellows are these that come after?' and, on
hearing that they are Falstaff's, observes 'I did never see such
pitiful rascals.' The explanation of their condition has already
been given us by their captain:

> I have misused the King's press damnably. I have got, in
> exchange of a hundred and fifty soldiers, three hundred
> and odd pounds.

The details of this exchange Shakespeare has filled in for us
in Part two where Falstaff pays his first visit to Justice Shallow in Gloucestershire. Here as elsewhere in Part two, especially in the scenes at the Boar's Head Tavern, there is
turned for our inspection the more seamy side of the gay
bravery in which we have so far seen the Knight. We are
told what must have happened when Falstaff was raising his
company for Shrewsbury; but if the actual representation of

what took place is even more comic it is also more sobering. And Shakespeare was consistent in revealing to us Falstaff's most successful stroke of cozenage only in the very hour of his greatest defeat. We know that Falstaff was making a second visit to Justice Shallow for more than the sake of old acquaintance; but we learn of the success of the visit only after Falstaff, having just received from his former Prince public sentence of banishment, turns to Shallow to say,

Master Shallow, I owe you a thousand pound.

In Part two Shakespeare has felt it necessary to touch more realistically on those aspects of Falstaff's way of life that are calculated to make him unacceptable to those whose duty it is to maintain law and order. To emphasize this feature of his design Shakespeare makes Falstaff's first appearance in Part two his encounter with the Lord Chief Justice. His whole behaviour to the Chief Justice is, as Maurice Morgann observes, singularly insolent, for Falstaff knows that he can gain nothing here by flattery; impudence is his only resource, but he has encountered the embodiment of something not so easily put out of countenance. Falstaff relied on settling disputes by overwhelming his opponents with the dexterity of his wit; but the Lord Chief Justice was not interested in Falstaff's story that Mrs. Quickly had said her son was like his Lordship:

Sir John, Sir John, I am well acquainted with your manner of wrenching the true cause the false way. It is not a confident brow, nor the throng of words that come with such more than impudent sauciness from you, can thrust me from a level consideration.

And he adds more severely: 'You speak as having power to do wrong.' The Prince is able to enjoy the Falstaffian respect for nothing; but has no intention of tolerating it as King. When raffishness presumes to interrupt the necessary business of state the Lord Chief Justice consigns it to the Fleet.

It is unnecessary to regard the Lord Chief Justice as the Prince's good angel to whom the Prince owes his conversion. The Prince is conscious from the beginning of what he intends to do to those who fail to respect his person; he needs

no one to instruct him in his use of authority. Yet Shakespeare adapts the Prince's relations with the Lord Chief Justice to place beyond all doubt the new King's purposes.
Whether Shakespeare had when he began on the first Part
a clear notion of how he would treat the transformation of
the Prince to King and dispose of Falstaff must remain uncertain; when he started on the second Part however Shakespeare deliberately prepares for the new King's rejection of
his old companion. Falstaff is given such ample opportunity
to indulge his humour that the final scene is inevitable. The
man who enjoys making the world his dupe is himself the
biggest dupe of all.

This termination however satisfactory and indeed inevitable in one way and however cleverly staged by Shakespeare is not without its difficulties. If the two plays are
taken literally then the Prince's opening declaration of his intention to dismiss his cronies and his final disposal of them
raise the question of good faith and gentlemanly behaviour.
Beside such conduct the wheedling and cozenage of Falstaff
are almost venial; the Prince is the real villain of the piece.
But this was not Shakespeare's intention, it may be very
properly objected. Shakespeare is merely indicating to us at
the very start the inevitable outcome of Falstaff's way of life.
Shakespeare like his Prince was capable of enjoying the un-
limited scope for wit such an outlook as Falstaff's can provide; but the dramatist was too much a realist, too conscious
of the social implications of Falstaff's conduct to refrain from
putting it in its place in the context that Falstaff wished to
ignore. The Prince's warning is to be taken not so much as a
dramatic utterance as the author's outline of his plot.

That this latter view is the more satisfactory of the two
may be admitted. It still however leaves open to question the
artistry of Shakespeare's manner of preparation. So obvious
a statement of a dramatist's intentions inevitably infects the
action with a kind of unreality; our suspension of disbelief in
the fictional nature of the story is too peremptorily commanded to be given without question. Shakespeare himself
has had to direct us to look as his design in a particular way;
but this we feel would have been unnecessary had he been
able to transform his material to the complete embodiment

of his idea. To make therefore of the plot a parable that reveals the profounder promptings of Shakespeare's art is to ignore the compromise with his material that Shakespeare acknowledges in treating the Prince, even if only for a brief speech, as a chorus that will direct the audience to the author's intentions about the character. It is impossible to regard the Prince as Shakespeare's Prodigal Son unless we can so rewrite the parable that the Prodigal may say as he departs for the far country,

I'll so offend, to make offence a skill.

Any such suggestion would deprive the parable of all its significance; and the Prince's words make any comparison between Shakespeare's plays and the parable inadequate. Nor can we regard the influence of the Morality tradition as the shaping force in Shakespeare's treatment. We should have to regard the ruler in *The Cradle of Security* as merely pretending to sleep while Pride, Covetousness, and Luxury croon over his cradle, so that he might detain them till End-of-the-World and Last Judgment catch them in the act, were we to moralize Shakespeare's plot.

We must accept Shakespeare's scheme for his Prince as he has outlined it for us; but it is in its nature somewhat artificial and conventional. The Elizabethan audience was right in finding its enjoyment in the part of Falstaff, for it is here that Shakespeare's art is unconfined; and it is here too that the Prince himself finds his real freedom. Morgann has linked Falstaff and the Prince in a comparison that expresses their true relation:

There is a natural activity about Falstaff which, for want of proper employment shews itself in a kind of swell or bustle, which seems to correspond with his bulk, as if his mind had inflated his body, and demanded a habitation of no less circumference: Thus conditioned he rolls (in the language of *Ossian*) like a *Whale of Ocean*, scattering the smaller fry; but affording in his turn, noble contention to *Hal* and *Poins;* who, to keep up the allusion, I may be allowed on this occasion to compare to the Thresher and the Sword-fish.

To show the Prince hanging back from this sport in deference to some moral scruple we may attribute to him or in an attempt to give the plot the artistic coherence it does not possess is to ignore the substance of Shakespeare's work in pursuit of the shadow that goes with it. In a recent production it was noted that

> Prince Hal seems scarcely to enjoy Falstaff and rarely brings himself to bandy base comparisons with the rascal without introducing a covert threat.

And, adds the critic,

> Falstaff is more than half aware that his standing with the Prince is in doubt.

Had it been so, we may well ask why Falstaff so misjudged his coronation greeting. This is to take the heart out of the play in an attempt to provide it with a conscience. The Elizabethans knew better and their wholehearted enjoyment of the Knight shows not only a more human but a more artistic appreciation of Shakespeare's greatest comic character.

RUMOUR, *the Presenter*
KING HENRY THE FOURTH

HENRY, PRINCE OF WALES, *afterwards* HENRY V
PRINCE JOHN OF LANCASTER
PRINCE HUMPHREY OF GLOUCESTER
THOMAS, DUKE OF CLARENCE
  Sons of Henry IV

EARL OF NORTHUMBERLAND   SCROOP, ARCHBISHOP OF YORK
LORD MOWBRAY   LORD HASTINGS
LORD BARDOLPH   SIR JOHN COLVILLE
TRAVERS *and* MORTON, *retainers of Northumberland*
  Opposites against King Henry IV

EARL OF WARWICK   EARL OF WESTMORELAND
EARL OF SURREY   EARL OF KENT
GOWER   HARCOURT   BLUNT
  Of the King's party

LORD CHIEF JUSTICE   SERVANT, *to Lord Chief Justice*

SIR JOHN FALSTAFF   EDWARD POINS
BARDOLPH   PISTOL   PETO
  Irregular humourists

PAGE, *to Falstaff*

ROBERT SHALLOW *and* SILENCE, *country Justices*
DAVY, *servant to Shallow*

FANG *and* SNARE, *Sheriff's officers*

RALPH MOULDY, SIMON SHADOW, THOMAS WART, FRANCIS
  FEEBLE, PETER BULLCALF, *country soldiers*

FRANCIS, *a drawer*

LADY NORTHUMBERLAND   LADY PERCY, *Percy's widow*
HOSTESS QUICKLY, *of the Boar's Head, Eastcheap*
DOLL TEARSHEET

Lords, Attendants, Porter, Drawers, Beadles, Grooms, Servants, Speaker of the Epilogue

SCENE: *England*

The Second Part of
King Henry the Fourth

INDUCTION

Warkworth. Before NORTHUMBERLAND'S *castle*

Enter RUMOUR, *painted full of tongues*

RUMOUR. Open your ears; for which of you will stop
 The vent of hearing when loud Rumour speaks?
 I, from the orient to the drooping west,
 Making the wind my post-horse, still unfold
 The acts commenced on this ball of earth.
 Upon my tongues continual slanders ride,
 The which in every language I pronounce,
 Stuffing the ears of men with false reports.
 I speak of peace while covert enmity,
 Under the smile of safety, wounds the world;
 And who but Rumour, who but only I,
 Make fearful musters and prepar'd defence,
 Whiles the big year, swoln with some other grief,
 Is thought with child by the stern tyrant war,
 And no such matter? Rumour is a pipe
 Blown by surmises, jealousies, conjectures,
 And of so easy and so plain a stop
 That the blunt monster with uncounted heads,
 The still-discordant wav'ring multitude,
 Can play upon it. But what need I thus
 My well-known body to anatomize
 Among my household? Why is Rumour here?
 I run before King Harry's victory,
 Who, in a bloody field by Shrewsbury,
 Hath beaten down young Hotspur and his troops,
 Quenching the flame of bold rebellion
 Even with the rebels' blood. But what mean I

To speak so true at first? My office is
To noise abroad that Harry Monmouth fell
Under the wrath of noble Hotspur's sword,
And that the King before the Douglas' rage
Stoop'd his anointed head as low as death.
This have I rumour'd through the peasant towns
Between that royal field of Shrewsbury
And this worm-eaten hold of ragged stone,
Where Hotspur's father, old Northumberland,
Lies crafty-sick. The posts come tiring on,
And not a man of them brings other news
Than they have learnt of me. From Rumour's tongues
They bring smooth comforts false, worse than true wrongs.

Exit

ACT I. SCENE 1

Warkworth. Before NORTHUMBERLAND's *castle*

Enter LORD BARDOLPH

LORD BARDOLPH. Who keeps the gate here, ho?

The PORTER *opens the gate*

Where is the Earl?
PORTER. What shall I say you are?
LORD BARDOLPH. Tell thou the Earl
That the Lord Bardolph doth attend him here.
PORTER. His lordship is walk'd forth into the orchard.
Please it your honour knock but at the gate,
And he himself will answer.

Enter NORTHUMBERLAND

LORD BARDOLPH. Here comes the Earl.   *Exit* PORTER
NORTHUMBERLAND. What news, Lord Bardolph? Every
minute now
Should be the father of some stratagem.
The times are wild; contention, like a horse

284

Full of high feeding, madly hath broke loose
And bears down all before him.

LORD BARDOLPH. Noble Earl,
I bring you certain news from Shrewsbury.

NORTHUMBERLAND. Good, an God will!

LORD BARDOLPH. As good as heart can wish.
The King is almost wounded to the death;
And, in the fortune of my lord your son,
Prince Harry slain outright; and both the Blunts
Kill'd by the hand of Douglas; young Prince John,
And Westmoreland, and Stafford, fled the field;
And Harry Monmouth's brawn, the hulk Sir John,
Is prisoner to your son. O, such a day,
So fought, so followed, and so fairly won,
Came not till now to dignify the times,
Since Cæsar's fortunes!

NORTHUMBERLAND. How is this deriv'd?
Saw you the field? Came you from Shrewsbury?

LORD BARDOLPH. I spake with one, my lord, that came from
thence;
A gentleman well bred and of good name,
That freely rend'red me these news for true.

Enter TRAVERS

NORTHUMBERLAND. Here comes my servant Travers, whom
I sent
On Tuesday last to listen after news.

LORD BARDOLPH. My lord, I over-rode him on the way;
And he is furnish'd with no certainties
More than he haply may retail from me.

NORTHUMBERLAND. Now, Travers, what good tidings comes
with you?

TRAVERS. My lord, Sir John Umfrevile turn'd me back
With joyful tidings; and, being better hors'd,
Out-rode me. After him came spurring hard
A gentleman, almost forspent with speed,
That stopp'd by me to breathe his bloodied horse.
He ask'd the way to Chester; and of him
I did demand what news from Shrewsbury.
He told me that rebellion had bad luck,

And that young Harry Percy's spur was cold.
With that he gave his able horse the head
And, bending forward, struck his armed heels
Against the panting sides of his poor jade
Up to the rowel-head; and starting so,
He seem'd in running to devour the way,
Staying no longer question.

NORTHUMBERLAND. Ha! Again:
Said he young Harry Percy's spur was cold?
Of Hotspur, Coldspur? that rebellion
Had met ill luck?

LORD BARDOLPH. My lord, I'll tell you what:
If my young lord your son have not the day,
Upon mine honour, for a silken point
I'll give my barony. Never talk of it.

NORTHUMBERLAND. Why should that gentleman that rode
  by Travers
Give then such instances of loss?

LORD BARDOLPH. Who—he?
He was some hilding fellow that had stol'n
The horse he rode on and, upon my life,
Spoke at a venture. Look, here comes more news.

Enter MORTON

NORTHUMBERLAND. Yea, this man's brow, like to a title-leaf,
Foretells the nature of a tragic volume.
So looks the strand whereon the imperious flood
Hath left a witness'd usurpation.
Say, Morton, didst thou come from Shrewsbury?

MORTON. I ran from Shrewsbury, my noble lord;
Where hateful death put on his ugliest mask
To fright our party.

NORTHUMBERLAND. How doth my son and brother?
Thou tremblest; and the whiteness in thy cheek
Is apter than thy tongue to tell thy errand.
Even such a man, so faint, so spiritless,
So dull, so dread in look, so woe-begone,
Drew Priam's curtain in the dead of night
And would have told him half his Troy was burnt;
But Priam found the fire ere he his tongue,

286

And I my Percy's death ere thou report'st it.
This thou wouldst say: 'Your son did thus and thus;
Your brother thus; so fought the noble Douglas'—
Stopping my greedy ear with their bold deeds;
But in the end, to stop my ear indeed,
Thou hast a sigh to blow away this praise,
Ending with 'Brother, son, and all, are dead.'
MORTON. Douglas is living, and your brother, yet;
But for my lord your son—
NORTHUMBERLAND. Why, he is dead.
See what a ready tongue suspicion hath!
He that but fears the thing he would not know
Hath by instinct knowledge from others' eyes
That what he fear'd is chanced. Yet speak, Morton;
Tell thou an earl his divination lies,
And I will take it as a sweet disgrace
And make thee rich for doing me such wrong.
MORTON. You are too great to be by me gainsaid;
Your spirit is too true, your fears too certain.
NORTHUMBERLAND. Yet, for all this, say not that Percy's
dead.
I see a strange confession in thine eye;
Thou shak'st thy head, and hold'st it fear or sin
To speak a truth. If he be slain, say so:
The tongue offends not that reports his death;
And he doth sin that doth belie the dead,
Not he which says the dead is not alive.
Yet the first bringer of unwelcome news
Hath but a losing office, and his tongue
Sounds ever after as a sullen bell,
Rememb'red tolling a departing friend.
LORD BARDOLPH. I cannot think, my lord, your son is dead.
MORTON. I am sorry I should force you to believe
That which I would to God I had not seen;
But these mine eyes saw him in bloody state,
Rend'ring faint quittance, wearied and out-breath'd,
To Harry Monmouth, whose swift wrath beat down
The never-daunted Percy to the earth,
From whence with life he never more sprung up.
In few, his death—whose spirit lent a fire

287

Even to the dullest peasant in his camp—
Being bruited once, took fire and heat away
From the best-temper'd courage in his troops;
For from his metal was his party steeled;
Which once in him abated, all the rest
Turn'd on themselves, like dull and heavy lead.
And as the thing that's heavy in itself
Upon enforcement flies with greatest speed,
So did our men, heavy in Hotspur's loss,
Lend to this weight such lightness with their fear
That arrows fled not swifter toward their aim
Than did our soldiers, aiming at their safety,
Fly from the field. Then was that noble Worcester
Too soon ta'en prisoner; and that furious Scot,
The bloody Douglas, whose well-labouring sword
Had three times slain th' appearance of the King,
Gan vail his stomach and did grace the shame
Of those that turn'd their backs, and in his flight,
Stumbling in fear, was took. The sum of all
Is that the King hath won, and hath sent out
A speedy power to encounter you, my lord,
Under the conduct of young Lancaster
And Westmoreland. This is the news at full.
NORTHUMBERLAND. For this I shall have time enough to
    mourn.
In poison there is physic; and these news,
Having been well, that would have made me sick,
Being sick, have in some measure made me well;
And as the wretch whose fever-weak'ned joints,
Like strengthless hinges, buckle under life,
Impatient of his fit, breaks like a fire
Out of his keeper's arms, even so my limbs,
Weak'ned with grief, being now enrag'd with grief,
Are thrice themselves. Hence, therefore, thou nice crutch!
A scaly gauntlet now with joints of steel
Must glove this hand; and hence, thou sickly coif!
Thou art a guard too wanton for the head
Which princes, flesh'd with conquest, aim to hit.
Now bind my brows with iron; and approach
The ragged'st hour that time and spite dare bring

To frown upon th' enrag'd Northumberland!
Let heaven kiss earth! Now let not Nature's hand
Keep the wild flood confin'd! Let order die!
And let this world no longer be a stage
To feed contention in a ling'ring act;
But let one spirit of the first-born Cain
Reign in all bosoms, that, each heart being set
On bloody courses, the rude scene may end
And darkness be the burier of the dead!

LORD BARDOLPH. This strained passion doth you wrong, my
    lord.

MORTON. Sweet Earl, divorce not wisdom from your honour.
    The lives of all your loving complices
    Lean on your health; the which, if you give o'er
    To stormy passion, must perforce decay.
    You cast th' event of war, my noble lord,
    And summ'd the account of chance before you said
    'Let us make head.' It was your pre-surmise
    That in the dole of blows your son might drop.
    You knew he walk'd o'er perils on an edge,
    More likely to fall in than to get o'er;
    You were advis'd his flesh was capable
    Of wounds and scars, and that his forward spirit
    Would lift him where most trade of danger rang'd;
    Yet did you say 'Go forth'; and none of this,
    Though strongly apprehended, could restrain
    The stiff-borne action. What hath then befall'n,
    Or what hath this bold enterprise brought forth
    More than that being which was like to be?

LORD BARDOLPH. We all that are engaged to this loss
    Knew that we ventured on such dangerous seas
    That if we wrought out life 'twas ten to one;
    And yet we ventur'd, for the gain propos'd
    Chok'd the respect of likely peril fear'd;
    And since we are o'erset, venture again.
    Come, we will put forth, body and goods.

MORTON. 'Tis more than time. And, my most noble lord,
    I hear for certain, and dare speak the truth:
    The gentle Archbishop of York is up
    With well-appointed pow'rs. He is a man

Who with a double surety binds his followers.
My lord your son had only but the corpse,
But shadows and the shows of men, to fight;
For that same word 'rebellion' did divide
The action of their bodies from their souls;
And they did fight with queasiness, constrain'd,
As men drink potions; that their weapons only
Seem'd on our side, but for their spirits and souls
This word 'rebellion'—it had froze them up,
As fish are in a pond. But now the Bishop
Turns insurrection to religion.
Suppos'd sincere and holy in his thoughts,
He's follow'd both with body and with mind;
And doth enlarge his rising with the blood
Of fair King Richard, scrap'd from Pomfret stones;
Derives from heaven his quarrel and his cause;
Tells them he doth bestride a bleeding land,
Gasping for life under great Bolingbroke;
And more and less do flock to follow him.

NORTHUMBERLAND. I knew of this before; but, to speak truth,
This present grief had wip'd it from my mind.
Go in with me; and counsel every man
The aptest way for safety and revenge.
Get posts and letters, and make friends with speed—
Never so few, and never yet more need.   *Exeunt*

SCENE 2

London. A street

Enter SIR JOHN FALSTAFF, *with his* PAGE *bearing his sword and buckler*

FALSTAFF. Sirrah, you giant, what says the doctor to my water?

PAGE. He said, sir, the water itself was a good healthy water; but for the party that owed it, he might have moe diseases than he knew for.

FALSTAFF. Men of all sorts take a pride to gird at me. The

brain of this foolish-compounded clay, man, is not able to invent anything that intends to laughter, more than I invent or is invented on me. I am not only witty in myself, but the cause that wit is in other men. I do here walk before thee like a sow that hath overwhelm'd all her litter but one. If the Prince put thee into my service for any other reason than to set me off, why then I have no judgment. Thou whoreson mandrake, thou art fitter to be worn in my cap than to wait at my heels. I was never mann'd with an agate till now; but I will inset you neither in gold nor silver, but in vile apparel, and send you back again to your master, for a jewel—the juvenal, the Prince your master, whose chin is not yet fledge. I will sooner have a beard grow in the palm of my hand than he shall get one off his cheek; and yet he will not stick to say his face is a face-royal. God may finish it when he will, 'tis not a hair amiss yet. He may keep it still at a face-royal, for a barber shall never earn sixpence out of it; and yet he'll be crowing as if he had writ man ever since his father was a bachelor. He may keep his own grace, but he's almost out of mine, I can assure him. What said Master Dommelton about the satin for my short cloak and my slops?

PAGE. He said, sir, you should procure him better assurance than Bardolph. He would not take his band and yours; he liked not the security.

FALSTAFF. Let him be damn'd, like the Glutton; pray God his tongue be hotter! A whoreson Achitophel! A rascal-yea-forsooth knave, to bear a gentleman in hand, and then stand upon security! The whoreson smooth-pates do now wear nothing but high shoes, and bunches of keys at their girdles; and if a man is through with them in honest taking-up, then they must stand upon security. I had as lief they would put ratsbane in my mouth as offer to stop it with security. I look'd 'a should have sent me two and twenty yards of satin, as I am a true knight, and he sends me security. Well, he may sleep in security; for he hath the horn of abundance, and the lightness of his wife shines through it; and yet cannot he see, though he have his own lanthorn to light him. Where's Bardolph?

PAGE. He's gone into Smithfield to buy your worship a horse.

FALSTAFF. I bought him in Paul's, and he'll buy me a horse in Smithfield. An I could get me but a wife in the stews, I were mann'd, hors'd, and wiv'd.

Enter the LORD CHIEF JUSTICE *and* SERVANT

PAGE. Sir, here comes the nobleman that committed the Prince for striking him about Bardolph.

FALSTAFF. Wait close; I will not see him.

CHIEF JUSTICE. What's he that goes there?

SERVANT. Falstaff, an't please your lordship.

CHIEF JUSTICE. He that was in question for the robb'ry?

SERVANT. He, my lord; but he hath since done good service at Shrewsbury, and, as I hear, is now going with some charge to the Lord John of Lancaster.

CHIEF JUSTICE. What, to York? Call him back again.

SERVANT. Sir John Falstaff!

FALSTAFF. Boy, tell him I am deaf.

PAGE. You must speak louder; my master is deaf.

CHIEF JUSTICE. I am sure he is, to the hearing of anything good. Go, pluck him by the elbow; I must speak with him.

SERVANT. Sir John!

FALSTAFF. What! a young knave, and begging! Is there not wars? Is there not employment? Doth not the King lack subjects? Do not the rebels need soldiers? Though it be a shame to be on any side but one, it is worse shame to beg than to be on the worst side, were it worse than the name of rebellion can tell how to make it.

SERVANT. You mistake me, sir.

FALSTAFF. Why, sir, did I say you were an honest man? Setting my knighthood and my soldiership aside, I had lied in my throat if I had said so.

SERVANT. I pray you, sir, then set your knighthood and your soldiership aside; and give me leave to tell you you lie in your throat, if you say I am any other than an honest man.

FALSTAFF. I give thee leave to tell me so! I lay aside that which grows to me! If thou get'st any leave of me, hang me; if thou tak'st leave, thou wert better be hang'd. You hunt counter. Hence! Avaunt!

SERVANT. Sir, my lord would speak with you.

CHIEF JUSTICE. Sir John Falstaff, a word with you.

FALSTAFF. My good lord! God give your lordship good time of day. I am glad to see your lordship abroad. I heard say your lordship was sick; I hope your lordship goes abroad by advice. Your lordship, though not clean past your youth, hath yet some smack of age in you, some relish of the saltness of time; and I most humbly beseech your lordship to have a reverend care of your health.

CHIEF JUSTICE. Sir John, I sent for you before your expedition to Shrewsbury.

FALSTAFF. An't please your lordship, I hear his Majesty is return'd with some discomfort from Wales.

CHIEF JUSTICE. I talk not of his Majesty. You would not come when I sent for you.

FALSTAFF. And I hear, moreover, his Highness is fall'n into this same whoreson apoplexy.

CHIEF JUSTICE. Well, God mend him! I pray you let me speak with you.

FALSTAFF. This apoplexy, as I take it, is a kind of lethargy, an't please your lordship, a kind of sleeping in the blood, a whoreson tingling.

CHIEF JUSTICE. What tell you me of it? Be it as it is.

FALSTAFF. It hath it original from much grief, from study, and perturbation of the brain. I have read the cause of his effects in Galen; it is a kind of deafness.

CHIEF JUSTICE. I think you are fall'n into the disease, for you hear not what I say to you.

FALSTAFF. Very well, my lord, very well. Rather an't please you, it is the disease of not listening, the malady of not marking, that I am troubled withal.

CHIEF JUSTICE. To punish you by the heels would amend the attention of your ears; and I care not if I do become your physician.

FALSTAFF. I am as poor as Job, my lord, but not so patient. Your lordship may minister the potion of imprisonment to me in respect of poverty; but how I should be your patient to follow your prescriptions, the wise may make some dram of a scruple, or indeed a scruple itself.

CHIEF JUSTICE. I sent for you, when there were matters against you for your life, to come speak with me.

FALSTAFF. As I was then advis'd by my learned counsel in the laws of this land-service, I did not come.

CHIEF JUSTICE. Well, the truth is, Sir John, you live in great infamy.

FALSTAFF. He that buckles himself in my belt cannot live in less.

CHIEF JUSTICE. Your means are very slender, and your waste is great.

FALSTAFF. I would it were otherwise; I would my means were greater and my waist slenderer.

CHIEF JUSTICE. You have misled the youthful Prince.

FALSTAFF. The young Prince hath misled me. I am the fellow with the great belly, and he my dog.

CHIEF JUSTICE. Well, I am loath to gall a new-heal'd wound. Your day's service at Shrewsbury hath a little gilded over your night's exploit on Gadshill. You may thank th' unquiet time for your quiet o'erposting that action.

FALSTAFF. My lord—

CHIEF JUSTICE. But since all is well, keep it so: wake not a sleeping wolf.

FALSTAFF. To wake a wolf is as bad as smell a fox.

CHIEF JUSTICE. What! you are as a candle, the better part burnt out.

FALSTAFF. A wassail candle, my lord—all tallow; if I did say of wax, my growth would approve the truth.

CHIEF JUSTICE. There is not a white hair in your face but should have his effect of gravity.

FALSTAFF. His effect of gravy, gravy, gravy.

CHIEF JUSTICE. You follow the young Prince up and down, like his ill angel.

FALSTAFF. Not so, my lord. Your ill angel is light; but I hope he that looks upon me will take me without weighing. And yet in some respects, I grant, I cannot go—I cannot tell. Virtue is of so little regard in these costermongers' times that true valour is turn'd berod; pregnancy is made a tapster, and his quick wit wasted in giving reckonings;

all the other gifts appertinent to man, as the malice of this age shapes them, are not worth a gooseberry. You that are old consider not the capacities of us that are young; you do measure the heat of our livers with the bitterness of your galls; and we that are in the vaward of our youth, I must confess, are wags too.

CHIEF JUSTICE. Do you set down your name in the scroll of youth, that are written down old with all the characters of age? Have you not a moist eye, a dry hand, a yellow cheek, a white beard, a decreasing leg, an increasing belly? Is not your voice broken, your wind short, your chin double, your wit single, and every part about you blasted with antiquity? And will you yet call yourself young? Fie, fie, fie, Sir John!

FALSTAFF. My lord, I was born about three of the clock in the afternoon, with a white head and something a round belly. For my voice—I have lost it with hallooing and singing of anthems. To approve my youth further, I will not. The truth is, I am only old in judgment and understanding; and he that will caper with me for a thousand marks, let him lend me the money, and have at him. For the box of the ear that the Prince gave you—he gave it like a rude prince, and you took it like a sensible lord. I have check'd him for it; and the young lion repents—marry, not in ashes and sackcloth, but in new silk and old sack.

CHIEF JUSTICE. Well, God send the Prince a better companion!

FALSTAFF. God send the companion a better prince! I cannot rid my hands of him.

CHIEF JUSTICE. Well, the King hath sever'd you. I hear you are going with Lord John of Lancaster against the Archbishop and the Earl of Northumberland.

FALSTAFF. Yea; I thank your pretty sweet wit for it. But look you pray, all you that kiss my Lady Peace at home, that our armies join not in a hot day; for, by the Lord, I take but two shirts out with me, and I mean not to sweat extraordinarily. If it be a hot day, and I brandish anything but a bottle, I would I might never spit white again. There is not a dangerous action can peep out his head but I am thrust upon it. Well, I cannot last ever; but it was alway yet the trick of our English nation, if they have a good thing, to make it too common. If ye will needs say I am an old man, you should give me rest. I would to God my name were not so terrible to the enemy as it is. I were better to be eaten to death with a rust than to be scoured to nothing with perpetual motion.

CHIEF JUSTICE. Well, be honest, be honest; and God bless your expedition!

FALSTAFF. Will your lordship lend me a thousand pound to furnish me forth?

CHIEF JUSTICE. Not a penny, not a penny; you are too impatient to bear crosses. Fare you well. Commend me to my cousin Westmoreland.

Exeunt CHIEF JUSTICE *and* SERVANT

FALSTAFF. If I do, fillip me with a three-man beetle. A man can no more separate age and covetousness than 'a can part young limbs and lechery; but the gout galls the one, and the pox pinches the other; and so both the degrees prevent my curses. Boy!

PAGE. Sir?

FALSTAFF. What money is in my purse?

PAGE. Seven groats and two pence.

FALSTAFF. I can get no remedy against this consumption of the purse; borrowing only lingers and lingers it out, but the disease is incurable. Go bear this letter to my Lord of Lancaster; this to the Prince; this to the Earl of Westmoreland; and this to old Mistress Ursula, whom I have weekly sworn to marry since I perceiv'd the first white hair of my chin. About it; you know where to find me. [*Exit* PAGE] A pox of this gout! or, a gout of this pox! for the one or the other plays the rogue with my great toe. 'Tis no matter if I do halt; I have the wars for my colour, and my pension shall seem the more reasonable. A good wit will make use of anything. I will turn diseases to commodity.

Exit

SCENE 3

York. The ARCHBISHOP'S *palace*

Enter the ARCHBISHOP, THOMAS MOWBRAY *the* EARL
MARSHAL, LORD HASTINGS, *and* LORD BARDOLPH

ARCHBISHOP. Thus have you heard our cause and known our
    means;
  And, my most noble friends, I pray you all
  Speak plainly your opinions of our hopes—
  And first, Lord Marshal, what say you to it?
MOWBRAY. I well allow the occasion of our arms;
  But gladly would be better satisfied
  How, in our means, we should advance ourselves
  To look with forehead bold and big enough
  Upon the power and puissance of the King.
HASTINGS. Our present musters grow upon the file
  To five and twenty thousand men of choice;
  And our supplies live largely in the hope
  Of great Northumberland, whose bosom burns
  With an incensed fire of injuries.
LORD BARDOLPH. The question then, Lord Hastings, standeth
    thus:
  Whether our present five and twenty thousand
  May hold up head without Northumberland?
HASTINGS. With him, we may.
LORD BARDOLPH. Yea, marry, there's the point;
  But if without him we be thought too feeble,
  My judgment is we should not step too far
  Till we had his assistance by the hand;
  For, in a theme so bloody-fac'd as this,
  Conjecture, expectation, and surmise
  Of aids incertain, should not be admitted.
ARCHBISHOP. 'Tis very true, Lord Bardolph; for indeed
  It was young Hotspur's case at Shrewsbury.
LORD BARDOLPH. It was, my lord; who lin'd himself with
    hope,
  Eating the air and promise of supply,
  Flatt'ring himself in project of a power

Much smaller than the smallest of his thoughts;
And so, with great imagination
Proper to madmen, led his powers to death,
And, winking, leapt into destruction.
HASTINGS. But, by your leave, it never yet did hurt
To lay down likelihoods and forms of hope.
LORD BARDOLPH. Yes, if this present quality of war—
Indeed the instant action, a cause on foot—
Lives so in hope, as in an early spring
We see th' appearing buds; which to prove fruit
Hope gives not so much warrant, as despair
That frosts will bite them. When we mean to build,
We first survey the plot, then draw the model;
And when we see the figure of the house,
Then we must rate the cost of the erection;
Which if we find outweighs ability,
What do we then but draw anew the model
In fewer offices, or at least desist
To build at all? Much more, in this great work—
Which is almost to pluck a kingdom down
And set another up—should we survey
The plot of situation and the model,
Consent upon a sure foundation,
Question surveyors, know our own estate
How able such a work to undergo—
To weigh against his opposite; or else
We fortify in paper and in figures,
Using the names of men instead of men;
Like one that draws the model of a house
Beyond his power to build it; who, half through,
Gives o'er and leaves his part-created cost
A naked subject to the weeping clouds
And waste for churlish winter's tyranny.
HASTINGS. Grant that our hopes—yet likely of fair birth—
Should be still-born, and that we now possess'd
The utmost man of expectation,
I think we are so a body strong enough,
Even as we are, to equal with the King.
LORD BARDOLPH. What, is the King but five and twenty
thousand?

HASTINGS. To us no more; nay, not so much, Lord Bardolph;
    For his divisions, as the times do brawl,
    Are in three heads: one power against the French,
    And one against Glendower; perforce a third
    Must take up us. So is the unfirm King
    In three divided; and his coffers sound
    With hollow poverty and emptiness.
ARCHBISHOP. That he should draw his several strengths
      together
    And come against us in full puissance
    Need not be dreaded.
HASTINGS. If he should do so,
    He leaves his back unarm'd, the French and Welsh
    Baying at his heels. Never fear that.
LORD BARDOLPH. Who is it like should lead his forces hither?
HASTINGS. The Duke of Lancaster and Westmoreland;
    Against the Welsh, himself and Harry Monmouth;
    But who is substituted against the French
    I have no certain notice.
ARCHBISHOP. Let us on,
    And publish the occasion of our arms.
    The commonwealth is sick of their own choice;
    Their over-greedy love hath surfeited.
    An habitation giddy and unsure
    Hath he that buildeth on the vulgar heart.
    O thou fond many, with what loud applause
    Didst thou beat heaven with blessing Bolingbroke
    Before he was what thou wouldst have him be!
    And being now trimm'd in thine own desires,
    Thou, beastly feeder, art so full of him
    That thou provok'st thyself to cast him up.
    So, so, thou common dog, didst thou disgorge
    Thy glutton bosom of the royal Richard;
    And now thou wouldst eat thy dead vomit up,
    And howl'st to find it. What trust is in these times?
    They that, when Richard liv'd, would have him die
    Are now become enamour'd on his grave.
    Thou that threw'st dust upon his goodly head,
    When through proud London he came sighing on
    After th' admired heels of Bolingbroke,

Criest now 'O earth, yield us that king again,
And take thou this!' O thoughts of men accurs'd!
Past and to come seems best; things present, worst.
MOWBRAY. Shall we go draw our numbers, and set on?
HASTINGS. We are time's subjects, and time bids be gone.

Exeunt

ACT II. SCENE 1

London. A street

Enter HOSTESS *with two officers,* FANG *and* SNARE

HOSTESS. Master Fang, have you ent'red the action?
FANG. It is ent'red.
HOSTESS. Where's your yeoman? Is't a lusty yeoman? Will 'a
stand to't?
FANG. Sirrah, where's Snare?
HOSTESS. O Lord, ay! good Master Snare.
SNARE. Here, here.
FANG. Snare, we must arrest Sir John Falstaff.
HOSTESS. Yea, good Master Snare; I have ent'red him and all.
SNARE. It may chance cost some of our lives, for he will stab.
HOSTESS. Alas the day! take heed of him; he stabb'd me in
mine own house, and that most beastly. In good faith, 'a
cares not what mischief he does, if his weapon be out; he
will foin like any devil; he will spare neither man, woman,
nor child.
FANG. If I can close with him, I care not for his thrust.
HOSTESS. No, nor I neither; I'll be at your elbow.
FANG. An I but fist him once; an 'a come but within my
vice!
HOSTESS. I am undone by his going; I warrant you, he's an
infinitive thing upon my score. Good Master Fang, hold
him sure. Good Master Snare, let him not scape. 'A comes
continuantly to Pie-corner—saving your manhoods—to buy
a saddle; and he is indited to dinner to the Lubber's Head
in Lumbert Street, to Master Smooth's the silkman. I pray

you, since my exion is ent'red, and my case so openly
known to the world, let him be brought in to his answer.
A hundred mark is a long one for a poor lone woman to
bear; and I have borne, and borne, and borne; and have
been fubb'd off, and fubb'd off, and fubb'd off, from this
day to that day, that it is a shame to be thought on. There
is no honesty in such dealing; unless a woman should be
made an ass and a beast, to bear every knave's wrong.

Enter Sir John Falstaff, Page, *and* Bardolph

Yonder he comes; and that arrant malmsey-nose knave,
Bardolph, with him. Do your offices, do your offices, Master Fang and Master Snare; do me, do me, do me your
offices.

Falstaff. How now! whose mare's dead? What's the matter?

Fang. Sir John, I arrest you at the suit of Mistress Quickly.

Falstaff. Away, varlets! Draw, Bardolph. Cut me off the
villain's head. Throw the quean in the channel.

Hostess. Throw me in the channel! I'll throw thee in the
channel. Wilt thou? wilt thou? thou bastardly rogue!
Murder, murder! Ah, thou honeysuckle villain! wilt thou
kill God's officers and the King's? Ah, thou honey-seed
rogue! thou art a honey-seed; a man-queller and a woman-
queller.

Falstaff. Keep them off, Bardolph.

Fang. A rescue! a rescue!

Hostess. Good people, bring a rescue or two. Thou wot,
wot thou! thou wot, wot ta? Do, do, thou rogue! do, thou
hemp-seed!

Page. Away, you scullion! you rampallian! you fustilarian!
I'll tickle your catastrophe.

Enter the Lord Chief Justice *and his men*

Chief Justice. What is the matter? Keep the peace here, ho!

Hostess. Good my lord, be good to me. I beseech you,
stand to me.

Chief Justice. How now, Sir John! what, are you brawling
here?
Doth this become your place, your time, and business?
You should have been well on your way to York.

Stand from him, fellow; wherefore hang'st thou upon him?

HOSTESS. O my most worshipful lord, an't please your Grace, I am a poor widow of Eastcheap, and he is arrested at my suit.

CHIEF JUSTICE. For what sum?

HOSTESS. It is more than for some, my lord; it is for all—all I have. He hath eaten me out of house and home; he hath put all my substance into that fat belly of his. But I will have some of it out again, or I will ride thee a nights like a mare.

FALSTAFF. I think I am as like to ride the mare, if I have any vantage of ground to get up.

CHIEF JUSTICE. How comes this, Sir John? Fie! What man of good temper would endure this tempest of exclamation? Are you not ashamed to enforce a poor widow to so rough a course to come by her own?

FALSTAFF. What is the gross sum that I owe thee?

HOSTESS. Marry, if thou wert an honest man, thyself and the money too. Thou didst swear to me upon a parcel-gilt goblet, sitting in my Dolphin chamber, at the round table, by a sea-coal fire, upon Wednesday in Wheeson week, when the Prince broke thy head for liking his father to a singing-man of Windsor—thou didst swear to me then, as I was washing thy wound, to marry me and make me my lady thy wife. Canst thou deny it? Did not goodwife Keech, the butcher's wife, come in then and call me gossip Quickly? Coming in to borrow a mess of vinegar, telling us she had a good dish of prawns, whereby thou didst desire to eat some, whereby I told thee they were ill for a green wound? And didst thou not, when she was gone down stairs, desire me to be no more so familiarity with such poor people, saying that ere long they should call me madam? And didst thou not kiss me, and bid me fetch thee thirty shillings? I put thee now to thy book-oath. Deny it, if thou canst.

FALSTAFF. My lord, this is a poor mad soul, and she says up and down the town that her eldest son is like you. She hath been in good case, and, the truth is, poverty hath distracted her. But for these foolish officers, I beseech you I may have redress against them.

CHIEF JUSTICE. Sir John, Sir John, I am well acquainted with
your manner of wrenching the true cause the false way. It
is not a confident brow, nor the throng of words that
come with such more than impudent sauciness from you,
can thrust me from a level consideration. You have, as it
appears to me, practis'd upon the easy yielding spirit of
this woman, and made her serve your uses both in purse
and in person.

HOSTESS. Yea, in truth, my lord.

CHIEF JUSTICE. Pray thee, peace. Pay her the debt you owe
her, and unpay the villainy you have done with her; the
one you may do with sterling money, and the other with
current repentance.

FALSTAFF. My lord, I will not undergo this sneap without reply. You call honourable boldness impudent sauciness; if
a man will make curtsy and say nothing, he is virtuous.
No, my lord, my humble duty rememb'red, I will not be
your suitor. I say to you I do desire deliverance from these
officers, being upon hasty employment in the King's
affairs.

CHIEF JUSTICE. You speak as having power to do wrong; but
answer in th' effect of your reputation, and satisfy the
poor woman.

FALSTAFF. Come hither, hostess.

Enter GOWER

CHIEF JUSTICE. Now, Master Gower, what news?

GOWER. The King, my lord, and Harry Prince of Wales
Are near at hand. The rest the paper tells. [*Gives a letter*]

FALSTAFF. As I am a gentleman!

HOSTESS. Faith, you said so before.

FALSTAFF. As I am a gentleman! Come, no more words of it.

HOSTESS. By this heavenly ground I tread on, I must be fain
to pawn both my plate and the tapestry of my dining-
chambers.

FALSTAFF. Glasses, glasses, is the only drinking; and for thy
walls, a pretty slight drollery, or the story of the Prodigal,
or the German hunting, in water-work, is worth a thousand of these bed-hangers and these fly-bitten tapestries.
Let it be ten pound, if thou canst. Come, and 'twere not

for thy humours, there's not a better wench in England. Go, wash thy face, and draw the action. Come, thou must not be in this humour with me; dost not know me? Come, come, I know thou wast set on to this.

HOSTESS. Pray thee, Sir John, let it be but twenty nobles; i' faith, I am loath to pawn my plate, so God save me, la!

FALSTAFF. Let it alone; I'll make other shift. You'll be a fool still.

HOSTESS. Well, you shall have it, though I pawn my gown. I hope you'll come to supper. You'll pay me all together?

FALSTAFF. Will I live? [*To* BARDOLPH] Go, with her, with her; hook on, hook on.

HOSTESS. Will you have Doll Tearsheet meet you at supper?

FALSTAFF. No more words; let's have her.

Exeunt HOSTESS, BARDOLPH, *and* OFFICERS

CHIEF JUSTICE. I have heard better news.

FALSTAFF. What's the news, my lord?

CHIEF JUSTICE. Where lay the King to-night?

GOWER. At Basingstoke, my lord.

FALSTAFF. I hope, my lord, all's well. What is the news, my lord?

CHIEF JUSTICE. Come all his forces back?

GOWER. No; fifteen hundred foot, five hundred horse,
Are march'd up to my Lord of Lancaster,
Against Northumberland and the Archbishop.

FALSTAFF. Comes the King back from Wales, my noble lord?

CHIEF JUSTICE. You shall have letters of me presently.
Come, go along with me, good Master Gower.

FALSTAFF. My lord!

CHIEF JUSTICE. What's the matter?

FALSTAFF. Master Gower, shall I entreat you with me to dinner?

GOWER. I must wait upon my good lord here, I thank you, good Sir John.

CHIEF JUSTICE. Sir John, you loiter here too long, being you are to take soldiers up in counties as you go.

FALSTAFF. Will you sup with me, Master Gower?

CHIEF JUSTICE. What foolish master taught you these manners, Sir John?

FALSTAFF. Master Gower, if they become me not, he was a

fool that taught them me. This is the right fencing grace, my lord; tap for tap, and so part fair.

CHIEF JUSTICE. Now, the Lord lighten thee! Thou art a great fool.   *Exeunt*

SCENE 2

London. Another street

Enter PRINCE HENRY *and* POINS

PRINCE. Before God, I am exceeding weary.

POINS. Is't come to that? I had thought weariness durst not have attach'd one of so high blood.

PRINCE. Faith, it does me; though it discolours the complexion of my greatness to acknowledge it. Doth it not show vilely in me to desire small beer?

POINS. Why, a prince should not be so loosely studied as to remember so weak a composition.

PRINCE. Belike then my appetite was not princely got; for, by my troth, I do now remember the poor creature, small beer. But indeed these humble considerations make me out of love with my greatness. What a disgrace is it to me to remember thy name, or to know thy face to-morrow, or to take note how many pair of silk stockings thou hast— viz., these, and those that were thy peach-colour'd ones— or to bear the inventory of thy shirts—as, one for superfluity, and another for use! But that the tennis-court-keeper knows better than I; for it is a low ebb of linen with thee when thou keepest not racket there; as thou hast not done a great while, because the rest of thy low countries have made a shift to eat up thy holland. And God knows whether those that bawl out of the ruins of thy linen shall inherit his kingdom; but the midwives say the children are not in the fault; whereupon the world increases, and kindreds are mightily strengthened.

POINS. How ill it follows, after you have laboured so hard, you should talk so idly! Tell me, how many good young princes would do so, their fathers being so sick as yours at this time is?

PRINCE. Shall I tell thee one thing, Poins?

POINS. Yes, faith; and let it be an excellent good thing.

PRINCE. It shall serve among wits of no higher breeding than thine.

POINS. Go to; I stand the push of your one thing that you will tell.

PRINCE. Marry, I tell thee it is not meet that I should be sad, now my father is sick; albeit I could tell to thee—as to one it pleases me, for fault of a better, to call my friend—I could be sad and sad indeed too.

POINS. Very hardly upon such a subject.

PRINCE. By this hand, thou thinkest me as far in the devil's book as thou and Falstaff for obduracy and persistency: let the end try the man. But I tell thee my heart bleeds inwardly that my father is so sick; and keeping such vile company as thou art hath in reason taken from me all ostentation of sorrow.

POINS. The reason?

PRINCE. What wouldst thou think of me if I should weep?

POINS. I would think thee a most princely hypocrite.

PRINCE. It would be every man's thought; and thou art a blessed fellow to think as every man thinks. Never a man's thought in the world keeps the road-way better than thine. Every man would think me an hypocrite indeed. And what accites your most worshipful thought to think so?

POINS. Why, because you have been so lewd and so much engraffed to Falstaff.

PRINCE. And to thee.

POINS. By this light, I am well spoke on; I can hear it with mine own ears. The worst that they can say of me is that I am a second brother and that I am a proper fellow of my hands; and those two things, I confess, I cannot help. By the mass, here comes Bardolph.

Enter BARDOLPH *and* PAGE

PRINCE. And the boy that I gave Falstaff. 'A had him from me Christian; and look if the fat villain have not transform'd him ape.

BARDOLPH. God save your Grace!

PRINCE. And yours, most noble Bardolph!

POINS. Come, you virtuous ass, you bashful fool, must you be blushing? Wherefore blush you now? What a maidenly man-at-arms are you become! Is't such a matter to get a pottle-pot's maidenhead?

PAGE. 'A calls me e'en now, my lord, through a red lattice, and I could discern no part of his face from the window. At last I spied his eyes; and methought he had made two holes in the alewife's new petticoat, and so peep'd through.

PRINCE. Has not the boy profited?

BARDOLPH. Away, you whoreson upright rabbit, away!

PAGE. Away, you rascally Althæa's dream, away!

PRINCE. Instruct us, boy; what dream, boy?

PAGE. Marry, my lord, Althæa dreamt she was delivered of a firebrand; and therefore I call him her dream.

PRINCE. A crown's worth of good interpretation. There 'tis, boy.   *[Giving a crown]*

POINS. O that this blossom could be kept from cankers! Well, there is sixpence to preserve thee.

BARDOLPH. An you do not make him be hang'd among you, the gallows shall have wrong.

PRINCE. And how doth thy master, Bardolph?

BARDOLPH. Well, my lord. He heard of your Grace's coming to town. There's a letter for you.

POINS. Deliver'd with good respect. And how doth the martlemas, your master?

BARDOLPH. In bodily health, sir.

POINS. Marry, the immortal part needs a physician; but that moves not him. Though that be sick, it dies not.

PRINCE. I do allow this wen to be as familiar with me as my dog; and he holds his place, for look you how he writes.

POINS. *[Reads]* 'John Falstaff, knight'—Every man must know that as oft as he has occasion to name himself, even like those that are kin to the King; for they never prick their finger but they say 'There's some of the King's blood spilt.' 'How comes that?' says he that takes upon him not to conceive. The answer is as ready as a borrower's cap: 'I am the King's poor cousin, sir.'

PRINCE. Nay, they will be kin to us, or they will fetch it from Japhet. But the letter: *[Reads]* 'Sir John Falstaff,

knight, to the son of the King nearest his father, Harry
Prince of Wales, greeting.'

POINS. Why, this is a certificate.

PRINCE. Peace! [*Reads*] 'I will imitate the honourable Romans in brevity.'—

POINS. He sure means brevity in breath, short-winded.

PRINCE. [*Reads*] 'I commend me to thee, I commend thee,
and I leave thee. Be not too familiar with Poins; for he
misuses thy favours so much that he swears thou art to
marry his sister Nell. Repent at idle times as thou mayst,
and so farewell.

    Thine, by yea and no—which is as much as to say as
    thou usest him—JACK FALSTAFF with my familiars,
    JOHN with my brothers and sisters, and SIR JOHN with
    all Europe.'

POINS. My lord, I'll steep this letter in sack and make him
eat it.

PRINCE. That's to make him eat twenty of his words. But do
you use me thus, Ned? Must I marry your sister?

POINS. God send the wench no worse fortune! But I never
said so.

PRINCE. Well, thus we play the fools with the time, and the
spirits of the wise sit in the clouds and mock us. Is your
master here in London?

BARDOLPH. Yea, my lord.

PRINCE. Where sups he? Doth the old boar feed in the old
frank?

BARDOLPH. At the old place, my lord, in Eastcheap.

PRINCE. What company?

PAGE. Ephesians, my lord, of the old church.

PRINCE. Sup any women with him?

PAGE. None, my lord, but old Mistress Quickly and Mistress
Doll Tearsheet.

PRINCE. What pagan may that be?

PAGE. A proper gentlewoman, sir, and a kinswoman of my
master's.

PRINCE. Even such kin as the parish heifers are to the town
bull. Shall we steal upon them, Ned, at supper?

POINS. I am your shadow, my lord; I'll follow you.

PRINCE. Sirrah, you boy, and Bardolph, no word to your

master that I am yet come to town. There's for your
silence.

BARDOLPH. I have no tongue, sir.

PAGE. And for mine, sir, I will govern it.

PRINCE. Fare you well; go.   *Exeunt* BARDOLPH *and* PAGE
This Doll Tearsheet should be some road.

POINS. I warrant you, as common as the way between Saint
Albans and London.

PRINCE. How might we see Falstaff bestow himself to-night
in his true colours, and not ourselves be seen?

POINS. Put on two leathern jerkins and aprons, and wait
upon him at his table as drawers.

PRINCE. From a god to a bull? A heavy descension! It was
Jove's case. From a prince to a prentice? A low transformation! That shall be mine; for in everything the purpose must weigh with the folly. Follow me, Ned.

Exeunt

SCENE 3

Warkworth. Before the castle

Enter NORTHUMBERLAND, LADY NORTHUMBERLAND,
and LADY PERCY

NORTHUMBERLAND. I pray thee, loving wife, and gentle
daughter,
Give even way unto my rough affairs;
Put not you on the visage of the times
And be, like them, to Percy troublesome.

LADY NORTHUMBERLAND. I have given over, I will speak no
more.
Do what you will; your wisdom be your guide.

NORTHUMBERLAND. Alas, sweet wife, my honour is at pawn;
And but my going nothing can redeem it.

LADY PERCY. O, yet, for God's sake, go not to these wars!
The time was, father, that you broke your word,
When you were more endear'd to it than now;
When your own Percy, when my heart's dear Harry,
Threw many a northward look to see his father

Bring up his powers; but he did long in vain.
Who then persuaded you to stay at home?
There were two honours lost, yours and your son's.
For yours, the God of heaven brighten it!
For his, it stuck upon him as the sun
In the grey vault of heaven; and by his light
Did all the chivalry of England move
To do brave acts. He was indeed the glass
Wherein the noble youth did dress themselves.
He had no legs that practis'd not his gait;
And speaking thick, which nature made his blemish,
Became the accents of the valiant;
For those who could speak low and tardily
Would turn their own perfection to abuse
To seem like him: so that in speech, in gait,
In diet, in affections of delight,
In military rules, humours of blood,
He was the mark and glass, copy and book,
That fashion'd others. And him—O wondrous him!
O miracle of men!—him did you leave—
Second to none, unseconded by you—
To look upon the hideous god of war
In disadvantage, to abide a field
Where nothing but the sound of Hotspur's name
Did seem defensible. So you left him.
Never, O never, do his ghost the wrong
To hold your honour more precise and nice
With others than with him! Let them alone.
The Marshal and the Archbishop are strong.
Had my sweet Harry had but half their numbers,
To-day might I, hanging on Hotspur's neck,
Have talk'd of Monmouth's grave.
NORTHUMBERLAND. Beshrew your heart,
Fair daughter, you do draw my spirits from me
With new lamenting ancient oversights.
But I must go and meet with danger there,
Or it will seek me in another place,
And find me worse provided.
LADY NORTHUMBERLAND. O, fly to Scotland
Till that the nobles and the armed commons

Have of their puissance made a little taste.

LADY PERCY. If they get ground and vantage of the King,
Then join you with them, like a rib of steel,
To make strength stronger; but, for all our loves,
First let them try themselves. So did your son;
He was so suff'red; so came I a widow;
And never shall have length of life enough
To rain upon remembrance with mine eyes,
That it may grow and sprout as high as heaven,
For recordation to my noble husband.

NORTHUMBERLAND. Come, come, go in with me. 'Tis with
    my mind
As with the tide swell'd up unto his height,
That makes a still-stand, running neither way.
Fain would I go to meet the Archbishop,
But many thousand reasons hold me back.
I will resolve for Scotland. There am I,
Till time and vantage crave my company.   *Exeunt*

SCENE 4

London. The Boar's Head Tavern in Eastcheap

Enter FRANCIS *and another* DRAWER

FRANCIS. What the devil hast thou brought there—apple-
johns? Thou knowest Sir John cannot endure an apple-
john.

SECOND DRAWER. Mass, thou say'st true. The Prince once set
a dish of apple-johns before him, and told him there were
five more Sir Johns; and, putting off his hat, said 'I will
now take my leave of these six dry, round, old, withered
knights.' It ang'red him to the heart; but he hath forgot
that.

FRANCIS. Why, then, cover and set them down; and see if
thou canst find out Sneak's noise; Mistress Tearsheet
would fain hear some music.

Enter third DRAWER

THIRD DRAWER. Dispatch! The room where they supp'd is
too hot; they'll come in straight.

FRANCIS. Sirrah, here will be the Prince and Master Poins anon; and they will put on two of our jerkins and aprons; and Sir John must not know of it. Bardolph hath brought word.

THIRD DRAWER. By the mass, here will be old utis; it will be an excellent stratagem.

SECOND DRAWER. I'll see if I can find out Sneak.

Exeunt second and third DRAWERS

Enter HOSTESS *and* DOLL TEARSHEET

HOSTESS. I'faith, sweetheart, methinks now you are in an excellent good temperality. Your pulsidge beats as extraordinarily as heart would desire; and your colour, I warrant you, is as red as any rose, in good truth, la! But, i' faith, you have drunk too much canaries; and that's a marvellous searching wine, and it perfumes the blood ere one can say 'What's this?' How do you now?

DOLL. Better than I was—hem.

HOSTESS. Why, that's well said; a good heart's worth gold. Lo, here comes Sir John.

Enter FALSTAFF

FALSTAFF. [*Singing*] 'When Arthur first in court'—Empty the jordan. [*Exit* FRANCIS]—[*Singing*] 'And was a worthy king'—How now, Mistress Doll!

HOSTESS. Sick of a calm; yea, good faith.

FALSTAFF. So is all her sect; and they be once in a calm, they are sick.

DOLL. A pox damn you, you muddy rascal! Is that all the comfort you give me?

FALSTAFF. You make fat rascals, Mistress Doll.

DOLL. I make them! Gluttony and diseases make them: I make them not.

FALSTAFF. If the cook help to make the gluttony, you help to make the diseases, Doll. We catch of you, Doll, we catch of you; grant that, my poor virtue, grant that.

DOLL. Yea, joy, our chains and our jewels.

FALSTAFF. 'Your brooches, pearls, and ouches.' For to serve bravely is to come halting off; you know, to come off the

breach with his pike bent bravely, and to surgery bravely;
to venture upon the charg'd chambers bravely—

DOLL. Hang yourself, you muddy conger, hang yourself!

HOSTESS. By my troth, this is the old fashion; you two never
meet but you fall to some discord. You are both, i' good
truth, as rheumatic as two dry toasts; you cannot one bear
with another's confirmities. What the good-year! one must
bear, and that must be you. You are the weaker vessel, as
as they say, the emptier vessel.

DOLL. Can a weak empty vessel bear such a huge full hogs-
head? There's a whole merchant's venture of Bourdeaux
stuff in him; you have not seen a hulk better stuff'd in the
hold. Come, I'll be friends with thee, Jack. Thou art going
to the wars; and whether I shall ever see thee again or no,
there is nobody cares.

Re-enter FRANCIS

FRANCIS. Sir, Ancient Pistol's below and would speak with
you.

DOLL. Hang him, swaggering rascal! Let him not come
hither; it is the foul-mouth'dst rogue in England.

HOSTESS. If he swagger, let him not come here. No, by my
faith! I must live among my neighbours; I'll no swaggerers.
I am in good name and fame with the very best. Shut the
door. There comes no swaggerers here; I have not liv'd all
this while to have swaggering now. Shut the door, I pray
you.

FALSTAFF. Dost thou hear, hostess?

HOSTESS. Pray ye, pacify yourself, Sir John; there comes no
swaggerers here.

FALSTAFF. Dost thou hear? It is mine ancient.

HOSTESS. Tilly-fally, Sir John, ne'er tell me; and your ancient swagg'rer comes not in my doors. I was before Master Tisick, the debuty, t' other day; and, as he said to me
—'twas no longer ago than Wednesday last, i' good faith!—
'Neighbour Quickly,' says he—Master Dumbe, our minister, was by then—'Neighbour Quickly,' says he 'receive
those that are civil, for' said he 'you are in an ill name.'
Now 'a said so, I can tell whereupon. 'For' says he 'you
are an honest woman and well thought on, therefore take

heed what guests you receive. Receive' says he 'no swaggering companions.' There comes none here. You would
bless you to hear what he said. No, I'll no swagg'rers.

FALSTAFF. He's no swagg'rer, hostess; a tame cheater, i' faith;
you may stroke him as gently as a puppy greyhound. He'll
not swagger with a Barbary hen, if her feathers turn back
in any show of resistance. Call him up, drawer.

Exit FRANCIS

HOSTESS. Cheater, call you him? I will bar no honest man
my house, nor no cheater; but I do not love swaggering,
by my troth. I am the worse when one says 'swagger.'
Feel, masters, how I shake; look you, I warrant you.

DOLL. So you do, hostess.

HOSTESS. Do I? Yea, in very truth, do I, an 'twere an aspen
leaf. I cannot abide swagg'rers.

Enter PISTOL, BARDOLPH, *and* PAGE

PISTOL. God save you, Sir John!

FALSTAFF. Welcome, Ancient Pistol. Here, Pistol, I charge
you with a cup of sack; do you discharge upon mine
hostess.

PISTOL. I will discharge upon her, Sir John, with two bullets.

FALSTAFF. She is pistol-proof, sir; you shall not hardly offend
her.

HOSTESS. Come, I'll drink no proofs nor no bullets. I'll drink
no more than will do me good, for no man's pleasure, I.

PISTOL. Then to you, Mistress Dorothy; I will charge you.

DOLL. Charge me! I scorn you, scurvy companion. What!
you poor, base, rascally, cheating, lack-linen mate! Away,
you mouldy rogue, away! I am meat for your master.

PISTOL. I know you, Mistress Dorothy.

DOLL. Away, you cut-purse rascal! you filthy bung, away!
By this wine, I'll thrust my knife in your mouldy chaps,
an you play the saucy cuttle with me. Away, you bottle-
ale rascal! you basket-hilt stale juggler, you! Since when, I
pray you, sir? God's light, with two points on your shoulder? Much!

PISTOL. God let me not live but I will murder your ruff for
this.

FALSTAFF. No more, Pistol; I would not have you go off here. Discharge yourself of our company, Pistol.

HOSTESS. No, good Captain Pistol; not here, sweet captain.

DOLL. Captain! Thou abominable damn'd cheater, art thou not ashamed to be called captain? An captains were of my mind, they would truncheon you out, for taking their names upon you before you have earn'd them. You a captain! you slave, for what? For tearing a poor whore's ruff in a bawdy-house? He a captain! hang him, rogue! He lives upon mouldy stew'd prunes and dried cakes. A captain! God's light, these villains will make the word as odious as the word 'occupy'; which was an excellent good word before it was ill sorted. Therefore captains had need look to't.

BARDOLPH. Pray thee go down, good ancient.

FALSTAFF. Hark thee hither, Mistress Doll.

PISTOL. Not I! I tell thee what, Corporal Bardolph, I could tear her; I'll be reveng'd of her.

PAGE. Pray thee go down.

PISTOL. I'll see her damn'd first; to Pluto's damn'd lake, by this hand, to th' infernal deep, with Erebus and tortures vile also. Hold hook and line, say I. Down, down, dogs! down, faitors! Have we not Hiren here?

HOSTESS. Good Captain Peesel, be quiet; 'tis very late, i' faith; I beseek you now, aggravate your choler.

PISTOL. These be good humours, indeed! Shall packhorses,
And hollow pamper'd jades of Asia,
  Which cannot go but thirty mile a day,
Compare with Cæsars, and with Cannibals,
And Troiant Greeks? Nay, rather damn them with
King Cerberus; and let the welkin roar.
Shall we fall foul for toys?

HOSTESS. By my troth, Captain, these are very bitter words.

BARDOLPH. Be gone, good ancient; this will grow to a brawl anon.

PISTOL. Die men like dogs! Give crowns like pins! Have we not Hiren here?

HOSTESS. O' my word, Captain, there's none such here. What the good-year! do you think I would deny her? For God's sake, be quiet.

PISTOL. Then feed and be fat, my fair Calipolis.
  Come, give's some sack.
  'Si fortune me tormente sperato me contento.'
  Fear we broadsides? No, let the fiend give fire.
  Give me some sack; and, sweetheart, lie thou there.
                                        [*Laying down his sword*]
  Come we to full points here, and are etceteras nothings?
FALSTAFF. Pistol, I would be quiet.
PISTOL. Sweet knight, I kiss thy neaf. What! we have seen
  the seven stars.
DOLL. For God's sake thrust him down stairs; I cannot en-
  dure such a fustian rascal.
PISTOL. Thrust him down stairs! Know we not Galloway
  nags?
FALSTAFF. Quoit him down, Bardolph, like a shove-groat
  shilling. Nay, an 'a do nothing but speak nothing, 'a shall
  be nothing here.
BARDOLPH. Come, get you down stairs.
PISTOL. What! shall we have incision? Shall we imbrue?
                                        [*Snatching up his sword*]
  Then death rock me asleep, abridge my doleful days!
  Why, then, let grievous, ghastly, gaping wounds
  Untwine the Sisters Three! Come, Atropos, I say!
HOSTESS. Here's goodly stuff toward!
FALSTAFF. Give me my rapier, boy.
DOLL. I pray thee, Jack, I pray thee, do not draw.
FALSTAFF. Get you down stairs.
                                [*Drawing and driving* PISTOL *out*]
HOSTESS. Here's a goodly tumult! I'll forswear keeping
  house afore I'll be in these tirrits and frights. So; murder, I
  warrant now. Alas, alas! put up your naked weapons, put
  up your naked weapons.   *Exeunt* PISTOL *and* BARDOLPH
DOLL. I pray thee, Jack, be quiet; the rascal's gone. Ah, you
  whoreson little valiant villain, you!
HOSTESS. Are you not hurt i' th' groin? Methought 'a made
  a shrewd thrust at your belly.

Re-enter BARDOLPH

FALSTAFF. Have you turn'd him out a doors?

BARDOLPH. Yea, sir. The rascal's drunk. You have hurt him, sir, i' th' shoulder.

FALSTAFF. A rascal! to brave me!

DOLL. Ah, you sweet little rogue, you! Alas, poor ape, how thou sweat'st! Come, let me wipe thy face. Come on, you whoreson chops. Ah, rogue! i' faith, I love thee. Thou art as valorous as Hector of Troy, worth five of Agamemnon, and ten times better than the Nine Worthies. Ah, villain!

FALSTAFF. A rascally slave! I will toss the rogue in a blanket.

DOLL. Do, an thou dar'st for thy heart. An thou dost, I'll canvass thee between a pair of sheets.

Enter musicians

PAGE. The music is come, sir.

FALSTAFF. Let them play. Play, sirs. Sit on my knee, Doll. A rascal bragging slave! The rogue fled from me like quick-silver.

DOLL. I'faith, and thou follow'dst him like a church. Thou whoreson little tidy Bartholomew boar-pig, when wilt thou leave fighting a days and foining a nights, and begin to patch up thine old body for heaven?

Enter, behind, PRINCE HENRY *and* POINS *disguised as drawers*

FALSTAFF. Peace, good Doll! Do not speak like a death's-head; do not bid me remember mine end.

DOLL. Sirrah, what humour's the Prince of?

FALSTAFF. A good shallow young fellow. 'A would have made a good pantler; 'a would ha' chipp'd bread well.

DOLL. They say Poins has a good wit.

FALSTAFF. He a good wit! hang him, baboon! His wit's as thick as Tewksbury mustard; there's no more conceit in him than is in a mallet.

DOLL. Why does the Prince love him so, then?

FALSTAFF. Because their legs are both of a bigness, and 'a plays at quoits well, and eats conger and fennel, and drinks off candles' ends for flap-dragons, and rides the wild mare with the boys, and jumps upon join'd-stools, and swears with a good grace, and wears his boots very smooth, like unto the sign of the Leg, and breeds no bate with telling of discreet stories; and such other gambol faculties 'a has, that show a weak mind and an able body, for the which the Prince admits him. For the Prince himself is such another; the weight of a hair will turn the scales between their avoirdupois.

PRINCE. Would not this nave of a wheel have his ears cut off?

POINS. Let's beat him before his whore.

PRINCE. Look whe'er the wither'd elder hath not his poll claw'd like a parrot.

POINS. Is it not strange that desire should so many years outlive performance?

FALSTAFF. Kiss me, Doll.

PRINCE. Saturn and Venus this year in conjunction! What says th' almanac to that?

POINS. And look whether the fiery Trigon, his man, be not lisping to his master's old tables, his note-book, his counsel-keeper.

FALSTAFF. Thou dost give me flattering busses.

DOLL. By my troth, I kiss thee with a most constant heart.

FALSTAFF. I am old, I am old.

DOLL. I love thee better than I love e'er a scurvy young boy of them all.

FALSTAFF. What stuff wilt have a kirtle of? I shall receive money a Thursday. Shalt have a cap to-morrow. A merry song, come. 'A grows late; we'll to bed. Thou't forget me when I am gone.

DOLL. By my troth, thou't set me a-weeping, an thou say'st so. Prove that ever I dress myself handsome till thy return. Well, hearken a' th' end.

FALSTAFF. Some sack, Francis.

PRINCE. ⎫
POINS. ⎬ Anon, anon, sir.   [*Advancing*]

FALSTAFF. Ha! a bastard son of the King's? And art thou not Poins his brother?

PRINCE. Why, thou globe of sinful continents, what a life dost thou lead!

FALSTAFF. A better than thou. I am a gentleman: thou art a drawer.

PRINCE. Very true, sir, and I come to draw you out by the
ears.

HOSTESS. O, the Lord preserve thy Grace! By my troth,
welcome to London. Now the Lord bless that sweet face
of thine. O Jesu, are you come from Wales?

FALSTAFF. Thou whoreson mad compound of majesty, by
this light flesh and corrupt blood, thou art welcome.

[*Leaning his hand upon* DOLL]

DOLL. How, you fat fool! I scorn you.

POINS. My lord, he will drive you out of your revenge and
turn all to a merriment, if you take not the heat.

PRINCE. You whoreson candle-mine, you, how vilely did
you speak of me even now before this honest, virtuous,
civil gentlewoman!

HOSTESS. God's blessing of your good heart! and so she is,
by my troth.

FALSTAFF. Didst thou hear me?

PRINCE. Yea; and you knew me, as you did when you ran
away by Gadshill. You knew I was at your back, and
spoke it on purpose to try my patience.

FALSTAFF. No, no, no; not so; I did not think thou wast
within hearing.

PRINCE. I shall drive you then to confess the wilful abuse,
and then I know how to handle you.

FALSTAFF. No abuse, Hal, o' mine honour; no abuse.

PRINCE. Not—to dispraise me, and call me pantler, and
bread-chipper, and I know not what!

FALSTAFF. No abuse, Hal.

POINS. No abuse!

FALSTAFF. No abuse, Ned, i' th' world; honest Ned, none. I
disprais'd him before the wicked—that the wicked might
not fall in love with thee; in which doing, I have done the
part of a careful friend and a true subject; and thy father
is to give me thanks for it. No abuse, Hal; none, Ned,
none; no, faith, boys, none.

PRINCE. See now, whether pure fear and entire cowardice
doth not make thee wrong this virtuous gentlewoman to
close with us? Is she of the wicked? Is thine hostess here
of the wicked? Or is thy boy of the wicked? Or honest
Bardolph, whose zeal burns in his nose, of the wicked?

POINS. Answer, thou dead elm, answer.

FALSTAFF. The fiend hath prick'd down Bardolph irrecoverable; and his face is Lucifer's privy-kitchen, where he doth nothing but roast malt-worms. For the boy—there is a good angel about him; but the devil outbids him too.

PRINCE. For the women?

FALSTAFF. For one of them—she's in hell already, and burns poor souls. For th' other—I owe her money; and whether she be damn'd for that, I know not.

HOSTESS. No, I warrant you.

FALSTAFF. No, I think thou art not; I think thou art quit for that. Marry, there is another indictment upon thee for suffering flesh to be eaten in thy house, contrary to the law; for the which I think thou wilt howl.

HOSTESS. All vict'lers do so. What's a joint of mutton or two in a whole Lent?

PRINCE. You, gentlewoman—

DOLL. What says your Grace?

FALSTAFF. His Grace says that which his flesh rebels against.
[*Knocking within*]

HOSTESS. Who knocks so loud at door? Look to th' door there, Francis.

Enter PETO

PRINCE. Peto, how now! What news?

PETO. The King your father is at Westminster;
And there are twenty weak and wearied posts
Come from the north; and as I came along
I met and overtook a dozen captains,
Bare-headed, sweating, knocking at the taverns,
And asking every one for Sir John Falstaff.

PRINCE. By heaven, Poins, I feel me much to blame
So idly to profane the precious time,
When tempest of commotion, like the south,
Borne with black vapour, doth begin to melt
And drop upon our bare unarmed heads.
Give me my sword and cloak. Falstaff, good night.

Exeunt PRINCE, POINS, PETO, *and* BARDOLPH

FALSTAFF. Now comes in the sweetest morsel of the night,

and we must hence, and leave it unpick'd. [*Knocking within*] More knocking at the door!

Re-enter BARDOLPH

How now! What's the matter?

BARDOLPH. You must away to court, sir, presently;
A dozen captains stay at door for you.

FALSTAFF. [*To the* PAGE] Pay the musicians, sirrah.—Farewell, hostess; farewell, Doll. You see, my good wenches, how men of merit are sought after; the undeserver may sleep, when the man of action is call'd on. Farewell, good wenches. If I be not sent away post, I will see you again ere I go.

DOLL. I cannot speak. If my heart be not ready to burst! Well, sweet Jack, have a care of thyself.

FALSTAFF. Farewell, farewell.

Exeunt FALSTAFF *and* BARDOLPH

HOSTESS. Well, fare thee well. I have known thee these twenty-nine years, come peascod-time; but an honester and truer-hearted man—well, fare thee well.

BARDOLPH. [*Within*] Mistress Tearsheet!

HOSTESS. What's the matter?

BARDOLPH. [*Within*] Bid Mistress Tearsheet come to my master.

HOSTESS. O, run Doll, run, run, good Doll. Come. [*To* BARDOLPH] She comes blubber'd.—Yea, will you come, Doll? *Exeunt*

ACT III. SCENE 1

Westminster. The palace

Enter the KING *in his nightgown, with a page*

KING. Go call the Earls of Surrey and of Warwick;
But, ere they come, bid them o'er-read these letters
And well consider of them. Make good speed. *Exit page*
How many thousands of my poorest subjects

Are at this hour asleep! O sleep, O gentle sleep,
Nature's soft nurse, how have I frightened thee,
That thou no more will weigh my eyelids down,
And steep my senses in forgetfulness?
Why rather, sleep, liest thou in smoky cribs,
Upon uneasy pallets stretching thee,
And hush'd with buzzing night-flies to thy slumber,
Than in the perfum'd chambers of the great,
Under the canopies of costly state,
And lull'd with sound of sweetest melody?
O thou dull god, why liest thou with the vile
In loathsome beds, and leav'st the kingly couch
A watch-case or a common 'larum-bell?
Wilt thou upon the high and giddy mast
Seal up the ship-boy's eyes, and rock his brains
In cradle of the rude imperious surge,
And in the visitation of the winds,
Who take the ruffian billows by the top,
Curling their monstrous heads, and hanging them
With deafing clamour in the slippery clouds,
That with the hurly death itself awakes?
Canst thou, O partial sleep, give thy repose
To the wet sea-boy in an hour so rude;
And in the calmest and most stillest night,
With all appliances and means to boot,
Deny it to a king? Then, happy low, lie down!
Uneasy lies the head that wears a crown.

Enter WARWICK *and* SURREY

WARWICK. Many good morrows to your Majesty!
KING. Is it good morrow, lords?
WARWICK. 'Tis one o'clock, and past.
KING. Why then, good morrow to you all, my lords.
  Have you read o'er the letters that I sent you?
WARWICK. We have, my liege.
KING. Then you perceive the body of our kingdom
  How foul it is; what rank diseases grow,
  And with what danger, near the heart of it.
WARWICK. It is but as a body yet distempered;
  Which to his former strength may be restored

With good advice and little medicine.
My Lord Northumberland will soon be cool'd.
KING. O God! that one might read the book of fate,
  And see the revolution of the times
  Make mountains level, and the continent,
  Weary of solid firmness, melt itself
  Into the sea; and other times to see
  The beachy girdle of the ocean
  Too wide for Neptune's hips; how chances mock,
  And changes fill the cup of alteration
  With divers liquors! O, if this were seen,
  The happiest youth, viewing his progress through,
  What perils past, what crosses to ensue,
  Would shut the book and sit him down and die.
  'Tis not ten years gone
  Since Richard and Northumberland, great friends,
  Did feast together, and in two years after
  Were they at wars. It is but eight years since
  This Percy was the man nearest my soul;
  Who like a brother toil'd in my affairs
  And laid his love and life under my foot;
  Yea, for my sake, even to the eyes of Richard
  Gave him defiance. But which of you was by—
  [*To* WARWICK] You, cousin Nevil, as I may remember—
  When Richard, with his eye brim full of tears,
  Then check'd and rated by Northumberland,
  Did speak these words, now prov'd a prophecy?
  'Northumberland, thou ladder by the which
  My cousin Bolingbroke ascends my throne'—
  Though then, God knows, I had no such intent
  But that necessity so bow'd the state
  That I and greatness were compell'd to kiss—
  'The time shall come'—thus did he follow it—
  'The time will come that foul sin, gathering head,
  Shall break into corruption' so went on,
  Foretelling this same time's condition
  And the division of our amity.
WARWICK. There is a history in all men's lives,
  Figuring the natures of the times deceas'd;
  The which observ'd, a man may prophesy,

With a near aim, of the main chance of things
As yet not come to life, who in their seeds
And weak beginning lie intreasured.
Such things become the hatch and brood of time;
And, by the necessary form of this,
King Richard might create a perfect guess
That great Northumberland, then false to him,
Would of that seed grow to a greater falseness;
Which should not find a ground to root upon
Unless on you.

KING. Are these things then necessities?
Then let us meet them like necessities;
And that same word even now cries out on us.
They say the Bishop and Northumberland
Are fifty thousand strong.

WARWICK. It cannot be, my lord.
Rumour doth double, like the voice and echo,
The numbers of the feared. Please it your Grace
To go to bed. Upon my soul, my lord,
The powers that you already have sent forth
Shall bring this prize in very easily.
To comfort you the more, I have receiv'd
A certain instance that Glendower is dead.
Your Majesty hath been this fortnight ill;
And these unseasoned hours perforce must add
Unto your sickness.

KING. I will take your counsel.
And, were these inward wars once out of hand,
We would, dear lords, unto the Holy Land.   *Exeunt*

SCENE 2

Gloucestershire. Before JUSTICE SHALLOW'S *house*

Enter SHALLOW *and* SILENCE, *meeting;* MOULDY, SHADOW,
WART, FEEBLE, BULLCALF, *and servants behind*

SHALLOW. Come on, come on, come on; give me your hand,
sir; give me your hand, sir. An early stirrer, by the rood!
And how doth my good cousin Silence?

SILENCE. Good morrow, good cousin Shallow.

SHALLOW. And how doth my cousin, your bed-fellow? and your fairest daughter and mine, my god-daughter Ellen?

SILENCE. Alas, a black ousel, cousin Shallow!

SHALLOW. By yea and no, sir. I dare say my cousin William is become a good scholar; he is at Oxford still, is he not?

SILENCE. Indeed, sir, to my cost.

SHALLOW. 'A must, then, to the Inns o' Court shortly. I was once of Clement's Inn; where I think they will talk of mad Shallow yet.

SILENCE. You were call'd 'lusty Shallow' then, cousin.

SHALLOW. By the mass, I was call'd anything; and I would have done anything indeed too, and roundly too. There was I, and little John Doit of Staffordshire, and black George Barnes, and Francis Pickbone, and Will Squele a Cotsole man—you had not four such swinge-bucklers in all the Inns of Court again. And I may say to you we knew where the bona-robas were, and had the best of them all at commandment. Then was Jack Falstaff, now Sir John, a boy, and page to Thomas Mowbray, Duke of Norfolk.

SILENCE. This Sir John, cousin, that comes hither anon about soldiers?

SHALLOW. The same Sir John, the very same. I see him break Scoggin's head at the court gate, when 'a was a crack not thus high; and the very same day did I fight with one Sampson Stockfish, a fruiterer, behind Gray's Inn. Jesu, Jesu, the mad days that I have spent! and to see how many of my old acquaintance are dead!

SILENCE. We shall all follow, cousin.

SHALLOW. Certain, 'tis certain; very sure, very sure. Death, as the Psalmist saith, is certain to all; all shall die. How a good yoke of bullocks at Stamford fair?

SILENCE. By my troth, I was not there.

SHALLOW. Death is certain. Is old Double of your town living yet?

SILENCE. Dead, sir.

SHALLOW. Jesu, Jesu, dead! 'A drew a good bow; and dead! 'A shot a fine shoot. John a Gaunt loved him well, and betted much money on his head. Dead! 'A would have clapp'd i' th' clout at twelve score, and carried you a forehand shaft a fourteen and fourteen and a half, that it would have done a man's heart good to see. How a score of ewes now?

SILENCE. Thereafter as they be—a score of good ewes may be worth ten pounds.

SHALLOW. And is old Double dead?

Enter BARDOLPH, *and one with him*

SILENCE. Here come two of Sir John Falstaff's men, as I think.

SHALLOW. Good morrow, honest gentlemen.

BARDOLPH. I beseech you, which is Justice Shallow?

SHALLOW. I am Robert Shallow, sir, a poor esquire of this county, and one of the King's justices of the peace. What is your good pleasure with me?

BARDOLPH. My captain, sir, commends him to you; my captain, Sir John Falstaff—a tall gentleman, by heaven, and a most gallant leader.

SHALLOW. He greets me well, sir; I knew him a good backsword man. How doth the good knight? May I ask how my lady his wife doth?

BARDOLPH. Sir, pardon; a soldier is better accommodated than with a wife.

SHALLOW. It is well said, in faith, sir; and it is well said indeed too. 'Better accommodated!' It is good; yea, indeed, is it. Good phrases are surely, and ever were, very commendable. 'Accommodated!' It comes of accommodo. Very good; a good phrase.

BARDOLPH. Pardon, sir; I have heard the word. 'Phrase' call you it? By this day, I know not the phrase; but I will maintain the word with my sword to be a soldier-like word, and a word of exceeding good command, by heaven. Accommodated: that is, when a man is, as they say, accommodated; or, when a man is being—whereby 'a may be thought to be accommodated; which is an excellent thing.

Enter FALSTAFF

SHALLOW. It is very just. Look, here comes good Sir John.

Give me your good hand, give me your worship's good hand. By my troth, you like well and bear your years very well. Welcome, good Sir John.

FALSTAFF. I am glad to see you well, good Master Robert Shallow. Master Surecard, as I think?

SHALLOW. No, Sir John; it is my cousin Silence, in commission with me.

FALSTAFF. Good Master Silence, it well befits you should be of the peace.

SILENCE. Your good worship is welcome.

FALSTAFF. Fie! this is hot weather. Gentlemen, have you provided me here half a dozen sufficient men?

SHALLOW. Marry, have we, sir. Will you sit?

FALSTAFF. Let me see them, I beseech you.

SHALLOW. Where's the roll? Where's the roll? Where's the roll? Let me see, let me see, let me see. So, so, so, so, so—so, so—yea, marry, sir. Rafe Mouldy! Let them appear as I call; let them do so, let them do so. Let me see; where is Mouldy?

MOULDY. Here, an't please you.

SHALLOW. What think you, Sir John? A good-limb'd fellow; young, strong, and of good friends.

FALSTAFF. Is thy name Mouldy?

MOULDY. Yea, an't please you.

FALSTAFF. 'Tis the more time thou wert us'd.

SHALLOW. Ha, ha, ha! most excellent, i' faith! Things that are mouldy lack use. Very singular good! In faith, well said, Sir John; very well said.

FALSTAFF. Prick him.

MOULDY. I was prick'd well enough before, an you could have let me alone. My old dame will be undone now for one to do her husbandry and her drudgery. You need not to have prick'd me; there are other men fitter to go out than I.

FALSTAFF. Go to; peace, Mouldy; you shall go. Mouldy, it is time you were spent.

MOULDY. Spent!

SHALLOW. Peace, fellow, peace; stand aside; know you where you are? For th' other, Sir John—let me see. Simon Shadow!

FALSTAFF. Yea, marry, let me have him to sit under. He's like to be a cold soldier.

SHALLOW. Where's Shadow?

SHADOW. Here, sir.

FALSTAFF. Shadow, whose son art thou?

SHADOW. My mother's son, sir.

FALSTAFF. Thy mother's son! Like enough; and thy father's shadow. So the son of the female is the shadow of the male. It is often so indeed; but much of the father's substance!

SHALLOW. Do you like him, Sir John?

FALSTAFF. Shadow will serve for summer. Prick him; for we have a number of shadows fill up the muster-book.

SHALLOW. Thomas Wart!

FALSTAFF. Where's he?

WART. Here, sir.

FALSTAFF. Is thy name Wart?

WART. Yea, sir.

FALSTAFF. Thou art a very ragged wart.

SHALLOW. Shall I prick him, Sir John?

FALSTAFF. It were superfluous; for his apparel is built upon his back, and the whole frame stands upon pins. Prick him no more.

SHALLOW. Ha, ha, ha! You can do it, sir; you can do it. I commend you well. Francis Feeble!

FEEBLE. Here, sir.

FALSTAFF. What trade art thou, Feeble?

FEEBLE. A woman's tailor, sir.

SHALLOW. Shall I prick him, sir?

FALSTAFF. You may; but if he had been a man's tailor, he'd ha' prick'd you. Wilt thou make as many holes in an enemy's battle as thou hast done in a woman's petticoat?

FEEBLE. I will do my good will, sir; you can have no more.

FALSTAFF. Well said, good woman's tailor! well said, courageous Feeble! Thou wilt be as valiant as the wrathful dove or most magnanimous mouse. Prick the woman's tailor—well, Master Shallow, deep, Master Shallow.

FEEBLE. I would Wart might have gone, sir.

FALSTAFF. I would thou wert a man's tailor, that thou mightst mend him and make him fit to go. I cannot put him to a private soldier, that is the leader of so many thousands. Let that suffice, most forcible Feeble.

FEEBLE. It shall suffice, sir.

FALSTAFF. I am bound to thee, reverend Feeble. Who is next?

SHALLOW. Peter Bullcalf o' th' green!

FALSTAFF. Yea, marry, let's see Bullcalf.

BULLCALF. Here, sir.

FALSTAFF. Fore God, a likely fellow! Come, prick me Bullcalf till he roar again.

BULLCALF. O Lord! good my lord captain—

FALSTAFF. What, dost thou roar before thou art prick'd?

BULLCALF. O Lord, sir! I am a diseased man.

FALSTAFF. What disease hast thou?

BULLCALF. A whoreson cold, sir, a cough, sir, which I caught with ringing in the King's affairs upon his coronation day, sir.

FALSTAFF. Come, thou shalt go to the wars in a gown. We will have away thy cold; and I will take such order that thy friends shall ring for thee. Is here all?

SHALLOW. Here is two more call'd than your number. You must have but four here, sir; and so, I pray you, go in with me to dinner.

FALSTAFF. Come, I will go drink with you, but I cannot tarry dinner. I am glad to see you, by my troth, Master Shallow.

SHALLOW. O, Sir John, do you remember since we lay all night in the windmill in Saint George's Field?

FALSTAFF. No more of that, Master Shallow, no more of that.

SHALLOW. Ha, 'twas a merry night. And is Jane Nightwork alive?

FALSTAFF. She lives, Master Shallow.

SHALLOW. She never could away with me.

FALSTAFF. Never, never; she would always say she could not abide Master Shallow.

SHALLOW. By the mass, I could anger her to th' heart. She was then a bona-roba. Doth she hold her own well?

FALSTAFF. Old, old, Master Shallow.

SHALLOW. Nay, she must be old; she cannot choose but be

old; certain she's old; and had Robin Nightwork, **by old Nightwork**, before I came to Clement's Inn.

SILENCE. That's fifty-five year ago.

SHALLOW. Ha, cousin Silence, that thou hadst seen that that this knight and I have seen! Ha, Sir John, said I well?

FALSTAFF. We have heard the chimes at midnight, Master Shallow.

SHALLOW. That we have, that we have, that we have; in faith, Sir John, we have. Our watchword was 'Hem, boys!' Come, let's to dinner; come, let's to dinner. Jesus, the days that we have seen! Come, come.

Exeunt FALSTAFF *and the* JUSTICES

BULLCALF. Good Master Corporate Bardolph, stand my friend; and here's four Harry ten shillings in French crowns for you. In very truth, sir, I had as lief be hang'd, sir, as go. And yet, for mine own part, sir, I do not care; but rather because I am unwilling and, for mine own part, have a desire to stay with my friends; else, sir, I did not care for mine own part so much.

BARDOLPH. Go to; stand aside.

MOULDY. And, good Master Corporal Captain, for my old dame's sake, stand my friend. She has nobody to do anything about her when I am gone; and she is old, and cannot help herself. You shall have forty, sir.

BARDOLPH. Go to; stand aside.

FEEBLE. By my troth, I care not; a man can die but once; we owe God a death. I'll ne'er bear a base mind. An't be my destiny, so; an't be not, so. No man's too good to serve 's Prince; and, let it go which way it will, he that dies this year is quit for the next.

BARDOLPH. Well said; th'art a good fellow.

FEEBLE. Faith, I'll bear no base mind.

Re-enter FALSTAFF *and the* JUSTICES

FALSTAFF. Come, sir, which men shall I have?

SHALLOW. Four of which you please.

BARDOLPH. Sir, a word with you. I have three pound to free Mouldy and Bullcalf.

FALSTAFF. Go to; well.

SHALLOW. Come, Sir John, which four will you have?

FALSTAFF. Do you choose for me.

SHALLOW. Marry, then—Mouldy, Bullcalf, Feeble, and Shadow.

FALSTAFF. Mouldy and Bullcalf: for you, Mouldy, stay at home till you are past service; and for your part, Bullcalf, grow till you come unto it. I will none of you.

SHALLOW. Sir John, Sir John, do not yourself wrong. They are your likeliest men, and I would have you serv'd with the best.

FALSTAFF. Will you tell me, Master Shallow, how to choose a man? Care I for the limb, the thews, the stature, bulk, and big assemblance of a man! Give me the spirit, Master Shallow. Here's Wart; you see what a ragged appearance it is. 'A shall charge you and discharge you with the motion of a pewterer's hammer, come off and on swifter than he that gibbets on the brewer's bucket. And this same half-fac'd fellow, Shadow—give me this man. He presents no mark to the enemy; the foeman may with as great aim level at the edge of a penknife. And, for a retreat—how swiftly will this Feeble, the woman's tailor, run off! O, give me the spare men, and spare me the great ones. Put me a caliver into Wart's hand, Bardolph.

BARDOLPH. Hold, Wart. Traverse—thus, thus, thus.

FALSTAFF. Come, manage me your caliver. So—very well. Go to; very good; exceeding good. O, give me always a little, lean, old, chopt, bald shot. Well said, i' faith, Wart; th'art a good scab. Hold, there's a tester for thee.

SHALLOW. He is not his craft's master, he doth not do it right. I remember at Mile-end Green, when I lay at Clement's Inn—I was then Sir Dagonet in Arthur's show—there was a little quiver fellow, and 'a would manage you his piece thus; and 'a would about and about, and come you in and come you in. 'Rah, tah, tah!' would 'a say; 'Bounce!' would 'a say; and away again would 'a go, and again would 'a come. I shall ne'er see such a fellow.

FALSTAFF. These fellows will do well. Master Shallow, God keep you! Master Silence, I will not use many words with you: Fare you well! Gentlemen both, I thank you. I must a dozen mile to-night. Bardolph, give the soldiers coats.

SHALLOW. Sir John, the Lord bless you; God prosper your

affairs; God send us peace! At your return, visit our house; let our old acquaintance be renewed. Peradventure I will with ye to the court.

FALSTAFF. Fore God, would you would.

SHALLOW. Go to; I have spoke at a word. God keep you.

FALSTAFF. Fare you well, gentle gentlemen. [*Exeunt* JUS-TICES] On, Bardolph; lead the men away. [*Exeunt all but* FALSTAFF] As I return, I will fetch off these justices. I do see the bottom of Justice Shallow. Lord, Lord, how subject we old men are to this vice of lying! This same starv'd justice hath done nothing but prate to me of the wildness of his youth and the feats he hath done about Turnbull Street; and every third word a lie, duer paid to the hearer than the Turk's tribute. I do remember him at Clement's Inn, like a man made after supper of a cheese-paring. When 'a was naked, he was for all the world like a fork'd radish, with a head fantastically carved upon it with a knife. 'A was so forlorn that his dimensions to any thick sight were invisible. 'A was the very genius of famine; yet lecherous as a monkey, and the whores call'd him man-drake. 'A came ever in the rearward of the fashion, and sung those tunes to the overscutch'd huswifes that he heard the carmen whistle, and sware they were his fancies or his good-nights. And now is this Vice's dagger become a squire, and talks as familiarly of John a Gaunt as if he had been sworn brother to him; and I'll be sworn 'a ne'er saw him but once in the Tiltyard; and then he burst his head for crowding among the marshal's men. I saw it, and told John a Gaunt he beat his own name; for you might have thrust him and all his apparel into an eel-skin; the case of a treble hautboy was a mansion for him, a court—and now has he land and beeves. Well, I'll be acquainted with him if I return; and't shall go hard but I'll make him a philoso-pher's two stones to me. If the young dace be a bait for the old pike, I see no reason in the law of nature but I may snap at him. Let time shape, and there an end.   *Exit*

ACT IV. SCENE 1

Yorkshire. Within the Forest of Gaultree

Enter the ARCHBISHOP OF YORK, MOWBRAY,
HASTINGS, *and others*

ARCHBISHOP. What is this forest call'd?
HASTINGS. 'Tis Gaultree Forest, an't shall please your Grace.
ARCHBISHOP. Here stand, my lords, and send discoverers forth
  To know the numbers of our enemies.
HASTINGS. We have sent forth already.
ARCHBISHOP. 'Tis well done.
  My friends and brethren in these great affairs,
  I must acquaint you that I have receiv'd
  New-dated letters from Northumberland;
  Their cold intent, tenour, and substance, thus:
  Here doth he wish his person, with such powers
  As might hold sortance with his quality,
  The which he could not levy; whereupon
  He is retir'd, to ripe his growing fortunes,
  To Scotland; and concludes in hearty prayers
  That your attempts may overlive the hazard
  And fearful meeting of their opposite.
MOWBRAY. Thus do the hopes we have in him touch ground
  And dash themselves to pieces.

Enter a MESSENGER

HASTINGS. Now, what news?
MESSENGER. West of this forest, scarcely off a mile,
  In goodly form comes on the enemy;
  And, by the ground they hide, I judge their number
  Upon or near the rate of thirty thousand.
MOWBRAY. The just proportion that we gave them out.
  Let us sway on and face them in the field.

Enter WESTMORELAND

ARCHBISHOP. What well-appointed leader fronts us here?
MOWBRAY. I think it is my Lord of Westmoreland.
WESTMORELAND. Health and fair greeting from our general,
  The Prince, Lord John and Duke of Lancaster.

ARCHBISHOP. Say on, my Lord of Westmoreland, in peace,
  What doth concern your coming.
WESTMORELAND. Then, my lord,
  Unto your Grace do I in chief address
  The substance of my speech. If that rebellion
  Came like itself, in base and abject routs,
  Led on by bloody youth, guarded with rags,
  And countenanc'd by boys and beggary—
  I say, if damn'd commotion so appear'd
  In his true, native, and most proper shape,
  You, reverend father, and these noble lords,
  Had not been here to dress the ugly form
  Of base and bloody insurrection
  With your fair honours. You, Lord Archbishop,
  Whose see is by a civil peace maintain'd,
  Whose beard the silver hand of peace hath touch'd,
  Whose learning and good letters peace hath tutor'd,
  Whose white investments figure innocence,
  The dove, and very blessed spirit of peace—
  Wherefore you do so ill translate yourself
  Out of the speech of peace, that bears such grace,
  Into the harsh and boist'rous tongue of war;
  Turning your books to graves, your ink to blood,
  Your pens to lances, and your tongue divine
  To a loud trumpet and a point of war?
ARCHBISHOP. Wherefore do I this? So the question stands.
  Briefly to this end: we are all diseas'd
  And with our surfeiting and wanton hours
  Have brought ourselves into a burning fever,
  And we must bleed for it; of which disease
  Our late King, Richard, being infected, died.
  But, my most noble Lord of Westmoreland,
  I take not on me here as a physician;
  Nor do I as an enemy to peace
  Troop in the throngs of military men;
  But rather show awhile like fearful war
  To diet rank minds sick of happiness,
  And purge th' obstructions which begin to stop
  Our very veins of life. Hear me more plainly.
  I have in equal balance justly weigh'd

What wrongs our arms may do, what wrongs we suffer,
And find our griefs heavier than our offences.
We see which way the stream of time doth run
And are enforc'd from our most quiet there
By the rough torrent of occasion;
And have the summary of all our griefs,
When time shall serve, to show in articles;
Which long ere this we offer'd to the King,
And might by no suit gain our audience:
When we are wrong'd, and would unfold our griefs,
We are denied access unto his person,
Even by those men that most have done us wrong.
The dangers of the days but newly gone,
Whose memory is written on the earth
With yet appearing blood, and the examples
Of every minute's instance, present now,
Hath put us in these ill-beseeming arms;
Not to break peace, or any branch of it,
But to establish here a peace indeed,
Concurring both in name and quality.

WESTMORELAND. When ever yet was your appeal denied;
Wherein have you been galled by the King;
What peer hath been suborn'd to grate on you
That you should seal this lawless bloody book
Of forg'd rebellion with a seal divine,
And consecrate commotion's bitter edge?

ARCHBISHOP. My brother general, the commonwealth,
To brother born an household cruelty,
I make my quarrel in particular.

WESTMORELAND. There is no need of any such redress;
Or if there were, it not belongs to you.

MOWBRAY. Why not to him in part, and to us all
That feel the bruises of the days before,
And suffer the condition of these times
To lay a heavy and unequal hand
Upon our honours?

WESTMORELAND. O my good Lord Mowbray,
Construe the times to their necessities,
And you shall say, indeed, it is the time,
And not the King, that doth you injuries.

Yet, for your part, it not appears to me,
Either from the King or in the present time,
That you should have an inch of any ground
To build a grief on. Were you not restor'd
To all the Duke of Norfolk's signiories,
Your noble and right well-rememb'red father's?
MOWBRAY. What thing, in honour, had my father lost
That need to be reviv'd and breath'd in me?
The King that lov'd him, as the state stood then,
Was force perforce compell'd to banish him,
And then that Henry Bolingbroke and he,
Being mounted and both roused in their seats,
Their neighing coursers daring of the spur,
Their armed staves in charge, their beavers down,
Their eyes of fire sparkling through sights of steel,
And the loud trumpet blowing them together—
Then, then, when there was nothing could have stay'd
My father from the breast of Bolingbroke,
O, when the King did throw his warder down—
His own life hung upon the staff he threw—
Then threw he down himself, and all their lives
That by indictment and by dint of sword
Have since miscarried under Bolingbroke.
WESTMORELAND. You speak, Lord Mowbray, now you know
    not what.
The Earl of Hereford was reputed then
In England the most valiant gentleman.
Who knows on whom fortune would then have smil'd?
But if your father had been victor there,
He ne'er had borne it out of Coventry;
For all the country, in a general voice,
Cried hate upon him; and all their prayers and love
Were set on Hereford, whom they doted on,
And bless'd and grac'd indeed more than the King.
But this is mere digression from my purpose.
Here come I from our princely general
To know your griefs; to tell you from his Grace
That he will give you audience; and wherein
It shall appear that your demands are just,
You shall enjoy them, everything set off

That might so much as think you enemies.

MOWBRAY. But he hath forc'd us to compel this offer;
And it proceeds from policy, not love.

WESTMORELAND. Mowbray, you overween to take it so.
This offer comes from mercy, not from fear;
For, lo! within a ken our army lies—
Upon mine honour, all too confident
To give admittance to a thought of fear.
Our battle is more full of names than yours,
Our men more perfect in the use of arms,
Our armour all as strong, our cause the best;
Then reason will our hearts should be as good.
Say you not, then, our offer is compell'd.

MOWBRAY. Well, by my will we shall admit no parley.

WESTMORELAND. That argues but the shame of your offence:
A rotten case abides no handling.

HASTINGS. Hath the Prince John a full commission,
In very ample virtue of his father,
To hear and absolutely to determine
Of what conditions we shall stand upon?

WESTMORELAND. That is intended in the general's name.
I muse you make so slight a question.

ARCHBISHOP. Then take, my Lord of Westmoreland, this
schedule,
For this contains our general grievances.
Each several article herein redress'd,
All members of our cause, both here and hence,
That are insinewed to this action,
Acquitted by a true substantial form,
And present execution of our wills
To us and to our purposes confin'd—
We come within our awful banks again,
And knit our powers to the arm of peace.

WESTMORELAND. This will I show the general. Please you,
lords,
In sight of both our battles we may meet;
And either end in peace—which God so frame!—
Or to the place of diff'rence call the swords
Which must decide it.

ARCHBISHOP. My lord, we will do so.   *Exit* WESTMORELAND

MOWBRAY. There is a thing within my bosom tells me
  That no conditions of our peace can stand.
HASTINGS. Fear you not that: if we can make our peace
  Upon such large terms and so absolute
  As our conditions shall consist upon,
  Our peace shall stand as firm as rocky mountains.
MOWBRAY. Yea, but our valuation shall be such
  That every slight and false-derived cause,
  Yea, every idle, nice, and wanton reason,
  Shall to the King taste of this action;
  That, were our royal faiths martyrs in love,
  We shall be winnow'd with so rough a wind
  That even our corn shall seem as light as chaff,
  And good from bad find no partition.
ARCHBISHOP. No, no, my lord. Note this: the King is weary
  Of dainty and such picking grievances;
  For he hath found to end one doubt by death
  Revives two greater in the heirs of life;
  And therefore will he wipe his tables clean,
  And keep no tell-tale to his memory
  That may repeat and history his loss
  To new remembrance. For full well he knows
  He cannot so precisely weed this land
  As his misdoubts present occasion:
  His foes are so enrooted with his friends
  That, plucking to unfix an enemy,
  He doth unfasten so and shake a friend.
  So that this land, like an offensive wife
  That hath enrag'd him on to offer strokes,
  As he is striking, holds his infant up,
  And hangs resolv'd correction in the arm
  That was uprear'd to execution.
HASTINGS. Besides, the King hath wasted all his rods
  On late offenders, that he now doth lack
  The very instruments of chastisement;
  So that his power, like to a fangless lion,
  May offer, but not hold.
ARCHBISHOP. 'Tis very true;
  And therefore be assur'd, my good Lord Marshal,
  If we do now make our atonement well,

Our peace will, like a broken limb united,
Grow stronger for the breaking.
MOWBRAY. Be it so.
    Here is return'd my Lord of Westmoreland.

Re-enter WESTMORELAND

WESTMORELAND. The Prince is here at hand. Pleaseth your
    lordship
To meet his Grace just distance 'tween our armies?
MOWBRAY. Your Grace of York, in God's name then, set
    forward.
ARCHBISHOP. Before, and greet his Grace. My lord, we come.
                                      Exeunt

SCENE 2

Another part of the forest

Enter, from one side, MOWBRAY, *attended; after-*
wards, the ARCHBISHOP, HASTINGS, *and others; from*
the other side, PRINCE JOHN OF LANCASTER, WEST-
MORELAND, OFFICERS, *and others*

PRINCE JOHN. You are well encount'red here, my cousin
    Mowbray.
Good day to you, gentle Lord Archbishop;
And so to you, Lord Hastings, and to all.
My Lord of York, it better show'd with you
When that your flock, assembled by the bell,
Encircled you to hear with reverence
Your exposition on the holy text
Than now to see you here an iron man,
Cheering a rout of rebels with your drum,
Turning the word to sword, and life to death.
That man that sits within a monarch's heart
And ripens in the sunshine of his favour,
Would he abuse the countenance of the king,
Alack, what mischiefs might he set abroach
In shadow of such greatness! With you, Lord Bishop,
It is even so. Who hath not heard it spoken
How deep you were within the books of God?

To us the speaker in His parliament,
To us th' imagin'd voice of God himself,
The very opener and intelligencer
Between the grace, the sanctities of heaven,
And our dull workings. O, who shall believe
But you misuse the reverence of your place,
Employ the countenance and grace of heav'n
As a false favourite doth his prince's name,
In deeds dishonourable? You have ta'en up,
Under the counterfeited zeal of God,
The subjects of His substitute, my father,
And both against the peace of heaven and him
Have here up-swarm'd them.

ARCHBISHOP. Good my Lord of Lancaster,
I am not here against your father's peace;
But, as I told my Lord of Westmoreland,
The time misord'red doth, in common sense,
Crowd us and crush us to this monstrous form
To hold our safety up. I sent your Grace
The parcels and particulars of our grief,
The which hath been with scorn shov'd from the court,
Whereon this hydra son of war is born;
Whose dangerous eyes may well be charm'd asleep
With grant of our most just and right desires;
And true obedience, of this madness cur'd,
Stoop tamely to the foot of majesty.

MOWBRAY. If not, we ready are to try our fortunes
To the last man.

HASTINGS. And though we here fall down,
We have supplies to second our attempt.
If they miscarry, theirs shall second them;
And so success of mischief shall be born,
And heir from heir shall hold this quarrel up
Whiles England shall have generation.

PRINCE JOHN. You are too shallow, Hastings, much too shallow,
To sound the bottom of the after-times.

WESTMORELAND. Pleaseth your Grace to answer them directly
How far forth you do like their articles.

PRINCE JOHN. I like them all and do allow them well;
   And swear here, by the honour of my blood,
   My father's purposes have been mistook;
   And some about him have too lavishly
   Wrested his meaning and authority.
   My lord, these griefs shall be with speed redress'd;
   Upon my soul, they shall. If this may please you,
   Discharge your powers unto their several counties,
   As we will ours; and here, between the armies,
   Let's drink together friendly and embrace,
   That all their eyes may bear those tokens home
   Of our restored love and amity.
ARCHBISHOP. I take your princely word for these redresses.
PRINCE JOHN. I give it you, and will maintain my word;
   And thereupon I drink unto your Grace.
HASTINGS. Go, Captain, and deliver to the army
   This news of peace. Let them have pay, and part.
   I know it will please them. Hie thee, Captain.

                        Exit Officer

ARCHBISHOP. To you, my noble Lord of Westmoreland.
WESTMORELAND. I pledge your Grace; and if you knew
     what pains
   I have bestow'd to breed this present peace,
   You would drink freely; but my love to ye
   Shall show itself more openly hereafter.
ARCHBISHOP. I do not doubt you.
WESTMORELAND. I am glad of it.
   Health to my lord and gentle cousin, Mowbray.
MOWBRAY. You wish me health in very happy season,
   For I am on the sudden something ill.
ARCHBISHOP. Against ill chances men are ever merry;
   But heaviness foreruns the good event.
WESTMORELAND. Therefore be merry, coz; since sudden
     sorrow
   Serves to say thus, 'Some good thing comes to-morrow.'
ARCHBISHOP. Believe me, I am passing light in spirit.
MOWBRAY. So much the worse, if your own rule be true.

                        [Shouts within]

PRINCE JOHN. The word of peace is rend'red. Hark, how
   they shout!

MOWBRAY. This had been cheerful after victory.

ARCHBISHOP. A peace is of the nature of a conquest;
    For then both parties nobly are subdu'd,
    And neither party loser.

PRINCE JOHN. Go, my lord,
    And let our army be discharged too.

                         Exit WESTMORELAND

    And, good my lord, so please you let our trains
    March by us, that we may peruse the men
    We should have cop'd withal.

ARCHBISHOP. Go, good Lord Hastings,
    And, ere they be dismiss'd, let them march by.

                           Exit HASTINGS

PRINCE JOHN. I trust, lords, we shall lie to-night together.

Re-enter WESTMORELAND

    Now, cousin, wherefore stands our army still?

WESTMORELAND. The leaders, having charge from you to
    stand,
    Will not go off until they hear you speak.

PRINCE JOHN. They know their duties.

Re-enter HASTINGS

HASTINGS. My lord, our army is dispers'd already.
    Like youthful steers unyok'd, they take their courses
    East, west, north, south; or like a school broke up,
    Each hurries toward his home and sporting-place.

WESTMORELAND. Good tidings, my Lord Hastings; for the
    which
    I do arrest thee, traitor, of high treason;
    And you, Lord Archbishop, and you, Lord Mowbray,
    Of capital treason I attach you both.

MOWBRAY. Is this proceeding just and honourable?

WESTMORELAND. Is your assembly so?

ARCHBISHOP. Will you thus break your faith?

PRINCE JOHN. I pawn'd thee none:
    I promis'd you redress of these same grievances
    Whereof you did complain; which, by mine honour,
    I will perform with a most Christian care.
    But for you, rebels—look to taste the due

Meet for rebellion and such acts as yours.
Most shallowly did you these arms commence,
Fondly brought here, and foolishly sent hence.
Strike up our drums, pursue the scatt'red stray.
God, and not we, hath safely fought to-day.
Some guard these traitors to the block of death,
Treason's true bed and yielder-up of breath.　　*Exeunt*

SCENE 3

Another part of the forest

Alarum; excursions. Enter FALSTAFF *and*
COLVILLE, *meeting*

FALSTAFF. What's your name, sir? Of what condition are
you, and of what place, I pray?

COLVILLE. I am a knight sir; and my name is Colville of the
Dale.

FALSTAFF. Well then, Colville is your name, a knight is your
degree, and your place the Dale. Colville shall still be your
name, a traitor your degree, and the dungeon your place—
a place deep enough; so shall you be still Colville of the
Dale.

COLVILLE. Are not you Sir John Falstaff?

FALSTAFF. As good a man as he, sir, whoe'er I am. Do you
yield, sir, or shall I sweat for you? If I do sweat, they are
the drops of thy lovers, and they weep for thy death;
therefore rouse up fear and trembling, and do observance
to my mercy.

COLVILLE. I think you are Sir John Falstaff, and in that
thought yield me.

FALSTAFF. I have a whole school of tongues in this belly of
mine; and not a tongue of them all speaks any other word
but my name. An I had but a belly of any indifferency,
I were simply the most active fellow in Europe. My
womb, my womb, my womb undoes me. Here comes our
general.

Enter PRINCE JOHN OF LANCASTER, WESTMORELAND,
BLUNT, *and others*

PRINCE JOHN. The heat is past; follow no further now.
Call in the powers, good cousin Westmoreland.

Exit WESTMORELAND

Now, Falstaff, where have you been all this while?
When everything is ended, then you come.
These tardy tricks of yours will, on my life,
One time or other break some gallows' back.

FALSTAFF. I would be sorry, my lord, but it should be thus:
I never knew yet but rebuke and check was the reward
of valour. Do you think me a swallow, an arrow, or a bullet? Have I, in my poor and old motion, the expedition of
thought? I have speeded hither with the very extremest
inch of possibility; I have found'red nine score and odd
posts; and here, travel tainted as I am, have, in my pure
and immaculate valour, taken Sir John Colville of the Dale,
a most furious knight and valorous enemy. But what of
that? He saw me, and yielded; that I may justly say with
the hook-nos'd fellow of Rome—I came, saw, and overcame.

PRINCE JOHN. It was more of his courtesy than your deserving.

FALSTAFF. I know not. Here he is, and here I yield him; and
I beseech your Grace, let it be book'd with the rest of this
day's deeds; or, by the Lord, I will have it in a particular
ballad else, with mine own picture on the top on't, Colville
kissing my foot; to the which course if I be enforc'd, if
you do not all show like gilt twopences to me, and I, in the
clear sky of fame, o'ershine you as much as the full moon
doth the cinders of the element, which show like pins'
heads to her, believe not the word of the noble. Therefore
let me have right, and let desert mount.

PRINCE JOHN. Thine's too heavy to mount.

FALSTAFF. Let it shine, then.

PRINCE JOHN. Thine's too thick to shine.

FALSTAFF. Let it do something, my good lord, that may do
me good, and call it what you will.

PRINCE JOHN. Is thy name Colville?

COLVILLE. It is, my lord.

PRINCE JOHN. A famous rebel art thou, Colville.

FALSTAFF. And a famous true subject took him.

COLVILLE. I am, my lord, but as my betters are
  That led me hither. Had they been rul'd by me,
  You should have won them dearer than you have.
FALSTAFF. I know not how they sold themselves; but thou,
  like a kind fellow, gavest thyself away gratis; and I thank
  thee for thee.

Re-enter WESTMORELAND

PRINCE JOHN. Now, have you left pursuit?
WESTMORELAND. Retreat is made, and execution stay'd.
PRINCE JOHN. Send Colville, with his confederates,
  To York, to present execution.
  Blunt, lead him hence; and see you guard him sure.
                              Exeunt BLUNT *and others*
  And now dispatch we toward the court, my lords.
  I hear the King my father is sore sick.
  Our news shall go before us to his Majesty,
  Which, cousin, you shall bear to comfort him
  And we with sober speed will follow you.
FALSTAFF. My lord, I beseech you, give me leave to go
  through Gloucestershire; and, when you come to court,
  stand my good lord, pray, in your good report.
PRINCE JOHN. Fare you well, Falstaff. I, in my condition,
  Shall better speak of you than you deserve.
                              Exeunt all but FALSTAFF
FALSTAFF. I would you had but the wit; 'twere better than
  your dukedom. Good faith, this same young sober-blooded
  boy doth not love me; nor a man cannot make him laugh
  —but that's no marvel; he drinks no wine. There's never
  none of these demure boys come to any proof; for thin
  drink doth so over-cool their blood, and making many
  fish-meals, that they fall into a kind of male green-sickness;
  and then, when they marry, they get wenches. They are
  generally fools and cowards—which some of us should be
  too, but for inflammation. A good sherris-sack hath a twofold operation in it. It ascends me into the brain; dries me
  there all the foolish and dull and crudy vapours which
  environ it; makes it apprehensive, quick, forgetive, full of
  nimble, fiery, and delectable shapes; which delivered o'er
  to the voice, the tongue, which is the birth, becomes excel-

lent wit. The second property of your excellent sherris is the warming of the blood; which before, cold and settled, left the liver white and pale, which is the badge of pusillanimity and cowardice; but the sherris warms it, and makes it course from the inwards to the parts extremes. It illumineth the face, which, as a beacon, gives warning to all the rest of this little kingdom, man, to arm; and then the vital commoners and inland petty spirits muster me all to their captain, the heart, who, great and puff'd up with this retinue, doth any deed of courage—and this valour comes of sherris. So that skill in the weapon is nothing without sack, for that sets it a-work; and learning, a mere hoard of gold kept by a devil till sack commences it and sets it in act and use. Hereof comes it that Prince Harry is valiant; for the cold blood he did naturally inherit of his father, he hath, like lean, sterile, and bare land, manured, husbanded, and till'd, with excellent endeavour of drinking good and good store of fertile sherris, that he is become very hot and valiant. If I had a thousand sons, the first humane principle I would teach them should be to forswear thin potations and to addict themselves to sack.

Enter BARDOLPH

How now, Bardolph!

BARDOLPH. The army is discharged all and gone.

FALSTAFF. Let them go. I'll through Gloucestershire, and there will I visit Master Robert Shallow, Esquire. I have him already temp'ring between my finger and my thumb, and shortly will I seal with him. Come away.   *Exeunt*

SCENE 4

Westminster. The Jerusalem Chamber

Enter the KING, PRINCE THOMAS OF CLARENCE, PRINCE HUMPHREY OF GLOUCESTER, WARWICK, *and others*

KING. Now, lords, if God doth give successful end
To this debate that bleedeth at our doors,

We will our youth lead on to higher fields,
And draw no swords but what are sanctified.
Our navy is address'd, our power collected,
Our substitutes in absence well invested,
And everything lies level to our wish.
Only we want a little personal strength;
And pause us till these rebels, now afoot,
Come underneath the yoke of government.
WARWICK. Both which we doubt not but your Majesty
    Shall soon enjoy.
KING. Humphrey, my son of Gloucester,
    Where is the Prince your brother?
PRINCE HUMPHREY. I think he's gone to hunt, my lord, at
    Windsor.
KING. And how accompanied?
PRINCE HUMPHREY. I do not know, my lord.
KING. Is not his brother, Thomas of Clarence, with him?
PRINCE HUMPHREY. No, my good lord, he is in presence
    here.
CLARENCE. What would my lord and father?
KING. Nothing but well to thee, Thomas of Clarence.
    How chance thou art not with the Prince thy brother?
    He loves thee, and thou dost neglect him, Thomas.
    Thou hast a better place in his affection
    Than all thy brothers; cherish it, my boy,
    And noble offices thou mayst effect
    Of mediation, after I am dead,
    Between his greatness and thy other brethren.
    Therefore omit him not; blunt not his love,
    Nor lose the good advantage of his grace
    By seeming cold or careless of his will;
    For he is gracious if he be observ'd.
    He hath a tear for pity and a hand
    Open as day for melting charity;
    Yet notwithstanding, being incens'd, he is flint;
    As humorous as winter, and as sudden
    As flaws congealed in the spring of day.
    His temper, therefore, must be well observ'd.
    Chide him for faults, and do it reverently,
    When you perceive his blood inclin'd to mirth;

347

But, being moody, give him line and scope
Till that his passions, like a whale on ground,
Confound themselves with working. Learn this, Thomas,
And thou shalt prove a shelter to thy friends,
A hoop of gold to bind thy brothers in,
That the united vessel of their blood,
Mingled with venom of suggestion—
As, force perforce, the age will pour it in—
Shall never leak, though it do work as strong
As aconitum or rash gunpowder.

CLARENCE. I shall observe him with all care and love.
KING. Why art thou not at Windsor with him, Thomas?
CLARENCE. He is not there to-day; he dines in London.
KING. And how accompanied? Canst thou tell that?
CLARENCE. With Poins, and other his continual followers.
KING. Most subject is the fattest soil to weeds;
And he, the noble image of my youth,
Is overspread with them; therefore my grief
Stretches itself beyond the hour of death.
The blood weeps from my heart when I do shape,
In forms imaginary, th' unguided days
And rotten times that you shall look upon
When I am sleeping with my ancestors.
For when his headstrong riot hath no curb,
When rage and hot blood are his counsellors,
When means and lavish manners meet together,
O, with what wings shall his affections fly
Towards fronting peril and oppos'd decay!
WARWICK. My gracious lord, you look beyond him quite.
The Prince but studies his companions
Like a strange tongue, wherein, to gain the language,
'Tis needful that the most immodest word
Be look'd upon and learnt; which once attain'd,
Your Highness knows, comes to no further use
But to be known and hated. So, like gross terms,
The Prince will, in the perfectness of time,
Cast off his followers; and their memory
Shall as a pattern or a measure live
By which his Grace must mete the lives of other,
Turning past evils to advantages.

KING. 'Tis seldom when the bee doth leave her comb
In the dead carrion.

Enter WESTMORELAND

Who's here? Westmoreland?
WESTMORELAND. Health to my sovereign, and new happiness
Added to that that I am to deliver!
Prince John, your son, doth kiss your Grace's hand.
Mowbray, the Bishop Scroop, Hastings, and all,
Are brought to the correction of your law.
There is not now a rebel's sword unsheath'd,
But Peace puts forth her olive everywhere.
The manner how this action hath been borne
Here at more leisure may your Highness read,
With every course in his particular.
KING. O Westmoreland, thou art a summer bird,
Which ever in the haunch of winter sings
The lifting up of day.

Enter HARCOURT

Look here's more news.
HARCOURT. From enemies heaven keep your Majesty;
And, when they stand against you, may they fall
As those that I am come to tell you of!
The Earl Northumberland and the Lord Bardolph,
With a great power of English and of Scots,
Are by the shrieve of Yorkshire overthrown.
The manner and true order of the fight
This packet, please it you, contains at large.
KING. And wherefore should these good news make me
sick?
Will Fortune never come with both hands full,
But write her fair words still in foulest letters?
She either gives a stomach and no food—
Such are the poor, in health—or else a feast,
And takes away the stomach—such are the rich
That have abundance and enjoy it not.
I should rejoice now at this happy news;
And now my sight fails, and my brain is giddy.
O me! come near me now I am much ill.

PRINCE HUMPHREY. Comfort, your Majesty!

CLARENCE. O my royal father!

WESTMORELAND. My sovereign lord, cheer up yourself,
    look up.

WARWICK. Be patient, Princes; you do know these fits
  Are with his Highness very ordinary.
  Stand from him, give him air; he'll straight be well.

CLARENCE. No, no; he cannot long hold out these pangs.
  Th' incessant care and labour of his mind
  Hath wrought the mure that should confine it in
  So thin that life looks through, and will break out.

PRINCE HUMPHREY. The people fear me; for they do observe
  Unfather'd heirs and loathly births of nature.
  The seasons change their manners, as the year
  Had found some months asleep, and leapt them over.

CLARENCE. The river hath thrice flow'd, no ebb between;
  And the old folk, Time's doting chronicles,
  Say it did so a little time before
  That our great grandsire, Edward, sick'd and died.

WARWICK. Speak lower, Princes, for the King recovers.

PRINCE HUMPHREY. This apoplexy will certain be his end.

KING. I pray you take me up, and bear me hence
  Into some other chamber. Softly, pray.   *Exeunt*

SCENE 5

Westminster. Another chamber

The KING *lying on a bed;* CLARENCE, GLOUCESTER,
WARWICK, *and others in attendance*

KING. Let there be no noise made, my gentle friends;
  Unless some dull and favourable hand
  Will whisper music to my weary spirit.

WARWICK. Call for the music in the other room.

KING. Set me the crown upon my pillow here.

CLARENCE. His eye is hollow, and he changes much.

WARWICK. Less noise, less noise!

Enter PRINCE HENRY

PRINCE. Who saw the Duke of Clarence?

CLARENCE. I am here, brother, full of heaviness.

PRINCE. How now! Rain within doors, and none abroad!
 How doth the King?

PRINCE HUMPHREY. Exceeding ill.

PRINCE. Heard he the good news yet? Tell it him.

PRINCE HUMPHREY. He alt'red much upon the hearing it.

PRINCE. If he be sick with joy, he'll recover without physic.

WARWICK. Not so much noise, my lords. Sweet Prince,
 speak low;
 The King your father is dispos'd to sleep.

CLARENCE. Let us withdraw into the other room.

WARWICK. Will't please your Grace to go along with us?

PRINCE. No; I will sit and watch here by the King.

Exeunt all but the PRINCE

Why doth the crown lie there upon his pillow,
Being so troublesome a bedfellow?
O polish'd perturbation! golden care!
That keep'st the ports of slumber open wide
To many a watchful night! Sleep with it now!
Yet not so sound and half so deeply sweet
As he whose brow with homely biggen bound
Snores out the watch of night. O majesty!
When thou dost pinch thy bearer, thou dost sit
Like a rich armour worn in heat of day
That scald'st with safety. By his gates of breath
There lies a downy feather which stirs not.
Did he suspire, that light and weightless down
Perforce must move. My gracious lord! my father!
This sleep is sound indeed; this is a sleep
That from this golden rigol hath divorc'd
So many English kings. Thy due from me
Is tears and heavy sorrows of the blood
Which nature, love, and filial tenderness,
Shall, O dear father, pay thee plenteously.
My due from thee is this imperial crown,
Which, as immediate from thy place and blood,
Derives itself to me. [*Putting on the crown*] Lo where
 it sits—
Which God shall guard; and put the world's whole strength

Into one giant arm, it shall not force
This lineal honour from me. This from thee
Will I to mine leave as 'tis left to me.   *Exit*
KING. Warwick! Gloucester! Clarence!

Re-enter WARWICK, GLOUCESTER, CLARENCE

CLARENCE. Doth the King call?
WARWICK. What would your Majesty? How fares your
    Grace?
KING. Why did you leave me here alone, my lords?
CLARENCE. We left the Prince my brother here, my liege,
    Who undertook to sit and watch by you.
KING. The Prince of Wales! Where is he? Let me see him.
    He is not here.
WARWICK. This door is open; he is gone this way.
PRINCE HUMPHREY. He came not through the chamber
    where we stay'd.
KING. Where is the crown? Who took it from my pillow?
WARWICK. When we withdrew, my liege, we left it here.
KING. The Prince hath ta'en it hence. Go, seek him out.
    Is he so hasty that he doth suppose
    My sleep my death?
    Find him, my lord of Warwick; chide him hither.
                                                    Exit WARWICK

    This part of his conjoins with my disease
    And helps to end me. See, sons, what things you are!
    How quickly nature falls into revolt
    When gold becomes her object!
    For this the foolish over-careful fathers
    Have broke their sleep with thoughts,
    Their brains with care, their bones with industry;
    For this they have engrossed and pil'd up
    The cank'red heaps of strange-achieved gold;
    For this they have been thoughtful to invest
    Their sons with arts and martial exercises;
    When, like the bee, tolling from every flower
    The virtuous sweets,
    Our thighs with wax, our mouths with honey pack'd,
    We bring it to the hive, and, like the bees,
    Are murd'red for our pains. This bitter taste

Yields his engrossments to the ending father.

Re-enter WARWICK

Now where is he that will not stay so long
Till his friend sickness hath determin'd me?
WARWICK. My lord, I found the Prince in the next room,
Washing with kindly tears his gentle cheeks,
With such a deep demeanour in great sorrow,
That tyranny, which never quaff'd but blood,
Would, by beholding him, have wash'd his knife
With gentle eye-drops. He is coming hither.
KING. But wherefore did he take away the crown?

Re-enter PRINCE HENRY

Lo where he comes. Come hither to me, Harry.
Depart the chamber, leave us here alone.
                    Exeunt all but the KING *and the* PRINCE
PRINCE. I never thought to hear you speak again.
KING. Thy wish was father, Harry, to that thought.
I stay too long by thee, I weary thee.
Dost thou so hunger for mine empty chair
That thou wilt needs invest thee with my honours
Before thy hour be ripe? O foolish youth!
Thou seek'st the greatness that will overwhelm thee.
Stay but a little, for my cloud of dignity
Is held from falling with so weak a wind
That it will quickly drop; my day is dim.
Thou hast stol'n that which, after some few hours,
Were thine without offense; and at my death
Thou hast seal'd up my expectation.
Thy life did manifest thou lov'dst me not,
And thou wilt have me die assur'd of it.
Thou hid'st a thousand daggers in thy thoughts,
Which thou hast whetted on thy stony heart,
To stab at half an hour of my life.
What, canst thou not forbear me half an hour?
Then get thee gone, and dig my grave thyself;
And bid the merry bells ring to thine ear
That thou art crowned, not that I am dead.
Let all the tears that should bedew my hearse

Be drops of balm to sanctify thy head;
Only compound me with forgotten dust;
Give that which gave thee life unto the worms.
Pluck down my officers, break my decrees;
For now a time is come to mock at form—
Harry the Fifth is crown'd. Up, vanity:
Down, royal state. All you sage counsellors, hence.
And to the English court assemble now,
From every region, apes of idleness.
Now, neighbour confines, purge you of your scum.
Have you a ruffian that will swear, drink, dance,
Revel the night, rob, murder, and commit
The oldest sins the newest kind of ways?
Be happy, he will trouble you no more.
England shall double gild his treble guilt;
England shall give him office, honour, might;
For the fifth Harry from curb'd license plucks
The muzzle of restraint, and the wild dog
Shall flesh his tooth on every innocent.
O my poor kingdom, sick with civil blows!
When that my care could not withhold thy riots,
What wilt thou do when riot is thy care?
O, thou wilt be a wilderness again.
Peopled with wolves, thy old inhabitants!
PRINCE. O, pardon me, my liege! But for my tears,
The moist impediments unto my speech,
I had forestall'd this dear and deep rebuke
Ere you with grief had spoke and I had heard
The course of it so far. There is your crown,
And he that wears the crown immortally
Long guard it yours! [*Kneeling*] If I affect it more
Than as your honour and as your renown,
Let me no more from this obedience rise,
Which my most inward true and duteous spirit
Teacheth this prostrate and exterior bending!
God witness with me, when I here came in
And found no course of breath within your Majesty,
How cold it struck my heart! If I do feign,
O, let me in my present wildness die,
And never live to show th' incredulous world

The noble change that I have purposed!
Coming to look on you, thinking you dead—
And dead almost, my liege, to think you were—
I spake unto this crown as having sense,
And thus upbraided it: 'The care on thee depending
Hath fed upon the body of my father;
Therefore thou best of gold art worst of gold.
Other, less fine in carat, is more precious,
Preserving life in med'cine potable;
But thou, most fine, most honour'd, most renown'd,
Hast eat thy bearer up.' Thus, my most royal liege,
Accusing it, I put it on my head,
To try with it—as with an enemy
That had before my face murd'red my father—
The quarrel of a true inheritor.
But if it did infect my blood with joy,
Or swell my thoughts to any strain of pride;
If any rebel or vain spirit of mine
Did with the least affection of a welcome
Give entertainment to the might of it,
Let God for ever keep it from my head,
And make me as the poorest vassal is,
That doth with awe and terror kneel to it!
KING. O my son,
God put it in thy mind to take it hence,
That thou mightst win the more thy father's love,
Pleading so wisely in excuse of it!
Come hither, Harry; sit thou by my bed,
And hear, I think, the very latest counsel
That ever I shall breathe. God knows, my son,
By what by-paths and indirect crook'd ways
I met this crown; and I myself know well
How troublesome it sat upon my head:
To thee it shall descend with better quiet,
Better opinion, better confirmation;
For all the soil of the achievement goes
With me into the earth. It seem'd in me
But as an honour snatch'd with boist'rous hand;
And I had many living to upbraid
My gain of it by their assistances;

Which daily grew to quarrel and to bloodshed,
Wounding supposed peace. All these bold fears
Thou seest with peril I have answered;
For all my reign hath been but as a scene
Acting that argument. And now my death
Changes the mood; for what in me was purchas'd
Falls upon thee in a more fairer sort;
So thou the garland wear'st successively.
Yet, though thou stand'st more sure than I could do,
Thou art not firm enough, since griefs are green;
And all my friends, which thou must make thy friends,
Have but their stings and teeth newly ta'en out;
By whose fell working I was first advanc'd,
And by whose power I well might lodge a fear
To be again displac'd; which to avoid,
I cut them off; and had a purpose now
To lead out many to the Holy Land,
Lest rest and lying still might make them look
Too near unto my state. Therefore, my Harry,
Be it thy course to busy giddy minds
With foreign quarrels, that action, hence borne **out**,
May waste the memory of the former days.
More would I, but my lungs are wasted so
That strength of speech is utterly denied me.
How I came by the crown, O God, forgive;
And grant it may with thee in true peace live!
PRINCE. My gracious liege,
You won it, wore it, kept it, gave it me;
Then plain and right must my possession be;
Which I with more than with a common pain
'Gainst all the world will rightfully maintain.

Enter PRINCE JOHN OF LANCASTER, WARWICK, LORDS,
and others

KING. Look, look, here comes my John of Lancaster.
PRINCE JOHN. Health, peace, and happiness, to my **royal**
father!
KING. Thou bring'st me happiness and peace, son John;
But health, alack, with youthful wings is flown
From this bare wither'd trunk. Upon thy sight

My worldly business makes a period.
Where is my Lord of Warwick?
PRINCE. My Lord of Warwick!
KING. Doth any name particular belong
Unto the lodging where I first did swoon?
WARWICK. 'Tis call'd Jerusalem, my noble lord.
KING. Laud be to God! Even there my life must end.
It hath been prophesied to me many years,
I should not die but in Jerusalem;
Which vainly I suppos'd the Holy Land.
But bear me to that chamber; there I'll lie;
In that Jerusalem shall Harry die.   *Exeunt*

ACT V. SCENE 1

Gloucestershire. SHALLOW's *house*

Enter SHALLOW, FALSTAFF, BARDOLPH, *and* PAGE

SHALLOW. By cock and pie, sir, you shall not away to-night.
What, Davy, I say!
FALSTAFF. You must excuse me, Master Robert Shallow.
SHALLOW. I will not excuse you; you shall not be excus'd;
excuses shall not be admitted; there is no excuse shall serve;
you shall not be excus'd. Why, Davy!

Enter DAVY

DAVY. Here, sir.
SHALLOW. Davy, Davy, Davy, Davy; let me see, Davy; let
me see, Davy; let me see—yea, marry, William cook, bid
him come hither. Sir John, you shall not be excus'd.
DAVY. Marry, sir, thus: those precepts cannot be served; and,
again, sir—shall we sow the headland with wheat?
SHALLOW. With red wheat, Davy. But for William cook—
are there no young pigeons?
DAVY. Yes, sir. Here is now the smith's note for shoeing and
plough-irons.

SHALLOW. Let it be cast, and paid. Sir John, you shall not be
excused.

DAVY. Now, sir, a new link to the bucket must needs be had;
and, sir, do you mean to stop any of William's wages
about the sack he lost the other day at Hinckley fair?

SHALLOW. 'A shall answer it. Some pigeons, Davy, a couple
of short-legg'd hens, a joint of mutton, and any pretty little tiny kickshaws, tell William cook.

DAVY. Doth the man of war stay all night, sir?

SHALLOW. Yea, Davy; I will use him well. A friend i' th'
court is better than a penny in purse. Use his men well,
Davy; for they are arrant knaves and will backbite.

DAVY. No worse than they are backbitten, sir; for they have
marvellous foul linen.

SHALLOW. Well conceited, Davy—about thy business, Davy.

DAVY. I beseech you, sir, to countenance William Visor of
Woncot against Clement Perkes o' th' hill.

SHALLOW. There is many complaints, Davy, against that
Visor. That Visor is an arrant knave, on my knowledge.

DAVY. I grant your worship that he is a knave, sir; but yet
God forbid, sir, but a knave should have some countenance
at his friend's request. An honest man, sir, is able to speak
for himself, when a knave is not. I have serv'd your worship truly, sir, this eight years; an I cannot once or twice
in a quarter bear out a knave against an honest man, I
have but a very little credit with your worship. The knave
is mine honest friend, sir; therefore, I beseech you, let him
be countenanc'd.

SHALLOW. Go to; I say he shall have no wrong. Look about,
Davy. [*Exit* DAVY] Where are you, Sir John? Come,
come, come, off with your boots. Give me your hand,
Master Bardolph.

BARDOLPH. I am glad to see your worship.

SHALLOW. I thank thee with all my heart, kind Master Bardolph. [*To the* PAGE] And welcome, my tall fellow.
Come, Sir John.

FALSTAFF. I'll follow you, good Master Robert Shallow.
[*Exit* SHALLOW] Bardolph, look to our horses. [*Exeunt*
BARDOLPH *and* PAGE] If I were sawed into quantities, I
should make four dozen of such bearded hermits' staves as

Master Shallow. It is a wonderful thing to see the semblable coherence of his men's spirits and his. They, by observing of him, do bear themselves like foolish justices: he,
by conversing with them, is turned into a justice-like
serving-man. Their spirits are so married in conjunction
with the participation of society that they flock together in
consent, like so many wild geese. If I had a suit to Master
Shallow, I would humour his men with the imputation of
being near their master; if to his men, I would curry with
Master Shallow that no man could better command his
servants. It is certain that either wise bearing or ignorant
carriage is caught, as men take diseases, one of another;
therefore let men take heed of their company. I will devise
matter enough out of this Shallow to keep Prince Harry
in continual laughter the wearing out of six fashions,
which is four terms, or two actions; and 'a shall laugh
without intervallums. O, it is much that a lie with a slight
oath, and a jest with a sad brow will do with a fellow that
never had the ache in his shoulders! O, you shall see him
laugh till his face be like a wet cloak ill laid up!
SHALLOW. [*Within*] Sir John!
FALSTAFF. I come, Master Shallow; I come, Master Shallow.

Exit

SCENE 2

Westminster. The palace

Enter, severally, WARWICK, *and the*
LORD CHIEF JUSTICE

WARWICK. How now, my Lord Chief Justice; whither away?
CHIEF JUSTICE. How doth the King?
WARWICK. Exceeding well; his cares are now all ended.
CHIEF JUSTICE. I hope, not dead.
WARWICK. He's walk'd the way of nature;
And to our purposes he lives no more.
CHIEF JUSTICE. I would his Majesty had call'd me with him.
The service that I truly did his life

Hath left me open to all injuries.

WARWICK. Indeed, I think the young king loves you not.

CHIEF JUSTICE. I know he doth not, and do arm myself
To welcome the condition of the time,
Which cannot look more hideously upon me
Than I have drawn it in my fantasy.

Enter LANCASTER, CLARENCE, GLOUCESTER,
WESTMORELAND, *and others*

WARWICK. Here comes the heavy issue of dead Harry.
O that the living Harry had the temper
Of he, the worst of these three gentlemen!
How many nobles then should hold their places
That must strike sail to spirits of vile sort!

CHIEF JUSTICE. O God, I fear all will be overturn'd.

PRINCE JOHN. Good morrow, cousin Warwick, good morrow.

GLOUCESTER. ⎫
CLARENCE. ⎬ Good morrow, cousin.

PRINCE JOHN. We meet like men that had forgot to speak.

WARWICK. We do remember; but our argument
Is all too heavy to admit much talk.

PRINCE JOHN. Well, peace be with him that hath made us
heavy!

CHIEF JUSTICE. Peace be with us, lest we be heavier!

PRINCE HUMPHREY. O, good my lord, you have lost a friend
indeed;
And I dare swear you borrow not that face
Of seeming sorrow—it is sure your own.

PRINCE JOHN. Though no man be assur'd what grace to find,
You stand in coldest expectation.
I am the sorrier; would 'twere otherwise.

CLARENCE. Well, you must now speak Sir John Falstaff fair;
Which swims against your stream of quality.

CHIEF JUSTICE. Sweet Princes, what I did, I did in honour,
Led by th' impartial conduct of my soul;
And never shall you see that I will beg
A ragged and forestall'd remission.
If truth and upright innocency fail me,
I'll to the King my master that is dead,
And tell him who hath sent me after him.

WARWICK. Here comes the Prince.

Enter KING HENRY THE FIFTH, *attended*

CHIEF JUSTICE. Good morrow, and God save your Majesty!
KING. This new and gorgeous garment, majesty,
  Sits not so easy on me as you think.
  Brothers, you mix your sadness with some fear.
  This is the English, not the Turkish court;
  Not Amurath an Amurath succeeds,
  But Harry Harry. Yet be sad, good brothers,
  For, by my faith, it very well becomes you.
  Sorrow so royally in you appears
  That I will deeply put the fashion on,
  And wear it in my heart. Why, then, be sad;
  But entertain no more of it, good brothers,
  Than a joint burden laid upon us all.
  For me, by heaven, I bid you be assur'd,
  I'll be your father and your brother too;
  Let me but bear your love, I'll bear your cares.
  Yet weep that Harry's dead, and so will I;
  But Harry lives that shall convert those tears
  By number into hours of happiness.
BROTHERS. We hope no otherwise from your Majesty.
KING. You all look strangely on me; and you most.
  You are, I think, assur'd I love you not.
CHIEF JUSTICE. I am assur'd, if I be measur'd rightly,
  Your Majesty hath no just cause to hate me.
KING. No?
  How might a prince of my great hopes forget
  So great indignities you laid upon me?
  What, rate, rebuke, and roughly send to prison,
  Th' immediate heir of England! Was this easy?
  May this be wash'd in Lethe and forgotten?
CHIEF JUSTICE. I then did use the person of your father;
  The image of his power lay then in me;
  And in th' administration of his law,
  Whiles I was busy for the commonwealth,
  Your Highness pleased to forget my place,
  The majesty and power of law and justice,
  The image of the King whom I presented,

And struck me in my very seat of judgment;
Whereon, as an offender to your father,
I gave bold way to my authority
And did commit you. If the deed were ill,
Be you contented, wearing now the garland,
To have a son set your decrees at nought,
To pluck down justice from your awful bench,
To trip the course of law, and blunt the sword
That guards the peace and safety of your person;
Nay, more, to spurn at your most royal image,
And mock your workings in a second body.
Question your royal thoughts, make the case yours;
Be now the father, and propose a son;
Hear your own dignity so much profan'd,
See your most dreadful laws so loosely slighted,
Behold yourself so by a son disdain'd;
And then imagine me taking your part
And, in your power, soft silencing your son.
After this cold considerance, sentence me;
And, as you are a king, speak in your state
What I have done that misbecame my place,
My person, or my liege's sovereignty.
KING. You are right, Justice, and you weigh this well;
Therefore still bear the balance and the sword;
And I do wish your honours may increase
Till you do live to see a son of mine
Offend you, and obey you, as I did.
So shall I live to speak my father's words:
'Happy am I that have a man so bold
That dares do justice on my proper son;
And not less happy, having such a son
That would deliver up his greatness so
Into the hands of justice.' You did commit me;
For which I do commit into your hand
Th' unstained sword that you have us'd to bear;
With this remembrance—that you use the same
With the like bold, just, and impartial spirit
As you have done 'gainst me. There is my hand.
You shall be as a father to my youth;
My voice shall sound as you do prompt mine ear;

And I will stoop and humble my intents
To your well-practis'd wise directions.
And, Princes all, believe me, I beseech you,
My father is gone wild into his grave,
For in his tomb lie my affections;
And with his spirits sadly I survive,
To mock the expectation of the world,
To frustrate prophecies, and to raze out
Rotten opinion, who hath writ me down
After my seeming. The tide of blood in me
Hath proudly flow'd in vanity till now.
Now doth it turn and ebb back to the sea,
Where it shall mingle with the state of floods,
And flow henceforth in formal majesty.
Now call we our high court of parliament;
And let us choose such limbs of noble counsel,
That the great body of our state may go
In equal rank with the best govern'd nation;
That war, or peace, or both at once, may be
As things acquainted and familiar to us;
In which you, father, shall have foremost hand.
Our coronation done, we will accite,
As I before rememb'red, all our state;
And—God consigning to my good intents—
No prince nor peer shall have just cause to say,
God shorten Harry's happy life one day.   *Exeunt*

SCENE 3

Gloucestershire. SHALLOW's *orchard*

Enter FALSTAFF, SHALLOW, SILENCE, BARDOLPH,
the PAGE, *and* DAVY

SHALLOW. Nay, you shall see my orchard, where, in an ar-
bour, we will eat a last year's pippin of mine own graffing,
with a dish of caraways, and so forth. Come, cousin Silence. And then to bed.

FALSTAFF. Fore God, you have here a goodly dwelling and
rich.

SHALLOW. Barren, barren, barren; beggars all, beggars all, Sir
John—marry, good air. Spread, Davy, spread, Davy; well
said, Davy.

FALSTAFF. This Davy serves you for good uses; he is your
serving-man and your husband.

SHALLOW. A good varlet, a good varlet, a very good varlet,
Sir John. By the mass, I have drunk too much sack at supper. A good varlet. Now sit down, now sit down; come,
cousin.

SILENCE. Ah, sirrah! quoth-a—we shall   [*Singing*]

> Do nothing but eat and make good cheer,
> And praise God for the merry year;
> When flesh is cheap and females dear,
> And lusty lads roam here and there,
>   So merrily,
>   And ever among so merrily.

FALSTAFF. There's a merry heart! Good Master Silence, I'll
give you a health for that anon.

SHALLOW. Give Master Bardolph some wine, Davy.

DAVY. Sweet sir, sit; I'll be with you anon; most sweet sir,
sit. Master Page, good Master Page, sit. Proface! What
you want in meat, we'll have in drink. But you must bear;
the heart's all.   *Exit*

SHALLOW. Be merry, Master Bardolph; and, my little soldier
there, be merry.

SILENCE. [*Singing*]

> Be merry, be merry, my wife has all;
> For women are shrews, both short and tall;
> 'Tis merry in hall when beards wag all;
>   And welcome merry Shrove-tide.
> Be merry, be merry.

FALSTAFF. I did not think Master Silence had been a man of
this mettle.

SILENCE. Who, I? I have been merry twice and once ere
now.

Re-enter DAVY

DAVY. [*To* BARDOLPH] There's a dish of leather-coats for
you.

SHALLOW. Davy!

DAVY. Your worship! I'll be with you straight. [*To* BAR-DOLPH] A cup of wine, sir?

SILENCE. [*Singing*]

> A cup of wine that's brisk and fine,
> And drink unto the leman mine;
> And a merry heart lives long-a.

FALSTAFF. Well said, Master Silence.

SILENCE. An we shall be merry, now comes in the sweet o' th' night.

FALSTAFF. Health and long life to you, Master Silence!

SILENCE. [*Singing*]

> Fill the cup, and let it come,
> I'll pledge you a mile to th' bottom.

SHALLOW. Honest Bardolph, welcome; if thou want'st anything and wilt not call, beshrew thy heart. Welcome, my little tiny thief and welcome indeed too. I'll drink to Master Bardolph, and to all the cabileros about London.

DAVY. I hope to see London once ere I die.

BARDOLPH. An I might see you there, Davy!

SHALLOW. By the mass, you'll crack a quart together—ha! will you not, Master Bardolph?

BARDOLPH. Yea, sir, in a pottle-pot.

SHALLOW. By God's liggens, I thank thee. The knave will stick by thee, I can assure thee that. 'A will not out, 'a; 'tis true bred.

BARDOLPH. And I'll stick by him, sir.

SHALLOW. Why, there spoke a king. Lack nothing; be merry. [*One knocks at door*] Look who's at door there, ho! Who knocks?   *Exit* DAVY

FALSTAFF. [*To* SILENCE, *who has drunk a bumper*] Why, now you have done me right.

SILENCE. [*Singing*]

> Do me right,
> And dub me knight.
> Samingo.

Is't not so?

365

FALSTAFF. 'Tis so.

SILENCE. Is't so? Why then, say an old man can do somewhat.

Re-enter DAVY

DAVY. An't please your worship, there's one Pistol come from the court with news.

FALSTAFF. From the court? Let him come in.

Enter PISTOL

How now, Pistol?

PISTOL. Sir John, God save you!

FALSTAFF. What wind blew you hither, Pistol?

PISTOL. Not the ill wind which blows no man to good. Sweet knight, thou art now one of the greatest men in this realm.

SILENCE. By'r lady, I think 'a be, but goodman Puff of Barson.

PISTOL. Puff!

Puff in thy teeth, most recreant coward base!

Sir John, I am thy Pistol and thy friend,

And helter-skelter have I rode to thee;

And tidings do I bring, and lucky joys,

And golden times, and happy news of price.

FALSTAFF. I pray thee now, deliver them like a man of this world.

PISTOL. A foutra for the world and worldlings base!

I speak of Africa and golden joys.

FALSTAFF. O base Assyrian knight, what is thy news?

Let King Cophetua know the truth thereof.

SILENCE. [*Singing*] And Robin Hood, Scarlet, and John.

PISTOL. Shall dunghill curs confront the Helicons?

And shall good news be baffled?

Then, Pistol, lay thy head in Furies' lap.

SHALLOW. Honest gentleman, I know not your breeding.

PISTOL. Why, then, lament therefore.

SHALLOW. Give me pardon, sir. If, sir, you come with news from the court, I take it there's but two ways—either to utter them or conceal them. I am, sir, under the King, in some authority.

PISTOL. Under which king, Bezonian? Speak, or die.

SHALLOW. Under King Harry.
PISTOL. Harry the Fourth—or Fifth?
SHALLOW. Harry the Fourth.
PISTOL. A foutra for thine office!
  Sir John, thy tender lambkin now is King;
  Harry the Fifth's the man. I speak the truth.
  When Pistol lies, do this; and fig me, like
  The bragging Spaniard.
FALSTAFF. What, is the old king dead?
PISTOL. As nail in door. The things I speak are just.
FALSTAFF. Away, Bardolph! saddle my horse. Master Robert
  Shallow, choose what office thou wilt in the land, 'tis thine.
  Pistol, I will double-charge thee with dignities.
BARDOLPH. O joyful day!
  I would not take a knighthood for my fortune.
PISTOL. What, I do bring good news?
FALSTAFF. Carry Master Silence to bed. Master Shallow, my
  Lord Shallow, be what thou wilt—I am Fortune's steward.
  Get on thy boots; we'll ride all night. O sweet Pistol!
  Away, Bardolph! [*Exit* BARDOLPH] Come, Pistol, utter
  more to me; and withal devise something to do thyself
  good. Boot, boot, Master Shallow! I know the young King
  is sick for me. Let us take any man's horses: the laws of
  England are at my commandment. Blessed are they that
  have been my friends; and woe to my Lord Chief Justice!
PISTOL. Let vultures vile seize on his lungs also!
  'Where is the life that late I led?' say they.
  Why, here it is; welcome these pleasant days!   *Exeunt*

SCENE 4

London. A street

Enter BEADLES, *dragging in* HOSTESS QUICKLY *and*
DOLL TEARSHEET

HOSTESS. No, thou arrant knave; I would to God that I
  might die, that I might have thee hang'd. Thou hast drawn
  my shoulder out of joint.
FIRST BEADLE. The constables have delivered her over to me;

and she shall have whipping-cheer enough, I warrant her. There hath been a man or two lately kill'd about her.

DOLL. Nut-hook, nut-hook, you lie. Come on; I'll tell thee what, thou damn'd tripe-visag'd rascal, an the child I now go with do miscarry, thou wert better thou hadst struck thy mother, thou paper-fac'd villain.

HOSTESS. O the Lord, that Sir John were come! He would make this a bloody day to somebody. But I pray God the fruit of her womb miscarry!

FIRST BEADLE. If it do, you shall have a dozen of cushions again; you have but eleven now. Come, I charge you both go with me; for the man is dead that you and Pistol beat amongst you.

DOLL. I'll tell you what, you thin man in a censer, I will have you as soundly swing'd for this—you blue-bottle rogue, you filthy famish'd correctioner, if you be not swing'd, I'll forswear half-kirtles.

FIRST BEADLE. Come, come, you she knight-errant, come.

HOSTESS. O God, that right should thus overcome might! Well, of sufferance comes ease.

DOLL. Come, you rogue, come; bring me to a justice.

HOSTESS. Ay, come, you starv'd bloodhound.

DOLL. Goodman death, goodman bones!

HOSTESS. Thou atomy, thou!

DOLL. Come, you thin thing! come, you rascal!

FIRST BEADLE. Very well.   *Exeunt*

SCENE 5

Westminster. Near the Abbey

Enter GROOMS, *strewing rushes*

FIRST GROOM. More rushes, more rushes!

SECOND GROOM. The trumpets have sounded twice.

THIRD GROOM. 'Twill be two o'clock ere they come from the coronation. Dispatch, dispatch.   *Exeunt*

Trumpets sound, and the KING *and his train pass over the stage. After them enter* FALSTAFF, SHAL-LOW, PISTOL, BARDOLPH, *and page*

FALSTAFF. Stand here by me, Master Robert Shallow; I will make the King do you grace. I will leer upon him, as 'a comes by; and do but mark the countenance that he will give me.

PISTOL. God bless thy lungs, good knight!

FALSTAFF. Come here, Pistol; stand behind me. [*To* SHALLOW] O, if I had had time to have made new liveries, I would have bestowed the thousand pound I borrowed of you. But 'tis no matter; this poor show doth better; this doth infer the zeal I had to see him.

SHALLOW. It doth so.

FALSTAFF. It shows my earnestness of affection—

SHALLOW. It doth so.

FALSTAFF. My devotion—

SHALLOW. It doth, it doth, it doth.

FALSTAFF. As it were, to ride day and night; and not to deliberate, not to remember, not to have patience to shift me—

SHALLOW. It is best, certain.

FALSTAFF. But to stand stained with travel, and sweating with desire to see him; thinking of nothing else, putting all affairs else in oblivion, as if there were nothing else to be done but to see him.

PISTOL. 'Tis 'semper idem' for 'obsque hoc nihil est.' 'Tis all in every part.

SHALLOW. 'Tis so, indeed.

PISTOL. My knight, I will inflame thy noble liver
And make thee rage.
Thy Doll, and Helen of thy noble thoughts,
Is in base durance and contagious prison;
Hal'd thither
By most mechanical and dirty hand.
Rouse up revenge from ebon den with fell Alecto's snake,
For Doll is in. Pistol speaks nought but truth.

FALSTAFF. I will deliver her.

[*Shouts within, and the trumpets sound*]

PISTOL. There roar'd the sea, and trumpet-clangor sounds.

Enter the KING *and his train, the* LORD CHIEF JUSTICE
among them

FALSTAFF. God save thy Grace, King Hal; my royal Hal!

PISTOL. The heavens thee guard and keep, most royal imp of
    fame!

FALSTAFF. God save thee, my sweet boy!

KING. My Lord Chief Justice, speak to that vain man.

CHIEF JUSTICE. Have you your wits? Know you what 'tis
    you speak?

FALSTAFF. My king! my Jove! I speak to thee, my heart!

KING. I know thee not, old man. Fall to thy prayers.
  How ill white hairs become a fool and jester!
  I have long dreamt of such a kind of man,
  So surfeit-swell'd, so old, and so profane;
  But being awak'd, I do despise my dream.
  Make less thy body hence, and more thy grace;
  Leave gormandizing; know the grave doth gape
  For thee thrice wider than for other men—
  Reply not to me with a fool-born jest;
  Presume not that I am the thing I was,
  For God doth know, so shall the world perceive,
  That I have turn'd away my former self;
  So will I those that kept me company.
  When thou dost hear I am as I have been,
  Approach me, and thou shalt be as thou wast,
  The tutor and the feeder of my riots.
  Till then I banish thee, on pain of death,
  As I have done the rest of my misleaders,
  Not to come near our person by ten mile.
  For competence of life I will allow you,
  That lack of means enforce you not to evils;
  And, as we hear you do reform yourselves,
  We will, according to your strengths and qualities,
  Give you advancement. Be it your charge, my lord,
  To see perform'd the tenour of our word.
  Set on.   *Exeunt the* KING *and his train*

FALSTAFF. Master Shallow, I owe you a thousand pounds.

SHALLOW. Yea, marry, Sir John; which I beseech you to let
    me have home with me.

FALSTAFF. That can hardly be, Master Shallow. Do not you
    grieve at this; I shall be sent for in private to him. Look
    you, he must seem thus to the world. Fear not your ad-

vancements; I will be the man yet that shall make **you** great.

SHALLOW. I cannot perceive how, unless you give me your doublet, and stuff me out with straw. I beseech you, good Sir John, let me have five hundred of my thousand.

FALSTAFF. Sir, I will be as good as my word. This that you heard was but a colour.

SHALLOW. A colour that I fear you will die in, Sir John.

FALSTAFF. Fear no colours; go with me to dinner. Come, Lieutenant Pistol; come, Bardolph. I shall be sent for soon at night.

Re-enter PRINCE JOHN, *the* LORD CHIEF JUSTICE, *with officers*

CHIEF JUSTICE. Go, carry Sir John Falstaff to the Fleet;
Take all his company along with him.

FALSTAFF. My lord, my lord—

CHIEF JUSTICE. I cannot now speak. I will hear you soon.
Take them away.

PISTOL. Si fortuna me tormenta, spero me contenta.

Exeunt all but PRINCE JOHN *and the* LORD CHIEF JUSTICE

PRINCE JOHN. I like this fair proceeding of the King's.
He hath intent his wonted followers
Shall all be very well provided for;
But all are banish'd till their conversations
Appear more wise and modest to the world.

CHIEF JUSTICE. And so they are.

PRINCE JOHN. The King hath call'd his parliament, my lord.

CHIEF JUSTICE. He hath.

PRINCE JOHN. I will lay odds that, ere this year expire,
We bear our civil swords and native fire
As far as France. I heard a bird so sing,
Whose music, to my thinking, pleas'd the King.
Come, will you hence?   *Exeunt*

EPILOGUE

First my fear, then my curtsy, last my speech. My fear, is your displeasure; my curtsy, my duty; and my speech, to beg your pardons. If you look for a good speech now, you undo me; for what I have to say is of mine own making; and what, indeed, I should say will, I doubt, prove mine own marring. But to the purpose, and so to the venture. Be it known to you, as it is very well, I was lately here in the end of a displeasing play, to pray your patience for it and to promise you a better. I meant, indeed, to pay you with this; which if like an ill venture it come unluckily home, I break, and you, my gentle creditors, lose. Here I promis'd you I would be, and here I commit my body to your mercies. Bate me some, and I will pay you some, and, as most debtors do, promise you infinitely; and so I kneel down before you—but, indeed, to pray for the Queen.

If my tongue cannot entreat you to acquit me, will you command me to use my legs? And yet that were but light payment—to dance out of your debt. But a good conscience will make any possible satisfaction, and so would I. All the gentlewomen here have forgiven me. If the gentlemen will not, then the gentlemen do not agree with the gentlewomen, which was never seen before in such an assembly.

One word more, I beseech you. If you be not too much cloy'd with fat meat, our humble author will continue the story, with Sir John in it, and make you merry with fair Katherine of France; where, for anything I know, Falstaff shall die of a sweat, unless already 'a be killed with your hard opinions; for Oldcastle died a martyr and this is not the man. My tongue is weary; when my legs are too, I will bid you good night.

The Life of
King Henry the Fifth

KING HENRY THE FIFTH

THOSE who regard the cycle of Histories that begins with *Richard II* and ends with *Henry V* as the expression of a sustained evaluation of political conduct tend to regard *Henry V* as the work in which Shakespeare at last finds an ideal on which he can expatiate without qualification or reserve. All his earlier Histories had dealt with men unfitted in one way or another for the task of kingship: Henry VI was well-meaning but more in place in a hermitage than on the throne; Richard III and John were villains; Richard II irresponsible and incompetent; even Henry IV had a past that all his abilities and virtues could not live down. So checkered is the story as Shakespeare presents it of these kings that some have regarded his Histories as an exposure of the pretensions that seem to conceal themselves in the authority with which they were invested. Shakespeare, it is clear, did not follow the rule laid down for dramatists in a later age:

> We are to presume the greatest virtues, where we find the highest of rewards; and though it is not necessary that all Heroes should be Kings, yet undoubtedly all crown'd heads by Poetical right are Heroes.

Were we to accept this critical ruling, Shakespeare's Histories might well be treated as almost a satire on the ideals with which men delude themselves; for Shakespeare's kings are hardly heroes, if we except his Henry V. Here at last is the true king, the darling of his countrymen, the example to posterity, the man whom the Poet may take as his Hero without violation of the decorum the strictest critic may prescribe.

Shakespeare had before him in the Chronicles a king whom all united to glorify. Here is Holinshed's tribute:

> This Henrie was a king, of life without spot; a prince whome all men loved, and of none disdained; a capteine against whome fortune never frowned, nor mischance once spurned; whose people him so severe a iusticer both loved

377

and obeied, (and so humane withall,) that he left no
offense unpunished, nor freendship unrewarded; a terrour
to rebels, and suppressour of sedition; his vertues notable,
his qualities most praise-worthie.

And Holinshed finally pronounces him

a paterne in princehood, a lode-starre in honour, and
mirror of magnificence; the most highlie exalted in his life,
the more deepelie lamented at his death, and famous to the
world alwaie.

The captain who won so against the odds at Agincourt needs
no poet to keep alive his fame among men who can understand the qualities such a feat demands; yet it will hardly be
denied that Shakespeare gave to his fame wings that have
carried it "to states unborn" and that its translation into "accents still unknown" is in part at least because of the dramatist's tribute to the royal captain.

That the play is in one aspect Shakespeare's tribute to a
king whose memory Englishmen of the dramatist's day still
venerated cannot very reasonably be denied; for Shakespeare
has cast his piece into a form that requires the poet to speak
in his own person of the character on which the chief interest is focused. Shakespeare may, it has been suggested, have
spoken the choruses himself; this is not improbable, but even
if he played some other part it is his voice we hear in the
choruses, and his are the comments on his hero's actions.
Such an undramatic form of presentation is found nowhere
else in Shakespeare. Why we may ask should Shakespeare
have had recourse to such a device here and here only?
Henry's character is not in any way enigmatic, yet Shakespeare keeps directing our sympathies to the various aspects
of the King's virtues, while he leaves us elsewhere, even
when there is a mysterious complexity in the protagonist,
entirely to our own devices. This peculiarity of form critics
have tried to account for by arguing that Shakespeare now
saw his theme epically rather than dramatically. Henry is for
Shakespeare, it has been argued, what Aeneas is to Virgil, a
man with a mission of national importance and not merely a
character to be viewed dispassionately according to our pri-

vate predilections. Shakespeare rounds off his Histories by in part abandoning the dramatic mode and identifying his King in a manner, hitherto impossible, with the fortunes of England; hence the undisguised patriotic appeal of the whole production and the frank abandonment of a strictly dramatic form.

Were such a comparison acceptable even with qualifications, it might help us to understand the attitude adopted by many critics to the King. In spite of all Shakespeare's commendations, even in face of the instructions of the Chorus, there are commentators who can hardly find language forcible enough to express their disapproval of Henry whether as Prince or King. Shakespeare's hero is like Virgil's Aeneas denounced as a prig or a cad. The age of chivalry found Aeneas lacking in the instincts of a gentleman, and modern criticism is apt to see the Prince as Falstaff describes him to Doll Tearsheet: the Prince is just like Poins who has all the gambol faculties that show a weak mind and an able body.

Hazlitt's denunciation of Henry is historical:

In private, he seemed to have no idea of the common decencies of life, which he subjected to a kind of regal licence; in public affairs, he seemed to have no idea of any rule of right or wrong, but brute force, glossed over with a little religious hypocrisy and archiepiscopal advice. . . . His adventure on Gadshill was a prelude to the affair at Agincourt, only a bloodless one. . . . Henry, because he did not know how to govern his own kingdom, determined to make war upon his neighbours.

Yet Hazlitt tells us in his first sentence on the character of Henry that this monarch was not only a favourite with the English nation but "appears to have been also a favourite with Shakespeare." Hazlitt's character of Henry is derived from the play; we may well ask how Shakespeare came to give a "favourite" character so unpleasant a set of vices as that displayed for us by Hazlitt. We should have to suppose Shakespeare very much inferior to Hazlitt in moral insight to take Hazlitt's paradox at its face value.

Yeats is as paradoxical as Hazlitt in his statement of the dramatist's attitude. It seems

> Shakespeare cared little for the State, the source of all our judgments, apart from its shows and splendours, its turmoils and battles, its flamings out of the uncivilized heart.

Shakespeare, apparently, disliked civil war, and still didn't seem to care whether the ruler made a success of his task or not. The kind of success Shakespeare attributes to Henry seemed to Yeats the result of the King's commonplace vices. How the dramatist who thought as Yeats represents Shakespeare's thinking to us came to write *Henry V* must remain a mystery. Critics, Yeats felt, have the admiration for Henry "that school-boys have for the sailor or soldier hero of a romance in some boys' paper." What then shall we say of the dramatist who gives the critics so much excuse for their reactions?

Another Irish critic, a contemporary of Yeats, has suggested an answer to the question raised indirectly by the Irish poet. Bernard Shaw too has no great opinion of the King's character:

> One can hardly forgive Shakespeare for the worldly phase in which he tried to thrust such a Jingo hero as his Harry V down our throats. The combination of conventional propriety and brute masterfulness in his public capacity with a low-lived blackguardism in his private tastes is not a pleasant one. No doubt he is true to nature as a picture of what is by no means uncommon in English society, an able young Philistine inheriting high position and authority . . . who would have been quite in place if he had been born a game-keeper or a farmer.

Shakespeare must have failed badly with the victor of Agincourt if we feel that the King is "no assistant for a state" but better fitted to "keep a farm and carters." Yet Bernard Shaw has stressed an aspect of the play that explains in some measure why the reactions of the critic are often so opposed to those proposed for him by Shakespeare. The characters, Bernard Shaw observed, "are labelled and described and insisted upon with the roughest directness." It may seem strange to describe the method employed in the choruses as a rough directness, but the term must be taken relatively; with Hamlet in mind we can see how much more obvious and direct is the manner Shakespeare adopts in creating Henry. In *Henry V* Shakespeare is always calling on us to use our imagination; but he is very careful to leave as little as possible of the King to our imagination:

> O, now, who will behold
> The royal captain of this ruin'd Band
> Walking from watch to watch, from tent to tent,
> Let him cry 'Praise and glory on his head!'

Shakespeare here, as so often elsewhere in *Henry V*, is telling us; not, as he is in his greatest work, showing us. The subject perhaps made any other treatment in the space at his disposal impossible. But there is a natural aversion in human nature to being told anything, unless it seems to make for immediate profit of one kind or another; and critics are pleased to show how easily the events of the play could be fitted to quite a different cry from the 'Praise and glory on his head' asked for by Shakespeare. Shakespeare expects us to show a proper respect in the presence of the victor of Agincourt. There are doubtless many to-day who profess to despise such a path to glory as Henry trod. Shakespeare was quite aware there can be two sides to the question. He was for the moment interested to enforce one only; and that is doubtless why Falstaff was denied a part in his companion's most famous victory.

How necessary in the social economy of a nation are what Yeats describes as Henry's commonplace vices is suggested by Shakespeare in the play itself. Perhaps Shakespeare's most remarkable reference to current affairs is found in the chorus that introduces the fifth Act. The reference, as it is not only the chief evidence for dating the play but also a means of reminding us of the political conditions in which Shakespeare was writing such a piece as *Henry V*, well deserves the attention commentators have devoted to it. Shakespeare is describing Henry's return after the campaign and his reception by London. He begins by comparing it to the triumphant entry to Rome of some victorious Caesar:

The mayor and all his brethren in best sort—
Like to the senators of th' antique Rome,
With the plebeians swarming at their heels—
Go forth and fetch their conqu'ring Caesar in;

and then turning from the past to the present Shakespeare compares Henry's reception to the welcome that he trusts awaits Essex on his return from Ireland,

As, by a lower but loving likelihood,
Were now the General of our gracious Empress—
As in good time he may—from Ireland coming,
Bringing rebellion broached on his sword,
How many would the peaceful city quit
To welcome him! Much more, and much more cause,
Did they this Harry.

On 27 March 1599, Essex had left London amid the cheers and blessings of the citizens on his journey to Ireland where he was to command a force sufficient it was hoped to reduce the rebellious Tyrone and restore some semblance of order. By July Essex had little to show and had made no headway so far in Ulster where the main action was expected. The Queen was not satisfied, but there seemed still some hope that Essex might yet do better. Shakespeare's "As in good time he may" suggests that the public were beginning to wonder if all was well. By September Essex had effected nothing against Tyrone and when he received the Queen's reproof for his ill-management he handed over his command against the Queen's instructions and set out for London where he arrived with a small party of intimates on 28 September. Shakespeare's references must have been made between March and September 1599.

That Shakespeare's reference reflects his goodwill towards Essex and the hope that the general would wage a successful campaign we need not doubt. Southampton to whom the dramatist had dedicated his *Venus and Adonis* and *Lucrece* only some five or six years before this was with Essex and among his most devoted adherents. Shakespeare must have observed however the headstrong, misguided, and exceedingly foolish manner in which Essex had conducted himself in the period just before he was unwise enough to accept the Irish commission. Essex was contemptuous of the proposals that would have given the command to anyone but himself, although he had been warned by Bacon among others and had some misgivings in his own mind that the task would not enhance his position in the land. John Hayward had in February just before the start of the expedition published his indiscreet work on the reign of Henry IV, a work that was later to land the author in prison and cast suspicion on Essex, to whom it was dedicated, when he found himself at odds with the government. Shakespeare saw to it that his reference could bear no sinister interpretation or reflect unfavourably on the recipient of his good wishes. The dramatist does not flatter Essex by suggesting that his campaign in Ireland can be equated with that of Henry in France, and he clearly indicates the Earl's position as the Queen's emissary. Shakespeare's wishes for a happy outcome must have been spoken when there was still hope of success, though there is just a hint that hope had been slower of realization than the Earl's friends could have wished.

When one considers the sorry outcome of the affair to which Shakespeare wished success and the shadow that the infatuated and disloyal behaviour of Essex cast on the Queen's last years, it is not possible to suppose with any show of sense that Shakespeare regarded the determined, skilful, and prudent conduct of the soldierly Henry as an example of commonplace vice. What was needed in Shakespeare's day as always was a sense of comradeship and the loyalty to the common cause that Shakespeare saw or imagined he saw in Henry and the men of Agincourt. Of course there were scallywags there too, but their shrift is short when they presume too far. Yet Johnson has written their epitaph:

> Falstaff and Mrs. Quickly are dead; Nym and Bardolph are hanged; Gadshill was lost immediately after the robbery; Poins and Peto have vanished since, one knows not how; and Pistol is now beaten into obscurity. I believe every reader regrets their departure.

Shakespeare insists on having the best of both worlds. That is why Bernard Shaw can say that the characters are insisted upon with the roughest directness. Shakespeare shifts the point of view as it suits him, and we cannot find any standpoint that will allow us to see all the figures in the picture in satisfactory focus. To cry down the soldier for the sake of the humorists is as untrue to the Henry play as to regard Falstaff as the Prince's bad angel.

Johnson has in his last words on *Henry V* put the question that those who would offer a criticism of the play must answer:

> The lines given to the chorus have many admirers; but the truth is, that in them a little may be praised and much must be forgiven; nor can it easily be discovered why the intelligence given by the chorus is more necessary in this play than in many others where it is omitted.

Shakespeare had a point of view to put that he could not embody satisfactorily in his play; and this was so because he had in mind what was not strictly a dramatic idea. He was here both a dramatist and an Englishman; he had to make what he could of the material required to bring his sequence of plays to a conclusion, but he was contemplating the actions of his countrymen with the admiration not of a disinterested dramatist but of their panegyrist. In a panegyric even actions that may seem on reflection and long after the event somewhat open to criticism have to be represented in a form favourable to the subject of the encomium. That Shakespeare himself thought of Henry as a King that deserved the admiration of his countrymen we have every reason to believe, and he has said some memorable things that have helped to perpetuate the soldier's memory. The subject however did not lend itself to dramatic development and Shakespeare found it necessary to come forward in person as it were to impress on us the theme that the play itself cannot fully sustain.

CHORUS
KING HENRY THE FIFTH
DUKE OF GLOUCESTER ⎫ *brothers to the King*
DUKE OF BEDFORD ⎭
DUKE OF EXETER, *uncle to the King*
DUKE OF YORK, *cousin to the King*
EARL OF SALISBURY
EARL OF WESTMORELAND
EARL OF WARWICK
ARCHBISHOP OF CANTERBURY
BISHOP OF ELY

EARL OF CAMBRIDGE ⎫
LORD SCROOP ⎬ *conspirators against the King*
SIR THOMAS GREY ⎭

SIR THOMAS ERPINGHAM   GOWER ⎫ *officers in the*
FLUELLEN   MACMORRIS   JAMY ⎭ *King's army*

BATES   COURT   WILLIAMS ⎫ *soldiers in the King's army*
NYM   BARDOLPH   PISTOL ⎭

BOY   A HERALD

CHARLES THE SIXTH, *King of France*
LEWIS, *the Dauphin*   DUKE OF BURGUNDY
DUKE OF ORLEANS   DUKE OF BRITAINE
DUKE OF BOURBON   THE CONSTABLE OF FRANCE
RAMBURES ⎫ *French Lords*
GRANDPRÉ ⎭
GOVERNOR OF HARFLEUR   MONTJOY, *a French herald*
AMBASSADORS *to the King of England*

ISABEL, *Queen of France*
KATHERINE, *daughter to Charles and Isabel*
ALICE, *a lady attending her*
HOSTESS *of the Boar's Head, Eastcheap; formerly Mrs. Quickly, now married to Pistol*

Lords, Ladies, Officers, Soldiers, Messengers, Attendants

SCENE:
England and France

King Henry the Fifth

PROLOGUE

Enter CHORUS

CHORUS. O for a Muse of fire, that would ascend
    The brightest heaven of invention,
    A kingdom for a stage, princes to act,
    And monarchs to behold the swelling scene!
    Then should the warlike Harry, like himself,
    Assume the port of Mars; and at his heels,
    Leash'd in like hounds, should famine, sword, and fire,
    Crouch for employment. But pardon, gentles all,
    The flat unraised spirits that hath dar'd
    On this unworthy scaffold to bring forth
    So great an object. Can this cockpit hold
    The vasty fields of France? Or may we cram
    Within this wooden O the very casques
    That did affright the air at Agincourt?
    O, pardon! since a crooked figure may
    Attest in little place a million;
    And let us, ciphers to this great accompt,
    On your imaginary forces work.
    Suppose within the girdle of these walls
    Are now confin'd two mighty monarchies,
    Whose high upreared and abutting fronts
    The perilous narrow ocean parts asunder.
    Piece out our imperfections with your thoughts:
    Into a thousand parts divide one man,
    And make imaginary puissance;
    Think, when we talk of horses, that you see them
    Printing their proud hoofs i' th' receiving earth;
    For 'tis your thoughts that now must deck our kings,
    Carry them here and there, jumping o'er times,
    Turning th' accomplishment of many years
    Into an hour-glass; for the which supply,
    Admit me Chorus to this history;

Who prologue-like, your humble patience pray
Gently to hear, kindly to judge, our play.   *Exit*

ACT I. SCENE 1

London. An ante-chamber in the KING'S *palace*

Enter the ARCHBISHOP OF CANTERBURY *and the*
BISHOP OF ELY

CANTERBURY. My lord, I'll tell you: that self bill is urg'd
  Which in th' eleventh year of the last king's reign
  Was like, and had indeed against us pass'd
  But that the scambling and unquiet time
  Did push it out of farther question.
ELY. But how, my lord, shall we resist it now?
CANTERBURY. It must be thought on. If it pass against us,
  We lose the better half of our possession;
  For all the temporal lands which men devout
  By testament have given to the church
  Would they strip from us; being valu'd thus—
  As much as would maintain, to the King's honour,
  Full fifteen earls and fifteen hundred knights,
  Six thousand and two hundred good esquires;
  And, to relief of lazars and weak age,
  Of indigent faint souls, past corporal toil,
  A hundred alms-houses right well supplied;
  And to the coffers of the King, beside,
  A thousand pounds by th' year: thus runs the bill.
ELY. This would drink deep.
CANTERBURY. 'Twould drink the cup and all.
ELY. But what prevention?
CANTERBURY. The King is full of grace and fair regard.
ELY. And a true lover of the holy Church.
CANTERBURY. The courses of his youth promis'd it not.
  The breath no sooner left his father's body
  But that his wildness, mortified in him,
  Seem'd to die too; yea, at that very moment,

388

Consideration like an angel came
And whipp'd th' offending Adam out of him,
Leaving his body as a paradise
T'envelop and contain celestial spirits.
Never was such a sudden scholar made;
Never came reformation in a flood,
With such a heady currance, scouring faults;
Nor never Hydra-headed wilfulness
So soon did lose his seat, and all at once,
As in this king.

ELY. We are blessed in the change.

CANTERBURY. Hear him but reason in divinity,
And, all-admiring, with an inward wish
You would desire the King were made a prelate;
Hear him debate of commonwealth affairs,
You would say it hath been all in all his study;
List his discourse of war, and you shall hear
A fearful battle rend'red you in music.
Turn him to any cause of policy,
The Gordian knot of it he will unloose,
Familiar as his garter; that, when he speaks,
The air, a charter'd libertine, is still,
And the mute wonder lurketh in men's ears
To steal his sweet and honey'd sentences;
So that the art and practic part of life
Must be the mistress to this theoric;
Which is a wonder how his Grace should glean it,
Since his addiction was to courses vain,
His companies unletter'd, rude, and shallow,
His hours fill'd up with riots, banquets, sports;
And never noted in him any study,
Any retirement, any sequestration
From open haunts and popularity.

ELY. The strawberry grows underneath the nettle,
And wholesome berries thrive and ripen best
Neighbour'd by fruit of baser quality;
And so the Prince obscur'd his contemplation
Under the veil of wildness; which, no doubt,
Grew like the summer grass, fastest by night,
Unseen, yet crescive in his faculty.

CANTERBURY. It must be so; for miracles are ceas'd;
   And therefore we must needs admit the means
   How things are perfected.
ELY. But, my good lord,
   How now for mitigation of this bill
   Urg'd by the Commons? Doth his Majesty
   Incline to it, or no?
CANTERBURY. He seems indifferent
   Or rather swaying more upon our part
   Than cherishing th' exhibiters against us;
   For I have made an offer to his Majesty—
   Upon our spiritual convocation
   And in regard of causes now in hand,
   Which I have open'd to his Grace at large,
   As touching France—to give a greater sum
   Than ever at one time the clergy yet
   Did to his predecessors part withal.
ELY. How did this offer seem receiv'd, my lord?
CANTERBURY. With good acceptance of his Majesty;
   Save that there was not time enough to hear,
   As I perceiv'd his Grace would fain have done,
   The severals and unhidden passages
   Of his true titles to some certain dukedoms,
   And generally to the crown and seat of France,
   Deriv'd from Edward, his great-grandfather.
ELY. What was th' impediment that broke this off?
CANTERBURY. The French ambassador upon that instant
   Crav'd audience; and the hour, I think, is come
   To give him hearing: is it four o'clock?
ELY. It is.
CANTERBURY. Then go we in, to know his embassy;
   Which I could with a ready guess declare,
   Before the Frenchman speak a word of it.
ELY. I'll wait upon you, and I long to hear it.   *Exeunt*

SCENE 2

London. The Presence Chamber in the KING's *palace*

Enter the KING, GLOUCESTER, BEDFORD, EXETER, WARWICK,
WESTMORELAND, *and attendants*

KING HENRY. Where is my gracious Lord of Canterbury?
EXETER. Not here in presence.
KING HENRY. Send for him, good uncle.
WESTMORELAND. Shall we call in th' ambassador, my liege?
KING HENRY. Not yet, my cousin; we would be resolv'd,
  Before we hear him, of some things of weight
  That task our thoughts, concerning us and France.

Enter the ARCHBISHOP OF CANTERBURY *and*
the BISHOP OF ELY

CANTERBURY. God and his angels guard your sacred throne,
  And make you long become it!
KING HENRY. Sure, we thank you.
  My learned lord, we pray you to proceed,
  And justly and religiously unfold
  Why the law Salique, that they have in France,
  Or should or should not bar us in our claim;
  And God forbid, my dear and faithful lord,
  That you should fashion, wrest, or bow your reading,
  Or nicely charge your understanding soul
  With opening titles miscreate whose right
  Suits not in native colours with the truth;
  For God doth know how many, now in health,
  Shall drop their blood in approbation
  Of what your reverence shall incite us to.
  Therefore take heed how you impawn our person,
  How you awake our sleeping sword of war—
  We charge you, in the name of God, take heed;
  For never two such kingdoms did contend
  Without much fall of blood; whose guiltless drops
  Are every one a woe, a sore complaint,
  'Gainst him whose wrongs gives edge unto the swords
  That makes such waste in brief mortality.

Under this conjuration speak, my lord;
For we will hear, note, and believe in heart,
That what you speak is in your conscience wash'd
As pure as sin with baptism.
CANTERBURY. Then hear me, gracious sovereign, and you peers,
That owe yourselves, your lives, and services,
To this imperial throne. There is no bar
To make against your Highness' claim to France
But this, which they produce from Pharamond:
'In terram Salicam mulieres ne succedant'—
'No woman shall succeed in Salique land';
Which Salique land the French unjustly gloze
To be the realm of France, and Pharamond
The founder of this law and female bar.
Yet their own authors faithfully affirm
That the land Salique is in Germany,
Between the floods of Sala and of Elbe;
Where Charles the Great, having subdu'd the Saxons,
There left behind and settled certain French;
Who, holding in disdain the German women
For some dishonest manners of their life,
Establish'd then this law: to wit, no female
Should be inheritrix in Salique land;
Which Salique, as I said, 'twixt Elbe and Sala,
Is at this day in Germany call'd Meisen.
Then doth it well appear the Salique law
Was not devised for the realm of France;
Nor did the French possess the Salique land
Until four hundred one and twenty years
After defunction of King Pharamond,
Idly suppos'd the founder of this law;
Who died within the year of our redemption
Four hundred twenty-six; and Charles the Great
Subdu'd the Saxons, and did seat the French
Beyond the river Sala, in the year
Eight hundred five. Besides, their writers say,
King Pepin, which deposed Childeric,
Did, as heir general, being descended
Of Blithild, which was daughter to King Clothair,

Make claim and title to the crown of France.
Hugh Capet also, who usurp'd the crown
Of Charles the Duke of Lorraine, sole heir male
Of the true line and stock of Charles the Great,
To find his title with some shows of truth—
Though in pure truth it was corrupt and naught—
Convey'd himself as th' heir to th' Lady Lingare,
Daughter to Charlemain, who was the son
To Lewis the Emperor, and Lewis the son
Of Charles the Great. Also King Lewis the Tenth,
Who was sole heir to the usurper Capet,
Could not keep quiet in his conscience,
Wearing the crown of France, till satisfied
That fair Queen Isabel, his grandmother,
Was lineal of the Lady Ermengare,
Daughter to Charles the foresaid Duke of Lorraine;
By the which marriage the line of Charles the Great
Was re-united to the Crown of France.
So that, as clear as is the summer's sun,
King Pepin's title, and Hugh Capet's claim,
King Lewis his satisfaction, all appear
To hold in right and title of the female;
So do the kings of France unto this day,
Howbeit they would hold up this Salique law
To bar your Highness claiming from the female;
And rather choose to hide them in a net
Than amply to imbar their crooked titles
Usurp'd from you and your progenitors.

KING HENRY. May I with right and conscience make this
    claim?

CANTERBURY. The sin upon my head, dread sovereign!
For in the book of Numbers is it writ,
When the man dies, let the inheritance
Descend unto the daughter. Gracious lord,
Stand for your own, unwind your bloody flag,
Look back into your mighty ancestors.
Go, my dread lord, to your great-grandsire's tomb,
From whom you claim; invoke his warlike spirit,
And your great-uncle's, Edward the Black Prince,
Who on the French ground play'd a tragedy,

Making defeat on the full power of France,
Whiles his most mighty father on a hill
Stood smiling to behold his lion's whelp
Forage in blood of French nobility.
O noble English, that could entertain
With half their forces the full pride of France,
And let another half stand laughing by,
All out of work and cold for action!

ELY. Awake remembrance of these valiant dead,
And with your puissant arm renew their feats.
You are their heir; you sit upon their throne;
The blood and courage that renowned them
Runs in your veins; and my thrice-puissant liege
Is in the very May-morn of his youth,
Ripe for exploits and mighty enterprises.

EXETER. Your brother kings and monarchs of the earth
Do all expect that you should rouse yourself,
As did the former lions of your blood.

WESTMORELAND. They know your Grace hath cause and
means and might—
So hath your Highness; never King of England
Had nobles richer and more loyal subjects,
Whose hearts have left their bodies here in England
And lie pavilion'd in the fields of France.

CANTERBURY. O, let their bodies follow, my dear liege,
With blood and sword and fire to win your right!
In aid whereof we of the spiritualty
Will raise your Highness such a mighty sum
As never did the clergy at one time
Bring in to any of your ancestors.

KING HENRY. We must not only arm t' invade the French,
But lay down our proportions to defend
Against the Scot, who will make road upon us
With all advantages.

CANTERBURY. They of those marches, gracious sovereign,
Shall be a wall sufficient to defend
Our inland from the pilfering borderers.

KING HENRY. We do not mean the coursing snatchers only,
But fear the main intendment of the Scot,
Who hath been still a giddy neighbour to us;

For you shall read that my great-grandfather
Never went with his forces into France
But that the Scot on his unfurnish'd kingdom
Came pouring, like the tide into a breach,
With ample and brim fulness of his force,
Galling the gleaned land with hot assays,
Girdling with grievous siege castles and towns;
That England, being empty of defence,
Hath shook and trembled at th' ill neighbourhood.
CANTERBURY. She hath been then more fear'd than harm'd,
    my liege;
For hear her but exampled by herself:
When all her chivalry hath been in France,
And she a mourning widow of her nobles,
She hath herself not only well defended
But taken and impounded as a stray
The King of Scots; whom she did send to France,
To fill King Edward's fame with prisoner kings,
And make her chronicle as rich with praise
As is the ooze and bottom of the sea
With sunken wreck and sumless treasuries.
WESTMORELAND. But there's a saying, very old and true:

      'If that you will France win,
        Then with Scotland first begin.'

For once the eagle England being in prey,
To her unguarded nest the weasel Scot
Comes sneaking, and so sucks her princely eggs,
Playing the mouse in absence of the cat,
To tear and havoc more than she can eat.
EXETER. It follows, then, the cat must stay at home;
   Yet that is but a crush'd necessity,
Since we have locks to safeguard necessaries
And pretty traps to catch the petty thieves.
While that the armed hand doth fight abroad,
Th' advised head defends itself at home;
For government, though high, and low, and lower,
Put into parts, doth keep in one consent,
Congreeing in a full and natural close,
Like music.

CANTERBURY. Therefore doth heaven divide
  The state of man in divers functions,
  Setting endeavour in continual motion;
  To which is fixed as an aim or butt
  Obedience; for so work the honey bees,
  Creatures that by a rule in nature teach
  The act of order to a peopled kingdom.
  They have a king, and officers of sorts,
  Where some like magistrates correct at home;
  Others like merchants venture trade abroad;
  Others like soldiers, armed in their stings,
  Make boot upon the summer's velvet buds,
  Which pillage they with merry march bring home
  To the tent-royal of their emperor;
  Who, busied in his majesty, surveys
  The singing masons building roofs of gold,
  The civil citizens kneading up the honey,
  The poor mechanic porters crowding in
  Their heavy burdens at his narrow gate,
  The sad-ey'd justice, with his surly hum,
  Delivering o'er to executors pale
  The lazy yawning drone. I this infer,
  That many things, having full reference
  To one consent, may work contrariously;
  As many arrows loosed several ways
  Come to one mark, as many ways meet in one town,
  As many fresh streams meet in one salt sea,
  As many lines close in the dial's centre;
  So many a thousand actions, once afoot,
  End in one purpose, and be all well borne
  Without defeat. Therefore to France, my liege.
  Divide your happy England into four;
  Whereof take you one quarter into France,
  And you withal shall make all Gallia shake.
  If we, with thrice such powers left at home,
  Cannot defend our own doors from the dog,
  Let us be worried, and our nation lose
  The name of hardiness and policy.
KING HENRY. Call in the messengers sent from the Dauphin.
                                            Exeunt some attendants

Now are we well resolv'd; and, by God's help
And yours, the noble sinews of our power,
France being ours, we'll bend it to our awe,
Or break it all to pieces; or there we'll sit,
Ruling in large and ample empery
O'er France and all her almost kingly dukedoms,
Or lay these bones in an unworthy urn,
Tombless, with no remembrance over them.
Either our history shall with full mouth
Speak freely of our acts, or else our grave,
Like Turkish mute, shall have a tongueless mouth,
Not worshipp'd with a waxen epitaph.

Enter AMBASSADORS *of France*

Now are we well prepar'd to know the pleasure
Of our fair cousin Dauphin; for we hear
Your greeting is from him, not from the King.
AMBASSADOR. May't please your Majesty to give us leave
    Freely to render what we have in charge;
    Or shall we sparingly show you far off
    The Dauphin's meaning and our embassy?
KING HENRY. We are no tyrant, but a Christian king,
    Unto whose grace our passion is as subject
    As are our wretches fett'red in our prisons;
    Therefore with frank and with uncurbed plainness
    Tell us the Dauphin's mind.
AMBASSADOR. Thus then, in few.
    Your Highness, lately sending into France,
    Did claim some certain dukedoms in the right
    Of your great predecessor, King Edward the Third.
    In answer of which claim, the Prince our master
    Says that you savour too much of your youth,
    And bids you be advis'd there's nought in France
    That can be with a nimble galliard won;
    You cannot revel into dukedoms there.
    He therefore sends you, meeter for your spirit,
    This tun of treasure; and, in lieu of this,
    Desires you let the dukedoms that you claim
    Hear no more of you. This the Dauphin speaks.
KING HENRY. What treasure, uncle?

EXETER. Tennis-balls, my liege.

KING HENRY. We are glad the Dauphin is so pleasant
　　with us;
　　His present and your pains we thank you for.
　　When we have match'd our rackets to these balls,
　　We will in France, by God's grace, play a set
　　Shall strike his father's crown into the hazard.
　　Tell him he hath made a match with such a wrangler
　　That all the courts of France will be disturb'd
　　With chaces. And we understand him well,
　　How he comes o'er us with our wilder days,
　　Not measuring what use we made of them.
　　We never valu'd this poor seat of England;
　　And therefore, living hence, did give ourself
　　To barbarous licence; as 'tis ever common
　　That men are merriest when they are from home.
　　But tell the Dauphin I will keep my state,
　　Be like a king, and show my sail of greatness,
　　When I do rouse me in my throne of France;
　　For that I have laid by my majesty
　　And plodded like a man for working-days;
　　But I will rise there with so full a glory
　　That I will dazzle all the eyes of France,
　　Yea, strike the Dauphin blind to look on us.
　　And tell the pleasant Prince this mock of his
　　Hath turn'd his balls to gun-stones, and his soul
　　Shall stand sore charged for the wasteful vengeance
　　That shall fly with them; for many a thousand widows
　　Shall this his mock mock out of their dear husbands;
　　Mock mothers from their sons, mock castles down;
　　And some are yet ungotten and unborn
　　That shall have cause to curse the Dauphin's scorn.
　　But this lies all within the will of God,
　　To whom I do appeal; and in whose name,
　　Tell you the Dauphin, I am coming on,
　　To venge me as I may and to put forth
　　My rightful hand in a well-hallow'd cause.
　　So get you hence in peace; and tell the Dauphin
　　His jest will savour but of shallow wit,
　　When thousands weep more than did laugh at it.

Convey them with safe conduct. Fare you well.

Exeunt AMBASSADORS

EXETER. This was a merry message.

KING HENRY. We hope to make the sender blush at it.
Therefore, my lords, omit no happy hour
That may give furth'rance to our expedition;
For we have now no thought in us but France,
Save those to God, that run before our business.
Therefore let our proportions for these wars
Be soon collected, and all things thought upon
That may with reasonable swiftness add
More feathers to our wings; for, God before,
We'll chide this Dauphin at his father's door.
Therefore let every man now task his thought
That this fair action may on foot be brought. *Exeunt*

ACT II. PROLOGUE

Flourish. Enter CHORUS

CHORUS. Now all the youth of England are on fire,
And silken dalliance in the wardrobe lies;
Now thrive the armourers, and honour's thought
Reigns solely in the breast of every man;
They sell the pasture now to buy the horse,
Following the mirror of all Christian kings
With winged heels, as English Mercuries.
For now sits Expectation in the air,
And hides a sword from hilts unto the point
With crowns imperial, crowns, and coronets,
Promis'd to Harry and his followers.
The French, advis'd by good intelligence
Of this most dreadful preparation,
Shake in their fear and with pale policy
Seek to divert the English purposes.
O England! model to thy inward greatness,
Like little body with a mighty heart,
What mightst thou do that honour would thee do,

Were all thy children kind and natural!
But see thy fault! France hath in thee found out
A nest of hollow bosoms, which he fills
With treacherous crowns; and three corrupted men—
One, Richard Earl of Cambridge, and the second,
Henry Lord Scroop of Masham, and the third,
Sir Thomas Grey, knight, of Northumberland,
Have, for the gilt of France—O guilt indeed!—
Confirm'd conspiracy with fearful France;
And by their hands this grace of kings must die—
If hell and treason hold their promises,
Ere he take ship for France—and in Southampton.
Linger your patience on, and we'll digest
Th' abuse of distance, force a play.
The sum is paid, the traitors are agreed,
The King is set from London, and the scene
Is now transported, gentles, to Southampton;
There is the play-house now, there must you sit,
And thence to France shall we convey you safe
And bring you back, charming the narrow seas
To give you gentle pass; for, if we may,
We'll not offend one stomach with our play.
But, till the King come forth, and not till then,
Unto Southampton do we shift our scene.   *Exit*

SCENE 1

London. Before the Boar's Head Tavern, Eastcheap

Enter CORPORAL NYM *and* LIEUTENANT BARDOLPH

BARDOLPH. Well met, Corporal Nym.

NYM. Good morrow, Lieutenant Bardolph.

BARDOLPH. What, are Ancient Pistol and you friends yet?

NYM. For my part, I care not; I say little, but when time
shall serve, there shall be smiles—but that shall be as it
may. I dare not fight; but I will wink and hold out mine
iron. It is a simple one; but what though? It will toast
cheese, and it will endure cold as another man's sword
will; and there's an end.

BARDOLPH. I will bestow a breakfast to make you friends; and we'll be all three sworn brothers to France. Let't be so, good Corporal Nym.

NYM. Faith, I will live so long as I may, that's the certain of it; and when I cannot live any longer, I will do as I may. That is my rest, that is the rendezvous of it.

BARDOLPH. It is certain, Corporal, that he is married to Nell Quickly; and certainly she did you wrong, for you were troth-plight to her.

NYM. I cannot tell; things must be as they may. Men may sleep, and they may have their throats about them at that time; and some say knives have edges. It must be as it may; though patience be a tired mare, yet she will plod. There must be conclusions. Well, I cannot tell.

Enter PISTOL *and* HOSTESS

BARDOLPH. Here comes Ancient Pistol and his wife. Good Corporal, be patient here.

NYM. How now, mine host Pistol!

PISTOL. Base tike, call'st thou me host?
Now by this hand, I swear I scorn the term;
Nor shall my Nell keep lodgers.

HOSTESS. No, by my troth, not long; for we cannot lodge and board a dozen or fourteen gentlewomen that live honestly by the prick of their needles, but it will be thought we keep a bawdy-house straight. [NYM *draws*] O well-a-day, Lady, if he be not drawn! Now we shall see wilful adultery and murder committed.

BARDOLPH. Good Lieutenant, good Corporal, offer nothing here.

NYM. Pish!

PISTOL. Pish for thee, Iceland dog! thou prick-ear'd cur of Iceland!

HOSTESS. Good Corporal Nym, show thy valour, and put up your sword.

NYM. Will you shog off? I would have you solus.

PISTOL. 'Solus,' egregious dog? O viper vile!
The 'solus' in thy most mervailous face;
The 'solus' in thy teeth, and in thy throat,
And in thy hateful lungs, yea, in thy maw, perdy;

And, which is worse, within thy nasty mouth!
I do retort the 'solus' in thy bowels;
For I can take, and Pistol's cock is up,
And flashing fire will follow.

NYM. I am not Barbason: you cannot conjure me. I have an
humour to knock you indifferently well. If you grow foul
with me, Pistol, I will scour you with my rapier, as I may,
in fair terms; if you would walk off I would prick your
guts a little, in good terms, as I may, and that's the humour
of it.

PISTOL. O braggart vile and damned furious wight!
The grave doth gape and doting death is near;
Therefore exhale.   [PISTOL *draws*]

BARDOLPH. Hear me, hear me what I say: he that strikes the
first stroke I'll run him up to the hilts, as I am a soldier.
                                    [*Draws*]

PISTOL. An oath of mickle might; and fury shall abate.
            [PISTOL *and* NYM *sheathe their swords*]
Give me thy fist, thy fore-foot to me give;
Thy spirits are most tall.

NYM. I will cut thy throat one time or other, in fair terms;
that is the humour of it.

PISTOL. 'Couple a gorge!'
That is the word. I thee defy again.
O hound of Crete, think'st thou my spouse to get?
No; to the spital go,
And from the powd'ring tub of infamy
Fetch forth the lazar kite of Cressid's kind,
Doll Tearsheet she by name, and her espouse.
I have, and I will hold, the quondam Quickly
For the only she; and—pauca, there's enough.
Go to.

Enter the BOY

BOY. Mine host Pistol, you must come to my master; and
your hostess—he is very sick, and would to bed. Good
Bardolph, put thy face between his sheets, and do the
office of a warming-pan. Faith, he's very ill.

BARDOLPH. Away, you rogue.

HOSTESS. By my troth, he'll yield the crow a pudding one

of these days: the King has kill'd his heart. Good husband,
come home presently. _Exeunt_ Hostess _and_ Boy

BARDOLPH. Come, shall I make you two friends? We must to
France together; why the devil should we keep knives to
cut one another's throats?

PISTOL. Let floods o'erswell, and fiends for food howl on!

NYM. You'll pay me the eight shillings I won of you at
betting?

PISTOL. Base is the slave that pays.

NYM. That now I will have; that's the humour of it.

PISTOL. As manhood shall compound: push home.
[PISTOL _and_ NYM _draw_]

BARDOLPH. By this sword, he that makes the first thrust I'll
kill him; by this sword, I will.

PISTOL. Sword is an oath, and oaths must have their course.
[_Sheathes his sword_]

BARDOLPH. Corporal Nym, an thou wilt be friends, be
friends; an thou wilt not, why then be enemies with me
too. Prithee put up.

NYM. I shall have my eight shillings I won of you at
betting?

PISTOL. A noble shalt thou have, and present pay;
And liquor likewise will I give to thee,
And friendship shall combine, and brotherhood.
I'll live by Nym and Nym shall live by me.
Is not this just? For I shall sutler be
Unto the camp, and profits will accrue.
Give me thy hand.

NYM. [_Sheathing his sword_] I shall have my noble?

PISTOL. In cash most justly paid.

NYM. [_Shaking hands_] Well, then, that's the humour of't.

Re-enter HOSTESS

HOSTESS. As ever you come of women, come in quickly to
Sir John. Ah, poor heart! he is so shak'd of a burning
quotidian tertian that it is most lamentable to behold.
Sweet men, come to him.

NYM. The King hath run bad humours on the knight; that's
the even of it.

PISTOL. Nym, thou hast spoke the right;

His heart is fracted and corroborate.

NYM. The King is a good king, but it must be as it may; he passes some humours and careers.

PISTOL. Let us condole the knight; for, lambkins, we will live. *Exeunt*

SCENE 2

Southampton. A council-chamber

Enter EXETER, BEDFORD, *and* WESTMORELAND

BEDFORD. Fore God, his Grace is bold, to trust these traitors.

EXETER. They shall be apprehended by and by.

WESTMORELAND. How smooth and even they do bear them-
selves,
As if allegiance in their bosoms sat,
Crowned with faith and constant loyalty!

BEDFORD. The King hath note of all that they intend,
By interception which they dream not of.

EXETER. Nay, but the man that was his bedfellow,
Whom he hath dull'd and cloy'd with gracious favours—
That he should, for a foreign purse, so sell
His sovereign's life to death and treachery!

Trumpets sound. Enter the KING, SCROOP,
CAMBRIDGE, GREY, *and attendants*

KING HENRY. Now sits the wind fair, and we will aboard.
My Lord of Cambridge, and my kind Lord of Masham,
And you, my gentle knight, give me your thoughts.
Think you not that the pow'rs we bear with us
Will cut their passage through the force of France,
Doing the execution and the act
For which we have in head assembled them?

SCROOP. No doubt, my liege, if each man do his best.

KING HENRY. I doubt not that, since we are well persuaded
We carry not a heart with us from hence
That grows not in a fair consent with ours;
Nor leave not one behind that doth not wish
Success and conquest to attend on us.

CAMBRIDGE. Never was monarch better fear'd and lov'd
  Than is your Majesty. There's not, I think, a subject
  That sits in heart-grief and uneasiness
  Under the sweet shade of your government.
GREY. True: those that were your father's enemies
  Have steep'd their galls in honey, and do serve you
  With hearts create of duty and of zeal.
KING HENRY. We therefore have great cause of thankfulness,
  And shall forget the office of our hand
  Sooner than quittance of desert and merit
  According to the weight and worthiness.
SCROOP. So service shall with steeled sinews toil,
  And labour shall refresh itself with hope,
  To do your Grace incessant services.
KING HENRY. We judge no less. Uncle of Exeter,
  Enlarge the man committed yesterday
  That rail'd against our person. We consider
  It was excess of wine that set him on;
  And on his more advice we pardon him.
SCROOP. That's mercy, but too much security.
  Let him be punish'd, sovereign, lest example
  Breed, by his sufferance, more of such a kind.
KING HENRY. O, let us yet be merciful!
CAMBRIDGE. So may your Highness, and yet punish too.
GREY. Sir,
  You show great mercy if you give him life,
  After the taste of much correction.
KING HENRY. Alas, your too much love and care of me
  Are heavy orisons 'gainst this poor wretch!
  If little faults proceeding on distemper
  Shall not be wink'd at, how shall we stretch our eye
  When capital crimes, chew'd, swallow'd, and digested,
  Appear before us? We'll yet enlarge that man,
  Though Cambridge, Scroop, and Grey, in their dear care
  And tender preservation of our person,
  Would have him punish'd. And now to our French causes:
  Who are the late commissioners?
CAMBRIDGE. I one, my lord.
  Your Highness bade me ask for it to-day.
SCROOP. So did you me, my liege.

GREY. And I, my royal sovereign.

KING HENRY. Then, Richard Earl of Cambridge, there is
    yours;
  There yours, Lord Scroop of Masham; and, Sir Knight,
  Grey of Northumberland, this same is yours.
  Read them, and know I know your worthiness.
  My Lord of Westmoreland, and uncle Exeter,
  We will aboard to-night. Why, how now, gentlemen?
  What see you in those papers, that you lose
  So much complexion? Look ye how they change!
  Their cheeks are paper. Why, what read you there
  That have so cowarded and chas'd your blood
  Out of appearance?

CAMBRIDGE. I do confess my fault,
  And do submit me to your Highness' mercy.

GREY, SCROOP. To which we all appeal.

KING HENRY. The mercy that was quick in us but late
  By your own counsel is suppress'd and kill'd.
  You must not dare, for shame, to talk of mercy;
  For your own reasons turn into your bosoms
  As dogs upon their masters, worrying you.
  See you, my princes and my noble peers,
  These English monsters! My Lord of Cambridge here—
  You know how apt our love was to accord
  To furnish him with all appertinents
  Belonging to his honour; and this man
  Hath, for a few light crowns, lightly conspir'd,
  And sworn unto the practices of France
  To kill us here in Hampton; to the which
  This knight, no less for bounty bound to us
  Than Cambridge is, hath likewise sworn. But, O,
  What shall I say to thee, Lord Scroop, thou cruel,
  Ingrateful, savage, and inhuman creature?
  Thou that didst bear the key of all my counsels,
  That knew'st the very bottom of my soul,
  That almost mightst have coin'd me into gold,
  Wouldst thou have practis'd on me for thy use—
  May it be possible that foreign hire
  Could out of thee extract one spark of evil
  That might annoy my finger? 'Tis so strange

That, though the truth of it stands off as gross
As black and white, my eye will scarcely see it.
Treason and murder ever kept together,
As two yoke-devils sworn to either's purpose,
Working so grossly in a natural cause
That admiration did not whoop at them;
But thou, 'gainst all proportion, didst bring in
Wonder to wait on treason and on murder;
And whatsoever cunning fiend it was
That wrought upon thee so preposterously
Hath got the voice in hell for excellence;
And other devils that suggest by treasons
Do botch and bungle up damnation
With patches, colours, and with forms, being fetch'd
From glist'ring semblances of piety;
But he that temper'd thee bade thee stand up,
Gave thee no instance why thou shouldst do treason,
Unless to dub thee with the name of traitor.
If that same demon that hath gull'd thee thus
Should with his lion gait walk the whole world,
He might return to vasty Tartar back,
And tell the legions 'I can never win
A soul so easy as that Englishman's.'
O, how hast thou with jealousy infected
The sweetness of affiance! Show men dutiful?
Why, so didst thou. Seem they grave and learned?
Why, so didst thou. Come they of noble family?
Why, so didst thou. Seem they religious?
Why, so didst thou. Or are they spare in diet,
Free from gross passion or of mirth or anger,
Constant in spirit, not swerving with the blood,
Garnish'd and deck'd in modest complement,
Not working with the eye without the ear,
And but in purged judgment trusting neither?
Such and so finely bolted didst thou seem;
And thus thy fall hath left a kind of blot
To mark the full-fraught man and best indued
With some suspicion. I will weep for thee;
For this revolt of thine, methinks, is like
Another fall of man. Their faults are open.

Arrest them to the answer of the law;
And God acquit them of their practices!

EXETER. I arrest thee of high treason, by the name of Richard Earl of Cambridge.

I arrest thee of high treason, by the name of Henry Lord
Scroop of Masham.

I arrest thee of high treason, by the name of Thomas
Grey, knight, of Northumberland.

SCROOP. Our purposes God justly hath discover'd,
And I repent my fault more than my death;
Which I beseech your Highness to forgive,
Although my body pay the price of it.

CAMBRIDGE. For me, the gold of France did not seduce,
Although I did admit it as a motive
The sooner to effect what I intended;
But God be thanked for prevention,
Which I in sufferance heartily will rejoice,
Beseeching God and you to pardon me.

GREY. Never did faithful subject more rejoice
At the discovery of most dangerous treason
Than I do at this hour joy o'er myself,
Prevented from a damned enterprise.
My fault, but not my body, pardon, sovereign.

KING HENRY. God quit you in his mercy! Hear your
sentence.
You have conspir'd against our royal person,
Join'd with an enemy proclaim'd, and from his coffers
Receiv'd the golden earnest of our death;
Wherein you would have sold your king to slaughter,
His princes and his peers to servitude,
His subjects to oppression and contempt,
And his whole kingdom into desolation.
Touching our person seek we no revenge;
But we our kingdom's safety must so tender,
Whose ruin you have sought, that to her laws
We do deliver you. Get you therefore hence,
Poor miserable wretches, to your death;
The taste whereof God of his mercy give
You patience to endure, and true repentance
Of all your dear offences. Bear them hence.

ACT II. SCENE 2

Exeunt CAMBRIDGE, SCROOP, *and* GREY, *guarded*

Now, lords, for France; the enterprise whereof
Shall be to you as us like glorious.
We doubt not of a fair and lucky war,
Since God so graciously hath brought to light
This dangerous treason, lurking in our way
To hinder our beginnings; we doubt not now
But every rub is smoothed on our way.
Then, forth, dear countrymen; let us deliver
Our puissance into the hand of God,
Putting it straight in expedition.
Cheerly to sea; the signs of war advance;
No king of England, if not king of France!

Flourish. Exeunt

SCENE 3

Eastcheap. Before the Boar's Head tavern

Enter PISTOL, HOSTESS, NYM, BARDOLPH, *and* BOY

HOSTESS. Prithee, honey-sweet husband, let me bring thee
to Staines.

PISTOL. No; for my manly heart doth earn.
Bardolph, be blithe; Nym, rouse thy vaunting veins;
Boy, bristle thy courage up. For Falstaff he is dead,
And we must earn therefore.

BARDOLPH. Would I were with him, wheresome'er he is,
either in heaven or in hell!

HOSTESS. Nay, sure, he's not in hell: he's in Arthur's bosom,
if ever man went to Arthur's bosom. 'A made a finer end,
and went away an it had been any christom child; 'a
parted ev'n just between twelve and one, ev'n at the turning o' th' tide; for after I saw him fumble with the sheets,
and play with flowers, and smile upon his fingers' end, I
knew there was but one way; for his nose was as sharp as
a pen, and 'a babbl'd of green fields. 'How now, Sir John!'
quoth I 'What, man, be o' good cheer.' So 'a cried out
'God, God, God!' three or four times. Now I, to comfort
him, bid him 'a should not think of God; I hop'd there was

409

no need to trouble himself with any such thoughts yet. So 'a bade me lay more clothes on his feet; I put my hand into the bed and felt them, and they were as cold as any stone; then I felt to his knees, and so upward and upward, and all was as cold as any stone.

NYM. They say he cried out of sack.

HOSTESS. Ay, that 'a did.

BARDOLPH. And of women.

HOSTESS. Nay, that 'a did not.

BOY. Yes, that 'a did, and said they were devils incarnate.

HOSTESS. 'A could never abide carnation; 'twas a colour he never liked.

BOY. 'A said once the devil would have him about women.

HOSTESS. 'A did in some sort, indeed, handle women; but then he was rheumatic, and talk'd of the Whore of Babylon.

BOY. Do you not remember 'a saw a flea stick upon Bardolph's nose, and 'a said it was a black soul burning in hell?

BARDOLPH. Well, the fuel is gone that maintain'd that fire: that's all the riches I got in his service.

NYM. Shall we shog? The King will be gone from Southampton.

PISTOL. Come, let's away. My love, give me thy lips.
Look to my chattles and my moveables;
Let senses rule. The word is 'Pitch and Pay.'
Trust none;
For oaths are straws, men's faiths are wafer-cakes,
And Holdfast is the only dog, my duck.
Therefore, Caveto be thy counsellor.
Go, clear thy crystals. Yoke-fellows in arms,
Let us to France, like horse-leeches, my boys,
To suck, to suck, the very blood to suck.

BOY. And that's but unwholesome food, they say.

PISTOL. Touch her soft mouth and march.

BARDOLPH. Farewell, hostess.   *[Kissing her]*

NYM. I cannot kiss, that is the humour of it; but adieu.

PISTOL. Let housewifery appear; keep close, I thee command.

HOSTESS. Farewell; adieu.   *Exeunt*

SCENE 4

France. The KING's *palace*

Flourish. Enter the FRENCH KING, *the* DAUPHIN, *the* DUKES OF BERRI *and* BRITAINE, *the* CONSTABLE, *and others*

FRENCH KING. Thus comes the English with full power
    upon us;
  And more than carefully it us concerns
  To answer royally in our defences.
  Therefore the Dukes of Berri and of Britaine,
  Of Brabant and of Orleans, shall make forth,
  And you, Prince Dauphin, with all swift dispatch,
  To line and new repair our towns of war
  With men of courage and with means defendant;
  For England his approaches makes as fierce
  As waters to the sucking of a gulf.
  It fits us, then, to be as provident
  As fear may teach us, out of late examples
  Left by the fatal and neglected English
  Upon our fields.
DAUPHIN. My most redoubted father,
  It is most meet we arm us 'gainst the foe;
  For peace itself should not so dull a kingdom,
  Though war nor no known quarrel were in question,
  But that defences, musters, preparations,
  Should be maintain'd, assembled, and collected,
  As were a war in expectation.
  Therefore, I say, 'tis meet we all go forth
  To view the sick and feeble parts of France;
  And let us do it with no show of fear—
  No, with no more than if we heard that England
  Were busied with a Whitsun morris-dance;
  For, my good liege, she is so idly king'd,
  Her sceptre so fantastically borne
  By a vain, giddy, shallow, humorous youth,
  That fear attends her not.
CONSTABLE. O peace, Prince Dauphin!

You are too much mistaken in this king.
Question your Grace the late ambassadors
With what great state he heard their embassy,
How well supplied with noble counsellors,
How modest in exception, and withal
How terrible in constant resolution,
And you shall find his vanities forespent
Were but the outside of the Roman Brutus,
Covering discretion with a coat of folly;
As gardeners do with ordure hide those roots
That shall first spring and be most delicate.
DAUPHIN. Well, 'tis not so, my Lord High Constable;
But though we think it so, it is no matter.
In cases of defence 'tis best to weigh
The enemy more mighty than he seems;
So the proportions of defence are fill'd;
Which of a weak and niggardly projection
Doth like a miser spoil his coat with scanting
A little cloth.
FRENCH KING. Think we King Harry strong;
And, Princes, look you strongly arm to meet him.
The kindred of him hath been flesh'd upon us;
And he is bred out of that bloody strain
That haunted us in our familiar paths.
Witness our too much memorable shame
When Cressy battle fatally was struck,
And all our princes captiv'd by the hand
Of that black name, Edward, Black Prince of Wales;
Whiles that his mountain sire—on mountain standing,
Up in the air, crown'd with the golden sun—
Saw his heroical seed, and smil'd to see him,
Mangle the work of nature, and deface
The patterns that by God and by French fathers
Had twenty years been made. This is a stem
Of that victorious stock; and let us fear
The native mightiness and fate of him.

Enter a MESSENGER

MESSENGER. Ambassadors from Harry King of England
Do crave admittance to your Majesty.

FRENCH KING. We'll give them present audience. Go and
 bring them.   *Exeunt* MESSENGER *and certain* LORDS
 You see this chase is hotly followed, friends.
DAUPHIN. Turn head and stop pursuit; for coward dogs
 Most spend their mouths when what they seem to threaten
 Runs far before them. Good my sovereign,
 Take up the English short, and let them know
 Of what a monarchy you are the head.
 Self-love, my liege, is not so vile a sin
 As self-neglecting.

   Re-enter LORDS, *with* EXETER *and train*

FRENCH KING. From our brother of England?
EXETER. From him, and thus he greets your Majesty:
 He wills you, in the name of God Almighty,
 That you divest yourself, and lay apart
 The borrowed glories that by gift of heaven,
 By law of nature and of nations, 'longs
 To him and to his heirs—namely, the crown,
 And all wide-stretched honours that pertain,
 By custom and the ordinance of times,
 Unto the crown of France. That you may know
 'Tis no sinister nor no awkward claim,
 Pick'd from the worm-holes of long-vanish'd days,
 Nor from the dust of old oblivion rak'd,
 He sends you this most memorable line, [*Gives a paper*]
 In every branch truly demonstrative;
 Willing you overlook this pedigree.
 And when you find him evenly deriv'd
 From his most fam'd of famous ancestors,
 Edward the Third, he bids you then resign
 Your crown and kingdom, indirectly held
 From him, the native and true challenger.
FRENCH KING. Or else what follows?
EXETER. Bloody constraint; for if you hide the crown
 Even in your hearts, there will he rake for it.
 Therefore in fierce tempest is he coming,
 In thunder and in earthquake, like a Jove,
 That if requiring fail, he will compel;
 And bids you, in the bowels of the Lord,

Deliver up the crown; and to take mercy
On the poor souls for whom this hungry war
Opens his vasty jaws; and on your head
Turning the widows' tears, the orphans' cries,
The dead men's blood, the privy maidens' groans,
For husbands, fathers, and betrothed lovers,
That shall be swallowed in this controversy.
This is his claim, his threat'ning, and my message;
Unless the Dauphin be in presence here,
To whom expressly I bring greeting too.

FRENCH KING. For us, we will consider of this further;
To-morrow shall you bear our full intent
Back to our brother of England.

DAUPHIN. For the Dauphin:
I stand here for him. What to him from England?

EXETER. Scorn and defiance, slight regard, contempt,
And anything that may not misbecome
The mighty sender, doth he prize you at.
Thus says my king: an if your father's Highness
Do not, in grant of all demands at large,
Sweeten the bitter mock you sent his Majesty,
He'll call you to so hot an answer of it
That caves and womby vaultages of France
Shall chide your trespass and return your mock
In second accent of his ordinance.

DAUPHIN. Say, if my father render fair return,
It is against my will; for I desire
Nothing but odds with England. To that end,
As matching to his youth and vanity,
I did present him with the Paris balls.

EXETER. He'll make your Paris Louvre shake for it,
Were it the mistress court of mighty Europe;
And be assur'd you'll find a difference,
As we his subjects have in wonder found,
Between the promise of his greener days
And these he masters now. Now he weighs time
Even to the utmost grain; that you shall read
In your own losses, if he stay in France.

FRENCH KING. To-morrow shall you know our mind at full.

EXETER. Dispatch us with all speed, lest that our king

ACT II. SCENE 4

Come here himself to question our delay;
For he is footed in this land already.
FRENCH KING. You shall be soon dispatch'd with fair con-
  ditions.
A night is but small breath and little pause
To answer matters of this consequence.   *Flourish. Exeunt*

ACT III. PROLOGUE

Flourish. Enter CHORUS

CHORUS. Thus with imagin'd wing our swift scene flies,
  In motion of no less celerity
  Than that of thought. Suppose that you have seen
  The well-appointed King at Hampton pier
  Embark his royalty; and his brave fleet
  With silken streamers the young Phœbus fanning.
  Play with your fancies; and in them behold
  Upon the hempen tackle ship-boys climbing;
  Hear the shrill whistle which doth order give
  To sounds confus'd; behold the threaden sails,
  Borne with th' invisible and creeping wind,
  Draw the huge bottoms through the furrowed sea,
  Breasting the lofty surge. O, do but think
  You stand upon the rivage and behold
  A city on th' inconstant billows dancing;
  For so appears this fleet majestical,
  Holding due course to Harfleur. Follow, follow!
  Grapple your minds to sternage of this navy
  And leave your England as dead midnight still,
  Guarded with grandsires, babies, and old women,
  Either past or not arriv'd to pith and puissance;
  For who is he whose chin is but enrich'd
  With one appearing hair that will not follow
  These cull'd and choice-drawn cavaliers to France?
  Work, work your thoughts, and therein see a siege;
  Behold the ordnance on their carriages,

With fatal mouths gaping on girded Harfleur.
Suppose th' ambassador from the French comes back;
Tells Harry that the King doth offer him
Katherine his daughter, and with her to dowry
Some petty and unprofitable dukedoms.
The offer likes not; and the nimble gunner
With linstock now the devilish cannon touches,

[Alarum, and chambers go off]

And down goes all before them. Still be kind,
And eke out our performance with your mind.   *Exit*

SCENE 1

France. Before Harfleur

Alarum. Enter the KING, EXETER, BEDFORD, GLOUCESTER,
and soldiers with scaling-ladders

KING. Once more unto the breach, dear friends, once more;
  Or close the wall up with our English dead.
  In peace there's nothing so becomes a man
  As modest stillness and humility;
  But when the blast of war blows in our ears,
  Then imitate the action of the tiger:
  Stiffen the sinews, summon up the blood,
  Disguise fair nature with hard-favour'd rage;
  Then lend the eye a terrible aspect;
  Let it pry through the portage of the head
  Like the brass cannon: let the brow o'erwhelm it
  As fearfully as doth a galled rock
  O'erhang and jutty his confounded base,
  Swill'd with the wild and wasteful ocean.
  Now set the teeth and stretch the nostril wide;
  Hold hard the breath, and bend up every spirit
  To his full height. On, on, you noblest English,
  Whose blood is fet from fathers of war-proof—
  Fathers that like so many Alexanders
  Have in these parts from morn till even fought,
  And sheath'd their swords for lack of argument.
  Dishonour not your mothers; now attest

416

That those whom you call'd fathers did beget you.
Be copy now to men of grosser blood,
And teach them how to war. And you, good yeomen,
Whose limbs were made in England, show us here
The mettle of your pasture; let us swear
That you are worth your breeding—which I doubt not;
For there is none of you so mean and base
That hath not noble lustre in your eyes.
I see you stand like greyhounds in the slips,
Straining upon the start. The game's afoot:
Follow your spirit; and upon this charge
Cry 'God for Harry, England, and Saint George!'
                    [*Exeunt. Alarum, and chambers go off*]

SCENE 2

Before Harfleur

Enter NYM, BARDOLPH, PISTOL, *and* BOY

BARDOLPH. On, on, on, on, on! to the breach, to the breach!
NYM. Pray thee, Corporal, stay; the knocks are too hot, and
  for mine own part I have not a case of lives. The humour
  of it is too hot; that is the very plain-song of it.
PISTOL. The plain-song is most just; for humours do abound:

  Knocks go and come; God's vassals drop and die;
    And sword and shield
    In bloody field
   Doth win immortal fame.

BOY. Would I were in an alehouse in London! I would give
  all my fame for a pot of ale and safety.
PISTOL. And I:

   If wishes would prevail with me,
   My purpose should not fail with me,
    But thither would I hie.

BOY.   As duly, but not as truly,
     As bird doth sing on bough.

     Enter FLUELLEN

FLUELLEN. Up to the breach, you dogs!

Avaunt, you cullions! [*Driving them forward*]

PISTOL. Be merciful, great duke, to men of mould.

Abate thy rage, abate thy manly rage;

Abate thy rage, great duke.

Good bawcock, bate thy rage. Use lenity, sweet chuck.

NYM. These be good humours. Your honour wins bad humours. *Exeunt all but* BOY

BOY. As young as I am, I have observ'd these three swashers. I am boy to them all three; but all they three, though they would serve me, could not be man to me; for indeed three such antics do not amount to a man. For Bardolph, he is white-liver'd and red-fac'd; by the means whereof 'a faces it out, but fights not. For Pistol, he hath a killing tongue and a quiet sword; by the means whereof 'a breaks words and keeps whole weapons. For Nym, he hath heard that men of few words are the best men, and therefore he scorns to say his prayers lest 'a should be thought a coward; but his few bad words are match'd with as few good deeds; for 'a never broke any man's head but his own, and that was against a post when he was drunk. They will steal anything, and call it purchase. Bardolph stole a lute-case, bore it twelve leagues, and sold it for three halfpence. Nym and Bardolph are sworn brothers in filching, and in Calais they stole a fire-shovel; I knew by that piece of service the men would carry coals. They would have me as familiar with men's pockets as their gloves or their handkerchers; which makes much against my manhood, if I should take from another's pocket to put into mine; for it is plain pocketing up of wrongs. I must leave them and seek some better service; their villainy goes against my weak stomach, and therefore I must cast it up. *Exit*

Re-enter FLUELLEN, GOWER *following*

GOWER. Captain Fluellen, you must come presently to the mines; the Duke of Gloucester would speak with you.

FLUELLEN. To the mines! Tell you the Duke it is not so good to come to the mines; for, look you, the mines is not according to the disciplines of the war; the concavities of it is not sufficient. For, look you, th' athversary—you may discuss unto the Duke, look you—is digt himself four yard under the countermines; by Cheshu, I think 'a will plow up all, if there is not better directions.

GOWER. The Duke of Gloucester, to whom the order of the siege is given, is altogether directed by an Irishman—a very valiant gentleman, i' faith.

FLUELLEN. It is Captain Macmorris, is it not?

GOWER. I think it be.

FLUELLEN. By Cheshu, he is an ass, as in the world: I will verify as much in his beard; he has no more directions in the true disciplines of the wars, look you, of the Roman disciplines, than is a puppy-dog.

Enter MACMORRIS *and* CAPTAIN JAMY

GOWER. Here 'a comes; and the Scots captain, Captain Jamy, with him.

FLUELLEN. Captain Jamy is a marvellous falorous gentleman, that is certain, and of great expedition and knowledge in th' aunchient wars, upon my particular knowledge of his directions. By Cheshu, he will maintain his argument as well as any military man in the world, in the disciplines of the pristine wars of the Romans.

JAMY. I say gud day, Captain Fluellen.

FLUELLEN. God-den to your worship, good Captain James.

GOWER. How now, Captain Macmorris! Have you quit the mines? Have the pioneers given o'er?

MACMORRIS. By Chrish, la, tish ill done! The work ish give over, the trompet sound the retreat. By my hand, I swear, and my father's soul, the work ish ill done; it ish give over; I would have blowed up the town, so Chrish save me, la, in an hour. O, tish ill done, tish ill done; by my hand, tish ill done!

FLUELLEN. Captain Macmorris, I beseech you now, will you voutsafe me, look you, a few disputations with you, as partly touching or concerning the disciplines of the war, the Roman wars, in the way of argument, look you, and friendly communication; partly to satisfy my opinion, and partly for the satisfaction, look you, of my mind, as touching the direction of the military discipline, that is the point.

JAMY. It sall be vary gud, gud feith, gud captains bath; and I sall quit you with gud leve, as I may pick occasion; that sall I, marry.

MACMORRIS. It is no time to discourse, so Chrish save me. The day is hot, and the weather, and the wars, and the King, and the Dukes; it is no time to discourse. The town is beseech'd, and the trumpet call us to the breach; and we talk and, be Chrish, do nothing. 'Tis shame for us all, so God sa' me, 'tis shame to stand still; it is shame, by my hand; and there is throats to be cut, and works to be done; and there ish nothing done, so Chrish sa' me, la.

JAMY. By the mess, ere theise eyes of mine take themselves to slomber, ay'll de gud service, or I'll lig i' th' grund for it; ay, or go to death. And I'll pay't as valorously as I may, that sall I suerly do, that is the breff and the long. Marry, I wad full fain heard some question 'tween you tway.

FLUELLEN. Captain Macmorris, I think, look you, under your correction, there is not many of your nation—

MACMORRIS. Of my nation? What ish my nation? Ish a villain, and a bastard, and a knave, and a rascal. What ish my nation? Who talks of my nation?

FLUELLEN. Look you, if you take the matter otherwise than is meant, Captain Macmorris, peradventure I shall think you do not use me with that affability as in discretion you ought to use me, look you; being as good a man as yourself, both in the disciplines of war and in the derivation of my birth, and in other particularities.

MACMORRIS. I do not know you so good a man as myself; so Chrish save me, I will cut off your head.

GOWER. Gentlemen both, you will mistake each other.

JAMY. Ah! that's a foul fault.   [*A parley sounded*]

GOWER. The town sounds a parley.

FLUELLEN. Captain Macmorris, when there is more better opportunity to be required, look you, I will be so bold as to tell you I know the disciplines of war; and there is an end.   *Exeunt*

SCENE 3

Before the gates of Harfleur

Enter the GOVERNOR *and some citizens on the walls. Enter the* KING *and all his train before the gates*

KING HENRY. How yet resolves the Governor of the town?
This is the latest parle we will admit;
Therefore to our best mercy give yourselves
Or, like to men proud of destruction,
Defy us to our worst; for, as I am a soldier,
A name that in my thoughts becomes me best,
If I begin the batt'ry once again,
I will not leave the half-achieved Harfleur
Till in her ashes she lie buried.
The gates of mercy shall be all shut up,
And the flesh'd soldier, rough and hard of heart,
In liberty of bloody hand shall range
With conscience wide as hell, mowing like grass
Your fresh fair virgins and your flow'ring infants.
What is it then to me if impious war,
Array'd in flames, like to the prince of fiends,
Do, with his smirch'd complexion, all fell feats
Enlink'd to waste and desolation?
What is't to me when you yourselves are cause,
If your pure maidens fall into the hand
Of hot and forcing violation?
What rein can hold licentious wickedness
When down the hill he holds his fierce career?
We may as bootless spend our vain command
Upon th' enraged soldiers in their spoil,
As send precepts to the Leviathan
To come ashore. Therefore, you men of Harfleur,
Take pity of your town and of your people
Whiles yet my soldiers are in my command;
Whiles yet the cool and temperate wind of grace
O'erblows the filthy and contagious clouds
Of heady murder, spoil, and villainy.
If not—why, in a moment look to see

The blind and bloody soldier with foul hand
Defile the locks of your shrill-shrieking daughters;
Your fathers taken by the silver beards,
And their most reverend heads dash'd to the walls;
Your naked infants spitted upon pikes,
Whiles the mad mothers with their howls confus'd
Do break the clouds, as did the wives of Jewry
At Herod's bloody-hunting slaughtermen.
What say you? Will you yield, and this avoid?
Or, guilty in defence, be thus destroy'd?

GOVERNOR. Our expectation hath this day an end:
The Dauphin, whom of succours we entreated,
Returns us that his powers are yet not ready
To raise so great a siege. Therefore, great King,
We yield our town and lives to thy soft mercy.
Enter our gates; dispose of us and ours;
For we no longer are defensible.

KING HENRY. Open your gates. [*Exit* GOVERNOR] Come,
uncle Exeter,
Go you and enter Harfleur; there remain,
And fortify it strongly 'gainst the French;
Use mercy to them all. For us, dear uncle,
The winter coming on, and sickness growing
Upon our soldiers, we will retire to Calais.
To-night in Harfleur will we be your guest;
To-morrow for the march are we addrest.
[*Flourish. The* KING *and his train enter the town*]

SCENE 4

Rouen. The FRENCH KING'S *palace*

Enter KATHERINE *and* ALICE

KATHERINE. Alice, tu as été en Angleterre, et tu parles bien
le langage.
ALICE. Un peu, madame.
KATHERINE. Je te prie, m'enseignez; il faut que j'apprenne à
parler. Comment appelez-vous la main en Anglais?
ALICE. La main? Elle est appelée de hand.

KATHERINE. De hand. Et les doigts?

ALICE. Les doigts? Ma foi, j'oublie les doigts; mais je me souviendrai. Les doigts? Je pense qu'ils sont appelés de fingres; oui, de fingres.

KATHERINE. La main, de hand; les doigts, de fingres. Je pense que je suis le bon écolier; j'ai gagné deux mots d'Anglais vîtement. Comment appelez-vous les ongles?

ALICE. Les ongles? Nous les appelons de nails.

KATHERINE. De nails. Ecoutez; dites-moi si je parle bien: de hand, de fingres, et de nails.

ALICE. C'est bien dit, madame; il est fort bon Anglais.

KATHERINE. Dites-moi l'Anglais pour le bras.

ALICE. De arm, madame.

KATHERINE. Et le coude?

ALICE. D'elbow.

KATHERINE. D'elbow. Je m'en fais la répétition de tous les mots que vous m'avez appris dès à présent.

ALICE. Il est trop difficile, madame, comme je pense.

KATHERINE. Excusez-moi, Alice; écoutez: d'hand, de fingre, de nails, d'arma, de bilbow.

ALICE. D'elbow, madame.

KATHERINE. O Seigneur Dieu, je m'en oublie! D'elbow. Comment appelez-vous le col?

ALICE. De nick, madame.

KATHERINE. De nick. Et le menton?

ALICE. De chin.

KATHERINE. De sin. Le col, de nick; le menton, de sin.

ALICE. Oui. Sauf votre honneur, en vérité, vous prononcez les mots aussi droit que les natifs d'Angleterre.

KATHERINE. Je ne doute point d'apprendre, par la grace de Dieu, et en peu de temps.

ALICE. N'avez-vous pas déjà oublié ce que je vous ai enseigné?

KATHERINE. Non, je reciterai à vous promptement: d'hand, de fingre, de mails—

ALICE. De nails, madame.

KATHERINE. De nails, de arm, de ilbow.

ALICE. Sauf votre honneur, d'elbow.

KATHERINE. Ainsi dis-je; d'elbow, de nick, et de sin. Comment appelez-vous le pied et la robe?

ALICE. Le foot, madame; et le count.

KATHERINE. Le foot et le count. O Seigneur Dieu! ils sont
mots de son mauvais, corruptible, gros, et impudique, et
non pour les dames d'honneur d'user: je ne voudrais pro-
noncer ces mots devant les seigneurs de France pour tout
le monde. Foh! le foot et le count! Néanmoins, je reciterai
une autre fois ma leçon ensemble: d'hand, de fingre, de
nails, d'arm, d'elbow, de nick, de sin, de foot, le count.

ALICE. Excellent, madame!

KATHERINE. C'est assez pour une fois: allons-nous à dîner.

Exeunt

SCENE 5

The FRENCH KING'S *palace*

Enter the KING OF FRANCE, *the* DAUPHIN, DUKE OF
BRITAINE, *the* CONSTABLE OF FRANCE, *and others*

FRENCH KING. 'Tis certain he hath pass'd the river Somme.

CONSTABLE. And if he be not fought withal, my lord,
Let us not live in France; let us quit all,
And give our vineyards to a barbarous people.

DAUPHIN. O Dieu vivant! Shall a few sprays of us,
The emptying of our fathers' luxury,
Our scions, put in wild and savage stock,
Spirt up so suddenly into the clouds,
And overlook their grafters?

BRITAINE. Normans, but bastard Normans, Norman bastards!
Mort Dieu, ma vie! if they march along
Unfought withal, but I will sell my dukedom
To buy a slobb'ry and a dirty farm
In that nook-shotten isle of Albion.

CONSTABLE. Dieu de batailles! where have they this mettle?
Is not their climate foggy, raw, and dull;
On whom, as in despite, the sun looks pale,
Killing their fruit with frowns? Can sodden water,
A drench for sur-rein'd jades, their barley-broth,
Decoct their cold blood to such valiant heat?
And shall our quick blood, spirited with wine,

Seem frosty? O, for honour of our land,
Let us not hang like roping icicles
Upon our houses' thatch, whiles a more frosty people
Sweat drops of gallant youth in our rich fields—
Poor we call them in their native lords!

DAUPHIN. By faith and honour,
Our madams mock at us and plainly say
Our mettle is bred out, and they will give
Their bodies to the lust of English youth
To new-store France with bastard warriors.

BRITAINE. They bid us to the English dancing-schools
And teach lavoltas high and swift corantos,
Saying our grace is only in our heels
And that we are most lofty runaways.

FRENCH KING. Where is Montjoy the herald? Speed him
hence;
Let him greet England with our sharp defiance.
Up, Princes, and, with spirit of honour edged
More sharper than your swords, hie to the field:
Charles Delabreth, High Constable of France;
You Dukes of Orleans, Bourbon, and of Berri,
Alençon, Brabant, Bar, and Burgundy;
Jaques Chatillon, Rambures, Vaudemont,
Beaumont, Grandpré, Roussi, and Fauconbridge,
Foix, Lestrake, Bouciqualt, and Charolois;
High dukes, great princes, barons, lords, and knights,
For your great seats now quit you of great shames.
Bar Harry England, that sweeps through our land
With pennons painted in the blood of Harfleur.
Rush on his host as doth the melted snow
Upon the valleys, whose low vassal seat
The Alps doth spit and void his rheum upon;
Go down upon him, you have power enough,
And in a captive chariot into Rouen
Bring him our prisoner.

CONSTABLE. This becomes the great.
Sorry am I his numbers are so few,
His soldiers sick and famish'd in their march;
For I am sure, when he shall see our army,
He'll drop his heart into the sink of fear,

And for achievement offer us his ransom.

FRENCH KING. Therefore, Lord Constable, haste on Montjoy,
    And let him say to England that we send
    To know what willing ransom he will give.
    Prince Dauphin, you shall stay with us in Rouen.

DAUPHIN. Not so, I do beseech your Majesty.

FRENCH KING. Be patient, for you shall remain with us.
    Now forth, Lord Constable and Princes all,
    And quickly bring us word of England's fall.   *Exeunt*

SCENE 6

The English camp in Picardy

Enter CAPTAINS, *English and Welsh,* GOWER *and* FLUELLEN

GOWER. How now, Captain Fluellen! Come you from the
    bridge?

FLUELLEN. I assure you there is very excellent services com-
    mitted at the bridge.

GOWER. Is the Duke of Exeter safe?

FLUELLEN. The Duke of Exeter is as magnanimous as Aga-
    memnon; and a man that I love and honour with my soul,
    and my heart, and my duty, and my live, and my living,
    and my uttermost power. He is not—God be praised and
    blessed!—any hurt in the world, but keeps the bridge most
    valiantly, with excellent discipline. There is an aunchient
    Lieutenant there at the bridge—I think in my very con-
    science he is as valiant a man as Mark Antony; and he is a
    man of no estimation in the world; but I did see him do as
    gallant service.

GOWER. What do you call him?

FLUELLEN. He is call'd Aunchient Pistol.

GOWER. I know him not.

Enter PISTOL

FLUELLEN. Here is the man.

PISTOL. Captain, I thee beseech to do me favours.
    The Duke of Exeter doth love thee well.

FLUELLEN. Ay, I praise God; and I have merited some love
at his hands.

PISTOL. Bardolph, a soldier, firm and sound of heart,
And of buxom valour, hath by cruel fate
And giddy Fortune's furious fickle wheel,
That goddess blind,
That stands upon the rolling restless stone—

FLUELLEN. By your patience, Aunchient Pistol. Fortune is
painted blind, with a muffler afore her eyes, to signify to
you that Fortune is blind; and she is painted also with a
wheel, to signify to you, which is the moral of it, that she
is turning, and inconstant, and mutability, and variation;
and her foot, look you, is fixed upon a spherical stone,
which rolls, and rolls, and rolls. In good truth, the poet
makes a most excellent description of it: Fortune is an excellent moral.

PISTOL. Fortune is Bardolph's foe, and frowns on him;
For he hath stol'n a pax, and hanged must 'a be—
A damned death!
Let gallows gape for dog; let man go free,
And let not hemp his windpipe suffocate.
But Exeter hath given the doom of death
For pax of little price.
Therefore, go speak—the Duke will hear thy voice;
And let not Bardolph's vital thread be cut
With edge of penny cord and vile reproach.
Speak, Captain, for his life, and I will thee requite.

FLUELLEN. Aunchient Pistol, I do partly understand your
meaning.

PISTOL. Why then, rejoice therefore.

FLUELLEN. Certainly, Aunchient, it is not a thing to rejoice
at; for if, look you, he were my brother, I would desire
the Duke to use his good pleasure, and put him to execution; for discipline ought to be used.

PISTOL. Die and be damn'd! and figo for thy friendship!

FLUELLEN. It is well.

PISTOL. The fig of Spain!   *Exit*

FLUELLEN. Very good.

GOWER. Why, this is an arrant counterfeit rascal; I remember him now—a bawd, a cutpurse.

FLUELLEN. I'll assure you, 'a utt'red as prave words at the pridge as you shall see in a summer's day. But it is very well; what he has spoke to me, that is well, I warrant you, when time is serve.

GOWER. Why, 'tis a gull, a fool, a rogue, that now and then goes to the wars to grace himself, at his return into London, under the form of a soldier. And such fellows are perfect in the great commanders' names; and they will learn you by rote where services were done—at such and such a sconce, at such a breach, at such a convoy; who came off bravely, who was shot, who disgrac'd, what terms the enemy stood on; and this they con perfectly in the phrase of war, which they trick up with new-tuned oaths; and what a beard of the General's cut and a horrid suit of the camp will do among foaming bottles and ale-wash'd wits is wonderful to be thought on. But you must learn to know such slanders of the age, or else you may be marvellously mistook.

FLUELLEN. I tell you what, Captain Gower, I do perceive he is not the man that he would gladly make show to the world he is; if I find a hole in his coat I will tell him my mind. [*Drum within*] Hark you, the King is coming; and I must speak with him from the pridge.

Drum and colours. Enter the KING and his poor soldiers, and GLOUCESTER

God pless your Majesty!

KING HENRY. How now, Fluellen! Cam'st thou from the bridge?

FLUELLEN. Ay, so please your Majesty. The Duke of Exeter has very gallantly maintain'd the pridge; the French is gone off, look you, and there is gallant and most prave passages. Marry, th' athversary was have possession of the pridge; but he is enforced to retire, and the Duke of Exeter is master of the pridge; I can tell your Majesty the Duke is a prave man.

KING HENRY. What men have you lost, Fluellen!

FLUELLEN. The perdition of th' athversary hath been very great, reasonable great; marry, for my part, I think the Duke hath lost never a man, but one that is like to be executed for robbing a church—one Bardolph, if your Majesty know the man; his face is all bubukles, and whelks, and knobs, and flames o' fire; and his lips blows at his nose, and it is like a coal of fire, sometimes plue and sometimes red; but his nose is executed and his fire's out.

KING HENRY. We would have all such offenders so cut off. And we give express charge that in our marches through the country there be nothing compell'd from the villages, nothing taken but paid for, none of the French upbraided or abused in disdainful language; for when lenity and cruelty play for a kingdom the gentler gamester is the soonest winner.

Tucket. Enter MONTJOY

MONTJOY. You know me by my habit.

KING HENRY. Well then, I know thee; what shall I know of thee?

MONTJOY. My master's mind.

KING HENRY. Unfold it.

MONTJOY. Thus says my king. Say thou to Harry of England: Though we seem'd dead we did but sleep; advantage is a better soldier than rashness. Tell him we could have rebuk'd him at Harfleur, but that we thought not good to bruise an injury till it were full ripe. Now we speak upon our cue, and our voice is imperial: England shall repent his folly, see his weakness, and admire our sufferance. Bid him therefore consider of his ransom, which must proportion the losses we have borne, the subjects we have lost, the disgrace we have digested; which, in weight to re-answer, his pettiness would bow under. For our losses his exchequer is too poor; for th' effusion of our blood, the muster of his kingdom too faint a number; and for our disgrace, his own person kneeling at our feet but a weak and worthless satisfaction. To this add defiance; and tell him, for conclusion, he hath betrayed his followers, whose condemnation is pronounc'd. So far my king and master; so much my office.

KING HENRY. What is thy name? I know thy quality.

MONTJOY. Montjoy.

KING HENRY. Thou dost thy office fairly. Turn thee back,

And tell thy king I do not seek him now,
But could be willing to march on to Calais
Without impeachment; for, to say the sooth—
Though 'tis no wisdom to confess so much
Unto an enemy of craft and vantage—
My people are with sickness much enfeebled;
My numbers lessen'd; and those few I have
Almost no better than so many French;
Who when they were in health, I tell thee, herald,
I thought upon one pair of English legs
Did march three Frenchmen. Yet forgive me, God,
That I do brag thus; this your air of France
Hath blown that vice in me; I must repent.
Go, therefore, tell thy master here I am;
My ransom is this frail and worthless trunk;
My army but a weak and sickly guard;
Yet, God before, tell him we will come on,
Though France himself and such another neighbour
Stand in our way. There's for thy labour, Montjoy.
Go, bid thy master well advise himself.
If we may pass, we will; if we be hind'red,
We shall your tawny ground with your red blood
Discolour; and so, Montjoy, fare you well.
The sum of all our answer is but this:
We would not seek a battle as we are;
Nor as we are, we say, we will not shun it.
So tell your master.

MONTJOY. I shall deliver so. Thanks to your Highness. *Exit*
GLOUCESTER. I hope they will not come upon us now.
KING HENRY. We are in God's hand, brother, not in theirs.
March to the bridge, it now draws toward night;
Beyond the river we'll encamp ourselves,
And on to-morrow bid them march away.   *Exeunt*

SCENE 7

The French camp near Agincourt

Enter the CONSTABLE OF FRANCE, *the* LORD RAMBURES, *the* DUKE OF ORLEANS, *the* DAUPHIN, *with others*

CONSTABLE. Tut! I have the best armour of the world. Would it were day!

ORLEANS. You have an excellent armour; but let my horse have his due.

CONSTABLE. It is the best horse of Europe.

ORLEANS. Will it never be morning?

DAUPHIN. My Lord of Orleans and my Lord High Constable, you talk of horse and armour?

ORLEANS. You are as well provided of both as any prince in the world.

DAUPHIN. What a long night is this! I will not change my horse with any that treads but on four pasterns. Ça, ha! he bounds from the earth as if his entrails were hairs; le cheval volant, the Pegasus, chez les narines de feu! When I bestride him I soar, I am a hawk. He trots the air; the earth sings when he touches it; the basest horn of his hoof is more musical than the pipe of Hermes.

ORLEANS. He's of the colour of the nutmeg.

DAUPHIN. And of the heat of the ginger. It is a beast for Perseus: he is pure air and fire; and the dull elements of earth and water never appear in him, but only in patient stillness while his rider mounts him; he is indeed a horse, and all other jades you may call beasts.

CONSTABLE. Indeed, my lord, it is a most absolute and excellent horse.

DAUPHIN. It is the prince of palfreys; his neigh is like the bidding of a monarch, and his countenance enforces homage.

ORLEANS. No more, cousin.

DAUPHIN. Nay, the man hath no wit that cannot, from the rising of the lark to the lodging of the lamb, vary deserved praise on my palfrey. It is a theme as fluent as the sea: turn the sands into eloquent tongues, and my horse is argument for them all; 'tis a subject for a sovereign to reason on, and for a sovereign's sovereign to ride on; and for the world—familiar to us and unknown—to lay apart their particular functions and wonder at him. I once writ a sonnet in his praise and began thus: 'Wonder of nature'—

ORLEANS. I have heard a sonnet begin so to one's mistress.

DAUPHIN. Then did they imitate that which I compos'd to my courser; for my horse is my mistress.

ORLEANS. Your mistress bears well.

DAUPHIN. Me well; which is the prescript praise and perfection of a good and particular mistress.

CONSTABLE. Nay, for methought yesterday your mistress shrewdly shook your back.

DAUPHIN. So perhaps did yours.

CONSTABLE. Mine was not bridled.

DAUPHIN. O, then belike she was old and gentle; and you rode like a kern of Ireland, your French hose off and in your strait strossers.

CONSTABLE. You have good judgment in horsemanship.

DAUPHIN. Be warn'd by me, then: they that ride so, and ride not warily, fall into foul bogs. I had rather have my horse to my mistress.

CONSTABLE. I had as lief have my mistress a jade.

DAUPHIN. I tell thee, Constable, my mistress wears his own hair.

CONSTABLE. I could make as true a boast as that, if I had a sow to my mistress.

DAUPHIN. 'Le chien est retourné à son propre vomissement, et la truie lavée au bourbier.' Thou mak'st use of anything.

CONSTABLE. Yet do I not use my horse for my mistress, or any such proverb so little kin to the purpose.

RAMBURES. My Lord Constable, the armour that I saw in your tent to-night—are those stars or suns upon it?

CONSTABLE. Stars, my lord.

DAUPHIN. Some of them will fall to-morrow, I hope.

CONSTABLE. And yet my sky shall not want.

DAUPHIN. That may be, for you bear a many superfluously, and 'twere more honour some were away.

CONSTABLE. Ev'n as your horse bears your praises, who would trot as well were some of your brags dismounted.

DAUPHIN. Would I were able to load him with his desert!
Will it never be day? I will trot to-morrow a mile, and
my way shall be paved with English faces.

CONSTABLE. I will not say so, for fear I should be fac'd out
of my way; but I would it were morning, for I would
fain be about the ears of the English.

RAMBURES. Who will go to hazard with me for twenty
prisoners?

CONSTABLE. You must first go yourself to hazard ere you
have them.

DAUPHIN. 'Tis midnight; I'll go arm myself.   *Exit*

ORLEANS. The Dauphin longs for morning.

RAMBURES. He longs to eat the English.

CONSTABLE. I think he will eat all he kills.

ORLEANS. By the white hand of my lady, he's a gallant
prince.

CONSTABLE. Swear by her foot, that she may tread out the
oath.

ORLEANS. He is simply the most active gentleman of France.

CONSTABLE. Doing is activity, and he will still be doing.

ORLEANS. He never did harm that I heard of.

CONSTABLE. Nor will do none to-morrow: he will keep that
good name still.

ORLEANS. I know him to be valiant.

CONSTABLE. I was told that by one that knows him better
than you.

ORLEANS. What's he?

CONSTABLE. Marry, he told me so himself; and he said he
car'd not who knew it.

ORLEANS. He needs not; it is no hidden virtue in him.

CONSTABLE. By my faith, sir, but it is; never anybody saw it
but his lackey.
'Tis a hooded valour, and when it appears it will bate.

ORLEANS. Ill-wind never said well.

CONSTABLE. I will cap that proverb with 'There is flattery in
friendship.'

ORLEANS. And I will take up that with 'Give the devil his
due.'

CONSTABLE. Well plac'd! There stands your friend for the

devil; have at the very eye of that proverb with 'A pox of the devil!'

ORLEANS. You are the better at proverbs by how much 'A fool's bolt is soon shot.'

CONSTABLE. You have shot over.

ORLEANS. 'Tis not the first time you were overshot.

Enter a MESSENGER

MESSENGER. My Lord High Constable, the English lie within fifteen hundred paces of your tents.

CONSTABLE. Who hath measur'd the ground?

MESSENGER. The Lord Grandpré.

CONSTABLE. A valiant and most expert gentleman. Would it were day! Alas, poor Harry of England! he longs not for the dawning as we do.

ORLEANS. What a wretched and peevish fellow is this King of England, to mope with his fat-brain'd followers so far out of his knowledge!

CONSTABLE. If the English had any apprehension, they would run away.

ORLEANS. That they lack; for if their heads had any intellectual armour, they could never wear such heavy headpieces.

RAMBURES. That island of England breeds very valiant creatures; their mastiffs are of unmatchable courage.

ORLEANS. Foolish curs, that run winking into the mouth of a Russian bear, and have their heads crush'd like rotten apples! You may as well say that's a valiant flea that dare eat his breakfast on the lip of a lion.

CONSTABLE. Just, just! and the men do sympathise with the mastiffs in robustious and rough coming on, leaving their wits with their wives; and then give them great meals of beef and iron and steel; they will eat like wolves and fight like devils.

ORLEANS. Ay, but these English are shrewdly out of beef.

CONSTABLE. Then shall we find to-morrow they have only stomachs to eat, and none to fight. Now is it time to arm. Come, shall we about it?

ORLEANS. It is now two o'clock; but let me see—by ten We shall have each a hundred Englishmen. *Exeunt*

ACT IV. PROLOGUE

Enter CHORUS

CHORUS. Now entertain conjecture of a time
  When creeping murmur and the poring dark
  Fills the wide vessel of the universe.
  From camp to camp, through the foul womb of night,
  The hum of either army stilly sounds,
  That the fix'd sentinels almost receive
  The secret whispers of each other's watch.
  Fire answers fire, and through their paly flames
  Each battle sees the other's umber'd face;
  Steed threatens steed, in high and boastful neighs
  Piercing the night's dull ear; and from the tents
  The armourers accomplishing the knights,
  With busy hammers closing rivets up,
  Give dreadful note of preparation.
  The country cocks do crow, the clocks do toll,
  And the third hour of drowsy morning name.
  Proud of their numbers and secure in soul,
  The confident and over-lusty French
  Do the low-rated English play at dice;
  And chide the cripple tardy-gaited night
  Who like a foul and ugly witch doth limp
  So tediously away. The poor condemned English,
  Like sacrifices, by their watchful fires
  Sit patiently and inly ruminate
  The morning's danger; and their gesture sad
  Investing lank-lean cheeks and war-worn coats
  Presenteth them unto the gazing moon
  So many horrid ghosts. O, now, who will behold
  The royal captain of this ruin'd band
  Walking from watch to watch, from tent to tent,
  Let him cry 'Praise and glory on his head!'
  For forth he goes and visits all his host;
  Bids them good morrow with a modest smile,
  And calls them brothers, friends, and countrymen.
  Upon his royal face there is no note
  How dread an army hath enrounded him;

Nor doth he dedicate one jot of colour
Unto the weary and all-watched night;
But freshly looks, and over-bears attaint
With cheerful semblance and sweet majesty;
That every wretch, pining and pale before,
Beholding him, plucks comfort from his looks;
A largess universal, like the sun,
His liberal eye doth give to every one,
Thawing cold fear, that mean and gentle all
Behold, as may unworthiness define,
A little touch of Harry in the night.
And so our scene must to the battle fly;
Where—O for pity!—we shall much disgrace
With four or five most vile and ragged foils,
Right ill-dispos'd in brawl ridiculous,
The name of Agincourt. Yet sit and see,
Minding true things by what their mock'ries be.   *Exit*

SCENE 1

France. The English camp at Agincourt

Enter the KING, BEDFORD, *and* GLOUCESTER

KING HENRY. Gloucester, 'tis true that we are in great
     danger;
     The greater therefore should our courage be.
     Good morrow, brother Bedford. God Almighty!
     There is some soul of goodness in things evil,
     Would men observingly distil it out;
     For our bad neighbour makes us early stirrers,
     Which is both healthful and good husbandry.
     Besides, they are our outward consciences
     And preachers to us all, admonishing
     That we should dress us fairly for our end.
     Thus may we gather honey from the weed,
     And make a moral of the devil himself.

Enter ERPINGHAM

Good morrow, old Sir Thomas Erpingham:

A good soft pillow for that good white head
Were better than a churlish turf of France.

ERPINGHAM. Not so, my liege; this lodging likes me better,
Since I may say 'Now lie I like a king.'

KING HENRY. 'Tis good for men to love their present pains
Upon example; so the spirit is eased;
And when the mind is quick'ned, out of doubt
The organs, though defunct and dead before,
Break up their drowsy grave and newly move
With casted slough and fresh legerity.
Lend me thy cloak, Sir Thomas. Brothers both,
Commend me to the princes in our camp;
Do my good morrow to them, and anon
Desire them all to my pavilion.

GLOUCESTER. We shall, my liege.

ERPINGHAM. Shall I attend your Grace?

KING HENRY. No, my good knight:
Go with my brothers to my lords of England;
I and my bosom must debate awhile,
And then I would no other company.

ERPINGHAM. The Lord in heaven bless thee, noble Harry!

Exeunt all but the KING

KING HENRY. God-a-mercy, old heart! thou speak'st cheerfully.

Enter PISTOL

PISTOL. Qui va là?

KING HENRY. A friend.

PISTOL. Discuss unto me: art thou officer,
Or art thou base, common, and popular?

KING HENRY. I am a gentleman of a company.

PISTOL. Trail'st thou the puissant pike?

KING HENRY. Even so. What are you?

PISTOL. As good a gentleman as the Emperor.

KING HENRY. Then you are a better than the King.

PISTOL. The King's a bawcock and a heart of gold,
A lad of life, an imp of fame;
Of parents good, of fist most valiant.
I kiss his dirty shoe, and from heart-string
I love the lovely bully. What is thy name?

KING HENRY. Harry le Roy.

PISTOL. Le Roy! a Cornish name; art thou of Cornish crew?

KING HENRY. No, I am a Welshman.

PISTOL. Know'st thou Fluellen?

KING HENRY. Yes.

PISTOL. Tell him I'll knock his leek about his pate
Upon Saint Davy's day.

KING. Do not you wear your dagger in your cap that day,
lest he knock that about yours.

PISTOL. Art thou his friend?

KING HENRY. And his kinsman too.

PISTOL. The figo for thee, then!

KING HENRY. I thank you; God be with you!

PISTOL. My name is Pistol call'd.   *Exit*

KING HENRY. It sorts well with your fierceness.

Enter FLUELLEN *and* GOWER

GOWER. Captain Fluellen!

FLUELLEN. So! in the name of Jesu Christ, speak fewer. It is
the greatest admiration in the universal world, when the
true and aunchient prerogatifes and laws of the wars is not
kept: if you would take the pains but to examine the wars
of Pompey the Great, you shall find, I warrant you, that
there is no tiddle-taddle nor pibble-pabble in Pompey's
camp; I warrant you, you shall find the ceremonies of the
wars, and the cares of it, and the forms of it, and the
sobriety of it, and the modesty of it, to be otherwise.

GOWER. Why, the enemy is loud; you hear him all night.

FLUELLEN. If the enemy is an ass, and a fool, and a prating
coxcomb, is it meet, think you, that we should also, look
you, be an ass, and a fool, and a prating coxcomb? In your
own conscience, now?

GOWER. I will speak lower.

FLUELLEN. I pray you and beseech you that you will.

Exeunt GOWER *and* FLUELLEN

KING HENRY. Though it appear a little out of fashion,
There is much care and valour in this Welshman.

Enter three soldiers: JOHN BATES, ALEXANDER COURT,
and MICHAEL WILLIAMS

COURT. Brother John Bates, is not that the morning which breaks yonder?

BATES. I think it be; but we have no great cause to desire the approach of day.

WILLIAMS. We see yonder the beginning of the day, but I think we shall never see the end of it. Who goes there?

KING HENRY. A friend.

WILLIAMS. Under what captain serve you?

KING HENRY. Under Sir Thomas Erpingham.

WILLIAMS. A good old commander and a most kind gentleman. I pray you, what thinks he of our estate?

KING HENRY. Even as men wreck'd upon a sand, that look to be wash'd off the next tide.

BATES. He hath not told his thought to the King?

KING HENRY. No; nor it is not meet he should. For though I speak it to you, I think the King is but a man as I am: the violet smells to him as it doth to me; the element shows to him as it doth to me; all his senses have but human conditions; his ceremonies laid by, in his nakedness he appears but a man; and though his affections are higher mounted than ours, yet, when they stoop, they stoop with the like wing. Therefore, when he sees reason of fears, as we do, his fears, out of doubt, be of the same relish as ours are; yet, in reason, no man should possess him with any appearance of fear, lest he, by showing it, should dishearten his army.

BATES. He may show what outward courage he will; but I believe, as cold a night as 'tis, he could wish himself in Thames up to the neck; and so I would he were, and I by him, at all adventures, so we were quit here.

KING HENRY. By my troth, I will speak my conscience of the King: I think he would not wish himself anywhere but where he is.

BATES. Then I would he were here alone; so should he be sure to be ransomed, and a many poor men's lives saved.

KING HENRY. I dare say you love him not so ill to wish him here alone, howsoever you speak this, to feel other men's minds; methinks I could not die anywhere so contented as in the King's company, his cause being just and his quarrel honourable.

WILLIAMS. That's more than we know.

BATES. Ay, or more than we should seek after; for we know enough if we know we are the King's subjects. If his cause be wrong, our obedience to the King wipes the crime of it out of us.

WILLIAMS. But if the cause be not good, the King himself hath a heavy reckoning to make when all those legs and arms and heads, chopp'd off in a battle, shall join together at the latter day and cry all 'We died at such a place'—some swearing, some crying for a surgeon, some upon their wives left poor behind them, some upon the debts they owe, some upon their children rawly left. I am afeard there are few die well that die in a battle; for how can they charitably dispose of anything when blood is their argument? Now, if these men do not die well, it will be a black matter for the King that led them to it; who to disobey were against all proportion of subjection.

KING HENRY. So, if a son that is by his father sent about merchandise do sinfully miscarry upon the sea, the imputation of his wickedness, by your rule, should be imposed upon his father that sent him; or if a servant, under his master's command transporting a sum of money, be assailed by robbers and die in many irreconcil'd iniquities, you may call the business of the master the author of the servant's damnation. But this is not so: the King is not bound to answer the particular endings of his soldiers, the father of his son, nor the master of his servant; for they purpose not their death when they purpose their services. Besides, there is no king, be his cause never so spotless, if it come to the arbitrement of swords, can try it out with all unspotted soldiers: some peradventure have on them the guilt of premeditated and contrived murder; some, of beguiling virgins with the broken seals of perjury; some, making the wars their bulwark, that have before gored the gentle bosom of peace with pillage and robbery. Now, if these men have defeated the law and outrun native punishment, though they can outstrip men they have no wings to fly from God: war is His beadle, war is His vengeance; so that here men are punish'd for before-breach of the King's laws in now the King's quarrel. Where they feared the death they have borne life away; and where they would be safe they perish. Then if they die unprovided, no more is the King guilty of their damnation than he was before guilty of those impieties for the which they are now visited. Every subject's duty is the King's; but every subject's soul is his own. Therefore should every soldier in the wars do as every sick man in his bed—wash every mote out of his conscience; and dying so, death is to him advantage; or not dying, the time was blessedly lost wherein such preparation was gained; and in him that escapes it were not sin to think that, making God so free an offer, He let him outlive that day to see His greatness, and to teach others how they should prepare.

WILLIAMS. 'Tis certain, every man that dies ill, the ill upon his own head—the King is not to answer for it.

BATES. I do not desire he should answer for me, and yet I determine to fight lustily for him.

KING HENRY. I myself heard the King say he would not be ransom'd.

WILLIAMS. Ay, he said so, to make us fight cheerfully; but when our throats are cut he may be ransom'd, and we ne'er the wiser.

KING HENRY. If I live to see it, I will never trust his word after.

WILLIAMS. You pay him then! That's a perilous shot out of an elder-gun, that a poor and a private displeasure can do against a monarch! You may as well go about to turn the sun to ice with fanning in his face with a peacock's feather. You'll never trust his word after! Come, 'tis a foolish saying.

KING HENRY. Your reproof is something too round; I should be angry with you, if the time were convenient.

WILLIAMS. Let it be a quarrel between us if you live.

KING HENRY. I embrace it.

WILLIAMS. How shall I know thee again?

KING HENRY. Give me any gage of thine, and I will wear it in my bonnet; then if ever thou dar'st acknowledge it, I will make it my quarrel.

WILLIAMS. Here's my glove; give me another of thine.

KING HENRY. There.

WILLIAMS. This will I also wear in my cap; if ever thou

come to me and say, after to-morrow, 'This is my glove,'
by this hand I will take thee a box on the ear.

KING HENRY. If ever I live to see it, I will challenge it.

WILLIAMS. Thou dar'st as well be hang'd.

KING HENRY. Well, I will do it, though I take thee in the
King's company.

WILLIAMS. Keep thy word. Fare thee well.

BATES. Be friends, you English fools, be friends; we have
French quarrels enow, if you could tell how to reckon.

KING HENRY. Indeed, the French may lay twenty French
crowns to one they will beat us, for they bear them on
their shoulders; but it is no English treason to cut French
crowns, and to-morrow the King himself will be a clipper.

Exeunt soldiers

Upon the King! Let us our lives, our souls,
Our debts, our careful wives,
Our children, and our sins, lay on the King!
We must bear all. O hard condition,
Twin-born with greatness, subject to the breath
Of every fool, whose sense no more can feel
But his own wringing! What infinite heart's ease
Must kings neglect that private men enjoy!
And what have kings that privates have not too,
Save ceremony—save general ceremony?
And what art thou, thou idol Ceremony?
What kind of god art thou, that suffer'st more
Of mortal griefs than do thy worshippers?
What are thy rents? What are thy comings-in?
O Ceremony, show me but thy worth!
What is thy soul of adoration?
Art thou aught else but place, degree, and form,
Creating awe and fear in other men?
Wherein thou art less happy being fear'd
Than they in fearing.
What drink'st thou oft, instead of homage sweet,
But poison'd flattery? O, be sick, great greatness,
And bid thy ceremony give thee cure!
Thinks thou the fiery fever will go out
With titles blown from adulation?
Will it give place to flexure and low bending?

Canst thou, when thou command'st the beggar's knee,
Command the health of it? No, thou proud dream,
That play'st so subtly with a king's repose.
I am a king that find thee; and I know
'Tis not the balm, the sceptre, and the ball,
The sword, the mace, the crown imperial,
The intertissued robe of gold and pearl,
The farced title running fore the king,
The throne he sits on, nor the tide of pomp
That beats upon the high shore of this world—
No, not all these, thrice gorgeous ceremony,
Not all these, laid in bed majestical,
Can sleep so soundly as the wretched slave
Who, with a body fill'd and vacant mind,
Gets him to rest, cramm'd with distressful bread;
Never sees horrid night, the child of hell;
But, like a lackey, from the rise to set
Sweats in the eye of Phœbus, and all night
Sleeps in Elysium; next day, after dawn,
Doth rise and help Hyperion to his horse;
And follows so the ever-running year
With profitable labour, to his grave.
And but for ceremony, such a wretch,
Winding up days with toil and nights with sleep,
Had the fore-hand and vantage of a king.
The slave, a member of the country's peace,
Enjoys it; but in gross brain little wots
What watch the king keeps to maintain the peace
Whose hours the peasant best advantages.

Enter Erpingham

Erpingham. My lord, your nobles, jealous of your absence,
  Seek through your camp to find you.
King. Good old knight,
  Collect them all together at my tent:
  I'll be before thee.
Erpingham. I shall do't, my lord.   *Exit*
King. O God of battles, steel my soldiers' hearts,
  Possess them not with fear! Take from them now
  The sense of reck'ning, if th' opposed numbers

Pluck their hearts from them! Not to-day, O Lord,
O, not to-day, think not upon the fault
My father made in compassing the crown!
I Richard's body have interred new,
And on it have bestowed more contrite tears
Than from it issued forced drops of blood;
Five hundred poor I have in yearly pay,
Who twice a day their wither'd hands hold up
Toward heaven, to pardon blood; and I have built
Two chantries, where the sad and solemn priests
Sing still for Richard's soul. More will I do;
Though all that I can do is nothing worth,
Since that my penitence comes after all,
Imploring pardon.

Enter GLOUCESTER

GLOUCESTER. My liege!
KING HENRY. My brother Gloucester's voice? Ay;
  I know thy errand, I will go with thee;
  The day, my friends, and all things, stay for me. *Exeunt*

SCENE 2

The French camp

Enter the DAUPHIN, ORLEANS, RAMBURES, *and others*

ORLEANS. The sun doth gild our armour; up, my lords!
DAUPHIN. Montez à cheval! My horse! Varlet, laquais! Ha!
ORLEANS. O brave spirit!
DAUPHIN. Via! Les eaux et la terre—
ORLEANS. Rien puis? L'air et le feu.
DAUPHIN. Ciel! cousin Orleans.

Enter CONSTABLE

Now, my Lord Constable!
CONSTABLE. Hark how our steeds for present service neigh!
DAUPHIN. Mount them, and make incision in their hides,
  That their hot blood may spin in English eyes,
  And dout them with superfluous courage, ha!

RAMBURES. What, will you have them weep our horses'
    blood?
  How shall we then behold their natural tears?

Enter a MESSENGER

MESSENGER. The English are embattl'd, you French peers.
CONSTABLE. To horse, you gallant Princes! straight to horse!
  Do but behold yon poor and starved band,
  And your fair show shall suck away their souls,
  Leaving them but the shales and husks of men.
  There is not work enough for all our hands;
  Scarce blood enough in all their sickly veins
  To give each naked curtle-axe a stain
  That our French gallants shall to-day draw out,
  And sheathe for lack of sport. Let us but blow on them,
  The vapour of our valour will o'erturn them.
  'Tis positive 'gainst all exceptions, lords,
  That our superfluous lackeys and our peasants—
  Who in unnecessary action swarm
  About our squares of battle—were enow
  To purge this field of such a hilding foe;
  Though we upon this mountain's basis by
  Took stand for idle speculation—
  But that our honours must not. What's to say?
  A very little little let us do,
  And all is done. Then let the trumpets sound
  The tucket sonance and the note to mount;
  For our approach shall so much dare the field
  That England shall couch down in fear and yield.

Enter GRANDPRÉ

GRANDPRÉ. Why do you stay so long, my lords of France?
  Yond island carrions, desperate of their bones,
  Ill-favouredly become the morning field;
  Their ragged curtains poorly are let loose,
  And our air shakes them passing scornfully;
  Big Mars seems bankrupt in their beggar'd host,
  And faintly through a rusty beaver peeps.
  The horsemen sit like fixed candlesticks
  With torch-staves in their hand; and their poor jades

Lob down their heads, dropping the hides and hips,
The gum down-roping from their pale-dead eyes,
And in their pale dull mouths the gimmal'd bit
Lies foul with chaw'd grass, still and motionless;
And their executors, the knavish crows,
Fly o'er them, all impatient for their hour.
Description cannot suit itself in words
To demonstrate the life of such a battle
In life so lifeless as it shows itself.

CONSTABLE. They have said their prayers and they stay for
death.

DAUPHIN. Shall we go send them dinners and fresh suits,
And give their fasting horses provender,
And after fight with them?

CONSTABLE. I stay but for my guidon. To the field!
I will the banner from a trumpet take,
And use it for my haste. Come, come, away!
The sun is high, and we outwear the day.   *Exeunt*

SCENE 3

The English camp

Enter GLOUCESTER, BEDFORD, EXETER, ERPINGHAM, *with
all his host;* SALISBURY *and* WESTMORELAND

GLOUCESTER. Where is the King?

BEDFORD. The King himself is rode to view their battle.

WESTMORELAND. Of fighting men they have full three-score
thousand.

EXETER. There's five to one; besides, they all are fresh.

SALISBURY. God's arm strike with us! 'tis a fearful odds.
God bye you, Princes all; I'll to my charge.
If we no more meet till we meet in heaven,
Then joyfully, my noble Lord of Bedford,
My dear Lord Gloucester, and my good Lord Exeter,
And my kind kinsman—warriors all, adieu!

BEDFORD. Farewell, good Salisbury; and good luck go with
thee!

EXETER. Farewell, kind lord. Fight valiantly to-day;

And yet I do thee wrong to mind thee of it,
For thou art fram'd of the firm truth of valour.

Exit SALISBURY

BEDFORD. He is as full of valour as of kindness;
Princely in both.

Enter the KING

WESTMORELAND. O that we now had here
But one ten thousand of those men in England
That do no work to-day!
KING. What's he that wishes so?
My cousin Westmoreland? No, my fair cousin;
If we are mark'd to die, we are enow
To do our country loss; and if to live,
The fewer men, the greater share of honour.
God's will! I pray thee, wish not one man more.
By Jove, I am not covetous for gold,
Nor care I who doth feed upon my cost;
It yearns me not if men my garments wear;
Such outward things dwell not in my desires.
But if it be a sin to covet honour,
I am the most offending soul alive.
No, faith, my coz, wish not a man from England.
God's peace! I would not lose so great an honour
As one man more methinks would share from me
For the best hope I have. O, do not wish one more!
Rather proclaim it, Westmoreland, through my host,
That he which hath no stomach to this fight,
Let him depart; his passport shall be made,
And crowns for convoy put into his purse;
We would not die in that man's company
That fears his fellowship to die with us.
This day is call'd the feast of Crispian.
He that outlives this day, and comes safe home,
Will stand a tip-toe when this day is nam'd,
And rouse him at the name of Crispian.
He that shall live this day, and see old age,
Will yearly on the vigil feast his neighbours,
And say 'To-morrow is Saint Crispian.'
Then will he strip his sleeve and show his scars,

And say 'These wounds I had on Crispian's day.'
Old men forget; yet all shall be forgot,
But he'll remember, with advantages,
What feats he did that day. Then shall our names,
Familiar in his mouth as household words—
Harry the King, Bedford and Exeter,
Warwick and Talbot, Salisbury and Gloucester—
Be in their flowing cups freshly rememb'red.
This story shall the good man teach his son;
And Crispin Crispian shall ne'er go by,
From this day to the ending of the world,
But we in it shall be remembered—
We few, we happy few, we band of brothers;
For he to-day that sheds his blood with me
Shall be my brother; be he ne'er so vile,
This day shall gentle his condition;
And gentlemen in England now-a-bed
Shall think themselves accurs'd they were not here,
And hold their manhoods cheap whiles any speaks
That fought with us upon Saint Crispin's day.

Re-enter SALISBURY

SALISBURY. My sovereign lord, bestow yourself with speed:
The French are bravely in their battles set,
And will with all expedience charge on us.
KING HENRY. All things are ready, if our minds be so.
WESTMORELAND. Perish the man whose mind is backward
now!
KING HENRY. Thou dost not wish more help from England,
coz?
WESTMORELAND. God's will, my liege! would you and I
alone,
Without more help, could fight this royal battle!
KING HENRY. Why, now thou hast unwish'd five thousand
men;
Which likes me better than to wish us one.
You know your places. God be with you all!

Tucket. Enter MONTJOY

MONTJOY. Once more I come to know of thee, King Harry,

448

If for thy ransom thou wilt now compound,
Before thy most assured overthrow;
For certainly thou art so near the gulf
Thou needs must be englutted. Besides, in mercy,
The constable desires thee thou wilt mind
Thy followers of repentance, that their souls
May make a peaceful and a sweet retire
From off these fields, where, wretches, their poor bodies
Must lie and fester.
KING HENRY. Who hath sent thee now?
MONTJOY. The Constable of France.
KING HENRY. I pray thee bear my former answer back:
  Bid them achieve me, and then sell my bones.
  Good God! why should they mock poor fellows thus?
  The man that once did sell the lion's skin
  While the beast liv'd was kill'd with hunting him.
  A many of our bodies shall no doubt
  Find native graves; upon the which, I trust,
  Shall witness live in brass of this day's work.
  And those that leave their valiant bones in France,
  Dying like men, though buried in your dunghills,
  They shall be fam'd; for there the sun shall greet them
  And draw their honours reeking up to heaven,
  Leaving their earthly parts to choke your clime,
  The smell whereof shall breed a plague in France.
  Mark then abounding valour in our English,
  That, being dead, like to the bullet's grazing
  Break out into a second course of mischief,
  Killing in relapse of mortality.
  Let me speak proudly: tell the Constable
  We are but warriors for the working-day;
  Our gayness and our gilt are all besmirch'd
  With rainy marching in the painful field;
  There's not a piece of feather in our host—
  Good argument, I hope, we will not fly—
  And time hath worn us into slovenry.
  But, by the mass, our hearts are in the trim;
  And my poor soldiers tell me yet ere night
  They'll be in fresher robes, or they will pluck
  The gay new coats o'er the French soldiers' heads

And turn them out of service. If they do this—
As, if God please, they shall—my ransom then
Will soon be levied. Herald, save thou thy labour;
Come thou no more for ransom, gentle herald;
They shall have none, I swear, but these my joints;
Which if they have, as I will leave 'em them,
Shall yield them little, tell the Constable.
MONTJOY. I shall, King Harry. And so fare thee well:
Thou never shalt hear herald any more.   *Exit*
KING HENRY. I fear thou wilt once more come again for a
ransom.

Enter the DUKE OF YORK

YORK. My lord, most humbly on my knee I beg
The leading of the vaward.
KING HENRY. Take it, brave York. Now, soldiers, march
away;
And how thou pleasest, God, dispose the day!   *Exeunt*

SCENE 4

The field of battle

Alarum. Excursions. Enter FRENCH SOLDIER,
PISTOL, *and* BOY

PISTOL. Yield, cur!
FRENCH SOLDIER. Je pense que vous êtes le gentilhomme de
bonne qualité.
PISTOL. Cality! Calen o custure me! Art thou a gentleman?
What is thy name? Discuss.
FRENCH SOLDIER. O Seigneur Dieu!
PISTOL. O, Signieur Dew should be a gentleman.
Perpend my words, O Signieur Dew, and mark:
O Signieur Dew, thou diest on point of fox,
Except, O Signieur, thou do give to me
Egregious ransom.
FRENCH SOLDIER. O, prenez miséricorde; ayez pitié de moi!
PISTOL. Moy shall not serve; I will have forty moys;
Or I will fetch thy rim out at thy throat

In drops of crimson blood.

FRENCH SOLDIER. Est-il impossible d'échapper la force de ton bras?

PISTOL. Brass, cur?
Thou damned and luxurious mountain-goat,
Offer'st me brass?

FRENCH SOLDIER. O, pardonnez-moi!

PISTOL. Say'st thou me so? Is that a ton of moys?
Come hither, boy; ask me this slave in French
What is his name.

BOY. Ecoutez: comment êtes-vous appelé?

FRENCH SOLDIER. Monsieur le Fer.

BOY. He says his name is Master Fer.

PISTOL. Master Fer! I'll fer him, and firk him, and ferret him—discuss the same in French unto him.

BOY. I do not know the French for fer, and ferret, and firk.

PISTOL. Bid him prepare; for I will cut his throat.

FRENCH SOLDIER. Que dit-il, monsieur?

BOY. Il me commande à vous dire que vous faites vous prêt; car ce soldat ici est disposé tout à cette heure de couper votre gorge.

PISTOL. Owy, cuppele gorge, permafoy!
Peasant, unless thou give me crowns, brave crowns;
Or mangled shalt thou be by this my sword.

FRENCH SOLDIER. O, je vous supplie, pour l'amour de Dieu, me pardonner! Je suis gentilhomme de bonne maison. Gardez ma vie, et je vous donnerai deux cents écus.

PISTOL. What are his words?

BOY. He prays you to save his life; he is a gentleman of a good house, and for his ransom he will give you two hundred crowns.

PISTOL. Tell him my fury shall abate, and I
The crowns will take.

FRENCH SOLDIER. Petit monsieur, que dit-il?

BOY. Encore qu'il est contre son jurement de pardonner aucun prisonnier, néanmoins, pour les écus que vous l'avez promis, il est content à vous donner la liberté, le franchisement.

FRENCH SOLDIER. Sur mes genoux je vous donne mille remercîmens; et je m'estime heureux que je suis tombé entre les mains d'un chevalier, je pense, le plus brave, vaillant, et très distingué seigneur d'Angleterre.

PISTOL. Expound unto me, boy.

BOY. He gives you, upon his knees, a thousand thanks; and he esteems himself happy that he hath fall'n into the hands of one—as he thinks—the most brave, valorous, and thrice-worthy signieur of England.

PISTOL. As I suck blood, I will some mercy show.
Follow me. *Exit*

BOY. Suivez-vous le grand capitaine. *Exit* FRENCH SOLDIER
I did never know so full a voice issue from so empty a heart; but the saying is true—the empty vessel makes the greatest sound. Bardolph and Nym had ten times more valour than this roaring devil i' th' old play, that every one may pare his nails with a wooden dagger; and they are both hang'd; and so would this be, if he durst steal anything adventurously. I must stay with the lackeys, with the luggage of our camp. The French might have a good prey of us, if he knew of it; for there is none to guard it but boys. *Exit*

SCENE 5

Another part of the field of battle

Enter CONSTABLE, ORLEANS, BOURBON, DAUPHIN, *and* RAMBURES

CONSTABLE. O diable!

ORLEANS. O Seigneur! le jour est perdu, tout est perdu!

DAUPHIN. Mort Dieu, ma vie! all is confounded, all!
Reproach and everlasting shame
Sits mocking in our plumes. [*A short alarum*]
O méchante fortune! Do not run away.

CONSTABLE. Why, all our ranks are broke.

DAUPHIN. O perdurable shame! Let's stab ourselves.
Be these the wretches that we play'd at dice for?

ORLEANS. Is this the king we sent to for his ransom?

BOURBON. Shame, and eternal shame, nothing but shame!
Let us die in honour: once more back again;

And he that will not follow Bourbon now,
Let him go hence and, with his cap in hand
Like a base pander, hold the chamber-door
Whilst by a slave, no gentler than my dog,
His fairest daughter is contaminated.
CONSTABLE. Disorder, that hath spoil'd us, friend us now!
Let us on heaps go offer up our lives.
ORLEANS. We are enow yet living in the field
To smother up the English in our throngs,
If any order might be thought upon.
BOURBON. The devil take order now! I'll to the throng.
Let life be short, else shame will be too long.   *Exeunt*

SCENE 6

Another part of the field

Alarum. Enter the KING *and his train, with
prisoners;* EXETER, *and others*

KING HENRY. Well have we done, thrice-valiant coun-
trymen;
But all's not done—yet keep the French the field.
EXETER. The Duke of York commends him to your Majesty.
KING HENRY. Lives he, good uncle? Thrice within this hour
I saw him down; thrice up again, and fighting;
From helmet to the spur all blood he was.
EXETER. In which array, brave soldier, doth he lie
Larding the plain; and by his bloody side,
Yoke-fellow to his honour-owing wounds,
The noble Earl of Suffolk also lies.
Suffolk first died; and York, all haggled over,
Comes to him, where in gore he lay insteeped,
And takes him by the beard, kisses the gashes
That bloodily did yawn upon his face,
He cries aloud 'Tarry, my cousin Suffolk.
My soul shall thine keep company to heaven;
Tarry, sweet soul, for mine, then fly abreast;
As in this glorious and well-foughten field
We kept together in our chivalry.'

Upon these words I came and cheer'd him up;
He smil'd me in the face, raught me his hand,
And, with a feeble grip, says 'Dear my lord,
Commend my service to my sovereign.'
So did he turn, and over Suffolk's neck
He threw his wounded arm and kiss'd his lips;
And so, espous'd to death, with blood he seal'd
A testament of noble-ending love.
The pretty and sweet manner of it forc'd
Those waters from me which I would have stopp'd;
But I had not so much of man in me,
And all my mother came into mine eyes
And gave me up to tears.

KING HENRY. I blame you not;
For, hearing this, I must perforce compound
With mistful eyes, or they will issue too.   [*Alarum*]
But hark! what new alarum is this same?
The French have reinforc'd their scatter'd men.
Then every soldier kill his prisoners;
Give the word through.   *Exeunt*

SCENE 7

Another part of the field

Enter FLUELLEN *and* GOWER

FLUELLEN. Kill the poys and the luggage! 'Tis expressly against the law of arms; 'tis as arrant a piece of knavery, mark you now, as can be offert; in your conscience, now, is it not?

GOWER. 'Tis certain there's not a boy left alive; and the cowardly rascals that ran from the battle ha' done this slaughter; besides, they have burned and carried away all that was in the King's tent; wherefore the King most worthily hath caus'd every soldier to cut his prisoner's throat. O, 'tis a gallant King!

FLUELLEN. Ay, he was porn at Monmouth, Captain Gower. What call you the town's name where Alexander the Pig was born?

GOWER. Alexander the Great.

FLUELLEN. Why, I pray you, is not 'pig' great? The pig, or great, or the mighty, or the huge, or the magnanimous, are all one reckonings, save the phrase is a little variations.

GOWER. I think Alexander the Great was born in Macedon; his father was called Philip of Macedon, as I take it.

FLUELLEN. I think it is in Macedon where Alexander is porn. I tell you, Captain, if you look in the maps of the 'orld, I warrant you sall find, in the comparisons between Macedon and Monmouth, that the situations, look you, is both alike. There is a river in Macedon; and there is also moreover a river at Monmouth; it is call'd Wye at Monmouth, but it is out of my prains what is the name of the other river; but 'tis all one, 'tis alike as my fingers is to my fingers, and there is salmons in both. If you mark Alexander's life well, Harry of Monmouth's life is come after it indifferent well; for there is figures in all things. Alexander—God knows, and you know—in his rages, and his furies, and his wraths, and his cholers, and his moods, and his displeasures, and his indignations, and also being a little intoxicates in his prains, did, in his ales and his angers, look you, kill his best friend, Cleitus.

GOWER. Our king is not like him in that: he never kill'd any of his friends.

FLUELLEN. It is not well done, mark you now, to take the tales out of my mouth ere it is made and finished. I speak but in the figures and comparisons of it; as Alexander kill'd his friend Cleitus, being in his ales and his cups, so also Harry Monmouth, being in his right wits and his good judgments, turn'd away the fat knight with the great belly doublet; he was full of jests, and gipes, and knaveries, and mocks; I have forgot his name.

GOWER. Sir John Falstaff.

FLUELLEN. That is he. I'll tell you there is good men porn at Monmouth.

GOWER. Here comes his Majesty.

Alarum. Enter the KING, WARWICK, GLOUCESTER, EXETER, *and others, with prisoners. Flourish*

KING HENRY. I was not angry since I came to France

Until this instant. Take a trumpet, herald;
Ride thou unto the horsemen on yond hill;
If they will fight with us, bid them come down
Or void the field; they do offend our sight.
If they'll do neither, we will come to them
And make them skirr away as swift as stones
Enforced from the old Assyrian slings;
Besides, we'll cut the throats of those we have,
And not a man of them that we shall take
Shall taste our mercy. Go and tell them so.

Enter MONTJOY

EXETER. Here comes the herald of the French, my liege.
GLOUCESTER. His eyes are humbler than they us'd to be.
KING HENRY. How now! What means this, herald? know'st
    thou not
That I have fin'd these bones of mine for ransom?
Com'st thou again for ransom?
MONTJOY. No, great King;
    I come to thee for charitable licence,
    That we may wander o'er this bloody field
    To book our dead, and then to bury them;
    To sort our nobles from our common men;
    For many of our princes—woe the while!—
    Lie drown'd and soak'd in mercenary blood;
    So do our vulgar drench their peasant limbs
    In blood of princes; and their wounded steeds
    Fret fetlock deep in gore, and with wild rage
    Yerk out their armed heels at their dead masters,
    Killing them twice. O, give us leave, great King,
    To view the field in safety, and dispose
    Of their dead bodies!
KING HENRY. I tell thee truly, herald,
    I know not if the day be ours or no;
    For yet a many of your horsemen peer
    And gallop o'er the field.
MONTJOY. The day is yours.
KING HENRY. Praised be God, and not our strength, for it!
    What is this castle call'd that stands hard by?
MONTJOY. They call it Agincourt.

KING HENRY. Then call we this the field of Agincourt,
Fought on the day of Crispin Crispianus.

FLUELLEN. Your grandfather of famous memory, an't please
your Majesty, and your great-uncle Edward the Plack
Prince of Wales, as I have read in the chronicles, fought
a most prave pattle here in France.

KING HENRY. They did, Fluellen.

FLUELLEN. Your Majesty says very true; if your Majesties
is rememb'red of it, the Welshmen did good service in a
garden where leeks did grow, wearing leeks in their Monmouth caps; which your Majesty know to this hour is an
honourable badge of the service; and I do believe your
Majesty takes no scorn to wear the leek upon Saint Tavy's
day.

KING HENRY. I wear it for a memorable honour;
For I am Welsh, you know, good countryman.

FLUELLEN. All the water in Wye cannot wash your Majesty's Welsh plood out of your pody, I can tell you that.
Got pless it and preserve it as long as it pleases his Grace
and his Majesty too!

KING HENRY. Thanks, good my countryman.

FLUELLEN. By Jeshu, I am your Majesty's countryman, I
care not who know it; I will confess it to all the 'orld: I
need not be asham'd of your Majesty, praised be Got, so
long as your Majesty is an honest man.

Enter WILLIAMS

KING HENRY. God keep me so! Our heralds go with him:
Bring me just notice of the numbers dead
On both our parts. Call yonder fellow hither.

Exeunt heralds with MONTJOY

EXETER. Soldier, you must come to the King.

KING HENRY. Soldier, why wear'st thou that glove in thy
cap?

WILLIAMS. An't please your Majesty, 'tis the gage of one
that I should fight withal, if he be alive.

KING HENRY. An Englishman?

WILLIAMS. An't please your Majesty, a rascal that swagger'd
with me last night; who, if 'a live and ever dare to challenge this glove, I have sworn to take him a box o' th' ear;

457

or if I can see my glove in his cap—which he swore, as he was a soldier, he would wear if alive—I will strike it out soundly.

KING HENRY. What think you, Captain Fluellen, is it fit this soldier keep his oath?

FLUELLEN. He is a craven and a villain else, an't please your Majesty, in my conscience.

KING HENRY. It may be his enemy is a gentlemen of great sort, quite from the answer of his degree.

FLUELLEN. Though he be as good a gentleman as the Devil is, as Lucifier and Belzebub himself, it is necessary, look your Grace, that he keep his vow and his oath; if he be perjur'd, see you now, his reputation is as arrant a villain and a Jacksauce as ever his black shoe trod upon God's ground and his earth, in my conscience, la.

KING HENRY. Then keep thy vow, sirrah, when thou meet'st the fellow.

WILLIAMS. So I will, my liege, as I live.

KING HENRY. Who serv'st thou under?

WILLIAMS. Under Captain Gower, my liege.

FLUELLEN. Gower is a good captain, and is good knowledge and literatured in the wars.

KING HENRY. Call him hither to me, soldier.

WILLIAMS. I will, my liege.   *Exit*

KING HENRY. Here, Fluellen; wear thou this favour for me, and stick it in thy cap; when Alençon and myself were down together, I pluck'd this glove from his helm. If any man challenge this, he is a friend to Alençon and an enemy to our person; if thou encounter any such, apprehend him, an thou dost me love.

FLUELLEN. Your Grace does me as great honours as can be desir'd in the hearts of his subjects. I would fain see the man that has but two legs that shall find himself aggrief'd at this glove, that is all; but I would fain see it once, an please God of his grace that I might see.

KING HENRY. Know'st thou Gower?

FLUELLEN. He is my dear friend, an please you.

KING HENRY. Pray thee, go seek him, and bring him to my tent.

FLUELLEN. I will fetch him.   *Exit*
KING HENRY. My Lord of Warwick and my brother Glou-
   cester,
Follow Fluellen closely at the heels;
The glove which I have given him for a favour
May haply purchase him a box o' th' ear.
It is the soldier's: I, by bargain, should
Wear it myself. Follow, good cousin Warwick;
If that the soldier strike him, as I judge
By his blunt bearing he will keep his word,
Some sudden mischief may arise of it;
For I do know Fluellen valiant,
And touch'd with choler, hot as gunpowder,
And quickly will return an injury;
Follow, and see there be no harm between them.
Go you with me, uncle of Exeter.   *Exeunt*

SCENE 8

Before KING HENRY's *pavilion*

Enter GOWER *and* WILLIAMS

WILLIAMS. I warrant it is to knight you, Captain.

Enter FLUELLEN

FLUELLEN. God's will and his pleasure, Captain, I beseech
you now, come apace to the King: there is more good
toward you peradventure than is in your knowledge to
dream of.
WILLIAMS. Sir, know you this glove?
FLUELLEN. Know the glove? I know the glove is a glove.
WILLIAMS. I know this; and thus I challenge it. [*Strikes him*]
FLUELLEN. 'Sblood, an arrant traitor as any's in the universal
world, or in France, or in England!
GOWER. How now, sir! you villain!
WILLIAMS. Do you think I'll be forsworn?
FLUELLEN. Stand away, Captain Gower; I will give treason
his payment into plows, I warrant you.
WILLIAMS. I am no traitor.

FLUELLEN. That's a lie in thy throat. I charge you in his Majesty's name, apprehend him: he's a friend of the Duke Alençon's.

Enter WARWICK *and* GLOUCESTER

WARWICK. How now! how now! what's the matter?

FLUELLEN. My Lord of Warwick, here is—praised be God for it!—a most contagious treason come to light, look you, as you shall desire in a summer's day. Here is his Majesty.

Enter the KING *and* EXETER

KING HENRY. How now! what's the matter?

FLUELLEN. My liege, here is a villain and a traitor, that, look your Grace, has struck the glove which your Majesty is take out of the helmet of Alençon.

WILLIAMS. My liege, this was my glove: here is the fellow of it; and he that I gave it to in change promis'd to wear it in his cap; I promis'd to strike him if he did; I met this man with my glove in his cap, and I have been as good as my word.

FLUELLEN. Your Majesty hear now, saving your Majesty's manhood, what an arrant, rascally, beggarly, lousy knave it is; I hope your Majesty is pear me testimony and witness, and will avouchment, that this is the glove of Alençon that your Majesty is give me; in your conscience, now.

KING HENRY. Give me thy glove, soldier; look, here is the fellow of it.

'Twas I, indeed, thou promised'st to strike,

And thou hast given me most bitter terms.

FLUELLEN. An please your Majesty, let his neck answer for it, if there is any martial law in the world.

KING HENRY. How canst thou make me satisfaction?

WILLIAMS. All offences, my lord, come from the heart; never came any from mine that might offend your Majesty.

KING HENRY. It was ourself thou didst abuse.

WILLIAMS. Your Majesty came not like yourself: you appear'd to me but as a common man; witness the night, your garments, your lowliness; and what your Highness suffer'd under that shape I beseech you take it for your

own fault, and not mine; for had you been as I took you
for, I made no offence; therefore, I beseech your Highness
pardon me.

KING HENRY. Here, uncle Exeter, fill this glove with crowns,
And give it to this fellow. Keep it, fellow;
And wear it for an honour in thy cap
Till I do challenge it. Give him the crowns;
And, Captain, you must needs be friends with him.

FLUELLEN. By this day and this light, the fellow has mettle
enough in his belly: hold, there is twelve pence for you;
and I pray you to serve God, and keep you out of prawls,
and prabbles, and quarrels, and dissensions, and, I warrant
you, it is the better for you.

WILLIAMS. I will none of your money.

FLUELLEN. It is with a good will; I can tell you it will serve
you to mend your shoes. Come, wherefore should you be
so pashful? Your shoes is not so good. 'Tis a good silling,
I warrant you, or I will change it.

Enter an ENGLISH HERALD

KING HENRY. Now, herald, are the dead numb'red?

HERALD. Here is the number of the slaught'red French.

                          [*Gives a paper*]

KING HENRY. What prisoners of good sort are taken, uncle?

EXETER. Charles Duke of Orleans, nephew to the King;
John Duke of Bourbon, and Lord Bouciqualt;
Of other lords and barons, knights and squires,
Full fifteen hundred, besides common men.

KING HENRY. This note doth tell me of ten thousand French
That in the field lie slain; of princes in this number,
And nobles bearing banners, there lie dead
One hundred twenty-six; added to these,
Of knights, esquires, and gallant gentlemen,
Eight thousand and four hundred; of the which
Five hundred were but yesterday dubb'd knights.
So that, in these ten thousand they have lost,
There are but sixteen hundred mercenaries;
The rest are princes, barons, lords, knights, squires,
And gentlemen of blood and quality.
The names of those their nobles that lie dead:

Charles Delabreth, High Constable of France;
Jaques of Chatillon, Admiral of France;
The master of the cross-bows, Lord Rambures;
Great Master of France, the brave Sir Guichard Dolphin;
John Duke of Alençon; Antony Duke of Brabant,
The brother to the Duke of Burgundy;
And Edward Duke of Bar. Of lusty earls,
Grandpré and Roussi, Fauconbridge and Foix,
Beaumont and Marle, Vaudemont and Lestrake.
Here was a royal fellowship of death!
Where is the number of our English dead?
                    [HERALD *presents another paper*]
Edward the Duke of York, the Earl of Suffolk,
Sir Richard Kikely, Davy Gam, Esquire;
None else of name; and of all other men
But five and twenty. O God, thy arm was here!
And not to us, but to thy arm alone,
Ascribe we all. When, without stratagem,
But in plain shock and even play of battle,
Was ever known so great and little loss
On one part and on th' other? Take it, God,
For it is none but thine.
EXETER. 'Tis wonderful!
KING HENRY. Come, go we in procession to the village;
And be it death proclaimed through our host
To boast of this or take that praise from God
Which is his only.
FLUELLEN. Is it not lawful, an please your Majesty, to tell
how many is kill'd?
KING HENRY. Yes, Captain; but with this acknowledgment,
That God fought for us.
FLUELLEN. Yes, my conscience, he did us great good.
KING HENRY. Do we all holy rites:
Let there be sung 'Non nobis' and 'Te Deum';
The dead with charity enclos'd in clay—
And then to Calais; and to England then;
Where ne'er from France arriv'd more happy men. *Exeunt*

ACT V. PROLOGUE

Enter CHORUS

CHORUS. Vouchsafe to those that have not read the story
That I may prompt them; and of such as have,
I humbly pray them to admit th' excuse
Of time, of numbers, and due course of things,
Which cannot in their huge and proper life
Be here presented. Now we bear the King
Toward Calais. Grant him there. There seen,
Heave him away upon your winged thoughts
Athwart the sea. Behold, the English beach
Pales in the flood with men, with wives, and boys,
Whose shouts and claps out-voice the deep-mouth'd sea,
Which, like a mighty whiffler, fore the King
Seems to prepare his way. So let him land,
And solemnly see him set on to London.
So swift a pace hath thought that even now
You may imagine him upon Blackheath;
Where that his lords desire him to have borne
His bruised helmet and his bended sword
Before him through the city. He forbids it,
Being free from vainness and self-glorious pride;
Giving full trophy, signal, and ostent,
Quite from himself to God. But now behold
In the quick forge and working-house of thought,
How London doth pour out her citizens!
The mayor and all his brethren in best sort—
Like to the senators of th' antique Rome,
With the plebeians swarming at their heels—
Go forth and fetch their conqu'ring Cæsar in;
As, by a lower but loving likelihood,
Were now the General of our gracious Empress—
As in good time he may—from Ireland coming,
Bringing rebellion broached on his sword,
How many would the peaceful city quit
To welcome him! Much more, and much more cause,
Did they this Harry. Now in London place him—
As yet the lamentation of the French
Invites the King of England's stay at home;

463

The Emperor's coming in behalf of France
To order peace between them; and omit
All the occurrences, whatever chanc'd,
Till Harry's back-return again to France.
There must we bring him; and myself have play'd
The interim, by rememb'ring you 'tis past.
Then brook abridgment; and your eyes advance,
After your thoughts, straight back again to France.   *Exit*

SCENE 1

France. The English camp

Enter FLUELLEN *and* GOWER

GOWER. Nay, that's right; but why wear you your leek to-
day? Saint Davy's day is past.

FLUELLEN. There is occasions and causes why and wherefore
in all things. I will tell you, ass my friend, Captain Gower:
the rascally, scald, beggarly, lousy, pragging knave, Pistol
—which you and yourself and all the world know to be no
petter than a fellow, look you now, of no merits—he is
come to me, and prings me pread and salt yesterday, look
you, and bid me eat my leek; it was in a place where I
could not breed no contention with him; but I will be so
bold as to wear it in my cap till I see him once again, and
then I will tell him a little piece of my desires.

Enter PISTOL

GOWER. Why, here he comes, swelling like a turkey-cock.

FLUELLEN. 'Tis no matter for his swellings nor his turkey-
cocks. God pless you, Aunchient Pistol! you scurvy, lousy
knave, God pless you!

PISTOL. Ha! art thou bedlam? Dost thou thirst, base Troyan,
To have me fold up Parca's fatal web?
Hence! I am qualmish at the smell of leek.

FLUELLEN. I peseech you heartily, scurvy, lousy knave, at
my desires, and my requests, and my petitions, to eat, look
you, this leek; because, look you, you do not love it, nor

your affections, and your appetites, and your digestions,
does not agree with it, I would desire you to eat it.

PISTOL. Not for Cadwallader and all his goats.

FLUELLEN. There is one goat for you. [*Strikes him*] Will
you be so good, scald knave, as eat it?

PISTOL. Base Troyan, thou shalt die.

FLUELLEN. You say very true, scald knave—when God's will
is. I will desire you to live in the meantime, and eat your
victuals; come, there is sauce for it. [*Striking him again*]
You call'd me yesterday mountain-squire; but I will make
you to-day a squire of low degree. I pray you fall to; if
you can mock a leek, you can eat a leek.

GOWER. Enough, Captain, you have astonish'd him.

FLUELLEN. I say I will make him eat some part of my leek,
or I will peat his pate four days. Bite, I pray you, it is
good for your green wound and your ploody coxcomb.

PISTOL. Must I bite?

FLUELLEN. Yes, certainly, and out of doubt, and out of question too, and ambiguities.

PISTOL. By this leek, I will most horribly revenge—I eat and
eat, I swear—

FLUELLEN. Eat, I pray you; will you have some more sauce
to your leek? There is not enough leek to swear by.

PISTOL. Quiet thy cudgel: thou dost see I eat.

FLUELLEN. Much good do you, scald knave, heartily. Nay,
pray you throw none away; the skin is good for your
broken coxcomb. When you take occasions to see leeks
hereafter, I pray you mock at 'em; that is all.

PISTOL. Good.

FLUELLEN. Ay, leeks is good. Hold you, there is a groat to
heal your pate.

PISTOL. Me a groat!

FLUELLEN. Yes, verily and in truth, you shall take it; or
I have another leek in my pocket which you shall eat.

PISTOL. I take thy groat in earnest of revenge.

FLUELLEN. If I owe you anything I will pay you in cudgels;
you shall be a woodmonger, and buy nothing of me but
cudgels. God bye you, and keep you, and heal your pate.

Exit

PISTOL. All hell shall stir for this.

GOWER. Go, go: you are a counterfeit cowardly knave. Will you mock at an ancient tradition, begun upon an honourable respect, and worn as a memorable trophy of predeceased valour, and dare not avouch in your deeds any of your words? I have seen you gleeking and galling at this gentleman twice or thrice. You thought, because he could not speak English in the native garb, he could not therefore handle an English cudgel; you find it otherwise, and henceforth let a Welsh correction teach you a good English condition. Fare ye well. *Exit*

PISTOL. Doth Fortune play the huswife with me now?
News have I that my Nell is dead i' th' spital
Of malady of France;
And there my rendezvous is quite cut off.
Old I do wax; and from my weary limbs
Honour is cudgell'd. Well, bawd I'll turn,
And something lean to cutpurse of quick hand.
To England will I steal, and there I'll steal;
And patches will I get unto these cudgell'd scars,
And swear I got them in the Gallia wars. *Exit*

SCENE 2

France. The FRENCH KING's *palace*

Enter at one door, KING HENRY, EXETER, BEDFORD, GLOUCESTER, WARWICK, WESTMORELAND, *and other* LORDS; *at another, the* FRENCH KING, QUEEN ISABEL, *the* PRINCESS KATHERINE, ALICE, *and other* LADIES; *the* DUKE OF BURGUNDY, *and his train*

KING HENRY. Peace to this meeting, wherefore we are met!
Unto our brother France, and to our sister,
Health and fair time of day; joy and good wishes
To our most fair and princely cousin Katherine.
And, as a branch and member of this royalty,
By whom this great assembly is contriv'd,
We do salute you, Duke of Burgundy.
And, princes French, and peers, health to you all!

FRENCH KING. Right joyous are we to behold your face,

Most worthy brother England; fairly met!
So are you, princes English, every one.
QUEEN ISABEL. So happy be the issue, brother England,
  Of this good day and of this gracious meeting
  As we are now glad to behold your eyes—
  Your eyes, which hitherto have borne in them,
  Against the French that met them in their bent,
  The fatal balls of murdering basilisks;
  The venom of such looks, we fairly hope,
  Have lost their quality; and that this day
  Shall change all griefs and quarrels into love.
KING HENRY. To cry amen to that, thus we appear.
QUEEN ISABEL. You English princes all, I do salute you.
BURGUNDY. My duty to you both, on equal love,
  Great Kings of France and England! That I have labour'd
  With all my wits, my pains, and strong endeavours,
  To bring your most imperial Majesties
  Unto this bar and royal interview,
  Your mightiness on both parts best can witness.
  Since then my office hath so far prevail'd
  That face to face and royal eye to eye
  You have congreeted, let it not disgrace me
  If I demand, before this royal view,
  What rub or what impediment there is
  Why that the naked, poor, and mangled Peace,
  Dear nurse of arts, plenties, and joyful births,
  Should not in this best garden of the world,
  Our fertile France, put up her lovely visage?
  Alas, she hath from France too long been chas'd!
  And all her husbandry doth lie on heaps,
  Corrupting in it own fertility.
  Her vine, the merry cheerer of the heart,
  Unpruned dies; her hedges even-pleach'd,
  Like prisoners wildly overgrown with hair,
  Put forth disorder'd twigs; her fallow leas
  The darnel, hemlock, and rank fumitory,
  Doth root upon, while that the coulter rusts
  That should deracinate such savagery;
  The even mead, that erst brought sweetly forth
  The freckled cowslip, burnet, and green clover,

Wanting the scythe, all uncorrected, rank,
Conceives by idleness, and nothing teems
But hateful docks, rough thistles, kecksies, burs,
Losing both beauty and utility.
And as our vineyards, fallows, meads, and hedges,
Defective in their natures, grow to wildness;
Even so our houses and ourselves and children
Have lost, or do not learn for want of time,
The sciences that should become our country;
But grow, like savages—as soldiers will,
That nothing do but meditate on blood—
To swearing and stern looks, diffus'd attire,
And everything that seems unnatural.
Which to reduce into our former favour
You are assembled; and my speech entreats
That I may know the let why gentle Peace
Should not expel these inconveniences
And bless us with her former qualities.

KING HENRY. If, Duke of Burgundy, you would the peace
Whose want gives growth to th' imperfections
Which you have cited, you must buy that peace
With full accord to all our just demands;
Whose tenours and particular effects
You have, enschedul'd briefly, in your hands.

BURGUNDY. The King hath heard them; to the which as yet
There is no answer made.

KING HENRY. Well then, the peace,
Which you before so urg'd, lies in his answer.

FRENCH KING. I have but with a cursorary eye
O'erglanced the articles; pleaseth your Grace
To appoint some of your council presently
To sit with us once more, with better heed
To re-survey them, we will suddenly
Pass our accept and peremptory answer.

KING HENRY. Brother, we shall. Go, uncle Exeter,
And brother Clarence, and you, brother Gloucester,
Warwick, and Huntington, go with the King;
And take with you free power to ratify,
Augment, or alter, as your wisdoms best
Shall see advantageable for our dignity,

Any thing in or out of our demands;
And we'll consign thereto. Will you, fair sister,
Go with the princes or stay here with us?

QUEEN ISABEL. Our gracious brother, I will go with them;
Haply a woman's voice may do some good,
When articles too nicely urg'd be stood on.

KING HENRY. Yet leave our cousin Katherine here with us;
She is our capital demand, compris'd
Within the fore-rank of our articles.

QUEEN ISABEL. She hath good leave.

Exeunt all but the KING, KATHERINE, *and* ALICE

KING HENRY. Fair Katherine, and most fair,
Will you vouchsafe to teach a soldier terms
Such as will enter at a lady's ear,
And plead his love-suit to her gentle heart?

KATHERINE. Your Majesty shall mock me; I cannot speak
your England.

KING HENRY. O fair Katherine, if you will love me soundly
with your French heart, I will be glad to hear you confess
it brokenly with your English tongue. Do you like me,
Kate?

KATHERINE. Pardonnez-moi, I cannot tell vat is like me.

KING HENRY. An angel is like you, Kate, and you are like an
angel.

KATHERINE. Que dit-il? que je suis semblable à les anges?

ALICE. Oui, vraiment, sauf votre grace, ainsi dit-il.

KING HENRY. I said so, dear Katherine, and I must not blush
to affirm it.

KATHERINE. O bon Dieu! les langues des hommes sont
pleines de tromperies.

KING HENRY. What says she, fair one? that the tongues of
men are full of deceits?

ALICE. Oui, dat de tongues of de mans is be full of deceits—
dat is de Princess.

KING HENRY. The Princess is the better English-woman.
I'faith, Kate, my wooing is fit for thy understanding: I am
glad thou canst speak no better English; for if thou couldst,
thou wouldst find me such a plain king that thou wouldst
think I had sold my farm to buy my crown. I know no
ways to mince it in love, but directly to say 'I love you.'

Then, if you urge me farther than to say 'Do you in faith?' I wear out my suit. Give me your answer; i'faith, do; and so clap hands and a bargain. How say you, lady?

KATHERINE. Sauf votre honneur, me understand well.

KING HENRY. Marry, if you would put me to verses or to dance for your sake, Kate, why you undid me; for the one I have neither words nor measure, and for the other I have no strength in measure, yet a reasonable measure in strength. If I could win a lady at leap-frog, or by vaulting into my saddle with my armour on my back, under the correction of bragging be it spoken, I should quickly leap into a wife. Or if I might buffet for my love, or bound my horse for her favours, I could lay on like a butcher, and sit like a jack-an-apes, never off. But, before God, Kate, I cannot look greenly, nor gasp out my eloquence, nor I have no cunning in protestation; only downright oaths, which I never use till urg'd, nor never break for urging. If thou canst love a fellow of this temper, Kate, whose face is not worth sunburning, that never looks in his glass for love of anything he sees there, let thine eye be thy cook. I speak to thee plain soldier. If thou canst love me for this, take me; if not, to say to thee that I shall die is true—but for thy love, by the Lord, no; yet I love thee too. And while thou liv'st, dear Kate, take a fellow of plain and uncoined constancy; for he perforce must do thee right, because he hath not the gift to woo in other places; for these fellows of infinite tongue, that can rhyme themselves into ladies' favours, they do always reason themselves out again. What! a speaker is but a prater: a rhyme is but a ballad. A good leg will fall; a straight back will stoop; a black beard will turn white; a curl'd pate will grow bald; a fair face will wither; a full eye will wax hollow. But a good heart, Kate, is the sun and the moon; or, rather, the sun, and not the moon—for it shines bright and never changes, but keeps his course truly. If thou would have such a one, take me; and take me, take a soldier; take a soldier, take a king. And what say'st thou, then, to my love? Speak, my fair, and fairly, I pray thee.

KATHERINE. Is it possible dat I sould love de enemy of France?

KING HENRY. No, it is not possible you should love the enemy of France, Kate, but in loving me you should love the friend of France; for I love France so well that I will not part with a village of it; I will have it all mine. And, Kate, when France is mine and I am yours, then yours is France and you are mine.

KATHERINE. I cannot tell vat is dat.

KING HENRY. No, Kate? I will tell thee in French, which I am sure will hang upon my tongue like a new-married wife about her husband's neck, hardly to be shook off. Je quand sur le possession de France, et quand vous avez le possession de moi—let me see, what then? Saint Denis be my speed!— donc votre est France et vous êtes mienne. It is as easy for me, Kate, to conquer the kingdom as to speak so much more French: I shall never move thee in French, unless it be to laugh at me.

KATHERINE. Sauf votre honneur, le Français que vous parlez, il est meilleur que l'Anglais lequel je parle.

KING HENRY. No, faith, is't not, Kate; but thy speaking of my tongue, and I thine, most truly falsely, must needs be granted to be much at one. But, Kate, dost thou understand thus much English—Canst thou love me?

KATHERINE. I cannot tell.

KING HENRY. Can any of your neighbours tell, Kate? I'll ask them. Come, I know thou lovest me; and at night, when you come into your closet, you'll question this gentlewoman about me; and I know, Kate, you will to her dispraise those parts in me that you love with your heart. But, good Kate, mock me mercifully; the rather, gentle Princess, because I love thee cruelly. If ever thou beest mine, Kate, as I have a saving faith within me tells me thou shalt, I get thee with scambling, and thou must therefore needs prove a good soldier-breeder. Shall not thou and I, between Saint Denis and Saint George, compound a boy, half French, half English, that shall go to Constantinople and take the Turk by the beard? Shall we not? What say'st thou, my fair flower-de-luce?

KATHERINE. I do not know dat.

KING HENRY. No: 'tis hereafter to know, but now to promise; do but now promise, Kate, you will endeavour for your

French part of such a boy; and for my English moiety
take the word of a king and a bachelor. How answer you,
la plus belle Katherine du monde, mon tres chèr et divin
déesse?

KATHERINE. Your Majestee ave fausse French enough to deceive de most sage damoiselle dat is en France.

KING HENRY. Now, fie upon my false French! By mine
honour, in true English, I love thee, Kate; by which honour I
dare not swear thou lovest me; yet my blood begins to flatter
me that thou dost, notwithstanding the poor and untempering effect of my visage. Now beshrew my father's
ambition! He was thinking of civil wars when he got me;
therefore was I created with a stubborn outside, with an
aspect of iron, that when I come to woo ladies I fright
them. But, in faith, Kate, the elder I wax, the better I
shall appear: my comfort is, that old age, that ill layer-up
of beauty, can do no more spoil upon my face; thou hast
me, if thou hast me, at the worst; and thou shalt wear me,
if thou wear me, better and better. And therefore tell me,
most fair Katherine, will you have me? Put off your
maiden blushes; avouch the thoughts of your heart with
the looks of an empress; take me by the hand and say
'Harry of England, I am thine.' Which word thou shalt
no sooner bless mine ear withal but I will tell thee aloud
'England is thine, Ireland is thine, France is thine, and
Henry Plantagenet is thine'; who, though I speak it before
his face, if he be not fellow with the best king, thou shalt
find the best king of good fellows. Come, your answer in
broken music—for thy voice is music and thy English
broken; therefore, Queen of all, Katherine, break thy
mind to me in broken English, wilt thou have me?

KATHERINE. Dat is as it shall please de roi mon père.

KING HENRY. Nay, it will please him well, Kate—it shall please
him, Kate.

KATHERINE. Den it sall also content me.

KING HENRY. Upon that I kiss your hand, and I call you my
queen.

KATHERINE. Laissez, mon seigneur, laissez, laissez! Ma foi, je
ne veux point que vous abaissiez votre grandeur en baisant

la main d'une, notre seigneur, indigne serviteur; excusez-moi, je vous supplie, mon très puissant seigneur.

KING HENRY. Then I will kiss your lips, Kate.

KATHERINE. Les dames et demoiselles pour être baisées devant leur noces, il n'est pas la coutume de France.

KING HENRY. Madame my interpreter, what says she?

ALICE. Dat it is not be de fashion pour le ladies of France—I cannot tell vat is baiser en Anglish.

KING HENRY. To kiss.

ALICE. Your Majestee entendre bettre que moi.

KING HENRY. It is not a fashion for the maids in France to kiss before they are married, would she say?

ALICE. Oui, vraiment.

KING HENRY. O Kate, nice customs curtsy to great kings. Dear Kate, you and I cannot be confin'd within the weak list of a country's fashion; we are the makers of manners, Kate; and the liberty that follows our places stops the mouth of all find-faults—as I will do yours for upholding the nice fashion of your country in denying me a kiss; therefore, patiently and yielding. [*Kissing her*] You have witchcraft in your lips, Kate: there is more eloquence in a sugar touch of them than in the tongues of the French council; and they should sooner persuade Henry of England than a general petition of monarchs. Here comes your father.

Enter the FRENCH POWER *and the* ENGLISH LORDS

BURGUNDY. God save your Majesty! My royal cousin,
Teach you our princess English?

KING HENRY. I would have her learn, my fair cousin, how perfectly I love her; and that is good English.

BURGUNDY. Is she not apt?

KING HENRY. Our tongue is rough, coz, and my condition is not smooth; so that, having neither the voice nor the heart of flattery about me, I cannot so conjure up the spirit of love in her that he will appear in his true likeness.

BURGUNDY. Pardon the frankness of my mirth, if I answer you for that. If you would conjure in her, you must make a circle; if conjure up love in her in his true likeness, he must appear naked and blind. Can you blame her, then, being a maid yet ros'd over with the virgin crimson of modesty, if she deny the appearance of a naked blind boy in her naked seeing self? It were, my lord, a hard condition for a maid to consign to.

KING HENRY. Yet they do wink and yield, as love is blind and enforces.

BURGUNDY. They are then excus'd, my lord, when they see not what they do.

KING HENRY. Then, good my lord, teach your cousin to consent winking.

BURGUNDY. I will wink on her to consent, my lord, if you will teach her to know my meaning; for maids well summer'd and warm kept are like flies at Bartholomew-tide, blind, though they have their eyes; and then they will endure handling, which before would not abide looking on.

KING HENRY. This moral ties me over to time and a hot summer; and so I shall catch the fly, your cousin, in the latter end, and she must be blind too.

BURGUNDY. As love is, my lord, before it loves.

KING HENRY. It is so; and you may, some of you, thank love for my blindness, who cannot see many a fair French city for one fair French maid that stands in my way.

FRENCH KING. Yes, my lord, you see them perspectively, the cities turned into a maid; for they are all girdled with maiden walls that war hath never ent'red.

KING HENRY. Shall Kate be my wife?

FRENCH KING. So please you.

KING HENRY. I am content, so the maiden cities you talk of may wait on her; so the maid that stood in the way for my wish shall show me the way to my will.

FRENCH KING. We have consented to all terms of reason.

KING HENRY. Is't so, my lords of England?

WESTMORELAND. The king hath granted every article:
His daughter first; and then in sequel, all,
According to their firm proposed natures.

EXETER. Only he hath not yet subscribed this:
Where your Majesty demands that the King of France, having any occasion to write for matter of grant, shall name your Highness in this form and with this addition, in French, Notre très cher fils Henri, Roi d'Angleterre,

Héritier de France; and thus in Latin, Præclarissimus filius
noster Henricus, Rex Angliæ et Hæres Franciæ.

FRENCH KING. Nor this I have not, brother, so denied
But our request shall make me let it pass.

KING HENRY. I pray you, then, in love and dear alliance,
Let that one article rank with the rest;
And thereupon give me your daughter.

FRENCH KING. Take her, fair son, and from her blood raise
up
Issue to me; that the contending kingdoms
Of France and England, whose very shores look pale
With envy of each other's happiness,
May cease their hatred; and this dear conjunction
Plant neighbourhood and Christian-like accord
In their sweet bosoms, that never war advance
His bleeding sword 'twixt England and fair France.

LORDS. Amen!

KING HENRY. Now, welcome, Kate; and bear me witness all,
That here I kiss her as my sovereign queen.   [Flourish]

QUEEN ISABEL. God, the best maker of all marriages,
Combine your hearts in one, your realms in one!
As man and wife, being two, are one in love,
So be there 'twixt your kingdoms such a spousal
That never may ill office or fell jealousy,
Which troubles oft the bed of blessed marriage,
Thrust in between the paction of these kingdoms,
To make divorce of their incorporate league;
That English may as French, French Englishmen,
Receive each other. God speak this Amen!

ALL. Amen!

KING HENRY. Prepare we for our marriage; on which day,
My Lord of Burgundy, we'll take your oath,
And all the peers', for surety of our leagues.
Then shall I swear to Kate, and you to me,
And may our oaths well kept and prosp'rous be!

Sennet. Exeunt

KING HENRY V

EPILOGUE

Enter CHORUS

CHORUS. Thus far, with rough and all-unable pen,
Our bending author hath pursu'd the story,
In little room confining mighty men,
Mangling by starts the full course of their glory.
Small time, but, in that small, most greatly lived
This star of England. Fortune made his sword;
By which the world's best garden he achieved,
And of it left his son imperial lord.
Henry the Sixth, in infant bands crown'd king
Of France and England, did this king succeed;
Whose state so many had the managing
That they lost France and made his England bleed;
Which oft our stage hath shown; and, for their sake,
In your fair minds let this acceptance take.   *Exit*

The First Part of
King Henry the Sixth

THE FIRST PART OF
KING HENRY THE SIXTH

THE notion that Shakespeare may well have begun as an improver of the work of others must rest entirely on the evidence we can extract from the plays themselves, not on any assumptions about the state of Shakespeare's education when he came to London. The evidence must further be interpreted in light of what we know of the characteristics of genius; but as genius is always an extraordinary phenomenon conjecture has a latitude difficult to determine.

Turning to examine the evidence provided by the three parts of *Henry VI*, we find that at the close of the eighteenth century the earlier view that Shakespeare began by revising plays by other men seems confirmed in the most scholarly manner by the work of Malone. This distinguished scholar proved to the satisfaction of all but a very few of his contemporaries who were interested in such matters that the second and third parts of this play were built almost scene by scene on the earlier work of Greene, or Peele, or possibly Marlowe, as Malone later thought. This established, it was inevitable that the first part should be relegated to the same class of compositions; in this instance the original work had not been preserved as it had been, in Malone's opinion, for the two later parts, but the first part seemed on the face of it even less the unalloyed metal of Shakespeare's craft than the other two. If it were indeed proved that the second and third parts of *Henry VI* were not wholly Shakespeare's, the first part would have also to be regarded as in large part from another hand.

The evidence concerning the authorship of the second and third parts must be held over for examination in the discussion that is prefixed to these pieces. Meantime we must ask what may be conjectured about the authorship of 1 *Henry VI*.

What scholars generally accept as the first reference in

print to Shakespeare's 1 *Henry VI* stands in a work entitled *Pierce Penilesse His Supplication to the Devil*, published in London about September 1592. The author Thomas
Nashe was a graduate of Cambridge who came to town to
make his way as a man of letters and gained a reputation as
a wit and satirist and a writer of controversial pamphlets.
In his *Pierce Penilesse*, which is ostensibly a satire on avarice
and other deadly sins, Nashe finds occasion to drag in any
topic that seems for the moment to interest him. In the sec-
tion on Sloth he takes the opportunity of saying something
in favour of the theatres:

> the pollicie of Playes is very necessary, howsoever some
> shallow-braind censurers (not the deepest serchers into the
> secrets of government) mightily oppugne them. For
> whereas the afternoone being the idlest time of the day;
> wherein men that are their owne masters (as Gentlemen
> of the Court, the Innes of the Courte, and the number of
> Captaines and Souldiers about *London*) do wholy bestow
> themselves upon pleasure, and that pleasure they devide
> (how vertuously it skils not) either into gameing, follow-
> ing of harlots, drinking, or seeing a Playe: is it not then
> better (since of foure extreames all the world cannot keepe
> them but they will choose one) that they should betake
> them to the least, which is Playes?

This may seem a strange sort of commendation to bestow on
the theatre, but Nashe has to link up the topic somehow with
his discourse on the Vices; having, however, established some
sort of excuse for the transition he quickly changes his tune
and continues:

> Nay, what if I proove Playes to be no extreame; but a
> rare exercise of vertue? First, for the subject of them (for
> the most part) it is borrowed out of our English Chron-
> icles, wherein our forefathers valiant acts (that have live
> long buried in rustie brasse and worme-eaten bookes) are
> revived, and they themselves raised from the Grave of
> Oblivion, and brought to pleade their aged Honours in
> open presence: than which, what can be a sharper reproofe
> to these degenerate effeminate dayes of ours?

INTRODUCTION

How would it have joyed brave *Talbot* (the Terror of the French) to thinke that after he had lyne two hundred yeares in his Tombe, hee should triumphe againe on the Stage, and have his bones newe embalmed with the teares of ten thousand spectators at least (at severall times), who, in the Tragedian that represents his person, imagine they behold him fresh bleeding.

That Nashe is here referring to the play we now know as the first part of *Henry VI* seems very probable; and if the play on Henry the Sixth performed at the Rose in the spring of 1592 was Shakespeare's the reference could be taken as certain.

The Rose was a theatre on the south bank of the river built and owned by Philip Henslowe. Henslowe was not himself an actor or dramatist but a financier who saw there was money in the theatre and hired his building to companies at an agreed rate. Some of his Diaries, which are for the most part a record of his financial dealings, are still extant; and one set of entries covers the period from 19 February to 22 June, 1592 when Lord Strange's company occupied the Rose. On 3 March they performed a piece described in the Diary as 'Harry the VI' and Henslowe's share of the takings amounted to £3.16.8. Henslowe had, scholars agree, half the takings from the galleries; and the sum taken by Henslowe on this occasion, it is calculated, represents a full house. During their stay at the Rose Strange's company performed *Henry VI* fourteen times, almost always to good houses. The play was exceptionally popular.

Although Strange's company were occupying the Rose in 1592, Henslowe had other theatrical connections, for he was associated with Edward Alleyn, who was to marry his step-daughter Joan Woodward in October 1592. Alleyn was himself as a player the servant of the Lord Admiral but from about 1590 the companies were in a state of flux, and during the Strange season at the Rose Alleyn was acting with them. The repertory was drawn from plays owned by the Admiral's as well as by Strange's men. That *Henry VI* belonged to Strange's men seems indicated by its absence from Henslowe's entries after Strange's men left the Rose.

That the play was newly written for or newly acquired by Strange's men is indicated by the mark "ne" which Henslowe put against plays in these two categories. As what are now known as the second and third parts of *Henry VI* were, as Greene's attack on Shakespeare proves, on the stage by 22 June, and as Henslowe's entries almost certainly refer to the first part only, we have to explain, if possible, why the parts were in the hands of rival companies. Various guesses have been offered to explain this fact, for the circumstances in which the various companies found themselves at this time are obviously so complicated and so scantily documented that only guesses are possible. The guess now advanced is that Shakespeare wrote the second and third parts of *Henry VI* for Pembroke's men and that Strange's men acquired the Talbot play which Shakespeare had written before he joined Pembroke's men and that its revival was so successful because of the success of the second and third parts and the growing recognition of Shakespeare's powers as a dramatist. Strange's men would acquire their part not from Shakespeare himself but from the company for which he originally wrote it. As Shakespeare joined Strange's men when they became the Chamberlain's men the three parts were reunited, and the Talbot play was then adapted as the first part of the trilogy.

Professor Dover Wilson takes a very different view of the possibilities. He holds that Greene and Nashe, with Peele's help perhaps, wrote what we regard as the second and third parts of *Henry VI* and sold them to Pembroke's men; Shakespeare then revised both parts drastically for stage-production. Greene and Nashe then devised what is now the first part, but resenting Shakespeare's interference with their earlier versions now sold their new play to Strange's men. Here again, however, Shakespeare, although working and presumably acting with a rival company, was called in to give the work some finishing touches.

Professor Dover Wilson's story, it must be said, does not seem a likely one; our information, however, about the theatre world at the time is too imperfect to permit us to say that the actor and reviser who was working for Pembroke's men would not have been invited to revise or finish a new

play for Strange's company. The first part of *Henry VI,*
however, does seem an earlier and somewhat more primitive
piece than the succeeding parts; and in spite of the details
with which Professor Dover Wilson supports his contention
that it must have been composed after and not before 2 and
3 *Henry VI* the possibility that it was an earlier piece by
Shakespeare acquired in 1592 by Strange's men cannot be
ruled out. Henslowe's mark 'ne' was at times attached to
plays that had newly come into the repertory of the company performing at the Rose, although they had been earlier
staged elsewhere by another group of players; further
1 *Henry VI* itself though primitive when compared with
Shakespeare's later work does have about it something that
may be regarded as Shakespearean.

The peculiarly Shakespearean feature in 1 *Henry VI* is
what may be called its construction. This has been well
emphasized in his paper on *Construction in Shakespeare* by
Professor Hereward T. Price. Speaking of the opening scene
he observes:

> The scene appears to be simple, and it certainly has none
> of the profundity which Shakespeare was able to put into
> a play later on. But it does everything a first scene should
> do, it gives the situation: Henry the Fifth is dead, Henry
> the Sixth is a baby; the nobles are ready to fly at one an-
> other's throats, and each does what is right in his own
> eyes; Talbot is introduced, and his importance stressed; the
> treachery that is to strike him down and to cause the loss
> of France is foreshadowed. . . . Here is a scene full of
> matter and incident, condensed, swift, and clear, imposing
> as a stage spectacle, presenting the principal characters on
> the English side and introducing the principal motifs of the
> play, leading up to an important climax that suggests what
> the whole play is to be about—here Shakespeare shows that
> he is already a master of construction.

The next scene is at the French court and this provides the
contrast required to emphasize the theme of England's lack
of unity; here we have the new hope that gives unity to the
French counter-action. So throughout the play scene by
scene can be traced the main motifs of the play contrasted

and intertwined in ways that point to the careful planning on the dramatist's part.

The Suffolk-Margaret scenes have the appearance of insertions made to link this part with those written later. Even when writing 1 *Henry VI* Shakespeare may have had in mind the possibility of a sequel, although when he came to the actual writing of the second part he may have found it advisable to arrange his matter in a way that made some additions to the Talbot play necessary if the continuity was to be maintained.

The suggestion is, therefore, that 1 *Henry VI* is an early play by Shakespeare in which Talbot was the central figure. In construction and in the motifs developed the play shows features that are highly characteristic of Shakespeare's later work; nor are these features to be paralleled in the work of Greene, Nashe, or Peele. It seems most hazardous on the evidence of what may be regarded as accidental features that can be explained in various ways to suppose that Shakespeare was revising for two different companies work by Greene and Nashe. Could it be shown, however, that there was good evidence in the second and third parts of *Henry VI* that they were originally by Greene and Nashe the reasons so far given for regarding 1 *Henry VI* as an early work by Shakespeare would be open to serious criticism. One must turn, therefore, to an examination of 2 and 3 *Henry VI*, for the problem of the authorship of any one part cannot be separated from that of the others.

King Henry the Sixth

Duke of Gloucester, *uncle to the King, and Protector*

Duke of Bedford, *uncle to the King, and Regent of France*

Thomas Beaufort, Duke of Exeter, *great-uncle to the King*

Henry Beaufort, *great-uncle to the King,* Bishop of Winchester, *and afterwards* Cardinal

John Beaufort, Earl of Somerset, *afterwards Duke*

Richard Plantagenet, *son of Richard late Earl of Cambridge, afterwards* Duke of York

Earl of Warwick   Earl of Salisbury   Earl of Suffolk

Lord Talbot, *afterwards* Earl of Shrewsbury

John Talbot, *his son*

Edmund Mortimer, Earl of March

Sir John Fastolfe   Sir William Lucy

Sir William Glansdale   Sir Thomas Gargrave

Mayor of London

Woodville, *Lieutenant of the Tower*

Vernon, *of the White Rose or York faction*

Basset, *of the Red Rose or Lancaster faction*

A Lawyer   Gaolers, *to Mortimer*

Charles, *Dauphin, and afterwards King of France*

Reignier, Duke of Anjou, *and titular King of Naples*

Duke of Burgundy   Duke of Alençon

Bastard of Orleans   Governor of Paris

Master-Gunner of Orleans, *and his* Son

General of the French Forces *in Bordeaux*

A French Sergeant   A Porter

An Old Shepherd, *father to Joan la Pucelle*

Margaret, *daughter to Reignier, afterwards married to King Henry*   Countess of Auvergne

Joan la Pucelle, *commonly called* Joan of Arc

Lords, Warders of the Tower, Heralds, Officers, Soldiers, Messengers, English *and* French Attendants. Fiends *appearing to La Pucelle*

SCENE:

England and France

The First Part of
King Henry the Sixth

ACT I. SCENE 1

Westminster Abbey

Dead March. Enter the funeral of KING HENRY THE
FIFTH, *attended on by the* DUKE OF BEDFORD, *Regent of France, the* DUKE OF GLOUCESTER, *Protector, the* DUKE OF EXETER, *the* EARL OF WARWICK,
the BISHOP OF WINCHESTER

BEDFORD. Hung be the heavens with black, yield day to
　　night!
　Comets, importing change of times and states,
　Brandish your crystal tresses in the sky
　And with them scourge the bad revolting stars
　That have consented unto Henry's death!
　King Henry the Fifth, too famous to live long!
　England ne'er lost a king of so much worth.
GLOUCESTER. England ne'er had a king until his time.
　Virtue he had, deserving to command;
　His brandish'd sword did blind men with his beams;
　His arms spread wider than a dragon's wings;
　His sparkling eyes, replete with wrathful fire,
　More dazzled and drove back his enemies
　Than mid-day sun fierce bent against their faces.
　What should I say? His deeds exceed all speech:
　He ne'er lift up his hand but conquered.
EXETER. We mourn in black; why mourn we not in blood?
　Henry is dead and never shall revive.
　Upon a wooden coffin we attend;
　And death's dishonourable victory
　We with our stately presence glorify,
　Like captives bound to a triumphant car.

What! shall we curse the planets of mishap
That plotted thus our glory's overthrow?
Or shall we think the subtle-witted French
Conjurers and sorcerers, that, afraid of him,
By magic verses have contriv'd his end?
WINCHESTER. He was a king bless'd of the King of kings;
Unto the French the dreadful judgment-day
So dreadful will not be as was his sight.
The battles of the Lord of Hosts he fought;
The Church's prayers made him so prosperous.
GLOUCESTER. The Church! Where is it? Had not churchmen
  pray'd,
His thread of life had not so soon decay'd.
None do you like but an effeminate prince,
Whom like a school-boy you may overawe.
WINCHESTER. Gloucester, whate'er we like, thou art
  Protector
And lookest to command the Prince and realm.
Thy wife is proud; she holdeth thee in awe
More than God or religious churchmen may.
GLOUCESTER. Name not religion, for thou lov'st the flesh;
And ne'er throughout the year to church thou go'st,
Except it be to pray against thy foes.
BEDFORD. Cease, cease these jars and rest your minds in peace;
Let's to the altar. Heralds, wait on us.
Instead of gold, we'll offer up our arms,
Since arms avail not, now that Henry's dead.
Posterity, await for wretched years,
When at their mothers' moist'ned eyes babes shall suck,
Our isle be made a nourish of salt tears,
And none but women left to wail the dead.
Henry the Fifth, thy ghost I invocate:
Prosper this realm, keep it from civil broils,
Combat with adverse planets in the heavens.
A far more glorious star thy soul will make
Than Julius Cæsar or bright—

Enter a MESSENGER

MESSENGER. My honourable lords, health to you all!
Sad tidings bring I to you out of France,

Of loss, of slaughter, and discomfiture:
Guienne, Champagne, Rheims, Orleans,
Paris, Guysors, Poictiers, are all quite lost.
BEDFORD. What say'st thou, man, before dead Henry's corse?
　Speak softly, or the loss of those great towns
　Will make him burst his lead and rise from death.
GLOUCESTER. Is Paris lost? Is Rouen yielded up?
　If Henry were recall'd to life again,
　These news would cause him once more yield the ghost.
EXETER. How were they lost? What treachery was us'd?
MESSENGER. No treachery, but want of men and money.
　Amongst the soldiers this is muttered—
　That here you maintain several factions;
　And whilst a field should be dispatch'd and fought,
　You are disputing of your generals:
　One would have ling'ring wars, with little cost;
　Another would fly swift, but wanteth wings;
　A third thinks, without expense at all,
　By guileful fair words peace may be obtain'd.
　Awake, awake, English nobility!
　Let not sloth dim your honours, new-begot.
　Cropp'd are the flower-de-luces in your arms;
　Of England's coat one half is cut away.
EXETER. Were our tears wanting to this funeral,
　These tidings would call forth their flowing tides.
BEDFORD. Me they concern; Regent I am of France.
　Give me my steeled coat; I'll fight for France.
　Away with these disgraceful wailing robes!
　Wounds will I lend the French instead of eyes,
　To weep their intermissive miseries.

Enter a second MESSENGER

SECOND MESSENGER. Lords, view these letters full of bad
　mischance.
　France is revolted from the English quite,
　Except some petty towns of no import.
　The Dauphin Charles is crowned king in Rheims;
　The Bastard of Orleans with him is join'd;
　Reignier, Duke of Anjou, doth take his part;
　The Duke of Alençon flieth to his side.

EXETER. The Dauphin crowned king! all fly to him!
O, whither shall we fly from this reproach?
GLOUCESTER. We will not fly but to our enemies' throats.
Bedford, if thou be slack I'll fight it out.
BEDFORD. Gloucester, why doubt'st thou of my forwardness?
An army have I muster'd in my thoughts,
Wherewith already France is overrun.

Enter a third MESSENGER

THIRD MESSENGER. My gracious lords, to add to your
laments,
Wherewith you now bedew King Henry's hearse,
I must inform you of a dismal fight
Betwixt the stout Lord Talbot and the French.
WINCHESTER. What! Wherein Talbot overcame? Is't so?
THIRD MESSENGER. O, no; wherein Lord Talbot was
o'erthrown.
The circumstance I'll tell you more at large.
The tenth of August last this dreadful lord,
Retiring from the siege of Orleans,
Having full scarce six thousand in his troop,
By three and twenty thousand of the French
Was round encompassed and set upon.
No leisure had he to enrank his men;
He wanted pikes to set before his archers;
Instead whereof sharp stakes pluck'd out of hedges
They pitched in the ground confusedly
To keep the horsemen off from breaking in.
More than three hours the fight continued;
Where valiant Talbot, above human thought,
Enacted wonders with his sword and lance:
Hundreds he sent to hell, and none durst stand him;
Here, there, and everywhere, enrag'd he slew—
The French exclaim'd the devil was in arms;
All the whole army stood agaz'd on him.
His soldiers, spying his undaunted spirit,
'A Talbot! a Talbot!' cried out amain,
And rush'd into the bowels of the battle.
Here had the conquest fully been seal'd up
If Sir John Fastolfe had not play'd the coward.

He, being in the vaward—plac'd behind
With purpose to relieve and follow them—
Cowardly fled, not having struck one stroke;
Hence grew the general wreck and massacre.
Enclosed were they with their enemies.
A base Walloon, to win the Dauphin's grace,
Thrust Talbot with a spear into the back;
Whom all France, with their chief assembled strength,
Durst not presume to look once in the face.
BEDFORD. Is Talbot slain? Then I will slay myself,
For living idly here in pomp and ease,
Whilst such a worthy leader, wanting aid,
Unto his dastard foemen is betray'd.
THIRD MESSENGER. O no, he lives, but is took prisoner,
And Lord Scales with him, and Lord Hungerford;
Most of the rest slaughter'd or took likewise.
BEDFORD. His ransom there is none but I shall pay.
I'll hale the Dauphin headlong from his throne;
His crown shall be the ransom of my friend;
Four of their lords I'll change for one of ours.
Farewell, my masters; to my task will I;
Bonfires in France forthwith I am to make
To keep our great Saint George's feast withal.
Ten thousand soldiers with me I will take,
Whose bloody deeds shall make all Europe quake.
THIRD MESSENGER. So you had need; for Orleans is besieg'd;
The English army is grown weak and faint;
The Earl of Salisbury craveth supply
And hardly keeps his men from mutiny,
Since they, so few, watch such a multitude.
EXETER. Remember, lords, your oaths to Henry sworn,
Either to quell the Dauphin utterly,
Or bring him in obedience to your yoke.
BEDFORD. I do remember it, and here take my leave
To go about my preparation.   *Exit*
GLOUCESTER. I'll to the Tower with all the haste I can
To view th' artillery and munition;
And then I will proclaim young Henry king.   *Exit*
EXETER. To Eltham will I, where the young King is,
Being ordain'd his special governor;

And for his safety there I'll best devise.   *Exit*
WINCHESTER. [*Aside*] Each hath his place and function to
    attend:
I am left out; for me nothing remains.
But long I will not be Jack out of office.
The King from Eltham I intend to steal,
And sit at chiefest stern of public weal.   *Exeunt*

SCENE 2

France. Before Orleans

Sound a flourish. Enter CHARLES THE DAUPHIN, ALENÇON,
and REIGNIER, *marching with drum and soldiers*

CHARLES. Mars his true moving, even as in the heavens
So in the earth, to this day is not known.
Late did he shine upon the English side;
Now we are victors, upon us he smiles.
What towns of any moment but we have?
At pleasure here we lie near Orleans;
Otherwhiles the famish'd English, like pale ghosts,
Faintly besiege us one hour in a month.
ALENÇON. They want their porridge and their fat bull-
beeves.
Either they must be dieted like mules
And have their provender tied to their mouths,
Or piteous they will look, like drowned mice.
REIGNIER. Let's raise the siege. Why live we idly here?
Talbot is taken, whom we wont to fear;
Remaineth none but mad-brain'd Salisbury,
And he may well in fretting spend his gall—
Nor men nor money hath he to make war.
CHARLES. Sound, sound alarum; we will rush on them.
Now for the honour of the forlorn French!
Him I forgive my death that killeth me,
When he sees me go back one foot or flee.   *Exeunt*

Here alarum. They are beaten back by the English, with
great loss. Re-enter CHARLES, ALENÇON, *and* REIGNIER

CHARLES. Who ever saw the like? What men have I!
  Dogs! cowards! dastards! I would ne'er have fled
  But that they left me midst my enemies.
REIGNIER. Salisbury is a desperate homicide;
  He fighteth as one weary of his life.
  The other lords, like lions wanting food,
  Do rush upon us as their hungry prey.
ALENÇON. Froissart, a countryman of ours, records
  England all Olivers and Rowlands bred
  During the time Edward the Third did reign.
  More truly now may this be verified;
  For none but Samsons and Goliases
  It sendeth forth to skirmish. One to ten!
  Lean raw-bon'd rascals! Who would e'er suppose
  They had such courage and audacity?
CHARLES. Let's leave this town; for they are hare-brain'd
  slaves,
  And hunger will enforce them to be more eager.
  Of old I know them; rather with their teeth
  The walls they'll tear down than forsake the siege.
REIGNIER. I think by some odd gimmers or device
  Their arms are set, like clocks, still to strike on;
  Else ne'er could they hold out so as they do.
  By my consent, we'll even let them alone.
ALENÇON. Be it so.

Enter the BASTARD OF ORLEANS

BASTARD. Where's the Prince Dauphin? I have news for him.
CHARLES. Bastard of Orleans, thrice welcome to us.
BASTARD. Methinks your looks are sad, your cheer appall'd.
  Hath the late overthrow wrought this offence?
  Be not dismay'd, for succour is at hand.
  A holy maid hither with me I bring,
  Which, by a vision sent to her from heaven,
  Ordained is to raise this tedious siege
  And drive the English forth the bounds of France.
  The spirit of deep prophecy she hath,
  Exceeding the nine sibyls of old Rome:
  What's past and what's to come she can descry.
  Speak, shall I call her in? Believe my words,

For they are certain and unfallible.

CHARLES. Go, call her in. [*Exit* BASTARD] But first, to try
   her skill,
Reignier, stand thou as Dauphin in my place;
Question her proudly; let thy looks be stern;
By this means shall we sound what skill she hath.

Re-enter the BASTARD OF ORLEANS, *with*
JOAN LA PUCELLE

REIGNIER. Fair maid, is 't thou wilt do these wondrous feats?
PUCELLE. Reignier, is 't thou that thinkest to beguile me?
   Where is the Dauphin? Come, come from behind;
   I know thee well, though never seen before.
   Be not amaz'd, there's nothing hid from me.
   In private will I talk with thee apart.
   Stand back, you lords, and give us leave awhile.
REIGNIER. She takes upon her bravely at first dash.
PUCELLE. Dauphin, I am by birth a shepherd's daughter,
   My wit untrain'd in any kind of art.
   Heaven and our Lady gracious hath it pleas'd
   To shine on my contemptible estate.
   Lo, whilst I waited on my tender lambs
   And to sun's parching heat display'd my cheeks,
   God's Mother deigned to appear to me,
   And in a vision full of majesty
   Will'd me to leave my base vocation
   And free my country from calamity—
   Her aid she promis'd and assur'd success.
   In complete glory she reveal'd herself;
   And whereas I was black and swart before,
   With those clear rays which she infus'd on me
   That beauty am I bless'd with which you may see.
   Ask me what question thou canst possible,
   And I will answer unpremeditated.
   My courage try by combat if thou dar'st,
   And thou shalt find that I exceed my sex.
   Resolve on this: thou shalt be fortunate
   If thou receive me for thy warlike mate.
CHARLES. Thou hast astonish'd me with thy high terms.
   Only this proof I'll of thy valour make—

In single combat thou shalt buckle with me;
And if thou vanquishest, thy words are true;
Otherwise I renounce all confidence.

PUCELLE. I am prepar'd; here is my keen-edg'd sword,
Deck'd with five flower-de-luces on each side,
The which at Touraine, in Saint Katherine's churchyard,
Out of a great deal of old iron I chose forth.

CHARLES. Then come, o' God's name; I fear no woman.

PUCELLE. And while I live I'll ne'er fly from a man.

[*Here they fight and* JOAN LA PUCELLE *overcomes*]

CHARLES. Stay, stay thy hands; thou art an Amazon,
And fightest with the sword of Deborah.

PUCELLE. Christ's Mother helps me, else I were too weak.

CHARLES. Whoe'er helps thee, 'tis thou that must help me.
Impatiently I burn with thy desire;
My heart and hands thou hast at once subdu'd.
Excellent Pucelle, if thy name be so,
Let me thy servant and not sovereign be.
'Tis the French Dauphin sueth to thee thus.

PUCELLE. I must not yield to any rites of love,
For my profession's sacred from above.
When I have chased all thy foes from hence,
Then will I think upon a recompense.

CHARLES. Meantime look gracious on thy prostrate thrall.

REIGNIER. My lord, methinks, is very long in talk.

ALENÇON. Doubtless he shrives this woman to her smock;
Else ne'er could he so long protract his speech.

REIGNIER. Shall we disturb him, since he keeps no mean?

ALENÇON. He may mean more than we poor men do know;
These women are shrewd tempters with their tongues.

REIGNIER. My lord, where are you? What devise you on?
Shall we give o'er Orleans, or no?

PUCELLE. Why, no, I say; distrustful recreants!
Fight till the last gasp; I will be your guard.

CHARLES. What she says I'll confirm; we'll fight it out.

PUCELLE. Assign'd am I to be the English scourge.
This night the siege assuredly I'll raise.
Expect Saint Martin's summer, halcyon days,
Since I have entered into these wars.
Glory is like a circle in the water,

Which never ceaseth to enlarge itself
Till by broad spreading it disperse to nought.
With Henry's death the English circle ends;
Dispersed are the glories it included.
Now am I like that proud insulting ship
Which Cæsar and his fortune bare at once.
CHARLES. Was Mahomet inspired with a dove?
Thou with an eagle art inspired then.
Helen, the mother of great Constantine,
Nor yet Saint Philip's daughters were like thee.
Bright star of Venus, fall'n down on the earth,
How may I reverently worship thee enough?
ALENÇON. Leave off delays, and let us raise the siege.
REIGNIER. Woman, do what thou canst to save our honours;
Drive them from Orleans, and be immortaliz'd.
CHARLES. Presently we'll try. Come, let's away about it.
No prophet will I trust if she prove false.   *Exeunt*

SCENE 3

London. Before the Tower gates

Enter the DUKE OF GLOUCESTER, *with his serving-men
in blue coats*

GLOUCESTER. I am come to survey the Tower this day;
Since Henry's death, I fear, there is conveyance.
Where be these warders that they wait not here?
Open the gates; 'tis Gloucester that calls.
FIRST WARDER. [*Within*] Who's there that knocks so im-
periously?
FIRST SERVING-MAN. It is the noble Duke of Gloucester.
SECOND WARDER. [*Within*] Whoe'er he be, you may not be
let in.
FIRST SERVING-MAN. Villains, answer you so the Lord
Protector?
FIRST WARDER. [*Within*] The Lord protect him! so we
answer him.
We do no otherwise than we are will'd.

GLOUCESTER. Who willed you, or whose will stands but
　mine?
There's none Protector of the realm but I.
Break up the gates, I'll be your warrantize.
Shall I be flouted thus by dunghill grooms?
　　　　　[GLOUCESTER's *men rush at the Tower gates, and*
　　　　　　　WOODVILLE *the Lieutenant speaks within*]
WOODVILLE. [*Within*] What noise is this? What traitors
　have we here?
GLOUCESTER. Lieutenant, is it you whose voice I hear?
Open the gates; here's Gloucester that would enter.
WOODVILLE. [*Within*] Have patience, noble Duke, I may
　not open;
The Cardinal of Winchester forbids.
From him I have express commandment
That thou nor none of thine shall be let in.
GLOUCESTER. Faint-hearted Woodville, prizest him fore me?
Arrogant Winchester, that haughty prelate
Whom Henry, our late sovereign, ne'er could brook!
Thou art no friend to God or to the King.
Open the gates, or I'll shut thee out shortly.
SERVING-MEN. Open the gates unto the Lord Protector,
Or we'll burst them open, if that you come not quickly.

Enter to the PROTECTOR *at the Tower gates* WINCHESTER
and his men in tawny coats

WINCHESTER. How now, ambitious Humphry! What means
　this?
GLOUCESTER. Peel'd priest, dost thou command me to be
　shut out?
WINCHESTER. I do, thou most usurping proditor,
And not Protector of the King or realm.
GLOUCESTER. Stand back, thou manifest conspirator,
Thou that contrived'st to murder our dead lord;
Thou that giv'st whores indulgences to sin.
I'll canvass thee in thy broad cardinal's hat,
If thou proceed in this thy insolence.
WINCHESTER. Nay, stand thou back; I will not budge a foot.
This be Damascus; be thou cursed Cain,
To slay thy brother Abel, if thou wilt.

499

GLOUCESTER. I will not slay thee, but I'll drive thee back.
Thy scarlet robes as a child's bearing-cloth
I'll use to carry thee out of this place.
WINCHESTER. Do what thou dar'st; I beard thee to thy face.
GLOUCESTER. What! am I dar'd and bearded to my face?
Draw, men, for all this privileged place—
Blue-coats to tawny-coats. Priest, beware your beard;
I mean to tug it, and to cuff you soundly;
Under my feet I stamp thy cardinal's hat;
In spite of Pope or dignities of church,
Here by the cheeks I'll drag thee up and down.
WINCHESTER. Gloucester, thou wilt answer this before the
Pope.
GLOUCESTER. Winchester goose! I cry 'A rope, a rope!'
Now beat them hence; why do you let them stay?
Thee I'll chase hence, thou wolf in sheep's array.
Out, tawny-coats! Out, scarlet hypocrite!

Here GLOUCESTER'S *men beat out the* CARDINAL'S
men; and enter in the hurly-burly the MAYOR OF
LONDON *and his* OFFICERS

MAYOR. Fie, lords! that you, being supreme magistrates,
Thus contumeliously should break the peace!
GLOUCESTER. Peace, Mayor! thou know'st little of my wrongs:
Here's Beaufort, that regards nor God nor King,
Hath here distrain'd the Tower to his use.
WINCHESTER. Here's Gloucester, a foe to citizens;
One that still motions war and never peace,
O'ercharging your free purses with large fines;
That seeks to overthrow religion,
Because he is Protector of the realm,
And would have armour here out of the Tower,
To crown himself King and suppress the Prince.
GLOUCESTER. I will not answer thee with words, but blows.
[*Here they skirmish again*]
MAYOR. Nought rests for me in this tumultuous strife
But to make open proclamation.
Come, officer, as loud as e'er thou canst,
Cry.
OFFICER. [*Cries*] All manner of men assembled here in arms

this day against God's peace and the King's, we charge
and command you, in his Highness' name, to repair to
your several dwelling-places; and not to wear, handle, or
use, any sword, weapon, or dagger, henceforward, upon
pain of death.
GLOUCESTER. Cardinal, I'll be no breaker of the law;
But we shall meet and break our minds at large.
WINCHESTER. Gloucester, we'll meet to thy cost, be sure;
Thy heart-blood I will have for this day's work.
MAYOR. I'll call for clubs if you will not away.
This Cardinal's more haughty than the devil.
GLOUCESTER. Mayor, farewell; thou dost but what thou
    mayst.
WINCHESTER. Abominable Gloucester, guard thy head,
For I intend to have it ere long.
          Exeunt, severally, GLOUCESTER *and* WINCHESTER
                                with their servants
MAYOR. See the coast clear'd, and then we will depart.
Good God, these nobles should such stomachs bear!
I myself fight not once in forty year.   *Exeunt*

SCENE 4

France. Before Orleans

Enter, on the walls, the MASTER-GUNNER
OF ORLEANS *and his* BOY

MASTER-GUNNER. Sirrah, thou know'st how Orleans is
    besieg'd,
And how the English have the suburbs won.
BOY. Father, I know; and oft have shot at them,
Howe'er unfortunate I miss'd my aim.
MASTER-GUNNER. But now thou shalt not. Be thou rul'd
    by me.
Chief master-gunner am I of this town;
Something I must do to procure me grace.
The Prince's espials have informed me
How the English, in the suburbs close intrench'd,
Wont, through a secret grate of iron bars

In yonder tower, to overpeer the city,
And thence discover how with most advantage
They may vex us with shot or with assault.
To intercept this inconvenience,
A piece of ordnance 'gainst it I have plac'd;
And even these three days have I watch'd
If I could see them. Now do thou watch,
For I can stay no longer.
If thou spy'st any, run and bring me word;
And thou shalt find me at the Governor's.   *Exit*
Boy. Father, I warrant you; take you no care;
I'll never trouble you, if I may spy them.   *Exit*

> *Enter* Salisbury *and* Talbot *on the turrets, with*
> Sir William Glansdale, Sir Thomas Gargrave,
> *and others*

Salisbury. Talbot, my life, my joy, again return'd!
How wert thou handled being prisoner?
Or by what means got'st thou to be releas'd?
Discourse, I prithee, on this turret's top.
Talbot. The Earl of Bedford had a prisoner
Call'd the brave Lord Ponton de Santrailles;
For him was I exchang'd and ransomed.
But with a baser man of arms by far
Once, in contempt, they would have barter'd me;
Which I disdaining scorn'd, and craved death
Rather than I would be so vile esteem'd.
In fine, redeem'd I was as I desir'd.
But, O! the treacherous Fastolfe wounds my heart
Whom with my bare fists I would execute,
If I now had him brought into my power.
Salisbury. Yet tell'st thou not how thou wert entertain'd.
Talbot. With scoffs, and scorns, and contumelious taunts,
In open market-place produc'd they me
To be a public spectacle to all;
Here, said they, is the terror of the French,
The scarecrow that affrights our children so.
Then broke I from the officers that led me,
And with my nails digg'd stones out of the ground
To hurl at the beholders of my shame;

My grisly countenance made others fly;
None durst come near for fear of sudden death.
In iron walls they deem'd me not secure;
So great fear of my name 'mongst them was spread
That they suppos'd I could rend bars of steel
And spurn in pieces posts of adamant;
Wherefore a guard of chosen shot I had
That walk'd about me every minute-while;
And if I did but stir out of my bed,
Ready they were to shoot me to the heart.

Enter the Boy *with a linstock*

SALISBURY. I grieve to hear what torments you endur'd;
But we will be reveng'd sufficiently.
Now it is supper-time in Orleans:
Here, through this grate, I count each one
And view the Frenchmen how they fortify.
Let us look in; the sight will much delight thee.
Sir Thomas Gargrave and Sir William Glansdale,
Let me have your express opinions
Where is best place to make our batt'ry next.
GARGRAVE. I think at the North Gate; for there stand lords.
GLANSDALE. And I here, at the bulwark of the bridge.
TALBOT. For aught I see, this city must be famish'd,
Or with light skirmishes enfeebled.
                    [*Here they shoot and* SALISBURY *and* GARGRAVE
                                        fall down]
SALISBURY. O Lord, have mercy on us, wretched sinners!
GARGRAVE. O Lord, have mercy on me, woeful man!
TALBOT. What chance is this that suddenly hath cross'd us?
Speak, Salisbury; at least, if thou canst speak.
How far'st thou, mirror of all martial men?
One of thy eyes and thy cheek's side struck off!
Accursed tower! accursed fatal hand
That hath contriv'd this woeful tragedy!
In thirteen battles Salisbury o'ercame;
Henry the Fifth he first train'd to the wars;
Whilst any trump did sound or drum struck up,
His sword did ne'er leave striking in the field.
Yet liv'st thou, Salisbury? Though thy speech doth fail,

One eye thou hast to look to heaven for grace;
The sun with one eye vieweth all the world.
Heaven, be thou gracious to none alive
If Salisbury wants mercy at thy hands!
Bear hence his body; I will help to bury it.
Sir Thomas Gargrave, hast thou any life?
Speak unto Talbot; nay, look up to him.
Salisbury, cheer thy spirit with this comfort,
Thou shalt not die whiles—
He beckons with his hand and smiles on me,
As who should say 'When I am dead and gone,
Remember to avenge me on the French.'
Plantagenet, I will; and like thee, Nero,
Play on the lute, beholding the towns burn.
Wretched shall France be only in my name.
        [*Here an alarum, and it thunders and lightens*]
What stir is this? What tumult's in the heavens?
Whence cometh this alarum and the noise?

                Enter a MESSENGER

MESSENGER. My lord, my lord, the French have gather'd
    head.
The Dauphin, with one Joan la Pucelle join'd,
A holy prophetess new risen up,
Is come with a great power to raise the siege.
        [*Here* SALISBURY *lifteth himself up and groans*]
TALBOT. Hear, hear how dying Salisbury doth groan.
    It irks his heart he cannot be reveng'd.
    Frenchmen, I'll be a Salisbury to you.
    Pucelle or puzzel, dolphin or dogfish,
    Your hearts I'll stamp out with my horse's heels
    And make a quagmire of your mingled brains.
    Convey me Salisbury into his tent,
    And then we'll try what these dastard Frenchmen dare.
                                Alarum. Exeunt

SCENE 5

Before Orleans

Here an alarum again, and TALBOT *pursueth the*
DAUPHIN *and driveth him. Then enter* JOAN LA
PUCELLE *driving Englishmen before her. Then
enter* TALBOT

TALBOT. Where is my strength, my valour, and my force?
Our English troops retire, I cannot stay them;
A woman clad in armour chaseth them.

Enter LA PUCELLE

Here, here she comes. I'll have a bout with thee.
Devil or devil's dam, I'll conjure thee;
Blood will I draw on thee—thou art a witch—
And straightway give thy soul to him thou serv'st.
PUCELLE. Come, come, 'tis only I that must disgrace thee.
[Here they fight]
TALBOT. Heavens, can you suffer hell so to prevail?
My breast I'll burst with straining of my courage.
And from my shoulders crack my arms asunder,
But I will chastise this high-minded strumpet.
[They fight again]
PUCELLE. Talbot, farewell; thy hour is not yet come.
I must go victual Orleans forthwith.
[A short alarum; then enter the town with soldiers]
O'ertake me if thou canst; I scorn thy strength.
Go, go, cheer up thy hungry starved men;
Help Salisbury to make his testament.
This day is ours, as many more shall be.   *Exit*
TALBOT. My thoughts are whirled like a potter's wheel;
I know not where I am nor what I do.
A witch by fear, not force, like Hannibal,
Drives back our troops and conquers as she lists.
So bees with smoke and doves with noisome stench
Are from their hives and houses driven away.
They call'd us, for our fierceness, English dogs;
Now like to whelps we crying run away.
[A short alarum]

Hark, countrymen! Either renew the fight
Or tear the lions out of England's coat;
Renounce your soil, give sheep in lions' stead:
Sheep run not half so treacherous from the wolf,
Or horse or oxen from the leopard,
As you fly from your oft-subdued slaves.

[Alarum. Here another skirmish]

It will not be—retire into your trenches.
You all consented unto Salisbury's death,
For none would strike a stroke in his revenge.
Pucelle is ent'red into Orleans
In spite of us or aught that we could do.
O, would I were to die with Salisbury!
The shame hereof will make me hide my head.

Exit Talbot. *Alarum; retreat*

SCENE 6

Orleans

Flourish. Enter on the walls, La Pucelle, Charles,
Reignier, Alençon, *and soldiers*

Pucelle. Advance our waving colours on the walls;
Rescu'd is Orleans from the English.
Thus Joan la Pucelle hath perform'd her word.
Charles. Divinest creature, Astræa's daughter,
How shall I honour thee for this success?
Thy promises are like Adonis' gardens,
That one day bloom'd and fruitful were the next.
France, triumph in thy glorious prophetess.
Recover'd is the town of Orleans.
More blessed hap did ne'er befall our state.
Reignier. Why ring not out the bells aloud throughout the
town?
Dauphin, command the citizens make bonfires
And feast and banquet in the open streets
To celebrate the joy that God hath given us.
Alençon. All France will be replete with mirth and joy
When they shall hear how we have play'd the men.

ACT I. SCENE 6

CHARLES. 'Tis Joan, not we, by whom the day is won;
For which I will divide my crown with her;
And all the priests and friars in my realm
Shall in procession sing her endless praise.
A statelier pyramis to her I'll rear
Than Rhodope's of Memphis ever was.
In memory of her, when she is dead,
Her ashes, in an urn more precious
Than the rich jewell'd coffer of Darius,
Transported shall be at high festivals
Before the kings and queens of France.
No longer on Saint Denis will we cry,
But Joan la Pucelle shall be France's saint.
Come in, and let us banquet royally
After this golden day of victory.   *Flourish. Exeunt*

ACT II. SCENE 1

Before Orleans

Enter a FRENCH SERGEANT *and two* SENTINELS

SERGEANT. Sirs, take your places and be vigilant.
If any noise or soldier you perceive
Near to the walls, by some apparent sign
Let us have knowledge at the court of guard.
FIRST SENTINEL. Sergeant, you shall. [*Exit* SERGEANT] Thus
   are poor servitors,
When others sleep upon their quiet beds,
Constrain'd to watch in darkness, rain, and cold.

Enter TALBOT, BEDFORD, BURGUNDY, *and forces,
with scaling-ladders; their drums beating a dead
march*

TALBOT. Lord Regent, and redoubted Burgundy,
By whose approach the regions of Artois,
Wallon, and Picardy, are friends to us,
This happy night the Frenchmen are secure,

507

Having all day carous'd and banqueted;
Embrace we then this opportunity,
As fitting best to quittance their deceit,
Contriv'd by art and baleful sorcery.

BEDFORD. Coward of France, how much he wrongs his fame,
Despairing of his own arm's fortitude,
To join with witches and the help of hell!

BURGUNDY. Traitors have never other company.
But what's that Pucelle whom they term so pure?

TALBOT. A maid, they say.

BEDFORD. A maid! and be so martial!

BURGUNDY. Pray God she prove not masculine ere long,
If underneath the standard of the French
She carry armour as she hath begun.

TALBOT. Well, let them practise and converse with spirits:
God is our fortress, in whose conquering name
Let us resolve to scale their flinty bulwarks.

BEDFORD. Ascend, brave Talbot; we will follow thee.

TALBOT. Not all together; better far, I guess,
That we do make our entrance several ways;
That if it chance the one of us do fail
The other yet may rise against their force.

BEDFORD. Agreed; I'll to yond corner.

BURGUNDY. And I to this.

TALBOT. And here will Talbot mount or make his grave.
Now, Salisbury, for thee, and for the right
Of English Henry, shall this night appear
How much in duty I am bound to both.

[*The English scale the walls and cry 'Saint George!*
a Talbot!']

SENTINEL. Arm! arm! The enemy doth make assault.

The French leap o'er the walls in their shirts. Enter,
several ways, BASTARD, ALENÇON, REIGNIER, *half*
ready and half unready

ALENÇON. How now, my lords? What, all unready so?

BASTARD. Unready! Ay, and glad we 'scap'd so well.

REIGNIER. 'Twas time, I trow, to wake and leave our beds,
Hearing alarums at our chamber doors.

ALENÇON. Of all exploits since first I follow'd arms

Ne'er heard I of a warlike enterprise
More venturous or desperate than this.

BASTARD. I think this Talbot be a fiend of hell.

REIGNIER. If not of hell, the heavens, sure, favour him.

ALENÇON. Here cometh Charles; I marvel how he sped.

Enter CHARLES *and* LA PUCELLE

BASTARD. Tut! holy Joan was his defensive guard.

CHARLES. Is this thy cunning, thou deceitful dame?
Didst thou at first, to flatter us withal,
Make us partakers of a little gain
That now our loss might be ten times so much?

PUCELLE. Wherefore is Charles impatient with his friend?
At all times will you have my power alike?
Sleeping or waking, must I still prevail,
Or will you blame and lay the fault on me?
Improvident soldiers! Had your watch been good
This sudden mischief never could have fall'n.

CHARLES. Duke of Alençon, this was your default
That, being captain of the watch to-night,
Did look no better to that weighty charge.

ALENÇON. Had all your quarters been as safely kept
As that whereof I had the government,
We had not been thus shamefully surpris'd.

BASTARD. Mine was secure.

REIGNIER. And so was mine, my lord.

CHARLES. And, for myself, most part of all this night,
Within her quarter and mine own precinct
I was employ'd in passing to and fro
About relieving of the sentinels.
Then how or which way should they first break in?

PUCELLE. Question, my lords, no further of the case,
How or which way; 'tis sure they found some place
But weakly guarded, where the breach was made.
And now there rests no other shift but this—
To gather our soldiers, scatter'd and dispers'd,
And lay new platforms to endamage them.

Alarum. Enter an ENGLISH SOLDIER, *crying 'A
Talbot! A Talbot!' They fly, leaving their clothes
behind*

509

SOLDIER. I'll be so bold to take what they have left.
The cry of Talbot serves me for a sword;
For I have loaden me with many spoils,
Using no other weapon but his name.   *Exit*

SCENE 2

Orleans. Within the town

Enter TALBOT, BEDFORD, BURGUNDY, *a* CAPTAIN,
and others

BEDFORD. The day begins to break, and night is fled
Whose pitchy mantle over-veil'd the earth.
Here sound retreat and cease our hot pursuit.
                              [*Retreat sounded*]
TALBOT. Bring forth the body of old Salisbury
And here advance it in the market-place,
The middle centre of this cursed town.
Now have I paid my vow unto his soul;
For every drop of blood was drawn from him
There hath at least five Frenchmen died to-night.
And that hereafter ages may behold
What ruin happened in revenge of him,
Within their chiefest temple I'll erect
A tomb, wherein his corpse shall be interr'd;
Upon the which, that every one may read,
Shall be engrav'd the sack of Orleans,
The treacherous manner of his mournful death,
And what a terror he had been to France.
But, lords, in all our bloody massacre,
I muse we met not with the Dauphin's grace,
His new-come champion, virtuous Joan of Arc,
Nor any of his false confederates.
BEDFORD. 'Tis thought, Lord Talbot, when the fight began,
Rous'd on the sudden from their drowsy beds,
They did amongst the troops of armed men
Leap o'er the walls for refuge in the field.
BURGUNDY. Myself, as far as I could well discern
For smoke and dusky vapours of the night,

Am sure I scar'd the Dauphin and his trull,
When arm in arm they both came swiftly running,
Like to a pair of loving turtle-doves
That could not live asunder day or night.
After that things are set in order here,
We'll follow them with all the power we have.

Enter a MESSENGER

MESSENGER. All hail, my lords! Which of this princely train
  Call ye the warlike Talbot, for his acts
  So much applauded through the realm of France?
TALBOT. Here is the Talbot; who would speak with him?
MESSENGER. The virtuous lady, Countess of Auvergne,
  With modesty admiring thy renown,
  By me entreats, great lord, thou wouldst vouchsafe
  To visit her poor castle where she lies,
  That she may boast she hath beheld the man
  Whose glory fills the world with loud report.
BURGUNDY. Is it even so? Nay, then I see our wars
  Will turn into a peaceful comic sport,
  When ladies crave to be encount'red with.
  You may not, my lord, despise her gentle suit.
TALBOT. Ne'er trust me then; for when a world of men
  Could not prevail with all their oratory,
  Yet hath a woman's kindness overrul'd;
  And therefore tell her I return great thanks
  And in submission will attend on her.
  Will not your honours bear me company?
BEDFORD. No, truly; 'tis more than manners will;
  And I have heard it said unbidden guests
  Are often welcomest when they are gone.
TALBOT. Well then, alone, since there's no remedy,
  I mean to prove this lady's courtesy.
  Come hither, Captain. [*Whispers*] You perceive my mind?
CAPTAIN. I do, my lord, and mean accordingly.   *Exeunt*

SCENE 3

Auvergne. The castle

Enter the COUNTESS *and her* PORTER

COUNTESS. Porter, remember what I gave in charge;
And when you have done so, bring the keys to me.
PORTER. Madam, I will.   *Exit*
COUNTESS. The plot is laid; if all things fall out right,
I shall as famous be by this exploit
As Scythian Tomyris by Cyrus' death.
Great is the rumour of this dreadful knight,
And his achievements of no less account.
Fain would mine eyes be witness with mine ears
To give their censure of these rare reports.

Enter MESSENGER *and* TALBOT

MESSENGER. Madam, according as your ladyship desir'd,
By message crav'd, so is Lord Talbot come.
COUNTESS. And he is welcome. What! is this the man?
MESSENGER. Madam, it is.
COUNTESS. Is this the scourge of France?
Is this the Talbot, so much fear'd abroad
That with his name the mothers still their babes?
I see report is fabulous and false.
I thought I should have seen some Hercules,
A second Hector, for his grim aspect
And large proportion of his strong-knit limbs.
Alas, this is a child, a silly dwarf!
It cannot be this weak and writhled shrimp
Should strike such terror to his enemies.
TALBOT. Madam, I have been bold to trouble you;
But since your ladyship is not at leisure,
I'll sort some other time to visit you.   *[Going]*
COUNTESS. What means he now? Go ask him whither he
goes.
MESSENGER. Stay, my Lord Talbot; for my lady craves
To know the cause of your abrupt departure.
TALBOT. Marry, for that she's in a wrong belief,

I go to certify her Talbot's here.

Re-enter PORTER *with keys*

COUNTESS. If thou be he, then art thou prisoner.
TALBOT. Prisoner! To whom?
COUNTESS. To me, blood-thirsty lord
  And for that cause I train'd thee to my house.
  Long time thy shadow hath been thrall to me,
  For in my gallery thy picture hangs;
  But now the substance shall endure the like
  And I will chain these legs and arms of thine
  That hast by tyranny these many years
  Wasted our country, slain our citizens,
  And sent our sons and husbands captivate.
TALBOT. Ha, ha, ha!
COUNTESS. Laughest thou, wretch? Thy mirth shall turn to
  moan.
TALBOT. I laugh to see your ladyship so fond
  To think that you have aught but Talbot's shadow
  Whereon to practise your severity.
COUNTESS. Why, art not thou the man?
TALBOT. I am indeed.
COUNTESS. Then have I substance too.
TALBOT. No, no, I am but shadow of myself.
  You are deceiv'd, my substance is not here;
  For what you see is but the smallest part
  And least proportion of humanity.
  I tell you, madam, were the whole frame here,
  It is of such a spacious lofty pitch
  Your roof were not sufficient to contain 't.
COUNTESS. This is a riddling merchant for the nonce;
  He will be here, and yet he is not here.
  How can these contrarieties agree?
TALBOT. That will I show you presently.

Winds his horn; drums strike up; a peal of ordnance.
Enter soldiers

How say you, madam? Are you now persuaded
That Talbot is but shadow of himself?
These are his substance, sinews, arms, and strength,

With which he yoketh your rebellious necks,
Razeth your cities, and subverts your towns,
And in a moment makes them desolate.
COUNTESS. Victorious Talbot! pardon my abuse.
I find thou art no less than fame hath bruited,
And more than may be gathered by thy shape.
Let my presumption not provoke thy wrath,
For I am sorry that with reverence
I did not entertain thee as thou art.
TALBOT. Be not dismay'd, fair lady; nor misconster
The mind of Talbot as you did mistake
The outward composition of his body.
What you have done hath not offended me.
Nor other satisfaction do I crave
But only, with your patience, that we may
Taste of your wine and see what cates you have,
For soldiers' stomachs always serve them well.
COUNTESS. With all my heart, and think me honoured
To feast so great a warrior in my house.   *Exeunt*

SCENE 4

London. The Temple garden

Enter the EARLS OF SOMERSET, SUFFOLK, *and* WAR-
WICK; RICHARD PLANTAGENET, VERNON, *and another*
LAWYER

PLANTAGENET. Great lords and gentlemen, what means this
    silence?
Dare no man answer in a case of truth?
SUFFOLK. Within the Temple Hall we were too loud;
The garden here is more convenient.
PLANTAGENET. Then say at once if I maintain'd the truth;
Or else was wrangling Somerset in th' error?
SUFFOLK. Faith, I have been a truant in the law
And never yet could frame my will to it;
And therefore frame the law unto my will.
SOMERSET. Judge you, my Lord of Warwick, then, be-
    tween us.

WARWICK. Between two hawks, which flies the higher pitch;
    Between two dogs, which hath the deeper mouth;
    Between two blades, which bears the better temper;
    Between two horses, which doth bear him best;
    Between two girls, which hath the merriest eye—
    I have perhaps some shallow spirit of judgment;
    But in these nice sharp quillets of the law,
    Good faith, I am no wiser than a daw.
PLANTAGENET. Tut, tut, here is a mannerly forbearance:
    The truth appears so naked on my side
    That any purblind eye may find it out.
SOMERSET. And on my side it is so well apparell'd,
    So clear, so shining, and so evident,
    That it will glimmer through a blind man's eye.
PLANTAGENET. Since you are tongue-tied and so loath to
    speak,
    In dumb significants proclaim your thoughts.
    Let him that is a true-born gentleman
    And stands upon the honour of his birth,
    If he suppose that I have pleaded truth,
    From off this brier pluck a white rose with me.
SOMERSET. Let him that is no coward nor no flatterer,
    But dare maintain the party of the truth,
    Pluck a red rose from off this thorn with me.
WARWICK. I love no colours; and, without all colour
    Of base insinuating flattery,
    I pluck this white rose with Plantagenet.
SUFFOLK. I pluck this red rose with young Somerset,
    And say withal I think he held the right.
VERNON. Stay, lords and gentlemen, and pluck no more
    Till you conclude that he upon whose side
    The fewest roses are cropp'd from the tree
    Shall yield the other in the right opinion.
SOMERSET. Good Master Vernon, it is well objected;
    If I have fewest, I subscribe in silence.
PLANTAGENET. And I.
VERNON. Then, for the truth and plainness of the case,
    I pluck this pale and maiden blossom here,
    Giving my verdict on the white rose side.
SOMERSET. Prick not your finger as you pluck it off,

Lest, bleeding, you do paint the white rose red,
And fall on my side so, against your will.

VERNON. If I, my lord, for my opinion bleed,
Opinion shall be surgeon to my hurt
And keep me on the side where still I am.

SOMERSET. Well, well, come on; who else?

LAWYER. [*To* SOMERSET] Unless my study and my books be
false,
The argument you held was wrong in you;
In sign whereof I pluck a white rose too.

PLANTAGENET. Now, Somerset, where is your argument?

SOMERSET. Here in my scabbard, meditating that
Shall dye your white rose in a bloody red.

PLANTAGENET. Meantime your cheeks do counterfeit our
roses;
For pale they look with fear, as witnessing
The truth on our side.

SOMERSET. No, Plantagenet,
'Tis not for fear but anger that thy cheeks
Blush for pure shame to counterfeit our roses,
And yet thy tongue will not confess thy error.

PLANTAGENET. Hath not thy rose a canker, Somerset?

SOMERSET. Hath not thy rose a thorn, Plantagenet?

PLANTAGENET. Ay, sharp and piercing, to maintain his truth;
Whiles thy consuming canker eats his falsehood.

SOMERSET. Well, I'll find friends to wear my bleeding roses,
That shall maintain what I have said is true,
Where false Plantagenet dare not be seen.

PLANTAGENET. Now, by this maiden blossom in my hand,
I scorn thee and thy fashion, peevish boy.

SUFFOLK. Turn not thy scorns this way, Plantagenet.

PLANTAGENET. Proud Pole, I will, and scorn both him and
thee.

SUFFOLK. I'll turn my part thereof into thy throat.

SOMERSET. Away, away, good William de la Pole!
We grace the yeoman by conversing with him.

WARWICK. Now, by God's will, thou wrong'st him, Somer-
set;
His grandfather was Lionel Duke of Clarence,
Third son to the third Edward, King of England.

Spring crestless yeomen from so deep a root?
PLANTAGENET. He bears him on the place's privilege,
  Or durst not for his craven heart say thus.
SOMERSET. By Him that made me, I'll maintain my words
  On any plot of ground in Christendom.
  Was not thy father, Richard Earl of Cambridge,
  For treason executed in our late king's days?
  And by his treason stand'st not thou attainted,
  Corrupted, and exempt from ancient gentry?
  His trespass yet lives guilty in thy blood;
  And till thou be restor'd thou art a yeoman.
PLANTAGENET. My father was attached, not attainted;
  Condemn'd to die for treason, but no traitor;
  And that I'll prove on better men than Somerset,
  Were growing time once ripened to my will.
  For your partaker Pole, and you yourself,
  I'll note you in my book of memory
  To scourge you for this apprehension.
  Look to it well, and say you are well warn'd.
SOMERSET. Ay, thou shalt find us ready for thee still;
  And know us by these colours for thy foes—
  For these my friends in spite of thee shall wear.
PLANTAGENET. And, by my soul, this pale and angry rose,
  As cognizance of my blood-drinking hate,
  Will I for ever, and my faction, wear,
  Until it wither with me to my grave,
  Or flourish to the height of my degree.
SUFFOLK. Go forward, and be chok'd with thy ambition!
  And so farewell until I meet thee next.   *Exit*
SOMERSET. Have with thee, Pole. Farewell, ambitious Rich-
  ard.   *Exit*
PLANTAGENET. How I am brav'd, and must perforce endure
  it!
WARWICK. This blot that they object against your house
  Shall be wip'd out in the next Parliament,
  Call'd for the truce of Winchester and Gloucester;
  And if thou be not then created York,
  I will not live to be accounted Warwick.
  Meantime, in signal of my love to thee,
  Against proud Somerset and William Pole,

Will I upon thy party wear this rose;
And here I prophesy: this brawl to-day,
Grown to this faction in the Temple Garden,
Shall send between the Red Rose and the White
A thousand souls to death and deadly night.
PLANTAGENET. Good Master Vernon, I am bound to you
That you on my behalf would pluck a flower.
VERNON. In your behalf still will I wear the same.
LAWYER. And so will I.
PLANTAGENET. Thanks, gentle sir.
Come, let us four to dinner. I dare say
This quarrel will drink blood another day.   *Exeunt*

SCENE 5

The Tower of London

Enter MORTIMER, *brought in a chair, and* GAOLERS

MORTIMER. Kind keepers of my weak decaying age,
Let dying Mortimer here rest himself.
Even like a man new haled from the rack,
So fare my limbs with long imprisonment;
And these grey locks, the pursuivants of death,
Nestor-like aged in an age of care,
Argue the end of Edmund Mortimer.
These eyes, like lamps whose wasting oil is spent,
Wax dim, as drawing to their exigent;
Weak shoulders, overborne with burdening grief,
And pithless arms, like to a withered vine
That droops his sapless branches to the ground.
Yet are these feet, whose strengthless stay is numb,
Unable to support this lump of clay,
Swift-winged with desire to get a grave,
As witting I no other comfort have.
But tell me, keeper, will my nephew come?
FIRST KEEPER. Richard Plantagenet, my lord, will come.
We sent unto the Temple, unto his chamber;
And answer was return'd that he will come.
MORTIMER. Enough; my soul shall then be satisfied.

Poor gentleman! his wrong doth equal mine.
Since Henry Monmouth first began to reign,
Before whose glory I was great in arms,
This loathsome sequestration have I had;
And even since then hath Richard been obscur'd,
Depriv'd of honour and inheritance.
But now the arbitrator of despairs,
Just Death, kind umpire of men's miseries,
With sweet enlargement doth dismiss me hence.
I would his troubles likewise were expir'd,
That so he might recover what was lost.

Enter RICHARD PLANTAGENET

FIRST KEEPER. My lord, your loving nephew now is come.
MORTIMER. Richard Plantagenet, my friend, is he come?
PLANTAGENET. Ay, noble uncle, thus ignobly us'd,
  Your nephew, late despised Richard, comes.
MORTIMER. Direct mine arms I may embrace his neck
  And in his bosom spend my latter gasp.
  O, tell me when my lips do touch his cheeks,
  That I may kindly give one fainting kiss.
  And now declare, sweet stem from York's great stock,
  Why didst thou say of late thou wert despis'd?
PLANTAGENET. First, lean thine aged back against mine arm;
  And, in that ease, I'll tell thee my disease.
  This day, in argument upon a case,
  Some words there grew 'twixt Somerset and me;
  Among which terms he us'd his lavish tongue
  And did upbraid me with my father's death;
  Which obloquy set bars before my tongue,
  Else with the like I had requited him.
  Therefore, good uncle, for my father's sake,
  In honour of a true Plantagenet,
  And for alliance sake, declare the cause
  My father, Earl of Cambridge, lost his head.
MORTIMER. That cause, fair nephew, that imprison'd me
  And hath detain'd me all my flow'ring youth
  Within a loathsome dungeon, there to pine,
  Was cursed instrument of his decease.
PLANTAGENET. Discover more at large what cause that was,

For I am ignorant and cannot guess.
MORTIMER. I will, if that my fading breath permit
And death approach not ere my tale be done.
Henry the Fourth, grandfather to this king,
Depos'd his nephew Richard, Edward's son,
The first-begotten and the lawful heir
Of Edward king, the third of that descent;
During whose reign the Percies of the north,
Finding his usurpation most unjust,
Endeavour'd my advancement to the throne.
The reason mov'd these warlike lords to this
Was, for that—young Richard thus remov'd,
Leaving no heir begotten of his body—
I was the next by birth and parentage;
For by my mother I derived am
From Lionel Duke of Clarence, third son
To King Edward the Third; whereas he
From John of Gaunt doth bring his pedigree,
Being but fourth of that heroic line.
But mark: as in this haughty great attempt
They laboured to plant the rightful heir,
I lost my liberty, and they their lives.
Long after this, when Henry the Fifth,
Succeeding his father Bolingbroke, did reign,
Thy father, Earl of Cambridge, then deriv'd
From famous Edmund Langley, Duke of York,
Marrying my sister, that thy mother was,
Again, in pity of my hard distress,
Levied an army, weening to redeem
And have install'd me in the diadem;
But, as the rest, so fell that noble earl,
And was beheaded. Thus the Mortimers,
In whom the title rested, were suppress'd.
PLANTAGENET. Of which, my lord, your honour is the last.
MORTIMER. True; and thou seest that I no issue have,
And that my fainting words do warrant death.
Thou art my heir; the rest I wish thee gather;
But yet be wary in thy studious care.
PLANTAGENET. Thy grave admonishments prevail with me.
But yet methinks my father's execution

Was nothing less than bloody tyranny.

MORTIMER. With silence, nephew, be thou politic;
   Strong fixed is the house of Lancaster
   And like a mountain not to be remov'd.
   But now thy uncle is removing hence,
   As princes do their courts when they are cloy'd
   With long continuance in a settled place.

PLANTAGENET. O uncle, would some part of my young years
   Might but redeem the passage of your age!

MORTIMER. Thou dost then wrong me, as that slaughterer
   doth
   Which giveth many wounds when one will kill.
   Mourn not, except thou sorrow for my good;
   Only give order for my funeral.
   And so, farewell; and fair be all thy hopes,
   And prosperous be thy life in peace and war!   [*Dies*]

PLANTAGENET. And peace, no war, befall thy parting soul!
   In prison hast thou spent a pilgrimage,
   And like a hermit overpass'd thy days.
   Well, I will lock his counsel in my breast;
   And what I do imagine, let that rest.
   Keepers, convey him hence; and I myself
   Will see his burial better than his life.

      Exeunt GAOLERS, *bearing out the body of* MORTIMER
   Here dies the dusky torch of Mortimer,
   Chok'd with ambition of the meaner sort;
   And for those wrongs, those bitter injuries,
   Which Somerset hath offer'd to my house,
   I doubt not but with honour to redress;
   And therefore haste I to the Parliament,
   Either to be restored to my blood,
   Or make my ill th' advantage of my good.   *Exit*

KING HENRY VI. PART 1

ACT III. SCENE 1

London. The Parliament House

Flourish. Enter the KING, EXETER, GLOUCESTER, WARWICK, SOMERSET, *and* SUFFOLK; *the* BISHOP OF WINCHESTER, RICHARD PLANTAGENET, *and others.* GLOUCESTER *offers to put up a bill;* WINCHESTER *snatches it, and tears it*

WINCHESTER. Com'st thou with deep premeditated lines,
With written pamphlets studiously devis'd?
Humphrey of Gloucester, if thou canst accuse
Or aught intend'st to lay unto my charge,
Do it without invention, suddenly;
I with sudden and extemporal speech
Purpose to answer what thou canst object.
GLOUCESTER. Presumptuous priest, this place commands my
    patience,
Or thou shouldst find thou hast dishonour'd me.
Think not, although in writing I preferr'd
The manner of thy vile outrageous crimes,
That therefore I have forg'd, or am not able
Verbatim to rehearse the method of my pen.
No, prelate; such is thy audacious wickedness,
Thy lewd, pestiferous, and dissentious pranks,
As very infants prattle of thy pride.
Thou art a most pernicious usurer;
Froward by nature, enemy to peace;
Lascivious, wanton, more than well beseems
A man of thy profession and degree;
And for thy treachery, what's more manifest—
In that thou laid'st a trap to take my life,
As well at London Bridge as at the Tower?
Beside, I fear me, if thy thoughts were sifted,
The King, thy sovereign, is not quite exempt
From envious malice of thy swelling heart.
WINCHESTER. Gloucester, I do defy thee. Lords, vouchsafe
To give me hearing what I shall reply.
If I were covetous, ambitious, or perverse,

As he will have me, how am I so poor?
Or how haps it I seek not to advance
Or raise myself, but keep my wonted calling?
And for dissension, who preferreth peace
More than I do, except I be provok'd?
No, my good lords, it is not that offends;
It is not that that hath incens'd the Duke:
It is because no one should sway but he;
No one but he should be about the King;
And that engenders thunder in his breast
And makes him roar these accusations forth.
But he shall know I am as good—
GLOUCESTER. As good!
Thou bastard of my grandfather!
WINCHESTER. Ay, lordly sir; for what are you, I pray,
But one imperious in another's throne?
GLOUCESTER. Am I not Protector, saucy priest?
WINCHESTER. And am not I a prelate of the church?
GLOUCESTER. Yes, as an outlaw in a castle keeps,
And useth it to patronage his theft.
WINCHESTER. Unreverent Gloucester!
GLOUCESTER. Thou art reverend
Touching thy spiritual function, not thy life.
WINCHESTER. Rome shall remedy this.
WARWICK. Roam thither then.
SOMERSET. My lord, it were your duty to forbear.
WARWICK. Ay, see the bishop be not overborne.
SOMERSET. Methinks my lord should be religious,
And know the office that belongs to such.
WARWICK. Methinks his lordship should be humbler;
It fitteth not a prelate so to plead.
SOMERSET. Yes, when his holy state is touch'd so near.
WARWICK. State holy or unhallow'd, what of that?
Is not his Grace Protector to the King?
PLANTAGENET. [Aside] Plantagenet, I see, must hold his
tongue,
Lest it be said 'Speak, sirrah, when you should;
Must your bold verdict enter talk with lords?'
Else would I have a fling at Winchester.
KING HENRY. Uncles of Gloucester and of Winchester,

The special watchmen of our English weal,
I would prevail, if prayers might prevail,
To join your hearts in love and amity.
O, what a scandal is it to our crown
That two such noble peers as ye should jar!
Believe me, lords, my tender years can tell
Civil dissension is a viperous worm
That gnaws the bowels of the commonwealth.
    [*A noise within:* 'Down with the tawny coats!']
What tumult's this?
WARWICK. An uproar, I dare warrant,
Begun through malice of the Bishop's men.
      [*A noise again:* 'Stones! Stones!']

Enter the MAYOR OF LONDON, *attended*

MAYOR. O, my good lords, and virtuous Henry,
Pity the city of London, pity us!
The Bishop and the Duke of Gloucester's men,
Forbidden late to carry any weapon,
Have fill'd their pockets full of pebble stones
And, banding themselves in contrary parts,
Do pelt so fast at one another's pate
That many have their giddy brains knock'd out.
Our windows are broke down in every street,
And we for fear compell'd to shut our shops.

Enter in skirmish, the retainers of GLOUCESTER *and*
WINCHESTER, *with bloody pates*

KING HENRY. We charge you, on allegiance to ourself,
To hold your slaught'ring hands and keep the peace.
Pray, uncle Gloucester, mitigate this strife.
FIRST SERVING-MAN. Nay, if we be forbidden stones, we'll
fall to it with our teeth.
SECOND SERVING-MAN. Do what ye dare, we are as resolute.
        [*Skirmish again*]
GLOUCESTER. You of my household, leave this peevish broil,
And set this unaccustom'd fight aside.
THIRD SERVING-MAN. My lord, we know your Grace to be a
man
Just and upright, and for your royal birth

Inferior to none but to his Majesty;
And ere that we will suffer such a prince,
So kind a father of the commonweal,
To be disgraced by an inkhorn mate,
We and our wives and children all will fight
And have our bodies slaught'red by thy foes.
FIRST SERVING-MAN. Ay, and the very parings of our nails
Shall pitch a field when we are dead.   [Begin again]
GLOUCESTER. Stay, stay, I say!
And if you love me, as you say you do,
Let me persuade you to forbear awhile.
KING HENRY. O, how this discord doth afflict my soul!
Can you, my Lord of Winchester, behold
My sighs and tears and will not once relent?
Who should be pitiful, if you be not?
Or who should study to prefer a peace,
If holy churchmen take delight in broils?
WARWICK. Yield, my Lord Protector; yield, Winchester;
Except you mean with obstinate repulse
To slay your sovereign and destroy the realm.
You see what mischief, and what murder too,
Hath been enacted through your enmity;
Then be at peace, except ye thirst for blood.
WINCHESTER. He shall submit, or I will never yield.
GLOUCESTER. Compassion on the King commands me stoop,
Or I would see his heart out ere the priest
Should ever get that privilege of me.
WARWICK. Behold, my Lord of Winchester, the Duke
Hath banish'd moody discontented fury,
As by his smoothed brows it doth appear;
Why look you still so stern and tragical?
GLOUCESTER. Here, Winchester, I offer thee my hand.
KING HENRY. Fie, uncle Beaufort! I have heard you preach
That malice was a great and grievous sin;
And will not you maintain the thing you teach,
But prove a chief offender in the same?
WARWICK. Sweet King! The Bishop hath a kindly gird.
For shame, my Lord of Winchester, relent;
What, shall a child instruct you what to do?
WINCHESTER. Well, Duke of Gloucester, I will yield to thee;

Love for thy love and hand for hand I give.

GLOUCESTER [*Aside*] Ay, but, I fear me, with a hollow
  heart.—

See here, my friends and loving countrymen:
This token serveth for a flag of truce
Betwixt ourselves and all our followers.
So help me God, as I dissemble not!

WINCHESTER [*Aside*] So help me God, as I intend it not!

KING HENRY. O loving uncle, kind Duke of Gloucester,
How joyful am I made by this contract!
Away, my masters! trouble us no more;
But join in friendship, as your lords have done.

FIRST SERVING-MAN. Content: I'll to the surgeon's.

SECOND SERVING-MAN. And so will I.

THIRD SERVING-MAN. And I will see what physic the tavern
  affords.   *Exeunt servants*, MAYOR, &c.

WARWICK. Accept this scroll, most gracious sovereign;
Which in the right of Richard Plantagenet
We do exhibit to your Majesty.

GLOUCESTER. Well urg'd, my Lord of Warwick; for, sweet
  prince,
An if your Grace mark every circumstance,
You have great reason to do Richard right;
Especially for those occasions
At Eltham Place I told your Majesty.

KING HENRY. And those occasions, uncle, were of force;
Therefore, my loving lords, our pleasure is
That Richard be restored to his blood.

WARWICK. Let Richard be restored to his blood;
So shall his father's wrongs be recompens'd.

WINCHESTER. As will the rest, so willeth Winchester.

KING HENRY. If Richard will be true, not that alone
But all the whole inheritance I give
That doth belong unto the house of York,
From whence you spring by lineal descent.

PLANTAGENET. Thy humble servant vows obedience
And humble service till the point of death.

KING HENRY. Stoop then and set your knee against my foot;
And in reguerdon of that duty done
I girt thee with the valiant sword of York.

Rise, Richard, like a true Plantagenet,
And rise created princely Duke of York.
PLANTAGENET. And so thrive Richard as thy foes may fall!
And as my duty springs, so perish they
That grudge one thought against your Majesty!
ALL. Welcome, high Prince, the mighty Duke of York!
SOMERSET. [*Aside*] Perish, base Prince, ignoble Duke of
York!
GLOUCESTER. Now will it best avail your Majesty
To cross the seas and to be crown'd in France:
The presence of a king engenders love
Amongst his subjects and his loyal friends,
As it disanimates his enemies.
KING HENRY. When Gloucester says the word, King Henry
goes;
For friendly counsel cuts off many foes.
GLOUCESTER. Your ships already are in readiness.
                    Sennet. Flourish. Exeunt all but EXETER
EXETER. Ay, we may march in England or in France,
Not seeing what is likely to ensue.
This late dissension grown betwixt the peers
Burns under feigned ashes of forg'd love
And will at last break out into a flame;
As fest'red members rot but by degree
Till bones and flesh and sinews fall away,
So will this base and envious discord breed.
And now I fear that fatal prophecy
Which in the time of Henry nam'd the Fifth
Was in the mouth of every sucking babe:
That Henry born at Monmouth should win all,
And Henry born at Windsor should lose all.
Which is so plain that Exeter doth wish
His days may finish ere that hapless time.   *Exit*

SCENE 2

France. Before Rouen

Enter LA PUCELLE *disguis'd, with four soldiers dressed like countrymen, with sacks upon their backs*

PUCELLE. These are the city gates, the gates of Rouen,
Through which our policy must make a breach.
Take heed, be wary how you place your words;
Talk like the vulgar sort of market-men
That come to gather money for their corn.
If we have entrance, as I hope we shall,
And that we find the slothful watch but weak,
I'll by a sign give notice to our friends,
That Charles the Dauphin may encounter them.
FIRST SOLDIER. Our sacks shall be a mean to sack the city,
And we be lords and rulers over Rouen;
Therefore we'll knock.   [*Knocks*]
WATCH. [*Within*] Qui est là?
PUCELLE. Paysans, pauvres gens de France—
Poor market-folks that come to sell their corn.
WATCH. Enter, go in; the market-bell is rung.
PUCELLE. Now, Rouen, I'll shake thy bulwarks to the ground.

     [LA PUCELLE, *&c., enter the town*]

Enter CHARLES, BASTARD, ALENÇON, REIGNIER, *and forces*

CHARLES. Saint Denis bless this happy stratagem!
And once again we'll sleep secure in Rouen.
BASTARD. Here ent'red Pucelle and her practisants;
Now she is there, how will she specify
Here is the best and safest passage in?
ALENÇON. By thrusting out a torch from yonder tower;
Which once discern'd shows that her meaning is—
No way to that, for weakness, which she ent'red.

Enter LA PUCELLE, *on the top, thrusting out
a torch burning*

PUCELLE. Behold, this is the happy wedding torch

That joineth Rouen unto her countrymen,
But burning fatal to the Talbotites.   *Exit*
BASTARD. See, noble Charles, the beacon of our friend;
The burning torch in yonder turret stands.
CHARLES. Now shine it like a comet of revenge,
A prophet to the fall of all our foes!
ALENÇON. Defer no time, delays have dangerous ends;
Enter, and cry 'The Dauphin!' presently,
And then do execution on the watch.   *Alarum. Exeunt*

An alarum. Enter TALBOT *in an excursion*

TALBOT. France, thou shalt rue this treason with thy tears,
If Talbot but survive thy treachery.
Pucelle, that witch, that damned sorceress,
Hath wrought this hellish mischief unawares,
That hardly we escap'd the pride of France.   *Exit*

An alarum; excursions. BEDFORD *brought in sick in
a chair. Enter* TALBOT *and* BURGUNDY *without;
within,* LA PUCELLE, CHARLES, BASTARD, ALENÇON,
and REIGNIER, *on the walls*

PUCELLE. Good morrow, gallants! Want ye corn for bread?
I think the Duke of Burgundy will fast
Before he'll buy again at such a rate.
'Twas full of darnel—do you like the taste?
BURGUNDY. Scoff on, vile fiend and shameless courtezan.
I trust ere long to choke thee with thine own,
And make thee curse the harvest of that corn.
CHARLES. Your Grace may starve, perhaps, before that time.
BEDFORD. O, let no words, but deeds, revenge this treason!
PUCELLE. What will you do, good grey-beard? Break a
lance,
And run a tilt at death within a chair?
TALBOT. Foul fiend of France and hag of all despite,
Encompass'd with thy lustful paramours,
Becomes it thee to taunt his valiant age
And twit with cowardice a man half dead?
Damsel, I'll have a bout with you again,
Or else let Talbot perish with this shame.
PUCELLE. Are ye so hot, sir? Yet, Pucelle, hold thy peace;

If Talbot do but thunder, rain will follow.
         [The English party whisper together in council]
God speed the parliament! Who shall be the Speaker?
TALBOT. Dare ye come forth and meet us in the field?
PUCELLE. Belike your lordship takes us then for fools,
  To try if that our own be ours or no.
TALBOT. I speak not to that railing Hecate,
  But unto thee, Alençon, and the rest.
  Will ye, like soldiers, come and fight it out?
ALENÇON. Signior, no.
TALBOT. Signior, hang! Base muleteers of France!
  Like peasant foot-boys do they keep the walls,
  And dare not take up arms like gentlemen.
PUCELLE. Away, captains! Let's get us from the walls;
  For Talbot means no goodness by his looks.
  God b'uy, my lord; we came but to tell you
  That we are here.   *Exeunt from the walls*
TALBOT. And there will we be too, ere it be long,
  Or else reproach be Talbot's greatest fame!
  Vow, Burgundy, by honour of thy house,
  Prick'd on by public wrongs sustain'd in **France**,
  Either to get the town again or die;
  And I, as sure as English Henry lives
  And as his father here was conqueror,
  As sure as in this late-betrayed town
  Great Cœur-de-lion's heart was buried—
  So sure I swear to get the town or die.
BURGUNDY. My vows are equal partners with thy vows.
TALBOT. But ere we go, regard this dying prince,
  The valiant Duke of Bedford. Come, my lord,
  We will bestow you in some better place,
  Fitter for sickness and for crazy age.
BEDFORD. Lord Talbot, do not so dishonour me;
  Here will I sit before the walls of Rouen,
  And will be partner of your weal or woe.
BURGUNDY. Courageous Bedford, let us now persuade you.
BEDFORD. Not to be gone from hence; for once I read
  That stout Pendragon in his litter sick
  Came to the field, and vanquished his foes.
  Methinks I should revive the soldiers' hearts,

Because I ever found them as myself.

TALBOT. Undaunted spirit in a dying breast!
Then be it so. Heavens keep old Bedford safe!
And now no more ado, brave Burgundy,
But gather we our forces out of hand
And set upon our boasting enemy.
Exeunt against the town all but BEDFORD *and attendants*

An alarum; excursions. Enter SIR JOHN FASTOLFE,
and a CAPTAIN

CAPTAIN. Whither away, Sir John Fastolfe, in such haste?
FASTOLFE. Whither away? To save myself by flight:
We are like to have the overthrow again.
CAPTAIN. What! Will you fly, and leave Lord Talbot?
FASTOLFE. Ay,
All the Talbots in the world, to save my life.   *Exit*
CAPTAIN. Cowardly knight! ill fortune follow thee!
                              Exit into the town

Retreat; excursions. LA PUCELLE, ALENÇON, *and*
CHARLES *fly*

BEDFORD. Now, quiet soul, depart when heaven please,
For I have seen our enemies' overthrow.
What is the trust or strength of foolish man?
They that of late were daring with their scoffs
Are glad and fain by flight to save themselves.
    [BEDFORD *dies and is carried in by two in his chair*]

An alarum. Re-enter TALBOT, BURGUNDY, *and the rest*

TALBOT. Lost and recovered in a day again!
This is a double honour, Burgundy.
Yet heavens have glory for this victory!
BURGUNDY. Warlike and martial Talbot, Burgundy
Enshrines thee in his heart, and there erects
Thy noble deeds as valour's monuments.
TALBOT. Thanks, gentle Duke. But where is Pucelle now?
I think her old familiar is asleep.
Now where's the Bastard's braves, and Charles his gleeks?
What, all amort? Rouen hangs her head for grief
That such a valiant company are fled.

Now will we take some order in the town,
Placing therein some expert officers;
And then depart to Paris to the King,
For there young Henry with his nobles lie.
BURGUNDY. What wills Lord Talbot pleaseth Burgundy.
TALBOT. But yet, before we go, let's not forget
The noble Duke of Bedford, late deceas'd,
But see his exequies fulfill'd in Rouen.
A braver soldier never couched lance,
A gentler heart did never sway in court;
But kings and mightiest potentates must die,
For that's the end of human misery.   *Exeunt*

SCENE 3

The plains near Rouen

Enter CHARLES, *the* BASTARD, ALENÇON, LA PUCELLE,
and forces

PUCELLE. Dismay not, Princes, at this accident,
Nor grieve that Rouen is so recovered.
Care is no cure, but rather corrosive,
For things that are not to be remedied.
Let frantic Talbot triumph for a while
And like a peacock sweep along his tail;
We'll pull his plumes and take away his train,
If Dauphin and the rest will be but rul'd.
CHARLES. We have been guided by thee hitherto,
And of thy cunning had no diffidence;
One sudden foil shall never breed distrust.
BASTARD. Search out thy wit for secret policies,
And we will make thee famous through the world.
ALENÇON. We'll set thy statue in some holy place,
And have thee reverenc'd like a blessed saint.
Employ thee, then, sweet virgin, for our good.
PUCELLE. Then thus it must be; this doth Joan devise:
By fair persuasions, mix'd with sug'red words,
We will entice the Duke of Burgundy
To leave the Talbot and to follow us.

CHARLES. Ay, marry, sweeting, if we could do that,
France were no place for Henry's warriors;
Nor should that nation boast it so with us,
But be extirped from our provinces.
ALENÇON. For ever should they be expuls'd from France,
And not have title of an earldom here.
PUCELLE. Your honours shall perceive how I will work
To bring this matter to the wished end.
                              [*Drum sounds afar off*]
Hark! by the sound of drum you may perceive
Their powers are marching unto Paris-ward.

*Here sound an English march. Enter, and pass over
at a distance, TALBOT and his forces*

There goes the Talbot, with his colours spread,
And all the troops of English after him.

French march. Enter the DUKE OF BURGUNDY *and
his forces*

Now in the rearward comes the Duke and his.
Fortune in favour makes him lag behind.
Summon a parley; we will talk with him.
                              [*Trumpets sound a parley*]
CHARLES. A parley with the Duke of Burgundy!
BURGUNDY. Who craves a parley with the Burgundy?
PUCELLE. The princely Charles of France, thy countryman.
BURGUNDY. What say'st thou, Charles? for I am marching
    hence.
CHARLES. Speak, Pucelle, and enchant him with thy words.
PUCELLE. Brave Burgundy, undoubted hope of France!
    Stay, let thy humble handmaid speak to thee.
BURGUNDY. Speak on; but be not over-tedious.
PUCELLE. Look on thy country, look on fertile France,
    And see the cities and the towns defac'd
    By wasting ruin of the cruel foe;
    As looks the mother on her lowly babe
    When death doth close his tender dying eyes,
    See, see the pining malady of France;
    Behold the wounds, the most unnatural wounds,
    Which thou thyself hast given her woeful breast.

O, turn thy edged sword another way;
Strike those that hurt, and hurt not those that help!
One drop of blood drawn from thy country's bosom
Should grieve thee more than streams of foreign gore.
Return thee therefore with a flood of tears,
And wash away thy country's stained spots.
BURGUNDY. Either she hath bewitch'd me with her words,
Or nature makes me suddenly relent.
PUCELLE. Besides, all French and France exclaims on thee,
Doubting thy birth and lawful progeny.
Who join'st thou with but with a lordly nation
That will not trust thee but for profit's sake?
When Talbot hath set footing once in France,
And fashion'd thee that instrument of ill,
Who then but English Henry will be lord,
And thou be thrust out like a fugitive?
Call we to mind—and mark but this for proof:
Was not the Duke of Orleans thy foe?
And was he not in England prisoner?
But when they heard he was thine enemy
They set him free without his ransom paid,
In spite of Burgundy and all his friends.
See then, thou fight'st against thy countrymen,
And join'st with them will be thy slaughtermen.
Come, come, return; return, thou wandering lord;
Charles and the rest will take thee in their arms.
BURGUNDY. I am vanquished; these haughty words of hers
Have batt'red me like roaring cannon-shot
And made me almost yield upon my knees.
Forgive me, country, and sweet countrymen
And, lords, accept this hearty kind embrace.
My forces and my power of men are yours;
So, farewell, Talbot; I'll no longer trust thee.
PUCELLE. Done like a Frenchman—[Aside] turn and turn
again.
CHARLES. Welcome, brave Duke! Thy friendship makes us
fresh.
BASTARD. And doth beget new courage in our breasts.
ALENÇON. Pucelle hath bravely play'd her part in this,
And doth deserve a coronet of gold.

ACT III. SCENE 3

CHARLES. Now let us on, my lords, and join our powers,
And seek how we may prejudice the foe. *Exeunt*

SCENE 4

Paris. The palace

Enter the KING, GLOUCESTER, WINCHESTER, YORK,
SUFFOLK, SOMERSET, WARWICK, EXETER, VERNON,
BASSET, *and others. To them, with his soldiers,*
TALBOT

TALBOT. My gracious Prince, and honourable peers,
Hearing of your arrival in this realm,
I have awhile given truce unto my wars
To do my duty to my sovereign;
In sign whereof, this arm that hath reclaim'd
To your obedience fifty fortresses,
Twelve cities, and seven walled towns of strength,
Beside five hundred prisoners of esteem,
Lets fall his sword before your Highness' feet,
And with submissive loyalty of heart
Ascribes the glory of his conquest got
First to my God and next unto your Grace.   [*Kneels*]
KING HENRY. Is this the Lord Talbot, uncle Gloucester,
That hath so long been resident in France?
GLOUCESTER. Yes, if it please your Majesty, my liege.
KING HENRY. Welcome, brave captain and victorious lord!
When I was young, as yet I am not old,
I do remember how my father said
A stouter champion never handled sword.
Long since we were resolved of your truth,
Your faithful service, and your toil in war;
Yet never have you tasted our reward,
Or been reguerdon'd with so much as thanks,
Because till now we never saw your face.
Therefore stand up; and for these good deserts
We here create you Earl of Shrewsbury;
And in our coronation take your place.
     Sennet. Flourish. Exeunt all but VERNON *and* BASSET

535

VERNON. Now, sir, to you, that were so hot at sea,
Disgracing of these colours that I wear
In honour of my noble Lord of York—
Dar'st thou maintain the former words thou spak'st?
BASSET. Yes, sir; as well as you dare patronage
The envious barking of your saucy tongue
Against my lord the Duke of Somerset.
VERNON. Sirrah, thy lord I honour as he is.
BASSET. Why, what is he? As good a man as York!
VERNON. Hark ye: not so. In witness, take ye that.
                                        [*Strikes him*]
BASSET. Villain, thou knowest the law of arms is such
That whoso draws a sword 'tis present death,
Or else this blow should broach thy dearest blood.
But I'll unto his Majesty and crave
I may have liberty to venge this wrong;
When thou shalt see I'll meet thee to thy cost.
VERNON. Well, miscreant, I'll be there as soon as you;
And, after, meet you sooner than you would.   *Exeunt*

ACT IV. SCENE 1

Paris. The palace

Enter the KING, GLOUCESTER, WINCHESTER, YORK,
SUFFOLK, SOMERSET, WARWICK, TALBOT, EXETER,
the GOVERNOR OF PARIS, *and others*

GLOUCESTER. Lord Bishop, set the crown upon his head.
WINCHESTER. God save King Henry, of that name the Sixth!
GLOUCESTER. Now, Governor of Paris, take your oath—
                                        [GOVERNOR *kneels*]
That you elect no other king but him,
Esteem none friends but such as are his friends,
And none your foes but such as shall pretend
Malicious practices against his state.
This shall ye do, so help you righteous God!
                            Exeunt GOVERNOR *and his train*

536

ACT IV. SCENE 1

Enter SIR JOHN FASTOLFE

FASTOLFE. My gracious sovereign, as I rode from Calais,
  To haste unto your coronation,
  A letter was deliver'd to my hands,
  Writ to your Grace from th' Duke of Burgundy.
TALBOT. Shame to the Duke of Burgundy and thee!
  I vow'd, base knight, when I did meet thee next
  To tear the Garter from thy craven's leg, [*Plucking it off*]
  Which I have done, because unworthily
  Thou wast installed in that high degree.
  Pardon me, princely Henry, and the rest:
  This dastard, at the battle of Patay,
  When but in all I was six thousand strong,
  And that the French were almost ten to one,
  Before we met or that a stroke was given,
  Like to a trusty squire did run away;
  In which assault we lost twelve hundred men;
  Myself and divers gentlemen beside
  Were there surpris'd and taken prisoners.
  Then judge, great lords, if I have done amiss,
  Or whether that such cowards ought to wear
  This ornament of knighthood—yea or no.
GLOUCESTER. To say the truth, this fact was infamous
  And ill beseeming any common man,
  Much more a knight, a captain, and a leader.
TALBOT. When first this order was ordain'd, my lords,
  Knights of the Garter were of noble birth,
  Valiant and virtuous, full of haughty courage,
  Such as were grown to credit by the wars;
  Not fearing death nor shrinking for distress,
  But always resolute in most extremes.
  He then that is not furnish'd in this sort
  Doth but usurp the sacred name of knight,
  Profaning this most honourable order,
  And should, if I were worthy to be judge,
  Be quite degraded, like a hedge-born swain
  That doth presume to boast of gentle blood.
KING HENRY. Stain to thy countrymen, thou hear'st thy
  doom.

537

Be packing, therefore, thou that wast a knight;
Henceforth we banish thee on pain of death.

Exit FASTOLFE

And now, my Lord Protector, view the letter
Sent from our uncle Duke of Burgundy.
GLOUCESTER. [*Viewing the superscription*] What means his
Grace, that he hath chang'd his style?
No more but plain and bluntly 'To the King!'
Hath he forgot he is his sovereign?
Or doth this churlish superscription
Pretend some alteration in good-will?
What's here? [*Reads*] 'I have, upon especial cause,
Mov'd with compassion of my country's wreck,
Together with the pitiful complaints
Of such as your oppression feeds upon,
Forsaken your pernicious faction,
And join'd with Charles, the rightful King of France.'
O monstrous treachery! Can this be so—
That in alliance, amity, and oaths,
There should be found such false dissembling guile?
KING HENRY. What! Doth my uncle Burgundy revolt?
GLOUCESTER. He doth, my lord, and is become your foe.
KING HENRY. Is that the worst this letter doth contain?
GLOUCESTER. It is the worst, and all, my lord, he writes.
KING HENRY. Why then Lord Talbot there shall talk with
him
And give him chastisement for this abuse.
How say you, my lord, are you not content?
TALBOT. Content, my liege! Yes; but that I am prevented,
I should have begg'd I might have been employ'd.
KING HENRY. Then gather strength and march unto him
straight;
Let him perceive how ill we brook his treason.
And what offence it is to flout his friends.
TALBOT. I go, my lord, in heart desiring still
You may behold confusion of your foes. *Exit*

Enter VERNON *and* BASSET

VERNON. Grant me the combat, gracious sovereign.
BASSET. And me, my lord, grant me the combat too.

YORK. This is my servant: hear him, noble Prince.

SOMERSET. And this is mine: sweet Henry, favour him.

KING HENRY. Be patient, lords, and give them leave to speak.
Say, gentlemen, what makes you thus exclaim,
And wherefore crave you combat, or with whom?

VERNON. With him, my lord; for he hath done me wrong.

BASSET. And I with him; for he hath done me wrong.

KING HENRY. What is that wrong whereof you both
complain?
First let me know, and then I'll answer you.

BASSET. Crossing the sea from England into France,
This fellow here, with envious carping tongue,
Upbraided me about the rose I wear,
Saying the sanguine colour of the leaves
Did represent my master's blushing cheeks
When stubbornly he did repugn the truth
About a certain question in the law
Argu'd betwixt the Duke of York and him;
With other vile and ignominious terms—
In confutation of which rude reproach
And in defence of my lord's worthiness,
I crave the benefit of law of arms.

VERNON. And that is my petition, noble lord;
For though he seem with forged quaint conceit
To set a gloss upon his bold intent,
Yet know, my lord, I was provok'd by him,
And he first took exceptions at this badge,
Pronouncing that the paleness of this flower
Bewray'd the faintness of my master's heart.

YORK. Will not this malice, Somerset, be left?

SOMERSET. Your private grudge, my Lord of York, will out,
Though ne'er so cunningly you smother it.

KING HENRY. Good Lord, what madness rules in brainsick
men,
When for so slight and frivolous a cause
Such factious emulations shall arise!
Good cousins both, of York and Somerset,
Quiet yourselves, I pray, and be at peace.

YORK. Let this dissension first be tried by fight,
And then your Highness shall command a peace.

SOMERSET. The quarrel toucheth none but us alone;
  Betwixt ourselves let us decide it then.
YORK. There is my pledge; accept it, Somerset.
VERNON. Nay, let it rest where it began at first.
BASSET. Confirm it so, mine honourable lord.
GLOUCESTER. Confirm it so? Confounded be your strife;
  And perish ye, with your audacious prate!
  Presumptuous vassals, are you not asham'd
  With this immodest clamorous outrage
  To trouble and disturb the King and us?
  And you, my lords—methinks you do not well
  To bear with their perverse objections,
  Much less to take occasion from their mouths
  To raise a mutiny betwixt yourselves.
  Let me persuade you take a better course.
EXETER. It grieves his Highness. Good my lords, be friends.
KING HENRY. Come hither, you that would be combatants:
  Henceforth I charge you, as you love our favour,
  Quite to forget this quarrel and the cause.
  And you, my lords, remember where we are:
  In France, amongst a fickle wavering nation;
  If they perceive dissension in our looks
  And that within ourselves we disagree,
  How will their grudging stomachs be provok'd
  To wilful disobedience, and rebel!
  Beside, what infamy will there arise
  When foreign princes shall be certified
  That for a toy, a thing of no regard,
  King Henry's peers and chief nobility
  Destroy'd themselves and lost the realm of France!
  O, think upon the conquest of my father,
  My tender years; and let us not forgo
  That for a trifle that was bought with blood!
  Let me be umpire in this doubtful strife.
  I see no reason, if I wear this rose,   [Putting on a red rose]
  That any one should therefore be suspicious
  I more incline to Somerset than York:
  Both are my kinsmen, and I love them both.
  As well they may upbraid me with my crown,
  Because, forsooth, the King of Scots is crown'd.

But your discretions better can persuade
Than I am able to instruct or teach;
And, therefore, as we hither came in peace,
So let us still continue peace and love.
Cousin of York, we institute your Grace
To be our Regent in these parts of France.
And, good my Lord of Somerset, unite
Your troops of horsemen with his bands of foot;
And like true subjects, sons of your progenitors,
Go cheerfully together and digest
Your angry choler on your enemies.
Ourself, my Lord Protector, and the rest,
After some respite will return to Calais;
From thence to England, where I hope ere long
To be presented by your victories
With Charles, Alençon, and that traitorous rout.
                Flourish. Exeunt all but YORK, WARWICK,
                                    EXETER, VERNON
WARWICK. My Lord of York, I promise you, the King
Prettily, methought, did play the orator.
YORK. And so he did; but yet I like it not,
In that he wears the badge of Somerset.
WARWICK. Tush, that was but his fancy; blame him not;
I dare presume, sweet prince, he thought no harm.
YORK. An if I wist he did—but let it rest;
Other affairs must now be managed.
                        Exeunt all but EXETER
EXETER. Well didst thou, Richard, to suppress thy voice;
For had the passions of thy heart burst out,
I fear we should have seen decipher'd there
More rancorous spite, more furious raging broils,
Than yet can be imagin'd or suppos'd.
But howsoe'er, no simple man that sees
This jarring discord of nobility,
This shouldering of each other in the court,
This factious bandying of their favourites,
But that it doth presage some ill event.
'Tis much when sceptres are in children's hands;
But more when envy breeds unkind division:
There comes the ruin, there begins confusion.   *Exit*

SCENE 2

France. Before Bordeaux

Enter TALBOT, *with trump and drum*

TALBOT. Go to the gates of Bordeaux, trumpeter;
Summon their general unto the wall.

Trumpet sounds a parley. Enter, aloft, the GENERAL
OF THE FRENCH, *and others*

English John Talbot, Captains, calls you forth,
Servant in arms to Harry King of England;
And thus he would—Open your city gates,
Be humble to us, call my sovereign yours
And do him homage as obedient subjects,
And I'll withdraw me and my bloody power;
But if you frown upon this proffer'd peace,
You tempt the fury of my three attendants,
Lean famine, quartering steel, and climbing fire;
Who in a moment even with the earth
Shall lay your stately and air-braving towers,
If you forsake the offer of their love.
GENERAL OF THE FRENCH. Thou ominous and fearful owl of
death,
Our nation's terror and their bloody scourge!
The period of thy tyranny approacheth.
On us thou canst not enter but by death;
For, I protest, we are well fortified,
And strong enough to issue out and fight.
If thou retire, the Dauphin, well appointed,
Stands with the snares of war to tangle thee.
On either hand thee there are squadrons pitch'd
To wall thee from the liberty of flight,
And no way canst thou turn thee for redress
But death doth front thee with apparent spoil
And pale destruction meets thee in the face.
Ten thousand French have ta'en the sacrament
To rive their dangerous artillery
Upon no Christian soul but English Talbot.

Lo, there thou stand'st, a breathing valiant man,
Of an invincible unconquer'd spirit!
This is the latest glory of thy praise
That I, thy enemy, due thee withal;
For ere the glass that now begins to run
Finish the process of his sandy hour,
These eyes that see thee now well coloured
Shall see thee withered, bloody, pale, and dead.

                       [Drum afar off]

Hark! hark! The Dauphin's drum, a warning bell,
Sings heavy music to thy timorous soul;
And mine shall ring thy dire departure out.   *Exit*
TALBOT. He fables not; I hear the enemy.
Out, some light horsemen, and peruse their wings.
O, negligent and heedless discipline!
How are we park'd and bounded in a pale—
A little herd of England's timorous deer,
Maz'd with a yelping kennel of French curs!
If we be English deer, be then in blood;
Not rascal-like to fall down with a pinch,
But rather, moody-mad and desperate stags,
Turn on the bloody hounds with heads of steel
And make the cowards stand aloof at bay.
Sell every man his life as dear as mine,
And they shall find dear deer of us, my friends.
God and Saint George, Talbot and England's right,
Prosper our colours in this dangerous fight!   *Exeunt*

SCENE 3

Plains in Gascony

Enter YORK, *with trumpet and many soldiers. A*
MESSENGER *meets him*

YORK. Are not the speedy scouts return'd again
That dogg'd the mighty army of the Dauphin?
MESSENGER. They are return'd, my lord, and give it out
That he is march'd to Bordeaux with his power
To fight with Talbot; as he march'd along,

By your espials were discovered
Two mightier troops than that the Dauphin led,
Which join'd with him and made their march for
    Bordeaux.
YORK. A plague upon that villain Somerset
That thus delays my promised supply
Of horsemen that were levied for this siege!
Renowned Talbot doth expect my aid,
And I am louted by a traitor villain
And cannot help the noble chevalier.
God comfort him in this necessity!
If he miscarry, farewell wars in France.

Enter SIR WILLIAM LUCY

LUCY. Thou princely leader of our English strength,
Never so needful on the earth of France,
Spur to the rescue of the noble Talbot,
Who now is girdled with a waist of iron
And hemm'd about with grim destruction.
To Bordeaux, warlike Duke! to Bordeaux, York!
Else, farewell Talbot, France, and England's honour.
YORK. O God, that Somerset, who in proud heart
Doth stop my cornets, were in Talbot's place!
So should we save a valiant gentleman
By forfeiting a traitor and a coward.
Mad ire and wrathful fury makes me weep
That thus we die while remiss traitors sleep.
LUCY. O, send some succour to the distress'd lord!
YORK. He dies; we lose; I break my warlike word.
We mourn: France smiles. We lose: they daily get—
All long of this vile traitor Somerset.
LUCY. Then God take mercy on brave Talbot's soul,
And on his son, young John, who two hours since
I met in travel toward his warlike father.
This seven years did not Talbot see his son;
And now they meet where both their lives are done.
YORK. Alas, what joy shall noble Talbot have
To bid his young son welcome to his grave?
Away! vexation almost stops my breath,
That sund'red friends greet in the hour of death.

Lucy, farewell; no more my fortune can
But curse the cause I cannot aid the man.
Maine, Blois, Poictiers, and Tours, are won away
Long all of Somerset and his delay.   *Exit with forces*
LUCY. Thus, while the vulture of sedition
Feeds in the bosom of such great commanders,
Sleeping neglection doth betray to loss
The conquest of our scarce-cold conqueror,
That ever-living man of memory,
Henry the Fifth. Whiles they each other cross,
Lives, honours, lands, and all, hurry to loss.   *Exit*

SCENE 4

Other plains of Gascony

Enter SOMERSET, *with his forces; an* OFFICER *of*
TALBOT'S *with him*

SOMERSET. It is too late; I cannot send them now.
This expedition was by York and Talbot
Too rashly plotted; all our general force
Might with a sally of the very town
Be buckled with. The over-daring Talbot
Hath sullied all his gloss of former honour
By this unheedful, desperate, wild adventure.
York set him on to fight and die in shame.
That, Talbot dead, great York might bear the name.
OFFICER. Here is Sir William Lucy, who with me
Set from our o'er-match'd forces forth for aid.

Enter SIR WILLIAM LUCY

SOMERSET. How now, Sir William! Whither were you sent?
LUCY. Whither, my lord! From bought and sold Lord
Talbot,
Who, ring'd about with bold adversity,
Cries out for noble York and Somerset
To beat assailing death from his weak legions;
And whiles the honourable captain there
Drops bloody sweat from his war-wearied limbs

545

And, in advantage ling'ring, looks for rescue,
You, his false hopes, the trust of England's honour,
Keep off aloof with worthless emulation.
Let not your private discord keep away
The levied succours that should lend him aid,
While he, renowned noble gentleman,
Yield up his life unto a world of odds.
Orleans the Bastard, Charles, Burgundy,
Alençon, Reignier, compass him about,
And Talbot perisheth by your default.

SOMERSET. York set him on; York should have sent him aid.

LUCY. And York as fast upon your Grace exclaims,
Swearing that you withhold his levied host,
Collected for this expedition.

SOMERSET. York lies; he might have sent and had the horse.
I owe him little duty and less love,
And take foul scorn to fawn on him by sending.

LUCY. The fraud of England, not the force of France,
Hath now entrapp'd the noble-minded Talbot.
Never to England shall he bear his life,
But dies betray'd to fortune by your strife.

SOMERSET. Come, go; I will dispatch the horsemen straight;
Within six hours they will be at his aid.

LUCY. Too late comes rescue; he is ta'en or slain,
For fly he could not if he would have fled;
And fly would Talbot never, though he might.

SOMERSET. If he be dead, brave Talbot, then, adieu!

LUCY. His fame lives in the world, his shame in you.

Exeunt

SCENE 5

The English camp near Bordeaux

Enter TALBOT *and* JOHN *his son*

TALBOT. O young John Talbot! I did send for thee
To tutor thee in stratagems of war,
That Talbot's name might be in thee reviv'd
When sapless age and weak unable limbs

546

Should bring thy father to his drooping chair.
But—O malignant and ill-boding stars!—
Now thou art come unto a feast of death,
A terrible and unavoided danger;
Therefore, dear boy, mount on my swiftest horse,
And I'll direct thee how thou shalt escape
By sudden flight. Come, dally not, be gone.

JOHN. Is my name Talbot, and am I your son?
And shall I fly? O, if you love my mother,
Dishonour not her honourable name,
To make a bastard and a slave of me!
The world will say he is not Talbot's blood
That basely fled when noble Talbot stood.

TALBOT. Fly to revenge my death, if I be slain.

JOHN. He that flies so will ne'er return again.

TALBOT. If we both stay, we both are sure to die.

JOHN. Then let me stay; and, father, do you fly.
Your loss is great, so your regard should be;
My worth unknown, no loss is known in me;
Upon my death the French can little boast;
In yours they will, in you all hopes are lost.
Flight cannot stain the honour you have won;
But mine it will, that no exploit have done;
You fled for vantage, every one will swear;
But if I bow, they'll say it was for fear.
There is no hope that ever I will stay
If the first hour I shrink and run away.
Here, on my knee, I beg mortality,
Rather than life preserv'd with infamy.

TALBOT. Shall all thy mother's hopes lie in one tomb?

JOHN. Ay, rather than I'll shame my mother's womb.

TALBOT. Upon my blessing I command thee go.

JOHN. To fight I will, but not to fly the foe.

TALBOT. Part of thy father may be sav'd in thee.

JOHN. No part of him but will be shame in me.

TALBOT. Thou never hadst renown, nor canst not lose it.

JOHN. Yes, your renowned name; shall flight abuse it?

TALBOT. Thy father's charge shall clear thee from that stain.

JOHN. You cannot witness for me, being slain.
If death be so apparent, then both fly.

TALBOT. And leave my followers here to fight and die?
My age was never tainted with such shame.
JOHN. And shall my youth be guilty of such blame?
No more can I be severed from your side
Than can yourself yourself in twain divide.
Stay, go, do what you will, the like do I;
For live I will not if my father die.
TALBOT. Then here I take my leave of thee, fair son,
Born to eclipse thy life this afternoon.
Come, side by side together live and die;
And soul with soul from France to heaven fly.   *Exeunt*

SCENE 6

A field of battle

Alarum: excursions wherein JOHN TALBOT *is hemm'd
about, and* TALBOT *rescues him*

TALBOT. Saint George and victory! Fight, soldiers, fight.
The Regent hath with Talbot broke his word
And left us to the rage of France his sword.
Where is John Talbot? Pause and take thy breath;
I gave thee life and rescu'd thee from death.
JOHN. O, twice my father, twice am I thy son!
The life thou gav'st me first was lost and done
Till with thy warlike sword, despite of fate,
To my determin'd time thou gav'st new date.
TALBOT. When from the Dauphin's crest thy sword struck
fire,
It warm'd thy father's heart with proud desire
Of bold-fac'd victory. Then leaden age,
Quicken'd with youthful spleen and warlike rage,
Beat down Alençon, Orleans, Burgundy,
And from the pride of Gallia rescued thee.
The ireful bastard Orleans, that drew blood
From thee, my boy, and had the maidenhood
Of thy first fight, I soon encountered
And, interchanging blows, I quickly shed
Some of his bastard blood; and in disgrace

Bespoke him thus: 'Contaminated, base,
And misbegotten blood I spill of thine,
Mean and right poor, for that pure blood of mine
Which thou didst force from Talbot, my brave boy.'
Here purposing the Bastard to destroy,
Came in strong rescue. Speak, thy father's care;
Art thou not weary, John? How dost thou fare?
Wilt thou yet leave the battle, boy, and fly,
Now thou art seal'd the son of chivalry?
Fly, to revenge my death when I am dead:
The help of one stands me in little stead.
O, too much folly is it, well I wot,
To hazard all our lives in one small boat!
If I to-day die not with Frenchmen's rage,
To-morrow I shall die with mickle age.
By me they nothing gain an if I stay:
'Tis but the short'ning of my life one day.
In thee thy mother dies, our household's name,
My death's revenge, thy youth, and England's fame.
All these and more we hazard by thy stay;
All these are sav'd if thou wilt fly away.
JOHN. The sword of Orleans hath not made me smart;
These words of yours draw life-blood from my heart.
On that advantage, bought with such a shame,
To save a paltry life and slay bright fame,
Before young Talbot from old Talbot fly,
The coward horse that bears me fall and die!
And like me to the peasant boys of France,
To be shame's scorn and subject of mischance!
Surely, by all the glory you have won,
An if I fly, I am not Talbot's son;
Then talk no more of flight, it is no boot;
If son to Talbot, die at Talbot's foot.
TALBOT. Then follow thou thy desp'rate sire of Crete,
Thou Icarus; thy life to me is sweet.
If thou wilt fight, fight by thy father's side;
And, commendable prov'd, let's die in pride.   *Exeunt*

SCENE 7

Another part of the field

Alarum; excursions. Enter old TALBOT *led by a* SERVANT

TALBOT. Where is my other life? Mine own is gone.
O, where's young Talbot? Where is valiant John?
Triumphant death, smear'd with captivity,
Young Talbot's valour makes me smile at thee.
When he perceiv'd me shrink and on my knee,
His bloody sword he brandish'd over me,
And like a hungry lion did commence
Rough deeds of rage and stern impatience;
But when my angry guardant stood alone,
Tend'ring my ruin and assail'd of none,
Dizzy-ey'd fury and great rage of heart
Suddenly made him from my side to start
Into the clust'ring battle of the French;
And in that sea of blood my boy did drench
His overmounting spirit; and there died,
My Icarus, my blossom, in his pride.

Enter soldiers, bearing the body of JOHN TALBOT

SERVANT. O my dear lord, lo where your son is borne!
TALBOT. Thou antic Death, which laugh'st us here to scorn,
Anon, from thy insulting tyranny,
Coupled in bonds of perpetuity,
Two Talbots, winged through the lither sky,
In thy despite shall scape mortality.
O thou whose wounds become hard-favoured Death,
Speak to thy father ere thou yield thy breath!
Brave Death by speaking, whether he will or no;
Imagine him a Frenchman and thy foe.
Poor boy! he smiles, methinks, as who should say,
Had Death been French, then Death had died to-day.
Come, come, and lay him in his father's arms.
My spirit can no longer bear these harms.
Soldiers, adieu! I have what I would have,
Now my old arms are young John Talbot's grave. [*Dies*]

ACT IV. SCENE 7

Enter CHARLES, ALENÇON, BURGUNDY, BASTARD,
LA PUCELLE, *and forces*

CHARLES. Had York and Somerset brought rescue in,
We should have found a bloody day of this.
BASTARD. How the young whelp of Talbot's, raging wood,
Did flesh his puny sword in Frenchmen's blood!
PUCELLE. Once I encount'red him, and thus I said:
'Thou maiden youth, be vanquish'd by a maid.'
But with a proud majestical high scorn
He answer'd thus: 'Young Talbot was not born
To be the pillage of a giglot wench.'
So, rushing in the bowels of the French,
He left me proudly, as unworthy fight.
BURGUNDY. Doubtless he would have made a noble knight.
See where he lies inhearsed in the arms
Of the most bloody nurser of his harms!
BASTARD. Hew them to pieces, hack their bones asunder,
Whose life was England's glory, Gallia's wonder.
CHARLES. O, no; forbear! For that which we have fled
During the life, let us not wrong it dead.

Enter SIR WILLIAM LUCY, *attended; a* FRENCH
HERALD *preceding*

LUCY. Herald, conduct me to the Dauphin's tent,
To know who hath obtain'd the glory of the day.
CHARLES. On what submissive message art thou sent?
LUCY. Submission, Dauphin! 'Tis a mere French word:
We English warriors wot not what it means.
I come to know what prisoners thou hast ta'en,
And to survey the bodies of the dead.
CHARLES. For prisoners ask'st thou? Hell our prison is.
But tell me whom thou seek'st.
LUCY. But where's the great Alcides of the field,
Valiant Lord Talbot, Earl of Shrewsbury,
Created for his rare success in arms
Great Earl of Washford, Waterford, and Valence,
Lord Talbot of Goodrig and Urchinfield,
Lord Strange of Blackmere, Lord Verdun of Alton,
Lord Cromwell of Wingfield, Lord Furnival of Sheffield,

The thrice victorious Lord of Falconbridge,
Knight of the noble order of Saint George,
Worthy Saint Michael, and the Golden Fleece,
Great Marshal to Henry the Sixth
Of all his wars within the realm of France?

PUCELLE. Here's a silly-stately style indeed!
The Turk, that two and fifty kingdoms hath,
Writes not so tedious a style as this.
Him that thou magnifi'st with all these titles,
Stinking and fly-blown lies here at our feet.

LUCY. Is Talbot slain—the Frenchmen's only scourge,
Your kingdom's terror and black Nemesis?
O, were mine eye-balls into bullets turn'd,
That I in rage might shoot them at your faces!
O that I could but call these dead to life!
It were enough to fright the realm of France.
Were but his picture left amongst you here,
It would amaze the proudest of you all.
Give me their bodies, that I may bear them hence
And give them burial as beseems their worth.

PUCELLE. I think this upstart is old Talbot's ghost,
He speaks with such a proud commanding spirit.
For God's sake, let him have them; to keep them here,
They would but stink, and putrefy the air.

CHARLES. Go, take their bodies hence.

LUCY. I'll bear them hence; but from their ashes shall be
rear'd
A phœnix that shall make all France afeard.

CHARLES. So we be rid of them, do with them what thou
wilt.
And now to Paris in this conquering vein!
All will be ours, now bloody Talbot's slain.   *Exeunt*

ACT V. SCENE 1

London. The palace

Sennet. Enter the KING, GLOUCESTER, *and* EXETER

KING HENRY. Have you perus'd the letters from the Pope,
  The Emperor, and the Earl of Armagnac?
GLOUCESTER. I have, my lord; and their intent is this:
  They humbly sue unto your Excellence
  To have a godly peace concluded of
  Between the realms of England and of France.
KING HENRY. How doth your Grace affect their motion?
GLOUCESTER. Well, my good lord, and as the only means
  To stop effusion of our Christian blood
  And stablish quietness on every side.
KING HENRY. Ay, marry, uncle; for I always thought
  It was both impious and unnatural
  That such immanity and bloody strife
  Should reign among professors of one faith.
GLOUCESTER. Beside, my lord, the sooner to effect
  And surer bind this knot of amity,
  The Earl of Armagnac, near knit to Charles,
  A man of great authority in France,
  Proffers his only daughter to your Grace
  In marriage, with a large and sumptuous dowry.
KING HENRY. Marriage, uncle! Alas, my years are young
  And fitter is my study and my books
  Than wanton dalliance with a paramour.
  Yet call th' ambassadors, and, as you please,
  So let them have their answers every one.
  I shall be well content with any choice
  Tends to God's glory and my country's weal.

  Enter WINCHESTER *in Cardinal's habit as* CARDINAL
  BEAUFORT, *the* PAPAL LEGATE, *and two* AMBASSA-
  DORS

EXETER. What! Is my Lord of Winchester install'd
  And call'd unto a cardinal's degree?
  Then I perceive that will be verified
  Henry the Fifth did sometime prophesy:

'If once he come to be a cardinal,
He'll make his cap co-equal with the crown.'
KING HENRY. My Lords Ambassadors, your several suits
Have been consider'd and debated on.
Your purpose is both good and reasonable,
And therefore are we certainly resolv'd
To draw conditions of a friendly peace,
Which by my Lord of Winchester we mean
Shall be transported presently to France.
GLOUCESTER. And for the proffer of my lord your master,
I have inform'd his Highness so at large,
As, liking of the lady's virtuous gifts,
Her beauty, and the value of her dower,
He doth intend she shall be England's Queen.
KING HENRY. [*To* AMBASSADOR] In argument and proof of
which contract,
Bear her this jewel, pledge of my affection.
And so, my Lord Protector, see them guarded
And safely brought to Dover; where inshipp'd,
Commit them to the fortune of the sea.
                    Exeunt all but WINCHESTER *and the* LEGATE
WINCHESTER. Stay, my Lord Legate; you shall first receive
The sum of money which I promised
Should be delivered to his Holiness
For clothing me in these grave ornaments.
LEGATE. I will attend upon your lordship's leisure.
WINCHESTER. [*Aside*] Now Winchester will not submit, I
trow,
Or be inferior to the proudest peer.
Humphrey of Gloucester, thou shalt well perceive
That neither in birth or for authority
The Bishop will be overborne by thee.
I'll either make thee stoop and bend thy knee,
Or sack this country with a mutiny.   *Exeunt*

SCENE 2

France. Plains in Anjou

Enter CHARLES, BURGUNDY, ALENÇON, BASTARD,
REIGNIER, LA PUCELLE, *and* forces

CHARLES. These news, my lords, may cheer our drooping
  spirits:
'Tis said the stout Parisians do revolt
And turn again unto the warlike French.
ALENÇON. Then march to Paris, royal Charles of France,
  And keep not back your powers in dalliance.
PUCELLE. Peace be amongst them, if they turn to us;
  Else ruin combat with their palaces!

Enter a SCOUT

SCOUT. Success unto our valiant general,
  And happiness to his accomplices!
CHARLES. What tidings send our scouts? I prithee speak.
SCOUT. The English army, that divided was
  Into two parties, is now conjoin'd in one,
  And means to give you battle presently.
CHARLES. Somewhat too sudden, sirs, the warning is;
  But we will presently provide for them.
BURGUNDY. I trust the ghost of Talbot is not there.
  Now he is gone, my lord, you need not fear.
PUCELLE. Of all base passions fear is most accurs'd.
  Command the conquest, Charles, it shall be thine,
  Let Henry fret and all the world repine.
CHARLES. Then on, my lords; and France be fortunate!
                            Exeunt

SCENE 3

Before Angiers

Alarum; excursions. Enter LA PUCELLE

PUCELLE. The Regent conquers and the Frenchmen fly.
  Now help, ye charming spells and periapts;

And ye choice spirits that admonish me
And give me signs of future accidents;   [*Thunder*]
You speedy helpers that are substitutes
Under the lordly monarch of the north,
Appear and aid me in this enterprise!

Enter Fiends

This speedy and quick appearance argues proof
Of your accustom'd diligence to me.
Now, ye familiar spirits that are cull'd
Out of the powerful regions under earth,
Help me this once, that France may get the field.
      [*They walk and speak not*]
O, hold me not with silence over-long!
Where I was wont to feed you with my blood,
I'll lop a member off and give it you
In earnest of a further benefit,
So you do condescend to help me now.
      [*They hang their heads*]
No hope to have redress? My body shall
Pay recompense, if you will grant my suit.
      [*They shake their heads*]
Cannot my body nor blood sacrifice
Entreat you to your wonted furtherance?
Then take my soul—my body, soul, and all,
Before that England give the French the foil.
      [*They depart*]
See! they forsake me. Now the time is come
That France must vail her lofty-plumed crest
And let her head fall into England's lap.
My ancient incantations are too weak,
And hell too strong for me to buckle with.
Now, France, thy glory droopeth to the dust.   *Exit*

Excursions. Enter French and English, fighting. La
Pucelle *and* York *fight hand to hand;* La Pucelle
is taken. The French fly

York. Damsel of France, I think I have you fast.
Unchain your spirits now with spelling charms,
And try if they can gain your liberty.

A goodly prize, fit for the devil's grace!
See how the ugly witch doth bend her brows
As if, with Circe, she would change my shape!
PUCELLE. Chang'd to a worser shape thou canst not be.
YORK. O, Charles the Dauphin is a proper man:
No shape but his can please your dainty eye.
PUCELLE. A plaguing mischief light on Charles and thee!
And may ye both be suddenly surpris'd
By bloody hands, in sleeping on your beds!
YORK. Fell banning hag; enchantress, hold thy tongue.
PUCELLE. I prithee give me leave to curse awhile.
YORK. Curse, miscreant, when thou comest to the stake.

Exeunt

Alarum. Enter SUFFOLK, *with* MARGARET *in his hand*

SUFFOLK. Be what thou wilt, thou art my prisoner.

[*Gazes on her*]

O fairest beauty, do not fear nor fly!
For I will touch thee but with reverent hands;
I kiss these fingers for eternal peace,
And lay them gently on thy tender side.
Who art thou? Say, that I may honour thee.
MARGARET. Margaret my name, and daughter to a king,
The King of Naples—whosoe'er thou art.
SUFFOLK. An earl I am, and Suffolk am I call'd.
Be not offended, nature's miracle,
Thou art allotted to be ta'en by me.
So doth the swan her downy cygnets save,
Keeping them prisoner underneath her wings.
Yet, if this servile usage once offend,
Go and be free again as Suffolk's friend. [*She is going*]
O, stay! [*Aside*] I have no power to let her pass;
My hand would free her, but my heart says no.
As plays the sun upon the glassy streams,
Twinkling another counterfeited beam,
So seems this gorgeous beauty to mine eyes.
Fain would I woo her, yet I dare not speak.
I'll call for pen and ink, and write my mind.
Fie, de la Pole! disable not thyself;
Hast not a tongue? Is she not here thy prisoner?

Wilt thou be daunted at a woman's sight?
Ay, beauty's princely majesty is such
Confounds the tongue and makes the senses rough.
MARGARET. Say, Earl of Suffolk, if thy name be so,
What ransom must I pay before I pass?
For I perceive I am thy prisoner.
SUFFOLK. [*Aside*] How canst thou tell she will deny thy
suit,
Before thou make a trial of her love?
MARGARET. Why speak'st thou not? What ransom must I
pay?
SUFFOLK. [*Aside*] She's beautiful, and therefore to be woo'd;
She is a woman, therefore to be won.
MARGARET. Wilt thou accept of ransom—yea or no?
SUFFOLK. [*Aside*] Fond man, remember that thou hast a
wife;
Then how can Margaret be thy paramour?
MARGARET. I were best leave him, for he will not hear.
SUFFOLK. [*Aside*] There all is marr'd; there lies a cooling
card.
MARGARET. He talks at random; sure, the man is mad.
SUFFOLK. [*Aside*] And yet a dispensation may be had.
MARGARET. And yet I would that you would answer me.
SUFFOLK. [*Aside*] I'll win this Lady Margaret. For whom?
Why, for my King! Tush, that's a wooden thing!
MARGARET. He talks of wood. It is some carpenter.
SUFFOLK. [*Aside*] Yet so my fancy may be satisfied,
And peace established between these realms.
But there remains a scruple in that too;
For though her father be the King of Naples,
Duke of Anjou and Maine, yet is he poor,
And our nobility will scorn the match.
MARGARET. Hear ye, Captain—are you not at leisure?
SUFFOLK. [*Aside*] It shall be so, disdain they ne'er so much.
Henry is youthful, and will quickly yield.—
Madam, I have a secret to reveal.
MARGARET. [*Aside*] What though I be enthrall'd? He seems
a knight,
And will not any way dishonour me.
SUFFOLK. Lady, vouchsafe to listen what I say.

MARGARET. [*Aside*] Perhaps I shall be rescu'd by the French;
And then I need not crave his courtesy.
SUFFOLK. Sweet madam, give me hearing in a cause—
MARGARET. [*Aside*] Tush! women have been captivate ere
now.
SUFFOLK. Lady, wherefore talk you so?
MARGARET. I cry you mercy, 'tis but quid for quo.
SUFFOLK. Say, gentle Princess, would you not suppose
Your bondage happy, to be made a queen?
MARGARET. To be a queen in bondage is more vile
Than is a slave in base servility;
For princes should be free.
SUFFOLK. And so shall you,
If happy England's royal king be free.
MARGARET. Why, what concerns his freedom unto me?
SUFFOLK. I'll undertake to make thee Henry's queen,
To put a golden sceptre in thy hand
And set a precious crown upon thy head,
If thou wilt condescend to be my—
MARGARET. What?
SUFFOLK. His love.
MARGARET. I am unworthy to be Henry's wife.
SUFFOLK. No, gentle madam; I unworthy am
To woo so fair a dame to be his wife
And have no portion in the choice myself.
How say you, madam? Are ye so content?
MARGARET. An if my father please, I am content.
SUFFOLK. Then call our captains and our colours forth!
And, madam, at your father's castle walls
We'll crave a parley to confer with him.

Sound a parley. Enter REIGNIER *on the walls*

See, Reignier, see, thy daughter prisoner!
REIGNIER. To whom?
SUFFOLK. To me.
REIGNIER. Suffolk, what remedy?
I am a soldier and unapt to weep
Or to exclaim on fortune's fickleness.
SUFFOLK. Yes, there is remedy enough, my lord.
Consent, and for thy honour give consent,

Thy daughter shall be wedded to my king,
Whom I with pain have woo'd and won thereto;
And this her easy-held imprisonment
Hath gain'd thy daughter princely liberty.
REIGNIER. Speaks Suffolk as he thinks?
SUFFOLK. Fair Margaret knows
That Suffolk doth not flatter, face, or feign.
REIGNIER. Upon thy princely warrant I descend
To give thee answer of thy just demand.
Exit REIGNIER *from the walls*
SUFFOLK. And here I will expect thy coming.

Trumpets sound. Enter REIGNIER *below*

REIGNIER. Welcome, brave Earl, into our territories;
Command in Anjou what your Honour pleases.
SUFFOLK. Thanks, Reignier, happy for so sweet a child,
Fit to be made companion with a king.
What answer makes your Grace unto my suit?
REIGNIER. Since thou dost deign to woo her little worth
To be the princely bride of such a lord,
Upon condition I may quietly
Enjoy mine own, the country Maine and Anjou,
Free from oppression or the stroke of war,
My daughter shall be Henry's, if he please.
SUFFOLK. That is her ransom; I deliver her.
And those two counties I will undertake
Your Grace shall well and quietly enjoy.
REIGNIER. And I again, in Henry's royal name,
As deputy unto that gracious king,
Give thee her hand for sign of plighted faith.
SUFFOLK. Reignier of France, I give thee kingly thanks,
Because this is in traffic of a king.
[*Aside*] And yet, methinks, I could be well content
To be mine own attorney in this case.—
I'll over then to England with this news,
And make this marriage to be solemniz'd.
So, farewell, Reignier. Set this diamond safe
In golden palaces, as it becomes.
REIGNIER. I do embrace thee as I would embrace
The Christian prince, King Henry, were he here.

MARGARET. Farewell, my lord. Good wishes, praise, and
    prayers,
Shall Suffolk ever have of Margaret.   [*She is going*]
SUFFOLK. Farewell, sweet madam. But hark you, Margaret—
No princely commendations to my king?
MARGARET. Such commendations as becomes a maid,
    A virgin, and his servant, say to him.
SUFFOLK. Words sweetly plac'd and modestly directed.
    But, madam, I must trouble you again—
    No loving token to his Majesty?
MARGARET. Yes, my good lord: a pure unspotted heart,
    Never yet taint with love, I send the King.
SUFFOLK. And this withal.   [*Kisses her*]
MARGARET. That for thyself—I will not so presume
    To send such peevish tokens to a king.
                 Exeunt REIGNIER *and* MARGARET
SUFFOLK. O, wert thou for myself! But, Suffolk, stay;
    Thou mayst not wander in that labyrinth:
    There Minotaurs and ugly treasons lurk.
    Solicit Henry with her wondrous praise.
    Bethink thee on her virtues that surmount,
    And natural graces that extinguish art;
    Repeat their semblance often on the seas,
    That, when thou com'st to kneel at Henry's feet,
    Thou mayst bereave him of his wits with wonder.   *Exit*

SCENE 4

Camp of the DUKE OF YORK *in Anjou*

Enter YORK, WARWICK, *and others*

YORK. Bring forth that sorceress, condemn'd to burn.

Enter LA PUCELLE, *guarded, and a* SHEPHERD

SHEPHERD. Ah, Joan, this kills thy father's heart outright!
    Have I sought every country far and near,
    And, now it is my chance to find thee out,
    Must I behold thy timeless cruel death?
    Ah, Joan, sweet daughter Joan, I'll die with thee!

PUCELLE. Decrepit miser! base ignoble wretch!
I am descended of a gentler blood;
Thou art no father nor no friend of mine.
SHEPHERD. Out, out! My lords, an please you, 'tis not so;
I did beget her, all the parish knows.
Her mother liveth yet, can testify
She was the first fruit of my bach'lorship.
WARWICK. Graceless, wilt thou deny thy parentage?
YORK. This argues what her kind of life hath been—
Wicked and vile; and so her death concludes.
SHEPHERD. Fie, Joan, that thou wilt be so obstacle!
God knows thou art a collop of my flesh;
And for thy sake have I shed many a tear.
Deny me not, I prithee, gentle Joan.
PUCELLE. Peasant, avaunt! You have suborn'd this man
Of purpose to obscure my noble birth.
SHEPHERD. 'Tis true, I gave a noble to the priest
The morn that I was wedded to her mother.
Kneel down and take my blessing, good my girl.
Wilt thou not stoop? Now cursed be the time
Of thy nativity. I would the milk
Thy mother gave thee when thou suck'dst her breast
Had been a little ratsbane for thy sake.
Or else, when thou didst keep my lambs a-field,
I wish some ravenous wolf had eaten thee.
Dost thou deny thy father, cursed drab?
O, burn her, burn her! Hanging is too good.   *Exit*
YORK. Take her away; for she hath liv'd too long,
To fill the world with vicious qualities.
PUCELLE. First let me tell you whom you have condemn'd:
Not me begotten of a shepherd swain,
But issued from the progeny of kings;
Virtuous and holy, chosen from above
By inspiration of celestial grace,
To work exceeding miracles on earth.
I never had to do with wicked spirits.
But you, that are polluted with your lusts,
Stain'd with the guiltless blood of innocents,
Corrupt and tainted with a thousand vices,
Because you want the grace that others have,

You judge it straight a thing impossible
To compass wonders but by help of devils.
No, misconceived! Joan of Arc hath been
A virgin from her tender infancy,
Chaste and immaculate in very thought;
Whose maiden blood, thus rigorously effus'd,
Will cry for vengeance at the gates of heaven.
YORK. Ay, ay. Away with her to execution!
WARWICK. And hark ye, sirs; because she is a maid,
Spare for no fagots, let there be enow.
Place barrels of pitch upon the fatal stake,
That so her torture may be shortened.
PUCELLE. Will nothing turn your unrelenting hearts?
Then, Joan, discover thine infirmity
That warranteth by law to be thy privilege:
I am with child, ye bloody homicides;
Murder not then the fruit within my womb,
Although ye hale me to a violent death.
YORK. Now heaven forfend! The holy maid with child!
WARWICK. The greatest miracle that e'er ye wrought:
Is all your strict preciseness come to this?
YORK. She and the Dauphin have been juggling.
I did imagine what would be her refuge.
WARWICK. Well, go to; we'll have no bastards live;
Especially since Charles must father it.
PUCELLE. You are deceiv'd; my child is none of his:
It was Alençon that enjoy'd my love.
YORK. Alençon, that notorious Machiavel!
It dies, an if it had a thousand lives.
PUCELLE. O, give me leave, I have deluded you.
'Twas neither Charles nor yet the Duke I nam'd,
But Reignier, King of Naples, that prevail'd.
WARWICK. A married man! That's most intolerable.
YORK. Why, here's a girl! I think she knows not well—
There were so many—whom she may accuse.
WARWICK. It's sign she hath been liberal and free.
YORK. And yet, forsooth, she is a virgin pure.
Strumpet, thy words condemn thy brat and thee.
Use no entreaty, for it is in vain.

PUCELLE. Then lead me hence—with whom I leave my
curse:
May never glorious sun reflex his beams
Upon the country where you make abode;
But darkness and the gloomy shade of death
Environ you, till mischief and despair
Drive you to break your necks or hang yourselves!

Exit, guarded

YORK. Break thou in pieces and consume to ashes,
Thou foul accursed minister of hell!

Enter CARDINAL BEAUFORT, *attended*

CARDINAL. Lord Regent, I do greet your Excellence
With letters of commission from the King.
For know, my lords, the states of Christendom,
Mov'd with remorse of these outrageous broils,
Have earnestly implor'd a general peace
Betwixt our nation and the aspiring French;
And here at hand the Dauphin and his train
Approacheth, to confer about some matter.
YORK. Is all our travail turn'd to this effect?
After the slaughter of so many peers,
So many captains, gentlemen, and soldiers,
That in this quarrel have been overthrown
And sold their bodies for their country's benefit,
Shall we at last conclude effeminate peace?
Have we not lost most part of all the towns,
By treason, falsehood, and by treachery,
Our great progenitors had conquered?
O Warwick, Warwick! I foresee with grief
The utter loss of all the realm of France.
WARWICK. Be patient, York. If we conclude a peace,
It shall be with such strict and severe covenants
As little shall the Frenchmen gain thereby.

Enter CHARLES, ALENÇON, BASTARD, REIGNIER, *and others*

CHARLES. Since, lords of England, it is thus agreed
That peaceful truce shall be proclaim'd in France,
We come to be informed by yourselves
What the conditions of that league must be.

YORK. Speak, Winchester; for boiling choler chokes
  The hollow passage of my poison'd voice,
  By sight of these our baleful enemies.
CARDINAL. Charles, and the rest, it is enacted thus:
  That, in regard King Henry gives consent,
  Of mere compassion and of lenity,
  To ease your country of distressful war,
  An suffer you to breathe in fruitful peace,
  You shall become true liegemen to his crown;
  And, Charles, upon condition thou wilt swear
  To pay him tribute and submit thyself,
  Thou shalt be plac'd as viceroy under him,
  And still enjoy thy regal dignity.
ALENÇON. Must he be then as shadow of himself?
  Adorn his temples with a coronet
  And yet, in substance and authority,
  Retain but privilege of a private man?
  This proffer is absurd and reasonless.
CHARLES. 'Tis known already that I am possess'd
  With more than half the Gallian territories,
  And therein reverenc'd for their lawful king.
  Shall I, for lucre of the rest unvanquish'd,
  Detract so much from that prerogative
  As to be call'd but viceroy of the whole?
  No, Lord Ambassador; I'll rather keep
  That which I have than, coveting for more,
  Be cast from possibility of all.
YORK. Insulting Charles! Hast thou by secret means
  Us'd intercession to obtain a league,
  And now the matter grows to compromise
  Stand'st thou aloof upon comparison?
  Either accept the title thou usurp'st,
  Of benefit proceeding from our king
  And not of any challenge of desert,
  Or we will plague thee with incessant wars.
REIGNIER. [To CHARLES] My lord, you do not well in
    obstinacy
  To cavil in the course of this contract.
  If once it be neglected, ten to one

We shall not find like opportunity.

ALENÇON. [*To* CHARLES] To say the truth, it is your policy
To save your subjects from such massacre
And ruthless slaughters as are daily seen
By our proceeding in hostility;
And therefore take this compact of a truce,
Although you break it when your pleasure serves.

WARWICK. How say'st thou, Charles? Shall our condition
stand?

CHARLES. It shall;
Only reserv'd, you claim no interest
In any of our towns of garrison.

YORK. Then swear allegiance to his Majesty:
As thou art knight, never to disobey
Nor be rebellious to the crown of England—
Thou, nor thy nobles, to the crown of England.

[CHARLES *and the rest give tokens of fealty*]
So, now dismiss your army when ye please;
Hang up your ensigns, let your drums be still,
For here we entertain a solemn peace. *Exeunt*

SCENE 5

London. The palace

Enter SUFFOLK, *in conference with the* KING,
GLOUCESTER *and* EXETER

KING HENRY. Your wondrous rare description, noble Earl,
Of beauteous Margaret hath astonish'd me.
Her virtues, graced with external gifts,
Do breed love's settled passions in my heart;
And like as rigour of tempestuous gusts
Provokes the mightiest hulk against the tide,
So am I driven by breath of her renown
Either to suffer shipwreck or arrive
Where I may have fruition of her love.

SUFFOLK. Tush, my good lord! This superficial tale
Is but a preface of her worthy praise.
The chief perfections of that lovely dame,

Had I sufficient skill to utter them,
Would make a volume of enticing lines,
Able to ravish any dull conceit;
And, which is more, she is not so divine,
So full-replete with choice of all delights,
But with as humble lowliness of mind
She is content to be at your command—
Command, I mean, of virtuous chaste intents,
To love and honour Henry as her lord.
KING HENRY. And otherwise will Henry ne'er presume.
Therefore, my Lord Protector, give consent
That Marg'ret may be England's royal Queen.
GLOUCESTER. So should I give consent to flatter sin.
You know, my lord, your Highness is betroth'd
Unto another lady of esteem.
How shall we then dispense with that contract,
And not deface your honour with reproach?
SUFFOLK. As doth a ruler with unlawful oaths;
Or one that at a triumph, having vow'd
To try his strength, forsaketh yet the lists
By reason of his adversary's odds:
A poor earl's daughter is unequal odds,
And therefore may be broke without offence.
GLOUCESTER. Why, what, I pray, is Margaret more than
    that?
Her father is no better than an earl,
Although in glorious titles he excel.
SUFFOLK. Yes, my lord, her father is a king,
The King of Naples and Jerusalem;
And of such great authority in France
As his alliance will confirm our peace,
And keep the Frenchmen in allegiance.
GLOUCESTER. And so the Earl of Armagnac may do,
Because he is near kinsman unto Charles.
EXETER. Beside, his wealth doth warrant a liberal dower;
Where Reignier sooner will receive than give.
SUFFOLK. A dow'r, my lords! Disgrace not so your king,
That he should be so abject, base, and poor,
To choose for wealth and not for perfect love.
Henry is able to enrich his queen,

And not to seek a queen to make him rich.
So worthless peasants bargain for their wives,
As market-men for oxen, sheep, or horse.
Marriage is a matter of more worth
Than to be dealt in by attorneyship;
Not whom we will, but whom his Grace affects,
Must be companion of his nuptial bed.
And therefore, lords, since he affects her most,
It most of all these reasons bindeth us
In our opinions she should be preferr'd;
For what is wedlock forced but a hell,
An age of discord and continual strife?
Whereas the contrary bringeth bliss,
And is a pattern of celestial peace.
Whom should we match with Henry, being a king,
But Margaret, that is daughter to a king?
Her peerless feature, joined with her birth,
Approves her fit for none but for a king;
Her valiant courage and undaunted spirit,
More than in women commonly is seen,
Will answer our hope in issue of a king;
For Henry, son unto a conqueror,
Is likely to beget more conquerors,
If with a lady of so high resolve
As is fair Margaret he be link'd in love.
Then yield, my lords; and here conclude with me
That Margaret shall be Queen, and none but she.
KING HENRY. Whether it be through force of your report,
  My noble Lord of Suffolk, or for that
  My tender youth was never yet attaint
  With any passion of inflaming love,
  I cannot tell; but this I am assur'd,
  I feel such sharp dissension in my breast,
  Such fierce alarums both of hope and fear,
  As I am sick with working of my thoughts.
  Take therefore shipping; post, my lord, to France;
  Agree to any covenants; and procure
  That Lady Margaret do vouchsafe to come
  To cross the seas to England, and be crown'd
  King Henry's faithful and anointed queen.

For your expenses and sufficient charge,
Among the people gather up a tenth.
Be gone, I say; for till you do return
I rest perplexed with a thousand cares.
And you, good uncle, banish all offence:
If you do censure me by what you were,
Not what you are, I know it will excuse
This sudden execution of my will.
And so conduct me where, from company,
I may revolve and ruminate my grief.   *Exit*
GLOUCESTER. Ay, grief, I fear me, both at first and last.
                    Exeunt GLOUCESTER *and* EXETER
SUFFOLK. Thus Suffolk hath prevail'd; and thus he goes,
As did the youthful Paris once to Greece,
With hope to find the like event in love
But prosper better than the Troyan did.
Margaret shall now be Queen, and rule the King;
But I will rule both her, the King, and realm.   *Exit*

The Second Part of
King Henry the Sixth

THE SECOND AND THIRD PARTS OF
KING HENRY THE SIXTH

THE first reference in print to Shakespeare is still the subject of debate amongst scholars. What exactly did Greene
intend to tell the public about Shakespeare in the open letter
addressed to 'those Gentlemen his Quondam acquaintance,
that spend their wits in making plaies'? This letter Chettle
printed in the pamphlet which Greene wrote on his death-
bed. Greene was a bitter, disappointed, and ailing man; but
the letter was addressed to playwrights who must have
known the truth about the situation Greene was discussing
—some of them must have known Shakespeare personally and
may even have worked for the same theatrical company;
whatever Greene may have wished the public to read into
his attack, he would know that Marlowe, who was certainly
among those addressed, and Nashe and Peele, if they were
also included, could check his statements. The trouble, however, is that Greene's manner of expressing himself is not
without a certain ambiguity or confusion, and what may
have been obvious at sight to his fellow playwrights is still
puzzling to the modern reader. Greene's words have to be
studied in a context that extends beyond the letter itself and
even beyond the pamphlet that contains it.

It is necessary then to look once more at the passage in
which Greene warns three of his friends against the actors
and especially against Shakespeare:

> Base minded men all three of you, if by my miserie you
> be not warnd: for unto none of you (like mee) sought
> those burres to cleave: those Puppets (I meane) that spake
> from our mouths, those Anticks garnisht in our colours. Is
> it not strange, that I, to whom they all have beene behold-
> ing: is it not like that you, to whome they all have beene
> beholding, shall (were yee in that case as I am now) bee
> both at once of them forsaken? Yes trust them not: for

there is an upstart Crow, beautified with our feathers, that with his *Tygers hart wrapt in a Players hyde*, supposes he is as well able to bombast out a blanke verse as the best of you: and beeing an absolute *Iohannes fac totum*, is in his owne conceit the onely Shake-scene in a countrey. O that I might intreat your rare wits to be imploied in more profitable courses: and let those Apes imitate your past excellence, and never more acquaint them with your ad-mired inventions.

Greene concludes his admonition to the three dramatists he has so far addressed:

Whilest you may, seeke you better Maisters: for it is pittie men of such rare wits, should be subject to the pleasure of such rude groomes.

The same advice he gives to 'two more,' and then reflects on the treatment 'new-commers' are likely to receive at the hands of 'these painted monsters' as he calls the actors.

Greene's attack is chiefly directed against the actors: they have abandoned him in his distress, he declares, and they will behave in the same inhuman way, he prophesies, to Marlowe and the other dramatists when their services are no longer required. The actors are presented in a series of disparaging figures: they are 'burres' that stick to the dramatist as long as it suits them; they are 'Puppets,' for they can speak only what the dramatist puts into their mouths; they are 'Anticks garnisht in our colours,' the 'painted monsters' of a later pas-sage; they are 'buckram Gentlemen,' 'as changeable in minde, as in many attyres.'

This tirade against actors must be read in conjunction with earlier passages in the *Groatsworth of Witte*. There Roberto, who shades off towards the end of the pamphlet into Robert Greene himself, is offered help in his distress by a stranger who declares it is a pity men of learning should live in lack. The encounter is given in Greene's own words as follows:

Roberto wondring to heare such good wordes, for that this iron age affoordes few that esteeme of vertue; returnd him thankfull gratulations, and (urgde by necessitie) uttered his present griefe, beseeching his advise how he might be imployed.

Why Roberto should feel he has merited the esteem of a lover of virtue, it is hard to say; for Roberto has just been discarded by a courtezan whose partner he had been in fleecing the unwary. The admirer of virtue, however, replies:

Why, easily quoth hee, and greatly to your benefite: for men of my profession gette by schollers their whole living. What is your profession, said *Roberto?* Truly sir, saide hee, I am a player. A player, quoth *Roberto*, I tooke you rather for a Gentleman of great living, for if by outward habit men should be censured, I tell you, you would bee taken for a substantiall man. So I am where I dwell (quoth the player) reputed able at my proper cost to build a Windmill. What though the world once went hard with me, when I was faine to carry my playing Fardle a footeback; *Tempora mutantur*, I know you know the meaning of it better than I, but I thus conster it, its otherwise now; for my very share in playing apparell will not be sold for two hundred pounds.

Here in dialogue form is set out the main count in Greene's charge against the actors.

Greene's dissatisfaction with the financial relation between dramatist and actor was not first voiced by him in his *Groatsworth of Witte*. Some years before in the second part of his *Never Too Late* he had given a short sketch of the development of the drama from its classical origins to his own day. Plays, Greene would persuade us, were originally written by gentlemen for gentlemen; this ideal arrangement, however, was disturbed by the intrusion of worldly minded and avaricious men whose interest in the stage was prompted merely by greed of gain; and as the type of these lowminded fellows Greene selects the famous Roman actor Roscius that the reader may find, in the reproof Greene reports as directed at the actor by Cicero, classical precedent for Greene's own attitude. Greene's Cicero uses the terms Greene himself employs in his later attack on the actors:

Why *Roscius*, are thou proud with *Esops* Crow, being pranct with the glorie of others feathers? Of thy selfe thou canst say nothing, and if the Cobler hath taught thee to say *Ave Caesar*, disdain not thy tutor, because thou pratest in a Kings chamber.

The speaker is reminding the actor of his debt to the dramatist; of himself the actor can say nothing, yet on the actor the public bestows its applause and its money, while the dramatist has to be content with the beggarly pittance the actor condescends to pass on to him. In the *Groatsworth of Witte* the actor tells Roberto that he had been something of an author as well as an actor:

Nay more (quoth the Player) I can serve to make a pretie speech, for I was a countrey Author, passing at a Morrall, for twas I that pende the Morrall of mans witte, the Dialogue of Dives, and for seven yeers space was absolute Interpreter to the puppets. But now my Almanacke is out of date.

The old style of Morality that could be put together even by a country author would no longer meet the demands of the London stage; the type of play required was beyond the wit of Roberto's acquaintance; so the scholar turns dramatist to keep the actor in business. Yet the actors, as Greene's letter to his 'quondam acquaintance' asserts, are so forgetful of their debt that they have cast off in his need the man who has provided them with the very means of their livelihood. And the point of his advice to his friends is that they should give up their play-writing before the actors abandon them to the poverty and misery which is now Greene's own fate.

This warning against the ungrateful nature of actors is all the more necessary, Greene insinuates, for there is coming to the notice of the public an actor who not content with his mechanical calling presumes to intrude on the preserve of the dramatists. This actor is not like Roberto's friend, one who writes in the outmoded manner of the Moralities; he has the effrontery to challenge Greene and his friends in the new style of composition fashionable in the London theatres. The actors will naturally favour one of their own tribe, however inflated and bombastic his style, and rate him above his betters in scholarship and taste. Shakespeare, for there can be no doubt that he is the actor-dramatist Greene is scoffing at, will, however undeserving, take from better dramatists the fickle favours of the actors and drive Greene's friends all the more certainly to the destitution Greene foresees for them.

Greene affects to despise Shakespeare, first because he belongs to the despicable crew of actors, and then because he actually aspires to rival the dramatists and forgets his place and the insuperable handicap of his shameful origins.

Some distinguished Shakespearean scholars, however, find more than this in Greene's attack. There is the further accusation of plagiarism, they feel. Greene's anger is too vehement, they argue, to have been provoked by anything less: Greene, when he calls Shakespeare 'an upstart Crow, beautified with our feathers,' means, they argue, that Shakespeare has rewritten work first plotted and composed by Greene and one or other of his friends. It is true Greene uses this very expression in scoffing at the successful actor whose type he sees in Roscius; the actor whose success has made him forget that he is 'proud with Esops Crow, being pranct with the glorie of others feathers'; as Shakespeare was an actor he too was 'beautified' with the feathers of the dramatists, so that the expression need refer only to Shakespeare's part as an actor, an aspect of Shakespeare's career Greene was specially anxious to emphasize, for this separated Shakespeare from Greene's acquaintances, who were not actors, and placed him in the camp of those whom Greene wished to represent as the dishonest gang who preyed on Greene's friends as well as on Greene himself.

Professor Dover Wilson has attempted to strengthen the argument in favour of regarding Greene's words as a charge of literary plagiarism by pointing out that Horace in his *Epistle* to Julius Florus alludes to the fable of the crow and his borrowed plumage to illustrate the dangers of decking out one's verses with borrowings from the classics. Horace is chaffing Florus and his friends, who have gone East on the staff of Tiberius, on their literary activities, and he hints that Celsus, who is of the party, is too slavish an imitator of what may be called the standard authors. Horace, as his *Ars*

578

Poetica shows, had no objection to an author working on a familiar story, but the writer must make it his own; he must not, if he is handling a subject treated by the Greeks, translate word for word or follow like a mere copyist. This was obviously the tendency Horace detected in Celsus. As Professor Dover Wilson insists the Elizabethans sometimes recalled the words of Horace as they set themselves to retell some familiar story; Greene himself so introduces his version of the story of Susanna and the Elders, adding, however, that he presents 'another mans picture, but freshlie flourished with mine owne colours.' From this Professor Dover Wilson concludes that Greene in his reference to Shakespeare 'as beautified with our feathers' is recalling the phrase *furtivis coloribus* that Horace uses of Celsus. There must be some confusion of thought here on Greene's part, if this were so, for what Horace found fault with in Celsus was not his rehandling of familiar subjects but his slavish adaptation of other men's words and treatment; and Greene excuses himself by insisting that, unlike Celsus, he had provided his own colours. Are we entitled then to conclude that Shakespeare was, in Greene's judgment, guilty of the practice favoured by Celsus, that is of literal imitation; or that Shakespeare had, as Greene himself did, in retelling familiar stories, added his own colours; or that Shakespeare had not only borrowed his story but often his words as well? Professor Dover Wilson seems to imply that Greene is accusing Shakespeare on the last count; for he thinks that Shakespeare in his revision of 2 and 3 *Henry VI*, though he recast the language in places, retained much of the original verse and phraseology of Greene and Nashe. Greene then, Professor Dover Wilson argues, by saying Shakespeare is 'beautified with our feathers' means that Shakespeare has not only taken over his plots but at times his very language from Greene and his friend.

Greene's letter taken by itself does not enable us to determine whether the phrase 'beautified with our feathers' means that Shakespeare had taken over and refurbished work by Greene and others or merely points to Shakespeare as an actor. The letter, however, caused some stir in theatrical circles and prompted some comment on its tenour and content.

Greene died on 3 September 1592; his *Groatsworth of*

Witte was entered in the Stationers' Register on 20 September 1592 and must have been published just after the author's death. Although the title page attributes the work to Greene there were readers who thought they saw in the production the hand of Nashe, for Nashe had at an earlier date been associated with Greene; Nashe too had scoffed at the actors in his *Epistle* prefixed to Greene's *Menaphon* and had not spared to exercise his satirical wit on dramatists who wrote for a company that played in rivalry with the men to whom his friend Greene was then attached. That was in 1589. In 1592, however, Nashe was emphatic in his denial of any share in the *Groatsworth of Witte* and wrote, in an introductory *Epistle* to the second edition of his *Pierce Penilesse*, about October 1592:

> Other news I am advertised of, that a scald trivial lying pamphlet, cald *Greens* groats-worth of wit, is given out to be of my doing. God never have care of my soule, but utterly renounce me, if the least word or sillable in it proceeded from my pen, or if I were any way privie to the writing or printing of it.

Nashe was very ready to defend Greene's memory against Gabriel Harvey and other critics, but he disclaimed all connection with the *Groatsworth of Witte*. In calling it 'a scald trivial lying pamphlet' he even seems to imply it may not have been from Greene's own hand.

Nashe's assertion that he had no share in or knowledge of the work was confirmed by the man who saw the pamphlet through the press. The publisher when entering *The Groatsworth* in the Stationers' Register was aware that Greene's tirade might give rise to unpleasantness and had inserted as a measure of self-protection the clause 'uppon the perill of Henrye Chettle.' Chettle was a friend of Greene and had prepared the pamphlet for the printer. It was inevitable that on Chettle should fall much of the displeasure excited by the publication; such was the force of hostile criticism that he found it advisable to defend himself by explaining his part in the affair; this he did in an *Epistle* to the Gentlemen Readers which he prefixed to his pamphlet *Kind-Harts Dreame*, entered in the Stationers' Register on 8 December 1592. He excuses himself and he clears Nashe as follows:

> I had onely in the copy this share, it was il written as sometime *Greenes* hand was none of the best, licensd it must be, ere it could bee printed which could never be if it might not be read. To be briefe *I* writ it over, and as neare as *I* could, followed the copy, onely in that letter *I* put something out, but in the whole booke not a worde in, for I protest it was all *Greenes*, not mine nor Maister *Nashes*, as some unjustly have affirmed.

Earlier in the *Epistle* Chettle refers to two dramatists who had expressed their displeasure at Greene's references to them. It is clear from Chettle's own reply that he is referring to Marlowe and Shakespeare. Greene in his letter had addressed Marlowe as an acquaintance, but had taken upon himself to reproach Marlowe with atheism and with other offences that Chettle tells us he felt bound to omit. These latter charges Greene, so Chettle felt, had in 'some displeasure writ,' and as to publish them 'was intollerable' this is what Chettle put out. Even here then Chettle pleads he exercised the restraint that he has always shown in hindering 'the bitter inveying against schollers.' Further as he was not himself acquainted with Marlowe or Shakespeare he had no personal animus against them; Chettle, however, feels he owes no apology to Marlowe:

> With neither of them that take offence was I acquainted, and with one of them I care not if I never be.

To Shakespeare Chettle offers a full and frank apology:

> The other, whome at that time I did not so much spare, as since I wish I had, for that as I have moderated the heate of living writers, and might have usde my owne discretion (especially in such a case) the Author beeing dead, that I did not, I am as sory as if the originall fault had beene my fault, because my selfe have seen his demeanor no less civill than he exelent in the qualitie he professes: Besides, divers of worship have reported his uprightness of dealing,

which argues his honesty, and his facetious grace in writting, that aprooves his Art.

In considering this statement by Chettle we may put aside at once some of the conclusions that have been drawn from it. It does not prove that Shakespeare must have been a new recruit to the stage because Chettle was unacquainted with him. Chettle did not know Marlowe, although Marlowe had been a well known dramatist for at least five years before Chettle mentions him. Nor does it prove that Chettle interpreted Greene's words as a charge of plagiarism against Shakespeare. 'Honesty' to the Elizabethans had a wider connotation than it has to-day. Greene had put Shakespeare with the actors as one of a dishonest profession—Chettle's words about honesty indicate that gentlemen who knew Shakespeare regarded him as a man upright in his dealings and in no way dishonest. Chettle although unacquainted with Marlowe knew about him by report and respected, so he tells us, his scholarship; he had also seen Shakespeare's quality as an actor and his equally acceptable deportment off the stage, and Chettle now adds that Shakespeare is highly spoken of as a writer by gentlemen whose views are respected. Chettle does not in this distinguish between what he knew of Marlowe or Shakespeare before he copied out Greene's pamphlet and what he heard of them afterwards. Conclusions that require us to believe that Chettle had never seen or heard of Shakespeare till Greene's letter provoked public comment rest on no sure foundation.

Chettle's statement provides sound evidence for believing that by 1592 Shakespeare was already known as a gifted writer and that gentlemen who knew him respected him as a man. There is no suggestion in Chettle's words that Shakespeare had ever been accused of literary theft.

There is, however, one scrap of contemporary evidence that might be taken to imply that Greene had provided the groundwork on which other men built. It is found in a publication entitled *Greenes Funeralls* and published early in 1594. The title page ascribes it to 'R.B. *Gent*,' but who 'R.B.' was is still a mystery. The volume contains 14 'Sonnets,' though none is in what we call sonnet form. 'Sonnets' thirteen and

fourteen are by Richard Stonyhurst; they are included as expressions of the sentiments and faith appropriate to Greene's
death-bed. Other 'Sonnets' celebrate Greene's virtues and
graces:

Nor *Mouth*, nor *Minde*, nor *Muse* can halfe declare,
His *Life*, his *Love*, his *Laude*, so excellent they were.

'Sonnet' IX mentions Greene's literary gift and contains the
lines that have been used to support the contention that
Shakespeare revised work by Greene:

Greene, is the pleasing Object of an eie:
Greene, pleasde the eies of all that lookt uppon him.
Greene, is the ground of everie Painters die:
Greene, gave the ground, to all that wrote upon him.
Nay more the men, that so Eclipst his fame:
Purloynde his Plumes, can they deny the same?

To the question, Who were the men that 'Eclipst' Greene's
fame? the answers are various, but some would reckon
Shakespeare in the number. From this some commentators
conclude that R.B. is merely clarifying Greene's assertion
that Shakespeare was 'beautified with our feathers'; Shakespeare purloined Greene's verses.

R.B. does not mention Shakespeare, and the whole tenour
of the 'Sonnets' is so incoherent and rhapsodical, the picture
in them of Greene's life and character so different from what
we learn of him from other sources, that R.B.'s evidence,
even if we could be sure he meant to refer to Shakespeare,
would be suspect. We do not know to what men R.B. refers;
we have no grounds here for supposing that Shakespeare any
more than Marlowe wrote on the ground provided by
Greene. This is the only external evidence that can be cited
in support of the opinion that Greene accused Shakespeare of
rewriting early versions of 2 and 3 *Henry VI* that Greene
himself had sketched; but what R.B. says, even if we knew
precisely what it implied, is, as the 'Sonnets' as a whole make
clear, not evidence.

Malone, who first used Greene's letter as evidence that
Shakespeare's 2 and 3 *Henry VI* were rewritings of earlier
work by Greene, thought he had good external evidence for
this interpretation of Greene's attack on Shakespeare in two

publications now commonly referred to as *The Contention* and *The True Tragedy*. These Quartos were issued in 1594 and 1595 respectively. They treat of the same action as 2 and 3 *Henry VI*, introduce the same characters, and contain much verse in common with the Folio texts; 3 *Henry VI* has about 2,900 lines, and of these some 2,000 on Malone's reckoning are found, sometimes word for word, sometimes in various transformations, in *The True Tragedy*. The relation between the Quarto text and the Folio version, however it is explained, is a close one.

Malone at first regarded *The Contention* as an original work by Greene and *The True Tragedy* as Peele's; or alternatively that the two Quarto versions were the joint composition of Greene and Peele. Shakespeare had rewritten them as 2 and 3 *Henry VI*, and Greene, Malone thought, was pointing to something which Shakespeare had stolen when he refers to Shakespeare 'with his *Tygers hart wrapt in a Players hyde.*' The line

Oh Tygres Heart, wrapt in a Womans Hide

is found in 3 *Henry VI*, I, 4 and in *The True Tragedy*. Here Malone argued:

> Greene wishing to depreciate our author, very naturally quotes a line from one of the pieces Shakespeare had thus *re-written* . . . This line, with many others, Shakespeare adopted without any alteration.

But if anything can be taken as certain from Greene's expressions it is that the line is Shakespeare's and that Greene is quoting against Shakespeare a specimen of the kind of verse Greene professes to despise. Greene adds to the contempt he wishes to express by substituting 'Players' for 'Womans,' for to Greene the actors were the cruel tribe that preyed on the dramatists. The supposition that Shakespeare must have done Greene some personal wrong is not required by the context. The wrong Shakespeare had done Greene lay in his proving a better and more popular dramatist; Greene wrote spitefully of Marlowe even as he professed to claim his acquaintance, for the accusation so deliberately made of atheism and something worse cannot be explained away as a death-bed repentance; the man who knew he had squandered his own talent felt in the actor-dramatist's success the reproof that often takes the form of a vindictive jealousy.

The evidence Malone found in the Quartos of Greene's original authorship of these pieces is now generally discredited. Professor Dover Wilson, although he still accepts in the main Malone's reading of Greene's letter and regards it as a charge of plagiarism against Shakespeare, holds that *The Contention* and *The True Tragedy* are no more than pirated versions of 2 and 3 *Henry VI*. The Quarto versions were put together by actors who had played in 2 and 3 *Henry VI*; *The Contention* and *The True Tragedy* belong to the group of texts Pollard called the Bad Quarto and show all the marks of plays put together from memory and odd players' parts. The years that immediately followed the closing of the theatres in 1592 were hard for actors; companies that had flourished in London were hard put to it to make their way in the provinces; there was considerable reorganization on the re-opening of the theatres in 1594, and the temptation to earn a little by reconstructing a piece for performance in the provinces or for sale to the publishers was an open one. There is not a shred of evidence that *The True Tragedy* was in existence when Greene was quoting from 3 *Henry VI*; he quotes from it to belittle Shakespeare's style, and chooses a line that he can use against the player as well as the dramatist. Tyrwhitt who first introduced Greene's letter into the discussion of the authorship of *Henry VI* was in no doubt that it pointed at Shakespeare as their author. We now understand the circumstances in which such Bad Quartos as *The Contention* and *The True Tragedy* were put together and why they appeared after the plague years that so impoverished the actors. They provide no evidence about the conditions that provoked Greene to slander Shakespeare except this: they were the product of the years when the actors were in straits and when dramatists like Greene who lived, as he himself reports, from hand to mouth must also have felt the pinch. Greene lay dying in the early months of what must have been a specially lean period for those who were as he was already in poverty and distress.

Those who ignore the evidence that Greene's letter affords

of Shakespeare's authorship of 3 *Henry VI* and treat it as a claim by Greene to the authorship or at least to the planning and sketching of that work have no external evidence to support their contention, unless they care to regard R.B.'s strange effusion as corroborative testimony. They must rely on the evidence that 2 and 3 *Henry VI* themselves afford of multiple authorship and of revision by Shakespeare.

Much reading has been given to finding expressions, phrases, words, in 2 and 3 *Henry VI* that can be paralleled in the writings of Greene or Nashe. But from common phrases such as 'A crafty knave does need no broker,' or 'ruling the roast,' or expressions that refer to wives wearing the breeches, no safe conclusions may be drawn. Against this there is the very strong argument that if Greene sketched these plays he showed a mastery in construction that has no parallel elsewhere in his work. Shakespeare's skill in the co-ordination of his scenes has already been commented on in the Introduction to *King John*; 2 and 3 *Henry VI* show the dexterity that he was later to raise to mastery. To suppose Shakespeare had to learn from Greene an art that Greene never possessed himself in any notable degree seems inadmissible.

The man who planned these plays obviously thought like Shakespeare on what may be called the social and political issues raised by their historical matter. No one stresses more than Professor Dover Wilson himself this like-mindedness between the plotter of these plays and Shakespeare. Of the third part he says:

> it imposes the rhythm of art upon the ebb and flow of civil strife, and frames dramatic cosmos out of a chaos of historical events.

The man who laid the lines on which the action was to run had surveyed the ground carefully; and we are entitled to ask what evidence Greene's acknowledged work gives of such preparation. To say that Shakespeare revised the work and improved on the original author's design without attributing to Shakespeare the interest in the matter as set out by the Chroniclers that Greene is supposed to have had is to contradict the evidence that can be drawn from the work

elsewhere of Greene and Shakespeare. Professor Dover Wilson insists that the drafters or authors of *Henry VI* must
have had 'quite a little library of chronicles on the shelf';
and he argues that 'so active and voluminous a writer as
Greene must once have possessed a "study of books." ' But
Shakespeare was an even more active writer and as voluminous. Are we not entitled by the same token to suppose his
study was equally well furnished? Shakespeare to the end of
his working life showed his interest in history. Even his
Tragedies, though they are not Histories, are often drawn
from what were regarded as historical sources. Why we
should have to suppose that the man who plotted *Macbeth*
needed Greene to set out the design of *Henry VI* for him is
a question that has never been answered. Certainly *Henry
VI* is a much cruder and less intensively contrived work than
Macbeth, but the latter is the work of Shakespeare's maturity.
We have no right to suppose that his earlier pieces must contain alien elements because they are not the well wrought
dramas of his later years. The man who drafted *Henry VI*
worked like the man who wrote *Henry IV*, only without the
experience and craft with which the years were to crown
his endeavour. As Professor Dover Wilson observes, the historical material is worked into the plot of 2 *Henry VI*

> with no little skill, a skill evident also in certain additions
> to, or developments of, the source material.

To object

> that, despite all this careful contrivance, the details are
> often woefully lacking in care or even dramatic com-
> petence

is, if the charge were true and acceptable as evidence of
divided authorship, to argue that Shakespeare was not a very
competent reviser. This is having it both ways. If Shakespeare could let such 'incompetence' stand in his revision, he
was surely capable of such carelessness in his own composition. But we have no need of Greene to explain what lapses
there are; they are the evidence of youth and immaturity and
Henry VI was written when Shakespeare was still in his
twenties.

KING HENRY THE SIXTH
HUMPHREY, DUKE OF GLOUCESTER, *his uncle*
CARDINAL BEAUFORT, BISHOP OF WINCHESTER, *great-uncle to the King*
RICHARD PLANTAGENET, DUKE OF YORK
EDWARD *and* RICHARD, *his sons*   DUKE OF SOMERSET
DUKE OF SUFFOLK   DUKE OF BUCKINGHAM
LORD CLIFFORD
YOUNG CLIFFORD, *his son*
EARL OF SALISBURY   EARL OF WARWICK
LORD SCALES   LORD SAY
SIR HUMPHREY STAFFORD
WILLIAM STAFFORD, *his brother*
SIR JOHN STANLEY   VAUX
MATTHEW GOFFE
A LIEUTENANT, *a* SHIPMASTER, *a* MASTER'S MATE, *and* WALTER WHITMORE
TWO GENTLEMEN, *prisoners with Suffolk*
JOHN HUME *and* JOHN SOUTHWELL, *two priests*
ROGER BOLINGBROKE, *a conjurer*
A SPIRIT *raised by him*
THOMAS HORNER, *an armourer*
PETER, *his man*   CLERK OF CHATHAM
MAYOR OF SAINT ALBANS
SAUNDER SIMPCOX, *an impostor*
ALEXANDER IDEN, *a Kentish gentleman*
JACK CADE, *a rebel*
GEORGE BEVIS, JOHN HOLLAND, DICK THE BUTCHER, SMITH THE WEAVER, MICHAEL, *&c., followers of Cade*
TWO MURDERERS

MARGARET, *Queen to King Henry*
ELEANOR, *Duchess of Gloucester*
MARGERY JOURDAIN, *a witch*   WIFE *to Simpcox*

Lords, Ladies, *and* Attendants; Petitioners, Aldermen, *a* Herald, *a* Beadle, *a* Sheriff, Officers, Citizens, Prentices, Falconers, Guards, Soldiers, Messengers, *&c.*

SCENE:

England

The Second Part of King Henry the Sixth

ACT I. SCENE 1

London. The palace

Flourish of trumpets; then hautboys. Enter the KING, DUKE HUMPHREY OF GLOUCESTER, SALISBURY, WARWICK, *and* CARDINAL BEAUFORT, *on the one side; the* QUEEN, SUFFOLK, YORK, SOMERSET, *and* BUCKINGHAM, *on the other*

SUFFOLK. As by your high imperial Majesty
I had in charge at my depart for France,
As procurator to your Excellence,
To marry Princess Margaret for your Grace;
So, in the famous ancient city Tours,
In presence of the Kings of France and Sicil,
The Dukes of Orleans, Calaber, Bretagne, and Alençon,
Seven earls, twelve barons, and twenty reverend bishops,
I have perform'd my task, and was espous'd;
And humbly now upon my bended knee,
In sight of England and her lordly peers,
Deliver up my title in the Queen
To your most gracious hands, that are the substance
Of that great shadow I did represent:
The happiest gift that ever marquis gave,
The fairest queen that ever king receiv'd.
KING HENRY. Suffolk, arise. Welcome, Queen Margaret:
I can express no kinder sign of love
Than this kind kiss. O Lord, that lends me life,
Lend me a heart replete with thankfulness!
For thou hast given me in this beauteous face
A world of earthly blessings to my soul,
If sympathy of love unite our thoughts.

QUEEN. Great King of England, and my gracious lord,
The mutual conference that my mind hath had,
By day, by night, waking and in my dreams,
In courtly company or at my beads,
With you, mine alder-liefest sovereign,
Makes me the bolder to salute my king
With ruder terms, such as my wit affords
And over-joy of heart doth minister.

KING HENRY. Her sight did ravish, but her grace in speech,
Her words y-clad with wisdom's majesty,
Makes me from wond'ring fall to weeping joys,
Such is the fulness of my heart's content.
Lords, with one cheerful voice welcome my love.

ALL. [Kneeling] Long live Queen Margaret, England's happiness!

QUEEN. We thank you all. [Flourish]

SUFFOLK. My Lord Protector, so it please your Grace,
Here are the articles of contracted peace
Between our sovereign and the French King Charles,
For eighteen months concluded by consent.

GLOUCESTER. [Reads] 'Imprimis: It is agreed between the French King Charles and William de la Pole, Marquess of Suffolk, ambassador for Henry King of England, that the said Henry shall espouse the Lady Margaret, daughter unto Reignier King of Naples, Sicilia, and Jerusalem, and crown her Queen of England ere the thirtieth of May next ensuing.

Item: That the duchy of Anjou and the county of Maine shall be released and delivered to the King her father'— [Lets the paper fall]

KING HENRY. Uncle, how now!

GLOUCESTER. Pardon me, gracious lord;
Some sudden qualm hath struck me at the heart,
And dimm'd mine eyes, that I can read no further.

KING HENRY. Uncle of Winchester, I pray read on.

CARDINAL. [Reads] 'Item: It is further agreed between them that the duchies of Anjou and Maine shall be released and delivered over to the King her father, and she sent over of the King of England's own proper cost and charges, without having any dowry.'

ACT I. SCENE 1

KING HENRY. They please us well. Lord Marquess, kneel
   down.
We here create thee the first Duke of Suffolk,
And girt thee with the sword. Cousin of York,
We here discharge your Grace from being Regent
I' th' parts of France, till term of eighteen months
Be full expir'd. Thanks, uncle Winchester,
Gloucester, York, Buckingham, Somerset,
Salisbury, and Warwick;
We thank you all for this great favour done
In entertainment to my princely queen.
Come, let us in, and with all speed provide
To see her coronation be perform'd.
               Exeunt KING, QUEEN, *and* SUFFOLK

GLOUCESTER. Brave peers of England, pillars of the state,
To you Duke Humphrey must unload his grief—
Your grief, the common grief of all the land.
What! did my brother Henry spend his youth,
His valour, coin, and people, in the wars?
Did he so often lodge in open field,
In winter's cold and summer's parching heat,
To conquer France, his true inheritance?
And did my brother Bedford toil his wits
To keep by policy what Henry got?
Have you yourselves, Somerset, Buckingham,
Brave York, Salisbury, and victorious Warwick,
Receiv'd deep scars in France and Normandy?
Or hath mine uncle Beaufort and myself,
With all the learned Council of the realm,
Studied so long, sat in the Council House
Early and late, debating to and fro
How France and Frenchmen might be kept in awe?
And had his Highness in his infancy
Crowned in Paris, in despite of foes?
And shall these labours and these honours die?
Shall Henry's conquest, Bedford's vigilance,
Your deeds of war, and all our counsel die?
O peers of England, shameful is this league!
Fatal this marriage, cancelling your fame,
Blotting your names from books of memory,

Razing the characters of your renown,
Defacing monuments of conquer'd France,
Undoing all, as all had never been!

CARDINAL. Nephew, what means this passionate discourse,
This peroration with such circumstance?
For France, 'tis ours; and we will keep it still.

GLOUCESTER. Ay, uncle, we will keep it if we can;
But now it is impossible we should.
Suffolk, the new-made duke that rules the roast,
Hath given the duchy of Anjou and Maine
Unto the poor King Reignier, whose large style
Agrees not with the leanness of his purse.

SALISBURY. Now, by the death of Him that died for all,
These counties were the keys of Normandy!
But wherefore weeps Warwick, my valiant son?

WARWICK. For grief that they are past recovery;
For were there hope to conquer them again
My sword should shed hot blood, mine eyes no tears.
Anjou and Maine! myself did win them both;
Those provinces these arms of mine did conquer;
And are the cities that I got with wounds
Deliver'd up again with peaceful words?
Mort Dieu!

YORK. For Suffolk's duke, may he be suffocate,
That dims the honour of this warlike isle!
France should have torn and rent my very heart
Before I would have yielded to this league.
I never read but England's kings have had
Large sums of gold and dowries with their wives;
And our King Henry gives away his own
To match with her that brings no vantages.

GLOUCESTER. A proper jest, and never heard before,
That Suffolk should demand a whole fifteenth
For costs and charges in transporting her!
She should have stay'd in France, and starv'd in France,
Before—

CARDINAL. My Lord of Gloucester, now ye grow too hot:
It was the pleasure of my lord the King.

GLOUCESTER. My Lord of Winchester, I know your mind;
'Tis not my speeches that you do mislike,

But 'tis my presence that doth trouble ye.
Rancour will out: proud prelate, in thy face
I see thy fury; if I longer stay
We shall begin our ancient bickerings.
Lordings, farewell; and say, when I am gone,
I prophesied France will be lost ere long.   *Exit*
CARDINAL. So, there goes our Protector in a rage.
'Tis known to you he is mine enemy;
Nay, more, an enemy unto you all,
And no great friend, I fear me, to the King.
Consider, lords, he is the next of blood
And heir apparent to the English crown.
Had Henry got an empire by his marriage
And all the wealthy kingdoms of the west,
There's reason he should be displeas'd at it.
Look to it, lords; let not his smoothing words
Bewitch your hearts; be wise and circumspect.
What though the common people favour him,
Calling him 'Humphrey, the good Duke of Gloucester,'
Clapping their hands, and crying with loud voice
'Jesu maintain your royal excellence!'
With 'God preserve the good Duke Humphrey!'
I fear me, lords, for all this flattering gloss,
He will be found a dangerous Protector.
BUCKINGHAM. Why should he then protect our sovereign,
He being of age to govern of himself?
Cousin of Somerset, join you with me,
And all together, with the Duke of Suffolk,
We'll quickly hoise Duke Humphrey from his seat.
CARDINAL. This weighty business will not brook delay;
I'll to the Duke of Suffolk presently.   *Exit*
SOMERSET. Cousin of Buckingham, though Humphrey's pride
And greatness of his place be grief to us,
Yet let us watch the haughty cardinal;
His insolence is more intolerable
Than all the princes in the land beside;
If Gloucester be displac'd, he'll be Protector.
BUCKINGHAM. Or thou or I, Somerset, will be Protector,
Despite Duke Humphrey or the Cardinal.
                    Exeunt BUCKINGHAM *and* SOMERSET

593

SALISBURY. Pride went before, ambition follows him.
　While these do labour for their own preferment,
　Behoves it us to labour for the realm.
　I never saw but Humphrey Duke of Gloucester
　Did bear him like a noble gentleman.
　Oft have I seen the haughty Cardinal—
　More like a soldier than a man o' th' church,
　As stout and proud as he were lord of all—
　Swear like a ruffian and demean himself
　Unlike the ruler of a commonweal.
　Warwick my son, the comfort of my age,
　Thy deeds, thy plainness, and thy housekeeping,
　Hath won the greatest favour of the commons,
　Excepting none but good Duke Humphrey.
　And, brother York, thy acts in Ireland,
　In bringing them to civil discipline,
　Thy late exploits done in the heart of France
　When thou wert Regent for our sovereign,
　Have made thee fear'd and honour'd of the people:
　Join we together for the public good,
　In what we can, to bridle and suppress
　The pride of Suffolk and the Cardinal,
　With Somerset's and Buckingham's ambition;
　And, as we may, cherish Duke Humphrey's deeds
　While they do tend the profit of the land.
WARWICK. So God help Warwick, as he loves the land
　And common profit of his country!
YORK. And so says York—[Aside] for he hath greatest cause.
SALISBURY. Then let's make haste away and look unto the
　main.
WARWICK. Unto the main! O father, Maine is lost—
　That Maine which by main force Warwick did win,
　And would have kept so long as breath did last.
　Main chance, father, you meant; but I meant Maine,
　Which I will win from France, or else be slain.
　　　　　　　　　　　　　　Exeunt WARWICK and SALISBURY
YORK. Anjou and Maine are given to the French;
　Paris is lost; the state of Normandy
　Stands on a tickle point now they are gone.
　Suffolk concluded on the articles;

The peers agreed; and Henry was well pleas'd
To changes two dukedoms for a duke's fair daughter.
I cannot blame them all: what is't to them?
'Tis thine they give away, and not their own.
Pirates may make cheap pennyworths of their pillage,
And purchase friends, and give to courtezans,
Still revelling like lords till all be gone;
While as the silly owner of the goods
Weeps over them and wrings his hapless hands
And shakes his head and trembling stands aloof,
While all is shar'd and all is borne away,
Ready to starve and dare not touch his own.
So York must sit and fret and bite his tongue,
While his own lands are bargain'd for and sold.
Methinks the realms of England, France, and Ireland,
Bear that proportion to my flesh and blood
As did the fatal brand Althæa burnt
Unto the prince's heart of Calydon.
Anjou and Maine both given unto the French!
Cold news for me, for I had hope of France,
Even as I have of fertile England's soil.
A day will come when York shall claim his own;
And therefore I will take the Nevils' parts,
And make a show of love to proud Duke Humphrey,
And when I spy advantage, claim the crown,
For that's the golden mark I seek to hit.
Nor shall proud Lancaster usurp my right,
Nor hold the sceptre in his childish fist,
Nor wear the diadem upon his head,
Whose church-like humours fits not for a crown.
Then, York, be still awhile, till time do serve;
Watch thou and wake, when others be asleep,
To pry into the secrets of the state;
Till Henry, surfeiting in joys of love
With his new bride and England's dear-bought queen,
And Humphrey with the peers be fall'n at jars;
Then will I raise aloft the milk-white rose,
With whose sweet smell the air shall be perfum'd,
And in my standard bear the arms of York,
To grapple with the house of Lancaster;

And force perforce I'll make him yield the crown,
Whose bookish rule hath pull'd fair England down.   *Exit*

SCENE 2

The Duke of Gloucester's *house*

Enter Duke Humphrey *and his wife* Eleanor

DUCHESS. Why droops my lord, like over-ripen'd corn
Hanging the head at Ceres' plenteous load?
Why doth the great Duke Humphrey knit his brows,
As frowning at the favours of the world?
Why are thine eyes fix'd to the sullen earth,
Gazing on that which seems to dim thy sight?
What see'st thou there? King Henry's diadem,
Enchas'd with all the honours of the world?
If so, gaze on, and grovel on thy face
Until thy head be circled with the same.
Put forth thy hand, reach at the glorious gold.
What, is't too short? I'll lengthen it with mine;
And having both together heav'd it up,
We'll both together lift our heads to heaven,
And never more abase our sight so low
As to vouchsafe one glance unto the ground.
GLOUCESTER. O Nell, sweet Nell, if thou dost love thy lord,
Banish the canker of ambitious thoughts!
And may that thought, when I imagine ill
Against my king and nephew, virtuous Henry,
Be my last breathing in this mortal world!
My troublous dreams this night doth make me sad.
DUCHESS. What dream'd my lord? Tell me, and I'll requite it
With sweet rehearsal of my morning's dream.
GLOUCESTER. Methought this staff, mine office-badge in
    court,
Was broke in twain; by whom I have forgot,
But, as I think, it was by th' Cardinal;
And on the pieces of the broken wand
Were plac'd the heads of Edmund Duke of Somerset
And William de la Pole, first Duke of Suffolk.

This was my dream; what it doth bode God knows.

DUCHESS. Tut, this was nothing but an argument
  That he that breaks a stick of Gloucester's grove
  Shall lose his head for his presumption.
  But list to me, my Humphrey, my sweet Duke:
  Methought I sat in seat of majesty
  In the cathedral church of Westminster,
  And in that chair where kings and queens were crown'd;
  Where Henry and Dame Margaret kneel'd to me,
  And on my head did set the diadem.

GLOUCESTER. Nay, Eleanor, then must I chide outright.
  Presumptuous dame, ill-nurtur'd Eleanor!
  Art thou not second woman in the realm,
  And the Protector's wife, belov'd of him?
  Hast thou not worldly pleasure at command
  Above the reach or compass of thy thought?
  And wilt thou still be hammering treachery
  To tumble down thy husband and thyself
  From top of honour to disgrace's feet?
  Away from me, and let me hear no more!

DUCHESS. What, what, my lord! Are you so choleric
  With Eleanor for telling but her dream?
  Next time I'll keep my dreams unto myself
  And not be check'd.

GLOUCESTER. Nay, be not angry; I am pleas'd again.

Enter a MESSENGER

MESSENGER. My Lord Protector, 'tis his Highness' pleasure
  You do prepare to ride unto Saint Albans,
  Where as the King and Queen do mean to hawk.

GLOUCESTER. I go. Come, Nell, thou wilt ride with us?

DUCHESS. Yes, my good lord, I'll follow presently.

Exeunt GLOUCESTER *and* MESSENGER

  Follow I must; I cannot go before,
  While Gloucester bears this base and humble mind.
  Were I a man, a duke, and next of blood,
  I would remove these tedious stumbling-blocks
  And smooth my way upon their headless necks;
  And, being a woman, I will not be slack
  To play my part in Fortune's pageant.

Where are you there, Sir John? Nay, fear not, man,
We are alone; here's none but thee and I.

Enter HUME

HUME. Jesus preserve your royal Majesty!
DUCHESS. What say'st thou? Majesty! I am but Grace.
HUME. But, by the grace of God and Hume's advice,
  Your Grace's title shall be multiplied.
DUCHESS. What say'st thou, man? Hast thou as yet conferr'd
  With Margery Jourdain, the cunning witch of Eie,
  With Roger Bolingbroke, the conjurer?
  And will they undertake to do me good?
HUME. This they have promised, to show your Highness
  A spirit rais'd from depth of underground
  That shall make answer to such questions
  As by your Grace shall be propounded him.
DUCHESS. It is enough; I'll think upon the questions;
  When from Saint Albans we do make return
  We'll see these things effected to the full.
  Here, Hume, take this reward; make merry, man,
  With thy confederates in this weighty cause.   *Exit*
HUME. Hume must make merry with the Duchess' gold;
  Marry, and shall. But, how now, Sir John Hume!
  Seal up your lips and give no words but mum:
  The business asketh silent secrecy.
  Dame Eleanor gives gold to bring the witch:
  Gold cannot come amiss were she a devil.
  Yet have I gold flies from another coast—
  I dare not say from the rich Cardinal,
  And from the great and new-made Duke of Suffolk;
  Yet I do find it so; for, to be plain,
  They, knowing Dame Eleanor's aspiring humour,
  Have hired me to undermine the Duchess,
  And buzz these conjurations in her brain.
  They say 'A crafty knave does need no broker';
  Yet am I Suffolk and the Cardinal's broker.
  Hume, if you take not heed, you shall go near
  To call them both a pair of crafty knaves.
  Well, so its stands; and thus, I fear, at last
  Hume's knavery will be the Duchess' wreck,

And her attainture will be Humphrey's fall.
Sort how it will, I shall have gold for all.　　　*Exit*

SCENE 3

London. The palace

Enter three or four PETITIONERS, PETER,
the Armourer's man, being one

FIRST PETITIONER. My masters, let's stand close; my Lord
Protector will come this way by and by, and then we may
deliver our supplications in the quill.

SECOND PETITIONER. Marry, the Lord protect him, for he's a
good man, Jesu bless him!

Enter SUFFOLK *and* QUEEN

FIRST PETITIONER. Here 'a comes, methinks, and the Queen
with him. I'll be the first, sure.

SECOND PETITIONER. Come back, fool; this is the Duke of
Suffolk and not my Lord Protector.

SUFFOLK. How now, fellow! Wouldst anything with me?

FIRST PETITIONER. I pray, my lord, pardon me; I took ye for
my Lord Protector.

QUEEN. [*Reads*] 'To my Lord Protector!' Are your supplications to his lordship? Let me see them. What is thine?

FIRST PETITIONER. Mine is, an't please your Grace, against
John Goodman, my Lord Cardinal's man, for keeping my
house and lands, and wife and all, from me.

SUFFOLK. Thy wife too! That's some wrong indeed. What's
yours? What's here! [*Reads*] 'Against the Duke of Suffolk, for enclosing the commons of Melford.' How now,
sir knave!

SECOND PETITIONER. Alas, sir, I am but a poor petitioner of
our whole township.

PETER. [*Presenting his petition*] Against my master, Thomas
Horner, for saying that the Duke of York was rightful
heir to the crown.

QUEEN. What say'st thou? Did the Duke of York say he was
rightful heir to the crown?

PETER. That my master was? No, forsooth. My master said
that he was, and that the King was an usurper.

SUFFOLK. Who is there? [*Enter servant*] Take this fellow in,
and send for his master with a pursuivant presently. We'll
hear more of your matter before the King.

Exit servant with PETER

QUEEN. And as for you, that love to be protected
Under the wings of our Protector's grace,
Begin your suits anew, and sue to him.

[*Tears the supplications*]

Away, base cullions! Suffolk, let them go.

ALL. Come, let's be gone. *Exeunt*

QUEEN. My Lord of Suffolk, say, is this the guise,
Is this the fashions in the court of England?
Is this the government of Britain's isle,
And this the royalty of Albion's king?
What, shall King Henry be a pupil still,
Under the surly Gloucester's governance?
Am I a queen in title and in style,
And must be made a subject to a duke?
I tell thee, Pole, when in the city Tours
Thou ran'st a tilt in honour of my love
And stol'st away the ladies' hearts of France,
I thought King Henry had resembled thee
In courage, courtship, and proportion;
But all his mind is bent to holiness,
To number Ave-Maries on his beads;
His champions are the prophets and apostles;
His weapons, holy saws of sacred writ;
His study is his tilt-yard, and his loves
Are brazen images of canonized saints.
I would the college of the Cardinals
Would choose him Pope, and carry him to Rome,
And set the triple crown upon his head;
That were a state fit for his holiness.

SUFFOLK. Madam, be patient. As I was cause
Your Highness came to England, so will I
In England work your Grace's full content.

QUEEN. Beside the haughty Protector, have we Beaufort
The imperious churchman; Somerset, Buckingham,

And grumbling York; and not the least of these
But can do more in England than the King.
SUFFOLK. And he of these that can do most of all
Cannot do more in England than the Nevils;
Salisbury and Warwick are no simple peers.
QUEEN. Not all these lords do vex me half so much
As that proud dame, the Lord Protector's wife.
She sweeps it through the court with troops of ladies,
More like an empress than Duke Humphrey's wife.
Strangers in court do take her for the Queen.
She bears a duke's revenues on her back,
And in her heart she scorns our poverty;
Shall I not live to be aveng'd on her?
Contemptuous base-born callet as she is,
She vaunted 'mongst her minions t' other day
The very train of her worst wearing gown
Was better worth than all my father's lands,
Till Suffolk gave two dukedoms for his daughter.
SUFFOLK. Madam, myself have lim'd a bush for her,
And plac'd a quire of such enticing birds
That she will light to listen to the lays,
And never mount to trouble you again.
So, let her rest. And, madam, list to me,
For I am bold to counsel you in this:
Although we fancy not the Cardinal,
Yet must we join with him and with the lords,
Till we have brought Duke Humphrey in disgrace.
As for the Duke of York, this late complaint
Will make but little for his benefit.
So one by one we'll weed them all at last,
And you yourself shall steer the happy helm.

Sound a sennet. Enter the KING, DUKE HUMPHREY,
CARDINAL BEAUFORT, BUCKINGHAM, YORK, SOMER-
SET, SALISBURY, WARWICK, *and the* DUCHESS OF
GLOUCESTER

KING HENRY. For my part, noble lords, I care not which:
Or Somerset or York, all's one to me.
YORK. If York have ill demean'd himself in France,
Then let him be denay'd the regentship.

SOMERSET. If Somerset be unworthy of the place,
  Let York be Regent; I will yield to him.
WARWICK. Whether your Grace be worthy, yea or no,
  Dispute not that; York is the worthier.
CARDINAL. Ambitious Warwick, let thy betters speak.
WARWICK. The Cardinal's not my better in the field.
BUCKINGHAM. All in this presence are thy betters, Warwick.
WARWICK. Warwick may live to be the best of all.
SALISBURY. Peace, son! And show some reason, Buckingham,
  Why Somerset should be preferr'd in this.
QUEEN. Because the King, forsooth, will have it so.
GLOUCESTER. Madam, the King is old enough himself
  To give his censure. These are no women's matters.
QUEEN. If he be old enough, what needs your Grace
  To be Protector of his Excellence?
GLOUCESTER. Madam, I am Protector of the realm;
  And at his pleasure will resign my place.
SUFFOLK. Resign it then, and leave thine insolence.
  Since thou wert king—as who is king but thou?—
  The commonwealth hath daily run to wrack,
  The Dauphin hath prevail'd beyond the seas,
  And all the peers and nobles of the realm
  Have been as bondmen to thy sovereignty.
CARDINAL. The commons hast thou rack'd; the clergy's bags
  Are lank and lean with thy extortions.
SOMERSET. Thy sumptuous buildings and thy wife's attire
  Have cost a mass of public treasury.
BUCKINGHAM. Thy cruelty in execution
  Upon offenders hath exceeded law,
  And left thee to the mercy of the law.
QUEEN. Thy sale of offices and towns in France,
  If they were known, as the suspect is great,
  Would make thee quickly hop without thy head.
            Exit GLOUCESTER. *The* QUEEN *drops her fan*
  Give me my fan. What, minion, can ye not?
            [*She gives the* DUCHESS *a box on the ear*]
  I cry your mercy, madam; was it you?
DUCHESS. Was't I? Yea, I it was, proud Frenchwoman.
  Could I come near your beauty with my nails,
  I could set my ten commandments in your face.

KING HENRY. Sweet aunt, be quiet; 'twas against her will.
DUCHESS. Against her will, good King? Look to 't in time;
  She'll hamper thee and dandle thee like a baby.
  Though in this place most master wear no breeches,
  She shall not strike Dame Eleanor unreveng'd.   *Exit*
BUCKINGHAM. Lord Cardinal, I will follow Eleanor,
  And listen after Humphrey, how he proceeds.
  She's tickled now; her fume needs no spurs,
  She'll gallop far enough to her destruction.   *Exit*

Re-enter GLOUCESTER

GLOUCESTER. Now, lords, my choler being overblown
  With walking once about the quadrangle,
  I come to talk of commonwealth affairs.
  As for your spiteful false objections,
  Prove them, and I lie open to the law;
  But God in mercy so deal with my soul
  As I in duty love my king and country!
  But to the matter that we have in hand:
  I say, my sovereign, York is meetest man
  To be your Regent in the realm of France.
SUFFOLK. Before we make election, give me leave
  To show some reason, of no little force,
  That York is most unmeet of any man.
YORK. I'll tell thee, Suffolk, why I am unmeet:
  First, for I cannot flatter thee in pride;
  Next, if I be appointed for the place,
  My Lord of Somerset will keep me here
  Without discharge, money, or furniture,
  Till France be won into the Dauphin's hands.
  Last time I danc'd attendance on his will
  Till Paris was besieg'd, famish'd, and lost.
WARWICK. That can I witness; and a fouler fact
  Did never traitor in the land commit.
SUFFOLK. Peace, headstrong Warwick!
WARWICK. Image of pride, why should I hold my peace?

Enter HORNER, *the Armourer, and his man* PETER,
guarded

SUFFOLK. Because here is a man accus'd of treason:

Pray God the Duke of York excuse himself!

YORK. Doth any one accuse York for a traitor?

KING HENRY. What mean'st thou, Suffolk? Tell me, what
are these?

SUFFOLK. Please it your Majesty, this is the man
That doth accuse his master of high treason;
His words were these: that Richard Duke of York
Was rightful heir unto the English crown,
And that your Majesty was an usurper.

KING HENRY. Say, man, were these thy words?

HORNER. An't shall please your Majesty, I never said nor
thought any such matter. God is my witness, I am falsely
accus'd by the villain.

PETER. [Holding up his hands] By these ten bones, my lords,
he did speak them to me in the garret one night, as we
were scouring my Lord of York's armour.

YORK. Base dunghill villain and mechanical,
I'll have thy head for this thy traitor's speech.
I do beseech your royal Majesty,
Let him have all the rigour of the law.

HORNER. Alas, my lord, hang me if ever I spake the words.
My accuser is my prentice; and when I did correct him
for his fault the other day, he did vow upon his knees he
would be even with me. I have good witness of this;
therefore I beseech your Majesty, do not cast away an
honest man for a villain's accusation.

KING HENRY. Uncle, what shall we say to this in law?

GLOUCESTER. This doom, my lord, if I may judge:
Let Somerset be Regent o'er the French,
Because in York this breeds suspicion;
And let these have a day appointed them
For single combat in convenient place,
For he hath witness of his servant's malice.
This is the law, and this Duke Humphrey's doom.

SOMERSET. I humbly thank your royal Majesty.

HORNER. And I accept the combat willingly.

PETER. Alas, my lord, I cannot fight; for God's sake, pity
my case! The spite of man prevaileth against me. O Lord,
have mercy upon me, I shall never be able to fight a blow!
O Lord, my heart!

ACT I. SCENE 3

GLOUCESTER. Sirrah, or you must fight or else be hang'd.
KING HENRY. Away with them to prison; and the day of combat shall be the last of the next month.
Come, Somerset, we'll see thee sent away. *Flourish. Exeunt*

SCENE 4

London. The DUKE OF GLOUCESTER'S *garden*

Enter MARGERY JOURDAIN, *the witch; the two priests,* HUME *and* SOUTHWELL; *and* BOLINGBROKE

HUME. Come, my masters; the Duchess, I tell you, expects performance of your promises.
BOLINGBROKE. Master Hume, we are therefore provided; will her ladyship behold and hear our exorcisms?
HUME. Ay, what else? Fear you not her courage.
BOLINGBROKE. I have heard her reported to be a woman of an invincible spirit; but it shall be convenient, Master Hume, that you be by her aloft while we be busy below; and so I pray you go, in God's name, and leave us. [*Exit* HUME] Mother Jourdain, be you prostrate and grovel on the earth; John Southwell, read you; and let us to our work.

Enter DUCHESS *aloft, followed by* HUME

DUCHESS. Well said, my masters; and welcome all. To this gear, the sooner the better.
BOLINGBROKE. Patience, good lady; wizards know their times:
Deep night, dark night, the silent of the night,
The time of night when Troy was set on fire;
The time when screech-owls cry and ban-dogs howl,
And spirits walk and ghosts break up their graves—
That time best fits the work we have in hand.
Madam, sit you, and fear not: whom we raise
We will make fast within a hallow'd verge.

[*Here they do the ceremonies belonging, and make the circle;* BOLINGBROKE *or* SOUTHWELL *reads:* 'Con-

juro te,' &c. It thunders and lightens terribly; then
the SPIRIT riseth]

SPIRIT. Adsum.
MARGERY JOURDAIN. Asmath,
  By the eternal God, whose name and power
  Thou tremblest at, answer that I shall ask;
  For till thou speak thou shalt not pass from hence.
SPIRIT. Ask what thou wilt; that I had said and done.
BOLINGBROKE. [Reads] 'First of the king: what shall of him
  become?'
SPIRIT. The Duke yet lives that Henry shall depose;
  But him outlive, and die a violent death.
        [As the SPIRIT speaks, SOUTHWELL writes the answer]
BOLINGBROKE. 'What fates await the Duke of Suffolk?'
SPIRIT. By water shall he die and take his end.
BOLINGBROKE. 'What shall befall the Duke of Somerset?'
SPIRIT. Let him shun castles:
  Safer shall he be upon the sandy plains
  Than where castles mounted stand.
  Have done, for more I hardly can endure.
BOLINGBROKE. Descend to darkness and the burning lake;
  False fiend, avoid!   Thunder and lightning. Exit SPIRIT

    Enter the DUKE OF YORK and the DUKE OF
    BUCKINGHAM with their guard, and break in

YORK. Lay hands upon these traitors and their trash.
  Beldam, I think we watch'd you at an inch.
  What, madam, are you there? The King and commonweal
  Are deeply indebted for this piece of pains;
  My Lord Protector will, I doubt it not,
  See you well guerdon'd for these good deserts.
DUCHESS. Not half so bad as thine to England's king,
  Injurious Duke, that threatest where's no cause.
BUCKINGHAM. True, madam, none at all. What call you this?
  Away with them! let them be clapp'd up close,
  And kept asunder. You, madam, shall with us.
  Stafford, take her to thee.
  We'll see your trinkets here all forthcoming.
  All, away!

Exeunt, above, DUCHESS *and* HUME, *guarded; below,*
WITCH, SOUTHWELL *and* BOLINGBROKE, *guarded*

YORK. Lord Buckingham, methinks you watch'd her well.
A pretty plot, well chosen to build upon!
Now, pray, my lord, let's see the devil's writ.
What have we here? [*Reads*]
'The duke yet lives that Henry shall depose;
But him outlive, and die a violent death.'
Why, this is just
'Aio te, Æacida, Romanos vincere posse.'
Well, to the rest:
'Tell me what fate awaits the Duke of Suffolk?'
'By water shall he die and take his end.'
'What shall betide the Duke of Somerset?'
'Let him shun castles;
Safer shall he be upon the sandy plains
Than where castles mounted stand.'
Come, come, my lords;
These oracles are hardly attain'd,
And hardly understood.
The King is now in progress towards Saint Albans,
With him the husband of this lovely lady;
Thither go these news as fast as horse can carry them—
A sorry breakfast for my Lord Protector.
BUCKINGHAM. Your Grace shall give me leave, my Lord of
York,
To be the post, in hope of his reward.
YORK. At your pleasure, my good lord.
Who's within there, ho?

Enter a serving-man

Invite my Lords of Salisbury and Warwick
To sup with me to-morrow night. Away! *Exeunt*

ACT II. SCENE 1

Saint Albans

Enter the KING, QUEEN, GLOUCESTER, CARDINAL, *and* SUFFOLK, *with Falconers halloing*

QUEEN. Believe me, lords, for flying at the brook,
  I saw not better sport these seven years' day;
  Yet, by your leave, the wind was very high,
  And ten to one old Joan had not gone out.
KING HENRY. But what a point, my lord, your falcon made,
  And what a pitch she flew above the rest!
  To see how God in all His creatures works!
  Yea, man and birds are fain of climbing high.
SUFFOLK. No marvel, an it like your Majesty,
  My Lord Protector's hawks do tow'r so well;
  They know their master loves to be aloft,
  And bears his thoughts above his falcon's pitch.
GLOUCESTER. My lord, 'tis but a base ignoble mind
  That mounts no higher than a bird can soar.
CARDINAL. I thought as much; he would be above the clouds.
GLOUCESTER. Ay, my lord Cardinal, how think you by that?
  Were it not good your Grace could fly to heaven?
KING HENRY. The treasury of everlasting joy!
CARDINAL. Thy heaven is on earth; thine eyes and thoughts
  Beat on a crown, the treasure of thy heart;
  Pernicious Protector, dangerous peer,
  That smooth'st it so with King and commonweal.
GLOUCESTER. What, Cardinal, is your priesthood grown
    peremptory?
  Tantaene animis coelestibus irae?
  Churchmen so hot? Good uncle, hide such malice;
  With such holiness can you do it?
SUFFOLK. No malice, sir; no more than well becomes
  So good a quarrel and so bad a peer.
GLOUCESTER. As who, my lord?
SUFFOLK. Why, as you, my lord,
  An't like your lordly Lord's Protectorship.
GLOUCESTER. Why, Suffolk, England knows thine insolence.

QUEEN. And thy ambition, Gloucester.

KING HENRY. I prithee, peace,
Good Queen, and whet not on these furious peers;
For blessed are the peacemakers on earth.

CARDINAL. Let me be blessed for the peace I make
Against this proud Protector with my sword!

GLOUCESTER. [*Aside to* CARDINAL] Faith, holy uncle, would
'twere come to that!

CARDINAL. [*Aside to* GLOUCESTER] Marry, when thou dar'st.

GLOUCESTER. [*Aside to* CARDINAL] Make up no factious
numbers for the matter;
In thine own person answer thy abuse.

CARDINAL. [*Aside to* GLOUCESTER] Ay, where thou dar'st
not peep; an if thou dar'st,
This evening on the east side of the grove.

KING HENRY. How now, my lords!

CARDINAL. Believe me, cousin Gloucester,
Had not your man put up the fowl so suddenly,
We had had more sport. [*Aside to* GLOUCESTER] Come
with thy two-hand sword.

GLOUCESTER. True, uncle.

CARDINAL. [*Aside to* GLOUCESTER] Are ye advis'd? The east
side of the grove?

GLOUCESTER. [*Aside to* CARDINAL] Cardinal, I am with you.

KING HENRY. Why, how now, uncle Gloucester!

GLOUCESTER. Talking of hawking; nothing else, my lord.
[*Aside to* CARDINAL] Now, by God's Mother, priest,
I'll shave your crown for this,
Or all my fence shall fail.

CARDINAL. [*Aside to* GLOUCESTER] Medice, teipsum;
Protector, see to't well; protect yourself.

KING HENRY. The winds grow high; so do your stomachs,
lords.
How irksome is this music to my heart!
When such strings jar, what hope of harmony?
I pray, my lords, let me compound this strife.

Enter a TOWNSMAN *of Saint Albans, crying* 'A miracle!'

GLOUCESTER. What means this noise?
Fellow, what miracle dost thou proclaim?

TOWNSMAN. A miracle! A miracle!

SUFFOLK. Come to the King, and tell him what miracle.

TOWNSMAN. Forsooth, a blind man at Saint Albans shrine
Within this half hour hath receiv'd his sight;
A man that ne'er saw in his life before.

KING HENRY. Now God be prais'd that to believing souls
Gives light in darkness, comfort in despair!

Enter the MAYOR OF SAINT ALBANS *and his
brethren, bearing* SIMPCOX *between two in a chair;
his* WIFE *and a multitude following*

CARDINAL. Here comes the townsmen on procession
To present your Highness with the man.

KING HENRY. Great is his comfort in this earthly vale,
Although by his sight his sin be multiplied.

GLOUCESTER. Stand by, my masters; bring him near the
King;
His Highness' pleasure is to talk with him.

KING HENRY. Good fellow, tell us here the circumstance,
That we for thee may glorify the Lord.
What, hast thou been long blind and now restor'd?

SIMPCOX. Born blind, an't please your Grace.

WIFE. Ay indeed was he.

SUFFOLK. What woman is this?

WIFE. His wife, an't like your worship.

GLOUCESTER. Hadst thou been his mother, thou couldst have
better told.

KING HENRY. Where wert thou born?

SIMPCOX. At Berwick in the north, an't like your Grace.

KING HENRY. Poor soul, God's goodness hath been great to
thee.
Let never day nor night unhallowed pass,
But still remember what the Lord hath done.

QUEEN. Tell me, good fellow, cam'st thou here by chance,
Or of devotion, to this holy shrine?

SIMPCOX. God knows, of pure devotion; being call'd
A hundred times and oft'ner, in my sleep,
By good Saint Alban, who said 'Simpcox, come,
Come, offer at my shrine, and I will help thee.'

WIFE. Most true, forsooth; and many time and oft

Myself have heard a voice to call him so.

CARDINAL. What, art thou lame?

SIMPCOX. Ay, God Almighty help me!

SUFFOLK. How cam'st thou so?

SIMPCOX. A fall off of a tree.

WIFE. A plum tree, master.

GLOUCESTER. How long hast thou been blind?

SIMPCOX. O, born so, master!

GLOUCESTER. What, and wouldst climb a tree?

SIMPCOX. But that in all my life, when I was a youth.

WIFE. Too true; and bought his climbing very dear.

GLOUCESTER. Mass, thou lov'dst plums well, that wouldst venture so.

SIMPCOX. Alas, good master, my wife desir'd some damsons
And made me climb, with danger of my life.

GLOUCESTER. A subtle knave! But yet it shall not serve:
Let me see thine eyes; wink now; now open them;
In my opinion yet thou seest not well.

SIMPCOX. Yes, master, clear as day, I thank God and Saint Alban.

GLOUCESTER. Say'st thou me so? What colour is this cloak of?

SIMPCOX. Red, master; red as blood.

GLOUCESTER. Why, that's well said. What colour is my gown of?

SIMPCOX. Black, forsooth; coal-black as jet.

KING HENRY. Why, then, thou know'st what colour jet is of?

SUFFOLK. And yet, I think, jet did he never see.

GLOUCESTER. But cloaks and gowns before this day a many.

WIFE. Never before this day in all his life.

GLOUCESTER. Tell me, sirrah, what's my name?

SIMPCOX. Alas, master, I know not.

GLOUCESTER. What's his name?

SIMPCOX. I know not.

GLOUCESTER. Nor his?

SIMPCOX. No, indeed, master.

GLOUCESTER. What's thine own name?

SIMPCOX. Saunder Simpcox, an if it please you, master.

GLOUCESTER. Then, Saunder, sit there, the lying'st knave in

Christendom. If thou hadst been born blind, thou mightst as well have known all our names as thus to name the several colours we do wear. Sight may distinguish of colours; but suddenly to nominate them all, it is impossible. My lords, Saint Alban here hath done a miracle; and would ye not think his cunning to be great that could restore this cripple to his legs again?

SIMPCOX. O master, that you could!

GLOUCESTER. My masters of Saint Albans, have you not beadles in your town, and things call'd whips?

MAYOR. Yes, my lord, if it please your Grace.

GLOUCESTER. Then send for one presently.

MAYOR. Sirrah, go fetch the beadle hither straight.

Exit an attendant

GLOUCESTER. Now fetch me a stool hither by and by. [*A stool brought*] Now, sirrah, if you mean to save yourself from whipping, leap me over this stool and run away.

SIMPCOX. Alas, master, I am not able to stand alone!
You go about to torture me in vain.

Enter a BEADLE *with whips*

GLOUCESTER. Well, sir, we must have you find your legs. Sirrah beadle, whip him till he leap over that same stool.

BEADLE. I will, my lord. Come on, sirrah; off with your doublet quickly.

SIMPCOX. Alas, master, what shall I do? I am not able to stand.

After the BEADLE *hath hit him once, he leaps over the stool and runs away; and they follow and cry 'A miracle!'*

KING HENRY. O God, seest Thou this, and bearest so long?

QUEEN. It made me laugh to see the villain run.

GLOUCESTER. Follow the knave, and take this drab away.

WIFE. Alas, sir, we did it for pure need!

GLOUCESTER. Let them be whipp'd through every market town till they come to Berwick, from whence they came.

Exeunt MAYOR, BEADLE, WIFE, &c.

CARDINAL. Duke Humphrey has done a miracle to-day.

SUFFOLK. True; made the lame to leap and fly away.

GLOUCESTER. But you have done more miracles than **I**:
 You made in a day, my lord, whole towns to fly.

Enter BUCKINGHAM

KING HENRY. What tidings with our cousin Buckingham?
BUCKINGHAM. Such as my heart doth tremble to unfold:
 A sort of naughty persons, lewdly bent,
 Under the countenance and confederacy
 Of Lady Eleanor, the Protector's wife,
 The ringleader and head of all this rout,
 Have practis'd dangerously against your state,
 Dealing with witches and with conjurers,
 Whom we have apprehended in the fact,
 Raising up wicked spirits from under ground,
 Demanding of King Henry's life and death
 And other of your Highness' Privy Council,
 As more at large your Grace shall understand.
CARDINAL. And so, my Lord Protector, by this means
 Your lady is forthcoming yet at London.
 This news, I think, hath turn'd your weapon's edge;
 'Tis like, my lord, you will not keep your hour.
GLOUCESTER. Ambitious churchman, leave to afflict my heart.
 Sorrow and grief have vanquish'd all my powers;
 And, vanquish'd as I am, I yield to thee
 Or to the meanest groom.
KING HENRY. O God, what mischiefs work the wicked ones,
 Heaping confusion on their own heads thereby!
QUEEN. Gloucester, see here the tainture of thy nest;
 And look thyself be faultless, thou wert best.
GLOUCESTER. Madam, for myself, to heaven I do appeal
 How I have lov'd my King and commonweal;
 And for my wife I know not how it stands.
 Sorry I am to hear what I have heard.
 Noble she is; but if she have forgot
 Honour and virtue, and convers'd with such
 As, like to pitch, defile nobility,
 I banish her my bed and company
 And give her as a prey to law and shame,
 That hath dishonoured Gloucester's honest name.
KING HENRY. Well, for this night we will repose us here.

To-morrow toward London back again
To look into this business thoroughly
And call these foul offenders to their answers,
And poise the cause in justice' equal scales,
Whose beam stands sure, whose rightful cause prevails.

Flourish. Exeunt

SCENE 2

London. The DUKE OF YORK'S *garden*

Enter YORK, SALISBURY, *and* WARWICK

YORK. Now, my good Lords of Salisbury and Warwick,
Our simple supper ended, give me leave
In this close walk to satisfy myself
In craving your opinion of my title,
Which is infallible, to England's crown.
SALISBURY. My lord, I long to hear it at full.
WARWICK. Sweet York, begin; and if thy claim be good,
The Nevils are thy subjects to command.
YORK. Then thus:
Edward the Third, my lords, had seven sons;
The first, Edward the Black Prince, Prince of Wales;
The second, William of Hatfield; and the third,
Lionel Duke of Clarence; next to whom
Was John of Gaunt, the Duke of Lancaster;
The fifth was Edmund Langley, Duke of York;
The sixth was Thomas of Woodstock, Duke of Gloucester;
William of Windsor was the seventh and last.
Edward the Black Prince died before his father
And left behind him Richard, his only son,
Who, after Edward the Third's death, reign'd as king
Till Henry Bolingbroke, Duke of Lancaster,
The eldest son and heir of John of Gaunt,
Crown'd by the name of Henry the Fourth,
Seiz'd on the realm, depos'd the rightful king,
Sent his poor queen to France, from whence she came.
And him to Pomfret, where, as all you know,
Harmless Richard was murdered traitorously.
WARWICK. Father, the Duke hath told the truth;

Thus got the house of Lancaster the crown.
YORK. Which now they hold by force, and not by right;
 For Richard, the first son's heir, being dead,
 The issue of the next son should have reign'd.
SALISBURY. But William of Hatfield died without an heir.
YORK. The third son, Duke of Clarence, from whose line
 I claim the crown, had issue Philippe, a daughter,
 Who married Edmund Mortimer, Earl of March;
 Edmund had issue, Roger Earl of March;
 Roger had issue, Edmund, Anne, and Eleanor.
SALISBURY. This Edmund, in the reign of Bolingbroke,
 As I have read, laid claim unto the crown;
 And, but for Owen Glendower, had been king,
 Who kept him in captivity till he died.
 But, to the rest.
YORK. His eldest sister, Anne,
 My mother, being heir unto the crown,
 Married Richard Earl of Cambridge, who was
 To Edmund Langley, Edward the Third's fifth son, son.
 By her I claim the kingdom: she was heir
 To Roger Earl of March, who was the son
 Of Edmund Mortimer, who married Philippe,
 Sole daughter unto Lionel Duke of Clarence;
 So, if the issue of the elder son
 Succeed before the younger, I am King.
WARWICK. What plain proceedings is more plain than this?
 Henry doth claim the crown from John of Gaunt,
 The fourth son: York claims it from the third.
 Till Lionel's issue fails, his should not reign.
 It fails not yet, but flourishes in thee
 And in thy sons, fair slips of such a stock.
 Then, father Salisbury, kneel we together,
 And in this private plot be we the first
 That shall salute our rightful sovereign
 With honour of his birthright to the crown.
BOTH. Long live our sovereign Richard, England's King!
YORK. We thank you, lords. But I am not your king
 Till I be crown'd, and that my sword be stain'd
 With heart-blood of the house of Lancaster;
 And that's not suddenly to be perform'd,

But with advice and silent secrecy.
Do you as I do in these dangerous days:
Wink at the Duke of Suffolk's insolence,
At Beaufort's pride, at Somerset's ambition,
At Buckingham, and all the crew of them,
Till they have snar'd the shepherd of the flock,
That virtuous prince, the good Duke Humphrey;
'Tis that they seek; and they, in seeking that,
Shall find their deaths, if York can prophesy.

SALISBURY. My lord, break we off; we know your mind at
full.

WARWICK. My heart assures me that the Earl of Warwick
Shall one day make the Duke of York a king.

YORK. And, Nevil, this I do assure myself,
Richard shall live to make the Earl of Warwick
The greatest man in England but the King.   *Exeunt*

SCENE 3

London. A hall of justice

Sound trumpets. Enter the KING *and State: the*
QUEEN, GLOUCESTER, YORK, SUFFOLK, *and* SALIS-
BURY, *with guard, to banish the* DUCHESS. *Enter,*
guarded, the DUCHESS OF GLOUCESTER, MARGERY
JOURDAIN, HUME, SOUTHWELL, *and* BOLINGBROKE

KING HENRY. Stand forth, Dame Eleanor Cobham, Glou-
cester's wife:
In sight of God and us, your guilt is great;
Receive the sentence of the law for sins
Such as by God's book are adjudg'd to death.
You four, from hence to prison back again;
From thence unto the place of execution:
The witch in Smithfield shall be burnt to ashes,
And you three shall be strangled on the gallows.
You, madam, for you are more nobly born,
Despoiled of your honour in your life,
Shall, after three days' open penance done,
Live in your country here in banishment

With Sir John Stanley in the Isle of Man.

DUCHESS. Welcome is banishment; welcome were my death.

GLOUCESTER. Eleanor, the law, thou seest, hath judged thee.
I cannot justify whom the law condemns.

Exeunt the DUCHESS *and the other prisoners, guarded*

Mine eyes are full of tears, my heart of grief.
Ah, Humphrey, this dishonour in thine age
Will bring thy head with sorrow to the ground!
I beseech your Majesty give me leave to go;
Sorrow would solace, and mine age would ease.

KING HENRY. Stay, Humphrey Duke of Gloucester; ere
thou go,
Give up thy staff; Henry will to himself
Protector be; and God shall be my hope,
My stay, my guide, and lantern to my feet.
And go in peace, Humphrey, no less belov'd
Than when thou wert Protector to thy King.

QUEEN. I see no reason why a king of years
Should be to be protected like a child.
God and King Henry govern England's realm!
Give up your staff, sir, and the King his realm.

GLOUCESTER. My staff! Here, noble Henry, is my staff.
As willingly do I the same resign
As ere thy father Henry made it mine;
And even as willingly at thy feet I leave it
As others would ambitiously receive it.
Farewell, good King; when I am dead and gone,
May honourable peace attend thy throne!   *Exit*

QUEEN. Why, now is Henry King, and Margaret Queen,
And Humphrey Duke of Gloucester scarce himself,
That bears so shrewd a maim: two pulls at once—
His lady banish'd and a limb lopp'd off.
This staff of honour raught, there let it stand
Where it best fits to be, in Henry's hand.

SUFFOLK. Thus droops this lofty pine and hangs his sprays;
Thus Eleanor's pride dies in her youngest days.

YORK. Lords, let him go. Please it your Majesty,
This is the day appointed for the combat;
And ready are the appellant and defendant,
The armourer and his man, to enter the lists,

So please your Highness to behold the fight.

QUEEN. Ay, good my lord; for purposely therefore
Left I the court, to see this quarrel tried.

KING HENRY. A God's name, see the lists and all things fit;
Here let them end it, and God defend the right!

YORK. I never saw a fellow worse bested,
Or more afraid to fight, than is the appellant,
The servant of his armourer, my lords.

Enter at one door, HORNER, *the Armourer, and his*
NEIGHBOURS, *drinking to him so much that he is*
drunk; and he enters with a drum before him and
his staff with a sand-bag fastened to it; and at the
other door PETER, *his man, with a drum and sand-*
bag, and PRENTICES *drinking to him*

FIRST NEIGHBOUR. Here, neighbour Horner, I drink to you
in a cup of sack; and fear not, neighbour, you shall do
well enough.

SECOND NEIGHBOUR. And here, neighbour, here's a cup of
charneco.

THIRD NEIGHBOUR. And here's a pot of good double beer,
neighbour; drink, and fear not your man.

HORNER. Let it come, i'faith, and I'll pledge you all; and a
fig for Peter!

FIRST PRENTICE. Here, Peter, I drink to thee; and be not
afraid.

SECOND PRENTICE. Be merry, Peter, and fear not thy master:
fight for credit of the prentices.

PETER. I thank you all. Drink, and pray for me, I pray you;
for I think I have taken my last draught in this world.
Here, Robin, an if I die, I give thee my apron; and, Will,
thou shalt have my hammer; and here, Tom, take all the
money that I have. O Lord bless me, I pray God! for I
am never able to deal with my master, he hath learnt so
much fence already.

SALISBURY. Come, leave your drinking and fall to blows.
Sirrah, what's thy name?

PETER. Peter, forsooth.

SALISBURY. Peter? What more?

PETER. Thump.

SALISBURY. Thump? Then see thou thump thy master well.

HORNER. Masters, I am come hither, as it were, upon my
man's instigation, to prove him a knave and myself an
honest man; and touching the Duke of York, I will take
my death I never meant him any ill, nor the King, nor the
Queen; and therefore, Peter, have at thee with a downright blow!

YORK. Dispatch—this knave's tongue begins to double.
Sound, trumpets, alarum to the combatants!

[*Alarum. They fight and* PETER *strikes him down*]

HORNER. Hold, Peter, hold! I confess, I confess treason.

[*Dies*]

YORK. Take away his weapon. Fellow, thank God, and the
good wine in thy master's way.

PETER. O God, have I overcome mine enemies in this presence? O Peter, thou hast prevail'd in right!

KING HENRY. Go, take hence that traitor from our sight,
For by his death we do perceive his guilt;
And God in justice hath reveal'd to us
The truth and innocence of this poor fellow,
Which he had thought to have murder'd wrongfully.
Come, fellow, follow us for thy reward.

Sound a flourish. Exeunt

SCENE 4

London. A street

Enter DUKE HUMPHREY *and his men, in mourning cloaks*

GLOUCESTER. Thus sometimes hath the brightest day a cloud,
And after summer evermore succeeds
Barren winter, with his wrathful nipping cold;
So cares and joys abound, as seasons fleet.
Sirs, what's o'clock?

SERVING-MAN. Ten, my lord.

GLOUCESTER. Ten is the hour that was appointed me
To watch the coming of my punish'd duchess.
Uneath may she endure the flinty streets
To tread them with her tender-feeling feet.

Sweet Nell, ill can thy noble mind abrook
The abject people gazing on thy face,
With envious looks, laughing at thy shame,
That erst did follow thy proud chariot wheels
When thou didst ride in triumph through the streets.
But, soft! I think she comes, and I'll prepare
My tear-stain'd eyes to see her miseries.

Enter the DUCHESS OF GLOUCESTER *in a white sheet,
and a taper burning in her hand, with* SIR JOHN
STANLEY, *the* SHERIFF, *and* OFFICERS

SERVING-MAN. So please your Grace, we'll take her from the
sheriff.
GLOUCESTER. No, stir not for your lives; let her pass by.
DUCHESS. Come you, my lord, to see my open shame?
Now thou dost penance too. Look how they gaze!
See how the giddy multitude do point
And nod their heads and throw their eyes on thee;
Ah, Gloucester, hide thee from their hateful looks,
And, in thy closet pent up, rue my shame
And ban thine enemies, both mine and thine!
GLOUCESTER. Be patient, gentle Nell; forget this grief.
DUCHESS. Ah, Gloucester, teach me to forget myself!
For whilst I think I am thy married wife
And thou a prince, Protector of this land,
Methinks I should not thus be led along,
Mail'd up in shame, with papers on my back,
And follow'd with a rabble that rejoice
To see my tears and hear my deep-fet groans.
The ruthless flint doth cut my tender feet,
And when I start, the envious people laugh
And bid me be advised how I tread.
Ah, Humphrey, can I bear this shameful yoke?
Trowest thou that e'er I'll look upon the world
Or count them happy that enjoy the sun?
No; dark shall be my light and night my day;
To think upon my pomp shall be my hell.
Sometimes I'll say I am Duke Humphrey's wife,
And he a prince, and ruler of the land;
Yet so he rul'd, and such a prince he was,

As he stood by whilst I, his forlorn duchess,
Was made a wonder and a pointing-stock
To every idle rascal follower.
But be thou mild, and blush not at my shame,
Nor stir at nothing till the axe of death
Hang over thee, as sure it shortly will.
For Suffolk—he that can do all in all
With her that hateth thee and hates us all—
And York, and impious Beaufort, that false priest,
Have all lim'd bushes to betray thy wings,
And, fly thou how thou canst, they'll tangle thee.
But fear not thou until thy foot be snar'd,
Nor never seek prevention of thy foes.

GLOUCESTER. Ah, Nell, forbear! Thou aimest all awry.
I must offend before I be attainted;
And had I twenty times so many foes,
And each of them had twenty times their power,
All these could not procure me any scathe
So long as I am loyal, true, and crimeless.
Wouldst have me rescue thee from this reproach?
Why, yet thy scandal were not wip'd away,
But I in danger for the breach of law.
Thy greatest help is quiet, gentle Nell.
I pray thee sort thy heart to patience;
These few days' wonder will be quickly worn.

Enter a HERALD

HERALD. I summon your Grace to his Majesty's Parliament,
Holden at Bury the first of this next month.

GLOUCESTER. And my consent ne'er ask'd herein before!
This is close dealing. Well, I will be there.   *Exit* HERALD
My Nell, I take my leave—and, master sheriff,
Let not her penance exceed the King's commission.

SHERIFF. An't please your Grace, here my commission stays;
And Sir John Stanley is appointed now
To take her with him to the Isle of Man.

GLOUCESTER. Must you, Sir John, protect my lady here?

STANLEY. So am I given in charge, may't please your Grace.

GLOUCESTER. Entreat her not the worse in that I pray
You use her well; the world may laugh again,

And I may live to do you kindness if
You do it her. And so, Sir John, farewell.
DUCHESS. What, gone, my lord, and bid me not farewell!
GLOUCESTER. Witness my tears, I cannot stay to speak.
                    Exeunt GLOUCESTER *and servants*
DUCHESS. Art thou gone too? All comfort go with thee!
For none abides with me. My joy is death—
Death, at whose name I oft have been afeard,
Because I wish'd this world's eternity.
Stanley, I prithee go, and take me hence;
I care not whither, for I beg no favour,
Only convey me where thou art commanded.
STANLEY. Why, madam, that is to the Isle of Man,
There to be us'd according to your state.
DUCHESS. That's bad enough, for I am but reproach—
And shall I then be us'd reproachfully?
STANLEY. Like to a duchess and Duke Humphrey's lady;
According to that state you shall be us'd.
DUCHESS. Sheriff, farewell, and better than I fare,
Although thou hast been conduct of my shame.
SHERIFF. It is my office; and, madam, pardon me.
DUCHESS. Ay, ay, farewell; thy office is discharg'd.
Come, Stanley, shall we go?
STANLEY. Madam, your penance done, throw off this sheet,
And go we to attire you for our journey.
DUCHESS. My shame will not be shifted with my sheet.
No, it will hang upon my richest robes
And show itself, attire me how I can.
Go, lead the way; I long to see my prison.   *Exeunt*

ACT III. SCENE 1

The Abbey at Bury St. Edmunds

Sound a sennet. Enter the KING, *the* QUEEN, CARDI-
NAL, SUFFOLK, YORK, BUCKINGHAM, SALISBURY, *and*
WARWICK, *to the Parliament*

KING HENRY. I muse my Lord of Gloucester is not come.

'Tis not his wont to be the hindmost man,
Whate'er occasion keeps him from us now.
QUEEN. Can you not see, or will ye not observe
　The strangeness of his alter'd countenance?
　With what a majesty he bears himself;
　How insolent of late he is become,
　How proud, how peremptory, and unlike himself?
　We know the time since he was mild and affable,
　And if we did but glance a far-off look
　Immediately he was upon his knee,
　That all the court admir'd him for submission.
　But meet him now and be it in the morn,
　When every one will give the time of day,
　He knits his brow and shows an angry eye
　And passeth by with stiff unbowed knee,
　Disdaining duty that to us belongs.
　Small curs are not regarded when they grin,
　But great men tremble when the lion roars,
　And Humphrey is no little man in England.
　First note that he is near you in descent,
　And should you fall he is the next will mount;
　Me seemeth, then, it is no policy—
　Respecting what a rancorous mind he bears,
　And his advantage following your decease—
　That he should come about your royal person
　Or be admitted to your Highness' Council.
　By flattery hath he won the commons' hearts;
　And when he please to make commotion,
　'Tis to be fear'd they all will follow him.
　Now 'tis the spring, and weeds are shallow-rooted;
　Suffer them now, and they'll o'ergrow the garden
　And choke the herbs for want of husbandry.
　The reverent care I bear unto my lord
　Made me collect these dangers in the Duke.
　If it be fond, call it a woman's fear;
　Which fear if better reasons can supplant,
　I will subscribe, and say I wrong'd the Duke.
　My Lord of Suffolk, Buckingham, and York,
　Reprove my allegation if you can,
　Or else conclude my words effectual.

SUFFOLK. Well hath your Highness seen into this duke;
    And had I first been put to speak my mind,
    I think I should have told your Grace's tale.
    The Duchess, by his subornation,
    Upon my life, began her devilish practices;
    Or if he were not privy to those faults,
    Yet by reputing of his high descent—
    As next the King he was successive heir—
    And such high vaunts of his nobility,
    Did instigate the bedlam brainsick Duchess
    By wicked means to frame our sovereign's fall.
    Smooth runs the water where the brook is deep,
    And in his simple show he harbours treason.
    The fox barks not when he would steal the lamb.
    No, no, my sovereign, Gloucester is a man
    Unsounded yet, and full of deep deceit.
CARDINAL. Did he not, contrary to form of law,
    Devise strange deaths for small offences done?
YORK. And did he not, in his protectorship,
    Levy great sums of money through the realm
    For soldiers' pay in France, and never sent it?
    By means whereof the towns each day revolted.
BUCKINGHAM. Tut, these are petty faults to faults unknown
    Which time will bring to light in smooth Duke Hum-
    phrey.
KING HENRY. My lords, at once: the care you have of us,
    To mow down thorns that would annoy our foot,
    Is worthy praise; but shall I speak my conscience?
    Our kinsman Gloucester is as innocent
    From meaning treason to our royal person
    As is the sucking lamb or harmless dove:
    The Duke is virtuous, mild, and too well given
    To dream on evil or to work my downfall.
QUEEN. Ah, what's more dangerous than this fond affiance?
    Seems he a dove? His feathers are but borrow'd,
    For he's disposed as the hateful raven.
    Is he a lamb? His skin is surely lent him,
    For he's inclin'd as is the ravenous wolf.
    Who cannot steal a shape that means deceit?
    Take heed, my lord; the welfare of us all

Hangs on the cutting short that fraudful man.

Enter SOMERSET

SOMERSET. All health unto my gracious sovereign!
KING HENRY. Welcome, Lord Somerset. What news from
   France?
SOMERSET. That all your interest in those territories
   Is utterly bereft you; all is lost.
KING HENRY. Cold news, Lord Somerset; but God's will be
   done!
YORK. [*Aside*] Cold news for me; for I had hope of France
   As firmly as I hope for fertile England.
   Thus are my blossoms blasted in the bud,
   And caterpillars eat my leaves away;
   But I will remedy this gear ere long,
   Or sell my title for a glorious grave.

Enter GLOUCESTER

GLOUCESTER. All happiness unto my lord the King!
   Pardon, my liege, that I have stay'd so long.
SUFFOLK. Nay, Gloucester, know that thou art come too
   soon,
   Unless thou wert more loyal than thou art.
   I do arrest thee of high treason here.
GLOUCESTER. Well, Suffolk, thou shalt not see me blush
   Nor change my countenance for this arrest:
   A heart unspotted is not easily daunted.
   The purest spring is not so free from mud
   As I am clear from treason to my sovereign.
   Who can accuse me? Wherein am I guilty?
YORK. 'Tis thought, my lord, that you took bribes of France
   And, being Protector, stay'd the soldiers' pay;
   By means whereof his Highness hath lost France.
GLOUCESTER. Is it but thought so? What are they that think
   it?
   I never robb'd the soldiers of their pay
   Nor ever had one penny bribe from France.
   So help me God, as I have watch'd the night—
   Ay, night by night—in studying good for England!
   That doit that e'er I wrested from the King,

Or any groat I hoarded to my use,
Be brought against me at my trial-day!
No; many a pound of mine own proper store,
Because I would not tax the needy commons,
Have I dispursed to the garrisons,
And never ask'd for restitution.
CARDINAL. It serves you well, my lord, to say so much.
GLOUCESTER. I say no more than truth, so help me God!
YORK. In your protectorship you did devise
  Strange tortures for offenders, never heard of,
  That England was defam'd by tyranny.
GLOUCESTER. Why, 'tis well known that whiles I was Protector
  Pity was all the fault that was in me;
  For I should melt at an offender's tears,
  And lowly words were ransom for their fault.
  Unless it were a bloody murderer,
  Or foul felonious thief that fleec'd poor passengers,
  I never gave them condign punishment.
  Murder indeed, that bloody sin, I tortur'd
  Above the felon or what trespass else.
SUFFOLK. My lord, these faults are easy, quickly answer'd;
  But mightier crimes are laid unto your charge,
  Whereof you cannot easily purge yourself.
  I do arrest you in His Highness' name,
  And here commit you to my Lord Cardinal
  To keep until your further time of trial.
KING HENRY. My Lord of Gloucester, 'tis my special hope
  That you will clear yourself from all suspense.
  My conscience tells me you are innocent.
GLOUCESTER. Ah, gracious lord, these days are dangerous!
  Virtue is chok'd with foul ambition,
  And charity chas'd hence by rancour's hand;
  Foul subornation is predominant,
  And equity exil'd your Highness' land.
  I know their complot is to have my life;
  And if my death might make this island happy
  And prove the period of their tyranny,
  I would expend it with all willingness.
  But mine is made the prologue to their play;

For thousands more that yet suspect no peril
Will not conclude their plotted tragedy.
Beaufort's red sparkling eyes blab his heart's malice,
And Suffolk's cloudy brow his stormy hate;
Sharp Buckingham unburdens with his tongue
The envious load that lies upon his heart;
And dogged York, that reaches at the moon,
Whose overweening arm I have pluck'd back,
By false accuse doth level at my life.
And you, my sovereign lady, with the rest,
Causeless have laid disgraces on my head,
And with your best endeavour have stirr'd up
My liefest liege to be mine enemy;
Ay, all of you have laid your heads together—
Myself had notice of your conventicles—
And all to make away my guiltless life.
I shall not want false witness to condemn me
Nor store of treasons to augment my guilt.
The ancient proverb will be well effected:
'A staff is quickly found to beat a dog.'
CARDINAL. My liege, his railing is intolerable.
    If those that care to keep your royal person
    From treason's secret knife and traitor's rage
    Be thus upbraided, chid, and rated at,
    And the offender granted scope of speech,
    'Twill make them cool in zeal unto your Grace.
SUFFOLK. Hath he not twit our sovereign lady here
    With ignominious words, though clerkly couch'd,
    As if she had suborned some to swear
    False allegations to o'erthrow his state?
QUEEN. But I can give the loser leave to chide.
GLOUCESTER. Far truer spoke than meant: I lose indeed.
    Beshrew the winners, for they play'd me false!
    And well such losers may have leave to speak.
BUCKINGHAM. He'll wrest the sense, and hold us here all day.
    Lord Cardinal, he is your prisoner.
CARDINAL. Sirs, take away the Duke, and guard him sure.
GLOUCESTER. Ah, thus King Henry throws away his crutch
    Before his legs be firm to bear his body!
    Thus is the shepherd beaten from thy side,

And wolves are gnarling who shall gnaw thee first.
Ah, that my fear were false! ah, that it were!
For, good King Henry, thy decay I fear.   *Exit, guarded*
KING HENRY. My lords, what to your wisdoms seemeth best
  Do or undo, as if ourself were here.
QUEEN. What, will your Highness leave the Parliament?
KING HENRY. Ay, Margaret; my heart is drown'd with grief,
  Whose flood begins to flow within mine eyes;
  My body round engirt with misery—
  For what's more miserable than discontent?
  Ah, uncle Humphrey, in thy face I see
  The map of honour, truth, and loyalty!
  And yet, good Humphrey, is the hour to come
  That e'er I prov'd thee false or fear'd thy faith.
  What louring star now envies thy estate
  That these great lords, and Margaret our Queen,
  Do seek subversion of thy harmless life?
  Thou never didst them wrong, nor no man wrong;
  And as the butcher takes away the calf,
  And binds the wretch, and beats it when it strays,
  Bearing it to the bloody slaughter-house,
  Even so, remorseless, have they borne him hence;
  And as the dam runs lowing up and down,
  Looking the way her harmless young one went,
  And can do nought but wail her darling's loss,
  Even so myself bewails good Gloucester's case
  With sad unhelpful tears, and with dimm'd eyes
  Look after him, and cannot do him good,
  So mighty are his vowed enemies.
  His fortunes I will weep, and 'twixt each groan
  Say 'Who's a traitor? Gloucester he is none.'   *Exit*
QUEEN. Free lords, cold snow melts with the sun's hot
    beams:
  Henry my lord is cold in great affairs,
  Too full of foolish pity; and Gloucester's show
  Beguiles him as the mournful crocodile
  With sorrow snares relenting passengers;
  Or as the snake, roll'd in a flow'ring bank,
  With shining checker'd slough, doth sting a child
  That for the beauty thinks it excellent.

Believe me, lords, were none more wise than I—
And yet herein I judge mine own wit good—
This Gloucester should be quickly rid the world
To rid us from the fear we have of him.
CARDINAL. That he should die is worthy policy;
　But yet we want a colour for his death.
　'Tis meet he be condemn'd by course of law.
SUFFOLK. But, in my mind, that were no policy:
　The King will labour still to save his life;
　The commons haply rise to save his life;
　And yet we have but trivial argument,
　More than mistrust, that shows him worthy death.
YORK. So that, by this, you would not have him die.
SUFFOLK. Ah, York, no man alive so fain as I!
YORK. 'Tis York that hath more reason for his death.
　But, my Lord Cardinal, and you, my Lord of Suffolk,
　Say as you think, and speak it from your souls:
　Were't not all one an empty eagle were set
　To guard the chicken from a hungry kite
　As place Duke Humphrey for the King's Protector?
QUEEN. So the poor chicken should be sure of death.
SUFFOLK. Madam, 'tis true; and were't not madness then
　To make the fox surveyor of the fold?
　Who being accus'd a crafty murderer,
　His guilt should be but idly posted over,
　Because his purpose is not executed.
　No; let him die, in that he is a fox,
　By nature prov'd an enemy to the flock,
　Before his chaps be stain'd with crimson blood,
　As Humphrey, prov'd by reasons, to my liege.
　And do not stand on quillets how to slay him;
　Be it by gins, by snares, by subtlety,
　Sleeping or waking, 'tis no matter how,
　So he be dead; for that is good deceit
　Which mates him first that first intends deceit.
QUEEN. Thrice-noble Suffolk, 'tis resolutely spoke.
SUFFOLK. Not resolute, except so much were done,
　For things are often spoke and seldom meant;
　But that my heart accordeth with my tongue,
　Seeing the deed is meritorious,

And to preserve my sovereign from his foe,
Say but the word, and I will be his priest.
CARDINAL. But I would have him dead, my Lord of Suffolk,
Ere you can take due orders for a priest;
Say you consent and censure well the deed,
And I'll provide his executioner—
I tender so the safety of my liege.
SUFFOLK. Here is my hand the deed is worthy doing.
QUEEN. And so say I.
YORK. And I. And now we three have spoke it,
It skills not greatly who impugns our doom.

Enter a POST

POST. Great lords, from Ireland am I come amain
To signify that rebels there are up
And put the Englishmen unto the sword.
Send succours, lords, and stop the rage betime,
Before the wound do grow uncurable;
For, being green, there is great hope of help.
CARDINAL. A breach that craves a quick expedient stop!
What counsel give you in this weighty cause?
YORK. That Somerset be sent as Regent thither;
'Tis meet that lucky ruler be employ'd,
Witness the fortune he hath had in France.
SOMERSET. If York, with all his far-fet policy,
Had been the Regent there instead of me,
He never would have stay'd in France so long.
YORK. No, not to lose it all as thou hast done.
I rather would have lost my life betimes
Than bring a burden of dishonour home
By staying there so long till all were lost.
Show me one scar character'd on thy skin:
Men's flesh preserv'd so whole do seldom win.
QUEEN. Nay then, this spark will prove a raging fire,
If wind and fuel be brought to feed it with;
No more, good York; sweet Somerset, be still.
Thy fortune, York, hadst thou been Regent there,
Might happily have prov'd far worse than his.
YORK. What, worse than nought? Nay, then a shame take
all!

SOMERSET. And in the number, thee that wishest shame!

CARDINAL. My Lord of York, try what your fortune is.
  Th' uncivil kerns of Ireland are in arms
  And temper clay with blood of Englishmen;
  To Ireland will you lead a band of men,
  Collected choicely, from each county some,
  And try your hap against the Irishmen?

YORK. I will, my lord, so please his Majesty.

SUFFOLK. Why, our authority is his consent,
  And what we do establish he confirms;
  Then, noble York, take thou this task in hand.

YORK. I am content; provide me soldiers, lords,
  Whiles I take order for mine own affairs.

SUFFOLK. A charge, Lord York, that I will see perform'd.
  But now return we to the false Duke Humphrey.

CARDINAL. No more of him; for I will deal with him
  That henceforth he shall trouble us no more.
  And so break off; the day is almost spent.
  Lord Suffolk, you and I must talk of that event.

YORK. My Lord of Suffolk, within fourteen days
  At Bristol I expect my soldiers;
  For there I'll ship them all for Ireland.

SUFFOLK. I'll see it truly done, my Lord of York.

Exeunt all but YORK

YORK. Now, York, or never, steel thy fearful thoughts
  And change misdoubt to resolution;
  Be that thou hop'st to be; or what thou art
  Resign to death—it is not worth th' enjoying.
  Let pale-fac'd fear keep with the mean-born man
  And find no harbour in a royal heart.
  Faster than spring-time show'rs comes thought on thought,
  And not a thought but thinks on dignity.
  My brain, more busy than the labouring spider,
  Weaves tedious snares to trap mine enemies.
  Well, nobles, well, 'tis politicly done
  To send me packing with an host of men.
  I fear me you but warm the starved snake,
  Who, cherish'd in your breasts, will sting your hearts.
  'Twas men I lack'd, and you will give them me;
  I take it kindly. Yet be well assur'd

You put sharp weapons in a madman's hands.
Whiles I in Ireland nourish a mighty band,
I will stir up in England some black storm
Shall blow ten thousand souls to heaven or hell;
And this fell tempest shall not cease to rage
Until the golden circuit on my head,
Like to the glorious sun's transparent beams,
Do calm the fury of this mad-bred flaw.
And for a minister of my intent
I have seduc'd a headstrong Kentishman,
John Cade of Ashford,
To make commotion, as full well he can,
Under the title of John Mortimer.
In Ireland have I seen this stubborn Cade
Oppose himself against a troop of kerns,
And fought so long till that his thighs with darts
Were almost like a sharp-quill'd porpentine;
And in the end being rescu'd, I have seen
Him caper upright like a wild Morisco,
Shaking the bloody darts as he his bells.
Full often, like a shag-hair'd crafty kern,
Hath he conversed with the enemy,
And undiscover'd come to me again
And given me notice of their villainies.
This devil here shall be my substitute;
For that John Mortimer, which now is dead,
In face, in gait, in speech, he doth resemble.
By this I shall perceive the commons' mind,
How they affect the house and claim of York.
Say he be taken, rack'd, and tortured;
I know no pain they can inflict upon him
Will make him say I mov'd him to those arms.
Say that he thrive, as 'tis great like he will,
Why, then from Ireland come I with my strength,
And reap the harvest which that rascal sow'd;
For Humphrey being dead, as he shall be,
And Henry put apart, the next for me.   *Exit*

SCENE 2

Bury St. Edmunds. A room of state

Enter two or three MURDERERS *running over the stage,
from the murder of* DUKE HUMPHREY

FIRST MURDERER. Run to my Lord of Suffolk; let him know
  We have dispatch'd the Duke, as he commanded.
SECOND MURDERER. O that it were to do! What have we
  done?
  Didst ever hear a man so penitent?

Enter SUFFOLK

FIRST MURDERER. Here comes my lord.
SUFFOLK. Now, sirs, have you dispatch'd this thing?
FIRST MURDERER. Ay, my good lord, he's dead.
SUFFOLK. Why, that's well said. Go, get you to my house;
  I will reward you for this venturous deed.
  The King and all the peers are here at hand.
  Have you laid fair the bed? Is all things well,
  According as I gave directions?
FIRST MURDERER. 'Tis, my good lord.
SUFFOLK. Away! be gone.   *Exeunt* MURDERERS

Sound trumpets. Enter the KING, *the* QUEEN, CARDINAL,
SOMERSET, *with attendants*

KING HENRY. Go call our uncle to our presence straight;
  Say we intend to try his Grace to-day,
  If he be guilty, as 'tis published.
SUFFOLK. I'll call him presently, my noble lord.   *Exit*
KING HENRY. Lords, take your places; and, I pray you all,
  Proceed no straiter 'gainst our uncle Gloucester
  Than from true evidence, of good esteem,
  He be approv'd in practice culpable.
QUEEN. God forbid any malice should prevail
  That faultless may condemn a nobleman!
  Pray God he may acquit him of suspicion!
KING HENRY. I thank thee, Meg; these words content me
  much.

Re-enter SUFFOLK

How now! Why look'st thou pale? Why tremblest thou?
Where is our uncle? What's the matter, Suffolk?
SUFFOLK. Dead in his bed, my lord; Gloucester is dead.
QUEEN. Marry, God forfend!
CARDINAL. God's secret judgment! I did dream to-night
  The Duke was dumb and could not speak a word.
                            [*The* KING *swoons*]
QUEEN. How fares my lord? Help, lords! The King is dead.
SOMERSET. Rear up his body; wring him by the nose.
QUEEN. Run, go, help, help! O Henry, ope thine eyes!
SUFFOLK. He doth revive again; madam, be patient.
KING. O heavenly God!
QUEEN. How fares my gracious lord?
SUFFOLK. Comfort, my sovereign! Gracious Henry, comfort!
KING HENRY. What, doth my Lord of Suffolk comfort me?
  Came he right now to sing a raven's note,
  Whose dismal tune bereft my vital pow'rs;
  And thinks he that the chirping of a wren,
  By crying comfort from a hollow breast,
  Can chase away the first conceived sound?
  Hide not thy poison with such sug'red words;
  Lay not thy hands on me; forbear, I say,
  Their touch affrights me as a serpent's sting.
  Thou baleful messenger, out of my sight!
  Upon thy eye-balls murderous tyranny
  Sits in grim majesty to fright the world.
  Look not upon me, for thine eyes are wounding;
  Yet do not go away; come, basilisk,
  And kill the innocent gazer with thy sight;
  For in the shade of death I shall find joy—
  In life but double death, now Gloucester's dead.
QUEEN. Why do you rate my Lord of Suffolk thus?
  Although the Duke was enemy to him,
  Yet he most Christian-like laments his death;
  And for myself—foe as he was to me—
  Might liquid tears, or heart-offending groans,
  Or blood-consuming sighs, recall his life,
  I would be blind with weeping, sick with groans,

Look pale as primrose with blood-drinking sighs,
And all to have the noble Duke alive.
What know I how the world may deem of me?
For it is known we were but hollow friends:
It may be judg'd I made the Duke away;
So shall my name with slander's tongue be wounded,
And princes' courts be fill'd with my reproach.
This get I by his death. Ay me, unhappy!
To be a queen and crown'd with infamy!

KING HENRY. Ah, woe is me for Gloucester, wretched man!

QUEEN. Be woe for me, more wretched than he is.
What, dost thou turn away, and hide thy face?
I am no loathsome leper—look on me.
What, art thou like the adder waxen deaf?
Be poisonous too, and kill thy forlorn Queen.
Is all thy comfort shut in Gloucester's tomb?
Why, then Dame Margaret was ne'er thy joy.
Erect his statuë and worship it,
And make my image but an alehouse sign.
Was I for this nigh wreck'd upon the sea,
And twice by awkward wind from England's bank
Drove back again unto my native clime?
What boded this but well-forewarning wind
Did seem to say 'Seek not a scorpion's nest,
Nor set no footing on this unkind shore'?
What did I then but curs'd the gentle gusts,
And he that loos'd them forth their brazen caves;
And bid them blow towards England's blessed shore,
Or turn our stern upon a dreadful rock?
Yet Æolus would not be a murderer,
But left that hateful office unto thee.
The pretty-vaulting sea refus'd to drown me,
Knowing that thou wouldst have me drown'd on shore
With tears as salt as sea through thy unkindness;
The splitting rocks cow'r'd in the sinking sands
And would not dash me with their ragged sides,
Because thy flinty heart, more hard than they,
Might in thy palace perish Margaret.
As far as I could ken thy chalky cliffs,
When from thy shore the tempest beat us back,

I stood upon the hatches in the storm;
And when the dusky sky began to rob
My earnest-gaping sight of thy land's view,
I took a costly jewel from my neck—
A heart it was, bound in with diamonds—
And threw it towards thy land. The sea receiv'd it;
And so I wish'd thy body might my heart.
And even with this I lost fair England's view,
And bid mine eyes be packing with my heart,
And call'd them blind and dusky spectacles
For losing ken of Albion's wished coast.
How often have I tempted Suffolk's tongue—
The agent of thy foul inconstancy—
To sit and witch me, as Ascanius did
When he to madding Dido would unfold
His father's acts commenc'd in burning Troy!
Am I not witch'd like her? Or thou not false like him?
Ay me, I can no more! Die, Margaret,
For Henry weeps that thou dost live so long.

Noise within. Enter WARWICK, SALISBURY,
and many commons

WARWICK. It is reported, mighty sovereign,
 That good Duke Humphrey traitorously is murd'red
 By Suffolk and the Cardinal Beaufort's means.
 The commons, like an angry hive of bees
 That want their leader, scatter up and down
 And care not who they sting in his revenge.
 Myself have calm'd their spleenful mutiny
 Until they hear the order of his death.
KING HENRY. That he is dead, good Warwick, 'tis too true;
 But how he died God knows, not Henry.
 Enter his chamber, view his breathless corpse,
 And comment then upon his sudden death.
WARWICK. That shall I do, my liege. Stay, Salisbury,
 With the rude multitude till I return. *Exit*
 Exit SALISBURY *with the commons*
KING HENRY. O Thou that judgest all things, stay my
 thoughts—
 My thoughts that labour to persuade my soul

Some violent hands were laid on Humphrey's life!
If my suspect be false, forgive me, God;
For judgment only doth belong to Thee.
Fain would I go to chafe his paly lips
With twenty thousand kisses and to drain
Upon his face an ocean of salt tears
To tell my love unto his dumb deaf trunk;
And with my fingers feel his hand un-feeling;
But all in vain are these mean obsequies;
And to survey his dead and earthy image,
What were it but to make my sorrow greater?

Bed put forth with the body. Enter WARWICK

WARWICK. Come hither, gracious sovereign, view this body.
KING HENRY. That is to see how deep my grave is made;
For with his soul fled all my worldly solace,
For, seeing him, I see my life in death.
WARWICK. As surely as my soul intends to live
With that dread King that took our state upon Him
To free us from his Father's wrathful curse,
I do believe that violent hands were laid
Upon the life of this thrice-famed Duke.
SUFFOLK. A dreadful oath, sworn with a solemn tongue!
What instance gives Lord Warwick for his vow?
WARWICK. See how the blood is settled in his face.
Oft have I seen a timely-parted ghost,
Of ashy semblance, meagre, pale, and bloodless,
Being all descended to the labouring heart,
Who, in the conflict that it holds with death,
Attracts the same for aidance 'gainst the enemy,
Which with the heart there cools, and ne'er returneth
To blush and beautify the cheek again.
But see, his face is black and full of blood;
His eye-balls further out than when he liv'd,
Staring full ghastly like a strangled man;
His hair uprear'd, his nostrils stretch'd with struggling;
His hands abroad display'd, as one that grasp'd
And tugg'd for life, and was by strength subdu'd.
Look, on the sheets his hair, you see, is sticking;
His well-proportion'd beard made rough and rugged,

Like to the summer's corn by tempest lodged.
It cannot be but he was murd'red here:
The least of all these signs were probable.
SUFFOLK. Why, Warwick, who should do the Duke to
  death?
Myself and Beaufort had him in protection;
And we, I hope, sir, are no murderers.
WARWICK. But both of you were vow'd Duke Humphrey's
  foes;
And you, forsooth, had the good Duke to keep.
'Tis like you would not feast him like a friend;
And 'tis well seen he found an enemy.
QUEEN. Then you, belike, suspect these noblemen
As guilty of Duke Humphrey's timeless death.
WARWICK. Who finds the heifer dead and bleeding fresh,
And sees fast by a butcher with an axe,
But will suspect 'twas he that made the slaughter?
Who finds the partridge in the puttock's nest
But may imagine how the bird was dead,
Although the kite soar with unbloodied beak?
Even so suspicious is this tragedy.
QUEEN. Are you the butcher, Suffolk? Where's your knife?
Is Beaufort term'd a kite? Where are his talons?
SUFFOLK. I wear no knife to slaughter sleeping men;
But here's a vengeful sword, rusted with ease,
That shall be scoured in his rancorous heart
That slanders me with murder's crimson badge.
Say if thou dar'st, proud Lord of Warwickshire,
That I am faulty in Duke Humphrey's death.
              Exeunt CARDINAL, SOMERSET, *and others*
WARWICK. What dares not Warwick, if false Suffolk dare
  him?
QUEEN. He dares not calm his contumelious spirit,
Nor cease to be an arrogant controller,
Though Suffolk dare him twenty thousand times.
WARWICK. Madam, be still—with reverence may I say;
For every word you speak in his behalf
Is slander to your royal dignity.
SUFFOLK. Blunt-witted lord, ignoble in demeanour,
If ever lady wrong'd her lord so much,

Thy mother took into her blameful bed
Some stern untutor'd churl, and noble stock
Was graft with crab-tree slip, whose fruit thou art,
And never of the Nevils' noble race.
WARWICK. But that the guilt of murder bucklers thee,
  And I should rob the deathsman of his fee,
  Quitting thee thereby of ten thousand shames,
  And that my sovereign's presence makes me mild,
  I would, false murd'rous coward, on thy knee
  Make thee beg pardon for thy passed speech
  And say it was thy mother that thou meant'st,
  That thou thyself was born in bastardy;
  And, after all this fearful homage done,
  Give thee thy hire and send thy soul to hell,
  Pernicious blood-sucker of sleeping men.
SUFFOLK. Thou shalt be waking while I shed thy blood,
  If from this presence thou dar'st go with me.
WARWICK. Away even now, or I will drag thee hence.
  Unworthy though thou art, I'll cope with thee,
  And do some service to Duke Humphrey's ghost.
                    Exeunt SUFFOLK *and* WARWICK
KING HENRY. What stronger breastplate than a heart untainted?
  Thrice is he arm'd that hath his quarrel just;
  And he but naked, though lock'd up in steel,
  Whose conscience with injustice is corrupted.
                              [*A noise within*]
QUEEN. What noise is this?

       Re-enter SUFFOLK *and* WARWICK, *with their
                 weapons drawn*

KING. Why, how now, lords, your wrathful weapons
    drawn
  Here in our presence! Dare you be so bold?
  Why, what tumultuous clamour have we here?
SUFFOLK. The trait'rous Warwick, with the men of Bury,
  Set all upon me, mighty sovereign.

              Re-enter SALISBURY

SALISBURY. [*To the Commons within*] Sirs, stand apart, the
  King shall know your mind.

Dread lord, the commons send you word by me
Unless Lord Suffolk straight be done to death,
Or banished fair England's territories,
They will by violence tear him from your palace
And torture him with grievous ling'ring death.
They say by him the good Duke Humphrey died;
They say in him they fear your Highness' death;
And mere instinct of love and loyalty,
Free from a stubborn opposite intent,
As being thought to contradict your liking,
Makes them thus forward in his banishment.
They say, in care of your most royal person,
That if your Highness should intend to sleep
And charge that no man should disturb your rest,
In pain of your dislike or pain of death,
Yet, notwithstanding such a strait edict,
Were there a serpent seen with forked tongue
That slily glided towards your Majesty,
It were but necessary you were wak'd,
Lest, being suffer'd in that harmful slumber,
The mortal worm might make the sleep eternal.
And therefore do they cry, though you forbid,
That they will guard you, whe'er you will or no,
From such fell serpents as false Suffolk is;
With whose envenomed and fatal sting
Your loving uncle, twenty times his worth,
They say, is shamefully bereft of life.

COMMONS. [*Within*] An answer from the King, my Lord
  of Salisbury!

SUFFOLK. 'Tis like the commons, rude unpolish'd hinds,
  Could send such message to their sovereign;
  But you, my lord, were glad to be employ'd,
  To show how quaint an orator you are.
  But all the honour Salisbury hath won
  Is that he was the lord ambassador
  Sent from a sort of tinkers to the King.

COMMONS. [*Within*] An answer from the King, or we will
  all break in!

KING HENRY. Go, Salisbury, and tell them all from me
  I thank them for their tender loving care;

And had I not been cited so by them,
Yet did I purpose as they do entreat;
For sure my thoughts do hourly prophesy
Mischance unto my state by Suffolk's means.
And therefore by His Majesty I swear,
Whose far unworthy deputy I am,
He shall not breathe infection in this air
But three days longer, on the pain of death.

Exit SALISBURY

QUEEN. O Henry, let me plead for gentle Suffolk!
KING HENRY. Ungentle Queen, to call him gentle Suffolk!
No more, I say; if thou dost plead for him,
Thou wilt but add increase unto my wrath.
Had I but said, I would have kept my word;
But when I swear, it is irrevocable.
If after three days' space thou here be'st found
On any ground that I am ruler of,
The world shall not be ransom for thy life.
Come, Warwick, come, good Warwick, go with me;
I have great matters to impart to thee.

Exeunt all but QUEEN *and* SUFFOLK

QUEEN. Mischance and sorrow go along with you!
Heart's discontent and sour affliction
Be playfellows to keep you company!
There's two of you; the devil make a third,
And threefold vengeance tend upon your steps!
SUFFOLK. Cease, gentle Queen, these execrations,
And let thy Suffolk take his heavy leave.
QUEEN. Fie, coward woman and soft-hearted wretch,
Has thou not spirit to curse thine enemy?
SUFFOLK. A plague upon them! Wherefore should I curse
them?
Would curses kill as doth the mandrake's groan,
I would invent as bitter searching terms,
As curst, as harsh, and horrible to hear,
Deliver'd strongly through my fixed teeth,
With full as many signs of deadly hate,
As lean-fac'd Envy in her loathsome cave.
My tongue should stumble in mine earnest words,
Mine eyes should sparkle like the beaten flint,

Mine hair be fix'd an end, as one distract;
Ay, every joint should seem to curse and ban;
And even now my burden'd heart would break,
Should I not curse them. Poison be their drink!
Gall, worse than gall, the daintiest that they taste!
Their sweetest shade a grove of cypress trees!
Their chiefest prospect murd'ring basilisks!
Their softest touch as smart as lizards' stings!
Their music frightful as the serpent's hiss,
And boding screech-owls make the consort full!
All the foul terrors in dark-seated hell—
QUEEN. Enough, sweet Suffolk, thou torment'st thyself;
And these dread curses, like the sun 'gainst glass,
Or like an overcharged gun, recoil,
And turns the force of them upon thyself.
SUFFOLK. You bade me ban, and will you bid me leave?
Now, by the ground that I am banish'd from,
Well could I curse away a winter's night,
Though standing naked on a mountain top
Where biting cold would never let grass grow,
And think it but a minute spent in sport.
QUEEN. O, let me entreat thee cease! Give me thy hand,
That I may dew it with my mournful tears;
Nor let the rain of heaven wet this place
To wash away my woeful monuments.
O, could this kiss be printed in thy hand,
That thou might'st think upon these by the seal,
Through whom a thousand sighs are breath'd for thee!
So, get thee gone, that I may know my grief;
'Tis but surmis'd whiles thou art standing by,
As one that surfeits thinking on a want.
I will repeal thee or, be well assur'd,
Adventure to be banished myself;
And banished I am, if but from thee.
Go, speak not to me; even now be gone.
O, go not yet! Even thus two friends condemn'd
Embrace, and kiss, and take ten thousand leaves,
Loather a hundred times to part than die.
Yet now, farewell; and farewell life with thee!
SUFFOLK. Thus is poor Suffolk ten times banished,

Once by the King and three times thrice by thee,
'Tis not the land I care for, wert thou thence;
A wilderness is populous enough,
So Suffolk had thy heavenly company;
For where thou art, there is the world itself,
With every several pleasure in the world;
And where thou art not, desolation.
I can no more: Live thou to joy thy life;
Myself no joy in nought but that thou liv'st.

Enter VAUX

QUEEN. Whither goes Vaux so fast? What news, I prithee?
VAUX. To signify unto his Majesty
 That Cardinal Beaufort is at point of death;
 For suddenly a grievous sickness took him
 That makes him gasp, and stare, and catch the air,
 Blaspheming God, and cursing men on earth.
 Sometime he talks as if Duke Humphrey's ghost
 Were by his side; sometime he calls the King
 And whispers to his pillow, as to him,
 The secrets of his overcharged soul;
 And I am sent to tell his Majesty
 That even now he cries aloud for him.
QUEEN. Go tell this heavy message to the King. *Exit* VAUX
 Ay me! What is this world! What news are these!
 But wherefore grieve I at an hour's poor loss,
 Omitting Suffolk's exile, my soul's treasure?
 Why only, Suffolk, mourn I not for thee,
 And with the southern clouds contend in tears—
 Theirs for the earth's increase, mine for my sorrows?
 Now get thee hence: the King, thou know'st, is coming;
 If thou be found by me, thou art but dead.
SUFFOLK. If I depart from thee I cannot live;
 And in thy sight to die, what were it else
 But like a pleasant slumber in thy lap?
 Here could I breathe my soul into the air,
 As mild and gentle as the cradle-babe
 Dying with mother's dug between its lips;
 Where, from thy sight, I should be raging mad
 And cry out for thee to close up mine eyes,

To have thee with thy lips to stop my mouth;
So shouldst thou either turn my flying soul,
Or I should breathe it so into thy body,
And then it liv'd in sweet Elysium.
To die by thee were but to die in jest:
From thee to die were torture more than death.
O, let me stay, befall what may befall!

QUEEN. Away! Though parting be a fretful corrosive,
It is applied to a deathful wound.
To France, sweet Suffolk. Let me hear from thee;
For whereso'er thou art in this world's globe
I'll have an Iris that shall find thee out.

SUFFOLK. I go.

QUEEN. And take my heart with thee.   [*She kisses him*]

SUFFOLK. A jewel, lock'd into the woefull'st cask
That ever did contain a thing of worth.
Even as a splitted bark, so sunder we:
This way fall I to death.

QUEEN. This way for me.   *Exeunt severally*

SCENE 3

London. CARDINAL BEAUFORT's *bedchamber*

Enter the KING, SALISBURY, *and* WARWICK,
to the CARDINAL *in bed*

KING HENRY. How fares my lord? Speak, Beaufort, to thy
   sovereign.

CARDINAL. If thou be'st Death I'll give thee England's treasure,
Enough to purchase such another island,
So thou wilt let me live and feel no pain.

KING HENRY. Ah, what a sign it is of evil life
Where death's approach is seen so terrible!

WARWICK. Beaufort, it is thy sovereign speaks to thee.

CARDINAL. Bring me unto my trial when you will.
Died he not in his bed? Where should he die?
Can I make men live, whe'er they will or no?
O, torture me no more! I will confess.

Alive again? Then show me where he is;
I'll give a thousand pound to look upon him.
He hath no eyes, the dust hath blinded them.
Comb down his hair; look, look! it stands upright,
Like lime-twigs set to catch my winged soul!
Give me some drink; and bid the apothecary
Bring the strong poison that I bought of him.
KING HENRY. O Thou eternal Mover of the heavens,
Look with a gentle eye upon this wretch!
O, beat away the busy meddling fiend
That lays strong siege unto this wretch's soul,
And from his bosom purge this black despair!
WARWICK. See how the pangs of death do make him grin.
SALISBURY. Disturb him not, let him pass peaceably.
KING HENRY. Peace to his soul, if God's good pleasure be!
Lord Card'nal, if thou think'st on heaven's bliss,
Hold up thy hand, make signal of thy hope.
He dies, and makes no sign: O God, forgive him!
WARWICK. So bad a death argues a monstrous life.
KING HENRY. Forbear to judge, for we are sinners all.
Close up his eyes, and draw the curtain close;
And let us all to meditation.   *Exeunt*

ACT IV. SCENE 1

The coast of Kent

Alarum. Fight at sea. Ordnance goes off. Enter a
LIEUTENANT, *a* SHIPMASTER *and his* MATE, *and*
WALTER WHITMORE, *with sailors;* SUFFOLK *and*
other GENTLEMEN, *as prisoners*

LIEUTENANT. The gaudy, blabbing, and remorseful day
Is crept into the bosom of the sea;
And now loud-howling wolves arouse the jades
That drag the tragic melancholy night;
Who with their drowsy, slow, and flagging wings
Clip dead men's graves, and from their misty jaws

Breathe foul contagious darkness in the air.
Therefore bring forth the soldiers of our prize;
For, whilst our pinnace anchors in the Downs,
Here shall they make their ransom on the sand,
Or with their blood stain this discoloured shore.
Master, this prisoner freely give I thee;
And thou that art his mate make boot of this;
The other, Walter Whitmore, is thy share.

FIRST GENTLEMAN. What is my ransom, master, let me
know?

MASTER. A thousand crowns, or else lay down your head.

MATE. And so much shall you give, or off goes yours.

LIEUTENANT. What, think you much to pay two thousand
crowns,
And bear the name and port of gentlemen?
Cut both the villains' throats—for die you shall;
The lives of those which we have lost in fight
Be counterpois'd with such a petty sum!

FIRST GENTLEMAN. I'll give it, sir: and therefore spare my
life.

SECOND GENTLEMAN. And so will I, and write home for it
straight.

WHITMORE. I lost mine eye in laying the prize aboard,
[To SUFFOLK] And therefore, to revenge it, shalt thou die;
And so should these, if I might have my will.

LIEUTENANT. Be not so rash; take ransom, let him live.

SUFFOLK. Look on my George, I am a gentleman:
Rate me at what thou wilt, thou shalt be paid.

WHITMORE. And so am I: my name is Walter Whitmore.
How now! Why start'st thou? What, doth death affright?

SUFFOLK. Thy name affrights me, in whose sound is death.
A cunning man did calculate my birth
And told me that by water I should die;
Yet let not this make thee be bloody-minded;
Thy name is Gualtier, being rightly sounded.

WHITMORE. Gualtier or Walter, which it is I care not:
Never yet did base dishonour blur our name
But with our sword we wip'd away the blot;
Therefore, when merchant-like I sell revenge,
Broke be my sword, my arms torn and defac'd,

And I proclaim'd a coward through the world.

SUFFOLK. Stay, Whitmore, for thy prisoner is a prince,
  The Duke of Suffolk, William de la Pole.

WHITMORE. The Duke of Suffolk muffled up in rags?

SUFFOLK. Ay, but these rags are no part of the Duke:
  Jove sometime went disguis'd, and why not I?

LIEUTENANT. But Jove was never slain, as thou shalt be.

SUFFOLK. Obscure and lowly swain, King Henry's blood,
  The honourable blood of Lancaster,
  Must not be shed by such a jaded groom.
  Hast thou not kiss'd thy hand and held my stirrup,
  Bareheaded plodded by my foot-cloth mule,
  And thought thee happy when I shook my head?
  How often hast thou waited at my cup,
  Fed from my trencher, kneel'd down at the board,
  When I have feasted with Queen Margaret?
  Remember it, and let it make thee crestfall'n,
  Ay, and allay thus thy abortive pride,
  How in our voiding-lobby hast thou stood
  And duly waited for my coming forth.
  This hand of mine hath writ in thy behalf,
  And therefore shall it charm thy riotous tongue.

WHITMORE. Speak, Captain, shall I stab the forlorn swain?

LIEUTENANT. First let my words stab him, as he hath me.

SUFFOLK. Base slave, thy words are blunt, and so art thou.

LIEUTENANT. Convey him hence, and on our longboat's side
  Strike off his head.

SUFFOLK. Thou dar'st not, for thy own.

LIEUTENANT. Poole!

SUFFOLK. Poole?

LIEUTENANT. Ay, kennel, puddle, sink, whose filth and dirt
  Troubles the silver spring where England drinks;
  Now will I dam up this thy yawning mouth
  For swallowing the treasure of the realm.
  Thy lips, that kiss'd the Queen, shall sweep the ground;
  And thou that smil'dst at good Duke Humphrey's death
  Against the senseless winds shalt grin in vain,
  Who in contempt shall hiss at thee again;
  And wedded be thou to the hags of hell
  For daring to affy a mighty lord

Unto the daughter of a worthless king,
Having neither subject, wealth, nor diadem.
By devilish policy art thou grown great,
And, like ambitious Sylla, overgorg'd
With gobbets of thy mother's bleeding heart.
By thee Anjou and Maine were sold to France;
The false revolting Normans thorough thee
Disdain to call us lord; and Picardy
Hath slain their governors, surpris'd our forts,
And sent the ragged soldiers wounded home.
The princely Warwick, and the Nevils all,
Whose dreadful swords were never drawn in vain,
As hating thee, are rising up in arms;
And now the house of York—thrust from the crown
By shameful murder of a guiltless king
And lofty proud encroaching tyranny—
Burns with revenging fire, whose hopeful colours
Advance our half-fac'd sun, striving to shine,
Under the which is writ 'Invitis nubibus.'
The commons here in Kent are up in arms;
And to conclude, reproach and beggary
Is crept into the palace of our King,
And all by thee. Away! convey him hence.
SUFFOLK. O that I were a god, to shoot forth thunder
    Upon these paltry, servile, abject drudges!
    Small things make base men proud: this villain here,
    Being captain of a pinnace, threatens more
    Than Bargulus, the strong Illyrian pirate.
    Drones suck not eagles' blood but rob beehives.
    It is impossible that I should die
    By such a lowly vassal as thyself.
    Thy words move rage and not remorse in me.
    I go of message from the Queen to France:
    I charge thee waft me safely cross the Channel.
LIEUTENANT. Walter—
WHITMORE. Come, Suffolk, I must waft thee to thy death.
SUFFOLK. Gelidus timor occupat artus: it is thee I fear.
WHITMORE. Thou shalt have cause to fear before I leave
    thee.
    What, are ye daunted now? Now will ye stoop?

FIRST GENTLEMAN. My gracious lord, entreat him, speak him
    fair.

SUFFOLK. Suffolk's imperial tongue is stern and rough,
  Us'd to command, untaught to plead for favour.
  Far be it we should honour such as these
  With humble suit: no, rather let my head
  Stoop to the block than these knees bow to any
  Save to the God of heaven and to my king;
  And sooner dance upon a bloody pole
  Than stand uncover'd to the vulgar groom.
  True nobility is exempt from fear:
  More can I bear than you dare execute.

LIEUTENANT. Hale him away, and let him talk no more.

SUFFOLK. Come, soldiers, show what cruelty ye can,
  That this my death may never be forgot—
  Great men oft die by vile bezonians:
  A Roman sworder and banditto slave
  Murder'd sweet Tully; Brutus' bastard hand
  Stabb'd Julius Cæsar; savage islanders
  Pompey the Great; and Suffolk dies by pirates.

                Exit WALTER *with* SUFFOLK

LIEUTENANT. And as for these, whose ransom we have set,
  It is our pleasure one of them depart;
  Therefore come you with us, and let him go.

          Exeunt all but the FIRST GENTLEMAN

Re-enter WHITMORE *with* SUFFOLK's *body*

WHITMORE. There let his head and lifeless body lie,
  Until the Queen his mistress bury it.   *Exit*

FIRST GENTLEMAN. O barbarous and bloody spectacle!
  His body will I bear unto the King.
  If he revenge it not, yet will his friends;
  So will the Queen, that living held him dear.

                  Exit with the body

SCENE 2

Blackheath

Enter GEORGE BEVIS *and* JOHN HOLLAND

GEORGE. Come and get thee a sword, though made of a lath;
they have been up these two days.

JOHN. They have the more need to sleep now, then.

GEORGE. I tell thee Jack Cade the clothier means to dress the
commonwealth, and turn it, and set a new nap upon it.

JOHN. So he had need, for 'tis threadbare. Well, I say it was
never merry world in England since gentlemen came up.

GEORGE. O miserable age! Virtue is not regarded in handi-
craftsmen.

JOHN. The nobility think scorn to go in leather aprons.

GEORGE. Nay, more, the King's Council are no good
workmen.

JOHN. True; and yet it is said 'Labour in thy vocation';
which is as much to say as 'Let the magistrates be labouring men'; and therefore should we be magistrates.

GEORGE. Thou hast hit it; for there's no better sign of a
brave mind than a hard hand.

JOHN. I see them! I see them! There's Best's son, the tanner
of Wingham—

GEORGE. He shall have the skins of our enemies to make
dog's leather of.

JOHN. And Dick the butcher—

GEORGE. Then is sin struck down, like an ox, and iniquity's
throat cut like a calf.

JOHN. And Smith the weaver—

GEORGE. Argo, their thread of life is spun.

JOHN. Come, come, let's fall in with them.

Drum. Enter CADE, DICK THE BUTCHER, SMITH THE
WEAVER, *and a* SAWYER, *with infinite numbers*

CADE. We John Cade, so term'd of our supposed father—

DICK. [*Aside*] Or rather, of stealing a cade of herrings.

CADE. For our enemies shall fall before us, inspired with the spirit of putting down kings and princes—command silence.

DICK. Silence!

CADE. My father was a Mortimer—

DICK. [*Aside*] He was an honest man and a good bricklayer.

CADE. My mother a Plantagenet—

DICK. [*Aside*] I knew her well; she was a midwife.

CADE. My wife descended of the Lacies—

DICK. [*Aside*] She was, indeed, a pedlar's daughter, and sold many laces.

SMITH. [*Aside*] But now of late, not able to travel with her furr'd pack, she washes bucks here at home.

CADE. Therefore am I of an honourable house.

DICK. [*Aside*] Ay, by my faith, the field is honourable, and there was he born, under a hedge, for his father had never a house but the cage.

CADE. Valiant I am.

SMITH. [*Aside*] 'A must needs; for beggary is valiant.

CADE. I am able to endure much.

DICK. [*Aside*] No question of that; for I have seen him whipt three market days together.

CADE. I fear neither sword nor fire.

SMITH. [*Aside*] He need not fear the sword, for his coat is of proof.

DICK. [*Aside*] But methinks he should stand in fear of fire, being burnt i' th' hand for stealing of sheep.

CADE. Be brave, then, for your captain is brave, and vows reformation. There shall be in England seven halfpenny loaves sold for a penny; the three-hoop'd pot shall have ten hoops; and I will make it felony to drink small beer. All the realm shall be in common, and in Cheapside shall my palfrey go to grass. And when I am king—as king I will be—

ALL. God save your Majesty!

CADE. I thank you, good people—there shall be no money; all shall eat and drink on my score, and I will apparel them all in one livery, that they may agree like brothers and worship me their lord.

DICK. The first thing we do, let's kill all the lawyers.

CADE. Nay, that I mean to do. Is not this a lamentable thing,

that of the skin of an innocent lamb should be made parchment? That parchment, being scribbl'd o'er, should undo
a man? Some say the bee stings; but I say 'tis the bee's
wax; for I did but seal once to a thing, and I was never
mine own man since. How now! Who's there?

Enter some, bringing in the CLERK OF CHATHAM

SMITH. The clerk of Chatham. He can write and read and
cast accompt.
CADE. O monstrous!
SMITH. We took him setting of boys' copies.
CADE. Here's a villain!
SMITH. Has a book in his pocket with red letters in't.
CADE. Nay, then he is a conjurer.
DICK. Nay, he can make obligations and write court-hand.
CADE. I am sorry for't; the man is a proper man, of mine
honour; unless I find him guilty, he shall not die. Come
hither, sirrah, I must examine thee. What is thy name?
CLERK. Emmanuel.
DICK. They use to write it on the top of letters; 'twill go
hard with you.
CADE. Let me alone. Dost thou use to write thy name, or
hast thou a mark to thyself, like a honest plain-dealing
man?
CLERK. Sir, I thank God, I have been so well brought up
that I can write my name.
ALL. He hath confess'd. Away with him! He's a villain and
a traitor.
CADE. Away with him, I say! Hang him with his pen and
inkhorn about his neck.   *Exit one with the* CLERK

Enter MICHAEL

MICHAEL. Where's our General?
CADE. Here I am, thou particular fellow.
MICHAEL. Fly, fly, fly! Sir Humphrey Stafford and his
brother are hard by, with the King's forces.
CADE. Stand, villain, stand, or I'll fell thee down. He shall be
encount'red with a man as good as himself. He is but a
knight, is 'a?

MICHAEL. No.

CADE. To equal him, I will make myself a knight presently. [*Kneels*] Rise up, Sir John Mortimer. [*Rises*] Now have at him!

Enter SIR HUMPHREY STAFFORD *and* WILLIAM
his brother, with drum and soldiers

STAFFORD. Rebellious hinds, the filth and scum of Kent,
Mark'd for the gallows, lay your weapons down;
Home to your cottages, forsake this groom;
The King is merciful if you revolt.

WILLIAM STAFFORD. But angry, wrathful, and inclin'd to blood,
If you go forward; therefore yield or die.

CADE. As for these silken-coated slaves, I pass not;
It is to you, good people, that I speak,
O'er whom, in time to come, I hope to reign;
For I am rightful heir unto the crown.

STAFFORD. Villain, thy father was a plasterer;
And thou thyself a shearman, art thou not?

CADE. And Adam was a gardener.

WILLIAM STAFFORD. And what of that?

CADE. Marry, this: Edmund Mortimer, Earl of March,
Married the Duke of Clarence' daughter, did he not?

STAFFORD. Ay, sir.

CADE. By her he had two children at one birth.

WILLIAM STAFFORD. That's false.

CADE. Ay, there's the question; but I say 'tis true.
The elder of them being put to nurse,
Was by a beggar-woman stol'n away,
And, ignorant of his birth and parentage,
Became a bricklayer when he came to age.
His son am I; deny it if you can.

DICK. Nay, 'tis too true; therefore he shall be king.

SMITH. Sir, he made a chimney in my father's house, and the bricks are alive at this day to testify it; therefore deny it not.

STAFFORD. And will you credit this base drudge's words
That speaks he knows not what?

ALL. Ay, marry, will we; therefore get ye gone.

WILLIAM STAFFORD. Jack Cade, the Duke of York hath
taught you this.

CADE. [*Aside*] He lies, for I invented it myself—Go to, sirrah, tell the King from me that for his father's sake, Henry
the Fifth, in whose time boys went to span-counter for
French crowns, I am content he shall reign; but I'll be
Protector over him.

DICK. And furthermore, we'll have the Lord Say's head for
selling the dukedom of Maine.

CADE. And good reason; for thereby is England main'd and
fain to go with a staff, but that my puissance holds it up.
Fellow kings, I tell you that that Lord Say hath gelded the
commonwealth and made it an eunuch; and more than
that, he can speak French, and therefore he is a traitor.

STAFFORD. O gross and miserable ignorance!

CADE. Nay, answer if you can; the Frenchmen are our
enemies. Go to, then, I ask but this: can he that speaks
with the tongue of an enemy be a good counsellor, or no?

ALL. No, no; and therefore we'll have his head.

WILLIAM STAFFORD. Well, seeing gentle words will not
prevail,
Assail them with the army of the King.

STAFFORD. Herald, away; and throughout every town
Proclaim them traitors that are up with Cade;
That those which fly before the battle ends
May, even in their wives' and children's sight,
Be hang'd up for example at their doors.
And you that be the King's friends, follow me.
Exeunt the two STAFFORDS *and soldiers*

CADE. And you that love the commons follow me.
Now show yourselves men; 'tis for liberty.
We will not leave one lord, one gentleman;
Spare none but such as go in clouted shoon,
For they are thrifty honest men and such
As would—but that they dare not—take our parts.

DICK. They are all in order, and march toward us.

CADE. But then are we in order when we are most out of
order. Come, march forward. *Exeunt*

SCENE 3

Another part of Blackheath

Alarums to the fight, wherein both the STAFFORDS *are slain. Enter* CADE *and the rest*

CADE. Where's Dick, the butcher of Ashford?

DICK. Here, sir.

CADE. They fell before thee like sheep and oxen, and thou behavedst thyself as if thou hadst been in thine own slaughter-house; therefore thus will I reward thee—the Lent shall be as long again as it is, and thou shalt have a licence to kill for a hundred lacking one.

DICK. I desire no more.

CADE. And, to speak truth, thou deserv'st no less. [*Putting on* SIR HUMPHREY's *brigandine*] This monument of the victory will I bear, and the bodies shall be dragged at my horse heels till I do come to London, where we will have the mayor's sword borne before us.

DICK. If we mean to thrive and do good, break open the gaols and let out the prisoners.

CADE. Fear not that, I warrant thee. Come, let's march towards London. *Exeunt*

SCENE 4

London. The palace

Enter the KING *with a supplication, and the* QUEEN *with* SUFFOLK's *head; the* DUKE OF BUCKINGHAM, *and the* LORD SAY

QUEEN. Oft have I heard that grief softens the mind
And makes it fearful and degenerate;
Think therefore on revenge and cease to weep.
But who can cease to weep, and look on this?
Here may his head lie on my throbbing breast;
But where's the body that I should embrace?

BUCKINGHAM. What answer makes your Grace to the rebels'
supplication?

KING HENRY. I'll send some holy bishop to entreat;
For God forbid so many simple souls
Should perish by the sword! And I myself,
Rather than bloody war shall cut them short,
Will parley with Jack Cade their general.
But stay, I'll read it over once again.

QUEEN. Ah, barbarous villains! Hath this lovely face
Rul'd like a wandering planet over me,
And could it not enforce them to relent
That were unworthy to behold the same?

KING HENRY. Lord Say, Jack Cade hath sworn to have thy
head.

SAY. Ay, but I hope your Highness shall have his.

KING HENRY. How now, madam!
Still lamenting and mourning for Suffolk's death?
I fear me, love, if that I had been dead,
Thou wouldst not have mourn'd so much for me.

QUEEN. No, my love, I should not mourn, but die for thee.

Enter a MESSENGER

KING HENRY. How now! What news? Why com'st thou in
such haste?

MESSENGER. The rebels are in Southwark; fly, my lord!
Jack Cade proclaims himself Lord Mortimer,
Descended from the Duke of Clarence' house,
And calls your Grace usurper, openly,
And vows to crown himself in Westminster.
His army is a ragged multitude
Of hinds and peasants, rude and merciless;
Sir Humphrey Stafford and his brother's death
Hath given them heart and courage to proceed.
All scholars, lawyers, courtiers, gentlemen,
They call false caterpillars and intend their death.

KING HENRY. O graceless men! they know not what they do.

BUCKINGHAM. My gracious lord, retire to Killingworth
Until a power be rais'd to put them down.

QUEEN. Ah, were the Duke of Suffolk now alive,
These Kentish rebels would be soon appeas'd!

ACT IV. SCENE 4

KING HENRY. Lord Say, the traitors hate thee;
  Therefore away with us to Killingworth.
SAY. So might your Grace's person be in danger.
  The sight of me is odious in their eyes;
  And therefore in this city will I stay
  And live alone as secret as I may.

Enter another MESSENGER

SECOND MESSENGER. Jack Cade hath gotten London Bridge.
  The citizens fly and forsake their houses;
  The rascal people, thirsting after prey,
  Join with the traitor; and they jointly swear
  To spoil the city and your royal court.
BUCKINGHAM. Then linger not, my lord; away, take horse.
KING HENRY. Come Margaret; God, our hope, will succour
  us.
QUEEN. My hope is gone, now Suffolk is deceas'd.
KING HENRY. [*To* LORD SAY] Farewell, my lord, trust not the
  Kentish rebels.
BUCKINGHAM. Trust nobody, for fear you be betray'd.
SAY. The trust I have is in mine innocence,
  And therefore am I bold and resolute.   *Exeunt*

SCENE 5

London. The Tower

Enter LORD SCALES *upon the Tower, walking. Then
enter two or three* CITIZENS, *below*

SCALES. How now! Is Jack Cade slain?
FIRST CITIZEN. No, my lord, nor likely to be slain; for they
  have won the bridge, killing all those that withstand them.
  The Lord Mayor craves aid of your honour from the
  Tower, to defend the city from the rebels.
SCALES. Such aid as I can spare you shall command,
  But I am troubled here with them myself;
  The rebels have assay'd to win the Tower.
  But get you to Smithfield, and gather head,
  And thither I will send you Matthew Goffe;

Fight for your King, your country, and your lives;
And so, farewell, for I must hence again.   *Exeunt*

SCENE 6

London. Cannon street

Enter JACK CADE *and the rest, and strikes his staff*
on London Stone

CADE. Now is Mortimer lord of this city. And here, sitting
upon London Stone, I charge and command that, of the
city's cost, the pissing conduit run nothing but claret wine
this first year of our reign. And now henceforward it shall
be treason for any that calls me other than Lord Mortimer.

Enter a SOLDIER, *running*

SOLDIER. Jack Cade! Jack Cade!
CADE. Knock him down there.   [*They kill him*]
SMITH. If this fellow be wise, he'll never call ye Jack Cade
more; I think he hath a very fair warning.
DICK. My lord, there's an army gathered together in Smith-
field.
CADE. Come then, let's go fight with them. But first go and
set London Bridge on fire; and, if you can, burn down the
Tower too. Come, let's away.   *Exeunt*

SCENE 7

London. Smithfield

Alarums. MATTHEW GOFFE *is slain, and all the rest.*
Then enter JACK CADE, *with his company*

CADE. So, sirs. Now go some and pull down the Savoy;
others to th' Inns of Court; down with them all.
DICK. I have a suit unto your lordship.
CADE. Be it a lordship, thou shalt have it for that word.
DICK. Only that the laws of England may come out of your
mouth.

JOHN. [*Aside*] Mass, 'twill be sore law then; for he was thrust in the mouth with a spear, and 'tis not whole yet.

SMITH. [*Aside*] Nay, John, it will be stinking law; for his breath stinks with eating toasted cheese.

CADE. I have thought upon it; it shall be so. Away, burn all the records of the realm. My mouth shall be the Parliament of England.

JOHN. [*Aside*] Then we are like to have biting statutes, unless his teeth be pull'd out.

CADE. And henceforward all things shall be in common.

Enter a MESSENGER

MESSENGER. My lord, a prize, a prize! Here's the Lord Say, which sold the towns in France; he that made us pay one and twenty fifteens, and one shilling to the pound, the last subsidy.

Enter GEORGE BEVIS, *with the* LORD SAY

CADE. Well, he shall be beheaded for it ten times. Ah, thou say, thou serge, nay, thou buckram lord! Now art thou within point blank of our jurisdiction regal. What canst thou answer to my Majesty for giving up of Normandy unto Mounsieur Basimecu the Dauphin of France? Be it known unto thee by these presence, even the presence of Lord Mortimer, that I am the besom that must sweep the court clean of such filth as thou art. Thou hast most traitorously corrupted the youth of the realm in erecting a grammar school; and whereas, before, our forefathers had no other books but the score and the tally, thou hast caused printing to be us'd, and, contrary to the King, his crown, and dignity, thou hast built a paper-mill. It will be proved to thy face that thou hast men about thee that usually talk of a noun and a verb, and such abominable words as no Christian ear can endure to hear. Thou hast appointed justices of peace, to call poor men before them about matters they were not able to answer. Moreover, thou hast put them in prison, and because they could not read, thou hast hang'd them, when, indeed, only for that cause they have been most worthy to live. Thou dost ride in a foot-cloth, dost thou not?

SAY. What of that?

CADE. Marry, thou ought'st not to let thy horse wear a cloak, when honester men than thou go in their hose and doublets.

DICK. And work in their shirt too, as myself, for example, that am a butcher.

SAY. You men of Kent—

DICK. What say you of Kent?

SAY. Nothing but this: 'tis 'bona terra, mala gens.'

CADE. Away with him, away with him! He speaks Latin.

SAY. Hear me but speak, and bear me where you will.
    Kent, in the Commentaries Cæsar writ,
    Is term'd the civil'st place of all this isle.
    Sweet is the country, because full of riches;
    The people liberal, valiant, active, wealthy;
    Which makes me hope you are not void of pity.
    I sold not Maine, I lost not Normandy;
    Yet, to recover them, would lose my life.
    Justice with favour have I always done;
    Pray'rs and tears have mov'd me, gifts could never.
    When have I aught exacted at your hands,
    But to maintain the King, the realm, and you?
    Large gifts have I bestow'd on learned clerks,
    Because my book preferr'd me to the King,
    And seeing ignorance is the curse of God,
    Knowledge the wing wherewith we fly to heaven,
    Unless you be possess'd with devilish spirits
    You cannot but forbear to murder me.
    This tongue hath parley'd unto foreign kings
    For your behoof.

CADE. Tut, when struck'st thou one blow in the field?

SAY. Great men have reaching hands. Oft have I struck
    Those that I never saw, and struck them dead.

GEORGE. O monstrous coward! What, to come behind folks?

SAY. These cheeks are pale for watching for your good.

CADE. Give him a box o' th' ear, and that will make 'em red again.

SAY. Long sitting to determine poor men's causes
    Hath made me full of sickness and diseases.

CADE. Ye shall have a hempen caudle then, and the help of hatchet.

DICK. Why dost thou quiver, man?

SAY. The palsy, and not fear, provokes me.

CADE. Nay, he nods at us, as who should say 'I'll be even with you'; I'll see if his head will stand steadier on a pole, or no. Take him away, and behead him.

SAY. Tell me: wherein have I offended most?
Have I affected wealth or honour? Speak.
Are my chests fill'd up with extorted gold?
Is my apparel sumptuous to behold?
Whom have I injur'd, that ye seek my death?
These hands are free from guiltless bloodshedding,
This breast from harbouring foul deceitful thoughts.
O, let me live!

CADE. [*Aside*] I feel remorse in myself with his words; but I'll bridle it. He shall die, an it be but for pleading so well for his life.—Away with him! He has a familiar under his tongue; he speaks not o' God's name. Go, take him away, I say, and strike off his head presently, and then break into his son-in-law's house, Sir James Cromer, and strike off his head, and bring them both upon two poles hither.

ALL. It shall be done.

SAY. Ah, countrymen! if when you make your pray'rs,
God should be so obdurate as yourselves,
How would it fare with your departed souls?
And therefore yet relent and save my life.

CADE. Away with him, and do as I command ye. [*Exeunt some with* LORD SAY] The proudest peer in the realm shall not wear a head on his shoulders, unless he pay me tribute; there shall not a maid be married, but she shall pay to me her maidenhead ere they have it. Men shall hold of me in capite; and we charge and command that their wives be as free as heart can wish or tongue can tell.

DICK. My lord, when shall we go to Cheapside, and take up commodities upon our bills?

CADE. Marry, presently.

ALL. O, brave!

Re-enter one with the heads

CADE. But is not this braver? Let them kiss one another, for
they lov'd well when they were alive. Now part them
again, lest they consult about the giving up of some more
towns in France. Soldiers, defer the spoil of the city until
night; for with these borne before us instead of maces will
we ride through the streets, and at every corner have them
kiss. Away!   *Exeunt*

SCENE 8

Southwark

Alarum and retreat. Enter again CADE *and all his
rabblement*

CADE. Up Fish Street! down Saint Magnus' Corner! Kill and
knock down! Throw them into Thames! [*Sound a parley*]
What noise is this I hear? Dare any be so bold to sound
retreat or parley when I command them kill?

Enter BUCKINGHAM *and old* CLIFFORD, *attended*

BUCKINGHAM. Ay, here they be that dare and will disturb
thee.
And therefore yet relent, and save my life.
Know, Cade, we come ambassadors from the King
Unto the commons whom thou hast misled;
And here pronounce free pardon to them all
That will forsake thee and go home in peace.
CLIFFORD. What say ye, countrymen? Will ye relent
And yield to mercy whilst 'tis offer'd you,
Or let a rebel lead you to your deaths?
Who loves the King, and will embrace his pardon,
Fling up his cap and say 'God save his Majesty!'
Who hateth him and honours not his father,
Henry the Fifth, that made all France to quake,
Shake he his weapon at us and pass by.
ALL. God save the King! God save the King!
CADE. What, Buckingham and Clifford, are ye so brave?
And you, base peasants, do ye believe him? Will you needs

be hang'd with your pardons about your necks? Hath my sword therefore broke through London gates, that you should leave me at the White Hart in Southwark? I thought ye would never have given out these arms till you had recovered your ancient freedom. But you are all recreants and dastards, and delight to live in slavery to the nobility. Let them break your backs with burdens, take your houses over your heads, ravish your wives and daughters before your faces. For me, I will make shift for one; and so God's curse light upon you all!

ALL. We'll follow Cade, we'll follow Cade!

CLIFFORD. Is Cade the son of Henry the Fifth,
That thus you do exclaim you'll go with him?
Will he conduct you through the heart of France,
And make the meanest of you earls and dukes?
Alas, he hath no home, no place to fly to;
Nor knows he how to live but by the spoil,
Unless by robbing of your friends and us.
Were't not a shame that whilst you live at jar
The fearful French, whom you late vanquished,
Should make a start o'er seas and vanquish you?
Methinks already in this civil broil
I see them lording it in London streets,
Crying 'Villiago!' unto all they meet.
Better ten thousand base-born Cades miscarry
Than you should stoop unto a Frenchman's mercy.
To France, to France, and get what you have lost;
Spare England, for it is your native coast.
Henry hath money; you are strong and manly.
God on our side, doubt not of victory.

ALL. A Clifford! a Clifford! We'll follow the King and Clifford.

CADE. Was ever feather so lightly blown to and fro as this multitude? The name of Henry the Fifth hales them to an hundred mischiefs, and makes them leave me desolate. I see them lay their heads together to surprise me. My sword make way for me for here is no staying. In despite of the devils and hell, have through the very middest of you! and heavens and honour be witness that no want of resolution in me, but only my followers' base and ignominious treasons, makes me betake me to my heels.   *Exit*

BUCKINGHAM. What, is he fled? Go some, and follow him;
    And he that brings his head unto the King
    Shall have a thousand crowns for his reward.

Exeunt some of them

    Follow me, soldiers; we'll devise a mean
    To reconcile you all unto the King.   *Exeunt*

SCENE 9

Killingworth Castle

Sound trumpets. Enter KING, QUEEN, *and* SOMERSET,
on the terrace

KING HENRY. Was ever king that joy'd an earthly throne
    And could command no more content than I?
    No sooner was I crept out of my cradle
    But I was made a king, at nine months old.
    Was never subject long'd to be a king
    As I do long and wish to be a subject.

Enter BUCKINGHAM *and old* CLIFFORD

BUCKINGHAM. Health and glad tidings to your Majesty!
KING HENRY. Why, Buckingham, is the traitor Cade
    surpris'd?
    Or is he but retir'd to make him strong?

Enter, below, multitudes, with halters about their necks

CLIFFORD. He is fled, my lord, and all his powers do yield,
    And humbly thus, with halters on their necks,
    Expect your Highness' doom of life or death.
KING HENRY. Then, heaven, set ope thy everlasting gates,
    To entertain my vows of thanks and praise!
    Soldiers, this day have you redeem'd your lives,
    And show'd how well you love your Prince and country.
    Continue still in this so good a mind,
    And Henry, though he be infortunate,
    Assure yourselves, will never be unkind.
    And so, with thanks and pardon to you all,

I do dismiss you to your several countries.

ALL. God save the King! God save the King!

Enter a MESSENGER

MESSENGER. Please it your Grace to be advertised
The Duke of York is newly come from Ireland
And with a puissant and a mighty power
Of gallowglasses and stout kerns
Is marching hitherward in proud array,
And still proclaimeth, as he comes along,
His arms are only to remove from thee
The Duke of Somerset, whom he terms a traitor.

KING HENRY. Thus stands my state, 'twixt Cade and York distress'd;
Like to a ship that, having scap'd a tempest,
Is straightway calm'd, and boarded with a pirate;
But now is Cade driven back, his men dispers'd,
And now is York in arms to second him.
I pray thee, Buckingham, go and meet him
And ask him what's the reason of these arms.
Tell him I'll send Duke Edmund to the Tower—
And Somerset, we will commit thee thither
Until his army be dismiss'd from him.

SOMERSET. My lord,
I'll yield myself to prison willingly,
Or unto death, to do my country good.

KING HENRY. In any case be not too rough in terms,
For he is fierce and cannot brook hard language.

BUCKINGHAM. I will, my lord, and doubt not so to deal
As all things shall redound unto your good.

KING HENRY. Come, wife, let's in, and learn to govern better;
For yet may England curse my wretched reign.

Flourish. Exeunt

SCENE 10

Kent. IDEN'S *garden*

Enter CADE

CADE. Fie on ambitions! Fie on myself, that have a sword

and yet am ready to famish! These five days have I hid me in these woods and durst not peep out, for all the country is laid for me; but now am I so hungry that, if I might have a lease of my life for a thousand years, I could stay no longer. Wherefore, on a brick wall have I climb'd into this garden, to see if I can eat grass or pick a sallet another while, which is not amiss to cool a man's stomach this hot weather. And I think this word 'sallet' was born to do me good; for many a time, but for a sallet, my brain-pain had been cleft with a brown bill; and many a time, when I have been dry, and bravely marching, it hath serv'd me instead of a quart-pot to drink in; and now the word 'sallet' must serve me to feed on.

Enter IDEN

IDEN. Lord, who would live turmoiled in the court
And may enjoy such quiet walks as these?
This small inheritance my father left me
Contenteth me, and worth a monarchy.
I seek not to wax great by others' waning
Or gather wealth I care not with what envy;
Sufficeth that I have maintains my state,
And sends the poor well pleased from my gate.

CADE. Here's the lord of the soil come to seize me for a stray, for entering his fee-simple without leave. Ah, villain, thou wilt betray me, and get a thousand crowns of the King by carrying my head to him; but I'll make thee eat iron like an ostrich and swallow my sword like a great pin ere thou and I part.

IDEN. Why, rude companion, whatsoe'er thou be,
I know thee not; why then should I betray thee?
Is't not enough to break into my garden
And like a thief to come to rob my grounds,
Climbing my walls in spite of me the owner,
But thou wilt brave me with these saucy terms?

CADE. Brave thee? Ay, by the best blood that ever was broach'd, and beard thee too. Look on me well: I have eat no meat these five days, yet come thou and thy five men and if I do not leave you all as dead as a door-nail, I pray God I may never eat grass more.

IDEN. Nay, it shall ne'er be said, while England stands,
  That Alexander Iden, an esquire of Kent,
  Took odds to combat a poor famish'd man.
  Oppose thy steadfast-gazing eyes to mine;
  See if thou canst outface me with thy looks;
  Set limb to limb, and thou art far the lesser;
  Thy hand is but a finger to my fist,
  Thy leg a stick compared with this truncheon;
  My foot shall fight with all the strength thou hast,
  And if mine arm be heaved in the air,
  Thy grave is digg'd already in the earth.
  As for words, whose greatness answers words,
  Let this my sword report what speech forbears.

CADE. By my valour, the most complete champion that ever
  I heard! Steel, if thou turn the edge, or cut not out the
  burly bon'd clown in chines of beef ere thou sleep in thy
  sheath, I beseech God on my knees thou mayst be turn'd
  to hobnails. [*Here they fight;* CADE *falls*] O, I am slain!
  famine and no other hath slain me. Let ten thousand devils
  come against me, and give me but the ten meals I have
  lost, and I'd defy them all. Wither, garden, and be henceforth a burying place to all that do dwell in this house, because the unconquered soul of Cade is fled.

IDEN. Is't Cade that I have slain, that monstrous traitor?
  Sword, I will hallow thee for this thy deed
  And hang thee o'er my tomb when I am dead.
  Ne'er shall this blood be wiped from thy point,
  But thou shalt wear it as a herald's coat
  To emblaze the honour that thy master got.

CADE. Iden, farewell; and be proud of thy victory. Tell Kent
  from me she hath lost her best man, and exhort all the
  world to be cowards; for I, that never feared any, am
  vanquished by famine, not by valour.   [*Dies*]

IDEN. How much thou wrong'st me, heaven be my judge.
  Die, damned wretch, the curse of her that bare thee!
  And as I thrust thy body in with my sword,
  So wish I I might thrust thy soul to hell.
  Hence will I drag thee headlong by the heels
  Unto a dunghill, which shall be thy grave,
  And there cut off thy most ungracious head,

667

Which I will bear in triumph to the King,
Leaving thy trunk for crows to feed upon.   *Exit*

ACT V. SCENE 1

Fields between Dartford and Blackheath

Enter YORK, *and his army of Irish, with drum and colours*

YORK. From Ireland thus comes York to claim his right
And pluck the crown from feeble Henry's head:
Ring bells aloud, burn bonfires clear and bright,
To entertain great England's lawful king.
Ah, sancta majestas! who would not buy thee dear?
Let them obey that knows not how to rule;
This hand was made to handle nought but gold.
I cannot give due action to my words
Except a sword or sceptre balance it.
A sceptre shall it have, have I a soul,
On which I'll toss the flower-de-luce of France.

Enter BUCKINGHAM

[*Aside*] Whom have we here? Buckingham, to disturb me?
The King hath sent him, sure: I must dissemble.
BUCKINGHAM. York, if thou meanest well, I greet thee well.
YORK. Humphrey of Buckingham, I accept thy greeting.
Art thou a messenger, or come of pleasure?
BUCKINGHAM. A messenger from Henry, our dread liege,
To know the reason of these arms in peace;
Or why thou, being a subject as I am,
Against thy oath and true allegiance sworn,
Should raise so great a power without his leave,
Or dare to bring thy force so near the court.
YORK. [*Aside*] Scarce can I speak, my choler is so great.
O, I could hew up rocks and fight with flint,
I am so angry at these abject terms;

And now, like Ajax Telamonius,
On sheep or oxen could I spend my fury.
I am far better born than is the King,
More like a king, more kingly in my thoughts;
But I must make fair weather yet awhile,
Till Henry be more weak and I more strong.—
Buckingham, I prithee, pardon me
That I have given no answer all this while;
My mind was troubled with deep melancholy.
The cause why I have brought this army hither
Is to remove proud Somerset from the King,
Seditious to his Grace and to the state.
BUCKINGHAM. That is too much presumption on thy part;
But if thy arms be to no other end,
The King hath yielded unto thy demand:
The Duke of Somerset is in the Tower.
YORK. Upon thine honour, is he prisoner?
BUCKINGHAM. Upon mine honour, he is prisoner.
YORK. Then, Buckingham, I do dismiss my pow'rs.
Soldiers, I thank you all; disperse yourselves;
Meet me to-morrow in Saint George's field,
You shall have pay and everything you wish.
And let my sovereign, virtuous Henry,
Command my eldest son, nay, all my sons,
As pledges of my fealty and love.
I'll send them all as willing as I live:
Lands, goods, horse, armour, anything I have,
Is his to use, so Somerset may die.
BUCKINGHAM. York, I commend this kind submission.
We twain will go into his Highness' tent.

Enter the KING, *and attendants*

KING HENRY. Buckingham, doth York intend no harm to us,
That thus he marcheth with thee arm in arm?
YORK. In all submission and humility
York doth present himself unto your Highness.
KING HENRY. Then what intends these forces thou dost bring?
YORK. To heave the traitor Somerset from hence,
And fight against that monstrous rebel Cade,
Who since I heard to be discomfited.

Enter IDEN, *with* CADE's *head*

IDEN. If one so rude and of so mean condition
  May pass into the presence of a king,
  Lo, I present your Grace a traitor's head,
  The head of Cade, whom I in combat slew.
KING HENRY. The head of Cade! Great God, how just art
    Thou!
  O, let me view his visage, being dead,
  That living wrought me such exceeding trouble.
  Tell me, my friend, art thou the man that slew him?
IDEN. I was, an't like your Majesty.
KING HENRY. How art thou call'd? And what is thy degree?
IDEN. Alexander Iden, that's my name;
  A poor esquire of Kent that loves his king.
BUCKINGHAM. So please it you, my lord, 'twere not amiss
  He were created knight for his good service.
KING HENRY. Iden, kneel down. [*He kneels*] Rise up a knight.
  We give thee for reward a thousand marks,
  And will that thou thenceforth attend on us.
IDEN. May Iden live to merit such a bounty,
  And never live but true unto his liege!

Enter the QUEEN *and* SOMERSET

KING HENRY. See, Buckingham! Somerset comes with th'
    Queen:
  Go, bid her hide him quickly from the Duke.
QUEEN. For thousand Yorks he shall not hide his head,
  But boldly stand and front him to his face.
YORK. How now! Is Somerset at liberty?
  Then, York, unloose thy long-imprisoned thoughts
  And let thy tongue be equal with thy heart.
  Shall I endure the sight of Somerset?
  False king, why hast thou broken faith with me,
  Knowing how hardly I can brook abuse?
  King did I call thee? No, thou art not king;
  Not fit to govern and rule multitudes,
  Which dar'st not, no, nor canst not rule a traitor.
  That head of thine doth not become a crown;
  Thy hand is made to grasp a palmer's staff,

And not to grace an awful princely sceptre.
That gold must round engirt these brows of mine,
Whose smile and frown, like to Achilles' spear,
Is able with the change to kill and cure.
Here is a hand to hold a sceptre up,
And with the same to act controlling laws.
Give place. By heaven, thou shalt rule no more
O'er him whom heaven created for thy ruler.

SOMERSET. O monstrous traitor! I arrest thee, York,
Of capital treason 'gainst the King and crown.
Obey, audacious traitor; kneel for grace.

YORK. Wouldst have me kneel? First let me ask of these,
If they can brook I bow a knee to man.
Sirrah, call in my sons to be my bail: *Exit attendant*
I know, ere thy will have me go to ward,
They'll pawn their swords for my enfranchisement.

QUEEN. Call hither Clifford; bid him come amain,
To say if that the bastard boys of York
Shall be the surety for their traitor father.

Exit BUCKINGHAM

YORK. O blood-bespotted Neapolitan,
Outcast of Naples, England's bloody scourge!
The sons of York, thy betters in their birth,
Shall be their father's bail; and bane to those
That for my surety will refuse the boys!

Enter EDWARD *and* RICHARD PLANTAGENET

See where they come: I'll warrant they'll make it good.

Enter CLIFFORD *and his* SON

QUEEN. And here comes Clifford to deny their bail.

CLIFFORD. Health and all happiness to my lord the King!
[Kneels]

YORK. I thank thee, Clifford. Say, what news with thee?
Nay, do not fright us with an angry look.
We are thy sovereign, Clifford, kneel again;
For thy mistaking so, we pardon thee.

CLIFFORD. This is my King, York, I do not mistake;
But thou mistakes me much to think I do.
To Bedlam with him! Is the man grown mad?

KING HENRY. Ay, Clifford; a bedlam and ambitious humour
    Makes him oppose himself against his king.
CLIFFORD. He is a traitor; let him to the Tower,
    And chop away that factious pate of his.
QUEEN. He is arrested, but will not obey;
    His sons, he says, shall give their words for him.
YORK. Will you not, sons?
EDWARD. Ay, noble father, if our words will serve.
RICHARD. And if words will not, then our weapons shall.
CLIFFORD. Why, what a brood of traitors have we here!
YORK. Look in a glass, and call thy image so:
    I am thy king, and thou a false-heart traitor.
    Call hither to the stake my two brave bears,
    That with the very shaking of their chains
    They may astonish these fell-lurking curs.
    Bid Salisbury and Warwick come to me.

Enter the EARLS OF WARWICK *and* SALISBURY

CLIFFORD. Are these thy bears? We'll bait thy bears to death,
    And manacle the berard in their chains,
    If thou dar'st bring them to the baiting-place.
RICHARD. Oft have I seen a hot o'erweening cur
    Run back and bite, because he was withheld;
    Who, being suffer'd, with the bear's fell paw,
    Hath clapp'd his tail between his legs and cried;
    And such a piece of service will you do,
    If you oppose yourselves to match Lord Warwick.
CLIFFORD. Hence, heap of wrath, foul indigested lump,
    As crooked in thy manners as thy shape!
YORK. Nay, we shall heat you thoroughly anon.
CLIFFORD. Take heed, lest by your heat you burn yourselves.
KING HENRY. Why, Warwick, hath thy knee forgot to bow?
    Old Salisbury, shame to thy silver hair,
    Thou mad misleader of thy brainsick son!
    What, wilt thou on thy death-bed play the ruffian
    And seek for sorrow with thy spectacles?
    O, where is faith? O, where is loyalty?
    If it be banish'd from the frosty head,
    Where shall it find a harbour in the earth?
    Wilt thou go dig a grave to find out war

And shame thine honourable age with blood?
Why art thou old, and want'st experience?
Or wherefore dost abuse it, if thou hast it?
For shame! In duty bend thy knee to me,
That bows unto the grave with mickle age.

SALISBURY. My lord, I have considered with myself
The title of this most renowned duke,
And in my conscience do repute his Grace
The rightful heir to England's royal seat.

KING HENRY. Hast thou not sworn allegiance unto me?

SALISBURY. I have.

KING HENRY. Canst thou dispense with heaven for such an
oath?

SALISBURY. It is great sin to swear unto a sin;
But greater sin to keep a sinful oath.
Who can be bound by any solemn vow
To do a murd'rous deed, to rob a man,
To force a spotless virgin's chastity,
To reave the orphan of his patrimony,
To wring the widow from her custom'd right,
And have no other reason for this wrong
But that he was bound by a solemn oath?

QUEEN. A subtle traitor needs no sophister.

KING HENRY. Call Buckingham, and bid him arm himself.

YORK. Call Buckingham, and all the friends thou hast,
I am resolv'd for death or dignity.

CLIFFORD. The first I warrant thee, if dreams prove true.

WARWICK. You were best to go to bed and dream again
To keep thee from the tempest of the field.

CLIFFORD. I am resolv'd to bear a greater storm
Than any thou canst conjure up to-day;
And that I'll write upon thy burgonet,
Might I but know thee by thy household badge.

WARWICK. Now, by my father's badge, old Nevil's crest,
The rampant bear chain'd to the ragged staff,
This day I'll wear aloft my burgonet,
As on a mountain-top the cedar shows,
That keeps his leaves in spite of any storm,
Even to affright thee with the view thereof.

CLIFFORD. And from thy burgonet I'll rend thy bear

And tread it under foot with all contempt,
Despite the berard that protects the bear.
YOUNG CLIFFORD. And so to arms, victorious father,
To quell the rebels and their complices.
RICHARD. Fie! charity, for shame! Speak not in spite,
For you shall sup with Jesu Christ to-night.
YOUNG CLIFFORD. Foul stigmatic, that's more than thou canst
tell.
RICHARD. If not in heaven, you'll surely sup in hell.

Exeunt severally

SCENE 2

Saint Albans

Alarums to the battle. Enter WARWICK

WARWICK. Clifford of Cumberland, 'tis Warwick calls;
And if thou dost not hide thee from the bear,
Now, when the angry trumpet sounds alarum
And dead men's cries do fill the empty air,
Clifford, I say, come forth and fight with me.
Proud northern lord, Clifford of Cumberland,
Warwick is hoarse with calling thee to arms.

Enter YORK

How now, my noble lord! what, all a-foot?
YORK. The deadly-handed Clifford slew my steed;
But match to match I have encount'red him,
And made a prey for carrion kites and crows
Even of the bonny beast he lov'd so well.

Enter OLD CLIFFORD

WARWICK. Of one or both of us the time is come.
YORK. Hold, Warwick, seek thee out some other chase,
For I myself must hunt this deer to death.
WARWICK. Then, nobly, York; 'tis for a crown thou fight'st.
As I intend, Clifford, to thrive to-day,
It grieves my soul to leave thee unassail'd.   *Exit*

CLIFFORD. What seest thou in me, York? Why dost thou
    pause?
YORK. With thy brave bearing should I be in love
  But that thou art so fast mine enemy.
CLIFFORD. Nor should thy prowess want praise and esteem
  But that 'tis shown ignobly and in treason.
YORK. So let it help me now against thy sword,
  As I in justice and true right express it!
CLIFFORD. My soul and body on the action both!
YORK. A dreadful lay! Address thee instantly.
                             [*They fight and* CLIFFORD *falls*]
CLIFFORD. La fin couronne les œuvres.   [*Dies*]
YORK. Thus war hath given thee peace, for thou art still.
  Peace with his soul, heaven, if it be thy will!   *Exit*

Enter YOUNG CLIFFORD

YOUNG CLIFFORD. Shame and confusion! All is on the rout;
  Fear frames disorder, and disorder wounds
  Where it should guard. O war, thou son of hell,
  Whom angry heavens do make their minister,
  Throw in the frozen bosoms of our part
  Hot coals of vengeance! Let no soldier fly.
  He that is truly dedicate to war
  Hath no self-love; nor he that loves himself
  Hath not essentially, but by circumstance,
  The name of valour.   [*Sees his father's body*]
  O, let the vile world end
  And the premised flames of the last day
  Knit earth and heaven together!
  Now let the general trumpet blow his blast,
  Particularities and petty sounds
  To cease! Wast thou ordain'd, dear father,
  To lose thy youth in peace and to achieve
  The silver livery of advised age,
  And in thy reverence and thy chair-days thus
  To die in ruffian battle? Even at this sight
  My heart is turn'd to stone; and while 'tis mine
  It shall be stony. York not our old men spares;
  No more will I their babes. Tears virginal
  Shall be to me even as the dew to fire;

And beauty, that the tyrant oft reclaims,
Shall to my flaming wrath be oil and flax.
Henceforth I will not have to do with pity:
Meet I an infant of the house of York,
Into as many gobbets will I cut it
As wild Medea young Absyrtus did;
In cruelty will I seek out my fame.
Come, thou new ruin of old Clifford's house;
As did Æneas old Anchises bear,
So bear I thee upon my manly shoulders;
But then Æneas bare a living load,
Nothing so heavy as these woes of mine.

Exit with the body

Enter RICHARD *and* SOMERSET *to fight.* SOMERSET
is killed

RICHARD. So, lie thou there;
    For underneath an alehouse' paltry sign,
    The Castle in Saint Albans, Somerset
    Hath made the wizard famous in his death.
    Sword, hold thy temper; heart, be wrathful still:
    Priests pray for enemies, but princes kill.   *Exit*

Fight. Excursions. Enter KING, QUEEN, *and others*

QUEEN. Away, my lord! You are slow; for shame, away!
KING HENRY. Can we outrun the heavens? Good Margaret,
    stay.
QUEEN. What are you made of? You'll nor fight nor fly.
    Now is it manhood, wisdom, and defence,
    To give the enemy way, and to secure us
    By what we can, which can no more but fly.
                                          [*Alarum afar off*]
    If you be ta'en, we then should see the bottom
    Of all our fortunes; but if we haply scape—
    As well we may, if not through your neglect—
    We shall to London get, where you are lov'd,
    And where this breach now in our fortunes made
    May readily be stopp'd.

Re-enter YOUNG CLIFFORD

YOUNG CLIFFORD. But that my heart's on future mischief set,
I would speak blasphemy ere bid you fly;
But fly you must; uncurable discomfit
Reigns in the hearts of all our present parts.
Away, for your relief! and we will live
To see their day and them our fortune give.
Away, my lord, away! *Exeunt*

SCENE 3

Fields near Saint Albans

Alarum. Retreat. Enter YORK, RICHARD, WARWICK,
and soldiers, with drum and colours

YORK. Of Salisbury, who can report of him,
That winter lion, who in rage forgets
Aged contusions and all brush of time
And, like a gallant in the brow of youth,
Repairs him with occasion? This happy day
Is not itself, nor have we won one foot,
If Salisbury be lost.
RICHARD. My noble father,
Three times to-day I holp him to his horse,
Three times bestrid him, thrice I led him off,
Persuaded him from any further act;
But still where danger was, still there I met him;
And like rich hangings in a homely house,
So was his will in his old feeble body.
But, noble as he is, look where he comes.

Enter SALISBURY

SALISBURY. Now, by my sword, well hast thou fought to-
day!
By th' mass, so did we all. I thank you, Richard:
God knows how long it is I have to live,
And it hath pleas'd Him that three times to-day
You have defended me from imminent death.
Well, lords, we have not got that which we have;
'Tis not enough our foes are this time fled,

Being opposites of such repairing nature.
YORK. I know our safety is to follow them;
  For, as I hear, the King is fled to London
  To call a present court of Parliament.
  Let us pursue him ere the writs go forth.
  What says Lord Warwick? Shall we after them?
WARWICK. After them? Nay, before them, if we can.
  Now, by my faith, lords, 'twas a glorious day:
  Saint Albans' battle, won by famous York,
  Shall be eterniz'd in all age to come.
  Sound drum and trumpets and to London all;
  And more such days as these to us befall!   *Exeunt*

The Third Part of
King Henry the Sixth

KING HENRY THE SIXTH
EDWARD, PRINCE OF WALES, *his son*
LEWIS XI, *King of France*   DUKE OF SOMERSET
DUKE OF EXETER   EARL OF OXFORD
EARL OF NORTHUMBERLAND   EARL OF WESTMORELAND
LORD CLIFFORD
RICHARD PLANTAGENET, DUKE OF YORK
EDWARD, EARL OF MARCH, *afterwards*
   KING EDWARD IV
EDMUND, EARL OF RUTLAND   } *his sons*
GEORGE, *afterwards* DUKE OF CLARENCE
RICHARD, *afterwards* DUKE OF GLOUCESTER
DUKE OF NORFOLK   MARQUIS OF MONTAGUE
EARL OF WARWICK   EARL OF PEMBROKE
LORD HASTINGS   LORD STAFFORD
SIR JOHN MORTIMER   }
SIR HUGH MORTIMER   } *uncles to the Duke of York*
HENRY, EARL OF RICHMOND, *a youth*
LORD RIVERS, *brother to Lady Grey*
SIR WILLIAM STANLEY   SIR JOHN MONTGOMERY
SIR JOHN SOMERVILLE   TUTOR, *to Rutland*
MAYOR OF YORK   LIEUTENANT OF THE TOWER
A NOBLEMAN   TWO KEEPERS
A HUNTSMAN
A SON *that has killed his father*
A FATHER *that has killed his son*

QUEEN MARGARET
LADY GREY, *afterwards* QUEEN *to Edward IV*
BONA, *sister to the French Queen*

Soldiers, Attendants, Messengers, Watchmen, &c.

SCENE:

England and France

The Third Part of
King Henry the Sixth

ACT I. SCENE 1

London. The Parliament House

Alarum. Enter Duke of York, Edward, Richard, Norfolk, Montague, Warwick, *and soldiers, with white roses in their hats*

Warwick. I wonder how the King escap'd our hands.
York. While we pursu'd the horsemen of the north,
  He slily stole away and left his men;
  Whereat the great Lord of Northumberland,
  Whose warlike ears could never brook retreat,
  Cheer'd up the drooping army, and himself,
  Lord Clifford, and Lord Stafford, all abreast,
  Charg'd our main battle's front, and, breaking in,
  Were by the swords of common soldiers slain.
Edward. Lord Stafford's father, Duke of Buckingham,
  Is either slain or wounded dangerous;
  I cleft his beaver with a downright blow.
  That this is true, father, behold his blood.
Montague. And, brother, here's the Earl of Wiltshire's
    blood,
  Whom I encount'red as the battles join'd.
Richard. Speak thou for me, and tell them what I did.
                    [*Throwing down* Somerset's *head*]
York. Richard hath best deserv'd of all my sons.
  But is your Grace dead, my Lord of Somerset?
Norfolk. Such hope have all the line of John of Gaunt!
Richard. Thus do I hope to shake King Henry's head.
Warwick. And so do I. Victorious Prince of York,
  Before I see thee seated in that throne

Which now the house of Lancaster usurps,
I vow by heaven these eyes shall never close.
This is the palace of the fearful King,
And this the regal seat. Possess it, York;
For this is thine, and not King Henry's heirs'.

YORK. Assist me then, sweet Warwick, and I will;
For hither we have broken in by force.

NORFOLK. We'll all assist you; he that flies shall die.

YORK. Thanks, gentle Norfolk. Stay by me, my lords;
And, soldiers, stay and lodge by me this night.

[*They go up*]

WARWICK. And when the King comes, offer him no violence.
Unless he seek to thrust you out perforce.

YORK. The Queen this day here holds her parliament,
But little thinks we shall be of her council.
By words or blows here let us win our right.

RICHARD. Arm'd as we are, let's stay within this house.

WARWICK. The bloody parliament shall this be call'd,
Unless Plantagenet, Duke of York, be King,
And bashful Henry depos'd, whose cowardice
Hath made us by-words to our enemies.

YORK. Then leave me not, my lords; be resolute:
I mean to take possession of my right.

WARWICK. Neither the King, nor he that loves him best,
The proudest he that holds up Lancaster,
Dares stir a wing if Warwick shake his bells.
I'll plant Plantagenet, root him up who dares.
Resolve thee, Richard; claim the English crown.

[YORK *occupies the throne*]

Flourish. Enter KING HENRY, CLIFFORD, NORTHUM-
BERLAND, WESTMORELAND, EXETER, *and others, with
red roses in their hats*

KING HENRY. My lords, look where the sturdy rebel sits,
Even in the chair of state! Belike he means,
Back'd by the power of Warwick, that false peer,
To aspire unto the crown and reign as king.
Earl of Northumberland, he slew thy father;

And thine, Lord Clifford; and you both have vow'd revenge
On him, his sons, his favourites, and his friends.
NORTHUMBERLAND. If I be not, heavens be reveng'd on me!
CLIFFORD. The hope thereof makes Clifford mourn in steel.
WESTMORELAND. What, shall we suffer this? Let's pluck him down;
My heart for anger burns; I cannot brook it.
KING HENRY. Be patient, gentle Earl of Westmoreland.
CLIFFORD. Patience is for poltroons such as he;
He durst not sit there had your father liv'd.
My gracious lord, here in the parliament
Let us assail the family of York.
NORTHUMBERLAND. Well hast thou spoken, cousin; be it so.
KING HENRY. Ah, know you not the city favours them,
And they have troops of soldiers at their beck?
EXETER. But when the Duke is slain they'll quickly fly.
KING HENRY. Far be the thought of this from Henry's heart,
To make a shambles of the parliament house!
Cousin of Exeter, frowns, words, and threats,
Shall be the war that Henry means to use.
Thou factious Duke of York, descend my throne
And kneel for grace and mercy at my feet;
I am thy sovereign.
YORK. I am thine.
EXETER. For shame, come down; he made thee Duke of York.
YORK. 'Twas my inheritance, as the earldom was.
EXETER. Thy father was a traitor to the crown.
WARWICK. Exeter, thou art a traitor to the crown
In following this usurping Henry.
CLIFFORD. Whom should he follow but his natural king?
WARWICK. True, Clifford; and that's Richard Duke of York.
KING HENRY. And shall I stand, and thou sit in my throne?
YORK. It must and shall be so; content thyself.
WARWICK. Be Duke of Lancaster; let him be King.
WESTMORELAND. He is both King and Duke of Lancaster;
And that the Lord of Westmoreland shall maintain.
WARWICK. And Warwick shall disprove it. You forget
That we are those which chas'd you from the field,

And slew your fathers, and with colours spread
March'd through the city to the palace gates.
NORTHUMBERLAND. Yes, Warwick, I remember it to my grief;
And, by his soul, thou and thy house shall rue it.
WESTMORELAND. Plantagenet, of thee, and these thy sons,
Thy kinsmen, and thy friends, I'll have more lives
Than drops of blood were in my father's veins.
CLIFFORD. Urge it no more; lest that instead of words
I send thee, Warwick, such a messenger
As shall revenge his death before I stir.
WARWICK. Poor Clifford, how I scorn his worthless threats!
YORK. Will you we show our title to the crown?
If not, our swords shall plead it in the field.
KING HENRY. What title hast thou, traitor, to the crown?
Thy father was, as thou art, Duke of York;
Thy grandfather, Roger Mortimer, Earl of March:
I am the son of Henry the Fifth,
Who made the Dauphin and the French to stoop,
And seiz'd upon their towns and provinces.
WARWICK. Talk not of France, sith thou hast lost it all.
KING HENRY. The Lord Protector lost it, and not I:
When I was crown'd, I was but nine months old.
RICHARD. You are old enough now, and yet methinks you
lose.
Father, tear the crown from the usurper's head.
EDWARD. Sweet father, do so; set it on your head.
MONTAGUE. Good brother, as thou lov'st and honourest arms,
Let's fight it out and not stand cavilling thus.
RICHARD. Sound drums and trumpets, and the King will fly.
YORK. Sons, peace!
KING HENRY. Peace thou! and give King Henry leave to
speak.
WARWICK. Plantagenet shall speak first. Hear him, lords;
And be you silent and attentive too,
For he that interrupts him shall not live.
KING HENRY. Think'st thou that I will leave my kingly
throne,
Wherein my grandsire and my father sat?
No; first shall war unpeople this my realm;
Ay, and their colours, often borne in France,

And now in England to our heart's great sorrow,
Shall be my winding-sheet. Why faint you, lords?
My title's good, and better far than his.

WARWICK. Prove it, Henry, and thou shalt be King.

KING HENRY. Henry the Fourth by conquest got the crown.

YORK. 'Twas by rebellion against his king.

KING HENRY. [*Aside*] I know not what to say; my title's
weak.—
Tell me, may not a king adopt an heir?

YORK. What then?

KING HENRY. An if he may, then am I lawful King;
For Richard, in the view of many lords,
Resign'd the crown to Henry the Fourth,
Whose heir my father was, and I am his.

YORK. He rose against him, being his sovereign,
And made him to resign his crown perforce.

WARWICK. Suppose, my lords, he did it unconstrain'd,
Think you 'twere prejudicial to his crown?

EXETER. No; for he could not so resign his crown
But that the next heir should succeed and reign.

KING HENRY. Art thou against us, Duke of Exeter?

EXETER. His is the right, and therefore pardon me.

YORK. Why whisper you, my lords, and answer not?

EXETER. My conscience tells me he is lawful King.

KING HENRY. [*Aside*] All will revolt from me, and turn to
him.

NORTHUMBERLAND. Plantagenet, for all the claim thou lay'st,
Think not that Henry shall be so depos'd.

WARWICK. Depos'd he shall be, in despite of all.

NORTHUMBERLAND. Thou art deceiv'd. 'Tis not thy southern
power
Of Essex, Norfolk, Suffolk, nor of Kent,
Which makes thee thus presumptuous and proud,
Can set the Duke up in despite of me.

CLIFFORD. King Henry, be thy title right or wrong,
Lord Clifford vows to fight in thy defence.
May that ground gape, and swallow me alive,
Where I shall kneel to him that slew my father!

KING HENRY. O Clifford, how thy words revive my heart!

YORK. Henry of Lancaster, resign thy crown.

What mutter you, or what conspire you, lords?
WARWICK. Do right unto this princely Duke of York;
  Or I will fill the house with armed men,
  And over the chair of state, where now he sits,
  Write up his title with usurping blood.
                    [*He stamps with his foot and the*
                        soldiers show themselves]
KING HENRY. My Lord of Warwick, hear but one word:
  Let me for this my life-time reign as king.
YORK. Confirm the crown to me and to mine heirs,
  And thou shalt reign in quiet while thou liv'st.
KING HENRY. I am content. Richard Plantagenet,
  Enjoy the kingdom after my decease.
CLIFFORD. What wrong is this unto the Prince your son!
WARWICK. What good is this to England and himself!
WESTMORELAND. Base, fearful, and despairing Henry!
CLIFFORD. How hast thou injur'd both thyself and us!
WESTMORELAND. I cannot stay to hear these articles.
NORTHUMBERLAND. Nor I.
CLIFFORD. Come, cousin, let us tell the Queen these news.
WESTMORELAND. Farewell, faint-hearted and degenerate king,
  In whose cold blood no spark of honour bides.
NORTHUMBERLAND. Be thou a prey unto the house of York
  And die in bands for this unmanly deed!
CLIFFORD. In dreadful war mayst thou be overcome,
  Or live in peace abandon'd and despis'd!
                    Exeunt NORTHUMBERLAND, CLIFFORD,
                        and WESTMORELAND
WARWICK. Turn this way, Henry, and regard them not.
EXETER. They seek revenge, and therefore will not yield.
KING HENRY. Ah, Exeter!
WARWICK. Why should you sigh, my lord?
KING HENRY. Not for myself, Lord Warwick, but my son,
  Whom I unnaturally shall disinherit.
  But be it as it may. [*To* YORK] I here entail
  The crown to thee and to thine heirs for ever;
  Conditionally, that here thou take an oath
  To cease this civil war, and, whilst I live,
  To honour me as thy king and sovereign,
  And neither by treason nor hostility

687

To seek to put me down and reign thyself.

YORK. This oath I willingly take, and will perform.

[Coming from the throne]

WARWICK. Long live King Henry! Plantagenet, embrace him.

KING HENRY. And long live thou, and these thy forward sons!

YORK. Now York and Lancaster are reconcil'd.

EXETER. Accurs'd be he that seeks to make them foes!

[Sennet. Here they come down]

YORK. Farewell, my gracious lord; I'll to my castle.

WARWICK. And I'll keep London with my soldiers.

NORFOLK. And I to Norfolk with my followers.

MONTAGUE. And I unto the sea, from whence I came.

Exeunt the YORKISTS

KING HENRY. And I, with grief and sorrow, to the court.

Enter QUEEN MARGARET *and the* PRINCE OF WALES

EXETER. Here comes the Queen, whose looks bewray her anger.

I'll steal away.

KING HENRY. Exeter, so will I.

QUEEN MARGARET. Nay, go not from me; I will follow thee.

KING HENRY. Be patient, gentle queen, and I will stay.

QUEEN MARGARET. Who can be patient in such extremes?
Ah, wretched man! Would I had died a maid,
And never seen thee, never borne thee son,
Seeing thou hast prov'd so unnatural a father!
Hath he deserv'd to lose his birthright thus?
Hadst thou but lov'd him half so well as I,
Or felt that pain which I did for him once,
Or nourish'd him as I did with my blood,
Thou wouldst have left thy dearest heart-blood there
Rather than have made that savage duke thine heir,
And disinherited thine only son.

PRINCE OF WALES. Father, you cannot disinherit me.
If you be King, why should not I succeed?

KING HENRY. Pardon me, Margaret; pardon me, sweet son.
The Earl of Warwick and the Duke enforc'd me.

ACT I. SCENE 1

QUEEN MARGARET. Enforc'd thee! Art thou King and wilt
    be forc'd?
  I shame to hear thee speak. Ah, timorous wretch!
  Thou hast undone thyself, thy son, and me;
  And giv'n unto the house of York such head
  As thou shalt reign but by their sufferance.
  To entail him and his heirs unto the crown,
  What is it but to make thy sepulchre
  And creep into it far before thy time?
  Warwick is Chancellor and the lord of Calais;
  Stern Falconbridge commands the narrow seas;
  The Duke is made Protector of the realm;
  And yet shalt thou be safe? Such safety finds
  The trembling lamb environed with wolves.
  Had I been there, which am a silly woman,
  The soldiers should have toss'd me on their pikes
  Before I would have granted to that act.
  But thou prefer'st thy life before thine honour;
  And seeing thou dost, I here divorce myself,
  Both from thy table, Henry, and thy bed,
  Until that act of parliament be repeal'd
  Whereby my son is disinherited.
  The northern lords that have forsworn thy colours
  Will follow mine, if once they see them spread;
  And spread they shall be, to thy foul disgrace
  And utter ruin of the house of York.
  Thus do I leave thee. Come, son, let's away;
  Our army is ready; come, we'll after them.
KING HENRY. Stay, gentle Margaret, and hear me speak.
QUEEN MARGARET. Thou hast spoke too much already; get
    thee gone.
KING HENRY. Gentle son Edward, thou wilt stay with me?
QUEEN MARGARET. Ay, to be murder'd by his enemies.
PRINCE OF WALES. When I return with victory from the
    field
  I'll see your Grace; till then I'll follow her.
QUEEN MARGARET. Come, son, away; we may not linger
    thus.   *Exeunt* QUEEN MARGARET *and the* PRINCE
KING HENRY. Poor queen! How love to me and to her son
  Hath made her break out into terms of rage!

689

Reveng'd may she be on that hateful Duke,
Whose haughty spirit, winged with desire,
Will cost my crown, and like an empty eagle
Tire on the flesh of me and of my son!
The loss of those three lords torments my heart.
I'll write unto them, and entreat them fair;
Come, cousin, you shall be the messenger.
EXETER. And I, I hope, shall reconcile them all.   *Exeunt*

SCENE 2

Sandal Castle, near Wakefield, in Yorkshire

Flourish. Enter EDWARD, RICHARD, *and* MONTAGUE

RICHARD. Brother, though I be youngest, give me leave.
EDWARD. No, I can better play the orator.
MONTAGUE. But I have reasons strong and forcible.

Enter the DUKE OF YORK

YORK. Why, how now, sons and brother! at a strife?
    What is your quarrel? How began it first?
EDWARD. No quarrel, but a slight contention.
YORK. About what?
RICHARD. About that which concerns your Grace and us–
    The crown of England, father, which is yours.
YORK. Mine, boy? Not till King Henry be dead.
RICHARD. Your right depends not on his life or death.
EDWARD. Now you are heir, therefore enjoy it now.
    By giving the house of Lancaster leave to breathe,
    It will outrun you, father, in the end.
YORK. I took an oath that he should quietly reign.
EDWARD. But for a kingdom any oath may be broken:
    I would break a thousand oaths to reign one year.
RICHARD. No; God forbid your Grace should be forsworn.
YORK. I shall be, if I claim by open war.
RICHARD. I'll prove the contrary, if you'll hear me speak.
YORK. Thou canst not, son; it is impossible.
RICHARD. An oath is of no moment, being not took
    Before a true and lawful magistrate

That hath authority over him that swears.
Henry had none, but did usurp the place;
Then, seeing 'twas he that made you to depose,
Your oath, my lord, is vain and frivolous.
Therefore, to arms. And, father, do but think
How sweet a thing it is to wear a crown,
Within whose circuit is Elysium
And all that poets feign of bliss and joy.
Why do we linger thus? I cannot rest
Until the white rose that I wear be dy'd
Even in the lukewarm blood of Henry's heart.
YORK. Richard, enough; I will be King, or die.
Brother, thou shalt to London presently
And whet on Warwick to this enterprise.
Thou, Richard, shalt to the Duke of Norfolk
And tell him privily of our intent.
You, Edward, shall unto my Lord Cobham,
With whom the Kentishmen will willingly rise;
In them I trust, for they are soldiers,
Witty, courteous, liberal, full of spirit.
While you are thus employ'd, what resteth more
But that I seek occasion how to rise,
And yet the King not privy to my drift,
Nor any of the house of Lancaster?

Enter a MESSENGER

But, stay. What news? Why com'st thou in such post?
MESSENGER. The Queen with all the northern earls and lords
Intend here to besiege you in your castle.
She is hard by with twenty thousand men;
And therefore fortify your hold, my lord.
YORK. Ay, with my sword. What! think'st thou that we fear
them?
Edward and Richard, you shall stay with me;
My brother Montague shall post to London.
Let noble Warwick, Cobham, and the rest,
Whom we have left protectors of the King,
With pow'rful policy strengthen themselves
And trust not simple Henry nor his oaths.
MONTAGUE. Brother, I go; I'll win them, fear it not.

And thus most humbly I do take my leave. *Exit*

Enter SIR JOHN *and* SIR HUGH MORTIMER

YORK. Sir John and Sir Hugh Mortimer, mine uncles!
  You are come to Sandal in a happy hour;
  The army of the Queen mean to besiege us.
SIR JOHN. She shall not need; we'll meet her in the field.
YORK. What, with five thousand men?
RICHARD. Ay, with five hundred, father, for a need.
  A woman's general; what should we fear?

[A march afar off]

EDWARD. I hear their drums. Let's set our men in order,
  And issue forth and bid them battle straight.
YORK. Five men to twenty! Though the odds be great,
  I doubt not, uncle, of our victory.
  Many a battle have I won in France,
  When as the enemy hath been ten to one;
  Why should I not now have the like success? *Exeunt*

SCENE 3

Field of battle between Sandal Castle and Wakefield

Alarum. Enter RUTLAND *and his* TUTOR

RUTLAND. Ah, whither shall I fly to scape their hands?
  Ah, tutor, look where bloody Clifford comes!

Enter CLIFFORD *and soldiers*

CLIFFORD. Chaplain, away! Thy priesthood saves thy life.
  As for the brat of this accursed duke,
  Whose father slew my father, he shall die.
TUTOR. And I, my lord, will bear him company.
CLIFFORD. Soldiers, away with him!
TUTOR. Ah, Clifford, murder not this innocent child,
  Lest thou be hated both of God and man.

Exit, forced off by soldiers

CLIFFORD. How now, is he dead already? Or is it fear
  That makes him close his eyes? I'll open them.

RUTLAND. So looks the pent-up lion o'er the wretch
That trembles under his devouring paws;
And so he walks, insulting o'er his prey,
And so he comes, to rend his limbs asunder.
Ah, gentle Clifford, kill me with thy sword,
And not with such a cruel threat'ning look!
Sweet Clifford, hear me speak before I die.
I am too mean a subject for thy wrath;
Be thou reveng'd on men, and let me live.
CLIFFORD. In vain thou speak'st, poor boy; my father's blood
Hath stopp'd the passage where thy words should enter.
RUTLAND. Then let my father's blood open it again:
He is a man, and, Clifford, cope with him.
CLIFFORD. Had I thy brethren here, their lives and thine
Were not revenge sufficient for me;
No, if I digg'd up thy forefathers' graves
And hung their rotten coffins up in chains,
It could not slake mine ire nor ease my heart.
The sight of any of the house of York
Is as a fury to torment my soul;
And till I root out their accursed line
And leave not one alive, I live in hell.
Therefore—
RUTLAND. O, let me pray before I take my death!
To thee I pray: sweet Clifford, pity me.
CLIFFORD. Such pity as my rapier's point affords.
RUTLAND. I never did thee harm; why wilt thou slay me?
CLIFFORD. Thy father hath.
RUTLAND. But 'twas ere I was born.
Thou hast one son; for his sake pity me,
Lest in revenge thereof, sith God is just,
He be as miserably slain as I.
Ah, let me live in prison all my days;
And when I give occasion of offence
Then let me die, for now thou hast no cause.
CLIFFORD. No cause!
Thy father slew my father; therefore, die.   [*Stabs him*]
RUTLAND. Di faciant laudis summa sit ista tuae!   [*Dies*]
CLIFFORD. Plantagenet, I come, Plantagenet;
And this thy son's blood cleaving to my blade

Shall rust upon my weapon, till thy blood,
Congeal'd with this, do make me wipe off both.   *Exit*

SCENE 4

Another part of the field

Alarum. Enter the DUKE OF YORK

YORK. The army of the Queen hath got the field.
My uncles both are slain in rescuing me;
And all my followers to the eager foe
Turn back and fly, like ships before the wind,
Or lambs pursu'd by hunger-starved wolves.
My sons—God knows what hath bechanced them;
But this I know—they have demean'd themselves
Like men born to renown by life or death.
Three times did Richard make a lane to me,
And thrice cried 'Courage, father! fight it out.'
And full as oft came Edward to my side
With purple falchion, painted to the hilt
In blood of those that had encount'red him.
And when the hardiest warriors did retire,
Richard cried 'Charge, and give no foot of ground!'
And cried 'A crown, or else a glorious tomb!
A sceptre, or an earthly sepulchre!'
With this we charg'd again; but out alas!
We bodg'd again; as I have seen a swan
With bootless labour swim against the tide
And spend her strength with over-matching waves.
                              [*A short alarum within*]
Ah, hark! The fatal followers do pursue,
And I am faint and cannot fly their fury;
And were I strong, I would not shun their fury.
The sands are numb'red that make up my life;
Here must I stay, and here my life must end.

Enter QUEEN MARGARET, CLIFFORD, NORTHUMBER-
LAND, *the* PRINCE OF WALES, *and soldiers*

Come, bloody Clifford, rough Northumberland,

I dare your quenchless fury to more rage;
I am your butt, and I abide your shot.

NORTHUMBERLAND. Yield to our mercy, proud Plantagenet.

CLIFFORD. Ay, to such mercy as his ruthless arm
With downright payment show'd unto my father.
Now Phaethon hath tumbled from his car,
And made an evening at the noontide prick.

YORK. My ashes, as the phœnix, may bring forth
A bird that will revenge upon you all;
And in that hope I throw mine eyes to heaven,
Scorning whate'er you can afflict me with.
Why come you not? What! multitudes, and fear?

CLIFFORD. So cowards fight when they can fly no further;
So doves do peck the falcon's piercing talons;
So desperate thieves, all hopeless of their lives,
Breathe out invectives 'gainst the officers.

YORK. O Clifford, but bethink thee once again,
And in thy thought o'errun my former time;
And, if thou canst for blushing, view this face,
And bite thy tongue that slanders him with cowardice
Whose frown hath made thee faint and fly ere this!

CLIFFORD. I will not bandy with thee word for word,
But buckler with thee blows, twice two for one.

QUEEN MARGARET. Hold, valiant Clifford; for a thousand causes
I would prolong awhile the traitor's life.
Wrath makes him deaf; speak thou, Northumberland.

NORTHUMBERLAND. Hold, Clifford! do not honour him so much
To prick thy finger, though to wound his heart.
What valour were it, when a cur doth grin,
For one to thrust his hand between his teeth,
When he might spurn him with his foot away?
It is war's prize to take all vantages;
And ten to one is no impeach of valour.

[*They lay hands on* YORK, *who struggles*]

CLIFFORD. Ay, ay, so strives the woodcock with the gin.

NORTHUMBERLAND. So doth the cony struggle in the net.

YORK. So triumph thieves upon their conquer'd booty;
So true men yield, with robbers so o'er-match'd.

NORTHUMBERLAND. What would your Grace have done
    unto him now?
QUEEN MARGARET. Brave warriors, Clifford and Northum-
    berland,
Come, make him stand upon this molehill here
That raught at mountains with outstretched arms,
Yet parted but the shadow with his hand.
What, was it you that would be England's king?
Was't you that revell'd in our parliament
And made a preachment of your high descent?
Where are your mess of sons to back you now?
The wanton Edward and the lusty George?
And where's that valiant crook-back prodigy,
Dicky your boy, that with his grumbling voice
Was wont to cheer his dad in mutinies?
Or, with the rest, where is your darling Rutland?
Look, York: I stain'd this napkin with the blood
That valiant Clifford with his rapier's point
Made issue from the bosom of the boy;
And if thine eyes can water for his death,
I give thee this to dry thy cheeks withal.
Alas, poor York! but that I hate thee deadly,
I should lament thy miserable state.
I prithee grieve to make me merry, York.
What, hath thy fiery heart so parch'd thine entrails
That not a tear can fall for Rutland's death?
Why art thou patient, man? Thou shouldst be mad;
And I to make thee mad do mock thee thus.
Stamp, rave, and fret, that I may sing and dance.
Thou wouldst be fee'd, I see, to make me sport;
York cannot speak unless he wear a crown.
A crown for York!—and, lords, bow low to him.
Hold you his hands whilst I do set it on.
                 [Putting a paper crown on his head]
Ay, marry, sir, now looks he like a king!
Ay, this is he that took King Henry's chair,
And this is he was his adopted heir.
But how is it that great Plantagenet
Is crown'd so soon and broke his solemn oath?
As I bethink me, you should not be King

Till our King Henry had shook hands with death.
And will you pale your head in Henry's glory,
And rob his temples of the diadem,
Now in his life, against your holy oath?
O, 'tis a fault too too unpardonable!
Off with the crown and with the crown his head;
And, whilst we breathe, take time to do him dead.

CLIFFORD. That is my office, for my father's sake.

QUEEN MARGARET. Nay, stay; let's hear the orisons he
makes.

YORK. She-wolf of France, but worse than wolves of France,
Whose tongue more poisons than the adder's tooth!
How ill-beseeming is it in thy sex
To triumph like an Amazonian trull
Upon their woes whom fortune captivates!
But that thy face is visard-like, unchanging,
Made impudent with use of evil deeds,
I would assay, proud queen, to make thee blush.
To tell thee whence thou cam'st, of whom deriv'd,
Were shame enough to shame thee, wert thou not shame-
less.
Thy father bears the type of King of Naples,
Of both the Sicils and Jerusalem,
Yet not so wealthy as an English yeoman.
Hath that poor monarch taught thee to insult?
It needs not, nor it boots thee not, proud queen;
Unless the adage must be verified,
That beggars mounted run their horse to death.
'Tis beauty that doth oft make women proud;
But, God He knows, thy share thereof is small.
'Tis virtue that doth make them most admir'd;
The contrary doth make thee wond'red at.
'Tis government that makes them seem divine;
The want thereof makes thee abominable.
Thou art as opposite to every good
As the Antipodes are unto us,
Or as the south to the septentrion.
O tiger's heart wrapp'd in a woman's hide!
How couldst thou drain the life-blood of the child,
To bid the father wipe his eyes withal,

And yet be seen to bear a woman's face?
Women are soft, mild, pitiful, and flexible:
Thou stern, obdurate, flinty, rough, remorseless.
Bid'st thou me rage? Why, now thou hast thy wish;
Wouldst have me weep? Why, now thou hast thy will;
For raging wind blows up incessant showers,
And when the rage allays, the rain begins.
These tears are my sweet Rutland's obsequies;
And every drop cries vengeance for his death
'Gainst thee, fell Clifford, and thee, false Frenchwoman.

NORTHUMBERLAND. Beshrew me, but his passions move me so
    That hardly can I check my eyes from tears.

YORK. That face of his the hungry cannibals
    Would not have touch'd, would not have stain'd with
      blood;
    But you are more inhuman, more inexorable—
    O, ten times more—than tigers of Hyrcania.
    See, ruthless queen, a hapless father's tears.
    This cloth thou dipp'dst in blood of my sweet boy,
    And I with tears do wash the blood away.
    Keep thou the napkin, and go boast of this;
    And if thou tell'st the heavy story right,
    Upon my soul, the hearers will shed tears;
    Yea, even my foes will shed fast-falling tears
    And say 'Alas, it was a piteous deed!'
    There, take the crown, and with the crown my curse;
    And in thy need such comfort come to thee
    As now I reap at thy too cruel hand!
    Hard-hearted Clifford, take me from the world;
    My soul to heaven, my blood upon your heads!

NORTHUMBERLAND. Had he been slaughter-man to all my
    kin,
    I should not for my life but weep with him,
    To see how inly sorrow gripes his soul.

QUEEN MARGARET. What, weeping-ripe, my Lord Northum-
    berland?
    Think but upon the wrong he did us all,
    And that will quickly dry thy melting tears.

CLIFFORD. Here's for my oath, here's for my father's death.
                                  [*Stabbing him*]

ACT I. SCENE 4

QUEEN MARGARET. And here's to right our gentle-hearted
    king.   *[Stabbing him]*
YORK. Open Thy gate of mercy, gracious God!
    My soul flies through these wounds to seek out Thee.
                                         [Dies]
QUEEN MARGARET. Off with his head, and set it on York
    gates;
    So York may overlook the town of York.
                                Flourish. Exeunt

ACT II. SCENE 1

A plain near Mortimer's Cross in Herefordshire

A march. Enter EDWARD, RICHARD, *and their power*

EDWARD. I wonder how our princely father scap'd,
    Or whether he be scap'd away or no
    From Clifford's and Northumberland's pursuit.
    Had he been ta'en, we should have heard the news;
    Had he been slain, we should have heard the news;
    Or had he scap'd, methinks we should have heard
    The happy tidings of his good escape.
    How fares my brother? Why is he so sad?
RICHARD. I cannot joy until I be resolv'd
    Where our right valiant father is become.
    I saw him in the battle range about,
    And watch'd him how he singled Clifford forth.
    Methought he bore him in the thickest troop
    As doth a lion in a herd of neat;
    Or as a bear, encompass'd round with dogs,
    Who having pinch'd a few and made them cry,
    The rest stand all aloof and bark at him.
    So far'd our father with his enemies;
    So fled his enemies my warlike father.
    Methinks 'tis prize enough to be his son.
    See how the morning opes her golden gates
    And takes her farewell of the glorious sun.

How well resembles it the prime of youth,
  Trimm'd like a younker prancing to his love!
EDWARD. Dazzle mine eyes, or do I see three suns?
RICHARD. Three glorious suns, each one a perfect sun;
  Not separated with the racking clouds,
  But sever'd in a pale clear-shining sky.
  See, see! they join, embrace, and seem to kiss,
  As if they vow'd some league inviolable.
  Now are they but one lamp, one light, one sun.
  In this the heaven figures some event.
EDWARD. 'Tis wondrous strange, the like yet never heard of.
  I think it cites us, brother, to the field,
  That we, the sons of brave Plantagenet,
  Each one already blazing by our meeds,
  Should notwithstanding join our lights together
  And overshine the earth, as this the world.
  Whate'er it bodes, henceforward will I bear
  Upon my target three fair shining suns.
RICHARD. Nay, bear three daughters—by your leave I speak it,
  You love the breeder better than the male.

              Enter a MESSENGER, *blowing*

  But what art thou, whose heavy looks foretell
  Some dreadful story hanging on thy tongue?
MESSENGER. Ah, one that was a woeful looker-on
  When as the noble Duke of York was slain,
  Your princely father and my loving lord!
EDWARD. O, speak no more! for I have heard too much.
RICHARD. Say how he died, for I will hear it all.
MESSENGER. Environed he was with many foes,
  And stood against them as the hope of Troy
  Against the Greeks that would have ent'red Troy.
  But Hercules himself must yield to odds;
  And many strokes, though with a little axe,
  Hews down and fells the hardest-timber'd oak.
  By many hands your father was subdu'd;
  But only slaught'red by the ireful arm
  Of unrelenting Clifford and the Queen,
  Who crown'd the gracious Duke in high despite,
  Laugh'd in his face; and when with grief he wept,

The ruthless Queen gave him to dry his cheeks
A napkin steeped in the harmless blood
Of sweet young Rutland, by rough Clifford slain;
And after many scorns, many foul taunts,
They took his head, and on the gates of York
They set the same; and there it doth remain,
The saddest spectacle that e'er I view'd.

EDWARD. Sweet Duke of York, our prop to lean upon,
Now thou art gone, we have no staff, no stay.
O Clifford, boist'rous Clifford, thou hast slain
The flow'r of Europe for his chivalry;
And treacherously hast thou vanquish'd him,
For hand to hand he would have vanquish'd thee.
Now my soul's palace is become a prison.
Ah, would she break from hence, that this my body
Might in the ground be closed up in rest!
For never henceforth shall I joy again;
Never, O never, shall I see more joy.

RICHARD. I cannot weep, for all my body's moisture
Scarce serves to quench my furnace-burning heart;
Nor can my tongue unload my heart's great burden,
For self-same wind that I should speak withal
Is kindling coals that fires all my breast,
And burns me up with flames that tears would quench.
To weep is to make less the depth of grief.
Tears then for babes; blows and revenge for me!
Richard, I bear thy name; I'll venge thy death,
Or die renowned by attempting it.

EDWARD. His name that valiant duke hath left with thee;
His dukedom and his chair with me is left.

RICHARD. Nay, if thou be that princely eagle's bird,
Show thy descent by gazing 'gainst the sun;
For chair and dukedom, throne and kingdom, say:
Either that is thine, or else thou wert not his.

March. Enter WARWICK, MONTAGUE, *and their army*

WARWICK. How now, fair lords! What fare? What news
abroad?

RICHARD. Great Lord of Warwick, if we should recount
Our baleful news and at each word's deliverance

Stab poinards in our flesh till all were told,
The words would add more anguish than the wounds.
O valiant lord, the Duke of York is slain!
EDWARD. O Warwick, Warwick! that Plantagenet
  Which held thee dearly as his soul's redemption
  Is by the stern Lord Clifford done to death.
WARWICK. Ten days ago I drown'd these news in tears;
  And now, to add more measure to your woes,
  I come to tell you things sith then befall'n.
  After the bloody fray at Wakefield fought,
  Where your brave father breath'd his latest gasp,
  Tidings, as swiftly as the posts could run,
  Were brought me of your loss and his depart.
  I, then in London, keeper of the King,
  Muster'd my soldiers, gathered flocks of friends,
  And very well appointed, as I thought,
  March'd toward Saint Albans to intercept the Queen,
  Bearing the King in my behalf along;
  For by my scouts I was advertised
  That she was coming with a full intent
  To dash our late decree in parliament
  Touching King Henry's oath and your succession.
  Short tale to make—we at Saint Albans met,
  Our battles join'd, and both sides fiercely fought;
  But whether 'twas the coldness of the King,
  Who look'd full gently on his warlike queen,
  That robb'd my soldiers of their heated spleen,
  Or whether 'twas report of her success,
  Or more than common fear of Clifford's rigour,
  Who thunders to his captives blood and death,
  I cannot judge; but, to conclude with truth,
  Their weapons like to lightning came and went:
  Our soldiers', like the night-owl's lazy flight
  Or like an idle thresher with a flail,
  Fell gently down, as if they struck their friends.
  I cheer'd them up with justice of our cause,
  With promise of high pay and great rewards,
  But all in vain; they had no heart to fight,
  And we in them no hope to win the day;
  So that we fled: the King unto the Queen;

Lord George your brother, Norfolk, and myself,
In haste post-haste are come to join with you;
For in the marches here we heard you were
Making another head to fight again.

EDWARD. Where is the Duke of Norfolk, gentle Warwick?
And when came George from Burgundy to England?

WARWICK. Some six miles off the Duke is with the soldiers;
And for your brother, he was lately sent
From your kind aunt, Duchess of Burgundy,
With aid of soldiers to this needful war.

RICHARD. 'Twas odds, belike, when valiant Warwick fled.
Oft have I heard his praises in pursuit,
But ne'er till now his scandal of retire.

WARWICK. Nor now my scandal, Richard, dost thou hear;
For thou shalt know this strong right hand of mine
Can pluck the diadem from faint Henry's head
And wring the awful sceptre from his fist,
Were he as famous and as bold in war
As he is fam'd for mildness, peace, and prayer.

RICHARD. I know it well, Lord Warwick; blame me not.
'Tis love I bear thy glories makes me speak.
But in this troublous time what's to be done?
Shall we go throw away our coats of steel
And wrap our bodies in black mourning-gowns,
Numbering our Ave-Maries with our beads?
Or shall we on the helmets of our foes
Tell our devotion with revengeful arms?
If for the last, say 'Ay,' and to it, lords.

WARWICK. Why, therefore Warwick came to seek you out;
And therefore comes my brother Montague.
Attend me, lords. The proud insulting Queen,
With Clifford and the haught Northumberland,
And of their feather many moe proud birds,
Have wrought the easy-melting King like wax.
He swore consent to your succession,
His oath enrolled in the parliament;
And now to London all the crew are gone
To frustrate both his oath and what beside
May make against the house of Lancaster.
Their power, I think, is thirty thousand strong.

Now if the help of Norfolk and myself,
With all the friends that thou, brave Earl of March,
Amongst the loving Welshmen canst procure,
Will but amount to five and twenty thousand,
Why, Via! to London will we march amain,
And once again bestride our foaming steeds,
And once again cry 'Charge upon our foes!'
But never once again turn back and fly.

RICHARD. Ay, now methinks I hear great Warwick speak.
Ne'er may he live to see a sunshine day
That cries 'Retire!' if Warwick bid him stay.

EDWARD. Lord Warwick, on thy shoulder will I lean;
And when thou fail'st—as God forbid the hour!—
Must Edward fall, which peril heaven forfend.

WARWICK. No longer Earl of March, but Duke of York;
The next degree is England's royal throne,
For King of England shalt thou be proclaim'd
In every borough as we pass along;
And he that throws not up his cap for joy
Shall for the fault make forfeit of his head.
King Edward, valiant Richard, Montague,
Stay we no longer, dreaming of renown,
But sound the trumpets and about our task.

RICHARD. Then, Clifford, were thy heart as hard as steel,
As thou hast shown it flinty by thy deeds,
I come to pierce it or to give thee mine.

EDWARD. Then strike up drums. God and Saint George
for us!

Enter a MESSENGER

WARWICK. How now! what news?

MESSENGER. The Duke of Norfolk sends you word by me
The Queen is coming with a puissant host,
And craves your company for speedy counsel.

WARWICK. Why, then it sorts; brave warriors, let's away.

Exeunt

SCENE 2

Before York

Flourish. Enter KING HENRY, QUEEN MARGARET, *the* PRINCE OF WALES, CLIFFORD, NORTHUMBER- LAND, *with drum and trumpets*

QUEEN MARGARET. Welcome, my lord, to this brave town of
 York.
 Yonder's the head of that arch-enemy
 That sought to be encompass'd with your crown.
 Doth not the object cheer your heart, my lord?
KING HENRY. Ay, as the rocks cheer them that fear their
 wreck—
 To see this sight, it irks my very soul.
 Withhold revenge, dear God; 'tis not my fault,
 Nor wittingly have I infring'd my vow.
CLIFFORD. My gracious liege, this too much lenity
 And harmful pity must be laid aside.
 To whom do lions cast their gentle looks?
 Not to the beast that would usurp their den.
 Whose hand is that the forest bear doth lick?
 Not his that spoils her young before her face.
 Who scapes the lurking serpent's mortal sting?
 Not he that sets his foot upon her back,
 The smallest worm will turn, being trodden on,
 And doves will peck in safeguard of their brood.
 Ambitious York did level at thy crown,
 Thou smiling while he knit his angry brows.
 He, but a Duke, would have his son a king,
 And raise his issue like a loving sire:
 Thou, being a king, bless'd with a goodly son,
 Didst yield consent to disinherit him,
 Which argued thee a most unloving father.
 Unreasonable creatures feed their young;
 And though man's face be fearful to their eyes,
 Yet, in protection of their tender ones,
 Who hath not seen them—even with those wings
 Which sometime they have us'd with fearful flight—

Make war with him that climb'd unto their nest,
Offering their own lives in their young's defence?
For shame, my liege, make them your precedent!
Were it not pity that this goodly boy
Should lose his birthright by his father's fault,
And long hereafter say unto his child
'What my great-grandfather and grandsire got
My careless father fondly gave away'?
Ah, what a shame were this! Look on the boy;
And let his manly face, which promiseth
Successful fortune, steel thy melting heart
To hold thine own and leave thine own with him.

KING HENRY. Full well hath Clifford play'd the orator,
Inferring arguments of mighty force.
But, Clifford, tell me, didst thou never hear
That things ill got had ever bad success?
And happy always was it for that son
Whose father for his hoarding went to hell?
I'll leave my son my virtuous deeds behind;
And would my father had left me no more!
For all the rest is held at such a rate
As brings a thousand-fold more care to keep
Than in possession any jot of pleasure.
Ah, cousin York! would thy best friends did know
How it doth grieve me that thy head is here!

QUEEN MARGARET. My lord, cheer up your spirits; our foes
are nigh,
And this soft courage makes your followers faint.
You promis'd knighthood to our forward son:
Unsheathe your sword and dub him presently.
Edward, kneel down.

KING HENRY. Edward Plantagenet, arise a knight;
And learn this lesson: Draw thy sword in right.

PRINCE OF WALES. My gracious father, by your kingly leave,
I'll draw it as apparent to the crown,
And in that quarrel use it to the death.

CLIFFORD. Why, that is spoken like a toward prince.

Enter a MESSENGER

MESSENGER. Royal commanders, be in readiness;

For with a band of thirty thousand men
Comes Warwick, backing of the Duke of York,
And in the towns, as they do march along,
Proclaims him king, and many fly to him.
Darraign your battle, for they are at hand.

CLIFFORD. I would your Highness would depart the field:
The Queen hath best success when you are absent.

QUEEN MARGARET. Ay, good my lord, and leave us to our
fortune.

KING HENRY. Why, that's my fortune too; therefore I'll
stay.

NORTHUMBERLAND. Be it with resolution, then, to fight.

PRINCE OF WALES. My royal father, cheer these noble lords,
And hearten those that fight in your defence.
Unsheathe your sword, good father; cry 'Saint George!'

March. Enter EDWARD, GEORGE, RICHARD, WARWICK,
NORFOLK, MONTAGUE, *and soldiers*

EDWARD. Now, perjur'd Henry, wilt thou kneel for grace
And set thy diadem upon my head,
Or bide the mortal fortune of the field?

QUEEN MARGARET. Go rate thy minions, proud insulting
boy.
Becomes it thee to be thus bold in terms
Before thy sovereign and thy lawful king?

EDWARD. I am his king, and he should bow his knee.
I was adopted heir by his consent:
Since when, his oath is broke; for, as I hear,
You that are King, though he do wear the crown,
Have caus'd him by new act of parliament
To blot out me and put his own son in.

CLIFFORD. And reason too:
Who should succeed the father but the son?

RICHARD. Are you there, butcher? O, I cannot speak!

CLIFFORD. Ay, crook-back, here I stand to answer thee,
Or any he, the proudest of thy sort.

RICHARD. 'Twas you that kill'd young Rutland, was it not?

CLIFFORD. Ay, and old York, and yet not satisfied.

RICHARD. For God's sake, lords, give signal to the fight.

WARWICK. What say'st thou, Henry? Wilt thou yield the
crown?

QUEEN MARGARET. Why, how now, long-tongu'd Warwick!
Dare you speak?
When you and I met at Saint Albans last
Your legs did better service than your hands.

WARWICK. Then 'twas my turn to fly, and now 'tis thine.

CLIFFORD. You said so much before, and yet you fled.

WARWICK. 'Twas not your valour, Clifford, drove me
thence.

NORTHUMBERLAND. No, nor your manhood that durst make
you stay.

RICHARD. Northumberland, I hold thee reverently.
Break off the parley; for scarce I can refrain
The execution of my big-swol'n heart
Upon that Clifford, that cruel child-killer.

CLIFFORD. I slew thy father; call'st thou him a child?

RICHARD. Ay, like a dastard and a treacherous coward,
As thou didst kill our tender brother Rutland;
But ere sunset I'll make thee curse the deed.

KING HENRY. Have done with words, my lords, and hear me
speak.

QUEEN MARGARET. Defy them then, or else hold close thy
lips.

KING HENRY. I prithee give no limits to my tongue:
I am a king, and privileg'd to speak.

CLIFFORD. My liege, the wound that bred this meeting here
Cannot be cur'd by words; therefore be still.

RICHARD. Then, executioner, unsheathe thy sword.
By Him that made us all, I am resolv'd
That Clifford's manhood lies upon his tongue.

EDWARD. Say, Henry, shall I have my right, or no?
A thousand men have broke their fasts to-day
That ne'er shall dine unless thou yield the crown.

WARWICK. If thou deny, their blood upon thy head;
For York in justice puts his armour on.

PRINCE OF WALES. If that be right which Warwick says is
right,
There is no wrong, but every thing is right.

RICHARD. Whoever got thee, there thy mother stands;

For well I wot thou hast thy mother's tongue.
QUEEN MARGARET. But thou art neither like thy sire nor
    dam;
    But like a foul misshapen stigmatic,
    Mark'd by the destinies to be avoided,
    As venom toads or lizards' dreadful stings.
RICHARD. Iron of Naples hid with English gilt,
    Whose father bears the title of a king—
    As if a channel should be call'd the sea—
    Sham'st thou not, knowing whence thou art extraught,
    To let thy tongue detect thy base-born heart?
EDWARD. A wisp of straw were worth a thousand crowns
    To make this shameless callet know herself.
    Helen of Greece was fairer far than thou,
    Although thy husband may be Menelaus;
    And ne'er was Agamemmon's brother wrong'd
    By that false woman as this king by thee.
    His father revell'd in the heart of France,
    And tam'd the King, and made the Dauphin stoop;
    And had he match'd according to his state,
    He might have kept that glory to this day;
    But when he took a beggar to his bed
    And grac'd thy poor sire with his bridal day,
    Even then that sunshine brew'd a show'r for him
    That wash'd his father's fortunes forth of France
    And heap'd sedition on his crown at home.
    For what hath broach'd this tumult but thy pride?
    Hadst thou been meek, our title still had slept;
    And we, in pity of the gentle King,
    Had slipp'd our claim until another age.
GEORGE. But when we saw our sunshine made thy spring,
    And that thy summer bred us no increase,
    We set the axe to thy usurping root;
    And though the edge hath something hit ourselves,
    Yet know thou, since we have begun to strike,
    We'll never leave till we have hewn thee down,
    Or bath'd thy growing with our heated bloods.
EDWARD. And in this resolution I defy thee;
    Not willing any longer conference,
    Since thou deniest the gentle King to speak.

Sound trumpets; let our bloody colours wave,
And either victory or else a grave!
QUEEN MARGARET. Stay, Edward.
EDWARD. No, wrangling woman, we'll no longer stay;
These words will cost ten thousand lives this day. *Exeunt*

SCENE 3

*A field of battle between Towton and Saxton,
in Yorkshire*

Alarum; excursions. Enter WARWICK

WARWICK. Forspent with toil, as runners with a race,
I lay me down a little while to breathe;
For strokes receiv'd and many blows repaid
Have robb'd my strong-knit sinews of their strength,
And spite of spite needs must I rest awhile.

Enter EDWARD, *running*

EDWARD. Smile, gentle heaven, or strike, ungentle death;
For this world frowns, and Edward's sun is clouded.
WARWICK. How now, my lord. What hap? What hope of
good?

Enter GEORGE

GEORGE. Our hap is lost, our hope but sad despair;
Our ranks are broke, and ruin follows us.
What counsel give you? Whither shall we fly?
EDWARD. Bootless is flight: they follow us with wings;
And weak we are, and cannot shun pursuit.

Enter RICHARD

RICHARD. Ah, Warwick, why hast thou withdrawn thyself?
Thy brother's blood the thirsty earth hath drunk,
Broach'd with the steely point of Clifford's lance;
And in the very pangs of death he cried,
Like to a dismal clangor heard from far,
'Warwick, revenge! Brother, revenge my death.'
So, underneath the belly of their steeds,

That stain'd their fetlocks in his smoking blood,
The noble gentleman gave up the ghost.

WARWICK. Then let the earth be drunken with our blood.
I'll kill my horse, because I will not fly.
Why stand we like soft-hearted women here,
Wailing our losses, whiles the foe doth rage,
And look upon, as if the tragedy
Were play'd in jest by counterfeiting actors?
Here on my knee I vow to God above
I'll never pause again, never stand still,
Till either death hath clos'd these eyes of mine
Or fortune given me measure of revenge.

EDWARD. O Warwick, I do bend my knee with thine,
And in this vow do chain my soul to thine!
And ere my knee rise from the earth's cold face
I throw my hands, mine eyes, my heart to Thee,
Thou setter-up and plucker-down of kings,
Beseeching Thee, if with Thy will it stands
That to my foes this body must be prey,
Yet that Thy brazen gates of heaven may ope
And give sweet passage to my sinful soul.
Now, lords, take leave until we meet again,
Where'er it be, in heaven or in earth.

RICHARD. Brother, give me thy hand; and, gentle Warwick,
Let me embrace thee in my weary arms.
I that did never weep now melt with woe
That winter should cut off our spring-time so.

WARWICK. Away, away! Once more, sweet lords, farewell.

GEORGE. Yet let us all together to our troops,
And give them leave to fly that will not stay,
And call them pillars that will stand to us;
And if we thrive, promise them such rewards
As victors wear at the Olympian games.
This may plant courage in their quailing breasts,
For yet is hope of life and victory.
Forslow no longer; make we hence amain.   *Exeunt*

SCENE 4

Another part of the field

Excursions. Enter RICHARD *and* CLIFFORD

RICHARD. Now, Clifford, I have singled thee alone.
    Suppose this arm is for the Duke of York,
    And this for Rutland; both bound to revenge,
    Wert thou environ'd with a brazen wall.
CLIFFORD. Now, Richard, I am with thee here alone.
    This is the hand that stabbed thy father York;
    And this the hand that slew thy brother Rutland;
    And here's the heart that triumphs in their death
    And cheers these hands that slew thy sire and brother
    To execute the like upon thyself;
    And so, have at thee!   [*They fight*]

Enter WARWICK; CLIFFORD *flies*

RICHARD. Nay, Warwick, single out some other chase;
    For I myself will hunt this wolf to death.   *Exeunt*

SCENE 5

Another part of the field

Alarum. Enter KING HENRY *alone*

KING HENRY. This battle fares like to the morning's war,
    When dying clouds contend with growing light,
    What time the shepherd, blowing of his nails,
    Can neither call it perfect day nor night.
    Now sways it this way, like a mighty sea
    Forc'd by the tide to combat with the wind;
    Now sways it that way, like the selfsame sea
    Forc'd to retire by fury of the wind.
    Sometime the flood prevails, and then the wind;
    Now one the better, then another best;
    Both tugging to be victors, breast to breast,
    Yet neither conqueror nor conquered.

So is the equal poise of this fell war.
Here on this molehill will I sit me down.
To whom God will, there be the victory!
For Margaret my queen, and Clifford too,
Have chid me from the battle, swearing both
They prosper best of all when I am thence.
Would I were dead, if God's good will were so!
For what is in this world but grief and woe?
O God! methinks it were a happy life
To be no better than a homely swain;
To sit upon a hill, as I do now,
To carve out dials quaintly, point by point,
Thereby to see the minutes how they run—
How many makes the hour full complete,
How many hours brings about the day,
How many days will finish up the year,
How many years a mortal man may live.
When this is known, then to divide the times—
So many hours must I tend my flock;
So many hours must I take my rest;
So many hours must I contemplate;
So many hours must I sport myself;
So many days my ewes have been with young;
So many weeks ere the poor fools will ean;
So many years ere I shall shear the fleece:
So minutes, hours, days, months, and years,
Pass'd over to the end they were created,
Would bring white hairs unto a quiet grave.
Ah, what a life were this! how sweet! how lovely!
Gives not the hawthorn bush a sweeter shade
To shepherds looking on their silly sheep,
Than doth a rich embroider'd canopy
To kings that fear their subjects' treachery?
O yes, it doth; a thousand-fold it doth.
And to conclude: the shepherd's homely curds,
His cold thin drink out of his leather bottle,
His wonted sleep under a fresh tree's shade,
All which secure and sweetly he enjoys,
Is far beyond a prince's delicates—
His viands sparkling in a golden cup,

His body couched in a curious bed,
When care, mistrust, and treason waits on him.

Alarum. Enter a SON *that hath kill'd his Father, at
one door; and a* FATHER *that hath kill'd his Son, at
another door*

SON. Ill blows the wind that profits nobody.
This man whom hand to hand I slew in fight
May be possessed with some store of crowns;
And I, that haply take them from him now,
May yet ere night yield both my life and them
To some man else, as this dead man doth me.
Who's this? O God! It is my father's face,
Whom in this conflict I unwares have kill'd.
O heavy times, begetting such events!
From London by the King was I press'd forth;
My father, being the Earl of Warwick's man,
Came on the part of York, press'd by his master;
And I, who at his hands receiv'd my life,
Have by my hands of life bereaved him.
Pardon me, God, I knew not what I did.
And pardon, father, for I knew not thee.
My tears shall wipe away these bloody marks;
And no more words till they have flow'd their fill.
KING HENRY. O piteous spectacle! O bloody times!
Whiles lions war and battle for their dens,
Poor harmless lambs abide their enmity.
Weep, wretched man; I'll aid thee tear for tear;
And let our hearts and eyes, like civil war,
Be blind with tears and break o'ercharg'd with grief.

Enter FATHER, *bearing of his* SON

FATHER. Thou that so stoutly hath resisted me,
Give me thy gold, if thou hast any gold;
For I have bought it with an hundred blows.
But let me see. Is this our foeman's face?
Ah, no, no, no, it is mine only son!
Ah, boy, if any life be left in thee,
Throw up thine eye! See, see what show'rs arise,
Blown with the windy tempest of my heart

Upon thy wounds, that kills mine eye and heart!
O, pity, God, this miserable age!
What stratagems, how fell, how butcherly,
Erroneous, mutinous, and unnatural,
This deadly quarrel daily doth beget!
O boy, thy father gave thee life too soon,
And hath bereft thee of thy life too late!

KING HENRY. Woe above woe! grief more than common
   grief!
O that my death would stay these ruthful deeds!
O pity, pity, gentle heaven, pity!
The red rose and the white are on his face,
The fatal colours of our striving houses:
The one his purple blood right well resembles;
The other his pale cheeks, methinks, presenteth.
Wither one rose, and let the other flourish!
If you contend, a thousand lives must perish.

SON. How will my mother for a father's death
   Take on with me, and ne'er be satisfied!

FATHER. How will my wife for slaughter of my son
   Shed seas of tears, and ne'er be satisfied!

KING HENRY. How will the country for these woeful
   chances
Misthink the King, and not be satisfied!

SON. Was ever son so rued a father's death?

FATHER. Was ever father so bemoan'd his son?

KING HENRY. Was ever king so griev'd for subjects' woe?
   Much is your sorrow; mine ten times so much.

SON. I'll bear thee hence, where I may weep my fill.

                     Exit with the body

FATHER. These arms of mine shall be thy winding-sheet;
   My heart, sweet boy, shall be thy sepulchre,
For from my heart thine image ne'er shall go;
My sighing breast shall be thy funeral bell;
And so obsequious will thy father be,
Even for the loss of thee, having no more,
As Priam was for all his valiant sons.
I'll bear thee hence; and let them fight that will,
For I have murdered where I should not kill.

                     Exit with the body

KING HENRY. Sad-hearted men, much overgone with care,
Here sits a king more woeful than you are.

Alarums; excursions. Enter QUEEN MARGARET,
PRINCE OF WALES, *and* EXETER

PRINCE OF WALES. Fly, father, fly; for all your friends are
fled,
And Warwick rages like a chafed bull.
Away! for death doth hold us in pursuit.
QUEEN MARGARET. Mount you, my lord; towards Berwick
post amain.
Edward and Richard, like a brace of greyhounds
Having the fearful flying hare in sight,
With fiery eyes sparkling for very wrath,
And bloody steel grasp'd in their ireful hands,
Are at our backs; and therefore hence amain.
EXETER. Away! for vengeance comes along with them.
Nay, stay not to expostulate; make speed;
Or else come after. I'll away before.
KING HENRY. Nay, take me with thee, good sweet Exeter.
Not that I fear to stay, but love to go
Whither the Queen intends. Forward; away!   *Exeunt*

SCENE 6

Another part of the field

A loud alarum. Enter CLIFFORD, *wounded*

CLIFFORD. Here burns my candle out; ay, here it dies,
Which, whiles it lasted, gave King Henry light.
O Lancaster, I fear thy overthrow
More than my body's parting with my soul!
My love and fear glu'd many friends to thee;
And, now I fall, thy tough commixture melts,
Impairing Henry, strength'ning misproud York.
The common people swarm like summer flies;
And whither fly the gnats but to the sun?
And who shines now but Henry's enemies?
O Phœbus, hadst thou never given consent

That Phaethon should check thy fiery steeds,
Thy burning car never had scorch'd the earth!
And, Henry, hadst thou sway'd as kings should do,
Or as thy father and his father did,
Giving no ground unto the house of York,
They never then had sprung like summer flies;
I and ten thousand in this luckless realm
Had left no mourning widows for our death;
And thou this day hadst kept thy chair in peace.
For what doth cherish weeds but gentle air?
And what makes robbers bold but too much lenity?
Bootless are plaints, and cureless are my wounds.
No way to fly, nor strength to hold out flight.
The foe is merciless and will not pity;
For at their hands I have deserv'd no pity.
The air hath got into my deadly wounds,
And much effuse of blood doth make me faint.
Come, York and Richard, Warwick and the rest;
I stabb'd your fathers' bosoms: split my breast.

[He faints]

Alarum and retreat. Enter EDWARD, GEORGE, RICHARD,
MONTAGUE, WARWICK, and soldiers

EDWARD. Now breathe we, lords. Good fortune bids us
    pause
  And smooth the frowns of war with peaceful looks.
  Some troops pursue the bloody-minded Queen
  That led calm Henry, though he were a king,
  As doth a sail, fill'd with a fretting gust,
  Command an argosy to stem the waves.
  But think you, lords, that Clifford fled with them?
WARWICK. No, 'tis impossible he should escape;
  For, though before his face I speak the words,
  Your brother Richard mark'd him for the grave;
  And, whereso'er he is, he's surely dead.

[CLIFFORD groans, and dies]

RICHARD. Whose soul is that which takes her heavy leave?
  A deadly groan, like life and death's departing.
  See who it is.
EDWARD. And now the battle's ended,

If friend or foe, let him be gently used.

RICHARD. Revoke that doom of mercy, for 'tis Clifford;
  Who not contented that he lopp'd the branch
  In hewing Rutland when his leaves put forth,
  But set his murd'ring knife unto the root
  From whence that tender spray did sweetly spring—
  I mean our princely father, Duke of York.

WARWICK. From off the gates of York fetch down the head,
  Your father's head, which Clifford placed there;
  Instead whereof let this supply the room.
  Measure for measure must be answered.

EDWARD. Bring forth that fatal screech-owl to our house,
  That nothing sung but death to us and ours.
  Now death shall stop his dismal threat'ning sound,
  And his ill-boding tongue no more shall speak.

WARWICK. I think his understanding is bereft.
  Speak, Clifford, dost thou know who speaks to thee?
  Dark cloudy death o'ershades his beams of life,
  And he nor sees nor hears us what we say.

RICHARD. O, would he did! and so, perhaps, he doth.
  'Tis but his policy to counterfeit,
  Because he would avoid such bitter taunts
  Which in the time of death he gave our father.

GEORGE. If so thou think'st, vex him with eager words.

RICHARD. Clifford, ask mercy and obtain no grace.

EDWARD. Clifford, repent in bootless penitence.

WARWICK. Clifford, devise excuses for thy faults.

GEORGE. While we devise fell tortures for thy faults.

RICHARD. Thou didst love York, and I am son to York.

EDWARD. Thou pitied'st Rutland, I will pity thee.

GEORGE. Where's Captain Margaret, to fence you now?

WARWICK. They mock thee, Clifford; swear as thou wast
  wont.

RICHARD. What, not an oath? Nay, then the world goes hard
  When Clifford cannot spare his friends an oath.
  I know by that he's dead; and by my soul,
  If this right hand would buy two hours' life,
  That I in all despite might rail at him,
  This hand should chop it off, and with the issuing blood
  Stifle the villain whose unstanched thirst

York and young Rutland could not satisfy.

WARWICK. Ay, but he's dead. Off with the traitor's head,
And rear it in the place your father's stands.
And now to London with triumphant march,
There to be crowned England's royal King;
From whence shall Warwick cut the sea to France,
And ask the Lady Bona for thy queen.
So shalt thou sinew both these lands together;
And, having France thy friend, thou shalt not dread
The scatt'red foe that hopes to rise again;
For though they cannot greatly sting to hurt,
Yet look to have them buzz to offend thine ears.
First will I see the coronation;
And then to Brittany I'll cross the sea
To effect this marriage, so it please my lord.

EDWARD. Even as thou wilt, sweet Warwick, let it be;
For in thy shoulder do I build my seat,
And never will I undertake the thing
Wherein thy counsel and consent is wanting.
Richard, I will create thee Duke of Gloucester;
And George, of Clarence; Warwick, as ourself,
Shall do and undo as him pleaseth best.

RICHARD. Let me be Duke of Clarence, George of Gloucester;
For Gloucester's dukedom is too ominous.

WARWICK. Tut, that's a foolish observation.
Richard, be Duke of Gloucester. Now to London
To see these honours in possession.   *Exeunt*

ACT III. SCENE 1

A chase in the north of England

Enter two KEEPERS, *with cross-bows in their hands*

FIRST KEEPER. Under this thick-grown brake we'll shroud
  ourselves,
For through this laund anon the deer will come;
And in this covert will we make our stand,

Culling the principal of all the deer.

SECOND KEEPER. I'll stay above the hill, so both may shoot.

FIRST KEEPER. That cannot be; the noise of thy cross-bow
Will scare the herd, and so my shoot is lost.
Here stand we both, and aim we at the best;
And, for the time shall not seem tedious,
I'll tell thee what befell me on a day
In this self-place where now we mean to stand.

SECOND KEEPER. Here comes a man; let's stay till he be past.

Enter KING HENRY, *disguised, with a prayer-book*

KING HENRY. From Scotland am I stol'n, even of pure love,
To greet mine own land with my wishful sight.
No, Harry, Harry, 'tis no land of thine;
Thy place is fill'd, thy sceptre wrung from thee,
Thy balm wash'd off wherewith thou wast anointed.
No bending knee will call thee Cæsar now,
No humble suitors press to speak for right,
No, not a man comes for redress of thee;
For how can I help them and not myself?

FIRST KEEPER. Ay, here's a deer whose skin's a keeper's fee.
This is the quondam King; let's seize upon him.

KING HENRY. Let me embrace thee, sour adversity,
For wise men say it is the wisest course.

SECOND KEEPER. Why linger we? let us lay hands upon him.

FIRST KEEPER. Forbear awhile; we'll hear a little more.

KING HENRY. My Queen and son are gone to France for aid;
And, as I hear, the great commanding Warwick
Is thither gone to crave the French King's sister
To wife for Edward. If this news be true,
Poor queen and son, your labour is but lost;
For Warwick is a subtle orator,
And Lewis a prince soon won with moving words.
By this account, then, Margaret may win him;
For she's a woman to be pitied much.
Her sighs will make a batt'ry in his breast;
Her tears will pierce into a marble heart;
The tiger will be mild whiles she doth mourn;
And Nero will be tainted with remorse
To hear and see her plaints, her brinish tears.

Ay, but she's come to beg: Warwick, to give.
She, on his left side, craving aid for Henry:
He, on his right, asking a wife for Edward.
She weeps, and says her Henry is depos'd:
He smiles, and says his Edward is install'd;
That she, poor wretch, for grief can speak no more;
Whiles Warwick tells his title, smooths the wrong,
Inferreth arguments of mighty strength,
And in conclusion wins the King from her
With promise of his sister, and what else,
To strengthen and support King Edward's place.
O Margaret, thus 'twill be; and thou, poor soul,
Art then forsaken, as thou went'st forlorn!

SECOND KEEPER. Say, what art thou that talk'st of kings and
    queens?

KING HENRY. More than I seem, and less than I was born to:
    A man at least, for less I should not be;
    And men may talk of kings, and why not I?

SECOND KEEPER. Ay, but thou talk'st as if thou wert a king.

KING HENRY. Why, so I am—in mind; and that's enough.

SECOND KEEPER. But, if thou be a king, where is thy crown?

KING HENRY. My crown is in my heart, not on my head;
    Not deck'd with diamonds and Indian stones,
    Not to be seen. My crown is call'd content;
    A crown it is that seldom kings enjoy.

SECOND KEEPER. Well, if you be a king crown'd with
    content,
    Your crown content and you must be contented
    To go along with us; for as we think,
    You are the king King Edward hath depos'd;
    And we his subjects, sworn in all allegiance,
    Will apprehend you as his enemy.

KING HENRY. But did you never swear, and break an oath?

SECOND KEEPER. No, never such an oath; nor will not now.

KING HENRY. Where did you dwell when I was King of
    England?

SECOND KEEPER. Here in this country, where we now
    remain.

KING HENRY. I was anointed king at nine months old;
    My father and my grandfather were kings;

And you were sworn true subjects unto me;
And tell me, then, have you not broke your oaths?

FIRST KEEPER. No;
For we were subjects but while you were king.

KING HENRY. Why, am I dead? Do I not breathe a man?
Ah, simple men, you know not what you swear!
Look, as I blow this feather from my face,
And as the air blows it to me again,
Obeying with my wind when I do blow,
And yielding to another when it blows,
Commanded always by the greater gust,
Such is the lightness of you common men.
But do not break your oaths; for of that sin
My mild entreaty shall not make you guilty.
Go where you will, the King shall be commanded;
And be you kings: command, and I'll obey.

FIRST KEEPER. We are true subjects to the King, King
Edward.

KING HENRY. So would you be again to Henry,
If he were seated as King Edward is.

FIRST KEEPER. We charge you, in God's name and the
King's,
To go with us unto the officers.

KING HENRY. In God's name, lead; your King's name be
obey'd;
And what God will, that let your King perform;
And what he will, I humbly yield unto.   *Exeunt*

SCENE 2

London. The palace

Enter KING EDWARD, GLOUCESTER, CLARENCE,
and LADY GREY

KING EDWARD. Brother of Gloucester, at Saint Albans' field
This lady's husband, Sir Richard Grey, was slain,
His land then seiz'd on by the conqueror.
Her suit is now to repossess those lands;
Which we in justice cannot well deny,

Because in quarrel of the house of York
The worthy gentleman did lose his life.

GLOUCESTER. Your Highness shall do well to grant her suit;
It were dishonour to deny it her.

KING EDWARD. It were no less; but yet I'll make a pause.

GLOUCESTER. [*Aside to* CLARENCE] Yea, is it so?
I see the lady hath a thing to grant,
Before the King will grant her humble suit.

CLARENCE. [*Aside to* GLOUCESTER] He knows the game;
how true he keeps the wind!

GLOUCESTER. [*Aside to* CLARENCE] Silence!

KING EDWARD. Widow, we will consider of your suit;
And come some other time to know our mind.

LADY GREY. Right gracious lord, I cannot brook delay.
May it please your Highness to resolve me now;
And what your pleasure is shall satisfy me.

GLOUCESTER. [*Aside*] Ay, widow? Then I'll warrant you
all your lands,
An if what pleases him shall pleasure you.
Fight closer or, good faith, you'll catch a blow.

CLARENCE. [*Aside to* GLOUCESTER] I fear her not, unless she
chance to fall.

GLOUCESTER. [*Aside to* CLARENCE] God forbid that, for
he'll take vantages.

KING EDWARD. How many children hast thou, widow, tell
me.

CLARENCE. [*Aside to* GLOUCESTER] I think he means to beg
a child of her.

GLOUCESTER. [*Aside to* CLARENCE] Nay, then whip me;
he'll rather give her two.

LADY GREY. Three, my most gracious lord.

GLOUCESTER. [*Aside*] You shall have four if you'll be rul'd
by him.

KING EDWARD. 'Twere pity they should lose their father's
lands.

LADY GREY. Be pitiful, dread lord, and grant it, then.

KING EDWARD. Lords, give us leave; I'll try this widow's wit.

GLOUCESTER. [*Aside*] Ay, good leave have you; for you
will have leave
Till youth take leave and leave you to the crutch.

[GLOUCESTER *and* CLARENCE *withdraw*]

KING EDWARD. Now tell me, madam, do you love your
  children?

LADY GREY. Ay, full as dearly as I love myself.

KING EDWARD. And would you not do much to do them
  good?

LADY GREY. To do them good I would sustain some harm.

KING EDWARD. Then get your husband's lands, to do them
  good.

LADY GREY. Therefore I came unto your Majesty.

KING EDWARD. I'll tell you how these lands are to be got.

LADY GREY. So shall you bind me to your Highness'
  service.

KING EDWARD. What service wilt thou do me if I give them?

LADY GREY. What you command that rests in me to do.

KING EDWARD. But you will take exceptions to my boon.

LADY GREY. No, gracious lord, except I cannot do it.

KING EDWARD. Ay, but thou canst do what I mean to ask.

LADY GREY. Why, then I will do what your Grace commands.

GLOUCESTER. He plies her hard; and much rain wears the
  marble.

CLARENCE. As red as fire! Nay, then her wax must melt.

LADY GREY. Why stops my lord? Shall I not hear my task?

KING EDWARD. An easy task; 'tis but to love a king.

LADY GREY. That's soon perform'd, because I am a subject.

KING EDWARD. Why, then, thy husband's lands I freely give
  thee.

LADY GREY. I take my leave with many thousand thanks.

GLOUCESTER. The match is made; she seals it with a curtsy.

KING EDWARD. But stay thee—'tis the fruits of love I mean.

LADY GREY. The fruits of love I mean, my loving liege.

KING EDWARD. Ay, but, I fear me, in another sense.
  What love, thinkst thou, I sue so much to get?

LADY GREY. My love till death, my humble thanks, my
  prayers;
  That love which virtue begs and virtue grants.

KING EDWARD. No, by my troth, I did not mean such love.

LADY GREY. Why, then you mean not as I thought you did.

KING EDWARD. But now you partly may perceive my mind.

LADY GREY. My mind will never grant what I perceive
  Your Highness aims at, if I aim aright.
KING EDWARD. To tell thee plain, I aim to lie with thee.
LADY GREY. To tell you plain, I had rather lie in prison.
KING EDWARD. Why, then thou shalt not have thy husband's
  lands.
LADY GREY. Why, then mine honesty shall be my dower;
  For by that loss I will not purchase them.
KING EDWARD. Therein thou wrong'st thy children mightily.
LADY GREY. Herein your Highness wrongs both them and
  me.
  But, mighty lord, this merry inclination
  Accords not with the sadness of my suit.
  Please you dismiss me, either with ay or no.
KING EDWARD. Ay, if thou wilt say ay to my request;
  No, if thou dost say no to my demand.
LADY GREY. Then, no, my lord. My suit is at an end.
GLOUCESTER. The widow likes him not; she knits her brows.
CLARENCE. He is the bluntest wooer in Christendom.
KING EDWARD. [*Aside*] Her looks doth argue her replete
  with modesty;
  Her words doth show her wit incomparable;
  All her perfections challenge sovereignty.
  One way or other, she is for a king;
  And she shall be my love, or else my queen.
  Say that King Edward take thee for his queen?
LADY GREY. 'Tis better said than done, my gracious lord.
  I am a subject fit to jest withal,
  But far unfit to be a sovereign.
KING EDWARD. Sweet widow, by my state I swear to thee
  I speak no more than what my soul intends;
  And that is to enjoy thee for my love.
LADY GREY. And that is more than I will yield unto.
  I know I am too mean to be your queen,
  And yet too good to be your concubine.
KING EDWARD. You cavil, widow; I did mean my queen.
LADY GREY. 'Twill grieve your Grace my sons should call
  you father.
KING EDWARD. No more than when my daughters call thee
  mother.

Thou art a widow, and thou hast some children;
And, by God's Mother, I, being but a bachelor,
Have other some. Why, 'tis a happy thing
To be the father unto many sons.
Answer no more, for thou shalt be my queen.
GLOUCESTER. The ghostly father now hath done his shrift.
CLARENCE. When he was made a shriver, 'twas for shrift.
KING EDWARD. Brothers, you muse what chat we two have
    had.
GLOUCESTER. The widow likes it not, for she looks very sad.
KING EDWARD. You'd think it strange if I should marry her.
CLARENCE. To who, my lord?
KING EDWARD. Why, Clarence, to myself.
GLOUCESTER. That would be ten days' wonder at the least.
CLARENCE. That's a day longer than a wonder lasts.
GLOUCESTER. By so much is the wonder in extremes.
KING EDWARD. Well, jest on, brothers; I can tell you both
    Her suit is granted for her husband's lands.

Enter a NOBLEMAN

NOBLEMAN. My gracious lord, Henry your foe is taken
    And brought your prisoner to your palace gate.
KING EDWARD. See that he be convey'd unto the Tower.
    And go we, brothers, to the man that took him
    To question of his apprehension.
    Widow, go you along. Lords, use her honourably.
                              Exeunt all but GLOUCESTER
GLOUCESTER. Ay, Edward will use women honourably.
    Would he were wasted, marrow, bones, and all,
    That from his loins no hopeful branch may spring
    To cross me from the golden time I look for!
    And yet, between my soul's desire and me—
    The lustful Edward's title buried—
    Is Clarence, Henry, and his son young Edward,
    And all the unlook'd for issue of their bodies,
    To take their rooms ere I can place myself.
    A cold premeditation for my purpose!
    Why, then I do but dream on sovereignty;
    Like one that stands upon a promontory
    And spies a far-off shore where he would tread,

Wishing his foot were equal with his eye;
And chides the sea that sunders him from thence,
Saying he'll lade it dry to have his way—
So do I wish the crown, being so far off;
And so I chide the means that keeps me from it;
And so I say I'll cut the causes off,
Flattering me with impossibilities.
My eye's too quick, my heart o'erweens too much,
Unless my hand and strength could equal them.
Well, say there is no kingdom then for Richard;
What other pleasure can the world afford?
I'll make my heaven in a lady's lap,
And deck my body in gay ornaments,
And witch sweet ladies with my words and looks.
O miserable thought! and more unlikely
Than to accomplish twenty golden crowns.
Why, love forswore me in my mother's womb;
And, for I should not deal in her soft laws,
She did corrupt frail nature with some bribe
To shrink mine arm up like a wither'd shrub
To make an envious mountain on my back,
Where sits deformity to mock my body;
To shape my legs of an unequal size;
To disproportion me in every part,
Like to a chaos, or an unlick'd bear-whelp
That carries no impression like the dam.
And am I, then, a man to be belov'd?
O monstrous fault to harbour such a thought!
Then, since this earth affords no joy to me
But to command, to check, to o'erbear such
As are of better person than myself,
I'll make my heaven to dream upon the crown,
And whiles I live t' account this world but hell,
Until my misshap'd trunk that bear this head
Be round impaled with a glorious crown.
And yet I know not how to get the crown,
For many lives stand between me and home;
And I—like one lost in a thorny wood
That rents the thorns and is rent with the thorns,
Seeking a way and straying from the way

Not knowing how to find the open air,
But toiling desperately to find it out—
Torment myself to catch the English crown;
And from that torment I will free myself
Or hew my way out with a bloody axe.
Why, I can smile, and murder whiles I smile,
And cry 'Content!' to that which grieves my heart,
And wet my cheeks with artificial tears,
And frame my face to all occasions.
I'll drown more sailors than the mermaid shall;
I'll slay more gazers than the basilisk;
I'll play the orator as well as Nestor,
Deceive more slily than Ulysses could,
And, like a Sinon, take another Troy.
I can add colours to the chameleon,
Change shapes with Protheus for advantages,
And set the murderous Machiavel to school.
Can I do this, and cannot get a crown?
Tut, were it farther off, I'll pluck it down.   *Exit*

SCENE 3

France. The KING'S palace

Flourish. Enter LEWIS *the French King, his sister*
BONA, *his Admiral call'd* BOURBON; PRINCE EDWARD,
QUEEN MARGARET, *and the* EARL OF OXFORD. LEWIS
sits, and riseth up again

LEWIS. Fair Queen of England, worthy Margaret,
    Sit down with us. It ill befits thy state
    And birth that thou shouldst stand while Lewis doth sit.
QUEEN MARGARET. No, mighty King of France. Now
        Margaret
    Must strike her sail and learn a while to serve
    Where kings command. I was, I must confess,
    Great Albion's Queen in former golden days;
    But now mischance hath trod my title down
    And with dishonour laid me on the ground,
    Where I must take like seat unto my fortune,

And to my humble seat conform myself.

LEWIS. Why, say, fair Queen, whence springs this deep
    despair?

QUEEN MARGARET. From such a cause as fills mine eyes with
    tears

And stops my tongue, while heart is drown'd in cares.

LEWIS. Whate'er it be, be thou still like thyself,
    And sit thee by our side. [*Seats her by him*] Yield not thy
    neck
    To fortune's yoke, but let thy dauntless mind
    Still ride in triumph over all mischance.
    Be plain, Queen Margaret, and tell thy grief;
    It shall be eas'd, if France can yield relief.

QUEEN MARGARET. Those gracious words revive my droop-
    ing thoughts
    And give my tongue-tied sorrows leave to speak.
    Now therefore be it known to noble Lewis
    That Henry, sole possessor of my love,
    Is, of a king, become a banish'd man,
    And forc'd to live in Scotland a forlorn;
    While proud ambitious Edward Duke of York
    Usurps the regal title and the seat
    Of England's true-anointed lawful King.
    This is the cause that I, poor Margaret,
    With this my son, Prince Edward, Henry's heir,
    Am come to crave thy just and lawful aid;
    And if thou fail us, all our hope is done.
    Scotland hath will to help, but cannot help;
    Our people and our peers are both misled,
    Our treasure seiz'd, our soldiers put to flight,
    And, as thou seest, ourselves in heavy plight.

LEWIS. Renowned Queen, with patience calm the storm,
    While we bethink a means to break it off.

QUEEN MARGARET. The more we stay, the stronger grows
    our foe.

LEWIS. The more I stay, the more I'll succour thee.

QUEEN MARGARET. O, but impatience waiteth on true sorrow.
    And see where comes the breeder of my sorrow!

Enter WARWICK

KING HENRY VI. PART 3

LEWIS. What's he approacheth boldly to our presence?
QUEEN MARGARET. Our Earl of Warwick, Edward's greatest friend.
LEWIS. Welcome, brave Warwick! What brings thee to France? [*He descends. She ariseth*]
QUEEN MARGARET. Ay, now begins a second storm to rise;
For this is he that moves both wind and tide.
WARWICK. From worthy Edward, King of Albion,
My lord and sovereign, and thy vowed friend,
I come, in kindness and unfeigned love,
First to do greetings to thy royal person,
And then to crave a league of amity,
And lastly to confirm that amity
With nuptial knot, if thou vouchsafe to grant
That virtuous Lady Bona, thy fair sister,
To England's King in lawful marriage.
QUEEN MARGARET. [*Aside*] If that go forward, Henry's hope is done.
WARWICK. [*To* BONA] And, gracious madam, in our king's behalf,
I am commanded, with your leave and favour,
Humbly to kiss your hand, and with my tongue
To tell the passion of my sovereign's heart;
Where fame, late ent'ring at his heedful ears,
Hath plac'd thy beauty's image and thy virtue.
QUEEN MARGARET. King Lewis and Lady Bona, hear me speak
Before you answer Warwick. His demand
Springs not from Edward's well-meant honest love,
But from deceit bred by necessity;
For how can tyrants safely govern home
Unless abroad they purchase great alliance?
To prove him tyrant this reason may suffice,
That Henry liveth still; but were he dead,
Yet here Prince Edward stands, King Henry's son.
Look therefore, Lewis, that by this league and marriage
Thou draw not on thy danger and dishonour;
For though usurpers sway the rule a while
Yet heav'ns are just, and time suppresseth wrongs.
WARWICK. Injurious Margaret!

730

PRINCE OF WALES. And why not Queen?
WARWICK. Because thy father Henry did usurp;
  And thou no more art prince than she is queen.
OXFORD. Then Warwick disannuls great John of Gaunt,
  Which did subdue the greatest part of Spain;
  And, after John of Gaunt, Henry the Fourth,
  Whose wisdom was a mirror to the wisest;
  And, after that wise prince, Henry the Fifth,
  Who by his prowess conquered all France.
  From these our Henry lineally descends.
WARWICK. Oxford, how haps it in this smooth discourse
  You told not how Henry the Sixth hath lost
  All that which Henry the Fifth had gotten?
  Methinks these peers of France should smile at that.
  But for the rest: you tell a pedigree
  Of threescore and two years—a silly time
  To make prescription for a kingdom's worth.
OXFORD. Why, Warwick, canst thou speak against thy
    liege,
  Whom thou obeyed'st thirty and six years,
  And not betray thy treason with a blush?
WARWICK. Can Oxford that did ever fence the right
  Now buckler falsehood with a pedigree?
  For shame! Leave Henry, and call Edward king.
OXFORD. Call him my king by whose injurious doom
  My elder brother, the Lord Aubrey Vere,
  Was done to death; and more than so, my father,
  Even in the downfall of his mellow'd years,
  When nature brought him to the door of death?
  No, Warwick, no; while life upholds this arm,
  This arm upholds the house of Lancaster.
WARWICK. And I the house of York.
LEWIS. Queen Margaret, Prince Edward, and Oxford,
  Vouchsafe at our request to stand aside
  While I use further conference with Warwick.
                              [*They stand aloof*]
QUEEN MARGARET. Heavens grant that Warwick's words
    bewitch him not!
LEWIS. Now, Warwick, tell me, even upon thy conscience,
  Is Edward your true king? for I were loath

To link with him that were not lawful chosen.

WARWICK. Thereon I pawn my credit and mine honour.

LEWIS. But is he gracious in the people's eye?

WARWICK. The more that Henry was unfortunate.

LEWIS. Then further: all dissembling set aside,
   Tell me for truth the measure of his love
   Unto our sister Bona.

WARWICK. Such it seems
   As may beseem a monarch like himself.
   Myself have often heard him say and swear
   That this his love was an eternal plant
   Whereof the root was fix'd in virtue's ground,
   The leaves and fruit maintain'd with beauty's sun,
   Exempt from envy, but not from disdain,
   Unless the Lady Bona quit his pain.

LEWIS. Now, sister, let us hear your firm resolve.

BONA. Your grant or your denial shall be mine.
   [To WARWICK] Yet I confess that often ere this day,
   When I have heard your king's desert recounted,
   Mine ear hath tempted judgment to desire.

LEWIS. Then, Warwick, thus: our sister shall be Edward's.
   And now forthwith shall articles be drawn
   Touching the jointure that your king must make,
   Which with her dowry shall be counterpois'd.
   Draw near, Queen Margaret, and be a witness
   That Bona shall be wife to the English king.

PRINCE OF WALES. To Edward, but not to the English king.

QUEEN MARGARET. Deceitful Warwick, it was thy device
   By this alliance to make void my suit.
   Before thy coming, Lewis was Henry's friend.

LEWIS. And still is friend to him and Margaret.
   But if your title to the crown be weak,
   As may appear by Edward's good success,
   Then 'tis but reason that I be releas'd
   From giving aid which late I promised.
   Yet shall you have all kindness at my hand
   That your estate requires and mine can yield.

WARWICK. Henry now lives in Scotland at his ease,
   Where having nothing, nothing can he lose.
   And as for you yourself, our quondam queen,

You have a father able to maintain you,
And better 'twere you troubled him than France.
QUEEN MARGARET. Peace, impudent and shameless Warwick,
Proud setter up and puller down of kings!
I will not hence till with my talk and tears,
Both full of truth, I make King Lewis behold
Thy sly conveyance and thy lord's false love;
For both of you are birds of self-same feather.

[Post *blowing a horn within*]

LEWIS. Warwick, this is some post to us or thee.

Enter the POST

POST. My lord ambassador, these letters are for you,
Sent from your brother, Marquis Montague.
These from our King unto your Majesty.
And, madam, these for you; from whom I know not.

[*They all read their letters*]

OXFORD. I like it well that our fair Queen and mistress
Smiles at her news, while Warwick frowns at his.
PRINCE OF WALES. Nay, mark how Lewis stamps as he were
nettled.
I hope all's for the best.
LEWIS. Warwick, what are thy news? And yours, fair
Queen?
QUEEN MARGARET. Mine such as fill my heart with unhop'd
joys.
WARWICK. Mine full of sorrow and heart's discontent.
LEWIS. What, has your king married the Lady Grey?
And now, to soothe your forgery and his,
Sends me a paper to persuade me patience?
Is this th' alliance that he seeks with France?
Dare he presume to scorn us in this manner?
QUEEN MARGARET. I told your Majesty as much before.
This proveth Edward's love and Warwick's honesty.
WARWICK. King Lewis, I here protest in sight of heaven,
And by the hope I have of heavenly bliss,
That I am clear from this misdeed of Edward's—
No more my king, for he dishonours me,
But most himself, if he could see his shame.
Did I forget that by the house of York

My father came untimely to his death?
Did I let pass th' abuse done to my niece?
Did I impale him with the regal crown?
Did I put Henry from his native right?
And am I guerdon'd at the last with shame?
Shame on himself! for my desert is honour;
And to repair my honour lost for him
I here renounce him and return to Henry.
My noble Queen, let former grudges pass,
And henceforth I am thy true servitor.
I will revenge his wrong to Lady Bona,
And replant Henry in his former state.
QUEEN MARGARET. Warwick, these words have turn'd my
    hate to love;
    And I forgive and quite forget old faults,
    And joy that thou becom'st King Henry's friend.
WARWICK. So much his friend, ay, his unfeigned friend,
    That if King Lewis vouchsafe to furnish us
    With some few bands of chosen soldiers,
    I'll undertake to land them on our coast
    And force the tyrant from his seat by war.
    'Tis not his new-made bride shall succour him;
    And as for Clarence, as my letters tell me,
    He's very likely now to fall from him
    For matching more for wanton lust than honour
    Or than for strength and safety of our country.
BONA. Dear brother, how shall Bona be reveng'd
    But by thy help to this distressed queen?
QUEEN MARGARET. Renowned Prince, how shall poor Henry
    live
    Unless thou rescue him from foul despair?
BONA. My quarrel and this English queen's are one.
WARWICK. And mine, fair Lady Bona, joins with yours.
LEWIS. And mine with hers, and thine, and Margaret's.
    Therefore, at last, I firmly am resolv'd
    You shall have aid.
QUEEN MARGARET. Let me give humble thanks for all at
    once.
LEWIS. Then, England's messenger, return in post
    And tell false Edward, thy supposed king,

That Lewis of France is sending over masquers
To revel it with him and his new bride.
Thou seest what's past; go fear thy king withal.
BONA. Tell him, in hope he'll prove a widower shortly,
  I'll wear the willow-garland for his sake.
QUEEN MARGARET. Tell him my mourning weeds are laid
    aside,
  And I am ready to put armour on.
WARWICK. Tell him from me that he hath done me wrong,
  And therefore I'll uncrown him ere't be long.
  There's thy reward; be gone.   *Exit* POST
LEWIS. But, Warwick,
  Thou and Oxford, with five thousand men,
  Shall cross the seas and bid false Edward battle:
  And, as occasion serves, this noble Queen
  And Prince shall follow with a fresh supply.
  Yet, ere thou go, but answer me one doubt:
  What pledge have we of thy firm loyalty?
WARWICK. This shall assure my constant loyalty:
  That if our Queen and this young Prince agree,
  I'll join mine eldest daughter and my joy
  To him forthwith in holy wedlock bands.
QUEEN MARGARET. Yes, I agree, and thank you for your
    motion.
  Son Edward, she is fair and virtuous,
  Therefore delay not—give thy hand to Warwick;
  And with thy hand thy faith irrevocable
  That only Warwick's daughter shall be thine.
PRINCE OF WALES. Yes, I accept her, for she well deserves it;
  And here, to pledge my vow, I give my hand.
                    [*He gives his hand to* WARWICK]
LEWIS. Why stay we now? These soldiers shall be levied;
  And thou, Lord Bourbon, our High Admiral,
  Shall waft them over with our royal fleet.
  I long till Edward fall by war's mischance
  For mocking marriage with a dame of France.
                    Exeunt all but WARWICK
WARWICK. I came from Edward as ambassador,
  But I return his sworn and mortal foe.
  Matter of marriage was the charge he gave me,

But dreadful war shall answer his demand.
Had he none else to make a stale but me?
Then none but I shall turn his jest to sorrow.
I was the chief that rais'd him to the crown,
And I'll be chief to bring him down again;
Not that I pity Henry's misery,
But seek revenge on Edward's mockery.   *Exit*

ACT IV. SCENE 1

London. The palace

Enter GLOUCESTER, CLARENCE, SOMERSET, *and*
MONTAGUE

GLOUCESTER. Now tell me, brother Clarence, what think you
   Of this new marriage with the Lady Grey?
   Hath not our brother made a worthy choice?
CLARENCE. Alas, you know 'tis far from hence to France!
   How could he stay till Warwick made return?
SOMERSET. My lords, forbear this talk; here comes the King.

   Flourish. Enter KING EDWARD, *attended;* LADY
   GREY, *as Queen;* PEMBROKE, STAFFORD, HASTINGS,
   *and others. Four stand on one side, and four on the
   other*

GLOUCESTER. And his well-chosen bride.
CLARENCE. I mind to tell him plainly what I think.
KING EDWARD. Now, brother of Clarence, how like you our
   choice
   That you stand pensive as half malcontent?
CLARENCE. As well as Lewis of France or the Earl of
   Warwick,
   Which are so weak of courage and in judgment
   That they'll take no offence at our abuse.
KING EDWARD. Suppose they take offence without a cause;
   They are but Lewis and Warwick: I am Edward,
   Your King and Warwick's and must have my will.

GLOUCESTER. And shall have your will, because our King.
    Yet hasty marriage seldom proveth well.
KING EDWARD. Yea, brother Richard, are you offended too?
GLOUCESTER. Not I.
    No, God forbid that I should wish them sever'd
    Whom God hath join'd together; ay, and 'twere pity
    To sunder them that yoke so well together.
KING EDWARD. Setting your scorns and your mislike aside,
    Tell me some reason why the Lady Grey
    Should not become my wife and England's Queen.
    And you too, Somerset and Montague,
    Speak freely what you think.
CLARENCE. Then this is mine opinion: that King Lewis
    Becomes your enemy for mocking him
    About the marriage of the Lady Bona.
GLOUCESTER. And Warwick, doing what you gave in charge,
    Is now dishonoured by this new marriage.
KING EDWARD. What if both Lewis and Warwick be
        appeas'd
    By such invention as I can devise?
MONTAGUE. Yet to have join'd with France in such alliance
    Would more have strength'ned this our commonwealth
    'Gainst foreign storms than any home-bred marriage.
HASTINGS. Why, knows not Montague that of itself
    England is safe, if true within itself?
MONTAGUE. But the safer when 'tis back'd with France.
HASTINGS. 'Tis better using France than trusting France.
    Let us be back'd with God, and with the seas
    Which He hath giv'n for fence impregnable,
    And with their helps only defend ourselves.
    In them and in ourselves our safety lies.
CLARENCE. For this one speech Lord Hastings well deserves
    To have the heir of the Lord Hungerford.
KING EDWARD. Ay, what of that? it was my will and grant;
    And for this once my will shall stand for law.
GLOUCESTER. And yet methinks your Grace hath not done
        well
    To give the heir and daughter of Lord Scales
    Unto the brother of your loving bride.
    She better would have fitted me or Clarence;

737

But in your bride you bury brotherhood.

CLARENCE. Or else you would not have bestow'd the heir
Of the Lord Bonville on your new wife's son,
And leave your brothers to go speed elsewhere.

KING EDWARD. Alas, poor Clarence! Is it for a wife
That thou art malcontent? I will provide thee.

CLARENCE. In choosing for yourself you show'd your judgment,
Which being shallow, you shall give me leave
To play the broker in mine own behalf;
And to that end I shortly mind to leave you.

KING EDWARD. Leave me or tarry, Edward will be King,
And not be tied unto his brother's will.

QUEEN ELIZABETH. My lords, before it pleas'd his Majesty
To raise my state to title of a queen,
Do me but right, and you must all confess
That I was not ignoble of descent:
And meaner than myself have had like fortune.
But as this title honours me and mine,
So your dislikes, to whom I would be pleasing,
Doth cloud my joys with danger and with sorrow.

KING EDWARD. My love, forbear to fawn upon their frowns.
What danger or what sorrow can befall thee,
So long as Edward is thy constant friend
And their true sovereign whom they must obey?
Nay, whom they shall obey, and love thee too,
Unless they seek for hatred at my hands;
Which if they do, yet will I keep thee safe,
And they shall feel the vengeance of my wrath.

GLOUCESTER. [*Aside*] I hear, yet say not much, but think
the more.

Enter a POST

KING EDWARD. Now, messenger, what letters or what news
From France?

MESSENGER. My sovereign liege, no letters, and few words,
But such as I, without your special pardon,
Dare not relate.

KING EDWARD. Go to, we pardon thee; therefore, in brief,
Tell me their words as near as thou canst guess them.

What answer makes King Lewis unto our letters?

MESSENGER. At my depart, these were his very words:
  'Go tell false Edward, the supposed king,
  That Lewis of France is sending over masquers
  To revel it with him and his new bride.'

KING EDWARD. Is Lewis so brave? Belike he thinks me
  Henry.
  But what said Lady Bona to my marriage?

MESSENGER. These were her words, utt'red with mild
  disdain:
  'Tell him, in hope he'll prove a widower shortly,
  I'll wear the willow-garland for his sake.'

KING EDWARD. I blame not her: she could say little less;
  She had the wrong. But what said Henry's queen?
  For I have heard that she was there in place.

MESSENGER. 'Tell him' quoth she 'my mourning weeds are
  done,
  And I am ready to put armour on.'

KING EDWARD. Belike she minds to play the Amazon.
  But what said Warwick to these injuries?

MESSENGER. He, more incens'd against your Majesty
  Than all the rest, discharg'd me with these words:
  'Tell him from me that he hath done me wrong;
  And therefore I'll uncrown him ere't be long.'

KING EDWARD. Ha! durst the traitor breathe out so proud
  words?
  Well, I will arm me, being thus forewarn'd.
  They shall have wars and pay for their presumption.
  But say, is Warwick friends with Margaret?

MESSENGER. Ay, gracious sovereign; they are so link'd in
  friendship
  That young Prince Edward marries Warwick's daughter.

CLARENCE. Belike the elder; Clarence will have the younger.
  Now, brother king, farewell, and sit you fast,
  For I will hence to Warwick's other daughter;
  That, though I want a kingdom, yet in marriage
  I may not prove inferior to yourself.
  You that love me and Warwick, follow me.

                              Exit, and SOMERSET *follows*

GLOUCESTER. [*Aside*] Not I.

My thoughts aim at a further matter; I
Stay not for the love of Edward but the crown.
KING EDWARD. Clarence and Somerset both gone to
    Warwick!
Yet am I arm'd against the worst can happen;
And haste is needful in this desp'rate case.
Pembroke and Stafford, you in our behalf
Go levy men and make prepare for war;
They are already, or quickly will be landed.
Myself in person will straight follow you.

Exeunt PEMBROKE *and* STAFFORD

But ere I go, Hastings and Montague,
Resolve my doubt. You twain, of all the rest,
Are near to Warwick by blood and by alliance.
Tell me if you love Warwick more than me?
If it be so, then both depart to him:
I rather wish you foes than hollow friends.
But if you mind to hold your true obedience,
Give me assurance with some friendly vow,
That I may never have you in suspect.
MONTAGUE. So God help Montague as he proves true!
HASTINGS. And Hastings as he favours Edward's cause!
KING EDWARD. Now, brother Richard, will you stand by us?
GLOUCESTER. Ay, in despite of all that shall withstand you.
KING EDWARD. Why, so! then am I sure of victory.
Now therefore let us hence, and lose no hour
Till we meet Warwick with his foreign pow'r.   *Exeunt*

SCENE 2

A plain in Warwickshire

Enter WARWICK *and* OXFORD, *with French soldiers*

WARWICK. Trust me, my lord, all hitherto goes well;
    The common people by numbers swarm to us.

Enter CLARENCE *and* SOMERSET

But see where Somerset and Clarence comes.
Speak suddenly, my lords—are we all friends?

CLARENCE. Fear not that, my lord.
WARWICK. Then, gentle Clarence, welcome unto Warwick;
  And welcome, Somerset. I hold it cowardice
  To rest mistrustful where a noble heart
  Hath pawn'd an open hand in sign of love;
  Else might I think that Clarence, Edward's brother,
  Were but a feigned friend to our proceedings.
  But welcome, sweet Clarence; my daughter shall be thine.
  And now what rests but, in night's coverture,
  Thy brother being carelessly encamp'd,
  His soldiers lurking in the towns about,
  And but attended by a simple guard,
  We may surprise and take him at our pleasure?
  Our scouts have found the adventure very easy;
  That as Ulysses and stout Diomede
  With sleight and manhood stole to Rhesus' tents,
  And brought from thence the Thracian fatal steeds,
  So we, well cover'd with the night's black mantle,
  At unawares may beat down Edward's guard
  And seize himself—I say not 'slaughter him,'
  For I intend but only to surprise him.
  You that will follow me to this attempt,
  Applaud the name of Henry with your leader.
                    [*They all cry* 'Henry!']
  Why then, let's on our way in silent sort.
  For Warwick and his friends, God and Saint George!
                                        Exeunt

SCENE 3

Edward's camp, near Warwick

Enter three WATCHMEN, *to guard the* KING'S *tent*

FIRST WATCHMAN. Come on, my masters, each man take his
    stand;
  The King by this is set him down to sleep.
SECOND WATCHMAN. What, will he not to bed?
FIRST WATCHMAN. Why, no; for he hath made a solemn
    vow

Never to lie and take his natural rest
Till Warwick or himself be quite suppress'd.

SECOND WATCHMAN. To-morrow then, belike, shall be the day,
If Warwick be so near as men report.

THIRD WATCHMAN. But say, I pray, what nobleman is that
That with the King here resteth in his tent?

FIRST WATCHMAN. 'Tis the Lord Hastings, the King's chiefest friend.

THIRD WATCHMAN. O, is it so? But why commands the King
That his chief followers lodge in towns about him,
While he himself keeps in the cold field?

SECOND WATCHMAN. 'Tis the more honour, because more dangerous.

THIRD WATCHMAN. Ay, but give me worship and quietness;
I like it better than a dangerous honour.
If Warwick knew in what estate he stands,
'Tis to be doubted he would waken him.

FIRST WATCHMAN. Unless our halberds did shut up his passage.

SECOND WATCHMAN. Ay, wherefore else guard we his royal tent
But to defend his person from night-foes?

Enter WARWICK, CLARENCE, OXFORD, SOMERSET,
and French soldiers, silent all

WARWICK. This is his tent; and see where stand his guard.
Courage, my masters! Honour now or never!
But follow me, and Edward shall be ours.

FIRST WATCHMAN. Who goes there?

SECOND WATCHMAN. Stay, or thou diest.

WARWICK *and the rest cry all* 'Warwick! War-wick!' *and set upon the guard, who fly, crying* 'Arm! Arm!' WARWICK *and the rest following them*

The drum playing and trumpet sounding, re-enter WARWICK *and the rest, bringing the* KING *out in his gown, sitting in a chair.* GLOUCESTER *and* HASTINGS *fly over the stage*

SOMERSET. What are they that fly there?

WARWICK. Richard and Hastings. Let them go; here is the
Duke.

KING EDWARD. The Duke! Why, Warwick, when we
parted,
Thou call'dst me King?

WARWICK. Ay, but the case is alter'd.
When you disgrac'd me in my embassade,
Then I degraded you from being King,
And come now to create you Duke of York.
Alas, how should you govern any kingdom
That know not how to use ambassadors,
Nor how to be contented with one wife,
Nor how to use your brothers brotherly,
Nor how to study for the people's welfare,
Nor how to shroud yourself from enemies?

KING EDWARD. Yea, brother of Clarence, art thou here too?
Nay, then I see that Edward needs must down.
Yet, Warwick, in despite of all mischance,
Of thee thyself and all thy complices,
Edward will always bear himself as King.
Though fortune's malice overthrow my state,
My mind exceeds the compass of her wheel.

WARWICK. Then, for his mind, be Edward England's king;
[*Takes off his crown*]
But Henry now shall wear the English crown
And be true King indeed; thou but the shadow.
My Lord of Somerset, at my request,
See that forthwith Duke Edward be convey'd
Unto my brother, Archbishop of York.
When I have fought with Pembroke and his fellows,
I'll follow you and tell what answer
Lewis and the Lady Bona send to him.
Now for a while farewell, good Duke of York.

KING EDWARD. What fates impose, that men must needs
abide;
It boots not to resist both wind and tide.
[*They lead him out forcibly*]

OXFORD. What now remains, my lords, for us to do
But march to London with our soldiers?

WARWICK. Ay, that's the first thing that we have to do;
To free King Henry from imprisonment,
And see him seated in the regal throne.   *Exeunt*

SCENE 4

London. The palace

Enter QUEEN ELIZABETH *and* RIVERS

RIVERS. Madam, what makes you in this sudden change?
QUEEN ELIZABETH. Why, brother Rivers, are you yet to learn
What late misfortune is befall'n King Edward?
RIVERS. What, loss of some pitch'd battle against Warwick?
QUEEN ELIZABETH. No, but the loss of his own royal person.
RIVERS. Then is my sovereign slain?
QUEEN ELIZABETH. Ay, almost slain, for he is taken prisoner;
Either betray'd by falsehood of his guard
Or by his foe surpris'd at unawares;
And, as I further have to understand,
Is new committed to the Bishop of York,
Fell Warwick's brother, and by that our foe.
RIVERS. These news, I must confess, are full of grief;
Yet, gracious madam, bear it as you may:
Warwick may lose that now hath won the day.
QUEEN ELIZABETH. Till then, fair hope must hinder life's decay.
And I the rather wean me from despair
For love of Edward's offspring in my womb.
This is it that makes me bridle passion
And bear with mildness my misfortune's cross;
Ay, ay, for this I draw in many a tear
And stop the rising of blood-sucking sighs,
Lest with my sighs or tears I blast or drown
King Edward's fruit, true heir to th' English crown.
RIVERS. But, madam, where is Warwick then become?
QUEEN ELIZABETH. I am inform'd that he comes towards London
To set the crown once more on Henry's head.

Guess thou the rest: King Edward's friends must down.
But to prevent the tyrant's violence—
For trust not him that hath once broken faith—
I'll hence forthwith unto the sanctuary
To save at least the heir of Edward's right.
There shall I rest secure from force and fraud.
Come, therefore, let us fly while we may fly:
If Warwick take us, we are sure to die.   *Exeunt*

SCENE 5

A park near Middleham Castle in Yorkshire

Enter GLOUCESTER, LORD HASTINGS, SIR WILLIAM
STANLEY, *and others*

GLOUCESTER. Now, my Lord Hastings and Sir William
　　Stanley,
　　Leave off to wonder why I drew you hither
　　Into this chiefest thicket of the park.
　　Thus stands the case: you know our King, my brother,
　　Is prisoner to the Bishop here, at whose hands
　　He hath good usage and great liberty;
　　And often but attended with weak guard
　　Comes hunting this way to disport himself.
　　I have advertis'd him by secret means
　　That if about this hour he make this way,
　　Under the colour of his usual game,
　　He shall here find his friends, with horse and men,
　　To set him free from his captivity.

Enter KING EDWARD *and a* HUNTSMAN *with him*

HUNTSMAN. This way, my lord; for this way lies the game.
KING EDWARD. Nay, this way, man. See where the huntsmen
　　stand.
　　Now, brother of Gloucester, Lord Hastings, and the rest,
　　Stand you thus close to steal the Bishop's deer?
GLOUCESTER. Brother, the time and case requireth haste;
　　Your horse stands ready at the park corner.
KING EDWARD. But whither shall we then?

HASTINGS. To Lynn, my lord; and shipt from thence to
Flanders.

GLOUCESTER. Well guess'd, believe me; for that was my
meaning.

KING EDWARD. Stanley, I will requite thy forwardness.

GLOUCESTER. But wherefore stay we? 'Tis no time to talk.

KING EDWARD. Huntsman, what say'st thou? Wilt thou go
along?

HUNTSMAN. Better do so than tarry and be hang'd.

GLOUCESTER. Come then, away; let's ha' no more ado.

KING EDWARD. Bishop, farewell. Shield thee from Warwick's
frown,
And pray that I may repossess the crown.   *Exeunt*

SCENE 6

London. The Tower

Flourish. Enter KING HENRY, CLARENCE, WARWICK,
SOMERSET, *young* HENRY, EARL OF RICHMOND, OX-
FORD, MONTAGUE, LIEUTENANT OF THE TOWER, *and
attendants*

KING HENRY. Master Lieutenant, now that God and friends
Have shaken Edward from the regal seat
And turn'd my captive state to liberty,
My fear to hope, my sorrows unto joys,
At our enlargement what are thy due fees?

LIEUTENANT. Subjects may challenge nothing of their
sov'reigns;
But if an humble prayer may prevail,
I then crave pardon of your Majesty.

KING HENRY. For what, Lieutenant? For well using me?
Nay, be thou sure I'll well requite thy kindness,
For that it made my imprisonment a pleasure;
Ay, such a pleasure as incaged birds
Conceive when, after many moody thoughts,
At last by notes of household harmony
They quite forget their loss of liberty.
But, Warwick, after God, thou set'st me free,

And chiefly therefore I thank God and thee;
He was the author, thou the instrument.
Therefore, that I may conquer fortune's spite
By living low where fortune cannot hurt me,
And that the people of this blessed land
May not be punish'd with my thwarting stars,
Warwick, although my head still wear the crown,
I here resign my government to thee,
For thou art fortunate in all thy deeds.

WARWICK. Your Grace hath still been fam'd for virtuous,
And now may seem as wise as virtuous
By spying and avoiding fortune's malice,
For few men rightly temper with the stars;
Yet in this one thing let me blame your Grace,
For choosing me when Clarence is in place.

CLARENCE. No, Warwick, thou art worthy of the sway,
To whom the heav'ns in thy nativity
Adjudg'd an olive branch and laurel crown,
As likely to be blest in peace and war;
And therefore I yield thee my free consent.

WARWICK. And I choose Clarence only for Protector.

KING HENRY. Warwick and Clarence, give me both your
    hands.
Now join your hands, and with your hands your hearts,
That no dissension hinder government.
I make you both Protectors of this land,
While I myself will lead a private life
And in devotion spend my latter days,
To sin's rebuke and my Creator's praise.

WARWICK. What answers Clarence to his sovereign's will?

CLARENCE. That he consents, if Warwick yield consent,
For on thy fortune I repose myself.

WARWICK. Why, then, though loath, yet must I be content.
We'll yoke together, like a double shadow
To Henry's body, and supply his place;
I mean, in bearing weight of government,
While he enjoys the honour and his ease.
And, Clarence, now then it is more than needful
Forthwith that Edward be pronounc'd a traitor,
And all his lands and goods confiscated.

CLARENCE. What else? And that succession be determin'd.
WARWICK. Ay, therein Clarence shall not want his part.
KING HENRY. But, with the first of all your chief affairs,
    Let me entreat—for I command no more—
    That Margaret your Queen and my son Edward
    Be sent for to return from France with speed;
    For till I see them here, by doubtful fear
    My joy of liberty is half eclips'd.
CLARENCE. It shall be done, my sovereign, with all speed.
KING HENRY. My Lord of Somerset, what youth is that,
    Of whom you seem to have so tender care?
SOMERSET. My liege, it is young Henry, Earl of Richmond.
KING HENRY. Come hither, England's hope.

                                [Lays his hand on his head]

    If secret powers
    Suggest but truth to my divining thoughts,
    This pretty lad will prove our country's bliss.
    His looks are full of peaceful majesty;
    His head by nature fram'd to wear a crown,
    His hand to wield a sceptre; and himself
    Likely in time to bless a regal throne.
    Make much of him, my lords; for this is he
    Must help you more than you are hurt by me.

                    Enter a POST

WARWICK. What news, my friend?
POST. That Edward is escaped from your brother
    And fled, as he hears since, to Burgundy.
WARWICK. Unsavoury news! But how made he escape?
POST. He was convey'd by Richard Duke of Gloucester
    And the Lord Hastings, who attended him
    In secret ambush on the forest side
    And from the Bishop's huntsmen rescu'd him;
    For hunting was his daily exercise.
WARWICK. My brother was too careless of his charge.
    But let us hence, my sovereign, to provide
    A salve for any sore that may betide.
          Exeunt all but SOMERSET, RICHMOND, *and* OXFORD
SOMERSET. My lord, I like not of this flight of Edward's;
    For doubtless Burgundy will yield him help,

And we shall have more wars befor't be long.
As Henry's late presaging prophecy
Did glad my heart with hope of this young Richmond,
So doth my heart misgive me, in these conflicts,
What may befall him to his harm and ours.
Therefore, Lord Oxford, to prevent the worst,
Forthwith we'll send him hence to Brittany,
Till storms be past of civil enmity.
OXFORD. Ay, for if Edward repossess the crown,
  'Tis like that Richmond with the rest shall down.
SOMERSET. It shall be so; he shall to Brittany.
  Come therefore, let's about it speedily.   *Exeunt*

SCENE 7

Before York

Flourish. Enter KING EDWARD, GLOUCESTER, HASTINGS,
and soldiers

KING EDWARD. Now, brother Richard, Lord Hastings, and
    the rest,
  Yet thus far fortune maketh us amends,
  And says that once more I shall interchange
  My waned state for Henry's regal crown.
  Well have we pass'd and now repass'd the seas,
  And brought desired help from Burgundy;
  What then remains, we being thus arriv'd
  From Ravenspurgh haven before the gates of York,
  But that we enter, as into our dukedom?
GLOUCESTER. The gates made fast! Brother, I like not this;
  For many men that stumble at the threshold
  Are well foretold that danger lurks within.
KING EDWARD. Tush, man, abodements must not now
    affright us.
  By fair or foul means we must enter in,
  For hither will our friends repair to us.
HASTINGS. My liege, I'll knock once more to summon them.

Enter, on the walls, the MAYOR OF YORK *and*
his BRETHREN

MAYOR. My lords, we were forewarned of your coming
    And shut the gates for safety of ourselves,
    For now we owe allegiance unto Henry.
KING EDWARD. But, Master Mayor, if Henry be your King,
    Yet Edward at the least is Duke of York.
MAYOR. True, my good lord; I know you for no less.
KING EDWARD. Why, and I challenge nothing but my duke-
    dom,
    As being well content with that alone.
GLOUCESTER. [*Aside*] But when the fox hath once got in his
    nose,
    He'll soon find means to make the body follow.
HASTINGS. Why, Master Mayor, why stand you in a doubt?
    Open the gates; we are King Henry's friends.
MAYOR. Ay, say you so? The gates shall then be open'd.
                             [*He descends*]
GLOUCESTER. A wise stout captain, and soon persuaded!
HASTINGS. The good old man would fain that all were well,
    So 'twere not long of him; but being ent'red,
    I doubt not, I, but we shall soon persuade
    Both him and all his brothers unto reason.

Enter, below, the MAYOR *and two* ALDERMEN

KING EDWARD. So, Master Mayor. These gates must not be
    shut
    But in the night or in the time of war.
    What! fear not, man, but yield me up the keys;
                           [*Takes his keys*]
    For Edward will defend the town and thee,
    And all those friends that deign to follow me.

March. Enter MONTGOMERY *with drum and soldiers*

GLOUCESTER. Brother, this is Sir John Montgomery,
    Our trusty friend, unless I be deceiv'd.
KING EDWARD. Welcome, Sir John! But why come you in
    arms?
MONTGOMERY. To help King Edward in his time of storm,
    As every loyal subject ought to do.
KING EDWARD. Thanks, good Montgomery; but we now
    forget

Our title to the crown, and only claim
Our dukedom till God please to send the rest.
MONTGOMERY. Then fare you well, for I will hence again.
  I came to serve a king and not a duke.
  Drummer, strike up, and let us march away.
                    [*The drum begins to march*]
KING EDWARD. Nay, stay, Sir John, a while, and we'll debate
  By what safe means the crown may be recover'd.
MONTGOMERY. What talk you of debating? In few words:
  If you'll not here proclaim yourself our King,
  I'll leave you to your fortune and be gone
  To keep them back that come to succour you.
  Why shall we fight, if you pretend no title?
GLOUCESTER. Why, brother, wherefore stand you on nice
    points?
KING EDWARD. When we grow stronger, then we'll make
    our claim;
  Till then 'tis wisdom to conceal our meaning.
HASTINGS. Away with scrupulous wit! Now arms must rule.
GLOUCESTER. And fearless minds climb soonest unto crowns.
  Brother, we will proclaim you out of hand;
  The bruit thereof will bring you many friends.
KING EDWARD. Then be it as you will; for 'tis my right,
  And Henry but usurps the diadem.
MONTGOMERY. Ay, now my sovereign speaketh like himself;
  And now will I be Edward's champion.
HASTINGS. Sound trumpet; Edward shall be here proclaim'd.
  Come, fellow soldier, make thou proclamation.
                    [*Gives him a paper. Flourish*]
SOLDIER. [*Reads*] 'Edward the Fourth, by the grace of God,
  King of England and France, and Lord of Ireland, &c.'
MONTGOMERY. And whoso'er gainsays King Edward's right,
  By this I challenge him to single fight.
                    [*Throws down his gauntlet*]
ALL. Long live Edward the Fourth!
KING EDWARD. Thanks, brave Montgomery, and thanks unto
    you all;
  If fortune serve me, I'll requite this kindness.
  Now for this night let's harbour here in York;
  And when the morning sun shall raise his car

Above the border of this horizon,
We'll forward towards Warwick and his mates;
For well I wot that Henry is no soldier.
Ah, froward Clarence, how evil it beseems thee
To flatter Henry and forsake thy brother!
Yet, as we may, we'll meet both thee and Warwick.
Come on, brave soldiers; doubt not of the day,
And, that once gotten, doubt not of large pay. *Exeunt*

SCENE 8

London. The palace

Flourish. Enter KING HENRY, WARWICK, MONTAGUE, CLARENCE, OXFORD, *and* EXETER

WARWICK. What counsel, lords? Edward from Belgia,
With hasty Germans and blunt Hollanders,
Hath pass'd in safety through the narrow seas
And with his troops doth march amain to London;
And many giddy people flock to him.
KING HENRY. Let's levy men and beat him back again.
CLARENCE. A little fire is quickly trodden out,
Which, being suffer'd, rivers cannot quench.
WARWICK. In Warwickshire I have true-hearted friends,
Not mutinous in peace, yet bold in war;
Those will I muster up, and thou, son Clarence,
Shalt stir up in Suffolk, Norfolk, and in Kent,
The knights and gentlemen to come with thee.
Thou, brother Montague, in Buckingham,
Northampton, and in Leicestershire, shalt find
Men well inclin'd to hear what thou command'st.
And thou, brave Oxford, wondrous well belov'd,
In Oxfordshire shalt muster up thy friends.
My sovereign, with the loving citizens,
Like to his island girt in with the ocean
Or modest Dian circled with her nymphs,
Shall rest in London till we come to him.
Fair lords, take leave and stand not to reply.
Farewell, my sovereign.

ACT IV. SCENE 8

KING HENRY. Farewell, my Hector and my Troy's true
    hope.
CLARENCE. In sign of truth, I kiss your Highness' hand.
KING HENRY. Well-minded Clarence, be thou fortunate!
MONTAGUE. Comfort, my lord; and so I take my leave.
OXFORD. [*Kissing the* KING's *hand*] And thus I seal my truth
    and bid adieu.
KING HENRY. Sweet Oxford, and my loving Montague,
  And all at once, once more a happy farewell.
WARWICK. Farewell, sweet lords; let's meet at Coventry.
                Exeunt all but the KING *and* EXETER
KING HENRY. Here at the palace will I rest a while.
  Cousin of Exeter, what thinks your lordship?
  Methinks the power that Edward hath in field
  Should not be able to encounter mine.
EXETER. The doubt is that he will seduce the rest.
KING HENRY. That's not my fear; my meed hath got me
    fame:
  I have not stopp'd mine ears to their demands,
  Nor posted off their suits with slow delays;
  My pity hath been balm to heal their wounds,
  My mildness hath allay'd their swelling griefs,
  My mercy dried their water-flowing tears;
  I have not been desirous of their wealth,
  Nor much oppress'd them with great subsidies,
  Nor forward of revenge, though they much err'd.
  Then why should they love Edward more than me?
  No, Exeter, these graces challenge grace;
  And, when the lion fawns upon the lamb,
  The lamb will never cease to follow him.
          [*Shout within* 'A Lancaster! A Lancaster!']
EXETER. Hark, hark, my lord! What shouts are these?

Enter KING EDWARD, GLOUCESTER, *and soldiers*

KING EDWARD. Seize on the shame-fac'd Henry, bear him
    hence;
  And once again proclaim us King of England.
  You are the fount that makes small brooks to flow.
  Now stops thy spring; my sea shall suck them dry,
  And swell so much the higher by their ebb.

753

Hence with him to the Tower: let him not speak.

Exeunt some with KING HENRY

And, lords, towards Coventry bend we our course,
Where peremptory Warwick now remains.
The sun shines hot; and, if we use delay,
Cold biting winter mars our hop'd-for hay.
GLOUCESTER. Away betimes, before his forces join,
And take the great-grown traitor unawares.
Brave warriors, march amain towards Coventry. *Exeunt*

ACT V. SCENE 1

Coventry

Enter WARWICK, *the* MAYOR OF COVENTRY, *two*
MESSENGERS, *and others upon the walls*

WARWICK. Where is the post that came from valiant Ox-
ford?
How far hence is thy lord, mine honest fellow?
FIRST MESSENGER. By this at Dunsmore, marching hither-
ward.
WARWICK. How far off is our brother Montague?
Where is the post that came from Montague?
SECOND MESSENGER. By this at Daintry, with a puissant
troop.

Enter SIR JOHN SOMERVILLE

WARWICK. Say, Somerville, what says my loving son?
And by thy guess how nigh is Clarence now?
SOMERVILLE. At Southam I did leave him with his forces,
And do expect him here some two hours hence.

[*Drum heard*]

WARWICK. Then Clarence is at hand; I hear his drum.
SOMERVILLE. It is not his, my lord; here Southam lies.
The drum your Honour hears marcheth from Warwick.
WARWICK. Who should that be? Belike unlook'd for friends.
SOMERVILLE. They are at hand, and you shall quickly know.

ACT V. SCENE 1

March. Flourish. Enter KING EDWARD, GLOUCESTER, *and soldiers*

KING EDWARD. Go, trumpet, to the walls, and sound a parle.
GLOUCESTER. See how the surly Warwick mans the wall.
WARWICK. O unbid spite! Is sportful Edward come?
  Where slept our scouts or how are they seduc'd
  That we could hear no news of his repair?
KING EDWARD. Now, Warwick, wilt thou ope the city gates,
  Speak gentle words, and humbly bend thy knee,
  Call Edward King, and at his hands beg mercy?
  And he shall pardon thee these outrages.
WARWICK. Nay, rather, wilt thou draw thy forces hence,
  Confess who set thee up and pluck'd thee down,
  Call Warwick patron, and be penitent?
  And thou shalt still remain the Duke of York.
GLOUCESTER. I thought, at least, he would have said the
    King;
  Or did he make the jest against his will?
WARWICK. Is not a dukedom, sir, a goodly gift?
GLOUCESTER. Ay, by my faith, for a poor earl to give.
  I'll do thee service for so good a gift.
WARWICK. 'Twas I that gave the kingdom to thy brother.
KING EDWARD. Why then 'tis mine, if but by Warwick's
    gift.
WARWICK. Thou art no Atlas for so great a weight;
  And, weakling, Warwick takes his gift again;
  And Henry is my King, Warwick his subject.
KING EDWARD. But Warwick's king is Edward's prisoner.
  And, gallant Warwick, do but answer this:
  What is the body when the head is off?
GLOUCESTER. Alas, that Warwick had no more forecast,
  But, whiles he thought to steal the single ten,
  The king was slily finger'd from the deck!
  You left poor Henry at the Bishop's palace,
  And ten to one you'll meet him in the Tower.
KING EDWARD. 'Tis even so; yet you are Warwick still.
GLOUCESTER. Come, Warwick, take the time; kneel down,
    kneel down.
  Nay, when? Strike now, or else the iron cools.

WARWICK. I had rather chop this hand off at a blow,
  And with the other fling it at thy face,
  Than bear so low a sail to strike to thee.
KING EDWARD. Sail how thou canst, have wind and tide thy
    friend,
  This hand, fast wound about thy coal-black hair,
  Shall, whiles thy head is warm and new cut off,
  Write in the dust this sentence with thy blood:
  'Wind-changing Warwick now can change no more.'

Enter OXFORD, *with drum and colours*

WARWICK. O cheerful colours! See where Oxford comes.
OXFORD. Oxford, Oxford, for Lancaster!
            [*He and his forces enter the city*]
GLOUCESTER. The gates are open, let us enter too.
KING EDWARD. So other foes may set upon our backs.
  Stand we in good array, for they no doubt
  Will issue out again and bid us battle;
  If not, the city being but of small defence,
  We'll quickly rouse the traitors in the same.
WARWICK. O, welcome, Oxford! for we want thy help.

Enter MONTAGUE, *with drum and colours*

MONTAGUE. Montague, Montague, for Lancaster!
            [*He and his forces enter the city*]
GLOUCESTER. Thou and thy brother both shall buy this
    treason
  Even with the dearest blood your bodies bear.
KING EDWARD. The harder match'd, the greater victory.
  My mind presageth happy gain and conquest.

Enter SOMERSET, *with drum and colours*

SOMERSET. Somerset, Somerset, for Lancaster!
            [*He and his forces enter the city*]
GLOUCESTER. Two of thy name, both Dukes of Somerset,
  Have sold their lives unto the house of York;
  And thou shalt be the third, if this sword hold.

Enter CLARENCE, *with drum and colours*

WARWICK. And lo where George of Clarence sweeps along,

Of force enough to bid his brother battle;
With whom an upright zeal to right prevails
More than the nature of a brother's love.

CLARENCE. Clarence, Clarence, for Lancaster!

KING EDWARD. Et tu Brute—wilt thou stab Cæsar too?
A parley, sirrah, to George of Clarence.

        [*Sound a parley.* RICHARD *and* CLARENCE *whisper*]

WARWICK. Come, Clarence, come. Thou wilt if Warwick
    call.

CLARENCE. [*Taking the red rose from his hat and throwing
    it at* WARWICK]
Father of Warwick, know you what this means?
Look here, I throw my infamy at thee.
I will not ruinate my father's house,
Who gave his blood to lime the stones together,
And set up Lancaster. Why, trowest thou, Warwick,
That Clarence is so harsh, so blunt, unnatural,
To bend the fatal instruments of war
Against his brother and his lawful King?
Perhaps thou wilt object my holy oath.
To keep that oath were more impiety
Than Jephtha when he sacrific'd his daughter.
I am so sorry for my trespass made
That, to deserve well at my brother's hands,
I here proclaim myself thy mortal foe;
With resolution whereso'er I meet thee—
As I will meet thee, if thou stir abroad—
To plague thee for thy foul misleading me.
And so, proud-hearted Warwick, I defy thee,
And to my brother turn my blushing cheeks.
Pardon me, Edward, I will make amends;
And, Richard, do not frown upon my faults,
For I will henceforth be no more unconstant.

KING EDWARD. Now welcome more, and ten times more
    belov'd,
Than if thou never hadst deserv'd our hate.

GLOUCESTER. Welcome, good Clarence; this is brother-like.

WARWICK. O passing traitor, perjur'd and unjust!

KING EDWARD. What, Warwick, wilt thou leave the town
    and fight?

Or shall we beat the stones about thine ears?

WARWICK. Alas, I am not coop'd here for defence!
　I will away towards Barnet presently
　And bid thee battle, Edward, if thou dar'st.

KING EDWARD. Yes, Warwick, Edward dares and leads the
　way.
　Lords, to the field; Saint George and victory!

Exeunt YORKISTS

[*March.* WARWICK *and his company follow*]

SCENE 2

A field of battle near Barnet

Alarum and excursions. Enter KING EDWARD, *bringing
forth* WARWICK, *wounded*

KING EDWARD. So, lie thou there. Die thou, and die our fear;
　For Warwick was a bug that fear'd us all.
　Now, Montague, sit fast; I seek for thee,
　That Warwick's bones may keep thine company.　　*Exit*

WARWICK. Ah, who is nigh? Come to me, friend or foe,
　And tell me who is victor, York or Warwick?
　Why ask I that? My mangled body shows,
　My blood, my want of strength, my sick heart shows,
　That I must yield my body to the earth
　And, by my fall, the conquest to my foe.
　Thus yields the cedar to the axe's edge,
　Whose arms gave shelter to the princely eagle,
　Under whose shade the ramping lion slept,
　Whose top-branch overpeer'd Jove's spreading tree
　And kept low shrubs from winter's pow'rful wind.
　These eyes, that now are dimm'd with death's black veil,
　Have been as piercing as the mid-day sun
　To search the secret treasons of the world;
　The wrinkles in my brows, now fill'd with blood,
　Were lik'ned oft to kingly sepulchres;
　For who liv'd King, but I could dig his grave?
　And who durst smile when Warwick bent his brow?
　Lo now my glory smear'd in dust and blood!

My parks, my walks, my manors, that I had,
Even now forsake me; and of all my lands
Is nothing left me but my body's length.
Why, what is pomp, rule, reign, but earth and dust?
And live we how we can, yet die we must.

Enter OXFORD *and* SOMERSET

SOMERSET. Ah, Warwick, Warwick! wert thou as we are,
  We might recover all our loss again.
  The Queen from France hath brought a puissant power;
  Even now we heard the news. Ah, couldst thou fly!
WARWICK. Why then, I would not fly. Ah, Montague,
  If thou be there, sweet brother, take my hand,
  And with thy lips keep in my soul a while!
  Thou lov'st me not; for, brother, if thou didst,
  Thy tears would wash this cold congealed blood
  That glues my lips and will not let me speak.
  Come quickly, Montague, or I am dead.
SOMERSET. Ah, Warwick! Montague hath breath'd his last;
  And to the latest gasp cried out for Warwick,
  And said 'Commend me to my valiant brother.'
  And more he would have said; and more he spoke,
  Which sounded like a clamour in a vault,
  That mought not be distinguish'd; but at last,
  I well might hear, delivered with a groan,
  'O farewell, Warwick!'
WARWICK. Sweet rest his soul! Fly, lords, and save your-
    selves:
  For Warwick bids you all farewell, to meet in heaven.
                                              [*Dies*]
OXFORD. Away, away, to meet the Queen's great power!
                          [*Here they bear away his body*]

SCENE 3

Another part of the field

Flourish. Enter KING EDWARD *in triumph; with*
GLOUCESTER, CLARENCE, *and the rest*

KING EDWARD. Thus far our fortune keeps an upward
  course,
  And we are grac'd with wreaths of victory.
  But in the midst of this bright-shining day
  I spy a black, suspicious, threat'ning cloud
  That will encounter with our glorious sun
  Ere he attain his easeful western bed—
  I mean, my lords, those powers that the Queen
  Hath rais'd in Gallia have arriv'd our coast
  And, as we hear, march on to fight with us.
CLARENCE. A little gale will soon disperse that cloud
  And blow it to the source from whence it came;
  Thy very beams will dry those vapours up,
  For every cloud engenders not a storm.
GLOUCESTER. The Queen is valued thirty thousand strong,
  And Somerset, with Oxford, fled to her.
  If she have time to breathe, be well assur'd
  Her faction will be full as strong as ours.
KING EDWARD. We are advertis'd by our loving friends
  That they do hold their course toward Tewksbury;
  We, having now the best at Barnet field,
  Will thither straight, for willingness rids way;
  And as we march our strength will be augmented
  In every county as we go along.
  Strike up the drum; cry 'Courage!' and away. *Exeunt*

SCENE 4

Plains near Tewksbury

Flourish. March. Enter QUEEN MARGARET, PRINCE
EDWARD, SOMERSET, OXFORD, *and soldiers*

QUEEN MARGARET. Great lords, wise men ne'er sit and wail
  their loss,

But cheerly seek how to redress their harms.
What though the mast be now blown overboard,
The cable broke, the holding-anchor lost,
And half our sailors swallow'd in the flood;
Yet lives our pilot still. Is't meet that he
Should leave the helm and, like a fearful lad,
With tearful eyes add water to the sea
And give more strength to that which hath too much;
Whiles, in his moan, the ship splits on the rock,
Which industry and courage might have sav'd?
Ah, what a shame! ah, what a fault were this!
Say Warwick was our anchor; what of that?
And Montague our top-mast; what of him?
Our slaught'red friends the tackles; what of these?
Why, is not Oxford here another anchor?
And Somerset another goodly mast?
The friends of France our shrouds and tacklings?
And, though unskilful, why not Ned and I
For once allow'd the skilful pilot's charge?
We will not from the helm to sit and weep,
But keep our course, though the rough wind say no,
From shelves and rocks that threaten us with wreck,
As good to chide the waves as speak them fair.
And what is Edward but a ruthless sea?
What Clarence but a quicksand of deceit?
And Richard but a ragged fatal rock?
All these the enemies to our poor bark.
Say you can swim; alas, 'tis but a while!
Tread on the sand; why, there you quickly sink.
Bestride the rock; the tide will wash you off,
Or else you famish—that's a threefold death.
This speak I, lords, to let you understand,
If case some one of you would fly from us,
That there's no hop'd-for mercy with the brothers
More than with ruthless waves, with sands, and rocks.
Why, courage then! What cannot be avoided
'Twere childish weakness to lament or fear.
PRINCE OF WALES. Methinks a woman of this valiant spirit
   Should, if a coward hear her speak these words,
   Infuse his breast with magnanimity

And make him naked foil a man-at-arms.
I speak not this as doubting any here;
For did I but suspect a fearful man,
He should have leave to go away betimes,
Lest in our need he might infect another
And make him of the like spirit to himself.
If any such be here—as God forbid!—
Let him depart before we need his help.

OXFORD. Women and children of so high a courage,
And warriors faint! Why, 'twere perpetual shame.
O brave young Prince! thy famous grandfather
Doth live again in thee. Long mayst thou live
To bear his image and renew his glories!

SOMERSET. And he that will not fight for such a hope,
Go home to bed and, like the owl by day,
If he arise, be mock'd and wond'red at.

QUEEN MARGARET. Thanks, gentle Somerset; sweet Oxford,
thanks.

PRINCE OF WALES. And take his thanks that yet hath nothing
else.

Enter a MESSENGER

MESSENGER. Prepare you, lords, for Edward is at hand
Ready to fight; therefore be resolute.

OXFORD. I thought no less. It is his policy
To haste thus fast, to find us unprovided.

SOMERSET. But he's deceiv'd; we are in readiness.

QUEEN MARGARET. This cheers my heart, to see your forwardness.

OXFORD. Here pitch our battle; hence we will not budge.

Flourish and march. Enter, at a distance, KING EDWARD,
GLOUCESTER, CLARENCE, *and soldiers*

KING EDWARD. Brave followers, yonder stands the thorny
wood
Which, by the heavens' assistance and your strength,
Must by the roots be hewn up yet ere night.
I need not add more fuel to your fire,
For well I wot ye blaze to burn them out.
Give signal to the fight, and to it, lords.

ACT V. SCENE 4

QUEEN MARGARET. Lords, knights, and gentlemen, what I
  should say
My tears gainsay; for every word I speak,
Ye see, I drink the water of my eye.
Therefore, no more but this: Henry, your sovereign,
Is prisoner to the foe; his state usurp'd,
His realm a slaughter-house, his subjects slain,
His statutes cancell'd, and his treasure spent;
And yonder is the wolf that makes this spoil.
You fight in justice. Then, in God's name, lords,
Be valiant, and give signal to the fight.
                    Alarum, retreat, excursions. Exeunt

SCENE 5

Another part of the field

Flourish. Enter KING EDWARD, GLOUCESTER, CLAR-
ENCE, *and forces, with* QUEEN MARGARET, OX-
FORD, *and* SOMERSET, *prisoners*

KING EDWARD. Now here a period of tumultuous broils.
  Away with Oxford to Hames Castle straight;
  For Somerset, off with his guilty head.
  Go, bear them hence; I will not hear them speak.
OXFORD. For my part, I'll not trouble thee with words.
SOMERSET. Nor I, but stoop with patience to my fortune.
                    Exeunt OXFORD *and* SOMERSET, *guarded*
QUEEN MARGARET. So part we sadly in this troublous world,
  To meet with joy in sweet Jerusalem.
KING EDWARD. Is proclamation made that who finds Edward
  Shall have a high reward, and he his life?
GLOUCESTER. It is; and lo where youthful Edward comes.

Enter soldiers, with PRINCE EDWARD

KING EDWARD. Bring forth the gallant; let us hear him speak.
  What, can so young a man begin to prick?
  Edward, what satisfaction canst thou make
  For bearing arms, for stirring up my subjects,
  And all the trouble thou hast turn'd me to?

763

PRINCE OF WALES. Speak like a subject, proud ambitious
York.
Suppose that I am now my father's mouth;
Resign thy chair, and where I stand kneel thou,
Whilst I propose the self-same words to thee
Which, traitor, thou wouldst have me answer to.
QUEEN MARGARET. Ah, that thy father had been so resolv'd!
GLOUCESTER. That you might still have worn the petticoat
And ne'er have stol'n the breech from Lancaster.
PRINCE OF WALES. Let Æsop fable in a winter's night;
His currish riddle sorts not with this place.
GLOUCESTER. By heaven, brat, I'll plague ye for that word.
QUEEN MARGARET. Ay, thou wast born to be a plague to
men.
GLOUCESTER. For God's sake, take away this captive scold.
PRINCE OF WALES. Nay, take away this scolding crookback
rather.
KING EDWARD. Peace, wilful boy, or I will charm your
tongue.
CLARENCE. Untutor'd lad, thou art too malapert.
PRINCE OF WALES. I know my duty; you are all undutiful.
Lascivious Edward, and thou perjur'd George,
And thou misshapen Dick, I tell ye all
I am your better, traitors as ye are;
And thou usurp'st my father's right and mine.
KING EDWARD. Take that, the likeness of this railer here.
[*Stabs him*]
GLOUCESTER. Sprawl'st thou? Take that, to end thy agony.
[*Stabs him*]
CLARENCE. And there's for twitting me with perjury.
[*Stabs him*]
QUEEN MARGARET. O, kill me too!
GLOUCESTER. Marry, and shall.   [*Offers to kill her*]
KING EDWARD. Hold, Richard, hold; for we have done too
much.
GLOUCESTER. Why should she live to fill the world with
words?
KING EDWARD. What, doth she swoon? Use means for her
recovery.
GLOUCESTER. Clarence, excuse me to the King my brother.

I'll hence to London on a serious matter;
Ere ye come there, be sure to hear some news.
CLARENCE. What? what?
GLOUCESTER. The Tower! the Tower!   *Exit*
QUEEN MARGARET. O Ned, sweet Ned, speak to thy mother,
    boy!
　Canst thou not speak? O traitors! murderers!
　They that stabb'd Cæsar shed no blood at all,
　Did not offend, nor were not worthy blame,
　If this foul deed were by to equal it.
　He was a man: this, in respect, a child;
　And men ne'er spend their fury on a child.
　What's worse than murderer, that I may name it?
　No, no, my heart will burst, an if I speak—
　And I will speak, that so my heart may burst.
　Butchers and villains! bloody cannibals!
　How sweet a plant have you untimely cropp'd!
　You have no children, butchers, if you had,
　The thought of them would have stirr'd up remorse.
　But if you ever chance to have a child,
　Look in his youth to have him so cut off
　As, deathsmen, you have rid this sweet young prince!
KING EDWARD. Away with her; go, bear her hence perforce.
QUEEN MARGARET. Nay, never bear me hence; dispatch me
    here.
　Here sheathe thy sword; I'll pardon thee my death.
　What, wilt thou not? Then, Clarence, do it thou.
CLARENCE. By heaven, I will not do thee so much ease.
QUEEN MARGARET. Good Clarence, do; sweet Clarence, do
    thou do it.
CLARENCE. Didst thou not hear me swear I would not do it?
QUEEN MARGARET. Ay, but thou usest to forswear thyself.
　'Twas sin before, but now 'tis charity.
　What! wilt thou not? Where is that devil's butcher,
　Hard-favour'd Richard? Richard, where art thou?
　Thou art not here. Murder is thy alms-deed;
　Petitioners for blood thou ne'er put'st back.
KING EDWARD. Away, I say; I charge ye bear her hence.
QUEEN MARGARET. So come to you and yours as to this
    prince.   *Exit, led out forcibly*

KING EDWARD. Where's Richard gone?
CLARENCE. To London, all in post; and, as I guess,
  To make a bloody supper in the Tower.
KING EDWARD. He's sudden, if a thing comes in his head.
  Now march we hence. Discharge the common sort
  With pay and thanks; and let's away to London
  And see our gentle queen how well she fares.
  By this, I hope, she hath a son for me.   *Exeunt*

SCENE 6

London. The Tower

Enter KING HENRY *and* GLOUCESTER *with the*
LIEUTENANT, *on the walls*

GLOUCESTER. Good day, my lord. What, at your book so
  hard?
KING HENRY. Ay, my good lord—my lord, I should say
  rather.
  'Tis sin to flatter; 'good' was little better.
  'Good Gloucester' and 'good devil' were alike,
  And both preposterous; therefore, not 'good lord.'
GLOUCESTER. Sirrah, leave us to ourselves; we must confer.
                                        Exit LIEUTENANT
KING HENRY. So flies the reckless shepherd from the wolf;
  So first the harmless sheep doth yield his fleece,
  And next his throat unto the butcher's knife.
  What scene of death hath Roscius now to act?
GLOUCESTER. Suspicion always haunts the guilty mind:
  The thief doth fear each bush an officer.
KING HENRY. The bird that hath been limed in a bush
  With trembling wings misdoubteth every bush;
  And I, the hapless male to one sweet bird,
  Have now the fatal object in my eye
  Where my poor young was lim'd, was caught, and kill'd.
GLOUCESTER. Why, what a peevish fool was that of Crete
  That taught his son the office of a fowl!
  And yet, for all his wings, the fool was drown'd.
KING HENRY. I, Dædalus; my poor boy, Icarus;

Thy father, Minos, that denied our course;
The sun that sear'd the wings of my sweet boy,
Thy brother Edward; and thyself, the sea
Whose envious gulf did swallow up his life.
Ah, kill me with thy weapon, not with words!
My breast can better brook thy dagger's point
Than can my ears that tragic history.
But wherefore dost thou come? Is't for my life?
GLOUCESTER. Think'st thou I am an executioner?
KING HENRY. A persecutor I am sure thou art.
If murdering innocents be executing,
Why, then thou are an executioner.
GLOUCESTER. Thy son I kill'd for his presumption.
KING HENRY. Hadst thou been kill'd when first thou didst
  presume,
Thou hadst not liv'd to kill a son of mine.
And thus I prophesy, that many a thousand
Which now mistrust no parcel of my fear,
And many an old man's sigh, and many a widow's,
And many an orphan's water-standing eye—
Men for their sons, wives for their husbands,
Orphans for their parents' timeless death—
Shall rue the hour that ever thou wast born.
The owl shriek'd at thy birth—an evil sign;
The night-crow cried, aboding luckless time;
Dogs howl'd, and hideous tempest shook down trees;
The raven rook'd her on the chimney's top,
And chatt'ring pies in dismal discords sung;
Thy mother felt more than a mother's pain,
And yet brought forth less than a mother's hope,
To wit, an indigest deformed lump,
Not like the fruit of such a goodly tree.
Teeth hadst thou in thy head when thou wast born,
To signify thou cam'st to bite the world;
And if the rest be true which I have heard,
Thou cam'st—
GLOUCESTER. I'll hear no more. Die, prophet, in thy speech.
                                          [*Stabs him*]
For this, amongst the rest, was I ordain'd.
KING HENRY. Ay, and for much more slaughter after this.

O, God forgive my sins and pardon thee! [*Dies*]
GLOUCESTER. What, will the aspiring blood of Lancaster
Sink in the ground? I thought it would have mounted.
See how my sword weeps for the poor King's death.
O, may such purple tears be always shed
From those that wish the downfall of our house!
If any spark of life be yet remaining,
Down, down to hell; and say I sent thee thither—
        [*Stabs him again*]
I, that have neither pity, love, nor fear.
Indeed, 'tis true that Henry told me of;
For I have often heard my mother say
I came into the world with my legs forward.
Had I not reason, think ye, to make haste
And seek their ruin that usurp'd our right?
The midwife wonder'd; and the women cried
'O, Jesus bless us, he is born with teeth!'
And so I was, which plainly signified
That I should snarl, and bite, and play the dog.
Then, since the heavens have shap'd my body so,
Let hell make crook'd my mind to answer it.
I have no brother, I am like no brother;
And this word 'love,' which greybeards call divine,
Be resident in men like one another,
And not in me! I am myself alone.
Clarence, beware; thou keep'st me from the light,
But I will sort a pitchy day for thee;
For I will buzz abroad such prophecies
That Edward shall be fearful of his life;
And then to purge his fear, I'll be thy death.
King Henry and the Prince his son are gone.
Clarence, thy turn is next, and then the rest;
Counting myself but bad till I be best.
I'll throw thy body in another room,
And triumph, Henry, in thy day of doom.
        Exit with the body

SCENE 7

London. The palace

Flourish. Enter KING EDWARD, QUEEN ELIZABETH, CLARENCE, GLOUCESTER, HASTINGS, NURSE *with the young* PRINCE, *and attendants*

KING EDWARD. Once more we sit in England's royal throne,
  Repurchas'd with the blood of enemies.
  What valiant foemen, like to autumn's corn,
  Have we mow'd down in tops of all their pride!
  Three Dukes of Somerset, threefold renown'd
  For hardy and undoubted champions;
  Two Cliffords, as the father and the son;
  And two Northumberlands—two braver men
  Ne'er spurr'd their coursers at the trumpet's sound;
  With them the two brave bears, Warwick and Montague,
  That in their chains fetter'd the kingly lion
  And made the forest tremble when they roar'd.
  Thus have we swept suspicion from our seat
  And made our footstool of security.
  Come hither, Bess, and let me kiss my boy.
  Young Ned, for thee thine uncles and myself
  Have in our armours watch'd the winter's night,
  Went all afoot in summer's scalding heat,
  That thou might'st repossess the crown in peace;
  And of our labours thou shalt reap the gain.
GLOUCESTER. [*Aside*] I'll blast his harvest if your head were
    laid;
  For yet I am not look'd on in the world.
  This shoulder was ordain'd so thick to heave;
  And heave it shall some weight or break my back.
  Work thou the way—and that shall execute.
KING EDWARD. Clarence and Gloucester, love my lovely
    queen;
  And kiss your princely nephew, brothers both.
CLARENCE. The duty that I owe unto your Majesty
  I seal upon the lips of this sweet babe.

KING EDWARD. Thanks, noble Clarence; worthy brother,
    thanks.
GLOUCESTER. And that I love the tree from whence thou
    sprang'st,
    Witness the loving kiss I give the fruit.
    [*Aside*] To say the truth, so Judas kiss'd his master
    And cried 'All hail!' when as he meant all harm.
KING EDWARD. Now am I seated as my soul delights,
    Having my country's peace and brothers' loves.
CLARENCE. What will your Grace have done with Margaret?
    Reignier, her father, to the King of France
    Hath pawn'd the Sicils and Jerusalem,
    And hither have they sent it for her ransom.
KING EDWARD. Away with her, and waft her hence to
    France.
    And now what rests but that we spend the time
    With stately triumphs, mirthful comic shows,
    Such as befits the pleasure of the court?
    Sound drums and trumpets. Farewell, sour annoy!
    For here, I hope, begins our lasting joy.   *Exeunt*

The Tragedy of
King Richard the Third

KING RICHARD THE THIRD

THERE emerges from the confusion and anarchy of the
Wars of the Roses the dominating figure of Richard the
Third. The early death of Edward the Fourth left his children without the protection necessary in so unsettled a time,
and his brother Richard, who has already shown himself in
3 *Henry VI* the most ruthless and unscrupulous of York's
sons, has before him the ideal situation for the exercise of his
powers. Shakespeare is now free to concentrate attention on
one leading figure throughout and give his History something of the form of his later tragedies in which the protagonist provides the centre of interest.

Fortunately for Shakespeare the historical ground for this
reign had been prepared in a very exceptional manner. About
1513, in the reign of Henry the Eighth, Sir Thomas More
wrote a brief account of Richard's reign. More was a boy
of seven or so when Richard was killed at Bosworth, but he
was brought up in the household of Cardinal Morton who
played an important part in the events that led Richard to
the throne and finally to his death. Morton figures in Shakespeare's play as the Bishop of Ely, and as he was one of the
principal agents in Richard's overthrow his memories of that
dangerous time must have been unusually vivid. More had
also the testimony of his father and other leading citizens of
London of his father's generation to draw on. From such
sources More gained a knowledge of the period that enabled
him to leave us with a picture of Richard that must always
remain the most authoritative historical presentation of this
remarkable man. Shakespeare's play follows More's account
as far as it goes, for More broke off his narrative just as
Morton is persuading Buckingham to desert Richard, the
dramatist often doing little more than transpose into stage
terms situations that More had already made dramatic.

Rastell, More's nephew, had printed More's account in
1557, having added here and there to it short passages taken
from a parallel Latin version, also by More, that broke off
at Richard's coronation. Shakespeare had Rastell's version be-

fore him in Holinshed's Chronicle. Shakespeare also used Hall's Chronicle which gives a version of More's story interpolated with material from Polydore Vergil. This historian, an Italian who spent some fifty years in England, wrote a Latin history of England in the reigns of Henry VII and his son; like More, he provided material that the Chroniclers found useful in their account of Richard's reign. More's history of the reign although unfinished and rounded off in the Chronicles from other sources provided the groundwork of Shakespeare's treatment of the character of the king. Like Plutarch's *Lives* More's *History* is more concerned with character than event or at least more concerned to dwell on human motive and disposition and their contribution to events than to chronicle the mere happenings themselves. Shakespeare took full advantage of the material at his disposal to paint a portrait of this arch-villain that in its vigour and incisiveness makes us realize the energy and purpose of the original.

Shakespeare follows the example of his source in emphasizing the blindness and overweening confidence of those who in their reckless pursuit of their own selfish schemes ignore the dangers that hang over them. Richard finds it easy to exploit the differences that embitter those who stand about the dying king with one another; and Hastings and Buckingham are through their vanity or greed turned into useful tools of villainy, only to be disposed of when their temper no longer serves for the further work in hand. But the man to whom these misguided creatures fall as a prey is in his turn the victim of a nemesis that awaits those who are blind to all claims of morality or humanity. To emphasize this aspect of the situation Shakespeare retains Queen Margaret, the wife of Henry the Sixth, as a kind of choric figure who comes and goes freely commenting on the misfortunes of her enemies and recalling their indifference in their hours of success to the violence she and her husband and son had known in their defeat. Like a fury sent to supervise the destruction of her enemies she rejoices in their deaths:

> I am hungry for revenge,
> And now I cloy me with beholding it.

Edward the Fourth is dead and with him his sons, Clarence
too, and the kindred of the queen. Richard remains but his
fate she foresees with a kind of prophetic fury:

> Richard yet lives, hell's black intelligencer;
> Only reserv'd their factor to buy souls
> And send them thither. But at hand, at hand,
> Ensues his piteous and unpitied end.
> Earth gapes, hell burns, fiends roar, saints pray,
> To have him suddenly convey'd from hence.
> Cancel his bond of life, dear God, I pray,
> That I may live and say 'The dog is dead.'

From More the dramatist took the cunning and hypocriti-
cal policy characteristic of the villain, and emphasized it with
touches here and there from other sources, most notably in
the scene where Richard appears between two bishops when
Buckingham directs the Lord Mayor, Aldermen and citizens
in their petition to Richard that he take over the government
and title of king. Here Richard plays the hypocrite with a
happy abandon that goes beyond More's reading of the
King's character. Hereford thought that the real Richard
was like More's something more cautious in his tactics than
Shakespeare's 'for he had to deceive or master the trained
political intelligence of England.' The trained political intelligence of England, however, cuts as sorry and impotent a
figure in More's story as in Shakespeare's drama. In Shakespeare the citizens see the game Richard is playing as clearly
as More's Londoners, but they are just as powerless to contest Richard's progress to the throne. Shakespeare's Richard
shows the cynical audacity that experience shows is often
such a deceiver's best resource; he beguiles the public with
their own clap-trap; assuming the forms that pass current for
morality and sound doctrine, he deceives the stupid and
dares the wiser sort to challenge his integrity.

KING EDWARD THE FOURTH

EDWARD, PRINCE OF WALES,
   afterwards KING EDWARD V ⎱ *sons to the King*
RICHARD, DUKE OF YORK ⎰

GEORGE, DUKE OF CLARENCE
RICHARD, DUKE OF GLOUCESTER, ⎱ *brothers to the King*
   afterwards KING RICHARD III ⎰

A YOUNG SON OF CLARENCE (*Edward, Earl of Warwick*)

HENRY, EARL OF RICHMOND, *afterwards* KING HENRY VII

CARDINAL BOURCHIER, ARCHBISHOP OF CANTERBURY

THOMAS ROTHERHAM, ARCHBISHOP OF YORK

JOHN MORTON, BISHOP OF ELY   DUKE OF BUCKINGHAM

DUKE OF NORFOLK

EARL OF SURREY, *his son*

EARL RIVERS, *brother to King Edward's Queen*

MARQUIS OF DORSET *and* LORD GREY, *her sons*

EARL OF OXFORD   LORD HASTINGS   LORD LOVEL

LORD STANLEY, *called also* EARL OF DERBY

SIR THOMAS VAUGHAN

SIR RICHARD RATCLIFF   SIR WILLIAM CATESBY

SIR JAMES TYRREL   SIR JAMES BLOUNT

SIR WALTER HERBERT   SIR WILLIAM BRANDON

SIR ROBERT BRAKENBURY, *Lieutenant of the Tower*

CHRISTOPHER URSWICK, *a priest*   LORD MAYOR OF LONDON

SHERIFF OF WILTSHIRE   HASTINGS, *a pursuivant*

TRESSEL *and* BERKELEY, *gentlemen attending on Lady Anne*

ELIZABETH, *Queen to King Edward IV*

MARGARET, *widow of King Henry VI*

DUCHESS OF YORK, *mother to King Edward IV*

LADY ANNE, *widow of Edward, Prince of Wales, son to King
   Henry VI; afterwards married to the Duke of Gloucester*

A YOUNG DAUGHTER OF CLARENCE (*Margaret Plantagenet,
   Countess of Salisbury*)

Ghosts, *of Richard's victims*

Lords, Gentlemen, *and* Attendants; Priest, Scrivener, Page,
   Bishops, Aldermen, Citizens, Soldiers, Messengers, Murderers, Keeper

SCENE: *England*

King Richard the Third

ACT I. SCENE 1

London. A street

Enter RICHARD, DUKE OF GLOUCESTER, *solus*

GLOUCESTER. Now is the winter of our discontent
    Made glorious summer by this sun of York;
    And all the clouds that lour'd upon our house
    In the deep bosom of the ocean buried.
    Now are our brows bound with victorious wreaths;
    Our bruised arms hung up for monuments;
    Our stern alarums chang'd to merry meetings,
    Our dreadful marches to delightful measures.
    Grim-visag'd war hath smooth'd his wrinkled front,
    And now, instead of mounting barbed steeds
    To fright the souls of fearful adversaries,
    He capers nimbly in a lady's chamber
    To the lascivious pleasing of a lute.
    But I—that am not shap'd for sportive tricks,
    Nor made to court an amorous looking-glass—
    I—that am rudely stamp'd, and want love's majesty
    To strut before a wanton ambling nymph—
    I—that am curtail'd of this fair proportion,
    Cheated of feature by dissembling nature,
    Deform'd, unfinish'd, sent before my time
    Into this breathing world scarce half made up,
    And that so lamely and unfashionable
    That dogs bark at me as I halt by them—
    Why, I, in this weak piping time of peace,
    Have no delight to pass away the time,
    Unless to spy my shadow in the sun
    And descant on mine own deformity.
    And therefore, since I cannot prove a lover
    To entertain these fair well-spoken days,

I am determined to prove a villain
And hate the idle pleasures of these days.
Plots have I laid, inductions dangerous,
By drunken prophecies, libels, and dreams,
To set my brother Clarence and the King
In deadly hate the one against the other;
And if King Edward be as true and just
As I am subtle, false, and treacherous,
This day should Clarence closely be mew'd up—
About a prophecy which says that G
Of Edward's heirs the murderer shall be.
Dive, thoughts, down to my soul. Here Clarence comes.

Enter CLARENCE, *guarded, and* BRAKENBURY

Brother, good day. What means this armed guard
That waits upon your Grace?
CLARENCE. His Majesty,
  Tend'ring my person's safety, hath appointed
  This conduct to convey me to th' Tower.
GLOUCESTER. Upon what cause?
CLARENCE. Because my name is George.
GLOUCESTER. Alack, my lord, that fault is none of yours:
  He should, for that, commit your godfathers.
  O, belike his Majesty hath some intent
  That you should be new-christ'ned in the Tower.
  But what's the matter, Clarence? May I know?
CLARENCE. Yea, Richard, when I know; for I protest
  As yet I do not; but, as I can learn,
  He hearkens after prophecies and dreams,
  And from the cross-row plucks the letter G,
  And says a wizard told him that by G
  His issue disinherited should be;
  And, for my name of George begins with G,
  It follows in his thought that I am he.
  These, as I learn, and such like toys as these
  Hath mov'd his Highness to commit me now.
GLOUCESTER. Why, this it is when men are rul'd by women:
  'Tis not the King that sends you to the Tower;
  My Lady Grey his wife, Clarence, 'tis she
  That tempers him to this extremity.

Was it not she and that good man of worship,
Antony Woodville, her brother there,
That made him send Lord Hastings to the Tower,
From whence this present day he is delivered?
We are not safe, Clarence; we are not safe.
CLARENCE. By heaven, I think there is no man is secure
But the Queen's kindred, and night-walking heralds
That trudge betwixt the King and Mistress Shore.
Heard you not what an humble suppliant
Lord Hastings was, for her delivery?
GLOUCESTER. Humbly complaining to her deity
Got my Lord Chamberlain his liberty.
I'll tell you what—I think it is our way,
If we will keep in favour with the King,
To be her men and wear her livery:
The jealous o'er-worn widow, and herself,
Since that our brother dubb'd them gentlewomen,
Are mighty gossips in our monarchy.
BRAKENBURY. I beseech your Graces both to pardon me:
His Majesty hath straitly given in charge
That no man shall have private conference,
Of what degree soever, with your brother.
GLOUCESTER. Even so; an't please your worship, Brakenbury,
You may partake of any thing we say:
We speak no treason, man; we say the King
Is wise and virtuous, and his noble queen
Well struck in years, fair, and not jealous;
We say that Shore's wife hath a pretty foot,
A cherry lip, a bonny eye, a passing pleasing tongue;
And that the Queen's kindred are made gentlefolks.
How say you, sir? Can you deny all this?
BRAKENBURY. With this, my lord, myself have naught to do.
GLOUCESTER. Naught to do with Mistress Shore! I tell thee,
fellow,
He that doth naught with her, excepting one,
Were best to do it secretly alone.
BRAKENBURY. What one, my lord?
GLOUCESTER. Her husband, knave! Wouldst thou betray me?
BRAKENBURY. I do beseech your Grace to pardon me, and
withal

Forbear your conference with the noble Duke.

CLARENCE. We know thy charge, Brakenbury, and will
obey.

GLOUCESTER. We are the Queen's abjects and must obey.
Brother, farewell; I will unto the King;
And whatsoe'er you will employ me in—
Were it to call King Edward's widow sister—
I will perform it to enfranchise you.
Meantime, this deep disgrace in brotherhood
Touches me deeper than you can imagine.

CLARENCE. I know it pleaseth neither of us well.

GLOUCESTER. Well, your imprisonment shall not be long;
I will deliver or else lie for you.
Meantime, have patience.

CLARENCE. I must perforce. Farewell.

       Exeunt CLARENCE, BRAKENBURY, *and guard*

GLOUCESTER. Go tread the path that thou shalt ne'er return.
Simple, plain Clarence, I do love thee so
That I will shortly send thy soul to heaven,
If heaven will take the present at our hands.
But who comes here? The new-delivered Hastings?

Enter LORD HASTINGS

HASTINGS. Good time of day unto my gracious lord!

GLOUCESTER. As much unto my good Lord Chamberlain!
Well are you welcome to the open air.
How hath your lordship brook'd imprisonment?

HASTINGS. With patience, noble lord, as prisoners must;
But I shall live, my lord, to give them thanks
That were the cause of my imprisonment.

GLOUCESTER. No doubt, no doubt; and so shall Clarence too;
For they that were your enemies are his,
And have prevail'd as much on him as you.

HASTINGS. More pity that the eagles should be mew'd
Whiles kites and buzzards prey at liberty.

GLOUCESTER. What news abroad?

HASTINGS. No news so bad abroad as this at home:
The King is sickly, weak, and melancholy,
And his physicians fear him mightily.

GLOUCESTER. Now, by Saint John, that news is bad indeed.

O, he hath kept an evil diet long
And overmuch consum'd his royal person!
'Tis very grievous to be thought upon.
Where is he? In his bed?
HASTINGS. He is.
GLOUCESTER. Go you before, and I will follow you.

Exit HASTINGS

He cannot live, I hope, and must not die
Till George be pack'd with posthorse up to heaven.
I'll in to urge his hatred more to Clarence
With lies well steel'd with weighty arguments;
And, if I fail not in my deep intent,
Clarence hath not another day to live;
Which done, God take King Edward to his mercy,
And leave the world for me to bustle in!
For then I'll marry Warwick's youngest daughter.
What though I kill'd her husband and her father?
The readiest way to make the wench amends
Is to become her husband and her father;
The which will I—not all so much for love
As for another secret close intent
By marrying her which I must reach unto.
But yet I run before my horse to market.
Clarence still breathes; Edward still lives and reigns;
When they are gone, then must I count my gains.   *Exit*

SCENE 2

London. Another street

Enter corpse of KING HENRY THE SIXTH, *with
halberds to guard it;* LADY ANNE *being the
mourner, attended by* TRESSEL *and* BERKELEY

ANNE. Set down, set down your honourable load—
If honour may be shrouded in a hearse;
Whilst I awhile obsequiously lament
Th' untimely fall of virtuous Lancaster.
Poor key-cold figure of a holy king!
Pale ashes of the house of Lancaster!

Thou bloodless remnant of that royal blood!
Be it lawful that I invocate thy ghost
To hear the lamentations of poor Anne,
Wife to thy Edward, to thy slaughtered son,
Stabb'd by the self-same hand that made these wounds.
Lo, in these windows that let forth thy life
I pour the helpless balm of my poor eyes.
O, cursed be the hand that made these holes!
Cursed the heart that had the heart to do it!
Cursed the blood that let this blood from hence!
More direful hap betide that hated wretch
That makes us wretched by the death of thee
Than I can wish to adders, spiders, toads,
Or any creeping venom'd thing that lives!
If ever he have child, abortive be it,
Prodigious, and untimely brought to light,
Whose ugly and unnatural aspect
May fright the hopeful mother at the view,
And that be heir to his unhappiness!
If ever he have wife, let her be made
More miserable by the death of him
Than I am made by my young lord and thee!
Come, now towards Chertsey with your holy load,
Taken from Paul's to be interred there;
And still as you are weary of this weight
Rest you, whiles I lament King Henry's corse.
                    [*The bearers take up the coffin*]

Enter GLOUCESTER

GLOUCESTER. Stay, you that bear the corse, and set it down.
ANNE. What black magician conjures up this fiend
    To stop devoted charitable deeds?
GLOUCESTER. Villains, set down the corse; or, by Saint Paul,
    I'll make a corse of him that disobeys!
FIRST GENTLEMAN. My lord, stand back, and let the coffin
    pass.
GLOUCESTER. Unmanner'd dog! Stand thou, when I com-
    mand.
    Advance thy halberd higher than my breast,
    Or, by Saint Paul, I'll strike thee to my foot

And spurn upon thee, beggar, for thy boldness.

[The bearers set down the coffin]

ANNE. What, do you tremble? Are you all afraid?
  Alas, I blame you not, for you are mortal,
  And mortal eyes cannot endure the devil.
  Avaunt, thou dreadful minister of hell!
  Thou hadst but power over his mortal body,
  His soul thou canst not have; therefore, be gone.
GLOUCESTER. Sweet saint, for charity, be not so curst.
ANNE. Foul devil, for God's sake, hence and trouble us not;
  For thou hast made the happy earth thy hell,
  Fill'd it with cursing cries and deep exclaims.
  If thou delight to view thy heinous deeds,
  Behold this pattern of thy butcheries.
  O, gentlemen, see, see! Dead Henry's wounds
  Open their congeal'd mouths and bleed afresh.
  Blush, blush, thou lump of foul deformity,
  For 'tis thy presence that exhales this blood
  From cold and empty veins where no blood dwells;
  Thy deeds inhuman and unnatural
  Provokes this deluge most unnatural.
  O God, which this blood mad'st, revenge his death!
  O earth, which this blood drink'st, revenge his death!
  Either, heav'n, with lightning strike the murd'rer dead;
  Or, earth, gape open wide and eat him quick,
  As thou dost swallow up this good king's blood,
  Which his hell-govern'd arm hath butchered.
GLOUCESTER. Lady, you know no rules of charity,
  Which renders good for bad, blessings for curses.
ANNE. Villain, thou knowest nor law of God nor man:
  No beast so fierce but knows some touch of pity.
GLOUCESTER. But I know none, and therefore am no beast.
ANNE. O wonderful, when devils tell the truth!
GLOUCESTER. More wonderful when angels are so angry.
  Vouchsafe, divine perfection of a woman,
  Of these supposed crimes to give me leave
  By circumstance but to acquit myself.
ANNE. Vouchsafe, diffus'd infection of a man,
  Of these known evils but to give me leave
  By circumstance to accuse thy cursed self.

GLOUCESTER. Fairer than tongue can name thee, let me have
  Some patient leisure to excuse myself.

ANNE. Fouler than heart can think thee, thou canst make
  No excuse current but to hang thyself.

GLOUCESTER. By such despair I should accuse myself.

ANNE. And by despairing shalt thou stand excused
  For doing worthy vengeance on thyself
  That didst unworthy slaughter upon others.

GLOUCESTER. Say that I slew them not?

ANNE. Then say they were not slain.
  But dead they are, and, devilish slave, by thee.

GLOUCESTER. I did not kill your husband.

ANNE. Why, then he is alive.

GLOUCESTER. Nay, he is dead, and slain by Edward's hands.

ANNE. In thy foul throat thou liest: Queen Margaret saw
  Thy murd'rous falchion smoking in his blood;
  The which thou once didst bend against her breast,
  But that thy brothers beat aside the point.

GLOUCESTER. I was provoked by her sland'rous tongue
  That laid their guilt upon my guiltless shoulders.

ANNE. Thou wast provoked by thy bloody mind,
  That never dream'st on aught but butcheries.
  Didst thou not kill this king?

GLOUCESTER. I grant ye.

ANNE. Dost grant me, hedgehog? Then, God grant me too
  Thou mayst be damned for that wicked deed!
  O, he was gentle, mild, and virtuous!

GLOUCESTER. The better for the King of Heaven, that hath
  him.

ANNE. He is in heaven, where thou shalt never come.

GLOUCESTER. Let him thank me that holp to send him
  thither,
  For he was fitter for that place than earth.

ANNE. And thou unfit for any place but hell.

GLOUCESTER. Yes, one place else, if you will hear me name it.

ANNE. Some dungeon.

GLOUCESTER. Your bed-chamber.

ANNE. Ill rest betide the chamber where thou liest!

GLOUCESTER. So will it, madam, till I lie with you.

ANNE. I hope so.

GLOUCESTER. I know so. But, gentle Lady Anne,
To leave this keen encounter of our wits,
And fall something into a slower method—
Is not the causer of the timeless deaths
Of these Plantagenets, Henry and Edward,
As blameful as the executioner?
ANNE. Thou wast the cause and most accurs'd effect.
GLOUCESTER. Your beauty was the cause of that effect—
Your beauty that did haunt me in my sleep
To undertake the death of all the world
So I might live one hour in your sweet bosom.
ANNE. If I thought that, I tell thee, homicide,
These nails should rend that beauty from my cheeks.
GLOUCESTER. These eyes could not endure that beauty's
wreck;
You should not blemish it if I stood by.
As all the world is cheered by the sun,
So I by that; it is my day, my life.
ANNE. Black night o'ershade thy day, and death thy life!
GLOUCESTER. Curse not thyself, fair creature; thou art both.
ANNE. I would I were, to be reveng'd on thee.
GLOUCESTER. It is a quarrel most unnatural,
To be reveng'd on him that loveth thee.
ANNE. It is a quarrel just and reasonable,
To be reveng'd on him that kill'd my husband.
GLOUCESTER. He that bereft thee, lady, of thy husband
Did it to help thee to a better husband.
ANNE. His better doth not breathe upon the earth.
GLOUCESTER. He lives that loves thee better than he could.
ANNE. Name him.
GLOUCESTER. Plantagenet.
ANNE. Why, that was he.
GLOUCESTER. The self-same name, but one of better nature.
ANNE. Where is he?
GLOUCESTER. Here. [*She spits at him*] Why dost thou spit
at me?
ANNE. Would it were mortal poison, for thy sake!
GLOUCESTER. Never came poison from so sweet a place.
ANNE. Never hung poison on a fouler toad.
Out of my sight! Thou dost infect mine eyes.

GLOUCESTER. Thine eyes, sweet lady, have infected mine.
ANNE. Would they were basilisks to strike thee dead!
GLOUCESTER. I would they were, that I might die at once;
For now they kill me with a living death.
Those eyes of thine from mine have drawn salt tears,
Sham'd their aspects with store of childish drops—
These eyes, which never shed remorseful tear,
No, when my father York and Edward wept
To hear the piteous moan that Rutland made
When black-fac'd Clifford shook his sword at him;
Nor when thy warlike father, like a child,
Told the sad story of my father's death,
And twenty times made pause to sob and weep
That all the standers-by had wet their cheeks
Like trees bedash'd with rain—in that sad time
My manly eyes did scorn an humble tear;
And what these sorrows could not thence exhale
Thy beauty hath, and made them blind with weeping.
I never sued to friend nor enemy;
My tongue could never learn sweet smoothing word;
But, now thy beauty is propos'd my fee,
My proud heart sues, and prompts my tongue to speak.
                    [*She looks scornfully at him*]
Teach not thy lip such scorn; for it was made
For kissing, lady, not for such contempt.
If thy revengeful heart cannot forgive,
Lo here I lend thee this sharp-pointed sword;
Which if thou please to hide in this true breast
And let the soul forth that adoreth thee,
I lay it naked to the deadly stroke,
And humbly beg the death upon my knee.
        [*He lays his breast open; she offers at it with his sword*]
Nay, do not pause; for I did kill King Henry—
But 'twas thy beauty that provoked me.
Nay, now dispatch; 'twas I that stabb'd young Edward—
But 'twas thy heavenly face that set me on.
                    [*She falls the sword*]
Take up the sword again, or take up me.
ANNE. Arise, dissembler; though I wish thy death,
I will not be thy executioner.

GLOUCESTER. Then bid me kill myself, and I will do it.
ANNE. I have already.
GLOUCESTER. That was in thy rage.
  Speak it again, and even with the word
  This hand, which for thy love did kill thy love,
  Shall for thy love kill a far truer love;
  To both their deaths shalt thou be accessary.
ANNE. I would I knew thy heart.
GLOUCESTER. 'Tis figur'd in my tongue.
ANNE. I fear me both are false.
GLOUCESTER. Then never was man true.
ANNE. Well, well, put up your sword.
GLOUCESTER. Say, then, my peace is made.
ANNE. That shalt thou know hereafter.
GLOUCESTER. But shall I live in hope?
ANNE. All men, I hope, live so.
GLOUCESTER. Vouchsafe to wear this ring.
ANNE. To take is not to give.   *[Puts on the ring]*
GLOUCESTER. Look how my ring encompasseth thy finger,
  Even so thy breast encloseth my poor heart;
  Wear both of them, for both of them are thine.
  And if thy poor devoted servant may
  But beg one favour at thy gracious hand,
  Thou dost confirm his happiness for ever.
ANNE. What is it?
GLOUCESTER. That it may please you leave these sad designs
  To him that hath most cause to be a mourner,
  And presently repair to Crosby House;
  Where—after I have solemnly interr'd
  At Chertsey monast'ry this noble king,
  And wet his grave with my repentant tears—
  I will with all expedient duty see you.
  For divers unknown reasons, I beseech you,
  Grant me this boon.
ANNE. With all my heart; and much it joys me too
  To see you are become so penitent.
  Tressel and Berkeley, go along with me.
GLOUCESTER. Bid me farewell.
ANNE. 'Tis more than you deserve;
  But since you teach me how to flatter you,

Imagine I have said farewell already.

Exeunt two Gentlemen *with* Lady Anne

Gloucester. Sirs, take up the corse.

Gentlemen. Towards Chertsey, noble lord?

Gloucester. No, to White Friars; there attend my coming.

Exeunt all but Gloucester

Was ever woman in this humour woo'd?
Was ever woman in this humour won?
I'll have her; but I will not keep her long.
What! I that kill'd her husband and his father—
To take her in her heart's extremest hate,
With curses in her mouth, tears in her eyes,
The bleeding witness of my hatred by;
Having God, her conscience, and these bars against me,
And I no friends to back my suit at all
But the plain devil and dissembling looks,
And yet to win her, all the world to nothing!
Ha!
Hath she forgot already that brave prince,
Edward, her lord, whom I, some three months since,
Stabb'd in my angry mood at Tewksbury?
A sweeter and a lovelier gentleman—
Fram'd in the prodigality of nature,
Young, valiant, wise, and no doubt right royal—
The spacious world cannot again afford;
And will she yet abase her eyes on me,
That cropp'd the golden prime of this sweet prince
And made her widow to a woeful bed?
On me, whose all not equals Edward's moiety?
On me, that halts and am misshapen thus?
My dukedom to a beggarly denier,
I do mistake my person all this while.
Upon my life, she finds, although I cannot,
Myself to be a marv'llous proper man.
I'll be at charges for a looking-glass,
And entertain a score or two of tailors
To study fashions to adorn my body.
Since I am crept in favour with myself,
I will maintain it with some little cost.
But first I'll turn yon fellow in his grave,

And then return lamenting to my love.
Shine out, fair sun, till I have bought a glass,
That I may see my shadow as I pass.   *Exit*

SCENE 3

London. The palace

Enter QUEEN ELIZABETH, LORD RIVERS, *and* LORD
GREY

RIVERS. Have patience, madam; there's no doubt his Majesty
Will soon recover his accustom'd health.
GREY. In that you brook it ill, it makes him worse;
Therefore, for God's sake, entertain good comfort,
And cheer his Grace with quick and merry eyes.
QUEEN ELIZABETH. If he were dead, what would betide on
me?
GREY. No other harm but loss of such a lord.
QUEEN ELIZABETH. The loss of such a lord includes all
harms.
GREY. The heavens have bless'd you with a goodly son
To be your comforter when he is gone.
QUEEN ELIZABETH. Ah, he is young; and his minority
Is put unto the trust of Richard Gloucester,
A man that loves not me, nor none of you.
RIVER. Is it concluded he shall be Protector?
QUEEN ELIZABETH. It is determin'd, not concluded yet;
But so it must be, if the King miscarry.

Enter BUCKINGHAM *and* DERBY

GREY. Here come the Lords of Buckingham and Derby.
BUCKINGHAM. Good time of day unto your royal Grace!
DERBY. God make your Majesty joyful as you have been.
QUEEN ELIZABETH. The Countess Richmond, good my Lord
of Derby,
To your good prayer will scarcely say amen.
Yet, Derby, notwithstanding she's your wife
And loves not me, be you, good lord, assur'd
I hate not you for her proud arrogance.

DERBY. I do beseech you, either not believe
   The envious slanders of her false accusers;
   Or, if she be accus'd on true report,
   Bear with her weakness, which I think proceeds
   From wayward sickness and no grounded malice.
QUEEN ELIZABETH. Saw you the King to-day, my Lord of
   Derby?
DERBY. But now the Duke of Buckingham and I
   Are come from visiting his Majesty.
QUEEN ELIZABETH. What likelihood of his amendment,
   lords?
BUCKINGHAM. Madam, good hope; his Grace speaks
   cheerfully.
QUEEN ELIZABETH. God grant him health! Did you confer
   with him?
BUCKINGHAM. Ay, madam; he desires to make atonement
   Between the Duke of Gloucester and your brothers,
   And between them and my Lord Chamberlain;
   And sent to warn them to his royal presence.
QUEEN ELIZABETH. Would all were well! But that will
   never be.
   I fear our happiness is at the height.

Enter GLOUCESTER, HASTINGS, *and* DORSET

GLOUCESTER. They do me wrong, and I will not endure it.
   Who is it that complains unto the King
   That I, forsooth, am stern and love them not?
   By holy Paul, they love his Grace but lightly
   That fill his ears with such dissentious rumours.
   Because I cannot flatter and look fair,
   Smile in men's faces, smooth, deceive, and cog,
   Duck with French nods and apish courtesy,
   I must be held a rancorous enemy.
   Cannot a plain man live and think no harm
   But thus his simple truth must be abus'd
   With silken, sly, insinuating Jacks?
GREY. To who in all this presence speaks your Grace?
GLOUCESTER. To thee, that hast nor honesty nor grace.
   When have I injur'd thee? when done thee wrong,
   Or thee, or thee, or any of your faction?

A plague upon you all! His royal Grace—
Whom God preserve better than you would wish!—
Cannot be quiet scarce a breathing while
But you must trouble him with lewd complaints.

QUEEN ELIZABETH. Brother of Gloucester, you mistake the
　　matter.
The King, on his own royal disposition
And not provok'd by any suitor else—
Aiming, belike, at your interior hatred
That in your outward action shows itself
Against my children, brothers, and myself—
Makes him to send that he may learn the ground.

GLOUCESTER. I cannot tell; the world is grown so bad
That wrens make prey where eagles dare not perch.
Since every Jack became a gentleman,
There's many a gentle person made a Jack.

QUEEN ELIZABETH. Come, come, we know your meaning,
　　brother Gloucester:
You envy my advancement and my friends';
God grant we never may have need of you!

GLOUCESTER. Meantime, God grants that I have need of you.
Our brother is imprison'd by your means,
Myself disgrac'd, and the nobility
Held in contempt; while great promotions
Are daily given to ennoble those
That scarce some two days since were worth a noble.

QUEEN ELIZABETH. By Him that rais'd me to this careful
　　height
From that contented hap which I enjoy'd,
I never did incense his Majesty
Against the Duke of Clarence, but have been
An earnest advocate to plead for him.
My lord, you do me shameful injury
Falsely to draw me in these vile suspects.

GLOUCESTER. You may deny that you were not the mean
Of my Lord Hastings' late imprisonment.

RIVERS. She may, my lord; for—

GLOUCESTER. She may, Lord Rivers? Why, who knows
　　not so?
She may do more, sir, than denying that:

She may help you to many fair preferments
And then deny her aiding hand therein,
And lay those honours on your high desert.
What may she not? She may—ay, marry, may she—
RIVERS. What, marry, may she?
GLOUCESTER. What, marry, may she? Marry with a king,
A bachelor, and a handsome stripling too.
Iwis your grandam had a worser match.
QUEEN ELIZABETH. My Lord of Gloucester, I have too long
borne
Your blunt upbraidings and your bitter scoffs.
By heaven, I will acquaint his Majesty
Of those gross taunts that oft I have endur'd.
I had rather be a country servant-maid
Than a great queen with this condition—
To be so baited, scorn'd, and stormed at.

Enter old QUEEN MARGARET, *behind*

Small joy have I in being England's Queen.
QUEEN MARGARET. And less'ned be that small, God, I be-
seech Him!
Thy honour, state, and seat, is due to me.
GLOUCESTER. What! Threat you me with telling of the
King?
Tell him and spare not. Look what I have said
I will avouch't in presence of the King.
I dare adventure to be sent to th' Tow'r.
'Tis time to speak—my pains are quite forgot.
QUEEN MARGARET. Out, devil! I do remember them too
well:
Thou kill'dst my husband Henry in the Tower,
And Edward, my poor son, at Tewksbury.
GLOUCESTER. Ere you were queen, ay, or your husband
king,
I was a pack-horse in his great affairs,
A weeder-out of his proud adversaries,
A liberal rewarder of his friends;
To royalize his blood I spent mine own.
QUEEN MARGARET. Ay, and much better blood than his or
thine.

GLOUCESTER. In all which time you and your husband Grey
 Were factious for the house of Lancaster;
 And, Rivers, so were you. Was not your husband
 In Margaret's battle at Saint Albans slain?
 Let me put in your minds, if you forget,
 What you have been ere this, and what you are;
 Withal, what I have been, and what I am.
QUEEN MARGARET. A murd'rous villain, and so still thou art.
GLOUCESTER. Poor Clarence did forsake his father, Warwick,
 Ay, and forswore himself—which Jesu pardon!—
QUEEN MARGARET. Which God revenge!
GLOUCESTER. To fight on Edward's party for the crown;
 And for his meed, poor lord, he is mewed up.
 I would to God my heart were flint like Edward's,
 Or Edward's soft and pitiful like mine.
 I am too childish-foolish for this world.
QUEEN MARGARET. Hie thee to hell for shame and leave this
  world,
 Thou cacodemon; there thy kingdom is.
RIVERS. My Lord of Gloucester, in those busy days
 Which here you urge to prove us enemies,
 We follow'd then our lord, our sovereign king.
 So should we you, if you should be our king.
GLOUCESTER. If I should be! I had rather be a pedlar.
 Far be it from my heart, the thought thereof!
QUEEN ELIZABETH. As little joy, my lord, as you suppose
 You should enjoy were you this country's king,
 As little joy you may suppose in me
 That I enjoy, being the Queen thereof.
QUEEN MARGARET. As little joy enjoys the Queen thereof;
 For I am she, and altogether joyless.
 I can no longer hold me patient.   [*Advancing*]
 Hear me, you wrangling pirates, that fall out
 In sharing that which you have pill'd from me.
 Which of you trembles not that looks on me?
 If not that, I am Queen, you bow like subjects,
 Yet that, by you depos'd, you quake like rebels?
 Ah, gentle villain, do not turn away!
GLOUCESTER. Foul wrinkled witch, what mak'st thou in my
  sight?

QUEEN MARGARET. But repetition of what thou hast marr'd,
That will I make before I let thee go.
GLOUCESTER. Wert thou not banished on pain of death?
QUEEN MARGARET. I was; but I do find more pain in ban-
  ishment
Than death can yield me here by my abode.
A husband and a son thou ow'st to me;
And thou a kingdom; all of you allegiance.
This sorrow that I have by right is yours;
And all the pleasures you usurp are mine.
GLOUCESTER. The curse my noble father laid on thee,
When thou didst crown his warlike brows with paper
And with thy scorns drew'st rivers from his eyes,
And then to dry them gav'st the Duke a clout
Steep'd in the faultless blood of pretty Rutland—
His curses then from bitterness of soul
Denounc'd against thee are all fall'n upon thee;
And God, not we, hath plagu'd thy bloody deed.
QUEEN ELIZABETH. So just is God to right the innocent.
HASTINGS. O, 'twas the foulest deed to slay that babe,
And the most merciless that e'er was heard of!
RIVERS. Tyrants themselves wept when it was reported.
DORSET. No man but prophesied revenge for it.
BUCKINGHAM. Northumberland, then present, wept to see it.
QUEEN MARGARET. What, were you snarling all before I
  came,
Ready to catch each other by the throat,
And turn you all your hatred now on me?
Did York's dread curse prevail so much with heaven
That Henry's death, my lovely Edward's death,
Their kingdom's loss, my woeful banishment,
Should all but answer for that peevish brat?
Can curses pierce the clouds and enter heaven?
Why then, give way, dull clouds, to my quick curses!
Though not by war, by surfeit die your king,
As ours by murder, to make him a king!
Edward thy son, that now is Prince of Wales,
For Edward our son, that was Prince of Wales,
Die in his youth by like untimely violence!
Thyself a queen, for me that was a queen,

Outlive thy glory, like my wretched self!
Long mayest thou live to wail thy children's death,
And see another, as I see thee now,
Deck'd in thy rights, as thou art stall'd in mine!
Long die thy happy days before thy death;
And, after many length'ned hours of grief,
Die neither mother, wife, nor England's Queen!
Rivers and Dorset, you were standers by,
And so wast thou, Lord Hastings, when my son
Was stabb'd with bloody daggers. God, I pray him,
That none of you may live his natural age,
But by some unlook'd accident cut off!

GLOUCESTER. Have done thy charm, thou hateful wither'd
hag.

QUEEN MARGARET. And leave out thee? Stay, dog, for thou
shalt hear me.
If heaven have any grievous plague in store
Exceeding those that I can wish upon thee,
O, let them keep it till thy sins be ripe,
And then hurl down their indignation
On thee, the troubler of the poor world's peace!
The worm of conscience still be-gnaw thy soul!
Thy friends suspect for traitors while thou liv'st,
And take deep traitors for thy dearest friends!
No sleep close up that deadly eye of thine,
Unless it be while some tormenting dream
Affrights thee with a hell of ugly devils!
Thou elvish-mark'd, abortive, rooting hog,
Thou that wast seal'd in thy nativity
The slave of nature and the son of hell,
Thou slander of thy heavy mother's womb,
Thou loathed issue of thy father's loins,
Thou rag of honour, thou detested—

GLOUCESTER. Margaret!

QUEEN MARGARET. Richard!

GLOUCESTER. Ha?

QUEEN MARGARET. I call thee not.

GLOUCESTER. I cry thee mercy then, for I did think
That thou hadst call'd me all these bitter names.

QUEEN MARGARET. Why, so I did, but look'd for no reply.

O, let me make the period to my curse!

GLOUCESTER. 'Tis done by me, and ends in—Margaret.

QUEEN ELIZABETH. Thus have you breath'd your curse
against yourself.

QUEEN MARGARET. Poor painted queen, vain flourish of my
fortune!
Why strew'st thou sugar on that bottled spider
Whose deadly web ensnareth thee about?
Fool, fool! thou whet'st a knife to kill thyself.
The day will come that thou shalt wish for me
To help thee curse this poisonous bunch-back'd toad.

HASTINGS. False-boding woman, end thy frantic curse,
Lest to thy harm thou move our patience.

QUEEN MARGARET. Foul shame upon you! you have all
mov'd mine.

RIVERS. Were you well serv'd, you would be taught your
duty.

QUEEN MARGARET. To serve me well you all should do me
duty,
Teach me to be your queen and you my subjects.
O, serve me well, and teach yourselves that duty!

DORSET. Dispute not with her; she is lunatic.

QUEEN MARGARET. Peace, Master Marquis, you are malapert;
Your fire-new stamp of honour is scarce current.
O, that your young nobility could judge
What 'twere to lose it and be miserable!
They that stand high have many blasts to shake them,
And if they fall they dash themselves to pieces.

GLOUCESTER. Good counsel, marry; learn it, learn it, Marquis.

DORSET. It touches you, my lord, as much as me.

GLOUCESTER. Ay, and much more; but I was born so high,
Our aery buildeth in the cedar's top,
And dallies with the wind, and scorns the sun.

QUEEN MARGARET. And turns the sun to shade—alas! alas!
Witness my son, now in the shade of death,
Whose bright out-shining beams thy cloudy wrath
Hath in eternal darkness folded up.
Your aery buildeth in our aery's nest.
O God that seest it, do not suffer it;
As it is won with blood, lost be it so!

BUCKINGHAM. Peace, peace, for shame, if not for charity!
QUEEN MARGARET. Urge neither charity nor shame to me.
  Uncharitably with me have you dealt,
  And shamefully my hopes by you are butcher'd.
  My charity is outrage, life my shame;
  And in that shame still live my sorrow's rage!
BUCKINGHAM. Have done, have done.
QUEEN MARGARET. O princely Buckingham, I'll kiss thy hand
  In sign of league and amity with thee.
  Now fair befall thee and thy noble house!
  Thy garments are not spotted with our blood,
  Nor thou within the compass of my curse.
BUCKINGHAM. Nor no one here; for curses never pass
  The lips of those that breathe them in the air.
QUEEN MARGARET. I will not think but they ascend the sky
  And there awake God's gentle-sleeping peace.
  O Buckingham, take heed of yonder dog!
  Look when he fawns, he bites; and when he bites,
  His venom tooth will rankle to the death:
  Have not to do with him, beware of him;
  Sin, death, and hell, have set their marks on him,
  And all their ministers attend on him.
GLOUCESTER. What doth she say, my Lord of Buckingham?
BUCKINGHAM. Nothing that I respect, my gracious lord.
QUEEN MARGARET. What, dost thou scorn me for my gentle counsel,
  And soothe the devil that I warn thee from?
  O, but remember this another day,
  When he shall split thy very heart with sorrow,
  And say poor Margaret was a prophetess!
  Live each of you the subjects to his hate,
  And he to yours, and all of you to God's!   *Exit*
BUCKINGHAM. My hair doth stand an end to hear her curses.
RIVERS. And so doth mine. I muse why she's at liberty.
GLOUCESTER. I cannot blame her; by God's holy Mother,
  She hath had too much wrong; and I repent
  My part thereof that I have done to her.
QUEEN ELIZABETH. I never did her any to my knowledge.
GLOUCESTER. Yet you have all the vantage of her wrong.

I was too hot to do somebody good
That is too cold in thinking of it now.
Marry, as for Clarence, he is well repaid;
He is frank'd up to fatting for his pains;
God pardon them that are the cause thereof!
RIVERS. A virtuous and a Christian-like conclusion,
    To pray for them that have done scathe to us!
GLOUCESTER. So do I ever—[*Aside*] being well advis'd;
    For had I curs'd now, I had curs'd myself.

Enter CATESBY

CATESBY. Madam, his Majesty doth call for you,
    And for your Grace, and you, my gracious lords.
QUEEN ELIZABETH. Catesby, I come. Lords, will you go
    with me?
RIVERS. We wait upon your Grace.
                              Exeunt all but GLOUCESTER
GLOUCESTER. I do the wrong, and first begin to brawl.
    The secret mischiefs that I set abroach
    I lay unto the grievous charge of others.
    Clarence, who I indeed have cast in darkness,
    I do beweep to many simple gulls;
    Namely, to Derby, Hastings, Buckingham;
    And tell them 'tis the Queen and her allies
    That stir the King against the Duke my brother.
    Now they believe it, and withal whet me
    To be reveng'd on Rivers, Dorset, Grey;
    But then I sigh and, with a piece of Scripture,
    Tell them that God bids us do good for evil.
    And thus I clothe my naked villainy
    With odd old ends stol'n forth of holy writ,
    And seem a saint when most I play the devil.

Enter two MURDERERS

    But, soft, here come my executioners.
    How now, my hardy stout resolved mates!
    Are you now going to dispatch this thing?
FIRST MURDERER. We are, my lord, and come to have the
    warrant,
    That we may be admitted where he is.

GLOUCESTER. Well thought upon; I have it here about me.
                                          [*Gives the warrant*]
  When you have done, repair to Crosby Place.
  But, sirs, be sudden in the execution,
  Withal obdurate, do not hear him plead;
  For Clarence is well-spoken, and perhaps
  May move your hearts to pity, if you mark him.
FIRST MURDERER. Tut, tut, my lord, we will not stand to
    prate;
  Talkers are no good doers. Be assur'd
  We go to use our hands and not our tongues.
GLOUCESTER. Your eyes drop millstones when fools' eyes fall
    tears.
  I like you, lads; about your business straight;
  Go, go, dispatch.
FIRST MURDERER. We will, my noble lord.   *Exeunt*

SCENE 4

London. The Tower

Enter CLARENCE *and* KEEPER

KEEPER. Why looks your Grace so heavily to-day?
CLARENCE. O, I have pass'd a miserable night,
  So full of fearful dreams, of ugly sights,
  That, as I am a Christian faithful man,
  I would not spend another such a night
  Though 'twere to buy a world of happy days—
  So full of dismal terror was the time!
KEEPER. What was your dream, my lord? I pray you
    tell me.
CLARENCE. Methoughts that I had broken from the Tower
  And was embark'd to cross to Burgundy;
  And in my company my brother Gloucester,
  Who from my cabin tempted me to walk
  Upon the hatches. Thence we look'd toward England,
  And cited up a thousand heavy times,
  During the wars of York and Lancaster,
  That had befall'n us. As we pac'd along

Upon the giddy footing of the hatches,
Methought that Gloucester stumbled, and in falling
Struck me, that thought to stay him, overboard
Into the tumbling billows of the main.
O Lord, methought what pain it was to drown,
What dreadful noise of waters in my ears,
What sights of ugly death within my eyes!
Methoughts I saw a thousand fearful wrecks,
A thousand men that fishes gnaw'd upon,
Wedges of gold, great anchors, heaps of pearl,
Inestimable stones, unvalued jewels,
All scatt'red in the bottom of the sea;
Some lay in dead men's skulls, and in the holes
Where eyes did once inhabit there were crept,
As 'twere in scorn of eyes, reflecting gems,
That woo'd the slimy bottom of the deep
And mock'd the dead bones that lay scatt'red by.
KEEPER. Had you such leisure in the time of death
　To gaze upon these secrets of the deep?
CLARENCE. Methought I had; and often did I strive
　To yield the ghost, but still the envious flood
　Stopp'd in my soul and would not let it forth
　To find the empty, vast, and wand'ring air;
　But smother'd it within my panting bulk,
　Who almost burst to belch it in the sea.
KEEPER. Awak'd you not in this sore agony?
CLARENCE. No, no, my dream was lengthen'd after life.
　O, then began the tempest to my soul!
　I pass'd, methought, the melancholy flood
　With that sour ferryman which poets write of,
　Unto the kingdom of perpetual night.
　The first that there did greet my stranger soul
　Was my great father-in-law, renowned Warwick,
　Who spake aloud 'What scourge for perjury
　Can this dark monarchy afford false Clarence?'
　And so he vanish'd. Then came wand'ring by
　A shadow like an angel, with bright hair
　Dabbled in blood, and he shriek'd out aloud
　'Clarence is come—false, fleeting, perjur'd Clarence,
　That stabb'd me in the field by Tewksbury.

Seize on him, Furies, take him unto torment!'
With that, methoughts, a legion of foul fiends
Environ'd me, and howled in mine ears
Such hideous cries that, with the very noise,
I trembling wak'd, and for a season after
Could not believe but that I was in hell,
Such terrible impression made my dream.

KEEPER. No marvel, lord, though it affrighted you;
I am afraid, methinks, to hear you tell it.

CLARENCE. Ah, Keeper, Keeper, I have done these things
That now give evidence against my soul
For Edward's sake, and see how he requites me!
O God! If my deep prayers cannot appease Thee,
But Thou wilt be aveng'd on my misdeeds,
Yet execute Thy wrath in me alone;
O, spare my guiltless wife and my poor children!
Keeper, I prithee sit by me awhile;
My soul is heavy, and I fain would sleep.

KEEPER. I will, my lord. God give your Grace good rest.

[CLARENCE *sleeps*]

Enter BRAKENBURY *the Lieutenant*

BRAKENBURY. Sorrow breaks seasons and reposing hours,
Makes the night morning and the noontide night.
Princes have but their titles for their glories,
An outward honour for an inward toil;
And for unfelt imaginations
They often feel a world of restless cares,
So that between their titles and low name
There's nothing differs but the outward fame.

Enter the two MURDERERS

FIRST MURDERER. Ho! who's here?

BRAKENBURY. What wouldst thou, fellow, and how cam'st
thou hither?

FIRST MURDERER. I would speak with Clarence, and I came
hither on my legs.

BRAKENBURY. What, so brief?

SECOND MURDERER. 'Tis better, sir, than to be tedious. Let
him see our commission and talk no more.

[B<small>RAKENBURY</small> *reads it*]

B<small>RAKENBURY</small>. I am, in this, commanded to deliver
The noble Duke of Clarence to your hands.
I will not reason what is meant hereby,
Because I will be guiltless from the meaning.
There lies the Duke asleep; and there the keys.
I'll to the King and signify to him
That thus I have resign'd to you my charge.

F<small>IRST</small> M<small>URDERER</small>. You may, sir; 'tis a point of wisdom. Fare
you well.   *Exeunt* B<small>RAKENBURY</small> *and* K<small>EEPER</small>

S<small>ECOND</small> M<small>URDERER</small>. What, shall I stab him as he sleeps?

F<small>IRST</small> M<small>URDERER</small>. No; he'll say 'twas done cowardly, when
he wakes.

S<small>ECOND</small> M<small>URDERER</small>. Why, he shall never wake until the great
judgment-day.

F<small>IRST</small> M<small>URDERER</small>. Why, then he'll say we stabb'd him
sleeping.

S<small>ECOND</small> M<small>URDERER</small>. The urging of that word judgment hath
bred a kind of remorse in me.

F<small>IRST</small> M<small>URDERER</small>. What, art thou afraid?

S<small>ECOND</small> M<small>URDERER</small>. Not to kill him, having a warrant; but to
be damn'd for killing him, from the which no warrant can
defend me.

F<small>IRST</small> M<small>URDERER</small>. I thought thou hadst been resolute.

S<small>ECOND</small> M<small>URDERER</small>. So I am, to let him live.

F<small>IRST</small> M<small>URDERER</small>. I'll back to the Duke of Gloucester and
tell him so.

S<small>ECOND</small> M<small>URDERER</small>. Nay, I prithee, stay a little. I hope this
passionate humour of mine will change; it was wont to
hold me but while one tells twenty.

F<small>IRST</small> M<small>URDERER</small>. How dost thou feel thyself now?

S<small>ECOND</small> M<small>URDERER</small>. Faith, some certain dregs of conscience
are yet within me.

F<small>IRST</small> M<small>URDERER</small>. Remember our reward, when the deed's
done.

S<small>ECOND</small> M<small>URDERER</small>. Zounds, he dies; I had forgot the reward.

F<small>IRST</small> M<small>URDERER</small>. Where's thy conscience now?

S<small>ECOND</small> M<small>URDERER</small>. O, in the Duke of Gloucester's purse!

F<small>IRST</small> M<small>URDERER</small>. When he opens his purse to give us our
reward, thy conscience flies out.

SECOND MURDERER. 'Tis no matter; let it go; there's few or none will entertain it.

FIRST MURDERER. What if it come to thee again?

SECOND MURDERER. I'll not meddle with it—it makes a man a coward: a man cannot steal, but it accuseth him; a man cannot swear, but it checks him; a man cannot lie with his neighbour's wife, but it detects him. 'Tis a blushing shame-fac'd spirit that mutinies in a man's bosom; it fills a man full of obstacles: it made me once restore a purse of gold that—by chance I found. It beggars any man that keeps it. It is turn'd out of towns and cities for a dangerous thing; and every man that means to live well endeavours to trust to himself and live without it.

FIRST MURDERER. Zounds, 'tis even now at my elbow, per-suading me not to kill the Duke.

SECOND MURDERER. Take the devil in thy mind and believe him not; he would insinuate with thee but to make thee sigh.

FIRST MURDERER. I am strong-fram'd; he cannot prevail with me.

SECOND MURDERER. Spoke like a tall man that respects thy reputation. Come, shall we fall to work?

FIRST MURDERER. Take him on the costard with the hilts of thy sword, and then chop him in the malmsey-butt in the next room.

SECOND MURDERER. O excellent device! and make a sop of him.

FIRST MURDERER. Soft! he wakes.

SECOND MURDERER. Strike!

FIRST MURDERER. No, we'll reason with him.

CLARENCE. Where art thou, Keeper? Give me a cup of wine.

SECOND MURDERER. You shall have wine enough, my lord, anon.

CLARENCE. In God's name, what art thou?

FIRST MURDERER. A man, as you are.

CLARENCE. But not as I am, royal.

SECOND MURDERER. Nor you as we are, loyal.

CLARENCE. Thy voice is thunder, but thy looks are humble.

FIRST MURDERER. My voice is now the King's, my looks mine own.

CLARENCE. How darkly and how deadly dost thou speak!
  Your eyes do menace me. Why look you pale?
  Who sent you hither? Wherefore do you come?
SECOND MURDERER. To, to, to—
CLARENCE. To murder me?
BOTH MURDERERS. Ay, ay.
CLARENCE. You scarcely have the hearts to tell me so,
  And therefore cannot have the hearts to do it.
  Wherein, my friends, have I offended you?
FIRST MURDERER. Offended us you have not, but the King.
CLARENCE. I shall be reconcil'd to him again.
SECOND MURDERER. Never, my lord; therefore prepare to die.
CLARENCE. Are you drawn forth among a world of men
  To slay the innocent? What is my offence?
  Where is the evidence that doth accuse me?
  What lawful quest have given their verdict up
  Unto the frowning judge, or who pronounc'd
  The bitter sentence of poor Clarence' death?
  Before I be convict by course of law,
  To threaten me with death is most unlawful.
  I charge you, as you hope to have redemption
  By Christ's dear blood shed for our grievous sins,
  That you depart and lay no hands on me.
  The deed you undertake is damnable.
FIRST MURDERER. What we will do, we do upon command.
SECOND MURDERER. And he that hath commanded is our
  king.
CLARENCE. Erroneous vassals! the great King of kings
  Hath in the tables of his law commanded
  That thou shalt do no murder. Will you then
  Spurn at his edict and fulfil a man's?
  Take heed; for he holds vengeance in his hand
  To hurl upon their heads that break his law.
SECOND MURDERER. And that same vengeance doth he hurl
  on thee
  For false forswearing, and for murder too;
  Thou didst receive the sacrament to fight
  In quarrel of the house of Lancaster.
FIRST MURDERER. And like a traitor to the name of God
  Didst break that vow; and with thy treacherous blade

Unripp'dst the bowels of thy sov'reign's son.

SECOND MURDERER. Whom thou wast sworn to cherish and
defend.

FIRST MURDERER. How canst thou urge God's dreadful law
to us,
When thou hast broke it in such dear degree?

CLARENCE. Alas! for whose sake did I that ill deed?
For Edward, for my brother, for his sake.
He sends you not to murder me for this,
For in that sin he is as deep as I.
If God will be avenged for the deed,
O, know you yet He doth it publicly.
Take not the quarrel from His pow'rful arm;
He needs no indirect or lawless course
To cut off those that have offended Him.

FIRST MURDERER. Who made thee then a bloody minister
When gallant-springing brave Plantagenet,
That princely novice, was struck dead by thee?

CLARENCE. My brother's love, the devil, and my rage.

FIRST MURDERER. Thy brother's love, our duty, and thy
faults,
Provoke us hither now to slaughter thee.

CLARENCE. If you do love my brother, hate not me;
I am his brother, and I love him well.
If you are hir'd for meed, go back again,
And I will send you to my brother Gloucester,
Who shall reward you better for my life
Than Edward will for tidings of my death.

SECOND MURDERER. You are deceiv'd: your brother Gloucester hates you.

CLARENCE. O, no, he loves me, and he holds me dear.
Go you to him from me.

FIRST MURDERER. Ay, so we will.

CLARENCE. Tell him when that our princely father York
Bless'd his three sons with his victorious arm
And charg'd us from his soul to love each other,
He little thought of this divided friendship.
Bid Gloucester think of this, and he will weep.

FIRST MURDERER. Ay, millstones; as he lesson'd us to weep.

CLARENCE. O, do not slander him, for he is kind.

FIRST MURDERER. Right, as snow in harvest. Come, you deceive yourself:
'Tis he that sends us to destroy you here.
CLARENCE. It cannot be; for he bewept my fortune
And hugg'd me in his arms, and swore with sobs
That he would labour my delivery.
FIRST MURDERER. Why, so he doth, when he delivers you
From this earth's thraldom to the joys of heaven.
SECOND MURDERER. Make peace with God, for you must die,
my lord.
CLARENCE. Have you that holy feeling in your souls
To counsel me to make my peace with God,
And are you yet to your own souls so blind
That you will war with God by murd'ring me?
O, sirs, consider: they that set you on
To do this deed will hate you for the deed.
SECOND MURDERER. What shall we do?
CLARENCE. Relent, and save your souls.
FIRST MURDERER. Relent! No, 'tis cowardly and womanish.
CLARENCE. Not to relent is beastly, savage, devilish.
Which of you, if you were a prince's son,
Being pent from liberty as I am now,
If two such murderers as yourselves came to you,
Would not entreat for life?
My friend, I spy some pity in thy looks;
O, if thine eye be not a flatterer,
Come thou on my side and entreat for me—
As you would beg were you in my distress.
A begging prince what beggar pities not?
SECOND MURDERER. Look behind you, my lord.
FIRST MURDERER. [*Stabbing him*] Take that, and that. If all
this will not do,
I'll drown you in the malmsey-butt within.
Exit with the body
SECOND MURDERER. A bloody deed, and desperately dispatch'd!
How fain, like Pilate, would I wash my hands
Of this most grievous murder!

Re-enter FIRST MURDERER

FIRST MURDERER. How now, what mean'st thou that thou
  help'st me not?
  By heavens, the Duke shall know how slack you have
  been!
SECOND MURDERER. I would he knew that I had sav'd his
  brother!
  Take thou the fee, and tell him what I say;
  For I repent me that the Duke is slain.   *Exit*
FIRST MURDERER. So do not I. Go, coward as thou art.
  Well, I'll go hide the body in some hole,
  Till that the Duke give order for his burial;
  And when I have my meed, I will away;
  For this will out, and then I must not stay.   *Exit*

ACT II. SCENE 1

London. The palace

Flourish. Enter KING EDWARD *sick,* QUEEN ELIZ-
ABETH, DORSET, RIVERS, HASTINGS, BUCKINGHAM,
GREY, *and others*

KING EDWARD. Why, so. Now have I done a good day's
  work.
  You peers, continue this united league.
  I every day expect an embassage
  From my Redeemer to redeem me hence;
  And more at peace my soul shall part to heaven,
  Since I have made my friends at peace on earth.
  Hastings and Rivers, take each other's hand;
  Dissemble not your hatred, swear your love.
RIVERS. By heaven, my soul is purg'd from grudging hate;
  And with my hand I seal my true heart's love.
HASTINGS. So thrive I, as I truly swear the like!
KING EDWARD. Take heed you dally not before your king;
  Lest He that is the supreme King of kings
  Confound your hidden falsehood and award
  Either of you to be the other's end.

HASTINGS. So prosper I, as I swear perfect love!

RIVERS. And I, as I love Hastings with my heart!

KING EDWARD. Madam, yourself is not exempt from this;
Nor you, son Dorset; Buckingham, nor you:
You have been factious one against the other.
Wife, love Lord Hastings, let him kiss your hand;
And what you do, do it unfeignedly.

QUEEN ELIZABETH. There, Hastings; I will never more remember
Our former hatred, so thrive I and mine!

KING EDWARD. Dorset, embrace him; Hastings, love Lord Marquis.

DORSET. This interchange of love, I here protest,
Upon my part shall be inviolable.

HASTINGS. And so swear I.   [*They embrace*]

KING EDWARD. Now, princely Buckingham, seal thou this league
With thy embracements to my wife's allies,
And make me happy in your unity.

BUCKINGHAM. [*To the* QUEEN] Whenever Buckingham doth turn his hate
Upon your Grace, but with all duteous love
Doth cherish you and yours, God punish me
With hate in those where I expect most love!
When I have most need to employ a friend
And most assured that he is a friend,
Deep, hollow, treacherous, and full of guile,
Be he unto me! This do I beg of God
When I am cold in love to you or yours.

[*They embrace*]

KING EDWARD. A pleasing cordial, princely Buckingham,
Is this thy vow unto my sickly heart.
There wanteth now our brother Gloucester here
To make the blessed period of this peace.

BUCKINGHAM. And, in good time,
Here comes Sir Richard Ratcliff and the Duke.

Enter GLOUCESTER, *and* RATCLIFF

GLOUCESTER. Good morrow to my sovereign king and queen;

And, princely peers, a happy time of day!
KING EDWARD. Happy, indeed, as we have spent the day.
　Gloucester, we have done deeds of charity,
　Made peace of enmity, fair love of hate,
　Between these swelling wrong-incensed peers.
GLOUCESTER. A blessed labour, my most sovereign lord.
　Among this princely heap, if any here,
　By false intelligence or wrong surmise,
　Hold me a foe—
　If I unwittingly, or in my rage,
　Have aught committed that is hardly borne
　To any in this presence, I desire
　To reconcile me to his friendly peace:
　'Tis death to me to be at enmity;
　I hate it, and desire all good men's love.
　First, madam, I entreat true peace of you,
　Which I will purchase with my duteous service;
　Of you, my noble cousin Buckingham,
　If ever any grudge were lodg'd between us;
　Of you, and you, Lord Rivers, and of Dorset,
　That all without desert have frown'd on me;
　Of you, Lord Woodville, and, Lord Scales, of you;
　Dukes, earls, lords, gentlemen—indeed, of all.
　I do not know that Englishman alive
　With whom my soul is any jot at odds
　More than the infant that is born to-night.
　I thank my God for my humility.
QUEEN ELIZABETH. A holy day shall this be kept hereafter.
　I would to God all strifes were well compounded.
　My sovereign lord, I do beseech your Highness
　To take our brother Clarence to your grace.
GLOUCESTER. Why, madam, have I off'red love for this,
　To be so flouted in this royal presence?
　Who knows not that the gentle Duke is dead?
　　　　　　　　　　　　　　　　　[They all start]
　You do him injury to scorn his corse.
KING EDWARD. Who knows not he is dead! Who knows
　he is?
QUEEN ELIZABETH. All-seeing heaven, what a world is this!
BUCKINGHAM. Look I so pale, Lord Dorset, as the rest?

DORSET. Ay, my good lord; and no man in the presence
   But his red colour hath forsook his cheeks.
KING EDWARD. Is Clarence dead? The order was revers'd.
GLOUCESTER. But he, poor man, by your first order died,
   And that a winged Mercury did bear;
   Some tardy cripple bare the countermand
   That came too lag to see him buried.
   God grant that some, less noble and less loyal,
   Nearer in bloody thoughts, an not in blood,
   Deserve not worse than wretched Clarence did,
   And yet go current from suspicion!

Enter DERBY

DERBY. A boon, my sovereign, for my service done!
KING EDWARD. I prithee, peace; my soul is full of sorrow.
DERBY. I will not rise unless your Highness hear me.
KING EDWARD. Then say at once what is it thou requests.
DERBY. The forfeit, sovereign, of my servant's life;
   Who slew to-day a riotous gentleman
   Lately attendant on the Duke of Norfolk.
KING EDWARD. Have I a tongue to doom my brother's death,
   And shall that tongue give pardon to a slave?
   My brother kill'd no man—his fault was thought,
   And yet his punishment was bitter death.
   Who sued to me for him? Who, in my wrath,
   Kneel'd at my feet, and bid me be advis'd?
   Who spoke of brotherhood? Who spoke of love?
   Who told me how the poor soul did forsake
   The mighty Warwick and did fight for me?
   Who told me, in the field at Tewksbury
   When Oxford had me down, he rescued me
   And said 'Dear Brother, live, and be a king'?
   Who told me, when we both lay in the field
   Frozen almost to death, how he did lap me
   Even in his garments, and did give himself,
   All thin and naked, to the numb cold night?
   All this from my remembrance brutish wrath
   Sinfully pluck'd, and not a man of you
   Had so much grace to put it in my mind.
   But when your carters or your waiting-vassals

Have done a drunken slaughter and defac'd
The precious image of our dear Redeemer,
You straight are on your knees for pardon, pardon;
And I, unjustly too, must grant it you.   [DERBY *rises*]
But for my brother not a man would speak;
Nor I, ungracious, speak unto myself
For him, poor soul. The proudest of you all
Have been beholding to him in his life;
Yet none of you would once beg for his life.
O God, I fear thy justice will take hold
On me, and you, and mine, and yours, for this!
Come, Hastings, help me to my closet. Ah, poor Clarence!
                           Exeunt some with KING *and* QUEEN
GLOUCESTER. This is the fruits of rashness. Mark'd you not
    How that the guilty kindred of the Queen
    Look'd pale when they did hear of Clarence' death?
    O, they did urge it still unto the King!
    God will revenge it. Come, lords, will you go
    To comfort Edward with our company?
BUCKINGHAM. We wait upon your Grace.   *Exeunt*

SCENE 2

London. The palace

Enter the old DUCHESS OF YORK, *with the* SON *and*
DAUGHTER *of* CLARENCE

SON. Good grandam, tell us, is our father dead?
DUCHESS. No, boy.
DAUGHTER. Why do you weep so oft, and beat your breast,
    And cry 'O Clarence, my unhappy son!'?
SON. Why do you look on us, and shake your head,
    And call us orphans, wretches, castaways,
    If that our noble father were alive?
DUCHESS. My pretty cousins, you mistake me both;
    I do lament the sickness of the King,
    As loath to lose him, not your father's death;
    It were lost sorrow to wail one that's lost.
SON. Then you conclude, my grandam, he is dead.

The King mine uncle is to blame for it.
God will revenge it; whom I will importune
With earnest prayers all to that effect.
DAUGHTER. And so will I.
DUCHESS. Peace, children, peace! The King doth love you well.
Incapable and shallow innocents,
You cannot guess who caus'd your father's death.
SON. Grandam, we can; for my good uncle Gloucester
Told me the King, provok'd to it by the Queen,
Devis'd impeachments to imprison him.
And when my uncle told me so, he wept,
And pitied me, and kindly kiss'd my cheek;
Bade me rely on him as on my father,
And he would love me dearly as a child.
DUCHESS. Ah, that deceit should steal such gentle shape,
And with a virtuous vizor hide deep vice!
He is my son; ay, and therein my shame;
Yet from my dugs he drew not this deceit.
SON. Think you my uncle did dissemble, grandam?
DUCHESS. Ay, boy.
SON. I cannot think it. Hark! what noise is this?

Enter QUEEN ELIZABETH, *with her hair about her*
ears; RIVERS *and* DORSET *after her*

QUEEN ELIZABETH. Ah, who shall hinder me to wail and weep,
To chide my fortune, and torment myself?
I'll join with black despair against my soul
And to myself become an enemy.
DUCHESS. What means this scene of rude impatience?
QUEEN ELIZABETH. To make an act of tragic violence.
Edward, my lord, thy son, our king, is dead.
Why grow the branches when the root is gone?
Why wither not the leaves that want their sap?
If you will live, lament; if die, be brief,
That our swift-winged souls may catch the King's,
Or like obedient subjects follow him
To his new kingdom of ne'er-changing night.
DUCHESS. Ah, so much interest have I in thy sorrow

As I had title in thy noble husband!
I have bewept a worthy husband's death,
And liv'd with looking on his images;
But now two mirrors of his princely semblance
Are crack'd in pieces by malignant death,
And I for comfort have but one false glass,
That grieves me when I see my shame in him.
Thou art a widow, yet thou art a mother
And hast the comfort of thy children left;
But death hath snatch'd my husband from mine arms
And pluck'd two crutches from my feeble hands—
Clarence and Edward. O, what cause have I—
Thine being but a moiety of my moan—
To overgo thy woes and drown thy cries?
Son. Ah, aunt, you wept not for our father's death!
    How can we aid you with our kindred tears?
Daughter. Our fatherless distress was left unmoan'd;
    Your widow-dolour likewise be unwept!
Queen Elizabeth. Give me no help in lamentation;
    I am not barren to bring forth complaints.
    All springs reduce their currents to mine eyes
    That I, being govern'd by the watery moon,
    May send forth plenteous tears to drown the world!
    Ah for my husband, for my dear Lord Edward!
Children. Ah for our father, for our dear Lord Clarence!
Duchess. Alas for both, both mine, Edward and Clarence!
Queen Elizabeth. What stay had I but Edward? and he's
    gone.
Children. What stay had we but Clarence? and he's gone.
Duchess. What stays had I but they? and they are gone.
Queen Elizabeth. Was never widow had so dear a loss.
Children. Were never orphans had so dear a loss.
Duchess. Was never mother had so dear a loss.
    Alas, I am the mother of these griefs!
    Their woes are parcell'd, mine is general.
    She for an Edward weeps, and so do I:
    I for a Clarence weep, so doth not she.
    These babes for Clarence weep, and so do I:
    I for an Edward weep, so do not they.
    Alas, you three on me, threefold distress'd,

Pour all your tears! I am your sorrow's nurse,
And I will pamper it with lamentation.

DORSET. Comfort, dear mother. God is much displeas'd
That you take with unthankfulness his doing.
In common worldly things 'tis called ungrateful
With dull unwillingness to repay a debt
Which with a bounteous hand was kindly lent;
Much more to be thus opposite with heaven,
For it requires the royal debt it lent you.

RIVERS. Madam, bethink you, like a careful mother,
Of the young prince your son. Send straight for him;
Let him be crown'd; in him your comfort lives.
Drown desperate sorrow in dead Edward's grave,
And plant your joys in living Edward's throne.

Enter GLOUCESTER, BUCKINGHAM, DERBY, HASTINGS,
and RATCLIFF

GLOUCESTER. Sister, have comfort. All of us have cause
To wail the dimming of our shining star;
But none can help our harms by wailing them.
Madam, my mother, I do cry you mercy;
I did not see your Grace. Humbly on my knee
I crave your blessing.

DUCHESS. God bless thee; and put meekness in thy breast,
Love, charity, obedience, and true duty!

GLOUCESTER. Amen! [*Aside*] And make me die a good old
man!
That is the butt end of a mother's blessing;
I marvel that her Grace did leave it out.

BUCKINGHAM. You cloudy princes and heart-sorrowing
peers,
That bear this heavy mutual load of moan,
Now cheer each other in each other's love.
Though we have spent our harvest of this king,
We are to reap the harvest of his son.
The broken rancour of your high-swol'n hearts,
But lately splinter'd, knit, and join'd together,
Must gently be preserv'd, cherish'd, and kept.
Me seemeth good that, with some little train,
Forthwith from Ludlow the young prince be fet

Hither to London, to be crown'd our King.
RIVERS. Why with some little train, my Lord of Buck-
  ingham?
BUCKINGHAM. Marry, my lord, lest by a multitude
  The new-heal'd wound of malice should break out,
  Which would be so much the more dangerous
  By how much the estate is green and yet ungovern'd;
  Where every horse bears his commanding rein
  And may direct his course as please himself,
  As well the fear of harm as harm apparent,
  In my opinion, ought to be prevented.
GLOUCESTER. I hope the King made peace with all of us;
  And the compact is firm and true in me.
RIVERS. And so in me; and so, I think, in all.
  Yet, since it is but green, it should be put
  To no apparent likelihood of breach,
  Which haply by much company might be urg'd;
  Therefore I say with noble Buckingham
  That it is meet so few should fetch the Prince.
HASTINGS. And so say I.
GLOUCESTER. Then be it so; and go we to determine
  Who they shall be that straight shall post to Ludlow.
  Madam, and you, my sister, will you go
  To give your censures in this business?
              Exeunt all but BUCKINGHAM *and* GLOUCESTER
BUCKINGHAM. My lord, whoever journeys to the Prince,
  For God sake, let not us two stay at home;
  For by the way I'll sort occasion,
  As index to the story we late talk'd of,
  To part the Queen's proud kindred from the Prince.
GLOUCESTER. My other self, my counsel's consistory,
  My oracle, my prophet, my dear cousin,
  I, as a child, will go by thy direction.
  Toward Ludlow then, for we'll not stay behind.   *Exeunt*

SCENE 3

London. A street

Enter one CITIZEN *at one door, and another*
at the other

FIRST CITIZEN. Good morrow, neighbour. Whither away so
fast?
SECOND CITIZEN. I promise you, I scarcely know myself.
Hear you the news abroad?
FIRST CITIZEN. Yes, that the King is dead.
SECOND CITIZEN. Ill news, by'r lady; seldom comes the
better.
I fear, I fear 'twill prove a giddy world.

Enter another CITIZEN

THIRD CITIZEN. Neighbours, God speed!
FIRST CITIZEN. Give you good morrow, sir.
THIRD CITIZEN. Doth the news hold of good King Edward's
death?
SECOND CITIZEN. Ay, sir, it is too true; God help the while!
THIRD CITIZEN. Then, masters, look to see a troublous
world.
FIRST CITIZEN. No, no; by God's good grace, his son shall
reign.
THIRD CITIZEN. Woe to that land that's govern'd by a child.
SECOND CITIZEN. In him there is a hope of government,
Which, in his nonage, council under him,
And, in his full and ripened years, himself,
No doubt, shall then, and till then, govern well.
FIRST CITIZEN. So stood the state when Henry the Sixth
Was crown'd in Paris but at nine months old.
THIRD CITIZEN. Stood the state so? No, no, good friends,
God wot;
For then this land was famously enrich'd
With politic grave counsel; then the King
Had virtuous uncles to protect his Grace.
FIRST CITIZEN. Why, so hath this, both by his father and
mother.

THIRD CITIZEN. Better it were they all came by his father,
Or by his father there were none at all;
For emulation who shall now be nearest
Will touch us all too near, if God prevent not.
O, full of danger is the Duke of Gloucester!
And the Queen's sons and brothers haught and proud;
And were they to be rul'd, and not to rule,
This sickly land might solace as before.
FIRST CITIZEN. Come, come, we fear the worst; all will be
well.
THIRD CITIZEN. When clouds are seen, wise men put on
their cloaks;
When great leaves fall, then winter is at hand;
When the sun sets, who doth not look for night?
Untimely storms make men expect a dearth.
All may be well; but, if God sort it so,
'Tis more than we deserve or I expect.
SECOND CITIZEN. Truly, the hearts of men are full of fear.
You cannot reason almost with a man
That looks not heavily and full of dread.
THIRD CITIZEN. Before the days of change, still is it so;
By a divine instinct men's minds mistrust
Ensuing danger; as by proof we see
The water swell before a boist'rous storm.
But leave it all to God. Whither away?
SECOND CITIZEN. Marry, we were sent for to the justices.
THIRD CITIZEN. And so was I; I'll bear you company.
                                                    Exeunt

SCENE 4

London. The palace

Enter the ARCHBISHOP OF YORK, *the young* DUKE
OF YORK, QUEEN ELIZABETH, *and the* DUCHESS
OF YORK

ARCHBISHOP. Last night, I hear, they lay at Stony Stratford,
And at Northampton they do rest to-night;

To-morrow or next day they will be here.

DUCHESS. I long with all my heart to see the Prince.
I hope he is much grown since last I saw him.

QUEEN ELIZABETH. But I hear no; they say my son of York
Has almost overta'en him in his growth.

YORK. Ay, mother; but I would not have it so.

DUCHESS. Why, my good cousin, it is good to grow.

YORK. Grandam, one night as we did sit at supper,
My uncle Rivers talk'd how I did grow
More than my brother. 'Ay,' quoth my uncle Gloucester
'Small herbs have grace: great weeds do grow apace.'
And since, methinks, I would not grow so fast,
Because sweet flow'rs are slow and weeds make haste.

DUCHESS. Good faith, good faith, the saying did not hold
In him that did object the same to thee.
He was the wretched'st thing when he was young,
So long a-growing and so leisurely
That, if his rule were true, he should be gracious.

ARCHBISHOP. And so no doubt he is, my gracious madam.

DUCHESS. I hope he is; but yet let mothers doubt.

YORK. Now, by my troth, if I had been rememb'red,
I could have given my uncle's Grace a flout
To touch his growth nearer than he touch'd mine.

DUCHESS. How, my young York? I prithee let me hear it.

YORK. Marry, they say my uncle grew so fast
That he could gnaw a crust at two hours old.
'Twas full two years ere I could get a tooth.
Grandam, this would have been a biting jest.

DUCHESS. I prithee, pretty York, who told thee this?

YORK. Grandam, his nurse.

DUCHESS. His nurse! Why she was dead ere thou wast
born.

YORK. If 'twere not she, I cannot tell who told me.

QUEEN ELIZABETH. A parlous boy! Go to, you are too
shrewd.

ARCHBISHOP. Good madam, be not angry with the child.

QUEEN ELIZABETH. Pitchers have ears.

Enter a MESSENGER

ARCHBISHOP. Here comes a messenger. What news?

MESSENGER. Such news, my lord, as grieves me to report.
QUEEN ELIZABETH. How doth the Prince?
MESSENGER. Well, madam, and in health.
DUCHESS. What is thy news?
MESSENGER. Lord Rivers and Lord Grey
    Are sent to Pomfret, and with them
    Sir Thomas Vaughan, prisoners.
DUCHESS. Who hath committed them?
MESSENGER. The mighty Dukes,
    Gloucester and Buckingham.
ARCHBISHOP. For what offence?
MESSENGER. The sum of all I can, I have disclos'd.
    Why or for what the nobles were committed
    Is all unknown to me, my gracious lord.
QUEEN ELIZABETH. Ay me, I see the ruin of my house!
    The tiger now hath seiz'd the gentle hind;
    Insulting tyranny begins to jet
    Upon the innocent and aweless throne.
    Welcome, destruction, blood, and massacre!
    I see, as in a map, the end of all.
DUCHESS. Accursed and unquiet wrangling days,
    How many of you have mine eyes beheld!
    My husband lost his life to get the crown;
    And often up and down my sons were toss'd
    For me to joy and weep their gain and loss;
    And being seated, and domestic broils
    Clean over-blown, themselves the conquerors
    Make war upon themselves—brother to brother,
    Blood to blood, self against self. O, preposterous
    And frantic outrage, end thy damned spleen,
    Or let me die, to look on death no more!
QUEEN ELIZABETH. Come, come, my boy; we will to
    sanctuary.
    Madam, farewell.
DUCHESS. Stay, I will go with you.
QUEEN ELIZABETH. You have no cause.
ARCHBISHOP. [*To the* QUEEN] My gracious lady, go.
    And thither bear your treasure and your goods.
    For my part, I'll resign unto your Grace
    The seal I keep; and so betide to me

As well I tender you and all of yours!
Go, I'll conduct you to the sanctuary.   *Exeunt*

ACT III. SCENE 1

London. A street

The trumpets sound. Enter the PRINCE OF WALES,
GLOUCESTER, BUCKINGHAM, CATESBY, CARDINAL
BOURCHIER, *and others*

BUCKINGHAM. Welcome, sweet Prince, to London, to your
chamber.
GLOUCESTER. Welcome, dear cousin, my thoughts' sovereign.
The weary way hath made you melancholy.
PRINCE. No, uncle; but our crosses on the way
Have made it tedious, wearisome, and heavy.
I want more uncles here to welcome me.
GLOUCESTER. Sweet Prince, the untainted virtue of your
years
Hath not yet div'd into the world's deceit;
Nor more can you distinguish of a man
Than of his outward show; which, God He knows,
Seldom or never jumpeth with the heart.
Those uncles which you want were dangerous;
Your Grace attended to their sug'red words
But look'd not on the poison of their hearts.
God keep you from them and from such false friends!
PRINCE. God keep me from false friends! but they were
none.
GLOUCESTER. My lord, the Mayor of London comes to greet
you.

Enter the LORD MAYOR *and his train*

MAYOR. God bless your Grace with health and happy days!
PRINCE. I thank you, good my lord, and thank you all.
I thought my mother and my brother York
Would long ere this have met us on the way.

Fie, what a slug is Hastings, that he comes not
To tell us whether they will come or no!

Enter LORD HASTINGS

BUCKINGHAM. And, in good time, here comes the sweating
    lord.
PRINCE. Welcome, my lord. What, will our mother come?
HASTINGS. On what occasion, God He knows, not I,
    The Queen your mother and your brother York
    Have taken sanctuary. The tender Prince
    Would fain have come with me to meet your Grace,
    But by his mother was perforce withheld.
BUCKINGHAM. Fie, what an indirect and peevish course
    Is this of hers? Lord Cardinal, will your Grace
    Persuade the Queen to send the Duke of York
    Unto his princely brother presently?
    If she deny, Lord Hastings, go with him
    And from her jealous arms pluck him perforce.
CARDINAL. My Lord of Buckingham, if my weak oratory
    Can from his mother win the Duke of York,
    Anon expect him here; but if she be obdurate
    To mild entreaties, God in heaven forbid
    We should infringe the holy privilege
    Of blessed sanctuary! Not for all this land
    Would I be guilty of so deep a sin.
BUCKINGHAM. You are too senseless-obstinate, my lord,
    Too ceremonious and traditional.
    Weigh it but with the grossness of this age,
    You break not sanctuary in seizing him.
    The benefit thereof is always granted
    To those whose dealings have deserv'd the place
    And those who have the wit to claim the place.
    This Prince hath neither claim'd it nor deserv'd it,
    And therefore, in mine opinion, cannot have it.
    Then, taking him from thence that is not there,
    You break no privilege nor charter there.
    Oft have I heard of sanctuary men;
    But sanctuary children never till now.
CARDINAL. My lord, you shall o'errule my mind for once.
    Come on, Lord Hastings, will you go with me?

HASTINGS. I go, my lord.
PRINCE. Good lords, make all the speedy haste you may.
          Exeunt CARDINAL *and* HASTINGS
 Say, uncle Gloucester, if our brother come,
 Where shall we sojourn till our coronation?
GLOUCESTER. Where it seems best unto your royal self.
 If I may counsel you, some day or two
 Your Highness shall repose you at the Tower,
 Then where you please and shall be thought most fit
 For your best health and recreation.
PRINCE. I do not like the Tower, of any place.
 Did Julius Cæsar build that place, my lord?
BUCKINGHAM. He did, my gracious lord, begin that place,
 Which, since, succeeding ages have re-edified.
PRINCE. Is it upon record, or else reported
 Successively from age to age, he built it?
BUCKINGHAM. Upon record, my gracious lord.
PRINCE. But say, my lord, it were not regist'red,
 Methinks the truth should live from age to age,
 As 'twere retail'd to all posterity,
 Even to the general all-ending day.
GLOUCESTER. [*Aside*] So wise so young, they say, do never
 live long.
PRINCE. What say you, uncle?
GLOUCESTER. I say, without characters, fame lives long.
 [*Aside*] Thus, like the formal vice, Iniquity,
 I moralize two meanings in one word.
PRINCE. That Julius Cæsar was a famous man;
 With what his valour did enrich his wit,
 His wit set down to make his valour live.
 Death makes no conquest of this conqueror;
 For now he lives in fame, though not in life.
 I'll tell you what, my cousin Buckingham—
BUCKINGHAM. What, my gracious lord?
PRINCE. An if I live until I be a man,
 I'll win our ancient right in France again,
 Or die a soldier as I liv'd a king.
GLOUCESTER. [*Aside*] Short summers lightly have a forward
 spring.
   Enter HASTINGS, *young* YORK, *and the* CARDINAL

BUCKINGHAM. Now, in good time, here comes the Duke of
  York.
PRINCE. Richard of York, how fares our loving brother?
YORK. Well, my dread lord; so must I call you now.
PRINCE. Ay brother, to our grief, as it is yours.
  Too late he died that might have kept that title,
  Which by his death hath lost much majesty.
GLOUCESTER. How fares our cousin, noble Lord of York?
YORK. I thank you, gentle uncle. O, my lord,
  You said that idle weeds are fast in growth.
  The Prince my brother hath outgrown me far.
GLOUCESTER. He hath, my lord.
YORK. And therefore is he idle?
GLOUCESTER. O, my fair cousin, I must not say so.
YORK. Then he is more beholding to you than I.
GLOUCESTER. He may command me as my sovereign;
  But you have power in me as in a kinsman.
YORK. I pray you, uncle, give me this dagger.
GLOUCESTER. My dagger, little cousin? With all my heart!
PRINCE. A beggar, brother?
YORK. Of my kind uncle, that I know will give,
  And being but a toy, which is no grief to give.
GLOUCESTER. A greater gift than that I'll give my cousin.
YORK. A greater gift! O, that's the sword to it!
GLOUCESTER. Ay, gentle cousin, were it light enough.
YORK. O, then, I see you will part but with light gifts:
  In weightier things you'll say a beggar nay.
GLOUCESTER. It is too heavy for your Grace to wear.
YORK. I weigh it lightly, were it heavier.
GLOUCESTER. What, would you have my weapon, little
  lord?
YORK. I would, that I might thank you as you call me.
GLOUCESTER. How?
YORK. Little.
PRINCE. My Lord of York will still be cross in talk.
  Uncle, your Grace knows how to bear with him.
YORK. You mean, to bear me, not to bear with me.
  Uncle, my brother mocks both you and me;
  Because that I am little, like an ape,
  He thinks that you should bear me on your shoulders.

BUCKINGHAM. With what a sharp-provided wit he reasons!
To mitigate the scorn he gives his uncle
He prettily and aptly taunts himself.
So cunning and so young is wonderful.
GLOUCESTER. My lord, will't please you pass along?
Myself and my good cousin Buckingham
Will to your mother, to entreat of her
To meet you at the Tower and welcome you.
YORK. What, will you go unto the Tower, my lord?
PRINCE. My Lord Protector needs will have it so.
YORK. I shall not sleep in quiet at the Tower.
GLOUCESTER. Why, what should you fear?
YORK. Marry, my uncle Clarence' angry ghost.
My grandam told me he was murder'd there.
PRINCE. I fear no uncles dead.
GLOUCESTER. Nor none that live, I hope.
PRINCE. An if they live, I hope I need not fear.
But come, my lord; and with a heavy heart,
Thinking on them, go I unto the Tower.
              A sennet. Exeunt all but GLOUCESTER, BUCKINGHAM,
                                      and CATESBY
BUCKINGHAM. Think you, my lord, this little prating York
Was not incensed by his subtle mother
To taunt and scorn you thus opprobriously?
GLOUCESTER. No doubt, no doubt. O, 'tis a perilous boy;
Bold, quick, ingenious, forward, capable.
He is all the mother's, from the top to toe.
BUCKINGHAM. Well, let them rest. Come hither, Catesby.
Thou art sworn as deeply to effect what we intend
As closely to conceal what we impart.
Thou know'st our reasons urg'd upon the way.
What think'st thou? Is it not an easy matter
To make William Lord Hastings of our mind,
For the instalment of this noble Duke
In the seat royal of this famous isle?
CATESBY. He for his father's sake so loves the Prince
That he will not be won to aught against him.
BUCKINGHAM. What think'st thou then of Stanley? Will
    not he?
CATESBY. He will do all in all as Hastings doth.

BUCKINGHAM. Well then, no more but this: go, gentle Catesby,
And, as it were far off, sound thou Lord Hastings
How he doth stand affected to our purpose;
And summon him to-morrow to the Tower,
To sit about the coronation.
If thou dost find him tractable to us,
Encourage him, and tell him all our reasons;
If he be leaden, icy, cold, unwilling,
Be thou so too, and so break off the talk,
And give us notice of his inclination;
For we to-morrow hold divided councils,
Wherein thyself shalt highly be employ'd.

GLOUCESTER. Commend me to Lord William. Tell him, Catesby,
His ancient knot of dangerous adversaries
To-morrow are let blood at Pomfret Castle;
And bid my lord, for joy of this good news,
Give Mistress Shore one gentle kiss the more.

BUCKINGHAM. Good Catesby, go effect this business soundly.

CATESBY. My good lords both, with all the heed I can.

GLOUCESTER. Shall we hear from you, Catesby, ere we sleep?

CATESBY. You shall, my lord.

GLOUCESTER. At Crosby House, there shall you find us both.

Exit CATESBY

BUCKINGHAM. Now, my lord, what shall we do if we perceive
Lord Hastings will not yield to our complots?

GLOUCESTER. Chop off his head—something we will determine.
And, look when I am King, claim thou of me
The earldom of Hereford and all the movables
Whereof the King my brother was possess'd.

BUCKINGHAM. I'll claim that promise at your Grace's hand.

GLOUCESTER. And look to have it yielded with all kindness.
Come, let us sup betimes, that afterwards
We may digest our complots in some form.   *Exeunt*

SCENE 2

Before LORD HASTING's *house*

Enter a MESSENGER *to the door of* HASTINGS

MESSENGER. My lord, my lord!   [*Knocking*]
HASTINGS. [*Within*] Who knocks?
MESSENGER. One from the Lord Stanley.
HASTINGS. [*Within*] What is't o'clock?
MESSENGER. Upon the stroke of four.

Enter LORD HASTINGS

HASTINGS. Cannot my Lord Stanley sleep these tedious
   nights?
MESSENGER. So it appears by that I have to say.
  First, he commends him to your noble self.
HASTINGS. What then?
MESSENGER. Then certifies your lordship that this night
  He dreamt the boar had razed off his helm.
  Besides, he says there are two councils kept,
  And that may be determin'd at the one
  Which may make you and him to rue at th' other.
  Therefore he sends to know your lordship's pleasure—
  If you will presently take horse with him
  And with all speed post with him toward the north
  To shun the danger that his soul divines.
HASTINGS. Go, fellow, go, return unto thy lord;
  Bid him not fear the separated council:
  His honour and myself are at the one,
  And at the other is my good friend Catesby;
  Where nothing can proceed that toucheth us
  Whereof I shall not have intelligence.
  Tell him his fears are shallow, without instance;
  And for his dreams, I wonder he's so simple
  To trust the mock'ry of unquiet slumbers.
  To fly the boar before the boar pursues
  Were to incense the boar to follow us
  And make pursuit where he did mean no chase.
  Go, bid thy master rise and come to me;

And we will both together to the Tower,
Where, he shall see, the boar will use us kindly.
MESSENGER. I'll go, my lord, and tell him what you say.

Exit

Enter CATESBY

CATESBY. Many good morrows to my noble lord!
HASTINGS. Good morrow, Catesby; you are early stirring.
What news, what news, in this our tott'ring state?
CATESBY. It is a reeling world indeed, my lord;
And I believe will never stand upright
Till Richard wear the garland of the realm.
HASTINGS. How, wear the garland! Dost thou mean the
crown?
CATESBY. Ay, my good lord.
HASTINGS. I'll have this crown of mine cut from my
shoulders
Before I'll see the crown so foul misplac'd.
But canst thou guess that he doth aim at it?
CATESBY. Ay, on my life; and hopes to find you forward
Upon his party for the gain thereof;
And thereupon he sends you this good news,
That this same very day your enemies,
The kindred of the Queen, must die at Pomfret.
HASTINGS. Indeed, I am no mourner for that news,
Because they have been still my adversaries;
But that I'll give my voice on Richard's side
To bar my master's heirs in true descent,
God knows I will not do it to the death.
CATESBY. God keep your lordship in that gracious mind!
HASTINGS. But I shall laugh at this a twelve month hence,
That they which brought me in my master's hate,
I live to look upon their tragedy.
Well, Catesby, ere a fortnight make me older,
I'll send some packing that yet think not on't.
CATESBY. 'Tis a vile thing to die, my gracious lord,
When men are unprepar'd and look not for it.
HASTINGS. O monstrous, monstrous! And so falls it out
With Rivers, Vaughan, Grey; and so 'twill do
With some men else that think themselves as safe

As thou and I, who, as thou knowest, are dear
To princely Richard and to Buckingham.
CATESBY. The Princes both make high account of you—
   [*Aside*] For they account his head upon the bridge.
HASTINGS. I know they do, and I have well deserv'd it.

Enter LORD STANLEY

Come on, come on; where is your boar-spear, man?
Fear you the boar, and go so unprovided?
STANLEY. My lord, good morrow; good morrow, Catesby.
   You may jest on, but, by the holy rood,
   I do not like these several councils, I.
HASTINGS. My lord, I hold my life as dear as yours,
   And never in my days, I do protest,
   Was it so precious to me as 'tis now.
   Think you, but that I know our state secure,
   I would be so triumphant as I am?
STANLEY. The lords at Pomfret, when they rode from
      London,
   Were jocund and suppos'd their states were sure,
   And they indeed had no cause to mistrust;
   But yet you see how soon the day o'ercast.
   This sudden stab of rancour I misdoubt;
   Pray God, I say, I prove a needless coward.
   What, shall we toward the Tower? The day is spent.
HASTINGS. Come, come, have with you. Wot you what, my
      lord?
   To-day the lords you talk'd of are beheaded.
STANLEY. They, for their truth, might better wear their
      heads
   Than some that have accus'd them wear their hats.
   But come, my lord, let's away.

Enter HASTINGS, *a pursuivant*

HASTINGS. Go on before; I'll talk with this good fellow.
                              Exeunt STANLEY *and* CATESBY
   How now, Hastings! How goes the world with thee?
PURSUIVANT. The better that your lordship please to ask.
HASTINGS. I tell thee, man, 'tis better with me now
   Than when thou met'st me last where now we meet:

Then was I going prisoner to the Tower
By the suggestion of the Queen's allies;
But now, I tell thee—keep it to thyself—
This day those enemies are put to death,
And I in better state than e'er I was.
PURSUIVANT. God hold it, to your honour's good content!
HASTINGS. Gramercy, Hastings; there, drink that for me.

> [*Throws him his purse*]

PURSUIVANT. I thank your honour.   *Exit*

Enter a PRIEST

PRIEST. Well met, my lord; I am glad to see your honour.
HASTINGS. I thank thee, good Sir John, with all my heart.
  I am in your debt for your last exercise;
  Come the next Sabbath, and I will content you.

> [*He whispers in his ear*]

PRIEST. I'll wait upon your lordship.

Enter BUCKINGHAM

BUCKINGHAM. What, talking with a priest, Lord Chamberlain!
  Your friends at Pomfret, they do need the priest:
  Your honour hath no shriving work in hand.
HASTINGS. Good faith, and when I met this holy man,
  The men you talk of came into my mind.
  What, go you toward the Tower?
BUCKINGHAM. I do, my lord, but long I cannot stay there;
  I shall return before your lordship thence.
HASTINGS. Nay, like enough, for I stay dinner there.
BUCKINGHAM. [*Aside*] And supper too, although thou
  knowest it not.—
  Come, will you go?
HASTINGS. I'll wait upon your lordship.   *Exeunt*

SCENE 3

Pomfret Castle

Enter SIR RICHARD RATCLIFF, *with halberds, carrying the Nobles,* RIVERS, GREY, *and* VAUGHAN, *to death*

RIVERS. Sir Richard Ratcliff, let me tell thee this:
To-day shalt thou behold a subject die
For truth, for duty, and for loyalty.
GREY. God bless the Prince from all the pack of you!
A knot you are of damned blood-suckers.
VAUGHAN. You live that shall cry woe for this hereafter.
RATCLIFF. Dispatch; the limit of your lives is out.
RIVERS. O Pomfret, Pomfret! O thou bloody prison,
Fatal and ominous to noble peers!
Within the guilty closure of thy walls
Richard the Second here was hack'd to death;
And for more slander to thy dismal seat,
We give to thee our guiltless blood to drink.
GREY. Now Margaret's curse is fall'n upon our heads,
When she exclaim'd on Hastings, you, and I,
For standing by when Richard stabb'd her son.
RIVERS. Then curs'd she Richard, then curs'd she Buckingham,
Then curs'd she Hastings. O, remember, God,
To hear her prayer for them, as now for us!
And for my sister, and her princely sons,
Be satisfied, dear God, with our true blood,
Which, as thou know'st, unjustly must be spilt.
RATCLIFF. Make haste; the hour of death is expiate.
RIVERS. Come, Grey; come, Vaughan; let us here embrace.
Farewell, until we meet again in heaven.   *Exeunt*

SCENE 4

London. The Tower

Enter Buckingham, Derby, Hastings, *the* Bishop
of Ely, Ratcliff, Lovel, *with others and seat
themselves at a table*

Hastings. Now, noble peers, the cause why we are met
 Is to determine of the coronation.
 In God's name speak—when is the royal day?
Buckingham. Is all things ready for the royal time?
Derby. It is, and wants but nomination.
Bishop of Ely. To-morrow then I judge a happy day.
Buckingham. Who knows the Lord Protector's mind
 herein?
 Who is most inward with the noble Duke?
Bishop of Ely. Your Grace, we think, should soonest know
 his mind.
Buckingham. We know each other's faces; for our hearts,
 He knows no more of mine than I of yours;
 Or I of his, my lord, than you of mine.
 Lord Hastings, you and he are near in love.
Hastings. I thank his Grace, I know he loves me well;
 But for his purpose in the coronation
 I have not sounded him, nor he deliver'd
 His gracious pleasure any way therein.
 But you, my honourable lords, may name the time;
 And in the Duke's behalf I'll give my voice,
 Which, I presume, he'll take in gentle part.

Enter Gloucester

Bishop of Ely. In happy time, here comes the Duke himself.
Gloucester. My noble lords and cousins all, good morrow.
 I have been long a sleeper, but I trust
 My absence doth neglect no great design
 Which by my presence might have been concluded.
Buckingham. Had you not come upon your cue, my lord,
 William Lord Hastings had pronounc'd your part—
 I mean, your voice for crowning of the King.

GLOUCESTER. Than my Lord Hastings no man might be
bolder;
His lordship knows me well and loves me well.
My lord of Ely, when I was last in Holborn
I saw good strawberries in your garden there.
I do beseech you send for some of them.
BISHOP OF ELY. Marry and will, my lord, with all my heart.
Exit

GLOUCESTER. Cousin of Buckingham, a word with you.
[*Takes him aside*]
Catesby hath sounded Hastings in our business,
And finds the testy gentleman so hot
That he will lose his head ere give consent
His master's child, as worshipfully he terms it,
Shall lose the royalty of England's throne.
BUCKINGHAM. Withdraw yourself awhile; I'll go with you.
Exeunt GLOUCESTER *and* BUCKINGHAM
DERBY. We have not yet set down this day of triumph.
To-morrow, in my judgment, is too sudden;
For I myself am not so well provided
As else I would be, were the day prolong'd.

Re-enter the BISHOP OF ELY

BISHOP OF ELY. Where is my lord the Duke of Gloucester?
I have sent for these strawberries.
HASTINGS. His Grace looks cheerfully and smooth this
morning;
There's some conceit or other likes him well
When that he bids good morrow with such spirit.
I think there's never a man in Christendom
Can lesser hide his love or hate than he;
For by his face straight shall you know his heart.
DERBY. What of his heart perceive you in his face
By any livelihood he show'd to-day?
HASTINGS. Marry, that with no man here he is offended;
For, were he, he had shown it in his looks.

Re-enter GLOUCESTER *and* BUCKINGHAM

GLOUCESTER. I pray you all, tell me what they deserve
That do conspire my death with devilish plots

Of damned witchcraft, and that have prevail'd
Upon my body with their hellish charms?
HASTINGS. The tender love I bear your Grace, my lord,
Makes me most forward in this princely presence
To doom th' offenders, whosoe'er they be.
I say, my lord, they have deserved death.
GLOUCESTER. Then be your eyes the witness of their evil.
Look how I am bewitch'd; behold, mine arm
Is like a blasted sapling wither'd up.
And this is Edward's wife, that monstrous witch,
Consorted with that harlot strumpet Shore,
That by their witchcraft thus have marked me.
HASTINGS. If they have done this deed, my noble lord—
GLOUCESTER. If?—thou protector of this damned strumpet,
Talk'st thou to me of ifs? Thou art a traitor.
Off with his head! Now by Saint Paul I swear
I will not dine until I see the same.
Lovel and Ratcliff, look that it be done.
The rest that love me, rise and follow me.
                    Exeunt all but HASTINGS, LOVEL, *and* RATCLIFF
HASTINGS. Woe, woe, for England! not a whit for me;
For I, too fond, might have prevented this.
Stanley did dream the boar did raze our helms,
And I did scorn it and disdain to fly.
Three times to-day my foot-cloth horse did stumble,
And started when he look'd upon the Tower,
As loath to bear me to the slaughter-house.
O, now I need the priest that spake to me!
I now repent I told the pursuivant,
As too triumphing, how mine enemies
To-day at Pomfret bloodily were butcher'd,
And I myself secure in grace and favour.
O Margaret, Margaret, now thy heavy curse
Is lighted on poor Hastings' wretched head!
RATCLIFF. Come, come, dispatch; the Duke would be at
    dinner.
Make a short shrift; he longs to see your head.
HASTINGS. O momentary grace of mortal men,
Which we more hunt for than the grace of God!
Who builds his hope in air of your good looks

Lives like a drunken sailor on a mast,
Ready with every nod to tumble down
Into the fatal bowels of the deep.
LOVEL. Come, come, dispatch; 'tis bootless to exclaim.
HASTINGS. O bloody Richard! Miserable England!
I prophesy the fearfull'st time to thee
That ever wretched age hath look'd upon.
Come, lead me to the block; bear him my head.
They smile at me who shortly shall be dead.   *Exeunt*

SCENE 5

London. The Tower-walls

Enter GLOUCESTER *and* BUCKINGHAM *in rotten
armour, marvellous ill-favoured*

GLOUCESTER. Come, cousin, canst thou quake and change
    thy colour,
Murder thy breath in middle of a word,
And then again begin, and stop again,
As if thou were distraught and mad with terror?
BUCKINGHAM. Tut, I can counterfeit the deep tragedian;
Speak and look back, and pry on every side,
Tremble and start at wagging of a straw,
Intending deep suspicion. Ghastly looks
Are at my service, like enforced smiles;
And both are ready in their offices
At any time to grace my stratagems.
But what, is Catesby gone?
GLOUCESTER. He is; and, see, he brings the mayor along.

Enter the LORD MAYOR *and* CATESBY

BUCKINGHAM. Lord Mayor—
GLOUCESTER. Look to the drawbridge there!
BUCKINGHAM. Hark! a drum.
GLOUCESTER. Catesby, o'erlook the walls.
BUCKINGHAM. Lord Mayor, the reason we have sent—
GLOUCESTER. Look back, defend thee; here are enemies.
BUCKINGHAM. God and our innocence defend and guard us!

836

ACT III. SCENE 5

Enter Lovel *and* Ratcliff, *with* Hastings' *head*

GLOUCESTER. Be patient; they are friends—Ratcliff and Lovel.
LOVEL. Here is the head of that ignoble traitor,
  The dangerous and unsuspected Hastings.
GLOUCESTER. So dear I lov'd the man that I must weep.
  I took him for the plainest harmless creature
  That breath'd upon the earth a Christian;
  Made him my book, wherein my soul recorded
  The history of all her secret thoughts.
  So smooth he daub'd his vice with show of virtue
  That, his apparent open guilt omitted,
  I mean his conversation with Shore's wife—
  He liv'd from all attainder of suspects.
BUCKINGHAM. Well, well, he was the covert'st shelt'red
    traitor
  That ever liv'd.
  Would you imagine, or almost believe—
  Were't not that by great preservation
  We live to tell it—that the subtle traitor
  This day had plotted, in the council-house,
  To murder me and my good Lord of Gloucester.
MAYOR. Had he done so?
GLOUCESTER. What! think you we are Turks or Infidels?
  Or that we would, against the form of law,
  Proceed thus rashly in the villain's death
  But that the extreme peril of the case,
  The peace of England and our persons' safety,
  Enforc'd us to this execution?
MAYOR. Now, fair befall you! He deserv'd his death;
  And your good Graces both have well proceeded
  To warn false traitors from the like attempts.
  I never look'd for better at his hands
  After he once fell in with Mistress Shore.
BUCKINGHAM. Yet had we not determin'd he should die
  Until your lordship came to see his end—
  Which now the loving haste of these our friends,
  Something against our meanings, have prevented—
  Because, my lord, I would have had you heard
  The traitor speak, and timorously confess

837

The manner and the purpose of his treasons:
That you might well have signified the same
Unto the citizens, who haply may
Misconster us in him and wail his death.
MAYOR. But, my good lord, your Grace's words shall serve
As well as I had seen and heard him speak;
And do not doubt, right noble Princes both,
But I'll acquaint our duteous citizens
With all your just proceedings in this cause.
GLOUCESTER. And to that end we wish'd your lordship here,
T' avoid the the censures of the carping world.
BUCKINGHAM. Which since you come too late of our intent,
Yet witness what you hear we did intend.
And so, my good Lord Mayor, we bid farewell.

Exit LORD MAYOR

GLOUCESTER. Go, after, after, cousin Buckingham.
The Mayor towards Guildhall hies him in all post.
There, at your meet'st advantage of the time,
Infer the bastardy of Edward's children.
Tell them how Edward put to death a citizen
Only for saying he would make his son
Heir to the crown—meaning indeed his house,
Which by the sign thereof was termed so.
Moreover, urge his hateful luxury
And bestial appetite in change of lust,
Which stretch'd unto their servants, daughters, wives,
Even where his raging eye or savage heart
Without control lusted to make a prey.
Nay, for a need, thus far come near my person:
Tell them, when that my mother went with child
Of that insatiate Edward, noble York
My princely father then had wars in France
And, by true computation of the time,
Found that the issue was not his begot;
Which well appeared in his lineaments,
Being nothing like the noble Duke my father.
Yet touch this sparingly, as 'twere far off;
Because, my lord, you know my mother lives.
BUCKINGHAM. Doubt not, my lord, I'll play the orator
As if the golden fee for which I plead

Were for myself; and so, my lord, adieu.

GLOUCESTER. If you thrive well, bring them to Baynard's
   Castle;
   Where you shall find me well accompanied
   With reverend fathers and well learned bishops.

BUCKINGHAM. I go; and towards three or four o'clock
   Look for the news that the Guildhall affords.   *Exit*

GLOUCESTER. Go, Lovel, with all speed to Doctor Shaw.
   [*To* CATESBY] Go thou to Friar Penker. Bid them both
   Meet me within this hour at Baynard's Castle.

                                   Exeunt all but GLOUCESTER

   Now will I go to take some privy order
   To draw the brats of Clarence out of sight,
   And to give order that no manner person
   Have any time recourse unto the Princes.   *Exit*

SCENE 6

London. A street

Enter a SCRIVENER

SCRIVENER. Here is the indictment of the good Lord Hastings;
   Which in a set hand fairly is engross'd
   That it may be to-day read o'er in Paul's.
   And mark how well the sequel hangs together:
   Eleven hours I have spent to write it over,
   For yesternight by Catesby was it sent me;
   The precedent was full as long a-doing;
   And yet within these five hours Hastings liv'd,
   Untainted, unexamin'd, free, at liberty.
   Here's a good world the while! Who is so gross
   That cannot see this palpable device?
   Yet who's so bold but says he sees it not?
   Bad is the world; and all will come to nought,
   When such ill dealing must be seen in thought.   *Exit*

SCENE 7

London. Baynard's Castle

Enter GLOUCESTER *and* BUCKINGHAM, *at several doors*

GLOUCESTER. How now, how now! What say the citizens?
BUCKINGHAM. Now, by the holy Mother of our Lord,
The citizens are mum, say not a word.
GLOUCESTER. Touch'd you the bastardy of Edward's children?
BUCKINGHAM. I did; with his contract with Lady Lucy,
And his contract by deputy in France;
Th' insatiate greediness of his desire,
And his enforcement of the city wives;
His tyranny for trifles; his own bastardy,
As being got, your father then in France,
And his resemblance, being not like the Duke.
Withal I did infer your lineaments,
Being the right idea of your father,
Both in your form and nobleness of mind;
Laid open all your victories in Scotland,
Your discipline in war, wisdom in peace,
Your bounty, virtue, fair humility;
Indeed, left nothing fitting for your purpose
Untouch'd or slightly handled in discourse.
And when mine oratory drew toward end
I bid them that did love their country's good
Cry 'God save Richard, England's royal King!'
GLOUCESTER. And did they so?
BUCKINGHAM. No, so God help me, they spake not a word;
But, like dumb statuës or breathing stones,
Star'd each on other, and look'd deadly pale.
Which when I saw, I reprehended them,
And ask'd the Mayor what meant this wilful silence.
His answer was, the people were not used
To be spoke to but by the Recorder.
Then he was urg'd to tell my tale again.
'Thus saith the Duke, thus hath the Duke inferr'd'—
But nothing spoke in warrant from himself.

When he had done, some followers of mine own
At lower end of the hall hurl'd up their caps,
And some ten voices cried 'God save King Richard!'
And thus I took the vantage of those few—
'Thanks, gentle citizens and friends,' quoth I
'This general applause and cheerful shout
Argues your wisdoms and your love to Richard.'
And even here brake off and came away.
GLOUCESTER. What, tongueless blocks were they? Would
  they not speak?
Will not the Mayor then and his brethren come?
BUCKINGHAM. The Mayor is here at hand. Intend some fear;
  Be not you spoke with but by mighty suit;
  And look you get a prayer-book in your hand,
  And stand between two churchmen, good my lord;
  For on that ground I'll make a holy descant;
  And be not easily won to our requests.
  Play the maid's part: still answer nay, and take it.
GLOUCESTER. I go; and if you plead as well for them
  As I can say nay to thee for myself,
  No doubt we bring it to a happy issue.
BUCKINGHAM. Go, go, up to the leads; the Lord Mayor
  knocks.   *Exit* GLOUCESTER

Enter the LORD MAYOR, ALDERMEN, *and citizens*

Welcome, my lord. I dance attendance here;
I think the Duke will not be spoke withal.

Enter CATESBY

Now, Catesby, what says your lord to my request?
CATESBY. He doth entreat your Grace, my noble lord,
  To visit him to-morrow or next day.
  He is within, with two right reverend fathers,
  Divinely bent to meditation;
  And in no worldly suits would he be mov'd,
  To draw him from his holy exercise.
BUCKINGHAM. Return, good Catesby, to the gracious Duke;
  Tell him, myself, the Mayor and Aldermen,
  In deep designs, in matter of great moment,
  No less importing than our general good,

Are come to have some conference with his Grace.
CATESBY. I'll signify so much unto him straight.   *Exit*
BUCKINGHAM. Ah ha, my lord, this prince is not an Edward!
    He is not lolling on a lewd love-bed,
    But on his knees at meditation;
    Not dallying with a brace of courtezans,
    But meditating with two deep divines;
    Not sleeping, to engross his idle body,
    But praying, to enrich his watchful soul.
    Happy were England would this virtuous prince
    Take on his Grace the sovereignty thereof;
    But, sure, I fear we shall not win him to it.
MAYOR. Marry, God defend his Grace should say us nay!
BUCKINGHAM. I fear he will. Here Catesby comes again.

Re-enter CATESBY

    Now, Catesby, what says his Grace?
CATESBY. My lord,
    He wonders to what end you have assembled
    Such troops of citizens to come to him.
    His Grace not being warn'd thereof before,
    He fears, my lord, you mean no good to him.
BUCKINGHAM. Sorry I am my noble cousin should
    Suspect me that I mean no good to him.
    By heaven, we come to him in perfect love;
    And so once more return and tell his Grace.
                                              Exit CATESBY
    When holy and devout religious men
    Are at their beads, 'tis much to draw them thence,
    So sweet is zealous contemplation.

Enter GLOUCESTER *aloft, between two* BISHOPS.
CATESBY *returns*

MAYOR. See where his Grace stands 'tween two clergymen!
BUCKINGHAM. Two props of virtue for a Christian prince,
    To stay him from the fall of vanity;
    And, see, a book of prayer in his hand,
    True ornaments to know a holy man.
    Famous Plantagenet, most gracious Prince,
    Lend favourable ear to our requests,

And pardon us the interruption
Of thy devotion and right Christian zeal.
GLOUCESTER. My lord, there needs no such apology:
I do beseech your Grace to pardon me,
Who, earnest in the service of my God,
Deferr'd the visitation of my friends.
But, leaving this, what is your Grace's pleasure?
BUCKINGHAM. Even that, I hope, which pleaseth God above,
And all good men of this ungovern'd isle.
GLOUCESTER. I do suspect I have done some offence
That seems disgracious in the city's eye,
And that you come to reprehend my ignorance.
BUCKINGHAM. You have, my lord. Would it might please
your Grace,
On our entreaties, to amend your fault!
GLOUCESTER. Else wherefore breathe I in a Christian land?
BUCKINGHAM. Know then, it is your fault that you resign
The supreme seat, the throne majestical,
The scept'red office of your ancestors,
Your state of fortune and your due of birth,
The lineal glory of your royal house,
To the corruption of a blemish'd stock;
Whiles in the mildness of your sleepy thoughts,
Which here we waken to our country's good,
The noble isle doth want her proper limbs;
Her face defac'd with scars of infamy,
Her royal stock graft with ignoble plants,
And almost should'red in the swallowing gulf
Of dark forgetfulness and deep oblivion.
Which to recure, we heartily solicit
Your gracious self to take on you the charge
And kingly government of this your land—
Not as protector, steward, substitute,
Or lowly factor for another's gain;
But as successively, from blood to blood,
Your right of birth, your empery, your own.
For this, consorted with the citizens,
Your very worshipful and loving friends,
And by their vehement instigation,
In this just cause come I to move your Grace.

GLOUCESTER. I cannot tell if to depart in silence
Or bitterly to speak in your reproof
Best fitteth my degree or your condition.
If not to answer, you might haply think
Tongue-tied ambition, not replying, yielded
To bear the golden yoke of sovereignty,
Which fondly you would here impose on me;
If to reprove you for this suit of yours,
So season'd with your faithful love to me,
Then, on the other side, I check'd my friends.
Therefore—to speak, and to avoid the first,
And then, in speaking, not to incur the last—
Definitively thus I answer you:
Your love deserves my thanks, but my desert
Unmeritable shuns your high request.
First, if all obstacles were cut away,
And that my path were even to the crown,
As the ripe revenue and due of birth,
Yet so much is my poverty of spirit,
So mighty and so many my defects,
That I would rather hide me from my greatness—
Being a bark to brook no mighty sea—
Than in my greatness covet to be hid,
And in the vapour of my glory smother'd.
But, God be thank'd, there is no need of me—
And much I need to help you, were there need.
The royal tree hath left us royal fruit
Which, mellow'd by the stealing hours of time,
Will well become the seat of majesty
And make, no doubt, us happy by his reign.
On him I lay that you would lay on me—
The right and fortune of his happy stars,
Which God defend that I should wring from him.
BUCKINGHAM. My lord, this argues conscience in your
    Grace;
But the respects thereof are nice and trivial,
All circumstances well considered.
You say that Edward is your brother's son.
So say we too, but not by Edward's wife;
For first was he contract to Lady Lucy—

844

Your mother lives a witness to his vow—
And afterward by substitute betroth'd
To Bona, sister to the King of France.
These both put off, a poor petitioner,
A care-craz'd mother to a many sons,
A beauty-waning and distressed widow,
Even in the afternoon of her best days,
Made prize and purchase of his wanton eye,
Seduc'd the pitch and height of his degree
To base declension and loath'd bigamy.
By her, in his unlawful bed, he got
This Edward, whom our manners call the Prince.
More bitterly could I expostulate,
Save that, for reverence to some alive,
I give a sparing limit to my tongue.
Then, good my lord, take to your royal self
This proffer'd benefit of dignity;
If not to bless us and the land withal,
Yet to draw forth your noble ancestry
From the corruption of abusing times
Unto a lineal true-derived course.
MAYOR. Do, good my lord; your citizens entreat you.
BUCKINGHAM. Refuse not, mighty lord, this proffer'd love.
CATESBY. O, make them joyful, grant their lawful suit!
GLOUCESTER. Alas, why would you heap this care on me?
I am unfit for state and majesty.
I do beseech you, take it not amiss:
I cannot nor I will not yield to you.
BUCKINGHAM. If you refuse it—as, in love and zeal,
Loath to depose the child, your brother's son;
As well we know your tenderness of heart
And gentle, kind, effeminate remorse,
Which we have noted in you to your kindred
And egally indeed to all estates—
Yet know, whe'er you accept our suit or no,
Your brother's son shall never reign our king;
But we will plant some other in the throne
To the disgrace and downfall of your house;
And in this resolution here we leave you.
Come, citizens. Zounds, I'll entreat no more.

GLOUCESTER. O, do not swear, my lord of Buckingham.

Exeunt BUCKINGHAM, MAYOR, *and citizens*

CATESBY. Call him again, sweet Prince, accept their suit.
   If you deny them, all the land will rue it.
GLOUCESTER. Will you enforce me to a world of cares?
   Call them again. I am not made of stones,
   But penetrable to your kind entreaties,
   Albeit against my conscience and my soul.

Re-enter BUCKINGHAM *and the rest*

   Cousin of Buckingham, and sage grave men,
   Since you will buckle fortune on my back,
   To bear her burden, whe'er I will or no,
   I must have patience to endure the load;
   But if black scandal or foul-fac'd reproach
   Attend the sequel of your imposition,
   Your mere enforcement shall acquittance me
   From all the impure blots and stains thereof;
   For God doth know, and you may partly see,
   How far I am from the desire of this.
MAYOR. God bless your Grace! We see it, and will say it.
GLOUCESTER. In saying so, you shall but say the truth.
BUCKINGHAM. Then I salute you with this royal title—
   Long live King Richard, England's worthy King!
ALL. Amen.
BUCKINGHAM. To-morrow may it please you to be crown'd?
GLOUCESTER. Even when you please, for you will have it so.
BUCKINGHAM. To-morrow, then, we will attend your Grace;
   And so, most joyfully, we take our leave.
GLOUCESTER. [*To the* BISHOPS] Come, let us to our holy
   work again.
   Farewell, my cousin; farewell, gentle friends.   *Exeunt*

ACT IV. SCENE 1

London. Before the Tower

Enter QUEEN ELIZABETH, DUCHESS OF YORK, *and*
MARQUIS OF DORSET, *at one door;* ANNE, DUCHESS
OF GLOUCESTER, *leading* LADY MARGARET PLAN-
TAGENET, CLARENCE'S *young daughter, at another
door*

DUCHESS. Who meets us here? My niece Plantagenet,
  Led in the hand of her kind aunt of Gloucester?
  Now, for my life, she's wand'ring to the Tower,
  On pure heart's love, to greet the tender Princes.
  Daughter, well met.
ANNE. God give your Graces both
 ̇A happy and a joyful time of day!
QUEEN ELIZABETH. As much to you, good sister! Whither
  away?
ANNE. No farther than the Tower; and, as I guess,
  Upon the like devotion as yourselves,
  To gratulate the gentle Princes there.
QUEEN ELIZABETH. Kind sister, thanks; we'll enter all to-
  gether.

Enter BRAKENBURY

And in good time, here the lieutenant comes.
Master Lieutenant, pray you, by your leave,
How doth the Prince, and my young son of York?
BRAKENBURY. Right well, dear madam. By your patience,
  I may not suffer you to visit them.
  The King hath strictly charg'd the contrary.
QUEEN ELIZABETH. The King! Who's that?
BRAKENBURY. I mean the Lord Protector.
QUEEN ELIZABETH. The Lord protect him from that kingly
  title!
Hath he set bounds between their love and me?
I am their mother; who shall bar me from them?
DUCHESS. I am their father's mother; I will see them.
ANNE. Their aunt I am in law, in love their mother.
  Then bring me to their sights; I'll bear thy blame,

And take thy office from thee on my peril.
BRAKENBURY. No, madam, no. I may not leave it so;
    I am bound by oath, and therefore pardon me.   *Exit*

Enter STANLEY

STANLEY. Let me but meet you, ladies, one hour hence,
    And I'll salute your Grace of York as mother
    And reverend looker-on of two fair queens.
    [*To* ANNE] Come, madam, you must straight to West-
    minster,
    There to be crowned Richard's royal queen.
QUEEN ELIZABETH. Ah, cut my lace asunder
    That my pent heart may have some scope to beat,
    Or else I swoon with this dead-killing news!
ANNE. Despiteful tidings! O unpleasing news!
DORSET. Be of good cheer; mother, how fares your Grace?
QUEEN ELIZABETH. O Dorset, speak not to me, get thee
    gone!
    Death and destruction dogs thee at thy heels;
    Thy mother's name is ominous to children.
    If thou wilt outstrip death, go cross the seas,
    And live with Richmond, from the reach of hell.
    Go, hie thee, hie thee from this slaughter-house,
    Lest thou increase the number of the dead,
    And make me die the thrall of Margaret's curse,
    Nor mother, wife, nor England's counted queen.
STANLEY. Full of wise care is this your counsel, madam.
    Take all the swift advantage of the hours;
    You shall have letters from me to my son
    In your behalf, to meet you on the way.
    Be not ta'en tardy by unwise delay.
DUCHESS. O ill-dispersing wind of misery!
    O my accursed womb, the bed of death!
    A cockatrice hast thou hatch'd to the world,
    Whose unavoided eye is murderous.
STANLEY. Come, madam, come; I in all haste was sent.
ANNE. And I with all unwillingness will go.
    O, would to God that the inclusive verge
    Of golden metal that must round my brow

Were red-hot steel, to sear me to the brains!
Anointed let me be with deadly venom,
And die ere men can say 'God save the Queen!'

QUEEN ELIZABETH. Go, go, poor soul; I envy not thy glory.
To feed my humour, wish thyself no harm.

ANNE. No, why? When he that is my husband now
Came to me, as I follow'd Henry's corse;
When scarce the blood was well wash'd from his hands
Which issued from my other angel husband,
And that dear saint which then I weeping follow'd—
O, when, I say, I look'd on Richard's face,
This was my wish: 'Be thou' quoth I 'accurs'd
For making me, so young, so old a widow;
And when thou wed'st, let sorrow haunt thy bed;
And be thy wife, if any be so mad,
More miserable by the life of thee
Than thou hast made me by my dear lord's death.'
Lo, ere I can repeat this curse again,
Within so small a time, my woman's heart
Grossly grew captive to his honey words
And prov'd the subject of mine own soul's curse,
Which hitherto hath held my eyes from rest;
For never yet one hour in his bed
Did I enjoy the golden dew of sleep,
But with his timorous dreams was still awak'd.
Besides, he hates me for my father Warwick;
And will, no doubt, shortly be rid of me.

QUEEN ELIZABETH. Poor heart, adieu! I pity thy complaining.

ANNE. No more than with my soul I mourn for yours.

DORSET. Farewell, thou woeful welcomer of glory!

ANNE. Adieu, poor soul, that tak'st thy leave of it!

DUCHESS. [*To* DORSET] Go thou to Richmond, and good
    fortune guide thee!
    [*To* ANNE] Go thou to Richard, and good angels tend
    thee!
    [*To* QUEEN ELIZABETH] Go thou to sanctuary, and good
    thoughts possess thee!
    I to my grave, where peace and rest lie with me!
    Eighty odd years of sorrow have I seen,
    And each hour's joy wreck'd with a week of teen.

QUEEN ELIZABETH. Stay, yet look back with me unto the
  Tower.
Pity, you ancient stones, those tender babes
Whom envy hath immur'd within your walls,
Rough cradle for such little pretty ones.
Rude ragged nurse, old sullen playfellow
For tender princes, use my babies well.
So foolish sorrows bids your stones farewell.   *Exeunt*

SCENE 2

London. The palace

Sound a sennet. Enter RICHARD, *in pomp, as* KING;
BUCKINGHAM, CATESBY, RATCLIFF, LOVEL, *a* PAGE,
and others

KING RICHARD. Stand all apart. Cousin of Buckingham!
BUCKINGHAM. My gracious sovereign?
KING RICHARD. Give me thy hand.
           [*Here he ascendeth the throne. Sound*]
Thus high, by thy advice
And thy assistance, is King Richard seated.
But shall we wear these glories for a day;
Or shall they last, and we rejoice in them?
BUCKINGHAM. Still live they, and for ever let them last!
KING RICHARD. Ah, Buckingham, now do I play the touch,
  To try if thou be current gold indeed.
  Young Edward lives—think now what I would speak.
BUCKINGHAM. Say on, my loving lord.
KING RICHARD. Why, Buckingham, I say I would be King.
BUCKINGHAM. Why, so you are, my thrice-renowned lord.
KING RICHARD. Ha! am I King? 'Tis so; but Edward lives.
BUCKINGHAM. True, noble Prince.
KING RICHARD. O bitter consequence:
  That Edward still should live—true noble Prince!
  Cousin, thou wast not wont to be so dull.
  Shall I be plain? I wish the bastards dead.
  And I would have it suddenly perform'd.
  What say'st thou now? Speak suddenly, be brief.

BUCKINGHAM. Your Grace may do your pleasure.
KING RICHARD. Tut, tut, thou art all ice; thy kindness freezes.
  Say, have I thy consent that they shall die?
BUCKINGHAM. Give me some little breath, some pause, dear
  lord,
  Before I positively speak in this.
  I will resolve you herein presently.   *Exit*
CATESBY. [*Aside to another*] The King is angry; see, he
  gnaws his lip.
KING RICHARD. I will converse with iron-witted fools
                            [*Descends from the throne*]
  And unrespective boys; none are for me
  That look into me with considerate eyes.
  High-reaching Buckingham grows circumspect.
  Boy!
PAGE. My lord?
KING RICHARD. Know'st thou not any whom corrupting
  gold
  Will tempt unto a close exploit of death?
PAGE. I know a discontented gentleman
  Whose humble means match not his haughty spirit.
  Gold were as good as twenty orators,
  And will, no doubt, tempt him to anything.
KING RICHARD. What is his name?
PAGE. His name, my lord, is Tyrrel.
KING RICHARD. I partly know the man. Go, call him hither,
  boy.   *Exit* PAGE
  The deep-revolving witty Buckingham
  No more shall be the neighbour to my counsels.
  Hath he so long held out with me, untir'd,
  And stops he now for breath? Well, be it so.

                    Enter STANLEY

  How now, Lord Stanley! What's the news?
STANLEY. Know, my loving lord,
  The Marquis Dorset, as I hear, is fled
  To Richmond, in the parts where he abides. [*Stands apart*]
KING RICHARD. Come hither, Catesby. Rumour it abroad
  That Anne, my wife, is very grievous sick;
  I will take order for her keeping close.

                        851

Inquire me out some mean poor gentleman,
Whom I will marry straight to Clarence' daughter—
The boy is foolish, and I fear not him.
Look how thou dream'st! I say again, give out
That Anne, my queen, is sick and like to die.
About it; for it stands me much upon
To stop all hopes whose growth may damage me.

Exit CATESBY

I must be married to my brother's daughter,
Or else my kingdom stands on brittle glass.
Murder her brothers, and then marry her!
Uncertain way of gain! But I am in
So far in blood that sin will pluck on sin.
Tear-falling pity dwells not in this eye.

Re-enter PAGE, *with* TYRREL

Is thy name Tyrrel?
TYRREL. James Tyrrel, and your most obedient subject.
KING RICHARD. Art thou, indeed?
TYRREL. Prove me, my gracious lord.
KING RICHARD. Dar'st thou resolve to kill a friend of mine?
TYRREL. Please you;
But I had rather kill two enemies.
KING RICHARD. Why, then thou hast it. Two deep enemies,
Foes to my rest, and my sweet sleep's disturbers,
Are they that I would have thee deal upon.
Tyrrel, I mean those bastards in the Tower.
TYRREL. Let me have open means to come to them,
And soon I'll rid you from the fear of them.
KING RICHARD. Thou sing'st sweet music. Hark, come
hither, Tyrrel.
Go, by this token. Rise, and lend thine ear.   [*Whispers*]
There is no more but so: say it is done,
And I will love thee and prefer thee for it.
TYRREL. I will dispatch it straight.   *Exit*

Re-enter BUCKINGHAM

BUCKINGHAM. My lord, I have consider'd in my mind
The late request that you did sound me in.

KING RICHARD. Well, let that rest. Dorset is fled to Richmond.

BUCKINGHAM. I hear the news, my lord.

KING RICHARD. Stanley, he is your wife's son: well, look unto it.

BUCKINGHAM. My lord, I claim the gift, my due by promise,
For which your honour and your faith is pawn'd:
Th' earldom of Hereford and the movables
Which you have promised I shall possess.

KING RICHARD. Stanley, look to your wife; if she convey
Letters to Richmond, you shall answer it.

BUCKINGHAM. What says your Highness to my just request?

KING RICHARD. I do remember me: Henry the Sixth
Did prophesy that Richmond should be King,
When Richmond was a little peevish boy.
A king!—perhaps—

BUCKINGHAM. My lord—

KING RICHARD. How chance the prophet could not at that time
Have told me, I being by, that I should kill him?

BUCKINGHAM. My lord, your promise for the earldom—

KING RICHARD. Richmond! When last I was at Exeter,
The mayor in courtesy show'd me the castle
And call'd it Rugemount, at which name I started,
Because a bard of Ireland told me once
I should not live long after I saw Richmond.

BUCKINGHAM. My lord—

KING RICHARD. Ay, what's o'clock?

BUCKINGHAM. I am thus bold to put your Grace in mind
Of what you promis'd me.

KING RICHARD. Well, but what's o'clock?

BUCKINGHAM. Upon the stroke of ten.

KING RICHARD. Well, let it strike.

BUCKINGHAM. Why let it strike?

KING RICHARD. Because that like a Jack thou keep'st the stroke
Betwixt thy begging and my meditation.
I am not in the giving vein to-day.

BUCKINGHAM. May it please you to resolve me in my suit.

KING RICHARD. Thou troublest me; I am not in the vein.

Exeunt all but BUCKINGHAM

BUCKINGHAM. And is it thus? Repays he my deep service
With such contempt? Made I him King for this?
O, let me think on Hastings, and be gone
To Brecknock while my fearful head is on!   *Exit*

SCENE 3

London. The palace

Enter TYRREL

TYRREL. The tyrannous and bloody act is done,
The most arch deed of piteous massacre
That ever yet this land was guilty of.
Dighton and Forrest, who I did suborn
To do this piece of ruthless butchery,
Albeit they were flesh'd villains, bloody dogs,
Melted with tenderness and mild compassion,
Wept like two children in their deaths' sad story.
'O, thus' quoth Dighton 'lay the gentle babes'—
'Thus, thus,' quoth Forrest 'girdling one another
Within their alabaster innocent arms.
Their lips were four red roses on a stalk,
And in their summer beauty kiss'd each other.
A book of prayers on their pillow lay;
Which once,' quoth Forrest 'almost chang'd my mind;
But, O, the devil'—there the villain stopp'd;
When Dighton thus told on: 'We smothered
The most replenished sweet work of nature
That from the prime creation e'er she framed.'
Hence both are gone with conscience and remorse
They could not speak; and so I left them both,
To bear this tidings to the bloody King.

Enter KING RICHARD

And here he comes. All health, my sovereign lord!
KING RICHARD. Kind Tyrrel, am I happy in thy news?
TYRREL. If to have done the thing you gave in charge
Beget your happiness, be happy then,

For it is done.

KING RICHARD. But didst thou see them dead?

TYRREL. I did, my lord.

KING RICHARD. And buried, gentle Tyrrel?

TYRREL. The chaplain of the Tower hath buried them;
But where, to say the truth, I do not know.

KING RICHARD. Come to me, Tyrrel, soon at after supper,
When thou shalt tell the process of their death.
Meantime, but think how I may do thee good
And be inheritor of thy desire.
Farewell till then.

TYRREL. I humbly take my leave.   *Exit*

KING RICHARD. The son of Clarence have I pent up close;
His daughter meanly have I match'd in marriage;
The sons of Edward sleep in Abraham's bosom,
And Anne my wife hath bid this world good night.
Now, for I know the Britaine Richmond aims
At young Elizabeth, my brother's daughter,
And by that knot looks proudly on the crown,
To her go I, a jolly thriving wooer.

Enter RATCLIFF

RATCLIFF. My lord!

KING RICHARD. Good or bad news, that thou com'st in so
bluntly?

RATCLIFF. Bad news, my lord: Morton is fled to Richmond;
And Buckingham, back'd with the hardy Welshmen,
Is in the field, and still his power increaseth.

KING RICHARD. Ely with Richmond troubles me more near
Than Buckingham and his rash-levied strength.
Come, I have learn'd that fearful commenting
Is leaden servitor to dull delay;
Delay leads impotent and snail-pac'd beggary.
Then fiery expedition be my wing,
Jove's Mercury, and herald for a king!
Go, muster men. My counsel is my shield.
We must be brief when traitors brave the field.   *Exeunt*

SCENE 4

London. Before the palace

Enter old QUEEN MARGARET

QUEEN MARGARET. So now prosperity begins to mellow
And drop into the rotten mouth of death.
Here in these confines slily have I lurk'd
To watch the waning of mine enemies.
A dire induction am I witness to,
And will to France, hoping the consequence
Will prove as bitter, black, and tragical.
Withdraw thee, wretched Margaret. Who comes here?
[Retires]

Enter QUEEN ELIZABETH *and the* DUCHESS OF YORK

QUEEN ELIZABETH. Ah, my poor princes! ah, my tender babes!
My unblown flowers, new-appearing sweets!
If yet your gentle souls fly in the air
And be not fix'd in doom perpetual,
Hover about me with your airy wings
And hear your mother's lamentation.
QUEEN MARGARET. Hover about her; say that right for right
Hath dimm'd your infant morn to aged night.
DUCHESS. So many miseries have craz'd my voice
That my woe-wearied tongue is still and mute.
Edward Plantagenet, why art thou dead?
QUEEN MARGARET. Plantagenet doth quit Plantagenet,
Edward for Edward pays a dying debt.
QUEEN ELIZABETH. Wilt thou, O God, fly from such gentle lambs
And throw them in the entrails of the wolf?
When didst thou sleep when such a deed was done?
QUEEN MARGARET. When holy Harry died, and my sweet son.
DUCHESS. Dead life, blind sight, poor mortal living ghost,
Woe's scene, world's shame, grave's due by life usurp'd,
Brief abstract and record of tedious days,

Rest thy unrest on England's lawful earth, [*Sitting down*]
Unlawfully made drunk with innocent blood.
QUEEN ELIZABETH. Ah, that thou wouldst as soon afford a
grave
As thou canst yield a melancholy seat!
Then would I hide my bones, not rest them here.
Ah, who hath any cause to mourn but we?
[*Sitting down by her*]
QUEEN MARGARET. [*Coming forward*] If ancient sorrow be
most reverend,
Give mine the benefit of seniory,
And let my griefs frown on the upper hand.
If sorrow can admit society, [*Sitting down with them*]
Tell o'er your woes again by viewing mine.
I had an Edward, till a Richard kill'd him;
I had a husband, till a Richard kill'd him:
Thou hadst an Edward, till a Richard kill'd him;
Thou hadst a Richard, till a Richard kill'd him.
DUCHESS. I had a Richard too, and thou didst kill him;
I had a Rutland too, thou holp'st to kill him.
QUEEN MARGARET. Thou hadst a Clarence too, and Richard
kill'd him.
From forth the kennel of thy womb hath crept
A hell-hound that doth hunt us all to death.
That dog, that had his teeth before his eyes
To worry lambs and lap their gentle blood,
That foul defacer of God's handiwork,
That excellent grand tyrant of the earth
That reigns in galled eyes of weeping souls,
Thy womb let loose to chase us to our graves.
O upright, just, and true-disposing God,
How do I thank thee that this carnal cur
Preys on the issue of his mother's body
And makes her pew-fellow with others' moan!
DUCHESS. O Harry's wife, triumph not in my woes!
God witness with me, I have wept for thine.
QUEEN MARGARET. Bear with me; I am hungry for revenge,
And now I cloy me with beholding it.
Thy Edward he is dead, that kill'd my Edward;
The other Edward dead, to quit my Edward;

Young York he is but boot, because both they
Match'd not the high perfection of my loss.
Thy Clarence he is dead that stabb'd my Edward;
And the beholders of this frantic play,
Th' adulterate Hastings, Rivers, Vaughan, Grey,
Untimely smother'd in their dusky graves.
Richard yet lives, hell's black intelligencer;
Only reserv'd their factor to buy souls
And send them thither. But at hand, at hand,
Ensues his piteous and unpitied end.
Earth gapes, hell burns, fiends roar, saints pray,
To have him suddenly convey'd from hence.
Cancel his bond of life, dear God, I pray,
That I may live and say 'The dog is dead.'
QUEEN ELIZABETH. O, thou didst prophesy the time would
     come
That I should wish for thee to help me curse
That bottled spider, that foul bunch-back'd toad!
QUEEN MARGARET. I call'd thee then vain flourish of my
     fortune;
I call'd thee then poor shadow, painted queen,
The presentation of but what I was,
The flattering index of a direful pageant,
One heav'd a-high to be hurl'd down below,
A mother only mock'd with two fair babes,
A dream of what thou wast, a garish flag
To be the aim of every dangerous shot,
A sign of dignity, a breath, a bubble,
A queen in jest, only to fill the scene.
Where is thy husband now? Where be thy brothers?
Where be thy two sons? Wherein dost thou joy?
Who sues, and kneels, and says 'God save the Queen'?
Where be the bending peers that flattered thee?
Where be the thronging troops that followed thee?
Decline all this, and see what now thou art:
For happy wife, a most distressed widow;
For joyful mother, one that wails the name;
For one being su'd to, one that humbly sues;
For Queen, a very caitiff crown'd with care;
For she that scorn'd at me, now scorn'd of me;

For she being fear'd of all, now fearing one;
For she commanding all, obey'd of none.
Thus hath the course of justice whirl'd about
And left thee but a very prey to time,
Having no more but thought of what thou wast
To torture thee the more, being what thou art.
Thou didst usurp my place, and dost thou not
Usurp the just proportion of my sorrow?
Now thy proud neck bears half my burden'd yoke,
From which even here I slip my weary head
And leave the burden of it all on thee.
Farewell, York's wife, and queen of sad mischance;
These English woes shall make me smile in France.

QUEEN ELIZABETH. O thou well skill'd in curses, stay awhile
And teach me how to curse mine enemies!

QUEEN MARGARET. Forbear to sleep the nights, and fast the
days;
Compare dead happiness with living woe;
Think that thy babes were sweeter than they were,
And he that slew them fouler than he is.
Bett'ring thy loss makes the bad-causer worse;
Revolving this will teach thee how to curse.

QUEEN ELIZABETH. My words are dull; O, quicken them
with thine!

QUEEN MARGARET. Thy woes will make them sharp and
pierce like mine.   *Exit*

DUCHESS. Why should calamity be full of words?

QUEEN ELIZABETH. Windy attorneys to their client woes,
Airy succeeders of intestate joys,
Poor breathing orators of miseries,
Let them have scope; though what they will impart
Help nothing else, yet do they ease the heart.

DUCHESS. If so, then be not tongue-tied. Go with me,
And in the breath of bitter words let's smother
My damned son that thy two sweet sons smother'd.
The trumpet sounds; be copious in exclaims.

Enter KING RICHARD *and his train, marching with
drums and trumpets*

KING RICHARD. Who intercepts me in my expedition?

DUCHESS. O, she that might have intercepted thee,
By strangling thee in her accursed womb,
From all the slaughters, wretch, that thou hast done!
QUEEN ELIZABETH. Hidest thou that forehead with a golden
crown
Where't should be branded, if that right were right,
The slaughter of the Prince that ow'd that crown,
And the dire death of my poor sons and brothers?
Tell me, thou villain slave, where are my children?
DUCHESS. Thou toad, thou toad, where is thy brother
Clarence?
And little Ned Plantagenet, his son?
QUEEN ELIZABETH. Where is the gentle Rivers, Vaughan,
Grey?
DUCHESS. Where is kind Hastings?
KING RICHARD. A flourish, trumpets! Strike alarum, drums!
Let not the heavens hear these tell-tale women
Rail on the Lord's anointed. Strike, I say!

[Flourish. Alarums]

Either be patient and entreat me fair,
Or with the clamorous report of war
Thus will I drown your exclamations.
DUCHESS. Art thou my son?
KING RICHARD. Ay, I thank God, my father, and yourself.
DUCHESS. Then patiently hear my impatience.
KING RICHARD. Madam, I have a touch of your condition
That cannot brook the accent of reproof.
DUCHESS. O, let me speak!
KING RICHARD. Do, then; but I'll not hear.
DUCHESS. I will be mild and gentle in my words.
KING RICHARD. And brief, good mother; for I am in haste.
DUCHESS. Art thou so hasty? I have stay'd for thee,
God knows, in torment and in agony.
KING RICHARD. And came I not at last to comfort you?
DUCHESS. No, by the holy rood, thou know'st it well
Thou cam'st on earth to make the earth my hell.
A grievous burden was thy birth to me;
Tetchy and wayward was thy infancy;
Thy school-days frightful, desp'rate, wild, and furious;
Thy prime of manhood daring, bold, and venturous;

Thy age confirm'd, proud, subtle, sly, and bloody,
More mild, but yet more harmful-kind in hatred.
What comfortable hour canst thou name
That ever grac'd me with thy company?
KING RICHARD. Faith, none but Humphrey Hour, that call'd
    your Grace
To breakfast once forth of my company.
If I be so disgracious in your eye,
Let me march on and not offend you, madam.
Strike up the drum.
DUCHESS. I prithee hear me speak.
KING RICHARD. You speak too bitterly.
DUCHESS. Hear me a word;
    For I shall never speak to thee again.
KING RICHARD. So.
DUCHESS. Either thou wilt die by God's just ordinance
    Ere from this war thou turn a conqueror;
    Or I with grief and extreme age shall perish
    And never more behold thy face again.
    Therefore take with thee my most grievous curse,
    Which in the day of battle tire thee more
    Than all the complete armour that thou wear'st!
    My prayers on the adverse party fight;
    And there the little souls of Edward's children
    Whisper the spirits of thine enemies
    And promise them success and victory.
    Bloody thou art; bloody will be thy end.
    Shame serves thy life and doth thy death attend.   *Exit*
QUEEN ELIZABETH. Though far more cause, yet much less
    spirit to curse
    Abides in me; I say amen to her.
KING RICHARD. Stay, madam, I must talk a word with you.
QUEEN ELIZABETH. I have no moe sons of the royal blood
    For thee to slaughter. For my daughters, Richard,
    They shall be praying nuns, not weeping queens;
    And therefore level not to hit their lives.
KING RICHARD. You have a daughter call'd Elizabeth.
    Virtuous and fair, royal and gracious.
QUEEN ELIZABETH. And must she die for this? O, let her
    live,

And I'll corrupt her manners, stain her beauty,
Slander myself as false to Edward's bed,
Throw over her the veil of infamy;
So she may live unscarr'd of bleeding slaughter,
I will confess she was not Edward's daughter.
KING RICHARD. Wrong not her birth; she is a royal Princess.
QUEEN ELIZABETH. To save her life I'll say she is not so.
KING RICHARD. Her life is safest only in her birth.
QUEEN ELIZABETH. And only in that safety died her brothers.
KING RICHARD. Lo, at their birth good stars were opposite.
QUEEN ELIZABETH. No, to their lives ill friends were contrary.
KING RICHARD. All unavoided is the doom of destiny.
QUEEN ELIZABETH. True, when avoided grace makes destiny.
My babes were destin'd to a fairer death,
If grace had bless'd thee with a fairer life.
KING RICHARD. You speak as if that I had slain my cousins.
QUEEN ELIZABETH. Cousins, indeed; and by their uncle cozen'd
Of comfort, kingdom, kindred, freedom, life.
Whose hand soever lanc'd their tender hearts,
Thy head, all indirectly, gave direction.
No doubt the murd'rous knife was dull and blunt
Till it was whetted on thy stone-hard heart
To revel in the entrails of my lambs.
But that still use of grief makes wild grief tame,
My tongue should to thy ears not name my boys
Till that my nails were anchor'd in thine eyes;
And I, in such a desp'rate bay of death,
Like a poor bark, of sails and tackling reft,
Rush all to pieces on thy rocky bosom.
KING RICHARD. Madam, so thrive I in my enterprise
And dangerous success of bloody wars,
As I intend more good to you and yours
Than ever you or yours by me were harm'd!
QUEEN ELIZABETH. What good is cover'd with the face of heaven,

To be discover'd, that can do me good?

KING RICHARD. Th' advancement of your children, gentle
lady.

QUEEN ELIZABETH. Up to some scaffold, there to lose their
heads?

KING RICHARD. Unto the dignity and height of Fortune,
The high imperial type of this earth's glory.

QUEEN ELIZABETH. Flatter my sorrow with report of it;
Tell me what state, what dignity, what honour,
Canst thou demise to any child of mine?

KING RICHARD. Even all I have—ay, and myself and all
Will I withal endow a child of thine;
So in the Lethe of thy angry soul
Thou drown the sad remembrance of those wrongs
Which thou supposest I have done to thee.

QUEEN ELIZABETH. Be brief, lest that the process of thy
kindness
Last longer telling than thy kindness' date.

KING RICHARD. Then know, that from my soul I love thy
daughter.

QUEEN ELIZABETH. My daughter's mother thinks it with her
soul.

KING RICHARD. What do you think?

QUEEN ELIZABETH. That thou dost love my daughter from
thy soul.
So from thy soul's love didst thou love her brothers,
And from my heart's love I do thank thee for it.

KING RICHARD. Be not so hasty to confound my meaning.
I mean that with my soul I love thy daughter
And do intend to make her Queen of England.

QUEEN ELIZABETH. Well, then, who dost thou mean shall be
her king?

KING RICHARD. Even he that makes her Queen. Who else
should be?

QUEEN ELIZABETH. What, thou?

KING RICHARD. Even so. How think you of it?

QUEEN ELIZABETH. How canst thou woo her?

KING RICHARD. That would I learn of you,
As one being best acquainted with her humour.

QUEEN ELIZABETH. And wilt thou learn of me?

KING RICHARD. Madam, with all my heart.

QUEEN ELIZABETH. Send to her, by the man that slew her
    brothers,
    A pair of bleeding hearts; thereon engrave
    'Edward' and 'York.' Then haply will she weep;
    Therefore present to her—as sometimes Margaret
    Did to thy father, steep'd in Rutland's blood—
    A handkerchief; which, say to her, did drain
    The purple sap from her sweet brother's body,
    And bid her wipe her weeping eyes withal.
    If this inducement move her not to love,
    Send her a letter of thy noble deeds;
    Tell her thou mad'st away her uncle Clarence,
    Her uncle Rivers; ay, and for her sake
    Mad'st quick conveyance with her good aunt Anne.

KING RICHARD. You mock me, madam; this is not the way
    To win your daughter.

QUEEN ELIZABETH. There is no other way;
    Unless thou couldst put on some other shape
    And not be Richard that hath done all this.

KING RICHARD. Say that I did all this for love of her.

QUEEN ELIZABETH. Nay, then indeed she cannot choose but
    hate thee,
    Having bought love with such a bloody spoil.

KING RICHARD. Look what is done cannot be now amended.
    Men shall deal unadvisedly sometimes,
    Which after-hours gives leisure to repent.
    If I did take the kingdom from your sons,
    To make amends I'll give it to your daughter.
    If I have kill'd the issue of your womb,
    To quicken your increase I will beget
    Mine issue of your blood upon your daughter.
    A grandam's name is little less in love
    Than is the doating title of a mother;
    They are as children but one step below,
    Even of your metal, of your very blood;
    Of all one pain, save for a night of groans
    Endur'd of her, for whom you bid like sorrow.
    Your children were vexation to your youth;
    But mine shall be a comfort to your age.

The loss you have is but a son being King,
And by that loss your daughter is made Queen.
I cannot make you what amends I would,
Therefore accept such kindness as I can.
Dorset your son, that with a fearful soul
Leads discontented steps in foreign soil,
This fair alliance quickly shall call home
To high promotions and great dignity.
The King, that calls your beauteous daughter wife,
Familiarly shall call thy Dorset brother;
Again shall you be mother to a king,
And all the ruins of distressful times
Repair'd with double riches of content.
What! we have many goodly days to see.
The liquid drops of tears that you have shed
Shall come again, transform'd to orient pearl,
Advantaging their loan with interest
Of ten times double gain of happiness.
Go, then, my mother, to thy daughter go;
Make bold her bashful years with your experience;
Prepare her ears to hear a wooer's tale;
Put in her tender heart th' aspiring flame
Of golden sovereignty; acquaint the Princess
With the sweet silent hours of marriage joys.
And when this arm of mine hath chastised
The petty rebel, dull-brain'd Buckingham,
Bound with triumphant garlands will I come,
And lead thy daughter to a conqueror's bed;
To whom I will retail my conquest won,
And she shall be sole victoress, Cæsar's Cæsar.

QUEEN ELIZABETH. What were I best to say? Her father's
  brother
Would be her lord? Or shall I say her uncle?
Or he that slew her brothers and her uncles?
Under what title shall I woo for thee
That God, the law, my honour, and her love
Can make seem pleasing to her tender years?

KING RICHARD. Infer fair England's peace by this alliance.

QUEEN ELIZABETH. Which she shall purchase with still-last-
  ing war.

KING RICHARD. Tell her the King, that may command, entreats.

QUEEN ELIZABETH. That at her hands which the King's King forbids.

KING RICHARD. Say she shall be a high and mighty queen.

QUEEN ELIZABETH. To wail the title, as her mother doth.

KING RICHARD. Say I will love her everlastingly.

QUEEN ELIZABETH. But how long shall that title 'ever' last?

KING RICHARD. Sweetly in force unto her fair life's end.

QUEEN ELIZABETH. But how long fairly shall her sweet life last?

KING RICHARD. As long as heaven and nature lengthens it.

QUEEN ELIZABETH. As long as hell and Richard likes of it.

KING RICHARD. Say I, her sovereign, am her subject low.

QUEEN ELIZABETH. But she, your subject, loathes such sovereignty.

KING RICHARD. Be eloquent in my behalf to her.

QUEEN ELIZABETH. An honest tale speeds best being plainly told.

KING RICHARD. Then plainly to her tell my loving tale.

QUEEN ELIZABETH. Plain and not honest is too harsh a style.

KING RICHARD. Your reasons are too shallow and too quick.

QUEEN ELIZABETH. O, no, my reasons are too deep and dead—
Too deep and dead, poor infants, in their graves.

KING RICHARD. Harp not on that string, madam; that is past.

QUEEN ELIZABETH. Harp on it still shall I till heartstrings break.

KING RICHARD. Now, by my George, my garter, and my crown—

QUEEN ELIZABETH. Profan'd, dishonour'd, and the third usurp'd.

KING RICHARD. I swear—

QUEEN ELIZABETH. By nothing; for this is no oath:
Thy George, profan'd, hath lost his lordly honour;
Thy garter, blemish'd, pawn'd his knightly virtue;
Thy crown, usurp'd, disgrac'd his kingly glory.
If something thou wouldst swear to be believ'd,
Swear then by something that thou hast not wrong'd.

KING RICHARD. Then, by my self—

QUEEN ELIZABETH. Thy self is self-misus'd.
KING RICHARD. Now, by the world—
QUEEN ELIZABETH. 'Tis full of thy foul wrongs.
KING RICHARD. My father's death—
QUEEN ELIZABETH. Thy life hath it dishonour'd.
KING RICHARD. Why, then, by God—
QUEEN ELIZABETH. God's wrong is most of all.
  If thou didst fear to break an oath with Him,
  The unity the King my husband made
  Thou hadst not broken, nor my brothers died.
  If thou hadst fear'd to break an oath by Him,
  Th' imperial metal, circling now thy head,
  Had grac'd the tender temples of my child;
  And both the Princes had been breathing here,
  Which now, two tender bedfellows for dust,
  Thy broken faith hath made the prey for worms.
  What canst thou swear by now?
KING RICHARD. The time to come.
QUEEN ELIZABETH. That thou hast wronged in the time
  o'erpast;
  For I myself have many tears to wash
  Hereafter time, for time past wrong'd by thee.
  The children live whose fathers thou hast slaughter'd,
  Ungovern'd youth, to wail it in their age;
  The parents live whose children thou hast butcher'd,
  Old barren plants, to wail it with their age.
  Swear not by time to come; for that thou hast
  Misus'd ere us'd, by times ill-us'd o'erpast.
KING RICHARD. As I intend to prosper and repent,
  So thrive I in my dangerous affairs
  Of hostile arms! Myself myself confound!
  Heaven and fortune bar me happy hours!
  Day, yield me not thy light; nor, night, thy rest!
  Be opposite all planets of good luck
  To my proceeding!—if, with dear heart's love,
  Immaculate devotion, holy thoughts,
  I tender not thy beauteous princely daughter.
  In her consists my happiness and thine;
  Without her, follows to myself and thee,
  Herself, the land, and many a Christian soul,

Death, desolation, ruin, and decay.
It cannot be avoided but by this;
It will not be avoided but by this.
Therefore, dear mother—I must call you so—
Be the attorney of my love to her;
Plead what I will be, not what I have been;
Not my deserts, but what I will deserve.
Urge the necessity and state of times,
And be not peevish-fond in great designs.

QUEEN ELIZABETH. Shall I be tempted of the devil thus?

KING RICHARD. Ay, if the devil tempt you to do good.

QUEEN ELIZABETH. Shall I forget myself to be myself?

KING RICHARD. Ay, if your self's remembrance wrong yourself.

QUEEN ELIZABETH. Yet thou didst kill my children.

KING RICHARD. But in your daughter's womb I bury them;
Where, in that nest of spicery, they will breed
Selves of themselves, to your recomforture.

QUEEN ELIZABETH. Shall I go win my daughter to thy will?

KING RICHARD. And be a happy mother by the deed.

QUEEN ELIZABETH. I go. Write to me very shortly,
And you shall understand from me her mind.

KING RICHARD. Bear her my true love's kiss; and so, farewell.
                    Kissing her. Exit QUEEN ELIZABETH
Relenting fool, and shallow, changing woman!

Enter RATCLIFF; CATESBY *following*

How now! what news?

RATCLIFF. Most mighty sovereign, on the western coast
Rideth a puissant navy; to our shores
Throng many doubtful hollow-hearted friends,
Unarm'd, and unresolv'd to beat them back.
'Tis thought that Richmond is their admiral;
And there they hull, expecting but the aid
Of Buckingham to welcome them ashore.

KING RICHARD. Some light-foot friend post to the Duke of
Norfolk.
Ratcliff, thyself—or Catesby; where is he?

CATESBY. Here, my good lord.

KING RICHARD. Catesby, fly to the Duke.

ACT IV. SCENE 4

CATESBY. I will, my lord, with all convenient haste.
KING RICHARD. Ratcliff, come hither. Post to Salisbury;
When thou com'st thither—[*To* CATESBY] Dull, unmind-
ful villain,
Why stay'st thou here, and go'st not to the Duke?
CATESBY. First, mighty liege, tell me your Highness' pleasure,
What from your Grace I shall deliver to him.
KING RICHARD. O, true, good Catesby. Bid him levy straight
The greatest strength and power that he can make
And meet me suddenly at Salisbury.
CATESBY. I go.   *Exit*
RATCLIFF. What, may it please you, shall I do at Salisbury?
KING RICHARD. Why, what wouldst thou do there before I
go?
RATCLIFF. Your Highness told me I should post before.
KING RICHARD. My mind is chang'd.

Enter LORD STANLEY

Stanley, what news with you?
STANLEY. None good, my liege, to please you with the hear-
ing;
Nor none so bad but well may be reported.
KING RICHARD. Hoyday, a riddle! neither good nor bad!
What need'st thou run so many miles about,
When thou mayest tell thy tale the nearest way?
Once more, what news?
STANLEY. Richmond is on the seas.
KING RICHARD. There let him sink, and be the seas on him!
White-liver'd runagate, what doth he there?
STANLEY. I know not, mighty sovereign, but by guess.
KING RICHARD. Well, as you guess?
STANLEY. Stirr'd up by Dorset, Buckingham, and Morton,
He makes for England here to claim the crown.
KING RICHARD. Is the chair empty? Is the sword unsway'd?
Is the King dead, the empire unpossess'd?
What heir of York is there alive but we?
And who is England's King but great York's heir?
Then tell me what makes he upon the seas.
STANLEY. Unless for that, my liege, I cannot guess.
KING RICHARD. Unless for that he comes to be your liege,

You cannot guess wherefore the Welshman comes.
Thou wilt revolt and fly to him, I fear.
STANLEY. No, my good lord; therefore mistrust me not.
KING RICHARD. Where is thy power then, to beat him back?
Where be thy tenants and thy followers?
Are they not now upon the western shore,
Safe-conducting the rebels from their ships?
STANLEY. No, my good lord, my friends are in the north.
KING RICHARD. Cold friends to me. What do they in the
north,
When they should serve their sovereign in the west?
STANLEY. They have not been commanded, mighty King.
Pleaseth your Majesty to give me leave,
I'll muster up my friends and meet your Grace
Where and what time your Majesty shall please.
KING RICHARD. Ay, ay, thou wouldst be gone to join with
Richmond;
But I'll not trust thee.
STANLEY. Most mighty sovereign,
You have no cause to hold my friendship doubtful.
I never was nor never will be false.
KING RICHARD. Go, then, and muster men. But leave behind
Your son, George Stanley. Look your heart be firm,
Or else his head's assurance is but frail.
STANLEY. So deal with him as I prove true to you.   *Exit*

Enter a MESSENGER

MESSENGER. My gracious sovereign, now in Devonshire,
As I by friends am well advertised,
Sir Edward Courtney and the haughty prelate,
Bishop of Exeter, his elder brother,
With many moe confederates, are in arms.

Enter another MESSENGER

SECOND MESSENGER. In Kent, my liege, the Guilfords are in
arms;
And every hour more competitors
Flock to the rebels, and their power grows strong.

Enter another MESSENGER

THIRD MESSENGER. My lord, the army of great Buckingham—
KING RICHARD. Out on you, owls! Nothing but songs of
death? [*He strikes him*]
There, take thou that till thou bring better news.
THIRD MESSENGER. The news I have to tell your Majesty
Is that by sudden floods and fall of waters
Buckingham's army is dispers'd and scatter'd;
And he himself wand'red away alone,
No man knows whither.
KING RICHARD. I cry thee mercy.
There is my purse to cure that blow of thine.
Hath any well-advised friend proclaim'd
Reward to him that brings the traitor in?
THIRD MESSENGER. Such proclamation hath been made, my
lord.

Enter another MESSENGER

FOURTH MESSENGER. Sir Thomas Lovel and Lord Marquis
Dorset,
'Tis said, my liege, in Yorkshire are in arms.
But this good comfort bring I to your Highness—
The Britaine navy is dispers'd by tempest.
Richmond in Dorsetshire sent out a boat
Unto the shore, to ask those on the banks
If they were his assistants, yea or no;
Who answer'd him they came from Buckingham
Upon his party. He, mistrusting them,
Hois'd sail, and made his course again for Britaine.
KING RICHARD. March on, march on, since we are up in
arms;
If not to fight with foreign enemies,
Yet to beat down these rebels here at home.

Re-enter CATESBY

CATESBY. My liege, the Duke of Buckingham is taken—
That is the best news. That the Earl of Richmond
Is with a mighty power landed at Milford
Is colder tidings, yet they must be told.
KING RICHARD. Away towards Salisbury! While we reason
here

871

A royal battle might be won and lost.
Some one take order Buckingham be brought
To Salisbury; the rest march on with me.

Flourish. Exeunt

SCENE 5

LORD DERBY's *house*

Enter STANLEY *and* SIR CHRISTOPHER URSWICK

STANLEY. Sir Christopher, tell Richmond this from me:
That in the sty of the most deadly boar
My son George Stanley is frank'd up in hold;
If I revolt, off goes young George's head;
The fear of that holds off my present aid.
So, get thee gone; commend me to thy lord.
Withal say that the Queen hath heartily consented
He should espouse Elizabeth her daughter.
But tell me, where is princely Richmond now?
CHRISTOPHER. At Pembroke, or at Ha'rford west in Wales.
STANLEY. What men of name resort to him?
CHRISTOPHER. Sir Walter Herbert, a renowned soldier;
Sir Gilbert Talbot, Sir William Stanley,
Oxford, redoubted Pembroke, Sir James Blunt,
And Rice ap Thomas, with a valiant crew;
And many other of great name and worth;
And towards London do they bend their power,
If by the way they be not fought withal.
STANLEY. Well, hie thee to thy lord; I kiss his hand;
My letter will resolve him of my mind.
Farewell.

Exeunt

ACT V. SCENE 1

Salisbury. An open place

Enter the SHERIFF *and guard, with* BUCKINGHAM,
led to execution

BUCKINGHAM. Will not King Richard let me speak with
him?
SHERIFF. No, my good lord; therefore be patient.
BUCKINGHAM. Hastings, and Edward's children, Grey, and
Rivers,
Holy King Henry, and thy fair son Edward,
Vaughan, and all that have miscarried
By underhand corrupted foul injustice,
If that your moody discontented souls
Do through the clouds behold this present hour,
Even for revenge mock my destruction!
This is All-Souls' day, fellow, is it not?
SHERIFF. It is, my lord.
BUCKINGHAM. Why, then All-Souls' day is my body's
doomsday.
This is the day which in King Edward's time
I wish'd might fall on me when I was found
False to his children and his wife's allies;
This is the day wherein I wish'd to fall
By the false faith of him whom most I trusted;
This, this All-Souls' day to my fearful soul
Is the determin'd respite of my wrongs;
That high All-Seer which I dallied with
Hath turn'd my feigned prayer on my head
And given in earnest what I begg'd in jest.
Thus doth He force the swords of wicked men
To turn their own points in their masters' bosoms.
Thus Margaret's curse falls heavy on my neck.
'When he' quoth she 'shall split thy heart with sorrow,
Remember Margaret was a prophetess.'
Come lead me, officers, to the block of shame;
Wrong hath but wrong, and blame the due of blame.
Exeunt

SCENE 2

Camp near Tamworth

Enter RICHMOND, OXFORD, SIR JAMES BLUNT, SIR WALTER HERBERT, *and others, with drum and colours*

RICHMOND. Fellows in arms, and my most loving friends,
Bruis'd underneath the yoke of tyranny,
Thus far into the bowels of the land
Have we march'd on without impediment;
And here receive we from our father Stanley
Lines of fair comfort and encouragement.
The wretched, bloody, and usurping boar,
That spoil'd your summer fields and fruitful vines,
Swills your warm blood like wash, and makes his trough
In your embowell'd bosoms—this foul swine
Is now even in the centre of this isle,
Near to the town of Leicester, as we learn.
From Tamworth thither is but one day's march.
In God's name cheerly on, courageous friends,
To reap the harvest of perpetual peace
By this one bloody trial of sharp war.
OXFORD. Every man's conscience is a thousand men,
To fight against this guilty homicide.
HERBERT. I doubt not but his friends will turn to us.
BLUNT. He hath no friends but what are friends for fear,
Which in his dearest need will fly from him.
RICHMOND. All for our vantage. Then in God's name march.
True hope is swift and flies with swallow's wings;
Kings it makes gods, and meaner creatures kings. *Exeunt*

SCENE 3

Bosworth Field

Enter KING RICHARD *in arms, with* NORFOLK,
RATCLIFF, *the* EARL OF SURREY, *and others*

KING RICHARD. Here pitch our tent, even here in Bosworth
field.
My Lord of Surrey, why look you so sad?
SURREY. My heart is ten times lighter than my looks.
KING RICHARD. My Lord of Norfolk!
NORFOLK. Here, most gracious liege.
KING RICHARD. Norfolk, we must have knocks; ha! must we
not?
NORFOLK. We must both give and take, my loving lord.
KING RICHARD. Up with my tent! Here will I lie to-night;
[*Soldiers begin to set up the* KING'S *tent*]
But where to-morrow? Well, all's one for that.
Who hath descried the number of the traitors?
NORFOLK. Six or seven thousand is their utmost power.
KING RICHARD. Why, our battalia trebles that account;
Besides, the King's name is a tower of strength,
Which they upon the adverse faction want.
Up with the tent! Come, noble gentlemen,
Let us survey the vantage of the ground.
Call for some men of sound direction.
Let's lack no discipline, make no delay;
For, lords, to-morrow is a busy day.   *Exeunt*

Enter, on the other side of the field, RICHMOND, SIR
WILLIAM BRANDON, OXFORD, DORSET, *and others.*
Some pitch RICHMOND'S *tent*

RICHMOND. The weary sun hath made a golden set,
And by the bright tract of his fiery car
Gives token of a goodly day to-morrow.
Sir William Brandon, you shall bear my standard.
Give me some ink and paper in my tent.
I'll draw the form and model of our battle,
Limit each leader to his several charge,

And part in just proportion our small power.
My Lord of Oxford—you, Sir William Brandon—
And you, Sir Walter Herbert—stay with me.
The Earl of Pembroke keeps his regiment;
Good Captain Blunt, bear my good night to him,
And by the second hour in the morning
Desire the Earl to see me in my tent.
Yet one thing more, good Captain, do for me—
Where is Lord Stanley quarter'd, do you know?
BLUNT. Unless I have mista'en his colours much—
Which well I am assur'd I have not done—
His regiment lies half a mile at least
South from the mighty power of the King.
RICHMOND. If without peril it be possible,
Sweet Blunt, make some good means to speak with him
And give him from me this most needful note.
BLUNT. Upon my life, my lord, I'll undertake it;
And so, God give you quiet rest to-night!
RICHMOND. Good night, good Captain Blunt. Come, gen-
tlemen,
Let us consult upon to-morrow's business.
In to my tent; the dew is raw and cold.

[*They withdraw into the tent*]

Enter, to his tent, KING RICHARD, NORFOLK,
RATCLIFF, *and* CATESBY

KING RICHARD. What is't o'clock?
CATESBY. It's supper-time, my lord;
It's nine o'clock.
KING RICHARD. I will not sup to-night.
Give me some ink and paper.
What, is my beaver easier than it was?
And all my armour laid into my tent?
CATESBY. It is, my liege; and all things are in readiness.
KING RICHARD. Good Norfolk, hie thee to thy charge;
Use careful watch, choose trusty sentinels.
NORFOLK. I go, my lord.
KING RICHARD. Stir with the lark to-morrow, gentle Norfolk.
NORFOLK. I warrant you, my lord. *Exit*
KING RICHARD. Catesby!

CATESBY. My lord?

KING RICHARD. Send out a pursuivant-at-arms
　To Stanley's regiment; bid him bring his power
　Before sunrising, lest his son George fall
　Into the blind cave of eternal night.　　　*Exit* CATESBY
　Fill me a bowl of wine. Give me a watch.
　Saddle white Surrey for the field to-morrow.
　Look that my staves be sound, and not too heavy.
　Ratcliff!

RATCLIFF. My lord?

KING RICHARD. Saw'st thou the melancholy Lord Northum-
　berland?

RATCLIFF. Thomas the Earl of Surrey and himself,
　Much about cock-shut time, from troop to troop
　Went through the army, cheering up the soldiers.

KING RICHARD. So, I am satisfied. Give me a bowl of wine.
　I have not that alacrity of spirit
　Nor cheer of mind that I was wont to have.
　Set it down. Is ink and paper ready?

RATCLIFF. It is, my lord.

KING RICHARD. Bid my guard watch; leave me.
　Ratcliff, about the mid of night come to my tent
　And help to arm me. Leave me, I say.
　　　　　　　　　　Exit RATCLIFF. RICHARD *sleeps*

Enter DERBY *to* RICHMOND *in his tent;* LORDS *attending*

DERBY. Fortune and victory sit on thy helm!

RICHMOND. All comfort that the dark night can afford
　Be to thy person, noble father-in-law!
　Tell me, how fares our loving mother?

DERBY. I, by attorney, bless thee from thy mother,
　Who prays continually for Richmond's good.
　So much for that. The silent hours steal on,
　And flaky darkness breaks within the east.
　In brief, for so the season bids us be,
　Prepare thy battle early in the morning,
　And put thy fortune to the arbitrement
　Of bloody strokes and mortal-staring war.
　I, as I may—that which I would I cannot—
　With best advantage will deceive the time

And aid thee in this doubtful shock of arms;
But on thy side I may not be too forward,
Lest, being seen, thy brother, tender George,
Be executed in his father's sight.
Farewell; the leisure and the fearful time
Cuts off the ceremonious vows of love
And ample interchange of sweet discourse
Which so-long-sund'red friends should dwell upon.
God give us leisure for these rites of love!
Once more, adieu; be valiant, and speed well!
RICHMOND. Good lords, conduct him to his regiment.
I'll strive with troubled thoughts to take a nap,
Lest leaden slumber peise me down to-morrow
When I should mount with wings of victory.
Once more, good night, kind lords and gentlemen.

Exeunt all but RICHMOND

O Thou, whose captain I account myself,
Look on my forces with a gracious eye;
Put in their hands Thy bruising irons of wrath,
That they may crush down with a heavy fall
The usurping helmets of our adversaries!
Make us Thy ministers of chastisement,
That we may praise Thee in the victory!
To Thee I do commend my watchful soul
Ere I let fall the windows of mine eyes.
Sleeping and waking, O, defend me still!   [*Sleeps*]

Enter the GHOST *of young* PRINCE EDWARD,
son to HENRY THE SIXTH

GHOST. [*To* RICHARD] Let me sit heavy on thy soul to-
morrow!
Think how thou stabb'dst me in my prime of youth
At Tewksbury; despair, therefore, and die!
[*To* RICHMOND] Be cheerful, Richmond; for the wronged
souls
Of butcher'd princes fight in thy behalf.
King Henry's issue, Richmond, comforts thee.

Enter the GHOST *of* HENRY THE SIXTH

GHOST. [*To* RICHARD] When I was mortal, my anointed
body

By thee was punched full of deadly holes.
Think on the Tower and me. Despair, and die.
Harry the Sixth bids thee despair and die.
[*To* RICHMOND] Virtuous and holy, be thou conqueror!
Harry, that prophesied thou shouldst be King,
Doth comfort thee in thy sleep. Live and flourish!

Enter the GHOST *of* CLARENCE

GHOST. [*To* RICHARD] Let me sit heavy in thy soul to-
morrow!
I that was wash'd to death with fulsome wine,
Poor Clarence, by thy guile betray'd to death!
To-morrow in the battle think on me,
And fall thy edgeless sword. Despair and die!
[*To* RICHMOND] Thou offspring of the house of Lan-
caster,
The wronged heirs of York do pray for thee.
Good angels guard thy battle! Live and flourish!

Enter the GHOSTS *of* RIVERS, GREY, *and* VAUGHAN

GHOST OF RIVERS. [*To* RICHARD] Let me sit heavy in thy
soul to-morrow,
Rivers that died at Pomfret! Despair and die!
GHOST OF GREY. [*To* RICHARD] Think upon Grey, and let
thy soul despair!
GHOST OF VAUGHAN. [*To* RICHARD] Think upon Vaughan,
and with guilty fear
Let fall thy lance. Despair and die!
ALL. [*To* RICHMOND] Awake, and think our wrongs in
Richard's bosom
Will conquer him. Awake and win the day.

Enter the GHOST *of* HASTINGS

GHOST. [*To* RICHARD] Bloody and guilty, guiltily awake,
And in a bloody battle end thy days!
Think on Lord Hastings. Despair and die.
[*To* RICHMOND] Quiet untroubled soul, awake, awake!
Arm, fight, and conquer, for fair England's sake!

Enter the GHOSTS *of the two young* PRINCES

GHOSTS. [*To* RICHARD] Dream on thy cousins smothered in
the Tower.
Let us be lead within thy bosom, Richard,
And weigh thee down to ruin, shame, and death!
Thy nephews' souls bid thee despair and die.
[*To* RICHMOND] Sleep, Richmond, sleep in peace, and
wake in joy;
Good angels guard thee from the boar's annoy!
Live, and beget a happy race of kings!
Edward's unhappy sons do bid thee flourish.

Enter the GHOST *of* LADY ANNE, *his wife*

GHOST. [*To* RICHARD] Richard, thy wife, that wretched
Anne thy wife
That never slept a quiet hour with thee
Now fills thy sleep with perturbations.
To-morrow in the battle think on me,
And fall thy edgeless sword. Despair and die.
[*To* RICHMOND] Thou quiet soul, sleep thou a quiet sleep;
Dream of success and happy victory.
Thy adversary's wife doth pray for thee.

Enter the GHOST *of* BUCKINGHAM

GHOST. [*To* RICHARD] The first was I that help'd thee to the
crown;
The last was I that felt thy tyranny.
O, in the battle think on Buckingham,
And die in terror of thy guiltiness!
Dream on, dream on of bloody deeds and death;
Fainting, despair; despairing, yield thy breath!
[*To* RICHMOND] I died for hope ere I could lend thee aid;
But cheer thy heart and be thou not dismay'd:
God and good angels fight on Richmond's side;
And Richard falls in height of all his pride.
[*The* GHOSTS *vanish.* RICHARD *starts out of his dream*]
KING RICHARD. Give me another horse. Bind up my wounds.
Have mercy, Jesu! Soft! I did but dream.
O coward conscience, how dost thou afflict me!
The lights burn blue. It is now dead midnight.
Cold fearful drops stand on my trembling flesh.

What do I fear? Myself? There's none else by.
Richard loves Richard; that is, I am I.
Is there a murderer here? No—yes, I am.
Then fly. What, from myself? Great reason why—
Lest I revenge. What, myself upon myself!
Alack, I love myself. Wherefore? For any good
That I myself have done unto myself?
O, no! Alas, I rather hate myself
For hateful deeds committed by myself!
I am a villain; yet I lie, I am not.
Fool, of thyself speak well. Fool, do not flatter.
My conscience hath a thousand several tongues,
And every tongue brings in a several tale,
And every tale condemns me for a villain.
Perjury, perjury, in the high'st degree;
Murder, stern murder, in the dir'st degree;
All several sins, all us'd in each degree,
Throng to the bar, crying all 'Guilty! guilty!'
I shall despair. There is no creature loves me;
And if I die no soul will pity me:
And wherefore should they, since that I myself
Find in myself no pity to myself?
Methought the souls of all that I had murder'd
Came to my tent, and every one did threat
To-morrow's vengeance on the head of Richard.

Enter RATCLIFF

RATCLIFF. My lord!
KING RICHARD. Zounds, who is there?
RATCLIFF. Ratcliff, my lord; 'tis I. The early village-cock
    Hath twice done salutation to the morn;
    Your friends are up and buckle on their armour.
KING RICHARD. O Ratcliff, I have dream'd a fearful dream!
    What think'st thou—will our friends prove all true?
RATCLIFF. No doubt, my lord.
KING RICHARD. O Ratcliff, I fear, I fear.
RATCLIFF. Nay, good my lord, be not afraid of shadows.
KING RICHARD. By the apostle Paul, shadows to-night
    Have stuck more terror to the soul of Richard
    Than can the substance of ten thousand soldiers

Armed in proof and led by shallow Richmond.
'Tis not yet near day. Come, go with me;
Under our tents I'll play the eaves-dropper,
To see if any mean to shrink from me.   *Exeunt*

Enter the LORDS *to* RICHMOND *sitting in his tent*

LORDS. Good morrow, Richmond!
RICHMOND. Cry mercy, lords and watchful gentlemen,
  That you have ta'en a tardy sluggard here.
LORDS. How have you slept, my lord?
RICHMOND. The sweetest sleep and fairest-boding dreams
  That ever ent'red in a drowsy head
  Have I since your departure had, my lords.
  Methought their souls whose bodies Richard murder'd
  Came to my tent and cried on victory.
  I promise you my soul is very jocund
  In the remembrance of so fair a dream.
  How far into the morning is it, lords?
LORDS. Upon the stroke of four.
RICHMOND. Why, then 'tis time to arm and give direction.

HIS ORATION TO HIS SOLDIERS

More than I have said, loving countrymen,
The leisure and enforcement of the time
Forbids to dwell upon; yet remember this:
God and our good cause fight upon our side;
The prayers of holy saints and wronged souls,
Like high-rear'd bulwarks, stand before our faces;
Richard except, those whom we fight against
Had rather have us win than him they follow.
For what is he they follow? Truly, gentlemen,
A bloody tyrant and a homicide;
One rais'd in blood, and one in blood establish'd;
One that made means to come by what he hath,
And slaughtered those that were the means to help him;
A base foul stone, made precious by the foil
Of England's chair, where he is falsely set;
One that hath ever been God's enemy.
Then if you fight against God's enemy,
God will in justice ward you as his soldiers;

If you do sweat to put a tyrant down,
You sleep in peace, the tyrant being slain;
If you do fight against your country's foes,
Your country's foes shall pay your pains the hire;
If you do fight in safeguard of your wives,
Your wives shall welcome home the conquerors;
If you do free your children from the sword,
Your children's children quits it in your age.
Then, in the name of God and all these rights,
Advance your standards, draw your willing swords.
For me, the ransom of my bold attempt
Shall be this cold corpse on the earth's cold face;
But if I thrive, the gain of my attempt
The least of you shall share his part thereof.
Sound drums and trumpets boldly and cheerfully;
God and Saint George! Richmond and victory!   *Exeunt*

Re-enter KING RICHARD, RATCLIFF, *attendants,*
and forces

KING RICHARD. What said Northumberland as touching
  Richmond?
RATCLIFF. That he was never trained up in arms.
KING RICHARD. He said the truth; and what said Surrey
  then?
RATCLIFF. He smil'd, and said 'The better for our purpose.'
KING RICHARD. He was in the right; and so indeed it is.
                                          [*Clock strikes*]
  Tell the clock there. Give me a calendar.
  Who saw the sun to-day?
RATCLIFF. Not I, my lord.
KING RICHARD. Then he disdains to shine; for by the book
  He should have brav'd the east an hour ago.
  A black day will it be to somebody.
  Ratcliff!
RATCLIFF. My lord?
KING RICHARD. The sun will not be seen to-day;
  The sky doth frown and lour upon our army.
  I would these dewy tears were from the ground.
  Not shine to-day! Why, what is that to me
  More than to Richmond? For the selfsame heaven

That frowns on me looks sadly upon him.

Enter NORFOLK

NORFOLK. Arm, arm, my lord; the foe vaunts in the field.
KING RICHARD. Come, bustle, bustle; caparison my horse;
Call up Lord Stanley, bid him bring his power.
I will lead forth my soldiers to the plain,
And thus my battle shall be ordered:
My foreward shall be drawn out all in length,
Consisting equally of horse and foot;
Our archers shall be placed in the midst.
John Duke of Norfolk, Thomas Earl of Surrey,
Shall have the leading of this foot and horse.
They thus directed, we will follow
In the main battle, whose puissance on either side
Shall be well winged with our chiefest horse.
This, and Saint George to boot! What think'st thou,
    Norfolk?
NORFOLK. A good direction, warlike sovereign.
This found I on my tent this morning.
                              [*He sheweth him a paper*]
KING RICHARD. [*Reads*]
        'Jockey of Norfolk, be not so bold,
        For Dickon thy master is bought and sold.'
A thing devised by the enemy.
Go, gentlemen, every man unto his charge.
Let not our babbling dreams affright our souls;
Conscience is but a word that cowards use,
Devis'd at first to keep the strong in awe.
Our strong arms be our conscience, swords our law.
March on, join bravely, let us to it pell-mell;
If not to heaven, then hand in hand to hell.

HIS ORATION TO HIS ARMY

What shall I say more than I have inferr'd?
Remember whom you are to cope withal—
A sort of vagabonds, rascals, and runaways,
A scum of Britaines, and base lackey peasants,
Whom their o'er-cloyed country vomits forth
To desperate adventures and assur'd destruction.

You sleeping safe, they bring to you unrest;
You having lands, and bless'd with beauteous wives,
They would restrain the one, distain the other.
And who doth lead them but a paltry fellow,
Long kept in Britaine at our mother's cost?
A milk-sop, one that never in his life
Felt so much cold as over shoes in snow?
Let's whip these stragglers o'er the seas again;
Lash hence these over-weening rags of France,
These famish'd beggars, weary of their lives;
Who, but for dreaming on this fond exploit,
For want of means, poor rats, had hang'd themselves.
If we be conquered, let men conquer us,
And not these bastard Britaines, whom our fathers
Have in their own land beaten, bobb'd, and thump'd,
And, in record, left them the heirs of shame.
Shall these enjoy our lands? lie with our wives,
Ravish our daughters? [*Drum afar off*] Hark! I hear their
  drum.
Fight, gentlemen of England! Fight, bold yeomen!
Draw, archers, draw your arrows to the head!
Spur your proud horses hard, and ride in blood;
Amaze the welkin with your broken staves!

Enter a MESSENGER

What says Lord Stanley? Will he bring his power?
MESSENGER. My lord, he doth deny to come.
KING RICHARD. Off with his son George's head!
NORFOLK. My lord, the enemy is pass'd the marsh.
  After the battle let George Stanley die.
KING RICHARD. A thousand hearts are great within my
  bosom.
Advance our standards, set upon our foes;
Our ancient word of courage, fair Saint George,
Inspire us with the spleen of fiery dragons!
Upon them! Victory sits on our helms.   *Exeunt*

SCENE 4

Another part of the field

Alarum; excursions. Enter NORFOLK *and forces;*
to him CATESBY

CATESBY. Rescue, my Lord of Norfolk, rescue, rescue!
The King enacts more wonders than a man,
Daring an opposite to every danger.
His horse is slain, and all on foot he fights,
Seeking for Richmond in the throat of death.
Rescue, fair lord, or else the day is lost.

Alarums. Enter KING RICHARD

KING RICHARD. A horse! a horse! my kingdom for a horse!
CATESBY. Withdraw, my lord! I'll help you to a horse.
KING RICHARD. Slave, I have set my life upon a cast
And I will stand the hazard of the die.
I think there be six Richmonds in the field;
Five have I slain to-day instead of him.
A horse! a horse! my kingdom for a horse!　　　　*Exeunt*

SCENE 5

Another part of the field

Alarum. Enter RICHARD *and* RICHMOND; *they fight;*
RICHARD *is slain. Retreat and flourish. Enter* RICH-
MOND, DERBY *bearing the crown, with other* LORDS

RICHMOND. God and your arms be prais'd, victorious friends;
The day is ours, the bloody dog is dead.
DERBY. Courageous Richmond, well hast thou acquit thee!
Lo, here, this long-usurped royalty
From the dead temples of this bloody wretch
Have I pluck'd off, to grace thy brows withal.
Wear it, enjoy it, and make much of it.
RICHMOND. Great God of heaven, say Amen to all!
But, tell me is young George Stanley living.

DERBY. He is, my lord, and safe in Leicester town,
  Whither, if it please you, we may now withdraw us.
RICHMOND. What men of name are slain on either side?
DERBY. John Duke of Norfolk, Walter Lord Ferrers,
  Sir Robert Brakenbury, and Sir William Brandon.
RICHMOND. Inter their bodies as becomes their births.
  Proclaim a pardon to the soldiers fled
  That in submission will return to us.
  And then, as we have ta'en the sacrament,
  We will unite the white rose and the red.
  Smile heaven upon this fair conjunction,
  That long have frown'd upon their enmity!
  What traitor hears me, and says not Amen?
  England hath long been mad, and scarr'd herself;
  The brother blindly shed the brother's blood,
  The father rashly slaughter'd his own son,
  The son, compell'd, been butcher to the sire;
  All this divided York and Lancaster,
  Divided in their dire division,
  O, now let Richmond and Elizabeth,
  The true succeeders of each royal house,
  By God's fair ordinance conjoin together!
  And let their heirs, God, if thy will be so,
  Enrich the time to come with smooth-fac'd peace,
  With smiling plenty, and fair prosperous days!
  Abate the edge of traitors, gracious Lord,
  That would reduce these bloody days again
  And make poor England weep in streams of blood!
  Let them not live to taste this land's increase
  That would with treason wound this fair land's peace!
  Now civil wounds are stopp'd, peace lives again—
  That she may long live here, God say Amen!   *Exeunt*

The Famous
History of the Life of
King Henry the Eighth

KING HENRY THE EIGHTH

ACCIDENT has preserved for us the date of the first perform-ance of Shakespeare's last play. The accident to which we owe this information was the burning of the Globe on 29 June 1613, during the première of *Henry VIII*. A jocular but circumstantial account is preserved in a letter in which Sir Henry Wotton, who was one of the audience, describes the affair to a friend:

Now to let matters of state sleep. I will entertain you at the present with what hath happened this week at the Bankside. The King's players had a new play, called *All is True*, representing some principal pieces of the reign of Henry the Eighth, which was set forth with many extraor-dinary circumstances of pomp and majesty, even to the matting of the stage; the Knights of the Order with their Georges and Garters, the guards with their embroidered coats, and the like—sufficient in truth within a while to make greatness very familiar if not ridiculous. Now, King Henry making a masque at the Cardinal Wolsey's house, and certain cannons being shot off at his entry, some of the paper, or other stuff wherewith one of them was stopped, did light on the thatch, where being thought at first but an idle smoke, and their eyes more attentive to the show, it kindled inwardly, and ran round like a train, con-suming within less than an hour the whole house to the very ground. This was the fatal period of that virtuous fabrick; wherein yet nothing did perish but wood and straw, and a few forsaken cloaks; only one man had his breeches set on fire, that would perhaps have broiled him, if he had not by the benefit of a provident wit, put it out with a bottle of ale.

Other accounts of the fire make it clear that it broke out during the first performance of *Henry VIII*. Wotton refers to the play by its alternative title *All is True*, which a ballad

glances at in its refrain. *The Prologue* to the play preserved in the First Folio refers to the audience as

The first and happiest hearers of the town

and is obviously that spoken on the first performance; it confirms that the play could be referred to as *All is True*.

Shakespeare had written nothing since *The Tempest*, produced in 1611, and the production of *Henry VIII* in 1613 was something of an occasion, for it is clear that the audience was large and included distinguished social and literary figures. The actors on their side had spared no expense and so lavish and complete was their costuming that it seemed to Wotton extravagant or at least slightly out of place; the actors were too like the noblemen they impersonated.

Scholarly opinion to-day inclines to the view that the play was largely Fletcher's work; but the manner in which the Company produced the piece and the obvious interest its production had aroused in the public suggest that those who went to the Globe on 29 June expected to see Shakespeare returned from his retirement to grace once more the scenes of his former triumphs.

Two considerations have led scholars to the conclusion that the major hand in the piece is Fletcher's. *Henry VIII* is loose in construction when compared with Shakespeare's greater plays: it is as Wotton describes it 'some principal pieces from the reign of Henry the Eighth' rather than a closely integrated whole. It has, however, held the stage and been specially popular in those periods when lavish production was the primary consideration with actor-managers, that is, when it was staged in the realistically expensive manner that marked the first performance by Shakespeare's own company. The play's effectiveness as a stage spectacle has been proved by experience. Why we should suppose that Shakespeare was incapable or unwilling to design so effective a play in this kind for his company is a question that has yet to be answered. The usual excuse for introducing Fletcher is that Shakespeare was a tired man and unwilling to make a supreme effort; it is as fair to argue that Shakespeare if he were tired contented himself with what was for him a comparatively easy task, but brought to it his long experience of stage technique and produced what would suit the occasion. His judgment seems vindicated by the play's first reception as well as by its subsequent history in the theatre.

The second reason on which commentators rely for their ascription of most of the play to Fletcher is more technical. They argue that large portions of the play are in a form of verse eminently characteristic of Fletcher and without adequate parallels in Shakespeare's acknowledged work.

All the features in the verse attributed to Fletcher can be found in Shakespeare's own earlier plays; so far he had not used them in the more extreme manner employed in *Henry VIII*. There is no reason why Shakespeare should not have adopted on this occasion the easier manner favoured by Fletcher, and to insist that the composition must be Fletcher's leaves a number of simple questions unanswered. The most obvious is this: How does it happen that all the best known speeches happen to be Fletcher's? Buckingham's farewell, Wolsey's farewell, Cranmer's prophecy over the infant Elizabeth, are all in the Fletcher manner; but where does Fletcher achieve anything comparable elsewhere in that style? The tokens we are offered for inspection may be Fletcher's but the voice can hardly be other than Shakespeare's. This is most obvious in the *Prologue* itself which the metrical evidence would assign to Fletcher. Dr. Partridge is driven to suggest that the rising young dramatist put it forward to excuse a play that he did not expect would please, because he had had to finish not very successfully an unfinished sketch by Shakespeare. If this were true and expectations so low, one must ask why there was such an audience at the première and why the actors had gone to such expense. This was hardly the occasion for such excuses; whereas it would be natural for Shakespeare, whose comic vein so captivated his contemporaries, to warn his audience that the affairs of the reign were not to be treated in the comic style already associated with the monarch's doings but in the graver and more compassionate tone in keeping with the title *All is True*.

KING HENRY THE EIGHTH
CARDINAL WOLSEY   CARDINAL CAMPEIUS
CAPUCIUS, *Ambassador from the Emperor Charles V*
CRANMER, ARCHBISHOP OF CANTERBURY
DUKE OF NORFOLK   DUKE OF BUCKINGHAM
DUKE OF SUFFOLK   EARL OF SURREY
LORD CHAMBERLAIN   LORD CHANCELLOR
GARDINER, BISHOP OF WINCHESTER
BISHOP OF LINCOLN   LORD ABERGAVENNY
LORD SANDYS   SIR HENRY GUILDFORD
SIR THOMAS LOVELL   SIR ANTHONY DENNY
SIR NICHOLAS VAUX   SECRETARIES *to Wolsey*
CROMWELL, *servant to Wolsey*
GRIFFITH, *gentleman-usher to Queen Katharine*
THREE GENTLEMEN
DOCTOR BUTTS, *physician to the King*
GARTER KING-AT-ARMS
SURVEYOR *to the Duke of Buckingham*
BRANDON, *and a* SERGEANT-AT-ARMS
DOORKEEPER *of the Council chamber*
PORTER, *and his* MAN   PAGE *to Gardiner*
A CRIER

QUEEN KATHARINE, *wife to King Henry, afterwards divorced*
ANNE BULLEN, *her Maid of Honour, afterwards Queen*
AN OLD LADY, *friend to Anne Bullen*
PATIENCE, *woman to Queen Katharine*

Lord Mayor, Aldermen, Lords *and* Ladies *in the Dumb Shows;* Women *attending upon the Queen;* Scribes, Officers, Guards, *and other* Attendants; Spirits

SCENE:

London; Westminster; Kimbolton

King Henry the Eighth

THE PROLOGUE

I come no more to make you laugh; things now
That bear a weighty and a serious brow,
Sad, high, and working, full of state and woe,
Such noble scenes as draw the eye to flow,
We now present. Those that can pity here
May, if they think it well, let fall a tear:
The subject will deserve it. Such as give
Their money out of hope they may believe
May here find truth too. Those that come to see
Only a show or two, and so agree
The play may pass, if they be still and willing,
I'll undertake may see away their shilling
Richly in two short hours. Only they
That come to hear a merry bawdy play,
A noise of targets, or to see a fellow
In a long motley coat guarded with yellow,
Will be deceiv'd; for, gentle hearers, know,
To rank our chosen truth with such a show
As fool and fight is, beside forfeiting
Our own brains, and the opinion that we bring
To make that only true we now intend,
Will leave us never an understanding friend.
Therefore, for goodness sake, and as you are known
The first and happiest hearers of the town,
Be sad, as we would make ye. Think ye see
The very persons of our noble story
As they were living; think you see them great,
And follow'd with the general throng and sweat
Of thousand friends; then, in a moment, see
How soon this mightiness meets misery.
And if you can be merry then, I'll say
A man may weep upon his wedding-day.

KING HENRY VIII

ACT I. SCENE 1

London. The palace

Enter the DUKE OF NORFOLK *at one door; at the other, the* DUKE OF BUCKINGHAM *and the* LORD ABERGAVENNY

BUCKINGHAM. Good morrow, and well met. How have ye done
Since last we saw in France?
NORFOLK. I thank your Grace,
Healthful; and ever since a fresh admirer
Of what I saw there.
BUCKINGHAM. An untimely ague
Stay'd me a prisoner in my chamber when
Those suns of glory, those two lights of men,
Met in the vale of Andren.
NORFOLK. 'Twixt Guynes and Arde—
I was then present, saw them salute on horseback;
Beheld them, when they lighted, how they clung
In their embracement, as they grew together;
Which had they, what four thron'd ones could have weigh'd
Such a compounded one?
BUCKINGHAM. All the whole time
I was my chamber's prisoner.
NORFOLK. Then you lost
The view of earthly glory; men might say,
Till this time pomp was single, but now married
To one above itself. Each following day
Became the next day's master, till the last
Made former wonders its. To-day the French,
All clinquant, all in gold, like heathen gods,
Shone down the English; and to-morrow they
Made Britain India: every man that stood
Show'd like a mine. Their dwarfish pages were
As cherubins, all gilt; the madams too,
Not us'd to toil, did almost sweat to bear
The pride upon them, that their very labour

Was to them as a painting. Now this masque
Was cried incomparable; and th' ensuing night
Made it a fool and beggar. The two kings,
Equal in lustre, were now best, now worst,
As presence did present them: him in eye
Still him in praise; and being present both,
'Twas said they saw but one, and no discerner
Durst wag his tongue in censure. When these suns—
For so they phrase 'em—by their heralds challeng'd
The noble spirits to arms, they did perform
Beyond thought's compass, that former fabulous story,
Being now seen possible enough, got credit,
That Bevis was believ'd.
BUCKINGHAM. O, you go far!
NORFOLK. As I belong to worship, and affect
In honour honesty, the tract of ev'rything
Would by a good discourser lose some life
Which action's self was tongue to. All was royal:
To the disposing of it nought rebell'd;
Order gave each thing view. The office did
Distinctly his full function.
BUCKINGHAM. Who did guide—
I mean, who set the body and the limbs
Of this great sport together, as you guess?
NORFOLK. One, certes, that promises no element
In such a business.
BUCKINGHAM. I pray you, who, my lord?
NORFOLK. All this was ord'red by the good discretion
Of the right reverend Cardinal of York.
BUCKINGHAM. The devil speed him! No man's pie is freed
From his ambitious finger. What had he
To do in these fierce vanities? I wonder
That such a keech can with his very bulk
Take up the rays o' th' beneficial sun,
And keep it from the earth.
NORFOLK. Surely, sir,
There's in him stuff that puts him to these ends;
For, being not propp'd by ancestry, whose grace
Chalks successors their way, nor call'd upon
For high feats done to th' crown, neither allied

To eminent assistants, but spider-like,
Out of his self-drawing web, 'a gives us note
The force of his own merit makes his way—
A gift that heaven gives for him, which buys
A place next to the King.
ABERGAVENNY. I cannot tell
What heaven hath given him—let some graver eye
Pierce into that; but I can see his pride
Peep through each part of him. Whence has he that?
If not from hell, the devil is a niggard
Or has given all before, and he begins
A new hell in himself.
BUCKINGHAM. Why the devil,
Upon this French going out, took he upon him—
Without the privity o' th' King—t' appoint
Who should attend on him? He makes up the file
Of all the gentry; for the most part such
To whom as great a charge as little honour
He meant to lay upon; and his own letter,
The honourable board of council out,
Must fetch him in he papers.
ABERGAVENNY. I do know
Kinsmen of mine, three at the least, that have
By this so sicken'd their estates that never
They shall abound as formerly.
BUCKINGHAM. O, many
Have broke their backs with laying manors on 'em
For this great journey. What did this vanity
But minister communication of
A most poor issue?
NORFOLK. Grievingly I think
The peace between the French and us not values
The cost that did conclude it.
BUCKINGHAM. Every man,
After the hideous storm that follow'd, was
A thing inspir'd, and, not consulting, broke
Into a general prophecy—that this tempest,
Dashing the garment of this peace, aboded
The sudden breach on't.
NORFOLK. Which is budded out;

For France hath flaw'd the league, and hath attach'd
Our merchants' goods at Bordeaux.
ABERGAVENNY. Is it therefore
Th' ambassador is silenc'd?
NORFOLK. Marry, is't.
ABERGAVENNY. A proper title of a peace, and purchas'd
At a superfluous rate!
BUCKINGHAM. Why, all this business
Our reverend Cardinal carried.
NORFOLK. Like it your Grace,
The state takes notice of the private difference
Betwixt you and the Cardinal. I advise you—
And take it from a heart that wishes towards you
Honour and plenteous safety—that you read
The Cardinal's malice and his potency
Together; to consider further, that
What his high hatred would effect wants not
A minister in his power. You know his nature,
That he's revengeful; and I know his sword
Hath a sharp edge—it's long and't may be said
It reaches far, and where 'twill not extend,
Thither he darts it. Bosom up my counsel,
You'll find it wholesome. Lo, where comes that rock
That I advise your shunning.

Enter CARDINAL WOLSEY, *the purse borne before
him, certain of the guard, and two* SECRETARIES
with papers. The CARDINAL *in his passage fixeth his
eye on* BUCKINGHAM, *and* BUCKINGHAM *on him,
both full of disdain*

WOLSEY. The Duke of Buckingham's surveyor? Ha!
Where's his examination?
SECRETARY. Here, so please you.
WOLSEY. Is he in person ready?
SECRETARY. Ay, please your Grace.
WOLSEY. Well, we shall then know more, and Buckingham
Shall lessen this big look.
Exeunt WOLSEY *and his train*
BUCKINGHAM. This butcher's cur is venom-mouth'd, and I
Have not the power to muzzle him; therefore best

Not wake him in his slumber. A beggar's book
Outworths a noble's blood.
NORFOLK. What, are you chaf'd?
Ask God for temp'rance; that's th' appliance only
Which your disease requires.
BUCKINGHAM. I read in's looks
Matter against me, and his eye revil'd
Me as his abject object. At this instant
He bores me with some trick. He's gone to th' King;
I'll follow, and outstare him.
NORFOLK. Stay, my lord,
And let your reason with your choler question
What 'tis you go about. To climb steep hills
Requires slow pace at first. Anger is like
A full hot horse, who being allow'd his way,
Self-mettle tires him. Not a man in England
Can advise me like you; be to yourself
As you would to your friend.
BUCKINGHAM. I'll to the King,
And from a mouth of honour quite cry down
This Ipswich fellow's insolence; or proclaim
There's difference in no persons.
NORFOLK. Be advis'd:
Heat not a furnace for your foe so hot
That it do singe yourself. We may outrun
By violent swiftness that which we run at,
And lose by over-running. Know you not
The fire that mounts the liquor till't run o'er
In seeming to augment it wastes it? Be advis'd.
I say again there is no English soul
More stronger to direct you than yourself,
If with the sap of reason you would quench
Or but allay the fire of passion.
BUCKINGHAM. Sir,
I am thankful to you, and I'll go along
By your prescription; but this top-proud fellow—
Whom from the flow of gall I name not, but
From sincere motions, by intelligence,
And proofs as clear as founts in July when
We see each grain of gravel—I do know

To be corrupt and treasonous.

NORFOLK. Say not treasonous.

BUCKINGHAM. To th' King I'll say't, and make my vouch as
    strong
As shore of rock. Attend: this holy fox,
Or wolf, or both—for he is equal rav'nous
As he is subtle, and as prone to mischief
As able to perform't, his mind and place
Infecting one another, yea, reciprocally—
Only to show his pomp as well in France
As here at home, suggests the King our master
To this last costly treaty, th' interview
That swallowed so much treasure and like a glass
Did break i' th' wrenching.

NORFOLK. Faith, and so it did.

BUCKINGHAM. Pray, give me favour, sir; this cunning cardinal
    The articles o' th' combination drew
As himself pleas'd; and they were ratified
As he cried 'Thus let be' to as much end
As give a crutch to th' dead. But our Count-Cardinal
Has done this, and 'tis well; for worthy Wolsey,
Who cannot err, he did it. Now this follows,
Which, as I take it, is a kind of puppy
To th' old dam treason: Charles the Emperor,
Under pretence to see the Queen his aunt—
For 'twas indeed his colour, but he came
To whisper Wolsey—here makes visitation—
His fears were that the interview betwixt
England and France might through their amity
Breed him some prejudice; for from this league
Peep'd harms that menac'd him—privily
Deals with our Cardinal; and, as I trow—
Which I do well, for I am sure the Emperor
Paid ere he promis'd; whereby his suit was granted
Ere it was ask'd—but when the way was made,
And pav'd with gold, the Emperor thus desir'd,
That he would please to alter the King's course,
And break the foresaid peace. Let the King know,
As soon he shall by me, that thus the Cardinal
Does buy and sell his honour as he pleases,

And for his own advantage.

NORFOLK. I am sorry
To hear this of him, and could wish he were
Something mistaken in't.

BUCKINGHAM. No, not a syllable:
I do pronounce him in that very shape
He shall appear in proof.

Enter BRANDON, *a* SERGEANT-AT-ARMS *before him,
and two or three of the guard*

BRANDON. Your office, sergeant: execute it.

SERGEANT. Sir,
My lord the Duke of Buckingham, and Earl
Of Hereford, Stafford, and Northampton, I
Arrest thee of high treason, in the name
Of our most sovereign King.

BUCKINGHAM. Lo you, my lord,
The net has fall'n upon me! I shall perish
Under device and practice.

BRANDON. I am sorry
To see you ta'en from liberty, to look on
The business present; 'tis his Highness' pleasure
You shall to th' Tower.

BUCKINGHAM. It will help me nothing
To plead mine innocence; for that dye is on me
Which makes my whit'st part black. The will of heav'n
Be done in this and all things! I obey.
O my Lord Aberga'ny, fare you well!

BRANDON. Nay, he must bear you company.
[*To* ABERGAVENNY] The King
Is pleas'd you shall to th' Tower, till you know
How he determines further.

ABERGAVENNY. As the Duke said,
The will of heaven be done, and the King's pleasure
By me obey'd.

BRANDON. Here is warrant from
The King t' attach Lord Montacute and the bodies
Of the Duke's confessor, John de la Car,
One Gilbert Peck, his chancellor—

BUCKINGHAM. So, so!

ACT I. SCENE 1

These are the limbs o' th' plot; no more, I hope.
BRANDON. A monk o' th' Chartreux.
BUCKINGHAM. O, Nicholas Hopkins?
BRANDON. He.
BUCKINGHAM. My surveyor is false. The o'er-great Cardinal
Hath show'd him gold; my life is spann'd already.
I am the shadow of poor Buckingham,
Whose figure even this instant cloud puts on
By dark'ning my clear sun. My lord, farewell.   *Exeunt*

SCENE 2

London. The Council Chamber

Cornets. Enter KING HENRY, *leaning on the* CARDI-
NAL'S *shoulder, the* NOBLES, *and* SIR THOMAS
LOVELL, *with others. The* CARDINAL *places himself
under the* KING'S *feet on his right side*

KING. My life itself, and the best heart of it,
Thanks you for this great care; I stood i' th' level
Of a full-charg'd confederacy, and give thanks
To you that chok'd it. Let be call'd before us
That gentleman of Buckingham's. In person
I'll hear his confessions justify;
And point by point the treasons of his master
He shall again relate.

*A noise within, crying 'Room for the Queen!'
Enter the* QUEEN, *usher'd by the* DUKES OF NOR-
FOLK *and* SUFFOLK; *she kneels. The* KING *riseth
from his state, takes her up, kisses and placeth her
by him*

QUEEN KATHARINE. Nay, we must longer kneel: I am a
suitor.
KING. Arise, and take place by us. Half your suit
Never name to us: you have half our power.
The other moiety ere you ask is given;
Repeat your will, and take it.
QUEEN KATHARINE. Thank your Majesty.

903

That you would love yourself, and in that love
Not unconsidered leave your honour nor
The dignity of your office, is the point
Of my petition.
KING. Lady mine, proceed.
QUEEN KATHARINE. I am solicited, not by a few,
And those of true condition, that your subjects
Are in great grievance: there have been commissions
Sent down among 'em which hath flaw'd the heart
Of all their loyalties; wherein, although,
My good Lord Cardinal, they vent reproaches
Most bitterly on you as putter-on
Of these exactions, yet the King our master—
Whose honour Heaven shield from soil!—even he escapes
    not
Language unmannerly; yea, such which breaks
The sides of loyalty, and almost appears
In loud rebellion.
NORFOLK. Not almost appears—
It doth appear; for, upon these taxations,
The clothiers all, not able to maintain
The many to them 'longing, have put off
The spinsters, carders, fullers, weavers, who
Unfit for other life, compell'd by hunger
And lack of other means, in desperate manner
Daring th' event to th' teeth, are all in uproar,
And danger serves among them.
KING. Taxation!
Wherein? and what taxation? My Lord Cardinal,
You that are blam'd for it alike with us,
Know you of this taxation?
WOLSEY. Please you, sir,
I know but of a single part in aught
Pertains to th' state, and front but in that file
Where others tell steps with me.
QUEEN KATHARINE. No, my lord!
You know no more than others! But you frame
Things that are known alike, which are not wholesome
To those which would not know them, and yet must
Perforce be their acquaintance. These exactions,

Whereof my sovereign would have note, they are
Most pestilent to th' hearing; and to bear 'em
The back is sacrifice to th' load. They say
They are devis'd by you, or else you suffer
Too hard an exclamation.
KING. Still exaction!
    The nature of it? In what kind, let's know,
    Is this exaction?
QUEEN KATHARINE. I am much too venturous
    In tempting of your patience, but am bold'ned
    Under your promis'd pardon. The subjects' grief
    Comes through commissions, which compels from each
    The sixth part of his substance, to be levied
    Without delay; and the pretence for this
    Is nam'd your wars in France. This makes bold mouths;
    Tongues spit their duties out, and cold hearts freeze
    Allegiance in them; their curses now
    Live where their prayers did; and it's come to pass
    This tractable obedience is a slave
    To each incensed will. I would your Highness
    Would give it quick consideration, for
    There is no primer business.
KING. By my life,
    This is against our pleasure.
WOLSEY. And for me,
    I have no further gone in this than by
    A single voice; and that not pass'd me but
    By learned approbation of the judges. If I am
    Traduc'd by ignorant tongues, which neither know
    My faculties nor person, yet will be
    The chronicles of my doing, let me say
    'Tis but the fate of place, and the rough brake
    That virtue must go through. We must not stint
    Our necessary actions in the fear
    To cope malicious censurers, which ever
    As rav'nous fishes do a vessel follow
    That is new-trimm'd, but benefit no further
    Than vainly longing. What we oft do best,
    By sick interpreters, once weak ones, is
    Not ours, or not allow'd; what worst, as oft

Hitting a grosser quality, is cried up
For our best act. If we shall stand still,
In fear our motion will be mock'd or carp'd at,
We should take root here where we sit, or sit
State-statues only.

KING. Things done well
And with a care exempt themselves from fear:
Things done without example, in their issue
Are to be fear'd. Have you a precedent
Of this commission? I believe, not any.
We must not rend our subjects from our laws,
And stick them in our will. Sixth part of each?
A trembling contribution! Why, we take
From every tree lop, bark, and part o' th' timber;
And though we leave it with a root, thus hack'd,
The air will drink the sap. To every county
Where this is question'd send our letters with
Free pardon to each man that has denied
The force of this commission. Pray, look to't;
I put it to your care.

WOLSEY. [*Aside to the* SECRETARY] A word with you.
Let there be letters writ to every shire
Of the King's grace and pardon. The grieved commons
Hardly conceive of me—let it be nois'd
That through our intercession this revokement
And pardon comes. I shall anon advise you
Further in the proceeding.   *Exit* SECRETARY

Enter SURVEYOR

QUEEN KATHARINE. I am sorry that the Duke of Buckingham
Is run in your displeasure.

KING. It grieves many.
The gentleman is learn'd and a most rare speaker;
To nature none more bound; his training such
That he may furnish and instruct great teachers
And never seek for aid out of himself. Yet see,
When these so noble benefits shall prove
Not well dispos'd, the mind growing once corrupt,
They turn to vicious forms, ten times more ugly
Than ever they were fair. This man so complete,

Who was enroll'd 'mongst wonders, and when we,
Almost with ravish'd list'ning, could not find
His hour of speech a minute—he, my lady,
Hath into monstrous habits put the graces
That once were his, and is become as black
As if besmear'd in hell. Sit by us; you shall hear—
This was his gentleman in trust—of him
Things to strike honour sad. Bid him recount
The fore-recited practices, whereof
We cannot feel too little, hear too much.
WOLSEY. Stand forth, and with bold spirit relate what you,
   Most like a careful subject, have collected
   Out of the Duke of Buckingham.
KING. Speak freely.
SURVEYOR. First, it was usual with him—every day
   It would infect his speech—that if the King
   Should without issue die, he'll carry it so
   To make the sceptre his. These very words
   I've heard him utter to his son-in-law,
   Lord Aberga'ny, to whom by oath he menac'd
   Revenge upon the Cardinal.
WOLSEY. Please your Highness, note
   This dangerous conception in this point:
   Not friended by his wish, to your high person
   His will is most malignant, and it stretches
   Beyond you to your friends.
QUEEN KATHARINE. My learn'd Lord Cardinal,
   Deliver all with charity.
KING. Speak on.
   How grounded he his title to the crown
   Upon our fail? To this point hast thou heard him
   At any time speak aught?
SURVEYOR. He was brought to this
   By a vain prophecy of Nicholas Henton.
KING. What was that Henton?
SURVEYOR. Sir, a Chartreux friar,
   His confessor, who fed him every minute
   With words of sovereignty.
KING. How know'st thou this?
SURVEYOR. Not long before your Highness sped to France,

The Duke being at the Rose, within the parish
Saint Lawrence Poultney, did of me demand
What was the speech among the Londoners
Concerning the French journey. I replied
Men fear'd the French would prove perfidious,
To the King's danger. Presently the Duke
Said 'twas the fear indeed and that he doubted
'Twould prove the verity of certain words
Spoke by a holy monk 'that oft' says he
'Hath sent to me, wishing me to permit
John de la Car, my chaplain, a choice hour
To hear from him a matter of some moment;
Whom after under the confession's seal
He solemnly had sworn that what he spoke
My chaplain to no creature living but
To me should utter, with demure confidence
This pausingly ensu'd: "Neither the King nor's heirs,
Tell you the Duke, shall prosper; bid him strive
To gain the love o' th' commonalty; the Duke
Shall govern England." '

QUEEN KATHARINE. If I know you well,
    You were the Duke's surveyor, and lost your office
    On the complaint o' th' tenants. Take good heed
    You charge not in your spleen a noble person
    And spoil your nobler soul. I say, take heed;
    Yes, heartily beseech you.

KING. Let him on.
    Go forward.

SURVEYOR. On my soul, I'll speak but truth.
    I told my lord the Duke, by th' devil's illusions
    The monk might be deceiv'd, and that 'twas dangerous
        for him
    To ruminate on this so far, until
    It forg'd him some design, which, being believ'd,
    It was much like to do. He answer'd 'Tush,
    It can do me no damage'; adding further
    That, had the King in his last sickness fail'd,
    The Cardinal's and Sir Thomas Lovell's heads
    Should have gone off.

KING. Ha! what, so rank? Ah ha!

There's mischief in this man. Canst thou say further?

SURVEYOR. I can, my liege.

KING. Proceed.

SURVEYOR. Being at Greenwich,
After your Highness had reprov'd the Duke
About Sir William Bulmer—

KING. I remember
Of such a time: being my sworn servant,
The Duke retain'd him his. But on: what hence?

SURVEYOR. 'If' quoth he 'I for this had been committed—
As to the Tower I thought—I would have play'd
The part my father meant to act upon
Th' usurper Richard; who, being at Salisbury,
Made suit to come in's presence, which if granted,
As he made semblance of his duty, would
Have put his knife into him.'

KING. A giant traitor!

WOLSEY. Now, madam, may his Highness live in freedom,
And this man out of prison?

QUEEN KATHARINE. God mend all!

KING. There's something more would out of thee: what
say'st?

SURVEYOR. After 'the Duke his father' with the 'knife,'
He stretch'd him, and, with one hand on his dagger,
Another spread on's breast, mounting his eyes,
He did discharge a horrible oath, whose tenour
Was, were he evil us'd, he would outgo
His father by as much as a performance
Does an irresolute purpose.

KING. There's his period,
To sheath his knife in us. He is attach'd;
Call him to present trial. If he may
Find mercy in the law, 'tis his; if none,
Let him not seek't of us. By day and night!
He's traitor to th' height.   *Exeunt*

SCENE 3

London. The palace

Enter the LORD CHAMBERLAIN *and* LORD SANDYS

CHAMBERLAIN. Is't possible the spells of France should juggle
  Men into such strange mysteries?
SANDYS. New customs,
  Though they be never so ridiculous,
  Nay, let 'em be unmanly, yet are follow'd.
CHAMBERLAIN. As far as I see, all the good our English
  Have got by the late voyage is but merely
  A fit or two o' th' face; but they are shrewd ones;
  For when they hold 'em, you would swear directly
  Their very noses had been counsellors
  To Pepin or Clotharius, they keep state so.
SANDYS. They have all new legs, and lame ones. One would
    take it,
  That never saw 'em pace before, the spavin
  Or springhalt reign'd among 'em.
CHAMBERLAIN. Death! my lord,
  Their clothes are after such a pagan cut to't,
  That sure th' have worn out Christendom.

Enter SIR THOMAS LOVELL

  How now?
  What news, Sir Thomas Lovell?
LOVELL. Faith, my lord,
  I hear of none but the new proclamation
  That's clapp'd upon the court gate.
CHAMBERLAIN. What is't for?
LOVELL. The reformation of our travell'd gallants,
  That fill the court with quarrels, talk, and tailors.
CHAMBERLAIN. I am glad 'tis there. Now I would pray our
    monsieurs
  To think an English courtier may be wise,
  And never see the Louvre.
LOVELL. They must either,
  For so run the conditions, leave those remnants

Of fool and feather that they got in France,
With all their honourable points of ignorance
Pertaining thereunto—as fights and fireworks;
Abusing better men than they can be,
Out of a foreign wisdom—renouncing clean
The faith they have in tennis, and tall stockings,
Short blist'red breeches, and those types of travel,
And understand again like honest men,
Or pack to their old playfellows. There, I take it,
They may, cum privilegio, wear away
The lag end of their lewdness and be laugh'd at.
SANDYS. 'Tis time to give 'em physic, their diseases
Are grown so catching.
CHAMBERLAIN. What a loss our ladies
Will have of these trim vanities!
LOVELL. Ay, marry,
There will be woe indeed, lords: the sly whoresons
Have got a speeding trick to lay down ladies.
A French song and a fiddle has no fellow.
SANDYS. The devil fiddle 'em! I am glad they are going,
For sure there's no converting 'em. Now
An honest country lord, as I am, beaten
A long time out of play, may bring his plainsong
And have an hour of hearing; and, by'r Lady,
Held current music too.
CHAMBERLAIN. Well said, Lord Sandys;
Your colt's tooth is not cast yet.
SANDYS. No, my lord,
Nor shall not while I have a stump.
CHAMBERLAIN. Sir Thomas,
Whither were you a-going?
LOVELL. To the Cardinal's;
Your lordship is a guest too.
CHAMBERLAIN. O, 'tis true;
This night he makes a supper, and a great one,
To many lords and ladies; there will be
The beauty of this kingdom, I'll assure you.
LOVELL. That churchman bears a bounteous mind indeed,
A hand as fruitful as the land that feeds us;
His dews fall everywhere.

CHAMBERLAIN. No doubt he's noble;
  He had a black mouth that said other of him.
SANDYS. He may, my lord; has wherewithal. In him
  Sparing would show a worse sin than ill doctrine:
  Men of his way should be most liberal,
  They are set here for examples.
CHAMBERLAIN. True, they are so;
  But few now give so great ones. My barge stays;
  Your lordship shall along. Come, good Sir Thomas,
  We shall be late else; which I would not be,
  For I was spoke to, with Sir Henry Guildford,
  This night to be comptrollers.
SANDYS. I am your lordship's.   *Exeunt*

SCENE 4

London. The Presence Chamber in York Place

Hautboys. A small table under a state for the Cardinal, a longer table for the guests. Then enter ANNE
BULLEN, *and divers other* LADIES *and* GENTLEMEN,
as guests, at one door; at another door enter SIR
HENRY GUILDFORD

GUILDFORD. Ladies, a general welcome from his Grace
  Salutes ye all; this night he dedicates
  To fair content and you. None here, he hopes,
  In all this noble bevy, has brought with her
  One care abroad; he would have all as merry
  As, first, good company, good wine, good welcome,
  Can make good people.

  Enter LORD CHAMBERLAIN, LORD SANDYS, *and* SIR
  THOMAS LOVELL

  O, my lord, y'are tardy,
  The very thought of this fair company
  Clapp'd wings to me.
CHAMBERLAIN. You are young, Sir Harry Guildford.
SANDYS. Sir Thomas Lovell, had the Cardinal
  But half my lay thoughts in him, some of these

Should find a running banquet ere they rested
I think would better please 'em. By my life,
They are a sweet society of fair ones.
LOVELL. O that your lordship were but now confessor
To one or two of these!
SANDYS. I would I were;
They should find easy penance.
LOVELL. Faith, how easy?
SANDYS. As easy as a down bed would afford it.
CHAMBERLAIN. Sweet ladies, will it please you sit? Sir Harry,
Place you that side; I'll take the charge of this.
His Grace is ent'ring. Nay, you must not freeze:
Two women plac'd together makes cold weather.
My Lord Sandys, you are one will keep 'em waking:
Pray sit between these ladies.
SANDYS. By my faith,
And thank your lordship. By your leave, sweet ladies.
    [*Seats himself between* ANNE BULLEN *and another lady*]
If I chance to talk a little wild, forgive me;
I had it from my father.
ANNE. Was he mad, sir?
SANDYS. O, very mad, exceeding mad, in love too.
But he would bite none; just as I do now,
He would kiss you twenty with a breath.   [*Kisses her*]
CHAMBERLAIN. Well said, my lord.
So, now y'are fairly seated. Gentlemen,
The penance lies on you if these fair ladies
Pass away frowning.
SANDYS. For my little cure,
Let me alone.

    Hautboys. Enter CARDINAL WOLSEY, *attended; and
        takes his state*

WOLSEY. Y'are welcome, my fair guests. That noble lady
Or gentleman that is not freely merry
Is not my friend. This, to confirm my welcome—
And to you all, good health!   [*Drinks*]
SANDYS. Your Grace is noble.
Let me have such a bowl may hold my thanks
And save me so much talking.

913

WOLSEY. My Lord Sandys,
I am beholding to you. Cheer your neighbours.
Ladies, you are not merry. Gentlemen,
Whose fault is this?
SANDYS. The red wine first must rise
In their fair cheeks, my lord; then we shall have 'em
Talk us to silence.
ANNE. You are a merry gamester,
My Lord Sandys.
SANDYS. Yes, if I make my play.
Here's to your ladyship; and pledge it, madam,
For 'tis to such a thing—
ANNE. You cannot show me.
SANDYS. I told your Grace they would talk anon.
              [*Drum and trumpet. Chambers discharg'd*]
WOLSEY. What's that?
CHAMBERLAIN. Look out there, some of ye.   *Exit a* SERVANT
WOLSEY. What warlike voice,
And to what end, is this? Nay, ladies, fear not:
By all the laws of war y'are privileg'd.
                  Re-enter SERVANT
CHAMBERLAIN. How now! what is't?
SERVANT. A noble troop of strangers—
For so they seem. Th' have left their barge and landed,
And hither make, as great ambassadors
From foreign princes.
WOLSEY. Good Lord Chamberlain,
Go, give 'em welcome; you can speak the French tongue;
And pray receive 'em nobly and conduct 'em
Into our presence, where this heaven of beauty
Shall shine at full upon them. Some attend him.
    Exit CHAMBERLAIN *attended. All rise, and tables remov'd*
You have now a broken banquet, but we'll mend it.
A good digestion to you all; and once more
I show'r a welcome on ye; welcome all.

    Hautboys. Enter the KING, *and others, as maskers,*
    habited like shepherds, usher'd by the LORD CHAM-
    BERLAIN. *They pass directly before the* CARDINAL,
    and gracefully salute him

A noble company! What are their pleasures?

CHAMBERLAIN. Because they speak no English, thus they
 pray'd
 To tell your Grace, that, having heard by fame
 Of this so noble and so fair assembly
 This night to meet here, they could do no less,
 Out of the great respect they bear to beauty,
 But leave their flocks and, under your fair conduct,
 Crave leave to view these ladies and entreat
 An hour of revels with 'em.

WOLSEY. Say, Lord Chamberlain,
 They have done my poor house grace; for which I pay 'em
 A thousand thanks, and pray 'em take their pleasures.
  [*They choose ladies. The* KING *chooses* ANNE BULLEN]

KING. The fairest hand I ever touch'd! O beauty,
 Till now I never knew thee!   [*Music. Dance*]

WOLSEY. My lord!

CHAMBERLAIN. Your Grace?

WOLSEY. Pray tell 'em thus much from me:
 There should be one amongst 'em, by his person,
 More worthy this place than myself; to whom,
 If I but knew him, with my love and duty
 I would surrender it.

CHAMBERLAIN. I will, my lord.
         [*He whispers to the maskers*]

WOLSEY. What say they?

CHAMBERLAIN. Such a one, they all confess,
 There is indeed; which they would have your Grace
 Find out, and he will take it.

WOLSEY. Let me see, then.   [*Comes from his state*]
 By all your good leaves, gentlemen, here I'll make
 My royal choice.

KING. [*Unmasking*] Ye have found him, Cardinal.
 You hold a fair assembly; you do well, lord.
 You are a churchman, or, I'll tell you, Cardinal,
 I should judge now unhappily.

WOLSEY. I am glad
 Your Grace is grown so pleasant.

KING. My Lord Chamberlain,
 Prithee come hither: what fair lady's that?

CHAMBERLAIN. An't please your Grace, Sir Thomas Bullen's
    daughter—
    The Viscount Rochford—one of her Highness' women.
KING. By heaven, she is a dainty one. Sweet heart,
    I were unmannerly to take you out
    And not to kiss you. A health, gentlemen!
    Let it go round.
WOLSEY. Sir Thomas Lovell, is the banquet ready
    I' th' privy chamber?
LOVELL. Yes, my lord.
WOLSEY. Your Grace,
    I fear, with dancing is a little heated.
KING. I fear, too much.
WOLSEY. There's fresher air, my lord,
    In the next chamber.
KING. Lead in your ladies, ev'ry one. Sweet partner,
    I must not yet forsake you. Let's be merry:
    Good my Lord Cardinal, I have half a dozen healths
    To drink to these fair ladies, and a measure
    To lead 'em once again; and then let's dream
    Who's best in favour. Let the music knock it.

                        Exeunt, with trumpets

ACT II. SCENE 1

Westminster. A street

Enter two GENTLEMEN, *at several doors*

FIRST GENTLEMAN. Whither away so fast?
SECOND GENTLEMAN. O, God save ye!
    Ev'n to the Hall, to hear what shall become
    Of the great Duke of Buckingham.
FIRST GENTLEMAN. I'll save you
    That labour, sir. All's now done but the ceremony
    Of bringing back the prisoner.
SECOND GENTLEMAN. Were you there?
FIRST GENTLEMAN. Yes, indeed, was I.

SECOND GENTLEMAN. Pray, speak what has happen'd.

FIRST GENTLEMAN. You may guess quickly what.

SECOND GENTLEMAN. Is he found guilty?

FIRST GENTLEMAN. Yes, truly is he, and condemn'd upon't.

SECOND GENTLEMAN. I am sorry for't.

FIRST GENTLEMAN. So are a number more.

SECOND GENTLEMAN. But, pray, how pass'd it?

FIRST GENTLEMAN. I'll tell you in a little. The great Duke
Came to the bar; where to his accusations
He pleaded still not guilty, and alleged
Many sharp reasons to defeat the law.
The King's attorney, on the contrary,
Urg'd on the examinations, proofs, confessions,
Of divers witnesses; which the Duke desir'd
To have brought, viva voce, to his face;
At which appear'd against him his surveyor,
Sir Gilbert Peck his chancellor, and John Car,
Confessor to him, with that devil-monk,
Hopkins, that made this mischief.

SECOND GENTLEMAN. That was he
That fed him with his prophecies?

FIRST GENTLEMAN. The same.
All these accus'd him strongly, which he fain
Would have flung from him; but indeed he could not;
And so his peers, upon this evidence,
Have found him guilty of high treason. Much
He spoke, and learnedly, for life; but all
Was either pitied in him or forgotten.

SECOND GENTLEMAN. After all this, how did he bear himself?

FIRST GENTLEMAN. When he was brought again to th' bar to
hear
His knell rung out, his judgment, he was stirr'd
With such an agony he sweat extremely,
And something spoke in choler, ill and hasty;
But he fell to himself again, and sweetly
In all the rest show'd a most noble patience.

SECOND GENTLEMAN. I do not think he fears death.

FIRST GENTLEMAN. Sure, he does not;
He never was so womanish; the cause

He may a little grieve at.
SECOND GENTLEMAN. Certainly
   The Cardinal is the end of this.
FIRST GENTLEMAN. 'Tis likely,
   By all conjectures: first, Kildare's attainder,
   Then deputy of Ireland, who remov'd,
   Earl Surrey was sent thither, and in haste too,
   Lest he should help his father.
SECOND GENTLEMAN. That trick of state
   Was a deep envious one.
FIRST GENTLEMAN. At his return
   No doubt he will requite it. This is noted,
   And generally: whoever the King favours
   The Cardinal instantly will find employment,
   And far enough from court too.
SECOND GENTLEMAN. All the commons
   Hate him perniciously, and, o' my conscience,
   Wish him ten fathom deep: this Duke as much
   They love and dote on; call him bounteous Buckingham,
   The mirror of all courtesy—

   Enter BUCKINGHAM *from his arraignment; tip-staves
   before him; the axe with the edge towards him; halberds on each side; accompanied with* SIR THOMAS
   LOVELL, SIR NICHOLAS VAUX, SIR WILLIAM SANDYS,
   and common people, etc.

FIRST GENTLEMAN. Stay there, sir,
   And see the noble ruin'd man you speak of.
SECOND GENTLEMAN. Let's stand close, and behold him.
BUCKINGHAM. All good people,
   You that thus far have come to pity me,
   Hear what I say, and then go home and lose me.
   I have this day receiv'd a traitor's judgment,
   And by that name must die; yet, heaven bear witness,
   And if I have a conscience, let it sink me
   Even as the axe falls, if I be not faithful!
   The law I bear no malice for my death:
   'T has done, upon the premises, but justice.
   But those that sought it I could wish more Christians.
   Be what they will, I heartily forgive 'em;

Yet let 'em look they glory not in mischief
Nor build their evils on the graves of great men,
For then my guiltless blood must cry against 'em.
For further life in this world I ne'er hope
Nor will I sue, although the King have mercies
More than I dare make faults. You few that lov'd me
And dare be bold to weep for Buckingham,
His noble friends and fellows, whom to leave
Is only bitter to him, only dying,
Go with me like good angels to my end;
And as the long divorce of steel falls on me
Make of your prayers one sweet sacrifice,
And lift my soul to heaven. Lead on, a God's name.
LOVELL. I do beseech your Grace, for charity,
 If ever any malice in your heart
 Were hid against me, now to forgive me frankly.
BUCKINGHAM. Sir Thomas Lovell, I as free forgive you
 As I would be forgiven. I forgive all.
 There cannot be those numberless offences
 'Gainst me that I cannot take peace with. No black envy
 Shall mark my grave. Commend me to his Grace;
 And if he speak of Buckingham, pray tell him
 You met him half in heaven. My vows and prayers
 Yet are the King's, and, till my soul forsake,
 Shall cry for blessings on him. May he live
 Longer than I have time to tell his years;
 Ever belov'd and loving may his rule be;
 And when old time shall lead him to his end,
 Goodness and he fill up one monument!
LOVELL. To th' water side I must conduct your Grace;
 Then give my charge up to Sir Nicholas Vaux,
 Who undertakes you to your end.
VAUX. Prepare there;
 The Duke is coming; see the barge be ready;
 And fit it with such furniture as suits
 The greatness of his person.
BUCKINGHAM. Nay, Sir Nicholas,
 Let it alone; my state now will but mock me.
 When I came hither I was Lord High Constable
 And Duke of Buckingham; now, poor Edward Bohun.

Yet I am richer than my base accusers
That never knew what truth meant; I now seal it;
And with that blood will make 'em one day groan for't.
My noble father, Henry of Buckingham,
Who first rais'd head against usurping Richard,
Flying for succour to his servant Banister,
Being distress'd, was by that wretch betray'd
And without trial fell; God's peace be with him!
Henry the Seventh succeeding, truly pitying
My father's loss, like a most royal prince,
Restor'd me to my honours, and out of ruins
Made my name once more noble. Now his son,
Henry the Eighth, life, honour, name, and all
That made me happy, at one stroke has taken
For ever from the world. I had my trial,
And must needs say a noble one; which makes me
A little happier than my wretched father;
Yet thus far we are one in fortunes: both
Fell by our servants, by those men we lov'd most—
A most unnatural and faithless service.
Heaven has an end in all. Yet, you that hear me,
This from a dying man receive as certain:
Where you are liberal of your loves and counsels,
Be sure you be not loose; for those you make friends
And give your hearts to, when they once perceive
The least rub in your fortunes, fall away
Like water from ye, never found again
But where they mean to sink ye. All good people,
Pray for me! I must now forsake ye; the last hour
Of my long weary life is come upon me.
Farewell;
And when you would say something that is sad,
Speak how I fell. I have done; and God forgive me!

       Exeunt BUCKINGHAM *and train*

FIRST GENTLEMAN. O, this is full of pity! Sir, it calls,
 I fear, too many curses on their heads
 That were the authors.
SECOND GENTLEMAN. If the Duke be guiltless,
 'Tis full of woe; yet I can give you inkling
 Of an ensuing evil, if it fall,

Greater than this.

FIRST GENTLEMAN. Good angels keep it from us!
  What may it be? You do not doubt my faith, sir?
SECOND GENTLEMAN. This secret is so weighty, 'twill require
  A strong faith to conceal it.
FIRST GENTLEMAN. Let me have it;
  I do not talk much.
SECOND GENTLEMAN. I am confident.
  You shall, sir. Did you not of late days hear
  A buzzing of a separation
  Between the King and Katharine ?
FIRST GENTLEMAN. Yes, but it held not;
  For when the King once heard it, out of anger
  He sent command to the Lord Mayor straight
  To stop the rumour and allay those tongues
  That durst disperse it.
SECOND GENTLEMAN. But that slander, sir,
  Is found a truth now; for it grows again
  Fresher than e'er it was, and held for certain
  The King will venture at it. Either the Cardinal
  Or some about him near have, out of malice
  To the good Queen, possess'd him with a scruple
  That will undo her. To confirm this too,
  Cardinal Campeius is arriv'd and lately;
  As all think, for this business.
FIRST GENTLEMAN. 'Tis the Cardinal;
  And merely to revenge him on the Emperor
  For not bestowing on him at his asking
  The archbishopric of Toledo, this is purpos'd.
SECOND GENTLEMAN. I think you have hit the mark; but is't
    not cruel
  That she should feel the smart of this? The Cardinal
  Will have his will, and she must fall.
FIRST GENTLEMAN. 'Tis woeful.
  We are too open here to argue this;
  Let's think in private more.   *Exeunt*

SCENE 2

London. The palace

Enter the Lord Chamberlain *reading this letter*

Chamberlain. 'My lord,
  'The horses your lordship sent for, with all the care I
had, I saw well chosen, ridden, and furnish'd. They were
young and handsome, and of the best breed in the north.
When they were ready to set out for London, a man of
my Lord Cardinal's, by commission, and main power, took
'em from me, with this reason: his master would be serv'd
before a subject, if not before the King; which stopp'd
our mouths, sir.'

I fear he will indeed. Well, let him have them.
He will have all, I think.

Enter to the Lord Chamberlain *the* Dukes of
Norfolk *and* Suffolk

Norfolk. Well met, my Lord Chamberlain.
Chamberlain. Good day to both your Graces.
Suffolk. How is the King employ'd?
Chamberlain. I left him private,
  Full of sad thoughts and troubles.
Norfolk. What's the cause?
Chamberlain. It seems the marriage with his brother's wife
  Has crept too near his conscience.
Suffolk. No, his conscience
  Has crept too near another lady.
Norfolk. 'Tis so;
  This is the Cardinal's doing; the King-Cardinal,
  That blind priest, like the eldest son of fortune,
  Turns what he list. The King will know him one day.
Suffolk. Pray God he do! He'll never know himself else.
Norfolk. How holily he works in all his business!
  And with what zeal! For, now he has crack'd the league
  Between us and the Emperor, the Queen's great nephew,
  He dives into the King's soul and there scatters
  Dangers, doubts, wringing of the conscience,

Fears, and despairs—and all these for his marriage;
And out of all these to restore the King,
He counsels a divorce, a loss of her
That like a jewel has hung twenty years
About his neck, yet never lost her lustre;
Of her that loves him with that excellence
That angels love good men with; even of her
That, when the greatest stroke of fortune falls,
Will bless the King—and is not this course pious?
CHAMBERLAIN. Heaven keep me from such counsel! 'Tis most
    true
    These news are everywhere; every tongue speaks 'em,
    And every true heart weeps for't. All that dare
    Look into these affairs see this main end—
    The French King's sister. Heaven will one day open
    The King's eyes, that so long have slept upon
    This bold bad man.
SUFFOLK. And free us from his slavery.
NORFOLK. We had need pray, and heartily, for our deliver-
    ance;
    Or this imperious man will work us all
    From princes into pages. All men's honours
    Lie like one lump before him, to be fashion'd
    Into what pitch he please.
SUFFOLK. For me, my lords,
    I love him not, nor fear him—there's my creed;
    As I am made without him, so I'll stand,
    If the King please; his curses and his blessings
    Touch me alike; th'are breath I not believe in.
    I knew him, and I know him; so I leave him
    To him that made him proud—the Pope.
NORFOLK. Let's in;
    And with some other business put the King
    From these sad thoughts that work too much upon him.
    My lord, you'll bear us company?
CHAMBERLAIN. Excuse me,
    The King has sent me otherwhere; besides,
    You'll find a most unfit time to disturb him.
    Health to your lordships!
NORFOLK. Thanks, my good Lord Chamberlain.

Exit Lord Chamberlain; *and the* King *draws
the curtain and sits reading pensively*

Suffolk. How sad he looks; sure, he is much afflicted.

King. Who's there, ha?

Norfolk. Pray God he be not angry.

King Henry. Who's there, I say? How dare you thrust
yourselves
Into my private meditations?
Who am I, ha?

Norfolk. A gracious king that pardons all offences
Malice ne'er meant. Our breach of duty this way
Is business of estate, in which we come
To know your royal pleasure.

King. Ye are too bold.
Go to; I'll make ye know your times of business.
Is this an hour for temporal affairs, ha?

Enter Wolsey *and* Campeius *with a commission*

Who's there? My good Lord Cardinal? O my Wolsey,
The quiet of my wounded conscience,
Thou art a cure fit for a King. [*To* Campeius] You're
welcome,
Most learned reverend sir, into our kingdom.
Use us and it. [*To* Wolsey] My good lord, have great
care
I be not found a talker.

Wolsey. Sir, you cannot.
I would your Grace would give us but an hour
Of private conference.

King. [*To* Norfolk *and* Suffolk] We are busy; go.

Norfolk. [*Aside to* Suffolk] This priest has no pride in
him!

Suffolk. [*Aside to* Norfolk] Not to speak of!
I would not be so sick though for his place.
But this cannot continue.

Norfolk [*Aside to* Suffolk] If it do,
I'll venture one have-at-him.

Suffolk. [*Aside to* Norfolk] I another.

Exeunt Norfolk *and* Suffolk

Wolsey. Your Grace has given a precedent of wisdom

Above all princes, in committing freely
Your scruple to the voice of Christendom.
Who can be angry now? What envy reach you?
The Spaniard, tied by blood and favour to her,
Must now confess, if they have any goodness,
The trial just and noble. All the clerks,
I mean the learned ones, in Christian kingdoms
Have their free voices. Rome the nurse of judgment,
Invited by your noble self, hath sent
One general tongue unto us, this good man,
This just and learned priest, Cardinal Campeius,
Whom once more I present unto your Highness.
KING. And once more in mine arms I bid him welcome,
And thank the holy conclave for their loves.
They have sent me such a man I would have wish'd for.
CAMPEIUS. Your Grace must needs deserve all strangers'
    loves,
You are so noble. To your Highness' hand
I tender my commission; by whose virtue—
The court of Rome commanding—you, my Lord
Cardinal of York, are join'd with me their servant
In the unpartial judging of this business.
KING. Two equal men. The Queen shall be acquainted
Forthwith for what you come. Where's Gardiner?
WOLSEY. I know your Majesty has always lov'd her
So dear in heart not to deny her that
A woman of less place might ask by law—
Scholars allow'd freely to argue for her.
KING. Ay, and the best she shall have; and my favour
To him that does best. God forbid else. Cardinal,
Prithee call Gardiner to me, my new secretary;
I find him a fit fellow.   *Exit* WOLSEY

                Re-enter WOLSEY *with* GARDINER

WOLSEY. [*Aside to* GARDINER] Give me your hand: much
    joy and favour to you;
You are the King's now.
GARDINER. [*Aside to* WOLSEY] But to be commanded
For ever by your Grace, whose hand has rais'd me.
KING. Come hither, Gardiner.   [*Walks and whispers*]

CAMPEIUS. My Lord of York, was not one Doctor Pace
  In this man's place before him?
WOLSEY. Yes, he was.
CAMPEIUS. Was he not held a learned man?
WOLSEY. Yes, surely.
CAMPEIUS. Believe me, there's an ill opinion spread then,
  Even of yourself, Lord Cardinal.
WOLSEY. How! Of me?
CAMPEIUS. They will not stick to say you envied him
  And, fearing he would rise, he was so virtuous,
  Kept him a foreign man still; which so griev'd him
  That he ran mad and died.
WOLSEY. Heav'n's peace be with him!
  That's Christian care enough. For living murmurers
  There's places of rebuke. He was a fool,
  For he would needs be virtuous: that good fellow,
  If I command him, follows my appointment.
  I will have none so near else. Learn this, brother,
  We live not to be grip'd by meaner persons.
KING. Deliver this with modesty to th' Queen.

                                        Exit GARDINER
  The most convenient place that I can think of
  For such receipt of learning is Blackfriars;
  There ye shall meet about this weighty business—
  My Wolsey, see it furnish'd. O, my lord,
  Would it not grieve an able man to leave
  So sweet a bedfellow? But, conscience, conscience!
  O, 'tis a tender place! and I must leave her.   *Exeunt*

SCENE 3

London. The palace

Enter ANNE BULLEN *and an* OLD LADY

ANNE. Not for that neither. Here's the pang that pinches:
  His Highness having liv'd so long with her, and she
  So good a lady that no tongue could ever
  Pronounce dishonour of her—by my life,

She never knew harm-doing—O, now, after
So many courses of the sun enthroned,
Still growing in a majesty and pomp, the which
To leave a thousand-fold more bitter than
'Tis sweet at first t' acquire—after this process,
To give her the avaunt, it is a pity
Would move a monster.

OLD LADY. Hearts of most hard temper
Melt and lament for her.

ANNE. O, God's will! much better
She ne'er had known pomp; though't be temporal,
Yet, if that quarrel, fortune, do divorce
It from the bearer, 'tis a sufferance panging
As soul and body's severing.

OLD LADY. Alas, poor lady!
She's a stranger now again.

ANNE. So much the more
Must pity drop upon her. Verily,
I swear 'tis better to be lowly born
And range with humble livers in content
Than to be perk'd up in a glist'ring grief
And wear a golden sorrow.

OLD LADY. Our content
Is our best having.

ANNE. By my troth and maidenhead,
I would not be a queen.

OLD LADY. Beshrew me, I would,
And venture maidenhead for't; and so would you,
For all this spice of your hypocrisy.
You that have so fair parts of woman on you
Have too a woman's heart, which ever yet
Affected eminence, wealth, sovereignty;
Which, to say sooth, are blessings; and which gifts,
Saving your mincing, the capacity
Of your soft cheveril conscience would receive
If you might please to stretch it.

ANNE. Nay, good troth.

OLD LADY. Yes, troth and troth. You would not be a queen!

ANNE. No, not for all the riches under heaven.

OLD LADY. 'Tis strange: a threepence bow'd would hire me,
　　Old as I am, to queen it. But, I pray you,
　　What think you of a duchess? Have you limbs
　　To bear that load of title?
ANNE. No, in truth.
OLD LADY. Then you are weakly made. Pluck off a little;
　　I would not be a young count in your way
　　For more than blushing comes to. If your back
　　Cannot vouchsafe this burden, 'tis too weak
　　Ever to get a boy.
ANNE. How you do talk!
　　I swear again I would not be a queen
　　For all the world.
OLD LADY. In faith, for little England
　　You'd venture an emballing. I myself
　　Would for Carnarvonshire, although there long'd
　　No more to th' crown but that. Lo, who comes here?

Enter the LORD CHAMBERLAIN

CHAMBERLAIN. Good morrow, ladies. What were't worth
　　to know
　　The secret of your conference?
ANNE. My good lord,
　　Not your demand; it values not your asking.
　　Our mistress' sorrows we were pitying.
CHAMBERLAIN. It was a gentle business and becoming
　　The action of good women; there is hope
　　All will be well.
ANNE. Now, I pray God, amen!
CHAMBERLAIN. You bear a gentle mind, and heav'nly bless-
　　ings
　　Follow such creatures. That you may, fair lady,
　　Perceive I speak sincerely and high note's
　　Ta'en of your many virtues, the King's Majesty
　　Commends his good opinion of you to you, and
　　Does purpose honour to you no less flowing
　　Than Marchioness of Pembroke; to which title
　　A thousand pound a year, annual support,
　　Out of his grace he adds.

ANNE. I do not know
>   What kind of my obedience I should tender;
>   More than my all is nothing, nor my prayers
>   Are not words duly hallowed, nor my wishes
>   More worth than empty vanities; yet prayers and wishes
>   Are all I can return. Beseech your lordship,
>   Vouchsafe to speak my thanks and my obedience,
>   As from a blushing handmaid, to his Highness;
>   Whose health and royalty I pray for.

CHAMBERLAIN. Lady,
>   I shall not fail t'approve the fair conceit
>   The King hath of you. [*Aside*] I have perus'd her well:
>   Beauty and honour in her are so mingled
>   That they have caught the King; and who knows yet
>   But from this lady may proceed a gem
>   To lighten all this isle?—I'll to the King
>   And say I spoke with you.

ANNE. My honour'd lord!   *Exit* LORD CHAMBERLAIN

OLD LADY. Why, this it is: see, see!
>   I have been begging sixteen years in court—
>   Am yet a courtier beggarly—nor could
>   Come pat betwixt too early and too late
>   For any suit of pounds; and you, O fate!
>   A very fresh-fish here—fie, fie, fie upon
>   This compell'd fortune!—have your mouth fill'd up
>   Before you open it.

ANNE. This is strange to me.

OLD LADY. How tastes it? Is it bitter? Forty pence, no.
>   There was a lady once—'tis an old story—
>   That would not be a queen, that would she not,
>   For all the mud in Egypt. Have you heard it?

ANNE. Come, you are pleasant.

OLD LADY. With your theme I could
>   O'ermount the lark. The Marchioness of Pembroke!
>   A thousand pounds a year for pure respect!
>   No other obligation! By my life,
>   That promises moe thousands: honour's train
>   Is longer than his foreskirt. By this time
>   I know your back will bear a duchess. Say,

Are you not stronger than you were?
ANNE. Good lady,
 Make yourself mirth with your particular fancy,
 And leave me out on't. Would I had no being,
 If this salute my blood a jot; it faints me
 To think what follows.
 The Queen is comfortless, and we forgetful
 In our long absence. Pray, do not deliver
 What here y' have heard to her.
OLD LADY. What do you think me?   *Exeunt*

SCENE 4

London. A hall in Blackfriars

Trumpets, sennet, and cornets. Enter two VERGERS, *with short silver wands; next them, two* SCRIBES, *in the habit of doctors; after them, the* ARCHBISHOP OF CANTERBURY *alone; after him, the* BISHOPS OF LINCOLN, ELY, ROCHESTER, *and* SAINT ASAPH; *next them, with some small distance, follows a* GENTLEMAN *bearing the purse, with the great seal, and a Cardinal's hat; then two* PRIESTS, *bearing each a silver cross; then a* GENTLEMAN USHER *bareheaded, accompanied with a* SERGEANT-AT-ARMS *bearing a silver mace; then two* GENTLEMEN *bearing two great silver pillars; after them, side by side, the two* CARDINALS, WOLSEY *and* CAMPEIUS; *two* NOBLEMEN *with the sword and mace. Then enter the* KING *and* QUEEN *and their trains. The* KING *takes place under the cloth of state; the two* CARDINALS *sit under him as judges. The* QUEEN *takes place some distance from the* KING. *The* BISHOPS *place themselves on each side of the court, in manner of a consistory; below them the* SCRIBES. *The* LORDS *sit next the* BISHOPS. *The rest of the attendants stand in convenient order about the stage*

WOLSEY. Whilst our commission from Rome is read,
 Let silence be commanded.

KING. What's the need?
  It hath already publicly been read,
  And on all sides th' authority allow'd;
  You may then spare that time.
WOLSEY. Be't so; proceed.
SCRIBE. Say 'Henry King of England, come into the court.'
CRIER. Henry King of England, &c.
KING. Here.
SCRIBE. Say 'Katharine Queen of England, come into the
  court.'
CRIER. Katharine Queen of England, &c.

  The QUEEN *makes no answer, rises out of her chair,
  goes about the court, comes to the* KING, *and kneels
  at his feet; then speaks*

QUEEN KATHARINE. Sir, I desire you do me right and justice,
  And to bestow your pity on me; for
  I am a most poor woman and a stranger,
  Born out of your dominions, having here
  No judge indifferent, nor no more assurance
  Of equal friendship and proceeding. Alas, sir,
  In what have I offended you? What cause
  Hath my behaviour given to your displeasure
  That thus you should proceed to put me off
  And take your good grace from me? Heaven witness,
  I have been to you a true and humble wife,
  At all times to your will conformable,
  Ever in fear to kindle your dislike,
  Yea, subject to your countenance—glad or sorry
  As I saw it inclin'd. When was the hour
  I ever contradicted your desire
  Or made it not mine too? Or which of your friends
  Have I not strove to love, although I knew
  He were mine enemy? What friend of mine
  That had to him deriv'd your anger did I
  Continue in my liking? Nay, gave notice
  He was from thence discharg'd? Sir, call to mind
  That I have been your wife in this obedience
  Upward of twenty years, and have been blest
  With many children by you. If, in the course

And process of this time, you can report,
And prove it too against mine honour, aught,
My bond to wedlock or my love and duty,
Against your sacred person, in God's name,
Turn me away and let the foul'st contempt
Shut door upon me, and so give me up
To the sharp'st kind of justice. Please you, sir,
The King, your father, was reputed for
A prince most prudent, of an excellent
And unmatch'd wit and judgment; Ferdinand,
My father, King of Spain, was reckon'd one
The wisest prince that there had reign'd by many
A year before. It is not to be question'd
That they had gather'd a wise council to them
Of every realm, that did debate this business,
Who deem'd our marriage lawful. Wherefore I humbly
Beseech you, sir, to spare me till I may
Be by my friends in Spain advis'd, whose counsel
I will implore. If not, i' th' name of God,
Your pleasure be fulfill'd!

WOLSEY. You have here, lady,
And of your choice, these reverend fathers—men
Of singular integrity and learning,
Yea, the elect o' th' land, who are assembled
To plead your cause. It shall be therefore bootless
That longer you desire the court, as well
For your own quiet as to rectify
What is unsettled in the King.

CAMPEIUS. His Grace
Hath spoken well and justly; therefore, madam,
It's fit this royal session do proceed
And that, without delay, their arguments
Be now produc'd and heard.

QUEEN KATHARINE. Lord Cardinal,
To you I speak.

WOLSEY. Your pleasure, madam?

QUEEN KATHARINE. Sir,
I am about to weep; but, thinking that
We are a queen, or long have dream'd so, certain

The daughter of a king, my drops of tears
I'll turn to sparks of fire.

WOLSEY. Be patient yet.

QUEEN KATHARINE. I will, when you are humble; nay, be-
fore,
Or God will punish me. I do believe,
Induc'd by potent circumstances, that
You are mine enemy, and make my challenge
You shall not be my judge; for it is you
Have blown this coal betwixt my lord and me—
Which God's dew quench! Therefore I say again,
I utterly abhor, yea, from my soul
Refuse you for my judge, whom yet once more
I hold my most malicious foe and think not
At all a friend to truth.

WOLSEY. I do profess
You speak not like yourself, who ever yet
Have stood to charity and display'd th' effects
Of disposition gentle and of wisdom
O'ertopping woman's pow'r. Madam, you do me wrong:
I have no spleen against you, nor injustice
For you or any; how far I have proceeded,
Or how far further shall, is warranted
By a commission from the Consistory,
Yea, the whole Consistory of Rome. You charge me
That I have blown this coal: I do deny it.
The King is present; if it be known to him
That I gainsay my deed, how may he wound,
And worthily, my falsehood! Yea, as much
As you have done my truth. If he know
That I am free of your report, he knows
I am not of your wrong. Therefore in him
It lies to cure me, and the cure is to
Remove these thoughts from you; the which before
His Highness shall speak in, I do beseech
You, gracious madam, to unthink your speaking
And to say so no more.

QUEEN KATHARINE. My lord, my lord,
I am a simple woman, much too weak

T' oppose your cunning. Y'are meek and humble-mouth'd;
You sign your place and calling, in full seeming,
With meekness and humility; but your heart
Is cramm'd with arrogancy, spleen, and pride.
You have, by fortune and his Highness' favours,
Gone slightly o'er low steps, and now are mounted
Where pow'rs are your retainers, and your words,
Domestics to you, serve your will as't please
Yourself pronounce their office. I must tell you
You tender more your person's honour than
Your high profession spiritual; that again
I do refuse you for my judge and here,
Before you all, appeal unto the Pope,
To bring my whole cause 'fore his Holiness
And to be judg'd by him.

          [*She curtsies to the* KING, *and offers to depart*]

CAMPEIUS. The Queen is obstinate,
  Stubborn to justice, apt to accuse it, and
  Disdainful to be tried by't; 'tis not well.
  She's going away.
KING. Call her again.
CRIER. Katharine Queen of England, come into the court.
GENTLEMAN USHER. Madam, you are call'd back.
QUEEN KATHARINE. What need you note it? Pray you keep
    your way;
  When you are call'd, return. Now the Lord help!
  They vex me past my patience. Pray you pass on.
  I will not tarry; no, nor ever more
  Upon this business my appearance make
  In any of their courts.   *Exeunt* QUEEN *and her attendants*
KING. Go thy ways, Kate.
  That man i' th' world who shall report he has
  A better wife, let him in nought be trusted
  For speaking false in that. Thou art, alone—
  If thy rare qualities, sweet gentleness,
  Thy meekness saint-like, wife-like government,
  Obeying in commanding, and thy parts
  Sovereign and pious else, could speak thee out—
  The queen of earthly queens. She's noble born;

And like her true nobility she has
Carried herself towards me.
WOLSEY. Most gracious sir,
  In humblest manner I require your Highness
  That it shall please you to declare in hearing
  Of all these ears—for where I am robb'd and bound,
  There must I be unloos'd, although not there
  At once and fully satisfied—whether ever I
  Did broach this business to your Highness, or
  Laid any scruple in your way which might
  Induce you to the question on't, or ever
  Have to you, but with thanks to God for such
  A royal lady, spake one the least word that might
  Be to the prejudice of her present state,
  Or touch of her good person?
KING. My Lord Cardinal,
  I do excuse you; yea, upon mine honour,
  I free you from't. You are not to be taught
  That you have many enemies that know not
  Why they are so, but, like to village curs,
  Bark when their fellows do. By some of these
  The Queen is put in anger. Y'are excus'd.
  But will you be more justified? You ever
  Have wish'd the sleeping of this business; never desir'd
  It to be stirr'd; but oft have hind'red, oft,
  The passages made toward it. On my honour,
  I speak my good Lord Cardinal to this point,
  And thus far clear him. Now, what mov'd me to't,
  I will be bold with time and your attention.
  Then mark th' inducement. Thus it came—give heed to't:
  My conscience first receiv'd a tenderness,
  Scruple, and prick, on certain speeches utter'd
  By th' Bishop of Bayonne, then French ambassador,
  Who had been hither sent on the debating
  A marriage 'twixt the Duke of Orleans and
  Our daughter Mary. I' th' progress of this business,
  Ere a determinate resolution, he—
  I mean the Bishop—did require a respite
  Wherein he might the King his lord advertise
  Whether our daughter were legitimate,

Respecting this our marriage with the dowager,
Sometimes our brother's wife. This respite shook
The bosom of my conscience, enter'd me,
Yea, with a splitting power, and made to tremble
The region of my breast, which forc'd such way
That many maz'd considerings did throng
And press'd in with this caution. First, methought
I stood not in the smile of heaven, who had
Commanded nature that my lady's womb,
If it conceiv'd a male child by me, should
Do no more offices of life to't than
The grave does to the dead; for her male issue
Or died where they were made, or shortly after
This world had air'd them. Hence I took a thought
This was a judgment on me, that my kingdom,
Well worthy the best heir o' th' world, should not
Be gladded in't by me. Then follows that
I weigh'd the danger which my realms stood in
By this my issue's fail, and that gave to me
Many a groaning throe. Thus hulling in
The wild sea of my conscience, I did steer
Toward this remedy, whereupon we are
Now present here together; that's to say
I meant to rectify my conscience, which
I then did feel full sick, and yet not well,
By all the reverend fathers of the land
And doctors learn'd. First, I began in private
With you, my Lord of Lincoln; you remember
How under my oppression I did reek,
When I first mov'd you.
LINCOLN. Very well, my liege.
KING. I have spoke long; be pleas'd yourself to say
　　How far you satisfied me.
LINCOLN. So please your Highness,
　　The question did at first so stagger me—
　　Bearing a state of mighty moment in't
　　And consequence of dread—that I committed
　　The daring'st counsel which I had to doubt,
　　And did entreat your Highness to this course
　　Which you are running here.

KING. I then mov'd you,
  My Lord of Canterbury, and got your leave
  To make this present summons. Unsolicited
  I left no reverend person in this court,
  But by particular consent proceeded
  Under your hands and seals; therefore, go on,
  For no dislike i' th' world against the person
  Of the good Queen, but the sharp thorny points
  Of my alleged reasons, drives this forward.
  Prove but our marriage lawful, by my life
  And kingly dignity, we are contented
  To wear our mortal state to come with her,
  Katharine our queen, before the primest creature
  That's paragon'd o' th' world.
CAMPEIUS. So please your Highness,
  The Queen being absent, 'tis a needful fitness
  That we adjourn this court till further day;
  Meanwhile must be an earnest motion
  Made to the Queen to call back her appeal
  She intends unto his Holiness.
KING. [*Aside*] I may perceive
  These cardinals trifle with me. I abhor
  This dilatory sloth and tricks of Rome.
  My learn'd and well-beloved servant, Cranmer,
  Prithee return. With thy approach I know
  My comfort comes along.—Break up the court;
  I say, set on.   *Exeunt in manner as they enter'd*

ACT III. SCENE 1

London. The QUEEN's *apartments*

Enter the QUEEN *and her women, as at work*

QUEEN KATHARINE. Take thy lute, wench. My soul grows
  sad with troubles;
  Sing and disperse 'em, if thou canst. Leave working.

Song

Orpheus with his lute made trees,
And the mountain tops that freeze,
  Bow themselves when he did sing;
To his music plants and flowers
Ever sprung, as sun and showers
  There had made a lasting spring.

Every thing that heard him play,
Even the billows of the sea,
  Hung their heads and then lay by.
In sweet music is such art,
Killing care and grief of heart
  Fall asleep or hearing die.

Enter a GENTLEMAN

QUEEN KATHARINE. How now?
GENTLEMAN. An't please your Grace, the two great Cardinals
  Wait in the presence.
QUEEN KATHARINE. Would they speak with me?
GENTLEMAN. They will'd me say so, madam.
QUEEN KATHARINE. Pray their Graces
  To come near. [*Exit* GENTLEMAN] What can be their business
  With me, a poor weak woman, fall'n from favour?
  I do not like their coming. Now I think on't,
  They should be good men, their affairs as righteous;
  But all hoods make not monks.

Enter the two CARDINALS, WOLSEY *and* CAMPEIUS

WOLSEY. Peace to your Highness!
QUEEN KATHARINE. Your Graces find me here part of a housewife;
  I would be all, against the worst may happen.
  What are your pleasures with me, reverend lords?
WOLSEY. May it please you, noble madam, to withdraw
  Into your private chamber, we shall give you
  The full cause of our coming.
QUEEN KATHARINE. Speak it here;

938

There's nothing I have done yet, o' my conscience,
Deserves a corner. Would all other women
Could speak this with as free a soul as I do!
My lords, I care not—so much I am happy
Above a number—if my actions
Were tried by ev'ry tongue, ev'ry eye saw 'em,
Envy and base opinion set against 'em,
I know my life so even. If your business
Seek me out, and that way I am wife in,
Out with it boldly; truth loves open dealing.

WOLSEY. Tanta est erga te mentis integritas, regina serenis-
sima—

QUEEN KATHARINE. O, good my lord, no Latin!
I am not such a truant since my coming,
As not to know the language I have liv'd in;
A strange tongue makes my cause more strange, suspicious;
Pray speak in English. Here are some will thank you,
If you speak truth, for their poor mistress' sake:
Believe me, she has had much wrong. Lord Cardinal,
The willing'st sin I ever yet committed
May be absolv'd in English.

WOLSEY. Noble lady,
I am sorry my integrity should breed,
And service to his Majesty and you,
So deep suspicion, where all faith was meant.
We come not by the way of accusation
To taint that honour every good tongue blesses,
Nor to betray you any way to sorrow—
You have too much, good lady; but to know
How you stand minded in the weighty difference
Between the King and you, and to deliver,
Like free and honest men, our just opinions
And comforts to your cause.

CAMPEIUS. Most honour'd madam,
My Lord of York, out of his noble nature,
Zeal and obedience he still bore your Grace,
Forgetting, like a good man, your late censure
Both of his truth and him—which was too far—
Offers, as I do, in a sign of peace,
His service and his counsel.

QUEEN KATHARINE. [*Aside*] To betray me.—
  My lords, I thank you both for your good wills;
  Ye speak like honest men—pray God ye prove so!
  But how to make ye suddenly an answer,
  In such a point of weight, so near mine honour,
  More near my life, I fear, with my weak wit,
  And to such men of gravity and learning,
  In truth I know not. I was set at work
  Among my maids, full little, God knows, looking
  Either for such men or such business.
  For her sake that I have been—for I feel
  The last fit of my greatness—good your Graces,
  Let me have time and counsel for my cause.
  Alas, I am a woman, friendless, hopeless!
WOLSEY. Madam, you wrong the King's love with these
    fears;
  Your hopes and friends are infinite.
QUEEN KATHARINE. In England
  But little for my profit; can you think, lords,
  That any Englishman dare give me counsel?
  Or be a known friend, 'gainst his Highness' pleasure—
  Though he be grown so desperate to be honest—
  And live a subject? Nay, forsooth, my friends,
  They that must weigh out my afflictions,
  They that my trust must grow to, live not here;
  They are, as all my other comforts, far hence,
  In mine own country, lords.
CAMPEIUS. I would your Grace
  Would leave your griefs, and take my counsel.
QUEEN KATHARINE. How, sir?
CAMPEIUS. Put your main cause into the King's protection;
  He's loving and most gracious. 'Twill be much
  Both for your honour better and your cause;
  For if the trial of the law o'ertake ye
  You'll part away disgrac'd.
WOLSEY. He tells you rightly.
QUEEN KATHARINE. Ye tell me what ye wish for both—my
    ruin.
  Is this your Christian counsel? Out upon ye!
  Heaven is above all yet: there sits a Judge

That no king can corrupt.

CAMPEIUS. Your rage mistakes us.

QUEEN KATHARINE. The more shame for ye; holy men I
    thought ye,
Upon my soul, two reverend cardinal virtues;
But cardinal sins and hollow hearts I fear ye.
Mend 'em, for shame, my lords. Is this your comfort?
The cordial that ye bring a wretched lady—
A woman lost among ye, laugh'd at, scorn'd?
I will not wish ye half my miseries:
I have more charity; but say I warned ye.
Take heed, for heaven's sake take heed, lest at once
The burden of my sorrows fall upon ye.

WOLSEY. Madam, this is a mere distraction;
You turn the good we offer into envy.

QUEEN KATHARINE. Ye turn me into nothing. Woe upon ye,
And all such false professors! Would you have me—
If you have any justice, any pity,
If ye be any thing but churchmen's habits—
Put my sick cause into his hands that hates me?
Alas! has banish'd me his bed already,
His love too long ago! I am old, my lords,
And all the fellowship I hold now with him
Is only my obedience. What can happen
To me above this wretchedness? All your studies
Make me a curse like this.

CAMPEIUS. Your fears are worse.

QUEEN KATHARINE. Have I liv'd thus long—let me speak
    myself,
Since virtue finds no friends—a wife, a true one?
A woman, I dare say without vain-glory,
Never yet branded with suspicion?
Have I with all my full affections
Still met the King, lov'd him next heav'n, obey'd him,
Been, out of fondness, superstitious to him,
Almost forgot my prayers to content him,
And am I thus rewarded? 'Tis not well, lords.
Bring me a constant woman to her husband,
One that ne'er dream'd a joy beyond his pleasure,
And to that woman, when she has done most,

Yet will I add an honour—a great patience.

WOLSEY. Madam, you wander from the good we aim at.

QUEEN KATHARINE. My lord, I dare not make myself so
    guilty,
To give up willingly that noble title
Your master wed me to: nothing but death
Shall e'er divorce my dignities.

WOLSEY. Pray hear me.

QUEEN KATHARINE. Would I had never trod this English
    earth,
Or felt the flatteries that grow upon it!
Ye have angels' faces, but heaven knows your hearts.
What will become of me now, wretched lady?
I am the most unhappy woman living.
    [*To her* WOMEN] Alas, poor wenches, where are now
    your fortunes?
Shipwreck'd upon a kingdom, where no pity,
No friends, no hope; no kindred weep for me;
Almost no grave allow'd me. Like the lily,
That once was mistress of the field, and flourish'd,
I'll hang my head and perish.

WOLSEY. If your Grace
Could but be brought to know our ends are honest,
You'd feel more comfort. Why should we, good lady,
Upon what cause, wrong you? Alas, our places,
The way of our profession is against it;
We are to cure such sorrows, not to sow 'em.
For goodness' sake, consider what you do;
How you may hurt yourself, ay, utterly
Grow from the King's acquaintance, by this carriage.
The hearts of princes kiss obedience,
So much they love it; but to stubborn spirits
They swell and grow as terrible as storms.
I know you have a gentle, noble temper,
A soul as even as a calm. Pray think us
Those we profess, peace-makers, friends, and servants.

CAMPEIUS. Madam, you'll find it so. You wrong your virtues
With these weak women's fears. A noble spirit,
As yours was put into you, ever casts
Such doubts as false coin from it. The King loves you;

Beware you lose it not. For us, if you please
To trust us in your business, we are ready
To use our utmost studies in your service.
QUEEN KATHARINE. Do what ye will, my lords; and pray
    forgive me
If I have us'd myself unmannerly;
You know I am a woman, lacking wit
To make a seemly answer to such persons.
Pray do my service to his Majesty;
He has my heart yet, and shall have my prayers
While I shall have my life. Come, reverend fathers,
Bestow your counsels on me; she now begs
That little thought, when she set footing here,
She should have bought her dignities so dear.   *Exeunt*

SCENE 2

London. The palace

Enter the DUKE OF NORFOLK, *the* DUKE OF SUFFOLK,
the EARL OF SURREY, *and the* LORD CHAMBERLAIN

NORFOLK. If you will now unite in your complaints
    And force them with a constancy, the Cardinal
    Cannot stand under them: if you omit
    The offer of this time, I cannot promise
    But that you shall sustain moe new disgraces
    With these you bear already.
SURREY. I am joyful
    To meet the least occasion that may give me
    Remembrance of my father-in-law, the Duke,
    To be reveng'd on him.
SUFFOLK. Which of the peers
    Have uncontemn'd gone by him, or at least
    Strangely neglected? When did he regard
    The stamp of nobleness in any person
    Out of himself?
CHAMBERLAIN. My lords, you speak your pleasures.
    What he deserves of you and me I know;
    What we can do to him—though now the time

Gives way to us—I much fear. If you cannot
Bar his access to th' King, never attempt
Anything on him; for he hath a witchcraft
Over the King in's tongue.

NORFOLK. O, fear him not!
His spell in that is out; the King hath found
Matter against him that for ever mars
The honey of his language. No, he's settled,
Not to come off, in his displeasure.

SURREY. Sir,
I should be glad to hear such news as this
Once every hour.

NORFOLK. Believe it, this is true:
In the divorce his contrary proceedings
Are all unfolded; wherein he appears
As I would wish mine enemy.

SURREY. How came
His practices to light?

SUFFOLK. Most strangely.

SURREY. O, how, how?

SUFFOLK. The Cardinal's letters to the Pope miscarried,
And came to th' eye o' th' King; wherein was read
How that the Cardinal did entreat his Holiness
To stay the judgment o' th' divorce; for if
It did take place, 'I do' quoth he 'perceive
My king is tangled in affection to
A creature of the Queen's, Lady Anne Bullen.'

SURREY. Has the King this?

SUFFOLK. Believe it.

SURREY. Will this work?

CHAMBERLAIN. The King in this perceives him how he coasts
And hedges his own way. But in this point
All his tricks founder, and he brings his physic
After his patient's death: the King already
Hath married the fair lady.

SURREY. Would he had!

SUFFOLK. May you be happy in your wish, my lord!
For, I profess, you have it.

SURREY. Now, all my joy
Trace the conjunction!

SUFFOLK. My amen to't!

NORFOLK. All men's!

SUFFOLK. There's order given for her coronation;
Marry, this is yet but young, and may be left
To some ears unrecounted. But, my lords,
She is a gallant creature, and complete
In mind and feature. I persuade me from her
Will fall some blessing to this land, which shall
In it be memoriz'd.

SURREY. But will the King
Digest this letter of the Cardinal's?
The Lord forbid!

NORFOLK. Marry, amen!

SUFFOLK. No, no;
There be moe wasps that buzz about his nose
Will make this sting the sooner. Cardinal Campeius
Is stol'n away to Rome; hath ta'en no leave;
Has left the cause o' th' King unhandled, and
Is posted, as the agent of our Cardinal,
To second all his plot. I do assure you
The King cried 'Ha!' at this.

CHAMBERLAIN. Now, God incense him,
And let him cry 'Ha!' louder!

NORFOLK. But, my lord,
When returns Cranmer?

SUFFOLK. He is return'd, in his opinions; which
Have satisfied the King for his divorce,
Together with all famous colleges
Almost in Christendom. Shortly, I believe,
His second marriage shall be publish'd, and
Her coronation. Katharine no more
Shall be call'd queen, but princess dowager
And widow to Prince Arthur.

NORFOLK. This same Cranmer's
A worthy fellow, and hath ta'en much pain
In the King's business.

SUFFOLK. He has; and we shall see him
For it an archbishop.

NORFOLK. So I hear.

SUFFOLK. 'Tis so.

Enter WOLSEY *and* CROMWELL

The Cardinal!

NORFOLK. Observe, observe, he's moody.

WOLSEY. The packet, Cromwell,
Gave't you the King?

CROMWELL. To his own hand, in's bedchamber.

WOLSEY. Look'd he o' th' inside of the paper?

CROMWELL. Presently
He did unseal them; and the first he view'd,
He did it with a serious mind; a heed
Was in his countenance. You he bade
Attend him here this morning.

WOLSEY. Is he ready
To come abroad?

CROMWELL. I think by this he is.

WOLSEY. Leave me awhile.   *Exit* CROMWELL
[*Aside*] It shall be to the Duchess of Alençon,
The French King's sister; he shall marry her.
Anne Bullen! No, I'll no Anne Bullens for him;
There's more in't than fair visage. Bullen!
No, we'll no Bullens. Speedily I wish
To hear from Rome. The Marchioness of Pembroke!

NORFOLK. He's discontented.

SUFFOLK. May be he hears the King
Does whet his anger to him.

SURREY. Sharp enough,
Lord, for thy justice!

WOLSEY. [*Aside*] The late Queen's gentlewoman, a knight's
    daughter,
To be her mistress' mistress! The Queen's queen!
This candle burns not clear. 'Tis I must snuff it;
Then out it goes. What though I know her virtuous
And well deserving? Yet I know her for
A spleeny Lutheran; and not wholesome to
Our cause that she should lie i' th' bosom of
Our hard-rul'd King. Again, there is sprung up
An heretic, an arch one, Cranmer; one
Hath crawl'd into the favour of the King,
And is his oracle.

NORFOLK. He is vex'd at something.

946

ACT III. SCENE 2

Enter the KING, *reading of a schedule, and* LOVELL

SURREY. I would 'twere something that would fret the string,
  The master-cord on's heart!
SUFFOLK. The King, the King!
KING. What piles of wealth hath he accumulated
  To his own portion! And what expense by th' hour
  Seems to flow from him! How, i' th' name of thrift,
  Does he rake this together?—Now, my lords,
  Saw you the Cardinal?
NORFOLK. My lord, we have
  Stood here observing him. Some strange commotion
  Is in his brain: he bites his lip and starts,
  Stops on a sudden, looks upon the ground,
  Then lays his finger on his temple; straight
  Springs out into fast gait; then stops again,
  Strikes his breast hard; and anon he casts
  His eye against the moon. In most strange postures
  We have seen him set himself.
KING. It may well be
  There is a mutiny in's mind. This morning
  Papers of state he sent me to peruse,
  As I requir'd; and wot you what I found
  There—on my conscience, put unwittingly?
  Forsooth, an inventory, thus importing
  The several parcels of his plate, his treasure,
  Rich stuffs, and ornaments of household; which
  I find at such proud rate that it outspeaks
  Possession of a subject.
NORFOLK. It's heaven's will;
  Some spirit put this paper in the packet
  To bless your eye withal.
KING. If we did think
  His contemplation were above the earth
  And fix'd on spiritual object, he should still
  Dwell in his musings; but I am afraid
  His thinkings are below the moon, not worth
  His serious considering.

> [*The* KING *takes his seat and whispers* LOVELL,
>   *who goes to the* CARDINAL]

WOLSEY. Heaven forgive me!
Ever God bless your Highness!
KING. Good, my lord,
You are full of heavenly stuff, and bear the inventory
Of your best graces in your mind; the which
You were now running o'er. You have scarce time
To steal from spiritual leisure a brief span
To keep your earthly audit; sure, in that
I deem you an ill husband, and am glad
To have you therein my companion.
WOLSEY. Sir,
For holy offices I have a time; a time
To think upon the part of business which
I bear i' th' state; and nature does require
Her times of preservation, which perforce
I, her frail son, amongst my brethren mortal,
Must give my tendance to.
KING. You have said well.
WOLSEY. And ever may your Highness yoke together,
As I will lend you cause, my doing well
With my well saying!
KING. 'Tis well said again;
And 'tis a kind of good deed to say well;
And yet words are no deeds. My father lov'd you:
He said he did; and with his deed did crown
His word upon you. Since I had my office
I have kept you next my heart; have not alone
Employ'd you where high profits might come home,
But par'd my present havings to bestow
My bounties upon you.
WOLSEY. [Aside] What should this mean?
SURREY. [Aside] The Lord increase this business!
KING. Have I not made you
The prime man of the state? I pray you tell me
If what I now pronounce you have found true;
And, if you may confess it, say withal
If you are bound to us or no. What say you?
WOLSEY. My sovereign, I confess your royal graces,
Show'r'd on me daily, have been more than could
My studied purposes requite; which went

Beyond all man's endeavours. My endeavours,
Have ever come too short of my desires,
Yet fil'd with my abilities; mine own ends
Have been mine so that evermore they pointed
To th' good of your most sacred person and
The profit of the state. For your great graces
Heap'd upon me, poor undeserver, I
Can nothing render but allegiant thanks;
My pray'rs to heaven for you; my loyalty,
Which ever has and ever shall be growing,
Till death, that winter, kill it.

KING. Fairly answer'd!
A loyal and obedient subject is
Therein illustrated; the honour of it
Does pay the act of it, as, i' th' contrary,
The foulness is the punishment. I presume
That, as my hand has open'd bounty to you,
My heart dropp'd love, my pow'r rain'd honour, more
On you than any, so your hand and heart,
Your brain, and every function of your power,
Should, notwithstanding that your bond of duty,
As 'twere in love's particular, be more
To me, your friend, than any.

WOLSEY. I do profess
That for your Highness' good I ever labour'd
More than mine own; that am, have, and will be—
Though all the world should crack their duty to you,
And throw it from their soul; though perils did
Abound as thick as thought could make 'em, and
Appear in forms more horrid—yet my duty,
As doth a rock against the chiding flood,
Should the approach of this wild river break,
And stand unshaken yours.

KING. 'Tis nobly spoken.
Take notice, lords, he has a loyal breast,
For you have seen him open 't. Read o'er this;

[Giving him papers]

And after, this; and then to breakfast with
What appetite you have.

Exit the KING, *frowning upon the* CARDINAL; *the* NOBLES
throng after him, smiling and whispering

WOLSEY. What should this mean?
What sudden anger's this? How have I reap'd it?
He parted frowning from me, as if ruin
Leap'd from his eyes; so looks the chafed lion
Upon the daring huntsman that has gall'd him—
Then makes him nothing. I must read this paper;
I fear, the story of his anger. 'Tis so;
This paper has undone me. 'Tis th' account
Of all that world of wealth I have drawn together
For mine own ends; indeed to gain the popedom,
And fee my friends in Rome. O negligence,
Fit for a fool to fall by! What cross devil
Made me put this main secret in the packet
I sent the King? Is there no way to cure this?
No new device to beat this from his brains?
I know 'twill stir him strongly; yet I know
A way, if it take right, in spite of fortune,
Will bring me off again. What's this? 'To th' Pope.'
The letter, as I live, with all the business
I writ to's Holiness. Nay then, farewell!
I have touch'd the highest point of all my greatness,
And from that full meridian of my glory
I haste now to my setting. I shall fall
Like a bright exhalation in the evening,
And no man see me more.

> *Re-enter to* WOLSEY *the* DUKES OF NORFOLK *and*
> SUFFOLK, *the* EARL OF SURREY, *and the* LORD
> CHAMBERLAIN

NORFOLK. Hear the King's pleasure, Cardinal, who com-
mands you
To render up the great seal presently
Into our hands, and to confine yourself
To Asher House, my Lord of Winchester's,
Till you hear further from his Highness.
WOLSEY. Stay:
Where's your commission, lords? Words cannot carry
Authority so weighty.

SUFFOLK. Who dare cross 'em,
  Bearing the King's will from his mouth expressly?
WOLSEY. Till I find more than will or words to do it—
  I mean your malice—know, officious lords,
  I dare and must deny it. Now I feel
  Of what coarse metal ye are moulded—envy;
  How eagerly ye follow my disgraces,
  As if it fed ye; and how sleek and wanton
  Ye appear in every thing may bring my ruin!
  Follow your envious courses, men of malice;
  You have Christian warrant for 'em, and no doubt
  In time will find their fit rewards. That seal
  You ask with such a violence, the King—
  Mine and your master—with his own hand gave me;
  Bade me enjoy it, with the place and honours,
  During my life; and, to confirm his goodness,
  Tied it by letters-patents. Now, who'll take it?
SURREY. The King, that gave it.
WOLSEY. It must be himself then.
SURREY. Thou art a proud traitor, priest.
WOLSEY. Proud lord, thou liest.
  Within these forty hours Surrey durst better
  Have burnt that tongue than said so.
SURREY. Thy ambition,
  Thou scarlet sin, robb'd this bewailing land
  Of noble Buckingham, my father-in-law.
  The heads of all thy brother cardinals,
  With thee and all thy best parts bound together,
  Weigh'd not a hair of his. Plague of your policy!
  You sent me deputy for Ireland;
  Far from his succour, from the King, from all
  That might have mercy on the fault thou gav'st him;
  Whilst your great goodness, out of holy pity,
  Absolv'd him with an axe.
WOLSEY. This, and all else
  This talking lord can lay upon my credit,
  I answer is most false. The Duke by law
  Found his deserts; how innocent I was
  From any private malice in his end,
  His noble jury and foul cause can witness.

If I lov'd many words, lord, I should tell **you**
You have as little honesty as honour,
That in the way of loyalty and truth
Toward the King, my ever royal master,
Dare mate a sounder man than Surrey can be
And all that love his follies.

SURREY. By my soul,
Your long coat, priest, protects you; thou shouldst feel
My sword i' the life-blood of thee else. My lords,
Can ye endure to hear this arrogance?
And from this fellow? If we live thus tamely,
To be thus jaded by a piece of scarlet,
Farewell nobility! Let his Grace go forward
And dare us with his cap like larks.

WOLSEY. All goodness
Is poison to thy stomach.

SURREY. Yes, that goodness
Of gleaning all the land's wealth into one,
Into your own hands, Cardinal, by extortion;
The goodness of your intercepted packets
You writ to th' Pope against the King; your goodness,
Since you provoke me, shall be most notorious.
My Lord of Norfolk, as you are truly noble,
As you respect the common good, the state
Of our despis'd nobility, our issues,
Whom, if he live, will scarce be gentlemen—
Produce the grand sum of his sins, the articles
Collected from his life. I'll startle you
Worse than the sacring bell, when the brown wench
Lay kissing in your arms, Lord Cardinal.

WOLSEY. How much, methinks, I could despise this man,
But that I am bound in charity against it!

NORFOLK. Those articles, my lord, are in the King's hand;
But, thus much, they are foul ones.

WOLSEY. So much fairer
And spotless shall mine innocence arise,
When the King knows my truth.

SURREY. This cannot save you.
I thank my memory I yet remember
Some of these articles; and out they shall.

Now, if you can blush and cry guilty, Cardinal,
You'll show a little honesty.

WOLSEY. Speak on, sir;
I dare your worst objections. If I blush,
It is to see a nobleman want manners.

SURREY. I had rather want those than my head. Have at
you!
First, that without the King's assent or knowledge
You wrought to be a legate; by which power
You maim'd the jurisdiction of all bishops.

NORFOLK. Then, that in all you writ to Rome, or else
To foreign princes, 'Ego et Rex meus'
Was still inscrib'd; in which you brought the King
To be your servant.

SUFFOLK. Then, that without the knowledge
Either of King or Council, when you went
Ambassador to the Emperor, you made bold
To carry into Flanders the great seal.

SURREY. Item, you sent a large commission
To Gregory de Cassado, to conclude,
Without the King's will or the state's allowance,
A league between his Highness and Ferrara.

SUFFOLK. That out of mere ambition you have caus'd
Your holy hat to be stamp'd on the King's coin.

SURREY. Then, that you have sent innumerable substance,
By what means got I leave to your own conscience,
To furnish Rome and to prepare the ways
You have for dignities, to the mere undoing
Of all the kingdom. Many more there are,
Which, since they are of you, and odious,
I will not taint my mouth with.

CHAMBERLAIN. O my lord,
Press not a falling man too far! 'Tis virtue.
His faults lie open to the laws; let them,
Not you, correct him. My heart weeps to see him
So little of his great self.

SURREY. I forgive him.

SUFFOLK. Lord Cardinal, the King's further pleasure is—
Because all those things you have done of late,
By your power legatine within this kingdom,

Fall into th' compass of a præmunire—
That therefore such a writ be sued against you:
To forfeit all your goods, lands, tenements,
Chattels, and whatsoever, and to be
Out of the King's protection. This is my charge.
NORFOLK. And so we'll leave you to your meditations
    How to live better. For your stubborn answer
    About the giving back the great seal to us,
    The King shall know it, and, no doubt, shall thank you.
    So fare you well, my little good Lord Cardinal.
                       Exeunt all but WOLSEY

WOLSEY. So farewell to the little good you bear me.
    Farewell, a long farewell, to all my greatness!
    This is the state of man: to-day he puts forth
    The tender leaves of hopes; to-morrow blossoms
    And bears his blushing honours thick upon him;
    The third day comes a frost, a killing frost,
    And when he thinks, good easy man, full surely
    His greatness is a-ripening, nips his root,
    And then he falls, as I do. I have ventur'd,
    Like little wanton boys that swim on bladders,
    This many summers in a sea of glory;
    But far beyond my depth. My high-blown pride
    At length broke under me, and now has left me,
    Weary and old with service, to the mercy
    Of a rude stream, that must for ever hide me.
    Vain pomp and glory of this world, I hate ye;
    I feel my heart new open'd. O, how wretched
    Is that poor man that hangs on princes' favours!
    There is betwixt that smile we would aspire to,
    That sweet aspect of princes, and their ruin
    More pangs and fears than wars or women have;
    And when he falls, he falls like Lucifer,
    Never to hope again.

          Enter CROMWELL, *standing amazed*

    Why, how now, Cromwell!
CROMWELL. I have no power to speak, sir.
WOLSEY. What, amaz'd
    At my misfortunes? Can thy spirit wonder

A great man should decline? Nay, an you weep,
I am fall'n indeed.
CROMWELL. How does your Grace?
WOLSEY. Why, well;
   Never so truly happy, my good Cromwell.
   I know myself now, and I feel within me
   A peace above all earthly dignities,
   A still and quiet conscience. The King has cur'd me,
   I humbly thank his Grace; and from these shoulders,
   These ruin'd pillars, out of pity, taken
   A load would sink a navy—too much honour.
   O, 'tis a burden, Cromwell, 'tis a burden
   Too heavy for a man that hopes for heaven!
CROMWELL. I am glad your Grace has made that right use
   of it.
WOLSEY. I hope I have. I am able now, methinks,
   Out of a fortitude of soul I feel,
   To endure more miseries and greater far
   Than my weak-hearted enemies dare offer.
   What news abroad?
CROMWELL. The heaviest and the worst
   Is your displeasure with the King.
WOLSEY. God bless him!
CROMWELL. The next is that Sir Thomas More is chosen
   Lord Chancellor in your place.
WOLSEY. That's somewhat sudden.
   But he's a learned man. May he continue
   Long in his Highness' favour, and do justice
   For truth's sake and his conscience; that his bones
   When he has run his course and sleeps in blessings,
   May have a tomb of orphans' tears wept on him!
   What more?
CROMWELL. That Cranmer is return'd with welcome,
   Install'd Lord Archbishop of Canterbury.
WOLSEY. That's news indeed.
CROMWELL. Last, that the Lady Anne,
   Whom the King hath in secrecy long married,
   This day was view'd in open as his queen,
   Going to chapel; and the voice is now
   Only about her coronation.

WOLSEY. There was the weight that pull'd me down. O Cromwell,
 The King has gone beyond me. All my glories
 In that one woman I have lost for ever.
 No sun shall ever usher forth mine honours,
 Or gild again the noble troops that waited
 Upon my smiles. Go get thee from me, Cromwell;
 I am a poor fall'n man, unworthy now
 To be thy lord and master. Seek the King;
 That sun, I pray, may never set! I have told him
 What and how true thou art. He will advance thee;
 Some little memory of me will stir him—
 I know his noble nature—not to let
 Thy hopeful service perish too. Good Cromwell,
 Neglect him not; make use now, and provide
 For thine own future safety.
CROMWELL. O my lord,
 Must I then leave you? Must I needs forgo
 So good, so noble, and so true a master?
 Bear witness, all that have not hearts of iron,
 With what a sorrow Cromwell leaves his lord.
 The King shall have my service; but my prayers
 For ever and for ever shall be yours.
WOLSEY. Cromwell, I did not think to shed a tear
 In all my miseries; but thou hast forc'd me,
 Out of thy honest truth, to play the woman.
 Let's dry our eyes; and thus far hear me, Cromwell,
 And when I am forgotten, as I shall be,
 And sleep in dull cold marble, where no mention
 Of me more must be heard of, say I taught thee—
 Say Wolsey, that once trod the ways of glory,
 And sounded all the depths and shoals of honour,
 Found thee a way, out of his wreck, to rise in—
 A sure and safe one, though thy master miss'd it.
 Mark but my fall and that that ruin'd me.
 Cromwell, I charge thee, fling away ambition:
 By that sin fell the angels. How can man then,
 The image of his Maker, hope to win by it?
 Love thyself last; cherish those hearts that hate thee;
 Corruption wins not more than honesty.

Still in thy right hand carry gentle peace
To silence envious tongues. Be just, and fear not;
Let all the ends thou aim'st at be thy country's,
Thy God's, and truth's; then, if thou fall'st, O Cromwell,
Thou fall'st a blessed martyr!
Serve the King, and—prithee lead me in.
There take an inventory of all I have
To the last penny; 'tis the King's. My robe,
And my integrity to heaven, is all
I dare now call mine own. O Cromwell, Cromwell!
Had I but serv'd my God with half the zeal
I serv'd my King, he would not in mine age
Have left me naked to mine enemies.
CROMWELL. Good sir, have patience.
WOLSEY. So I have. Farewell
    The hopes of court! My hopes in heaven do dwell. *Exeunt*

ACT IV. SCENE 1

A street in Westminster

Enter two GENTLEMEN, *meeting one another*

FIRST GENTLEMAN. Y'are well met once again.
SECOND GENTLEMAN. So are you.
FIRST GENTLEMAN. You come to take your stand here, and behold
    The Lady Anne pass from her coronation?
SECOND GENTLEMAN. 'Tis all my business. At our last encounter
    The Duke of Buckingham came from his trial.
FIRST GENTLEMAN. 'Tis very true. But that time offer'd sorrow;
    This, general joy.
SECOND GENTLEMAN. 'Tis well. The citizens,
    I am sure, have shown at full their royal minds—
    As, let 'em have their rights, they are ever forward—
    In celebration of this day with shows,

Pageants, and sights of honour.

FIRST GENTLEMAN. Never greater,
Nor, I'll assure you, better taken, sir.

SECOND GENTLEMAN. May I be bold to ask what that
    contains,
That paper in your hand?

FIRST GENTLEMAN. Yes; 'tis the list
Of those that claim their offices this day,
By custom of the coronation.
The Duke of Suffolk is the first, and claims
To be High Steward; next, the Duke of Norfolk,
He to be Earl Marshal. You may read the rest.

SECOND GENTLEMAN. I thank you, sir; had I not known
    those customs,
I should have been beholding to your paper.
But, I beseech you, what's become of Katharine,
The Princess Dowager? How goes her business?

FIRST GENTLEMAN. That I can tell you too. The Archbishop
Of Canterbury, accompanied with other
Learned and reverend fathers of his order,
Held a late court at Dunstable, six miles off
From Ampthill, where the Princess lay; to which
She was often cited by them, but appear'd not.
And, to be short, for not appearance and
The King's late scruple, by the main assent
Of all these learned men, she was divorc'd,
And the late marriage made of none effect;
Since which she was removed to Kimbolton,
Where she remains now sick.

SECOND GENTLEMAN. Alas, good lady!   [*Trumpets*]
The trumpets sound. Stand close, the Queen is coming.
                              [*Hautboys*]

THE ORDER OF THE CORONATION

1. *A lively flourish of trumpets.*
2. *Then two* JUDGES.
3. LORD CHANCELLOR, *with purse and mace before him.*
4. CHORISTERS *singing.*   [*Music*]
5. MAYOR OF LONDON, *bearing the mace. Then* GARTER, *in*

his coat of arms, and on his head he wore a gilt copper crown.

6. MARQUIS DORSET, *bearing a sceptre of gold, on his head a demi-coronal of gold. With him, the* EARL OF SURREY, *bearing the rod of silver with the dove, crowned with an earl's coronet. Collars of Esses.*

7. DUKE OF SUFFOLK, *in his robe of estate, his coronet on his head, bearing a long white wand, as High Steward. With him, the* DUKE OF NORFOLK, *with the rod of marshalship, a coronet on his head. Collars of Esses.*

8. *A canopy borne by four of the* CINQUE-PORTS; *under it the* QUEEN *in her robe; in her hair richly adorned with pearl, crowned. On each side her, the* BISHOPS OF LONDON *and* WINCHESTER.

9. *The old* DUCHESS OF NORFOLK, *in a coronal of gold. wrought with flowers, bearing the* QUEEN'S *train.*

10. *Certain* LADIES *or* COUNTESSES, *with plain circlets of gold without flowers.*

> *Exeunt, first passing over the stage in order and state, and then a great flourish of trumpets*

SECOND GENTLEMAN. A royal train, believe me. These I know.
 Who's that that bears the sceptre?
FIRST GENTLEMAN. Marquis Dorset;
 And that the Earl of Surrey, with the rod.
SECOND GENTLEMAN. A bold brave gentleman. That should be
 The Duke of Suffolk?
FIRST GENTLEMAN. 'Tis the same—High Steward.
SECOND GENTLEMAN. And that my Lord of Norfolk?
FIRST GENTLEMAN. Yes.
SECOND GENTLEMAN. [*Looking on the* QUEEN] Heaven bless thee!
 Thou hast the sweetest face I ever look'd on.
 Sir, as I have a soul, she is an angel;
 Our king has all the Indies in his arms,
 And more and richer, when he strains that lady;
 I cannot blame his conscience.
FIRST GENTLEMAN. They that bear
 The cloth of honour over her are four barons

Of the Cinque-ports.

SECOND GENTLEMAN. Those men are happy; and so are all
are near her.

I take it she that carries up the train
Is that old noble lady, Duchess of Norfolk.

FIRST GENTLEMAN. It is; and all the rest are countesses.

SECOND GENTLEMAN. Their coronets say so. These are stars
indeed,

And sometimes falling ones.

FIRST GENTLEMAN. No more of that.

Exit Procession, with a great flourish of trumpets

Enter a third GENTLEMAN

God save you, sir! Where have you been broiling?

THIRD GENTLEMAN. Among the crowds i' th' Abbey, where
a finger

Could not be wedg'd in more; I am stifled
With the mere rankness of their joy.

SECOND GENTLEMAN. You saw
The ceremony?

THIRD GENTLEMAN. That I did.

FIRST GENTLEMAN. How was it?

THIRD GENTLEMAN. Well worth the seeing.

SECOND GENTLEMAN. Good sir, speak it to us.

THIRD GENTLEMAN. As well as I am able. The rich stream
Of lords and ladies, having brought the Queen
To a prepar'd place in the choir, fell off
A distance from her, while her Grace sat down
To rest awhile, some half an hour or so,
In a rich chair of state, opposing freely
The beauty of her person to the people.
Believe me, sir, she is the goodliest woman
That ever lay by man; which when the people
Had the full view of, such a noise arose
As the shrouds make at sea in a stiff tempest,
As loud, and to as many tunes; hats, cloaks—
Doublets, I think—flew up, and had their faces
Been loose, this day they had been lost. Such joy
I never saw before. Great-bellied women,
That had not half a week to go, like rams

In the old time of war, would shake the press,
And make 'em reel before 'em. No man living
Could say 'This is my wife' there, all were woven
So strangely in one piece.
SECOND GENTLEMAN. But what follow'd?
THIRD GENTLEMAN. At length her Grace rose, and with
    modest paces
  Came to the altar, where she kneel'd, and saintlike
  Cast her fair eyes to heaven, and pray'd devoutly.
  Then rose again, and bow'd her to the people;
  When by the Archbishop of Canterbury
  She had all the royal makings of a queen:
  As holy oil, Edward Confessor's crown,
  The rod, and bird of peace, and all such emblems
  Laid nobly on her; which perform'd, the choir,
  With all the choicest music of the kingdom,
  Together sung 'Te Deum.' So she parted,
  And with the same full state pac'd back again
  To York Place, where the feast is held.
FIRST GENTLEMAN. Sir,
  You must no more call it York Place: that's past:
  For since the Cardinal fell that title's lost.
  'Tis now the King's, and call'd Whitehall.
THIRD GENTLEMAN. I know it;
  But 'tis so lately alter'd that the old name
  Is fresh about me.
SECOND GENTLEMAN. What two reverend bishops
  Were those that went on each side of the Queen?
THIRD GENTLEMAN. Stokesly and Gardiner: the one of
    Winchester,
  Newly preferr'd from the King's secretary;
  The other, London.
SECOND GENTLEMAN. He of Winchester
  Is held no great good lover of the Archbishop's,
  The virtuous Cranmer.
THIRD GENTLEMAN. All the land knows that;
  However, yet there is no great breach. When it comes,
  Cranmer will find a friend will not shrink from him.
SECOND GENTLEMAN. Who may that be, I pray you?
THIRD GENTLEMAN. Thomas Cromwell,

A man in much esteem with th' King, and truly
A worthy friend. The King has made him Master
O' th' Jewel House,
And one, already, of the Privy Council.
SECOND GENTLEMAN. He will deserve more.
THIRD GENTLEMAN. Yes, without all doubt.
Come, gentlemen, ye shall go my way, which
Is to th' court, and there ye shall be my guests:
Something I can command. As I walk thither,
I'll tell ye more.
BOTH. You may command us, sir.   *Exeunt*

SCENE 2

Kimbolton

Enter KATHARINE, *Dowager, sick; led between*
GRIFFITH, *her Gentleman Usher, and* PATIENCE, *her*
woman

GRIFFITH. How does your Grace?
KATHARINE. O Griffith, sick to death!
My legs like loaden branches bow to th' earth,
Willing to leave their burden. Reach a chair.
So—now, methinks, I feel a little ease.
Didst thou not tell me, Griffith, as thou led'st me,
That the great child of honour, Cardinal Wolsey,
Was dead?
GRIFFITH. Yes, madam; but I think your Grace,
Out of the pain you suffer'd, gave no ear to't.
KATHARINE. Prithee, good Griffith, tell me how he died.
If well, he stepp'd before me, happily,
For my example.
GRIFFITH. Well, the voice goes, madam;
For after the stout Earl Northumberland
Arrested him at York and brought him forward,
As a man sorely tainted, to his answer,
He fell sick suddenly, and grew so ill
He could not sit his mule.
KATHARINE. Alas, poor man!

GRIFFITH. At last, with easy roads, he came to Leicester,
  Lodg'd in the abbey; where the reverend abbot,
  With all his covent, honourably receiv'd him;
  To whom he gave these words: 'O father Abbot,
  An old man, broken with the storms of state,
  Is come to lay his weary bones among ye;
  Give him a little earth for charity!'
  So went to bed; where eagerly his sickness
  Pursu'd him still. And three nights after this,
  About the hour of eight—which he himself
  Foretold should be his last—full of repentance,
  Continual meditations, tears, and sorrows,
  He gave his honours to the world again,
  His blessed part to heaven, and slept in peace.
KATHARINE. So may he rest; his faults lie gently on him!
  Yet thus far, Griffith, give me leave to speak him,
  And yet with charity. He was a man
  Of an unbounded stomach, ever ranking
  Himself with princes; one that, by suggestion,
  Tied all the kingdom. Simony was fair play;
  His own opinion was his law. I' th' presence
  He would say untruths, and be ever double
  Both in his words and meaning. He was never,
  But where he meant to ruin, pitiful.
  His promises were, as he then was, mighty;
  But his performance, as he is now, nothing.
  Of his own body he was ill, and gave
  The clergy ill example.
GRIFFITH. Noble madam,
  Men's evil manners live in brass: their virtues
  We write in water. May it please your Highness
  To hear me speak his good now?
KATHARINE. Yes, good Griffith;
  I were malicious else.
GRIFFITH. This Cardinal,
  Though from an humble stock, undoubtedly
  Was fashion'd to much honour from his cradle.
  He was a scholar, and a ripe and good one;
  Exceeding wise, fair-spoken, and persuading;
  Lofty and sour to them that lov'd him not,

But to those men that sought him sweet as summer.
And though he were unsatisfied in getting—
Which was a sin—yet in bestowing, madam,
He was most princely: ever witness for him
Those twins of learning that he rais'd in you,
Ipswich and Oxford! One of which fell with him,
Unwilling to outlive the good that did it;
The other, though unfinish'd, yet so famous,
So excellent in art, and still so rising,
That Christendom shall ever speak his virtue.
His overthrow heap'd happiness upon him;
For then, and not till then, he felt himself,
And found the blessedness of being little.
And, to add greater honours to his age
Than man could give him, he died fearing God.
KATHARINE. After my death I wish no other herald,
No other speaker of my living actions,
To keep mine honour from corruption,
But such an honest chronicler as Griffith.
Whom I most hated living, thou hast made me,
With thy religious truth and modesty,
Now in his ashes honour. Peace be with him!
Patience, be near me still, and set me lower:
I have not long to trouble thee. Good Griffith,
Cause the musicians play me that sad note
I nam'd my knell, whilst I sit meditating
On that celestial harmony I go to.

[Sad and solemn music]
GRIFFITH. She is asleep. Good wench, let's sit down quiet,
For fear we wake her. Softly, gentle Patience.

THE VISION

Enter, solemnly tripping one after another, six
PERSONAGES *clad in white robes, wearing on their
heads garlands of bays, and golden vizards on their
faces; branches of bays or palm in their hands. They
first congee unto her, then dance; and, at certain
changes, the first two hold a spare garland over her
head, at which the other four make reverent curt-*

sies. Then the two that held the garland deliver the same to the other next two, who observe the same order in their changes, and holding the garland over her head; which done, they deliver the same garland to the last two, who likewise observe the same order; at which, as it were by inspiration, she makes in her sleep signs of rejoicing, and holdeth up her hands to heaven. And so in their dancing vanish, carrying the garland with them. The music continues

KATHARINE. Spirits of peace, where are ye? Are ye all gone?
  And leave me here in wretchedness behind ye?
GRIFFITH. Madam, we are here.
KATHARINE. It is not you I call for.
  Saw ye none enter since I slept?
GRIFFITH. None, madam.
KATHARINE. No? Saw you not, even now, a blessed troop
  Invite me to a banquet; whose bright faces
  Cast thousand beams upon me, like the sun?
  They promis'd me eternal happiness,
  And brought me garlands, Griffith, which I feel
  I am not worthy yet to wear. I shall, assuredly.
GRIFFITH. I am most joyful, madam, such good dreams
  Possess your fancy.
KATHARINE. Bid the music leave,
  They are harsh and heavy to me.   [*Music ceases*]
PATIENCE. Do you note
  How much her Grace is alter'd on the sudden?
  How long her face is drawn! How pale she looks,
  And of an earthly cold! Mark her eyes.
GRIFFITH. She is going, wench. Pray, pray.
PATIENCE. Heaven comfort her!

Enter a MESSENGER

MESSENGER. An't like your Grace—
KATHARINE. You are a saucy fellow.
  Deserve we no more reverence?
GRIFFITH. You are to blame,
  Knowing she will not lose her wonted greatness,

To use so rude behaviour. Go to, kneel.

MESSENGER. I humbly do entreat your Highness' pardon;
My haste made me unmannerly. There is staying
A gentleman, sent from the King, to see you.

KATHARINE. Admit him entrance, Griffith; but this fellow
Let me ne'er see again.   *Exit* MESSENGER

Enter LORD CAPUCIUS

If my sight fail not,
You should be Lord Ambassador from the Emperor,
My royal nephew, and your name Capucius.

CAPUCIUS. Madam, the same—your servant.

KATHARINE. O, my Lord,
The times and titles now are alter'd strangely
With me since first you knew me. But, I pray you,
What is your pleasure with me?

CAPUCIUS. Noble lady,
First, mine own service to your Grace; the next,
The King's request that I would visit you,
Who grieves much for your weakness, and by me
Sends you his princely commendations
And heartily entreats you take good comfort.

KATHARINE. O my good lord, that comfort comes too late,
'Tis like a pardon after execution:
That gentle physic, given in time, had cur'd me;
But now I am past all comforts here, but prayers.
How does his Highness?

CAPUCIUS. Madam, in good health.

KATHARINE. So may he ever do! and ever flourish
When I shall dwell with worms, and my poor name
Banish'd the kingdom! Patience, is that letter
I caus'd you write yet sent away?

PATIENCE. No, madam.   [*Giving it to* KATHARINE]

KATHARINE. Sir, I most humbly pray you to deliver
This to my lord the King.

CAPUCIUS. Most willing, madam.

KATHARINE. In which I have commended to his goodness
The model of our chaste loves, his young daughter—
The dews of heaven fall thick in blessings on her!—
Beseeching him to give her virtuous breeding—

She is young, and of a noble modest nature;
I hope she will deserve well—and a little
To love her for her mother's sake, that lov'd him,
Heaven knows how dearly. My next poor petition
Is that his noble Grace would have some pity
Upon my wretched women that so long
Have follow'd both my fortunes faithfully;
Of which there is not one, I dare avow—
And now I should not lie—but will deserve,
For virtue and true beauty of the soul,
For honesty and decent carriage,
A right good husband, let him be a noble;
And sure those men are happy that shall have 'em.
The last is for my men—they are the poorest,
But poverty could never draw 'em from me—
That they may have their wages duly paid 'em,
And something over to remember me by.
If heaven had pleas'd to have given me longer life
And able means, we had not parted thus.
These are the whole contents; and, good my lord,
By that you love the dearest in this world,
As you wish Christian peace to souls departed,
Stand these poor people's friend, and urge the King
To do me this last right.
CAPUCIUS. By heaven, I will,
  Or let me lose the fashion of a man!
KATHARINE. I thank you, honest lord. Remember me
  In all humility unto his Highness;
  Say his long trouble now is passing
  Out of this world. Tell him in death I bless'd him,
  For so I will. Mine eyes grow dim. Farewell,
  My lord. Griffith, farewell. Nay, Patience,
  You must not leave me yet. I must to bed;
  Call in more women. When I am dead, good wench,
  Let me be us'd with honour; strew me over
  With maiden flowers, that all the world may know
  I was a chaste wife to my grave. Embalm me,
  Then lay me forth; although unqueen'd, yet like
  A queen, and daughter to a king, inter me.
  I can no more.   *Exeunt, leading* KATHARINE

ACT V. SCENE 1

London. A gallery in the palace

Enter GARDINER, BISHOP OF WINCHESTER, *a* PAGE *with a torch before him, met by* SIR THOMAS LOVELL

GARDINER. It's one o'clock, boy, is't not?

BOY. It hath struck.

GARDINER. These should be hours for necessities,
Not for delights; times to repair our nature
With comforting repose, and not for us
To waste these times. Good hour of night, Sir Thomas!
Whither so late?

LOVELL. Came you from the King, my lord?

GARDINER. I did, Sir Thomas, and left him at primero
With the Duke of Suffolk.

LOVELL. I must to him too,
Before he go to bed. I'll take my leave.

GARDINER. Not yet, Sir Thomas Lovell. What's the matter?
It seems you are in haste. An if there be
No great offence belongs to't, give your friend
Some touch of your late business. Affairs that walk—
As they say spirits do—at midnight, have
In them a wilder nature than the business
That seeks despatch by day.

LOVELL. My lord, I love you;
And durst commend a secret to your ear
Much weightier than this work. The Queen's in labour,
They say in great extremity, and fear'd
She'll with the labour end.

GARDINER. The fruit she goes with
I pray for heartily, that it may find
Good time, and live; but for the stock, Sir Thomas,
I wish it grubb'd up now.

LOVELL. Methinks I could
Cry thee amen; and yet my conscience says
She's a good creature, and, sweet lady, does
Deserve our better wishes.

GARDINER. But, sir, sir—
  Hear me, Sir Thomas. Y'are a gentleman
  Of mine own way; I know you wise, religious;
  And, let me tell you, it will ne'er be well—
  'Twill not, Sir Thomas Lovell, take't of me—
  Till Cranmer, Cromwell, her two hands, and she,
  Sleep in their graves.
LOVELL. Now, sir, you speak of two
  The most remark'd i' th' kingdom. As for Cromwell,
  Beside that of the Jewel House, is made Master
  O' th' Rolls, and the King's secretary; further, sir,
  Stands in the gap and trade of moe preferments,
  With which the time will load him. Th' Archbishop
  Is the King's hand and tongue, and who dare speak
  One syllable against him?
GARDINER. Yes, yes, Sir Thomas,
  There are that dare; and I myself have ventur'd
  To speak my mind of him; and indeed this day,
  Sir—I may tell it you—I think I have
  Incens'd the lords o' th' Council, that he is—
  For so I know he is, they know he is—
  A most arch heretic, a pestilence
  That does infect the land; with which they moved
  Have broken with the King, who hath so far
  Given ear to our complaint—of his great grace
  And princely care, foreseeing those fell mischiefs
  Our reasons laid before him—hath commanded
  To-morrow morning to the Council board
  He be convented. He's a rank weed, Sir Thomas,
  And we must root him out. From your affairs
  I hinder you too long—good night, Sir Thomas.
LOVELL. Many good nights, my lord; I rest your servant.
                      Exeunt GARDINER *and* PAGE

  Enter the KING *and the* DUKE OF SUFFOLK

KING. Charles, I will play no more to-night;
  My mind's not on't; you are too hard for me.
SUFFOLK. Sir, I did never win of you before.
KING. But little, Charles;
  Nor shall not, when my fancy's on my play.

Now, Lovell, from the Queen what is the news?

LOVELL. I could not personally deliver to her
What you commanded me, but by her woman
I sent your message; who return'd her thanks
In the great'st humbleness, and desir'd your Highness
Most heartily to pray for her.

KING. What say'st thou, ha?
To pray for her? What, is she crying out?

LOVELL. So said her woman; and that her suff'rance made
Almost each pang a death.

KING. Alas, good lady!

SUFFOLK. God safely quit her of her burden, and
With gentle travail, to the gladding of
Your Highness with an heir!

KING. 'Tis midnight, Charles;
Prithee to bed; and in thy pray'rs remember
Th' estate of my poor queen. Leave me alone,
For I must think of that which company
Will not be friendly to.

SUFFOLK. I wish your Highness
A quiet night, and my good mistress will
Remember in my prayers.

KING. Charles, good night.   *Exit* SUFFOLK

Enter SIR ANTHONY DENNY

Well, sir, what follows?

DENNY. Sir, I have brought my lord the Archbishop,
As you commanded me.

KING. Ha! Canterbury?

DENNY. Ay, my good lord.

KING. 'Tis true. Where is he, Denny?

DENNY. He attends your Highness' pleasure.

KING. Bring him to us.   *Exit* DENNY

LOVELL. [*Aside*] This is about that which the bishop spake.
I am happily come hither.

Re-enter DENNY, *with* CRANMER

KING. Avoid the gallery.   [LOVELL *seems to stay*]
Ha! I have said. Be gone.
What!   *Exeunt* LOVELL *and* DENNY

CRANMER. [*Aside*] I am fearful—wherefore frowns he thus?
'Tis his aspect of terror. All's not well.
KING. How now, my lord? You do desire to know
Wherefore I sent for you.
CRANMER. [*Kneeling*] It is my duty
T'attend your Highness' pleasure.
KING. Pray you, arise,
My good and gracious Lord of Canterbury.
Come, you and I must walk a turn together;
I have news to tell you; come, come, give me your hand.
Ah, my good lord, I grieve at what I speak,
And am right sorry to repeat what follows.
I have, and most unwillingly, of late
Heard many grievous—I do say, my lord,
Grievous—complaints of you; which, being consider'd,
Have mov'd us and our Council that you shall
This morning come before us; where I know
You cannot with such freedom purge yourself
But that, till further trial in those charges
Which will require your answer, you must take
Your patience to you and be well contented
To make your house our Tow'r. You a brother of us,
It fits we thus proceed, or else no witness
Would come against you.
CRANMER. I humbly thank your Highness
And am right glad to catch this good occasion
Most throughly to be winnowed where my chaff
And corn shall fly asunder; for I know
There's none stands under more calumnious tongues
Than I myself, poor man.
KING. Stand up, good Canterbury;
Thy truth and thy integrity is rooted
In us, thy friend. Give me thy hand, stand up;
Prithee let's walk. Now, by my holidame,
What manner of man are you? My lord, I look'd
You would have given me your petition that
I should have ta'en some pains to bring together
Yourself and your accusers, and to have heard you
Without indurance further.
CRANMER. Most dread liege,

The good I stand on is my truth and honesty;
If they shall fail, I with mine enemies
Will triumph o'er my person; which I weigh not,
Being of those virtues vacant. I fear nothing
What can be said against me.

KING. Know you not
How your state stands i' th' world, with the whole world?
Your enemies are many, and not small; their practices
Must bear the same proportion; and not ever
The justice and the truth o' th' question carries
The due o' th' verdict with it; at what ease
Might corrupt minds procure knaves as corrupt
To swear against you? Such things have been done.
You are potently oppos'd, and with a malice
Of as great size. Ween you of better luck,
I mean in perjur'd witness, than your Master,
Whose minister you are, whiles here He liv'd
Upon this naughty earth? Go to, go to;
You take a precipice for no leap of danger,
And woo your own destruction.

CRANMER. God and your Majesty
Protect mine innocence, or I fall into
The trap is laid for me!

KING. Be of good cheer;
They shall no more prevail than we give way to.
Keep comfort to you, and this morning see
You do appear before them; if they shall chance,
In charging you with matters, to commit you,
The best persuasions to the contrary
Fail not to use, and with what vehemency
Th' occasion shall instruct you. If entreaties
Will render you no remedy, this ring
Deliver them, and your appeal to us
There make before them. Look, the good man weeps!
He's honest, on mine honour. God's blest Mother!
I swear he is true-hearted, and a soul
None better in my kingdom. Get you gone,
And do as I have bid you.

Exit CRANMER

He has strangled his language in his tears.

ACT V. SCENE 1

Enter OLD LADY

GENTLEMAN. [*Within*] Come back; what mean you?
OLD LADY. I'll not come back; the tidings that I bring
  Will make my boldness manners. Now, good angels
  Fly o'er thy royal head, and shade thy person
  Under their blessed wings!
KING. Now, by thy looks
  I guess thy message. Is the Queen deliver'd?
  Say ay, and of a boy.
OLD LADY. Ay, ay, my liege;
  And of a lovely boy. The God of Heaven
  Both now and ever bless her! 'Tis a girl,
  Promises boys hereafter. Sir, your queen
  Desires your visitation, and to be
  Acquainted with this stranger; 'tis as like you
  As cherry is to cherry.
KING. Lovell!

Enter LOVELL

LOVELL. Sir?
KING. Give her an hundred marks. I'll to the Queen.   *Exit*
OLD LADY. An hundred marks? By this light, I'll ha' more!
  An ordinary groom is for such payment.
  I will have more, or scold it out of him.
  Said I for this the girl was like to him! I'll
  Have more, or else unsay't; and now, while 'tis hot,
  I'll put it to the issue.   *Exeunt*

SCENE 2

Lobby before the Council Chamber

Enter CRANMER, ARCHBISHOP OF CANTERBURY

CRANMER. I hope I am not too late; and yet the gentleman
  That was sent to me from the Council pray'd me
  To make great haste. All fast? What means this? Ho!
  Who waits there? Sure you know me?

Enter KEEPER

KEEPER. Yes, my lord;
  But yet I cannot help you.
CRANMER. Why?
KEEPER. Your Grace must wait till you be call'd for.

Enter DOCTOR BUTTS

CRANMER. So.
BUTTS. [*Aside*] This is a piece of malice. I am glad
  I came this way so happily; the King
  Shall understand it presently.   *Exit*
CRANMER. [*Aside*] 'Tis Butts,
  The King's physician; as he pass'd along,
  How earnestly he cast his eyes upon me!
  Pray heaven he sound not my disgrace! For certain,
  This is of purpose laid by some that hate me—
  God turn their hearts! I never sought their malice—
  To quench mine honour; they would shame to make me
  Wait else at door, a fellow councillor,
  'Mong boys, grooms, and lackeys. But their pleasures
  Must be fulfill'd, and I attend with patience.

Enter the KING *and* BUTTS *at a window above*

BUTTS. I'll show your Grace the strangest sight—
KING. What's that, Butts?
BUTTS. I think your Highness saw this many a day.
KING. Body a me, where is it?
BUTTS. There my lord:
  The high promotion of his Grace of Canterbury;
  Who holds his state at door, 'mongst pursuivants,
  Pages, and footboys.
KING. Ha, 'tis he indeed.
  Is this the honour they do one another?
  'Tis well there's one above 'em yet. I had thought
  They had parted so much honesty among 'em—
  At least good manners—as not thus to suffer
  A man of his place, and so near our favour,
  To dance attendance on their lordships' pleasures,
  And at the door too, like a post with packets.
  By holy Mary, Butts, there's knavery!
  Let 'em alone, and draw the curtain close;
  We shall hear more anon.   *Exeunt*

SCENE 3

The Council Chamber

A Council table brought in, with chairs and stools, and placed under the state. Enter Lord Chancellor, *places himself at the upper end of the table on the left hand, a seat being left void above him, as for Canterbury's seat.* Duke of Suffolk, Duke of Norfolk, Surrey, Lord Chamberlain, Gardiner, *seat themselves in order on each side;* Cromwell *at lower end, as secretary.* Keeper *at the door*

Chancellor. Speak to the business, master secretary;
　Why are we met in council?
Cromwell. Please your honours,
　The chief cause concerns his Grace of Canterbury.
Gardiner. Has he had knowledge of it?
Cromwell. Yes.
Norfolk. Who waits there?
Keeper. Without, my noble lords?
Gardiner. Yes.
Keeper. My Lord Archbishop;
　And has done half an hour, to know your pleasures.
Chancellor. Let him come in.
Keeper. Your Grace may enter now.

Cranmer *approaches the Council table*

Chancellor. My good Lord Archbishop, I am very sorry
　To sit here at this present, and behold
　That chair stand empty; but we all are men,
　In our own natures frail and capable
　Of our flesh; few are angels; out of which frailty
　And want of wisdom, you, that best should teach us,
　Have misdemean'd yourself, and not a little,
　Toward the King first, then his laws, in filling
　The whole realm by your teaching and your chaplains—
　For so we are inform'd—with new opinions,
　Divers and dangerous; which are heresies,
　And, not reform'd, may prove pernicious.

GARDINER. Which reformation must be sudden too,
  My noble lords; for those that tame wild horses
  Pace 'em not in their hands to make 'em gentle,
  But stop their mouth with stubborn bits and spur 'em
  Till they obey the manage. If we suffer,
  Out of our easiness and childish pity
  To one man's honour, this contagious sickness,
  Farewell all physic; and what follows then?
  Commotions, uproars, with a general taint
  Of the whole state; as of late days our neighbours,
  The upper Germany, can dearly witness,
  Yet freshly pitied in our memories.

CRANMER. My good lords, hitherto in all the progress
  Both of my life and office, I have labour'd,
  And with no little study, that my teaching
  And the strong course of my authority
  Might go one way, and safely; and the end
  Was ever to do well. Nor is there living—
  I speak it with a single heart, my lords—
  A man that more detests, more stirs against,
  Both in his private conscience and his place,
  Defacers of a public peace than I do.
  Pray heaven the King may never find a heart
  With less allegiance in it! Men that make
  Envy and crooked malice nourishment
  Dare bite the best. I do beseech your lordships
  That, in this case of justice, my accusers,
  Be what they will, may stand forth face to face
  And freely urge against me.

SUFFOLK. Nay, my lord,
  That cannot be; you are a councillor,
  And by that virtue no man dare accuse you.

GARDINER. My lord, because we have business of more
    moment,
  We will be short with you. 'Tis his Highness' pleasure
  And our consent, for better trial of you,
  From hence you be committed to the Tower;
  Where, being but a private man again,
  You shall know many dare accuse you boldly,
  More than, I fear, you are provided for.

CRANMER. Ah, my good Lord of Winchester, I thank you;
    You are always my good friend; if your will pass,
    I shall both find your lordship judge and juror,
    You are so merciful. I see your end—
    'Tis my undoing. Love and meekness, lord,
    Become a churchman better than ambition;
    Win straying souls with modesty again,
    Cast none away. That I shall clear myself,
    Lay all the weight ye can upon my patience,
    I make as little doubt as you do conscience
    In doing daily wrongs. I could say more,
    But reverence to your calling makes me modest.
GARDINER. My lord, my lord, you are a sectary;
    That's the plain truth. Your painted gloss discovers,
    To men that understand you, words and weakness.
CROMWELL. My Lord of Winchester, y'are a little,
    By your good favour, too sharp; men so noble,
    However faulty, yet should find respect
    For what they have been; 'tis a cruelty
    To load a falling man.
GARDINER. Good Master Secretary,
    I cry your honour mercy; you may, worst
    Of all this table, say so.
CROMWELL. Why, my lord?
GARDINER. Do not I know you for a favourer
    Of this new sect? Ye are not sound.
CROMWELL. Not sound?
GARDINER. Not sound, I say.
CROMWELL. Would you were half so honest!
    Men's prayers then would seek you, not their fears.
GARDINER. I shall remember this bold language.
CROMWELL. Do.
    Remember your bold life too.
CHANCELLOR. This is too much;
    Forbear, for shame, my lords.
GARDINER. I have done.
CROMWELL. And I.
CHANCELLOR. Then thus for you, my lord: it stands agreed,
    I take it, by all voices, that forthwith
    You be convey'd to th' Tower a prisoner;

There to remain till the King's further pleasure
Be known unto us. Are you all agreed, lords?
ALL. We are.
CRANMER. Is there no other way of mercy,
But I must needs to th' Tower, my lords?
GARDINER. What other
Would you expect? You are strangely troublesome.
Let some o' th' guard be ready there.

Enter the guard

CRANMER. For me?
Must I go like a traitor thither?
GARDINER. Receive him,
And see him safe i' th' Tower.
CRANMER. Stay, good my lords,
I have a little yet to say. Look there, my lords;
By virtue of that ring I take my cause
Out of the gripes of cruel men and give it
To a most noble judge, the King my master.
CHAMBERLAIN. This is the King's ring.
SURREY. 'Tis no counterfeit.
SUFFOLK. 'Tis the right ring, by heav'n. I told ye all,
When we first put this dangerous stone a-rolling,
'Twould fall upon ourselves.
NORFOLK. Do you think, my lords,
The King will suffer but the little finger
Of this man to be vex'd?
CHAMBERLAIN. 'Tis now too certain;
How much more is his life in value with him!
Would I were fairly out on't!
CROMWELL. My mind gave me,
In seeking tales and informations
Against this man—whose honesty the devil
And his disciples only envy at—
Ye blew the fire that burns ye. Now have at ye!

Enter the KING *frowning on them; he takes his seat*

GARDINER. Dread sovereign, how much are we bound to
heaven
In daily thanks, that gave us such a prince;

Not only good and wise but most religious;
One that in all obedience makes the church
The chief aim of his honour and, to strengthen
That holy duty, out of dear respect,
His royal self in judgment comes to hear
The cause betwixt her and this great offender.

KING. You were ever good at sudden commendations,
Bishop of Winchester. But know I come not
To hear such flattery now, and in my presence
They are too thin and bare to hide offences.
To me you cannot reach you play the spaniel,
And think with wagging of your tongue to win me;
But whatsoe'er thou tak'st me for, I'm sure
Thou hast a cruel nature and a bloody.
[To CRANMER] Good man, sit down. Now let me see the
    proudest
He that dares most but wag his finger at thee.
By all that's holy, he had better starve
Than but once think this place becomes thee not.

SURREY. May it please your Grace—

KING. No, sir, it does not please me.
I had thought I had had men of some understanding
And wisdom of my Council; but I find none.
Was it discretion, lords, to let this man,
This good man—few of you deserve that title—
This honest man, wait like a lousy footboy
At chamber door? and one as great as you are?
Why, what a shame was this! Did my commission
Bid ye so far forget yourselves? I gave ye
Power as he was a councillor to try him,
Not as a groom. There's some of ye, I see,
More out of malice than integrity,
Would try him to the utmost, had ye mean;
Which ye shall never have while I live.

CHANCELLOR. Thus far,
My most dread sovereign, may it like your Grace
To let my tongue excuse all. What was purpos'd
Concerning his imprisonment was rather—
If there be faith in men—meant for his trial
And fair purgation to the world, than malice,

I'm sure, in me.

KING. Well, well, my lords, respect him;
Take him, and use him well, he's worthy of it.
I will say thus much for him: if a prince
May be beholding to a subject, I
Am for his love and service so to him.
Make me no more ado, but all embrace him;
Be friends, for shame, my lords! My Lord of Canterbury,
I have a suit which you must not deny me:
That is, a fair young maid that yet wants baptism;
You must be godfather, and answer for her.

CRANMER. The greatest monarch now alive may glory
In such an honour; how may I deserve it,
That am a poor and humble subject to you?

KING. Come, come, my lord, you'd spare your spoons. You shall have
Two noble partners with you: the old Duchess of Norfolk
And Lady Marquis Dorset. Will these please you?
Once more, my Lord of Winchester, I charge you,
Embrace and love this man.

GARDINER. With a true heart
And brother-love I do it.

CRANMER. And let heaven
Witness how dear I hold this confirmation.

KING. Good man, those joyful tears show thy true heart.
The common voice, I see, is verified
Of thee, which says thus: 'Do my Lord of Canterbury
A shrewd turn and he's your friend for ever.'
Come, lords, we trifle time away; I long
To have this young one made a Christian.
As I have made ye one, lords, one remain;
So I grow stronger, you more honour gain.   *Exeunt*

SCENE 4

The palace yard

Noise and tumult within. Enter PORTER *and his* MAN

PORTER. You'll leave your noise anon, ye rascals. Do you

take the court for Paris garden? Ye rude slaves, leave your gaping.

[*Within*: Good master porter, I belong to th' larder.]

PORTER. Belong to th' gallows, and be hang'd, ye rogue! Is this a place to roar in? Fetch me a dozen crab-tree staves, and strong ones; these are but switches to 'em. I'll scratch your heads. You must be seeing christenings? Do you look for ale and cakes here, you rude rascals?

MAN. Pray, sir, be patient; 'tis as much impossible,
Unless we sweep 'em from the door with cannons,
To scatter 'em as 'tis to make 'em sleep
On May-day morning; which will never be.
We may as well push against Paul's as stir 'em.

PORTER. How got they in, and be hang'd?

MAN. Alas, I know not: how gets the tide in?
As much as one sound cudgel of four foot—
You see the poor remainder—could distribute,
I made no spare, sir.

PORTER. You did nothing, sir.

MAN. I am not Samson, nor Sir Guy, nor Colbrand,
To mow 'em down before me; but if I spar'd any
That had a head to hit, either young or old,
He or she, cuckold or cuckold-maker,
Let me ne'er hope to see a chine again;
And that I would not for a cow, God save her!

[*Within*: Do you hear, master porter?]

PORTER. I shall be with you presently, good master puppy. Keep the door close, sirrah.

MAN. What would you have me do?

PORTER. What should you do, but knock 'em down by th' dozens? Is this Moorfields to muster in? Or have we some strange Indian with the great tool come to court, the women so besiege us? Bless me, what a fry of fornication is at door! On my Christian conscience, this one christening will beget a thousand: here will be father, godfather, and all together.

MAN. The spoons will be the bigger, sir. There is a fellow somewhat near the door, he should be a brazier by his face, for, o' my conscience, twenty of the dog-days now reign in's nose; all that stand about him are under the line,

they need no other penance. That fire-drake did I hit three
times on the head, and three times was his nose discharged
against me; he stands there like a mortar-piece, to blow us.
There was a haberdasher's wife of small wit near him, that
rail'd upon me till her pink'd porringer fell off her head,
for kindling such a combustion in the state. I miss'd the
meteor once, and hit that woman, who cried out 'Clubs!'
when I might see from far some forty truncheoners draw
to her succour, which were the hope o' th' Strand, where
she was quartered. They fell on; I made good my place.
At length they came to th' broomstaff to me; I defied 'em
still; when suddenly a file of boys behind 'em, loose shot,
deliver'd such a show'r of pebbles that I was fain to draw
mine honour in and let 'em win the work: the devil was
amongst 'em, I think surely.

PORTER. These are the youths that thunder at a playhouse
and fight for bitten apples; that no audience but the tribulation of Tower-hill or the limbs of Limehouse, their dear
brothers, are able to endure. I have some of 'em in Limbo
Patrum, and there they are like to dance these three days;
besides the running banquet of two beadles that is to come.

Enter the LORD CHAMBERLAIN

CHAMBERLAIN. Mercy o' me, what a multitude are here!
They grow still too; from all parts they are coming,
As if we kept a fair here! Where are these porters,
These lazy knaves? Y'have made a fine hand, fellows.
There's a trim rabble let in: are all these
Your faithful friends o' th' suburbs? We shall have
Great store of room, no doubt, left for the ladies,
When they pass back from the christening.

PORTER. An't please your honour,
We are but men; and what so many may do,
Not being torn a pieces, we have done.
An army cannot rule 'em.

CHAMBERLAIN. As I live,
If the King blame me for't, I'll lay ye all
By th' heels, and suddenly; and on your heads
Clap round fines for neglect. Y'are lazy knaves;
And here ye lie baiting of bombards, when

Ye should do service. Hark! the trumpets sound;
Th' are come already from the christening.
Go break among the press and find a way out
To let the troops pass fairly, or I'll find
A Marshalsea shall hold ye play these two months.
PORTER. Make way there for the Princess.
MAN. You great fellow,
Stand close up, or I'll make your head ache.
PORTER. You i' th' camlet, get up o' th' rail;
I'll peck you o'er the pales else.   *Exeunt*

SCENE 5

The palace

Enter TRUMPETS, *sounding; then two* ALDERMEN,
LORD MAYOR, GARTER, CRANMER, DUKE OF NOR-
FOLK, *with his marshal's staff,* DUKE OF SUFFOLK,
*two Noblemen bearing great standing-bowls for the
christening gifts; then four Noblemen bearing a
canopy, under which the* DUCHESS OF NORFOLK,
godmother, bearing the CHILD *richly habited in a
mantle, &c., train borne by a* LADY; *then follows
the* MARCHIONESS DORSET, *the other godmother, and*
LADIES. *The troop pass once about the stage, and*
GARTER *speaks*

GARTER. Heaven, from thy endless goodness, send prosperous life, long and ever-happy, to the high and mighty
Princess of England, Elizabeth!

Flourish. Enter KING *and guard*

CRANMER. [*Kneeling*] And to your royal Grace and the
good Queen!
My noble partners and myself thus pray:
All comfort, joy, in this most gracious lady,
Heaven ever laid up to make parents happy,
May hourly fall upon ye!
KING. Thank you, good Lord Archbishop.
What is her name?

CRANMER. Elizabeth.

KING. Stand up, lord.   [*The* KING *kisses the child*]
  With this kiss take my blessing: God protect thee!
  Into whose hand I give thy life.

CRANMER. Amen.

KING. My noble gossips, y'have been too prodigal;
  I thank ye heartily. So shall this lady,
  When she has so much English.

CRANMER. Let me speak, sir,
  For heaven now bids me; and the words I utter
  Let none think flattery, for they'll find 'em truth.
  This royal infant—heaven still move about her!—
  Though in her cradle, yet now promises
  Upon this land a thousand thousand blessings,
  Which time shall bring to ripeness. She shall be—
  But few now living can behold that goodness—
  A pattern to all princes living with her,
  And all that shall succeed. Saba was never
  More covetous of wisdom and fair virtue
  Than this pure soul shall be. All princely graces
  That mould up such a mighty piece as this is,
  With all the virtues that attend the good,
  Shall still be doubled on her. Truth shall nurse her,
  Holy and heavenly thoughts still counsel her;
  She shall be lov'd and fear'd. Her own shall bless her:
  Her foes shake like a field of beaten corn,
  And hang their heads with sorrow. Good grows with her;
  In her days every man shall eat in safety
  Under his own vine what he plants, and sing
  The merry songs of peace to all his neighbours.
  God shall be truly known; and those about her
  From her shall read the perfect ways of honour,
  And by those claim their greatness, not by blood.
  Nor shall this peace sleep with her; but as when
  The bird of wonder dies, the maiden phœnix
  Her ashes new create another heir
  As great in admiration as herself,
  So shall she leave her blessedness to one—
  When heaven shall call her from this cloud of darkness—
  Who from the sacred ashes of her honour

Shall star-like rise, as great in fame as she was,
And so stand fix'd. Peace, plenty, love, truth, terror,
That were the servants to this chosen infant,
Shall then be his, and like a vine grow to him;
Wherever the bright sun of heaven shall shine,
His honour and the greatness of his name
Shall be, and make new nations; he shall flourish,
And like a mountain cedar reach his branches
To all the plains about him; our children's children
Shall see this and bless heaven.

KING. Thou speakest wonders.

CRANMER. She shall be, to the happiness of England,
An aged princess; many days shall see her,
And yet no day without a deed to crown it.
Would I had known no more! But she must die—
She must, the saints must have her—yet a virgin;
A most unspotted lily shall she pass
To th' ground, and all the world shall mourn her.

KING. O Lord Archbishop,
Thou hast made me now a man; never before
This happy child did I get anything.
This oracle of comfort has so pleas'd me
That when I am in heaven I shall desire
To see what this child does, and praise my Maker.
I thank ye all. To you, my good Lord Mayor,
And you, good brethren, I am much beholding;
I have receiv'd much honour by your presence,
And ye shall find me thankful. Lead the way, lords;
Ye must all see the Queen, and she must thank ye,
She will be sick else. This day, no man think
Has business at his house; for all shall stay.
This little one shall make it holiday. *Exeunt*

THE EPILOGUE

'Tis ten to one this play can never please
All that are here. Some come to take their ease
And sleep an act or two; but those, we fear,
W'have frighted with our trumpets; so, 'tis clear,

They'll say 'tis nought; others to hear the city
Abus'd extremely, and to cry 'That's witty!'
Which we have not done neither; that, I fear,
All the expected good w'are like to hear
For this play at this time is only in
The merciful construction of good women;
For such a one we show'd 'em. If they smile
And say 'twill do, I know within a while
All the best men are ours; for 'tis ill hap
If they hold when their ladies bid 'em clap.

Glossary

GLOSSARY

ABATE, to blunt, *Rich.* 3, 5.v; 2 *Hen.* 4, 1.i; to lessen, *Hen.* 5, 2.i.

ABHOR, to loathe, *John,* 4.iii; to reject, *Hen.* 8, 2.iv.

ABJECT, *adj.,* despised, *Hen.* 8, 1.i; *sub.,* contemptible thing, *Rich.* 3, 1.i.

ABODE, to foretell, *Hen.* 8, 1.i.

ABODEMENT, bad omen, 3 *Hen.* 6, 4.vii.

ABORTIVES, untimely births, *John,* 3.iv.

ABRIDGEMENT, what cuts short the story or time, *Hen.* 5, 5.*Prol.*

ABROACH, *to set abroach,* to set going, *Rich.* 3, 1.iii.

ABROOK, to tolerate, 2 *Hen.* 6, 2.iv.

ABSEY-BOOK, a book to teach the ABC of a subject, *John,* 1.i.

ABSOLUTE, perfect, *Hen.* 5, 3.vii; complete, 1 *Hen.* 4, 4.iii.

ABSTRACT, 'a chip of the old block,' *John,* 2.i; summary, *Rich.* 3, 4.iv.

ACCENT, word, *John,* 5.vi.

ACCITE, to summon, 2 *Hen.* 4, 5.ii; to excite, 2 *Hen.* 4, 2.ii.

ACCOMMODATE, to furnish or equip, 2 *Hen.* 4, 3.ii.

ACCOMPLICE, comrade (but not in crime), 1 *Hen.* 6, 5.ii.

ACCOMPLISH, to arm completely, *Hen.* 5, 4.*Prol.*; to furnish, *Rich.* 2, 2.i.

ACCRUE, to grow, *Hen.* 5, 2.i.

ACHIEVEMENT, acquisition, 2 *Hen.* 4, 4.v.

ACHILLES' SPEAR, the rust from it curing Telephus, 2 *Hen.* 6, 5.i.

ACHITOPHEL, ringleader in Absalom's rebellion against David, 2 *Hen.* 4, 1.ii.

ACONITUM, poison from wolf's-bane, 2 *Hen.* 4, 4.iv.

ACQUITTANCE, to acquit, *Rich.* 3, 3.vii.

ADAM, *the offending Adam,* the sinfulness inherited by mankind as Adam's descendants, *Hen.* 5, 1.i.

ADAMANT, very hard substance, 1 *Hen.* 6, 1.iv.

ADDICTION, natural inclination, *Hen.* 5, 1.i.

ADDITION, description or title acquired, *Hen.* 5, 5.ii.

ADDRESS, to prepare, *Hen.* 5, 3.iii.

ADJUNCT, connected, *John,* 3.iii.

ADMIRAL, flagship, 1 *Hen.* 4, 3.iii.

ADMIRATION, astonishment, *Hen.* 5, 2.ii.

ADVANTAGE, *with advantages,* with additions, *Hen.* 5, 4.iii.

ADVERTISE, instruct, *Hen.* 8, 2.iv.

ADVERTISEMENT, information, warning, 1 *Hen.* 4, 3.ii; 1 *Hen.* 4, 4.i.

ADVICE, thought, *Hen.* 5, 2.ii.

AERY, nest and young of eagle, *Rich.* 3, 1.iii; *John,* 5.ii.

AFFECT, to desire, 2 *Hen.* 4, 4.v; to imitate, *John,* 1.i.

AFFECTION, inclination, 1 *Hen.* 4, 3.ii.

AFFIANCE, trust, 2 *Hen.* 6, 3.i.

AFFY, to betroth, 2 *Hen.* 6, 4.i.

A-FRONT, abreast, 1 *Hen.* 4, 2.iv.

AGATE, small figure like that cut on stone of seal-ring, 2 *Hen.* 4, 1.ii.

AGGRAVATE, *aggravate the note,* to add to the stigma, *Rich.* 2, 1.i.

AGUE, malaria, *John,* 3.iv.

AIM (from archery), term of encouragement, *John,* 2.i.

ALDERLIEFEST, dearest of all, 2 *Hen.* 6, 1.i.

ALECTO, one of the Furies, 2 *Hen.* 4, 5.v.

ALL-CHANGING, causing complete change, *John,* 2.i.

ALLEGIANT, loyal, *Hen.* 8, 3.ii.

ALL-HALLOWN SUMMER, summer lasting into winter and so vigour of manhood in age, 1 *Hen.* 4, 1.ii.

ALL-HATING, full of hate, *Rich.* 2, 5.v.

ALL-SOULS' DAY, 2nd Nov., *Rich.* 3, 5.i.

ALMANAC, calendar, 2 *Hen.* 4, 2.iv.

ALMS-DEED, charity, 3 *Hen.* 6, 5.v.

ALMS-MAN, man living on alms, *Rich.* 2, 3.iii.

AMORT, *all amort,* almost dead, 1 *Hen.* 6, 3.ii.

AMPLY, fully, *Hen.* 5, 1.ii.

ANATOMY, skeleton; *fell anatomy,* Death, *John,* 3.iv.

ANCIENT, from ensign or standard-bearer, so the officer or his flag, 1 *Hen.* 4, 4.ii.

ANGEL, gold coin stamped with im-

988

age of angel, worth about ten shillings, *John*, 2.i.

ANTIC, *the antic*, Death who mocks like a jester, *Rich.* 2, 3.ii.

APPELLANT, challenger, *Rich.* 2, 1.iii.

APPLE-JOHN, a sound but withered-looking apple, 1 *Hen.* 4, 1.iii.

APPLIANCE, remedy, *Hen.* 8, 1.i.

APPOINTMENT, direction, *Hen.* 8, 2.ii.

APPREHENSIVE, quick to understand, 2 *Hen.* 4, 4.iii.

APPROBATION, confirmation, *Hen.* 5, 1.ii.

ARBITREMENT, decision, *Rich.* 3, 5.iii; inquiry, 1 *Hen.* 4, 4.i.

ARCH, outstanding, *Rich.* 3, 4.iii.

ARGO, *ergo*, therefore, 2 *Hen.* 6, 4.ii.

ARGUMENT, subject of talk, 1 *Hen.* 4, 2.ii.

ARTHUR (i) *Arthur's show*, display of archery by London company called Prince Arthur's Knights, 2 *Hen.* 4, 3.ii; (ii) *Arthur's bosom*, malapropism for Abraham's bosom, *Hen.* 5, 2.iii.

ASSAY, attack, *Hen.* 5, 1.ii.

ASTRAEA, goddess of Justice, 1 *Hen.* 6, 1.vi.

ATONE, unite, reconcile, *Rich.* 2, 1.i.

ATROPOS, one of the Fates, 2 *Hen.* 4, 2.iv.

ATTAINDER, dishonouring charge, *Rich.* 2, 4.i.

BACKSWORD-MAN, a single-stick performer, 2 *Hen.* 4, 3.ii.

BAFFLE, to proclaim one a perjured knight, 1 *Hen.* 4, 1.ii.

BAIT, to set on dogs to worry an animal, as in a baiting-place, 2 *Hen.* 6, 5.i.

BALK'D, piled up, 1 *Hen.* 4, 1.i.

BAN, curse, 2 *Hen.* 6, 3.ii.

BANDITTO, outlaw, 2 *Hen.* 6, 4.i.

BANDY, to exchange blows or words or looks (as strokes in a rally at tennis), 3 *Hen.* 6, 1.iv.

BANE, ruin, 2 *Hen.* 6, 5.i.

BANK, to take in (as banker at card game), *John*, 5.ii.

BARBASON, a devil, *Hen.* 5, 2.i.

BARBED, protected on breast and flanks, of horse, *Rich.* 3, 1.i.

BARTHOLOMEW, -*tide*, 24th August, *Hen.* 5, 5.ii; *boar-pig*, kind sold at Bartholomew fair, 2 *Hen.* 4, 2.iv.

BASE-STRING, string of lowest pitch, 1 *Hen.* 4, 2.iv.

BASE-COURT, lower court of castle (as *basse-cour* in French), *Rich.* 2, 3.iii.

BASILISCO, character in play of 'Soliman and Perseda,' *John*, 1.i.

BASILISK, the fabled cockatrice that kills with its look, *Rich.* 3, 1.ii; cannon, *Hen.* 5, 5.ii.

BASIMECU, corruption of 'baissez ma queue,' 2 *Hen.* 6, 4.vii.

BASTARD, sweet wine from Spain, 1 *Hen.* 4, 2.iv.

BATE, *noun*, strife, 2 *Hen.* 4, 2.iv.

BATE, beat or flutter like a bird's wings, 1 *Hen.* 4, 4.i; to weaken, *Hen.* 5, 3.ii.

BAVIN, brushwood, easily kindled, 1 *Hen.* 4, 3.ii.

BAWCOCK, stout fellow (French, *beau coq*), *Hen.* 5, 3.ii.

BAY, *at bay*, when the hunted animal has to turn and face the pursuers, 1 *Hen.* 6, 4.ii.

BEADSMAN, one living on an endowment set aside to provide prayers for the benefactor, *Rich.* 2, 3.ii.

BEAR-HERD or BEAR-WARD (berrord), one who keeps a bear for exhibition, 2 *Hen.* 4, 1.ii; 2 *Hen.* 6, 5.i.

BEARING-CLOTH, christening robe, 1 *Hen.* 6, 1.iii.

BEAVER, face-piece of helmet, 2 *Hen.* 4, 4.i; the helmet as a whole, 1 *Hen.* 4, 4.i.

BEDLAM, (i) an asylum, the word being derived from Bethlehem, the name of the London hospital, 2 *Hen.* 6, 5.i; (ii) a crazed person, *John*, 2.i.

BEETLE, a heavy rammer for flattening earth, 2 *Hen.* 4, 1.ii.

BEFORE-BREACH, earlier violation, *Hen.* 5, 4.i.

BEHOVE, befit, 2 *Hen.* 6, 1.i.

BELDAM, a grandmother, old woman, 1 *Hen.* 4, 3.i.

BELL (book and candle), expression used in excommunication, *John*, 3.iii.

BENCH, the seat of authority, or those who sit in it, 2 *Hen.* 4, 5.ii.

BENEVOLENCE, a loan exacted by the king on the pretext that the payment is a gesture of goodwill, *Rich.* 2, 2.i.

BEREFT, taken from, 2 *Hen.* 6, 3.i.

BEROD, BERRORD, *see* BEAR-HERD.

BESHREW (a good-natured imprecation), plague on or curse whatever follows, *John*, 5.v.

BESPEAK, order beforehand, 1 *Hen.* 4, 1.ii.

BESTED, *worse bested*, in worse state, 2 *Hen.* 6, 2.iii.

BEST-TEMPER'D (as of metal), truest, 2 *Hen.* 4, 1.i.

BEVIS, of Southampton, of whom

prodigies were told by the early romancers, *Hen.* 8, 1.i.

BEZONIAN, a needy rascal, 2 *Hen.* 6, 4.i.

BIAS, the unsymmetrical shape of the bowl that makes its course oblique, so an influence, *John,* 2.i; and phrases of related meaning.

BIGAMY, marriage with a widow as in *Rich.* 3, 3.vii.

BIGGEN, night-cap, 2 *Hen.* 4, 4.v.

BILL, a weapon like a pole-axe, *Rich.* 2, 3.ii.

BLANK, a document to be filled in as the holder decides (*cp.* blank cheque), *Rich.* 2, 2.i.

BLISTER'D, puffed out, *Hen.* 8, 1.iii.

BLOW, to puff up, 1 *Hen.* 4, 4.ii.

BLUE-BOTTLE, the beadle, because of his blue coat, 2 *Hen.* 4, 5.iv.

BLUE-CAPS, the Scots with their blue-bonnets, 1 *Hen.* 4, 2.iv.

BODGE, to give way, 3 *Hen.* 6, 1.iv.

BOLT, short blunt-headed arrow, *Hen.* 5, 3.vii.

BOLT, to sift, *Hen.* 5, 2.ii.

BOLTER, for sifting flour, 1 *Hen.* 4, 3.iii.

BOLTING-HUTCH, the bin into which the flour falls when sifted from the bran, 1 *Hen.* 4, 2.iv.

BOMBARD, leather bottle for drink, 1 *Hen.* 4, 2.iv.

BOMBAST, cotton-wool stuffing, 1 *Hen.* 4, 2.iv.

BONA-ROBA, showy wanton, 2 *Hen.* 4, 3.ii.

BONES, *goodman bones*, skeleton-like (because he was very thin), 2 *Hen.* 4, 5.iv.

BOOT, something extra thrown in, *Rich.* 3, 4.iv; plunder, 2 *Hen.* 6, 4.i.

BOOTLESS, unsuccessful, 1 *Hen.* 4, 3.i.

BOSKY, with trees and undergrowth.

BOTCH, to patch, *Hen.* 5, 2.ii.

BOTTLED, *bottled spider*, swollen, bloated, *Rich.* 3, 1.iii.

BOTTOM, (i) valley, 1 *Hen.* 4, 3.i; (ii) ship, *John,* 2.i.

BRABBLER, brawler, *John,* 5.ii.

BRACE, a pair, 3 *Hen.* 6, 2.v.

BRACH, a kind of hound, 1 *Hen.* 4, 3.i.

BRAWL, *do brawl*, because of the troubles, 2 *Hen.* 4, 1.iii.

BRAWN, a boar fattened for the table, so of Falstaff, 2 *Hen.* 4, 1.i.

BRAZIER, worker in brass, *Hen.* 8, 5.iv.

BREEDING, pedigree, descent, 2 *Hen.* 4, 5.iii.

BRIEF, letter, 1 *Hen.* 4, 4.iv; summary, *John,* 2.i.

BROACH, to pierce (broach a cask), *Hen.* 5, 5.*Prol.*; open a discussion, or enter on some business, *Hen.* 8, 2.iv.

BROKEN MUSIC, music in parts (but punningly), *Hen.* 5, 5.ii.

BROKING PAWN, lodgment in dishonest hands, *Rich.* 2, 2.i.

BROOCH, an ornament, jewel, *Rich.* 2, 5.v.

BROODED, brooding (but maybe misprint for *broad-ey'd*), *John,* 3.iii.

BRUIT, *noun,* report, hearsay, 3 *Hen.* 6, 4.vii; *verb,* publish broadcast, 1 *Hen.* 6, 2.iii.

BUBUKLE, a portmanteau word from 'bubo,' an abscess, and carbuncle, *Hen.* 5, 3.vi.

BUCK, the pile of soiled clothes for washing, 2 *Hen.* 6, 4.ii.

BUCKLER, shield, 2 *Hen.* 6, 3.ii.

BUCKRAM, coarse linen specially treated, 1 *Hen.* 4, 2.iv.

BUFF, strong leather from ox-hide, used for jacket of soldiers, bailiffs, 1 *Hen.* 4, 1.ii.

BUG, a thing causing fear, 3 *Hen.* 6, 5.ii.

BULLY, often prefixed to express admiration or affection, *Hen.* 5, 4.i.

BUNG, pick-purse, 2 *Hen.* 4, 2.iv.

BURGONET, light helmet, 2 *Hen.* 6, 5.i.

BUSKY, 1 *Hen.* 4, 5.i; *see* BOSKY.

BUSS, *noun* and *verb,* kiss, 2 *Hen.* 4, 2.iv.

BUTT, target at archery, 3 *Hen.* 6, 1.iv.

BUZZARD, a hawk of a type useless for falconry, *Rich.* 3, 1.i.

CACODEMON, evil spirit, *Rich.* 3, 1.iii.

CADDIS-GARTER, garter of cheap tape, 1 *Hen.* 4, 2.iv.

CADE, herring-barrel, 2 *Hen.* 6, 4.ii.

CAGE, prison, 2 *Hen.* 6, 4.ii.

CAITIFF, slave, *Rich.* 3, 4.iv.

CALAMITY, misery, *Rich.* 3, 4.iv.

CALIPOLIS, wife of Muly Mahamet in Peele's 'Alcazar,' 2 *Hen.* 4, 2.iv.

CALIVER, musket, 1 *Hen.* 4, 4.ii.

CALL, decoy, *John,* 3.iv.

CALLET, contemptuous term for a woman, 3 *Hen.* 6, 2.ii.

CALYDON, *the Prince of Calydon*, Meleager whose life depended on his mother Althaea's keeping a log unburnt, 2 *Hen.* 6, 1.i.

CAMBYSES VEIN, in the style of the old play 'Cambises King of Percia,' 1 *Hen.* 4, 2.iv.

GLOSSARY

CANARY, sweet wine from the Canaries, 2 *Hen.* 4, 2.iv.

CANDLE-MINE, heap of tallow, 2 *Hen.* 4, 2.iv.

CANKER, ulcer-like evil or sore, 2 *Hen.* 6, 1.ii.

CANKER'D, evil-minded, *John*, 2.i.

CANON, church law, then any rule, God's law at *John*, 2.i.

CANSTICK, candlestick, 1 *Hen.* 4, 3.i.

CANTLE, a part cut out, 1 *Hen.* 4, 3.i.

CANVASS, to toss in a sheet, so to entertain, 2 *Hen.* 4, 2.iv; to punish, 1 *Hen.* 6, 1.iii.

CAP, cardinal's hat, *Hen.* 8, 3.ii.

CAPABLE, *of wounds*, liable by nature to, 2 *Hen.* 4, 1.i; able, *Rich.* 3, 3.i.

CAPET, Hugh Capet founded Capetian dynasty in 987 A.D., *Hen.* 5, 1.ii.

CAPITAL, principal, *Hen.* 5, 5.ii.

CAPITULATE, draw up articles of agreement, 1 *Hen.* 4, 3.ii.

CARAT, measure of purity of gold, 2 *Hen.* 4, 4.v.

CARBONADO, meat prepared for cooking by scoring with knife, 1 *Hen.* 4, 5.iii.

CARD, to adulterate drink, 1 *Hen.* 4, 3.ii.

CARDER, one who combs out defects in wool, *Hen.* 8, 1.ii.

CARDINAL, *cardinal virtues*, justice, prudence, temperance, fortitude, on which the others depend, *Hen.* 8, 3.i.

CAREER, course, *Rich.* 2, 1.ii.

CAREFUL, full of cares, *Rich.* 3, 1.iii.

CARNATION, flesh colour, *Hen.* 5, 2.iii.

CARRION, as good as dead, *Hen.* 5, 4.ii.

CART, that carries criminals to execution, 1 *Hen.* 4, 2.iv.

CAST, of dice, *Rich.* 3, 5.iv.

CATASTROPHE, end of tragedy, so end of body at 2 *Hen.* 4, 2.i.

CAUDLE, warm drink for invalid, so *hempen caudle*, to cure victim by hanging, 2 *Hen.* 6, 4.vii.

CENSURE, judgment, 2 *Hen.* 6, 1.iii.

CEINTURE, girdle, *John*, 4.iii.

CERTAINLY, *certainly resolved*, firmly determined, 1 *Hen.* 6, 5.i.

CESS, assessment, reckoning, 1 *Hen.* 4, 2.i.

CHACE (tennis term), an unreturned ball's second impact upon the floor, *Hen.* 5, 1.ii.

CHAMBER, London (*camera regis*), *Rich.* 3, 3.i.

CHANGELING, turncoat, 1 *Hen.* 4, 5.i.

CHANNEL, gutter, 2 *Hen.* 4, 2.i.

CHARACTER, *noun*, writing; *verb*, to write, 2 *Hen.* 6, 3.i.

CHARNECO, wine, 2 *Hen.* 6, 2.iii.

CHARTER'D, privileged, *Hen.* 5, 1.i.

CHARTREUX, the Charterhouse in London, *Hen.* 8, 1.i.

CHEATER, originally 'escheator,' an officer who looked after 'escheats' (forfeits or fines), then simply a swindler as at 2 *Hen.* 4, 2.iv.

CHEVERIL, flexible leather, easily manipulated, *Hen.* 8, 2.iii.

CHEWET, a jackdaw, and so applied to the talkative, 1 *Hen.* 4, 5.i.

CHOICE, *men of choice*, picked men, 2 *Hen.* 4, 1.iii; *choice-drawn*, specially picked, *Hen.* 5, 3.Prol.

CHOLER, bile (one of the four humours) which in excess causes anger, *Rich.* 2, 1.i.

CHOP, thrust suddenly, *Rich.* 3, 1.iv.

CHOPS, fat face, 1 *Hen.* 4, 1.ii.

CHRISTOM, *christom child*, a child still in its christening-robe, *Hen.* 5, 2.iii.

CHUFF, dull miserly sort, 1 *Hen.* 4, 2.ii.

CINQUE-PORTS, five English channel ports, *Hen.* 8, 4.i.

CIPHER, a mere figure, little or nothing in itself, but which may in its place signify much, *Hen.* 5, 1.Prol.

CIRCE, the enchantress, a draught from whose cup turned men to swine, 1 *Hen.* 6, 5.iii.

CIRCUIT, diadem, 2 *Hen.* 6, 3.i.

CIRCUMSTANCE, *by circumstance*, by a consideration of the circumstances, *Rich.* 3, 1.ii; *such circumstance*, unnecessary detail, 2 *Hen.* 6, 1.i.

CITAL, *blushing cital*, as if calling to account one ashamed of his conduct, 1 *Hen.* 4, 5.ii.

CITE, to summon before a court, *Hen.* 8, 4.i.

CLARET, *claret wine*, a light-red wine (now restricted to red wine from Bordeaux), 2 *Hen.* 6, 4.vi.

CLERK, scholar, *Hen.* 8, 2.ii; *clerkly*, in scholarly style, 2 *Hen.* 6, 3.i.

CLINQUANT, glittering, *Hen.* 8, 1.i.

CLIP, embrace, *John*, 5.ii; 1 *Hen.* 4, 3.i.

CLIPPER, one who pares off the edges of coin of the realm, *Hen.* 5, 4.i.

CLOSE, (i) *noun*, grapple, 1 *Hen.* 4, 1.i; (ii) *adj.*, secretive, 1 *Hen.* 4, 2.iii.

CLOUT, mark at archery, 2 *Hen.* 4, 3.ii.

GLOSSARY

CLOUTED, *clouted shoon,* hobnailed, 2 *Hen.* 6, 4.ii.

CLUTCH, to close or clench, *John,* 2.i.

COAL, *carry coals,* engage in dirty work, *Hen.* 5, 3.ii.

COAST, *coasts and hedges,* makes his way indirectly or secretly, *Hen.* 8, 3.ii.

COAT, *herald's coat,* tabard, 1 *Hen.* 4, 4.ii.

COCK, perversion of 'God,' in oaths, 2 *Hen.* 4, v.i.

COCKATRICE, *see* BASILISK.

COG, cheat, wheedle, *Rich.* 3, 1.iii.

COGNIZANCE, a device worn by a gentleman's retainers, so a token, 1 *Hen.* 6, 2.iv.

COIL, troublesome affair, *John,* 2.i.

COLBRAND, Danish giant, conquered by Sir Guy of Warwick, *Hen.* 8, 5.iv.

COLLECT, deduce from observation, 2 *Hen.* 6, 3.i.

COLOSSUS, huge bronze statue of Apollo at harbour of Rhodes, 1 *Hen.* 4, 5.i.

COLOUR, (often) deceitful appearance, pretence, *Hen.* 8, 1.i.

COLT, to trick, 1 *Hen.* 4, 2.ii.

COMBINATION, alliance, treaty, *Hen.* 8, 1.i.

COMFORTLESS, disconsolate, *Hen.* 8, 2.iii.

COMMENCE, confer the power to act, 2 *Hen.* 4, 4.iii.

COMMODITY, profit, *John,* 2.i; merchandise, 2 *Hen.* 6, 4.vii.

COMMON-HACKNEY'D, cheapened, 1 *Hen.* 4, 3.ii.

COMMOTION, rebellion, 2 *Hen.* 6, 3.i.

COMMUNITY, familiarity, 1 *Hen.* 4, 3.ii.

COMPANION, often contemptuously as at 2 *Hen.* 4, 2.iv.

COMPARATIVE, ready with unflattering comparisons, 1 *Hen.* 4, 1.ii; one who would compare himself with another in rank and so affect familiarity, 1 *Hen.* 4, 3.ii.

COMPARE, challenge comparison with, 2 *Hen.* 4, 2.iv.

COMPASSIONATE, appealing for pity, *Rich.* 2, 1.iii.

COMPETITOR, partner, associate, *Rich.* 3, 4.iv.

COMPLEMENT, completeness in appearance and social graces, *Hen.* 5, 2.ii.

COMPLEXION, appearance as governed by the predominant 'humour,' *Rich.* 2, 3.ii.

COMPLIMENT, social form, *John,* 1.i.

CON, learn, *Hen.* 5, 3.vi.

CONCEIT, idea, *Hen.* 8, 2.iii; play of mind, 2 *Hen.* 4, 2.iv.

CONCEITED, *well conceited,* aptly put, 2 *Hen.* 4, 5.i.

CONCEIVE, understand, 2 *Hen.* 4, 2.ii.

CONDIGN, *condign punishment,* well deserved, 2 *Hen.* 6, 3.i.

CONDUCT, guard, 2 *Hen.* 6, 2.iv.

CONGREE, uniting harmoniously, *Hen.* 5, 1.ii.

CONGREET, exchange greetings, *Hen.* 5, 5.ii.

CONJUNCTION, assembled force, 1 *Hen.* 4, 4.i; *in conjunction,* together (as planets may seem together in the sky), 2 *Hen.* 4, 2.iv.

CONSCIENCE, knowledge (shading off when of right and wrong into modern meaning), 2 *Hen.* 6, 3.i.

CONSENT, harmony, *Hen.* 5, 1.ii.

CONSIDERATE, thoughtful, *Rich.* 3, 4.ii.

CONSIGN, set the seal on, 2 *Hen.* 4, 5.ii.

CONSISTORY, assembly place, college of cardinals, *Hen.* 8, 2.iv.

CONSORT, company of musicians, 2 *Hen.* 6, 3.ii.

CONSTABLE, 'Master of the horse,' a principal officer, *Hen.* 5, 2.iv.

CONVENTICLE, secret meeting of conspirators, 2 *Hen.* 6, 3.i.

CONVERSATIONS, behaviour, 2 *Hen.* 4, 5.v.

CONVERSION, promotion, *John,* 1.i.

CONVEY, slang for steal, *Rich.* 3, 4.i.

CONVOCATION, assembly of clergy, *Hen.* 5, 1.i.

CONY, rabbit, 3 *Hen.* 6, 1.iv.

CORANTO, a dance, *Hen.* 5, 3.v.

CORINTH, CORINTHIAN, life in Corinth was supposed to be particularly gay, 1 *Hen.* 4, 2.iv.

CORNET, body of mounted troops, 1 *Hen.* 6, 4.iii.

CORPORAL, a senior rank in Shakespeare's day, 1 *Hen.* 4, 4.ii.

COSTARD, head, from name for large apple, *Rich.* 3, 1.iv.

COTSWOLD, COTSALL, this district in Gloucestershire was famous for its coursing contests, 2 *Hen.* 4, 3.ii.

COUNTER, used with *hunting* when dogs follow the scent in the wrong direction; play on this meaning and counter = debtors' prison in 2 *Hen.* 4, 1.ii.

COURAGE, disposition, 3 *Hen.* 6, 2.ii.

COURT-HAND, style of script used in legal documents, 2 *Hen.* 6, 4.ii.

COUSIN, COZ, a relative of some kind, or courtesy title, *John,* 3.iii.

COZEN, to cheat, *Rich.* 2, 2.ii.

GLOSSARY

CRACKER, boaster, *John*, 2.i.

CRANK, to zigzag, 1 *Hen.* 4, 3.i.

CRAZE, to break, *Rich.* 3, 4.iv.

CRESSET, metal container for inflammable material, 1 *Hen.* 4, 3.i.

CROOK-BACK, hunchback, 3 *Hen.* 6, 1.iv.

CROSS, money, silver coin stamped with cross, 2 *Hen.* 4, 1.ii.

CROSS-ROW, the alphabet, the row in the primer containing it being marked with a cross, *Rich.* 3, 1.i.

CRUDY, curdled, 2 *Hen.* 4, 4.iii.

CRY AIM, 'good shot!' *John* 2.i.

CULLION, low fellow, *Hen.* 5, 3.ii.

CULVERIN, cannon, long in proportion to its calibre, 1 *Hen.* 4, 2.iii.

CUNNING (i) *noun*, knowledge, skill; (ii) *adj.*, learned, clever (not always in bad sense as to-day), 2 *Hen.* 6, 1.ii.

CURIOUS, finely made, 3 *Hen.* 6, 2.v.

CURST, sharp in tone or temper, 2 *Hen.* 6, 3.ii.

CURTLE-AXE, kind of cutlass, *Hen.* 5, 4.ii.

CUSHES, thigh-armour, 1 *Hen.* 4, 4.i.

CUT, working-horse or gelding, 1 *Hen.* 4, 2.i.

DAFF, put off, thrust aside, 1 *Hen.* 4, 4.i.

DAGONET, Arthur's fool, 2 *Hen.* 4, 3.ii.—*see* Arthur's show.

DAMASCUS, regarded as the place where Cain killed Abel, 1 *Hen.* 6, 1.iii.

DARE (fowling term), to render the bird immobile by dazzling it by some device, *Hen.* 5, 4.ii.

DARNEL, a weed infesting corn, 1 *Hen.* 6, 3.ii.

DARRAIGN, set in order, 3 *Hen.* 6, 2.ii.

DAUB, to colour, to conceal, *Rich.* 3, 3.v.

DEARTH, scarcity, famine, *Rich.* 3, 3.iii.

DECK, pack of cards, 3 *Hen.* 6, 5.i.

DECOCT, heat up, *Hen.* 5, 3.v.

DEGREE, step, rank, *Hen.* 5, 4.i.

DEMISE, transmit, *Rich.* 3, 4.iv.

DENIER, French copper coin of small value, *Rich.* 3, 1.ii.

DEPOSE (i) set aside, *Rich.* 2, 3.ii; (ii) assert on oath, 3 *Hen.* 6, 1.ii; (iii) examine on oath, *Rich.* 2, 1.iii.

DEPUTATION, office of deputy, 1 *Hen.* 4, 4.iii.

DERACINATE, uproot, *Hen.* 5, 5.ii.

DESCANT, comment (from the term that refers to the upper and more elaborate part of a musical composition), *Rich.* 3, 3.vii.

DESTINIES, the three Fates who spin or cut the thread of life, *Rich.* 2, 1.ii.

DETERMINATE, purposed, conclusive, *Hen.* 8, 2.iv.

DETERMINATION, decision, 1 *Hen.* 4, 4.iii.

DETERMINE, end, 2 *Hen.* 4, 4.v.

DIAL, watch, 1 *Hen.* 4, 5.ii.

DIFFIDENCE, distrust, 1 *Hen.* 6, 3.iii.

DIGRESS, to transgress, *Rich.* 2, 5.iii.

DIM, pale, *John*, 3.iv.

DINT, *by dint of sword*, by the blow of war, 2 *Hen.* 4, 4.i.

DISCERNER, one with capacity of judging, *Hen.* 8, 1.i.

DISCIPLINE, skill in war, *John*, 2.i.

DISCOLOUR, cause to blush, 2 *Hen.* 4, 2.ii.

DISCOMFORTABLE, discouraging, *Rich.* 2, 3.ii.

DISCONTENT, one not satisfied with his conditions, 1 *Hen.* 4, 5.i.

DISCOVER, to reveal what is known to the speaker, 1 *Hen.* 6, 2.v; to find out, *Rich.* 2, 2.iii.

DISCOVERY, revelation, *Hen.* 5, 2.ii.

DISCREET, indiscreet, 2 *Hen.* 4, 2.iv.

DISGRACEFUL, without grace, 1 *Hen.* 6, 1.i.

DISLIKE, discord, 1 *Hen.* 4, 5.i.

DISMAL, ill-boding, unlucky, 2 *Hen.* 6, 3.ii.

DISPARK, open land to public use, *Rich.* 2, 3.i.

DISPENSATION, exemption from some law, 1 *Hen.* 6, 5.iii (here from his marriage promise).

DISPLEASURE, *your displeasure with the king*, your offending the king, *Hen.* 8, 3.ii.

DISPOSE, *noun*, disposal, *John*, 1.i; *verb*, arrange, *John*, 3.iv.

DISTEMPER, drunkenness, *Hen.* 5, 2.ii.

DISTEMPERATURE, lack of order and so inclemency in weather or illness in man, 1 *Hen.* 4, 3.i.

DISTRAIN, to take legal possession of goods, etc., to cover debt, to take over, *Rich.* 2, 2.iii; 1 *Hen.* 6, 1.iii.

DISTRESSFUL, earned by toil and sweat, *Hen.* 5, 4.i.

DISTRUSTFUL, diffident, 1 *Hen.* 6, 1.ii.

DIVERS, diverse, unorthodox in *Hen.* 8, 5.iii.

DIVISION, decorative elaboration of a musical theme, 1 *Hen.* 4, 3.i.

DOG-DAYS, from July to Mid-August, when Sirius the dog-star rising with the sun was supposed to add to its heat, *Hen.* 8, 5.iv.

GLOSSARY

DOIT, a Dutch coin of small value, 2 *Hen. 6*, 3.i.

DOOM, judgment, 2 *Hen. 6*, 3.i; *day of doom, doomsday,* day of one's death, 3 *Hen. 6*, 5.vi.

DOUBLE-FATAL, the yew yielding the wood for the bow and also poisonous berries, *Rich. 2*, 3.ii.

DOUBLET AND HOSE, the dress of a man when physically active, 2 *Hen. 6*, 4.vii, implies that plain men have to go simply dressed without a cloak, although the gentleman's horse is warm.

DOUBTLESS, free from fear or suspicion, *John*, 4.i.

DOUT, extinguish, *Hen. 5*, 4.ii.

DOWLAS, coarse linen, 1 *Hen. 4*, 3.iii.

DOWNS, sea between Goodwin Sands and Kent, 2 *Hen. 6*, 4.i.

DRAFF, pig-wash, 1 *Hen. 4*, 4.ii.

DRAWER, tapster, 1 *Hen. 4*, 2.iv.

DRESS, to train a horse, *Rich. 2*, 5.v.

DROLLERY, an amusing picture, 2 *Hen. 4*, 2.i.

DRONE, a pipe giving a single fixed note; a Lincolnshire bagpipe has one (the Scottish three), 1 *Hen. 4*, 1.ii.

DROPSY, *swollen parcel of dropsies,* puffed out as if with watery swellings, 1 *Hen. 4*, 2.iv.

DURANCE, the ideas of lasting material or of imprisonment are played on at 1 *Hen. 4*, 1.ii.

DUTY, *duties of a man,* respect due to a brave soldier, 1 *Hen. 4*, 5.ii.

EAGER, sharp, cutting, physically or mentally, *Rich. 2*, 1.i.

EAGERLY, relentlessly, *Hen. 8*, 4.ii.

EAN, to give birth, 3 *Hen. 6*, 2.v.

EAR, plough, cultivate, *Rich. 2*, 3.ii.

EARN, yearn, *Hen. 5*, 2.iii.

EARNEST, token payment as pledge of some service or obligation, *Hen. 5*, 5.i.

EFFEMINATE, gentle, *Rich. 3*, 3.vii.

EGREGIOUS, notable (used by Pistol at *Hen. 5*, 2.i).

ELBOW, *rub the elbow,* show pleasure, 1 *Hen. 4*, 5.i.

ELDER-GUN, child's toy gun, *Hen. 5*, 4.i.

ELEMENT, earth, air, fire or water, for from these everything was compounded, *Hen. 5*, 3.vii; the sky, so *the cinders of the element* are the stars, 2 *Hen. 4*, 4.iii; as each element was inhabited by its appropriate kind, *one that promises no element in such a business,* implies that the cardinal was engaged in a business hardly expected of him, *Hen. 8*, 1.i.

ELM, the elm tree used as a prop for vines, *dead elm,* a poor prop, 2 *Hen. 4*, 2.iv.

ELSE, *see else yourself,* see for yourself (if you doubt), *John*, 4.i.

ELVISH-MARK'D, deformed at birth by bad fairies, *Rich. 3*, 1.iii.

EMBLAZE, to set forth to all as a herald could, 2 *Hen. 6*, 4.x.

EMBOSSED, swollen, 1 *Hen. 4*, 3.iii.

EMMANUEL, 'God is with us,' often put at the head of documents, 2 *Hen. 6*, 4.ii.

ENCHAS'D, set as with precious stones, 2 *Hen. 6*, 1.ii.

ENFEOFF'D, became the vassal of, gave himself up to, 1 *Hen. 4*, 3.ii.

ENGRAFFED TO, closely attached to, 2 *Hen. 4*, 2.ii.

ENGROSS (i) to set out in official hand, *Rich. 3*, 3.vi; (ii) to acquire largely or exclusively, 2 *Hen. 4*, 4.v; to make fat, *Rich. 3*, 3.vii.

ENGROSSMENTS, acquisitions, 2 *Hen. 4*, 4.v.

ENJOY, possess, *John*, 2.i.

ENLARGEMENT, release from confinement, 1 *Hen. 4*, 3.i.

ENTAIL, to give as an inalienable possession, 3 *Hen. 6*, 1.i.

ENTERTAIN, receive, 2 *Hen. 6*, 4.ix.

EPHESIAN, a boon companion (heedless of what Paul told the Ephesians), 2 *Hen. 4*, 2.ii.

ERRONEOUS, wandering from right, 3 *Hen. 6*, 2.v.

ESPERANCE, the Percy motto, and Percy's battle cry, 1 *Hen. 4*, 5.ii.

ESTRIDGE, ostrich, 1 *Hen. 4*, 4.i.

EVIDENCE, witness, *Rich. 3*, 1.iv.

EXACTLY, completely, *Rich. 2*, 1.i.

EXCEPTION, *how modest in exception,* reasonable in his expression of disapproval, *Hen. 5*, 2.iv.

EXECUTION, performance of some desire or intent, 3 *Hen. 6*, 2.ii.

EXEMPT, separated from, free from, 1 *Hen. 6*, 2.iv and 3.i.

EXHALATION, meteor, *John*, 3.iv.

EXHALE, draw (your sword), *Hen. 5*, 2.i.

EXHIBITERS, those presenting a bill in parliament, *Hen. 5*, 1.i.

EXIGENT, end, 1 *Hen. 6*, 2.v.

EXORCISM, the calling up of spirits, 2 *Hen. 6*, 1.iv.

EXPECT, await, 1 *Hen. 6*, 5.iii.

EXPEDIENCE, haste, purpose requiring haste, *Rich. 2*, 2.i, 1 *Hen. 4*, 1.i.

EXPIATE, (literally) ended—the hour

of execution has come, *Rich.* 3, 3.iii.

EXPOSTULATE, to discuss, 3 *Hen.* 6, 2.v.

EXTEMPORAL, unpremeditated, 1 *Hen.* 6, 3.i.

EXTIRP, to weed out, 1 *Hen.* 6, 3.iii.

EXTRAUGHT, descended, 3 *Hen.* 6, 2.ii.

FACE, to trim a garment, to give a false appearance to, 1 *Hen.* 4, 5.i.

FACE ROYAL, refers to effigy on gold coin called 'a royal,' 2 *Hen.* 4, 1.ii.

FACT, what has been done, action, 1 *Hen.* 6, 4.i; *in the fact*, in the act, 2 *Hen.* 6, 2.i.

FAIN, glad, contented, forced, 2 *Hen.* 4, 2.i.

FAITORS, rascals (part of Pistol's rant), 2 *Hen.* 4, 2.iv.

FALCHION, a scimitar-like weapon, 3 *Hen.* 6, 1.iv.

FALSELY, mistakenly, *John*, 4.ii.

FAME, rumour, 1 *Hen.* 6, 2.iii; reputation, 1 *Hen.* 6, 2.i.

FANTASIED, moved by imaginary fears, *John*, 4.ii.

FANTASTIC, merely in the fancy, *Rich.* 2, 1.iii.

FANTASTICALLY, *fantastically carved*, grotesquely-shaped, 2 *Hen.* 4, 3.ii.

FANTASY, mere fancy, 1 *Hen.* 4, 5.iv; delirious thoughts, *John*, 5.vii.

FARCED, stuffed out with the appearance of dignity, *Hen.* 5, 4.i.

FAR-FET, far-fetched, remote and inapplicable, 2 *Hen.* 6, 3.i.

FARM, *in farm*, with its revenue at his disposal subject to a payment for the privilege, *Rich.* 2, 2.i.

FASHION, to give a false shape or turn to, *Hen.* 5, 1.ii.

FAT, hot, stuffy, 1 *Hen.* 4, 2.iv.

FATAL, *the Thracian fatal steeds:* Rhesus king of Thrace came to the help of the Trojans; as an oracle had declared that Troy would never fall if his horses grazed on Trojan grass, the Greeks, Ulysses and Diomede, prevented this by slaying the king and capturing the horses; so the steeds are the instruments of fate, 3 *Hen.* 6, 4.ii.

FATHER-IN-LAW, stepfather at *Rich.* 3, 5.iii.

FAVOUR, mercy, 2 *Hen.* 6, 4.vii; charm, 2 *Hen.* 6, 1.ii; token of someone's favour, *Rich.* 2, 5.iii; features, *Rich.* 2, 4.i.

FEALTY, loyalty, 2 *Hen.* 6, 5.i.

FEATURE, figure (not face), *Rich.* 3, 1.i.

FEE-SIMPLE, land held on the most absolute form of tenure by owner or his heirs, 2 *Hen.* 6, 4.x.

FENNEL, herb used in fish-sauce; serpents were supposed to like fennel, which became a symbol of flattery, 2 *Hen.* 4, 2.iv.

FERN-SEED, reputed to make the possessor invisible, 1 *Hen.* 4, 2.i.

FEW, *in few*, in few words, *Hen.* 5, 1.ii.

FICO, FIG, FIGO, contemptuous expression, often accompanied by insulting gesture, 2 *Hen.* 4, 5.iii.

FIELD, pun on field of coat-of-arms, a common field at 2 *Hen.* 6, 4.ii.

FIERCE, proud, 2 *Hen.* 6, 4.ix.

FIFTEENTH, the fifteenth part of personal property levied as tax, 2 *Hen.* 6, 1.i.

FIGURE, appearance, real, imaginary, or assumed, *Hen.* 8, 1.i; emblems, analogies, *Hen.* 5, 4.vii.

FILE, list, *Hen.* 8, 1.i.

FIND, *you have found me*, discovered in me the qualities indicated, 1 *Hen.* 4, 1.iii.

FINE, end, 1 *Hen.* 6, 1.iv.

FINSBURY, *Finsbury Fields*, a resort of Londoners, 1 *Hen.* 4, 3.i.

FIRE-DRAKE, meteor, and so in slang a red nose, *Hen.* 8, 5.iv.

FIRK, beat, *Hen.* 5, 4.iv.

FIT, spasm or attack of some disease or illness, *John*, 3.iv; trick of grimacing, *Hen.* 8, 1.iii.

FLAP-DRAGON, something served in flaming spirits to be gulped down, 2 *Hen.* 4, 2.iv.

FLAW, gust of wind, or passion, 2 *Hen.* 6, 3.i; snowstorm, 2 *Hen.* 4, 4.iv.

FLESH, to give a hound the flesh of the victim to rouse its keenness, so to introduce an untried soldier to bloodshed, *John*, 5.i; *flesh his sword*, use it in his first fight, 1 *Hen.* 6, 4.vii; *flesh'd*, accustomed to bloodshed, *Rich.* 3, 4.iii.

FLOCKS, tufts of wool, 1 *Hen.* 4, 2.i.

FLOURISH, embellishment, *Rich.* 3, 1.iii.

FLOWER-DE-LUCE, the lily of the French coat of arms, and so applied by Henry to Katherine, *Hen.* 5, 5.ii.

FOIL (i) setting of a jewel, so something that shows up the value of an act or accomplishment, 1 *Hen.* 4, 1.ii; (ii) *the foil*, overthrow, 1 *Hen.* 6, 5.iii.

GLOSSARY

Foin, thrust with rapier, 2 *Hen.* 4, 2.i.

Fond, foolish, doting, *Rich.* 2, 5.ii.

Fondly, foolishly, 2 *Hen.* 4, 4.ii.

Foot, *upon the foot of fear*, in flight, 1 *Hen.* 4, 5.v.

Foot-cloth, saddle-cloth hanging almost to ground, 2 *Hen.* 6, 4.i.

Forecast, forethought, 3 *Hen.* 6, 5.i.

Forehand, *forehand shaft*, short-range arrow, 2 *Hen.* 4, 3.ii.

Forespent, *vanities forespent*, former follies, *Hen.* 5, 2.iv.

Forestall'd, *forestall'd remission*, a pardon for some earlier act not requiring excuse, *Hen.* 5, 5.ii.

Forfeit, to hand over a person to death, 1 *Hen.* 6, 4.iii.

Forgetive (perhaps from 'forge'), shaping, inventive, 2 *Hen.* 4, 4.iii.

Forked, as with two legs, 2 *Hen.* 4, 3.ii.

Forslow, delay, 3 *Hen.* 6, 2.iii.

Forspent, exhausted, 2 *Hen.* 4, 1.i.

Forthcoming, as exhibits in the law court, 1 *Hen.* 6, 1.iv.

Fortitude, bodily power, 1 *Hen.* 6, 2.i.

Fox, a sword (some makes were marked with a wolf's head), *Hen.* 5, 4.iv.

Fracted, broken, *Hen.* 5, 2.i.

Frank, sty, 2 *Hen.* 4, 2.ii; *frank'd*, shut up as in a sty, *Rich.* 3, 1.iii.

Franklin, freeholder but not numbered among the county families, 1 *Hen.* 4, 2.i.

Fraught, laden, *full-fraught man*, complete with manly virtues, *Hen.* 5, 2.ii.

Frontier, advanced fort, 1 *Hen.* 4, 2.iii.

Fub, cheat, 1 *Hen.* 4, 1.ii.

Fuller, cloth-cleaner, *Hen.* 8, 1.ii.

Furniture, equipment, 2 *Hen.* 6, 1.iii.

Fustian (i) coarse cloth; (ii) ranting, 2 *Hen.* 4, 2.iv.

Fustilarian (comic formation), 2 *Hen.* 4, 2.i.

Gage, pledge, as glove thrown down to pledge the owner to meet in contest whoever picks it up, *Rich.* 2, 4.i.

Gait, walk, *Hen.* 8, 3.ii.

Gainsay, contradict, 2 *Hen.* 4, 1.i.

Galen, Greek who became physician to the Emperor Marcus Aurelius; his voluminous writings on medical topics were authoritative in Shakespeare's day, 1 *Hen.* 4, 1.ii.

Gall, bile; as the liver was supposed to provide the capacity for resentment and courage, *Hen.* 5, 2.ii.

Gallant-springing, *gallant-springing brave Plantagenet*, like the sprig of broom, the badge of his house, *Rich.* 3, 1.iv.

Gallian, French, 1 *Hen.* 6, 5.iv.

Galliard, a lively dance usually in triple time, *Hen.* 5, 1.ii.

Gallowglass, heavy-armed footman in army of Irish or from Scottish isles, 2 *Hen.* 6, 4.ix.

Gambol, horse-play, *Hen.* 5, 2.iv.

Gaping, bawling, *Hen.* 8, 5.iv.

Garb, manner, *Hen.* 5, 5.i.

Gawds, gay trifles, *John*, 3.iii.

Gear, business, 2 *Hen.* 6, 1.iv.

Genius, the spirit that is assigned to each individual as a guardian, so peculiar bent or nature; or the embodiment of some characteristic feature, 2 *Hen.* 4, 3.ii.

Gentle, of good birth, *Rich.* 3, 1.iii.

Gentleness, courtesy, *Hen.* 8, 2.iv.

Gentry, *exempt from ancient gentry*, deprived of noble rank, 1 *Hen.* 6, 2.iv.

George, small figure of St. George slaying the dragon worn as a pendant by Knights of the Garter as part of their insignia, *Rich.* 3, 4.iv.

Gesture, bearing, *Hen.* 5, 4.Prol.

Ghost, corpse, 2 *Hen.* 6, 3.ii.

Ghostly, concerned with spiritual welfare, 3 *Hen.* 6, 3.ii.

Gib, *gib cat*, tom-cat, 1 *Hen.* 4, 1.ii.

Giglot, wanton, 1 *Hen.* 6, 4.vii.

Gimmaled, jointed, *Hen.* 5, 4.ii.

Gimmer, links in mechanism of clock, 1 *Hen.* 6, 1.ii.

Glass, hour glass, 1 *Hen.* 6, 4.ii.

Gleaned, *gleaned land*, deprived of its defenders, *Hen.* 5, 1.ii.

Gleek, to joke, gibe, 1 *Hen.* 6, 3.ii.

Gloss, explanation, excuse, so fair outward show, *Hen.* 8, 5.iii.

Gloze, to explain, *Hen.* 5, 1.ii; to comment deceitfully, *Rich.* 2, 2.i.

Gobbet, portions of flesh, 2 *Hen.* 6, 4.i.

God-a-mercy, God reward you; as a reply to *good-den* (God give you good even) at *John*, 1.i.

Good-nights, slumber-songs, 2 *Hen.* 4, 3.ii.

Good year, a common exclamation, without any particular meaning, used as an expletive at 2 *Hen.* 4, 2.iv.

Goose, see Winchester goose.

GORBELLIED, fat, overfed, 1 *Hen.* 4, 2.ii.

GORDIAN KNOT, an oracle foretold that the man who could unloose this intricate knot, in the acropolis of Gordium, would be ruler of the East; Alexander the Great cut it; so of solving a problem, *Hen.* 5, 1.i.

GOSSIP, one associated with parents at baptism of their child, a godparent, *Hen.* 8, 5.v; friend, woman fond of idle talk, *Rich.* 3, 1.i.

GOSSIPING, enjoying the 'gossips' feast,' so of pleasant social intercourse, *John*, 5.ii.

GOVERNMENT, self-control, conduct, 1 *Hen.* 4, 3.i.

GOWN, nightgown, 2 *Hen.* 4, 3.ii.

GRACIOUS, attractive, beautiful, *John*, 3.iv.

GRAFT, to insert shoots and so to incorporate, *Rich.* 3, 3.iv.

GRAFTER, the tree from which the shoot for grafting has been taken, *Hen.* 5, 3.v.

GRAMERCY, expression of thanks, *Rich.* 3, 3.ii.

GRAMMAR-SCHOOL, a school founded to give instruction in Latin, the language of the Church or learned professions, 2 *Hen.* 6, 4.vii.

GRATE, to fret, annoy, 2 *Hen.* 4, 4.i.

GRATULATE, to greet and cheer, *Rich.* 3, 4.i.

GREAT, *great belly doublet*, one stuffed with lining; but Falstaff provided the stuffing himself, *Hen.* 5, 4.vii.

GREENLY, pale with love, *Hen.* 5, 5.ii.

GREEN-SICKNESS, bloodless condition, 2 *Hen.* 4, 4.iii.

GRIEF, grievance, *Hen.* 8, 1.ii.

GRIEVANCE, inconvenience, affliction, 2 *Hen.* 4, 4.i.

GROAT, fourpenny piece, *John*, 1.i.

GROUND, the theme in the bass over which the descant (*q.v.*) is constructed, so the subject to be elaborated, *Rich.* 3, 3.vii.

GROWTH, size, bulk, 2 *Hen.* 4, 1.ii.

GRUDGE, *grudge one thought*, harbour any grudge or ill-will, 1 *Hen.* 6, 3.i; *grudging stomachs*, resentful tempers, 1 *Hen.* 6, 4.i.

GUARD, trimming to a garment; *guarded*, trimmed, *Hen.* 8, Prol., *velvet-guards*, the women wearing them, 1 *Hen.* 4, 3.i.

GUARDANT, protector, 1 *Hen.* 6, 4.vii.

GUERDON'D, rewarded, 3 *Hen.* 6, 3.iii.

GUIDON, pennant, *Hen.* 5, 4.ii.

GUILTLESS, *guiltless blood-shedding*, shedding the blood of the guiltless, 2 *Hen.* 6, 4.vii.

GUISE, style, custom, 2 *Hen.* 6, 1.iii.

GULL, dupe, *Rich.* 3, 1.iii.

GUM, *gummed velvet*, velvet doctored with gum, to give inferior stuff a show, 1 *Hen.* 4, 2.ii.

GURNET, fish with large head, 1 *Hen.* 4, 4.ii.

GUY, Guy of Warwick who slew the Danish giant Colbrand, *Hen.* 8, 5.iv.

GYVES, fetters, 1 *Hen.* 4, 4.ii.

HABILIMENTS, costume, dress, *Rich.* 2, 1.iii.

HABIT, costume, *Hen.* 5, 3.vi.

HAGGLED, with many wounds, *Hen.* 5, 4.vi.

HAIR, character, 1 *Hen.* 4, 4.i.

HALBERD, axe-like weapon with long handle, *Rich.* 3, 1.ii.

HALCYON (from Halcyone, changed with her husband Ceyx to a type of kingfisher; their breeding season in winter was supposed to be favoured with fine weather), calm, happy, 1 *Hen.* 6, 1.ii.

HALF-FACED, thin faced (like the profile on the groat, a thin coin), *John*, 1.i; half seen, 2 *Hen.* 6, 4.i.

HALF-KIRTLE, skirt, 2 *Hen.* 4, 5.iv.

HALF SWORD, most closely engaged, 1 *Hen.* 4, 2.iv.

HALL, *The Hall*, Westminster Hall, the scene of such trials, *Hen.* 8, 2.i.

HALLOWMAS, 1st Nov. (All Saints' Day), *Rich.* 2, 5.i.

HAND, *made a fair hand*, done well, sarcastically at *Hen.* 8, 5.iv.

HAPLY, fortunately, 2 *Hen.* 6, 5.ii; perhaps, 2 *Hen.* 6, 3.i.

HARBOUR, lodging, 2 *Hen.* 6, 3.i.

HARD-FAVOUR'D, ugly, *Hen.* 5, 5.i.

HARDIMENT, *changing hardiment*, matching his adversary's prowess, 1 *Hen.* 4, 1.iii.

HARLOTRY, a hussy (with no suggestion of lack of chastity), 1 *Hen.* 4, 3.i.

HARNESS, armour, so armed men at 1 *Hen.* 4, 3.ii.

HARRY TEN SHILLINGS, half-sovereign coined in reign of Henry VII, 2 *Hen.* 4, 3.ii.

HATCH, the lower half of a divided door; *o'er the hatch*, to enter without opening the lower half, so irregularly, hence of an illegitimate child, *John*, 1.i.

HAUGHT, haughty, 3 *Hen.* 6, 2.i.

HAUGHTY, ambitious, *Rich.* 3, 4.ii.

GLOSSARY

HAUNCH, *haunch of winter*, the rear of winter, 2 *Hen.* 4, 4.iv.

HAUTBOY, early form of oboe, 2 *Hen.* 4, 3.ii.

HAVOC, general slaughter or destruction, *John*, 2.i.

HAZARD, game with dice, *Hen.* 5, 3.vii; risk, *Rich.* 3, 5.iv; term from tennis indicating a scoring stroke, *Hen.* 5, 1.ii.

HEAD, muster of men, usually soldiers, *John*, 5.ii.

HEADLAND, part of field left, for convenience of working, unploughed till the very end, 2 *Hen.* 4, 5.i.

HEARKEN, *hearken'd for*, long'd for, 1 *Hen.* 4, 5.iv.

HEARSE, coffin, *Rich.* 3, 1.ii.

HEAVENS, the roof carried on posts above the Elizabethan stage, 1 *Hen.* 6, 1.i.

HECATE, divinity of classical antiquity, associated with ghost world and later with witchcraft as at 1 *Hen.* 6, 3.ii, where Joan is regarded as a witch.

HEIGHT, *careful height*, position or rank burdened with anxieties, *Rich.* 3, 1.iii.

HEINOUSLY, shamefully, 1 *Hen.* 4, 3.iii.

HEIR, *heir apparent*, the King's eldest son, the undoubted heir, 1 *Hen.* 4, 1.ii; used also at 2 *Hen.* 6, 1.i.

HEMP-SEED, destined for the hangman's hempen rope, 2 *Hen.* 4, 2.i.

HERALD, an officer who was recognized as a privileged messenger between kings in time of war; later responsible for regulating precedence among nobility, ordering ceremonies, making proclamations.

HERB OF GRACE, rue, *Rich.* 2, 3.iv.

HEST, command, decision, 1 *Hen.* 4, 2.iii.

HIDE, protect, *John*, 2.i.

HILDING, inferior sort, 2 *Hen.* 4, 1.i.

HIND, female deer, *Rich.* 3, 2.iv.

HIREN, pun on 'iron' and Hyrin (Irene), a character in a play by Peele, 2 *Hen.* 4, 2.iv.

HIT, *hitting a grosser quality*, pleasing the thickwitted, *Hen.* 8, 1.ii.

HOLE, *hole in his coat*, a fault, *Hen.* 5, 3.vi.

HOLIDAME, an oath (on holy relics), reduced by Shakespeare's time to a mere asseveration, *Hen.* 8, 5.i.

HOLIDAY, impertinent amid the serious scene of war, 1 *Hen.* 4, 1.iii.

HOLY-ROOD DAY, 14th Sept., the feast of the Holy Cross, 1 *Hen.* 4, 1.i.

HOME, *pay us home*, discharge the debt as though he were wiping out an injury, 1 *Hen.* 4, 1.iii.

HONEY-SEED, for homicide, 2 *Hen.* 4, 2.i.

HOOD, to blindfold hawk (when unhooded it bates), *Hen.* 5, 3.vii.

HOOP, *the three-hooped pot*, a quart pot (which Cade promises to enlarge), 2 *Hen.* 6, 4.ii.

HOSE, includes various types of breeches and clothing (not stockings) for the lower limbs, 1 *Hen.* 4, 2.iv.

HULL, to furl sails and drift with the tide (*Tw. Night*, 1.v), so of the mind, *Hen.* 8, 2.iv.

HUMOROUS, governed by a humour (*q.v.*), changeable, *John*, 3.i.

HUMOUR, corresponding to the four elements (earth, air, fire, water) were the four humours—black bile, blood, bile, phlegm. According as one or other predominated in a man's system so his temperament was choleric or phlegmatic or melancholy, and his complexion in keeping. The term was overworked, and parodied in Nym's use of it, e.g. *Mer. Wives Win.*, 1.i; the Prince implies they are in morbid excess in Falstaff, 1 *Hen.* 4, 2.iv.

HYDRA, many-headed monster, 1 *Hen.* 4, 5.iv.

HYPERION, god of the sun, *Hen.* 5, 4.i.

HYRCANIA, south-east shore of Caspian sea; regarded as wild country and home of savage beasts (Virgil mentions tigers of Hyrcania), 3 *Hen.* 6, 1.iv.

ICARUS, son of Daedalus; father and son imprisoned by Minos of Crete escaped by using artificial wings; Icarus flew too near the sun, the wax of his wings melted and he fell into the Aegean Sea, 3 *Hen.* 6, 5.vi.

ICELAND DOG, type of pet dog, used in derision at *Hen.* 5, 2.i.

IDEA, image, *Rich.* 3, 3.vii.

IGNOBLE, *ignoble plants*, implying that Edward's children were not of noble descent but bastards, *Rich.* 3, 3.vii.

IGNOMINY, IGNOMY, disgrace, 1 *Hen.* 4, 5.iv.

ILLUSION, trick, *Hen.* 8, 1.ii.

ILLUSTRATE, describe, *Hen.* 8, 3.ii.

IMAGERY, figures in hangings, *Rich.* 2, 5.ii.

IMAGINARY, imaginative, *Hen.* 5, *Prol.*

IMBAR, to defend, *Hen.* 5, 1.ii. [2.iv.

IMBRUE, cover with blood, 2 *Hen.* 4,

IMMANITY, inhumanity, 1 *Hen.* 6, 5.i. [3, 4.i.

IMMURE, to put within walls, *Rich.*

IMP, child, 2 *Hen.* 4, 5.v; *verb* (term from falconry), to engraft feathers in a damaged wing, *Rich.* 2, 2.i.

IMPALE, encircle, 3 *Hen.* 6, 3.ii.

IMPEACH, charge, ground of question, 3 *Hen.* 6, 1.iv. [3.vi.

IMPEACHMENT, interference, *Hen.* 5,

IMPORT, importance, 1 *Hen.* 6, 1.i; *verb*, to have as burden, or concerning, *Rich.* 3, 3.vii.

IMPORTANCE, importunity, *John*, 2.i.

IMPOSE, laid upon (as a sin), *Hen.* 5, 4.i.

IMPOSITION, charge, *Rich.* 3, 3.vii.

IMPRESE, device, family crest, *Rich.* 2, 3.i. [*Hen.* 4, 1.i.

IMPRESS, call up or levy for war, 1

IMPUGN, question the decision, 2 *Hen.* 6, 3.i.

IMPUTATION, report, 2 *Hen.* 4, 5.i.

INCAPABLE, unable to realise, *Rich.* 3, 2.ii. [2.iii.

INCARNATE, in human form, *Hen.* 5,

INCISION, to let blood (as with the surgeon's knife), *Rich.* 2, 1.i.

INCOMPREHENSIBLE, boundless, 1 *Hen.* 4, 1.ii.

INCONTINENT, at once, *Rich.* 2, 5.vi.

INCORPORATE, bound up together, *Hen.* 5, 5.ii.

INDENT (from zigzag tear on matching halves of agreement), make a pact with, 1 *Hen.* 4, 1.iii.

INDEX, catalogue of contents of work, so indication of what is to follow, *Rich.* 3, 2.ii.

INDIES, the riches of the Indies were fabulous, *Hen.* 8, 4.i.

INDIFFERENT, impartial, *Rich.* 2, 2.iii.

INDIGESTED, unshaped, 3 *Hen.* 6, 5.vi.

INDIGNITY, unworthy act, 1 *Hen.* 4, 3.ii. [3, 1.iv.

INDIRECT, treacherous, unjust, *Rich.*

INDIRECTION, crooked course, *John*, 3.i.

INDIRECTLY, casually, 1 *Hen.* 4, 1.iii.

INDUCTION, first step, 1 *Hen.* 4, 3.i.

INDUE, furnish, *John*, 4.ii. [2.i.

INDUSTRIOUS, in all seriousness, *John*,

INDUSTRY, skill, 3 *Hen.* 6, 5.iv.

INFALLIBLE, certain, 2 *Hen.* 6, 2.ii.

INFANT STATE, the rank of the child (Arthur), *John*, 2.i.

INFECTION, *of a man*, unfinished specimen, *Rich.* 3, 1.ii.

INFER, to produce evidence or reason for some conclusion or course, *Rich.* 3, 3.vii.

INFLAMMATION, fired by drink, 2 *Hen.* 4, 4.iii. [1.i.

INHABITABLE, uninhabitable, *Rich.* 2,

INIQUITY, character in morality play, *Rich.* 3, 3.i. [1.iv.

INJURIOUS, defamatory, 2 *Hen.* 6,

INJURIES, offences, 3 *Hen.* 6, 4.i.

INKHORN, *inkhorn mate*, a bookish fellow, 1 *Hen.* 6, 3.i.

INLAND, part least exposed to raids, so even the least stirring members of the body respond to sherris, 2 *Hen.* 4, 4.iii.

INNS OF COURT, the residences of the law societies that have the exclusive right to call men to the bar; in Elizabeth's reign attended by many gentlemen who had no intention of practising law, 2 *Hen.* 4, 3.ii.

INNOVATION, *hurlyburly innovation*, revolution, 1 *Hen.* 4, 5.i.

INSENSIBLE, not perceived by the senses, 1 *Hen.* 4, 5.i. [*Hen.* 4, 4.i.

INSINEW'D, active in the affair, 2

INSINUATE, to assume a cordial form of address, *Rich.* 2, 4.i.

INSTANCE, reason, *Rich.* 3, 3.ii; proof, 2 *Hen.* 4, 3.i. [2.iv.

INSULT, to triumph over, *Rich.* 3,

INTELLIGENCE, information, so of spy, *John*, 4.ii; 1 *Hen.* 4, 4.iii.

INTELLIGENCER, informer, God's messenger at 2 *Hen.* 4, 4.ii.

INTEMPERATURE, misconduct, 1 *Hen.* 4, 3.ii. [3, 3.v.

INTENDING, expressing (falsely), *Rich.*

INTERCHANGEABLY, each having the bond signed by all the others, *Rich.* 2, 5.ii.

INTEREST, right, title, 1 *Hen.* 4, 3.ii.

INTERROGATORIES, questions as to a witness or accused, *John*, 3.i.

INVEST, to provide (as with garments), 2 *Hen.* 4, 4.v.

INVESTMENTS, attire, 2 *Hen.* 4, 4.i.

IRIS, goddess who acted as messenger, 2 *Hen.* 6, 3.ii. [4.i.

IRRECONCIL'D, unpardoned, *Hen.* 5,

ISSUE, weep, *Hen.* 5, 4.vi.

ITERATION, repetition of scripture, for the Prince has just quoted *Proverbs*, 1 *Hen.* 4. 1.ii.

IWIS, assuredly, *Rich.* 3, 1.iii.

JACK, often used to indicate contempt, *Rich.* 3, 1.iii; figure on clock, *Rich.* 3, 4.ii.

JACK-AN-APES, a monkey, *Hen.* 5, 5.ii.

JADE, poor kind of horse; *jaded,*

GLOSSARY

treated like a jade, or reduced to that level, *Hen.* 8, 3.ii; lowly, 2 *Hen.* 6, 4.i.

JAUNCE, *jauncing*, as the rider rises and falls in the saddle, *Rich.* 2, 5.v.

JEALOUS, concerned for, *Hen.* 5, 4.i.

JEALOUSY, suspicion, *Hen.* 5, 2.ii.

JERKIN, sleeveless jacket worn over doublet, for hard wear, often made of leather, 2 *Hen.* 4, 2.ii.

JERUSALEM, heaven, 3 *Hen.* 6, 5.v.

JET, *jet upon*, treat with arrogant assumption of superiority, *Rich.* 3, 2.iv.

JOCKEY, familiar form of Jack or John, *Rich.* 3, 5.iii.

JORDAN, chamber-pot, 1 *Hen.* 4, 2.i.

JOURNEY-BATED, worn out by travelling, 1 *Hen.* 4, 4.iii.

JUMP, to agree with, *Rich.* 3, 3.i.

JUTTY, overhang, *Hen.* 5, 3.i.

JUVENAL, youth, 2 *Hen.* 4, 1.ii.

KECKSY, hemlock-like weed, *Hen.* 5, 5.ii.

KEECH, roll of fat; of butcher's wife, 2 *Hen.* 4, 2.i; of butcher's son, *Hen.* 8, 1.i.

KEN, range of vision, 2 *Hen.* 4, 4.i; sight, 2 *Hen.* 6, 3.ii.

KENDAL GREEN, coarse cloth made in Westmoreland, 1 *Hen.* 4, 2.iv.

KENNEL, channel, gutter, 2 *Hen.* 6, 4.i.   [*Rich.* 2, 2.i.

KERN, light-armed Irish soldier,

KEY-COLD, dead, *Rich.* 3, 1.ii.

KICKSHAWS, fancy trifle of food or deportment, 2 *Hen.* 4, 5.i.

KINDRED, *kindred tears*, tears of those related, *Rich.* 3, 2.ii.

KINDLY, according to nature, unfeigned, 2 *Hen.* 4, 4.v; according to his kind (the bishop being reproved for lack of charity), 1 *Hen.* 6, 3.i.

KIRTLE, skirt, 2 *Hen.* 4, 2.iv.

KITE, term expressing abhorrence, *Hen.* 5, 2.i.

KNOT, plot in garden, *Rich.* 2, 3.iv.

LACKEY, to follow merely for hire, *Rich.* 3, 5.iii.   [3.ii.

LADE, empty by ladling, 3 *Hen.* 6,

LAG, late, *Rich.* 3, 2.i.

LAMENTABLE, *lamentable rheum*, tears of sorrow, *John*, 3.i.

LANDRAKERS, thieves, 1 *Hen.* 4, 2.i.

LAP, to wrap, *Rich.* 3, 2.i.

LARD, to fatten, enrich, 1 *Hen.* 4, 2.ii.

LARGESS, gifts of money, *Rich.* 2, 1.iv.

LATE, *late commissioners*, recently

appointed, *Hen.* 5, 2.ii; *of late days*, recently, *Hen.* 8, 2.i.

LATH, *dagger of lath*, of wood (the weapon of the Vice in the morality plays), 1 *Hen.* 4, 2.iv.

LATTER, last, 1 *Hen.* 6, 2.v.

LATTICE, *red lattice*, indicated alehouse, 2 *Hen.* 4, 2.ii.

LAUD, praise and glory, 2 *Hen.* 4, 4.v.   [3.i.

LAUND, clearing in forest, 3 *Hen.* 6,

LAVISHLY, arbitrarily, 2 *Hen.* 4, 4.ii.

LAVOLT, LAVOLTA, lively dance for pairs, *Hen.* 5, 3.v.

LAW, *the canon of the law*, the law of God, *John*, 2.i.

LAY, wager, 2 *Hen.* 6, 5.ii.

LAZAR, a leper or an afflicted person, *Hen.* 5, 1.i.

LAZY, sluggish, 3 *Hen.* 6, 2.i.

LEADING, generalship, 1 *Hen.* 4, 4.iii.

LEAN, unfertile, unfurnished, 1 *Hen.* 4, 1.ii.

LEAPING-HOUSE, brothel, 1 Hen. 4, 1.ii.

LEARN, to teach, *Rich.* 2, 4.i.

LEASH, *leash of drawers*, three tapsters (for hounds were three to a leash), 1 *Hen.* 4, 2.iv.

LEATHER-COAT, russet apple, 2 *Hen.* 4, 5.iii.

LEER, smile familiarly, 2 *Hen.* 4, 5.v.

LEG, *my leg*, bow, 1 *Hen.* 4, 2.iv.

LEGERITY, alacrity, *Hen.* 5, 4.i.

LEGION, name taken by unclean spirit in Mark, v.9, 'for we are many'; so host of friends, *Hen.* 5, 2.ii.

LEGITIMATION, legitimacy, *John*, 1.i.

LEISURE, *spiritual leisure*, religious meditation, *Hen.* 8, 3.ii.

LEMAN, sweetheart, 2 *Hen.* 4, 5.iii.

LENT, forty days fast before Easter, when meat was supposed to be excluded from one's diet, 2 *Hen.* 4, 2.iv.

LET, *noun*, impediment, *Hen.* 5, 5.ii.

LETHE, 'the river of oblivion' in the underworld whose waters caused forgetfulness of one's past existence, 2 *Hen.* 4, 5.ii.

LETTER, *letters patents*, open letters from crown conferring rights and privileges, *Rich.* 2, 2.i.

LEVEL, *noun*, aim (from gunnery), *Hen.* 8, 1.ii; *verb*, aim at, *Rich.* 3, 4.iv.   [3.ii.

LEWD, of the baser sort, 1 *Hen.* 4,

LIABLE, subject to, influenced by, *John*, 2.i.

LIBEL, lying publication, *Rich.* 3, 1.i.

LIBERAL, becoming the free man or gentleman, 3 *Hen.* 6, 1.ii.

GLOSSARY

LIBERTINE, *charter'd libertine,* entitled to go as it pleases, *Hen.* 5, 1.i.

LIEF, beloved, 2 *Hen.* 6, 3.i; *had as lief,* would as willingly, 2 *Hen.* 4, 1.ii.

LIEGE, overlord, king, 2 *Hen.* 6, 3.i.

LIEGEMAN, vassal, 1 *Hen.* 4, 2.iv.

LIFTING, *lifting up of day,* daybreak, 2 *Hen.* 6, 4.iv.

LIGHTEN, enlighten, 2 *Hen.* 4, 2.i.

LIKE, *like well,* look well, 2 *Hen.* 4, 3.ii.   [*Hen.* 4, 3.ii.

LIKELIHOOD, like to promise well, 1

LIKING, *in some liking,* in reasonable health, 1 *Hen.* 4, 3.iii.

LIMBO, *Limbo patrum,* the unbaptised and the virtuous pagans were received here after death; slang for prison, *Hen.* 8, 5.iv.

LIME, to snare, as a bird with birdlime, 2 *Hen.* 6, 1.iii; to doctor wine or sack with lime, 1 *Hen.* 4, 2.iv.

LINE, *under the line,* as if at the equator (because of the heat), *Hen.* 8, 5.iv.

LINE, to strengthen, 1 *Hen.* 4, 2.iii.

LINEAL, *lineal entrance,* entrance by right of descent, *John,* 2.i.

LINK, torch, 1 *Hen.* 4, 3.iii.

LINSTOCK, staff supporting the, match with which the gunner touched off the cannon, *Hen.* 5, 3. Prol.

LIONS, on coat of arms, 1 *Hen.* 6, 1.v.

LIQUOR, oil (to keep boots waterproof), so, with pun on 'boots' = plunder, authority will keep the thieves from falling foul of the law, 1 *Hen.* 4, 2.i.

LISTS, space enclosed for combat, 2 *Hen.* 6, 2.iii.

LITHER, yielding, 1 *Hen.* 6, 4.vii.

LIVELIHOOD, life, animation, *Rich.* 3, 3.iv.

LIVER, regarded as seat of more violent passions; love, courage, anger, 2 *Hen.* 4, 4.iii.

LIVERY, *sue my livery,* to take legal proceedings to have his inheritance restored to him, *Rich.* 2, 2.iii.

LODGE, *lodg'd,* flatten'd, 2 *Hen.* 6, 3.ii.

LONDON-STONE (the central milestone of Roman London from which distances were reckoned), ancient stone in Cannon Street, 2 *Hen.* 6, 4.vi.

LONG-STAFF, *sixpenny strikers,* those who would commit robbery with violence for petty sums, 1 *Hen.* 4, 2.i.   [4, 3.iii.

LONG-WINDED, sound in wind, 1 *Hen.*

LOOK, used before 'who,' 'what,' 'when,' 'how' to form indefinite relatives; *Look when he fawns, he bites,* whenever he fawns, *Rich.* 3, 1.iii.   [8, 5.iv.

LOOSE, *loose shot,* skirmishers, *Hen.*

LOP, smaller branches, *Hen.* 8, 1.ii.

LOSE, forget, *Hen.* 8, 2.i.

LOUTED, scorned and ill-used, 1 *Hen.* 6, 4.iii.   [*Rich.* 2, 3.ii.

LOWER, *lower world,* the earth,

LUCRE, gain, *for lucre of the rest,* in a desire to gain the rest, 1 *Hen.* 6, 5.iv.

LUGGAGE, baggage, *Hen.* 5, 4.iv.

LUMP, as of clay for the potter's shaping at *Hen.* 8, 2.ii.

LUTE, stringed instrument like a guitar, 1 *Hen.* 4, 3.i.

LUXURIOUS, lascivious, *Hen.* 5, 4.iv.

MACHIAVEL, regarded as the type of ruthless schemer, 3 *Hen.* 6, 3.ii.

MAD, *madding Dido,* distracted by love, 2 *Hen.* 6, 3.ii.

MAD-BRED, *mad-bred flaw,* produced by madness, 2 *Hen.* 6, 3.i.

MAGNANIMOUS, great-hearted, 2 *Hen.* 4, 3.ii.

MAID MARIAN, personage in the morris dance, 1 *Hen.* 4, 3.iii.

MAIL, *mailed Mars,* in armour, 1 *Hen.* 4, 4.i; *mail'd up,* shrouded in, 2 *Hen.* 6, 2.iv.

MAIM, disabling blow, 1 *Hen.* 4, 4.i.

MAIN, the number nominated before casting the dice at the game of hazard, 1 *Hen.* 4, 4.i; so *main chance,* 2 *Hen.* 4, 3.i.

MAINLY, violently, 1 *Hen.* 4, 2.iv.

MAINTENANCE, carriage, action, 1 *Hen.* 4, 5.iv.

MAJOR, *your major,* major premise in syllogism (a parody of scholastic argument), 1 *Hen.* 4, 2.iv.

MAJORITY, pre-eminence, 1 *Hen.* 4, 3.ii.   [1.iii.

MALAPERT, presumptuous, *Rich.* 3,

MALCONTENT, disgruntled, 3 *Hen.* 6, 4.i.

MALEVOLENT, *malevolent in all aspects,* terms from astrology, where a star may be described as exerting a harmful influence, 1 *Hen.* 4, 1.i.

MALICIOUS, *malicious day,* day of violence, *John,* 2.i.

MALIGNANT, *malignant stars,* exerting evil influence, 1 *Hen.* 6, 4.v.

MALMSEY, sweet wine, *Rich.* 3, 1.iv.

MALT-WORM, boozer, 2 *Hen.* 4, 2.iv.

MAMMET, doll, 1 *Hen.* 4, 2.iii.

MAN, to provide a man-servant, 2 *Hen.* 4, 1.ii.

GLOSSARY

MAN-QUELLER, murderer, 2 *Hen.* 4, 2.i.

MANAGE, training or handling of a horse, *Hen.* 8, 5.iii.

MANDRAKE, the root was thought to resemble the shape of a man and shriek when torn from the earth, 2 *Hen.* 6, 3.ii; 2 *Hen.* 4, 1.ii.

MANNER, the stolen article when found on the thief, so caught in the act, 1 *Hen.* 4, 2.iv.

MANUAL, *manual seal*, his gauntlet is as a warrant or pledge sealed with his own hand, *Rich.* 2, 4.i.

MARCHES, the English districts adjacent to Scotland and Wales, *Hen.* 5, 1.ii.

MARE, nightmare, 2 *Hen.* 4, 2.i; *wild mare*, see-saw, 2 *Hen.* 4, 2.iv.

MARK, a sum of money (not a coin) value 13s. 4d., *Hen.* 8, 5.i.

MARKET, *the market bell is rung*, so the market is opened, 1 *Hen.* 6, 2.ii.

MARQUESS, rank below duke and above earl, 2 *Hen.* 6, 1.i.

MARSHALSEA, the prison in Southwark, *Hen.* 8, 5.iv.

MARTIN, *Saint Martin's summer*, supposed to run from about 23rd Oct. to 11th Nov., St. Martin's day, 1 *Hen.* 6, 1.ii.

MARTLEMAS, Martinmas, 11th Nov.; animals that could not be fed through the winter were killed at this season, 2 *Hen.* 4, 2.ii.

MASTER, captain of merchant but navigator of war-ship, 2 *Hen.* 6, 4.i.

MATE, *verb*, outwit, 2 *Hen.* 6, 3.i; match, *Hen.* 8, 3.ii; *noun*, officer under the master, 2 *Hen.* 6, 4.i.

MAZED, bewildering, *Hen.* 8, 2.iv.

MEAN, moderation, 1 *Hen.* 6, 1.ii.

MEANING, intention, *Rich.* 3, 3.v.

MEASURE, *measure of revenge*, adequate revenge, 3 *Hen.* 6, 2.iii; so *measure for measure*, 3 *Hen.* 6, 2.vi.   [1.ii.

MECHANIC, manual worker, *Hen.* 5,

MECHANICAL, sometimes used disparagingly, 2 *Hen.* 6, 1.iii.

MEDICINE, *medicine potable*, drug containing gold, supposed to be like the elixir of life, 2 *Hen.* 4, 4.v.

MEED, merit, 3 *Hen.* 6, 2.i.

MELANCHOLY, of various kinds (*see As You Like*, 4.i), *John*, 3.iii.

MEMORIZE, make to be remembered, *Hen.* 8, 3.ii.

MEND, *I cannot mend it*, do anything to improve the matter, *Rich.* 2, 2.iv.

MERCURY, messenger of the gods, so messenger, *Rich.* 3, 2.i.   [3.ii.

MERE, complete, absolute, *Hen.* 8,

MERIT, reward, *Rich.* 2, 1.iii.

MESS, four, usual number in subdivisions of company at banquet, 3 *Hen.* 6, 1.iv.

METAL, METTLE, *the metal of your pasture*, the courage of your country, *Hen.* 5, 3.ii.

METE, measure, 2 *Hen.* 4, 4.iv.

METEOR, supposed to be of vapours drawn up by the sun, hence *an exhaled meteor*, 1 *Hen.* 4, 5.i.

MEW, shut up, *Rich.* 3, 1.i.

MICHER, truant, 1 *Hen.* 4, 2.iv.

MICKLE, *cp.* Scots 'muckle,' great, *Hen.* 5, 2.i.

MILE-END GREEN, where train-bands drilled, 2 *Hen.* 4, 3.ii.

MILLINER, vendor of gloves, hats, etc., 1 *Hen.* 4, 1.iii.

MINCING, affectation, *Hen.* 8, 2.iii.

MINION, favourite, but used contemptuously at 2 *Hen.* 6, 1.iii.

MINISTER, *noun*, agent, 2 *Hen.* 6, 3.i; *verb*, effect, *Hen.* 8, 1.i.

MINOTAUR, the monster that devoured the captives in the labyrinth at Crete, 1 *Hen.* 6, 5.iii.

MISCHIEF, misfortune, 1 *Hen.* 6, 5.iii.

MISCONCEIVED, wrongly judged, 1 *Hen.* 6, 5.iv.

MISCREATE, *titles miscreate*, spurious claims, *Hen.* 5, 1.ii.

MISPRISION, mistaking, 1 *Hen.* 4, 1.iii.

MISPROUD, overweening, 3 *Hen.* 6, 2.vi.

MISTEMPER'D, diseased, as if the 'humours' (*q.v.*) had become badly mixed, *John*, 5.i.

MISTRESS, chief, *Hen.* 5, 2.iv.

MISTRUST, *mistrust no parcel of my fear*, anticipate in no way what I fear for the future, 3 *Hen.* 6, 5.vi.

MOCKERY, pretence, *Hen.* 5, 4.*Prol.*

MODE (from music), *changes the mode*, comment will be based on a different note, 2 *Hen.* 4, 4.v.

MODEL, plan, 2 *Hen.* 4, 1.iii; copy, *Rich.* 2, 1.ii; imperfect manifestation of, *Hen.* 5, 2.*Prol.*

MODERN, ordinary, commonplace, *John*, 3.iv.

MODEST, reasonable, *Hen.* 5, 2.ii.

MODESTLY, without exaggeration, 1 *Hen.* 4, 5.ii.   [2.ii.

MODESTY, proper regard, 1 *Hen.* 6,

MODULE, lifeless image, *John*, 5.vii.

MOE, more, *John*, 5.iv.

MOIETY, half, but any share at 1 *Hen.* 4, 3.i.

MOLDWARP, mole, 1 *Hen.* 4, 3.i.

MONMOUTH CAP, commonly worn by soldiers and sailors, *Hen.* 5, 4.vii.

MOOD, anger, *Hen.* 5, 4.vii.

MOOR DITCH, *melancholy of Moor Ditch*, occasioned by the smell of the ditch, especially when being cleaned out, 1 *Hen.* 4, 1.ii.

MOORFIELDS, where the train-bands mustered for exercise, *Hen.* 8, 5.iv.

MOPE, wander in body or mind, *Hen.* 5, 3.vii.

MORAL, emblem, *Hen.* 5, 3.vi; *moralize*, signify, *Rich.* 3, 3.i.

MORISCO, a morris-dancer (supposed of Moorish origin), 2 *Hen.* 6, 3.i.

MORRIS-DANCE, costume dance of fantastic kind; characters included Robin Hood, Maid Marian, *Hen.* 5, 2.iv.

MORTALITY, death, 1 *Hen.* 6, 4.v.

MORTAL-STARING, with deadly gaze, *Rich.* 3, 5.iii.

MORTIFIED, reduced to the condition of death, *Hen.* 5, 1.i.

MOTE, evil spot, *Hen.* 5, 4.i.

MOTIVE, organ endowed with motion; *the slavish motive of recanting fear*, tongue, *Rich.* 2, 1.i.

MOTLEY, fool's costume, *Hen.* 8,*Prol.*

MOULD, earth, *Hen.* 5, 3.ii.

MOULTEN, having moulted, 1 *Hen.* 4, 3.i.

MOUSE, to seize in the jaws and rend, *John*, 2.i.

MUNITION, war material, *John*, 5.ii.

MURE, wall, 2 *Hen.* 4, 4.iv.

MUSIC, musicians, *Hen.* 8, 4.ii.

MUTINE, mutineer, *John*, 2.i.

MUTINY, contend, *Rich.* 2, 2.i.

MUTUAL, *mutual ranks*, united in common cause, 1 *Hen.* 4, 1.i.

NAG, *Galloway nags*, Scottish ponies, but of wanton wenches at 2 *Hen.* 4, 2.iv.

NAME, leading part, 1 *Hen.* 6, 4.iv.

NAPKIN, handkerchief, 3 *Hen.* 6, 1.iv.

NATURAL, patriotic, *Hen.* 5, 2.*Prol.*

NATURE, the promptings of humane feeling, 2 *Hen.* 4, 4.v.

NAUGHT, wantonly, *Rich.* 3, 1.i.

NAVE, hub of wheel, *nave of a wheel*, this fat knave, 2 *Hen.* 4, 2.iv.

NEAF, fist, 2 *Hen.* 4, 2.iv.

NEAT, animal, ox, cow, calf, 3 *Hen.* 6, 2.i.

NECK, where hangman's rope fitted, *Hen.* 5, 4.viii.

NEEDFUL, requiring supplies, 3 *Hen.* 6, 2.i.

NEMESIS, goddess of just vengeance, 1 *Hen.* 6, 4.vii.

NEPHEW, a relation—cousin, etc., 1 *Hen.* 6, 2.v.

NET, intricate argument, *Hen.* 5, 1.ii.

NETHER-STOCKS, stockings, 1 *Hen.* 4, 2.iv.

NEUTER, neutral, *Rich.* 2, 2.iii.

NICE, coy, shy, mannerly, fastidious; *makes nice of no vile hold*, doesn't hesitate to use it, *John*, 3.iv.

NICELY, subtly, ingeniously, *Rich.* 2, 2.i.

NIECE, grand-daughter, *Rich.* 3, 4.i.

NICHOLAS, patron-saint, of boys and scholars; *Saint Nicholas' clerks*, highway robbers, 1 *Hen.* 4, 2.i.

NOBLESSE, sense of honour, *Rich.* 2, 4.i.

NOBLE, a gold coin worth 6s. 8d., *Rich.* 2, 1.i. [2.iii.

NONAGE, youth, minority, *Rich.* 3,

NOISE, often applied to musical sounds; the men who make the noise, the band, 2 *Hen.* 4, 2.iv.

NONCE, for this particular purpose or occasion, 1 *Hen.* 4, 1.ii.

NOOK-SHOTTEN, all corners and angles, *Hen.* 5, 3.v.

NOTE, guilt (as if marked by brand on his body or noted by some authority), *Rich.* 2, 1.i. [2.iv.

NOT-PATED, hair cut short, 1 *Hen.* 4,

NOURISH, nurse, 1 *Hen.* 6, 1.i.

NUT-HOOK, beadle, 2 Hen. 4, 5.iv.

O, *this wooden O*, the theatre (perhaps the Globe), *Hen.* 5, 1.*Prol.* (cp. *the little O*, the globe itself, the earth, *Ant. and Cleo.*, 5.ii).

OB., abbreviation of 'obolus,' a halfpenny, 1 *Hen.* 4, 2.iv.

OBEDIENT, *obedient orb*, path of obedience, 1 *Hen.* 4, 5.i.

OBJECT, bring forward in accusation, 1 *Hen.* 6, 3.i.

OBJECTION, accusation, 2 *Hen.* 6, 1.iii.

OBLIGATION, bond, 2 *Hen.* 6, 4.ii.

OBLOQUY, shame, 1 *Hen.* 6, 2.v.

OBSCENE, abominable, *Rich.* 2, 4.i.

OBSEQUIOUS, duty to or love for the dead, 3 *Hen.* 6, 2.v.

OBSERVANCE, attention required by respect, homage, 2 *Hen.* 4, 4.iii.

OBSERVE, to show respect to, 2 *Hen.* 4, 4.iv.

OCCASION, happenings, 2 *Hen.* 4, 4.i; chance to blame, *John*, 4.ii.

OCCUPY, *as odious as the word 'occupy,'* because it was employed largely in an indecent sense (e.g. *Rom. and Jul.*, 2.iv), 2 *Hen.* 4, 2.iv.

O'ERBLOW, blows away, *Hen.* 5, 3.iii.

O'ERWHELM, overspread, by being

drawn down over the eye, *Hen. 5*, 3.i.

OFFEND, harm, *John*, 4.i.

OFFER, attack, 2 *Hen.* 4, 4.i.

OFFICE, function, service, *Rich.* 2, 2.ii; the functionary, *Hen.* 8, 1.i; *offices*, quarters in house where domestic needs are provided for, *Rich.* 2, 1.ii.

OMIT, forget, 2 *Hen.* 6, 3.ii. [2.i.

ONEYER, meaning doubtful, 1 *Hen.* 4,

OPENER, one who reveals, 2 *Hen.* 4, 4.ii.

OPINION, public judgment, 2 *Hen.* 4, 5.ii; self-conceit, 1 *Hen.* 4, 3.i.

OPPOSE, *opposed continent*, opposite bank, 1 *Hen.* 4, 3.i.

OPPOSITE, adversary, 2 *Hen.* 6, 5.iii; *adj.*, hostile, unfriendly, 2 *Hen.* 6, 3.ii.

ORB, the circle or sphere in which the planets were supposed to move, so of human place and order, 1 *Hen.* 4, 5.i.

ORDER, manner, 2 *Hen.* 6, 3.ii; *verb*, to arrange, direct, *John*, 5.i.

ORDINANCE, what has been ordained in the past or is ordained for the future, *Hen.* 5, 2.iv; divine decree, *Rich.* 3, 4.iv; cannon, *Hen.* 5, 2.iv.

ORIGINAL, origin, 2 *Hen.* 4, 1.ii.

ORISON, prayer, 3 *Hen.* 6, 1.iv.

ORNAMENTS, *grave ornaments*, the cardinal's robes, 1 *Hen.* 6, 5.i.

OSTENT, show, appearance, *Hen.* 5, 5.*Prol.*

OSTENTATION, display, 2 *Hen.* 4, 2.ii.

OUCHES, ornaments, 2 *Hen.* 4, 2.iv.

OUGHT, owed, 1 *Hen.* 4, 3.iii.

OUSEL, blackbird, 2 *Hen.* 4, 3.ii.

OUTDARE, defy, *Rich.* 2, 1.i.

OVERSCUTCH'D HUSWIFES, well whipped whores, so hardened to the trade, 2 *Hen.* 4, 3.ii.

OVERSHOT, worsted, *Hen.* 5, 3.vii.

OVERWEEN, presume too much, 2 *Hen.* 4, 4.i.

OWE, to possess, *John*, 4.i.

OX-HEAD, *set an ox-head*, make a cuckold, *John*, 2.i.

PACE, to train (as of horses), discipline, *Hen.* 8, 5.iii.

PAGEANT, a show, *Hen.* 8, 4.i.

PAINFUL, *painful field*, where toil is one's lot, *Hen.* 5, 4.iii.

PAINFULLY, with labour, *John*, 2.i.

PAINTED, specious, false, *John*, 3.i.

PAINTED CLOTH, canvas hangings painted with figures and moral sentences were a cheap substitute for figured tapestries, 2 *Hen.* 4, 2.i.

PALE, palisade, *Hen.* 8, 5.iv; *verb*, to

encircle, 3 *Hen.* 6, 1.iv (with the crown).

PALFREY, horse, 2 *Hen.* 6, 4.ii.

PALISADO, defence work of stakes, 1 *Hen.* 4, 2.iii.

PALLET, bed, 2 *Hen.* 4, 3.i.

PALMER, pilgrim, 2 *Hen.* 6, 5.i.

PANTLER, pantry-man, 2 *Hen.* 4, 2.iv.

PAPER, to serve with a writ or communication, *Hen.* 8, 1.i; writing describing the offence, 2 *Hen.* 6, 2.iv.

PARAGON, *paragon'd*, regarded as perfect example of kind, *Hen.* 8, 2.iv.

PARCA, Pistol's reference to the web of life spun by the Fates, *Hen.* 5, 5.i.

PARCEL, *the parcel of a reckoning*, an item in the bill, 1 *Hen.* 4, 2.iv; *parcell'd*, particular, *Rich.* 3, 2.ii.

PARIS BALLS, tennis balls, *Hen.* 5, 2.iv.

PARIS GARDEN, a bear-garden (for in this liberty on the Bankside was situated the ring for bear baiting), *Hen.* 8, 5.iv. [4.ii.

PARK'D, shut in, like game, 1 *Hen.* 6,

PARLE, PARLEY, call to amicable discussion, *Rich.* 2, 1.i; *verb*, to confer, *John*, 2.i.

PARLOUS, perilous, shrewd, *Rich.* 3, 2.iv. [1.iii.

PARMACETI, spermaceti, 1 *Hen.* 4,

PARTAKER, supporter, 1 *Hen.* 6, 2.iv.

PARTED, *timely-parted*, dead from natural causes, 2 *Hen.* 6, 3.ii.

PARTICULAR, *a particular ballad*, referring to one special person, 2 *Hen.* 4, 4.iii; *particular knowledge*, personal knowledge, *Hen.* 5, 3.ii.

PARTICULARITIES, private exclaims, 2 *Hen.* 6, 5.ii.

PARTS, outward appearance, *John*, 1.i, *Hen.* 8, 2.iii; quality, *Hen.* 5, 5.ii.

PARTIAL, *a partial slander*, the accusation of partiality, *Rich.* 2, 1.iii.

PARTIALIZE, affect with partiality, *Rich.* 2, 1.i.

PARTLET, *Dame Partlet*, traditional name for the hen, 1 *Hen.* 4, 3.iii.

PARTY-VERDICT, individual's contribution to common decision, *Rich.* 2, 1.iii. [6, 4.ii.

PASS, *I pass not*, do not care, 2 *Hen.*

PASSAGE, *passages of life*, habitual acts, 1 *Hen.* 4, 3.ii.

PASSING, surpassing, 3 *Hen.* 6, 5.i.

PASSION, physical or mental pain, 1 *Hen.* 4, 3.i; love, 3 *Hen.* 6, 3.iii.

PASSIONATE, grieving, *John*, 2.i; compassionate, *Rich.* 3, 1.iv.

PATIENCE, *with your patience*, with your permission, 1 *Hen.* 6, 2.iii.

GLOSSARY

PATRONAGE, maintain, protect, 1 *Hen.* 6, 3.i.

PATTERN, precedent, *John*, 3.iv; example, *Rich.* 3, 1.ii.

PAUL'S, *known as well as Paul's,* as familiar as the old St. Paul's cathedral which was the 'Bond Street of London' till the days of the Commonwealth, the haunt of idlers and centre of commerce, 1 *Hen.* 4, 2.iv.

PAUNCH, belly, 1 *Hen.* 4, 2.iv.

PAX, representation of the Crucifixion, or reliquary, kissed by the celebrant and people at mass, *Hen.* 5, 3.vi.

PEACE, *of the peace,* a justice of the peace (with pun on silence), 2 *Hen.* 4, 3.ii.

PEACH, to give away one's confederates, 1 *Hen.* 4, 2.ii.

PEASCOD-TIME, the time of year for peas, 2 *Hen.* 4, 2.iv.

PECK, *you o'er the pales,* pitch you over the railings, *Hen.* 8, 5.iv.

PEEL'D, tonsured, 1 *Hen.* 6, 1.iii.

PEEVISH-FOND, foolishly perverse, *Rich.* 3, 4.iv. [*John,* 2.i.

PEISE, *peised well,* well balanced, PELICAN (the pelican was supposed to feed her young with her blood), *Rich.* 2, 2.i.

PELTING, paltry, *Rich.* 2, 2.i.

PEPIN, father of Charlemagne, and so someone who lived long ago, *Hen.* 8, 1.iii.

PERCEIVE, see through, *Hen.* 8, 3.ii.

PERDURABLE, lasting, *Hen.* 5, 4.v.

PERDY (*French,* par dieu), *Hen.* 5, 2.i.

PEREMPTORY, determined, *John,* 2.i.

PERFECT, certain, 2 *Hen.* 4, 3.i; *perfect wrong,* absolute injustice, *John,* 3.i.

PERFORCE, forcibly, 3 *Hen.* 6, 1.i.

PERIAPT, a charm carried on the person, 1 *Hen.* 6, 5.iii.

PERIOD, end, limit, 1 *Hen.* 6, 4.ii.

PERISH, kill, 2 *Hen.* 6, 3.ii.

PERJUR'D, forsworn, 3 *Hen.* 6, 5.v.

PERORATION, studied harangue, 2 *Hen.* 6, 1.i.

PERPEND, ponder, *Hen.* 5, 4.iv.

PERSPECTIVE, a picture that appeared coherent and intelligible only from one particular point of view, *Rich.* 2, 2.ii.

PERSPECTIVELY, as through a perspective or distorting glass, *Hen.* 5, 5.ii.

PERTURBATION, cause of disquiet, 2 *Hen.* 4, 4.v.

PERUSE, *peruse their wings,* examine

the flanks of the enemy, 1 *Hen.* 6, 4.ii. [4.iv.

PEW, *pew-fellow,* associate, *Rich.* 3, PHILIP, name for sparrow, *John,* 1.i.

PHILIP, SAINT, *Saint Philip's daughters,* the daughters of Philip the Evangelist (Acts xxi, 8-9) had the gift of prophecy, 1 *Hen.* 6, 1.ii.

PHILOSOPHER, *philosopher's two stones,* even better than the philosopher's stone that was supposed to turn base metals to gold, 2 *Hen.* 4, 3.ii.

PHOEBUS, the sun-god, 1 *Hen,* 4, 1.ii.

PHOENIX, a unique wonder, *Hen.* 8, 5.v.

PICKED, affecting the superiority of the well-travelled, *John,* 1.i.

PICKING, *picking grievances,* so trivial that they have had to be searched for, 2 *Hen.* 4, 4.i.

PICK-THANK, toady, 1 *Hen.* 4, 3.ii.

PIE, magpie, 3 *Hen.* 6, 5.vi.

PILL, plunder by politic or physical means, *Rich.* 3, 1.iii.

PINES, makes unwholesome, *Rich.* 2, 5.i.

PINK'D, *pink'd porringer,* a fancy perforated cap, *Hen.* 8, 5.v.

PISMIRE, ant, 1 *Hen.* 4, 1.iii.

PISSING CONDUIT, well-known conduit on Cornhill, 2 *Hen.* 6, 4.vi.

PITCH, height, 2 *Hen.* 6, 2.i. [2.iii.

PITCH AND PAY, cash down, *Hen.* 5, PITEOUS, compassionate, *Rich.* 2, 5.iii.

PITH, strength, *Hen.* 5, 3.*Prol.; pithless,* weak, 1 *Hen.* 6, 2.v.

PLAINING, lamenting, *Rich.* 2, 1.iii.

PLAIN-SONG, *the very plain-song of it,* the simple truth, *Hen.* 5, 3.ii.

PLATE, to cover with armour, *Rich.* 2, 1.iii.

PLATFORMS, schemes, 1 *Hen.* 6, 2.i.

PLEASANT, jocular, *Hen.* 5, 1.ii.

PLEASURE, *come of pleasure,* of your own will, 2 *Hen.* 6, 5.i; *speak your pleasures,* speak your mind freely, *Hen.* 8, 3.ii.

PLENTIES, abundance of the 'good things' of life, *Hen.* 5, 5.ii.

PLUCK, *pluck off a little,* come down from duchess to countess, *Hen.* 8, 2.iii. [*Rich.* 2, 4.i.

PLUME, *plume-pluck'd,* dispossessed, POCKET UP, endure, *John,* 3.i.

POINT, *point of war,* trumpet-call, 2 *Hen.* 4, 4.i; lace for keeping hose attached to doublet, 1 *Hen.* 4, 2.iv (pun on 'point' = sword-point); (in falconry) the height to which the hawk climbs before striking, 2 *Hen.* 6, 2.i.

POINT-BLANK, *within point-blank,* so

near as to make a hit certain, 2 *Hen.* 6, 4.vii.

POISE, weigh, 2 *Hen.* 6, 2.i.

POLICY, *cause of policy*, political problem, *Hen.* 5, 1.i; *secret policies*, stratagems, 1 *Hen.* 6, 3.iii.

POLITIC, prudent, 1 *Hen.* 6, 2.v.

POLITICIAN, a political intriguer, 1 *Hen.* 4, 1.iii.

POMGARNET, pomegranate, rooms in inns often having names, 1 *Hen.* 4, 2.iv.

POPULARITY, contact with the common people, 1 *Hen.* 4, 3.ii.

PORING, *poring dark*, play on *poring* and *pouring*, where *poring* means straining one's eyes to see, *Hen.* 5, 4.*Prol.* [3.i.

PORPENTINE, porcupine, 2 *Hen.* 6,

PORRIDGE, pottage or soup, 1 *Hen.* 6, 1.ii.

PORRINGER, small bowl, used of a cap at *Hen.* 8, 5.iv.

PORT (i) gate, 2 *Hen.* 4, 4.v; (ii) bearing, *Hen.* 5, 1.*Prol.*

PORTAGE, port-holes, *Hen.* 5, 3.i.

PORTLY, dignified, 1 *Hen.* 4, 2.iv.

POSITIVELY, without dubiety, *Rich.* 3, 4.ii.

POST, courier, 2 *Hen.* 6, 1.iv; *in post*, in haste (as with post-horses), *Rich.* 2, 2.i.

POSTERN, side-door, *Rich.* 2, 5.v.

POST-HASTE, as speedily as possible, *Rich.* 2, 1.ii; *haste-post-haste*, 3 *Hen.* 6, 2.i.

POTENTS, potentates, *John*, 2.i.

POTTLE-POT, two-quart measure, so tankard, 2 *Hen.* 4, 2.ii.

POULTER, poulterer, 1 *Hen.* 4, 2.iv.

POUNCET-BOX, perforated scent-box. 1 *Hen.* 4, 1.iii.

POWDER, salt, 1 *Hen.* 4, 5.iv; *powdering-tub*, brine-tub (used of treatment for venereal disease), *Hen.* 5, 2.i.

PRACTIC, practical, *Hen.* 5, 1.i.

PRACTICE, intrigue, treachery, *John*, 4.iii.

PRACTISANT, performer of a stratagem, 1 *Hen.* 6, 3.ii.

PRACTISE, use some device, *Hen.* 5, 2.ii; plot, *John*, 4.i.

PRÆMUNIRE, *compass of a præmunire*, open to a charge of maintaining papal authority in England, *Hen.* 8, 3.ii.

PRECEDENT, original, *Rich.* 3, 3.vi; previous example, *Hen.* 8, 1.ii.

PRECEPT, writ containing orders, 2 *Hen.* 4, 5.i.

PRECINCT, area where one exercises authority, 1 *Hen.* 6, 2.i.

PRECISE, scrupulous, 2 *Hen.* 4, 2.iii.

PREDICAMENT, situation, 1 *Hen.* 4, 1.iii.

PREDOMINANT, in the ascendant or influential position, 2 *Hen.* 6, 3.i.

PREFER, bring forward, offer, 1 *Hen.* 6, 3.i; bring to notice of, 2 *Hen.* 6, 4.vii.

PREFERMENT, promotion, advantage, 2 *Hen.* 6, 1.i.   [1.ii.

PREGNANCY, ingenuity, wit, 2 *Hen.* 4,

PREMEDITATION, *cold premeditation*, discouraging consideration for any future scheme, 3 *Hen.* 6, 3.ii.

PREMISED, sent before their time, 2 *Hen.* 6, 5.ii.

PREPARATIONS, armed forces, *Hen.* 5, 2.iv.

PREPOSTEROUSLY, against the nature of man, *Hen.* 5, 2.ii.

PREROGATIVE, precedence, royal right, 1 *Hen.* 6, 5.iv.

PRESAGE, prophecy, sign of future happenings, presentiment, *John* 1.i; *Rich.* 2, 2.ii.

PRESCRIPT, *prescript praise*, praise as required by the subject of it, *Hen.* 5, 3.vii.

PRESCRIPTION, title founded on usage or antiquity, 3 *Hen.* 6, 3.iii.

PRESENCE, person, 1 *Hen.* 4, 3.ii; company, *Rich.* 2, 4.i; presence-chamber, *Hen.* 8, 3.i.

PRESENT, immediate, *Hen.* 8, 1.ii.

PRESENTATION, show, mere appearance, *Rich.* 3, 4.iv.

PRESENTLY, immediately, *John*, 2.i.

PRESS, authority to impress soldiers, 1 *Hen.* 4, 4.ii.

PRESS, *press'd to death*, refers to the pressing to death, with weights, of accused who would not plead, *Rich.* 2, 3.iv.

PRETEND, claim, assert, 3 *Hen.* 6, 4.vii; purpose, 1 *Hen.* 6, 4.i; indicate, 1 *Hen.* 6, 4.i.

PREVAIL, avail, *Hen.* 5, 3.ii.

PREVENT, anticipate, 1 *Hen.* 6, 4.i.

PREVENTION, interference, anticipatory counteraction, 2 *Hen.* 6, 2.iv.

PRICK, *noun*, mark on dial of clock, against hour, 3 *Hen.* 6, 1.iv; *verb*, mark off on a list, 2 *Hen.* 4, 3.ii.

PRIDE, wealth of ornament, *Hen.* 8, 1.i.

PRIEST, *be his priest*, be present at his last moments, murder him, 2 *Hen.* 6, 3.i.

PRIME, *no primer business*, no more important, *Hen.* 8, 1.ii.

PRIMERO, card-game, *Hen.* 8, 5.i.

PRISTINE, former, ancient, *Hen.* 5, 3. ii.

GLOSSARY

PRIVILEGE, justification, explanation, *John*, 4.iii; favour, 1 *Hen.* 6, 3.i; immunity, 1 *Hen.* 6, 5.iv.

PRODIGIOUS, unnatural, ominous, *Rich.* 3, 1.ii; so *prodigiously*, *John*, 3.i.

PRODITOR, traitor, 1 *Hen.* 6, 1.iii.

PROFACE, may it do you good! (formula before a meal), 2 *Hen.* 4, 5.iii.

PROGENY, race, 1 *Hen.* 6, 5.iv; descent, 1 *Hen.* 6, 3.iii.

PROLONG, postpone, *Rich.* 3, 3.iv.

PROOF, of armour, fitness to be put to the proof, impenetrability, *Rich.* 2, 1.iii.

PROPER, *a proper fellow of my hands*, active and fit, 2 *Hen.* 4, 2.ii.

PROPERLY, for my own part (or, perhaps, more to the point), *John*, 2.i.

PROPERTIED, made a mere tool or agent, *John*, 5.ii.

PROPOSE, put before your mind, 2 *Hen.* 4, 5.ii.

PROSPECT, sight, *John*, 2.i.

PROSTRATE, submissive, 2 *Hen.* 4, 4.v.

PROTEST, protestation, 1 *Hen.* 4, 3.i.

PROTEUS, sea-god who assumed various forms, 3 *Hen.* 6, 3.ii.

PROVOKE, drive, 1 *Hen.* 6, 5.v.

PRUNE, preen, 1 *Hen.* 4, 1.i.

PUDDING, stuffing, 1 *Hen.* 4, 2.iv.

PUISSANCE, power, army, *John*, 3.i; strength, 2 *Hen.* 6, 4.ii.

PUKE-STOCKING, cloth stocking, 1 *Hen.* 4, 2.iv.

PULSIDGE, pulse, 2 *Hen.* 4, 2.iv.

PURBLIND, half-blind, 1 *Hen.* 6, 2.iv.

PURCHASE, acquire, *Rich.* 2, 1.iii.

PURCHAS'D, acquired as opposed to possession by descent, *what in me was purchas'd* (the crown, not acquired by hereditary right), 2 *Hen.* 4, 4.v.   [8, 5.iii.

PURGATION, clearance of guilt, *Hen.*

PURPOSE, proposal, 1 *Hen.* 4, 4.iii.

PURSUIVANT, assistant to herald, messenger, *Rich.* 3, 3.iv.

PUSH, attack, 1 *Hen.* 4, 3.ii.

PUTTOCK, bird of prey, kite, 2 *Hen.* 6, 3.ii.

PUZZEL, a drab, 1 *Hen.* 6, 1.iv.

PYRAMIS, pyramid, 1 *Hen.* 6, 1.vi.

QUAINT, clever, 2 *Hen.* 6, 3.ii; ingenious, 1 *Hen.* 6, 4.i.

QUAINTLY, artfully, 3 *Hen.* 6, 2.v.

QUALIFY, to moderate, *John*, 5.i.

QUALITY, nature, 2 *Hen.* 4, 5.ii; profession, *Hen.* 5, 3.vi.

QUANTITY, *sawed into quantities*, pieces, 2 *Hen.* 4, 5.i.   [3.ii.

QUARREL, cause for strife, 2 *Hen.* 6,

QUARTER, area of camp or town assigned to a body of troops, 1 *Hen.*

6, 2.i; *keep good quarter*, watchful guard, *John*, 5.v.

QUARTERING, *quartering steel*, weapons that kill, 1 *Hen.* 6, 4.ii.

QUEAN, female, scold, 2 *Hen.* 4, 2.i.

QUEASINESS, with poor stomach for the business, 2 *Hen.* 4, 1.i.

QUEST, those empanelled at an enquiry, jury, *Rich.* 3, 1.iv.

QUESTION, *noun*, discussion, 2 *Hen.* 4, 1.i; *was in question*, under examination, 2 *Hen.* 4, 1.ii; *verb*, discuss, dispute, *Hen.* 8, 1.i.

QUICK, living, *Rich.* 3, 1.ii.

QUICKEN, bring to life, *Rich.* 3, 4.iv.

QUIDDITIES, subtle insinuations, 1 *Hen.* 4, 1.ii.   [6, 1.iii.

QUILL, *in the quill*, in a body, 2 *Hen.*

QUILLET, legal quibbles, 2 *Hen.* 6, 3.i.

QUIP, retort, sharp remark, 1 *Hen.* 4, 1.ii.

QUIT, to free, *Hen.* 8, 5.i; free oneself from, 1 *Hen.* 4, 3.ii; to requite, 3 *Hen.* 6, 3.iii.

QUITTANCE, like for like, 2 *Hen.* 4, 1.i; recompense, *Hen.* 5, 2.ii.

QUIVER, agile, 2 *Hen.* 4, 3.ii.

QUOIF, close-fitting cap, 2 *Hen.* 4, 1.i.

QUOIT, cast, 2 *Hen.* 4, 2.iv.

QUONDAM, former, 3 *Hen.* 6, 3.i.

QUOTE, mark out, *John*, 4.ii.

QUOTIDIAN, a fever that recurs daily, *quotidian tertian*, Mistress Quickly's terminology (a tertian fever recurred every second day), *Hen.* 5, 2.i.

RABBIT-SUCKER, baby rabbit, 1 *Hen.* 4, 2.iv.

RACE, course, *John*, 3.iii.

RACK, *verb*, stretch, torture, 2 *Hen.* 6, 3.i; tax to the limit, 2 *Hen.* 6, 1.iii.

RACKING, *the rack*, clouds drifting with the wind, so *racking clouds*, 3 *Hen.* 6, 2.i.

RAGAMUFFIN, *my ragamuffins*, tattered company, 1 *Hen.* 4, 5.iii.

RAGE, martial ardour, *John*, 2.i; ungovern'd temper, 1 *Hen.* 4, 3.i.

RAGE, *verb*, talk deliriously, *John*, 5.vii.

RAGING-WOOD, raging mad, 1 *Hen.* 6, 4.vii.

RAMPALLIAN, of a woman, scoundrel, 2 *Hen.* 4, 2.i.

RAMPING, rampant, on hind legs in fighting attitude, 1 *Hen.* 4, 3.i.

RANGE, to rank with, *Hen.* 8, 2.iii.

RANK, *rank minds*, diseased, as if surfeited with too good a diet, 2 *Hen.* 4, 4.i; excessively malevolent, *Hen.* 8, 1.ii.

RANKLE, inflict a wound that festers, *Rich.* 2, 1.iii.

RANSACK, plundering, *John,* 3.iv.

RASCAL, a lean and worthless deer, so term of contempt, 1 *Hen.* 6, 1.ii.   [4.iv.

RASH, sudden in operation, 2 *Hen.* 4,

RATE, price, *Hen.* 8, 1.i; estimation, *Hen.* 8, 3.ii.   [5.vi.

RATHER, *the rather,* the sooner, *John,*

RAVEL, *ravel out,* disentangle, *Rich.* 2, 4.i.

RAW, untrained, *Rich.* 2, 2.iii; *rawly left,* unprovided for, *Hen.* 5, 4.i.

RAW-BONED, because of extreme leanness, 1 *Hen.* 6, 1.ii.

RAZE, obliterate, 2 *Hen.* 6, 1.i; pluck off, *Rich.* 3, 3.iv; lay flat, 1 *Hen.* 6, 2.iii.

REACH, *verb, raught* (participle), taken hold of, 2 *Hen.* 6, 2.iii; attain to in numbers, 1 *Hen.* 4, 4.i.

READ, give instruction of learned kind, 1 *Hen.* 4, 3.i.

RE-ANSWER, afford compensation, *Hen.* 5, 3.vi.

REASON, *noun,* observation, *Hen.* 8, 5.i; cause, *Rich.* 3, 5.iii; *verb,* discuss, *Hen.* 5, 3.vii.

REBUKE, restrain, master, *Hen.* 5, 3.vi.

RECEIPT, sum received, *Rich.* 2. 1.i.

RECEIVE, believe, *Hen.* 8, 2.i.

RECKLESS, regardless of duty, 3 *Hen.* 6, 5.vi.

RECKONING, *all one reckonings,* equal, *Hen.* 5, 4.vii.

RECLAIM, subdue, 1 *Hen.* 6, 3.iv.

RECOMFORTURE, consolation, *Rich.* 3, 4.iv.   [2.iii.

RECORDATION, testimony, 2 *Hen.* 4,

RECORD, witness, *Rich.* 2, 1.i; *in record,* as history tells, *Rich.* 3, 5.iii.

RECORDER, city magistrate, *Rich.* 3, 3.vii.

RECOURSE, admittance, *Rich.* 3, 3.v.

RECURE, to restore to soundness, *Rich.* 3, 3.vii.

REDBREAST, *redbreast teacher,* one who teaches robins to sing, 1 *Hen.* 4, 3.i.

REDEEM, ransom, 2 *Hen.* 6, 4.ix; *redeeming time,* making up for past faults, 1 *Hen.* 4, 1.ii; deliver, *John,* 3.iv.   [*Hen.* 4, 2.ii.

RED LATTICE, window of alehouse, 2

REDOUBTED, regarded with fear, used as form of respect, *Rich.* 2, 3.iii.

REDRESS, satisfaction for injury, 2 *Hen.* 4, 2.i; *verb,* to find remedy for, 3 *Hen.* 6, 5.iv.

REDUCE, bring again, *Rich.* 3, 5.v.

RE-EDIFY, rebuild, extend, *Rich.* 3, 3.i.

REEKING, ascending like the smoke from incense, *Hen.* 5, 4.iii.

REFLEX, direct, 1 *Hen.* 6, 5.iv.

REFUGE, excuse, 1 *Hen.* 6, 5.iv; *verb,* hide away, *Rich.* 2, 5.v.

REGARD, self-regard, 1 *Hen.* 6, 4.v; estimation, 1 *Hen.* 4, 4.iii.

REGENERATE, born again, *Rich.* 2, 1.iii.

REGENT, ruler, *Rich.* 2, 2.i.   [2, 1.iii.

REGREET, to greet, greet again, *Rich.*

REGUERDON, *noun,* reward, 1 *Hen.* 6, 3.i; *verb,* to reward, 1 *Hen.* 6, 3.iv.

RELAPSE, *killing in relapse of mortality,* deadly though dead, *Hen.* 5, 4.iii.   [*Hen.* 6, 3.i.

RELENTING, being moved to pity, 2

RELIGIOUS, conscientious, *Hen.* 8, 4.ii.

RELISH, *noun,* kind, *Hen.* 5, 4.i.

REMAIN, dwell, 3 *Hen.* 6, 3.iii.

REMEMBER, *as I before remember'd,* said previously, *Hen.* 5, 5.ii; *been remember'd,* thought of it, *Rich.* 3, 2.iv.

REMEMBRANCE, *unkind remembrance,* of his memory for failing to recognize the voice of a friend, *John,* 5.ii; epitaph, *Hen.* 5, 1.ii; reminder, *Hen.* 5, 5.ii.

REMISSION, pardon, *Hen.* 5, 5.ii.

REMORSE, pity, 2 *Hen.* 6, 4.vii; *remorseful,* compassionate, *Rich.* 3, 1.ii; *remorseless,* without pity, 3 *Hen.* 6, 1.iv.

REMOVE, dispose of, 1 *Hen.* 6, 2.v; *any soul remov'd,* any stranger, 1 *Hen.* 4, 4.i.   [1 *Hen.* 4, 4.i.

RENDEZ-VOUS, meeting place, refuge,

RENOUNCE, disown, 3 *Hen.* 6, 3.iii.

RENOWN, to make famous, *Hen.* 5, 1.ii.

REPAIR, *noun,* resort, 3 *Hen.* 6, 5.i; *verb, opposites of such repairing nature,* an enemy so quick to recover, 2 *Hen.* 6, 5.iii.

REPEAL, *repeals himself,* returns from banishment on his own authority, *Rich.* 2, 2.ii; revoke, 3 *Hen.* 6, 1.i.

REPETITION, reference to the past, *John,* 2.i.   [3, 4.iii.

REPLENISHED, full, complete, *Rich.*

REPRISAL, prize, 1 *Hen.* 4, 4.i.

REPROACH, shame, 2 *Hen.* 6, 2.iv.

REPROACHFULLY, shamefully, 2 *Hen.* 6, 2.iv.

REPROOF, disproof, 1 *Hen.* 4, 1.ii.

REPROVE, disprove, 2 *Hen.* 6, 3.i.

REPUGN, resist, 1 *Hen.* 6, 4.i.

REPUTE, value, 2 *Hen.* 6, 3.i.

REPUTING, boasting, 2 *Hen.* 6, 3.i.

REQUIRE, to request, *Hen.* 8, 2.iv.

REQUIRING, request, *Hen.* 5, 2.iv.

RESERVE, *only reserved,* with this one

exception, 1 *Hen.* 6, 5.iv; *only reserved their factor*, preserved only to do hell's business, *Rich.* 3, 4.iv.

RESOLVE, dissolve, *John*, 5.iv; free from doubt, answer a question, 3 *Hen.* 6, 2.i; *resolv'd correction*, purposed chastisement, 2 *Hen.* 4, 4.i.

RESPECT, consideration, 1 *Hen.* 4, 4.iii; *in respect of*, because of, 1 *Hen.* 4, 2.iii.

RESPECTIVE, courteous, *John*, 1.i.

RESPITE, delay, 1 *Hen.* 6, 4.i; *determin'd respite*, appointed end of the time (in which my crimes went unpunished), *Rich.* 3, 5.i.

REST, term from card game of primero signifying the stake on which the game turned, the loss of which ended the game—what is at stake, *Hen.* 5, 2.i.

REST, *full of rest*, so of renewed strength, 1 *Hen.* 4, 4.iii. [3, 5.iii.

RESTRAIN, deny possession of, *Rich.*

RETAIN, *retain'd him his*, regarded the gentleman as his retainer, *Hen.* 8, 1.ii.

RETIREMENT, *a comfort of retirement*, support in the event of withdrawal, 1 *Hen.* 4, 4.i.

RETORT, give back, *Hen.* 5, 2.i.

RETREAT, *retreat is made*, the pursuit is called off, 2 *Hen.* 4, 4.iii.

RETURN, *noun*, reply, *Hen.* 5, 2.iv; *verb*, to send as an answer, *Rich.* 2, 3.iii. [4, 3.ii.

REVENGEMENT, punishment, 1 *Hen.*

REVERENCE, *saving your reverence*, with all due respect, 1 *Hen.* 4, 2.iv.

REVERSION, *in reversion*, in the future, as if by legal right, *Rich.* 2, 1.iv. [*Hen.* 8, 1.ii.

REVOKEMENT, recall of instructions,

REVOLUTION, *revolution of the times*, changes made by time, 2 *Hen.* 4, 3.i. [*Hen.* 6, 5.v.

REVOLVE, turn over in the mind, 1

RHEUM, a flow of tears, saliva, etc., *John*, 3.i.

RID, kill'd, 3 *Hen.* 6, 5.v; *willingness rids way*, makes light of the journey, 3 *Hen.* 6, 5.iii.

RIGHT, *right for right*, measure for measure, *Rich.* 3, 4.iv; *a little from the right*, illegitimately, *John*, 1.i; *adv.*, exactly, *Rich.* 3, 1.iv.

RIGOL, circle, *golden rigol*, crown, 2 *Hen.* 4, 4.v.

RIM, lining of belly, *Hen.* 5, 4.iv.

RIPE, *weeping-ripe*, about to weep, 3 *Hen.* 6, 1.iv.

RIVAGE, shore, *Hen.* 5, 3.Prol.

RIVO, a toper's exclamation, 1 *Hen.* 4, 2.iv.

ROAD, stage of a journey, *Hen.* 8, 4.ii; inroad, *Hen.* 5, 1.ii.

ROGUE, sometimes as term of endearment, 2 *Hen.* 4, 2.iv.

ROOD, crucifix, 2 *Hen.* 4, 3.ii.

ROOK, squat, 3 *Hen.* 6, 5.vi. [5.v.

ROOM, place allotted one, *Rich.* 2,

ROOTING, digging up, *Rich.* 3, 1.iii.

ROPE, for hanging or beating, so a cry of abuse, 1 *Hen.* 6, 1.iii. [3.v.

ROPING, hanging as a rope, *Hen.* 5,

ROUND, *too round*, out-spoken to the point of rudeness, *Hen.* 5, 4.i; *round fines*, substantial sums, *Hen.* 8, 5.iv; *verb*, to whisper, *John*, 2.i.

ROUNDLY, unceremoniously or freely, *Rich.* 2, 2.i.

ROUNDURE, circuit, *John*, 2.i.

ROUT, a gang, 2 *Hen.* 4, 4.ii.

ROYAL, gold coin, value 10 shillings, 1 *Hen.* 4, 1.ii; (punning on royal = 10 shillings, noble = 6s. 8d., difference = 40 pence = ten groats), *Rich.* 2, 5.v.

ROYALTY, *that high royalty*, the crown, *John*, 4.ii; emblem of dignity, *Rich.* 2, 2.iii.

RUB, *noun*, impediment (from game of bowls), *Rich.* 2, 3.iv; *John*, 3.iv.

RUDE, unformed, *John*, 5.vii; *rudely stamped*, so deformed, *Rich.* 3, 1.i.

RUE, pity, 2 *Hen.* 6, 2.iv.

RUG-HEADED, shaggy-hair'd, *Rich.* 2, 2.i. [3, 4.iv.

RUNAGATE, deserter, fugitive, *Rich.*

RUSH, *more rushes*, rushes being used to form a carpet in rooms or for a royal procession, 2 *Hen.* 4, 5.v.

RUTH, pity, *Rich.* 2, 3.iv; *ruthful*, pitiable, 3 *Hen.* 6, 2.v.

SABA, Queen of Sheba; 'Saba' is the spelling used in the Bishops' Bible, *Hen.* 8, 5.v.

SACK, a white wine of sherry class from Spain or Canaries, 1 *Hen.* 4, 1.ii.

SACRAMENT, *to take the sacrament*, to confirm an oath or pledge, *John*, 5.ii.

SACRING BELL, during Mass, the bell rung at elevation of Host; or bell calling to morning prayer, *Hen.* 8, 3.ii.

SAD, serious, grave, *Hen.* 5, 4.i; *sad-ey'd*, of serious countenance, *Hen.* 5, 1.ii; *sadness*, gravity, 3 *Hen.* 6, 3.ii.

SAIL, ships, *armado of convicted sail*, defeated fleet, *John*, 3.iv.

SALAMANDER, fabled to live in fire, so

of toper's red face, 1 *Hen.* 4, 3.iii.

SALIQUE, *salique law,* law limiting succession to heirs male, *Hen.* 5, 1.i.

SALLET (i) salad, 2 *Hen.* 6, 4.x; (ii) light helmet, 2 *Hen.* 6, 4.x.

SALUTE, excite, please, *Hen.* 8, 2.iii.

SANDY, *sandy hour,* hour marked by the falling sand in hour-glass, 1 *Hen.* 6, 4.ii.

SANGUINE, *sanguine coward,* the red colour in his face due not to courage but drink, 1 *Hen.* 4, 2.iv.

SANS, without, *John,* 5.vi.

SARCENET, fine silk (saracenic); *sarcenet surety for thy oaths,* like a shopkeeper's wife, 1 *Hen.* 4, 3.i.

SATURN, *Saturn and Venus in conjunction,* an unusual happening, as these planets are seldom in conjunction; Saturn was one of the older gods, so the comparison reflects on Falstaff's age, 2 *Hen.* 4, 2.iv.

SAVAGERY, rank vegetation, *Hen.* 5, 5.ii; inhumanity, *John,* 4.iii.

SAVING, *saving your reverence,* with all due respect, 1 *Hen.* 4, 2.iv.

SAVOUR, smell, *John,* 4.iii.

SAVOY, ancient palace in Strand, 2 *Hen.* 6, 4.vii.

SAW, precept, 2 *Hen.* 6, 1.iii.

SAY, serge, 2 *Hen.* 6, 4.vii.

'SBLOOD, by God's blood, *Hen.* 5, 4.viii.

SCAFFOLD, stage, *Hen.* 5, 1.*Prol.*

SCALD, scurvy, *Hen.* 5, 5.i.

SCAMBLE, scramble, *John,* 4.iii.

SCANDALIZED, victims of scandal, 1 *Hen.* 4, 1.iii. [5, 2.iv.

SCANT, to grudge, to withhold, *Hen.*

SCARLET, *scarlet sin,* for the cardinal's robes are scarlet, and Isaiah uses this colour of sin, *Hen.* 8, 3.ii.

SCATHE, injury, *John,* 2.i.

SCHEDULE, document, 2 *Hen.* 4, 4.i.

SCHOOL, *school of tongues,* shoal of tongues, for his belly would identify him in any part of the world, 2 *Hen.* 4, 4.iii.

SCIENCE, knowledge; *sciences,* studies, *Hen.* 5, 5.ii. [3.v.

SCION, cutting for grafting, *Hen.* 5,

SCONCE, fort, *Hen.* 5, 3.vi.

SCOPE, aim, *Rich.* 2, 3.iii; *scope of nature,* any extreme manifestation, *John,* 3.iv.

SCORE, *the score and the tally,* reckonings kept by notching a stick, 2 *Hen.* 6, 4.vii; *on my score,* in debt, 2 *Hen.* 4, 2.i.

SCOT, *scot and lot,* in full, 1 *Hen.* 4, 5.iv.

SCRAPING, careful of the pence, *Rich.* 2, 5.iii.

SCRIPTURE, writing (with reference to holy writ), *Rich.* 3, 1.iii.

SCROYLE, rascal, *John,* 2.i.

SCRUPLE, third of a dram, apothecaries' weight; Falstaff plays on this and its meaning as 'doubt' or 'objection' at 2 *Hen.* 4, 1.ii.

SCRUPULOUS, *scrupulous wit,* undecided, because it weighs everything too anxiously, 3 *Hen.* 6, 4.vii.

SCULLION, kitchen drudge, 2 *Hen.* 4, 2.i.

SEA-COAL, pit coal (not charcoal), so called being brought to London by sea from Newcastle, 2 *Hen.* 4, 2.i.

SEAL, *seal'd up my expectation,* confirmed my thoughts, 2 *Hen.* 4, 4.v.

SEARCHING, *searching terms,* invective, 2 *Hen.* 6, 3.ii; *searching wine,* intoxicating, 2 *Hen.* 4, 2.iv.

SEAT, to settle, *Hen.* 5, 1.ii; *seated,* on the throne, 3 *Hen.* 6, 3.i.

SECONDARY, a subordinate, *John,* 5.ii.

SECT, womankind, 2 *Hen.* 4, 2.iv.

SECURE, *adj.,* free from all suspicion or care, 1 *Hen.* 6, 2.i; *adv., securely perish,* feeling too safe to take precautions, *Rich.* 2, 2.i.

SECURITY, heedless confidence, *Rich.* 2, 3.ii.

SEE, *see the coronation,* see to, provide for, 3 *Hen.* 6, 2.vi.

SEEMING, appearance, outward show true or false, *Hen.* 8, 2.iv.

SELF, *self-drawing,* drawn from himself, *Hen.* 8, 1.i; *self-affrighted,* frightened at himself, *Rich.* 2, 3.ii.

SEMBLABLE, similar, 2 *Hen.* 4, 5.i; *semblably,* similarly, 1 *Hen.* 4, 5.iii.

SENNET (in stage directions), trumpet notes to mark entrance or exit of a procession, *Hen.* 8, 2.iv.

SENSELESS, without power of feeling; *senseless conjuration,* addressed to the inanimate earth, *Rich.* 2, 3.ii.

SENSIBLE, *sensible of grief,* capable of feeling grief (with play on sensible meaning 'reasonable'), *John,* 3.iv; *sensible of courtesy,* alive to compliment, 1 *Hen.* 4, 5.iv.

SENTENCE, moral saying, maxim, *Hen.* 5, 1.i. [1.iv.

SEPTENTRION, the north, 3 *Hen.* 6,

SEQUEL, *in sequel,* following in due order, *Hen.* 5, 5.ii; the sequence of events, *Rich.* 3, 3.vi.

SEQUESTRATION, seclusion, imprisonment, 1 *Hen.* 6, 2.v.

SET, stake; *Who sets me else?* Who puts down a stake (challenge) against me? *Rich.* 2, 4.i; *set off*, forgotten, 2 *Hen.* 4, 4.i. [2.ii.

SETTER, spy for thieves, 1 *Hen.* 4,

SEVERAL, *adj.*, *several parcels*, various items, *Hen.* 8, 3.ii; *noun*, *severals*, particulars, *Hen.* 5, 1.i.

SHADOW, portrait, 1 *Hen.* 6, 2.iii.

SHAG, hairy, *shag-hair'd kern*, 3 *Hen.* 6, 3.i.

SHAKE, *shook my head*, (perhaps) nod, 2 *Hen.* 6, 4.i.

SHALE, shell, *Hen.* 5, 4.ii.

SHALLOW, without discernment, stupid, *Rich.* 3, 4.iv; *shallowly*, without proper thought, 2 *Hen.* 4, 4.ii. [3, 1.iv.

SHAMEFAC'D, modest, backward, *Rich.*

SHAPE, *shape of likelihood*, reasonable conjecture, 1 *Hen.* 4, 1.i.

SHEARMAN, cloth-cutter, 2 *Hen.* 6, 4.ii.

SHEER, pure, *Rich.* 2, 5.iii.

SHELVES, sandbanks, 3 *Hen.* 6, 5.iv.

SHERRIS, sack, from Xeres in Spain, 2 *Hen.* 4, 4.iii.

SHIFT, trick, *John*, 4.iii.

SHIVERS, fragments, *Rich.* 2, 4.i.

SHOAL, shallow, *Hen.* 8, 3.ii.

SHOCK, shatter, *John*, 5.vii.

SHOG OFF, move away (so that the rivals might be alone together), *Hen.* 5, 2.i.

SHOON, shoes, 2 *Hen.* 6, 4.ii.

SHOT, reckoning; *shot-free*, without paying, 1 *Hen.* 4, 5.iii.

SHOTTEN, *shotten herring*, herring that has shed its roe and is of little value, 1 *Hen.* 4, 2.iv.

SHOULDER'D, *almost shoulder'd in the swallowing gulf*, all but completely sunk, *Rich.* 3, 3.viii.

SHOVE-GROAT, *shove-groat shilling* (same as an *Edward shovel-board*, *Mer. Wives Win.*, 1.i), smooth shilling for game of shove-half-penny, 2 *Hen.* 4, 2.iv.

SHREWD, shrewish, *Rich.* 3, 2.iv; malicious, *Hen.* 8, 5.iii; evil, *John*, 5.v.

SHREWDLY, *shrewdly out of beef*, exceedingly short of, *Hen.* 5, 3.vii.

SHRIEVE, sheriff, 2 *Hen.* 4, 4.iv.

SHRIFT, confession and absolution, 3 *Hen.* 6, 3.ii.

SHRIVER, one who hears confession and gives absolution, used ironically at 3 *Hen.* 6, 3.ii.

SHROUD, shelter, 3 *Hen.* 6, 3.i.

SHROUDS, ropes supporting mast, *John*, 5.vii.

SIBYL, prophetess, 1 *Hen.* 6, 1.ii.

SICIL, *both the Sicils*, Sicily and Naples, 3 *Hen.* 6, 1.iv.

SICK, *sick service*, service during illness, *John*, 4.i; *sicken'd their estates*, reduced by their expenditure, *Hen.* 8, 1.i.

SIGHT, *sights of steel*, visors, 2 *Hen.* 4, 4.i; *sightless stains*, unsightly, *John*, 3.i.

SIGN, *signs of war*, ensigns, *Hen.* 5, 2.ii; *sign of the leg*, bootmaker's sign, 2 *Hen.* 4, 2.iv.

SIGNAL, token, 1 *Hen.* 6, 2.iv.

SIGNIFICANT, *in dumb significants*, in silent acts that will make clear one's opinion, 1 *Hen.* 6, 2.iv.

SIGNORIES, estates, *Rich.* 2, 3.i.

SILLY, helpless, defenceless, 3 *Hen.* 6, 2.v.

SINEW, *a rated sinew*, an important power, 1 *Hen.* 4, 4.iv.

SINFULLY, *sinfully miscarry*, drown with his sins unforgiven, *Hen.* 5, 4.i.

SINGLE, *the single ten*, the plain ten (as contrasted with the courtly king), 3 *Hen.* 6, 5.i; *verb*, to pick out from the herd, 3 *Hen.* 6, 2.iv.

SINISTER, illegitimate, *Hen.* 5, 2.iv.

SIR, before Christian name of priest, *Rich.* 3, 3.ii.

SISTER, *Sisters Three*, the three Fates, 2 *Hen.* 4, 2.iv. [2 *Hen.* 6, 3.i.

SKILL, *it skills not*, it is no matter,

SKIMBLE-SKAMBLE, confused and meaningless, 1 *Hen.* 4, 3.i.

SKIRR, scurry, *Hen.* 5, 4.vii.

SLAKE, lessen, 3 *Hen.* 6, 1.iii.

SLEIGHT, stratagem, 3 *Hen.* 6, 4.ii.

SLOPS, wide breeches, 2 *Hen.* 4, 1.ii.

SLUG, snail, so slow-coach, *Rich.* 3, 3.i.

SMOCK, woman's undergarment, so a woman, 1 *Hen.* 6, 1.ii.

SMOKE, *smoke your skin-coat*, beat, *John*, 2.i.

SMOOTH, flatter, *Rich.* 3, 1.iii.

SMOOTH-PATES, close-cropped like Puritan tradesmen, 2 *Hen.* 4, 1.ii.

SMUG, smooth, 1 *Hen.* 4, 3.i.

SNEAP, snub, 2 *Hen.* 4, 2.i.

SNORT, snore, 1 *Hen.* 4, 2.iv.

SNUFF, *to take snuff*, to resent, 1 *Hen.* 4, 1.iii (with play on meanings of 'snuff').

SODDEN, *sodden water . . . barley-broth*, beer, *Hen.* 5, 3.v.

SOLACE, enjoy health again, *Rich.* 3, 2.iii.

SOLE, unique, *John*, 4.iii.

SOLEMNITY, festivity, *John*, 2.i.

SOLICIT, move, persuade, *Rich.* 2, 1.ii.

SONANCE, sound, *tucket sonance*, call (on the trumpet) for action, *Hen.* 5, 4.ii.

GLOSSARY

SOOTH, truth, *Hen.* 5, 3.vi; flattery, *Rich.* 2, 3.iii.

SOOTHERS, flatterers, 1 *Hen.* 4, 4.i.

SOP, cake or wafer in wine, *Rich.* 3, 1.iv.

SOPHISTER, one who makes wrong appear right, 2 *Hen.* 6, 5.i.

SORT, *noun*, rank, *Hen.* 5, 4.viii; gang, *Rich.* 2, 4.i; *verb*, ordain, *Rich.* 3, 2.iii; *sort occasion*, contrive events, *Rich.* 3, 2.ii; happen, 2 *Hen.* 6, 1.ii; *ill sorted*, associated with lewd terms, 2 *Hen.* 4, 2.iv.

SORTANCE, agreement, 2 *Hen.* 4, 4.i.

SOUL, *soul of adoration*, the real and inner nature of this worship, *Hen.* 5, 4.i.

SOUL-FEARING, causing fear to the soul, *John*, 2.i.

SOUSE, swoop down on (as a hawk), *John*, 5.ii.

SOUS'D, *sous'd gurnet*, fish treated in brine, 1 *Hen.* 4, 4.ii.

SPAN-COUNTER, game in which a coin is thrown to hit or lie beside another, 2 *Hen.* 6, 4.ii.

SPANISH-POUCH, cheap pouch at innkeeper's girdle, 1 *Hen.* 4, 2.iv.

SPEAK, speak on behalf of, *Hen.* 8, 2.iv.

SPECTACLES, the eyes, 2 *Hen.* 6, 3.ii.

SPECULATION, *idle speculation*, inactive looking on, *Hen.* 5, 4.ii.

SPEED, *be your speed*, help you to prosper, 1 *Hen.* 4, 3.i.

SPHERE, the orbit of a planet, so of path of duty, *John*, 5.vii.

SPHERICAL, round, *Hen.* 5, 3.vi.

SPIRITUALTY, clergy, *Hen.* 5, 1.ii.

SPITAL, hospital, *Hen.* 5, 5.i.

SPITE, vexation, 1 *Hen.* 4, 3.i.

SPLEEN, regarded as seat of anger, pugnacity, violent laughter, *John*, 2.i; 1 *Hen.* 4, 5.ii.

SPLINTER, join (as with splints), *Rich.* 3, 2.ii.

SPOIL, destruction, 1 *Hen.* 4, 3.iii; to carry away, 3 *Hen.* 6, 2.ii.

SPOON, *you'd spare your spoons*, spoons being given as christening presents, *Hen.* 8, 5.iii.

SPORTFUL, wanton, 3 *Hen.* 6, 5.i.

SPRINGHALT, leg-disease in horse, *Hen.* 8, 1.iii.

SQUIER, carpenter's rule, 1 *Hen.* 4, 2.ii. [5.iii.

STAFF, *staves*, lance shafts, *Rich.* 3, STAGGER, perplex, *Hen.* 8, 2.iv.

STALE, dupe, 3 *Hen.* 6, 3.iii.

STAMP, recognized character or standing (as the mint's stamp makes coin current), *Rich.* 3, 1.iii.

STAND, withstand, 1 *Hen.* 6, 1.i; *it stands me much upon*, it is very much my concern, *Rich.* 3, 4.ii.

STAR, *seven stars*, Pleiades, 1 *Hen.* 4, 1.ii.

STARTING-HOLE, refuge, 1 *Hen.* 4, 2.iv.

STARVED, skinny, 2 *Hen.* 4, 3.ii.

STATE, rank, 3 *Hen.* 6, 2.ii; *the state of floods*, the majesty of the sea, 2 *Hen.* 4, 5.ii; canopy of state, *Hen.* 8, 1.iv. (Scene Dir.).

STAY, a sudden check (which in a horse may shake the rider), *John*, 2.i; support, *John*, 5.vii.   [4.i.

STERLING, of current value, *Rich.* 2,

STERN, *at chiefest stern*, as in control, 1 *Hen.* 6, 1.i; *to sternage of*, astern of, *Hen.* 5, 3.*Prol.*

STICK, hesitate, 2 *Hen.* 4, 1.ii.

STIFF, *stiff-borne action*, unbendingly ventured on, 2 *Hen.* 4, 1.i.

STIGMATIC, marked out as wicked by some deformity, 2 *Hen.* 6, 5.i.

STILL, *adverb*, always; *still-breeding*, continually multiplying, *Rich.* 2, 5.v; *adj.*, continual, *Rich.* 3, 4.iv.

STINT, to cause to cease, *Hen.* 8, 1.ii.

STOCK, *nether stocks*, stockings, 1 *Hen.* 4, 2.iv.

STOCK-FISH, dried cod, softened before cooking with beating, applied to lean person, 1 *Hen.* 4, 2.iv.

STOMACH, inclination, *Hen.* 5, 3.ii; courage, ambition, 2 *Hen.* 4, 1.i; anger, 2 *Hen.* 6, 2.i.   [5, 4.i.

STOOP, to descend upon prey, *Hen.*

STOUT, bold, 2 *Hen.* 6, 1.i; *stoutly*, resolutely, 3 *Hen.* 6, 2.v.

STRAIN, race, *Hen.* 5, 2.iv; *strain of pride*, perhaps both in musical sense and sense of distension, 2 *Hen.* 4, 4.v; *strain too far*, go farther than facts warrant, 1 *Hen.* 4, 4.i; *strained*, excessive, 2 *Hen.* 4, 1.i.

STRAITER, *no straiter*, not more strictly, 2 *Hen.* 6, 3.ii; *straitly*, strictly, *Rich.* 3, 1.i.

STRANGE, extraordinary, 2 *Hen.* 4, 1.i; *strange-achieved*, by unusual exertion, 2 *Hen.* 4, 4.v.

STRANGENESS, aloofness, 2 *Hen.* 6, 3.i.

STRAPPADO, a punishment in which the victim is hoisted by a rope, let fall, and then brought up with a jerk, to dislocate his joints, 1 *Hen.* 4, 2.iv.   [6, 2.v.

STRATAGEM, act of violence, 3 *Hen.*

STRENGTH, army, 2 *Hen.* 6, 3.i.

STRIKE, lower sail, *Rich.* 2, 2.i; *strike sail to*, yield to, 2 *Hen.* 4, 5.ii.

STRONG, resolute, *Rich.* 2, 5.iii.

STROSSERS, *strait strossers*, narrow trousers, *Hen.* 5, 3.vii.

GLOSSARY

STUBBORN, rough, *Hen.* 5, 5.ii.

STUDIED, *so loosely studied*, so inclined to low desires, 2 *Hen.* 4, 2.ii; painstaking, *Hen.* 8, 3.ii; *studious*, diligent, 1 *Hen.* 6, 2.v; *studiously*, carefully, 1 *Hen.* 6, 3.1.

STYLE, title, 1 *Hen.* 6, 4.vii.

SUBORN, induce, *Rich.* 3, 4.iii; *subornation*, prompting, 2 *Hen.* 6, 3.i.

SUBSCRIBE, sign to, *Hen.* 5, 5.ii; assess, *Rich.* 2, 1.iv; agree, yield, 1 *Hen.* 6, 2.iv.   [2 *Hen.* 4, 1.iii.

SUBSTITUTED, leader in place of king,

SUCCESS, issue, result, *Rich.* 3, 4.iv; *success of mischief*, disastrous consequences, 2 *Hen.* 4, 4.i.

SUCCESSIVE, by right of succession, 2 *Hen.* 6, 3.i; *successively*, by inheritance, 2 *Hen.* 4, 4.v.

SUFFER, *being suffer'd*, uncheck'd, 3 *Hen.* 6, 4.viii; *by his sufferance*, by pardoning him, *Hen.* 5, 2.ii; *sufferance*, suffering for crime, *Hen.* 5, 2.ii; forbearance, *Hen.* 5, 3.vi.

SUFFICIENT, able, 2 *Hen.* 4, 3.ii.

SUGGEST, persuade, instruct, *Hen.* 8, 1.i; seduce, *Hen.* 5, 2.ii.   [4.iii.

SUGGESTION, incitement, 1 *Hen.* 4,

SUIT, dress, *Hen.* 5, 4.ii.

SUMMER, *well summer'd*, favourably treated, *Hen.* 5, 5.ii.

SUNDAY, the day citizens wore their best clothes, 1 *Hen.* 4, 3.i.

SUPERFLUOUS, overflowing, *Hen.* 5, 4.ii; extravagant, *Hen.* 8, 1.i.

SUPERSCRIPTION, address, 1 *Hen.* 6, 4.i.

SUPPLY, reinforcement, 1 *Hen.* 6, 1.i.

SURE, secure, *Rich.* 3, 3.ii.

SURETY, security, *John*, 5.vii.

SURMOUNT, excel, 1 *Hen.* 6, 5.iii.

SUR-REIN'D, overridden, *Hen.* 5, 3.v.

SURVEYOR, manager of estate, *Hen.* 8, 1.i.

SUSPECT, suspicion, *Rich.* 3, 1.iii.

SUSPIRE, breathe, 2 *Hen.* 4, 4.v.

SUTLER, camp follower, *Hen.* 5, 2.i.

SWINGE, thrash, 2 *Hen.* 4, 5.iv.

SWINGE-BUCKLERS, bold sparks, 2 *Hen.* 4, 3.ii.

SWORD-AND-BUCKLER, arms of lower ranks, so, as epithet, common, 1 *Hen.* 4, 1.iii.

SYMPATHISE, share nature, *Hen.* 5, 3.vii; accord with, *Rich.* 2, 5.i.

SYMPATHY, *if that thy valour stand on sympathy*, insists on fighting only an equal in rank, *Rich.* 2, 4.i; conformity, 2 *Hen.* 6, 1.i.

TABLE(-s), *noun*, wood or canvas for painting on, *John*, 2.i; note-book (so, *table-book*), 2 *Hen.* 4, 2.iv.

TAFFETA, a fine lustrous silk, 1 *Hen.* 4, 1.ii.

TAINT, *noun*, corruption, *Hen.* 8, 5.iii; *tainture*, evil state, 2 *Hen.* 6, 2.i; *verb*, discredit, *Hen.* 8, 3.i; to be affected, 3 *Hen.* 6, 3.i.

TAKE, *take my death*, take my dying oath, 2 *Hen.* 6, 2.iii; *take on*, be offended, 3 *Hen.* 6, 2.v.

TALL, of a fine specimen of manhood, 1 *Hen.* 4, 1.iii.

TALLY, stick notched according to debt contracted, 2 *Hen.* 6, 4.vii.

TARDY-GAITED, slow footed, *Hen.* 5, 4.*Prol.*   [4.i.

TARRE, to incite (as a dog), *John*,

TARTAR, Tartarus, hell, *Hen.* 5, 2.ii.

TASK, tax, 1 *Hen.* 4, 4.iii; challenge, 1 *Hen.* 4, 5.ii.

TASTE, *who did not taste to him?* acted as taster to provide against poisoning, *John*, 5.vi.

TAWNY-COAT, colour of livery of Bishop's men, 1 *Hen.* 6, 1.iii.

TEEM, *teeming womb*, fruitful, *Rich.* 2, 2.i.

TEEN, grief, *Rich.* 3, 4.i.

TELL, *tell the clock*, count the strokes, *Rich.* 3, 5.iii.

TEMPER, soften up as one might wax, 2 *Hen.* 4, 4.iii; *temper clay with blood*, moisten, 2 *Hen.* 6, 3.i.

TEMPLE, *Temple Hall*, that of Inner Temple, as at 1 *Hen.* 6, 2.iv and 1 *Hen.* 4, 3.iii. The Inner and Middle Temple were two of the Inns of Court (*q.v.*).

TEMPORAL, secular, *Hen.* 5, 1.i.

TEMPORIZE, come to terms, *John*, 5.ii.

TENDER (i) regard, 1 *Hen.* 4, 5.iv; (ii) offer, *John*, 5.vii.

TENTH, tax on personal property, 1 *Hen.* 6, 5.v.

TERMAGANT, a ranting part in the Mystery cycles, thought to be a Mohammedan deity, 1 *Hen.* 4, 5.iv.

TERTIAN, occurring every other day, *Hen.* 5, 2.i.

TESTER, sixpence, 2 *Hen.* 4, 3.ii.

TETCHY, peevish, *Rich.* 3, 4.iv.

THICK, *thick-ey'd*, dim unheeding eyes, 1 *Hen.* 4, 2.iii; *speaking thick*, fast, 2 *Hen.* 4, 2.iii.

THRACIAN, *Thracian fatal steeds*, see FATAL.

THREAD, *vital thread*, thread of life, spun and cut by the Fates, *Hen.* 5, 3.vi; *threaden*, woven, *Hen.* 5, 3.*Prol.*

THREE-FARTHINGS, a thin silver coin,

1013

Elizabeth's effigy having a rose as ornament, *John*, 1.i.

THREE-HOOPED, the quart pot had three hoops, Cade promises to extend it to ten, 2 *Hen.* 6, 4.ii.

THREE-MAN, requiring three men, as *three-man beetle* (*q.v.*), 2 *Hen.* 4, 1.ii.

THRIFT, profit, *Hen.* 8, 3.ii.

THROE, pain, *Hen.* 8, 2.iv.

THWART, *thwarting stars*, the misfortune that is my lot, 3 *Hen.* 6, 4.vi.

TICKLE, so delicately adjusted as to be unsafe, 2 *Hen.* 6, 1.i.

TIDE, *high tides*, important seasons or festivals, *John*, 3.i.

TIMELESS, untimely, 1 *Hen.* 6, 5.iv; *timely-parted*, having died from natural causes, not by violence, 2 *Hen.* 6, 3.ii.

TIRE, *tire on*, to devour (as bird of prey), 3 *Hen.* 6, 1.i.

TITHE, to levy a tenth, *John*, 3.i.

TITLE, description; *a proper title of peace*, where it is implied that that is not the proper name for it, *Hen.* 8, 1.i; possession, *John*, 1.i.

TOAST, piece of toast in wine, 2 *Hen.* 4, 2.iv.

TOLL, take as toll, 2 *Hen.* 4, 4.v.

TONGUE, the English language, 1 *Hen.* 4, 3.i.

TO-NIGHT, last night, *Hen.* 5, 3.vii.

TOOTH, *colt's tooth*, implying he has still the inclinations of youth, *Hen.* 8, 1.iii.

TOP, head, 2 *Hen.* 6, 1.ii.

Toss, to impale and raise aloft, 2 *Hen.* 6, 5.i.

TOUCH, *noun*, inward sense or feeling, *Rich.* 3, 1.ii; touchstone, *Rich.* 3, 4.ii; hint, *Hen.* 8, 5.i; *verb*, to test, *John*, 3.i; to infect, *John*, 5.vii.

TOWARD, oncoming, brave, 3 *Hen.* 6, 2.ii; in train, 2 *Hen.* 4, 2.iv.

TOWER, the falcon's climb before it swoops, 2 *Hen.* 6, 2.i.

TRACE, *my joy trace the conjunction*, follow, go with, the marriage, *Hen.* 8, 3.ii.

TRACT, track, *Rich.* 3, 5.iii.

TRADED, practised, *John*, 4.iii; *trade-fallen*, unemployed, 1 *Hen.* 4, 4.ii.

TRADITIONAL, old-fashioned, *Rich.* 3, 3.i.

TRAIN, to entice, *John*, 3.iv; 1 *Hen.* 6, 2.iii.

TRAVERSE, soldier's drill order, 2 *Hen.* 4, 3.ii.

TREATY, amicable offer, *John*, 2.i.

TRIBULATION, *of Tower-hill*, toughs, *Hen.* 8, 5.iv.

TRICK, *noun*, inherited characteristic, 1 *Hen.* 4, 5.ii, *John*, 1.i; custom, 2 *Hen.* 4, 1.ii; *verb, trick up*, dress up, *Hen.* 5, 3.vi.

TRIGON, the twelve signs of the Zodiac were grouped in threes (trigons) to correspond to earth, air, water, fire, 2 *Hen.* 4, 2.iv; when the three superior planets are together in Aries, Leo, or Sagittarius they form a fiery Trigon.

TRIM, *trimm'd in thine own desires*, having got your wish, 2 *Hen.* 4, 1.iii.

TRISTFUL, sad, 1 *Hen.* 4, 2.iv.

TRIUMPH, occasion of public rejoicing or recreation, 3 *Hen.* 6, 5.vii.

TROYAN, TROJAN, cant term for companion in drinking or thieving, 1 *Hen.* 4, 2.i.

TRUMPET, trumpeter, 3 *Hen.* 6, 5.i.

TRUTH, faith, 3 *Hen.* 6, 4.viii.

TUB, in which patients with venereal disease were sweated, *Hen.* 5, 2.i.

TUCK, rapier, 1 *Hen.* 4, 2.iv. [4.ii.

TUCKET, signal on trumpet, *Hen.* 5,

TULLY, Cicero, 2 *Hen.* 6, 4.i.

TURK, Sultan of Turkey, *Hen.* 5, 5.ii; *Turk Gregory*, perhaps Pope Gregory VII (Hildebrand), 1 *Hen.* 4, 5.iii.

TURNBULL STREET, in Clerkenwell, the haunt of prostitutes and loose characters, 2 *Hen.* 4, 3.ii.

TWELVE SCORE, in yards the length of an archery range, 2 *Hen.* 4, 3.ii.

TYRANT, usurper, 3 *Hen.* 6, 3.iii.

UMBER, earthy, brown colour; *umber'd*, showing dark in the firelight, *Hen.* 5, 4.Prol. [Epil.

UNABLE, weak, inadequate, *Hen.* 5,

UNADVIS'D, inconsiderate, *John*, 2.i.

UNAVOIDED, not to be escaped, *Rich.* 3, 4.iv.

UNCLEANLY, *uncleanly scruples*, improper doubts, *John*, 4.i.

UNCOINED, *uncoined constancy*, pure metal needing no formal stamp to give it worth, *Hen.* 5, 5.ii.

UNCOLTED, his horse (colt) being stolen—punning on colt = trick, 1 *Hen.* 4, 2.ii. [2.iv.

UNDER-SKINKER, tapster, 1 *Hen.* 4,

UNDERWROUGHT, dealt underhandedly with, *John*, 2.i.

UNDOUBTED, fearless, 3 *Hen.* 6, 5.vii.

UNEATH, scarcely, 2 *Hen.* 6, 2.iv.

UNEVEN, disturbing, 1 *Hen.* 4, 1.i.

UNFATHER'D, unnatural (begotten by demons), 2 *Hen.* 4, 4.iv.

GLOSSARY

UNFELT, *unfelt imagination,* 'the proud dream of pomp' that can't ease the senses, *Rich.* 3, 1.iv; *unfelt thanks,* thanks still to find expression in palpable form, *Rich.* 2, 2.iii.

UNFIRM, distracted, 2 *Hen.* 4, 1.iii.

UNGRACIOUS, insincere, *Rich.* 2, 2.iii.

UNHAPPINESS, wickedness, *Rich.* 3, 1.ii.

UNHAIR'D, too young for a beard, *John,* 5.ii.

UNKIND, unnatural, 1 *Hen.* 6, 4.i.

UNKNOWN, not to be disclosed, *Rich.* 3, 1.ii.

UNOWED, ownerless, *John,* 4.iii.

UNPROVIDED, unprepared for judgment, *Hen.* 5, 4.i; unarm'd, *Rich.* 3, 3.ii. [4.ii.

UNRESPECTIVE, thoughtless, *Rich.* 3,

UNSORTED, ill-chosen, 1 *Hen.* 4, 2.iv.

UNTAINTED, uncharged with crime, *Rich.* 3, 3.vi.

UNTEMPERING, unsoftening, unwinning, *Hen.* 5, 5.ii.

UNTHRIFT, prodigal, *Rich.* 2, 2.iii.

UNTRIMMED, (perhaps) with her hair hanging loose, *John,* 3.i.

UNVALUED, priceless, *Rich.* 3, 1.iv.

UNVEXED, peaceful, *John,* 2.i.

UNWASH'D, so hasty that there is no time for washing, 1 *Hen.* 4, 3.iii.

UNYOK'D, *unyok'd humour,* unrestrained mood, 1 *Hen.* 4, 1.ii.

URN, for grave at *Hen.* 5, 1.ii.

USE, profit, *John,* 5.iv; *Hen.* 5, 2.ii; *make use now,* take the chance of promotion, *Hen.* 8, 3.ii; regular practice, 3 *Hen.* 6, 1.iv.

UTIS, week beginning with a feast-day, so frolic, 2 *Hen.* 4, 2.iv.

VAIL, lower in token of submission, 1 *Hen.* 6, 5.iii.

VARLET, squire, *Hen.* 5, 4.ii; but often used abusively, 2 *Hen.* 4, 2.i.

VAULTAGE, space resembling vaulted structure, *Hen.* 5, 2.iv. [4.iii.

VAWARD, advance-guard, *Hen.* 5,

VELVET-GUARDS, *see* GUARD.

VENT, *vent of hearing,* ear, 2 *Hen.* 4, *Ind.*

VERBATIM, orally, 1 *Hen.* 6, 3.i.

VERGE, circle, limit, 1 *Hen.* 6, 1.iv.

VERIFY, affirm, 1 *Hen.* 6, 1.ii.

VIA, *interj.,* go on, 3 *Hen.* 6, 2.i.

VICE: The Vice was a character in the Morality plays, presented often as a buffoon, *Rich.* 3, 3.i.

VIEW, *this royal view,* this royal assembly, *Hen.* 5, 5.ii.

VIGIL, eve of a feast-day, *Hen.* 5, 4.iii.

VILLIAGO, villain, slave, 2 *Hen.* 6, 4.viii.

VIRTUE, valour, 1 *Hen.* 4, 2.iv; excellence, 1 *Hen.* 4, 3.i; power, *John,* 5.vii.

VIRTUOUS, essential, 2 *Hen.* 4, 4.v.

VISIT, afflict, 1 *Hen.* 4, 4.i; punish, *John,* 2.i.

VISITATION (in two senses) affliction and visit, 2 *Hen.* 4, 3.i.

VOICE, *a woman's voice,* her opinion, words, *Hen.* 5, 5.ii; rumour, *Hen.* 8, 3.ii; reputation, *Hen.* 5, 2.ii; vote, authority, *Rich.* 3, 3.iv.

VOIDING-LOBBY, waiting-room, 2 *Hen.* 6, 4.i.

VOLUNTARY, volunteers, *John,* 2.i.

VOUCH, testimony, *Hen.* 8, 1.i.

VOUCHSAFE, deign to accept, *Hen.* 8, 2.iii.

VULGAR, *our vulgar,* the rank and file, *Hen.* 5, 4.vii; *vulgar air,* common to all, *John,* 2.i.

WAFT, carry by sea, *John,* 2.i; convey ('by water I should die'), 2 *Hen.* 6, 4.i.

WAGE, hazard, *John,* 1.i.

WALK, *this close walk,* garden-path, 2 *Hen.* 6, 2.ii.

WALL-EY'D, discolouration of eye, giving it threatening look, *John,* 4.iii.

WANT, lack; *the utterance of a brace of tongues must needs want pleading for,* even a pair of tongues cannot plead sufficiently for, *John,* 4.i.

WANTON, self-indulgent, *Rich.* 2, 5.iii; unmanly, 2 *Hen.* 4, 1.i; *wantonness,* the pleasure of self-pity, *John,* 4.i.

WARD, defensive posture, 1 *Hen.* 4, 2.iv; division of city, 1 *Hen.* 4, 3.iii; prison, 2 *Hen.* 6, 5.i; to protect, *Rich.* 3, 5.iii.

WARDER, baton of rank, *Rich.* 2, 1.iii.

WARM, well-off, 1 *Hen.* 4, 4.ii.

WAR-PROOF, proved valiant in war, *Hen.* 5, 3.i.

WARRANT, *warrant death,* give assurance of death, 1 *Hen.* 6, 2.v; *I warrant her.* I can promise her, 2 *Hen.* 4, 5.iv; *nothing spake in warrant from himself,* on his own authority, *Rich.* 3, 3.vii. [1.iii.

WARRANTISE, authority, 1 *Hen.* 6,

WASSAIL (originally the salutation on drinking), carousing; *wassail candle,* specially large, to last out the feast, 2 *Hen.* 4, 1.ii.

WASTE, *noun,* what is damaged (as in legal sense of damage to an estate by tenant), *Rich.* 2, 2.i; desolation, *Hen.* 5, 1.ii.

WASTEFUL, devouring, *Hen.* 5, 3.i.

WATCH, timepiece, *Rich.* 2, 5.v; in same line *watches* refers to period of guard (watch), the sleepless sighs of sentinel, which like the jars of the pendulum record on the dial.

WATCH-CASE, (perhaps) sentry-box, 2 *Hen.* 4, 3.i.

WATCHFUL, sleepless, in time's service, *John*, 4.i.

WATERING, drinking, 1 *Hen.* 4, 2.iv.

WATER-WORK, water-colours, 2 *Hen.* 4, 2.i.

WATERY, *watery moon*, as governing the tides, *Rich.* 3, 2.ii.

WAXEN, *waxen epitaph*, a record soon obliterated, *Hen.* 5, 1.ii.

WAY, persuasion, outlook, *Hen.* 8, 5.i.

WEAL, state, 1 *Hen.* 6, 3.i.

WEATHER, *two women plac'd together makes cold weather*, poor fun at a feast, *Hen.* 8, 1.iv.

WEED, garment, 3 *Hen.* 6, 3.iii.

WEEN, to expect, *Hen.* 8, 5.i.

WEIGH, regard, *Hen.* 8, 5.i; *weigh out*, outweigh, *Hen.* 8, 3.i.

WELKIN, sky, *John*, 5.ii.

WELL-APPOINTED, well equipped, 2 *Hen.* 4, 1.i.

WELL-RESPECTED, *well-respected honour*, well considered, not mere vanity, 1 *Hen.* 4, 4.iii.

WHEESON, Whitsun, 2 *Hen.* 4, 2.i.

WHELK, pimple, *Hen.* 5, 3.vi.

WHIFFLER, official who goes ahead of procession to clear the way, *Hen.* 5, 5.*Prol.*

WHIPPING-CHEER, HAVE, be served with the lash, 2 *Hen.* 4, 5.iv.

WHOLESOME, helpful, *Hen.* 8, 3.ii.

WILD, wooded district, 1 *Hen.* 4, 2.i.

WILD-MARE, see-saw, 2 *Hen.* 4, 2.iv.

WILFUL-BLAME, deliberately culpable, 1 *Hen.* 4, 3.i.

WILLOW, *willow garland*, as sign of disappointment in love, 3 *Hen.* 6, 4.i.

WINCHESTER GOOSE (the liberty of the Bankside, under the jurisdiction of the Bishop of Winchester, sheltered many brothels; so the disease and its victims were named after him), 1 *Hen.* 6, 1.iii.

WINCOT, Wilmecot (home of Shakespeare's mother), 2 *Hen.* 4, 5.i.

WIND, *keeps the wind*, term from stalking game, so that animal may not scent huntsman, 3 *Hen.* 6, 3.ii.

WINK AT, ignore, *Hen.* 5, 2.ii.

WINNOW'D, tried, tested, *Hen.* 8, 5.i.

WIRY, *wiry friends*, hairs, *John*, 3.iv.

WIT, to know, 1 *Hen.* 6, 2.v.

WITHERS, *wrung in the withers*, with shoulder-ridge galled by the saddle, 1 *Hen.* 4, 2.i.

WITTY, wise, 3 *Hen.* 6, 1.ii.

WOE, grieved, 2 *Hen.* 6, 3.ii.

WONDER, to marvel, *Hen.* 8, 1.i; to admire, 2 *Hen.* 6, 1.i.

WONDERS, miracles, 1 *Hen.* 6, 5.iv.

WONT, to be accustomed, 1 *Hen.* 6, 1.iv.

WOOD, mad, frantic, 1 *Hen.* 6, 4.vii; *wooden*, foolish, 1 *Hen.* 6, 5.iii.

WORD, *at a word*, as I intend to do, 2 *Hen.* 4, 3.ii.

WORK, *see* WROUGHT.

WORKING, causing a working of the feelings, *Hen.* 8, *Prol.*

WORLD, *the world may laugh again*, fortune may favour me again, 2 *Hen.* 6, 2.iv. [6, 3.ii.

WORM, *deadly worm*, snake, 2 *Hen.*

WORSHIP, dignity; *as I belong to worship*, to the nobility, so entitled to respect, *Hen.* 8, 1.i; *worship of revenge*, the honour of exacting the penalty for this murder, *John*, 4.iii. [3.iv.

WORSHIPFUL, reverently, *Rich.* 3,

WORTHY, deserved, of praise or blame, *Rich.* 3, 1.ii.

WOT (i) know, *Hen.* 5, 4.i; (ii) wilt, *wot ta*, wilt thou, 2 *Hen.* 4, 2.i.

WRANGLER, opponent, *Hen.* 5, 1.ii.

WRATH, impetuosity, 2 *Hen.* 4, 1.i; *wrathful*, furious, *Rich.* 2, 1.iii.

WREST, take by violence or fraud, 2 *Hen.* 6, 3.i; misconstrue, 2 *Hen.* 4, 4.ii.

WRIT, document; *devil's writ*, his Scripture (as opposed to Holy Writ), 2 *Hen.* 6, 1.iv.

WRITE, *writ man*, entitled to reckon himself a man, 2 *Hen.* 4, 1.ii.

WRITHLED, wrinkled, 1 *Hen.* 6, 2.iii.

WROUGHT, endeavoured, *Hen.* 8, 3.ii.

YEA-FORSOOTH, mealy-mouthed, 2 *Hen.* 4, 1.ii.

YCLAD, clad, 2 *Hen.* 6, 1.i.

YEDWARD, Edward, 1 *Hen.* 4, 1.ii.

YEARN, grieve, *Hen.* 5, 4.iii.

YEOMAN, soldier (from the reputation the yeoman class had won in war), *Hen.* 5, 3.i.

YOKE, *noun*, pair, 2 *Hen.* 4, 3.ii; *verb*, in marriage, 3 *Hen.* 6, 4.i.

YOUNKER, novice, simpleton, 1 *Hen.* 4, 3.iii.

ZOUNDS, by God's wounds, *John*, 2.i.